THE LATER
CORRESPONDENCE
OF
GEORGE III

IN FIVE VOLUMES

VOLUME V

THE LATER
CORRESPONDENCE
OF
GEORGE III

PUBLISHED BY AUTHORITY OF
HER MAJESTY QUEEN ELIZABETH II

EDITED BY
A. ASPINALL C.V.O.

Emeritus Professor of Modern History in the University of Reading

IN FIVE VOLUMES
VOLUME V
JANUARY 1808 TO DECEMBER 1810

CAMBRIDGE
AT THE UNIVERSITY PRESS
1970

Published by the Syndics of the Cambridge University Press
Bentley House, 200 Euston Road, London N.W.1
American Branch: 32 East 57th Street, New York, N.Y.10022

Library of Congress Catalogue Card Number: 62–52516

Standard Book Number: 521 07451 7

Printed in Great Britain
at the University Printing House, Cambridge
(Brooke Crutchley, University Printer)

PREFACE

IT is my pleasant duty once more to express my thanks to all the owners of MSS. which are quoted in this volume, either in the text or in footnotes, for my indebtedness to them; and also to the Syndics and staff of the Cambridge University Press. I am most grateful, too, to Mr Mackworth-Young, C.V.O., Her Majesty's Librarian, and to Miss Jane Langton, M.V.O., Registrar of the Archives, and her staff, for their valuable assistance and advice. The Rev. S. B.-R. Poole has again been good enough to read the proofs of this volume.

The references in the letters to the murderous attack on the Duke of Cumberland by his valet Sellis suggest that it might be useful to explain why the Duke's alleged confession to the murder of his valet has been omitted. It forms no part of the King's correspondence; it is far too long to be quoted in a footnote; and, to avoid wasteful expense, it will be printed only in the forthcoming volume (VII) of *The Correspondence of George, Prince of Wales*.

This final volume of the King's correspondence contains an Index to the whole series, and has been considerably enlarged; also, a few errors in the Indexes to the earlier volumes have been corrected.

On page 665 of volume I a few errors in the first volume of the *Letters of King George IV* are corrected. It may be useful to correct another: No. 151, page 151. The date should probably be the 28th (the MS. has been re-checked, and though the very badly written date looks like the 20th, new evidence rules out this possibility). Lord Liverpool wrote to Lord Lonsdale on the 24th: 'I understand Sir James Graham declines standing for Liverpool...Colonel Congreve would be a very proper candidate for such a place and very likely to be successful. Colonel Congreve will set out for Liverpool tomorrow and I shall be much obliged to you if you could give him any assistance and support in your power' (Lonsdale MSS.).

A. ASPINALL

Highlands,
Belle Vue,
Maughold,
Isle of Man

CONTENTS

CORRIGENDA

Volume I

Page 60, note 6, *read* Dalhousie, 8th Earl of (d. 1787).
Page 635, No. 816, line 24, *read* Gemappe.

Volume II

Page 66, paragraph 5, line 2, *read* Ferrand.

Volume III

Page xxvii, column 4, *read* Liverpool.
Page 94, No. 1786, 18 July letter, line 3, *read* Pluto.
Page 102, note 1, for Emmett *read* Emmet.
Page 107, note 5. George Ellis was probably born in 1754, not 1753 as in *D.N.B.*
Page 119. The footnote should refer to Alexander Marsden, for whom see Volume IV, page 133, note 1.
Page 127, No. 1830, last paragraph, line 3, *read* w[h]ere.
Page 187, note 2, line 4, for Cornwallis *read* Fitzwilliam.
Page 219, line 4, delete the reference to note 1.
Page 228, column 2, *read* Camelford.
Page 261, penultimate line, *read* letters.
Page 331 note, line 1, *read* Alexei.
Page 378, note 1, line 3, *read* Huntingford.
Page 389, note 2, and Index, page 669, for Swedish *read* Danish.
Page 444, note 3, line 2, *read* 16 Oct. 1804 (correcting *G.E.C.*)
Page 467, note 5, line 3, *read* Lieutenant.
Page 507, note 3, line 1, *read* ministerial.

Volume IV

Page 328, note 1, last line, for G.C.B. *read* K.B.

Index under Popham, for 1762 *read* 1760, as in Volume III.
Index to Volumes I, II and III, under Princess Mary, Duchess of Gloucester, for 1834 read 1857, as in Volume I, page 124 note.
Index to Volumes II and III, under Lady Augusta Murray, for 1818 read 1830, as in II, 150n.

INTRODUCTION

THE appointment of Lieutenant-Colonel Taylor as the King's private secretary in 1805 produced a marked change in the contents and character of the Sovereign's correspondence. Copies of replies to letters received were then generally preserved —all, of course, on account of the King's blindness, in Taylor's own hand—and the originals too had merely the King's signature, in an increasingly illegible scrawl. There is evidence that Taylor did not copy every outgoing letter: Canning's private papers afford ample testimony as to occasional gaps. One other point is worth making. When the King's eyesight failed and it became evident that he could no longer read letters but had to have them read to him,[1] Ministers became increasingly careless about their handwriting, and in general took less trouble with both spelling and grammatical construction, and it is obvious that they no longer made a practice of reading over what they had written.

There was no marked deterioration in the King's health until the final onset of insanity in the autumn of 1810. In 1807 he was still hoping that the removal of the cataract would relieve him from the dreadful certainty of blindness, but the oculist seems to have considered the case hopeless, and the operation was not attempted. 'Phipps', wrote the well-informed Marquess of Buckingham (21 June 1807), 'certainly endeavours to soothe his uneasiness by hopes of recovering his eye[sight] by couching, which in truth he has no real intention of attempting.' Four months later the Marquess was told that hope had been abandoned. 'All couching must be absolutely out of the question, for the operation in his particular case would almost to a certainty *be fatal*.' He went on: 'The alternative is total blindness, and when that is complete, another question will arise respecting his faculties which very seldom survive a blindness of that description. You will from any medical man find that this question is very doubtful.'

At the beginning of 1808 the Duke of Portland's health was in such a poor state that his colleagues felt they could not long continue without a more efficient head. He was often unable to attend to business and seemed to be so much broken down that his speedy resignation was apparently inevitable. Lord Malmesbury said that he had often been with the Duke when he thought he would have died in his chair. 'His powers of attention were so weakened that he could neither read a paper nor listen for a while without becoming drowsy and falling asleep.' Reports were in circulation that Lord Chatham was to succeed the Duke. Robert Dundas, and probably others, thought that the Earl was not entirely fit for the Premiership. Bathurst, for example, believed that Chatham would be less practicable than the Duke, yet on the whole he seemed to be the best choice and was the person whom the King would prefer. Mutual jealousies made a solution of the succession problem as difficult as it was to be in April 1827 after Lord Liverpool's breakdown. In any

---

[1] The reference on p. 295 (No. 3901) to his reading a document need not be taken literally. Taylor probably read it to him.

case the choice of a new Prime Minister lay not with the Cabinet but with the King, and the Marquess of Buckingham remarked, with pardonable exaggeration, 'The King is master, and the House of Commons will support Dr. Simmons as his Minister if he will name him.' Colonel J. W. Gordon, the Duke of York's military secretary, said much the same in September 1809: 'If the King chose to give his confidence fully and decidedly to a chimney sweeper, and that the fellow had pretty good nerves, he might govern this country in spite of any opposition that might be offered.' Neither of these commentators, then, had much respect for the House of Commons as it was then constituted. The Colonel went on: 'From what I have seen of the House of Commons, and having considered the general composition of that Assembly a good deal, both collectively and individually, I certainly have the most inexpressible contempt for it, and am convinced that a man of good parts, and more than common nerves, could have it as much under his thumb as Napoleon has his Senate. That Assembly is governed by the clamour of the day or by the insolence of some demagogue who is himself led by a flippant news-writer... I have less respect for that Assembly than for so many noisy chattering schoolboys, and I long to see them under proper discipline.'

Some observers of the scene thought, indeed, that the King's choice might fall on Lord Wellesley, but others, knowing that the 'Sultanized Englishman' would seek to control him, were of a different opinion. Perceval, Chatham, Hawkesbury, and probably others, disliked Wellesley, partly because they thought him really attached to Lord Grenville, partly because they believed that if he entered the Cabinet, he, with Canning, would try to eject them.

Without effective control by the Duke of Portland—indeed, there was virtually no control at all—the Government was a 'Government of Departments', a situation which produced inefficiency, extravagance and intrigue. Canning's manner in the House of Commons and the language of his friends outside showed only too clearly how little he approved of what was going on, how plainly it was his ambition to play more than a subordinate part, in the belief that his vast ability and almost unrivalled oratorical powers entitled him to play the first part. Canning and Perceval, remarked Lord Temple, 'hate each other cordially as they always did'. Tierney thought that if only Canning had any weight or authority in the country he might shake off Perceval, who, in his view, had fallen remarkably low in the estimation of politicians because of his incapacity to manage either the House of Commons or the country's finances (24 May 1808). But Tierney believed that Perceval could do better without Canning than Canning could do without Perceval, with the result that Canning had to submit and derive what satisfaction he could from the thought that his rival was cutting a poor figure.

Perceval could see no solution of this problem of prime-ministerial control, composed as the Cabinet then was. 'Our Administration is so constituted that, let us change our head how we please, it is impossible, or next to impossible, that we should have such a controlling power as you [i.e. Huskisson] have been used to see exist with advantage, and consequently wish for again. There never can be the sort of acquiescence amongst us in control as there naturally was, and necessarily was, under Mr. Pitt. Mr. Pitt must have felt, and his colleagues must have felt also, that he had such comprehensive talents and powers that he was himself essentially the Government in all its Departments—that he could form a Government almost of himself, and each of his colleagues must have felt that Mr. Pitt could do without him, though he could not do without Mr. Pitt. Yet even under these circumstances I have understood from you that Mr. Pitt could not in all Departments control expenditure as he wished. But the present Government is so constituted with so many of equal or nearly equal pretensions, with respect to personal weight in the Government and importance to its continuance, by the share of public opinion for talent and character which attach on such an individual's belonging to it may contribute to the whole [*sic*]—that the Government, under whatever head, must to a great degree be and remain a Government of Departments. It is not because the Duke of Portland is at our head that the Government is a Government of Departments, but it is because the Government is and must be essentially a Government of Departments that the Duke of Portland is at our head and is the best head possibly that we could have. I very much doubt us continuing long under any other. There are more than one among us who might by saying, "If you will not do so and so I will resign," bring the Government to very great difficulty if not nearly to an end.' (21 Aug. 1809.)

Writing to Lord Lonsdale in November 1808 Robert Ward suggested that the mischief of no controlling head of the Cabinet had become fatal by the lack of understanding not only between Canning and Perceval, but also between Castlereagh and Chatham. The War Office, he believed, was responsible for the difficulties which General Moore was experiencing in the Peninsula, difficulties which were soon to end with Moore's tragic death at Corunna. Lord Wellesley too spoke of the general paralysis of Government—and referred, interestingly enough, not merely to the absence of a controlling authority but also to the struggle occasioned by the various adverse interests and failings of the Royal family. And Robert Ward remarked in April 1808, 'If anything can destroy this country it will be the state of parties and the folly of our Princes.' The intrigues of the Duke of Cumberland in particular caused much adverse comment.

For an Opposition member Tierney was exceptionally well informed about ministerial dissensions. He told Grey in December 1808 that Castlereagh was not likely to continue long as Secretary of State, and that Mulgrave too held the Admiralty by a weak tenure. On the other hand Tierney derived no great satisfaction from the weak state of the Ministry. He did not believe that the country had any confidence in the Opposition, whose disjointed state arose out of Fox's death, Lord Howick's translation to the House of Lords, and opposing views on the conduct of the war and the desirability of further peace negotiations. The choice of George Ponsonby as leader of the Party in the Commons following Howick's removal to the Lords was a compromise which was soon seen to be unsatisfactory, and his leadership, though it lasted until his death in 1817, was never more than nominal. Tierney confessed (16 May 1808), 'As a Party (in the House of Commons at least) we are completely disbanded...We have numbers sufficient to make two or even three respectable Oppositions, but it is impossible to mould us into *one*. We have neither leader nor concert, nor, as a whole, the means of obtaining either

...For any rational purpose we are worse than inefficient.' He could not believe that a Government with no effective Prime Minister could last more than two years, but neither could he see how it was to be overthrown by so disjointed an Opposition. So his paradoxical conclusion was that it could neither live nor die. (10 Nov. 1808.) A few weeks later the leading Whigs were even discussing the idea of a qualified secession from Parliament, in spite of its admitted futility in 1798. Lord Henry Petty would have none of it. 'I am convinced', he told Grey (21 Dec. 1808), 'that no determination could be taken more exposed to unfavourable construction, and more calculated to deprive us as a Party of whatever there might be of public confidence in its leaders than that of *secession* in an unqualified sense.' In February 1809, whilst the investigation into the conduct of the Duke of York was being conducted, Tierney suggested that nothing could keep Ministers in their places for a week but the state of the Opposition.

Various proposals had been made in 1808 to strengthen the Government. For obvious reasons no one put forward the one satisfactory solution—that Portland should resign in favour of an efficient head. Though not outstandingly able, Lord Bathurst was one of the most disinterested of politicians and therefore one of the most respected, and on 30 July 1808 with his usual generosity he again offered to put the Board of Trade at the Duke's disposal, for Lord Harrowby's acceptance. Harrowby's presence in the Cabinet, he said, was most desirable. He wrote to Harrowby, 'It is not the very critical state of public affairs, of which, indeed, you would have a still stronger impression if you were in the Cabinet, that now induces me again to press your acceptance.' Charles Long, one of the Paymasters-General, was asked to consider the idea of taking the office of President of the India Board when Robert Dundas's removal to Dublin Castle was thought of in the event of Sir Arthur Wellesley's resignation of the Irish Secretaryship. Long, however, declined the conditional offer. Had Wellesley resigned his civil office on going to the Peninsula in 1808, Dundas would probably have been his successor, and the embarrassing question of his father's return to office would have arisen. In fact it was discussed. In June Bathurst believed that Melville was 'most impatient' to be in office again; he had written to Eldon saying that if he were not placed in office before the end of the Session he should consider himself as placed on the shelf. He had always been anxious to be given the option of returning to the Admiralty, provided that it was the King's wish that he should do so. Indeed, Pitt had appointed Lord Barham as his successor in April 1805 precisely with the idea of facilitating Melville's return there at no great distance of time, when public feeling against him had died down, and after another general election. Melville had hoped that Portland would reappoint Barham (in his eighty-first year!) in March 1807 with the same idea in mind, and with a new House of Commons, different in composition from that which had condemned Melville, soon to be summoned. The Duke's failure to follow Pitt's example had seemed to indicate that it was not the intention either of the King or of his Ministers to make further use of Melville's services, though Charles Long reported to Lord Lonsdale in January 1808 that some Ministers agreed with him in thinking that Melville should be brought back. Robert Dundas blamed Portland's 'inertness' for the failure to bring the question of his father's return to office before the Cabinet in 1808, but he also thought that Liverpool would be affronted if it were hinted that he needed Melville's assistance in the House of Lords.

Melville claimed that he had uniformly shown his devotion to the King in supporting his Ministers, consistent, that is, with a life of retirement (he could not afford to keep up a house in London as well as Dunira, his Scottish home). He had tried to avoid involving them in renewed controversy by asking for the restoration of his name to the Privy Council, and it was only at the earnest importunity of Lady Melville, his son Robert, and the Lord Chief Baron of the Exchequer (Robert Dundas) that he had eventually acquiesced in their determination to raise the matter. With one exception he had approved all the ministerial measures, and especially the controversial operations at Copenhagen and in the Tagus, which, he said, had put the country upon an eminence 'from which it is enabled to baffle the hostile and futile combinations of its enemies'. Only on the subject of India had he felt the least anxiety, fearing that a real threat to the security of the Empire was there developing: a threat which was not being taken sufficiently seriously. 'If either Russia or the Turks or even the Court of Persia had remained in amity and friendship with Great Britain, I could have figured many modes of meeting the gigantic confederacy that I am afraid is formed; but, with a combination of all those Powers against us...nothing less than the utmost exertions of the full force and energies of this country are adequate to ward off the blow.' One reason why no offer was made to Melville in 1808 was that Lord Wellesley would have been outraged if any change that did not include him had been made.

The possibility of the return of the Addingtons to the fold was not seriously considered. Melville was confident in January 1808 that the King would have no such wish, and he recalled a remark which the King had made to him early in 1805 after Pitt had taken Sidmouth back into the Cabinet. 'He said to me, "You, of course, have heard what Mr. Pitt is doing about Addington." I told him I had. "Since Mr. Pitt wished it, I had not objected to it if he confined the proposition to some situation which flattered his vanity without giving him any efficient business to execute, but if Mr. Pitt had made any proposition of that kind I must have entered my protest against it." These were his very words, and I have often thought of them when I have heard people amusing themselves with the idea of his being the favourite Minister of the King on whom he rested his hopes.'

Sidmouth communicated his own views to his brother Hiley in November 1808. He spoke of his 'strong and increasing repugnance to office, arising from various causes (amongst the rest from the present state of my family) and my fixed determination never to return to it except under the positive obligation of public duty... I could not admit the existence of such an obligation unless I was to be placed in a situation of perfect and unqualified responsibility.'

Ministers were at loggerheads on both domestic and foreign issues, some calculated to arouse the deepest passions—such as the appointment of the rabid ultra-Protestant Dr Duigenan to a seat at the Irish Privy Council Board, which Canning indignantly denounced as 'full of evil', and for which Lord Liverpool, the Home Secretary, was responsible.

The correspondence illustrates afresh Cabinet divisions on such important questions as the controversial Convention of Cintra. Canning's outspoken criticism of its provisions, shared to some extent by the King, anticipated the quarrel with Castlereagh which culminated in that desperate encounter on Putney Heath in September 1809, with disastrous consequences to both of them and to the Government.

If Melville was correct in thinking that Ministers were underestimating the danger to the British Empire in India, he could not have accused them of indifference to the danger that might arise from the extension of French power from the Old World to the New, after the French occupation of Spain. Action was contemplated, with the King's entire approval, but on account of the country's limited military resources the expedition to South America which had been planned was diverted to the Peninsula to support the Spanish Rising.

Such questions as the trade war, as defined by the Orders-in-Council, and the difficulties with the United States arising out of the British insistence on the right to search American vessels for British deserters, were warmly debated in Parliament but they aroused comparatively little interest in the country. 'We hear no more about the Orders-in-Council and the American embargo than if such things did not exist,' said Tierney (16 May 1808). People were really interested in questions arising out of public expenditure and taxation. Henry Bankes's Offices in Reversion Bill was designed both to increase the power of Parliament and of public opinion at the expense of the Executive, and to reduce expenditure on sinecures. When his Bill was first introduced in the 1807 Session Ministers did not oppose it in the Commons, fearing that their popularity might suffer; but the Peers, who had no popularity to lose, threw it out, and among the majority were the Duke of Cumberland and his friend the Lord Chancellor. Bankes introduced a similar Bill in 1808; again it passed the Commons, Perceval being prepared to accept it, but in the Lords the ultras were determined to defeat it, and their position was strengthened by the King's refusal on 3 March to make known his approval of the Government's acceptance of the measure. Ministers therefore could not rely on the support of the 'Household Brigade'. The incomplete identification of Court and Administration was, then, another source of the Government's weakness. The King refused to instruct the Household to vote with Ministers, and there is no evidence that he complied with Lord Hawkesbury's request that the Archbishop of Canterbury should be asked to remind the Bishops of their obligation to the Government. Ministers were thwarted, too, by the Duke of Cumberland, the unofficial leader of the ultra Peers. Lord Camden wrote to Hawkesbury on 2 March: 'I have seen a Peer who has this day seen the Duke of Cumberland, who is taking the utmost pains to endeavour to enlist Peers to throw out the Bill, and no time should be lost in speaking to people.' And Hawkesbury, the leader of the House of Lords, wrote to Portland on the 2nd: 'I think it of most essential consequence to the character of the Government that you should lose no time in having a full explanation with the Duke of York, and of informing him most explicitly in what manner his conduct and that of the Duke of Cumberland is viewed by all upon the present occasion.' He said that he had received the most positive assurances from the King that the conduct of the Household and his family in general the previous evening was not only unauthorised by him but without his previous knowledge, and that he had never expressed to them his own hostility to the Bill.

The Government was further embarrassed by the attitude of the episcopal bench. The Bishop of Elphin wrote, very humbly and apologetically, to the Duke of Portland on the 9th: 'If I had had *any light* on the subject or been favoured originally with your Grace's wishes about the Reversion Bill, I most undoubtedly would have complied with them. But being left entirely to myself, and hating all changes in the Constitution, and particularly a reduction of the power of the Crown, and seeing Lord Arden [Perceval's brother] etc. and all the Bishops voting for the rejection of the Bill, I fell in with the stream and voted with them. On Monday I promised to vote against the Bill and am afraid I cannot get released from my engagement. It is an unfortunate case but it shall never happen again, as I will always take care in future to learn your Grace's sentiments respecting any Bill of the least importance.' In Committee the ultras defeated the Bill on an amendment to limit the prohibition of reversions to 1 June 1810. Beyond this compromise Ministers were not prepared to go, and on the third reading they voted with the ultras to defeat it by 120 votes to 48. Writing to Lord Malmesbury on 11 March, Camden commented: 'We had another division upon the Reversion Bill yesterday and it was of the same complexion as the last, vizt., "the Court against the Government," the Government conceiving they had *at least* the King's acquiescence in the line they took... This business will have given the Government a considerable shake.'

The other Royal Dukes were a source of only minor embarrassment to Ministers. The Duke of Kent told the King that his character and reputation would suffer if he was not to be allowed to resume his station at Gibraltar, but the King persisted in his refusal to reinstate him. The Duke, nevertheless, did not think of acting politically in opposition to his father's Ministers, to whom his application was forwarded. His influence with Canning might have borne fruit but for the blow-up in September 1809. Whilst playing no part in Opposition politics, the Duke revealed his political sympathies when he said that the Perceval Cabinet was undeserving the confidence of the country. The Duke was confident that the new Government (which refused to pay his bills) would not last long, and he remarked, 'It is devoutly to be hoped they will not.' The Duke of Sussex failed to persuade Perceval that a sum of £25,000 which he owed Lady Augusta Murray should be paid out of public funds.

In August 1808 the Duke of Cumberland was refused a military command in the Peninsula; he was too much of an ultra, too friendly with Lord Eldon, to contemplate opposition. It was disgraceful, he said, that none of the King's sons was with the Army. And the Duke of Clarence was denied a naval command in the Mediterranean.

At the beginning of 1809 Portland still had no thought of resigning, and the speculations about his successor were premature. Throughout the 1808 parliamentary session the independent members had been lukewarm in their support of Ministers, continuing it only because they had no confidence in the Whig Opposition. The belief was still prevalent that in the event of a change the King's choice would probably fall on Lord Chatham, but whatever prospects of the Premiership he might have had were finally blasted by the Walcheren fiasco, which ended his political career.

But before the ministerial crisis developed in the late summer the Mary Anne Clarke affair threatened seriously to affect the Royal family. Though there was no proof that the Duke of York was privy to his mistress's corrupt sale of military commissions, his association with a person who was not much better than a street woman compelled him to resign his office of Commander-in-Chief. 'With the degradation of our Princes,' wrote the Marquess of Buckingham, 'the ruin of the Monarchy is necessarily connected.' The Jacobins, as Tories described the Radical reformers, took full advantage of the situation to criticise not only the Monarchy but the whole Establishment. They tried to prove that corruption existed everywhere, and that only a drastic reform of the country's institutions would remedy the evil. Especially noteworthy was the extraordinary alliance of Jacobins and 'Saints' (the 'moral' part of Society, said Lord Liverpool, who, however, hoped that this alliance would break up when Wilberforce and his friends became aware of the lengths to which the Jacobins would try to carry them in their zeal for reform). Lord Eldon had no great respect for Wilberforce's little group. They were always thinking for themselves, yet they never knew their own minds, and on the whole their support was a mischievous one. 'I won't call them Saints,' he said. Some years earlier Wilberforce had toyed with the idea of Parliamentary Reform, being half inclined to consider the House of Lords a useless body because the Peers opposed the abolition of the slave trade, and because their influence over the composition of the House of Commons (with its large pro-slave-trade representation) was sufficiently notorious and extensive.

The Reformers raised a great outcry against various corrupt practices: ministerial interference with parliamentary elections and improper use of Government patronage; and Bills were introduced, supported but not always initiated by them, to reduce the pension list, abolish sinecures, prevent the granting of offices in reversion and reform Parliament. Commenting on the consequences of the enquiry into the Duke of York's conduct, Charles Long remarked, 'We have let, as it were, the whole people into the body of the House of Commons. The Gallery has almost as much influence as the House itself, and the newspapers are almost becoming the Government of the country. This state of things puts me in mind of what Burke once said to me, that I should live to see the Constitution itself destroyed by the licentiousness of the Press. I hope he was not prophetic in this instance, but I think great strides have been made towards effecting this purpose. Do not think me an alarmist, but the want of a leader on any side to whom any person looks up is a most serious calamity to the country.'

The King was naturally deeply distressed at the exposure of his son's relationship with Mrs Clarke, but he was confident that the Duke's conduct had not been corrupt, and most anxious that he should not be removed from his command and thus disgraced. The Prince of Wales, as usual, pursued a course different from that of the King, and sent a message to his brother saying that he should be 'neutral'.[1]

[1] For a detailed account of the Prince's equivocal behaviour see his *Early Correspondence*, vol. VI.

The extent of Mrs Clarke's influence over the Duke was sufficiently proved, but the inference that she could induce him to enter into her corrupt practices was unjustified.

'The more one hears of the No Popery Cabinet,' wrote Lord Holland (3 Oct. 1809), 'the more one perceives that it was the most wrangling, squabbling, quarrelsome set ever got together, and that the only way of going on at all was letting every man manage his own Department at the risk or rather with the certainty of one Minister counteracting the views of the other.' The events of 1808 foreshadowed the break-up of the Government in September 1809. Without the co-ordinating and controlling hand of an efficient Prime Minister, disputes within the Cabinet could not indefinitely be kept within bounds.

Canning had for long been dissatisfied with Castlereagh's management of the War Department. He had complained that Castlereagh had committed Ministers to the defence of Sir John Moore without making this line of conduct a Cabinet measure. The Ministry, he said, in his letter of 24 March 1809 to the Duke of Portland, had sunk in public estimation because of the Convention of Cintra, the failure of Moore's campaign in Spain, and the 'spirit of compromise' which prevented decisive action. To others he complained of the 'general tone of concession' adopted by Perceval in the management of the House of Commons, and Charles Long, who remained in office in October, admitted that this policy had 'really let down the dignity of the Government'. 'The Government,' said Canning, 'as at present constituted, does not appear to me equal to the great task which it has to perform,' and if the necessary changes could not be made, he should wish to retire. He did not demand Castlereagh's removal: Castlereagh's name was not even mentioned until a later date, and the suggestion that he should be removed did not originate with Canning. 'My representation', said Canning later, 'was on the general state of the Government... My only demand was for permission to retire myself. Whatever particular questions of arrangement followed afterwards arose, not from demands of mine, but from suggestions or proposals to me.'

At the Duke's suggestion Canning went to see him at Bulstrode on 4 April, staying there until the 8th. The conversations were preceded by some preliminary discussions between Canning and his closest friends. Lord Boringdon was then at Bath, but was kept informed of what was passing at Gloucester Lodge by Lord Granville Leveson-Gower. Boringdon's own view of what Canning ought to say to the Duke was as follows: He must get the Duke to agree that the Government was in a 'depressed' state. Something must be done to remedy the situation. In view of the disunion of the Opposition (Grenvilles and Foxites were at loggerheads on some important points) the King should be pressed to make an overture to Lord Grey, and Canning should conduct the negotiation. 'The experiment, if made in a manly manner, can give no just cause of offence to Canning's colleagues; and its failure, while it may become a means of rousing the torpor, quickening the activity and giving some sort of unity to the operations of Government, will also afford a very powerful consideration for Canning's not incurring an Opposition

(xvii)

pilgrimage which I am sure eventually he would not like, and the termination of which, no one could foresee.'

Boringdon feared that Canning's resignation would be the outcome of the conversations at Bulstrode, but he hoped that Canning would not retire without obtaining for him his wished-for promotion in the peerage. His 'late misfortune' (he had just divorced his adulterous wife) made him anxious to see his promotion accelerated: it would afford some consolation to a deeply wounded spirit. But much more important than the question of an Earldom—which he obtained only in 1815, still through Canning's intervention—was the view he confidently put forward that the King would never consent to Canning's elevation to the Premiership.

Granville Leveson learnt something of the course of the Bulstrode conversations when he saw Canning on Sunday, 9 April, but he did not care to communicate to Boringdon, in a letter which might be tampered with by inquisitive people in the Post Office, the details of what passed. He wrote (10 April): 'The D. of P. was disposed to do whatever he recommended. It appears that two or three different schemes of arrangement had been suggested; these the Duke was to take into consideration and on Tuesday they were to dine together at Burlington House and to finally determine what should be proposed to the King at the Levée the following day. By one of the proposed plans of arrangement Lord Chatham would be placed at the head of the Treasury and the old Duke go to the Presidency of the Council; Lord C[astlereagh] turn out into his original nothingness; Lord Wellesley take Castlereagh's place and Lord Mulgrave the Ordnance—but these are details which cannot be written.'

At Bulstrode the Duke asked Canning to suspend the execution of his intention to resign, saying that he wished to consult some members of the Cabinet before giving any advice to the King. The Duke returned to town and took Camden into his confidence: Camden, as Castlereagh's uncle, would be the fittest person to inform him of the coming change in his situation. Then, on 16 April, Portland discussed the matter with Bathurst, again, under a strict pledge of secrecy. About that time Canning, at the Duke's request, himself disclosed the matter, in confidence, to Bathurst, who strongly urged him to defer his resignation beyond the termination of the Easter Recess, to the close of the parliamentary session, when new arrangements could be more conveniently made. Canning felt unable to promise this but agreed to do nothing until the House of Commons had decided what action, if any, should be taken on the charge brought against Castlereagh that he had improperly disposed of Indian patronage. It was on 25 April that the Whig Lord Archibald Hamilton brought forward a Motion accusing Castlereagh of having in 1805 placed at Lord Clancarty's disposal an East India writership to enable Clancarty to get a seat in the Commons. The general expectation was that the division would be so unfavourable as to necessitate Castlereagh's resignation, and Canning thought that Castlereagh should have spared the Government embarrassment by resigning before the division. The Motion was defeated by 216 votes to 167.

Castlereagh was soon exposed to another damaging attack. On 5 and 11 May Maddocks charged him with having improperly sought to influence the vote of one of the members. Quintin Dick had bought a seat, for Cashel, through the agency of the Secretary of the Treasury, Henry Wellesley. On the important question of the Duke of York, Castlereagh, it was alleged, had intimated to Dick that unless he voted with Ministers instead of according to his own conscience he would have to resign his seat. Dick chose to go out of Parliament. The Motion was defeated by 310 votes to 85, but the minority included the votes of some highly respected, independent people like Wilberforce (on important issues the quality of the voting was often as important as the numbers). Canning, incidentally, thought that, in spite of the result, some atonement was due to the public. When it became clear that Castlereagh's resignation or dismissal would not follow, Canning became more urgent, telling Portland that he should resign if nothing was to be done.

There was no secrecy about other arrangements which were being made. Robert Dundas was to succeed Sir Arthur Wellesley as Irish Secretary, but, on the score of ill health, Harrowby declined Dundas's place at the India Board with a seat in the Cabinet. The offer of the Board of Control was then made to Charles Yorke, who, however, asked for the Secretaryship at War which Sir James Pulteney was thinking of vacating. Lord Hardwicke (24 April) had no objection to his brother's return to office without a seat in the Cabinet, provided that it was accompanied by a union of parties (Hardwicke was acting with Lord Grenville). He would wish to see Perceval with two or at most three of his colleagues united with 'some of the best men of the Opposition party'. But the condition proved to be impossible of fulfilment and in the end Portland had to appoint Granville Leveson.

Lord Boringdon, too, was anxious to see Canning and Lord Grey united for both public and personal reasons, and he made the interesting comment (4 April): 'The King is a good life for ten years. He never was better, and Canning may be assured that though the King might even like to see him high in office, yet to his being Prime Minister he never will consent.' He offered no explanation of this statement, but one may be reasonably sure that Canning's support of Catholic relief was an important contributory cause of the King's alleged veto. Canning himself obviously knew of the King's objections to him, for Mrs Canning was well aware of them, and she considered them not insurmountable. Boringdon wrote to Granville Leveson, probably on 7 April (the letter is undated): 'I am more concerned than surprised at Mrs Canning's sentiments. The ground of her error, I doubt not, is amiable—I mean attachment to Canning, and a conviction that the obstacles which *we* see to his attainment of the highest objects may and will be surmounted.' The King's objection to the idea of a Canning premiership may well have been strengthened when he learnt of Canning's threat to resign, which was calculated to break up the Government and involve the Crown in a whole sea of troubles in which the Catholic question might again come prominently forward.

On either 3 or 4 May Bathurst generously but vainly offered to put his own office at the Duke's disposal in order to facilitate a Cabinet reshuffle. On the 4th the Duke asked him to urge Canning to refrain from taking a step which would be dangerous to the country, and further expressed the hope that he, Bathurst, would succeed to the Premiership. By that time Camden had been informed of what had been going on, and Eldon was soon to be. The expedition to Walcheren, which was designed to destroy the French warships and arsenal at Antwerp, was then being prepared, and it was felt to be most unfair to Castlereagh, the Minister immediately responsible for the military side of the expedition, to drive him from office at that moment. Just before 5 May Bathurst proposed that Castlereagh should not be dismissed but put in charge of colonial and Indian affairs, Wellesley taking his place. But some of the Cabinet Ministers who were then in the secret thought it an absurd proposal. All were agreed that Canning's resignation must be prevented. He was proposing to resign because Castlereagh had not been moved from the War Department. Castlereagh would therefore have been exposed to fresh attacks in Parliament which the Government would have been too weak to resist. If, however, Castlereagh was dismissed he would be punished after acquittal by the House of Commons on other charges than inefficiency as a War Minster, and Perceval, for one, was not prepared to acquiesce in such manifest injustice.

On 5 May the Duke told Canning that he meant to lay the whole matter before the King the following Wednesday, the 10th. He did so, and the King said he would consider the situation. As this was a verbal communication there is no mention of it in the correspondence. On Wednesday the 31st Canning had an audience of the King and tendered his resignation. He was ordered to remain in office until the King should have had time to decide what should be done.

On or about 8 June Portland told Canning that the King had authorised him to effect a partial change in the War Department at the end of the session. That part of it which was connected with political correspondence was to be transferred to the Foreign Office, and the business of 'another office, then vacant' (Canning evidently meant the Board of Control, which Harrowby accepted on 28 June, two days after Bathurst had let him into the secret whilst they were dining together at Wimbledon). Various plans, in fact, had been considered. One was for the abolition of the Third Secretaryship of State, whereby the war business was to be transferred to the Foreign Office and the colonial business to the Home Department. This plan, however, was felt to be inconvenient in that it would deprive Castlereagh of his seat in the Cabinet, and, too, the public service might suffer. By another plan, that part of the war which related to the Peninsula was to be transferred to the Foreign Office, and by still another, the Foreign Secretary was to assume full responsibility for the management of the war in Europe, Castlereagh being left only with the colonial business, and compensated with the office of President of the India Board. Such an arrangement, however, was likely to be altogether unacceptable to Castlereagh, and to be disliked by the public, whose sympathy he had alienated following the disclosures in the debate about the East India writership. So the India Board was offered to Sir John Anstruther.

Camden had been taken into the Duke's confidence on 28 April, and shortly afterwards the King told Eldon, at the same time giving orders that no other member of the Cabinet should be let into the secret before the prorogation of Parliament. Further disclosures, the King felt, might cause dissensions amongst his confidential servants.

On 13 June Canning wrote to Portland protesting strongly against further delay. If the expedition were successful nothing would appear more unjust than to remove the War Minister immediately upon the accomplishment of a successful enterprise; but if it failed it would appear as if he were being made a sacrifice to public disappointment. Moreover, Canning strongly represented the unfairness of allowing Castlereagh to carry on this important business without his being apprised of the determination to remove him. Portland, however, took upon himself all the blame that might attach to such proceeding, and the King gave positive orders that no disclosure should yet be made to Castlereagh.

On 15 June the Cabinet approved the Walcheren plans, and Chatham's appointment was agreed to by the King the next day. Soon afterwards Chatham was taken into confidence by the Duke. He felt much embarrassed; he thought the concealment from Castlereagh unfair and, mentioning it to Canning, Canning agreed that it was so, yet both reluctantly acquiesced in the continuance of the concealment because the King had ordered it so. Chatham, accepting the military command not from inclination but from a sense of duty, embarked for the Continent.

On 18 June Portland told Canning that Wellesley was to be brought into the Cabinet, but, a day or two later, the Duke informed him that Castlereagh was unlikely to agree to this. On the 21st the older plan, whereby the work of the War Department was to be redistributed, was resurrected, and the King directed the Duke to inform Castlereagh, through Camden, of the projected change. On the 22nd, the day after the prorogation of Parliament, Portland let Perceval into the secret. Perceval said he could not acquiesce in the justice of the measure, especially since the expedition, of which Castlereagh was the principal architect, had just been approved by the Cabinet. And Perceval thought that the other members of the Cabinet ought not to have been kept in the dark.

Remarkably enough, the leading members of the Opposition, at least as early as 18 June, were aware of what was going on, at a time when only three members of the Cabinet besides the Duke and Canning (Camden, Bathurst and Eldon) were in the secret. Tierney's informant was probably Colonel J. W. Gordon, who had been the Duke of York's Military Secretary. Gordon was in close touch with the Duke of Cumberland, who passed on information coming from Lord Eldon. Tierney knew in mid-June in general terms what the King had said to Canning on 31 May. Tierney believed that not only Castlereagh but Mulgrave and Westmorland would soon be removed; that Portland wished to resign and that Camden would be ready to do so when called upon. All this, he told Grey, came from authority. 'Our friend has been hard at work for the last fortnight, and owns that he is in close communication with the Chancellor, and that he is instructed by him to endeavour to make use of me...He has put the question direct to me whether I think you would listen to a proposition to fill up a certain number of places with persons of your own selection, meaning a fair proportion in the Cabinet, assuring me that if my opinion was that you would, he had no doubt he would bring the negotiation about immediately. To this my answer has been that in the different conversations he has had with me he already knew my sentiments on this subject, and that he was as good a judge as myself of your views and dispositions. Beyond that I declined to say anything...As to myself I have, to very earnest solicitations to the overtures of Government, and to the strongest assurance that I might name my own terms, given for answer that any separate dealing with me for a junction with Ministers was entirely out of the question.'

On 20 June Tierney informed Grey that he had again 'fallen in' with 'our friend', who 'complains grievously of me for having thrown cold water on his plans'. Tierney was told that he would soon hear a great deal more and that Charles Long would probably be the person to communicate it. Grey (23 June) thought it very strange that an overture should have been made which tended directly to break up the Government without any certainty that the consequential negotiations would prove successful. He considered it likely that the places of the Ministers threatened with eviction would be filled from supporters of the Administration. In any case he would not treat on the basis suggested, and he repeated this on the 27th: 'The fundamental principle with me must be the dissolution of the present Administration before any terms can be listened to. Any hint, therefore, at a negotiation which is to proceed upon the ground of our being taken in by them, much more if it rests on the idea of a separation of Lord Grenville and me, I should wish, as far as I am concerned, to be stopped at once, and decisively.'

On 27 June Granville Leveson accepted the office of Secretary at War with a seat in the Cabinet. Canning wrote to him that day, very indignantly, 'You were utterly duped this morning and made to dupe me; I will not be made such a fool as Lord Camden and Lord Bathurst propose.' 'I have not the slightest doubt that Castlereagh knows everything, just as well as you and I do,' he went on. 'If he does not, how does the project of concealment for the next quarter of a year tally with Perceval's complaints of the concealment already practised?' He thought that Camden and Bathurst had decided that it was unnecessary that Castlereagh should be informed, and that further stalling until a week or two of the meeting of Parliament would answer. By that time the result of the expedition would be known. 'They trust then I cannot leave them, for *shame* if unsuccessful, and will not, from *policy* if successful.' He concluded, 'I am sorry the Duke of Portland should have lent himself to such a trick, and I cannot think the King will approve of it. But if he does I have no remedy but the one.' Next day, the 28th, Portland tried to explain matters to Canning and to soothe his ruffled feelings. It was his letter of the previous day, he said, that had caused a misunderstanding. He had had no intention of deferring the intimation to Castlereagh until the outcome of the expedition was known. 'But I thought...that it was the King's intention that *that* intimation should *not* be given to Lord C. *till the expedition had sailed, and that it should be made by him as immediately after as possible, and in the first instance by Lord Camden.* It therefore seemed to me perfectly indifferent whether the communication of his Majesty's sentiments was made to Lord Camden this or the last week. And further, that you could not be committed or subjected to any future embarrassment or difficulty by the communication to Lord Castlereagh being deferred till *the departure* of the expedition. I therefore consulted Lord Camden's convenience and my own in withholding the communication from him, *and it is only this morning and at the Queen's House* that I made him acquainted with the King's wishes, and by so doing I find that I have fully answered his Majesty's expectations. One fortnight more at furthest will in all probability be the longest time that Lord Castlereagh will remain uninformed of the King's wishes. And if *that* should still appear to be putting off the communication to too distant a time I am very ready to take it again into consideration and to be guided by the advice of such of our friends as are apprized of the circumstances, and submit the whole to his Majesty's determination.' Earlier that day Canning had an audience of the King and once more vainly tendered his resignation.

There now seemed little prospect of averting the dissolution of the Government. Bathurst asked his friend Harrowby to try to avert the catastrophe. For more than a year Harrowby had thought that Castlereagh's removal from the House of Commons and his being called up to the House of Lords would be very desirable both for the Government and for himself. He felt that although the reserve hitherto practised towards Castlereagh had placed his colleagues in a painful situation, they had been led to it by motives of kindness towards him, and that if Canning had resigned whilst Parliament was sitting the Government would have been overturned. Harrowby was sure that the right course was to continue to keep Castlereagh in the dark until the Walcheren expedition had sailed; to do so was painful, but justifiable on public grounds.

Nothing more, in any case could then be done because Portland again fell seriously ill and was still in bed on 5 July, though just well enough to see Canning on the 4th. Canning told his wife (5 July) that he was 'really very angry' at the Duke's 'apparent shuffling and twaddling'. The Duke had thought of another plan. Camden, who had repeatedly expressed his readiness to surrender his office, should be asked to resign; Castlereagh, with, of course, a peerage, should take his place as President of the Council, and Wellesley should succeed Castlereagh as War Secretary, still, however, going to Spain, as already arranged, as our Ambassador, Canning temporarily doing the duties of the War Department during the summer. Harrowby thought this an admirable plan; it was calculated to strengthen the Cabinet at its weakest point and place Castlereagh in an important position in the House of Lords. He himself had been ready, though rather reluctantly in view of his continuing ill health, to enter the Cabinet either without office or as President of the Board of Control, after receiving an assurance that the duties of that office were not so heavy as they had been. He strongly objected on principle to Cabinet Ministers without portfolios: this mode of entry 'opened the door to claims which a Minister must find it difficult to resist but more objectionable still to admit'. On 28 June Harrowby's acceptance of the India Board was announced at a Cabinet dinner, and he was rewarded for his self-sacrifice with an Earldom.

Portland wanted to know whether his new plan would satisfy Canning, or whether he would insist on Castlereagh's going out altogether. Canning asked for a few hours for consideration. He wrote to his wife: 'I feel that I could not without great *savageness* insist upon Castlereagh's entire removal, nor without some inconsistency after agreeing to try the King's proposal. So I think I shall say "yes" today, and I shall like getting Chuckle [Camden] out prodigiously.' He added, 'I am not sure that I do not like Camden's going out *better* than I should like Castlereagh's, especially if we can keep him out of the Cabinet, which I trust we may.'

(xxiii)

But Perceval thoroughly disapproved the new plan, and refused to pledge himself to support an arrangement decisive of Castlereagh's fate until he knew how Castlereagh would receive it. Lord Liverpool had already ('some days' before 11 July) heard from one or other of his colleagues something of what was going on, and Canning took him into his confidence on the 11th. Liverpool said that if he were asked to decide which of the two—Canning and Castlereagh—would have to go, it was beyond comparison of more importance to the Government that Canning should remain in office. On the other hand, he agreed with Perceval that it would be unjust and unnecessarily harsh to force Castlereagh out of office whilst the expedition was in progress. If it was determined that he should not see it through, he should not have been allowed to prepare it. Reporting this conversation to his wife, Canning said: 'He (Hawkesbury) knew very well that this was no fault of *mine*. He did me justice, and so did everybody in the Cabinet with whom he had talked upon the subject—but though it was not owing to me, the embarrassment was not the less real nor the less severe upon Castlereagh, and he (H.), who came to the consideration of the matter in its *present* state, without any knowledge of its progress or any responsibility for the difficulties in which it is involved, must judge of it as he finds it—and so judging, he could not but in fairness own that he should, if Castlereagh called out "injustice" and "cruelty" and resigned rather than submit to the change, be compelled to own that he had reason on his side and to join in supporting him.' If the expedition succeeded, said Liverpool, Castlereagh's removal could be represented to him merely as an expedient to strengthen the Government by securing Wellesley. If it failed, Castlereagh would be told that this misfortune 'in addition to the former misfortunes of his War administration' made it necessary that he should retire. Canning said he would agree to the postponement on receiving an assurance 'not in the name of the Duke only but of all the Cabinet, that the change shall take place at the end of the expedition, *end how it will*'. Canning heard from his friend Granville Leveson that Camden, now that it was proposed to accept his offer of resignation, was extremely reluctant to depart, and considered that a great sacrifice had been extorted from him.

Liverpool, like Camden, was ready to make sacrifices in order to keep the Government together. He would let Castlereagh have his office, with a peerage and the leadership of the House of Lords, and would resign from the Cabinet too. And Bathurst thought that Westmorland would be willing to resign the Privy Seal, making way for Lord Melville, and Wellesley would take the War Department. John Fordyce's office of Surveyor-General of Crown Lands might well provide 'a fine retreat' for Westmorland, especially if it could be given for life.

A peerage for Castlereagh was mentioned because Canning insisted that he should leave the House of Commons as well as the War Department. Canning further insisted that Liverpool's generous proposal was unacceptable: it was 'out of the question' that Wellesley should succeed to the War Secretaryship with Castlereagh as Leader in the House of Lords. 'This would not do at all.' 'It is very handsome of poor Hawksy.,' said Canning, 'but he is the person in the Government whom I should least like to lose, the one whom I like best, next to Leveson, and think one of the most useful if not the most so, and so I told him. His whole behaviour in this business has been manly and fair.' It is pleasant to think that the enmity which had disturbed their relationship in 1804 had ceased to exist, and that Canning had come to appreciate Liverpool's good qualities.

Later (21 Sept.) Castlereagh told his father that he could not have accepted Camden's office of Lord President. 'If I could have lent myself to such an idea I should well have deserved all the mortification that has been prepared for me.'

On 16 July the Duke told Canning that the King had given orders that the reserve which had been practised towards Castlereagh must be continued, and Canning naturally replied, two days later, 'It would ill become me to presume to question the propriety of it. But in justice to myself I cannot forbear to request of your Grace that it may be remembered, whenever hereafter this concealment shall be alleged (as I doubt not it will) *against me*, as an act of injustice towards Lord Castlereagh, that it did not originate in my suggestion—that so far from desiring it I conceived, however erroneously, Lord Camden to be the sure channel of communication to Lord Castlereagh, and that up to a very late period I believed such communication to have been actually made.' The Duke replied that he was ready to avow that the 'reserve' had originated with himself, and that he was willing to take the whole of the blame that may have been incurred. He could not understand why Canning should have thought that Castlereagh should have been informed of his intended removal—for the King, having accepted the Duke's advice, had ordered those to whom the secret had been confided, to continue the concealment.

The expedition sailed on 28 July. 'If it succeeds in all its parts,' said Canning (11 Aug.), 'it *will* be a great thing done.' On Wednesday, 2 August, Canning had 'a very satisfactory talk' with the King. In its course he discovered that the Duke had apparently misrepresented Canning's attitude to his (Portland's) plan early in July whereby Canning, retaining the Foreign Secretaryship, should temporarily take over part of the duties of the War Secretary until Wellesley's return from Spain. Canning told his wife of what had passed at his audience: 'I wanted very much an opportunity of letting him know that I had been perfectly ready to agree to *his* plan, but that when another was proposed to be substituted in its room which did not give to me any additional power or business I could not contend for the one which did, without appearing to be actuated by *that* motive. He was very much struck with this, and said, "Why, the Duke told me that you said you could not undertake it, that your hands were so full already that you could not do more." "No such thing, I assure your Majesty. The Duke must have misapprehended me. I did say indeed that when Parliament met I should perhaps find difficulty, but I distinctly and repeatedly said that I was ready to obey your Majesty's commands and to do my best, and that during the Recess I apprehended no difficulty at all." Was this blunder, or trick in the old Duke? I wonder. I went on to say that if I had had *my choice* I would have taken the War Dept. according to H.My.'s plan, rather than not—that the change of plan was not of my suggestion in any degree—that on the contrary I had written to the Duke about the time of the rising of Parliament disclaiming any wish to have to do with the expedition but claiming the Spanish correspondence immediately, and that with the north of Germany *if* anything should ripen there. "Aye," said he, "and whoever has the other Dept., *that must* be in *your* hands still; that cannot be separated from the Foreign Office."' 'All very gracious,' concluded Canning.

On 11 August, as the Duke was going in his carriage to Bulstrode, he had an epileptic fit. He made a partial recovery, but the King began seriously to think of replacing him. The awkwardnesses and jealousies which recent events had produced made it more difficult to carry on the Government without assistance. Camden thought that the only outside help then within reach could come from Melville or Sidmouth; there were objections to both, and the taking in of either would make the other 'a mortal enemy'. If, as was expected, Castlereagh resigned, many of his friends in and out of office would be 'less than lukewarm'. If Canning went out the Government could hardly survive. Camden therefore suggested (17 Aug.) that the King might be asked to consider the idea of an overture to the Opposition.

Towards the end of July the King had authorised Portland to invite Camden to inform Castlereagh of the projected changes, but Camden had expressed such extreme reluctance to be the channel of communication that the Duke ceased to urge him and offered to undertake this disagreeable duty himself. The King told him that since some of his colleagues objected to the measure, their views must be ascertained before any further steps were taken. Nothing was done because the Duke fell gravely ill on the 11th. His family wanted him to resign, but he ignored their strongly expressed wishes because of the difficulty of finding a successor. He told his private secretary, William Dacres Adams, that his colleagues expected him to inform them that he could not continue in office much longer, and to ask them to decide whom he might propose to the King as their future head. It had already been a subject of 'anxious and serious consultation amongst them', but, said Dacres Adams (26 Aug.), reporting a conversation with Arbuthnot, 'I could not make out that they had brought it to any point, for he once said that he should not at all wonder if the Duke's death should totally overthrow the Administration— and yet I thought he [Arbuthnot] had some one person in his head whom *Perceval's* party, at least, from which he gathers his intelligence, would prefer.' The Duke was confident that no Administration under Chatham could last a month, and it was certain that Perceval would not act under him as Chancellor of the Exchequer. Bathurst did not seem to be quite out of the question, though there were many objections to him. Arbuthnot considered Canning the best speaker in the House of Commons, but he spoke only on his own subjects, was no financier, had not much general information, and had no party in the country. The Duke was then much better, but it was obvious, said Dacres Adams, that his colleagues now wanted to get rid of him.

On 28 August, whilst Perceval was writing to Canning and suggesting that Harrowby might be an acceptable Prime Minister, Harrowby himself entered the room and, the idea being mentioned to him, he peremptorily put it aside. Perceval therefore had to abandon it and start another letter to Canning. He said that the precarious state of the Duke's health made it very desirable that his colleagues should be prepared with a plan, and though Robert Dundas had already given 'conditional *notice to quit*' and his defection along with his Scottish friends would be a serious matter, he, Perceval, was nevertheless hopeful that the existing Government could be remodelled from, in the main, existing materials. All his colleagues, he added, wished Castlereagh to remain with them. What did Canning think?

Canning wanted to know whether the Duke had intimated a disposition to resign, since his last illness, and whether the Duke knew that his colleagues were discussing the future of the Ministry. Next day, the 29th, Perceval told Canning that the answer to both questions was No. 'The Duke's probable disposition...is collected solely from what he had told me himself of his actual offer of resignation at an earlier period of the year.' 'No arrangement could appear useful or satisfactory which you did not cordially approve.' Consequently Perceval thought that until Canning's views were known, no communication with the Duke was necessary. Canning replied (on the 29th), saying that, after what had passed between him and the Duke at Easter, he felt a peculiar difficulty in ever again originating the subject with the Duke, and still more in discussing it with others, without the Duke's authorisation.

Canning then discussed the situation with his friends Charles Bagot, Charles Ellis, Boringdon and Granville Leveson (Huskisson was not yet one of his intimates), and on the 30th he wrote to his wife, telling her what he proposed to say to Perceval. 'A Minister, and that Minister in the House of Commons, is essential to the well carrying on of the King's Government in these times. It would be idle to pretend not to see that in the present frame of the Administration the choice of such a Minister must lie between two persons, yourself and me. I am not so presumptuous as to expect that you should acquiesce in *my* being that Minister. And on the other hand, I hope and trust that you will not consider it as any deficiency in esteem or kindness on my part that I should not be disposed to retain my situation under any First Minister in the House of Commons. But I can sincerely accompany this declaration with another—that if that character shall devolve upon *you*, I shall in retiring from my office, carry with me the most perfect goodwill and good humour —and (I will not say a *pledge*—because a pledge of that sort no man should give) but a disposition cordially to support, out of office, a Government so constituted.' He went on: 'This is my notion, and most of those whom I have mentioned agree in it. Leveson especially thinks that it will bring things to the right issue. But I have not seen Charles Ellis, and I want my own dearest love's full opinion.'

The King saw Canning that day, presumably at the Levée, but all the conversation that Canning reported to his wife was confined to one observation: 'Knobbs told me today that he had found out she [Lady Boringdon] was an apothecary's daughter at Lynn—and laughed.'

Perceval told Canning (on the 30th) that the King too had said that in view of the Duke's state of health his colleagues should be considering what to do. Would this remove Canning's difficulties? Whereas Canning had apparently been prepared to serve under Lord Chatham, that solution was now obviously out of the question and he repeated in substance what he had already outlined to his wife. Perceval replied the same day (the 31st). Neither would serve under the other as Prime Minister, and Perceval, whilst agreeing that the First Minister ought to be in the Commons, expressed the hope that the Government might be kept together with a Peer at the head. He wished to consult others before deciding what to do about

Canning's claims to the Premiership. Liverpool agreed (3 September) that as he was Leader of the House of Commons, and therefore the second man in the Government, he would sacrifice more by serving under Canning than Canning would sacrifice by serving under him. 'If *you two* cannot agree upon a *third*, some fundamental change must take place.' He explained: 'I cannot think that Canning by consenting to your being *Minister* would bring any personal degradation upon himself. It would make no alteration either in *his office* or in his *present station* in the House of Commons, and if in consequence of the other arrangements he should be the only Secretary of State in that House, the nature of his office and the character of his talents would secure to him a degree of consideration in the House, in the Government and in the country upon the whole perhaps not inferior to your own. But by your consenting to *his* becoming *Minister* you would relinquish both your *present office* and your *present station* in the House of Commons. There is no other office which you would be disposed to accept which would give you any relative weight or consequence there or would make your situation as second to him at all to be compared to his situation as second to you . . . I can add in confidence that I am convinced this latter arrangement would meet with other difficulties which would prove at this time unsurmountable.' 'What these are I do not know,' Perceval commented, in an endorsement.

On the 3rd Portland received another letter from Canning respecting the substitution of Wellesley for Castlereagh at the War Office. He said that 'the pressure in point of time' was becoming much more urgent, and that 'the period was arrived, according to H.M.'s gracious promise, communicated to him by me, that Lord Wellesley was to be called to the office of Secretary of State' (Portland was quoting Canning in a letter to Perceval). The Duke commented, 'No consideration will induce me to proceed farther in this most unfortunate transaction until I shall receive the King's farther commands, which I shall not ask for 'till I pay my duty to his Majesty in person on next Wednesday.'

The situation had suddenly become tense again because of the arrival on the 2nd of the news that Sir Arthur Wellesley had retreated across the Tagus, and that Lord Chatham had announced his determination to return home without attacking Antwerp. This meant that the Walcheren expedition had ended in disaster and disgrace, and Canning's letter to Portland at once followed.

Perceval had called on Canning a day or two earlier, repeating in greater detail what he had said in his letter: 'that if his own feelings alone and not his reputation and what others might feel for him were concerned, he would serve under me as Secretary of State, for the Home Department for instance, the only political office for which (he says) he can think himself fit, in the House of Commons. This,' Canning wrote to his wife (1 Sept.), '*I* own, *I* could not bear. It would *hurt me for him*. It would be a great humiliation. My wish was that he should be a Peer and President of the Council. But a Peerage he tells me he could not take. It would be ruinous to his family. Nothing could be more candid, more manly, more modest and more kind than Perceval's whole behaviour. The person whom he had in contemplation after Harrowby was Lord Bathurst. I once had him in contemplation. Perhaps he would be the best for such an arrangement if such an arrangement would do. But the other is the only one that is fit for the times. Perceval's difficulty about the Peerage, however, throws an unforeseen and most formidable difficulty in the way. For I *cannot* consent to his being disgraced even if upon reflection he should come prepared to say he will take the Home Department in the House of Commons.'

On 4 September Perceval suggested to Portland the one solution which would prevent a blow-up with Castlereagh: the Government should be remodelled entirely and Castlereagh need know nothing of what had been happening. The Duke expressed his readiness to resign in order to 'prevent the explosion that threatens us'. On the 6th Portland saw Canning and told him that if he insisted on Castlereagh's resignation, other members of the Cabinet would go out; and the Duke proposed that he himself should resign and Castlereagh be removed to some other office. Canning agreed not to press for the fulfilment of the King's promise, but said that he must resign with the Duke, whose decision to retire would create new difficulties.

On the 6th the Duke tendered his resignation at the Levée, and the King said he would accept it as soon as a successor had been selected. Bathurst too saw the King that day; the King told him he was anxious to keep Canning as being essential to the Government, but that if he had to choose between him and Perceval, he would choose Perceval, who was 'the most straightforward man he had almost ever known'. The Duke told Canning that he was resigning as a means of facilitating a Cabinet reconstruction, and that unless this step was taken other members of the Government might go. Canning thereupon refused to attend the Cabinet meeting on the 7th when Foreign Office business was to be discussed, and wrote to the Duke that day saying that he would not be the cause of the King's losing the services of anyone except Castlereagh, and desired his own resignation might be accepted. During the next few days he busied himself winding up arrears of official business but felt unable to make himself responsible for any new matter. (On 19 September, however, he did attend a Cabinet meeting to lay before it the draft of a despatch to Lord Wellesley. 'All this time,' he wrote to Granville Leveson that day, 'I have heard nothing from the King or from anybody in his name, and therefore do not regularly know whether I am out or in.')

On the evening of the 7th, at dinner, Castlereagh pressed Camden so strongly about Canning's absence from the Cabinet meeting, and asked questions which could hardly be answered without persisting in a concealment which Camden felt had lasted too long, that he had to tell him nearly the whole story, 'softened in many respects'. The promise made with respect to Wellesley was not mentioned. Camden told Bathurst next day: 'He received it firmly and reasonably but I think he conceives *me* to have acted unkindly to him in suffering an expedition to take place when I knew the ground on which he stood. I have felt this circumstance so much myself that I am not surprised at his feeling it, and it certainly is very painful to me and only excusable on my part from the representations made to me of the danger which might accrue from his being informed of the state of things at that time.'

On the 8th Castlereagh tendered his resignation to the King; according to custom he remained in office, like Canning, until his successor was appointed. As early as the 12th Perceval began canvassing for support, as if the King's choice had already fallen on him; and on the 13th the King instructed him to consult his colleagues about ways and means of remodelling the Government. He believed that the King would advise him to make an overture to Lord Grey. 'We must make the best battle we can,' he had said (9 Sept.), almost anticipating failure, 'rather than desert' the King. He urged Robert Dundas, who had pledged himself to support Canning, to come to no decision before hearing from him again, and he enquired of the Speaker (on the 12th) whether there was the least prospect of his accepting a Secretaryship of State. On the other hand he now completely ignored Portland, who resented being kept in the dark about what was going on. The Duke had to rely on Canning for information. He deprecated the idea of a junction with the Whigs and believed that the Government could be reconstructed from existing materials. Perceval's brother Lord Arden thought that the approach to Grey was the least objectionable of any that could be made. 'You must not write as if the cause was at all hopeless without his assistance,' he advised, 'for if you do he will assuredly require carte blanche.' If Grey proved unreasonable and the King asked Ministers to stand by him, Arden was confident that the battle could be won. His diagnosis proved to be accurate: 'Bad as the times are, and lowered as the King's authority and influence is, I still think that the constitutional prerogative, his Majesty's character and steady resolution will (as they have often proved before) be sufficient to uphold an Administration of his own choice that mean nothing but the public good, and are resolved to stand by and support the Crown— but then there must be no wavering, no more concessions to levellers and reformers.'

Canning's long account of his audience of the King on 13 September is printed in the correspondence, and he summarised it in a letter to his wife. He was no longer prepared, as he had been in the spring, to serve with Perceval under Lord Chatham or any other Peer, consequently the King had to choose between him and Perceval. He must have known that, in view of the King's dislike of him, his chances of success were negligible. The King, who told him he would seriously consider the matter, was at first a little agitated, but 'afterwards grew quite calm and patient and good humoured'. Portland and then Perceval preceded him. He told his wife: 'When I came into the Closet the King began upon all sorts of subjects with most perfect good humour and kindness, but rather, I suppose, wishing to avoid this. However, when he had run himself down I began with saying that the D. of P. had told me what had passed between them—that I had therefore the less to say to his Majesty—but that I was sure his Majesty would hear what I thought it my duty to say to him with his accustomed goodness. He encouraged me to go on, and then on I went to a most complete and full exposition of all my views and feelings... He heard me throughout with a patience, a kindness and generally speaking a degree of approbation beyond what I could have expected. I told him that I of course expected no decision on so important a question today. He said it *was* important, that he would consider of it most seriously; that all that I had stated was clear and plain, and that he gave me credit for the openness and sincerity of my conduct—that he was sorry that the necessity of such a statement had arisen, but thought I did my duty in making it to him—and thanked me.' Canning concluded: 'If my own love asks me what will be the result, really I cannot tell, but I rather think the more probable is—really I hardly know which is the more probable—but this I think is assured—that *if* I go out I go out without quarrelling with Knobbs, and that was the grand point of all.'

Tierney as usual knew a good deal of what was going on, and on 13 September informed Grey that, at a meeting the previous evening, Perceval, Eldon and Liverpool had decided that he (Grey) and Grenville must be sent for immediately and offered six or seven seats in the Cabinet. Tierney's informant was his friend Colonel J. W. Gordon, to whom Perceval's private secretary, J. C. Herries (afterwards, 1827, Chancellor of the Exchequer) had communicated the news. Tierney thought that Canning would have to 'knock under', that Bathurst would be Prime Minister, and that the King would probably not consent to Wellesley's introduction into the Cabinet, partly from personal dislike, partly because he was one of Canning's political friends. 'If the Ministers were anything but what they are,' he wrote again to Grey (15 Sept.), 'they would go out of themselves, and if the country was anything but what it is, it would turn them out, but such is the nature of the one and the other that the Government will be allowed to hang together.'

Sir Thomas Plumer, the Solicitor-General, warned Perceval on the 14th that his supporters in the Commons would react unfavourably to an overture to the Whig Opposition. He ought carefully to examine the list of M.P.s with the aid of his experienced political 'jockies'—such as Huskisson and Charles Long. The resignations of Canning and Castlereagh would mean loss of support; the 'Scotch Legion' would defect if Lord Melville were not taken in; many other members would disapprove of a junction with the Whigs; many good friends would be alienated by having to make way for a new party. How many could be gained to balance such losses? 'It is of the last importance to consider this again and again before you take an irrevocable step which may sink and degrade your own party and elevate your opponents.' In view of the state of public opinion, still under the influence of the 'Wardle mania', to dissolve Parliament might be quite risky. Huskisson, said Plumer, had 'correct knowledge of the state of the House of Commons and the leanings and connections and opinions of everyone in it, superior to what I believe anyone else possesses'. This warning may well have been reinforced by Robert Dundas's reply (15th) to Perceval's fishing letter of the 12th: he would not wish to adopt any course that might be at variance with his father's views.

Perceval went on canvassing for support. Sturges-Bourne, one of the Lords of the Treasury, was sent for on the 14th, but replied that he should act with Canning, who was fairly confident on the 15th that Huskisson too would follow him. Charles Long told Canning, also on the 15th, that the whole inclination of his mind was to go with him, as Pitt's truest successor, and that his patron, Lord Lonsdale, was similarly inclined. The statement was then accurate, but in the end the Earl adhered to Perceval. George Rose was sent for by Bathurst; Granville Leveson (much to his surprise) was questioned by Harrowby. Canning was anxiously awaiting the outcome of events, and wondering to what extent Perceval would be successful as a recruiting sergeant. 'The suspense is most certainly very nervous,' he told his wife on the 15th. 'It must end on Wednesday. Meantime I see nobody—of Cabinet I mean— except the poor old D. But I understand constant meetings and co-jobberations (as Lady Crewe would call them) are going on at P.'s. Castgh. has disappeared as through a trapdoor. Chuckle (Camd.) called upon me yesterday by (his) appointment to explain why he had not broke the matter to Castgh. sooner—and to say the truth he cleared himself of any fault in that particular.' As late as the 20th Canning expressed his willingness to form a Government. He told Portland that he could have done so easily a week earlier; it was daily becoming more difficult, but even then he would undertake it 'with a good prospect of success'.

Perceval discussed the situation with the King on the 19th, three days before the King replied to the Cabinet Minute of the 18th. The Catholic question completely filled the King's mind and conscience, and Perceval had great difficulty in persuading him to sanction an overture to the Whigs. Grey and Grenville would never give a written pledge (which Pitt had given in 1804 and which Grenville had refused to give in March 1807) that Catholic emancipation would be left in abeyance. Perceval tried to reassure the King by telling him that if a Coalition Ministry was formed, the Catholic question would not be supported as a Cabinet measure (and that, in fact, was to be precisely the situation in 1827 when the Lansdowne Whigs coalesced with Canning). To insist on such a pledge would at once ensure the failure of the negotiations. 'Then,' replied the King, 'I am driven to the wall and would be deserted.' Perceval told him that if they made an ineffectual attempt to form a Ministry on their own, they would be defeated and would be unable to stand between him and the wall. 'Then,' said the King, 'they [the Whigs] should take the Government to themselves.' He would have nothing to do with it; they should not have his name. 'Oh, Sir,' replied Perceval, 'what an extremity your Majesty is contemplating! What would become of your Majesty's country?' After Perceval had assured the King that a coalition would mean the shelving of a Catholic Relief Bill, the King expressed great reluctance to send for Grenville as well as Grey, and wished to try Grey first, but when Perceval told him that to send for Grenville afterwards would be even more unpleasant, he appeared to acquiesce, but repeated his objections to an overture to the Opposition because of the Catholic question.

Before the King sent a considered reply to the Cabinet Minute, Castlereagh challenged Canning to a duel, and the famous meeting took place on Putney Heath on the 21st: that is, after more than a week's perfectly cool deliberation by Castlereagh and consultation with his friends. Castlereagh communicated his views to his Under-Secretary, Edward Cooke, on the 16th. His resignation did not mean that he would necessarily refuse office in the next Administration. True, his confidence in his colleagues had been badly shaken, but if the King expressly commanded him to resume office he was ready to do so, provided that he approved of those who would be associated with him. He had no preference for any particular office but, he added, 'circumstances have placed all accommodation in this respect beyond the reach of my consideration and control...I wish it distinctly to be understood that in whatever respects the campaigns in Spain and Holland (however glorious to the British army) have in their result disappointed our hopes...that I cannot submit to charge myself with any excessive portion of the blame (if any blame at all exists) which may be thrown upon these failures.' He therefore concluded (and the statement explains why he was not in Perceval's Cabinet): 'If my colleagues, whose support and confidence I had no reason to doubt accompanied me throughout my late anxious and laborious duties, are either *unable* or *unwilling* to sustain me in that situation, I desire in that case only the privilege of being allowed to defend out of office my own public character and conduct.'

Castlereagh was almost as critical of the conduct of his colleagues who had been prepared to stand by him as he was of Canning himself, who had been made 'absolute master' of his fate. He spoke of the 'infatuation and folly' of those who called themselves his friends, who had placed him in a situation full of danger and of dishonour. 'Preserve me from my friends, and I shall not fear my enemies.' Referring to the idea of covering his fall by giving him his uncle's office of President of the Council, he said, 'I should well have deserved all the mortification that has been prepared for me...if I could have lent myself to such an idea.'

Castlereagh, then, did not act without due deliberation, and it was not until 19 September that he finally decided to challenge his enemy to a duel. Edward Cooke declared, 'I combatted for a long time against my judgment the decision his own mind had taken.' Colonel J. W. Gordon, who was also consulted, gave it as his opinion that nothing had passed which would justify a hostile meeting. The challenge, sent on the 19th through his second, Lord Yarmouth, was worded in a manner which precluded discussion. Charles Ellis, Canning's closest friend, acted as *his* second, after Henry Wellesley had declined to do so. On the night of the 20th the two seconds met at Henry Wellesley's house and tried in vain to reach a settlement. Ellis said that in his opinion Castlereagh was proposing to take a step which had no justification. Canning had not originally demanded Castlereagh's dismissal from the War Department; his first letter to Portland had been the consequence of his dissatisfaction at the general state of the Government. The time of effecting the change in the War Department was not left at his option, nor was it of his choice. Castlereagh's friends were equally guilty; it was they who had insisted on the concealment (and so had the King). Castlereagh admitted that Portland's conduct was as bad as, if not worse than, Canning's, but *he* did not have to fight because of his age and infirmity, and it was felt that Canning had aggravated his offence by taking advantage of the Duke's failings as a cover for intrigue. Castlereagh's friends had insisted that nothing should be done until the return of the expedition—in spite of Canning's warning that the outcome of Walcheren might be such as to render the execution of the arrangement still more unpleasant to Castlereagh's feelings.

Yarmouth reported Charles Ellis's facts to Castlereagh, but they produced no change in his feelings. Canning wrote to his wife a letter of farewell and made his Will. The meeting took place about 6 a.m. the next morning (the 21st) at Lord Yarmouth's cottage on Putney Heath. It was arranged that the two combatants should fire at the same moment, Ellis saying that Canning had no pretension whatever to the first fire. Yarmouth said to him, 'I conclude it is not your wish to render this business more desperate than is necessary,' and, Ellis agreeing, the distance was fixed at twelve paces, the longest of which there was any precedent. When Canning was given the pistol Ellis said to Yarmouth, 'I must cock it for him for I cannot trust him to do it himself. He has never fired a pistol in his life.' Ellis then took Yarmouth aside and said he thought that the affair should be settled on the ground that the concealment had taken place by the King's command (a fact which, out of loyalty to the Sovereign, was never publicly revealed). This statement was flatly disregarded, and Castlereagh thought it was quite improper to bring it forward at that awkward moment. The first shot was fired; both parties missed. Yarmouth suggested to Castlereagh that the matter had gone far enough. But Canning felt unable to offer further explanation or an apology; he said that he had no grievance against Castlereagh, and that Castlereagh must decide when he was satisfied. Yarmouth observed to Ellis, 'It is a pity, then, as no mischief is yet done, that Mr Canning did not fire in the air—the business might then have stopped here. I fear now they must fire another shot, but I hope you will agree with me, whatever may be the result of this shot, not to allow the business to proceed further.' Ellis replied, 'It can on no account be allowed to proceed further.'

The second shot hit Canning in the fleshy part of the thigh, the bullet going straight through without touching either a bone or an artery. Castlereagh himself assisted Canning in walking into Yarmouth's house. Two hours later Canning was back at Gloucester Lodge, lying quietly on a sofa, without fever and with very little pain, writing reassuringly to his Leigh cousins and being looked after by Charles Ellis until the arrival of Mrs Canning from Hinckley. When he was well enough to attend the Levée the King 'was as kind as possible. He made me point out to him on his own thigh the precise place of my wound, and said (which is more than I expected) that I could not do otherwise than I did in accepting the challenge, though he mortally disapproves of duels.' Canning added (11 Oct.), 'He expressed the greatest regret at my going out of office.'

Everyone naturally regretted the meeting at Putney. Perceval was critical of Castlereagh's conduct, telling Portland on the 21st, 'Surely Castlereagh misconceived the case very much, and I fear this event must lead to a detail of explanation and exposure that it is most desirable to avoid.' Lord Buckinghamshire, who shared his friend Sidmouth's dislike of Canning, had a certain sympathy for him. On being shown a confidential memorandum by Edward Cooke which embodied Castlereagh's case, he commented, 'If Lord Castlereagh's statement be well founded, much as I reprobate Canning's conduct, I hardly know why he was so pointedly distinguished from some of his colleagues.' William Brodrick, who remained in office at the Treasury Board, was shown the relevant correspondence from March onwards, and wrote to Arbuthnot, 'The impression made upon my mind by these letters is that Canning is exonerated from much blame for his conduct towards Castlereagh. It appears to me that the latter has more reason to complain of the Duke of Portland and Lord Camden, who have erred from good nature and weakness, than he has of Canning.' Lord Liverpool blamed chiefly the Duke, who, he said, had 'most unfairly' extracted from the King the promise that Castlereagh should be removed without the knowledge of most of his Cabinet colleagues. Sidmouth declared, 'A base and insulting injury was offered to Lord Castlereagh, but his nearest friend in the Cabinet...was the person of whose conduct he had the greatest reason to complain.' Robert Dundas criticised Canning for his bid for the Premiership, not for his earlier actions: 'Every day only serves to confirm the first impression which I felt on hearing of Canning's *exclusive* claim, because I am satisfied it will be prejudicial to his character in the estimation of the country. It is the more provoking, because on perusing the whole of his correspondence with the Duke of Portland and Perceval, it appears to me to be the only point or proposition which he has stated (except one or two connected with it) which he can have any cause to repent or regret.' Dundas, however, even as late as 21 September, told Perceval that he had been perfectly willing to serve under Canning as Prime Minister, and still was, if the King desired him to form a Coalition Ministry. He was equally willing to serve under Perceval, but said that if either of the two tried to form a Government from amongst themselves, the basis would be too narrow and he himself could take no part.

On 23 September Perceval, having received the King's authorisation written the previous day, wrote identical letters to Lords Grey and Grenville, inviting them to come to town to discuss the formation of 'an extended and combined Administration'. Replying from Boconnoc, his Cornish home, on the 25th, Grenville accepted the invitation to London, construing it as 'official signification of his Majesty's pleasure'. Grey refused, on the ground that the invitation did not come from the King himself. Expecting the summons, he had already decided to turn a deaf ear to anything but a direct message from the Sovereign, and his friend Lord Lauderdale, writing to him on the 23rd, fully agreed. Grey would have insisted on full latitude in forming another Government, but Lauderdale warned him that he could not go further and demand unlimited support for measures (a demand which would in effect, if acceded to, have abolished the Sovereign's preliminary veto over legislation). The country, said Lauderdale, remembering the events of March 1807, would construe such a demand into forcing Catholic emancipation down the King's throat. To oppose him on a matter of conscience would have the appearance of harshness and be most impolitic, especially at such a time; and he added: 'If you look to the mischiefs that have been done to the country within these two years it it would be profligate to do anything which, by raising a cry, might empower these people to go on.' Lauderdale thought that Grey should content himself with stipulating for a moderate Relief Bill with adequate safeguards for the Establishment, and in particular the King must have the right to veto the appointment of Catholic Bishops. The King's fears would then be set at rest, and in view of the schism in Ireland on the subject of the Veto, that solution would be the best for the country. Lauderdale, however, was surely deluding himself in thinking that the King could be induced to accept even this modest proposal. Thomas Grenville, too, thought that if the King himself were to make overtures to the Whig Lords, with limitations and restrictions on the Catholic question, they would disgrace themselves by accepting office on such terms; by refusing such an offer they would enable their Tory opponents to raise the old cry of Church and King, and inflame the people into the belief that they must rally round their aged and suffering Sovereign against the Whig Lords, the Pope and the Whore of Babylon. However wicked, the cry would be piously promoted and zealously sustained in every parish in the country.

Grey had no wish for office. He 'trembled' at the mere thought of 'the dreadful responsibility of being called upon to take any share in the Government'. The country's situation appalled him even as a spectator: three British armies and twenty millions of money had been squandered within nine months, he said. 'Certain ruin...must result from a perseverance in the fatal system of the two last years.' He considered the proposition for a junction as 'utterly inadmissible' and, anxious to show the steadiness of his resolution and to put an end to the false hopes and speculations to which his appearance in London would give rise, he decided, with just a little misgiving as to the rightness of his course of action, to remain at Howick. Grenville, thinking that a refusal to come to town might be liable to misconstruction, Perceval's letter being, possibly, a signification of the King's pleasure, and that his journey would have the advantage of affording easy communication with friends, set off for London. He thought it just possible that he and Grey would receive commands from the King himself to form a Government, but he also feared that the summons meant nothing more than 'a miserable trick for laying ground to appeal to the country against our unreasonableness'. Grey trusted to Perceval's honour not to make an unfair representation to the King of his answer but, to secure himself against all possible danger he asked Tierney to arrange that his reply to Perceval did actually reach the King through 'our friend'— Colonel Gordon evidently—either through the Duke of York or the Duke of Cumberland. To make assurance doubly sure, Tierney gave a copy of the letter to Lord George Cavendish, who undertook to put it into the hands of the 'quite friendly' Duke of York; the Duke would see to it that it was read 'at headquarters with proper emphasis'.

On the 25th Grey replied to Perceval's letter: a coalition was out of the question, and he told the Prince of Wales, 'It was impossible for me to hope that I could act usefully...in conjunction with men who came into office on the principles of the late Administration.' Grenville sent his final reply from London on the 29th, after hearing of Grey's decision: a union could be considered only as a dereliction of public principle.

Grenville correctly surmised that the indisposition towards any real change was still very great at Windsor, the Catholic question being the formidable difficulty. And information which Grey received from an authoritative quarter supported this view. He said that when Perceval and Liverpool took to the King the drafts of the letters to the two Lords on 23 September (the letters were despatched late that night) the King laid a positive injunction on them not to trouble him with any further communication on the subject until the whole had been definitely settled. 'This', said Grey, 'could only be meant to preclude any personal intercourse with Lord Grenville and myself, and as a mark to the public of the extreme reluctance with which he was brought to authorize any application to us.'

Grey himself would have wished to avoid an initial confrontation with the King on the Catholic question, saying that it would have been inadvisable to risk creating divisions in public opinion at that stage. But he could not have consented to the exclusion of that question from all consideration. 'When I said a full explanation must take place, I meant as to how much weight might be conceded, or what securities might be provided in carrying the measure, to satisfy the King's mind and to obviate the objections which are generally made to it. But it never came into my head that a doubt could be entertained as to the necessity of *some* arrangement on this subject. If this resolution is to be considered as a positive bar during the King's life I must submit to it, for there is no earthly inducement that can engage me to abandon it.'

But the views of the two Lords were not held by all their friends, and this division of opinion continued until the Relief Act of 1829 settled the matter. Tierney, for one, refused to pledge himself in this sense (and he showed his consistency by taking office under Canning in 1827). He wrote to Grey: 'Supposing the demand of a pledge to be abandoned, the question then arising for consideration amongst ourselves will be, shall Catholic emancipation (guarding the Established Church by such securities as may be thought reasonable and sufficient) be brought forward? If that be decided in the affirmative and pronounced indispensable as the condition of taking office, and the King be resolved not to agree to it, then, before I commit myself to a course of action and systematic Party opposition I must be convinced that by so doing I have a reasonable prospect of carrying the point contended for by getting the sense of the country with me against the prejudices of the Crown, and making my way by numbers...If the general sense of the country...is...with the King I must be forgiven if I pause before I commit myself, in the present state of public affairs and in a House of Commons such as exists at this day, to a system of regular opposition.'

Lord Holland was well satisfied with the outcome. His view had been that the Whigs should not take office without insisting on their own terms and making the King 'eat humble pie'. Lord Morpeth rejoiced that his friends were to have nothing to do with 'the champions of Protestant ascendancy, the instigators of the cry of No Popery'.

Sidmouth thought that Grenville's determination to take his stand on the ground he took in March 1807 meant that he made even Perceval's weak Government impregnable, for neither Parliament nor public opinion would tolerate an attempt to force the King to capitulate. The events of 1810 showed how far from impregnable was the Government's position in the House of Commons, yet it was not in vain that the King now called on his Ministers to stand by him. Grenville thought the country would support them: 'I do not see why they should not succeed as well as before.' Perceval's position was far from hopeless. The Government had been badly mutilated by the defection of Canning and his friends, and of Castlereagh with a smaller number of adherents. 'We are no longer the sole representatives of Mr Pitt,' Perceval had to admit. 'The magic of that name is in a great degree dissolved.' He got to the heart of the matter when he said, 'The principle on which we must rely to keep us together and give us the assistance of floating strength, is the public sentiment of loyalty and attachment to the King. Among the independent part of the House, the country gentlemen, the representatives of popular boroughs, we shall find our saving strength or our destruction.' This illustrates once more the accuracy of the statement that the Governments of this period were defeated not by their enemies but by their friends.

The Opposition itself was in no position to defeat anybody. It hardly existed. Writing to Grey on 26 October, Tierney tried to answer his question whether an Opposition could be formed, and if so, whether it would be prudent to take that step. Tierney had to admit that great numbers had fallen off amongst those who had formerly acted with them, and if the Whig leaders had formed a Ministry with Perceval and his friends, many of their supporters would have remained on the Opposition benches—as actually happened in 1827 when the Lansdowne Whigs coalesced with Canning. 'The party which was formed when we came out of office', said Tierney, 'is in my view of things at an end.' If most of the Whigs decided against taking office during the King's reign unless they were empowered to carry a Catholic Relief Bill, Tierney would not belong to such a party: 'not only because I should hold it to be madness to embark on a crusade against the power of the Crown and the sense of the country united, but because I should not think myself warranted systematically to oppose a Government, if I overthrow which, I cannot replace'.

On 2 October the King, accepting the Cabinet's unanimous advice, commissioned Perceval to succeed Portland as First Lord of the Treasury, and he kissed hands on the 4th. Following the precedent set by Lord North in 1770, he did not vacate his seat: it was not a new appointment but merely an advancement at the same Board. 'This appears to me very absurd,' remarked the ex-Speaker, Lord Sidmouth, 'as it does to Hatsell' (the Clerk of the House). But Perceval's view was supported by the Lord Chancellor and by Speaker Abbot (and this was decisive). Perceval had no intention of remaining Chancellor of the Exchequer, and he ultimately did so only because his efforts to find one proved unsuccessful. The Duke of Richmond, who was prepared strenuously to stand by the King in an attempt to continue 'the old Pittite system', regretted that the choice had not fallen either on Harrowby or on Bathurst. Lord Lowther told his father Lord Lonsdale that Perceval had 'neither weight or character sufficient to lead the House of Commons', and he added, 'Ministers appear to have no confidence one with another.'

The reconstruction of the Government took two months. Perceval at once invited Portland to remain in the Cabinet without office. The Duke agreed to stay, but he died before the end of the month. Lord Liverpool somewhat reluctantly moved to the War Department. Castlereagh was naturally not invited to return there nor was he offered any other office: he would have refused such an offer in any case. Richard Ryder succeeded Liverpool as Home Secretary. Eldon, Westmorland and Camden remained where they were. Continuing ill health compelled Harrowby to resign the Board of Control and to refuse Bathurst's generous offer to relinquish to him the less arduous post of President of the Board of Trade. Harrowby remained in the Cabinet without portfolio. After protracted negotiations Robert Dundas succeeded him at the India Board and was brought into the Cabinet. The initial suggestion was that Dundas should succeed Castlereagh as Secretary of State. He was fit for any situation, said the Duke of Richmond, who, as Lord Lieutenant of Ireland, had learnt to appreciate his talents.

But Dundas found himself awkwardly situated. As early as 17 September he had told his father, 'If there is any intention to patch up the form of a new Administration out of the remnants of the present, I certainly will not belong to it or continue in office.' His father raised difficulties. Earlier in the year Melville had expressed the hope that he might again be offered a place, though he admitted, 'If any proposition comes, it is most probable it will be so late as to render the acceptance of it undignified and of course impossible.' His financial situation was still not easy. He told Lord Lonsdale on 15 July that he had long since lost all desire for office, but at that moment he might have felt that there was no prospect of its being offered. Perceval now proposed to give him an Earldom as a mark of the King's approbation of his past services, but expressed regret that he could not invite him to take office because such an invitation would give offence to 'certain descriptions of persons in the House of Commons'—in other words, to 'Saints' and country gentlemen. Perceval was also afraid of Addresses pouring in from the provinces in protest against the appointment of a man who had suffered impeachment. In the end (8 Oct.) the Earldom was declined, but six days earlier Melville had warned his son against accepting the War Secretaryship until he knew who were to be his colleagues and what situations they were to fill. And on 8 October Melville told him he must never forget that he was 'connected with a great and powerful interest which has long wished, and that too very recently, for my return to office as essential to their having any confidence in the Administration even at a period when it was stronger than it is likely now to be. I cannot take it upon me to predict what may be their feelings on the present occasion. I shall see the Duke of Buccleuch, Lord Lonsdale and other friends soon. I trust they will all cordially concur with me in the sentiments I have already conveyed to you.' Melville, in any case, would prefer to see his son at the head of the Board of Control (with all its India patronage) than with the Seals of the War Secretaryship.

Dundas was much hurt by his father's letter, but said he could not accept office without his father's consent. On 24 October he received from his father a letter which almost compelled him to refuse office, and it apparently marked the end of Melville's determination to support the King. Perceval was much distressed, and Eldon no longer felt able to see his way through the enveloping cloud; if Dundas failed them and the 'Scotch Legion' went against them, the Government stood no chance of survival. Two days later, however, Dundas received another letter which gave him full liberty to act as he thought right, but it was suggested that he ought to return to the India Board. He told Perceval he would take that office. Perceval wanted him in the Cabinet, but a decision on this point was postponed until Melville came to town. 'We shall all go on heartily together now,' said Dundas with great satisfaction, and he accepted a seat in the Cabinet. Charles Long remarked, 'I wish he had been placed as at first intended. The present arrangement is the best that could be made under the circumstances, but Lord

Liverpool will not make so good a War Minister as Robert Dundas. The War Minister should certainly be in the House of Commons.'

When Chatham returned from the Continent he announced that he would attend no more Cabinet meetings until his colleagues had approved his conduct during the campaign. Then on 19 September he received from the King a letter in which his conduct was given a general approval. He therefore considered himself as entirely blameless and proceeded to transact business as usual. But he involved the King personally in a highly controversial manner, setting up the King's opinion as superseding that of his colleagues. On 14 October he had written a defence of his conduct of the expedition, and this Narrative, dated the 15th, was presented to the King, unknown to the Cabinet, on 15 January 1810. If he had kept secret the fact that he had given this paper privately to the King, all might have been well, but he chose to inform his Staff and the Generals who had served under him. Moreover, his *Narrative* tended not merely to vindicate his own conduct but to throw blame on the commander of the fleet, Sir Richard Strachan. Perceval was in no position to be unduly censorious and Chatham was allowed to stay, but the parliamentary investigation that quickly followed compelled him to resign on 7 March. The King would have liked him to remain Master-General, but in any case Mulgrave would not have continued in office with him.

Charles Yorke was still too poor to quarrel with his brother Lord Hardwicke, who supported Grenville, and he refused the Foreign Secretaryship, the War Secretaryship, the office of Secretary at War, and the Chancellorship of the Exchequer, much to Perceval's dismay. It was a cruel aggravation of the Government's misfortunes, he said.

It was not until December that Bathurst was relieved of the burden of the Foreign Secretaryship. On 5 October Perceval wrote to Wellesley offering him the Seals. The Marquess hastened home from Spain, arriving in London on 28 November, and soon afterwards went to Gloucester Lodge to see Canning. A misunderstanding had to be removed. Wellesley had been given the erroneous impression that Canning had resigned because he was not to be Prime Minister. After hearing Canning's explanation he admitted that he had been deceived, that Canning's motives were 'clear' and his conduct 'consistent throughout'. Canning accused Perceval of trickery, but it was Wellesley-Pole who had caused misunderstanding. Wellesley was under the erroneous impression that Perceval had written to Canning offering to serve under Wellesley as Prime Minister, if he would too, and that Canning had deprived him of the Premiership by insisting that the Prime Minister must be in the Commons. Wellesley, in fact, had been wrongly informed by his brother, Wellesley-Pole. Wellesley had already accepted the Foreign Secretaryship, the news of his acceptance arriving a few days before he landed at Portsmouth.

At first there was no intention of inviting the support of the Sidmouth party. The 'Scotch Legion' was more numerous, and the Government could not have both. Robert Dundas, whilst recognising the extent of Perceval's difficulties, told Harrowby that he was very doubtful about the feelings of his friends. 'I will not answer for them,' he said. 'It would undoubtedly be a material object to attain it if we do not purchase it too dearly. A *hearty* support is in general more useful than an occasional display of members.' Charles Long declared that if Sidmouth came in he would deprive the Government of as much strength as he brought with him.

On 5 October Perceval sent Chatham to discuss matters with Sidmouth. Chatham said he was not charged with an *overture*. Perceval wished to suspend filling up the remaining vacancies until he knew the disposition of Sidmouth and of his friends in the House of Commons, who alone, it was admitted, were in Perceval's contemplation. The only offices likely to be available were those which had been filled by Huskisson, Wellesley-Pole and Sturges-Bourne. Bragge-Bathurst and Benjamin Hobhouse were mentioned as possible recruits, but not Hiley Addington nor Vansittart. Bragge-Bathurst could have had the office of Secretary at War with a seat in the Cabinet, it was later intimated. If the overture had proved successful Sidmouth would have insisted on a Cabinet office for Buckinghamshire too, but Sidmouth had to bear the mortification of hearing from Perceval himself on 7 October that amongst some of the Government's warmest supporters, 'of the old Pitt connexion', there were several who were so prejudiced against his coming in that an offer would completely alienate them and perhaps drive them into Canning's camp. And there were others 'whose election between the seceders from the late Administration and those who remain is not yet decisively made and pledged,' who might choose to withhold their support. 'Some men's minds are so loose and unsettled at this moment, every feather may sway them.' Perceval could only express the hope that this unfavourable impression would wear off. Bragge-Bathurst made the interesting comment that the prejudice against his brother-in-law possibly came from the 'highest quarter'.

Sidmouth heard from Lord Chatham that Lord Lonsdale was one of the prejudiced people, and this was his explanation, fanciful though it may have been: 'This disposition...arose from my refusal to continue him his accustomed patronage after he had ceased to support my Government.' A more likely explanation is that Lonsdale had never forgiven him his treatment of Pitt in 1805.

Writing to Bragge-Bathurst, Sidmouth declared: 'The rest of the malcontents alluded to by Perceval consist, I dare say, of persons whose names would probably occur to you if you were to ask yourself who were the sourest, the shabbiest or the silliest of the supporters of the late Government.' His friends who, like all other party formations, believed in hunting in a pack, were outraged by Perceval's attempts to 'pick off individuals', as Wellington later characterised such tactics. Buckinghamshire thought that Perceval had acted 'upon the vilest principle that ever a public man ventured to found his proceedings', and that he would do well to 'expand his mind beyond the narrow limits of the Inns of Court'. Vansittart, who could have had the Chancellorship of the Exchequer, earned the gratitude of his friends by refusing to separate himself from them; and Davies Giddy, on the advice of Lord De Dunstanville, rejected an offer of the Secretaryship of the India Board. Hiley thought that Perceval had been 'blinded by vaulting ambition' or 'dazzled by royal favour'.

The overture, then, was singularly maladroit if not insulting. Sidmouth said in reply that a Government adequate to the crisis could not be formed without the assistance of Grey and Grenville and, in view of his own proscription, was inadmissible. 'By degrading and discrediting myself and my friends it would...utterly destroy our means of being really useful.'

In the end Perceval had to retain the Chancellorship of the Exchequer, the office having been successively refused by Charles Yorke, Vansittart, Palmerston, Milnes, George Rose and Charles Long. Its relative unimportance at that time, when the First Lord of the Treasury was in the Commons, is indicated by the fact that it was not necessarily considered a Cabinet one.

Three weeks before the opening of the parliamentary session, when Ministers had to encounter their first trial of strength in the debate on the Address, Richard Ryder thought that they had a reasonable chance of survival, provided that they were firm enough not to be frightened by the prospect of being left occasionally in a minority. He feared that the generally prevailing impression of the Ministry's weakness and the ill success of the war in the Peninsula and the Low Countries were likely to cause the absence of many 'speculators' who would wish to see what was going to happen before committing themselves. And it was well known that many Government supporters disavowed a regular party connection: that situation, indeed, always prevailed, these people keeping the Government of the day in being chiefly out of consideration for the King. Lord Seaforth, whilst regretting that the King had been advised to consider the Catholic question of vital importance, felt he would have to give his vote to save the King from annoyance and disturbance on that subject; and, as for the 'miserably unfortunate expeditions', he declared, 'Whatever turn things take I am resolute for one to adhere to the King and to lend my feeble voice for the support of his prerogatives and rights.' 'The battle', remarked the Duke of Richmond, 'is not merely for place but for the King.'

Lord Powis was not one of the 'speculators' but, being on friendly terms with Sidmouth, was certainly one of the 'doubtfuls', and he had declined an offer of a seat at the Board of Control for his son Lord Clive. He wished Ministers well, but would not engage to support them because in his judgment they were too weak to stand and they had not done all they could have done to secure the support of Sidmouth and Melville. Richard Ryder, to whom he confided his views, told him that if all the friends of Administration took the same line there would indeed be no chance of survival, and that it would be impossible to gain the support of *both* Sidmouth and Melville. And Ryder gently hinted that the part he was proposing to take was not the most fitting for a great aristocrat (he had five members in the House of Commons). But Sidmouth's follower Vansittart thought that Lord Powis had shown 'great firmness', and Sidmouth acknowledged that his conduct towards him had been very handsome. Powis and his friends, it was said, would not attend at the beginning of the Session.

Nor was Wilberforce a 'speculator', but he was not satisfied that the Government was strong enough to weather all storms; he favoured the idea of 'a general union of parties', and he believed that Perceval was deceiving himself if he hoped to be able to play the game Pitt had played in 1784. Wilberforce and his friends were never altogether popular with any Administration because their support on difficult questions could not be depended upon. Lord Eldon thus referred to them: 'I won't call them Saints, but I mean those gentlemen who are always thinking for themselves and yet never know their own minds.' Their support was upon the whole 'a mischievous support', he added. 'I am sure it was so to Pitt. I am sure he thought so though he could not disengage himself from them; and I am sure it was so to Sidmouth. You [Perceval] know better than I do what it was to the last Administration.'

As for the Opposition, it was still a disorganised band, without a recognised leader (it seemed doubtful at one moment whether George Ponsonby would continue to be accepted as such, even in a nominal capacity), as unpopular in the country as it had been in 1807, hopelessly divided on the question whether the forthcoming Catholic Petition should be supported with or without qualification, and whether, in the unlikely event of office coming their way, the Catholic question should or should not be made a *sine qua non* of acceptance of place. Grey thought that the King would have to send either for Sidmouth or for Wellesley. Grenville believed he would have to surrender to the Whigs. Tierney too was reasonably confident that the Government would be defeated on the Address at the opening of the Session (23 Jan.). But the Opposition's ground was not well chosen. The general attack on the late Administration for its conduct of the war meant that both Canning and Castlereagh had to defend policies for which they had been responsible, with the result that the Government had an unexpectedly large majority of 96 (263 to 167). Wilberforce's friends, and such of Sidmouth's as attended, also supported Ministers. The Prince of Wales had announced his intention of continuing his policy of 'neutrality', by which he meant, suggested Tierney, that Tyrwhitt and McMahon were not to vote, 'and that he is to tell everybody he wishes the Administration at the devil!'

Canning could not see his way at all clearly. Perceval, he believed, could not go on; the King, he was confident, would risk anything rather than send for Grenville. 'Yet,' he went on, 'if the King were to send to *me* I do not see how I could honestly undertake for forming a Government, and if Wellesley were to get the formation of it and offer me the House of Commons, I protest, I know not how to think of taking such an inheritance from Perceval with this inquiry in full cry. In short, if any superior power could say to me, "choose what you will", I hardly know how my choice would be made.' So he would go on warily and moderately, making as 'few more' enemies as possible.

The precarious nature of the Government's majority in the Commons was revealed on 26 January when Lord Portchester carried a Motion for an enquiry into the policy and conduct of the expedition to the Scheldt by 195 votes to 186. The majority consisted of the Opposition, the Sidmouths, the 'Saints', the Castlereaghs and some country gentlemen who usually supported Ministers. Wilberforce's speech was considered particularly mischievous, and 'the whole calendar of Saints' voted against. Canning's friends on this occasion voted with Ministers. Lord Hertford's members and the Carlton House members, McMahon and Tyrwhitt, stayed away.

The enquiry into the conduct of the expedition followed and, with the consequential debates, lasted from 2 February to 30 March. 'It is quite clear', wrote Richard Ryder (31 Jan.), 'that inquiry could not have been resisted with effect, and it must now take its course.' He expected to see Ministers frequently in a minority, but he was confident there would be no change of Government. A few hours after delivering these opinions he saw Ministers defeated three times on the question of the composition of the new Committee to enquire into Public Expenditure; and Perceval had to abandon his opposition to Henry Bankes's Bill to make permanent the Act to suspend the granting of offices in reversion. 'Mr. Bankes and his friends did as they pleased,' Denis Browne reported to the Duke of Richmond. 'He has made himself the master *over* the Government. . . *Finance questions* are the *rocks* on which those I presume to call our friends will be lost. The spirit of the times goes decidedly against sinecure employments, and the rage is for public economy.' The country gentlemen who usually supported the Ministers of the King's own choice were having to take note of their constituents' cry for reform and retrenchment; and Robert Ward regretted that a 'Jacobinical' spirit seemed to possess a considerable portion of the independent part of the House. 'In regard to our friends,' he told Lord Lonsdale, 'it must be confessed there is far too much indifference to any trouble in our defence. . .in the way of attendance to make it probable we can carry anything with vigour.' The Duke of Richmond was certain that the comfort of the King's life depended on the fate of Perceval's Ministry. The 'Saints' always did harm, he said, but he did not believe that they and other lukewarm friends would be willing to bring in the Opposition and embitter the King.

On 6 March Whitbread carried against the Government a Resolution which amounted to a censure on Lord Chatham for unconstitutionally abusing the privilege of access to the King in the matter of his Narrative. The voting was 221 to 188. Amongst the majority were nearly forty who usually supported Ministers, and the Prince, notwithstanding his professions of neutrality, sent his members to vote with the Whigs. Next day, after the Levée, Chatham reluctantly resigned. 'Some of the Opposition', wrote Charles Long (7 March), 'are very ready to take Lord Chatham by the hand. . .and to represent his colleagues as having deserted him, and I have reason to think he is not disinclined to adopt this opinion. I know he has complained much of the newspapers, and considers the Treasury (however unfairly) as responsible for all the attacks that have been made upon him in the ministerial ones.' Perceval rejoiced that Chatham had taken this necessary step voluntarily, 'rather than that it should be forced upon him by what the Government in general might have felt necessary'.

Chatham's colleagues felt that his censure was undeserved, yet they considered he had acted unfairly by them. Bathurst referred to his 'unfortunate jealous disposition, of which his brother frequently felt the effects'. But time softened hard feelings, and when the Earl of Dartmouth was dying in October 1810 Perceval thought of offering Chatham the office of Lord Chamberlain without a seat in the Cabinet. There was then a notion that it might be right to do something for 'Pitt's brother in distress' and, incidentally, such an appointment was calculated to 'keep the Duke of Rutland right'.

It was at once rumoured that Mulgrave was to succeed Chatham as Master-General of the Ordnance and Charles Yorke to take Mulgrave's place at the Admiralty, possibly with a Peerage to save him the expense of a county election. A by-election was due, in any case, following Yorke's acceptance of a Tellership of the Exchequer. A contest in Cambridgeshire would have been unavoidable after Lord Francis Godolphin Osborne came forward as an Opposition candidate; consequently Yorke withdrew and his brother offered to buy him a seat for the duration of the Parliament, whether he accepted a Cabinet office or not. In the end (27 April) he was returned for the Eliot borough of St Germans, his brother Sir Joseph making way for him.

The office of Master-General, however, was first offered to Lord Pembroke, a Lieutenant-General who had served with distinction under the Duke of York in the Flanders campaign in 1794. Pembroke declined it. Canning had not yet completely lived down the unpopularity he had incurred by his treatment of Castlereagh, but the studiously moderate tone he had recently adopted in Parliament was bringing the country gentlemen round. Yet his restless ambition made him an object of suspicion to those whose situation would be unfavourably affected by his return to office. At times he seemed to care little about his prospects. He told his wife on 7 April: 'As to office I know not what to say or what to wish. I am more indifferent than I was about it, but then the keeping a party even of twelve together is more toil and trouble than could well be imagined.' And he was now disillusioned about Wellesley, whose idleness at the Foreign Office was becoming generally known and deplored. Canning even thought they might get rid of him: they were becoming suspicious of him, especially when he demanded Canning's reinstatement in office; and his 'vices and shameless profligacy' were calculated to destroy whatever confidence the King still had in him. 'He is...running himself down, that is certain,' said Canning regretfully.

On the conduct of the Expedition two main questions were at issue: first, its policy—on which Ministers were certain of the support of Castlereagh and Canning; second, the delay in the evacuation of Walcheren—on which both of them were free to vote as they pleased. But before the critical division at the end of March Perceval decided to make overtures to the 'floating parties' as soon as the fate of the Government had been decided in the House of Commons. Wellesley-Pole was confident that only a simultaneous offer to Sidmouth, Castlereagh and Canning would give Ministers the prospect of more strength. His brother, Lord Wellesley, was ready to facilitate matters either by going out or by changing his office. Camden was willing to resign the Presidentship of the Council, Mulgrave the Admiralty, Ryder the Home Secretaryship, and Perceval the Exchequer. Perceval had no intention of making another approach to Grey and Grenville: he was determined to remained Prime Minister at all costs, to ignore defeats in Parliament and to resign only on a motion of censure. Wellesley, seeing the King on 21 March, represented to him the necessity of a change and told him he would be no party to any arrangement which excluded Canning.

The motion of censure was defeated on 31 March by 275 votes to 227, and the other divisions were also favourable. Castlereagh voted with Ministers, Sidmouth's friends against, Canning with. His friends, with his concurrence, voted different ways—two with Ministers, five against; and two went away. Charles Long commented: 'We ought to have had a few more; three or four went away of ours, not expecting a division... The result of the whole is this, that after deducting from the Opposition those who do not belong to them, and reckoning the Sidmouth party as Opposition, they are about 200 strong, which is more powerful than is compatible with carrying on the Government with any sort of facility, but what is to be done I know not with a view to strengthening it.'

Nothing was done for three weeks. Most members of the Cabinet were reluctant to apply to Canning after all that had happened, and no one favoured an overture to Canning alone. In the end Wellesley's plan of a combined approach to the three parties was accepted, the arrangement being that Perceval should ascertain the feelings of Sidmouth and Castlereagh, and Wellesley should sound Canning. On Sunday 22 April Yorke was sent to interview Sidmouth, and stayed with him until the Tuesday. Sidmouth rejected the invitation without a moment's hesitation; his friend Vansittart said later that it carried with it so much absurdity that it was difficult to believe it was seriously made. Sidmouth's negative attitude meant that it was then useless to make any approach to Castlereagh, who would not have come in with Canning except on the principle of re-uniting all the remains of Pitt's friends. Canning's reply to Wellesley was strictly confidential and so was not communicated to Perceval. Since the other two groups were not prepared to join, the reply was irrelevant. It looked, then, as if hatreds were never to be appeased, enemies never to be reconciled.

Canning's party was the most respectable of the three, and possibly the largest (the Whigs gave Sidmouth only eight members in the Commons, but as they described Vansittart as 'Opposition' the number was an underestimate, whilst Lord Kingston's figure of 30 votes, even if Peers were included, seems excessive). But of Canning's friends Huskisson was the only one fit for high office, and he made it known that he had an 'invincible repugnance' to being Chancellor of the Exchequer (even seventeen years later he refused the office). Lord Granville Leveson-Gower, indeed, had been in the Cabinet for a few weeks in 1809, but he was not a dedicated politician (he was a great gambler, and he had a fascination which women found irresistible), and in any case he would have been afraid to take office and run the risk of losing his county seat at the by-election. It was very doubtful whether Canning would have had the support in office of his brother-in-law, the new Duke of Portland, even though Canning would have undertaken to release him from this form of imprisonment after serving one year 'if he grew tired'. The Duke's reluctance to shackle himself was again to be revealed in April 1827 when Canning at long last reached the summit of his ambition, and needed the Duke as a 'sleeping partner in the firm'.

The idea of another application—to Sidmouth and Castlereagh alone—was next canvassed, but rejected because Wellesley vetoed it. Consequently Perceval had to make up his mind as a matter of necessity to meet Parliament again with only trifling changes. On the ground that the Government had failed to secure additional strength Dundas refused to be transferred to the Admiralty (28 April) and plainly intimated that he should soon resign altogether and take the 'Scotch Legion' (23 regular attenders in the House of Commons, said Wellesley-Pole) with him, unless strength could be obtained. 'My continuing in it', he told Perceval (28 April), 'will depend upon our all agreeing to sacrifice our predilections in favour of particular individuals and our repugnance to others, to the sole object of forming such an Administration as will maintain a high station in public opinion and carry on the public business with vigour and efficiency.' He was particularly anxious to see Canning again in office. There was no demand for office for his father, but the Duke of Richmond believed that something would have to be done for Lord Melville if the support of the 'northern members' was to continue.

Lord Mulgrave, then, was transferred from the Admiralty to the Ordnance, Perceval disregarding Bathurst's earnest recommendation of Lord Harrington as Master-General: an appointment which would have opened for the Duke of Richmond the additional office of Commander-in-Chief in Ireland, the Duke's salary as Lord Lieutenant being notoriously inadequate to meet expenses. And Charles Yorke was induced to go to the Admiralty. His sinecure had made him financially independent of his brother, but even so there was no question of his undertaking another contest in Cambridgeshire, and he was re-elected for St Germans on 25 May. It was an unpopular appointment: he had made himself obnoxious to the Press by clearing the Gallery of the House of Commons on 26 January, just before the enquiry into the conduct of the Walcheren expedition was opened. Yorke, moreover, had exposed himself to Whig criticism by taking the sinecure office which, it was suggested, ought to have been given to Wellington, whose pension would thereby have been saved to the public.

'Perceval', wrote Wellesley-Pole (28 April), 'does not seem to have an idea that any change in his situation could make it more easy to form a strong Administration. I do suppose no person could be found to tell him this, though certainly almost everybody thinks it.' He added, 'We have nothing for it but to stick to the vessel till she sinks, which I expect she will do very speedily.' Pole should have known that it was out of consideration for the King that Perceval was determined to remain Prime Minister until events forced him to retire. It never came to that. The Government was never in real danger after the crucial divisions on 31 March: the independent members were not prepared to bring in the Whigs. But Lord Lowther made the interesting comment, in a letter to his father, that votes were sometimes lost owing to the inefficiency of Arbuthnot, the new Secretary of the Treasury, who was chiefly responsible for parliamentary management. 'Arbuthnot is perfectly *useless*: he is not acquainted with one-third of the House and sits perfectly idle.' A better system of procuring attendance was needed, and members should not be allowed to leave the House before the divisions.

Two further efforts to secure the 'floating parties' were made during the next few months. On 12 June Wellesley, with Perceval's knowledge and consent, tried unsuccessfully to persuade Sidmouth to join the Government in company with Canning. His objections were not personal, but he thought that the proposed junction would be injurious to the character of the Administration. Two days later Wellesley told Perceval that an effort should then be made to secure Canning, and as a contribution to this end he himself would make way for Canning at the Foreign Office, and either take some other post or remain in the Cabinet temporarily without portfolio. Perceval agreed to summon a Cabinet meeting to consider the matter, but pressure of business delayed a discussion for several weeks. When Wellesley again offered to give up his office, it was objected that no overture to Castlereagh too had been proposed. Wellesley replied that that was no fault of his; he had never ceased to urge the propriety of making an overture to both simultaneously; he himself had offered to be the channel of communication, but the offer had not been accepted. Perceval said that nothing had been done because he thought it would be useless, but if the Cabinet decided that the attempt should be made, he would do what he could. The Cabinet decided unanimously that an effort should be made to strengthen the Government. The next question was this: as Sidmouth had already refused to join, should a joint offer now be made to Canning and Castlereagh? To this Yorke objected: because of his obligations to Sidmouth (who had appointed him Home Secretary in 1803) he could not consent to Sidmouth's complete exclusion, so he would resign. Wellesley said he would press nothing which should force Yorke in honour to resign, and after further discussion Yorke agreed to stay. Then Camden objected to any proposal to Canning; he would never be a party to it, but he would favour a proposal to Castlereagh and Sidmouth jointly. Wellesley at once said that if the Cabinet accepted this suggestion *he* should resign, whereupon that idea was abandoned, and the Cabinet then decided on a joint proposal to Canning and Castlereagh, Camden alone voting against. Next, Wellesley asked to be allowed to give up his office to Canning. This provoked a long and violent discussion. Almost everyone opposed the idea. They would have Canning back at the Foreign Office as a proposition in isolation, but it would not do, because they could not have Castlereagh back in *his* former office, and to make a distinction between them would display a partiality which they wished to avoid, and Castlereagh would certainly reject such a proposal. Neither, then, should be invited to resume the office he had previously held: on this point the Cabinet was unanimous except for Wellesley's vote.

What offices, then, were to be offered? Ryder wished to retire altogether, Camden was ready to give up his office, and Liverpool was willing to become President of the Council (but the Cabinet had decided that the War Secretaryship should not be changed). Yorke refused to move to it from the Admiralty so as to make his office disposable. An obvious arrangement would have been to make Wellesley Lord President and Liverpool Foreign Secretary, but they probably considered that that proposal would have been very offensive to Canning.

Another question to be decided was this: If one rejected the proposal and the other accepted, was the accession of the one to be acceptable? This put Wellesley in a difficulty because he wished Castlereagh's refusal to be decided differently from Canning's. The prevailing impression seemed to be that if Castlereagh could not be secured no offer should be made to Canning, so he did not press this point to a vote; had he done so he would probably have been supported only by Dundas and Mulgrave. He was not prepared to acquiesce in the idea of taking in Castlereagh alone, and when he stressed the importance of securing Canning, even if alone, for the stability it would give to the Government, Bathurst remarked, 'Oh, yes. I think as highly as you and anyone can of the value of that accession—not in the House of Commons only—but in this room—we should feel the value of it every day that we met. But my doubt is this—whether Canning's accession *alone* to the present Government would not lead to a change of the basis of the Government itself.' Bathurst evidently meant that such a change would lead to Wellesley's becoming Prime Minister—and that, undoubtedly, was the Marquess's ultimate ambition. Eldon too was strongly opposed to a single proposal, which he felt would throw into decided opposition the party left out. The details of these confidential Cabinet discussions were revealed by Wellesley to his friend Canning, who, behind the scenes, was the chief mover in all that was happening in connection with his proposed return to office.

Perceval's letter to Castlereagh was leisurely drafted and despatched on 22 August. He and Dundas were confident that the reply would be negative, and they were right. Wellesley was of a different opinion. The correspondence is printed in Walpole's *Perceval*, II, 144–56, and so need be only briefly referred to. The Admiralty and the Home Secretaryship were the offices offered to the two of them, to be filled, if possible, by an arrangement between themselves. On 4 September Castlereagh declined office. On the 25th Canning in effect did so too, saying, however, that if Wellesley's earlier suggestion that he should have the Foreign Secretaryship were repeated, Wellesley himself remaining in the Cabinet and places being found for Canning's friends, that proposition would be accepted. In particular Canning would have insisted on a proper provision for Huskisson. An offer of the Chancellorship would not have been made a *sine qua non*, though Canning thought Perceval unfit for that office, and said he should not choose to belong to a Government in which the finances were exclusively in Perceval's hands.

At the beginning of October, by which time the negotiations were at an end, the King was apparently in good health, but the shock of his daughter Amelia's fatal illness proved too much for his mind to bear. His secretary, Taylor, reported on the 8th that 'his valuable health is not affected by this severe and painful trial'. But by the 25th, eight days before his daughter died, unmistakable symptoms of insanity again appeared, though for almost a week the news was kept from the general public, who were led to believe that he was suffering from a severe cold. His doctors believed that the derangement had been brought on by grief and anxiety at the Princess's dreadful sufferings. Whether he suffered from the hereditary disorder porphyria is a matter not for the historian but for medical experts to decide, and as the theory has provoked controversy the opinion of a non-medical person is worth little. Whatever the cause, the symptoms of insanity were unmistakable, but to describe the King as being permanently insane after mid-October 1810 is misleading in the sense that he often had short, quite lucid intervals. He understood the nature of Princess Amelia's Will. He told Perceval in November of his determination to give his Ministers full support so long as they were firm and stood by him, and he very shrewdly observed that if that fact were made known, it would fix many people in their politics who would otherwise be inclined to waver.

Though obviously impaired by his illness, the King's influence remained a reality—so long as any hope remained of his ultimate recovery. Fear of his father's wrath if he did recover alone prevented the Prince of Wales from changing his Ministers on becoming Regent in February 1811. The prospect of having to face his father when unpleasant questions had to be discussed had always terrified the Prince, and not without cause, for the King had been apt to fly into paroxysms of rage on such occasions, frightening to all who had to witness them. If the Prince had dismissed the Ministers of his father's choice and had brought in his old Whig friends instead—men who despaired of victory and who were prepared to make peace on terms which would have left Napoleon master of the Continent—men who were prepared to endanger the Constitution in Church and State by passing a Catholic Relief Act—he would hardly have dared to face his father's wrath in the event of his recovery.

THE PORTLAND MINISTRY,
MARCH 1807–SEPTEMBER 1809

THE CABINET

	March–April 1807	June 1809	17 July 1809
First Lord of the Treasury	Portland	Portland	Portland
Chancellor of the Exchequer	*Spencer Perceval*[1] (26 March)	*Perceval*[1]	*Perceval*[1]
Lord Privy Seal	Earl of Westmorland (25 March)	Westmorland	Westmorland
Lord President of the Council	Earl Camden (26 March)	Camden	Camden
Lord Chancellor	Lord Eldon (1 April)	Eldon	Eldon
Home Secretary	Lord Hawkesbury (25 March)[2]	Liverpool	Liverpool
Foreign Secretary	*George Canning* (25 March)	*Canning*	*Canning*
Secretary for War and the Colonies	*Visc. Castlereagh* (25 March)	*Castlereagh*	*Castlereagh*
First Lord of the Admiralty	Lord Mulgrave (4 April)	Mulgrave	Mulgrave
President of the Board of Control			Earl of Harrowby
Master-General of the Ordnance	Earl of Chatham	Chatham	Chatham
President of the Board of Trade	Earl Bathurst[3] (26 March)	Bathurst[3]	Bathurst[3]
Secretary at War		*Lord Granville Leveson-Gower*	*Lord G. Leveson-Gower*

[1] Perceval was also Chancellor of the Duchy of Lancaster (from 30 March 1807).
[2] Earl of Liverpool from 17 December 1808.
[3] Bathurst was also Master of the Mint.

Junior Lords of the Treasury	Marquess of Titchfield, Wm. Eliot, Sturges-Bourne
16 Sept. 1807	Wm. Eliot, Sturges-Bourne, John Foster, Richard Ryder
2 Dec. 1807	Wm. Eliot, Sturges-Bourne, Foster, Wm. Brodrick
Secretaries of the Treasury	Wm. Huskisson (1 Apr. 1807–7 Dec. 1809) and Henry Wellesley (1 Apr. 1807–5 Apr. 1809)
	Huskisson and Chas. Arbuthnot (from 6 Apr. 1809)
Junior Lords of the Admiralty	James Gambier, Sir Richard Bickerton, Wm. Johnstone Hope, Robert Ward, Lord Palmerston, James Buller
9 May 1808	Sir R. Bickerton, W. Johnstone Hope, Robert Ward, Palmerston, Buller, Wm. Domett
30 March 1809	Bickerton, Ward, Palmerston, Buller, Domett, Robert Moorsom

Secretary of the Admiralty	Wm. Marsden, Wm. Wellesley-Pole (from 27 June 1807)
Under-Secretaries of State	
Home Department	Chas. Cecil Cope Jenkinson and John Beckett
Foreign Department	George Hammond and Visc. Fitzharris
19 Aug. 1807	Hammond and Charles Bagot
War and the Colonies	Edward Cooke and Chas. Wm. Stewart
3 May 1809	Edward Cooke and Frederick John Robinson
President of the Board of Control	Robert Dundas (to July 1809)
Commissioners of the Board of Control	Lord Lovaine, Lord Teignmouth, Thos. Wallace, George Johnstone
17 July 1809	Robert Dundas, Lovaine, Wallace, Lord Teignmouth, Lord Binning
Secretary to the Board of Control	George Peter Holford
Secretary at War	Lieut-Gen. Sir James Murray Pulteney
Lieutenant-General of the Ordnance	Sir Thomas Trigge
Surveyor-General of the Ordnance	Lieut.-Col. James Murray Hadden
Clerk of the Ordnance	Wm. Wellesley-Pole, Cropley Ashley Cooper (from 21 July 1807)
Storekeeper of the Ordnance	Mark Singleton
Surveyor-General of Woods and Forests	Lord Robert Spencer, Lord Glenbervie (from 9 Dec. 1807)
Surveyor-General of Crown Lands	John Fordyce
Paymasters-General	Chas. Long and Lord Charles Henry Somerset
Treasurer of the Navy	George Rose
Postmasters-General	Earl of Sandwich and Earl of Chichester
Vice-President of the Board of Trade	George Rose
Judge Advocate-General	Nathaniel Bond and Richard Ryder (from 28 Nov. 1807)
Master of the Rolls	Sir William Grant
Attorney-General	Sir Vicary Gibbs
Solicitor-General	Sir Thos. Plumer
Lord Advocate of Scotland	Archibald Colquhoun
Solicitor-General of Scotland	David Boyle

Lord Lieutenant	Duke of Richmond
Chief Secretary	Sir Arthur Wellesley; Robert Saunders Dundas (from 13 Apr. 1809)
Lord Chancellor	Lord Manners
Chancellor of the Exchequer	John Foster
Attorney-General	William Saurin
Solicitor-General	Charles Kendal Bushe
Under-Secretaries of State	
Civil Department	James Trail and Sir Charles Saxton (from 6 Sept. 1808)
Military Department	Sir E. B. Littlehales

THE PERCEVAL MINISTRY,
4 OCTOBER 1809—11 MAY 1812

THE CABINET

	Oct.–Nov. 1809	6 Dec. 1809	May 1810	March–April 1812
First Lord of the Treasury[1] Chancellor of the Exchequer	} Spencer Perceval[1] (4 Oct.)	Perceval[1]	Perceval[1]	Perceval[1]
Lord Privy Seal	E. of Westmorland	Westmorland	Westmorland	Westmorland
Lord President of Council	Earl Camden	Camden	Camden	Visct. Sidmouth (8 April)
Lord Chancellor	Lord Eldon	Eldon	Eldon	Eldon
Home Secretary	Richard Ryder (1 Nov.)	Ryder	Ryder	Ryder
Foreign Secretary	Earl Bathurst[2] (11 Oct.)	Marquess Wellesley	Wellesley	Castlereagh (4 March)
Secretary for War & Colonies	Earl of Liverpool	Liverpool	Liverpool	Liverpool
First Lord of Admiralty	Lord Mulgrave	Mulgrave	Charles Philip Yorke (1 May)	2nd Visct. Melville (24 March)
President of Board of Control	Robert Dundas[3] (13 Nov.)	Dundas	Dundas (2nd Visct. Melville, 29 May 1811)	E. of Buckinghamshire (7 April)
Master-General of Ordnance	Earl of Chatham	Chatham (to March 1810)	Lord Mulgrave (1 May)	
President of Board of Trade	Earl Bathurst	Bathurst	Bathurst	Bathurst
Ministers without portfolio	Duke of Portland (d. 30 Oct.)			Earl Camden (after 8 April)
	Earl of Harrowby (Nov.)	Harrowby	Harrowby	Harrowby

Junior Lords of the Treasury	John Foster, Wm. Brodrick, Wm. Eliot, Earl of Desart, Snowdon Barne
23 June 1810	Foster, Brodrick, Eliot, Barne, Berkeley Paget
31 Dec. 1811	Brodrick, Barne, B. Paget, Richard Wellesley (to Feb. 1812),Wm. Wellesley-Pole
Secretaries of the Treasury	Richard Wharton[4] and Chas. Arbuthnot

[1] Also Chancellor of the Duchy of Lancaster.

[2] Bathurst retained the Presidentship of the Board of Trade whilst he was Foreign Secretary *ad interim*, the duties of the office being performed by George Rose, the Vice-President. On 7 Oct. Perceval told the King that Harrowby would go to the Board of Trade whilst Bathurst was temporarily at the Foreign Office, but this proposal did not actually take effect.   [3] Seat in the Cabinet, c. 4 Nov. 1809.

[4] 'Huskisson is out, and so is Hammond.' (Tierney to Grey, 3 Oct. 1809.) Huskisson's resignation did not take effect until 7 Dec. 1809.

Junior Lords of the Admiralty	Sir Richard Bickerton, Robert Ward, James Buller, Wm. Domett, Robert Moorsom, Visct. Lowther
4 May 1810	Bickerton, Ward, Buller, Domett, Moorsom, Lowther
3 July 1810	Bickerton, Ward, Buller, Domett, Sir Joseph Sydney Yorke, Frederick John Robinson[1]
17 June 1811	Bickerton, Buller, Domett, Yorke, Robinson, Lord Walpole
25 March 1812	Domett, Yorke, Robinson, Walpole, Wm. Dundas, George Johnstone Hope
Secretary of the Admiralty	John Wilson Croker
Under-Secretaries of State	
Home Department	John Beckett
	Chas. Cecil Cope Jenkinson (to *c.* end Oct. 1809)
27 Feb. 1810	Henry Goulburn, *vice* Jenkinson
Foreign Department	Wm. Hamilton
13 Dec. 1809	Chas. Culling Smith, *vice* Geo. Hammond[2]
28 Feb. 1812	Edward Cooke, *vice* Culling Smith
War and the Colonies	Frederick John Robinson
c. 1 Nov. 1809	Chas. Cecil Cope Jenkinson
c. June 1810	Lieut.-Col. Henry E. Bunbury, *vice* Robinson
June 1810	Robert Peel, *vice* Jenkinson
Commissioners of the Board of Control	Lord Lovaine, Lord Teignmouth, Thos. Wallace, Lord Francis Almeric Spencer[3]
7 July 1810	Lovaine, Teignmouth, Wallace, Visct. Lowther
7 April 1812	Lovaine, Teignmouth, Wallace, Visct. Lowther, John Sullivan
Secretary to the Board of Control	George Peter Holford; Sir Patrick Murray (from 6 Jan. 1810)
Secretary at War	Visct. Palmerston
Lieut.-Gen. of the Ordnance	General Sir Thomas Trigge
Surveyor-Gen. of the Ordnance	Lieut.-Col. James Murray Hadden
20 July 1810	Rear-Admiral Robert Moorsom
Clerk of the Ordnance	Cropley Ashley Cooper
June 1811	Robert Ward
Storekeeper of the Ordnance	Mark Singleton

[1] Robinson told Hardwicke on 4 June that, after much hesitation, he had accepted Yorke's offer. (Add. MSS. 35648, f. 406.)   [2] See p. 711, n. 4.

[3] Spencer 'never attended the Board; of course was never sworn'. 'It has been said that his name was inserted in the Patent without his consent' (the Commission, dated 13 Nov. 1809 and gazetted on the 7th, has these dockets). (India Office Records: Board of Control, Compilations and Misc. F./5/1.) Information ex Miss S. R. Johnson.

Surveyor-Gen. of Woods and Forests	Lord Glenbervie[1]
Paymasters-General	Chas. Long and Lord Chas. Henry Somerset
Treasurer of the Navy	George Rose
Postmasters-General	Earl of Sandwich and Earl of Chichester
Vice-President of the Board of Trade	George Rose
Judge Advocate-General	Chas. Manners-Sutton
Master of the Rolls	Sir William Grant
Attorney-General	Sir Vicary Gibbs
Solicitor-General	Sir Thomas Plumer
Lord Advocate of Scotland	Archibald Colquhoun
Solicitor-General of Scotland	David Boyle (to Feb. 1811)
	David Monypenny

THE IRISH GOVERNMENT

Lord Lieutenant	Duke of Richmond
Chief Secretary	Wm. Wellesley-Pole
Lord Chancellor	Lord Manners
Chancellor of the Exchequer	John Foster
June 1811	Wm. Wellesley-Pole
Attorney-General	Wm. Saurin
Solicitor-General	Charles Kendal Bushe
Under-Secretaries of State[2]	
Civil Department	Sir Charles Saxton
Military Department	Sir E. B. Littlehales

THE KING'S HOUSEHOLD, 1802-10[3]

Lord Steward	Earl of Dartmouth (from Aug. 1802); Earl of Aylesford (from May 1804)
Lord Chamberlain	Marquess of Salisbury; Earl of Dartmouth (from 6 June 1804)
Treasurer	Viscount Stopford; Lord Ossulston (from 12 Feb. 1806); Viscount Stopford[4] (from 31 March 1807)
Groom of the Stole	Duke of Roxburghe (d. 19 March 1804); Earl of Winchilsea and Nottingham (from 6 June 1804)

[1] The office was re-named First Commissioner of Woods and Forests, July 1810.
[2] Charles William Flint was Under-Secretary of State at the Irish Office in London.
[3] This period has been selected to illustrate the extent to which the Household was changed on a change of Ministry.
[4] Lord Stopford succeeded as Earl of Courtown, 30 March 1810.

Master of the Horse	Earl of Chesterfield;
	Marquess of Hertford (from July 1804);
	Earl of Carnarvon (from Feb. 1806);
	Duke of Montrose (from March 1807)
Captain of the Band of Gentlemen Pensioners	Viscount Falmouth;
	Lord St John (from Feb. 1806);
	Visc. Falmouth (from *c.* March 1807–died 11 Feb. 1808);
	Earl of Mount-Edgcumbe (from 19 March 1808)
Captain of the Yeomen of the Guard	Earl of Aylesford;
	Lord Pelham (from 6 June 1804);
	Earl of Macclesfield (from 27 June 1804)
Comptroller	Lord Chas. Henry Somerset;
	Lord George Thynne (from *c.* 2 June 1804)
Vice-Chamberlain	Charles Francis Greville;[1]
	Lord John Thynne (from 11 July 1804)
Master of the Buckhounds	Earl of Sandwich;
	Earl of Albemarle (from Feb. 1806);
	Marquess Cornwallis (from May 1807)
Master of the Household	Sir Henry Strachey;
	William Kenrick (from 27 June 1810)

[1] In the Official History of Parliament (*The House of Commons, 1754–1790*, II, 550, by Sir Lewis Namier and J. Brooke), it is erroneously stated that Greville was Vice-Chamberlain until his death in 1809.

THE CORRESPONDENCE

[*Foreign Office, 31 Dec. 1807.*] Mr. Canning humbly begs leave to acquaint your Majesty that the Prince Starhemberg has called upon him today to announce the instructions which he has received, not directly from his Court but through Count Metternich from Bonaparte at Milan to propose to the British Government the immediate sending of Plenipotentiaries to Paris to treat for a peace with France & the other nations engaged in the war against Great Britain.

Prince Starhemberg is not authorized to propose any basis of negotiation: and though he appears inclined to take upon himself to offer the mediation of the Emperor of Austria, Mr Canning is satisfied from the conversation which passed between Prince Starhemberg & him that Prince Starhemberg has not even heard from Vienna by this occasion, & that his latest orders from thence are of the 30th of October & contained only a general injunction to him to act according to the suggestions of the French Government.

Prince Starhemberg had not been able to prepare his official Note today but has promised to deliver it to Mr. Canning tomorrow. (13310–1)

[*The King's reply, Windsor Castle, 1 Jan. 1808.*] The King has received Mr. Canning's letter & his M. is convinced that his Ministers will see with him the danger of admitting or acting upon any proposal of negociation which is unaccompanied by the statement of a basis. (13311)

[*From Canning, Foreign Office, 1 Jan.*] Mr. Canning humbly submits for your Majesty's royal approbation the draft of the Treaty of Subsidy proposed to be negotiated between your Majesty & the King of Sweden. (13315)

[*From Canning, Foreign Office, 1 Jan.*] Mr. Canning humbly lays before your Majesty a copy of the official Note which Prince Starhemberg has transmitted to him today. The original Note Mr. Canning has been under the necessity of returning to Prince Starhemberg in order that a most important omission in it may be supplied by that Minister—an omission which, grammatically, makes the sense imperfect, & which might be filled up in any one of three or four ways, each very different from the other. The sentence as now written runs thus 'comptant sur la sincerité de S.M.B.M.'—'n'hesite pas de proposer'—without specifying *who* it is that '*n'hesite pas*'. It may be the Emperor of Austria—it may be France— or it may be only Prince Starhemberg himself—or lastly the blank may be to be filled up by the word '*on*'—which is employed in a subsequent part of the paper, where Prince Starhemberg is at a loss in whose name to speak. In this uncertainty Mr. Canning did not venture to supply the omission by conjecture. But neither did he think it right on account of a circumstance apparently so trifling, to withhold from your Majesty the perusal of the paper as it now stands, and Prince

I-2

Starhemberg not having yet returned the original corrected, Mr. Canning has humbly presumed to send a copy to your Majesty. (13313–4)

[*The King's reply, Windsor Castle, 2 Jan. 1807* [*1808*].] The King was well assured that Mr. Canning would not be imposed upon by so palpable a trick as that which Prince Stahremberg appears to have intended by the omission in his official Note, & H.M. very much approves of Mr. Canning's having returned it to him for correction. This circumstance naturally tends to confirm H.M. in his opinion of the deception attending a proposal of negociation which, in the outset, is made in terms so loose & uncertain.

The King approves of the proposed Treaty of Subsidy with the King of Sweden. (12570)

[*From Canning, Foreign Office, 2 Jan.*] Mr. Canning humbly lays before your Majesty the altered Note received from Prince Starhemberg this morning, together with the copy of a letter which Mr. Canning has thought it right to address to Prince Starhemberg on the receipt of it. Mr. Canning at the same time takes the liberty of returning the copy of the Note sent to your Majesty yesterday, in order that your Majesty may have the opportunity of comparing the passages which have been changed. It will not escape your Majesty's observation that Prince Starhemberg does not now say *by whom* he is charged to propose the sending Plenipotentiaries to Paris. (13316–7)

[*The King's reply, Windsor Castle, 3 Jan.*] The King agrees with Mr. Canning in opinion that Prince Starhemberg has not been sufficiently explicit in his second Note which indeed varies little from that which was returned for correction, & H.M. is sensible of the propriety of Mr. Canning's insisting upon a more distinct declaration of the authority under which Prince Starhemberg acts. (13317)

3580   THE DUKE OF PORTLAND *to the* KING, *and the reply*

[*Bulstrode, Saturday, 2 Jan. 1808.*] In obedience to the commands which the Duke of Portland has received from her Majesty he humbly presumes to lay before your Majesty the name of the Revd. Mr. Charles Digby,[1] eldest son of the late Mr Stephen Digby, her Majesty's Vice-Chamberlain, as a proper person to fill the Stall at Windsor lately become vacant by the death of the late Dr. Lockman.[2] (13318)

[*The King's reply, Windsor Castle, 3 Jan.*] The King has received with great satisfaction the Duke of Portland's recommendation of the Revd. Mr. Charles Digby for the vacant Stall at Windsor. Independent of the excellent character

[1] Rector of Chiselborough, 1807, and of Bishop's Caundle, Dorset, 1810; Canon of Windsor, 1808. His mother was Lady Lucy Strangways Fox (1748–87), daughter of Stephen, Earl of Ilchester, who married Col. Stephen Digby (1742–1800) in 1771. (1775–1841.)
[2] John Lockman, D.D., F.R.S.

which Mr. Digby bears, his M. looks back with pleasure to the education which he received at Eton & at Christ Church, & he is glad that the Duke of Portland has had it in his power to meet the Queen's wishes upon this occasion. (13319)

3581   *Letters from* GEORGE CANNING *to the* KING, *and the replies*

[*Sunday, 3 Jan. 1808*.] Mr. Canning humbly begs leave to acquaint your Majesty that Prince Starhemberg has replied to Mr. Canning's letter of yesterday by a private letter, assuring him that the alterations made in the official Note have been made solely with the view of rendering it more respectful to your Majesty; and requesting Mr. Canning to accept & lay before your Majesty the second edition of the Note as that which Prince Starhemberg wishes to have considered as official. Mr. Canning has not thought it necessary to press Prince Starhemberg farther at present, conceiving that the obvious want of any due authority to act, as Prince Starhemberg has acted, will furnish the best ground for the official answer to the official Note of Prince Starhemberg.[1] (13320–1)

[*From Canning, Foreign Office, 4 Jan.*] Mr. Canning humbly transmits to your Majesty a letter from the King of Sweden, delivered to him (together with its copy) by Mr. de Brinkmann.[2] (13322)

[*From Canning, Foreign Office, 5 Jan.*] Mr. Canning humbly begs leave to submit to your Majesty the name of Mr. Francis Hill, late your Majesty's Secretary of Legation at Copenhagen, for the appointment of Secretary of Legation to the Mission to the Court of Portugal at the Brazils. (13323)

[*The King's reply, Windsor Castle, 6 Jan.*] The King acquiesces in Mr. Canning's recommendation of Mr. Francis Hill for the situation of Secretary of Legation to the Court of Portugal at the Brazils. (13324)

[*From Canning, Foreign Office, 6 Jan.*] Mr. Canning humbly submits for your Majesty's royal approbation the draft of the answer proposed to be returned to the official Note presented by Prince Starhemberg. Mr. Canning at the same time lays before your Majesty the extracts of letters from France which he took the liberty of mentioning to your Majesty as having been communicated to him in confidence by M. Alopeus. (13325)

[1] Lieutenant-Colonel Taylor wrote to Canning from Windsor on the 4th: 'Baron Jacobi's object was, as I suspected, a private application to the King for pecuniary aid to the King of Prussia, but he yesterday confined himself to asking me how he was to proceed & to whom apply. I told him that I knew no other than the official channel through which he could submit any proposal to the King, and he was more easily satisfied than I expected. He means now to apply to you but not to make his application the subject of any official representation. He gave me a greater dose of politics than I have had for years, not excepting even from my friend Sir John McPherson, & went over the whole history of the blunders committed by his own Court; but as he talked incessantly himself he gave me little opportunity of *committing any indiscretion*. The King has not replied to your letter of yesterday, considering its contents as matter of information, but you may perhaps be glad to know that his M. expressed his entire approbation of the grounds upon which you have thought it more advisable not to press Prince Starhemberg any further.' (Harewood MSS.)   [2] Brinkman in Harewood MSS. (Copy.)

[*The King's reply, Windsor Castle, 7 Jan.*] The King highly approves of the official answer which Mr. Canning has prepared to Prince Starhemberg's Note & H.M. has read with great interest the extracts of letters from France. (13326)

[*From Canning, Foreign Office, 7 Jan.*] Mr. Canning humbly presumes to trouble your Majesty a second time with the draft of the official answer to Prince Starhemberg, in consequence of a slight alteration in the concluding part of it, since it was submitted for your Majesty's gracious approbation.

As the passage now stands, it states that Prince Starhemberg '*not having*' exhibited any proof of his commission from France &c., your Majesty '*has not directed*' Mr. Canning to 'authorize him to speak in your Majesty's name'&c.— which may probably appear more definitive & be less likely to invite a reply from Prince Starhemberg than in the shape in which it stood before, which was, that '*until* Prince Starg. should exhibit "such proof" &c. your Majesty *would not direct*, &c.' (13327–8)

[*The King's reply, Windsor Castle, 8 Jan.*] The King considers that Mr. Canning has improved the answer to Prince Starhemberg's Note by an alteration which renders it more conclusive. (13328)

3582   VISCOUNT CASTLEREAGH *to the* KING

[*Wilderness,*[1] *9 Jan. 1808.*] Lord Castlereagh begs leave humbly to lay before your Majesty the accompanying letter address'd to your Majesty by the King of Persia, which has been transmitted to him by Mr Dundas for that purpose. (13329)

3583   THE DUKE OF PORTLAND *to the* KING, *and the reply*

[*Burlington House, Monday, 11 Jan. 1808.*] The Duke of Portland most humbly begs to assure your Majesty that his Royal Highness the Duke of York's trustees have put into his hands a statement of his Royal Highness's affairs, by which it appears that a sum of twenty thousand pounds is requisite to relieve his Royal Highness from the immediate pressure of some very urgent & embarrassing demands, to the liquidation of which an appropriation of his Royal Highness's income will not admit a sufficient part of it to be applied. But as his Royal Highness the Duke of York was the only Prince of your Majesty's royal House who did not partake of the liberality which your Majesty was graciously pleased last year to extend to all the younger branches of it, a circumstance of which your Majesty may possibly not be aware, the Duke of Portland is encouraged to hope that your Majesty will not be disposed to blame him for bringing that circumstance under your consideration, & for presuming to inform your Majesty that the droits of

[1] Lord Camden's seat in Kent. He was Castlereagh's uncle, his sister Frances having married the 1st Marquess of Londonderry in 1775.

Admiralty continue to afford to your Majesty the same means of extending your benevolence to his Royal Highness the Duke of York which they did last year to the other Princes of your Majesty's royal House. With this view therefore the Duke of Portland has had a warrant prepared for the issue of twenty thousand pounds to the Duke of York's trustees which is herewith submitted with all humility to your Majesty, as the Duke of Portland most humbly conceives that the consideration of the forbearance which has been hitherto manifested by his Royal Highness the Duke of York to trespass upon the generosity of your Majesty, & the perseverance with which he has exerted himself for the purpose of extricating himself from the embarrassments in which he is involved will dispose your Majesty to extend the same degree of liberality to his Royal Highness which your Majesty has already shewn to the other branches of your Majesty's royal family.[1] (16777)

[*The King's reply, Windsor Castle, 12 Jan.*] The King has signed the warrant for the issue of £20,000 to the Duke of York, & the Duke of Portland cannot doubt of the satisfaction which H.M. feels in acquiescing in his proposal to afford such relief for which he rejoices that the necessary funds still exist. (16779)

3584 *Letters from* LORD HAWKESBURY *to the* KING, *and the replies*

[*London, 12 Jan. 1808.*] Lord Hawkesbury begs leave most humbly to submit to your Majesty a petition he has received from Mr. Bacon[2] and requests your Majesty's commands as to the answer to be returned to it. (13330)

[1] Thomas Coutts had written to William Adam, one of the Duke of York's trustees, on 27 Sept. 1807: 'I augur everything that is ill from his Royal Hs. not writing in answer to your letter. He cannot bear the thoughts of retrenching, & I fear nothing will bring him to look his affairs full in the face 'till they are past recovery. Lady Bute seemed by a letter I had from her on entering Scotland to wish it might pass to the Duke's eye as if we had never heard anything of it from her. Her reason is a good one, viz. that it would, if noticed, seem like a contrived plan among us & lose the possibility of effect. Mr. Kendal brought to the Strand since I left it the bills for 3000—

which, with 1400 brought, makes	£4400—of 1249 he says he	
will bring a bill for	1000—in about ten days.	
The remainder of this	249—he expects in Novem.	
of the 500 stock at Byefleet	100—he expects in a fortnight.	
The remaining	400—and also the	
timber unsold valued	351—he cannot reckon upon	
	———	
till Christmas	6500—This is the whole	
except the Oatlands	4000—for stock & crops	
	———	
in all	10500	

With respect to the last article, £4000, he says the offer for the farm is only £1000 a year & £1500 demanded; and the stock cannot be realised 'till an agreement takes place of which he sees no prospect. Neither can the crops be sold 'till then but at a great disadvantage. Therefore beyond the 6500 I see little hopes of my reimbursement tho' I cannot see why the crops should be kept—or how it can be profitable to keep them...'

'P.S. I must notice to you that immediately on hearing of the drafts being refused, I wrote to the Strand & desired if Mr. Dickie found the amount of these drafts between [now] & Xmas did not exceed 4 or 5000, to pay them on his Rl. Hs. word to replace it for the Xmas quarter. But his R.H. seem'd to decline the assistance.' (Blair Adam MSS.)

[2] Either John Bacon (1777–1859), sculptor, or John Bacon (1738–1816) who worked in the first-fruits department of the office of Queen Anne's Bounty.

[*The King's reply, Windsor Castle, 13 Jan.*] The King acquaints Lord Hawkesbury that, as the Governors of the Bank of Ireland appear desirous of employing Mr. Bacon in the execution of the statue to be there erected, his M. has not any objection to his being named. (13331)

[*From Lord Hawkesbury, London, 13 Jan.*] Lord Hawkesbury begs leave most humbly to submit to your Majesty a letter which he has received this evening from Earl Grey[1] and to request your Majesty's commands on what day and at what time your Majesty will be please[d] to receive Earl Grey for the purpose stated in his letter.[2] (13332)

[*The King's reply, Queen's Palace, 14 Jan.*] The King desires that Lord Hawkesbury will appoint Earl Grey to attend here on Wednesday next the 26th inst. for the purpose stated in his letter. (13337)

3585   *Letters from* GEORGE CANNING *to the* KING, *and the reply*

[*Foreign Office, 13 Jan. 1808.*] Mr. Canning humbly lays before your Majesty two Notes received this evening from Prince Starhemberg. By one of them in answer to Mr. Canning's letter of this morning, your Majesty will perceive that Prince Starhemberg admits that he has received no dispatches from his Court of a later date than the 30th October, & that all his late proceedings therefore must have been without instructions. Mr. Canning conceives the discovery of this circumstance to have determined Prince Starhemberg to apply for his passports instead of deferring to do so, as Mr. Canning had heard he intended. (13333)

[*The King's reply, Queen's Palace, 14 Jan.*] The King has read the communications from Prince Starhemberg and Mr. Canning's notes to him of which he entirely approves. H.M. considers that Prince Starhemberg's immediate application for passports will relieve Mr. Canning from the embarassment of a verbal communication which might be misrepresented. (13334)

[*From Canning, Foreign Office, 15 Jan.*] Mr. Canning humbly submits for your Majesty's royal approbation the draft of a letter from your Majesty to the Prince Regent of Portugal. (13338)

[1] Lord Howick had succeeded his father as 2nd Earl Grey on 14 Nov. 1807. Tierney had written to Grey on 26 Nov. 1807: 'Will the death of your father make it necessary for you, either on account of your uncle or the giving up the Order to the King, to come to town soon?' (Howick MSS.) The first Earl Grey had been a K.B. since Jan. 1783. Tierney wrote again, on 1 Dec. 1807: 'Since receiving your letter this morning I have seen Lord Hawkesbury who says you need put yourself to no inconvenience about delivering up your father's Ribband. To remove any appearance of inattention on your part he will mention to the King your application to him, and take the delay upon himself. I dare say he would excuse you if you stayed in Northumberland till next summer.' (*Ibid.*) 'The Ribbon', said Lord Holland (30 Nov.), 'cannot be disposed of till that ceremony [the return of the insignia] is over.' (*Ibid.*)
[2] Missing.

3586 LORD HAWKESBURY *to the* KING, *and the reply*

[*London, 14 Jan. 1808.*] Lord Hawkesbury begs leave most humbly to submit to your Majesty the statement respecting criminals which Lord Hawkesbury took the liberty of mentioning to your Majesty yesterday. These accounts, except No. 3, have all been put together and printed for the first time. The two first numbers will bring before your Majesty in a short compass the state of crimes and capital punishments in the Metropolis and county of Middlesex from the year 1749 to the present period, and the result appears to be very satisfactory. The two last numbers will enable your Majesty to judge of the comparative state of different parts of England and Wales, not only as far as respects offenders of all descriptions, but likewise in regard to that class of your Majesty's subjects who receive parochial relief. (13335)

[*The King's reply, Queen's Palace, 15 Jan.*] The King acknowledges the receipt of Lord Hawkesbury's letter and the accompanying statement which appears to H.M. to be a very interesting document & very clearly & satisfactorily drawn up. (13336)

3587 *Letters from* VISCOUNT CASTLEREAGH *to the* KING, *and the reply*

[*St. James Sqre., 15 Jan. 1808.*] Your Majesty's confidential servants have authorized Lord Castlereagh humbly to submit for your Majesty's approbation the accompanying instructions to Major-General Spencer, and they humbly hope that the reasons assign'd therein will appear to your Majesty sufficient to justify the directions which it appears to them of importance to give to that officer at the present moment.[1] (13339)

[*The King's reply, Queen's Palace, 16 Jan. 1808.*] The King approves of the instructions which Lord Castlereagh has submitted for M. General Spencer, and his Majesty considers them very proper & very applicable to present circumstances. (13340)

[*From Lord Castlereagh, Downing St., Tuesday, 19 Jan., 3 p.m.*] Lord Castlereagh has the satisfaction humbly to acquaint your Majesty that the Island of Madeira surrender'd upon capitulation to M. General Beresford without resistance on the 26th[2] ult. The departure of the Royal Family for the Brazils was known at Madeira before the surrender. Lord Castlereagh submits to your Majesty the Articles of Capitulation, together with M. Genl. Beresford's dispatches. (13342)

---

[1] Not in Castlereagh's own hand. After his return from Copenhagen, Spencer was sent to the Mediterranean with about 5,000 men, to co-operate with Sir John Moore against the Russian fleet in the Tagus, and to attack the French fleet at Cadiz and the Spanish fleet at Port Mahon. Bad weather delayed his arrival at Gibraltar until March. When the Spaniards rose against the French invaders he left Port Mahon and sailed to Cadiz. Finally, in Aug., after the surrender of Dupont's army at Baylen (19 July) made it unnecessary for Spencer to remain near Cadiz, he joined Sir Arthur Wellesley's force at the mouth of the Mondego, and was second in command at Roliça and Vimiero.

[2] Altered from 27th.

[*Admiralty, 19 Jan. 1808.*] Lord Mulgrave has the honour humbly to report to your Majesty the happy event of the capture of the Island of Madeira on the 24th[1] inst. [*sic*]. Lord Mulgrave has the honour to transmit the Articles of Capitulation. (13343)

3589 *Letters from* LORD HAWKESBURY *to the* KING, *and the replies*

[*London, 19 Jan. 1808.*] Lord Hawkesbury begs leave most humbly to inform your Majesty that he has received a letter from the Archbishop of York elect to request your Majesty's permission to allow him to do hommage tomorrow for the Archbishoprick of York. (13341)

[*From Lord Hawkesbury, London, 19 Jan.*] Lord Hawkesbury begs leave most humbly to submit to your Majesty the draft of the Speech of the Lords Commissioners to the Houses of Parliament in your Majesty's name for your Majesty's most gracious consideration.[2] (13344)

[*The King's reply, Queen's Palace, 20 Jan.*] The King has read the draft of the Speech which Lord Hawkesbury has submitted, which, upon the whole, he approves. His M. indeed thinks it rather long, and that it has been usual hitherto more to touch upon than to discuss the points to which it refers, but the King does not feel this objection to be so strong as to induce him to wish to curtail the Speech. His Majesty has altered one expression which appeared to him inconsistent with the language which the Crown is in the habit of holding, but if Lord Hawkesbury should think any other words preferable to those which he has substituted, his Majesty has not any objection to his using them.

The King will receive the Archbishop of York elect this day. (13345)

[*From Lord Hawkesbury, Charles Street, 21 [22] Jan.*] Lord Hawkesbury begs leave most humbly to submit to your Majesty the Minutes of the House of Lords, and to inform your Majesty that the debate went off very satisfactorily. Lord Sidmouth and the Earl of Buckinghamshire spoke very decidedly against the Copenhagen expedition. There was no division.[3]

Lord Hawkesbury begs leave likewise to inform your Majesty that the Lord

---

[1] Altered from (?) 25th to (?) 24th.

[2] The speech was submitted to the King for approval not by the Duke of Portland, the Prime Minister, but by Hawkesbury as Home Secretary. He was also Leader of the House of Lords.

[3] *Parl. Deb.* x, 1–36 (the debate on the Lords Commissioners' Speech at the opening of the Session). The letter must have been written on the 22nd, since the debate went on until about 3 a.m. Lord Grey had this to say about it: 'The debate was most triumphant on our side. Ld. Sidmouth, who seems to have declared open war against the present Administration, spoke, contrary to his usual custom, extremely well, and Ld. Grenville's was I think almost the best speech I ever heard in my life. On the other side nothing could be more contemptible; Hawkesbury's was a flow of roaring nonsense; and absurdity and folly were never more completely exemplified than in Ld. Mulgrave.' (Howick MSS.) Lord Erskine privately remarked that if Hell had not already existed, Providence would now create it to punish Ministers for that damnable expedition.

Steward of your Majesty's Household will wait upon your Majesty tomorrow at two, if that time would not be inconvenient to your Majesty, to receive the Address of the House of Lords. (13346)

[*The King's reply, Queen's Palace, 22 Jan.*] The King has received much satisfaction from Lord Hawkesbury's report of last night's proceedings in the House of Lords, and his Majesty will be prepared to receive the Lord Steward with the Address at any hour this day which may be most convenient to him, as he is not going out. The King desires Lord Hawkesbury will previously send him the answer. (13360)

[*From Lord Hawkesbury, Charles Street, 22 Jan.*] Lord Hawkesbury begs leave most humbly to submit to your Majesty the answer to the Address of the House of Lords. (13364)

3590   *Letters from* SPENCER PERCEVAL *to the* KING, *and the reply*

[*Friday, 1.30 a.m., 22 Jan. 1808.*] Mr. Perceval acquaints your Majesty that the Address from the House of Commons to your Majesty upon the Speech which your Majesty commanded the Lords Commssrs. to deliver to Parliament has been carried without any Amendment being proposed. It was moved for by Lord Hamilton,[1] who proved himself to be a young man of very great ability, and distinguished himself by a very good speech delivered in an extremely good manner. It was seconded by Mr. Chs. Ellis who also spoke very ably and well upon the various topics to which the Speech referred.[2]

Lord Milton spoke first from the other side of the House, at no great length. Mr. Ponsonby followed him and took the course of complaining of the want of information upon the subject of the Copenhagen expedition, and tho' he declined moving any Amendment or even giving a negative to the Address, declared his intention of speaking more fully upon the subject when he would make a Motion for the production of information. Mr. Milnes, whom your Majesty may remember to have spoken two or three times with very great force in the last Session, spoke at considerable length and with great powers & ingenuity in support of the Address. Mr. Whitbread followed Mr. Milnes, and Mr. Secretary Canning, Mr. Whitbread. Mr. Canning, observing upon the strange line which was taken by the other side, adapted however the course of his speech to it; and as it was not intended by the other side to enter much into the debate at that time, but rather to give notice of an intention to renew it on a subsequent occasion, he went shortly thro' the points of the argument upon the subject of the Copenhagen expedition with his usual force & ability; but confined himself rather to pointing out the course of the argument than fully detailing it. He was followed by Lord Henry

---

[1] James, Viscount Hamilton (1786–1814), son of the 1st Marquess of Abercorn (1756–1818). Styled Viscount Hamilton, 1786–1814. M.P. for Dungannon, 1807–7; for Liskeard, 1807–12. The *Complete Peerage* wrongly states that he was elected for Dungannon in 1805.

[2] *Gent. Mag.*, 1808, 1, 66, declared, 'There was nothing remarkable in the speeches of either.'

Petty, Mr. and Mr. [*sic*] Bragg Bathurst. Mr. Bathurst lamented the want of that information which he thought ought to have been produced and was not satisfied with the sufficiency of the reasons which had been urged by Mr. Canning for witholding it.

Mr Windham followed Mr Bathurst, to whom Mr Perceval replied, and the debate ended with two very violent speeches from Mr Sheridan, and Mr Montagu Mathew.[1] They did not however think proper to take any means of obtaining the sense of the House, which Mr Perceval can only ascribe to the conviction which they felt that the sense of the House was very decidedly in support of the Address as it was moved, and Mr Perceval hopes he may present this night's proceeding to his Majesty as a good earnest of the support which his Majesty's Government is likely to meet with from the Ho. of Commons in the present Session.[2] (13361–2)

[*The King's reply, Queen's Palace, 22 Jan.*] The King has received with great pleasure the very satisfactory report which Mr Perceval has been enabled to make of the proceedings in the House of Commons last night; and as there will not be any delay in reporting the Address, his Majesty desires Mr Perceval will acquaint Lord Stopford[3] that he will be prepared to receive from him the Address of the House of Commons at ten o'clock tomorrow morning, previous to which he desires Mr Perceval will send his Majesty the answer, observing that, in addressing the House of Commons, unless it be in the House of Lords, the King's expression is 'Gentlemen', and not 'Gentlemen of the House of Commons.' (13363)

[1] Montagu James Mathew (1773–1819), Whig M.P. for Tipperary, 1806–19. Second son of Francis, 1st Earl of Landaff [I.] (?1738–1806). Cornet, 1792; Lieutenant, 1793; Lieutenant-Colonel, 1794; Colonel, 1794; Major-General, 1808; Lieutenant-General, 1813. He was said to be 'a disgrace to Ireland'.
[2] *Parl. Deb.*, X, 37–82; Colchester, II, 137. Writing to the Duke of Richmond on the 22nd, Sir Arthur Wellesley, the Irish Secretary, commented on the debate: 'The Parlt. met yesterday. Lord Hamilton moved & Ellis seconded the Address in the House of Commons, & both spoke remarkably well. Mills [*sic*] also spoke well, otherwise there was nothing remarkable in the debate excepting a drunken speech from Sheridan towards morning, & a blackguard one from Montague Matthew, who, with the figure of an Irish giant & the voice of a stentor, charged Perceval with treason to 5 millions of Irish Catholics, & me with corruption at the Tipperary election, at which I had spent the public money. George Ponsonby appeared as Leader, but he made but a bad figure. Notwithstanding that you will see that the Speech lays open the whole ground of the Copenhagen expedition, that Ministers declared they would produce no papers upon the subject, & that the Address specifically pledges the House to an approbation of the measure, the Opposition were afraid to divide, no Amendment was moved, & Ponsonby gave notice that he should take another opportunity of bringing the subject forward by a Motion for the production of papers. At the same time I suspect that they are stronger upon the question than they are themselves aware of, & I should not be surprized if we had a debate & division tonight upon the Report of the Address. The Addingtons were decidedly with them, & I understand that the Duke of Norfolk moved an Amendment in the Lords. He was suspected of an intention to join Govt.' (Richmond MSS. 65/835.)
 Writing to his wife, Lord Grey remarked: 'I hear from all quarters that the debate was uncommonly bad. Your uncle's [George Ponsonby's] speech seems to have given satisfaction but John [Lord Ponsonby] and some others, whose anxiety perhaps inclined them to see it in an unfavourable light, have conveyed to me that it was not very good. In general his appointment has been received far beyond my expectation. Whitbread I hear spoke well and Sheridan made a speech, drunk, at the end of the debate, in which amongst much absurdity there were some good things, and which seems to be in general to be praised. Everybody without exception tells me that Canning and Perceval both did very ill, particularly the former.' (Howick MSS.)
[3] Treasurer of the Household.

[*From Perceval, Downing Str.,*[1] *Saturday morng.* [*23 Jan.*].] Mr. Perceval knows not what to say for having neglected to send to his Majy. the accompanying paper before his return from the House last night. He prepared it before he went to the House of Commons, but did not send it lest he should have something to communicate to his Majesty on the subject of the debate yesterday eveng. But that debate having gone off with little or no novelty in it, Mr. Perceval did not think it necessary to trouble his Majy. with any account of it, and from this circumstance he did not think again of his Majesty's reply till he saw it this morning.[2] (13365–6)

3591   *Letters from* VISCOUNT CASTLEREAGH *to the* KING, *and the reply*

[*Stanmore, 30 Jan. 1808.*] Lord Castlereagh humbly begs leave to submit for your Majesty's approbation the accompanying instructions to M. Genl. Spencer. As the force to be assembled in Sicily, when the whole now proceeding there shall arrive, will amount to not less than 16,000 effective rank & file, exclusive of the 4 British regts. under M. Genl. Spencer's orders, it is submitted that these regts. should not under present circumstances proceed on to Sicily, but remain in garrison either at Ceuta, or Gibralter applicable according to circumstances, either to N. America, or other distant services. In the event of Ceuta falling, and their being employ'd in the first instance to garrison that fortress, should these regiments be elsewhere required, they can be relieved in the whole or in part by troops from home whose sp[h]ere of service is more limited.

Your Majesty's servants are humbly of opinion that it is not desireable under present circumstances to appropriate a larger force than 16,000 men for the defence of Sicily, regard being had to the various demands for disposeable force in other quarters. (13367–8)

[*From Castlereagh, Stanmore, 30 Jan.*] The Earl of Londonderry, being solicitous to pay his duty to your Majesty at your Majesty's Levée, has desired Lord Castlereagh humbly to solicit your Majesty's permission that he may attend at the Queen's House on Wednesday next for that purpose. (13369)

---

1 Perceval had hitherto, since the formation of the Government, written from Lincoln's Inn Fields. Writing to Lord Sidmouth on 23 September from Tunbridge Wells, Lord Ellenborough explained the change of address: 'I had a letter from Perceval about ten days ago telling me that he was going into the Downing Street house, the Duke of Portland having given it up to him, and offering me in a very civil manner his house in Lincoln's Inn Fields if it would suit me, for any term, longer or shorter, that I might choose. I declined it as my object is to fix in a situation nearer Westminster Hall....The circumstance of his removing to the Downing Street house shews, I think, that he either contemplates the continuance of the Duke of Portland at the head of the Treasury (which I had thought as improbable an event as it is unfit and disgraceful) or contemplates himself as the probable successor to the Duke in the event of a change.' (Sidmouth MSS.) Perceval slept at No. 10 for the first time on 19 Oct. Shortly afterwards Huskisson, Joint Secretary of the Treasury (he was in the main the Financial Secretary), went to live at the official residence of the Chancellor of the Exchequer, whilst Robert Dundas, President of the Board of Control, moved into the house which had been occupied by Sir Charles Morgan.

2 *Parl. Deb.* x, 83–94 (the debate on the Address in answer to the Lords Commissioners' Speech. The 'accompanying paper' was the King's answer to the Address.

[*The King's reply, Windsor Castle, 31 Jan.*] The King approves of the instructions to M. Genl. Spencer which Lord Castlereagh has now submitted and of the distribution proposed for the regiments under his command.

His M. will receive the Earl of Londonderry on Wednesday next. (13368)

3592 LORD HAWKESBURY *to the* KING, *and the reply*

[*Charles Street, 31 Jan. 1808.*] Lord Hawkesbury begs leave most humbly to submit to your Majesty whether as Wednesday is the day on which the Sheriffs of England and Wales will be nominated for the present year, the Princes of your Majesty's Royal Family should be summon'd to the Council. The Lord Chancellor suggested this for your Majesty's consideration, and the Lord President would not take any steps for summoning their Royal Highnesses until he had received your Majesty's commands on the subject. It appears that some of their Royal Highnesses have attended this ceremony on former occasions, but Lord Hawkesbury has not been able to learn whether it was in consequence of any special summons for that purpose. (13370)

[*The King's reply, Windsor Castle, 1 Feb.*] The King acquaints Lord Hawkesbury that he is correct in his conclusion that it has not been usual for the Princes of his Majesty's family to attend the Council when the Sheriffs are nominated. They may have been present accidentally but never in consequence of any special summons, which the King considers unnecessary upon this occasion. (13371)

3593 THE MARQUESS OF THOMOND *to the* KING

[*London, 2 Feb. 1808.*] I humbly venture to approach your Majesty with a request, and I am emboldened to do so in consequence of what your Majesty was graciously pleased to say on my application a few years ago for the honour of being appointed one of your Majesty's Lords of the Bedchamber.

The office of Master of the Robes being now vacant by the death of Lord Selsea,[1] I humbly solicit your Majesty to confer on me the honour of that appointment. With the deepest feeling of attachment to your Majesty's person, and the most unbounded sense of your Majesty's goodness, I am [etc.].[2] (13372)

3594 SPENCER PERCEVAL *to the* KING, *and the reply*

[*Thursday morng., 5 a.m., 4 Feb. 1808.*] Mr. Perceval acquaints your Majesty that the House is just up, having divided 253 to 108 against the Motions made by Mr Ponsonby for earlier papers relative to the information which your Majesty's

[1] James Peachey, Baron Selsey (1723–1808), 2nd son of Sir John Peachey, 2nd Bart. M.P. for Seaford, 1755–68. Succeeded his brother as 4th Baronet, 1765; created a peer, 13 Aug. 1794. Groom of the Bedchamber to George, Prince of Wales, 1751–60; to him when King, 1760–91; Master of the Robes 1791–1808; died 1 Feb.

[2] General Harcourt was appointed. Lord Thomond died eight days after making his application: he was run over by a cart in Grosvenor Square after falling from his horse.

Government might have received with regard to the disposition of the Danish Government. The debate turned almost wholly upon the Danish expedition and from its nature did not admit of a great deal of novelty. Mr Canning answered Mr Ponsonby in a speech of considerable length & detail and of very great ability indeed, and he made a very great impression upon the House. Mr. Windham followed Mr Canning. Mr Milnes spoke again, and very well, but not at so much length or perhaps with quite so much effect as before.[1]

Lord Palmerston spoke for the first time and very well. Mr Bragg Bathurst & Mr Whitbread both spoke for the production of the papers, Ld Granville Leveson against, stating his opinion fully (having been called upon by Mr Whitbread) that the Danish expedition did not occasion the war with Russia. Lord Castlereagh shewed that he was well recovered, as he took a very useful part in the debate at a very late hour, and was fully equal to the exertion. Mr Thos. Grenville spoke a few words distinguishing, or endeavouring to distinguish the Lisbon expedition under Ld. St. Vincent & Genl. Simcoe from the similarity in principle which was said to exist between that measure as intended & the Copenhagen measure as executed. The debate closed by a short reply from Mr Ponsonby, and Mr Perceval can venture to assure your Majesty that the whole impression of the debate was as favorable as the result of it in the numbers of the division.[2] (13373–4)

[1] Palmerston thought that Milnes's object in speaking again was to show that he was as good in reply as on preparation. 'His speech was a bad one.' (Bulwer's *Palmerston*, I, 80; and see Lady Holland's *Journal*, II, 240.)

[2] *Parl. Deb.* x, 252–310, where the list of the minority is given. About forty members were believed to have paired off. (Colchester, II, 138.) Palmerston wrote: 'I was tempted by some evil spirit to make a fool of myself for the entertainment of the House last night. However, I thought it was a good opportunity of breaking the ice, although one should flounder a little in doing so, as it was impossible to talk any very egregious nonsense upon so good a cause. Canning's speech was one of the most brilliant and convincing I ever heard; it lasted near three hours. He carried the House with him throughout, and I have scarcely ever heard such loud and frequent cheers. Ponsonby was dull and heavy, and neither Windham nor Whitbread were as good as usual; in fact, Canning's speech was so powerful that it gave a decisive turn to the debate. Lord Granville Leveson made a very good speech, and stated an important fact—that all the impartial people in Russia and other parts of the Continent, as far as he had any opportunity of collecting their sentiments, highly applauded, instead of condemning, our Danish expedition. Our division was not as large as I expected. The Opposition were not more numerous, but we were less so than I expected.' (Bulwer, I, 80–1.)

Lord Grey was in the House, and wrote to his wife: 'Your uncle's speech was really very good and was felt to be so by the House, tho' I do not say that it was exempt from faults, but I hear from everybody that it has given general satisfaction, and even John, who you know is very difficult, and on this occasion from nervousness and anxiety was doubly so, was not dissatisfied with it. Canning's speech will I have no doubt be very much celebrated. It certainly was eloquent and powerful, at least the parts I heard of it, but for audacious misrepresentation and even for positive falsehood I never heard it equalled. I only heard a small part of the rest of the debate which, upon the whole, I am afraid was not favourable to Opposition.' (Howick MSS.) Though Ponsonby had spoken before, this, said Lady Holland, was considered as a debut. 'His friends were rather anxious, as his forte lies more in reply than in the opening of a business. However, he acquitted himself well, and people seem to be generally satisfied with him.' (Lady Holland's *Journal*, II, 239.)

The brief report of Thomas Grenville's 'few words' hardly brings out the point made by Perceval but Windham said that the 1806 expedition to the Tagus, whose purpose had been to prevent the Portuguese fleet from falling into French hands, had been recalled because it proved to be unnecessary. The Portuguese fleet was not to have been seized until the Portuguese Government had refused British assistance to defend its territory, until a French army had invaded Portugal, and until it had become perfectly clear that if Britain did not take possession of the fleet, France would do so.

[The King's reply, Windsor Castle, 4 Feb.] The King acknowledges the receipt of Mr Perceval's letter & his M. has learnt with great pleasure from it that the debate in the House of Commons last night proved in every point of view so satisfactory. (13374)

3595 VISCOUNT CASTLEREAGH *to the* KING, *and the reply*

[St. James's Sq., 4 Feb. 1808.] Lord Castlereagh humbly begs leave to present, on the part of the Chairman & Deputy Chairman of the East India Company,[1] to your Majesty, the accompanying gold medal, struck in commemoration of the reduction of Seringapatam in the last Mysore war,[2] and of which they humbly request your Majesty's gracious acceptance. (13375)

[The King's reply, Windsor Castle, 5 Feb.] The King has received Lord Castlereagh's letter with the accompanying communication & medal sent by the Chairman & Deputy Chairman of the East India Company & his Majesty desires Lord Castlereagh will assure them that he is sensible of their attention in presenting the medal to him. (13376)

3596 SPENCER PERCEVAL *to the* KING, *and the reply*

[Downing Str., Sat. morng., 1.45 a.m. [6 Feb. 1808].] Mr Perceval acquaints your Majesty that the debate of this evening in the House of Commons took place upon a Motion made by Mr Perceval for the House going into a Committee of Ways & Means to consider of the Orders-in-Council. Lord Henry Petty opposed the Motion upon the grounds of the illegality of those Orders as contrary to the law of nations, as well as contrary to the statute law of the land; Mr Perceval answered him; and Dr Laurence followed Mr Perceval on the same side of the question with Lord Henry Petty. To Dr Laurence the Master of the Rolls replied, and in one of those luminous and convincing speeches for which he has been so frequently distinguished, he so satisfactorily and convincingly disposed of Dr Laurence's arguments, that tho' Mr Windham & Sir Arthur Pigott both spoke after him there was no necessity for prolonging the debate & the House without a division adopted Mr Perceval's Motion. Mr Perceval has the more satisfaction in giving to your Majesty the report of this debate because he has been given to understand that these Orders-in-Council were considered by the Opposition as likely to afford them one of the best opportunities which were likely to occur of making some impression upon the House and the country to the prejudice of the measures of your Maj.'s Government—and Mr. Perceval thinks that the discussion of this evening has set those Orders so completely in their right light that

[1] Edward Parry and Charles Grant. Charles Grant (1746–1823), M.P. for Invernessshire, 1802–18, had been in the service of the East India Company for many years, and was the father of Lord Glenelg.
[2] In 1799 when Tipu was defeated and killed.

there is no chance of their being able now to make any impression upon the public against them at all.[1] (14039–40)

[*The King's reply, Windsor Castle, 6 Feb.*] The King is very glad to learn from Mr Perceval's report that the debate of last night in the House of Commons upon the Orders-in-Council has tended so effectually to place those Orders in their right light & that the Master of the Rolls has with his usual sagacity felt the propriety of giving his opinion upon this occasion. (13377)

3597   THE DUKE OF KENT *to the* KING, *and the reply*

[*Windsor Castle, 6 Feb. 1808.*] The letters received by the mail just arrived from the Mediterranean, having brought the certain information that orders had reached Algeziras from Madrid, immediately to make such preparations in the neighbour-hood of Gibraltar as put beyond all doubt the intention of the enemy to besiege it, I could not under such circumstances reconcile it to my feelings, were I to delay a moment in not only assuring your Majesty of my readiness instantly to go out there, but in earnestly solliciting your sanction for my resuming the duties attached to the commission I have the honor of holding as Governor of that fortress. To your Majesty who yourself possess so nice a sense of honor, it is quite unnecessary for me to represent that, on the result of your decision upon this request, which I beg leave, in the most dutiful yet in the strongest manner to press upon your attention, everything most dear to me in life, I mean, my character as a man and my professional credit as a soldier, are at stake: I will not therefore presume to say more than that I place these in your Majesty's hands with no less confidence in your justice, as my Sovereign, than in your indulgence as my parent.

With every sentiment of the most devoted attachment, and of the most dutiful respect I have the honor [etc.]. (46351).

[*The King's reply, Windsor Castle, 9 Feb.*] The King has received the Duke of Kent's letter, and, while he is sensible of the propriety of the motives which have influenced him in his application to be allowed to resume the actual government of Gibraltar at this moment, his Majesty regrets that he should feel under the necessity of declining to acquiesce in it, although in referring to past occurrences he has no hesitation in again assuring the Duke of Kent that he is persuaded that the circumstances which produced his removal from Gibraltar may be attributed to over zeal on his part. The King has also been made aware of the Duke of Kent's wish to obtain, under certain restrictions, the command in the Mediterranean in the event of his return to Gibraltar not being deemed adviseable, and his Majesty is much concerned that various considerations should occur upon this occasion which do not, in his opinion, admit of his sanctioning such an arrangement.[2] (13380)

[1] *Parl. Deb.*, x, 314–40.
[2] If the letters were correctly dated, it is a fair assumption that the King consulted the Duke of York before replying.

3598   LORD MULGRAVE *to the* KING

[*Admiralty, 7 Feb. 1808.*] Lord Mulgrave has the honour to transmit to your Majesty dispatches from Sir Alexander Cockrane stating the surrender of the Danish Islands in the West Indies. Lord Mulgrave begs your Majesty's permission most humbly to congratulate your Majesty on the happy circumstance of the conquest having been atchieved without any effusion of blood. (13378)

3599   VISCOUNT CASTLEREAGH *to the* KING

[*St James's Square, 7 Feb. 1808.*] Lord Castlereagh begs leave to lay before your Majesty the translation of a letter which has been address'd to your Majesty by the Nabob of Arcot. The original having been entrusted to Lord William Bentinck, Lord Castlereagh has also the honor humbly to transmit it to your Majesty.[1] (13379)

3600   LORD HAWKESBURY *to the* KING

[*Charles Street, 11 Feb. 1808.*] Lord Hawkesbury begs leave most humbly to submit to your Majesty the Minutes of the House of Lords. There was no division on any of Lord Grey's Motions for papers, part of which was not opposed.[2] Lord

Though the Duke was unable to perform his duties as Governor of Gibraltar, he continued to receive pay and allowances:

Pay as General & Governor at £8 p. day			£2920
Deduct 1/6 in the pound	£219		
Do one day's pay in the year	8		
		227	
			£2693 0 0
Deduct Property Tax of 10 p.c. on the residue			269 6 0
			£2423 14 0
Contingent allowance as Governor, provided for in the War Office Estimate	£950		
Deduct Property Tax at 10 p.c.	95		
			855 0 0
Extra allowance from the revenues of Gibraltar	£2800		
Deduct Property Tax at 10 p.c.	280		
			2520 0 0
General Total to receive			£5798 14 0

The pay as General & Governor and the Contingent Allowance are payable regularly from the Military Chest at Gibraltar 25 March, 25 June, 25 Septr. & 25 December.

The Extra Allowance is paid half-yearly 30 June and 30 December. (46357–8)

[1] Bentinck had just returned to England, having been recalled from Madras by the Court of Directors following the mutiny at Vellore.

[2] Grey wished for the production of papers relative to the mediation offered by Russia and Austria. Castlereagh was prepared to produce many, but not all, of the papers moved for. Grey explained his purpose in a letter on the 5th: 'The object...is to enable me to make a statement in refutation of the charges brought against the late Government. This has been perhaps delayed too long, but the scandalous misrepresentations, not to say falsehoods, resorted to by Canning in the H. of Commons made it impossible to put off the justification which we owe to ourselves and to the country any longer. It is impossible for any person unacquainted with the facts to conceive the length of audacious falsehoods to which he has gone. If I had been in the House of Commons at the time I hardly know how I could have spoken of it without violating the rules of Parliamentary decorum. The heat occasioned by all this is becoming very great, and will probably produce some violence in the H. of Commons, but the

Hutchinson made another attempt to read letters which had passed between him and your Majesty's servants,[1] but he was called to order, and after some warm debate he at last desisted from his purpose.[2] (13381)

3601   GENERAL WILLIAM HARCOURT *to the* KING

[*Brighton, 12 Feb. 1808.*] So many and so great have been the favours and personal kindness I have ever received from your Majesty, that nothing can encrease my attachment or gratitude, nor any circumstance lessen it; yet as I formerly presumed to apply to your Majesty for the situation of Master of the Robes, I take the liberty now to remind your Majesty of my humble wishes to be removed to that office which your Majesty has generally disposed of to the eldest Groom of your Bedchamber; a situation which I have had the honour of holding about your Majesty's person for several years. With the most profound respect and attachment I have the honour to be [etc.].[3] (13386)

3602   VISCOUNT CASTLEREAGH *to the* KING, *and the reply*

[*St James's Sq., 16 Feb. 1808.*] The colony of Sierra Leone on the coast of Africa having been transfer'd by Act of Parliament from the Sierra Leone Company and placed under your Majesty's controul—Lord Castlereagh humbly begs leave to recommend Mr. Thomas Thompson[4] to be appointed Governor of that Settlement. (13391)

[*The King's reply, Windsor Castle, 17 Feb.*] The King [acquiesces[5]] in Lord Castlereagh's recommendation of Mr. Thomas Thompson to be Governor of the Colony of Sierra Leone. (13392)

3603   *Letters from* LORD HAWKESBURY *to the* KING, *and the reply*

[*Charles Street, 16 Feb. 1808.*] Lord Hawkesbury begs leave most humbly to submit to your Majesty the Minutes of the House of Lords and at the same time

gravity of the H. of Lords will prevent this, but not, I hope, so as to diminish the effect of a strong exposure of the most violent system of misrepresentation and falsehood ever practised.' (Howick MSS.)

[1] Lord Hutchinson had been sent to treat with Prussia at the end of 1806, had signed a peace treaty with Prussia on 28 Jan. 1807, and had left the neighbourhood of Memel on 20 July 1807 for Russia.

[2] *Parl. Deb.*, x, 431–49.

[3] His wishes were soon gratified (see No. 3751), and he was Master of the Robes until 1809 when he succeeded his brother as Master of the Horse to the Queen, an office which he retained until her death (*Courier*, 1 May 1809). He first appears in the Red Book as the First Groom of the Bedchamber in 1802.

[4] Thomas Perronet Thompson (1783–1869), a son of Thomas Thompson (1754–1828), merchant and banker of Hull, and M.P. for Midhurst, 1807–18. Entered the army, 1806, after four years' service in the navy. He owed his appointment to the influence of Wilberforce, a friend of his father. The Sierra Leone Company had been founded in 1791 to establish a settlement there for liberated slaves from Nova Scotia and also with the idea of introducing civilisation into that part of Africa from which slaves were drawn for transshipment to America and the West Indies. This philanthropic enterprise failed to prosper and Sierra Leone became a Crown Colony in 1807. Thompson proved to be an unsuitable Governor and he was soon recalled.   [5] Word omitted.

to inform your Majesty that the debate went off very favourably. Earl Bathurst and the Lord Chancellor made two excellent speeches. Lord Grenville spoke in answer to the Chancellor two hours and a half but did not appear to make any particular impression. Lord Hawkesbury regrets to say that the House is not as well attended as it should be under such circumstances.[1] (13393)

[*The King's reply, Windsor Castle, 16 Feb.*] The King acknowledges the receipt of Lord Hawkesbury's letter & the Minutes of the House of Lords from which his Majesty has learnt with pleasure that the debate upon the Orders-in-Council was so favourable. (13394)

[*From Lord Hawkesbury, Charles Street, 18 Feb.*] Lord Hawkesbury begs leave most humbly to submit to your Majesty the Minutes of the House of Lords. It is with considerable regret that Lord Hawkesbury is under the necessity of informing your Majesty that at an early hour in the day your Majesty's Government were outvoted on a question for the production of a paper embarrassing to your Majesty's Govt.[2] The great and pernicious activity of the Opposition renders it necessary for Lord Hawkesbury in duty to your Majesty most humbly to state to you that your Majesty's Govt. is not adequately supported in the House of Lords either by your Majesty's Household or by the Bishops, and that it is of the utmost importance that your Majesty should communicate your wishes and expectations on the subject to the Lord Chamberlain and to the Archbishop of Canterbury.

Lord Hawkesbury trusts to your Majesty's goodness in excusing this humble representation on his part, but as a great part of the labour of conducting your Majesty's Govt. in the House of Lords falls unavoidably upon Lord Hawkesbury he hopes he may be allowed to say that he feels it of the greatest importance to the credit and ease of your Majesty's Government that in times like the present he should appear to have the the [*sic*] constant and active support in the House of Lords of all those persons who hold offices in your Majesty's Household as well as of those who must be sensible how much the security of the establishment in Church and State is connected with the support of your Majesty's Govt. (13397–8)

3604 LORD MULGRAVE *to the* KING, *and the reply*

[*Admiralty, 18 Feb. 1808.*] Lord Mulgrave humbly begs leave to solicit your Majesty's gracious indulgence for an omission in the Admiralty Office, in consequence of which the dispatches received from Vice Admirally [*sic*] Sir John

[1] *Parl. Deb.*, x, 465–86 (15 Feb.). The list of the minority is given, the numbers being, excluding proxies, 61 *v*. 30; with proxies, 106 *v*. 48. Hawkesbury may have been referring obliquely to the poor attendance of the 'Household troops', as he was compelled to do openly in the next letter.

[2] *Parl. Deb.*, x, 641–2. Hawkesbury unsuccessfully resisted Grenville's Motion for the production of information which would justify the statement contained in the recent Orders-in-Council that the French Government was executing its own Decree against British trade with increased rigour. The voting was 47 to 38, and the list of the majority is given in column 642, the Duke of Gloucester being one of the 47.

Duckworth & Rear-Admiral Sir Samuel Hood were not this morning submitted to your Majesty. The accounts are vague and unsatisfactory—a line of battle ship & a frigate, supposed to be part of the Rochfort squadron, had chased your Majesty's ship Comus on the 24th of January; in consequence of this intelligence Sir John Duckworth had determined on the 27th of January to proceed to the West Indies with his squadron of five sail of the line, of which three are three-deck ships. The French ships were seen Latitude 33° 50, Longitude 21. (13395)

[*The King's reply, Windsor Castle, 19 Feb.*] The King acquaints Lord Mulgrave that the delay which occurred accidentally in the transmission of the intelligence from Sir John Duckworth was immaterial, as his Majesty was aware of the substance, and as the information is in general so vague. (13396)

3605   SPENCER PERCEVAL *to the* KING, *and the reply*

[*Downg. St., 18 [sic] Feb. 1808.*] Mr Perceval acquaints your Majesty that the second reading of the Bill for carrying into effect the Orders-in-Council came on this evening and it lasted till a $\frac{1}{4}$ p. 3 when the House divided 214 to 94 for the second reading.

Mr Eden began the debate against the Bill, and the Advocate General[1] answered him; the Advocate General took a very enlarged and able view of the whole subject and seemed to give great satisfaction. Lord Temple, Mr Hibbert, and Mr Wm. Smith spoke against it & Mr Rose for it, and the debate went on with a very long and certainly a very able speech of Ld. Henry Petty against the Bill, which was answered by Lord Castlereagh. Mr Perceval acquaints yr. Majesty that it was committed for this day, when the House will probably have a renewed debate upon it.[2] (13401)

[*The King's reply, Windsor Castle, 19 Feb.*] The King acknowledges the receipt of Mr Perceval's letter & is glad to hear that the second reading of the Bill for carrying into effect the Orders-in-Council was carried by so respectable a majority. (13402)

3606   GEORGE CANNING *to the* KING, *and the reply*

[*Foreign Office, 20 Feb. 1808.*] Mr. Canning humbly lays before your Majesty an original dispatch from the King of Sweden to M. Adlerberg, communicated by that Minister to Mr Canning this day, in which his Swedish Majesty expresses his strong sense of your Majesty's conduct towards him, & especially of the distinguished manner in which your Majesty has been pleased to make mention of the King of Sweden in the Speech delivered by your Majesty's commands at the

[1] Sir John Nicholl.
[2] *Parl. Deb.*, x, 665–684. The letter must have been written after 3.30 a.m. on the 19th. 'Petty', wrote Lord Grey on the 19th, 'is universally said to have made one of the best speeches that ever was heard.' (Howick MSS.)

opening of the present Session of Parliament.[1] Mr. Adlerberg was directed to take the most certain means for bringing this letter under your Majesty's notice: but Mr Canning has been able to satisfy the Swedish Minister with the promise of submitting it to your Majesty without soliciting of your Majesty an audience for Mr. Adlerberg in person. (13403–4)

[*The King's reply, Windsor Castle, 21 Feb.*] The King approves of Mr Canning having persuaded Mr Adlerberg to allow him to submit the King of Sweden's letter, and his Majesty desires that Mr Canning will write an ostensible letter to Mr Adlerberg, expressive of the favorable sentiments which he entertains for the King of Sweden & of the interest which he takes in his success. (13404)

3607   *Letters from the* DUKE OF PORTLAND *to the* KING, *and the replies*

[*Burlington House, Tuesday night, 23 Feb. 1808.*] At the unanimous request of your Majesty's confidential servants, the Duke of Portland most humbly begs leave to lay before your Majesty a statement of the circumstances to which the family of the late Viscount Lake is reduced by the melancholy event of his un-expected and untimely death.[2] The fortunes which his property has enabled him to leave to his five daughters,[3] amount only to fifteen hundred pounds each. To his second son,[4] who is Lieutenant-Colonel of the 29th Foot, he has left three thousand pounds. To his third son,[5] who is in your Majesty's Royal Navy, he has given five thousand pounds—and the residue of his property, which, after deduct-ing a legacy of one thousand pounds to his brother, Mr. Warwick Lake,[6] and legacies of two hundred and one hundred pounds to two of his servants, and discharging a mortgage of four thousand pounds charged on his landed estate[7] in Buckinghamshire, which produces about eight hundred pounds a year, and defray-

[1] 'The King of Sweden has resisted every attempt to induce him to abandon his alliance with Great Britain...and his Majesty entertains no doubt that you will feel with him the sacredness of the duty which the firmness and fidelity of the King of Sweden impose upon his Majesty, and that you will concur in enabling his Majesty to discharge it in a manner worthy of this country.' (*Parl. Deb.*, x, 4.)

[2] Lord Lake, who, on his return to England from India had been made a Viscount (4 Nov. 1807), caught a severe cold whilst attending the court martial on General Whitelocke, and died of its effects on 21 Feb. He gambled away most of his money. Michael Angelo Taylor said he had come back home with only £40,000 to provide for a wife and seven children. (*Parl. Deb.*, x, 790.)

[3] Anna Maria (d. 1837), who married Richard Borough (cr. Baronet, Nov. 1813); Annabella d. 1831), who in 1803 married John Brooks (*Collins' Peerage*; Joseph Brookes, according to *Burke's Peerage*); Elizabeth, who in 1806 married Sir John Harvey, K.C.B.; Frances; and Anne (who married only in 1812).

[4] George Augustus Frederick Lake (1781–1808). Page to the Prince of Wales. Lieutenant-Colonel, 1803. Killed at Roliça in the Peninsular War, 17 Aug. 1808. In the Red Book for 1806 he was described as Deputy Adjutant General in the East Indies.

[5] Warwick Lake (d. 1848). Lieutenant, 1804; Commander, 1806; Captain, Sept. 1808. Succeeded his brother Francis Gerard as 3rd Viscount Lake, 1836. In 1810 he was dismissed the service by sentence of court martial for an act of gross cruelty to a seaman, Richard Jeffery—abandoning him on a desert island in the West Indies—when in command of the sloop *Recruit*. See No. 4126. He succeeded to a pension of £2,000 a year on his brother's death.

[6] He had been one of the Prince of Wales's Grooms of the Bedchamber until the Prince's indebted-ness forced him to cut down his establishment (d. 1821).

[7] Aston Clinton, near Aylesbury.

ing the debts and funeral expences, is settled upon his eldest son;[1] and it is estimated may produce about twenty thousand pounds—so that the representative of the late Lord Lake will not be in possession of an income of quite two thousand pounds a year to support those honours which your Majesty was graciously pleased to confer as the reward of his father's distinguished services.

The reflections which arise out of the circumstances which the Duke of Portland has been desired to submit to the consideration of your Majesty, dispose your Majesty's confidential servants to recommend with all humility to your Majesty's superior wisdom to make such a provision for the present Lord Lake and his successors in the title as it has been customary for your Majesty, in your great benevolence, to grant in similar cases; the usual amount of which has been two thousand pounds a year for the lives of the grantee, and the next two in succession —and in case this suggestion should be so fortunate as to receive the sanction of your Majesty's approbation it is humbly hoped that your Majesty will be pleased to direct Lord Viscount Castlereagh, and Lord Hawkesbury to prepare a proper Message from your Majesty to the two Houses of Parliament, in order to enable your Majesty to carry your gracious intentions into effect.[2] (13412–4)

[*The King's reply, Windsor Castle, 24 Feb.*] Under the circumstances which the Duke of Portland has represented, the King readily acquiesces in what is proposed in regard to making a suitable provision for the present Lord Lake, at the same time that his Majesty trusts that his Ministers will admit this instance as a further proof of the impropriety of granting Peerages where there is not any property to support the rank. The King must upon this occasion advert particularly to the situation in which the daughters of the late Lord Lake have been left. Two of them are unmarried, were recommended to his Majesty by Lord Lake at his death-bed, and have strong claims to his protection. (13415)

[*From the Duke of Portland, ? 26 Feb.*[3]] The Duke of Portland having been most unfortunately prevented from paying his duty to your Majesty on Wednesday last, is under the necessity of resorting to this mode of acquainting your Majesty that in pursuance of your Majesty's commands to Count Munster, he has received the copy of a letter[4] from his Serene Highness the Duke of Brunswick-Oels to your Majesty, in which, after stating the extreme distress to which he and his family are reduced, his Serene Highness implores your Majesty to grant him an annual pecuniary allowance until his hereditary dominions shall be restored to him. The Duke of Portland therefore most humbly requests that your Majesty's pleasure may be signified to him in this respect. Your Majesty is apprized that two

[1] Francis Gerard, 2nd Viscount Lake (1772–1836). Lieutenant-Colonel, 1st Foot Guards, 1798; Colonel, 1808; Major-General, 1811; Lieutenant-General, 1821. A Lord of the Bedchamber, 1813, 1820–30.

[2] The King's Message, embodying these proposals, was presented to the House of Commons on 24 Feb. (*Parl. Deb.*, x, 711.)

[3] Parts of this letter came to be separated, hence the peculiar numbering of the folios. The first paragraph is clearly answered by the King's letter of the 27th. There could not very well be separate letters here, for the first sheet has no date or address.

[4] No. 3578.

thousand pounds have been remitted, according to the directions of her Royal Highness the Duchess of Brunswick, for the use of Prince George and Prince Augustus of Brunswick,[1] the expences of whose maintenance the Duke of Portland understands it to be her Royal Highness's opinion that that sum will be very sufficient to defray for the next three quarters or perhaps the whole of the ensuing year. But as the Duke of Brunswick-Oels has a family,[2] and an encreasing one, to provide for, the Duke of Portland cannot but be apprehensive of the inadequacy of such a provision in the case of his Serene Highness, and therefore submits with all humility to your Majesty the expediency of requesting her Royal Highness the Duchess of Brunswick's opinion respecting the amount of the provision which your Majesty may be disposed to allow to the Duke of Brunswick. (13579–80)

[*Burlington House, Friday night, 26 Feb. 1808.*] The disposition which your Majesty has at different times been graciously pleased to intimate, to bestow some mark of your royal favour on the Earl of Mount Edgcumbe,[3] encourages the Duke of Portland to submit to your Majesty the propriety of appointing that Earl to the command of the Band of Gentlemen Pensioners, now vacant by the death of the late Viscount Falmouth.[4] The Duke of Portland is well assured that it is an employment which will be most gratefully accepted by Lord Mount Edgcumbe; and he feels it his duty to add that Lord Mount Edgcumbe's loyalty and zealous attachment to your Majesty, and the liberality and steadiness with which he constantly supports the measures of your Majesty's Government, very justly entitle him to such a mark of distinction.

The Duke of Portland humbly begs leave to offer to your Majesty's consideration two other noble persons who have expressed their anxiety to bear some distinguishing mark of your Majesty's royal favour, namely, the Earl of Aberdeen,[5]

[1] The Duke's surviving brothers, (1769–1811) and (1770–1820) respectively, who renounced their rights to the succession on their father's death in 1806. Neither of them married: they were imbeciles. The Princess of Wales, of course, was their sister.

[2] He had two sons, Charles (1804–73) and William (1806–84).

[3] Richard, 2nd Earl of Mount Edgcumbe (1764–1839), succeeded his father on 4 Feb. 1795. Styled Viscount Valletort, 1789–95. M.P. for Lostwithiel, 1790–1; for Fowey, 1791–5; Captain of the Gentlemen Pensioners, 1808–12.　　　　　　　　[4] On 11 Feb. 1808.

[5] George Gordon, 4th Earl of Aberdeen (1784–1860). Succeeded his grandfather, 30 Aug. 1801. Styled Lord Haddo, 1791–1801. Scottish Representative Peer, 1806–18. K.T., 16 March 1808. Ambassador to Austria, 1813–14; Plenipotentiary at Châtillon-sur-Seine and at Paris, 1814; U.K. Peerage as Viscount Gordon, 1 June 1814. Chancellor of the Duchy of Lancaster, Jan.–June 1828; Foreign Secretary, June 1828–Nov. 1830, and 1841–6. Prime Minister, 1852–5. Lord Aberdeen had written to Lord Melville on 23 June 1807: 'I must inform you of my having seen the Duke of Portland lately on the subject of the Green Ribbon; after a great deal of persuasion and conversation with Lord Abercorn I agreed to speak to him (for it was my wish to have postponed it until a future occasion). He was very civil, spoke doubtingly about the present vacancy, but of his own accord promised the next, if this could not be obtained without interfering with any arrangement already made. I need not of course say that this is for your own eye.' (Melville MSS.)

As yet, this young man had little to recommend him for a mark of the King's favour. He had evidently wished to be in Parliament, but spoke rather contemptuously of politicians. Writing to Hudson Gurney on 8 October 1809, when Perceval was forming his Ministry, he said : 'These changes and intrigues of Ministers give me little trouble. The trade is so contemptible that a wise man must despise it, and so nefarious that an honest man must abhor it. Yet after all it is possible I may become one of the gang. Such is our consistency!' (Gurney MSS.)

who is a candidate for the Green Ribbon which has been so long vacant,[1] for which he has no competitor, and to which he has acquired some degree of pretension at least by his having repeatedly taken occasion to support the measures of your Majesty's Government in the House of Lords, and having acquitted himself with no inconsiderable share of credit upon every such occasion. The Viscount Strangford is the other candidate for a similar mark of favour. He has represented in so forcible a manner the advantage which would be derived to the management of your Majesty's concerns at the Court of Brazil by his returning there with the decorations of the Order of the Bath, and the Duke of Portland is so well aware of the impression which such marks of your Majesty's favour never fail to make on the publick mind in foreign Courts, that he cannot with justice withhold his assent to Lord Strangford's opinion and wishes in that respect, and he therefore cannot but express his humble but anxious hope that your Majesty may condescend to grant Lord Strangford's request.[2]

The next subject on which the Duke of Portland has to trouble your Majesty is the Lieutenancy of the county of Norfolk, which, notwithstanding the many objections to which the appointment is liable, it is so evidently and decidedly the unanimous opinion of all your Majesty's confidential servants that your Majesty's interest and the success of your Majesty's business in the House of Commons require should be placed in the hands of Lord Suffield[3] or his eldest son Mr. Harbord,[4] that it would be inexcusable in the Duke of Portland not only not to acquiesce in it, but to abstain from humbly recommending to your Majesty to accede to it. The state of Lord Suffield's health is such as to make it all but impossible for him to attend your Majesty in Council to take the oaths of office. Objectionable therefore as it is, the Duke of Portland most humbly submits to your Majesty that it will be less so to appoint Mr Harbord to the Lieutenancy, who is capable of performing the duties of it, than his father, and upon that ground the Duke of Portland rests his hope that your Majesty may condescend to permit the appointment to be made out in the name of Mr Harbord. The vacancy of this Lieutenancy has been twice made the subject of observation in the House of Commons by Mr Windham, and that circumstance has occasioned the rest of your Majesty's servants to urge the Duke of Portland to make this representation to your Majesty without further delay; which he very seriously regrets, as it deprives him of stating to your Majesty several circumstances relative to it which it would have been a great relief to the Duke of Portland's mind to have laid before your Majesty previous to this measure's taking place.

There remains at present only one other circumstance on which it is necessary for the Duke of Portland to request your Majesty's pleasure, and that respects the disposal of the Rectory of Sigglesthorne in the East Riding of Yorkshire, which the Duke of Portland humbly begs leave to solicit your Majesty to have the

[1] That is, since the death of the Earl of Galloway on 13 Nov. 1806.
[2] K.B., 16 March 1808.
[3] Sir Harbord Harbord (1734–1810), created Baron Suffield, 21 Aug. 1786. M.P. for Norwich, 1756–86.
[4] William Assheton Harbord (1766–1821) succeeded his father as 2nd Baron Suffield, 4 Feb. 1810. M.P. for Ludgershall, 1790–6; for Plympton, 1807–10. Lord Lieutenant of Norfolk, 1808–21.

goodness to bestow on his nephew Mr William Bentinck,[4] who has lately obtained priest's Orders, and the decency and regularity of whose character and behaviour encourage the Duke of Portland to hope will not disgrace his profession. (13416-20)

[*The King's reply, Windsor Castle, 27 Feb.*] The King does not object to the Duke of Portland's taking the Duchess of Brunswick's opinion as to the amount of the provision which may be absolutely necessary for the Duke of Oels, which his Majesty conceives should be merely temporary.

The King acquiesces in the recommendation of Lord Mount Edgecumbe, Lord Aberdeen and Lord Strangford for the several marks of favor specified; in the nomination of Mr Harbord to the Lieutenancy of the county of Norfolk, and in the disposal of the Rectory of Sigglesthorne to Mr. William Bentinck. (13421)

3608 *Letters from* LORD MULGRAVE *to the* KING
[*Admiralty, 28 Feb. 1808.*] Lord Mulgrave has the honour to acquaint your Majesty that a telegraph message was received at the Admiralty this evening, stating that Sir Richard Strachan had gone to the Medeterranean [*sic*]. (13422)

[*Admiralty, 29 Feb.*] Lord Mulgrave has the honour to acquaint your Majesty that by a telegraph message received this morning it is stated that the French squadron has gone into Toulon. (13423)

3609 VISCOUNT CASTLEREAGH *to the* KING, *and the reply*
[*Downing Street, 29 Feb. 1808.*] Your Majesty's confidential servants having taken into their most serious consideration the state of your Majesty's army as it now stands regulated under the provisions introduced into the Mutiny Act in the year 1806, and the arrangements consequent thereupon, beg leave humbly to submit for your Majesty's approbation the propriety of proposing a clause in the Mutiny Act of the present year for enabling recruits inlisting into your Majesty's service, to engage for unlimited service if they shall think fit to do so. Your Majesty's servants are humbly of opinion that it may under all the circumstances be adviseable to confine themselves in the present Session to the simple measure of an option, as above submitted, leaving it for consideration at a future period what system of re-inlistment it may be adviseable to apply to the men actually serving. They conceive this question may be postponed with the less prejudice to the efficiency of your Majesty's army, as none of the men inlisted under the late Act will be entitled to their discharges before the year 1813.

Lord Castlereagh begs permission to lay before your Majesty a memorandum of the present state of the army as it stands augmented under the Acts of the last Session. By a return received subsequently to that upon which the present statement was prepared, it appears that the number of men levied for the militia,

4 See No. 2777.

as well as of men transfer'd to the line, exceeds the amount therein taken credit for—the former may be estimated at nearly 40,000, and the latter at 24,000 men. (13424–5)

[*The King's reply*, *Windsor Castle*, *1 March*.] The King is glad to learn from Lord Castlereagh's letter that his Ministers have come to the resolution of introducing a clause into the ensuing Mutiny Act for enabling recruits to engage for unlimited service, which his Majesty trusts will prove one step towards remedying the evils now subsisting. (13456)

3610 SPENCER PERCEVAL *to the* KING, *and the reply*

[*Dowg. Str.*, *Tuesday morg.* [*1 March 1808*].] Mr Perceval acquaints your Majesty that the House agreed in a Committee to an Address to your Majesty to grant a pension of £2000 pr anm. to Lord Lake, and the two next in succession to the title, giving a retrospect to the date of the grant to the day of the victory at Delhi[1]—upon a division of 202 to 15. There had been a previous division upon the question of confining the grant to take effect from the day of the death of the late Lord Lake, but that limitation was negatived by 206 to 21.

The House then proceeded to take into consideration the three Resolutions which Mr Perceval incloses herewith. They were introduced by a long speech by Mr Whitbread, who was followed by Mr Ponsonby, who agreed in the two first Resolutions with Mr Whitbread, but moved the previous question upon the third. The debate was in some degree curious from this circumstance of Mr Ponsonby's opposing the third Resolution, but in other respects it was far from interesting. Mr Secretary Canning made a very able speech, and a Col. Brathbrook[2] [*sic*], a young member, spoke very much against the Motions—as did Mr Ward[3] for them. The business lasted to a very late hour, it being between 4 & 5 before the House separated.[4] (13452)

[1] Lord Lake's army had captured Delhi on 11 Sept. 1803.
[2] This should be Blachford. Barrington Pope Blachford (*d.* 1816), nephew of Sir John Barrington, was M.P. for Newtown (Isle of Wight), 1807–16, and a Lord of the Admiralty, August 1814–May 1816. This was his maiden speech. In March 1810 he joined Canning's small party as his 'izth man'. His country seat was Osborne, Isle of Wight. He was said to possess a fine stud, and one of his horses usually ran at Winchester, of which Races he was Steward in 1806.
He was certainly not a Colonel in the Army. Some months later he accompanied Sir Arthur Wellesley to the Peninsula 'as a traveller' ('as an amateur', Canning said later), and Wellesley wrote on 23 June: 'I will take care of him…He shall see everything that is to be seen, and he can then return to England when he will be tired of us. If he should take a commission in the army, he would be obliged to stay longer than is now his intention or than would suit his other views and objects.'
[3] John William Ward, 1st Earl of Dudley (1781–1833). M.P. for Downton, 1802–3; for Worcestershire, 1803–6; for Petersfield, 1806–7; for Wareham, 1807–12; for Ilchester, 1812–18; for Bossiney, 1819–23. Foreign Secretary, April 1827–May 1828. Succeeded his father as 4th Viscount Dudley and Ward, 25 April 1823; created Earl of Dudley, 5 Oct. 1827. One of Canning's political friends later.
[4] *Parl. Deb.*, x, 786–869 (29 Feb.); Colchester, ii, 140 (where the numbers on the first division are wrongly given).

RESOLVED. That it is the opinion of this House that the conditions stipulated by his Majesty's Ministers for the acceptance of the mediation offered by the Emperor of Russia were inexpedient and impolitic. Ayes 70. Noes 210.

That it is the opinion of this House that the conduct of his Maj.'s Ministers on the subject of the mediation of the Emperor of Austria was unwise & impolitic, & not calculated to ascertain how far the restoration of the blessings of peace might or might not have been attained through the means of such mediation. Ayes 67, Noes 211.

That there is nothing in the present circumstances of the war which ought to preclude his Majesty from embracing any fair opportunity of acceding to or commencing a negociation with the enemy on a footing of equality for the termination of hostilities on terms of justice & honour.

To which the previous question was moved and on a division the Ayes 58, Noes 217.[1] (13453)

[*The King's reply, Windsor Castle, 1 March.*] The King is much pleased to learn from Mr Perceval's report that the divisions upon the Resolutions moved by Mr Whitbread were so favourable. His Majesty considers Mr Ponsonby's opposition to the third Resolution as strongly indicating a want of union in the party. (13454)

[1] There had been a meeting at Ponsonby's house on the 28th at which Whitbread had reluctantly agreed to a softening of his strongly expressed Resolutions in favour of peace. But, said Lord Grey, 'Windham and others strongly objected to the Motion even in this form, and the consequence is that the original Resolutions are resumed. We go therefore into the H. of Commons quite divided. On the two first Resolutions, though I don't like even them, your uncle [Ponsonby] will support him. But on the third he will declare his opinion of the impropriety of moving it now, and support the previous question. This is most unfortunate if not fatal to the party, and the more provoking as we were going on so well, and had such a fair game before us in both Houses. Whitbread's conduct in forcing on this Motion under the present circumstances I can never approve, but as far as relates to modifications of the question and to accepting it in the form and adopting the alterations which, with a view to union, we had proposed, it has latterly been certainly very conciliatory.' (Howick MSS. To Lady Grey, 29 Feb.) Grey was more critical of Ponsonby than of Whitbread, who had 'shown a great disposition to conciliate by adapting his Motion to the opinions of others and in striking out the passages which were most objected to. But the unfortunate and unexpected turn which the meeting at your uncle's took on Sunday night, and what passed in yesterday's debate has produced a degree of discontent and division amongst our friends which I rather hope than expect to see recovered. The fault seems in part to be attributable to your uncle's want of management at the meeting...He has not met with that sort of assistance which he had a right to expect, but has on the contrary found his embarrassments increased by jealousies amongst those to whom he was obliged to look for support, and too often, I fear, by a disposition in some to urge their own personal objects without considering the interests of the Party in which they are engaged.' The meeting at Ponsonby's, he said, broke up without anything being settled, but the line which Ponsonby took in the debate on the third Resolution was disapproved by most of the Opposition members, who consequently voted with Whitbread. The result, Grey feared, would be fatal to party unity and to its power and consequence. (1 March.)

Whitbread had written to Creevey on 21 Feb.: 'Will you do me the favour to exert all your powers of collection to obtain a good attendance of our friends for Monday the 29th. "on Mr. Whitbread's Motion respecting the Russian and Austrian mediations, when a division will certainly take place." Pray send me a list of persons to whom I could write. Do you think I may venture upon Coke? I send you a copy of the Resolutions such as I have submitted to George Ponsonby for consideration and observation. I hope you will approve them.' (Creevey typescript.)

3611 VISCOUNT CASTLEREAGH *to the* KING, *and the reply*

[*St James's Sqr.*, *1 March 1808*.] Lord Castlereagh begs leave humbly to lay before your Majesty a letter he has received from Captain Paget[1] of the Cambrian and requests to be honor'd with your Majesty's commands with respect to the disposal of the Emperor of Morocco's present.[2] (13455)

[*The King's reply*, *Windsor Castle*, *2 March*.] The King desires that Lord Castlereagh will order the lioness mentioned in Captain Paget's letter to be sent to the Tower. (13455)

3612 LORD HAWKESBURY *to the* KING, *and the reply*

[*Charles Street*, *1 March* [*1808*], *2.30 a.m.*] Lord Hawkesbury begs leave most humbly to submit to your Majesty the Minutes of the House of Lords and trust[s] that your Majesty will feel satisfied with the attendance and the division this night.[3] (13458)

[*Enclosure*]

The Order of the Day being read for the Lords to be summoned, it was moved to resolve,

That previous to the 11th of November last his Majesty's Government was not in possession of any proof or sufficient ground of belief that the United States of America had acquiesced in, or submitted to, or intended to acqueisce in or submit to the execution of such parts of the French Decree of November 21st 1806 as purported to impose upon neutral commerce restraints inconsistent with the Law of Nations.

For the Motion	Against it
1 Lord St. John of Bletsoe	2 Earl Graham, who moved the previous Qun.
3 Lord Holland	4 Lord Mulgrave
5 Lord Holland to explain	6 Lord Mulgrave to explain
7 Lord Auckland	8 Lord Redesdale
9 Lord Lauderdale	10 Lord Privy Seal
11 Earl Grey	12 Lord Hawkesbury
13 Lord Grenville	14 Lord Stewart of Garlies

Upon the question put that this Question be now put
Tellers
Lord Lauderdale ⎱ content 24; proxies 23. Total, 47
Ld. Mulgrave ⎰ not content 66, proxies 61. Tot. 127
Resolved in the negative. (13460)

[*The King's reply*, *Windsor Castle*, *1 March*.] The King has received great pleasure from the information conveyed to him by Lord Hawkesbury that the attendance & division in the House of Lords were so good last night. (13458)

---

[1] Charles Paget. [2] Not in Castlereagh's hand.
[3] The debate on 29 Feb. in the Lords is not mentioned in *Parl. Deb.*

[*Burlington House, Tuesday, 1 March 1808, 6.20 p.m.*] In obedience to the commands which the Duke of Portland has received from her Royal Highness the Duchess of Brunswick to convey to your Majesty the enclosed letter from her Royal Highness he has the honor to transmit it herewith. (13457)

[*The King's reply, Windsor Castle, 2 March.*] The King encloses to the Duke of Portland a copy of the Duchess of Brunswick's letter in regard to a temporary provision to be made for the Duke of Brunswick. (13457)

[*From the Duke of Portland, Burlington House, Wednesday, 2 March.*[1]] The Duke of Portland most humbly begs leave to acquaint your Majesty that he received in due course the letter your Majesty was graciously pleased to write to him, inclosing a copy of the Duchess of Brunswick's letter to your Majesty, in regard to the temporary provision to be made for the Duke of Brunswick; respecting the amount of which he is enabled in consequence of your Majesty's permission, to lay before your Majesty the sentiments of her Royal Highness.

It is her Royal Highness's opinion that an allowance at the rate of three thousand pounds a year, if it shall be necessary to continue it for such a period, will be a sufficient provision for the Duke of Brunswick-Oels; and the Duke of Portland therefore submits with the utmost deference to your Majesty that two thousand pounds should be advanced to his Serene Highness immediately out of the same fund and in the same manner in which it was remitted to his brothers Prince George and Prince Augustus of Brunswick, with an intimation which may be communicated to him by Major Fleischer, the gentleman who brought over the letter the Duke of Brunswick addressed to your Majesty upon the state of his affairs, that he is only to consider this act of your Majesty's generosity as a temporary alleviation of his actual embarrassments, and is not to entertain the expectation of its being a regular and permanent settlement.

Should this suggestion be so fortunate as to receive the sanction of your Majesty's approbation, the Duke of Portland has concerted means with Mr. Secretary Canning for its being carried into immediate effect, either to the full extent of the annual provision which her Royal Highness the Duchess of Brunswick has thought sufficient, or in any other proportion which your Majesty may deem expedient.

The experience which the Duke of Portland has had of your Majesty's condescension and readiness to listen to any representations which a sense of what is due to their own characters may induce any of your subjects to be desirous of laying before your Majesty, will not suffer him to let the proceeding respecting the Reversion Bill which took place last night in the House of Lords pass unnoticed.[2] He acknowledges, with the highest sense of gratitude, the justice which

---

[1] This letter is referred to in Turberville's *Welbeck Abbey*, ii. 296 n., but there wrongly dated the 8th.
[2] On 24 March 1807 Henry Bankes, Chairman of the Committee of the House of Commons appointed to look into the public expenditure and suggest measures of economical reform, moved a Resolution 'That no office, place, employment or salary in any part of his Majesty's dominions, ought

your Majesty was pleased to do to his conduct in the Audience which your Majesty gave Lord Hawkesbury today in your Closet; but until your Majesty had expressed your opinion of the correctness with which the Duke of Portland has conducted himself respecting that measure, he could not but feel, to their utmost extent, all those painfull sensations which an event, so brought about, was formed to produce; to the very great injury of your Majesty's affairs, to the discredit of your Administration, and to the disgrace of the Duke of Portland's character both in a publick and private point of view. If, as he has now the consolation to learn from Lord Hawkesbury, the Duke of Portland did not misapprehend or mis-represent your Majesty's sentiments, and that in consideration of the circumstances which it was the Duke of Portland's duty to lay before your Majesty, your Majesty deemed it adviseable to acquiesce in the middle measure recommended to your Majesty by a very considerable majority of your confidential servants,[1] the

hereafter to be granted in 'reversion'. (*Parl. Deb.*, ix, 179.) The Resolution was agreed to, and Bankes, Horner and Sturges-Bourne were appointed to prepare and introduce a Bill embodying it. After the general election Bankes was given leave to introduce a Bill (29 June), which passed the Commons on 9 July, but on 4 Aug. it was rejected by the Lords. (*Ibid.*, ix, 1049.*) On 25 Jan. 1808 Bankes brought in another, similar Bill, and it passed the House of Commons, again without opposition from the Government, on 1 Feb. (*Parl. Deb.*, x, 96–100, 194–5.) On 1 March it was read a second time in the Lords by a majority of eight (69 *v.* 61). On the 10th the House decided to go into Committee on the Bill, the voting being 84 to 84, Lord Arden again leading the ultras who opposed the Bill. The voting allowed the Bill to go into Committee (*ibid.*, x, 1053) but the Bill was thrown out during the debate on the third reading, by 128 votes to 48 (*ibid.*, col. 1087) on the 15th.

[1] This is explained in the following notes or minutes by the Cabinet Ministers, from 7 Feb. onwards (Welbeck MSS.):

Lord Hawkesbury's Minute, 7 Feb. 1808: 'His Majesty's confidential servants are desired to deliver in writing their opinion as to the course which it may be most proper to adopt with respect to the Reversion Bill in its progress through the House of Lords. Whether under all the circumstances under which that Bill has passed the House of Commons and has been sent up to the House of Lords, it would be most expedient that his Majesty's servants in the House of Lords

1. should determine to give their support to the Bill subject only to such critical alterations in it as would not interfere with its principle; or

2. whether they should endeavour to persuade the House to reject the Bill; or

3. whether they should propose to the House of Lords to pass it for the period of two or three years with a view of having the general question undecided for the present but for the purpose of preventing the grant of any offices in Reversion during that interval, which in consequence of the en-quiries now depending in the House of Commons, it might be thought expedient either to abolish or to regulate.'

The Duke of Portland's note: 'Upon a full consideration of all the circumstances under which the Rever-sion Bill has reached its present stage in the House of Lords, I am of opinion that it will be most expe-dient *not* to endeavour to reject it, but to suffer it to pass, limiting its duration to the space of one or more years so as to leave a reasonable time for the Committee of Finance to pursue their enquiries into the fitness of the measure now depending.

Lord Camden's note: 'If the question were between rejecting or passing the Reversion Bill (with such critical alterations only as are necessary) my opinion would be for *rejecting* it. If the question were between *rejecting* the Bill or adopting a middle line and *passing* the Bill for a limited period of one or two years, I should also be for *rejecting* it, and I am inclined to think that it will be much more easy to persuade the House of Lords to reject than to pass the Bill. If, however, the difficulties apprehended in the other House should outweigh this consideration, and that such of his Majesty's Ministers as are necessarily best acquainted with the temper and disposition of the House of Commons represent the measure of rejection as too hazardous, and that it is conceived that serious embarrassment and incon-venience would thereby arise to the conduct of the King's affairs in Parliament, and that in consequence the prevailing opinion of the Cabinet should be to advise his Majesty to concede upon this point, and that a question should then arise, as between passing the Bill for a limited time or passing it as it is, I

Duke of Portland cannot but hope and anxiously entreat your Majesty to let those sentiments be known, that a stop may be put to those inferences which it must be acknowledged there are but too many and too obvious circumstances to justify, and that it may no longer be said that your Ministers have either imposed upon your Majesty or misrepresented your intentions, and that those who are disposed to support your Majesty's Government may no longer be intimidated from doing

should be for doing the latter, because I conceive the sacrifice of a principle is much the same in either case, while in the one it appears to be gratuitous but in the other there would at least be a prospect of its obtaining the advantages which on prudential grounds are sought from concession. If the intention of the Committee of Finance went no further than to prevent the granting reversions of certain offices until the final report of the Committee, an Address to the King would, I apprehend, have been more material.'

Lord Chatham's note: 'The House of Commons, having twice passed the Reversion Bill, and the King's Ministers in that House having twice acquiesced in it, I should think it most expedient to pass the Bill in the House of Lords; but if the difficulties which have arisen or may arise in the House of Lords and elsewhere are thought by his Majesty or the Cabinet to be paramount to those which may be felt from the House of Commons and the country taking an unfavourable opinion of the intentions of government with respect to objects of patronage, I acquiesce in the determination (if such should be the mark) of passing the Bill for only a limited period, which I think should not be less than two years.'

Lord Westmorland's note: 'My impression is for the rejection of the Bill and I have my doubts whether the wisest policy is not to resist this encroaching system in the first instance; however, on the ground stated in the Minute it may perhaps be expedient to pass it for one or two years.'

Canning's note: 'I am strongly impressed with the apprehension that the rejection of the Bill in the House of Lords by the influence of Government would produce a state of things in the House of Commons highly embarrassing. I should like best that Government should not interfere *at all*, if that course were possible, which, however, it may not be; next best, that it should be able to prevent all opposition to the passing of the Bill. But in that case I agree with Lord Chatham in thinking that the Bill must be passed as it is. I do not think we should gain anything by Government *originating* an alternative without visible necessity. In case of an opposition being made to the Bill without or against the consent of Government, and of that opposition appearing considerable enough to warrant a compromise, I think Government may fairly prepare the compromise and in that case I think the passing the Bill for two years the most advisable measure.'

Lord Castlereagh's note: 'As far as I understand the probable effects of this Bill if passed into a Law, I am inclined to consider its fate as a question more of *party* than of *political* importance. In the former view, so far as the interests of the Government and consequently those of the Crown depend upon the temper and feelings of the House of Commons and of the public at large, I should wish the Bill to be supported in the Lords, being of opinion that its rejection there may and will probably render the Finance Committee more enterprising and unmanageable. If however those who best understand the state of that House are of opinion that this cannot be either successfully undertaken or attempted without lowering the House of Peers, I should imagine Government will be strong enough in the Commons to resist any further attempt tending to commit the two Houses. We must not, however, flatter ourselves that the middle course will be considered by the proposers of the Bill as proceeding from any other feelings than those of ultimate hostility to its principle, and as it is understood the Bill in itself originated as a compromise in the Committee, being acquiesced in by the more moderate to avoid propositions of *direct abolition of offices*, it is not unlikely, if the Act is passed only for a limited time on the express ground of leaving such a course open to the Committee, that they may take us at our word, and send us a plan of reduction. Perhaps the whole scheme when unfolded might be more easily dealt with and rejected than the immediate proposition in question. If, however, by conciliating and strengthening the hands of friends on that Committee, Government could be saved from having such a task ultimately cast upon them, I should think the advantages of such a course greater than the evils of the Bill in *the times* in which we are now acting.'

Perceval's note: 'I agree with Lord Castlereagh that the Bill is of much greater importance as a *party* than a *public* measure, and upon the best consideration which I can give the subject I cannot think the passing of the Bill would be attended with any inconvenience to the Crown which would be equal to the effect of the impression unfavourable to the Government in point of character which the rejection, or proposed alteration of it, would under all the circumstances at present create. It is felt that with the desire of rejecting the Bill, supposing that desire strongly to exist, we are in a difficulty, but it should so in this instance by being assured that unless they vote for the rejection of the Reversion Bill, they will incur your Majesty's highest displeasure. As the Duke of Portland's sentiments respecting that Bill are fully known to your Majesty, and as your Majesty therefore will not attribute his anxiety for the success of the measure which Lord Hawkesbury is to propose, to any other motive than his devoted attachment to your Majesty's interests, and the success and facility of your Government, he feels it too much his duty to shrink from making this

not be considered as a difficulty which is greater now than it would have been had we endeavoured to meet it at an earlier period. Our difficulty began with our Government. Could we have resisted the Bill *wisely* before the dissolution? Interrupting that and other measures of the Finance Committee by the dissolution, could we have gone wisely to the country without a sort of pledge that the dissolution was not, as our enemies charged, aimed at these measures? Could we, after the dissolution and in the new Parliament wisely or consistently before we knew our situation, have taken a step which would by many have been construed as forfeiting our pledge? And the same question has recurred hitherto in every stage of this measure. We are more assured perhaps of our strength now than we were before, and so far the time may be more favourable, but with a view to character, if it was determined to have resisted the measure, it should have been resisted sooner. We should indeed at any time have had a considerable inconvenience to have encountered, but we should have had the credit of encountering it with more openness and manliness. As however the feelings of many of his Majesty's servants are in principle decidedly against passing the Bill in its present shape, I think in a choice of inconveniencies that the passing it for two years (but it must be for *two* years at least) is preferable to rejecting it.'

Lord Bathurst's note: 'I am for passing the Bill with such verbal alterations only as are necessary. Because I do not think it really affects the prerogatives of the Crown and tends ultimately to increase its influence, and because the passing the Bill in this manner gives us the best chances of keeping the Financial Committee in good order, and the best means of opposing their disorder.'

Lord Mulgrave's note, 5 March 1808: 'The course of proceeding which has already prevailed seems to preclude the full consideration of the principle on which such a Bill should be met. I think the Bill innocent with respect to the permanent influence on the interests of the Crown. I dislike it as the first measure of a system of innovation, provided against the influence of the Crown, which in its present state is barely (if it is at all) sufficient to maintain a firm and efficient administration of public affairs. The only question which now remains is whether the adoption of the Bill as it is will operate to quiet the spirit of innovation, and to confirm the good disposition of the moderate persons in the Committee of Finance, who are said to have produced this Bill with great exertion, as a compromise to avert more violent measures. If that party should be disappointed or mortified they may join cordially in more troublesome and possibly more popular proposals of reform. I know not, and have no means of forming an opinion, never having received any information or having been called upon for my sentiments on the expediency or rather necessity of reviving and recommending the Finance Committee, but as that measure was taken I have no doubt on a full and sound conviction on the minds of those who were capable of forming a competent judgment I must be of opinion that the same necessity which obliged the establishment of that Committee requires also that it should in some degree be satisfied and deferred to, for it would obviously have been better to fight the existence of the Committee once for all than to fight its ends and objects (which will rise upon the contest) every day: the honour of the House of Lords I do not think the House of Lords seriously involved in the question under all the circumstances of the rejection of the Bill by surprise last year [*sic*], but if the Government now comes forward and that the Committee should be roused to acrimony, and that any considerable body in the House of Commons should support their propositions, the Houses will be involved in a contest which the Government will not be able to guide or to control, and the friends of Government may be driven into strong opposing parties in the different Houses. I am therefore of opinion that the Bill should pass as it is, and should be made the instrument of supporting the propriety of resisting further encroachments. When the whole of his Majesty's servants may take an active and uniform part in both Houses and meet the measure (whatever it may be) at the outset, passing the Bill will maintain the line of non-interference hitherto adopted; proposing the middle (or any other) measure will look like an endeavour to compromise by your interference when you could not succeed in rejecting underhand and without shewing yourselves.' (Welbeck MSS.)

Perceval's note, 5 March 1808: 'Acquaint his Majesty that upon the receipt of his note he feels himself authorised *to disclaim* on his Majesty's part that his Majesty has given any opinion or taken any step to oppose the Amendment suggested by his Majesty's Government to the Reversion Bill.'

representation to your Majesty, and relies with confidence on your Majesty's justice and liberality for pardoning his presumption.[1] (13461–6)

[*The King's reply, Windsor Castle, 3 March.*] The King has received the Duke of Portland's letter and desires to assure him that he has been and continues willing to do justice to the motives which have given rise to the line of conduct which the Duke of Portland has taken in regard to the Reversion Bill, and to the feeling under which he has found himself obliged to support the measure. Aware of this, his Majesty has abstained from taking any part whatsoever upon this occasion, although he can never deny that he regrets that it should have been adopted; he has continued silent throughout its progress, and has no intention of departing from a course which has appeared to him most consistent with propriety and with his own dignity, whilst it is no less fair to those concerned.[2]

The King approves of the arrangement proposed for the Duke of Brunswick. (13467)

[1] 'We had last night a most curious scene in the House of Lords. The Princes, four in number, came down in force with all the Household troops and Bishops, and endeavoured to throw out the Reversion Bill on the question of going into the Committee. They beat us in the numbers present, but, the majority of proxies being on our side, we were equal upon the whole, and according to the established usage of the House of Lords the question was therefore decided in the negative, so that the Motion made by the enemies of the Bill for discharging the order for the Committee was lost. In the Committee Hawkesbury moved an Amendment to limit the duration of the Bill to two years. To this we of course objected, and as the courtiers voted with us for the sake of ultimately throwing out the Bill, as the Ministers had pledged themselves to vote against it if the Amendment was not carried, the latter were left by themselves and only divided 21. This shows what the real strength of the Party now in power is without the Court. After this the Bill passed the Committee without any Amendment, and is to be read a third time on Tuesday when I suppose it will be thrown out. Nothing can shew the degraded state of the Administration more strongly than what has happened on this occasion. The previous debate was a very good one on our side, and I have had great compliments on my speech in which I really felt that I had made a considerable impression on the House. I gave the Bishops and the Princes a severe lecture, though not half so severe as it would have been if I had not been afraid of giving a loose to all that I had in my mind to say.' (Howick MSS.) Grey wrote again, on the 18th: 'The explanation of what passed on the Reversion Bill which I do not wonder has puzzled you is as follows: We were of course for the Bill. The Ministers were in their hearts against it, but to avoid the unpopularity of a direct opposition to it, hit upon the expedient of proposing that it should be limited in its duration to two years, without which alteration they declared they must be against it. They therefore voted with us for going into a Committee where this alteration was to be proposed. They there moved this as an Amendment, to which Lord Holland and I objected as making the Bill worse, but declared we did not mean to press our objection (feeling that the Bill would be lost if the Amendment was negatived) though if we were compelled to vote we must do so in support of the Bill as it stood. We did not intend therefore to divide, but the courtiers, who had the Ministers pledged to oppose the Bill if the Amendment was lost, divided the House and voted with us against the Amendment, and the Ministers were left as I told you in a minority of only 21. The Bill therefore passed the Committee without alteration and on the third reading was opposed both by the Court and the Administration and thrown out accordingly.' (*Ibid.*)

[2] Lord Camden, writing to Lord Malmesbury on the 11th, had this interesting comment to make on the Cabinet's difficulties over the Reversion Bill: 'We had another division upon the Reversion Bill yesterday and it was of the same complexion as the last, vizt. "the Court against the Government", the Government conceiving they had *at least* the King's acquiescence in the line they took. I delivered your proxy in the same manner in which I gave my vote, and I thought myself authorised so to do from my having told you I had so done on a similar occasion when I saw you at the Duke of Portland's, and which conduct I conceived you to approve. I should have had no doubt whatever on my mind upon this subject, if Lord Fitzharris had not called me out prior to the division and asked me if I conceived myself authorised to give your proxy, upon which I mentioned to him the circumstance I have

[*Charles Street, 3 March 1808.*] Lord Hawkesbury begs leave most humbly to submit to your Majesty the Minutes of the House of Lords of this night. The only speakers were Lord Darnley and Lord Holland on one side and Lord Eliot and Lord Boringdon on the other. Lord Eliot made a very sensible and impressive speech against the Address proposed by Lord Darnley and afterwards proposed the Resolution of Approbation which was carried by 124 to 57.[1] (13468)

[*The King's reply, Windsor Castle, 4 March.*] The King acknowledges the receipt of Lord Hawkesbury's letter and the accompanying Minute of the House of Lords and is glad to hear that the proceedings were so satisfactory last night. (13478)

observed upon *above*, and he desired me to decide as I thought best. I accordingly gave your proxy and I hope to hear I have acted as you meant I should upon this occasion. The Third Reading is to take place on Tuesday. I believe I shall not attend but I should like to know what you wish to be done with your vote on that occasion.

'P.S. This business will have given the Government a considerable shake.' (Malmesbury MSS.)

Lord Malmesbury replied, from Bath, on the 13th: 'You certainly gave my proxy in the way that you were fully authorised to do. I was under the full persuasion that the King was aware of and acquiesced in the line Government took. It was with that impression on my mind that I spoke as I did when we met at the Duke of Portland's, and Fitzharris's having applied to you arose solely from my not having, through inadvertence, acquainted him with what had paased there, and probably from his not being sure in what way you yourself intended to give your vote. I confess too the manifest opposition of the Court to the Reversion Bill a little staggers my opinion, not because I feel like a courtier or as to the merits of the measure itself which in good truth I consider as one of no very great import, but from the very serious and fatal consequences which might attend a breach or even a diminution of mutual confidence between his Majesty and his present Government. I speak not of personal consequences, for they could not reach me, but under the most internal [?] conviction that, if by any unfortunate event, the present Ministers were to be dismissed or to be placed in a situation that would compel them to resign, the safety and very existence of the country must be most fearfully endangered. With this view of the business I need not say that I am glad to hear you think of staying away on Tuesday; I should be very sorry that my vote should differ from yours on this or on any occasion. At the same time and after having said what I have, if the Duke of Portland thinks differently and makes a strong and decided point of resisting at all hazards the wishes of the Court, I certainly should think it right and my clear duty to act as he desires, and as you probably have the same feeling, may I request of you to consult him in my name and if you please to shew him this letter? The idea you fling out in your P.S. that this business will have given the Government a considerable shake, confirms me in what I have written, and makes me deprecate as one of the greatest evils which could befall us, the effect of any possible difference between the King and his Government.' (*Ibid.*)

There is a final reference to this Bill in Camden's letter of the 17th: 'We have been kept so hard at work, that I really had not time to inform you of the use I made of your proxy on the 3rd Reading of the Reversion Bill. As the Amendment we proposed in the Committee was not adopted the Government voted against the 3rd Reading and I gave your *vote* accordingly. I am not yet aware what steps the House of Commons will take but I think we shall take care not to be so awkwardly circumstanced again.' (*Ibid.*)

[1] *Parl. Deb.*, x, 873–7 (a debate on the expedition to Copenhagen; the numbers there are given as 125 to 57). The Resolution approving the Government's measures was as follows: 'That this House, considering the Declarations laid before them by his Majesty's command, the state to which the Continent was reduced in consequence of the negotiations and Peace of Tilsit; the avowed determination of the French Government to exclude the British flag from every port of Europe, and to combine all the Powers of the Continent in a general confederacy against the maritime rights and political existence of Great Britain, most highly approves the prompt and vigorous measures which were adopted by his Majesty for the purpose of removing out of the reach of his Majesty's enemies the fleet and naval resources of Denmark.' (*H. of L. J.*, XLVI, 466.)

Grey commented: 'Holland made an exceedingly good speech...and as only Boringdon answered it, the debate ended there at nine o'clock.' (Howick MSS.)

3615 VISCOUNT CASTLEREAGH *to the* KING, *and the reply*

[*Downing Street, 3 March* [*1808*].] Lord Castlereagh has the satisfaction humbly to acquaint your Majesty that the transports and victuallers (amounting to 25 sail'd) which were separated from M. General Spencer's armament in the heavy gales on the 29th & 30th of last Decr. and did not return to a British port, have *all* arrived in safety at Gibraltar on the 23rd January, which accounts satisfactorily for the whole of the fleet which sail'd under convoy of Sir C. Cotton from Portsmouth on the 18th of Decr. (13476)

[*The King's reply, Windsor Castle, 4 March*.] The King has received great satisfaction from Lord Castlereagh's report of the safe arrival at Gibraltar of all the transports which were separated from M. General Spencer's armament. (13477)

3616 LORD MULGRAVE *to the* KING, *and the reply*

[*Admiralty, 4 March 1808*.] Lord Mulgrave has the honour to submit to your Majesty further dispatches relating to the Rochefort squadron, received this day from the Medeterranean [*sic*]. (13479)

[*The King's reply, Windsor Castle, 5 March*.] The King returns his thanks to Lord Mulgrave for his communication of the intelligence received relative to the Rochefort squadron. (13483)

3617 SPENCER PERCEVAL *to the* KING, *and the reply*

[*4 March 1808*.] Mr Perceval acquaints your Majesty that the debate of the evening began with a long conversation upon the propriety of receiving a Petition from Liverpool against the Bill for carrying into effect the Orders-in-Council, and which was rejected upon the same ground on which a similar Petition was rejected on the former evening, namely, that it was against a Bill for raising duties and that it was contrary to the practice of Parliament to receive a Petition against such a Bill. Upon the division the numbers were Noes 111, Ayes 57.[1]

After this Mr Adam made his Motion against Mr Secretary Canning. The Resolutions which he moved Mr Perceval herewith incloses. Mr Canning was heard in his place, and retired from the House. Mr Windham followed in support of the charge. Mr Perceval answered him and moved the orders of the day. Mr Whitbread followed Mr Perceval, and Ld. Caslereagh [*sic*], Mr Whitbread, and Mr Sturgess Bourne on the same side with Lord Castlereagh [*sic*], when Mr Adam replied, and the House divided against the Resolution 168 to 67.[2] (13480)

[1] *Parl. Deb.*, x, 896–98. See also cols. 889–95 (3 March), and Colchester, II, 141, where, on page 140 the debate on 3 March is dated 30 Feb.

[2] *Parl. Deb.*, x, 898–919. Canning was accused of having read to the House despatches from Ministers at Foreign Courts, none of which had then been communicated to the House by the King's commands, and some of which the House had determined should not be produced.

[*The King's reply, Windsor Castle, 5 March.*] The King acknowledges the receipt of Mr Perceval's report of last night's debate and is happy that the proceedings upon Mr. Adam's Motion ended so satisfactorily. (13484)

3618 GEORGE CANNING *to the* KING

[*Foreign Office, 7 March 1808.*] Mr. Canning humbly submits for your Majesty's royal approbation the draft of a Message to both Houses of Parliament, relative to the Swedish Treaty of Subsidy.[1] (13485)

3619 CHARLES HERBERT[2] *to the* KING

[*Endorsed 7 March 1808.*] The office of Master of the Robes to your Majesty being vacant, I humbly presume to request the appointment. It will add to the obligations I am under to your Majesty, but cannot encrease the sincere attachment with which I have served your Majesty upwards of thirty years.[3] (13486)

3620 *Letters from* SPENCER PERCEVAL *to the* KING, *and the replies*

[*Downg. Str., 12.30 a.m. Wedny. morng.* [*9 March 1808*].] Mr. Perceval acquaints your Majesty that Lord Castlereagh moved a clause this evening in the Committee on the Mutiny Bill, for enabling the recruit to inlist at his option either for unlimited service or for seven years. The clause was opposed at considerable length by Mr Windham & supported by Sr. J. Pulteney and Genl. Tarleton, and the Committee divided upon it, Ayes 169 and Noes 100.[4] (13487)

[*The King's reply, Windsor Castle, 9 March.*] The King acknowledges the receipt of Mr Perceval's letter from which his Majesty is glad to learn that the clause in the Mutiny Bill has been carried. (13488)

[*From Perceval, Downing Street, 6.30 Saty. morng.* [*12 March*].] Mr. Perceval has the satisfaction at length to acquaint your Majesty that the Bill for carrying into execution the Orders-in-Council has been passed this morning at a little before 6 o'clock, after a second day's debate on the Third Reading. Mr Perceval did not trouble your Majesty with any account of the preceding day's debate as

---

[1] On the 10th Canning presented to the House the following Message: 'His Majesty thinks it proper to acquaint the House of Commons that the King of Sweden having resisted every threat that had been employed to induce him to join the hostile continental confederacy against Great Britain, and having thereby exposed his dominions to increasing and imminent danger, his Majesty felt it his duty to afford that monarch the most prompt and efficacious support and assistance. His Majesty has, therefore, entered into a Convention with the King of Sweden, a copy of which he has directed to be laid before the House, and he relies on the wisdom and liberality of his faithful Commons that they will enable his Majesty to make good his engagements with an ally of such approved firmness and fidelity.'
[2] Charles Herbert (1743–1816), second son of the Hon. William Herbert (c. 1696–1757), he being the fifth son of Thomas, 8th Earl of Pembroke. M.P. for Wilton, 1775–80, and 1806–16. Groom of the Bedchamber, 1777–1816.   [3] See No. 71.   [4] *Parl. Deb.*, x, 980–91 (8 March).

he had not the power to report any progress. On the first day Sir Wm. Scott began the debate which had been delayed till near 9 o'clock before it commenced and he made a most able & powerful argument upon the legality of the Orders. The same side of the question was supported by Mr Stephen,[1] a new member, whom your Majesty may have heard of as the author of the pamphlet called *War in Disguise*, and who made a very able speech upon the subject. About three o'clock the Opposition began moving to adjourn, which it was thought adviseable if possible to resist. But after two hours spent in fruitless discussion & frequent divisions upon the Res. of adjournment, it was at last agreed to upon an understanding that the debate should certainly come on again and not be interrupted. It accordingly came on again yesterday afternoon about six o'clock and continued till about 6 this morning. The debate was all upon the old ground, and was only to be remarked for two very good speeches from the Solicitor-General & Mr. Canning. The Attorney-General was prepared to have spoken, but he had no favorable opportunity.[2] (13495)

[*The King's reply, Windsor Castle, 12 March.*] The King is much pleased to learn from Mr Perceval's letter that the Bill for carrying into effect the Orders-in-Council has at length been passed. H.M. has observed with great regret the spirit of chicane which has been shewn by the Opposition upon this & other occasions, which causes so great an interruption to business & so much fatigue to those concerned. (13496)

3621   GEORGE CANNING *to the* KING

[*Foreign Office, 12 March 1808.*] Mr. Canning humbly submits for your Majesty's royal approbation the draft of an Agreement proposed to be concluded with the Portuguese Minister respecting the Island of Madeira. (13497)

3622   *Letters from the* DUKE OF PORTLAND[3] *to the* KING, *and the replies*

[*Burlington House, Sunday, 13 March 1808.*] In consequence of the vacancy of the Lieutenancy of the County of Dorset which has lately taken place, the Duke of Portland begs leave to acquaint your Majesty that he has been desired by the Earl of Digby[4] to lay with all humility before yourMajesty the offer of his services to fill that office, and to express to your Majesty his most anxious hope that the zealous and uniform attachment he has manifested to your Majesty's royal person

[1] James Stephen (1758–1832), M.P. for Tralee, 1808–12; for East Grinstead, 1812–15; Wilberforce's brother-in-law and a member of the 'Clapham Sect'. His famous pamphlet (1805) denounced the evasions of the British trade regulations by neutral traders, and it was believed to have suggested the Orders-in-Council.

[2] *Parl. Deb.*, x, 1056–68 (10 March); 1072–6 (11th).

[3] His two letters are not in his own hand.

[4] Edward, 2nd Earl Digby (1773–1856). Succeeded his father, 25 Sept. 1793. Lord Lieutenant of Dorset, 1808–56.

and Government, and the steadiness and constancy with which he has endeavoured to tread in the same steps which he presumes procured for his father[1] the distinction he now solicits, and which his gratitude cannot but lead him to infer must have disposed your Majesty to bestow so many signal favours on other branches of his family, may incline your Majesty to grant his request. A similar application has been made to the Duke of Portland on the part of the Earl of Ilchester,[2] who is just become capable of fulfilling the duties of that office by having completed his twenty-first year on last Sunday the 6th inst.[3] but independently of that circumstance, the testimony which the Duke of Portland's experience of the Earl of Digby's conduct calls upon him to submit to your Majesty's consideration in favour of that Earl, makes the Duke of Portland feel it to be a matter of duty to represent, with the utmost deference to your Majesty's superior judgement, his humble opinion that the Earl of Digby's conduct, exclusively of the respectability of his family, justly entitles him to the preference he prays for, and that such a mark of your Majesty's approbation of it will greatly tend to the advantage of your Majesty's service.

The Duke of Portland takes this opportunity of informing your Majesty that the Rectory of Wadingham in the county of Lincoln, a benefice in the gift of your Majesty, is lately become vacant by the death of Dr. Barker,[4] Master of Christ's College in the University of Cambridge, and that, among the persons whom he has been desired to recommend to your Majesty, Mr Cooper,[5] a Fellow of St. John's College in that University, has united in his favour the wishes of the Earl of Macclesfield, the Earl of Powis and his son Lord Clive, Lords Palmerston and Hinchingbrook,[6] and Mr Fane,[7] one of the members for Oxfordshire; and that in so strong a manner as not only to warrant but to oblige the Duke of Portland to consider it a matter of duty to recommend Mr Cooper to your Majesty for this piece of preferment.

As the Duke of Portland believes that your Majesty has generally been pleased to admit to a seat in your Privy Council such persons as your Majesty has graciously thought fit to send on foreign Missions with the double rank of Envoys Extraordinary and Ministers Plenipotentiary, the Duke of Portland presumes to lay before your Majesty the humble hope of the Lord Viscount Strangford, that

---

[1] Henry Digby (1731–93), M.P. for Ludgershall, 1755–61; for Wells, 1761–5. Succeeded his brother as 7th Baron Digby [I.], 1757; created Baron Digby [G.B.], 1765, and Earl Digby [G.B.], 1 Nov. 1790. Lord Lieutenant of Dorset from 1771 until his death. See No. 3914.

[2] Henry Stephen, 3rd Earl of Ilchester (1787–1858), styled Lord Stavordale until 5 Sept. 1802, when he succeeded his father as Earl. Captain of the Yeomen of the Guard, 1835–41; Lord Lieutenant of Somerset, 1837–9.

[3] According to the *Complete Peerage* and also *Collins' Peerage* he was born on 21 Feb. 1787.

[4] John Barker, D.D. (c. 1727–1808), Master of Christ's College, Cambridge, 1780–1808; Vice-Chancellor, 1780–1.

[5] William Cooper (c. 1770–1856). Fellow of St. John's, Cambridge, 1794–1810; Rector of West Rasen, Lincs., 1809–56; Rector of Waddingham, 1808–56; domestic Chaplain to the Earl of Macclesfield; Chaplain to Queen Adelaide, 1830; Chaplain-in-ordinary to Queen Victoria.

[6] George John, 6th Earl of Sandwich (1773–1818), styled Viscount Hinchingbrooke from 29 Nov. 1790, on the death of his elder brother, to 6 June 1814, when he succeeded his father as 6th Earl. M.P. for Huntingdon, 1794–1814.

[7] John Fane (1751–1824), M.P. for Oxfordshire, 1796–1824. An anti-Catholic, he generally supported the Tory Governments of the period.

that honour may be conferred upon him before his departure on his Mission to the Brazils; and as the Duke of Portland has been given to understand that it is your Majesty's intention to invest Lord Strangford with the Order of the Bath on next Wednesday, the Duke of Portland ventures to suggest Lord Strangford's being admitted, on the same day, to a seat at the Council Board. (13498–01)

[*The King's reply, Windsor Castle, 14 March.*] The King entirely agrees with the Duke of Portland that of the two candidates for the Lieutenancy of the county of Dorset the Earl of Digby is the most eligible, and that the office will be placed in his hands with great advantage. His Majesty approves of Mr Cooper's being appointed to the Rectory of Wadingham, and acquiesces in the Duke of Portland's proposal that Lord Strangford should be admitted to a seat at the Privy Council on Wednesday next. (13504)

[*From the Duke of Portland, Burlington House, Monday, 14 March.*] The Duke of Portland, having received information that a Canonry of Windsor is become vacant by the death of Dr Duval,[1] considers it to be his duty to lose no time in acquainting your Majesty that on the day after your Majesty was graciously pleased to confer a Prebend of Canterbury on Dr. Marlow,[2] the Prince of Wales directed his pleasure to be signified to the Duke of Portland that Mr. Blomberg,[3] one of his Royal Highness's Chaplains, might be offered to your Majesty's consideration for the Prebend so disposed of, and his Royal Highness, being informed that that Prebend was no longer vacant, was further pleased to intimate his wishes that whenever a similar opportunity occurred of providing for Mr. Blomberg, that gentleman's name might be submitted to your Majesty's consideration. Notwithstanding therefore the respective applications from the Earl of Courtown in favour of his son,[4] from the Earl of Lonsdale in behalf of Dr. Gretton,[5] and from the Marquess Wellesley for Dr. Goodall,[6] which have been already laid before your Majesty, and several others which the Duke of Portland's indisposition has hitherto prevented him from submitting to your Majesty, he humbly conceives it to be indispensably his duty in the first instance to make your Majesty acquainted with what he supposes will be the wishes of his Royal Highness the Prince of Wales, in consequence of the opening of a Stall at Windsor, which has just taken place. (13502–3)

[1] Philip Duval, D.D., F.R.S., Prebendary of Worcester, 1767–72; Rector of Broadwas, Worcs., 1768; Chaplain to the Duke of Gloucester; Vicar of Twickenham, 1792–1808.
[2] Dr. Michael Marlow (*c.* 1759–1828). President of St. John's, Oxford, 1795–1828; Vice-Chancellor, 1798–1802; Vicar of St. Giles's, Oxford; Rector of Handborough, Oxon., 1795; Prebendary of Canterbury, 1808.
[3] The Rev. Frederick William Blomberg (1761–1847), Rector of Shepton Mallet, Somerset, 1787–1833; Prebendary of Bristol, 1790–1828; Private Secretary to the Prince of Wales from about 1785 to March 1795 when Tyrwhitt succeeded him; Chaplain to the Prince, 1793; Vicar of Bradford, Wilts., 1793–9 and 1808–33; Vicar of Banwell, Somerset, 1799–1808; appointed Clerk of the Closet to the Prince, Jan. 1808; Prebendary of Westminster, April 1808–1822; Prebendary of St. Paul's, 1822–47.
[4] The Rev. Richard Bruce Stopford (1774–1844). See No. 3014.
[5] George Gretton (*c.* 1754–1820). D.D., 1791. Vicar of Townstall, 1799–1804; Rector of Hedsor, Bucks., 1803; Vicar of Upton Bishop, Hereford, 30 March 1810; Prebendary of Hereford, 1818; Dean of Hereford, 1809–20; Chaplain to the King.   [6] Joseph Goodall (1760–1840). See No. 2559.

[*The King's reply, Windsor Castle, 15 March.*] The King has received the Duke of Portland's letter and must observe that of the several candidates for the vacant Canonry of Windsor who are therein named, it appears to his Majesty that Doctor Goodall, having been for several years at the head of one of the great Public Schools in the Kingdom, bearing a most excellent character, independent of his acknowledged merit as a scholar, has the strongest pretensions to attention. The King wishes well to Mr. Stopford, and has heard favorable mention made of Doctor Gretton. Mr. Blomberg's application having been made generally for any Prebend, his Majesty conceives that it may be reserved for such vacancy as may occur in one of the other Cathedrals. (13506)

3623   GEORGE CANNING *to the* KING, *and the reply*

[*Foreign Office, 14 March 1808.*] Mr. Canning humbly lays before your Majesty a letter received by him from M. de la Châtre, together with drafts of letters proposed by M. de la Châtre to be written in the name of Louis XVIII to the Emperor of Russia & the King of Sweden on the subject of the bringing over the French Queen & the Duchesse d'Angoulême from Mittau to England. (13505)

[*The King's reply, Windsor Castle, 15 March.*] The King has received the papers which Mr. Canning has submitted, from which his Majesty is sorry to learn that Louis the 18th is desirous of assembling the whole of his family in England, but however inconvenient this may prove, his Majesty does not feel that he can with due regard to humanity & to the melancholy situation of those concerned, resist their wishes, at the same time that he trusts means will be taken to prevent their near residence to London.[1] (13505)

3624   LORD HAWKESBURY *to the* KING, *and the reply*

[*Charles Street, 15 March 1808.*] Lord Hawkesbury begs leave most humbly to inform your Majesty that the Bishop of Carlisle[2] will attend tomorrow to do homage and the Earl of Aberdeen and Lord Strangford will attend at the same time to be invested with the Orders of the Thistle and the Bath with which your Majesty has been graciously pleased to announce your royal intention of honouring them. (13507)

[*The King's reply, Queen's Palace, 16 March.*] The King approves of Lord Hawkesbury's having appointed the Bishop of Carlisle and Lords Aberdeen and Strangford to attend here this day, and his Majesty takes it for granted that Lord

---

[1] 'The Duke of Portland or Lord Liverpool', wrote Glenbervie (25 Jan. 1808), 'tells Lord Bayning that the King never mentions the King of France, offended no doubt at his unannounced arrival in this kingdom, his refusal of an asylum in Holyrood House, and his breach of the regulation that he should not approach within fifty miles of London. He avowedly came to England by the advice of the King of Sweden, and, by that advice, without giving any previous notice, because, as his Swedish Majesty stated to him, he would certainly be refused permission to come if his intention should be communicated to this Government.' (*Glenbervie Journals*, II, 12.)   [2] Samuel Goodenough.

Hawkesbury has given due notice to the Knights of the Bath to attend for the investment of Lord Strangford. Not less than two Knights of the Thistle should also be required to attend for the investment of Lord Aberdeen, which should take precedence of the Bath. (13507)

3625   SPENCER PERCEVAL *to the* KING, *and the reply*

[*Downg. Str., 15 March, Tuesday morng. [1808].*] Mr Perceval has the satisfaction to acquaint yr. Majesty that the Mutiny Bill with Lord Castlereagh's clause giving to the recruit an option of inlisting for life, was passed at a little before one o'clock this morning. An Amendment was moved by Mr Calcraft to leave out that clause, and the House divided upon that Amendment, Ayes 116, Noes 189. Mr Windham supported his old argument at considerable length and was very well answered by Lord Castlereagh.[1] (13509)

[*The King's reply, Windsor Castle, 15 March.*] The King is glad to hear from Mr Perceval's report that the Mutiny Bill passed last night, & that his Ministers are relieved from further discussion on that subject. (13509)

3626   GEORGE CANNING *to the* KING, *and the reply*

[*Foreign Office, 19 March 1808.*] Mr. Canning humbly submits to your Majesty a note presented by M. Adlerberg the Swedish Minister, announcing the wish of the King of Sweden to give to Lord Kelly,[2] whom his Swedish Majesty has personally known during his Lordship's residence at Gottenburgh, the Order of Vasa; & requesting your Majesty's gracious permission for Lord Kelly to accept & wear that mark of his Swedish Majesty's favour.[3] (13513)

[*The King's reply, Windsor Castle, 20 March.*] The King has received Mr Canning's letter and the note annexed from Mr Adlerberg, and his Majesty acquiesces in the wish therein expressed that Lord Kelly should be permitted to accept & wear the Order of Vasa. (13514)

3627   THE DUKE OF PORTLAND *to the* KING,[4] *and the reply*

[*Burlington House, Monday, 21 March 1808.*] Mr. Bankes having given notice in the House of Commons of his intention to bring in a new Bill upon the subject of reversionary grants of offices, the Duke of Portland feels it his indispensable duty most humbly to represent to your Majesty that your Majesty's confidential servants will be under the necessity of taking some part upon this measure in the course of a very few days.

[1] *Parl. Deb.*, x, 1080–5 (14 March).
[2] The 9th Earl of Kellie (c. 1745–1828). See No. 2963.
[3] On the 19th a copy of a message from the Admiralty Office was sent to the King: 'Telegraph message received at half past six p.m. from *Deal*: The Prussian Ambassador at Dover not allowed to land at Calais.' (13512.)   [4] Not in the Duke's own hand.

It has been observed to the Duke of Portland, when Mr Bankes gave the notice abovementioned, that in adverting to the fate of his former Bill, he stated in the strongest manner his sense of the publick injury which might arise out of any quarrel between the two Houses at any time, but particularly at the present, and expressed a clear opinion that the House would therefore willingly concur in modifying their former measure, even to the extent of giving up some points which they might prefer to retain, provided they had a prospect, without losing the essential object of that measure, of avoiding any unpleasant differences between these two branches of the Legislature.

Notwithstanding this statement, however, your Majesty's servants in the House of Commons incline to be of opinion that it is most probable that he will propose his measure in a shape in which the Lords cannot receive it, consistently with the opinion which they expressed against Lord Hawkesbury's Amendment in the Committee of the House of Lords. The Chancellor of the Exchequer therefore feels very apprenhensive of the probability of your Majesty's confidential servants in the House of Commons being under the embarrassment of having a measure proposed to them in the shape in which Lord Hawkesbury's Amendment would have left the former Bill, which, if opposed by your Majesty's servants in the House [of] Commons, will be construed as manifesting a difference of opinion which never existed on that subject, between them and their colleagues in the House of Lords; and, if supported by them, would be sending back to the House of Lords a measure of which that House has already expressed its decided disapprobation.

The objection, however, that may be fairly taken to returning to the Lords a measure so recently rejected by them, may be considered as sufficiently strong to justify your Majesty's servants in the House of Commons for now opposing the very measure which their colleagues proposed a few days ago in the House of Lords. But then, with a view to the present state and temper of the House of Commons, your Majesty's servants there are of opinion that that cannot be done safely, nor without material prejudice to your Majesty's service, unless they are prepared to state something which they will consent to do, which shall answer, in some degree at least, the object to which the House of Commons has already shewn that it attaches so much importance—and the Chancellor of the Exchequer feels it a duty which he owes, not only to his colleagues but most especially to your Majesty, to express very distinctly his opinion with respect to the effect which he apprehends may be produced upon the temper of the House of Commons, were an attempt made to resist altogether the renewal of any Bill upon the subject of reversionary grants.

The majorities by which your Majesty's Government is enabled to carry its measures at present in the House of Commons, are unquestionably very considerable; but he thinks himself indispensably called upon to state to your Majesty that the number in those majorities which consists of persons whose opinions are influenced in a great degree by considerations which lead them to coincide in such a measure as Mr Bankes will propose, is very great, and if your Majesty's Ministers were to take any part upon such a measure as this, which should alienate the support of this description of persons, the numbers would be very much diminished: and although those of your Majesty's servants who are most connected with Mr Bankes are confident that nothing is further from his meaning than to produce any constitutional mischief, and that he would endeavour to prevent any such mischief from arising out of the Committee of Finance, he would himself be much soured at it; and should the œconomical sentiment of the House of Commons prevail against your Majesty's Ministers on a question of this nature, that Committee would gain a degree of strength which your Majesty's servants might feel the greatest difficulty in afterwards resisting, should it attempt any measure of real danger.

The course, therefore, which the Chancellor of the Exchequer thinks it incumbent upon him to wish to have submitted to your Majesty, is this, that your Majesty's servants in the House of Commons should endeavour to amend Mr Bankes's Bill in such a manner as to render it sufficiently different from that which was rejected by the Lords to reconcile the passing of it to the character and consistency of that House, and at the same time sufficiently applicable to whatever there is of plausibility in the arguments by which the Bills have been supported, to induce the House of Commons to concur in the measure.

The two points which have made the strongest impression on the House of Commons are stated by the Chancellor of the Exchequer to be the following. First, that reversionary grants not being noticed at the time when they are made, the persons who ought to be responsible, in publick character or otherwise, for advising them, are often out of reach of publick censure before the knowledge of the grant reaches the publick notice—and secondly, that a reversionary grant conferring an interest in offices which may last for a great length of time, precludes during that period the opportunity of alteration or reduction, however necessary in any such offices, and at the present moment particularly, when enquiries are going on under a direct recommendation from your Majesty for the purpose of the œconomical reduction of expenditure, grants should not be made which should disappoint the good effects of those enquiries.

To obviate these objections, therefore, the Chancellor of the Exchequer is anxious to have it submitted to your Majesty that a clause should be introduced in the Bill to be brought in by Mr. Bankes, which should make it necessary for the validity of a reversionary grant that it should be published as other grants usually are in the London Gazette within a limited period from its date; and also a clause to enact that all grants of reversions which may be made within the next two years (in order to give time for the Committee to have suggested any necessary reform) should be made and taken to be made with the intention that they should be subject to any such alteration, reduction, or abolition, as your Majesty, with the advice of both Houses of Parliament, might think proper to enact with respect to such offices within the said space of two years from the passing of the Act.

But your Majesty's servants so strongly feel that, upon this subject or any of a similar nature, before any such measure as has now been submitted to your Majesty is adopted and supported by them, or before any further determination can be taken upon it, it is their duty to apprize your Majesty of the necessity which they feel themselves to be under of entertaining some proposition of this nature, that they have unanimously desired the Duke of Portland to represent the above-mentioned circumstances to your Majesty in order that your Majesty may be enabled to signify your pleasure thereupon when your Majesty next thinks proper to come to town, when he has reason to hope that the re-establishment of his health will allow him to pay his duty to your Majesty. But if he should be so unfortunate as to be disappointed in this expectation, he is authorized by the Lord Chancellor humbly to ask your Majesty's permission for him to attend you, in order to take your Majesty's commands upon this subject. (13515–24)

[*The King's reply, Windsor Castle, 22 March.*] The King acknowledges the receipt of the Duke of Portland's letter and although he regrets that the subject of reversionary grants is again brought forward, his Majesty is sensible of the manner in which the Duke of Portland has entered into it. The King will be ready to speak to him upon it tomorrow if he should be well enough to attend at the Queen's Palace, which his Majesty trusts he will not venture, unless the day is favorable. Should the Duke of Portland be absent, the King will converse with the Chancellor upon the subject. (13533)

3628   SPENCER PERCEVAL *to the* KING, *and the reply*

[*Downing Str., Tuesday morng., 6 a.m.* [*22 March 1808*].] Mr. Perceval acquaints your Majesty that Mr. Sharp's Motion for an Address to your Majesty to convey the censure and disapprobation of the Ho. of Commons upon the expedition to Copenhagen led to a very long debate which lasted till past 5 o'clock this morning. The Address was negatived by 224 to 64. Mr. Stuart Wortley[1] moved a Resolution of approbation as soon as the Address was negatived. The greater part of the argument was of course very much the same with that which has been frequently urged before, and the debate was not particularly worth notice, except that Mr. Secretary Canning made a most extremely able speech upon it.

On the Motion of approbation the Ayes were 216 and the Noes 61.[2] (13527)

[*The King's reply, Windsor Castle, 22 March.*] The King is very happy to learn from Mr Perceval's report that the majority in the House of Commons has been so respectable upon a question which so immediately affects the conduct of his Government, and H.M. rejoyces that it afforded to Mr Canning an opportunity of distinguishing himself. (13527)

[1] James Archibald Stuart-Wortley-Mackenzie, 1st Baron Wharncliffe (1776–1845). M.P. for Bossiney, 1802–18; for Yorkshire, 1818–26. Second son of John, 3rd Earl of Bute, the Prime Minister, and brother of the 1st Marquess of Bute. Took additional name of Wortley after that of Stuart, 17 Jan. 1795, and that of Mackenzie in 1826; served in Army, 1790–1801, retiring as Lieutenant-Colonel. Peerage, 12 July 1826. Lord Privy Seal, Dec. 1834–April 1835; Lord President of the Council, Sept. 1841–5. Pitt had promised him a U.K. peerage, but had died before he was in a position to implement it. Pitt had made a similar promise to Lord Hopetoun (who got his U.K. Barony on 3 Feb. 1809), and had promised that Lord Dalkeith should be called to the House of Lords (which he was, on 11 April 1807, in his father's Barony of Tynedale).

[2] *Parl. Deb.*, x, 1185–1235. The Princess of Wales and Lady Glenbervie attended the debate. (Colchester, II, 147.)

[*Charles Street, 22 March 1808.*] Lord Hawkesbury begs leave most humbly to submit to your Majesty a dispatch with its enclosures which has been received from his Grace the Lord Lieutenant of Ireland, together with the draft of the answer which Lord Hawkesbury proposes to return to it, if it shall meet with your Majesty's gracious approbation. (13534)

[*The King's reply, Windsor Castle, 23 March.*] The King approves of the answer to the Lord Lieutenant of Ireland of which Lord Hawkesbury has submitted the draft to his Majesty with the dispatches to which it refers. (13535)

[*From Lord Hawkesbury, Charles Street, 24 March.*] Lord Hawkesbury begs leave most humbly to submit to your Majesty a Minute of Cabinet.

Lord Hawkesbury is concerned to be under the necessity of informing your Majesty that the Duke of Portland was prevented by indisposition from attending the Cabinet, but Lord Hawkesbury has every reason to believe that his Grace's sentiments concur intirely with the enclosed Minute. (13539)

[*Enclosure*]
[*Cabinet Minute, 24 March.*]
Present: The Lord Chancellor, the Lord President, the Lord Privy Seal, the Earl of Chatham, the Lord Bathurst, Viscount Castlereagh, Lord Mulgrave, Mr Secy Canning, Mr Perceval, Lord Hawkesbury.

The Lord Chancellor having communicated to your Majesty's confidential servants the substance of the conversation with which your Majesty was pleased to honour him yesterday on the subject of Mr Bankes's intended Motion in the House of Commons on the subject of grants of reversion, they could not but deem it to be their first duty to your Majesty most anxiously to consider whether they could not, without material prejudice to your Majesty's service, effectually oppose Mr Bankes's intended proposition, without offering any other on the same subject to the consideration of that House.

Mr. Bankes, they understand, means to move that all grants of reversion should be suspended for two years.

That proposition your Majesty's confidential servants are of opinion under present circumstances ought to be resisted, and without detailing other reasons upon which that opinion is founded, the fact that the House of Lords has so recently refused to agree to such a prohibition they humbly think sufficiently justifies such opinion.

On the other hand, upon a very serious consideration of what hath been represented to your Majesty's servants now assembled, by such of them as are members of the House of Commons, of the sentiments and feelings of that House upon this subject, your Majesty's confidential servants, however desirous to resist the Motion altogether, cannot, consistently with their sense of duty to your Majesty, forbear most humbly to state that they are apprehensive that if the proposed Motion could be effectually resisted in the House of Commons (of which doubts may be most seriously entertained) it could not be resisted without great prejudice to your Majesty's general service, unless they were enabled to offer some other proposition to the House which it might be enduced to adopt.

In considering what other proposition might with your Majesty's permission be offer'd to the House, they have been governed by a conviction that it is their duty to exert their utmost endeavours not to allow your Majesty's present rights as to granting reversions to be affected in the slightest degree beyond what the most scrupulous and zealous consideration of what upon the whole under present circumstances might most conduce to the preservation of your Majesty's interests would seem to warrant.

Actuated by such sentiments, they concur in thinking that it might be adviseable to admit that in such grants of reversions as shall in a time to be limitted be hereafter made, there shall be a clause declaring that the grant is intended to be made subject to such provisions as to abolition & regulation in all respects of the office and its emoluments, as your Majesty with the advice of Parliament may, in a time also to be limitted, think it proper to establish. This they humbly submit is not a prohibition to grant, nor a suspension of the power of granting reversions. It amounts on the one hand to an intimation to the grantee that he takes the grant subject to the condition therein expressed. It removes that ground of complaint on his part if your Majesty and Parliament should think fit to abolish or regulate the office, which has hitherto impeded those regulations which even your Majesty's wisdom might approve, when the grantee has had no other notice of his situation but such as he might derive from his own notions of the general law of the country. Your Majesty's servants on the other hand entertain a confidence that your Majesty would be fully supported whenever in your Majesty's wisdom you should be pleased to think that alterations should not be made, or that such as may be proposed should not be adopted.

It has further occurr'd that there could be no reasonable objection to admitting the same publication to be made in the Gazette of your Majesty's gracious acts of favour when offices are granted in reversion, as is always made when your Majesty is pleased to confer on any of your subjects offices in possession.

Having with every sense of duty to your Majesty represented these their sentiments, your Majesty's confidential servants humbly request that your Majesty would be graciously pleased to signify how far they may be at liberty to consider their view of this subject as meeting your Majesty's approbation under the difficult circumstances in which they are placed. They beg leave to inform your Majesty at the same time that Mr Bankes intends bringing forward his Motion in the House of Commons on Monday next. (13540–3)

[*The King's reply, Windsor Castle, 25 March.*] The King has received Lord Hawkesbury's letter and the accompanying Minute of Cabinet, and upon consideration of what is therein represented and of what has been stated by those of his confidential servants who are in the House of Commons as connected with the intended Motion of Mr. Bankes, his Majesty has determined to acquiesce in the unanimous proposal of his Cabinet that a Bill should be offered to the House upon the subject of reversionary grants of pensions which shall contain the two clauses specified in the Minute. (13539)

[*From Lord Hawkesbury, Charles Street, 25 March.*] Lord Hawkesbury begs leave most humbly to submit to your Majesty the Minutes of the House of Lords and has the satisfaction of informing your Majesty that the Bill for the furtherance of the Orders-in-Council has passed the House of Lords.[1] (13544)

[*The King's reply, Windsor Castle, 26 March.*] The King has learnt with much satisfaction from Lord Hawkesbury's report that the Bill for the Orders-in-Council has at length passed the House of Lords. (13544)

3630   SPENCER PERCEVAL *to the* KING, *and the reply*
[*Downing St., 25 March 1808.*] Mr Perceval acquaints your Majesty that he has received an application from the Rector of Castleford humbly soliciting your Majesty's gracious assistance towards defraying part of the expence of erecting a school house in that parish. The ground for presuming to make this prayer to your Majesty rests upon the Rectory of the parish being in your Majesty's gift in right of your Majesty's Duchy of Lancaster.[2]

Mr. Perceval incloses the letter which he has received upon this subject, that your Majesty may be able to determine whether it is a case in which your Majesty should be graciously pleased to order Mr Perceval to authorise the Treasurer of yr. Majesty's Duchy to pay such sum as yr. Majy. may think fit in furtherance of the above object. (13550)

[*The King's reply, Windsor Castle, 25 March.*] The King approves of Mr Perceval's authorizing the Treasurer of the Duchy of Lancaster to pay such sum towards the expence of erecting a School House of [*sic*] Castleford as he shall conceive to be proper. (13551)

3631   ADMIRAL ROBERT DIGBY *to the* KING
[*Mintern[e][3], 26 March 1808.*] The state of my health for some time past has depriv'd me of the happiness of attending on your Majesty, and, as I have no hope of being able to do my duty in future, I beg your Majesty's permission, whenever it may be convenient, to resign my situation of Groom of the Bedchamber, ever keeping in mind, with the most sincere gratitude, your Majesty's gracious favors to me and to all our family. (13552)

[1] *Parl. Deb.*, x, 1254–5.
[2] Castleford, of course, is in the West Riding, near Leeds.
[3] In Dorset, the seat of the Earls of Digby.

3632   LORD HAWKESBURY *to the* KING, *and the reply*

[*Charles Street, 26 March 1808.*] Lord Hawkesbury begs leave most humbly to submit to your Majesty the letters which he has received from the City Remembrancer.[1] If your Majesty should think proper to receive the City on Wednesday next, your Majesty would perhaps appoint some previous day to receive the Sheriffs at Windsor in order to announce to them your gracious intention.

Lord Hawkesbury has ventured to transmit to your Majesty a private letter which he has received from the City Remembrancer, who is a most loyal subject and an excellent man, and though Lord Hawkesbury cannot attempt to advise your Majesty to depart from the rule you have been pleased to lay down to receive the City of London at the Queen's Palace only by deputation, yet he humbly submits to your Majesty that it may be adviseable under the present circumstances not to limit the numbers too narrowly, and your Majesty may possibly be induced to allow Lord Hawkesbury to settle with the City Remembrancer what numbers shall be permitted to attend your Majesty with the Address upon the present occasion. (13553)

[*The King's reply, Windsor Castle, 27 March.*] In reply to Lord Hawkesbury's letter, the King acquaints him that in the present state of his eyes, it is impossible for him to receive the Address of the City at St. James's, but his Majesty will not object to the deputation being more numerous than the last, & leaves it to Lord Hawkesbury to settle the numbers with the City Remembrancer who is a well disposed man. He may also be informed that the King will receive the Address on Wednesday next at two at the Queen's Palace, & that the Sheriffs may attend here on Tuesday next at that hour. (13554)

3633   GEORGE CANNING *to the* KING, *and the reply*

[*Foreign Office, 26 March 1808, 3.30 p.m.*] Mr. Canning feels it to be his duty to lose no time in humbly acquainting your Majesty that intelligence has been received this morning that his Majesty the King of Denmark[2] died suddenly at Rendsburgh on the 13th instant. The Prince Royal was proclaimed on the 16th at Copenhagen by the title of Frederick the Sixth.[3] (13555)

[*The King's reply, 26 March.*] The King returns his thanks to Mr Canning for the early communication of the intelligence received of the death of the King of Denmark. (13555)

3634   VISCOUNT CASTLEREAGH *to the* KING, *and the reply*

[*St James's Sq., 28 March 1808.*] Lord Castlereagh has been desired by the Duke of Orleans to represent to your Majesty that the precarious state of his

---

[1] Timothy Tyrrell.   [2] Christian VII (1749–1808).
[3] Frederick VI (1768–1839). On 31 July 1790 he married Sophia Frederica (1767–1852), daughter of the Landgrave Charles of Hesse-Cassel (1744–1836).

brother Count Beaujolais's health has induced his physicians to recommend his immediate removal to a warmer climate. They have particularly advised that he should reside for some time at Malta, and the Duke of Orleans, who proposes to accompany his brother, requests your Majesty's gracious permission to carry into effect the plan which has been suggested for Count Beaujolais' restoration. Should your Majesty be pleased to signify your pleasure to this effect, Lord Castlereagh understands from Lord Mulgrave that the Duke of Orleans and Count Beaujolais may be accomodated with a passage to the Mediterranean, without inconvenience to your Majesty's service, in a frigate now under orders for that station. (13560–1)

[*The King's reply, Windsor Castle, 29 March.*] The King does not object to the application which the Duke of Orleans has made through Lord Castlereagh to be allowed to accompany his brother to Malta and to reside there for the benefit of the latter's health.[1] (13561)

3635   *Letters from the* DUKE OF PORTLAND[2] *to the* KING, *and the replies*

[*Burlington House, Monday, 28 March 1808.*] A vacancy having taken place in the Chapter of Westminster by the death of Doctor Smith,[3] it is become the Duke of Portland's duty, in obedience to the commands which he has received to that effect from his Royal Highness the Prince of Wales, to lay before your Majesty the name of Mr Blomberg, the same gentleman who was submitted to your Majesty's consideration on the last vacancy of a Stall at Windsor.

The Duke of Portland feels it at the same time incumbent upon him most humbly to acquaint your Majesty that very pressing applications have been made to him to submit to your Majesty the names of the following persons, who are considered by their respective patrons to be not undeserving of such a mark of your Majesty's royal favor. By the advocates in behalf of publick education, and the friends of Westminster School in particular, he is urged to offer to your Majesty the name of *Doctor Carey,* the Headmaster of that seminary, who, since his appointment to it, has distinguished himself very much to its advantage, and to the entire satisfaction of all those who are interested in its prosperity. *The Dean of Exeter,*[4] the income of whose Deanery is stated by his brother-in-law the Duke of Beaufort not to exceed £500 pr anm. and who is father of a family of ten children, is most anxiously offered by that Duke as an object worthy of your Majesty's consideration, not only upon account of his character, but on the incompetency of his means to support his numerous and increasing family. The Earl of Lonsdale no less anxiously interests himself for *Doctor Gretton,* whose

---

[1] The Count (1779–1808) died there on 30 May.

[2] Not in the Duke's hand.

[3] Samuel Smith (*c.* 1731–1808). Rector of Walpole St Andrew, Norfolk, 1762–85; Headmaster of Westminster, 1764–88; Rector of Dry Drayton, Cambs., 1785; Prebendary of Westminster, 1787–1808, and of Peterborough, 1787–1808.

[4] Charles Talbot, D.D. (1769–1823). He married the Duke of Beaufort's eldest sister, Lady Elizabeth Somerset (*d.* 1836) in 1796. Dean of Exeter until March 1809.

name was submitted to your Majesty on occasion of the late vacancy at Windsor,[1] in consequence of the obligation which Lord Lonsdale feels himself under to that gentleman, for the attention he paid to the education of Lord Lowther.[2] The Earl of Bridgewater[3] is also very solicitous that the name of *Mr. Todd*,[4] the very ingenious editor of Spencer and of Milton and a person of considerable eminence in the literary line, should be brought under your Majesty's notice. Lord Hawkesbury feels the greatest possible anxiety in behalf of his relation *Mr John Jenkinson*,[5] the only person of the ecclesiastical profession with whom he is connected by relationship, and the Duke of Portland must request your Majesty's permission to observe that Lord Hawkesbury's exertions in your Majesty's service have been so uniform, so usefull, and so important that it would be difficult for Lord Hawkesbury to form a wish which the Duke of Portland would not feel that his duty to your Majesty required him to contribute his utmost endeavours to the accomplishment of. The Duke of Marlborough's instances have not been less urgent in behalf of *Mr. Hind*, whom the Duke qualifies with the denomination of his friend, states his having been his domestick chaplain for some years, and having been abroad with one of the Duke's sons. The Lord Viscount Cathcart is not less interested in behalf of his brother *Mr. Cathcart*,[6] whose case is no less anxiously supported by his nephew the Earl of Mansfield. Nor are the merits of *Doctor Andrewes*,[7] the Rector of St. James's, represented with less energy and earnestness by Lord Boringdon, who, notwithstanding the personal obligations he states himself to be under to that gentleman, very justly wishes to rest his hopes of obtaining the distinction he presses the Duke of Portland to sollicit of your Majesty for *Doctor Andrewes*, on the services which have been rendered by him in his publick capacity.

[1] See No. 3622.

[2] William, 2nd Earl of Lonsdale (1787–1872), styled Viscount Lowther from 7 April 1807, when his father, Lord Lonsdale, was created Earl, until 19 March 1844, when he succeeded his father. M.P. for Cockermouth, 1808–13; for Westmorland, 1813–31; for Dunwich, 1832; for Westmorland, 1832–41. A Lord of the Admiralty, 1809; a Commissioner for India, 1810–18; a Lord of the Treasury, 1813–27; Chief Commissioner of Woods and Forests, 1828–30; Vice-President of the Board of Trade, 1834–5, and Treasurer of the Navy, 1834–5; Postmaster-General, 1841–5; Lord President of the Council, Feb.–Dec. 1852. Summoned, 8 Sept. 1841, to the House of Lords, *v.p.*, in his father's Barony.

[3] John William Egerton, 7th Earl of Bridgewater (1753–1823), succeeded his cousin Francis, 3rd Duke of Bridgewater, as Earl on 8 March 1803. Entered the army, 1771; Captain, 1776; Major, 1779; Lieutenant-Colonel, 1790; Colonel, 1793; Major-General, 1795; Lieutenant-General, 1802; General, 1812. M.P. for Morpeth, 1777–80; for Brackley, 1780–1803. Great efforts were made but without success to induce him to move the Address at the opening of the parliamentary session in Jan. 1809. (W. Dacres Adams MSS. Charles Long to Adams, 9 Jan.)

[4] Henry John Todd (1763–1845). Edited the *Poetical Works of Milton*, 1801; an edition of Spenser, 1805, and of Johnson's Dictionary, 1818. Rector of All Hallows, Lombard Street, 1801–10; domestic Chaplain to the Earl of Bridgewater, April 1803. Royal Chaplain, 1812. He held various preferments, owing some of them to the Earl.

[5] John Banks Jenkinson (1781–1840), whose father was the 1st Lord Liverpool's brother. Prebendary of Worcester, Aug. 1808; Dean of Worcester, 1817; Bishop of St. David's, 1825–40; Dean of Durham, 1827–40.

[6] The Rev. Archibald Hamilton Cathcart (1764–1841), Prebendary of York. His sister Louisa (1758–1843) married David, Earl of Mansfield (1727–96) as his second wife (1776), and her son David William was the 3rd Earl (1777–1840).

[7] The Rev. Gerrard Andrewes (1750–1825), Rector of St. James's, Piccadilly; Dean of Canterbury, 1809; refused offer of Bishopric of Chester, 1812.

As the Duke of Portland has now laid before your Majesty a summary of all the applications which have been made to him for a Prebendal Stall at Westminster exclusively, and finds the amount of them to be so numerous, he desists from trespassing further upon your Majesty at the present moment by the addition of those which have been made generally for ecclesiastical dignities of the same description, without any specification of the Cathedral or Chapter to which a preference would be given. (13562–7)

[*The King's reply, Windsor Castle, 29 March.*] The King has received the Duke of Portland's letter and considers the vacancy which has arisen in the Chapter of Westminster as affording a good opportunity of relieving the Duke of Portland from the difficulties under which he is placed, by the Prince of Wales's application in favor of Mr. Blomberg, upon whom it therefore appears desireable that his choice should fall upon this occasion. (13567)

[*From the Duke of Portland, Burlington House, Tuesday, 29 March.*] The Duke of Portland begs leave most humbly to represent to your Majesty that he has collected it to be the opinion of several of your Majesty's confidential servants, & particularly of the Earl Bathurst & of those who are in the habit of attending to the business of the Committee of Council for Trade, that your Majesty's service in that respect would derive considerable advantage from the assistance of Lord Redesdale's experience & great knowledge, & the D. of Portland has reason to beleive that Lord Redesdale is perfectly disposed to obey any commands to that effect which your Majesty may think proper to lay upon him. The D. of Portland therefore submits with all deference to your Majesty's superior judgement the expedience of appointing Lord Redesdale a member of the Committee of Council for Trade & Plantations, & in case your Majesty shall be pleased to approve the appointment, of directing Ld. Redesdale to attend at the Queen's Palace tomorrow in order to his having the honor of kissing your Majesty's hands in consequence of it.

The Duke of Portland most humbly acquaints your Majesty that he lost no time in informing the Prince of Wales of your Majesty's determination in consequence of his Royal Highness's wishes, to confer the vacant Prebend of Westminster on Mr Blomberg. (13568–9)

[*The King's reply, Windsor Castle, 30 March.*] The King approves of the Duke of Portland's proposal that Lord Redesdale should be appointed a member of the Committee of Trade, and of his attending at the Queen's Palace this day in consequence. (13569)

[*From the Duke of Portland, Burlington House, Wednesday, 30 March.*] The Duke of Portland humbly conceives it to be his duty to lay before your Majesty a letter which he has received from the Prince of Wales in answer to the communication made to his Royal Highness by the Duke of Portland of your Majesty's gracious intentions to confer the vacant Prebend of Westminster on Mr Blomberg

—for which his Royal Highness commands the Duke of Portland to lay him at your Majesty's feet, with the humble expression of his gratitude. (13577)

[*The King's reply, Windsor Castle, 31 March.*] The King acknowledges the receipt of the Duke of Portland's letter, inclosing one from the Prince of Wales to him, which his Majesty returns. (13578)

[*From the Duke of Portland, Burlington House, Monday, 4 April.*] The Duke of Portland having received from the Lord President, at so late an hour as makes the Duke of Portland apprehend that the Offices of the Secretaries of State are shut, a letter and packet addressed to your Majesty, presumes to take upon himself to transmit them to your Majesty in order to obviate the delay which must necessarily be incurred by waiting for the usual mode of their being conveyed to your Majesty. (13581)

[*The King's reply, Windsor Castle, 5 April.*] The King transmits to the Duke of Portland Lord Camden's letter and the accompanying proposed establishment of the Office of Privy Council, which, as it will doubtless produce an addition of expence, his Majesty conceives to be a subject of consideration for his Treasury. If it should meet with their concurrence, the King will agree to what is proposed, and Lord Camden may consult with the Duke of Portland upon the subject before he comes to him tomorrow.[1] (13582)

3636   GEORGE CANNING *to the* KING

[*Foreign Office, 4 Apr. 1808.*] Mr. Canning humbly lays before your Majesty the two notes which he humbly mentioned to your Majesty on Wednesday as having been delivered by Prince Castelcicala: and submits at the same time for your Majesty's royal approbation the draft of an answer to them. (13583)

3637   *Letters from* SPENCER PERCEVAL *to the* KING, *and the replies*

[*Downg. Street, Monday, 4 April 1808.*] Mr Perceval acquaints your Majesty that the Chr. of the Exchequer, with the approbation of your Maj.'s servants in Ireland, has prepared a Bill to extend to that part of the United Kingdom the

---

[1] The following letter from Portland to Perceval, 5 April, is of interest: 'I have often stated to you the difficulty I felt in proposing to the King the grant of a new pension as long as *that* which he authorized me to promise Mr. Chas. Greville, his former Vice-Chamberlain, remained to be granted. I send you enclosed a copy of his Majesty's letter to me upon the subject, & leave it to your candor to say whether with such a paper in my possession & having on the strength of it repeatedly given my testimony of H.M.'s intentions in favor of Mr. G., I can with any propriety or sense of what the King owes to himself overlook Mr. Greville when the pension fund is in a state to provide for others.
'P.S. From the manner in which the King's note is worded, it would naturally be supposed that Mr. Greville wished to quit his employment & that Lord John Thynne wished to obtain it. It is therefore necessary to apprize you that the case was directly the reverse; there was certainly nothing that Mr. G. wished less & I believe that Ld. John was by no means anxious to be his successor [i.e. in May 1804].' (Perceval MSS.)

provisions of an Act which passed in the 9th year of yr. Maj.'s reign. That Act is generally known by the name of the Nullum Tempus Act. It was passed for the purpose of quieting the possession of the subject against such old and dormant claims of the Crown as had not been enjoyed in fact for the last 60 years. This Statute has not yet been extended to Ireland, but it is not fit that such a Bill should proceed without your Majesty's previous approbation, which, if your Majesty should be graciously pleased to give it, it will be Mr Perceval's duty to signify. The rights to which such an Act will principally apply are rights to small fee-farm rents reserved on old grants. The great hardship in enforcing them after they have been long unclaimed is, first, that purchasers have come into possession without a knowledge of the existence of these rents as a charge upon their property, and thus they find their purchases charged with burthens which they did not know of when they purchased, and which the negligence of your Majesty's servants in not collecting them had suffered to fall into oblivion; and secondly, as the property remains at law liable not only for the annual payment, as it accrues in future, but also for the arrears, the immediate demand is in many instances very heavy. For the arrears having been accumulating for very many years, the amount which was originally and in its annual demand very small, has swelled to a very large sum in proportion to the value of the property out of which it is due. An instance of this description has been mentioned to Mr. Perceval where a rent of this description is due from a small living, and where the present incumbent has been called upon to pay the arrears that amount to more than the annual value of his living; arrears too which had accrued wholly in the time of his predecessor. With a view to such cases, therefore, it is further proposed that not only the principle of the Statute above referred to should be enacted as law for Ireland, but that it should be further provided that the ecclesiastical proprietor should not be answerable for the arrears of such rent where they have become due in the time of his predecessor.

If yr. Majesty should desire further explanation upon this subject, previous to your Majesty's signifying your pleasure upon it, it will be in sufficient time for every purpose that Mr. Perceval should receive your Majesty's pleasure upon it at the Queen's House on Wednesday next.[1] (13584–5)

[*From Perceval, Downg. Street, Monday, 4 April, 12 p.m.*] Mr Perceval acquaints your Majesty that Mr Bidulph's Motion to remove Mr Wharton[2] from being a member of the Finance Committee, on account of his holding a place of emolument as Chairman of the Committee of Ways and Means, was negatived by the House upon a division of 70 to 21; and indeed it was so extravagant a proposition that Mr Perceval would hardly have thought it necessary to have troubled your Majesty with this letter for the single purpose of communicating the fate of such a Motion, but Mr Perceval feels it his duty to inform your Majesty that in con-

[1] An Act was passed during the Session embodying Perceval's proposal (48 Geo. III, *c.* 47: 'An Act for quieting possessions and confirming defective titles in Ireland, and limiting the right of the Crown to sue in manner therein mentioned; and for the relief of incumbents in respect of arrears due to the Crown during the incumbency of their predecessors.')

[2] Richard Wharton (1764–1828). M.P. for Durham, 1802–4, 1806–20. Chairman of the Committee of Ways and Means, 1808; Joint Secretary of the Treasury, 1809–14. See *Parl. Deb.*, x, 1309–15.

sequence of the opinions which he has collected from various quarters in the Ho. of Commons, he begins seriously to apprehend that there will be found very great difficulty in prevailing upon a considerable number of the friends of Government, especially those who are representatives of populous places, to vote for the Amendment intended, with your Majesty's acquiescence, to be proposed in Mr Bankes's Bill tomorrow, and consequently that there is considerable danger of the Bill being carried as it will be moved by Mr Bankes.

Mr Perceval's apprehension upon this subject does not end with the Bill; he fears that if your Majesty's servants should be outvoted upon this point, such success on the part of the Committee of Finance will give them a very great and dangerous encrease of influence and strength. For when those gentlemen who generally support your Majesty's Government, shall have been once prevailed upon to vote against it upon such a point, in compliance with popular clamour, they may be carried by the Committee to support its views on other questions, against some of which at least, it may be very desireable to reserve the strength of yr. Majesty's Government in the House of Commons unimpaired, and unprejudiced by previous defeat.

Your Majesty is already apprized that it is Mr. Bankes's intention to propose, as his new Bill,[1] the very provision which Lord Hawkesbury moved in the Committee of the Ho. of Lords, of suspending the power of granting reversions for two years. As this proposal was rejected by the Lords, it has been thought that returning it to the Lords in the shape of a new Bill might lead to a quarrel between the two Houses, and therefore your Majesty's servants proposed for your Majesty's consideration the measure of amending Mr Bankes's Bill, in which your Majesty was graciously pleased to acquiesce. Mr Bankes will not come into that Amendment, and there is a strong sensation in the House of Commons against it. But Mr Bankes will consent so far to vary his Bill from the shape in which it was presented to the Lords in their Committee, as to propose the suspension of the grant of any reversions for *one* year instead of *two*, in the hope, as he says, that this alteration may reconcile the Lords to passing it without injury to their consistency.

Mr Perceval feels the difficulty and embarrassment in which a defeat upon this Bill will place your Majesty's service to be so great, that tho' he has not yet had the opportunity of consulting any other of his colleagues except Lord Castlereagh & Mr Canning, he has thought it his duty, previous to his meeting them in Cabinet tomorrow, to state these circumstances to your Majesty in order that he might be able to lay before his colleagues your Majesty's pleasure upon this point, how far your Majesty would approve in the event of its being thought by your Majesty's servants in the House of Lords that the limitation to which Mr Bankes will consent, would reconcile that House to the adoption of the Bill that your Majesty's servants, in the House of Commons, should, to avoid the difficulty and embarrassment which they foresee from the probability of a defeat, agree to the Bill with the limitation to which Mr Bankes will consent. Mr Perceval is anxious that your Majesty should be assured that he would not have ventured to forward this communication to your Majesty without previously consulting his colleagues, if

[1] Introduced, 28 March. (*Parl. Deb.*, x, 1259–68.)

he had not felt that there would be no time to hear from your Majesty after having consulted with them, before the question must come on in the Committee of the House of Commons tomorrow. (13586–8)

[*The King's reply, Windsor Castle, 5 April.* [1808].] The King has learnt with great concern from Mr Perceval that from the temper and disposition of the majority of the House of Commons there is reason to apprehend that the opposition to Mr. Bankes's Motion in its present shape would be insufficient, and his Majesty is satisfied that Mr Perceval will agree with him upon the incalculable mischief which attends the existence of a Committee of Finance originally instituted for bad purposes, and whose influence is such as to become formidable to Government, and to assume a controul in the House of Commons. It is this reflection which is chiefly painful to the King upon this occasion, not the simple question at issue. If, however, under the circumstances which Mr Perceval has stated, he should find that his Majesty's servants in the House of Lords consider it necessary to subscribe to the Bill with the limitation now proposed by Mr Bankes, the King will not withhold his consent, confident as he is that Mr Perceval and his other servants in the House of Commons will not go one step further in their concession than shall appear to them to be an act of the strictest necessity, under the unfortunate considerations affecting this question.[1]

His Majesty consents to the extension to Ireland of the Act known by the name of the Nullum Tempus Act. (13589)

[*From Perceval, Downg. Street, 5 April.*] Mr Perceval acquaints your Majesty that no business came on in the House of Commons this evening, as the ballot for the Election Committee which was appointed for today failed to be procured, three members being wanted, tho' there were not less than 180 present.[2] (13590)

[1] The Duke of Portland wrote to the Duke of Rutland on 2 April: 'The indulgence I have uniformly experienced from your Grace and the support with which you have no less uniformly distinguished his Majesty's Administration entitle me to hope that you will not only excuse the liberty I am now taking but that you will have the goodness to comply with the request which I make you (at the instance of our friends in the House of Commons) to use your influence with such members of that House as have the pleasure of being now with your Grace to prevail upon them to set out on the receipt of this in order to their being able to attend on Monday when Mr. Bankes's Bill respecting *reversionary grants* will be the subject of debate. Your Grace I dare say has been apprised that Mr. Bankes has brought the *exact same* Bill into the House of Commons which was rejected by the Lords, with the addition only of the limitation in point of time which was equally rejected by them—and you will therefore, I hope, think that it was a proceeding too offensive to the House of Lords to be submitted to. Such was the opinion of the King's servants, and two clauses have been drawn for the purpose of obviating the objections to which the Bill is liable on the part of the Lords and on the part of the Crown. They have been submitted to his Majesty and have received his Majesty's consent, and will accordingly be proposed by Mr. Perceval in the House of Commons on *Monday next.* But such is the wildness of the House upon this subject that the most serious apprehensions are entertained of Government being able to resist Mr. Bankes's Bill with effect unless the utmost exertions are made by the friends of Government in support of the clauses the object of which I have stated to you. I therefore most earnestly entreat your Grace's assistance upon this occasion and trust that the circumstances I have had the honour of laying before you will induce you to exert your influence in prevailing upon such members of the House of Commons as are now at Belvoir to attend in their places on the *day after tomorrow*, *viz. Monday the 4th instant.* I trust your Grace will forgive this intrusion.' (Rutland MSS.)

[2] The House was, as usual, counted before the Newry Election Committee was balloted for, and 185 members were present. The customary procedure was as follows: Forty-nine members' names were

[*From Perceval, Downg. Str., Wednesday evg., 6 April.*] Mr Perceval acquaints your Majesty that the debate on the Reversion Bill did not come on this day. Upon Mr Bankes's proposing to bring it on Mr Tierney[1] objected, because there was no Order of the Day or notice for going on with it: the notice for yesterday having fallen by means of the House not meeting. In this objection he was well founded according to the usual practice of the House on such occasions, unless there is a general consent to waive the necessity of a fresh notice. Mr Perceval expressed not only his readiness to have consented to Mr Bankes's proposition, but his anxiety to have entered into the consideration of the Bill, because he wished as soon as possible to clear away that misunderstanding which had been so industriously circulated as to his intention of opposing, and endeavouring to defeat the Bill. That the principle on which he meant to act with regard to it was to take care that the Bill when returned to the Lords should be so materially different in substance as well as form, as not to make it necessary for the Lords to reject it with a view to maintain their own consistency; and he wished therefore to know what Amendments would be proposed by Mr Bankes, and to prove what would be satisfactory to himself by proceeding without delay into the Comee. upon the Bill; but that he must admit, if this was opposed, the practice of the House afforded good ground for the objection. The Speaker confirmed this opinion from the Chair, and Mr Bankes therefore moved to commit the Bill for tomorrow. Mr Tierney & Mr Calcraft then asked Mr Perceval & Mr Bankes what were the Amendments which they proposed to make. Mr Perceval said he had already expressed the principle on which he should either propose Amendments or accede to Amendments proposed by others, and that he could not state what he had to move till he heard what was moved by Mr Bankes. Mr Bankes only answered generally; and then

drawn by lot to serve on the Committee. In the course of the drawing the names of many other members drawn were set aside as exempt from service on these unpopular Committees (i.e., members who were sixty years of age and upwards, members against whom other Election Petitions were pending or who were themselves petitioners; members who had already served on an Election Committee during the Session, or who were then serving on such Committees; members who had voted at the election under dispute; members who pleaded illness, and whose excuses were supported by a medical certificate; members in the Forces who might be called away on duty; members with judicial duties, like the Master of the Rolls; most, but not all, Ministers of the Crown. If 49 names could not be obtained either because of poor attendance or because of the large number claiming exemption, the House had to adjourn immediately, further efforts being made on each succeeding day. When the necessary 49 were obtained, the number was reduced to 13 by challenging from either side, the final number being 15, one other member being nominated by each side. Decisions were far from being impartial; complete impartiality had to wait until the trial of controverted elections was transferred to the Judges in 1868.

[1] Tierney was one of the Whig casualties at the 1807 general election, but the Earl of Bandon, joint patron with the Duke of Devonshire of the borough of Bandon (each alternately nominating the Member) resurrected him in August 1807, the by-election being occasioned by Lord Boyle's succession to his father as Earl of Shannon (20 May 1807). Sir Arthur Wellesley, the Irish Secretary, wrote to the Lord Lieutenant of Ireland, the Duke of Richmond (6 July 1807): 'I now write to apprise you that Long has informed me that Tierney is to be brought into Parliament for Bandon. Lord Bandon is the proprietor of this borough, and he is the brother-in-law of Lord Shannon, with whom he has always hitherto acted in politics. Would it be possible for you to prevail upon Lord Shannon to interfere to prevent Lord Bandon from returning Tierney? If you could it would be considered a great service here.' (N.L.I., Richmond MSS.) Tierney wrote to Grey on 25 Sept. 1808: 'I am afraid there has been sad work at Youghal in an attempt of the Duke of Devonshire's agents to get the borough from Lord Shannon. I wish it may not injure Ponsonby's strength in the County, and put Bandon further out of the Duke's reach than ever.' (Howick MSS.)

Mr Whitbread said that for his part, tho he should not oppose Mr Bankes's Amendment in the Committee, yet his objection was to any limitation as to time, or any alteration from the former Bill, and that therefore in some future stage he should propose to restore it to its former state. No notice was taken of this observation, but Mr Perceval thinks that such a Motion as Mr Whitbread expressed his intention to make will a little help to open people's eyes to what these measures may lead to; and upon the whole has no hesitation is stating that he thinks the result of the conversation, the substance of which he has briefly detailed, will prove a favorable introduction to the business of the debate tomorrow. (13591-2)

[*The King's reply, Queen's Palace, 7 April.*] The King is glad to hear from Mr Perceval's letter that what passed last night in the House of Commons affords hopes of a less unpleasant result of the discussion on the Reversion Bill. His Majesty conceives that it will be very material to watch the progress of any difference of sentiment which may arise among its original supporters, and not to neglect any opportunity of pointing out to those who are otherwise well inclined where the cloven foot is shewn. (13592)

3638   VISCOUNT CASTLEREAGH *to the* KING,[1] *and the reply*

[*St. James's Square, 6 April 1808.*] Lord Castlereagh begs permission humbly to submit for your Majesty's approbation the accompanying Minute agreed to by your Majesty's confidential servants, after having taken into their consideration the legislative provisions which at present subsist on the subject of internal defence.

Lord Castlereagh has the honour at the same time of laying before your Majesty an outline of the manner in which it is proposed to constitute the local militia, which your Majesty's confidential servants humbly conceive will provide for the country when carried into effect a more secure and permanent description of defence (resting as it will do on the provisions of positive law) than that which depends for its support altogether on the voluntary zeal of individuals. They deem it however expedient, considering the present numbers and efficiency of the volunteers, to continue to give every countenance and support to the existing corps so long as they may be found willing to continue their services, upon such conditions as your Majesty may think fit to prescribe to them; and that the local militia should only be progressively established in proportion as the volunteers may be found to relax in their attention to their military duties. (13593-4)

[*Cabinet Minute (Enclosure).*]

At a meeting of Cabinet held at Burlington House the 5th April 1808

Present: The Lord Chancellor, Lord President, Lord Privy Seal, the Duke of Portland, Earl Chatham, Earl Bathurst, Lord Hawkesbury, Lord Mulgrave, Mr Canning, Mr. Perceval, Viscount Castlereagh.

[1] Not in Castlereagh's own hand (but the Minute is).

It was resolved humbly to recommend to his Majesty that a Bill should be introduced into Parliament for the purpose of enabling his Majesty to direct a levy of local militia to take place in the respective counties, to the extent of any deficiencies that either now or hereafter may exist, in their quota of volunteers, as settled under the provisions of Mr Yorke's Defence Act, at six times the militia.

That the Training Bill should not be carried into execution with a view to the general training of the people, but that in the event of an adequate emergency arising, its provisions should be had recourse to for the purpose of selecting and preparing a sufficient number of them to serve in his Majesty's regular and militia forces, in case of actual invasion. (13595–6)

[*The King's reply, Windsor Castle, 6 April.*] The King has received Lord Castlereagh's letter and the accompanying Minute of Cabinet respecting the levy and establishment of a local militia, and his Majesty will approve of this or any other measure which may tend effectually to strengthen the means of defence of the country without bearing too hard upon the community at large. (13594)

3639 GEORGE CANNING *to the* KING

[*Foreign Office, 6 Apr. 1808.*] Mr. Canning humbly submits for your Majesty's royal approbation the draft of an answer from your Majesty to the letter received by your Majesty from the King of Sweden. (13597)

3640 *Letters from* SPENCER PERCEVAL *to the* KING, *and the replies*

[*Downg. St., 7 April 1808.*] Mr Perceval acquaints your Majesty that Mr Bankes's Reversion Bill past thro' the Committee this evening without any division. Mr Bankes proposed his alterations and Mr Perceval thinks the Bill will certainly be returned into the House of Lords materially different both in form and substance from that which was last rejected. Instead of being a Bill to *abolish* the power of granting reversions generally and entirely, it will be a Bill to suspend the granting of them for a year & to six weeks after the meeting of the then next Session of Parliament—and instead of its proceeding upon a recital of the expediency to abolish these reversions without any reason assigned, which was one objection strongly stated in the Lords, it will now recite the expediency with a *view to enquiries now pending* in the House of Commons to suspend the powers, and therefore whatever objections any of their Lordships may still feel and retain to the Bill in its present shape, at least they will not be able to consider it as a measure forced upon them the same in form or the same in substance as the former. Mr Perceval however has to regret that Mr Bankes stated that he adopted these alterations only because the Bill so altered was all that he could now accomplish, but that he hoped the House would not lose sight of the original measure.

Mr Tierney & Mr Whitbread were both against any limitation, and Mr Whitbread has given notice of his intention of moving tomorrow to extend the limitation to some very long period in order to bring the Bill as near as possible to its former shape—and Mr Perceval expects that he will have to report to your Majesty no unsatisfactory division upon that Motion should it be made tomorrow.[1] (13598–9)

[*The King's reply, Queen's Palace, 8 April.*] The King acknowledges the receipt of Mr Perceval's report of what passed in the House of Commons last night, and his Majesty trusts that Mr Perceval will not be disappointed in his hopes that the matter now in agitation will terminate more satisfactorily than he had reason to expect. (13599)

[*From Perceval, Downing Street, 8 April.*] Mr Perceval acquaints your Majesty that upon a Motion made by Mr Whitbread for the production of a declaration delivered by the Russian pelinpotentiaries [*sic*] to Lord Granville Leveson upon the signature of the Treaty of Alliance against France in 1805 and also for a private letter of Lord Granville Leveson to Mr Canning to which some allusion had been made, the former paper was agreed to be produced, and Mr Canning took the opportunity of explaining the circumstances attending that transaction in a manner completely to remove all the impression which had been attempted to be made on the public, as if there had been any indifference manifested on that occasion by your Majesty's other servants to the maritime rights of the country, and in a very masterly manner exposed the absurdity of the arguments by which the production of the private letter was attempted to be enforced. Upon this later part of the Motion the House divided 115[2] to 50 against its production.

After this was over the Reversion Bill was reported—but Mr Whitbread declined making his Motion of which he had given notice last night, deferring his intention till the third reading on Monday.[3] (13602–3)

[*The King's reply, Windsor Castle, 9 April.*] The King acknowledges the receipt of Mr Perceval's report of last night's proceedings in the House of Commons. (13603)

3641 VISCOUNT CASTLEREAGH *to the* KING

[*? 10 April 1808.*] Lord Castlereagh begs leave to submit to your Majesty a Memorandum which was prepared for the information of Cabinet, with respect to the present state of the Army at home and abroad.[4] (13670)

MEMORANDUM

[*Downing Street, 10 April 1808.*] Lord Castlereagh in compliance with the desire expressed at the last meeting of Cabinet on the South American question, circulates such information as may enable his colleagues to form a judgment how far the various services at home and abroad are at present adequately provided for, and whether there are any and what means applicable to other objects.

---

[1] *Parl. Deb.*, x, 1329–45.   [2] The correct number is 114.   [3] *Parl. Deb.*, x, 1353–68.
[4] Docketed, probably wrongly, 21 May 1808. The note may well be a covering letter to the Memorandum that follows.   [4] Not in his own hand.

The paper No. 1 compares the present effective force with the numbers required by the Commander-in-Chief in January 1804 for the several stations at home and abroad. It also shews how those services have stood in point of provision on the 1st of January in the intervening years 1805, 1806 & 1807.

The paper No. 2 shews the composition of the army at home; the regiments that have proceeded to the Baltic are marked (x). The regiments on foreign service are with a few exceptions on very high establishments. The Duke of York's requisition was made when the volunteer force was only forming, and when the French army was assembled in force upon the coast. (13609–10)

[*Enclosure*]

STATEMENT of Effective Force at home and abroad at the periods of January 1804, 1805, 1806, 1807 and 1st April 1808, compared with amount required by the Commander-in-Chief's letter of 13th Jany 1808.

Stations	Effectives January 1804	Effectives January 1805	Effectives January 1806	Effectives January 1807	Effectives 1st April 1808	Force required by Commander in Chief in letter of 13th Jany 1804 [*sic*]
Great Britain	127,000	129,580	114,247	119,076	130,661	143,000
Ireland	34,000	53,510	38,050	50,520	58,944	54,000
Islands	8,007	7,408	7,686	6,966	9,051	8,000
Home Army	169,007	190,498	159,983	176,562	A198,656	205,000
Leeward Islands	11,141	12,640	13,575	13,908	19,746	14,100
Jamaica	4,080	4,175	4,849	3,912	5,062	B 8,000
East Indies	15,197	15,818	18,235	17,764	24,137	17,560
Ceylon	4,350	5,042	6,026	5,658	5,062	4,000
Gibraltar	3,722	4,586	5,301	5,707	6,511	5,000
Malta	5,421	6,490	11,240	4,800	5,090	5,000
North America	3,361	4,194	5,149	4,808	9,144	5,000
Cape of G. Hope	—	—	4,312	4,655	6,027	—
Sicily	—	—	—	17,278	16,185	—
Madeira	—	—	—	—	1,981	—
South America	—	—	—	10,759	—	—
Continent	—	—	D21,139	—	C11,500	—
General Spencer	—	—	—	—	4,000	—
Army abroad	47,272	52,945	89,826	89,265	114,445	58,660
Army at home	169,007	190,498	159,983	176,562	198,656	205,000
Total Force	216,279	243,443	249,809	265,827	313,101	E263,660

Remarks

A Including the annual draft from the Irish Militia from 4 to 5,000 men may be expected to be added in the course of the year to the Regular Army at home.

B The Commander-in-Chief proposed this force for Jamaica in consideration of the then state of St Domingo.

C Corps under Sir John Moore.

D Corps under Lord Cathcart.

E The Duke of York urges in his letter the importance in addition to filling up the deficiency then existing in the army of 47,381 men, as compared with his estimate that 20,000 men more should

[*Charles Street, 11 April 1808.*] Lord Hawkesbury begs leave most humbly to submit to your Majesty that the Duke of Gordon is desirous of resigning the Lord Lieutenancy of the county of Aberdeen in favor of his son, the Marquis of Huntley, and if your Majesty should be graciously pleased to approve of this arrangement they will attend at the Queen's Palace on Wednesday next for the purpose of giving effect to it. (13612)

[*The King's reply, Windsor Castle, 12 April.*] The King approves of the arrangement proposed in Lord Hawkesbury's letter respecting the Lieutenancy of the county of Aberdeen, and of the Duke of Gordon's & Lord Huntley's attending at the Queen's Palace tomorrow in consequence. (13612)

3643 SPENCER PERCEVAL *to the* KING, *and the reply*

[*Downing Str., Tuesday, 3.30 a.m.* [*12 April 1808*].] Mr Perceval acquaints your Majesty that the Reversion Bill has been read a third time this morning, and has passed with those Amendments which Mr Perceval announced to your Majesty before. The debate has been principally in the hands of persons not in your Majesty's service. Amendments were moved by Lord Porchester to bring the Bill back to the state in which Mr Bankes introduced it by leaving out the recitals in the Preamble and restoring the *prohibition* in the room of the *suspension* —and also (with the view of ensuring an early debate upon the subject of it in the next Session) by limiting the duration of it, confining it to 6 weeks after the commencement of the next Session. Mr Bankes opposed these Amendments— Mr Tierney supported them—and the debate went on principally amongst those who are generally in opposition to your Majesty's Government, differing among themselves—except that Lord Grantham's brother Mr Robinson, Sr. J. Pulteney, Mr Stephen & Mr Willoughby[1] supported Mr Bankes, and Sir Francis Burdett spoke after Mr Stephen, and was followed by Mr Windham, who supported the Amendments, merely upon his objection to the particular use of yr. Majesty's prerogative in granting reversions, but he very manfully opposed all the extravagant opinions by which the Bill had been recommended as promising relief to the people, and as leading to further reform. Mr Sheridan followed him, replying

be provided for offensive operations, carrying the deficiency to 67,381 of the total force required to 283,660 men.

The Army now exceeds by 29,441 men the total force required, including the disposeable force of 20,000 men.

N.B. Corps for S. America may be furnish'd as follows:

Surplus force at Gibraltar	4,000
-do- Leeward Islands	4,000
-do- eventually No. America	4,000
From home	3,000
From Madeira	1,000
	16,000

(13671)

---

[1] Henry Willoughby (1780–1849), M.P. for Newark, 1805–31; nephew of Henry, Baron Midleton (*d.* 1800).

to him with considerable vehemence & warmth[1]; and with a few words from Mr. W. Smith the debate closed. The House was very thin for such a subject and the numbers were 112 to 60 against the Amendments. Your Majesty's confidential servants had no manner of occasion to take any part in the debate, and the Bill has now left the House of Commons, amended, as Mr Perceval trusts, not only in a way to reconcile it to the character & consistency of the Ho. of Lords, if they should adopt it, but in a manner in which it has led to a division and difference amongst those who are desirous of pressing forward reform thro' the Finance Committee—and Mr Perceval trusts he is not mistaken when he expresses his belief to his Majesty that the fate of this Bill now, if it should succeed in the House of Lords, instead of weakening the means of your Majesty's servants to resist any measure which may really be found objectionable as proposed by the Finance Committee, will rather have strengthened them; altho' undoubtedly the thinness of the House does not shew any great disposition on the part of the friends of Government to give their active support to it upon a measure connected with the subject of reform.[2] (13384–5)

[*The King's reply, Windsor Castle, 12 April.*] The King has received much pleasure from Mr Perceval's report of last night's debate in the House of Commons, and from the opinion which it conveys that the general appearance of the disposition and proceedings is more satisfactory than there had been reason to expect a short time since. (13613)

3644   LORD HAWKESBURY *to the* KING, *and the reply*

[*Charles Street, 14 April 1808.*] Lord Hawkesbury begs leave most humbly to acquaint your Majesty that the Comte d'Artois has applied for your Majesty's permission that the Duc d'Angoulême may be allowed to proceed in one of your Majesty's ships of war, which are destined for the Baltic, to Gothenburg for the purpose of endeavouring to bring away the Queen of France and the Duchess of Angoulême from the Russian dominions. Lord Hawkesbury has communicated with Lord Mulgrave on the subject, who sees no objection to the proposal of accomodating the Duc d'Angoulême and of giving the necessary instructions for that purpose. Lord Hawkesbury begs leave therefore to submit to your Majesty whether your Majesty would be pleased to authorise Lord Hawkesbury to give to the Lords of the Admiralty the authority to carry this proposal into effect. (13614)

[*The King's reply, Windsor Castle, 15 April.*] The King approves of Lord Hawkesbury's authorizing the Lords of the Admiralty to accomodate the Duke d'Angoulême in one of the ships of war destined for the Baltic. (13615)

[1] Sheridan may have had too much to drink; members on his own side often complained of his lack of sobriety, as Whitbread, for example, writing to Lord Grey the following 16 June: 'You will see by the papers that Sheridan, in concert with Canning, & against the wish & advice of all his friends, has been making a Motion about Spain. He did all he could to create a cry for himself as distinguished from all of us, but he was so exceedingly drunk he could hardly articulate. A more disgraceful exhibition was seldom if ever witnessed, but it served to make mischief.' (Howick MSS.)

[2] *Parl. Deb.*, XI, 18–29.

[*Bulstrode, Sunday, 17 April 1808.*] The Duke of Portland having acquainted the Marchioness Townshend with your Majesty's munificent intentions towards her, has received a letter from her, which in justice to her he humbly begs leave to lay before your Majesty; and in compliance with the verbal request which has been made to him by Lady Rumbold[1] he presumes to offer to your Majesty her most gratefull thanks for the very great & seasonable relief which your Majesty's liberality has afforded her & her large family, who would soon have been destitute of the almost common necessaries of life but for the interposition of your Majesty's bounty.

Information having been given to the Duke of Portland of the vacancy of a Stall at Worcester by the death of Mr Fountaine,[2] the knowledge of Lord Hawkesbury's sollicitude to obtain that situation for his near relation Mr John Jenkinson, (of whose character the Duke of Portland has received the most satisfactory testimonials) inclines him to hope that your Majesty will not disapprove the preference which the Duke of Portland cannot but consider Lord Hawkesbury to be intitled by the zeal, the abilities, and firmness which he has manifested & the important services he has render'd to your Majesty in the course of the present Session; & that your Majesty will think him worthy of having his wishes gratified in this instance. Independent of the considerations which the Duke of Portland has felt it his duty to submit to your Majesty, the only competitors for the Stall in question are a gentleman of the name of *Woollen*,[3] who is a friend of the Earl Poulett's[4] in the borough of Bridgewater; & a *Mr Barker*, who has been recommended by Lord Edward Somerset,[5] & who would be willing to resign a living

[1] Sir George Berriman Rumbold, 2nd Bart. (1764–1807), the son of Sir Thomas Rumbold, married in Nov. 1783 Caroline, daughter of James Hearne of Waterford, and they had two sons and four daughters. He had died at Königsberg on 15 Dec. 1807. On 11 Oct. 1809 she married Admiral Sir Sidney Smith, and died in Paris, 16 May 1826. Sir Thomas Rumbold had bequeathed the bulk of his property, not to his son but to his children by his second wife. The Duke of Kent referred to Lady Rumbold's marriage, in a letter to his friend Lieutenant-Colonel Wright on 23 Nov. 1809: 'Adverting to what you say of Mr. Spencer Smith, I am led to inform you, if you should not yet be apprized of it, that Sir Sydney himself has at length turn'd Benedict, having recently led to the Altar the gay widow Lady Rumbold, relict of our quondam Minister at Hamburgh, whom the French seized and carried off with his papers some years since. His marriage is itself very odd (for he had for years been supposed to have obtained all he could wish or expect from the lady) [and] was rendered the more singular by his driving direct from Church, where he was married, to the Levée, to be presented upon his marriage.' (46421–4)

[2] Thomas Fountaine (*c.* 1737–1815), Vicar of Old Windsor, 1771; Chaplain in Ordinary to the King, 1772; Prebendary of Worcester, 1774; Rector of North Tidworth, Wilts., 1780–8; Vicar of Bromsgrove, Worcs., 1788–1815; Vicar of Tarrington, Herefs., 1789–1815. The report of his death was inaccurate. He died in May 1815. According to the post-1808 Red Books John Banks Jenkinson was made a Prebendary in 1808, though there was no vacancy, and though the Duke of Portland said on 20 June 1808 that Mr. Jenkinson's hopes had been disappointed. (No. 3672.)

[3] The Rev. William Wollen (*c.* 1760–1844), Rector of Bridgwater with Chilton, 1788, and Vicar of Kilton, Somerset, 1815–44.

[4] John, 4th Earl Poulett (1756–1819), styled Viscount Hinton from 1764 until 14 April 1788, when he succeeded his father. K.T., 30 May 1794. A Lord of the Bedchamber, Nov. 1795–Jan. 1819. Lord Lieutenant of Somerset, 1792–1819.

[5] Lord Robert Edward Henry Somerset (1776–1842), fourth son of the 5th Duke of Beaufort. M.P. for Monmouth, 1799–1802; for Gloucestershire, 1803–31; for Cirencester, 1834–7. Entered the army, 1793; Captain, 1794; Major, 1799; Lieutenant-Colonel, 1800; Colonel, 1810; Major-General, 1813; Lieutenant-General, 1825; General, 1841. K.C.B., 1815; G.C.B., 1834.

which he says may be made worth £500 a year, should your Majesty think fit to give him the Prebend of Worcester. (13617–8)

[*Enclosure*]

[*The Marchioness Townshend to the Duke of Portland, Weymouth Street, 16 April.*]
I take the first moment in my power to express to your Grace, how much I feel his Majesty's great goodness to me; at the same time I am fully sensible that all I can say upon this occasion is, & would be very inadequate to the sense I have of the King's condescending kindness in bestowing upon me such a mark of his royal favor, and that too, under the impression which his Majesty so justly and so graciously entertains of Lord Townshend's never ceasing attachment to his royal person.

Lord Townshend was in truth, my Lord, one of his Majesty's most zealous and attached subjects, and to know that I receive from his Majesty such a testimony of his belief that he was so, makes this bounty of his Majesty the more valuable to me.[1]

Your Grace will add to the obligation I am under to you, my Lord, for the kind part you have taken on this occasion, if you will convey to his Majesty my grateful and humble acknowledgment of his condescending goodness to me. (13616)

[*The King's reply, Windsor Castle, 18 April.*] The King acknowledges the receipt of the Duke of Portland's letter and that inclosed from Lady Townshend, & his Majesty approves of Mr Jenkinson's succeeding to the vacant Stall at Worcester. (13618)

3646   VISCOUNT CASTLEREAGH *to the* KING, *and the reply*

[*Downing St., 17 April 1808.*] Your Majesty's confidential servants having taken into their consideration the pressing demands of your Majesty's ally the King of Sweeden for military succours, and the important influence the immediate presence of a British corps in the Baltick, (acting in conjunction with your Majesty's Fleet) may have in animating the Sweedish nation to the defence of their country against the common enemy, have determined humbly to recommend to your Majesty, that a corps of 10,000 men should be for[th]with sent, under the orders of Lt.-Genl. Moore to Gottenburgh with orders to co-operate in defence of that part of the Sweedish frontier against invasion, either from the side of Norway or the opposite coast. Your Majesty's servants humbly recommend that it should be distinctly explain'd to his Sweedish Majesty that this corps is intended to be employ'd on the coast under the immediate orders of your Majesty's own officers, and not to be detach'd into the interior or in separation from your Majesty's Fleet, and that it is at all times to be subject to be withdrawn should your Majesty's service more pressingly require its presence in any other quarter. Your Majesty's servants conceive the effect of sending this corps to Gottenburg will be to check

[1] The Marquess had died on 14 Sept. 1807.

any attempts against Sweeden from Norway—to preserve our commercial communication with the Continent, and to secure to your Majesty's Fleet a safe port to retire to in case of stress of weather, whilst it will liberate a considerable proportion of the Sweedish army which may then be applied to other objects. (13619–20)

[*The King's reply, Windsor Castle, 18 April.*] The King, being sensible of the necessity of supporting the King of Sweden, approves of the proposal submitted by Lord Castlereagh for sending to Scania ten thousand men, under the restrictions as to their disposal which are specified. (13620)

3647   GEORGE CANNING *to the* KING, *and the reply*

[*Hinckley,*[1] *19 April 1808.*] Mr. Canning humbly submits for your Majesty's royal approbation the drafts of instructions to Lord Strangford.

He humbly begs leave at the same time to request your Majesty's royal pleasure for assigning to Lord Robert FitzGerald, late your Majesty's Envoy Extraordinary & Minister Plenipotentiary at the Court of Lisbon, a pension of £2000 pr. an. *nominal.* This is a larger proportion of the appointments than has usually been assigned to Ministers of that character, but Mr Canning is induced humbly to recommend to your Majesty's gracious consideration such an allowance to Lord Robert FitzGerald in consequence of his having served your Majesty twenty years.[2]

Mr Canning most humbly requests your Majesty's gracious permission to be absent from town during the holidays, not having had an opportunity of seeing his family since the beginning of November. He apprehended that your Majesty

[1] Canning's seat in Leicestershire which he had recently purchased; he had given up South Hill Park, near Bracknell, Berks.

[2] Canning treated him with great indulgence. He had been absent from Lisbon on leave, 16 Sept.–19 Oct. 1804, and again, May–Oct. 1805; he had left Lisbon on 22 May 1806, and Lord Strangford, who had been Chargé d'Affaires during Fitzgerald's absences, and Minister Plenipotentiary *ad int.*, Jan.–Nov. 1807, delivered Lord Robert's recall at Rio de Janeiro, 25 July 1808. On 24 Nov. 1807 Canning wrote to the Duke of Richmond, to whom Fitzgerald had written, evidently to press his claims: 'I was disposed to deal quite fairly by him (as indeed he has already had sufficient proof) and ...no interest was necessary to induce me to do so. You must understand that *I* did not put Lord Strangford where he is, nor make him Minister. He was made so by the former Administration and, I *believe*, in order to allow of Lord Robert remaining in England and attending Parliament. Lord Robert's leave of absence has been beyond all precedent, and I have prolonged it at his desire, which, considering that he receives his full appointment all the time, is more than I would have ventured to do for any private friend of my own or any political friend of mine. I found him with a leave of absence which, at his request, I prolonged to him: and though I did once think of sending him back at the beginning of the discussion which has led to the emigration to the Brazils, I desisted from that intention upon the conviction, which I am sure was well founded, that the sending *any* new person to Lisbon at that time would have been prejudicial. I mention this only because I would do justice to Lord Robert's readiness to return when I proposed it to him in the summer. As it is, however, I can only act upon what *has* been the course of events, not upon what *might* have been. I shall be most happy at any time when it is in my power to consult Lord Robert Fitzgerald's interests, but I am sure you will agree with me that at a moment, and in a case so singularly important and interesting as the present, I cannot and ought not to act upon any ground of personal favour, and that thinking it (as I do) essential to the public service, I am bound to send Lord Strangford to the Brazils.' (Richmond MSS.)

did not intend to be in town this week: or he would not have presumed to leave town without your Majesty's previous permission. (13621–2)

[*The King's reply, Windsor Castle, 21 April.*] The King acquiesces in Mr Canning's proposal that Lord Robert Fitzgerald should receive a pension of £2000 per ann. nominal, and his Majesty is glad that Mr Canning can avail himself of the present moment to gain a little respite from his fatiguing duties. (13622)

3648   LORD MULGRAVE *to the* KING, *and the reply*

[*Admiralty, 20 April 1808.*] Lord Mulgrave has the honour to acquaint your Majesty (with great regret) that Admiral Lord Gardner in consequence of very severe indisposition finds himself unable to continue the arduous duties of his command, which that meritorious officer therefore humbly solicits your Majesty's gracious permission to resign. Lord Mulgrave humbly begs leave to submit to your Majesty's gracious consideration the appointment of Admiral Lord Gambier to succeed Admiral Lord Gardner in the command of the Channel Fleet. (13623)

[*The King's reply, Windsor Castle, 21 April.*] The King has learnt with much regret from Lord Mulgrave's letter that the state of Lord Gardner's health is such as to oblige him to resign the command of the Channel Fleet, and under this circumstance his Majesty is sensible that the choice of a successor could not fall upon a more proper person than Lord Gambier, whose gallantry & abilities have been tried and who will do credit to any command intrusted to him. (13624)

3649   THE DUKE OF PORTLAND *to the* KING, *and the reply*

[*Bulstrode, Thursday, 21 April 1808.*] Your Majesty's confidential servants have long entertained the most anxious apprehensions that the growing influence of France must at no distant period give to that Power the command of the wealth and resources of the Spanish provinces of South America, in addition to the uncontrolled dominion it already exercises over all the naval & military resources of the continent of Europe. As long as there was an hope that the duration of this most alarming influence might only be temporary, or that its extent might be limited, your Majesty's servants could not but consider any system of measures which might tend to loosen the connection of those colonies with their parent state as too hazardous an experiment to admit of its being submitted to your Majesty. But as the late events at Madrid and the intire occupation of Spain by French troops, have placed not only the powers of that Government but the person of its King in the hands and at the disposal of the enemy, so that whatever orders France may think fit to dictate with respect to the Spanish colonies may now be issued in the name of his Catholick Majesty, and that it is but too probable that the interval may be short between the seizure by France of the Spanish Government at home & the occupation by the same Power of its colonies abroad, the case appears to be totally alter'd, and the question no longer turns upon what is due to the preservation of an old-established Government, but upon what may be necessary to prevent the inordinate growth of a tyrannical usurped power.

Under these circumstances your Majesty's confidential servants are of opinion that it is become their indispensible duty most humbly to represent to your Majesty that in their judgement the essential interests of your Majesty's Empire demand that no time should be lost in exerting every endeavour to prevent the dominion of France from being extended over the Spanish colonies, and that with that view no means should be neglected that can animate those colonies & impress them with a just sense of the manner in which their Sovereign has been betrayed, and of the chains which they are forging for themselves.

Should such a determination on the part of the British Government be deferred 'till the political and military agents of the enemy have been introduced, under the sanction of his Catholick Majesty's name, into the principal fortresses belonging to Spain in the West Indies and South America, it will then perhaps be too late to prevent France from possessing herself of the intire resources of those provinces & directing them against your Majesty's Empire and the territories of the Portuguese monarchy in that quarter of the world—and your Majesty's servants cannot disguise from themselves or conceal from your Majesty the alarm with which they contemplate the possible union of all the wealth and power both of the New and Old World concentrated in the hands of France & directed against your Majesty's dominions. Unbounded as their confidence is in the bravery and attachment of your Majesty's people and in the extensive resources of your Majesty's Empire, they humbly conceive that the first principles of self-preservation require that the safety of your Majesty's dominions should not be exposed to so new and so formidable a danger, if it is possible by any means to prevent or to counteract it.

On a subject of such importance your Majesty's servants have deemed it more consistent with the respect & deference which they owe to your Majesty's superior judgement to bring the general principle under your Majesty's consideration in the first instance, it appearing to them to deserve a separate examination and decision than to embarass it with detailed suggestions of the measures necessary for giving it effect, should it be so fortunate as to receive the sanction of your Majesty's royal approbation—and the Duke of Portland has been desired by them to request your Majesty's permission to attend your Majesty in order to lay any further information before your Majesty which your Majesty may think fit to require respecting the motives by which the deliberations of your Majesty's servants have been influenced upon this arduous and important measure, and to receive any commands which your Majesty may be pleased to lay upon them respecting it. (13625–7)

[*The King's reply, Windsor Castle, 22 April.*] The King is fully sensible of the importance of the considerations which the Duke of Portland has submitted to him, and as the principle upon which his confidential servants are now disposed to recommend an expedition to the Spanish settlements in South America appears to his Majesty self-evident and perfectly justifiable by the circumstances under which it would be undertaken, he will not at present trouble the Duke of Portland to attend him for the purpose of further explaining the motives, but will wait until the project has been more fully digested and the arrangements proposed for its execution can be detailed. As the success of the measure must depend upon the adoption and application of the principle upon which it is grounded, and not upon forcible means which would be inconsistent with its spirit, his Majesty trusts that no very considerable force will be required for carrying it into effect at a moment when it has been deemed adviseable to detail ten thousand men to the assistance of Sweden. (13628)

3650 WILLIAM MORTON PITT *to* LORD RIVERS

[*23 April 1808.*] His Majesty having several years ago been graciously pleased to express an interest in the success of the efforts of the magistrates of the county of Dorset, relative to the building our new gaol and improving the system of its internal police, and having also permitted me from time to time to submit to him our annual publications, I beg the favor of you, when next you go to Windsor,[1] to lay at his Majesty's feet the statements sent you herewith, which complete the series of those documents to the 24th of June last.

The objects most worthy of remark are these: that the whole sum of £10,000 borrowed in aid of the county rates for the building of this prison, and all interest money due thereon, has been paid off—that the manufactures carried on have not only contributed very considerably towards the maintenance and support of the establishment, but have also proved the means of increasing the industry and amending the morals of a large proportion of those who have been in confinement, and that the number of persons committed, tried, & sentenced, and especially sentenced to death, has (when the population of our county is taken into consideration) been highly creditable to the county. (13629–30)

3651 GEORGE CANNING *to the* KING, *and the reply*

[*Hinckley, 23 April 1808.*] Mr. Canning humbly transmits to your Majesty copies of dispatches from the Swedish Minister at Koenigsberg to his Court, which have been confidentially communicated to him by M. Adlerberg.

The whole of these communications is extremely interesting: but as they are rather voluminous, your Majesty will perhaps be graciously pleased to pardon Mr. Canning if he presumes to point out those of the dates of the 13th & 14th of March as peculiarly deserving of your Majesty's attention. (13631)

[*The King's reply, Windsor Castle, 25 April.*] The King acknowledges the receipt of Mr Canning's letter, and as he states the communications from Mr Adlerberg to be interesting and they appear voluminous his Majesty will keep them until tomorrow. (13632)

[1] Lord Rivers was a Lord of the Bedchamber; he lived at Rushmore Lodge, Dorset, and at Strathfield Saye until the estate was purchased by the nation for the Duke of Wellington.

3652 LORD MULGRAVE *to the* KING, *and the reply*

[*Admiralty, 24 April 1808.*] Lord Mulgrave has the honour humbly to submit for your Majesty's gracious approbation the appointment of Capt. Sir Harry Neale, Bt. to be First Captain of the Channel Fleet under the command of Admiral Lord Gambier.

Lord Mulgrave has the honour to transmit to your Majesty the substance of very voluminous dispatches received from the Medeterranean. (13633)

[*The King's reply, Windsor Castle, 25 April.*] The King is satisfied that Lord Mulgrave could not have submitted the name of a more proper person to be First Captain of the Channel Fleet than Sir Harry Neale, and his Majesty intirely approves of that appointment. (13633)

3653 GEORGE CANNING *to the* KING, *and the reply*

[*Foreign Office, 25 April 1808.*] Mr. Canning, in humbly submitting to your Majesty a Note which he has this day received from Mr. Pinckney,[1] signifying the arrival of his credentials as Minister Plenipotentiary of the United States of America, humbly requests to receive your Majesty's pleasure whether it would be agreeable to your Majesty to admit Mr. Pinckney to an audience for the purpose of presenting his credentials on Wednesday.

Mr. Canning humbly requests for Mr. Rose your Majesty's permission to be presented to your Majesty on his return from America on the same day.[2] (13634)

[*The King's reply, Windsor Castle, 27 April.*] The King approves of Mr. Canning's desiring Mr. Pinckney & Mr. Rose to attend at the Queen's Palace tomorrow at the usual hour. (13635)

3654 VISCOUNT CASTLEREAGH *to the* KING, *and the reply*

[*St. James's Sq., 1 May 1808.*] Lord Castlereagh begs leave to acquaint your Majesty that the troops under Lt.-Genl. Sir J. Moore's orders will be prepared in the course of tomorrow to put to sea both from the Downs and Harwich, and as the wind is now fair, Lord Castlereagh requests to receive your Majesty's permission that they may be directed to proceed to their destination forthwith. (13636)

[*The King's reply, Windsor Castle, 2 May.*] The King has received Lord Castlereagh's letter and his Majesty approves of the troops under Sir John Moore's orders proceeding to their destination forthwith. (13637)

---

[1] William Pinkney (1764–1822). Attorney-General of Maryland, 1805–6. Joint Commissioner with James Monroe to treat with the British Government on questions of impressments and reparations. Eventually they signed a Treaty which, remarkably enough, did not bind the British Government. President Jefferson angrily repudiated it, yet when Monroe returned home in Oct. 1807, Pinkney remained as Minister. During the next four years he attempted unsuccessfully to obtain redress for the attack of the *Leopard* on the *Chesapeake*, and the repeal of the Orders-in-Council.

[2] See No. 3549.

[*From Canning, 2 May 1808*.] Mr. Canning humbly submits for your Majesty's royal approbation the drafts of some additional dispatches to Lord Strangford, [with] which, if your Majesty should be graciously pleased to approve, Lord Strangford will leave town for Portsmouth tomorrow. (13638)

[*The King's reply, Windsor Castle, 3 May*.] The King approves of the additional instructions to Lord Strangford which Mr. Canning has submitted. (13639)

[*From Canning, 6 May*.] Mr Canning feels it his duty humbly to acquaint your Majesty that he has this day seen Mr Pinckney, the American Minister, who waited upon him for the purpose of stating only 'that he had *no* communication to make from his Government. He had fully expected that the Orage would have brought him instructions from his Government, & ample information from General Armstrong, the American Minister at Paris. But General Armstrong had left him wholly uninformed of what had passed between him & the French Government, & indeed of the nature of the instructions which he (General Armstrong) had received by the Orage.

'Mr. Pinckney however had no doubt that those instructions related to the French Decrees against neutral commerce, & that had General Armstrong been able to procure any relaxation of those Decrees, he, Mr Pinckney, would have been informed of his success & would have been instructed to apply to the British Government for a revocation of the Orders-in-Council. He infers from General Armstrong's silence the failure of his attempt to prevail upon the French Govt. to relax, and presumes that in consequence of that failure Genl. Armstrong has taken upon himself to withhold the conditional instructions intended for Mr Pinckney.

'All the intelligence that Mr Pinckney has collected from Mr Nourse & Mr Lewis, the two gentlemen charged with the dispatches to France & England, confirms Mr Pinckney in the opinion that Bonaparte is determined to persevere in enforcing his Decrees with the utmost rigour, even at the hazard of a rupture with America.

'It is not true that General Armstrong had applied for passports for himself or for any of his countrymen.' (13640–1)

[*The King's reply, Windsor Castle, 7 May*.] The King acknowledges the receipt of Mr Canning's communication of the statement made by Mr Pinckney which appears to convey a very probable account of the circumstances connected with Mr Nourse's Mission to Paris. (13645)

3656 LORD ELDON *to the* KING

[*6 May 1808*.] The Lord Chancellor, having communicated his Majesty's gracious intentions to Mr. Sert. Bailey,[1] that gentleman has accepted the office which his

---

[1] Sir John Bayley (1763–1841), now made a Judge of the Court of King's Bench.

Majesty proposed to confer upon him, with a high sense of the honour done him & a resolution to manifest it in a faithful discharge of the great duties of that office. The Lord Chancellor has taken leave herewith to transmit an immediate warrant for his appointment, to be signed by his Majesty, if he shall graciously so please. (13642)

3657 *Letters from* SPENCER PERCEVAL *to the* KING, *and the replies*

[*6 May 1808.*] Mr Perceval acquaints your Majesty that a debate took place this eveng. in the Ho of Commons which was continued till 2 o'clock, upon the subject of the vote to the College of Maynooth in Ireland. The original sum which had been voted to this College by the Irish Parliament was £8000—and the same sum had been continued to be voted annually since the Union, and was calculated to maintain & educate 200 persons to be brought up for the R. Catholic priesthood. The late Administration proposing an increase of this establishment to 400, had added £1000 to the former sum, which was given in the last year. This additional grant had been so applied as to encrease the buildings of the College so far as to enable the College to contain 50 more students. As it did not appear adviseable to carry on the intended measure which the late Administration projected in this establishment, and as it seemed at the same time to be a hard measure to refuse them the means of maintaining the number which the buildings already complete would contain, it was proposed to add to the original sum of 8000, a sufficient addition to maintain the additional students—making the whole £9250.

This was strongly opposed by Sr. J. [*sic*] Tempest,[1] Ld Henry Petty, Mr. Montagu Mathew, Mr Grattan, Mr Williams Wynne, and some others who pressed for £13000, and supported by Sr. Arthur Wellesley, Mr Perceval, Mr Wilberforce, Mr Steven,[2] Mr Duigenan, &c.

The House divided 106 to 87[3] against the Motion which the Opposition made for the recommitment of the Resolution, with the view of enlarging the grant.

And then they moved to adjourn the further consideration of the Resolution, when the House divided again, against the adjournment 112 to 82—and then the original Resolution for £9250 was carried.[4] (13643-4)

[1] Presumably Sir Henry Vane-Tempest (1771–1813), M.P. for Durham, 1794–1800; for Durham County, 1807–13. Succeeded his father as 2nd Baronet, 7 June 1794. His speech is not reported in the *Debates.*

[2] James Stephen.

[3] The number is wrongly given as 82 in *Parl. Deb.*

[4] *Parl. Deb.* XI, 121–9 (5 May). A poor report. Lady Holland wrote on the 7th: 'Petty's speech was as good as his former famous one. He dwelt upon secret influence and the compromise. Lord Porchester attacked the Saints without misercorde. He called them a 'set of men who were *canonized by anticipation,* rallied and galled Wilberforce who talked of *us.* Neither Lord Castlereagh nor Mr. Canning were present. Perceval apologised for their absence and said the sentiments of the former were sufficiently known not to render a second vote necessary, and he did not *doubt* if the latter had been present he would have supported him and voted.... There will be another discussion as your friends are so much elated at the division and general impression of the debate. The majority was only 19: the numbers were given erroneously in the papers.' (Howick MSS.)

[*The King's reply, Windsor Castle, 6 May.*] The King acknowledges the receipt of Mr Perceval's letter, from which his Majesty is glad to learn that the Resolution for the limited grant of £9250 to Maynooth College was carried in the House of Commons last night. (13644)

[*From Perceval, Downing Street, 9 May.*] Mr Perceval transmits to your Majesty two Messages for your Majesty's signature, for the purpose of calling upon the Houses of Parliament to enable your Majesty to execute your gracious intention of conferring upon her R. Hss. the Dutchess of Brunswick a pension of ten thousand pounds pr anm.[1] (13646)

[*From Perceval, Downing Street, 9 May, 11.30 p.m.*] Mr Perceval acquaints your Majesty that a Motion was this evening made in the Ho. of Commons by Mr Calcraft for the purpose of criminating the Admiralty for neglecting to supply the squadron under Sr. R. Strachan with sufficient provisions & stores in the last winter. He moved several Resolutions of fact, intending to follow them with a Resolution of censure. Mr Wellesley-Pole answered him, went very fully & ably thro' the whole case, and shewed that the deficiency of the supply was not owing to any want of attention or exertion on the part of the Admiralty, but to a continued succession of weather which prevented the ships from this country sailing for the purpose of conveying that supply. He was answered by Sr. Chs. Poole [*sic*], who was followed by Mr. R. Ward, to whom Mr Ponsonby replied & closed the debate. The division was taken upon the previous qu. when there were against the Motion 144, and for it 69.[2] (13647)

[*The King's reply, Windsor Castle, 10 May.*] The King returns the Messages which he has signed, and his Majesty is glad to hear from Mr Perceval's report that the division in the House of Commons upon Mr Calcraft's Motion was so respectable. (13648)

[*From Perceval* [*11 May (Endorsement)*].] Mr Perceval has the satisfaction to acquaint your Majesty that the vote which he had the pleasure of proposing to the Committee of the House of Commons for a pension of ten thousand pounds pr. anm. to H.R.H. the Dutchess of Brunswick out of the Consolidated Fund was unanimously and cordially acceded to.

The House afterwards proceeded upon a Motion of Mr Barham to address your Majesty for the correspondence which had taken place between the Lord Lieut. of Ireland and your Maj.'s Secretary of State upon the subject of Doctor Duigenan's appointment to the Privy Council in Ireland. In the course of the debate the other evening upon the vote for the sum of money to the Rom. Cathc. College of Maynooth, Doctor Duigenan had certainly used some very strong

[1] Perceval presented the King's Message to the House of Commons on the 10th. No specific sum was mentioned. (*Parl. Deb.*, XI, 141.) See 48 George III, cap. 59: 'An Act for enabling his Majesty to settle an annuity on her Royal Highness the Duchess of Brunswick-Wolfenbüttel.'

[2] *Parl. Deb.*, XI, 132–9. The numbers should be 146 to 69 (*H. of C. J.*, LXIII, 304). The minority is wrongly given as 57 in Colchester, II, 149.

expressions against the Ro. Ca.'s of Ireland, and upon that occasion notice was immediately given by Mr Barham of his intention of moving some question upon Dr. Duigenan's appointment to the Privy Council.

This Motion it was thought essentially necessary to resist. Sr. A. Wellesley stated the grounds upon which Dr Duigenan was appointed, namely, to assist as a civilian in many questions which arise before the Privy Council. The colour given by the Opposition to the appointment was that it was intended as a mere insult and outrage upon the R. Catholic feelings, as he was known to be their very violent enemy. Mr Claudius Beresford[1] stated the strong ground of opposition to the particular Motion, that it was destructive of the freedom of debate. Upon this ground the debate was left on the part of your Majesty's Ministers, who thought it right not to be drawn into any discussion upon R. Cathc. questions which it was the object of the Opposition to provoke. Mr Tierney, Sr. J. Newport, Ld Henry Petty, Mr Windham, & Mr. Whitbread all spoke, endeavouring by all means to provoke some one of yr. Majesty's Ministers to speak, which however they resolutely resisted. At length the House divided 174 to 107 against the Motion of Mr Barham.[2] (13650–1)

[1] John Claudius Beresford (1766–1846), M.P. for Dublin, 1801–4; for Waterford County, 1806–11. A supporter of the Portland Ministry.

[2] *Parl. Deb.*, XI, 143–57, where the numbers are wrongly given as 179 to 107, majority 67. The numbers are wrongly given as 172 to 107 in Colchester, II, 149. Canning wrote to the Lord Lieutenant of Ireland on the 27th: '. . . As both these acts [the reduction of the Maynooth grant and the appointment of Dr. Duigenan to the Privy Council] must have had your Grace's concurrence, and as my acquiescence in one of them (the Maynooth grant) was obtained entirely by the assurance that your Grace had recommended it, I am persuaded there must be more good and less mischief in them than to *my* mind there appears to be. But I am therefore especially anxious to learn from yourself the view which you have taken of both subjects. The reduction of the Maynooth grant was justified—in Cabinet—upon the ground of the sufficiency of the number of priests, already provided for, to supply the annual demand, and upon the want of a sufficient control in the Government of Ireland over the conduct of the Establishment. The latter of these arguments would have led more naturally to an improvement in the manner of superintending and controlling the Establishment, and would at most have justified the suspension of the grant (if *otherwise* proper) until the consent of the Governors or Trustees should have been obtained to such improvement. The former, if correct, was undoubtedly, of itself, sufficient. But I understand it was afterwards contradicted and almost abandoned, and at best not clearly made out, in the House of Commons; and I understand that the arguments *there* used (for I myself was not present at the debate) were directed principally or solely against the nature and principles of the institution itself, and were such as, if they were to be acted upon at all, would have gone rather to the subversion of the system altogether, than merely to the limitation—and as (if I had been present) it would have been impossible for me, with my opinions, and with the recollection that the institution was Pitt's, not to have openly combated and disavowed. I certainly never would have consented to the reduction had I imagined that it was to be defended by arguments which went to justify the abolition. I heard nothing stated on your Grace's authority, or certainly saw nothing in that letter of your Grace's which was communicated to me, that went such a length.

'The appointment of Dr. Duigenan was so entirely unknown to me that when I heard of the allusions to it in the House of Commons on the Maynooth debate, I utterly disbelieved the fact. Upon inquiry from Hawkesbury I learnt the truth of it: as also (what indeed I should never have doubted) the fact that it had originated *here*; how, when, why, I am yet to learn. Nothing could equal my astonishment and dismay when I found the charge to be a true one. Had I been in the House of Commons when it was first urged, I should have contradicted it upon a venture. I *was* there when it was urged as matter of accusation, and your Grace will have seen what a figure the Government made upon that occasion. For *my* part my silence proceeded from the plain and single cause that there was nothing to be said in defence of the appointment, and that I did not wish to say how little I thought it could be defended. Taken by itself, it is full of evil, but coupled with Maynooth, it gives a new character of hostility to that measure which, alone, it might not have exhibited. It is in vain to assure the world or the House of

[*The King's reply, Queen's Palace, 12 May.*] The King acknowledges the receipt of Mr Perceval's report of the proceedings in the House of Commons. (13651)

3658 GEORGE CANNING *to the* KING

[*Foreign Office, 11 May 1808.*] Mr Canning humbly submits for your Majesty's royal approbation the draft of a letter from your Majesty to the King of Prussia, in answer to a letter of the King of Prussia notifying the birth of a Princess,[1] which was received by the Gottenburgh mail last week. As Baron Jacobi will probably soon quit this country on his return home (the King of Sweden appearing to have consented to his passing through Sweden) Mr Canning has thought it his duty to prepare this letter, to be sent by Baron Jacobi, if your Majesty shall be graciously pleased to approve of it. (13649)

Commons that the two things have nothing to do with each other. They *do* tell upon each other, and so strongly, that had the Maynooth reduction been in other respects right, it would, in my opinion, have become wrong from the single circumstance of Duigenan's contemporary honours. Together, they hung about our necks and weighed us down in the debate of Wednesday: and what would otherwise have been a triumphant and most advantageous debate, was (to my apprehension) as much the reverse as any debate concluding with a certain and large majority could be. Nothing, to be sure, could alter the result of the debate. The fate of the motion was certain. But the credit of the Government, and the grace with which it resisted a Catholic Motion, depended upon its being manifest to the world that the Government was the unwilling agitator of such questions, that the stirring of it was a wanton and unprovoked measure on the part of the Catholics and their advisers. Had the name of the Catholics never been heard within the walls of the House of Commons this session, *till* produced on Grattan's Motion, I am persuaded the indignation excited by the conduct of Opposition would have been unbounded. As it was, the Government was *upon the defensive*, and the vote, though a zealous, was not a cheerful one. I doubt if there were ten men who voted with us that would not have wished Maynooth and Duigenan undone.

'I have opened myself thus freely to your Grace upon these points (according to the spirit of the promise exchanged between us when you set out for Ireland last year) because I really think them in their character and their consequences of the most vital importance to the Government; and I most anxiously wish to hear from your Grace in return your individual opinions upon them, because I think it possible that hitherto your Grace may have considered yourself as reflecting back the collected and unanimous sense of the Government here on both these subjects, and may not have been aware of any diversity of feeling upon them either in the Government or in the public. Next to your *opinions*. I should be desirous of learning whether your Grace thinks the Privy Councillorship irretrievable. Here, I am told that your Grace's public letter of recommendation has been received, and the King's answer returned. Nothing therefore but formalities are wanting to complete the transaction. Would it be possible, with Duigenan's consent (I know not that it could be obtained—but if it could) still to postpone the completion—sine die?

'With respect to the Maynooth grant, are there grounds for the step which has been taken other than those to which I have referred? If there be, what are they? If not, would it not be better to set about endeavouring to remedy the main objection to the extended grant (or to any grant at all), the insufficiency of the control of Government over the Establishment by some negotiation with the Trustees—such as, if it succeeded, might justify the restoration of what has now been cut off, and if it failed might justify the defalcation? Surely the £3000 is not worth the trouble and discredit of an *annual* question upon a point on which Government are divided.' (Richmond MSS.)

[1] Princess Louisa, born on 1 Feb. (1808–70). On 21 May 1825 she married Prince Frederick (1797–1881), second son of William I, King of the Netherlands.

[*St. James's Sq., 13 May 1808.*] His Royal Highness the Duke of Kent in his letter of yesterday's date having desired that a letter received by Lord Castlereagh from his Royal Highness of the 22d ult. should be laid before your Majesty, Lord Castlereagh deems it his duty humbly to submit to your Majesty the correspondence which has pass'd between his Royal Highness and Lord Castlereagh subsequent to that period. Lord Castlereagh begs leave to state to your Majesty that having on the receipt of his Royal Highness's letter communicated it to your Majesty's confidential servants, their opinion was that without your Majesty's express commands, it was not competent for them collectively to deliberate upon the subject, and that without your Majesty's pleasure being first received, no individual servant of your Majesty was authorized to state what had or had not been a matter of deliberation in your Majesty's councils. (13652–3)

[*The King's reply, Windsor Castle, 14 May.*] The King has received Lord Castlereagh's letter and the accompanying correspondence with the Duke of Kent, which his Majesty had hoped, from what Lord Castlereagh had said to him on Wednesday last, it would not have been necessary to submit to him. Since, however, the Duke of Kent has again desired that it should, his Majesty is induced to refer to the answer which he returned on the 9th of Feby last to the Duke of Kent's direct application to be permitted to resume the command at Gibraltar, in which the King stated 'that while he is sensible of the propriety of the motives which have influenced the Duke of Kent in his application, his Majesty regrets that he should feel under the necessity of declining to acquiesce in it, although, in referring to past occurrences, he has no hesitation in again assuring the Duke of Kent that he is persuaded that the circumstances which produced his removal from Gibraltar may be attributed to over-zeal on his part.' The King has only to add that he does not think it necessary, after what he has quoted above, to authorize his Ministers to take into their consideration the Duke of Kent's present application. (13654)

[*From Castlereagh, Downing Street, 16 May.*] Lord Castlereagh by the desire of your Majesty's confidential servants begs leave humbly to submit the accompanying instructions for your Majesty's approbation. On the arrival of the 91st Regt. at Gibraltar it is conceived a corps of 6000 men may without hazard to the garrison be detach'd, which force in the judgment of those best acquainted with Minorca, will in all probability secure the capture or destruction of the enemy's squadron in Port Mahon, provided the blockade of that harbour has been previously establish'd and reinforcements are prevented by your Majesty's Fleet from being thrown in from Majorca.

Your Majesty's confidential servants do not consider this temporary appropriation of M.-Genl. Spencer's corps, as likely to interfere with operations in South America, should your Majesty hereafter deem it adviseable so to employ them; as the state of the seasons in that quarter would not render it desireable to move them from Gibraltar before the middle of August with a view to such a service. (13655–6)

3660 SPENCER PERCEVAL *to the* KING, *and the reply*

[*Downing Street, 17 May 1808.*] Mr Perceval acquaints your Majesty that by certain Acts still in force provision was made for selling certain quit rents and other small rents, manerial rights and other unproductive property, part of the land revenue of the Crown, for the purpose of producing a fund for the payment of the land tax upon the estate of the Crown. Under these Acts such quantity of property has been sold, and is now vested in the Funds, as is supposed to be sufficient for redeeming all the remaining part of such land tax, and consequently it is thought that the legal authority under those Acts has ceased, since no more money is wanted for the purpose for which alone the sale was authorised. But as much of the property of this description is entirely unproductive to the land revenue, and what is productive is attended with more expence in the collection than its produce is worth, and is also liable from time to time to be lost by inattention to the collection of it, it is thought desireable that the power of selling it should be revived and continued. To this power it will be adviseable to add provisions for enabling the exchange of small parcels of property lying detached from other property of the Crown and intermingled with the estates of other individuals. Similar provisions are much wanted and would be highly beneficial in your Majesty's Duchy of Lancaster estate, and are much recommended to Mr Perceval by Mr Harper.

In addition to these considerations it has been long recommended to the Treasury by your Majesty's Land Revenue Office to obtain powers to authorise the sale of the Forest of Brecon in South Wales. This is a forest on which there is no timber, and where the property of the Crown has been subject to so much encroachment that the establishing by legal proof the rights of the Crown would be attended not only with very heavy expence but also with extreme dissatisfaction in the district: and though the parties who have made these encroachments would resist any attempt by legal means to dispossess them, yet they would be very glad to give a valuable consideration for procuring a settlement and security of their titles.

All these objects seem to be of considerable importance, and have been frequently and strongly recommended to your Majesty's Treasury by the Surveyor-General of Crown Lands.[1] Mr Perceval would therefore wish to be permitted by your Majesty to give your Majesty's consent for the introduction of a Bill to effectuate these purposes as well with respect to the Duchy of Lancaster as to the land revenue of the Crown.

This opportunity would be taken for amending the Act for letting the Crown estates as far as respects certain inconveniences which have been experienced in

---

[1] John Fordyce.

the leasing of houses and curtileges annexed thereto. Provision will be made to secure the produce of these sales to your Majesty and your heirs in the same manner and subject to the same provisions as now apply to the estates themselves. (13657–9)

[*The King's reply, Windsor Castle, 18 May.*] The King acquiesces in Mr. Perceval's proposal for the introduction of a Bill to effectuate the purposes mentioned in his letter connected with the Duchy of Lancaster and the land revenue of the Crown, his Majesty having full confidence in Mr. Perceval's judgement as to the advantage & utility of the measure.

The King also acknowledges the receipt of Mr. Perceval's report[1] of last night's proceedings in the House of Commons. (13659)

3661 VISCOUNT CASTLEREAGH *to the* KING, *and the reply*

[*St James's Sq., 18 May 1808.*] Lord Castlereagh begs leave to submit to your Majesty the accompanying letters which have pass'd between his Royal Highness the Duke of Kent and Lord Castlereagh since the former part of the correspondence was laid before your Majesty. (13660)

[*The King's reply, Windsor Castle, 19 May.*] The King acknowledges the receipt of Lord Castlereagh's letter and the accompanying letters which have passed between him and the Duke of Kent since the 12th inst. (13661)

3662 SPENCER PERCEVAL *to the* KING

[*Downg. St., Wednesday morng.* [*18 May 1808*].] Mr Perceval acquaints your Majesty that Sir Thos. Turton's Motion against Lord Wellesley & Ld. Powys on the subject of their proceedings toward the Nabob of the Carnatic, came on yesterday evening in the House of Co. Sr Thomas spoke about 4 hours & ½. He was followed by Mr. Wallace, Lord A. Hamilton & Col. Allen,[2] Mr Wallace and Col. Allen opposing his Motion and Ld. Archibald supporting it. These speeches last[ed] till about ¼ p. one this morning when the debate was adjourned till this day sennight.[3] (13662)

3663 THE DUKE OF PORTLAND *to the* KING,[4] *and the reply*

[*Burlington House, Friday, 20 May 1808.*] The Duke of Portland is desired by the Earl of Romney to lay him at your Majesty's feet, and to represent to your Majesty, in consideration of the state of his health which disqualifies him from

[1] No. 3662.
[2] Sir Alexander Allan (*c.* 1764–1820). M.P. for Berwick-on-Tweed, 1803–6, 1807–20. He belonged to the Addington party. Baronetcy, 31 July 1819.
[3] *Parl. Deb.*, XI, 315–92 (17 May). Perceval meant Tuesday the 24th. The Speaker said that Turton spoke for four hours 'without a pause or hesitation' (Colchester, II, 149).
[4] Not in the Duke's own hand.

active service, and upon account of other circumstances which are incompatible with that constant residence in the county of Kent which the duties of his station as your Majesty's Lieutenant appear to him to require, that he feels himself called upon most humbly to request your Majesty's permission that he may resign that office. And as it is one which, in the present state of the kingdom, the Duke of Portland presumes to think will be considered by your Majesty to be of too much importance to remain any longer vacant than is absolutely necessary, he most humbly submits to your Majesty the Earl of Camden's wishes that he may be thought worthy by your Majesty of succeeding to that employment—a wish which the Duke of Portland ventures to hope may not appear unreasonable to your Majesty, considering that the Earls of Thanet, Stanhope, Guilford, and Darnley, together with the Viscount Sydney and Lord Amherst, are the only Peers of a sufficient age to execute that office.

The Duke of Portland humbly hopes that your Majesty will condescend to pardon him for presuming to suggest that, if your Majesty shall be graciously pleased to assent to the Earl Camden's wishes, or to confer the Lieutenancy of the county of Kent on any other person, directions may be given for his appointment to take place the next time that your Majesty shall think fit to order a Council to be summoned at the Queen's Palace; but seeing the extreme anxiety of the Earl of Romney to be released from the duties of the Lieutenancy, the Duke of Portland could not resist the Earl's importunity to have this suggestion submitted to your Majesty. (13667–9)

[*The King's reply, Windsor Castle, 21 May.*] The King approves of the Duke of Portland's recommendation of Earl Camden to succeed to the Lieutenancy of the county of Kent upon the resignation of Lord Romney, which his Majesty regrets is produced by the state of his health. Earl Camden may take the oaths on Wednesday next as proposed by the Duke of Portland. (13669)

3664   VISCOUNT CASTLEREAGH *to the* KING

[*St James's Sq., 26 May 1808.*] Lord Castlereagh begs leave to submit for your Majesty's approbation the accompanying appointment of Edward Barnes Esqre[1] to be Lt.-Governor of Dominica. This gentleman has been recommended to Lord Castlereagh by Mr Rose as at present resident within the Island and well qualified to take charge of the Government in the event of its devolving upon him.

Lord Castlereagh has reason to suppose that before this time B.-General Montgomery,[2] whom your Majesty was graciously pleased to approve of as Governor, has arrived from Demerary at Dominica. (13679)

[1] Ensign, 1792; Lieutenant, 1793; Major, 1800; Lieutenant-Colonel, 46th Foot, 1807; Colonel, 1810; Major-General, 1813; Lieutenant-General, 1825. K.C.B., 1815; G.C.B., 1831. Lieutenant-Governor of Dominica, 1808–12. (1776–1838). Governor of Ceylon, 1824–31; Commander-in-Chief in India, 1832–3. M.P. for Sudbury, 1834–5 and 1837–8.

[2] James Montgomerie (1755–1829). Colonel, 1802; Major-General, 1808; Lieutenant-General, 1814. M.P. for Ayrshire, 1818–29. He succeeded William Lukin as Governor of Dominica.

[*Thursday morng.* [*26 May 1808*], *4.30.*] Mr Perceval acquaints your Majesty that Mr Grattan brought forward his Motion upon the Roman Catholic Petition yesterday evg. by moving that it should be referred to a Committee of the Whole House. He opened it in a manner extremely temperate and conciliatory, and received from all quarters of the House strong testimony of the proper spirit which he manifested in this manner. Mr Canning spoke after him, opposing the consideration of the question upon the grounds of the marked impolicy of the discussion at the present time, as being calculated to produce the very contrary effect from that conciliation which Mr. G. expected. The debate went on then in the following manner. Mr Windham followed Mr. Canning for the Petition, Lord Pollington[1] against it—Lord Milton & Mr Maurice Fitzgerald for, Lord Castlereagh against, Ld Hy. Petty, Sr J. Hippisley and Mr Eliot for, Mr Wilberforce against. Mr Martin of Galway & Mr Ponsonby for, Mr Yorke, Genl. Archdall & Mr Perceval against, and Mr Whitbread for. It was at the time Mr Whitbread sat down, it was a ¼ p. 4 o'clock [*sic*], and Mr Hutchinson moved an adjournment which was supported by Mr Montagu Mathew and Mr Herbert; the House divided, for the adjournment 118, against it 298. After this division Coll Hutchinson went on with the debate, and the House divided on the original Motion—at ½ p. 5 o'clock: against the Committee 281—for it 128.[2] (13680)

[1] John Savile, 3rd Earl of Mexborough (1783–1860), styled Viscount Pollington until 3 Feb. 1830, when he succeeded his father as Earl. M.P. for Pontefract, 1807–12, 1812–26, 1831–2.

[2] *Parl. Deb.*, XI, 549–638; Colchester, II, 150. Tierney had written to Grey on the 24th: 'On the Catholic question tomorrow, as far as I learn, we shall divide but badly. Many are, or pretend to be, afraid of giving a vote which may endanger their election interests, while on the other hand I do not hear of more than four or five Irish members from the ministerial side who are likely to support us. Add to this that, as far as I am informed, no letters have yet been sent round.' (Howick MSS.)

Lady Holland wrote to Grey on the 27th: 'C. Ellis told me that the great clamour which arose after Grattan finished his speech was from the Opposition who pulled down their own friends to prevent their speaking in order that the question might be put before Ministers spoke, and then when Mr. Canning spoke there was a cry which proceeded from curiosity, all of which, he added, Canning did not mind. Grattan's speech is allowed by all to have been quite beautiful and his character of Fox very fine; Mr. Canning's merely an anticipation of what he expected Petty's speech would be, and a bad reply. Wilberforce...and Sir John Hippisley were coughed down. Mr. Whitbread's speech...was, they say, considering the lateness of the hour, very well heard.' (Howick MSS.)

Whitbread wrote to Grey on the 26th: 'Our debate was very satisfactory. Grattan made a most admirable speech, & the Gallery was cleared for a division immediately on his sitting down, as none of the Ministers rose to say a word. At last Canning rose amidst the shouts & groans of the House, & made what you yourself would have deemed a most contemptible & miserable figure. The Gallery were readmitted when he began. He was followed by Windham, & the debate went on till six this morning. An adjournment was proposed by Kit Hutchinson & negatived on a division, after which he spoke. Geo. Ponsonby spoke very well indeed, & so did Lord Henry [Petty]. I suppose by what I hear I was tolerably successful. I have seen Lord Fingall this morning, who appears exceedingly pleased. The temper of the House is evidently better disposed to the consideration of the question, & the fact announced by Grattan & Ponsonby that the Catholics would allow the King a negative upon the appointment of their Bishops made a great impression. Duigenan was muzzled, Sr. Wm. Scott was present & did not speak. I taunted him.' (Howick MSS.)

Grey wrote to Whitbread from Howick on the 29th: 'I read with the greatest pleasure last night the debate on the Catholic question, or rather Grattan's speech, for in the *Globe*, the only paper that I take, nothing else was given tolerably. Tierney tells me you never spoke so well, & I hope you feel, notwithstanding, that there does not live a person who can more sincerely rejoice in your success than I do. My own disgust at politics can never make me indifferent to any increase of your reputation, & even

[*The King's reply, Windsor Castle, 25 [26] May.*] The King acknowledges the receipt of Mr Perceval's report of last night's proceedings in the House of Commons, and his Majesty is glad that the divisions upon the Roman Catholic Petition have proved as favorable as Mr Perceval seemed to expect, and that the adjournment was resisted, which would have produced another long night. (13681)

3666 LORD HAWKESBURY *to the* KING, *and the reply*

[*Charles Street, Saturday morn., 5 a.m.* [*28 May 1808*].] Lord Hawkesbury begs leave most humbly to submit to your Majesty the Minutes of the House of Lords.

The general impression of the debate appear'd to Lord Hawkesbury to be favourable, but Lord Erskine and the Bishop of Norwich[1] supported the Motion, much to the surprise of the House, and the Earl of Essex, Lord Bulkeley, Lord Glastonbury,[2] the Earl of Fortescue and Lord Carrington,[3] who had voted against the question on a former occasion, voted or gave their proxies in favour of it this night. (13684)

[*The King's reply, Windsor Castle, 28 May.*] The King acknowledges the receipt of Lord Hawkesbury's report of the proceedings in the House of Lords last night. His Majesty rejoyces that the general impression of the debate was favorable, but learnt with much surprize that the Bishop of Norwich and Lord Erskine, and

when pursuing a course that I cannot approve whatever adds to the opinion of your talents is gratifying to me. In a debate so imperfectly given except as to the speech of the mover, it is not fair to suppose from what I read in the paper, that anything material was omitted. But in the short outline given of Petty's & Windham's speeches, they do not appear to me to have taken the best ground in the attack made by the Ministers upon our conduct last year. Upon this I certainly should have liked to have spoken for myself had it been possible.' (Howick MSS.)

Whitbread wrote to Grey on 6 June: 'I hope you have heard of the general satisfaction expressed at the debate on the Catholick question. Ld. Fingall called on me the day after our debate & was in the highest spirits. The conduct of Ministers did as much service as the best of our speeches. I heard on Friday morning that Canning had given so much offence to the Court by his speech that he was certainly to go out, & Wellesley to succeed him. He has scarcely appeared in the House since, & on Sr. Home Popham's night he was there for a minute during the debate & went away again. It is said he has been unwell with a tooth & rheumatic pain in his head, but he has not kept to his house. My performance on the Catholic night was very much praised by my friends, & much more than it deserves, but it happened to be adapted to the period of the debate at which it was spoken, & contained a sharp attack upon Wilberforce, which was much wanted, & highly relished by the House. I endeavoured to state the case for your Administration better than I thought it had been stated either by Windham or Petty; but you alone could have done yourself justice. Windham's was no *speech*, neither was Petty's, although very good, both of them, in their way, but the odd conduct on the other side changed all preconcerted schemes in the heads of the different speakers on our side: mine completely; for I had confidently expected an adjournment, & intended to speak on the second day, but it was all very well as it was.' (*Ibid.*)

1 Henry Bathurst (1744–1837). Prebendary of Durham, 1795; Bishop of Norwich, 1805–37.
2 James Grenville, Baron Glastonbury (1742–1825), M.P. for Thirsk, 1765–68; for Buckingham, 1770–90; for Buckinghamshire, 1790–97. Created a peer, 20 Oct. 1797. A Lord of the Treasury, March 1782–March 1783; a member of the Board of Trade, 1784–1825. His father, James, was a brother of George Grenville, the Prime Minister.
3 Lord Carrington had changed sides politically, too. He had owed his peerage to his friend Pitt, but then, as Lord Glenbervie remarked, he had subsequently become 'one of the most eager of the partisans of Lord Grenville and consequently, then, of Fox.' (Glenbervie MS. Journal, 1 Dec. 1809.) The list of Peers voting on 13 May 1805 is not given in the *Parl. Deb.*, IV, 843.

even that Lord Moira,[1] had upon this occasion voted in favor of the Catholic Petition.[2] (13684)

3667 *Letters from* VISCOUNT CASTLEREAGH *to the* KING, *and the reply*

[*St. James's Square, 1 June 1808.*] Lord Castlereagh begs leave to submit for your Majesty's approbation the accompanying instructions to Sir John Moore. (13687)

[*From Castlereagh, St James's Square, 1 June.*] Your Majesty's confidential servants have authorized Lord Castlereagh to submit for your Majesty's approbation the accompanying arrangement of force, with a view to service on the coast of Spain or eventually in South America, should no favorable opening present itself in Europe for their exertions.

Your Majesty's servants in looking to a provision of force which may admit of operations being carried on both in the River of Plate and the Northern Provinces, beg leave to reserve for future consideration the possible expediency of directing the whole force against Mexico according to the information that may hereafter be received. (13688)

[*The King's reply, Queen's Palace, 2 June.*] The King approves of the instructions to Sir John Moore which Lord Castlereagh has submitted. His Majesty also approves of the arrangement of force intended for service on the coast of Spain or eventually in South America, & desires that Lord Castlereagh will send him a copy of this paper, as it may be annexed to that which he received from him a few days since. (13689)

3668 THE DUKE OF PORTLAND *to the* KING,[3] *and the reply*

[*Burlington House, Thursday, 2 June 1808.*] The enquiry which your Majesty was pleased to make yesterday of the Duke of Portland respecting the means he had to submit to your Majesty of filling the See of Worcester and supplying the vacancy which the melancholy event of the late Bishop's death[4] had created on that Bench, appears to the Duke of Portland to render it his indispensable duty to lay before your Majesty the result of his endeavour to procure that information which might best enable your Majesty to make choice of such a person as should be most likely to compensate the loss your Majesty has sustained by being deprived

---

[1] As Hawkesbury had not mentioned Moira, the King must have heard of Moira's speech from another source, but why he should have been surprised at Moira's support of Catholic relief (assuming that he did mean Moira and not someone else) is inexplicable, for the Prince made no attempt to change Moira's vote on this question.

[2] *Parl. Deb.*, XI, 643–95. Erskine, though a Whig, and Lord Chancellor in the Grenville Ministry, had opposed Catholic emancipation whilst in office. None of the Royal Dukes supported Lord Grenville's Motion, which was defeated by 161 votes to 74.

[3] Not in the Duke's own hand.

[4] Dr. Hurd died on 28 May, and he was succeeded by the Bishop of Hereford, Dr. Ffolliott Herbert Walker Cornewall.

of that most excellent Prelate. And it is with great concern that the Duke of Portland has to observe that the choice is so limited that among all those Bishops who can be supposed to wish for a translation, there is but one whose character and conduct are considered by the best and most conscientious friends of the Church to be free from some exception or other to which it could be wished the successor of the late Bishop Hurd should not be liable—and that is the Bishop of Hereford, the correctness of whose life, as the Duke of Portland is assured, will in all respects bear the strictest scrutiny, whose learning is equal to that of any of his brethren, whose disinterestedness and liberality have distinguished him through life, whose temper and manners render him equally beloved and respected, and who is much wished for by the principal gentry as well as clergy of that county, who more than any other people feel and lament the loss of their late Bishop, whom they were in the habits [*sic*] of consulting and advising with upon their private as well as publick concerns, and who from the knowledge which the Bishop of Hereford's situation afforded them the means of obtaining of his character, have universally expressed a disposition to transfer to him the confidence they were in the habit of placing in their late Diocesan—a circumstance which, considering the state of political opinions in the county of Worcester, the Duke of Portland feels it his duty to observe to your Majesty is one of real importance to your Majesty's interests. The Duke of Portland has further to observe that the Bishop of Hereford is the only Bishop upon the Bench who possesses this advantage; but if in other respects there was any other candidate for the See of Worcester whose claims were superior or even equal to those of the Bishop of Hereford, the Duke of Portland would not lay the stress he does upon the estimation in which the Bishop of Hereford has the good fortune to be held by the gentlemen of Worcestershire—being willing to suppose that another Bishop, who was his equal in all other respects, would not be long before he would secure to himself all the respect which is due to his situation. But without any intention to depretiate any other candidate for this See who may have offered himself to your Majesty's consideration, the Duke of Portland cannot conceal his apprehensions that the only person who to his knowledge aspires to it does not possess those qualifications that will put him upon a level with the Bishop of Hereford.

As the Duke of Portland has now conscientiously fulfilled the duties which, by the situation in which your Majesty has thought fit to place him, were required of him upon this occasion, he has only to submit to whatever may be your Majesty's pleasure, and to pray your Majesty to pardon the freedom with which his zeal for your Majesty's service may have urged him to lay his sentiments upon this subject before your Majesty. (13696–700)

[*The King's reply, Queen's Palace, 3 June.*] The King desires the Duke of Portland will be assured that he is too sensible of the respectability of the Bishop of Hereford's character to allow any private partiality which his Majesty may feel towards another candidate to stand in the way of his claims to succeed to the late excellent Bishop of Worcester. (13700)

[*Foreign Office, 7 June 1808.*] Mr. Canning most humbly submits for your Majesty's royal signature Messages to the two Houses of Parliament to accompany the Treaty concluded between your Majesty & his Sicilian Majesty.[1] (13705)

[*From Canning, Foreign Office, Wed., 8 June, 2.30 p.m.*] Mr Canning thinks it his duty to lose no time in humbly acquainting your Majesty that there have arrived here this morning two Deputies to your Majesty from the States of the Province of Asturias in Spain, to implore your Majesty's gracious assistance in the struggle which they are determined to make against the usurpation of Bonaparte. These gentlemen left Oviedo (the capital of the Province) on the 26th of May, & embarked on the 30th at Gijon in an open boat, from which they were taken up by a British privateer cruizing off that coast, & brought to Falmouth. They are furnished with full powers in the name of the States of Asturias, & with a letter to your Majesty, both of which (with translations) Mr Canning humbly transmits herewith. The Deputies express their confident persuasion that the neighbouring provinces of Leon & Gallicia have by this time made common cause with that of Asturias, & that the spirit will spread rapidly throughout Spain. But their commission is from their own Province only. Mr Canning adds the translations of two Proclamations issued by the Junta to the people of Asturias. (13706–7)

[*The King's reply, Windsor Castle, 8 June.*] The King acknowledges the receipt of Mr Canning's very important and interesting communication of this day with the accompanying papers brought by the Deputies from the Province of Asturias. His Majesty cannot but feel willing to afford every support to those loyal subjects of the Spanish monarchy who are desirous of opposing unjust usurpation, but he conceives that nothing should be done hastily, and that it will be adviseable to wait for further advices from Sir Hew Dalrymple and Admiral Purvis, while every preparation may be made to give effect to the decision which may ultimately be taken. (13707)

3670 LORD HAWKESBURY *to the* KING, *and the reply*

[*Charles Street, 9 June 1808.*] Lord Hawkesbury begs leave most humbly to submit to your Majesty at the request of the Earl of Lonsdale the copy of the Memoir which he has directed to be printed of the reign of King James the 2d by his ancestor Lord Viscount Lonsdale,[2] who held the office of Lord Privy Seal in the reign of King William the third. Lord Hawkesbury trusts at the same time that he shall receive your Majesty's forgiveness for transmitting the copy of a letter which was addressed to him by the Earl of Lonsdale together with the book,

[1] The Message to the Commons, intimating that a treaty of alliance and subsidy had been concluded, is in *Parl. Deb.*, XI, 845 (10 June)—as is also the Treaty, signed at Palermo on 30 March.
[2] Sir John Lowther, 1st Viscount Lonsdale (1655–1700). First Lord of the Treasury, March–Nov. 1690; Lord Privy Seal, 1699–1700. His *Memoirs of the Reign of James II*, privately printed, 1808.

and which explains the Earl of Lonsdale's motives for requesting Lord Hawkesbury to solicit your Majesty's permission for laying this work before your Majesty. (13708)

[*The King's reply, Windsor Castle, 10 June.*] The King desires that Lord Hawkesbury will convey to the Earl of Lonsdale his thanks for a book which, being written by so distinguished a man as the first Viscount Lonsdale, cannot fail to be interesting. His Majesty also conceives that this[1] publication may prove particularly useful at this moment when works[2] probably of a different tendency are in circulation. (13709)

3671 SPENCER PERCEVAL *to the* KING, *and the reply*

[*Downg. St., Saturday morg.* [*11 June 1808*].] Mr. Perceval acquaints your Majesty that the Local Militia Bill passed the House of Co. after a long sitting till about ½ p. 2 o'clock this morning by a very large majority.[3]

Mr Perceval transmits for your Majesty's signature, if it meets with your Majesty's approbation, the Message[4] to the Lords & Commons whereon to found the Vote of Credit for the service of the present year. (13710)

[*The King's reply, Windsor Castle, 11 June.*] The King is glad to learn from Mr Perceval that the Local Militia Bill has at length passed the House of Commons in so satisfactory a manner. His Majesty returns the Messages which he has signed. (13711)

3672 GEORGE CANNING *to the* KING, *and the reply*

[*Foreign Office, 11 June 1808.*] Mr Canning most humbly submits for your Majesty's royal approbation the draft of a Note, prepared after a full consultation of your Majesty's confidential servants, as an answer to the letter addressed to your Majesty by the General Junta of the Principality of Asturias. Mr. Canning is humbly to submit to your Majesty the opinion of your Majesty's confidential servants that though it would have been highly desirable that some further intelligence should have been received from Cadiz or Gibraltar before the answer to the Deputies from Asturias had been sent off, yet that the danger of delay in a moment so critical was of all things most material to be avoided.

He is also to state to your Majesty, as one consideration which mainly influenced the judgement of your Majesty's servants, a circumstance which was not known to Mr. Canning at the time of his first writing to your Majesty upon this subject —that the assembly of the Junta of the Asturias is a regular & legitimate assembly, met together according to the established constitution of that Principality, & not

---

[1] 'its'. (Lonsdale MSS.)
[2] 'books'. (Lonsdale MSS.)
[3] *Parl. Deb.*, XI, 849–57 (10 June). The majority for the Third Reading was 78 (104 *v.* 26).
[4] *Ibid.*, col. 858 (13 June).

an assembly suddenly self-constituted in the exigency of the moment. The Junta was actually sitting in the discharge of its regular functions at the moment when the report of the events at Bayonne & of the usurpation of the Crown of Spain by Bonaparte occasioned them to take the resolution in pursuance of which they have thrown themselves upon your Majesty's protection.

Mr. Canning thinks it his duty to return to your Majesty the letter of the Junta & the full powers of the Deputies, in order that your Majesty may have them under your consideration together with the draft of the proposed answer. (13712-3)

[*The King's reply, Windsor Castle, 12 June.*] The King has received Mr Canning's letter and the accompanying draft of the answer to the Spanish Deputies which his Majesty entirely approves, as it appears to him sufficiently cautious & perfectly appropriate to circumstances. (13714)

3673   THE DUKE OF PORTLAND *to the* KING,[1] *and the reply*

[*Burlington House, Monday, 20 June 1808.*] The Duke of Portland humbly begs leave to acquaint your Majesty that in pursuance of your Majesty's commands he intimated his opinion to the Bishop of Bristol,[2] that your Majesty would not be disinclined to translate him to the See of Hereford; to which he replied that such an event would perfectly satisfy his wishes, and that his gratitude for so important a mark of your Majesty's favour would only end with his existence. Upon this the Duke of Portland told the Bishop that his sentiments should be submitted to your Majesty, and that he might hold himself in readiness to attend your Majesty at the Queen's Palace on Wednesday next, when it was probable that your Majesty would be graciously pleased to permit him to kiss your royal hands for the Bishoprick of Hereford. The advancement of the Bishop to so much more valuable a See than that of Bristol naturally leads the Duke of Portland to suppose that your Majesty will not suffer him to retain the Deanry of Gloucester, and in that case the Duke of Portland presumes to offer to your Majesty's consideration for that preferment Mr. Plumtre,[3] a Prebendary of Worcester and a most worthy clergyman, who had the care of the Earl Bathurst's education for several years to his perfect satisfaction and that of his family, and who has been long known and esteemed by the Duke of Portland for the perfect orthodoxy of his character in all respects; and should your Majesty be pleased to assent to this proposal in favour of Mr Plumtre, the Duke of Portland ventures with the utmost humility to suggest to your Majesty that an opening in the Chapter of Worcester would be made for obviating the disappointment which Lord Hawkesbury's relation Mr John Jenkinson suffered when your Majesty was pleased to destine for him the Stall in that Cathedral which was supposed to be vacant by the death of Mr. Fountaine.[4]

Though the Duke of Portland cannot pretend to delude himself so far as to

---

[1] Note in the Duke's own hand.   [2] John Luxmoore.
[3] John Plumptre. See No. 297.   [4] See No. 3645.

believe that Dr Mansel[1] is entitled to that decided preference which it is the Duke of Portland's anxious wish should be the case of those persons whom it is his duty to offer to your Majesty's consideration as being worthy to be placed upon the Episcopal Bench—his enquiries have not led him to discover any such objections to that gentleman as make it necessary for him to resist the very earnest and anxious sollicitations of the Chancellor of the Exchequer to submit Dr Mansel to your Majesty's superior wisdom as a proper person to fill the See of Bristol; and when the Duke of Portland considers the important situation which Mr. Perceval occupies in your Majesty's Councils, the assiduity and zeal which he has uniformly manifested upon all occasions in every situation with which he has been entrusted by your Majesty, his known attachment to the principles of our happy Constitution in Church as well as in State—when all these circumstances are considered, together with the opinion which the Duke of Portland knows Mr Perceval entertains of Dr. Mansel's principles and conduct, and the advantages which he conscientiously believes the University of Cambridge, as well as Trinity College, has derived from Dr Mansel's exertions since he has been placed at the head of that House, the Duke of Portland cannot but feel it a sort of duty he owes to your Majesty to bring Dr. Mansel again under your Majesty's consideration, and once more to lay before your Majesty Mr Perceval's solicitations in his behalf.[2]

(13723–7)

[*The King's reply, Windsor Castle, 21 June.*] The King is glad to hear that the Bishop of Bristol is so well satisfied with his translation to the See of Hereford and he approves of his attending at the Queen's Palace tomorrow. His Majesty

---

[1] See No. 1734.

[2] The Duke had written to Perceval on the 16th: 'I have no doubt that the King will consent to the promotion of Dr. Mansel to the Bench, but I am very sorry to tell you that H.M. started such a variety of objections to Dr. M.—'s being placed there that I did not think it advisable to press the matter farther on H.M. than to obtain his permission to bring the subject again under his consideration, which he granted me in these words: "If you *continue to think so*, you may when you will," meaning, as you will naturally infer, that if I continued to think Dr. M. the fittest person to place on the Bench I might propose him again—& with that our conversation ended.' (Perceval MSS.)

Portland wrote a remarkable letter to the Duke of Rutland on 21 June: 'The interest your Grace takes in the advancement of the honour and fortune of the Dean of Bristol [Dr. Bowyer Edward Sparke], and the recollection of what has passed between us respecting him, were too strongly impressed upon my mind to suffer me without extreme reluctance to yield to other claims that preference to which I consider him to be so highly entitled. But when your Grace is informed that this concession has been made to the pressing instances of Mr. Perceval, and that he urged me to it by every possible motive which could influence me; when the personal sacrifices he made in accepting his present situation, the services he has rendered to his Majesty in that capacity, and I must add the impossibility of relieving his Majesty from the embarrassment in which he was involved last year at the time of changing his Administration unless Mr. Perceval had consented to abandon his own profession and renounce the fair prospect it offered him are taken into consideration, I have the confidence, and I owe it to the candour I have so often experienced on the part of your Grace, to believe that they will be admitted by you as a justification of the determination I formed to recommend Mr. Perceval's friend Dr. Mansel to his Majesty for the See of Bristol which will be vacated by that Bishop's translation to the Bishopric of Hereford, and that you will not blame me for having given way under such circumstances. I have stated to your Grace without reserve the facts which have induced me to recommend to his Majesty the gratification of Mr. Perceval upon this occasion and on them I must wholly rely not only for my justification but for their disposing your Grace to give me credit for the assurances I beg leave to offer you of the anxiety with which I shall look for an opportunity of promoting your wishes.' (Rutland MSS.)

also acquiesces in the nominations which the Duke of Portland has recommended in succession to the Bishop of Bristol. (13727)

3674   *Letters from* LORD HAWKESBURY *to the* KING, *and the replies*

[*Charles Street, 22 June 1808.*] Lord Hawkesbury begs leave most humbly to submit to your Majesty the Minutes of the House of Lords of this night. The Opposition brought to town every person to whom they could apply on the occasion, and Lord Hawkesbury is sorry to be obliged to say that there was a very indifferent attendance on the side of Government, notwithstanding the notice which Lord Grenville had given of his intention so many days before.[1] (13728)

[*The King's reply, Windsor Castle, 23 June.*] The King is sorry to learn from Lord Hawkesbury that the attendance on the side of Government in the House of Lords was so indifferent last night. At the same time, if the Peers had no other summons than Lord Grenville's notice his Majesty cannot be surprized that many should have kept away, as he never knew any occasion upon which it was not more or less necessary to urge their attendance. (13728)

[*From Lord Hawkesbury, Charles Street, 23 June.*] Lord Hawkesbury begs leave most humbly to assure your Majesty that the most urgent and particular summonses were sent out by him for an attendance in the House of Lords yesterday, and that he spoke to the Archbishop of Canterbury more than a week ago to secure a good attendance of the Bishops on that day. Lord Hawkesbury is particularly anxious that your Majesty should not suppose that he has been remiss upon such an occasion, but if persons connected with Government will leave London before the close of the Session and will not themselves feel any anxiety about what is going forward in Parliament, it is very difficult with every exertion on the part of your Majesty's servants to secure a proper attendance, particularly as the Opposition have it in their power to determine upon the question on which they will make their greatest exertion. Neither the Marquis Cornwallis, the Earl of Chichester, the Earl of Sandwich nor Lord Amherst[2] were in the House of Lords last night; indeed the two former have not been in the House three times in the course of the present Session. (13731)

[*The King's reply, Windsor Castle, 24 June.*] The King has received Lord Hawkesbury's letter and is satisfied that there has not been any want of attention on his part towards ensuring a proper attendance in the House of Lords, and his Majesty has no doubt that every opportunity will be taken by Lord Hawkesbury to impress upon those who are deficient the absolute necessity of their shewing greater zeal in the support of his Government. (13732)

[1] *Parl. Deb.*, XI, 976–88. Grenville's Motion for providing for the admission of Catholics to the offices of Director and Governor of the Bank of Ireland, in the Bill for renewing the Bank's Charter, was lost by 101 votes to 63. The figures are inaccurately printed.

[2] Holding the offices, respectively, of Master of the Buckhounds, Joint Postmaster-General, Joint Postmaster-General, and Lord of the Bedchamber. Ascot Races had started on the 21st.

[*Downg. St., Friday morn.* [*24 June 1808*], *3.30 a.m.*] Mr Perceval informs your Majesty that the Ho. of Co. has just determined to bring in a separate Bill to carry into effect the vote in favor of Mr Palmer.[1] The numbers were 186 to 63.

Mr Perceval opened the debate, and was followed by Mr Palmer,[2] Sir Thos. Turton & Mr Windham. Mr Hawkins Brown answered Mr Windham. Mr Tierney followed Mr Brown, & Mr Bankes Mr Tierney. Mr Ponsonby & Mr Whitbread spoke also against the Motion, Mr Canning for it and Mr Perceval closed the debate. Mr Perceval has great satisfaction in giving your Majesty the account of the division & the numbers, as he thinks the division may be considered not only as terminating the labours of the Session but terminating them with a very creditable & satisfactory majority.[3] (13733)

[*The King's reply, Windsor Castle, 24 June.*] The King has learnt with great satisfaction from Mr Perceval that the result of last night's debate in the House of Commons has proved in every point of view so favorable, and his Majesty highly commends the exertions which have procured so respectable an attendance of members at this advanced season. (13733)

3676 LORD MULGRAVE *to the* KING, *and the reply*

[*Admiralty, 26 June 1808, 2 p.m.*] Lord Mulgrave has the honour to acquaint your Majesty that Capt. Tremlet[4] of your Majesty's ship Alcmene has this instant arrived at the Admiralty with two Spanish Deputies from the Province of Galicia. The substance of the information brought by Capt. Tremlet Lord Mulgrave has the honour humbly to offer to your Majesty's attention, as he has received it verbally from that officer amongst other important intelligence. Lord Mulgrave has the honour to submit an extract from a Spanish newspaper giving an account of a successful action between a French squadron and your Majesty's ships in the Medeterranean in which the force of the enemy is stated to have been entirely destroy'd. The Spanish account does not give any detail of the numbers on either side. (13738]

[*The King's reply, Windsor Castle, 26 June.*] The King acknowledges the receipt of Lord Mulgrave's letter with the very satisfactory intelligence brought by Captain Trimlet [*sic*] of the Alcmene. His M. sincerely hopes that the report of a successful action fought by his fleet in the Mediterranean may be confirmed. (13739)

---

[1] John Palmer (1742–1818), who in 1785 had secured the conveyance of the mails by stage coaches. Comptroller-General of the Post Office from 1786 to 1793, when he was compulsorily retired on a pension following a quarrel with the Postmaster-General, Lord Walsingham. After a protracted struggle he secured £50,000 as compensation (1813). On 14 June the House had resolved that he should be paid £54,702 0s. 7d. (*Parl. Deb.*, XI, 1010.) He sat for Bath, 1801–8.

[2] Charles Palmer (1777–1851), John Palmer's son. Entered the Army, 1796; Major, 1805; Lieutenant-Colonel, 1810; Colonel, 1814; Major-General, 1825. Whig M.P. for Bath (succeeding his father, 2 Feb.), 1808–26, and 1830–7. A.D.C. to the Prince Regent, Feb. 1811.

[3] *Parl. Deb.*, XI, 1010–42.

[4] William Henry Brown Tremlett. Lieutenant, 1795; Captain, 1802; Rear-Admiral, 1837.

[*Foreign Office, 26 June 1808.*] Mr Canning humbly submits to your Majesty the request of Sir John Stepney,[1] formerly one of your Majesty's Ministers abroad, & now residing in the Austrian dominions, to be permitted to wear your Majesty's uniform during his residence on the Continent. (13734)

[*From Canning, Sunday, 26 June.*] Mr. Canning most humbly acquaints your Majesty that two Deputies from the Kingdom of Galicia have this day arrived in London with a letter to your Majesty which, with a translation, Mr Canning humbly transmits to your Majesty. The accounts which these gentlemen bring of the state of affairs in Spain are highly satisfactory, as shewing that the spirit of resistance to France has pervaded a greater portion of the Kingdoms and Provinces of Spain than any former reports had described. It appears to be certain that in addition to the Principality of Asturias, the Kingdoms of Galicia & Leon have actually embodied troops, which are on their march to the Castiles, for the purpose of opposing the French before their re-inforcements can be received. The amount at which these troops are estimated is so large that Mr Canning hardly ventures to state it to your Majesty, but the Deputies aver that Galicia alone has furnished fifty thousand soldiers, of whom twenty four thousand are regular disciplined troops.

In addition to these facts (which they state as from their own knowledge) the Deputies *report* that the Spanish garrison of Oporto, consisting of 8000 men, had seized & imprisoned the French Commandant of that place; & were themselves marching to join the loyal Spanish army: that Andalusia, Valencia, & Catalonia were in determined resistance to the new French Government of Spain—that near Cadiz the Marquis de Solano[2] had been murdered in a popular commotion in consequence of his supposed acquiescence in the orders of Murat,[3] & of some acts of violence which he had directed as Governor of Cadiz against the citizens of that place;—that one of the principal officers of the Government of Valencia & the Governor of Carthagena had likewise suffered the same fate.

The Deputies also bring a Gazette published at Oviedo on the 11th of June (a translated extract of which Mr Canning thinks it his duty to transmit to your Majesty, though hardly relying upon its authenticity) containing an account of a naval action said to have taken place on the 24th of last month near Carthagena between a British squadron and a squadron of the enemy which was endeavouring to carry supplies into that port. (13736–7)

[*The King's reply, Windsor Castle, 27 June.*] The King acknowledges the receipt of Mr Canning's letter and the accompanying papers which are certainly very

---

[1] Sir John Stepney (1743–1811). Succeeded his father as 8th Baronet, 1772. M.P. for Monmouth, 1767–88. Envoy to Saxony, 1776–82; to Prussia, 1782–4.

[2] The Governor of Cadiz. He was murdered as a traitor to the national cause: he had hesitated to attack the French warships in Cadiz harbour.

[3] Joachim Murat (1771–1815). In 1808 he became King of the Two Sicilies, Napoleon having offered him the Portuguese throne as an alternative, but he was never able to gain Sicily, occupied by a British force. Shot by the Allies after Napoleon's final overthrow.

satisfactory as they shew that the spirit of resistance to France is diffusing itself more generally throughout Spain. The account of the naval action fought on the 24th May is so vague that it is impossible to rely upon its correctness.

His Majesty acquiesces in Sir John Stepney's wish to be permitted to wear his uniform upon the Continent. (13735)

[*From Canning, Foreign Office, 28 June.*] Mr Canning most humbly submits for your Majesty's royal approbation a draft, prepared after a meeting of your Majesty's confidential servants this day, of the answer proposed to be returned to the Deputies from the Kingdom of Galicia. (13740)

3678 LORD ELDON *to the* KING

[*29 June 1808.*] The Lord Chancellor offers his very humble duty to your Majesty, and has the honor to transmit a Commission for passing Bills tomorrow to receive your Majesty's Sign Manual, if your Majesty shall graciously so think fit.

The Lord Chancellor at the same time takes leave to lay before your Majesty the names of the Judges & the respective Circuits which, with your Majesty's permission, it is proposed they should respectively attend at the ensuing Assizes —and also a list of the Sergts. and others, whose names it is intended, if your Majesty so pleases, to insert in the respective Commissions. The Lord Chancellor humbly hopes that your Majesty's goodness will excuse his not having personally attended at the Queen's House today to lay these papers before your Majesty, the Chancellor having been detained in the House of Lords in hearing a cause which it was very important to finish before the close of the Session. (13741–2)

3679 SIR HENRY STRACHEY *to the* KING

[*Board of Green Cloth, 29 June 1808.*] Sir Henry Strachey is always averse to occasion your Majesty any trouble respecting any of the Royal Gardens, altho' circumstances of a difficult nature to determine upon sometimes occur. At present he feels it his duty to inform your Majesty that, in consequence of a representation from his Royal Highness the Duke of Kent that a little alteration and improvement in the small piece of ground annexed to the Pavilion at Hampton Court (consisting of one acre, three roods and four perches, called the Bowling Green) was requisite, he went to inspect the spot and, after consulting Mr. Padley, who gave him an estimate of the expence to be incurred, directed the improvement to be made. The work has accordingly been performed by Mr. Padley in a very satisfactory manner as far as Sir Henry Strachey could judge when he went a few days ago to view it.

The extra labor, together with the expence of new gravel and cutting & carting turf, amounting in the whole to sixty one pounds, six shillings (which is less than the estimate) has been paid by Mr. Padley. Sir Henry Strachey therefore presumes to submit to your Majesty's consideration the propriety of his reimbursing Mr. Padley that sum at the Board of Green Cloth.

He has the satisfaction to add that he now and at all other times has observed the gardens, including the curious vine under the care of Mr. Padley, in perfect good condition.[1] (16783)

3680 THE DUKE OF PORTLAND *to the* KING, *and the reply*

[*Burlington House, Wednesday night, 29 June 1808.*] It is with great concern the Duke of Portland finds himself under the necessity of laying before your Majesty a circumstance with which he has just been acquainted, by which the pecuniary interests of the Duke of Sussex are very materially affected & which, from the place in which it has happened, has operated very unpleasantly upon the feelings of his Royal Highness the Prince of Wales.

A debt having been contracted by the Duke of Sussex which his Royal Highness is unable to discharge, property belonging to his Royal Highness, which by permission of his Royal Highness the Prince of Wales had been deposited in Carlton House, has been resorted to & seized by the creditor, & will be publickly sold in the course of tomorrow at *Carlton House* under an execution by the Sheriff unless an offer is made to purchase it at a price exceeding £1500, that sum having been already bid for it by the plaintiff. These distressfull circumstances have occasioned the Duke of Portland to be called upon for assistance & relief—and his sense of the extreme difficulty of affording them made him lose no time in conferring with the Chancellor of the Exchequer, by whom he is very sorry to acquaint your Majesty that his apprehensions have been confirmed in their utmost extent. It appears upon the most anxious investigation that there is no fund whatever to which resort can be had for the relief of the Duke of Sussex's distress except *the Civil List*, & *that* is far from being in such a state of affluence as not to render it a part of the D. of Portland's duty, at the time that he points it out to your Majesty, most humbly to observe that it will not admit of being disposed of with that liberality which such an occasion as the present would make desireable; nor can he consistently with that duty forbear from stating his apprehensions to your Majesty that if it shall be your Majesty's pleasure to direct *that* relief to be administered to the Duke of Sussex which may put an end to his present embarrassment, that other demands may be made upon his Royal Highness, full as large, if not a much larger, amount than that which is the immediate cause of the present distress. Considering also the state of the Civil List the Duke of Portland cannot avoid submitting to your Majesty the expediency of requiring the sums (if any) which your Majesty may order to be issued from that Fund in aid of the Duke of Sussex to be repaid by certain installments out of his Royal Highness's allowance & in such sums as your Majesty shall think fit.

The Duke of Portland most humbly & anxiously implores your Majesty's pardon for having presumed to lay the above circumstances before your Majesty & for the liberty he has taken in submitting to your Majesty his sentiments respecting them; & he ventures to hope that he shall not be disappointed, in consideration

---

[1] Endorsed, 'Answered 30th June—approved.'

of the motives which urged him to propose these measures & the sense of duty which has compelled him to recur to the latter. (16781–2)

[*The King's reply, Queen's Palace, 30 June.*] The King has not learnt without great concern the circumstances relating to the Duke of Sussex's affairs, of which the Duke of Portland's letter has conveyed to him the first intimation. His Majesty is sensible of the considerate manner in which the Duke of Portland has entered into so unpleasant a matter and of his readiness to suggest the only arrangement which, in his Majesty's opinion, can meet so pressing a case, and of which he approves. (16784)

3681   SIR JAMES PULTENEY *to the* KING

[*War Office, 30 June 1808.*] The Secretary at War, understanding that the Commissioners of Military Enquiry have presented to the King their Sixth Report which relates to the War Office, requests that his Majesty will be pleased to allow him the perusal thereof when his Majesty has done with it. The Secretary at War would not trouble the King for this Report but that the copy presented to the House of Commons is in the hands of the printer, and will not be ready for some time. (13746)

3682   *Letters from* LORD MULGRAVE *to the* KING, *and the replies*

[*Admiralty, 30 June, 9 p.m.* [*1808*].] Lord Mulgrave has the honour most humbly to submit to your Majesty the intelligence just received from Admiral Sir Charles Cotton, dated June 12th. The French troops in Lisbon are not more than four thousand, who are totally seperated from the Spaniards; the populace are highly enraged against the French, and Admiral Sir Charles Cotton expresses a confident persuasion that five or six thousand of your Majesty's troops might effect a landing, gain possession of the of [*sic*] forts on the Tagus and in conjunction with your Majesty's Fleet gain possession of the whole of the maritime means in the Tagus. (13743)

[*From Lord Mulgrave, Admiralty, 30 June.*] Lord Mulgrave has the honour most humbly to represent to your Majesty that a Bill is depending in the House of Lords intituled 'An Act to prevent the right of presentation to the Rectory and Parish of Simonburne in the county of Northumberland from lapsing for a limited time', which Bill cannot pass through the remaining stages without the sanction of your Majesty's most gracious consent. The object of the law will be to provide for the division of that most extensive & unweildy parish into several parishes, & to provide a due reward and encouragement to the meritorious & long professional services of naval chaplains. Lord Mulgrave humbly begs to receive your Majesty's pleasure whether he may signify to the House of Lords your Majesty's gracious consent to the progress of the Bill. (13744–5)

[*The King's reply, Queen's Palace, 1 July.*] The King authorizes Lord Mulgrave to signify to the House of Lords his consent to the progress of the Bill which has reference to the Rectory and Parish of Simonburne in Northumberland. His Majesty acknowledges the receipt of the very satisfactory intelligence from Sir Charles Cotton. (13745)

[*From Lord Mulgrave, Admiralty, 1 July.*] Lord Mulgrave has the honour humbly to submit to your Majesty dispatches received at one this day from Admiral Purvis, & brought by Lt. Talbot[1] of the Encounter brig. By these dispatches it appears that after a short negociation with the Commander in Cadiz, an agreement had been concluded & a signal establish'd for the entrance of your Majesty's Fleet into Cadiz for the purpose of capturing the French squadron in that harbour, said to consist of five sail of the line, one frigate & one corvette.[2] The dispatch of Admiral Purvis is dated on the 6th of June. Lieutenant Talbot left the Fleet of Admiral Purvis at one p.m. on the 7th of June at which time four of your Majesty's line of battle ships under Capt. Sir John Gore had pilots on board for the harbour; other pilots (as Lt. Talbot understood) were coming off for the service of four more line of battle ships at daylight. On the eighth of June Lt. Talbot heard a cannonading in the direction of Cadiz, which he supposes to have been occasioned by the entrance of your Majesty's ships into that harbour.

Lt. Talbot has been greatly delayed by adverse winds. (13747–8)

[*The King's reply, Windsor Castle, 1 July.*] The King acknowledges the receipt of Lord Mulgrave's letter of this day and the accompanying dispatches from Admiral Purvis, which appear to his Majesty to offer every prospect of the French ships in Cadiz harbour being captured without material loss to his own forces in that quarter. (13748)

3683   LORD HAWKESBURY *to the* KING, *and the reply*

[*London, 2 July 1808.*] Lord Hawkesbury begs leave most humbly to submit to your Majesty the draft of the Speech[3] proposed by your Majesty's confidential servants, to be made by the Lords Commissioners on the occasion of proroguing the Parliament, for your Majesty's gracious consideration.

---

[1] James Hugh Talbot. Lieutenant, 1796.

[2] This was the remnant of Villeneuve's fleet, which, under the command of Admiral Rosilly, had been in harbour at Cadiz since Trafalgar. He surrendered on 14 June. About the same time Napoleon abandoned his invasion of England design.

[3] *Parl. Deb.*, XI, 1139–41 (4 July). Tierney wrote to Grey on the 12th: 'The Session has at last happily been brought to an end, at which I most sincerely and heartily rejoice, and so I believe does everyone else. The Members whether in Administration or Opposition seemed to be tired of one another, and the public tired of us all. Never was there within the same space of time so much debating and so little interest excited; such an abundance of speeches and such an indifference towards the speakers. The House of Commons has sunk in general estimation beyond what you can imagine, and, unless it can recover its importance it will soon become worse than useless.' (Howick MSS.) The Speaker wrote: 'The most laborious Session for hours of sitting ever known within living memory of the oldest members or officers of the House. There were 111 sitting days, amounting to 829 hours, averaging seven and a half hours a day. Since Easter to the close of the Session rarely less than ten or eleven hours every day.' (Colchester, II, 158.)

Lord Hawkesbury begs leave at the same time to submit to your Majesty the draft of an Order-in-Council for the suspension of hostilities between your Majesty and the Spanish dominions which has been approved by your Majesty's Advocate General, and if it shall meet with your Majesty's approbation might receive your Majesty's confirmation-in-Council before the reading of the Speech on Monday next. (13749)

[*The King's reply, Windsor Castle, 3 July.*] The King approves of the draft of the Speech which Lord Hawkesbury has submitted, and it has only occurred to him that as the word Europe has been twice introduced in reference to the designs of the enemy it might in the first instance be changed for the expression of 'the common enemy of all ancient and established Governments'.

His Majesty also approves of the proposed Order-in-Council which he will confirm tomorrow before reading the Speech. (13750)

[*From Lord Hawkesbury, Whitehall, 4 July.*] Lord Hawkesbury begs leave most humbly to submit to your Majesty a letter which he has received from his Grace the Duke of Richmond, inclosing a Memorial address'd to him by several Lords invested with the ensigns of the Order of St. Patrick, and begging that an Installation may be held at Dublin at an early period. Lord Hawkesbury requests to receive your Majesty's commands, whether your Majesty will be graciously pleased to approve of the recommendation of the Lord Lieutenant in favour of the representation above stated. (13751)

[*The King's reply, Windsor Castle, 6 July.*] The King acquiesces in the Duke of Richmond's desire to hold an Installation of the Knights of St Patrick & authorizes Lord Hawkesbury to acquaint him that he may fix his own time for it. (13752)

3684 LORD MULGRAVE *to the* KING, *and the reply*

[*Admiralty, 5 July 1808.*] Lord Mulgrave has the honour humbly to submit to your Majesty a letter from Vice-Admiral Sir James Saumarez, enclosing the copy of a dispatch received by that officer from your Majesty's Envoy at the Court of Stockholm; the nature & object of the message from the King of Sweden restraining the departure of Sir John Moore from Stockholm, remain unexplained. There can, however, be no doubt that Sir James Saumarez, upon the intimation which he has received, will take every necessary precaution for the security of your Majesty's forces if, contrary to all rational grounds of probability, the step taken by the King of Sweden should prove to have been adopted with any hostile or offensive intention.[1] (13753)

· [1] Sweden was now at war with Russia and the Russians overran Finland in Feb. 1808. On the arrival of General Moore's 10,000 troops at Göteborg, on 17 May, he was not allowed to land them, and Gustavus IV, who summoned him to Stockholm, insisted on the adoption of offensive measures which were irreconcilable with the British Government's instructions. Moore was for a time placed under arrest, but he soon contrived to escape, and returned to England with his army.

[*The King's reply, Windsor Castle, 6 July.*] The King acknowledges the receipt of Lord Mulgrave's letter and the accompanying communication from Sir James Saumarez, which, however extraordinary the circumstance to which it relates, has occasioned more concern than surprize to his Majesty. (13754)

3685 VISCOUNT CASTLEREAGH *to the* KING, *and the reply*

[*St. James's Sq., 5 July 1808, 11 p.m.*] Lord Castlereagh humbly submits for your Majesty's approbation the instructions which have appear'd to your Majesty's confidential servants the most adviseable to be adopted under the information received from Sweden, which will have been laid before your Majesty by Lord Mulgrave. They are humbly of opinion that it may be most prudent not to suffer the transaction as it at present comes before your Majesty, to interrupt the course of measures which your Majesty had previously determined to pursue, as there will remain in your Majesty's power ample means of vindicating hereafter, should it be necessary, any proceeding on the part of the King of Sweeden [*sic*], of which, upon full information, your Majesty may be of opinion that you have just cause of complaint. (13755–6)

[*The King's reply, Windsor Castle, 6 July.*] The King approves of the instructions which Lord Castlereagh has submitted for Sir John Moore & Sir John Hope[1] & entirely agrees with his Ministers that the transaction referred to, as it now stands, should not produce any measures on his Majesty's part which may cause irritation. (13756)

3686 *Letters from* GEORGE CANNING *to the* KING, *and the replies*

[*Foreign Office, 5 July 1808.*] Mr. Canning humbly transmits to your Majesty a letter from the King of Sweden to your Majesty, which was this day delivered to him by the Swedish Minister; together with a paper containing the King of Sweden's account of the last conference between his Swedish Majesty & General Moore. Mr. Adlerberg did not avow any knowledge of the transaction alluded to in the letters received by Lord Mulgrave from Sir James Saumarez (which Lord Mulgrave lays before your Majesty)—though Mr. Canning has little doubt, from Mr. Adlerberg's apparent embarrassment & anxiety, that he was at least indistinctly apprized of it. Mr. Canning did not mention that transaction to Mr Adlerberg, not having an opportunity, when he saw that Minister, of communicating with the rest of your Majesty's confidential servants upon it.

Mr. Canning is now most humbly to submit to your Majesty the humble opinion of your Majesty's servants that Mr Canning should see Mr Adlerberg again tomorrow & should state to him the circumstances reported in Mr. Thornton's letter to Sir James Saumarez, & Sir James Saumarez's letter to Lord Mul-

---

[1] John Hope, 4th Earl of Hopetown (1765–1823), who became a Lieutenant-General in 1808, was second in command of the army sent to Sweden. He was not a K.B. until 26 April 1809. The 'Sir' may be a slip pf the pen after the 'Sir' in Moore. Cf. No. 3687.

grave, & require a distinct explanation of them: & that upon Mr Adlerberg's denying (as he probably will) any knowledge of them, or at least the having received any instructions upon them, Mr. Canning should inform Mr. Adlerberg that it is impossible for your Majesty to return any answer whatever to the letter from the King of Sweden until this matter shall be cleared up; & that in the event of General Moore's continued detention at Stockholm, not only the troops will be withdrawn (as they will be at all events in consequence of the King of Sweden's refusal to permit their disembarkation) but the subsidy will also be discontinued, & your Majesty's Fleet directed to confine its operations to the defence of the trade of your Majesty's subjects; & that Mr. Thornton will at the same time also be instructed to quit Stockholm: but that your Majesty is most unwilling to believe that such extremities can be necessary, & most desirous of receiving a satisfactory explanation. (13757–8)

[*The King's reply, Windsor Castle, 6 July.*] The King entirely approves of what Mr. Canning has submitted as most adviseable to be done, and of the proposed communication to Mr. Adlerberg under the very unpleasant circumstances which have been reported to Lord Mulgrave by Sir James Saumarez. (13759)

[*From Canning, Foreign Office, 6 July.*] Mr. Canning humbly acquaints your Majesty that he has this day seen Mr Adlerberg & interrogated him respecting his knowledge of the transaction at Stockholm: of which Mr. Adlerberg did not admit himself to be fully informed, though he had heard that the King of Sweden had sent a message to General Moore requesting him to continue his residence at Stockholm until fresh instructions should be received from his Court. Subsequently to this message Mr. Adlerberg understood that Colonel Murray had had an interview either with the King of Sweden or his Minister in which everything was amicably arranged. Under the present uncertainty Mr Canning informed Mr Adlerberg that your Majesty could not return an answer to the King of Sweden's letter: and, if contrary to your Majesty's wishes & expectations, the report received from Gottenburgh should turn out to be true, your Majesty would feel yourself compelled not only to withdraw the army (for which orders were gone) but to direct your Majesty's Fleet to discontinue its co-operation with that of Sweden. Farther than this Mr Canning did not think it prudent to go, as Mr Adlerberg expressed himself (though upon insufficient grounds) convinced of the amicable adjustment of whatever difference had arisen. For the same reason your Majesty's confidential servants have humbly conceived that it would be expedient to defer sending instructions to Mr. Thornton until Friday, in the hope of receiving more precise & satisfactory intelligence before that day. (13762–3)

[*From Canning, Foreign Office, 6 July.*] Mr. Canning humbly submits to your Majesty that it has been thought advisable, in consequence of your Majesty's Order-in-Council re-opening the intercourse with Spain, & for the purpose of diminishing as much as possible the demand upon the Admiralty for small vessels, to re-establish a communication by packets between Spain & Great Britain. And this establishment appearing to afford an opportunity of placing a person of confidence at a port in Spain, & in relation with the local Government without a public diplomatic character; & Mr. Stuart,[1] late your Majesty's Secretary of Embassy at St. Petersburgh, having offered to undertake this service, Mr. Canning humbly submits for your Majesty's royal approbation the accompanying drafts relating to Mr. Stuart's appointment. (13760–1)

[*The King's reply, Windsor Castle, 7 July.*] The King highly approves of the communication made by Mr. Canning to Mr. Adlerberg, in consequence of the latter's reply to his questions, and his Majesty agrees that it will be adviseable to wait for further information from Mr Thornton before any instructions are sent to him. The King also approves of the appointment of Mr Stewart, and of the instructions under which he proceeds to Corunna. (13761)

3687   *Letters from* VISCOUNT CASTLEREAGH *to the* KING, *and the reply*

[*St. James's Square, 6 July 1808, 10 p.m.*] In submitting the accompanying dispatch to your Majesty, Lord Castlereagh begs permission humbly to acquaint your Majesty that it was not received till this evening, although by its date and contents it apparently ought to have been deliver'd on Monday evening. Lord Castlereagh is not at present enabled to offer to your Majesty any explanation of the circumstances which have led to this extraordinary detention of Sir J. Hope's dispatch. (13764)

[*From Castlereagh, St. James's Square, 7 July.*] In submitting the accompanying dispatches to your Majesty from Sir J. Moore, Lord Castlereagh humbly begs leave to acquaint your Majesty that directions have been given for the troops on their arrival off Yarmouth to proceed immediately to the Downs with a view to the immediate landing and refreshment of the corps, after the long period they have pass'd on board of transports, from which, however, Lt.-Col. Murray reports that their health has not apparently suffer'd.

Lord Castlereagh has also to lay before your Majesty the dispatches received this evening from Sir Hew Dalrymple and Major-General Spencer. (13769)

[*The King's reply, Windsor Castle, 8 July.*] The King approves of the orders which Lord Castlereagh proposes should be given for the disposal of Sir John Moore's corps upon its arrival at Yarmouth, and, under all the embarrassing circumstances connected with its stay in the Baltic, his Majesty cannot but sincerely rejoyce that it has been extricated from a situation so unpleasant. (13770)

3688   GEORGE CANNING *to the* KING, *and the reply*

[*Foreign Office, 7 July 1808.*] Mr. Canning, in humbly laying before your Majesty the dispatch received this day from Mr. Thornton, has to submit to your Majesty

---

[1] Charles Stuart, Secretary of Embassy, 1804–8, and Minister Plenipotentiary *ad int.*, 1806–7. He arrived at Corunna and was presented to the Junta of Galicia on 20 July.

the humble opinion of your Majesty's confidential servants (formed after deliberation upon this dispatch, & those received at the same time from General Moore by Lord Castlereagh) that no step should be taken on your Majesty's part in this very delicate & embarrassing affair until intelligence shall have been received from Stockholm of a date subsequent to General Moore's departure; or at least until it shall be known what representations Mr. Adlerberg may have been instructed to make upon the subject. The dispatches to Mr. Adlerberg having been entrusted by the King of Sweden to Colonel Murray upon an understanding that he should deliver them himself, Mr. Canning has not thought it right to take them out of that officer's possession; but he cannot doubt that Mr. Adlerberg will solicit an interview with him as soon as he receives them. (13765–6)

[*The King's reply*, *Windsor Castle*, *8 July*.] The King approves of what is submitted in Mr Canning's letter in regard to the conduct to be observed in the unpleasant transaction with Sweden. (13766)

3689   LORD MULGRAVE *to the* KING, *and the reply*

[*Admiralty*, *7 July 1808*.] Lord Mulgrave has the honour to transmit to your Majesty dispatches received this night from V. Admiral Lord Collingwood, R. Admiral Purvis and Admiral Sir Charles Cotton. Lord Mulgrave most humbly reports to your Majesty that the dispatches of Lord Collingwood of the earliest dates have little that can now be interesting except the circumstances herein humbly stated. In a dispatch of the 29th of May Lord Collingwood details information receiv'd by him from Sir Hew Dalrymple, by which it appears that the Spanish General Castagnos, commanding before Gibraltar, had declared that in the event of the destruction of the Spanish Royal Family now prisoners in France, the Archduke Charles of Austria would be invited to ascend the Throne of Spain. In consequence of this information Lord Collingwood had sent the Amphion frigate to Trieste, & had even written a letter to the Archduke to inform him that one of your Majesty's best appointed frigates was ready off that port for his reception, if required by his R. Highness being invited to Spain.

30th May.—Don Jeane Miguel de Vives, Governor-Genl. of the Balearic Islands, writes to Lord Collingwood to desire that an officer may be sent to treat of such measures as the interests of Great Britain & the Kingdom of Majorca may require; Lord Collingwood's instructions to V. Admiral Thornborough on this occasion contained stipulations for the military occupation of posts on the Island of Minorca, and for the surrender of the Spanish ships in Triest[e], which his Lordship has cancelled on his arrival at Gibraltar on the 8th of June where he learned the generous system of support and protection to the Spanish nation adopted by your Majesty.

Admiral Purvis in a dispatch dated June 11th states that the Spanish Governor of Cadiz having summoned the French Admiral Rosali to surrender; on his refusal a fire from batteries was opened on the French ships on the 10th in the evening which continued till $\frac{1}{2}$ past seven, and then remained quiet all night.

Vice-Admiral Lord Collingwood off Cadiz June 12th says the French Admiral had proposed terms of capitulation offerring to dismantle his ships; all conditions short of surrender had been rejected by the Spaniards, in consequence of the irritation of the populace against the French, which restrains the Governor from venturing to admit any terms short of unconditional submission: Lt-Col. Sir George Smith,[1] who had resided some days at Cadiz, represents the higher orders as not manifesting the same ardour in the cause as that which animates the people; from this information and the unsettled state of the Government, Lord Collingwood deems it expedient to use circumspection in his intercourse with them. He states that Deputies are coming to your Majesty from the Junta at Seville. Lord Collingwood has left V. Admiral Thornborough & Rear-Admiral Sir R. Strachan to watch the French at Toulon, and R. Admiral Martin[2] to watch the Spaniards at Minorca. The dispatch of Admiral Sir Charles Cotton of the 18th of June is so clear & concise that a précis must be nearly a transcript. The dispatches came to Plymouth in the Alphea cutter. Lord Mulgrave humbly represents that there has not been time to translate the Spanish papers.[3] (13767–8)

[1] For him see *Castlereagh Corresp.*, VII, 149. (6 June 1808). It was stated that he was to remain at Cadiz, to communicate between the Spanish and British Generals.

[2] Sir George Martin (1764–1847). Lieutenant, 1780; Captain, 1783; Rear-Admiral, Nov. 1805; Vice-Admiral, July 1810; Admiral, 1821. Knighted, 1814; K.C.B., 1815; G.C.B., 1821; G.C.M.G., 1836.

[3] General Castaños had been harassing the French in Andalusia and largely contributed to the capitulation of Dupont's army of 18,000 men at Baylen in mid-July, but on 23 November following, his Andalusian army, combined with that of Aragon under Palafox, was badly defeated by Lannes at Tudela, quarrels between the two Generals largely contributing to the disaster. The remnants of Castaños' forces were lucky to escape. 'No words', wrote the Duke of Kent to his friend Colonel Charles Stevenson (26 March 1809), 'can express the affliction I feel when I contemplate his sad reverse of fortune, aggravated if possible by the bitter reflection that it is chiefly to be ascribed to his mistaken loyalty to his Sovereign, which no consideration could induce him to depart from.' The Duke had been hoping that Castaños, whom he described as his 'good friend', would be able to use his influence to facilitate his return to Gibraltar as Governor. The Duke wrote, in continuation of the above letter: 'Before I conclude my answer to your several communications, I shall just advert to the reason given by Castanos for not having taken any steps with the Junta to engage them to apply for my return to Gibraltar, in order to observe, that as the influence, the power of which was then dreaded, is now at an end, & Mr. Frere is the particular friend of Mr. Canning, who I am sure is well inclin'd to me, I am confident, if the Junta could be moved to express to him that my return at this juncture, to Gibraltar, would be considered by them as a compliment to the King of Spain, & the Spanish nation, as being a proof of the King of England's friendly sentiments, such an intimation, coming officially to the Secy. of State for the Foreign Department, could not fail of producing the desired effect, especially at this particular moment. It would therefore be well for you to consult with Vialé how this can be effected, & above all to confine the application, as I wish it had been in the first instance, to the single point of my return to Gibraltar, which I will candidly own to you, would satisfy me as completely at the first, as if it were united to the general command in the Mediterranean.' (46391–4)

In subsequent letters to Lieutenant-Colonel Robert Wright, the Duke of Kent referred to the subject of his return to Gibraltar: 'Altho' his Majesty's Ministers may have told the Spanish Deputies that his Majesty would not consent to that taking place, I should still much wish the attempt to be made, for I am pretty confident that that is the language of the Ministers and not of the King, and this I will thank you to lose no time in intimating to Vialé, to whom I have no leisure to write by the present conveyance.' (46395–7 [23 June 1809])

[5 Sept. 1809.] 'The correctness of the opinion convey'd in your letter of the 29th June upon the measure of writing to Mr. Frere on the object I have still so much at heart to effect (my return to Gibraltar) is proved by that gentleman's answer to Vialé, as copied on to your letter of the 31st July. I only hope that from the politeness of the answer, and the just precaution you took to get Vialé to impress on his mind the communication as confidential, we may be warranted in inferring that he will

[*The King's reply, Windsor Castle, 8 July.*] The King acknowledges the receipt
of Lord Mulgrave's letter containing so clear and satisfactory a précis of the
intelligence received from Cadiz, Gibraltar & Lisbon. (13773)

3690 GEORGE CANNING *to the* KING, *and the reply*

[*Foreign Office, 8 July 1808.*] Mr. Canning most humbly submits for your
Majesty's royal approbation the draft of a dispatch to Mr Thornton, prepared
after communicating to your Majesty's confidential servants the substance of his
conference with the Swedish Minister.¹ Nothing material passed in the conference
with Mr Adlerberg beyond what is mentioned in this draft, except that Mr. Adlerberg professed to have received instructions to request the recall of Mr. Thornton,
especially on the ground of the Note which Mr Thornton had addressed to Mr.
Ehrensteim¹ [*sic*] declining his S. My.'s invitation of Colonel Murray to Haga.

This request Mr. Adlerberg, however, was not authorized to state in writing,
& he readily acquiesced in Mr. Canning's suggestion that it would be impossible
that your Majesty should be expected to take any such step upon *one* part of the

keep the secret, and if he could not promote the matter, that he would do nothing to impede it. You
are of course apprized that the Junta have authorized their Minister here to state to Mr. Canning their
wish that his Majesty would direct me to resume the command at Gibraltar, & to continue my residence
there during these critical times, and to add, if the King would condescend to grant their request, they
should consider it an additional proof of the interest he took in the support of the success of the endeavours of the loyal subjects of Ferdinand the 7th to maintain his rights against the attempts of the
Corsican invader. But I fear it has not yet produced an effect, altho' from a conversation I recently
had with Mr. Canning, I have reason to hope that he is disposed, as far as lies in his power, to promote
my views: I therefore by no means give the matter up, indeed I never shall to the last, as my return
to my station always will be the first wish of my heart on every account: I lament much that I have
no acquaintance with the Marquis of Wellesley, as I am well aware that if I could get him to take the
thing up, he would not abandon it till he had carried the point, but my being an entire stranger to him,
you must be aware precludes the possibility of my addressing myself to him, which otherwise I should
have had no hesitation in doing.' He added, 'I shall be delighted to find that your expectations as to
the reappointment of my worthy friend Castanos to the command at Algeciras, may be realised, for I
am certain he will spare no exertion with the Junta to effect my return, knowing from experience the
harmony that would result from it.' (46401–4)

[9 Sept. 1809.] 'I have this day receivd your letter of the 15th ulto. covering one from Mr. Browne:
my last will have apprized you of the correctness of the inference which you had drawn from the perusal
of that gentleman's communication to Vialé, and that the Supreme Junta had authorized their Minister
here to press my return to my Government, as a measure that would be peculiarly acceptable to the
Spanish Government in every sense; but altho' I have reason to believe that the despatch containing
the instructions to that effect was received here full a fortnight since, I have not yet had the most distant
hint given me from any quarter relative to it, which I own is both surprising & disheartening; but it
is possible that the atchievements of our expedition against Antwerp, and the critical position which
Lord Wellington has got into, may so occupy the attention of Ministers, whose plans must be shaken
by these events, as to oblige such minor objects to be at this time overlookd.' (46405–6)

[6 Oct. 1809.] 'I sincerely hope that your expectation of seeing our excellent friend General Castanos
replace Cuesta, may be realized, as perhaps it may give a helping hand to my business, which my friend
Mr. Canning's retiring from office, has at least for the present paralized, but be assured I never will rest
till I have somehow or another accomplish'd it, be it in *one two three*, or even *ten* years hence.' (46407–10)

[11 Dec. 1809.] 'I...[have] little or no prospect of returning to the Rock while the present people
are in office, altho' you may depend upon it that I will never omit a single opportunity of urging my
right to resume my command.' (46425–9)

¹ Baron d' Ehrenstein, the Swedish Foreign Minister (*d.* 1829). For him see Bagot, *Canning and
his Friends*, I, 282–4.

recent transactions at Stockholm, until the general character of the whole should be more clearly explained & understood. (13774–5)

[*The King's reply, Windsor Castle, 9 July.*] The King approves of the dispatch to Mr. Thornton of which Mr. Canning has submitted the draft. (13775)

3691 LORD MULGRAVE *to the* KING, *and the reply*

[*Admiralty, 11 July 1808.*] Lord Mulgrave has the honour humbly to submit to your Majesty the substance of the accompanying dispatches received this morning from V. Admiral Lord Collingwood & Admiral Sir Charles Cotton, which Lord Mulgrave humbly conceives to be of sufficient interest to be transmitted to your Majesty without delay.

Lord Collingwood reports that the French squadron in the Caraccas had struck their colours to the Spaniards at 7 o'clock in the morning of the 14th June; the Spanish colours were immediately hoisted on board the French ships. The French ships had not materially suffered, & the loss of men on both sides had been very considerable; dated off Cadiz, June 14th 1808. The Spanish Admiral is one of the Deputies about to proceed to England in yr. M. ship Revenge.

The dispatches from Sir Charles Cotton come down to the 24th June; they confirm the reports of a general spirit of animosity against the French in Portugal, in many parts of which the re-establishment of the Government of the Prince Regent has been formally proclaimed. By a letter from Capt. Creghe[1] of your Majesty's ship Eclipse dated Oporto 20th June, it appears that owing to the weak & undetermined conduct of Don D'Oliviera, Governor of Oporto (now confined as a traitor) the French had been enabled to re-establish their authority, which had been maintained till the 16th of June, the day of Corpus Christi, when an attempt having been made to substitute the French flag for that of Portugal which had usually been carried in the religious procession of the day, the people were incensed to such a degree that the whole population of the place rose, broke open the depots, supplied themselves with 25,000 stand of arms &c, together with the regular troops, formed a determined & enthusiastick army: every man either being French or suspected of favouring the French interests was arrested. The Bishop of Oporto was elected Governor & 20,000 men had been sent out to meet the French, who had pushed a corps of 900 men within six leagues of Oporto. The Provinces of Tras des Montes, Entre Duoro & Minho, and the northern part of Biera had risen in arms to the amount (as it is said) of 100,000 men exclusive of the force in Oporto. The President of the Senate of Viana writes on the 19th of June to Sir Charles Cotton soliciting your Majesty's protection, and the appearance of British ships of war in the provinces of Entre Duoro & Minho over which he presides.

Genl. Spencer arrived off Lisbon in the Scout brig on the 24th of June, and after communicating with Admiral Sir C. Cotton returned to join his forces off Cape St. Vincent it appeared by information received from three Hanoverian

[1] George Adey Creyke, Lieutenant, 1803; Commander, 1804.

deserters who reached the Hibernia on the 22d of June that Junot[1] had concentrated his forces near Lisbon in such numbers as to render success in landing with so small a corps of forces as that under the command of Genl. Spencer very doubtful.

By a letter from Capt. Digby[2] of the Cossack [*sic*] dated off St. Audeco 25th June, it appears that the French entered that place on the 23d previous to which the boats of the Cosack [*sic*] & the Comet had spiked & disabled all the guns in Fort St. Salvador de Ano and Fort Ledra, & destroyed the magazine of 500 barrels of powder. As the boats quitted the shore the French cavalry appeared on the hills. The letter of M. Sataro to Sir Chas. Cotton of the 20th June contains interesting intelligence respecting the force at Lisbon. These dispatches came to Plymouth in the Primrose. (13776–7)

[*The King's reply, Windsor Castle, 11 July.*] The King acknowledges the receipt of Lord Mulgrave's letter containing the abstract of the interesting intelligence received from Lord Collingwood & Sir Charles Cotton which, as far as it goes, appears to his Majesty very satisfactory. (13778)

3692   GEORGE CANNING *to the* KING

[*Foreign Office, 14 July 1808.*] Mr. Canning humbly transmits to your Majesty a letter received this day from the Duke of Orleans at Malta, which, Mr. Canning is concerned to learn from a letter to himself which accompanied this to your Majesty, contains an account of the death of the Count de Beaujolais.[3] (13787)

3693   *Letters from* VISCOUNT CASTLEREAGH *to the* KING, *and a reply*

[*St. James's Square, 14 July 1808.*] Your Majesty's confidential servants, having fully deliberated upon the present critical and important state of affairs in Spain & Portugal, are deeply impress'd with a sense that they should fail in their duty to your Majesty if they did not humbly recommend to your Majesty to employ such an amount of force in that quarter as may provide not only for the reduction of the enemy's force in the Tagus, but also may admit of such a detachment being made towards Cadiz without prejudice to the main operation as may be sufficient not only to give security to that place if it should be threaten'd, but may even facilitate the reduction of the French corps under Genl. Dupont which has enter'd Andalusia.

With this view they humbly beg leave to submit for your Majesty's gracious consideration that 5000 men be immediately embark'd to proceed off the Tagus with the least possible delay, and also that the force under Lt.-Genl. Sir John

---

[1] Andoche Junot (1771–1813), commander of the French army in Portugal, 1807. Created Duc d'Abrantès and Marshal of France. Defeated by Wellesley at Vimiero and concluded the Convention of Cintra.

[2] George Digby. Lieutenant, 1800; Captain, 1806.

[3] He died on 30 May. See No. 3634.

Moore, so soon as the transports are revictual'd, do proceed to the same destination. The whole force to be employ'd in that quarter, including M. Genl. Spencer's, will then amount to about 30,000 men which, it is humbly conceived, will admit of 10,000 men being employ'd on the side of Cadiz, without prejudice to the operation against the Tagus.

With respect to the arrangement of the command, upon conference with his Royal Highness the Commander-in-Chief, it is humbly submitted to your Majesty, as it is probable that the force may act in two separate corps, whether the superintending command might not be advantageously continued in Lt.-Genl. Sir Hew Dalrymple, who might be directed to leave the garrison of Gibraltar in charge of M. Genl. Drummond[1] and to repair himself either to Lisbon or Cadiz as the service might require, taking upon himself the command of the whole force, and distributing it according as circumstances should point out, as most for the advantage of the common cause.

The favorable opinion your Majesty has been pleased to express of the Lt.-General's judgment and conduct under the trying circumstances in which he has latterly been placed—the knowledge he must possess of the views and characters of those who are now at the head of affairs in Spain, and the degree in which he appears to have conciliated and to possess their confidence are considerations which have induced your Majesty's confidential servants to be of opinion that upon the whole your Majesty's views cannot be more advantageously promoted under present circumstances than by continuing the command in Sir H. Dalrymple, with Lt. Genl. Sir H. Burrard second in command. The station these officers hold in your Majesty's service will admit of the most active and distinguish'd young officers being brought forward under them, which will give your Majesty the benefit of their enterprize and ability without departing from that attention to standing in the service which your Majesty was pleased to signify your commands should be attended to in any arrangement that was to be submitted for your Majesty's approbation.[2] (13781–4)

[*From Lord Castlereagh, St. James's Sq., 14 July.*] Lord Castlereagh humbly begs leave to acquaint your Majesty that he finds from Sir J. Gore that the reason the transports to be sent from Gibraltar to bring the Spanish garrisons from Majorca and Minorca to the Continent were countermanded, was the arrival of intelligence at Cadiz that they had already been pass'd over to Valencia. This circumstance was not explain'd to Lord Collingwood, and appear'd upon the face of his last dispatches as open to some suspicion. The general report Sir John Gore makes of the progress of affairs in Andalusia is highly encouraging, and he considers Genl. Dupont's corps to be in a very critical predicament. (13785–6)

[1] Some months later the Duke of Kent was in correspondence with General Drummond, to whom he wrote, after a long delay, in April 1809. He referred to this letter in a letter to his friend Lieutenant-Colonel Robert Wright, 28 April 1809: 'I trust the communication of my grateful acknowledgments for the kind attention shewn by him to the interests of the Duke of Orleans' sister, in consequence of the letter I wrote to him upon that subject, will not be the less acceptable...' (46391–4)

[2] A quarrel between Castlereagh and Sir John Moore over questions of strategy meant that Moore was not put in command of the combined forces. See No. 3697.

[*The King's reply, Windsor Castle, 15 July.*] The King approves of the arrangement which is submitted in Lord Castlereagh's minute for the distribution of the forces to be employed in the support of Spain & Portugal and of that which regards the command, his Majesty being satisfied that Sir Hew Dalrymple, from his experience & knowledge of the Spaniards, will prove well calculated for the general direction of affairs, while he cannot have a more zealous and more steady second in command than Sir Harry Burrard. (13788)

3694   LORD HAWKESBURY *to the* KING, *and the reply*

[*Charles Street, 15 July 1808.*] Lord Hawkesbury begs leave most humbly to submit to your Majesty a letter which he has received from the City Remembrancer, and to request your Majesty's commands whether it would be convenient to your Majesty to receive the Sheriffs of London and Middlesex at Windsor at any hour on Monday so that your Majesty may be attended with the Address when your Majesty comes to town on Wednesday next. (13790)

[*The King's reply, Windsor Castle, 16 July.*] The King desires Lord Hawkesbury will appoint the Sheriffs of London and Middlesex to be here on Monday next at two o'clock, when his M. will acquaint them that he will receive the Address on Wednesday at the Queen's Palace. (13791)

3695   *Letters from* GEORGE CANNING *to the* KING, *and the replies*

[*Foreign Office, 16 July 1808.*] Mr. Canning in humbly submitting to your Majesty the drafts of dispatches proposed to be sent to Mr. Thornton, begs permission humbly to state to your Majesty that the dispatch dated the 10th of June is the transcript of a *private* letter written by Mr. Canning to Mr. Thornton at that time, before it appeared to Mr. Canning that things were sufficiently mature to allow of his submitting to your Majesty such opinions in the shape of formal instructions, though it seemed highly expedient that Mr. Thornton should sound the dispositions of the Swedish Ministers as early as possible upon the subject. Mr. Thornton appears to have done this very properly: & as there is an allusion to his conversation in Baron D'Ehrensteim's official Note, Mr Canning has thought it fair to Mr. Thornton to convert the private letter on which that conversation was in fact founded into the shape of an official dispatch, to remain on record in Mr. Thornton's correspondence. (13792–3)

[*From Canning, Foreign Office, 16 July.*] Mr Canning humbly acquaints your Majesty that he has this day seen the Deputies from Seville, whose account of the state of & prospect of affairs in Spain is more encouraging than any which has yet been received here, particularly as it tends to prove a degree of union & consistency in the proceedings of the different Juntas which appeared more than anything else to be requisite for the success of the Spanish cause.

Mr. Canning humbly conceives that your Majesty will forgive him for mentioning, as particularly likely to give satisfaction to your Majesty, that the Andalusian Deputies expressed themselves anxious above all other things to avoid in the conduct of their affairs any appearance of imitation of what had passed in the Revolution of France. This sentiment, they said, had made them studiously reject any forms or phrases or even words which had obtained particular signification or currency in the course of that Revolution. (13794–5)

[*The King's reply, Windsor Castle, 17 July.*] The King approves of the instructions to Mr Thornton and of Mr Canning's having converted into an official dispatch his private letter of the 10th June. His Majesty has also learnt with much pleasure the particulars which have been stated to Mr Canning by the Deputies of Seville. (13795)

[*From Canning, Foreign Office, 20 July.*] Mr. Canning most humbly transmits to your Majesty the paper of Mr. Gentz which Count Münster mentioned to your Majesty, and which he has learnt from Count Münster that your Majesty would be pleased to have the opportunity of reading at your Majesty's leisure. (13798)

[*The King's reply, Windsor Castle, 28 July.*] The King returns his thanks to Mr. Canning for the communication of Mr. Gentz's manuscript of which the most interesting parts have been read to him. (13798)

3696 *Letters from* VISCOUNT CASTLEREAGH *to the* DUKE OF YORK, *and the reply*

[*Stanmore Park, 24 July 1808. Most Secret.*] I observe the 4 regiments ordered to assemble at Cork do not much exceed 3,000 men. As a corps somewhat more substantial than this prepared to move from that point might under certain circumstances be of importance, I should be much obliged to your Royal Highness to make such further selection from the regiments serving in Ireland as will carry this corps to 5,000 rank & file.

As Sir David Baird is now in Ireland perhaps your Royal Highness would see no objection to charge him with the preparation and embarkation of this force. Whether it may be hereafter deemed advisable to combine it with the troops under orders from England, or to employ it on any separate object, the services of that officer might be advantageous in either case.[1]

I have taken measures to accelerate the arrival of the transports, and shall be obliged by your Royal Highness having the goodness to inform me by what day you think the troops may be assembled in the neighbourhood of Cork for embarkation. (13802)

[1] Sir David Baird was sent out with 13,000 troops to reinforce Sir John Moore's small army, and he landed at Corunna in mid-October. In June Sir Arthur Wellesley, who had been promoted to Lieutenant-General on 25 April, was appointed to command a force assembled at Cork and instructed to proceed to Portugal to co-operate with the Spanish and Portuguese commanders. His force sailed from Cork on 12 July and disembarked at Mondego Bay, more than 100 miles north of the Tagus.

[*From Castlereagh to the Duke, Stanmore Park, 24 July (Copy). Most secret & Confidential.*] Our intelligence from the enemy's coast states that all the troops have been moved from thence towards Spain and that the duty is now performed at Boulogne by a few sailors and conscripts. If, under the cover of augmenting our force in Spain, we could land the force now under orders in England near that port, I am sanguine in thinking we might either destroy the flotilla &c. or if we found any impediments from closed works which cannot be judged of from the examination of our cruizers, that we might withdraw before the enemy could form an army in the interior to move upon us, having, I believe, little else to compose it but National Guards, and the force on the spot not being of a magnitude or quality that could embarrass materially either the landing or reembarking, more especially, if we could succeed in masking the attack to the moment of execution.

As the bringing troops from Ireland is always a matter of great delay and uncertainty and their coming to the eastward would in a great measure serve to bring our views into suspicion, I should be glad [if] your R. Highness would consider what the utmost means are that could be put in motion from hence for a short operation of this nature—reserving it of course till the last moment, previous to the armament sailing, and taking our measures previously for moving them with rapidity, and embarking them instantly, might we not take 2 additional battalions of the Guards, leaving only one in London for the moment?

If from 12 to 15,000 men could thus be brought to act suddenly on Boulogne, I should deem our prospect of success better than if we waited to assemble a larger armament; and the services of the regiments not included in the return of troops destined for distant service might be considered as to be limited to this single effort, after which, in the event either of success or failure, they might resume their positions at home. (13803–4)

[*The Duke of York's reply, Stable Yard, 25 July (Copy).*] I take the earliest opportunity to acknowledge the receipt of your Lordship's two letters of yesterday by a special messenger, the first marked *most secret*, desiring that the corps under orders at Cork be augmented to five thousand rank and file, and suggesting Sir David Baird being appointed to the command of them—the second marked *most secret and confidential*, proposing that a force from twelve to fifteen thousand men should be without delay held in readiness to embark with a view to an operation against Boulogne, of which force you mention the whole of the Guards, except one battalion to be left in London, composing a part.

With regard to the first letter, I will take care to order the three second battalions of the 23d, 31 and 81 to be immediately moved towards Cork, all of whom being now encamped upon the Currah or in Dublin, will arrive at Cork in ten days from the time they receive the order, and as Sir David Baird is an officer of great merit, I can have no difficulty in compliance with your Lordship's wishes in recommending to his Majesty to order him upon this service, but I should not think that I fulfilled my duty if I did not transmit to your Lordship upon this occasion the copy of a letter which I received on Saturday from Lord Harrington[1] respecting the want of regular forces in Ireland.

In regard to your Lordship's second letter, I transmit to you the list of every battalion in England above five hundred men, which, with the two Brigades of Guards of five thousand men, will only make a force together of ten thousand rank and file (2d Battn. 4th, 2d Battn. 7th, 1st Battn. 43d, 2d Battn. 59th, 2d Battn. 87, 1 Battn. 88th and eleven companies of the 95th) to which I must however add that the 1st Battn. 43d is but just recovering from the effects of the opthalmia, and the 87th and 88th are at this moment considerably affected by it, which three battalions are the strongest of the whole of those of the line.

With respect to your Lordship's suggestion of augmenting this force by taking two out of the three battalions of Guards doing duty in London, I beg strongly to represent to your Lordship in the first place, that upon the strength of these three battalions are borne all the sick, all the recruits and all the worn-out men of the whole Brigade. These Battalions therefore, if ordered to march, and those men of course deducted from them, would be considerably weaker than your Lordship can possibly be aware of; and, in the next place, the duty of London is such that it would be totally impossible for the single battalion then remaining with the addition of the men of the other two who would be thus left behind, to perform it, and from the above statement your Lordship will yourself see how impossible it would be to find any other troops to assist them.

As I shall be anxious for an early opportunity of conferring with your Lordship upon this most important subject, I will, if you have no objection, call upon you tomorrow at your house in St. James's Square at twelve o'clock. (13805–6)

[*Enclosure*]

[*The Earl of Harrington to the Duke of York, Camp Curragh of Kildare, 18 July.*] I have the honor to acknowledge the receipt of your Royal Highness's letter of the 13th inst. and have given the necessary orders for the march of the regiments therein mentioned. Were the policy of collecting a large force in the south of Europe even less obvious, it is not within my province to argue on the general distribution of his Majesty's troops. It may not, however, I trust be thought presumptuous that I should on this occasion call your Royal Highness's serious attention to the state of the military force remaining in Ireland, and to the danger of leaving its internal no less than external defence, in the hands of the militia of the country, who at a time when the minds of the lower class of the people are agitated by discontents and alienated from the common interests of the Empire, may possibly, feeling themselves masters, throw the balance when an opportunity offers, on the wrong side. (13796)

3697 *Letters from* VISCOUNT CASTLEREAGH *to the* KING, *and the replies*

[*Downing Street, 26 July 1808.*] Lord Castlereagh when he has the honor to attend your Majesty tomorrow will beg leave humbly to lay before your Majesty

---

[1] Commander of the Forces in Ireland.

the circumstances to which the accompanying letters refer, and which he now submits to your Majesty, in conformity to the opinion of your Majesty's confidential servants.

Lord Castlereagh has with all humility to state to your Majesty on their part that it has not been without much hesitation that they have been enabled to determine with respect to the course which it became them to take at the present moment upon a subject in their judgment of much delicacy and importance; and the knowledge of which, they seem of opinion, could not with propriety be withheld from your Majesty.

Your Majesty's confidential servants humbly apprehend the present to be the first instance in which an officer of your Majesty's army going on service has thought fit to express himself in such terms, and on grounds so unfounded, with respect to the conduct of your Majesty's Government, either collectively or individually; and whilst your Majesty's confidential servants have upon full consideration come to a determination not to advise your Majesty to make any change in the arrangement which your Majesty has been graciously pleased to approve for the command of the troops now actually embark'd for service, they cannot avoid expressing an humble but anxious hope that the determination they have so come to may not be productive of future prejudice to your Majesty's service.[1] (13808-9)

[*The King's reply*, *Windsor Castle*, *27 July*.] The King regrets very much that any unpleasant circumstances should have occurred between Lord Castlereagh and Sir John Moore, but as the latter has given an assurance that what has passed will not diminish his zeal in any service in which he may be employed, his Majesty cannot but approve the determination to which his Ministers have come not to suffer what is represented in Lord Castlereagh's letter to affect the military arrangements which had already been made. (13809)

[1] Moore wrote, 12 Jan. 1808: 'I understand that some members of the Cabinet...disapproved my conduct in Sicily and inferred from the strong manner in which I expressed myself in my official correspondence that I was violent in my conduct. I thought it necessary, in my first interview with Lord Castlereagh, to explain myself on this subject.... The Duke of York has stood my friend in all the attempts to traduce me, and I have been told that the King has not allowed himself to be influenced. I believe my enemies in the Cabinet are confined to two or three individuals whose voices, though they may have weight there, are not in point of character either for sense or dignity such as to give me the smallest concern whether my conduct be approved by them or not.' (*Diary of Sir John Moore*, II, 201–2.) Ministers, he said, did everything in their power to give the command in Portugal to Wellesley, but he was so young a Lieutenant-General that the Duke of York had objected to it, and, afraid of disgusting the Army by such an appointment, they had given it up. 'Disappointed in their favourite object, they were determined it should not be given to me, and to prevent the possibility of its falling to me, Sir Harry Burrard was named as second.' (*Ibid.*, II, 239–40.)

On 22 July Castlereagh wrote to Moore: 'I think it right that you should not leave England without hearing from me that I have communicated to the King's Ministers...the complaint which you made to me in our last interview, of "unhandsome and unworthy treatment" received by you on the part of the King's Government and on mine, in the mode of carrying their measures into effect. At the same time that this complaint is felt by them as it is by me to be unfounded, I have to assure you that had not the arrangements of the Army been so far advanced as that they could not be undone without considerable detriment to his Majesty's service, there would have been every disposition on their part humbly to have advised his Majesty to relieve you from a situation in which you appeared to consider yourself to have been placed without a due attention to your feeling as an officer.' (II, 251.)

[*From Castlereagh, Downing Street, 28 July.*] Lord Castlereagh has humbly to submit to your Majesty that your Majesty's confidential servants having fully consider'd the course of events in Spain, together with the objects to which under certain circumstances that part of your Majesty's disposeable army, not already order'd upon service, might be applicable, do not as yet feel themselves prepared to offer to your Majesty any advice with respect to the actual destination of that force; but as time may be of the utmost moment in rendering their services useful to the common cause, Lord Castlereagh has to submit in their name for your Majesty's approbation, that every preliminary measure of preparation for enabling the above force to proceed on service, except that of actually embarking the men, should be proceeded on with all possible dispatch in order that as little interval as possible may intervene between any decision your Majesty may be pleased to come to with respect to the employment of the troops and the period of carrying your Majesty's commands into execution. (13810–11)

[*The King's reply, Windsor Castle, 29 July.*] The King approves of what is submitted in Lord Castlereagh's letter, his Majesty considering it most advantageous that the troops not actually ordered upon service should be kept in a state of preparation until the application of them can be directed by the general information received. (13811)

3698 *Letters from* GEORGE CANNING *to the* KING, *and the reply*

[*Foreign Office, 29 July 1808.*] Mr. Canning most humbly presumes to submit to your Majesty the letter to M. Novissiltzoff[1] which, if not disapproved by your Majesty, he proposes to send tomorrow in the manner which he humbly mentioned to your Majesty, to St. Petersburgh. (13813)

[*From Canning, Foreign Office, 29 July.*] Mr. Canning, at the same time that he lays before your Majesty a letter received by him from the Count d'Avaray, inclosing two notes of the French King, humbly submits for your Majesty's royal consideration, the draft of the answer proposed to be returned to Count d'Avaray: in which it has been thought right (subject to your Majesty's approbation) that your Majesty's name should be kept entirely out of question. (13812)

[*The King's reply, Windsor Castle, 30 July.*] The King approves of the answer which Mr Canning has prepared for the Comte d'Avaray, and his Majesty returns him thanks for the communication of his private letter to M. de Novosiltzoff. (13812)

3699 THE DUKE OF CUMBERLAND *to the* KING, *and the reply*

[*St. James's, 30 July 1808.*] At such a moment as the present it is the duty of every man to offer his services, and as I understand there is a great additional

---

[1] Count Novossilzoff, the Russian diplomat.

force of your Majesty's troops ordered for embarkation, let me entreat your Majesty's permission to accompany the cavalry, being ready to serve in any situation, my anxiety being only to prove to you my zeal for the service. (47207)

[*The King's reply, Windsor Castle, 1 Aug.*] The King has received the Duke of Cumberland's letter and is sensible of the zeal which has prompted him to make an offer of his services at the present moment, but his Majesty fears that he cannot, by a compliance with the Duke of Cumberland's wishes, set aside the arrangements which have been made for the command of the troops which have proceeded upon foreign service.[1] (47207)

[1] The King may or may not have consulted the Cabinet Ministers at some time on the question of a military command for the Duke of Cumberland. What is certain is that the Duke had little use for the Prime Minister. He wrote to Eldon on 5 May 1807: 'Will you dine tête à tête with me on Thursday at *six* o'clock, as I wish to show the correspondence between the Duke of Portland and myself in which I cannot disguise to you I think *he* has behaved *very ill* to me, and considering all the *abuse* I have met with in *Parliament* and from various members of my own family, for having *stood by the present Ministers* I really think I am entitled to a different conduct from *him*.' (Eldon MSS.)

The Duke strongly criticised the appointment of Sir John Moore to serve in the Peninsula under Sir Hew Dalrymple and Sir Harry Burrard, who, after their return home, left Moore as Commander-in-Chief. The Duke wrote to Eldon, 14 Oct. 1808: 'I understand the state of things with the Army is most lamentable and that the spirit of *cabal and party* reigns very high among them all, so much so that...many of the Generals have returned perfectly disgusted with all that has been going on, and certainly when the last decision of Government becomes known there they doubt as well as myself that any alteration for the better will be produced....The origin of all the evil that has occurred I affirm has been from the pusillanimity of the Cabinet (excuse the expression), for had the Ministers not been frightened by newspapers they would not have hesitated sending out the Commander-in-Chief who, from his station in life and rank in the Army was the proper person for that command, but, fearing the attacks of papers, they sacrifice the good of the Army and appointed a man perfectly inadequate to the situation both from his want of capacity and want of *experience*...I see every objection to that appointment and no one reason for it except what I term PATCHING UP. Such an appointment is in every respect derogatory to the honour and character of this country and must necessarily disgust the Army. I understand the Army at large and the Generals unanimously say the Commander-in-Chief ought to go, but I doubt the Ministers have strength of mind, nerves or constitution to do that, though I think in my conscience *he* could on ALL accounts be the properest person. In the first place has not Moore acted *ill* wherever he has had the chief command? In Sicily his conduct was such that he was recalled, and certainly his exit from Sweden cannot be termed very honourable to a Commander-in-Chief, but even had he been the completest Julius Caesar existing I maintain that where he is going it will not do. The grandees of Spain require a man of very high rank (has he that?); a man of conciliatory manners, suaviter in modo and fortiter in re (is he that?). Neither does he possess. Then in the name of God what can induce the Cabinet to make such an appointment? If the Cabinet is determined that the Duke of York should not go then in my humble opinion they ought to send Lord Moira and propose to him his taking the supreme command. There is a man of rank, a full General, and a person who might either go in Chief or act as second to the Commander-in-Chief. Should, however, he go in the supreme command then the door is open for other Generals to serve, and at least *I* might have an opportunity of serving my country, which I long for, and really it is a disgraceful thing that in such a great cause as this, that *none* of the King's sons are with the Army. If, by any means, my dear Lord, you would effect *this* for me that I might serve one campaign, which in that case I would do, I should feel an eternal obligation to you. I really feel unhappier than words can express at being forced to remain at home when *all* my men are going. You can easily feel for a man whose whole soul is bent on the glory and welfare of his country....I have been advised to speak to Castlereagh but I *will not*. I do not think him worthy of any communication of that sort.' (*Ibid.*)

[*Foreign Office, 4 Aug. 1808.*] Mr. Canning humbly lays before your Majesty a letter addressed to him by the Junta of the Principality of Asturias, containing an offer to your Majesty of some Spanish sheep of the finest breed in that country. Mr. Canning humbly solicits your Majesty's commands as to the answer which your Majesty would be graciously pleased to have returned to an offer, which, as it is evidently intended to express in a manner which they conceive to be agreeable to your Majesty the gratitude & affection of the Asturians, he humbly presumes your Majesty cannot have any hesitation in accepting. (13817)

[*The King's reply, Windsor Castle, 5 Aug.*] The King desires that Mr Canning will convey to the Junta of Asturias his sense of their attention to him in offering the Spanish sheep described in their letter which H.M. has no hesitation in accepting as a proof of their attachment, and he further desires that Mr Canning will communicate with the Admiralty in regard to the directions to be given for the safe conveyance of the sheep to this country. (13818)

[*From Canning, Foreign Office, 5 Aug.*] Mr. Canning did not trouble your Majesty with the letters from Ali Pacha & Sidkey Effendi now laid before your Majesty, until he could at the same time humbly submit for your Majesty's royal approbation the drafts of the answers proposed to be returned to them. (13819)

[*The King's reply, Windsor Castle, 6 Aug.*] The King approves of the answer which Mr Canning has prepared to the letters of Ali Pacha & Sydkey Effendi. (13820)

3701 CHARLES BAGOT[1] *to the* KING

[*Foreign Office, 8 Aug. 1808, 5 p.m.*] Mr. Bagot, in the absence of Mr. Secretary Canning, who has been forced suddenly to leave London on account of the dangerous illness of the Dean of Hereford,[2] feels it to be his duty to lose no time in humbly transmitting to your Majesty dispatches which have been received this morning from Mr. Stuart at Corunna. (13821)

[1] Sir Charles Bagot (1781–1843), brother of William, 2nd Baron Bagot. M.P. for Castle Rising, 1807–8; Under-Secretary of State for Foreign Affairs, Aug. 1807–Oct. 1809; Minister to the U.S.A., 1816–19; Ambassador to Russia, 1820–4, and to the Netherlands, 1824–32. Governor-General of Canada, 1841–3. G.C.B., 1820. He applied to his friend Canning for the Under-Secretaryship in March 1807, but was too late—Canning had made the offer to Lord Fitzharris. 'I doubt whether he would have done for me,' wrote Canning on 26 March. (Harewood MSS.) But the following August, when Fitzharris resigned, being 'worn down by the fatigue and attendance', Bagot was appointed, and on the 29th Canning wrote: 'Bagot does very well—very willingly at least. But he is not equal to F. No, nothing like it.' (*Ibid.*) See, too, Bagot, *Canning and his Friends*, I, 239–44, for the rigorous nature of the duties of the situation and for its incompatibility, in practice, with a seat in Parliament. And, on this latter point, Colchester, *Diary and Corresp.*, II, 136.

[2] Canning's uncle, the Rev. William Leigh, who for many years lived at Ashbourne in Derbyshire. He died at Yarmouth on the 11th.

[*London, 16 Aug. 1808.*] Lord Hawkesbury begs leave most humbly to submit to your Majesty several letters from his Grace the Lord Lieutenant of Ireland, together with a report of Mr Justice Mayne,[1] and the papers relating to the same proceeding on the tryal of Major Campbell of the 21st Regiment, convicted of murder for having killed Capt. Boyd of the same Regiment in a duel at Armagh in the month of June 1807. The case being of an unusual nature, the Lord Lieutenant has thought it his duty to transmit it for your Majesty's determination. Lord Hawkesbury has submitted these papers to the consideration of your Majesty's confidential servants. They are fully sensible of the delicacy which unavoidably belongs to questions of this description, but the present case appears to stand upon very particular grounds, and does not necessarily involve the consideration of any of those general principles which might occasion difficulties in other instances of the same nature.

This is the case of a duel, fought at night, in a room, at an unusually short distance (not more than seven paces) and without the intervention of any friends, as seconds, though persons without difficulty might have been procured to have acted in that capacity. The provocation given by the deceased to the prisoner, though it might have required explanation and satisfaction, does not appear to have been of that nature as to have called for any proceeding so unusual according to the understood laws of honour, and it appears clearly from the evidence for the prosecution, uncontradicted by the prisoner, that the time, mode and place of the contest were forced upon the deceased by the prisoner, against the representations and remonstrances of the deceased, who was anxious that the duel should be deferr'd for some hours to enable him to settle his affairs and to procure the advantage of the presence of a friend.

It appears likewise that this unfortunate event took place not in the first moment of passion but after a sufficient period had elapsed from the time of the provocation to give the parties the opportunity of deliberating on what had passed, and regulating their conduct by reflection.

Under all these circumstances Lord Hawkesbury has the painful but unavoidable duty of humbly submitting to your Majesty as the opinion of your Majesty's confidential servants that this is a case in which it would not be adviseable, according to the evidence as it appears before them, for your Majesty to interpose to prevent the law from taking its course. (13822–3)

[*The King's reply, Windsor Castle, 17 Aug.*] The King has received Lord Hawkesbury's letter and the accompanying papers, and, under the aggravated circumstances of Major Campbell's case, H.M. feels under the painful necessity of declining to interfere to prevent the law taking its course.[2] (13826)

[1] Edward Mayne, Judge of the Common Pleas [I.].

[2] The Duke of Richmond wrote to Lord Hawkesbury from Phoenix Park on 5 Aug.: 'Lord Harrington [Commander-in-Chief in Ireland] doubts about putting the sentence of the court martial into execution. I do not wish to interfere with his command, but if he does not punish them, then others will be encouraged to follow the example. I am still of opinion we shall never quiet the thing till a

[*Foreign Office, 16 Aug. 1808.*] Mr. Canning feels it his duty humbly to lay before your Majesty a letter which he has received from Seid Achmet Effendi, the person deputed by Ali Pacha to bring proposals of peace from the Ottoman Porte; relative to a misunderstanding which appears to have taken place on the Terrace at Windsor on Sunday evening: together with Mr Canning's answer to that letter. (13825)

[*The King's reply, Windsor Castle, 17 Aug.*] The King had not heard of the circumstance mentioned in Seid Achmet Effendi's letter and entirely approves of Mr Canning's reply. (13825)

3704   *Letters from* LORD MULGRAVE *to the* KING, *and the replies*

[*Admiralty, 22 Aug. 1808.*] Lord Mulgrave has the honour most humbly to submit to your Majesty's gracious approbation the name of Capt. Columbine, an officer of science, & great professional knowledge, to be inserted in the Commission to be appointed for surveying all the coast of Africa to which the trade of the African Company and the Sierra Leone Company have extended. (13831)

[*The King's reply, Windsor Castle, 23 Aug.*] The King approves of Captain Columbine's name being inserted in the Commission for surveying that part of the coast of Africa which is mentioned in Lord Mulgrave's letter. (13832)

[*From Lord Mulgrave, Admiralty, 23 Aug.*] Lord Mulgrave begs your Majesty's gracious permission to lay at your Majesty's feet his humble congratulations on the event of the deliverance of ten thousand Spanish troops from the power & influence of the enemy, through the exertions of a squadron of your Majesty's fleet under the command of Rear-Admiral Keats. The Spanish troops with their General, the Marquis de la Romana, are on the Island of Langeland in the Great Belt awaiting the arrival of transports from England for their conveyance into Spain. The dispatches of Rear-Admiral Keats are at once so full & so concise that Lord Mulgrave most humbly conceives that he could not submit a précis for your Majesty's perusal without omitting some interesting or important circumstance

punishment has taken place.' (Add. MSS. 38568, f. 173.) Major Campbell was hanged at Armagh on the 24th.

Sir Arthur Wellesley, the Irish Secretary, wrote to the Duke of Richmond on 22 May from London: 'General Macdonald sent me the papers on Major Campbell's case to read, and I was clearly of opinion that you could not do that which they wished me to urge you to do; vizt., promise him a pardon in case he should be convicted. Indeed I doubt whether a pardon can be given to him in any event. I spoke to Lord Hawkesbury upon the subject last summer when you wrote to me, but he appeared then to think that an Irish Jury would not convict him, and that it would not be possible to lay the case before the King for his commands without having further details. I will now mention the subject again, and will try to get the papers again from Macdonald; but in case I should not succeed, I wish you would send over any statement of the case which you may have.' (Wellington, *Civil Corresp. and Memoranda* [*Ireland*], p. 426.)

of a transaction the beneficial influence of which may be expected to extend far beyond its more immediate impression in Great Britain & in Spain.¹ (13833–4)

[*Lieut.-Colonel Taylor's reply, Windsor Castle, 23 Aug., 9 p.m.*] The King being at this moment engaged has ordered me to acknowledge the receipt of your Lordship's letter and to thank you for the early communication of the important dispatches from Sir James Saumarez & Rear-Admiral Keats. His M. has commanded me to assure your Lordship that the important event of the deliverance of so large a proportion of the Spanish troops from the power of the enemy has afforded to him a degree of satisfaction which H.M. would find it difficult to express, & that he is truly sensible of the beneficial influence of so interesting a transaction. (13835–6)

3705 LORD HAWKESBURY *to the* KING

[*Whitehall, 23 Aug. 1808.*] Lord Hawkesbury begs leave most humbly to submit to your Majesty for your royal signature the warrant for enabling the Judges or Lords of Session in Scotland to sit in two divisions, which warrant has been approved by the Lord Chancellor as conformable to the provisions of the Act of the last Session of Parliament.² (13837)

3706 GEORGE CANNING *to the* KING, *and the reply*

[*Foreign Office, 24 Aug. 1808.*] Mr. Canning most humbly submits to your Majesty the letter received by him from Baron Jacobi, & the draft of the answer proposed (with your Majesty's royal approbation) to be returned to it.

He lays before your Majesty at the same time (according to your Majesty's gracious permission) copies of Lord Granville Leveson's letters to Baron Stedingk & to Count Stadion.³

Mr. Canning has to ask your Majesty's forgiveness for having omitted to mention to your Majesty before the application stated in the enclosed private letter from Mr Hill,⁴ your Majesty's Envoy at the Court of Cagliari, to have been made to him from Lucien Bonaparte⁵ for a passport to enable him to proceed to the United States of America—which passport Mr Hill appears, after much deliberation, to have granted. (13838)

¹ The French, under Bernadotte, had had about 35,000 French, Spanish and Dutch troops in Jutland and the Danish islands for possible service against Gustavus IV of Sweden. Unrest developed among the Spanish contingent when news arrived of the rising in Spain against the French invaders, and, helped by the British Admiral, about 10,000 of them contrived to escape from the archipelago on British ships, the remainder being disarmed by Bernadotte or by the Danes.
² 48 George III, cap. 151: 'An Act concerning the administration of justice in Scotland, and concerning appeals to the House of Lords.' See *Parl. Deb.*, XI, 142, 973, 1062–84.
³ Count Stadion was at this time the Austrian Foreign Minister.
⁴ William Hill was Minister to Sardinia, 1808–24. The Sardinian Court had withdrawn from Rome to Cagliari, and returned to Turin only at the end of the war.
⁵ Lucien Bonaparte (1775–1840) had refused offers of the crowns of Italy and Spain, and, being less submissive to the Emperor than his other brothers, was discarded as useless. In 1810 he took ship for America, but fell into British hands and was kept in honourable captivity at Ludlow and Thorngrove, Worcestershire, for the rest of the war.

of an answer to Baron Jacobi's letter which Mr Canning has submitted with the copies of those addressed by Lord Granville Leveson to Baron Stedingh & to Count Stadion. (13839)

3707   *Letters from the* DUKE OF PORTLAND *to the* KING,[1] *and the replies*

[*Burlington House, Thursday, 25 Aug. 1808.*] The deliverance of the Spanish troops from the power of Bonaparte has caused such general satisfaction among all ranks of your Majesty's subjects, and the publick expressions of obligation to the officer to whose conduct that measure was entrusted, are so universal that the Duke of Portland would not think himself justified in withholding from your Majesty the expectations which he finds to be entertained by persons of all descriptions, that your Majesty will graciously condescend to bestow upon Admiral Keats some mark of your Majesty's royal favor. The Duke of Portland was confirmed in this opinion by the concurrence in the same sentiments which was manifested today at the meeting of your Majesty's confidential servants, and has been induced by the instances made to him by them to represent these circumstances to your Majesty, and to submit to your Majesty's superior judgment the material advantage which in their humble opinions could not fail to result from rewarding the very important and meritorious service which Admiral Keats has performed, by conferring on him the Order of the Bath. The Duke of Portland therefore ventures to hope that the motives which have urged him to lay these facts before your Majesty, will dispose your Majesty to be so gracious as to pardon his presumption. (13840–1)

[*The King's reply, Windsor Castle, 26 Aug.*] The Duke of Portland having so strongly pressed the bestowing immediately upon Admiral Keats a mark of the King's favor, his Majesty will not withhold his consent altho' he still thinks that it would have been more adviseable to have postponed rewarding him until the end of the campaign. (13842)

[*From the Duke of Portland, Bulstrode, Friday, 26 Aug.*] The Duke of Portland most anxiously hopes that your Majesty will graciously condescend to beleive that he could not hesitate an instant in deferring to your Majesty's superior judgement with respect to the time of rewarding Rear-Admiral Keats, & that the Duke of Portland therefore cannot but feel it to be his duty religiously to abstain from mentioning the Rear-Admiral's name until the time prescribed by your Majesty shall have elapsed.

After much investigation & consideration for the purpose of appointing a Commissary-General for your Majesty's army in Portugal & Spain, Mr. Erskine, one of the Comptrollers of Army Accounts, has appeared to be so much better qualified for the duties of that station than any other person who would consent to undertake it, that the Duke of Portland ventures humbly to offer him to your

---

[1] Not in the Duke's own hand.

Majesty for that appointment, & as it is very desireable in case he shall be approved of by your Majesty that he should proceed to his post as expeditiously as possible, the Duke of Portland has presumed to send herewith the necessary Commission for Mr Erskine's appointment which is most humbly submitted for your Majesty's royal signature. (13843–4)

[*The King's reply, Windsor Castle, 27 Aug.*] The King entirely approves of the Duke of Portland's recommendation of Mr Erskine for the situation of Commissary-General to the Army in Portugal & in Spain, and his Majesty has signed the Commission for his appointment. (13844)

3708   GEORGE CANNING *to the* KING, *and the reply*

[*Foreign Office, 26 Aug. 1808.*] Mr. Canning humbly submits to your Majesty's royal consideration the draft of an instruction which (after communication with the rest of your Majesty's servants) Mr Canning has prepared to Mr. Hill, your Majesty's Minister at Cagliari, on the subject of the passport solicited by Lucien Bonaparte. Mr. Hill's communication of this fact having been made in a private letter to Mr. Canning, Mr. Canning has not referred to that communication. (13845)

[*The King's reply, Windsor Castle, 27 Aug.*] The King approves of the instruction which Mr. Canning has prepared for Mr. Hill on the subject of the application made by Lucien Bonaparte for a passport. (13846)

3709   VISCOUNT CASTLEREAGH *to the* KING

[*Stanmore Park, 30 Aug. 1808.*] In consequence of the Act lately pass'd for the abolition of the slave trade, and the changes thereby occasion'd in the commercial intercourse of your Majesty's subjects with the coast of Africa, it has been deem'd expedient to institute an enquiry into the possibility of opening trade in other articles with that continent before a decision is submitted to your Majesty with respect to the settlements and forts establish'd on the African coast. With this view the accompanying warrant is humbly laid before your Majesty for your Majesty's royal signature by Lord Castlereagh. (13847)

3710   GEORGE CANNING *to the* KING, *and the reply*

[*Foreign Office, 31 Aug. 1808.*] Mr. Canning humbly submits for your Majesty's approbation the draft of a note to the Chev. de Souza, which he humbly mentioned to your Majesty this morning: as also the draft of an instruction proposed to be sent to Mr. Stuart at Coruna, in consequence of the confusion which has unluckily arisen from a misapprehension either in the Junta of Galicia or in some of the military officers employed in Spain. (13848)

[*The King's reply, Windsor Castle, 1 Sept.*] The King approves of the notes to Mr. de Souza and the instructions to Mr Stewart of which Mr Canning has submitted the drafts. (13849)

3711 VISCOUNT CASTLEREAGH *to the* KING

[*Downing Street, 1 Sepr. 1808.*] Lord Castlereagh has humbly to acquaint your Majesty that your Majesty's confidential servants, having taken into their most serious consideration the state of the war now carrying on in Spain and Portugal, are humbly of opinion that it may be expedient, so soon as your Majesty's forces shall have deliver'd Portugal from the dominion of the enemy, to direct the efforts of your Majesty's arms, in as considerable force as may be consistent with leaving an adequate garrison in Lisbon and in the forts on the Tagus, to the north of Spain, there to be join'd by the 10,000 men now ready for embarcation at home, and to cooperate with the armies of Spain in expelling the enemy from the Peninsula.

They are induced humbly to recommend this line of operations, as preferable to a forward movement through Portugal into the interior of Spain, as it will keep your Majesty's army more closely in connection with the Fleet, and consequently with its supplies. It will render their line of operations much less extended, and whilst it will facilitate communication from home with the army on service, it will render their return &c overland more easy when the proposed service shall have been effected.

Including the 10,000 men now in readiness to proceed from hence, your Majesty's confidential servants humbly conceive that after appropriating an adequate force for the immediate security of Portugal, a corps of 30,000 men, with a proportion of cavalry, may be brought if necessary to act in the north of Spain. To this force may ultimately be added the 10,000 Spanish troops from the Baltick, and they cannot but flatter themselves, if the Spanish nation shall continue to make the efforts which they have hitherto done and which the occasion requires, that the accession of 30,000 British and 10,000 Spanish regular troops to their exertions against the enemy in that quarter, must not only accelerate his expulsion from Spain, but may also contribute, if his retreat shall be delay'd, to the destruction of a considerable proportion of his army.

With a view of accelerating as far as circumstances will permit the execution of this operation, they humbly beg leave to submit for your Majesty's gracious approbation, that the accompanying instructions be sent to Lt.-Genl. Sir Hew Dalrymple; and in order that the troops to proceed from hence may be held in a more collected state of readiness to be detach'd, according to the intelligence that may hereafter be received of the progress of operations in Portugal and of the period when the force from thence can be expected to reach the north of Spain, your Majesty's servants beg leave humbly to recommend that the troops at Cork should be order'd to embark and proceed to Plymouth, there to be met by the proportion of the 10,000 men which are under orders in this country—by assembling the force at that station, it will be more immediately within your

Majesty's disposition, than in its present divided state, and there is every reason to hope that before the whole can be collected there, your Majesty may find yourself possess'd of sufficient information to decide upon its ulterior destination.[1] (13851–3)

[*From Castlereagh, Coombe Wood, Thursday night, 12 p.m.* [*1 Sept. 1808*].] Lord Castlereagh in submitting to your Majesty the accompanying dispatches from Lt.-Genl. Sir Harry Burrard and Lt.-Genl. Sir Arthur Wellesley, has the satisfaction humbly to acquaint your Majesty that previous to Capt. Campbell's[2] departure on the 22nd (who was charged with the dispatches) General Kellerman[3] had arrived with a flag of truce to treat for a capitulation of the French army in Portugal. (13850)

[*The King's reply, Windsor Castle, 2 Sept.*] The King has received with great satisfaction the dispatches which Lord Castlereagh has forwarded to him from Sir Henry Burrard & Sir Arthur Wellesley with the intelligence of two successful actions fought in Portugal which are so honorable to the officers & troops engaged. His Majesty considers them as a very happy beginning & trusts that the service will be completed in the same manner. The King approves of what is suggested in Lord Castlereagh's letter for the further application of the disposeable force collected here and in Portugal when that Kingdom shall have been cleared of the enemy, & of the instructions which are in consequence prepared for Sir Hew Dalrymple. (13854)

3712   THE DUKE OF PORTLAND *to the* KING, *and the reply*

[*Bulstrode, Saturday, 3 Sept. 1808.*] The Duke of Portland most humbly submits for your Majesty's royal signature the warrant for the pensions which your

---

[1] The British expeditionary force landed in Mondego Bay on 1 and 2 Aug., and, when reinforced to a total strength of 30,000 men, was placed under the command, not of Sir Arthur Wellesley, who had brought 9,000 troops from Ireland (the Commander-in-Chief and some members of the Cabinet disliking the Wellesley family), but of Sir Hew Dalrymple, with Sir Harry Burrard second in command. Wellesley would be only fourth, for Sir John Moore, whose force from the Baltic was also sent to Portugal, was his senior. On 17 Aug. Wellesley, who commanded a division, fought a successful action against a small French force at Roliça, north of Lisbon; and on the 21st he severely mauled Junot's army which attacked him at Vimiero, near Torres Vedras. Wellesley would have turned the French retreat into something like a rout, but at that moment he was superseded by Burrard, who had just landed, and, a few hours later, Burrard was in turn superseded by Dalrymple from Gibraltar, who had seen no active service since 1794. To their surprise Junot sent in a flag of truce to treat for the evacuation of Portugal by the French under a Convention. By the terms of the so-called Convention of Cintra (30 Aug.), which Wellesley himself reluctantly approved (in order to save Lisbon from destruction by the French) and signed, Junot's army was not only allowed to leave Portugal but was actually conveyed in British ships to La Rochelle; and the Russian fleet in the Tagus, commanded by Admiral Siniavin, by a separate Convention, was surrendered to Sir Charles Cotton.
  Wellesley found the Convention 'objectionable in many parts', but, he added, 'I approve of allowing the French to evacuate Portugal, because I see clearly that we cannot get them out of Portugal otherwise, under existing circumstances.'
[2] A.D.C. to Sir Arthur Wellesley. He arrived at Portsmouth from Lisbon on the 1st with the news of Junot's defeat.
[3] François Étienne Kellermann (1770–1835), son of Christophe Kellermann, Duke of Valmy and Marshal of France.

Majesty has been graciously pleased to grant to the Earl of Portmore,[1] Sr. William Dolben, Mr. Watson & Mr. Charles Mace, (the first of which two last mentioned persons had been long your Majesty's Consul at Venice, the other had been employed by your Majesty in the same capacity in one of the Barbary States[2]), Mrs. Matra, the widow of a person who had served your Majesty in a similar situation;[3] Lady Rooke,[4] the relict of Sir Giles Rooke, one of your Majesty's Justices of your Court of Common Pleas; and Miss Morell, the daughter of a person eminent for his literary character. Two other warrants are also submitted to your Majesty, one for part of a pension of £1000 net pr ann. which your Majesty was graciously pleased to grant to Sir Robert Milnes,[5] as a reward for his services as Governor of Martinico & Lieutenant-Governor of Lower Canada, and as a compensation for the loss he suffer'd both in his health & fortune during his residence in both those places, but particularly so in the last of them, and a similar grant of a contingent pension of £600 pr. ann to his wife in case she shall survive him.

The Duke of Portland most anxiously hopes that your Majesty will not deem him too presumptuous in most humbly requesting to be permitted to lay at your Majesty's feet his most dutifull congratulations on the glorious & important successes of your Majesty's arms in Portugal. (13855–6)

[*The King's reply, Windsor Castle, 3 Sept.*[6]] The King has signed the warrants which have been submitted by the Duke of Portland. His Majesty rejoyces in the late events in Portugal as promising farther success to the enterprize in which he has engaged. (13856)

3713   VISCOUNT CASTLEREAGH *to the* KING, *and the reply*

[*Downing Street, 4 Sept. 1808.*] Humbly trusting that the peculiar circumstances of the case may induce your Majesty to excuse the present intrusion, Lord Castlereagh begs leave to submit for your Majesty's approbation the accompanying draft to Lt.-Genl. Sir Hew Dalrymple, as transmitting to that officer the communication received from the Chevr. de Souza, together with Mr. Canning's answer, should that answer be honor'd with your Majesty's sanction. (13859)

[1] William Charles Colyear, 3rd Earl of Portmore [S.] (*c.* 1747–1823). Succeeded his father, 5 July 1785.
[2] Algiers (*c.* 1795).
[3] J. Maria Matra, Consul at Tunis.
[4] Sir Giles Rooke (1743–1808). King's Serjeant, 1793; Judge of the Court of Common Pleas, 1793–1808. Knighted, 1793. He married Harriet Sophia Burrard (*d.* 1839), daughter of Colonel William Burrard. He died on 7 March.
[5] Created Baronet, 21 March 1801. Malmesbury thus reported Portland's statement to him on 23 April 1807: 'No pensions were ever given to Governors on quitting their government....He had been trying, but in vain, to find a precedent, in order to give one to Sir R. Milnes, his relation by marriage, and now returning to Canada.' (Malmesbury, *Diaries and Corresp.*, IV, 385.) Charlotte Frances (*d.* 1850), daughter of John Albert, Count Bentinck (1737–75) married Sir Robert Shore Milnes (*d.* 1837) in 1785.
Another pension, of £500 a year, was granted to Milnes and his wife on 2 Jan. 1809, on their joint lives. See No. 3763.   [6] Endorsed by Taylor, the 4th.

[*The King's reply, Windsor Castle, 4 Sept.*] The King highly approves of Lord Castlereagh's letter to Sir Hew Dalrymple relative to the communication from M. de Souza, which, in regard to the alledged Convention his Majesty hopes, for the honor of this country, may prove incorrect. (13860)

3714 *Letters from* GEORGE CANNING *to the* KING, *and the replies*

[*Foreign Office, 4 Sept. 1808, 4 p.m.*] Mr. Canning most humbly intreats your Majesty's pardon for intruding upon your Majesty at an unusual hour. But it has appeared, after consultation with such of your Majesty's confidential servants as are in town, so essential that the accompanying communication from the Chevr. de Souza should be immediately answered, that Mr Canning has thought it his duty to lose no time in laying it before your Majesty; & in humbly submitting for your Majesty's royal approbation the draft of the answer proposed to be returned to it, in order that, if approved by your Majesty, that answer may be forwarded without delay to your Majesty's commanders in Portugal.

Mr. Canning is extremely sorry that one of the papers referred to in M. de Souza's note as having been delivered to Mr Hammond is not to be found at this moment, but it is not very important for your Majesty's view of the material points of M. de Souza's communication. (13857–8)

[*The King's reply, Windsor Castle, 4 Sept.*] Although the King can hardly bring himself to believe that any British officers could, under the circumstances in which Sir Hew Dalrymple and Sir Arthur Wellesley were placed, think of agreeing to such a Convention as that of which M. de Souza has sent a copy, his Majesty has observed with regret that Sir Hew Dalrymple's letter appears, from its style, genuine. The King can never sanction such a proceeding if unfortunately it should have any existence, and he entirely approves of the letter which Mr. Canning has written to M. de Souza respecting the communication of the Bishop of Oporto to the Russian Admiral which he must call treacherous. (13858)

[*From Canning, Foreign Office, 6 Sept.*] Mr. Canning humbly submits for your Majesty's royal consideration the draft of instructions proposed to be transmitted by the Brazil packet to Lord Strangford.

He also humbly lays before your Majesty a communication received this day from Prince Castelcicala, with respect to the subject of which, as well as to the step which Mr Drummond has taken in inducing his Sicilian Majesty to send the young Prince Leopold[1] of Sicily to Gibraltar, Mr Canning will most humbly beg leave to take your Majesty's pleasure tomorrow.

---

[1] Leopold, Prince of Salerno (1790–1851), youngest surviving son of King Ferdinand I. On 28 July 1816 he married Clementine (1798–1881), daughter of Francis I, Emperor of Austria. In Nov. 1809 the Duke of Kent heard that the sister of the Duke of Orleans might marry Prince Leopold. He wrote to his friend Lieutenant-Colonel Robert Wright on the 23rd: 'The report you communicate...respecting the plans of the Duke of Orleans, and his sister [*b.* 1777], have I own afforded me infinite astonishment, altho' I cannot deny having understood from my illustrious friend that both the King and Queen of Naples had intimated their wish that he might marry the Princess their daughter, yet, from the manner

He submits at the same time the translation of a letter to your Majesty from the Kingdom of Galicia brought by the Spanish frigate La Proba, bound for the River of Plate, & having on board the Governor of Monte Video. (13861–2)

[*The King's reply, Windsor Castle, 7 Sept.*] The King very much approves of the instructions to Lord Strangford of which Mr. Canning has submitted the drafts. (13862)

[*From Canning, Foreign Office, 7 Sept.*] Mr. Canning humbly lays before your Majesty the letter in which the Duke of Orleans gives an account of his proceedings in Sicily.

Mr. Canning has to intreat your Majesty's forgiveness for having forgotten today, as well as on last Wednesday, to mention to your Majesty that he had received from Mr. Pinckney a Note containing the formal proposal on the part of his Government to withdraw the embargo as against this country if your Majesty would consent to withdraw the Orders-in-Council. Mr. Canning does not trouble your Majesty with the Note itself until he can at the same time humbly submit for your Majesty's royal approbation an answer containing a statement of the reasons for which it is humbly apprehended by your Majesty's confidential servants that your Majesty could not consent to this proposal. (13863–4)

[*The King's reply, Windsor Castle, 8 Sept.*] The King fully admits the propriety of Mr Canning's not sending Mr Pinckney's note until the proposed answer could be transmitted. The Duke of Orleans' papers being voluminous, his Majesty has kept them back for the day. (13864)

3715 VISCOUNT CASTLEREAGH *to the* KING, *and the reply*
[*Downing Street, 7 Sept. 1808.*] Lord Castlereagh having submitted to your Majesty in person the reasons which have induced your Majesty's confidential servants humbly to advise your Majesty to direct your Majesty's Commanders in the West Indies to endeavor to procure the cession of Martinique on certain conditions, has now the honor of laying before your Majesty for your gracious consideration the accompanying instruction to that effect. (13865)

[*The King's reply, Windsor Castle, 8 Sept.*] The King approves the instruction which Lord Castlereagh has prepared for his Majesty's Commanders in the West Indies respecting Martinique. (13866)

in which he spoke of that affair, I never conceived that he would accept of it, and am at this moment rather inclin'd to be incredulous, but wonders never cease, and I do not see why this event, so considered, should not take place, as well as any other that one is least prepared to expect. As to the marriage of Mademoiselle with Prince Leopold, the disparity of age is the greatest if not the only objection to it, but there are precedents for similar ones in many of the Catholic Courts, where it is the custom for uncles and neices, nephews and aunts, & vice versa to intermarry. I only hope if the thing is to take place it will be for their mutual happiness, for I am very sincerely attach'd to the Duke, and his sister I have always heard spoken of as a most amiable young woman.' (46421–4)

[*Admiralty, 10 Sept. 1808.*] Lord Mulgrave has the honour humbly to submit to your Majesty some interesting dispatches received this day from the Baltick, the substance of which is stated in the précis.

In the event of an action with so considerable a fleet as that which Russia has sent out, an additional force may become necessary for maintaining the established stations in the Baltick: with this view the three sail of the line which have been employ'd under the command of Vice-Admiral Russel for the blockade of the Texel have been this day taken from under the command of that officer & ordered to proceed without delay to join Sir James Saumarez; which Lord Mulgrave most humbly hopes may receive your Majesty's gracious approbation, as the enemy's ships cannot come out of the Texel during the neap tides, and the necessary force may be reassembled under Vice-Admiral Russel in the course of the ensuing ten days. (13867)

[*The King's reply, Windsor Castle, 11 Sept.*] The King has received Lord Mulgrave's letter and entirely approves of the arrangement which he has made for sending a reinforcement to Vice Adl. Sir James Saumarez, which his Majesty hopes will reach the Baltick very opportunely. (13868)

3717 GEORGE CANNING *to the* KING, *and the reply*

[*Hinckley, 12 Sept. 1808.*] Mr. Canning humbly lays before your Majesty a second letter which he has received from the Duke of Orleans; & at the same time humbly submits the draft of an answer to his Serene Highness's two letters for your Majesty's royal approbation. (13869)

[*The King's reply, Windsor Castle, 14 Sept.*] The King has received Mr. Canning's letter and the accompanying communications from the Duke of Orleans, the proposed answer to which appears to his Majesty very proper. (13869)

3718 LORD HAWKESBURY *to the* KING

[*London, 14 Sept. 1808.*] Lord Hawkesbury begs leave most humbly to submit to your Majesty the Memorial which he had the honour of mentioning to you today. Lord Hawkesbury knows nothing of the writer, and the greater part of the Memorial is scarcely deserving your Majesty's attention, but Lord Hawkesbury has ascertained that the copy of the warrant of your Majesty of the 3d of Jany. 1767 is correct, and as that part of the Memorial relates to a claim of right or justice Lord Hawkesbury humbly submits to your Majesty whether your Majesty would not direct that it should be laid before the Attorney and Solicitor-General for their opinion upon it. (13870)

[*Admiralty, 15 Sept. 1808.*] Lord Mulgrave has the honour most humbly to report to your Majesty the arrival of Capt. Halsted,[1] Capt. of the Fleet under the command of Admiral Sir Charles Cotton with the dispatches which Lord Mulgrave has the honour to transmit to your Majesty. The Russian ships of war are to be held in deposit by your Majesty till six months after a peace with Russia, the officers & seamen to be sent unconditionally to Russia in ships of war or other proper vessels to be provided without delay.[2] The precarious state of the weather on the dangerous coast of Portugal, where transports could not remain in safety, & which the British fleet might have been obliged to quit, has hastened the measures, as it should seem, of the capitulation with the land forces of France. It appears by the report of Capt. Halsted that Sir Charles Cotton absolutely refused to admit the proposed neutrality of the Tagus or to become a party to any capitulation unless the forts at the mouth of the Tagus should be placed in the full occupation of your Majesty's troops, & that no French flag should fly near the anchorage of your Majesty's fleet. Lord Mulgrave humbly begs your Majesty's gracious indulgence for sending this news at an unseasonable hour. (13873–4)

[*The King's reply, Windsor Castle, 16 Sept.*] The King has received Lord Mulgrave's letter and the accompanying dispatches from Sir Charles Cotton, and H.M. rejoyces that Sir Charles Cotton has, under all the circumstances which have occurred in Portugal, and the difficulties which attended them, so properly supported the honor of this country and of the service, by refusing to accede to any terms short of the removal of the Russian ships of war to British ports. (13880)

3720   *Letters from* VISCOUNT CASTLEREAGH *to the* KING, *and the replies*

[*Downing Street, 15 Septr.* [*1808*], *6 p.m.*] Lord Castlereagh has humbly to submit to your Majesty dispatches received this day at 4 o'clock p.m. from Lt.-Genl. Sir Hew Dalrymple.

Whilst your Majesty's confidential servants cannot but express to your Majesty the deep disappointment they feel at the terms which have been conceded to the enemy, they deem it their duty humbly to represent to your Majesty that they do not perceive that there is any sufficient ground upon which they could advise your Majesty to oppose any obstacles to the Conventions agreed to being carried into effect.

In addition to what is stated in Sir Hew Dalrymple's letter with respect to the difficulty of preserving the communications with, and subsisting the army, in the event of protracted operations being carried on towards Lisbon whilst the Tagus remain'd in possession of the enemy, Capt. Halkett[3] describes the situation of a

---

[1] Sir Lawrence William Halsted (*d.* 1841). Lieutenant, 1781; Captain, 1791; Rear-Admiral, 1810; Vice-Admiral, 1814; Admiral, 1830. K.C.B., 1815; G.C.B., 1837.

[2] The British Admiral, that is, successfully objected to Junot's stipulation that the Russian fleet in the Tagus should be allowed to leave unmolested.

[3] Sir Peter Halkett (*d.* Oct. 1839, aged 74). Lieutenant, 1789; Captain, 1794; Rear-Admiral, 1812. Succeeded his brother as Baronet, 26 Jan. 1837. Cf. Halsted, No. 3719.

large fleet of transports as exposed to great danger whilst off that coast, particularly during the gales of wind naturally to be expected in the course of the month of September.

Your Majesty's confidential servants having appointed tomorrow for taking this important subject into their consideration, Lord Castlereagh will take the earliest opportunity of submitting to your Majesty the result of their deliberations. (13871–2)

[*The King's reply, Windsor Castle, 16 Sept.*] The King has received Lord Castle-reagh's letter and the accompanying dispatches from Sir Hew Dalrymple, and H.M. must lament that it should have been necessary to grant such terms to the French troops in Portugal. It only remains to be ascertained whether that necessity did actually exist to the full extent and whether the difficulties could or could not have been obviated. It appears satisfactory that no stipulation whatever is made in the Convention with General Junot for the Russian ships, as this seeming sacrifice by the French of their Allies may produce divisions between them. (13883)

[*From Castlereagh, Downing Street, 16 Sept.*] The equipments for the movement of your Majesty's disposeable force being now completed, Lord Castlereagh begs permission humbly to lay before your Majesty a statement of their nature and extent, together with the amount of force that will remain applicable to purposes of defence at home and abroad. (13877)

[*From Castlereagh, Downing Street, 16 Sepr.*] Your Majesty's confidential servants having taken into their most serious consideration the dispatches yesterday received from Lt. Genl. Sir Hew Dalrymple, have deem'd it their duty to submit humbly for your Majesty's royal approbation the accompanying drafts to be address'd to that officer. (13875)

[*The King's reply, Windsor Castle, 17 Sept.*] The King approves of the letters which Lord Castlereagh has prepared for transmission to Sir Hew Dalrymple and his Majesty acknowledges the receipt of the statement of the amount of his forces offensive and defensive. (13876)

3721 LORD MULGRAVE *to the* KING, *and the reply*

[*Admiralty, 16 Sept. 1808.*] Lord Mulgrave has the honour most humbly to submit to your Majesty's gracious consideration the draft of a dispatch to be sent by the Secretary to the Admiralty, addressed to Adl. Sir Charles Cotton, if it should receive your Majesty's sanction.

Lord Mulgrave has the honour at the same time to transmit to your Majesty dispatches this day received from V.-Adl. Sir James Saumarez & R. Admiral Sir Saml. Hood detailing the capture & destruction of a Russian line of battle ship by your Majesty's ships Centaur & Implacable, in the presence & in defiance of the whole body of the Russian fleet, by an exertion of the characteristic valour, enterprize, skill & nautical science of your Majesty's Navy, which have never been excelled, as Lord Mulgrave most humbly conceives. By private accounts it appears that the Swedish fleet have been strongly impressed with a just admiration of this distinguished action, and with an animated & respectful spirit of emulation.

Lord Mulgrave begs leave most humbly to submit to your Majesty Capt. Isaac Schomberg,[1] an officer of science & experience, to succeed Sir Robert Barlow[2] as Deputy Comptroller of the Navy. (13878–9)

[*The King's reply, Windsor Castle, 17 Sept.*] The King has received with very sensible satisfaction the communication from Lord Mulgrave of the capture and destruction of a Russian line of battle ship in the Baltic by the extraordinary exertions and gallantry of Sir Samuel Hood, Captains Martin[3] & Webley,[4] their officers & crew. Sir Samuel Hood has long been known to his Majesty and his conduct upon this occasion must if possible strengthen the high opinion which his Majesty has ever entertained of his character.

The King approves of the proposed letter to Sir Charles Cotton and of the appointment of Captain Schomberg to succeed Sir Robert Barlow. (13879)

3722 GEORGE CANNING *to the* KING, *and the reply*

[*Hinckley, 16 Sept. 1808.*] Mr. Canning humbly lays before your Majesty two notes received from the Prince Castelcicala; & submits for your Majesty's royal approbation the drafts of the answers which he has prepared to them; in conformity, as he humbly hopes, to your Majesty's commands as received by him on Wednesday last.

Mr. Canning takes the liberty humbly to remind your Majesty (in reference to the second of the two drafts herewith sent) that Mr. St. Clair, the Frenchman whose influence in the councils of the Court of Palermo has been so often the subject of representation, & whose wife is at Paris & in the household (as Mr Canning has been informed) of one of Buonaparte's relations, is one of the persons who have accompanied Prince Leopold to Gibraltar.

Mr. Canning also humbly submits to your Majesty the draft of a dispatch to Mr. Drummond. (13881–2)

[*The King's reply, Windsor Castle, 18 Sept.*] The King approves of the letters to Prince Castelcicala and to Mr. Drummond of which Mr. Canning has submitted the drafts. (13882)

[1] Lieutenant, 1777; Captain, 1790. (1753–1813).

[2] Lieutenant, 1778; Captain, 1793; Rear-Admiral, 1823; Admiral, 1840. Knighted, 1801; K.C.B., 1820; G.C.B., 1842. Deputy-Comptroller of the Navy, 1806–8; Commissioner of Chatham Dockyard, 1808. (1757–1843).

[3] Sir Thomas Byam Martin (1773–1854). Lieutenant, 1790; Captain, 1793; Rear-Admiral, 1811; Vice-Admiral, 1819; Admiral, 1830. K.C.B., 1815; G.C.B., 1830. M.P. for Plymouth, 1818–32. Deputy-Comptroller of the Navy, 1815; Comptroller, 1816–31. In 1808 he commanded the *Implacable*.

[4] William Henry Webley (later, Webley Parry). Lieutenant, 1790; Captain, 1802; Rear-Admiral, 1837 (*d.* 1837). In 1808 he commanded the *Centaur*.

3723   *Letters from* Viscount Castlereagh *to the* King, *and the replies*

[*St. James's Sq., 17 Sept. 1808.*] Lord Castlereagh begs leave again to submit to your Majesty the draft to Sir Hew Dalrymple, of which your Majesty was graciously pleased to approve, with two alterations, the one for the purpose of noticing the objections to having permitted the French in any respect to negotiate for the Russian fleet; the other to express the hope, which your Majesty is entitled to entertain, that in the execution of the Convention, undisguised plunder shall not be suffer'd to be withdrawn from Portugal under the mark of private property. (13884)

[*The King's reply, Windsor Castle, 18 Sept.*] The King considers the alterations Lord Castlereagh has proposed in the dispatch to Sir Hew Dalrymple to be a very material improvement. (13885)

[*From Castlereagh, St. James's Sq., 21 Sept.*] Lord Castlereagh having humbly submitted to your Majesty the reasons which have induced your Majesty's confidential servants to be of opinion that Sir Hew Dalrymple should be immediately directed to return to England, now lays before your Majesty for your Majesty's consideration, the accompanying drafts to be substituted in the room of those of which your Majesty was graciously pleased before to approve on the same subject. (13887)

[*The King's reply, Windsor Castle, 22 Sept.*] The King approves of the dispatches to Sir Hew Dalrymple which Lord Castlereagh has proposed to be substituted for those before submitted, his Majesty considering it very fair towards Sir Hew Dalrymple to give him an early opportunity of personally explaining his conduct. (13888)

3724   George Canning *to the* King, *and the reply*

[*Foreign Office, 22 Sept. 1808.*] Mr. Canning humbly lays before your Majesty the official letter addressed to him by the American Minister on the subject of your Majesty's Orders-in-Council of the 7th of Janry. & 11th of November 1807; & most humbly submits the drafts of an answer to it for your Majesty's royal approbation. (13889)

[*The King's reply, Windsor Castle, 23 Sept.*] The King approves of Mr. Canning's proposed answers to Mr Pinckney's late communications, and his Majesty considers them as placing the question between this country and America in a very clear point of view. (13890)

3725   *Letters from* Viscount Castlereagh *to the* King

[*St. James's Sq., 23 Sept. 1808.*] Your Majesty's confidential servants having taken into their consideration the future application of your Majesty's disposeable force, feel it their duty humbly to recommend to your Majesty that a corps of not less than 30,000 men, to be composed of the troops now collecting at Falmouth, and the force which may be drawn from Portugal, without prejudice to the security of that country, should be assembled for service, under the orders of Lt.-Genl. Sir John Moore, in the north of Spain. Your Majesty's confidential servants humbly hope that although Sir John Moore's standing in the Army is not such as your Majesty would probably wish for so high a command, that under all the circumstances of the case it may at the present moment be most for the advantage of your Majesty's service that in the arrangements to be made, the Staff of your Majesty's Army abroad, as recently settled by your Majesty, should be disturbed as little as possible. Whatever there may be to lament in the termination of the late operations in Portugal, your Majesty's confidential servants humbly conceive will only operate on your Majesty's mind as an additional motive for encreased exertion in support of the common cause. (13891–2)

[*From Castlereagh, St. James's Sq., 23 Sepr.*] Lord Castlereagh, in laying before your Majesty dispatches this day received from Lt.-Col. Doyle[1] at Madrid, is induced humbly to hope that although this officer has certainly travel'd beyond the line of his original destination, that in the present unexampled state of Spain, his zeal may induce your Majesty to sanction, in the absence of all more regular authority, the step he has taken for facilitating the movements of the troops from Madrid, at a moment so peculiarly critical, in support of the Arragonian army at Saragossa.

Lord Castlereagh is fully sensible how desireable it is that such an interference on the part of your Majesty's military servants should terminate as early as possible, but he trusts that during the late extraordinary crisis, and before your Majesty deem'd it suitable to send into Spain persons more regularly accredited, that the officers whom your Majesty has been graciously pleased to employ there for the purpose of collecting military information, have on more than one occasion seasonably interposed to give an advantageous impulse to the exertions of the Spanish nation, and that in this light the responsibility which Lt.-Col. Doyle has ventured to incur may not in the peculiar circumstances of the moment be disapproved by your Majesty. (13893–4)

3726 MEMORANDUM [*unsigned*]

[*Horse Guards, 23 Sept. 1808.*] The Convention which has been made in Portugal, in however unpleasant a light it may be viewed, having terminated all operations in that Kingdom, it becomes of the greatest consequence speedily to decide in what manner to employ the British troops most advantageously for the common good, and particularly for the assistance of the Spaniards in the great cause in which they are engaged. This assistance can be afforded but in two ways, either by such a diversion as may oblige Buonaparte to draw off a part of the forces

---

[1] Sir Charles William Doyle (1770–1842). Lieutenant, 1793; Lieutenant-Colonel, 1805; Colonel, 1813; Major-General, 1819; Lieutenant-General, 1837. Knighted, 1815; K.C.H., 1821; G.C.H., 1837.

destined against Spain, or by sending the British troops to Spain itself to take a part in the defence of that country.

For many reasons too long and unnecessary to be detailed in this paper, a diversion on some other part of the Continent, if it was possible, would be preferable, but in the present unfortunate state of the Continent when every country except Spain is either under the immediate tyranny of Buonaparte or so completely humbled and reduced as to be nearly if not full as much under his controul—there remains no place where a British force could be sent which could venture to receive it, & if it even does possess resources enough to make sufficient stand against the French so as to enable us to put our troops in a state to take the field.

It therefore appears evident from the foregoing observation that the only assistance which can effectually be given to the Spaniards is in Spain itself. As yet success has crowned the efforts of the Spaniards, and the French have been under the necessity of abandoning above three-quarters of that Kingdom and concentrating the remains of their forces behind the Ebro, in order to wait for the reinforcements which they expect, and which by all accounts are daily arriving. However we may admire the successful efforts which the Spaniards have made, we cannot delude ourselves so much as not to acknowledge that these successes have been greatly facilitated, if not wholly owing, to their great superiority in numbers as well as to the complete want of precaution of the French, and to their considering the general rising of an insulted people as mere partial popular tumults which would disperse and submit at the first appearance of a military force, thereby scattering their troops and allowing them to be beat in detail. Neither can we for a moment put in competition the Spanish troops, brave as they are, but mostly raw undisciplined levies, with the French army enured to war for the last fifteen years. Neither can we expect that the French will continue to commit the same military errors as they have hitherto done, & from the known character of Buonaparte, whose ambitious mind will never brook the being, for the first time, at least in Europe, foiled in any of his vast projects of universal dominion, we may be convinced that there is no effort he will not make to reduce Spain and to repossess himself of the riches and resources of that country. We may therefore conclude that his next efforts will be made in considerable force and upon some systematick plan, to which the present positions of the contending armies give him great advantage.

The French are concentrated upon the Ebro, their right upon Burgos and their left to Malager, having the country in the front of their centre entirely open, while the Spanish troops who are *actually* opposed to him are divided into two different corps under different Generals, perfectly separated from each other owing to the want of cavalry which obliged them to abandon the plain country and to occupy the mountains—the one in the Asturias & Galicia—the other considerably in front of Saragossa. It is therefore in the power of the enemy, under present circumstances, to make a great effort with their undivided force upon either of these corps, and in all probability without a chance of their mutual co-operation.

It is not my object in this paper to enter into a reasoning upon that plan of campaign which it would be most adviseable to adopt, but it is clear from the foregoing observations that the most efficient assistance which can be given to Spain is a corps of troops which can act with effect upon the plains. But it is equally as evident that such a corps must be strong enough to defend itself and competent to resist any effort which the enemy could venture to make against it. We should also consider that it must be upon this corps in case any great misfortune was to happen to the Spaniards, that the whole must rally. Any body of troops therefore short of this would, in my opinion, be of little essential use to the great cause, when on the contrary, being incapable of acting alone and consequently involved in the operations of the Spanish commanders, it would in the event of reverse, subject us to very great loss and discredit without any real advantage to our Allies.

Having thus given an outline of my opinion upon this subject as briefly as the importance of it would admit, I subjoin a sketch of the number of troops which might actually be employed upon this service, should it be judged advisable, without materially diminishing the number which are still at home. There are at present in Portugal—

Cavalry	1,640	
34 battalions of infantry	29,806	
Of this force the 20 Light Dragoons	327	
and 8 battalions of infantry should		
remain in Portugal	6,231	

The disposable force would then be—	Cavalry	Infantry
Now in Portugal	1,313	23,575
Force under orders	3,200	11,419
Force from Sicily	—	8,000
To this may be added the Second Brigade		
of Guards	—	2,434
and four regiments of cavalry	2,560	—
Total	7,073	45,428

When to this you add *four* battalions of infantry, which could be spared, and the Artillery, it will form a corps of above 60,000 men. (13895–9)

3727   *Letters from* VISCOUNT CASTLEREAGH *to the* KING, *and the replies*

[*St. James's Square, 24 Sept. 1808.*] Lord Castlereagh humbly submits to your Majesty dispatches received from Sir D. Baird and M.-Genl. Broderick,[1] communicating intelligence of an unfavorable nature, but in such general terms as to render it impossible to form any precise judgment either of the extent of the

[1] John Brodrick (1765–1842), sixth son of George, 3rd Viscount Midleton. Colonel, 1801; Brigadier-General, 1804; Major-General, 1808; Lieutenant-General, 1813; General, 1830.

disaster which is stated to have befallen General Blake's[1] army, or of the force which the enemy may have push'd forward to Valladolid. The last letters from M. General Leith[2] are dated from St. Andero on the 11th.; those from Adml. De Courcey[3] from Corunna come down as low as the 19th.

Your Majesty's confidential servants, under the circumstances of the case, have not conceived it possible for them to do more (in consequence of Sir D. Baird's application for instructions) than humbly to advise your Majesty to direct that officer, in the event of his finding himself obliged to re-embark without orders from Sir J. Moore, to proceed to the Tagus there to obey such instructions as he may receive from that officer for the direction of his conduct.

Sir D. Baird expected his corps to be assembled at Astorga on the 28th; Sir J. Moore's force, with the exception of a part of the column which moved by Elvas (in which, however, the cavalry and the artillery were included) would arrive in the vicinity of Salamanca on the 24th—the rear of Genl. Hope's column, consisting of the cavalry, was at Villa Vicosa on the 1st of Novr., which by the route they were to march is about 280 miles from Salamanca; supposing them on an average to advance at the rate of 10 miles a day, they might be expected to reach the point of assembly about the end of the month. (13900–1)

[*The King's reply, Windsor Castle, 24 Sept.*] The King approves of the proposal which is made in Lord Castlereagh's letter for sending to Spain a British force of not less than 30,000 men to be placed under the command of Sir John Moore. His Majesty is sensible of that officer's abilities, but must regret that he is not of higher standing in the army, when selected for so extensive a command, although he is willing to admit that the desire not to make any material alteration in the present Staff arrangements warrants the appointment as a matter of necessity.

The King considers that, under all the circumstances which are represented by Lt.-Col. Doyle he is excusable in having taken upon himself a degree of responsibility which his instructions did not authorize. (13902)

[*From Castlereagh, St. James's Sq., 24 Sept.*] Lord Castlereagh humbly requests that B. Genl. Dickens[4] may receive your Majesty's permission, in compliance with his request, to return to England, and that Lord Castlereagh may be allowed to express your Majesty's appreciation of his conduct in the execution of the service confided to him. (13903)

[1] Joachim Blake, the Spanish General commanding the Spanish army of 50,000 men in Galicia, was defeated by Marshal Bessières at Medina de Rio Seco on 14 July. The French thereby gained command of the Douro, enabling them to cut communications between Galicia and the southern Provinces.

[2] Sir James Leith (1763–1816). Colonel, 1794; Brigadier-General, 1804; Major-General, 1808; Lieutenant-General, 1813; Governor of the Leeward Islands, 1814. K.B., 1813; G.C.B., 1815. For his letters from Santander, etc. see *Castlereagh Corresp.*, VII, 220–40.

[3] Michael de Courcy (*d.* 1824), a son of John, 25th Lord Kingsale. Lieutenant, 1776; Captain, 1783; Rear-Admiral, 1805; Vice-Admiral, 1810; Admiral, 1821.

[4] Baron Decken. For his letters from Oporto (18 Aug.–25 Nov. 1808), see *Castlereagh Corresp.*, VII, 167–77.

[*The King's reply, Windsor Castle, 25 Sept.*] In consequence of Lord Castlereagh's letter the King agrees to B. General Dicken's application for leave to return to England. (13903)

3728 *Letters from* GEORGE CANNING *to the* KING, *and the reply*

[*Foreign Office, 24 Sept. 1808.*] Mr. Canning humbly lays before your Majesty a letter from the King of Sweden to your Majesty which has been this day delivered to him by Mr. Adlerberg. Mr. Canning is very sorry to see that this letter (of which a copy was communicated to him by Mr. Adlerberg) falls short of the description given of it to him by Mr. Thornton, who was taught to expect that it would contain either a satisfactory explanation of the affair of General Moore—or some sufficient apology for it. The letter to your Majesty referred to in this letter of the King of Sweden was not answered by your Majesty because the account of the affair of Genl. Moore arrived here at the same time with it.

Mr. Canning humbly lays before your Majesty the copy of another letter from the King of Sweden to your Majesty which Mr Adlerberg is charged to present in person together with the flag of the Russian ship taken by Sir Samuel Hood. Mr. Canning has represented to Mr. Adlerberg the inconvenience of bringing the flag itself to the Queen's Palace. But as your Majesty had proposed at all events to receive the Foreign Ministers on Wednesday, perhaps your Majesty would not object to his being permitted on that occasion to present the letter to your Majesty in compliance with the King of Sweden's orders. (13904–5)

[*The King's reply, Windsor Castle, 25 Sept.*] The justice of Mr. Canning's observation upon the King of Sweden's letter renders it unnecessary for the King to make any comment upon it. His Majesty has therefore only to approve of Mr Adlerberg's coming to the Queen's Palace on Wednesday next to present the other letter. (13906)

[*From Canning, Foreign Office, 27 Sept.*] Mr. Canning humbly takes the liberty of transmitting to your Majesty the names of the several Spanish Generals & Deputies whom your Majesty has been graciously pleased to allow Mr Canning to present to your Majesty at the Levée tomorrow.

The Portuguese Minister requests your Majesty's permission to present to your Majesty the Viscount de Pralsamao, son of M. de Pinto, so long Minister at this Court, & three officers lately arrived from Portugal.

The Swedish Minister will be accompanied by Lt.-Col. Gyllenskjold, Aide-de-camp de Marine to his Swedish Majesty, the officer charged by H.S.M. to deliver the Russian flag captured by Sir Samuel Hood—together with a letter to your Majesty. The flag Mr. Canning has already received, & the letter he has prevailed upon Mr. Adlerberg to direct to be delivered to him by Col. Gyllenskjold tomorrow, without troubling your Majesty for an audience.

Mr. Canning also humbly begs your Majesty's permission to present Mr Frere to your Majesty, on his appointment to a special mission to Spain.[1] (13910–11)

[*Enclosure*]

List

Marquis de la Romana
Lt.-Col. O'Donnell. Aide de Camp
M. de las Heras (Intendant with the rank of Colonel)

Andalusians

Genl. Don Adrian Jacome
Adml. Don Juan Ruiz Apodaca
Don Adrian Jacome (nephew of Genl. Jacome)
Don Lorenzo Noriega ⎫
Don Rafael Lobo ⎭ Lts. of the Navy

Asturians

Visct. Matarrosa
Don Andres Angel de la Vega

Galician

Don Francisco Sangro

M. de Sangro being indisposed probably will not be at the Levée. (13912)

3729 VISCOUNT CASTLEREAGH *to the* KING, *and the reply*
[*St. James's Square, 27 Sepr. 1808.*] For the reasons stated in the accompanying draft to Lt.-Genl. Sir D. Baird, your Majesty's confidential servants humbly recommend to your Majesty that the armament assembling at Falmouth under the orders of that officer should be directed to proceed to its destination so soon as the convoy from Cork shall arrive, every part of the equipment having already moved from the river, the Downs and Portsmouth to Falmouth. (13913)

[*The King's reply, Windsor Castle, 28 Sept.*] The King approves of the instructions for Lieut.-General Sir David Baird which Lord Castlereagh has submitted. (13913)

3730 GEORGE CANNING *to the* KING,[2] *and the reply*
[*Foreign Office, 28 Sept. 1808.*] The majority of your Majesty's confidential servants having humbly submitted to your Majesty, through Lord Castlereagh, their opinion that, under all the circumstances attending the Convention

---

[1] John Hookham Frere arrived at Corunna on 19 Oct. and at Madrid on 17 Nov. He presented his letter of credence to the President of the Supreme Junta at Aranjuez on 14 Nov.
[2] There is an inaccurate version of this letter in *Castlereagh Corresp.*, VI, 455. Cf. Canning's letter to Perceval, 17 Sept. 1808, in Walpole's *Perceval*, I, 294 (but very inaccurately transcribed from Perceval MSS., and wrongly dated the 16th).

concluded with the French army in Portugal, there appeared no ground for interposing, on the part of your Majesty, any obstacle to the execution of that Convention: Mr. Canning (who was not present at that meeting of your Majesty's confidential servants at which this decision was taken) having conceived an opinion differing in some essential points from that which has been submitted to your Majesty, & continuing, after the most painful & anxious deliberation, still to retain that opinion, feels it his duty humbly to lay before your Majesty an exposition of the principles on which it is founded. He most humbly assures your Majesty that he has no other motive or object in this statement than a conscientious discharge of his duty to your Majesty, & that he has presumed to trouble your Majesty in writing, principally that he may be enabled to communicate to his colleagues the statement which he makes to your Majesty on a subject on which he has the misfortune to differ from so many of them in opinion.

Mr. Canning fully admits that all engagements taken on the behalf of your Majesty by persons completely authorized to enter into such engagements ought to be fulfilled (so far as it is in your Majesty's power rightfully to fulfill them) however repugnant to your Majesty's feelings, & however inconvenient to your Majesty's interests. But Mr. Canning cannot persuade himself that the competency of a Commander-in-Chief of your Majesty's armies to enter into stipulations in your Majesty's name, is altogether unlimited; or that it extends to political as well as to military objects. Mr. Canning humbly conceives that the competency of a Commander-in-Chief of your Majesty's armies is limited by the very nature of his trust & office, & that it is further limited (like all legitimate power) by the rules of justice.

Consistently with these principles, Mr. Canning abstains from raising any question upon those Articles of the Convention which affect, however prejudicially, the interests & honour of Great Britain alone. Even for those stipulations which affect the interests of other Powers, remotely or incidentally, & through acts which your Majesty has the undoubted right & power to do, such as the conveyance of the French troops to France & of the Russian sailors to Russia, Mr. Canning professes to see no remedy. But where stipulations are contracted, the execution of which can only be obtained by your Majesty through a coercive controul to be exercised over other independent Powers, or where the thing stipulated is flagrantly unjust, Mr Canning does presume most humbly to conceive that such stipulations must be held to have been contracted without your Majesty's authority.

The 18th Article of the Convention engages for the restoration by the Spaniards (in return for the Spanish troops in the Tagus) of all French subjects, civil as well as military, not taken in arms but now detained in Spain. If the execution of this Article is understood to be binding upon your Majesty, perhaps a question could hardly have been devised more likely to produce disagreement between your Majesty & Spain; or one in which your Majesty would probably be more unwilling to interfere; considering that your Majesty has, from the beginning of the present war, uniformly resisted a principle of exchange by which France has attempted to confound civil with military captivity. But if (as may be contended) the engagement is merely personal to Sir Hew Dalrymple, & he alone is answerable for carrying it into effect, such an engagement appears to Mr Canning to be absolutely null—and if such were the construction adopted by your Majesty, it appears to Mr. Canning that such construction ought to have been unequivocally declared.

The first of the additional Articles contains nearly the same stipulation for the release by the Portuguese of all civil prisoners belonging to France; with these additional aggravations, that such release is to be without exchange, although the French have Portuguese in their possession, both civil & military, to a great amount; & that the Portuguese authorities were not consulted upon the subject. Is your Majesty bound to enforce the execution of these stipulations?

The stipulations in Articles 16 & 17 for a year's security to the property, & perpetual impunity to the persons, of the adherents of France in Portugal, appears liable to no less objection. That security & impunity might justly be promised so long as the British Army must of necessity remain in military possession of Portugal: but to extend them to a period within which the Portuguese Government must in all probability be re-established, is to place your Majesty in the situation of dictating as a conqueror to your Majesty's Ally the terms upon which alone he is to be permitted to recover his dominions. It is to make your Majesty the instrument of protecting & maintaining a French party in Portugal in defiance of the lawful Government of that country.

But far more injurious to your Majesty's honour, & too likely in its execution to prove in the highest degree distressing to your Majesty's feelings, is the stipulation in the 5th Article for securing what is denominated the private property of the French army.

There are two constructions given to this Article: one, that it does *not* include unlawful plunder; the other, that it admits of no discrimination. The former construction rests principally on the word of honour of the French General. The latter is unfortunately countenanced by those words of the Article itself which stipulate full security for the purchasers of what the French may sell: for where was the necessity of security to the purchaser, unless the right of the seller to his property were acknowledged to be equivocal? If the latter construction be merely *possible*, it does appear to Mr. Canning that too early or too distinct an explanation could not have been given of your Majesty's sentiments upon it. That the Portuguese will patiently endure the embarkation of all the fruits of French rapine & sacrilege is hardly credible: and if your Majesty is indeed bound to sanction the inforcing of the execution of this stipulation, *in that sense*, it may probably be to be enforced by means which cannot be thought of without horror. It was, & still continues to be the humble opinion of Mr. Canning that your Majesty is *not* so bound. He humbly conceives that your Majesty could have no imaginable right to the plunder of Portugal, unless your Majesty had been resolved to conquer Portugal for yourself, instead of recovering it for your Majesty's Ally: he thinks that, your Majesty possessing no such right, no military commander of your Majesty's could pledge your Majesty to the assumption & exercise of a power essentially unjust: and that when an engagement taken in your Majesty's name has stipulated that for your Majesty of which your Majesty cannot sanction the execution without doing violence & wrong, your Majesty might, without scruple or hesitation declare such a stipulation to be void.

Mr. Canning will not add to the length of this paper further than to intreat most humbly your Majesty's gracious indulgence & forgiveness for the trouble which he has thus presumed to give your Majesty; & for the imperfect manner in which he has endeavoured to convey to your Majesty opinions, which he felt too strongly to think himself justified in withholding them from your Majesty on a subject of so much importance.[1] (13914–9)

[*The King's reply, Windsor Castle, 29 Sept.*] The King acknowledges the receipt of Mr Canning's letter containing so full & clear a statement of his sentiments upon the Convention which has been concluded with the French army in Portugal. (13919)

3731 VISCOUNT CASTLEREAGH *to the* KING, *and the reply*

[*St. James's Square, 29 Sepr. 1808.*] Lord Castlereagh humbly begs leave to lay before your Majesty a Proclamation issued at Lisbon on the 10th inst. which he has received in a private letter from B. Genl. Stewart.[2] Although Sir H. Dalrymple has not transmitted this important document, nor indeed any information connected with the measures in progress in execution of the Convention, Lord Castlereagh cannot doubt the authenticity of the paper thus transmitted.

B. Genl. Stewart states that Generals Junot and Kellerman had publish'd a Counter-Proclamation, which he does not however transmit. As the Proclamation now sent is sign'd by Kellerman, it does not seem possible for him any further to cavil upon the true intent and meaning of the 5th Article, which it is to be hoped through the exertions of the Committee charged with the separation of the property of the enemy from the plunder of the Prince Regent and his subject[s] may be divested of its most objectionable consequences. (13920–1)

[1] The letter was read to the Cabinet at a meeting on the 27th. Canning wrote to Perceval from Hinckley on the 16th, at 2.30 p.m.: 'I cannot swallow the article of "property" to be carried off by the French army. What *property* can they have but plunder? I dislike it, because it puts us in the wrong with Portugal—& depend upon it, will make us odious there—& give us a more difficult game to play there than we have ever yet had. Heaven defend me from a special mission of Souza's to complain of this sacrifice of their interests...

'There can be no doubt I think that we ought to take this as a great event—and accordingly I am about to make the bell ringers here drunk. They cannot ring worse after that encouragement than they have been doing of their own accord.' (Perceval MSS.)

He wrote again, on the 24th, from the Foreign Office: 'I fear we have lost Portugal for ever, instead of gaining it now—that we were better off the day before the battle of Vimiera than we are since the signing of the Convention—& finally that if the 96 waggon loads of plate which are understood to be packed at Lisbon are included in the 5th of article [*sic*]—& if the Danish & other ships afloat in the Tagus are *not* prize (as I understand from Capt. Halstead) & only the Portugueze *are*—we have incurred a heavier loss & a heavier disgrace than any that British arms or British faith ever sustained.' (*Ibid.*)

[2] Castlereagh's half-brother.

[*The King's reply, Windsor Castle, 30 Sept.*] The King is glad to find from the nature of the printed Proclamation issued at Lisbon which Lord Castlereagh has sent to him that the 5th Article of the Convention does not bear the construction which it was here apprehended might be applied to it. (13921)

3732 LORD MULGRAVE *to the* KING, *and the reply*

[*Admiralty, 29 Sept. 1808.*] Lord Mulgrave has the honour to transmit to your Majesty dispatches received this day from Admiral Sir Charles Cotton, enclosing two Articles proposed by the Russian Admiral Siniavin, and acceded to, by Sir Charles Cotton, subsequent to the conclusion and transmission of the Convention of the 3d of September. Lord Mulgrave begs leave most humbly to submit for your Majesty's gracious consideration, the opinion of your Majesty's servants, that no principle of good faith requires the adoption of those Articles as they do not in any respect come within the description of explanatory Articles, but on the contrary bear the character of a supplementary Convention, framed after the full conclusion of a complete & final instrument. Your Majesty's servants are therefore humbly of opinion that the Articles being in themselves objectionable, it would be expedient to declare them void & of no effect. The condition of the first Article they humbly conceive to be inadmissible, inasmuch as the flag of an hostile Power ought not to be permitted to be displayed in any port of your Majesty's dominions.

The condition of the second Article which stipulates that 'the Russian ships of war shall be restored in the state in which they are actually delivered up,' would impose upon your Majesty the engagement (at whatever expence) to keep the Russian ships in constant repair during the war, or to incur the heavy charge of refitting at the return of peace ships which, from the materials of which they are constructed, are liable to very considerable decay in a state of ordinary [*sic*]. Under these circumstances, Lord Mulgrave most humbly submits to your Majesty whether he should, without delay, notify to Admiral Siniavin that the Convention of the 3d of September, being a complete and perfect instrument, concluded and ratified, no supplementary Convention can be admitted; that the Russian colours must be removed without delay; that, at the same time, the Admiral and the Captains of the several ships will be at full liberty to come on shore, if such be their wish: that no repairs can be given to the Russian ships in your Majesty's arsenals, but that a Russian Commissary will be admitted to reside in each ship, for the purpose of ascertaining that they suffer no wilful injury whilst they remain in your Majesty's custody. (13922–3)

[*The King's reply, Windsor Castle, 30 Sept.*] The King agrees with his Ministers that the Supplementary Articles granted by Sir Charles Cotton to Admiral Siniavin cannot in propriety, be sanctioned, and his Majesty highly approves of the communication which Lord Mulgrave proposes to make upon the subject to Admiral Siniavin. (13923)

[*Foreign Office, 30 Septr. 1808.*] Mr. Canning humbly acquaints your Majesty that Mr. Adlerberg has this day communicated to Mr. Canning his own recall, & the appointment of Mr. Brinkmann to succeed him in the situation of Swedish Minister at this Court. Mr. Adlerberg is appointed to Spain.

Mr. Adlerberg has it in command from the King of Sweden to solicit your Majesty's permission for Sir Samuel Hood & the other officers of your Majesty's Fleet engaged in the action in which the Russian ship was taken, to accept some honorary marks of his Swedish Majesty's favour, proportioned to their respective ranks, which his Swedish Majesty is desirous of bestowing upon them.[1] (13924–5)

[*The King's reply, Windsor Castle, 1 Oct.*] The King has received Mr. Canning's letter and his Majesty approves of Sir Samuel Hood and the other officers engaged in the action with the Russian fleet in the Baltic accepting the honorary marks of favor with which the King of Sweden is disposed to reward their gallant conduct. (13925)

[*From Canning, Foreign Office, 2 Oct.*] Mr. Canning humbly submits for your Majesty's royal consideration the draft of a Credential Letter for Mr. Frere, which (the case of his mission being so perfectly new & not provided for by any precedent) Mr. Canning would not presume to submit for your Majesty's signature until it had been previously considered & approved by your Majesty.

Mr. Canning submits also the draft of a letter to the President of the Central Junta, or other supreme authority exercising the executive power of the Government in the name & on the behalf of his Catholick Majesty, Ferdinand the Seventh.[2] (13926)

[*The King's reply, Windsor Castle, 3 Oct.*] The King approves of the Credential Letter for Mr. Frere of which Mr. Canning has submitted the draft and also of the letter proposed to be written to the President of the Central Junta of Spain. (13927)

[*From Canning, Foreign Office, 4 Oct.*] Mr. Canning humbly submits for your Majesty's royal consideration the draft of the general instructions to Mr. Frere, which, if graciously approved by your Majesty, will be prepared for your Majesty's royal signature; but which, from the novelty of the case, he has found it necessary to vary in a considerable degree from the ordinary form. (13928)

[*The King's reply, Windsor Castle, 5 Oct.*] The King approves of the proposed general instructions for Mr. Frere with the alterations which are submitted by Mr. Canning. (13929)

---

[1] Hood was awarded the Grand Cross of the Order of the Sword.

[2] Ferdinand VII (1784–1833) was deposed by Napoleon after his father Charles IV (1748–1819) had abdicated and run away.

[*From Canning, Foreign Office, 5 Oct.*] Mr. Canning humbly entreats your Majesty's gracious forgiveness in having omitted to pay his duty to your Majesty at the Queen's Palace today—having been detained in preparing despatches to Mr. Frere, & having arrived at the Queen's Palace the moment after your Majesty had left it. Mr. Canning humbly submits to your Majesty the general instructions to Mr. Frere for your Majesty's royal signature.

The dispatches received this night from Mr Stuart do not appear in Mr. Canning's judgement to vary those instructions but to point out in a still stronger light the necessity of inforcing the formation of a central Government in Spain. (13930)

[*From Canning, Foreign Office, 6 Oct.*] Mr. Canning most humbly submits for your Majesty's royal approbation the draft of additional instructions proposed to be given to Mr. Frere. (13931)

[*The King's reply, Windsor Castle, 7 Oct.*] The King approves of the additional instructions to Mr. Frere which Mr. Canning has submitted. (13931)

3734 VISCOUNT CASTLEREAGH *to the* KING

[*St. James's Square, 7 Oct. 1808.*] Lord Castlereagh has humbly to submit to your Majesty the accompanying letters received from Lt.-Genl. Sir Arthur Wellesley, as explanatory of the circumstances under which he solicited and obtain'd leave of absence from the Commander of your Majesty's forces in Portugal.[1] (13932)

3735 LORD HAWKESBURY *to the* KING, *and the reply*

[*London, 11 Oct. 1808.*] Lord Hawkesbury begs leave most humbly to submit to your Majesty a draft of the answer which it is proposed by your Majesty's confidential servants should be returned by your Majesty to the City Address tomorrow. (13933)

[*The King's reply, Windsor Castle, 12 Oct.*] The King entirely approves of the proposed answer to the Address of the City of London which Lord Hawkesbury has submitted. (13933)

[1] Robert Ward wrote to his patron Lord Lonsdale on the 10th: 'On his [Wellesley's] arrival he was sent to by that pushing fellow Stockdale who, with great professions of admiration, hoped to be honoured by publishing anything he might please to draw up in his defence—to which Sir Arthur replied that he meant to publish nothing whatever, knowing no doubt the people of England would very soon do him justice.' (Lonsdale MSS.)

'It appears to me to be quite impossible we can go on as we are now constituted,' Wellesley wrote to Sir John Moore on 17 Sept. 'The Commander-in-Chief must be changed, and the country and the army naturally turn their eyes to you as their Commander.' Wellesley arrived in London on 6 Oct.

3736 *Letters from* GEORGE CANNING *to the* KING

[*Foreign Office, 12 Oct. 1808.*] Mr. Canning humbly submits for your Majesty's gracious approbation the draft of an answer from your Majesty to the King of Sweden's letter, which accompanied the Russian flag. (13934)

[*Foreign Office, 13 Oct.*] Mr. Canning most humbly submits for your Majesty's royal signature the letter from your Majesty to the King of Sweden, with the alteration made in it by your Majesty. (13936)

3737 SPENCER PERCEVAL *to the* KING, *and the reply*

[*Downg. St., 13 Oct. 1808.*] Mr. Perceval humbly takes leave to inclose to his Majesty a short statement of the comparative produce of the Consolidated Fund for the quarters ending Oct. 10 1807 and 1808. His Majesty will thereby be gratified to see that the produce of the present year as well as the excess beyond the charge is greater than it was in the former year. This account appears to Mr Perceval so very satisfactory considering all the circumstances which have attended the present situation [of] affairs that he humbly trusts his Majesty will think it sufficient to justify him in troubling his Majesty with that communication. (13937)

[*The King's reply, Windsor Castle, 14 Oct.*] The King has received with much pleasure from Mr Perceval the statement of the comparative produce of the Consolidated Fund for the October quarters in 1807 & 1808 which presents so satisfactory a report of the public revenue. (13938)

3738 *Letters from* VISCOUNT CASTLEREAGH *to the* KING, *and the reply*

[*St. James's Square, 13 Oct. 1808.*] Lord Castlereagh humbly submits for your Majesty's royal approbation the accompanying instructions to your Majesty's Commanders in Portugal and Sicily. (13935)

[*From Lord Castlereagh, St. James's Square, 13 Oct.*] Lord Castlereagh humbly requests your Majesty's permission to absent himself from town for some days. He proposes to go to Dover, but will hold himself in readiness to return either upon Sir Hew Dalrymple's arrival, or upon any other publick business that may arise. (13940)

[*The King's reply, Windsor Castle, 14 Oct.*] The King approves of the instructions for the commanders of his forces in Portugal and in Sicily, and his Majesty has not any objection to Lord Castlereagh absenting himself from London for a few days. (13940)

3739 GEORGE CANNING *to the* KING

[*Foreign Office, 14 Oct. 1808.*] Mr. Canning humbly lays before your Majesty an extract of the letter which he humbly mentioned to your Majesty on Wednesday, as having been received by Baron Raigersfeldt from Count Stadion. (13941)

3740 LORD MULGRAVE *to the* KING, *and the reply*

[*Admiralty, 14 Oct. 1808.*] Lord Mulgrave has the honour to transmit to your Majesty a dispatch from Vice-Admiral Sir James Saumarez brought to the Admiralty this day by Capt. Martin of the Implacable; together with a narrative of the recent operations in the Baltick, drawn up by that officer. Lord Mulgrave humbly hopes that it may appear to your Majesty that nothing which zeal could suggest or activity effect has been omitted by Vice-Admiral Saumarez and the officers under his command; and that the escape of the enemy has been owing solely to the impracticability of attacking them in their position at Baltick port [*sic*].

Lord Mulgrave most humbly conceives that considering the relative circumstances of the naval Powers of the Baltick it may be highly expedient not only for the protection of the trade of your Majesty's subjects, but for the security of Sweden at the opening of the Baltick in the spring, that a considerable squadron of your Majesty's ships should pass the winter at Marstrand; from whence they would watch the motions of the Danes and interrupt their communication with Norway; they would be at the same time ready to follow the progress of the thaw into the Baltick, & effectually prevent any attempt which Russia (from the superior condition of her navy) might meditate against Sweden before a fleet could arrive from England. The presence of a British naval force in a Swedish port during the winter would not only give confidence to the Swedish nation, but would probably remove from the mind of the King of Sweden any impression of dissatisfaction or apprehension which may have been created by the return to Russia of the seamen under the command of Admiral Siniavin.

Under these impressions Lord Mulgrave begs leave most humbly to propose to your Majesty that five sail of the line, under the command of Rear-Admiral Sir Richard Keats, should be stationed in the port of Marstrand (which is not frozen during the winter) with instructions for the performance of the several services herein humbly submitted for your Majesty's consideration. (13942–3)

[*The King's reply, 15 Oct.*] The King is satisfied that the escape of the Russian fleet can never be ascribed to any want of zeal or activity on the part of Sir James Saumarez and the officers under his command. His Majesty approves of Lord Mulgrave's proposal that five sail of the line should be stationed in the port of Marstrand during the winter. (13943)

3741   LORD HAWKESBURY *to the* KING, *and the reply*

[*Walmer Castle, 14 Oct. 1808.*] Lord Hawkesbury begs leave most humbly to submit to your Majesty that there does not appear to your Majesty's confidential servants to be any business which need render it necessary for your Majesty to give yourself the trouble of coming to town on Wednesday next if your Majesty shall be pleased to put off your next private Levée till Wednesday the 26 instant. (13944)

[*The King's reply, Windsor Castle, 16 Oct.*] The King has received Lord Hawkesbury's letter, and as there is no probability of any business on Wednesday next, his Majesty will not go to town. (13944)

3742   LORD MULGRAVE *to the* KING, *and the reply*

[*Admiralty, 15 Oct. 1808.*] Lord Mulgrave begs your Majesty's gracious permission to go to Cheltenham for a fortnight for the benefit of his health. (13945)

[*The King's reply, Windsor Castle, 16 Oct.*] The King readily acquiesces in Lord Mulgrave's wish to go to Cheltenham & hopes that a fortnight's stay there will be of benefit to his health. (13945)

3743   *Letters from* GEORGE CANNING *to the* KING, *and the replies*

[*Foreign Office, 19 Oct. 1808, 1 p.m.*] Mr. Canning most humbly requests your Majesty's forgiveness for intruding on your Majesty at an unusual hour with the notice just received by telegraph at the Admiralty of the arrival of 300 of your Majesty's Asturian sheep at Portsmouth, a copy of which telegraph message, as transmitted to him from the Admiralty, Mr. Canning humbly takes the liberty of subjoining.[1] (13946)

[*From Canning, Foreign Office, 21 Oct., 5.30 p.m.*] Mr. Canning, though he very unwillingly presumes to break in upon your Majesty with this intelligence at an unusual hour, yet feels it his duty to lose no time in humbly acquainting your Majesty that two messengers from *Erfurth*, (French & Russian) have arrived in the Downs, & are on their way up to London. This intelligence is just received by telegraph from Deal.[2] (13947)

[1] Taylor replied to this note at 6 p.m. that day: 'The King has honored me with his commands to acknowledge your letter and to return you thanks for the immediate information of the arrival of part of his merino sheep at Portsmouth. Also to acquaint you that his Majesty has ordered Mr. Snart to proceed to Portsmouth to give the necessary directions for the further disposal of the sheep & that he is the bearer of a letter to Commissioner Grey on the subject. The King observed that it was not in his power to take any steps previous to the arrival of the sheep, as he was ignorant to what port they would be sent, or when they were likely to quit Gijon.' (Harewood MSS.)

[2] Taylor replied to this note at 9.30 p.m. that day: 'The King has commanded me to acknowledge the receipt of your letter and to say that although the arrival of messengers from Erfurth is unexpected, his Majesty is persuaded that any communication from that quarter can only be intended as one of those tricks by which Buonaparte endeavors to impose upon the public mind.' (Harewood MSS.)

[*From Canning, Bruton Street, Friday night, 21 Oct.*] Mr. Canning humbly lays before your Majesty two letters which he has received by the Russian & French messengers, whose arrival he humbly announced to your Majesty today, the one from Count Nicholas Romanzoff, the other from Mr. Champagny:[1] as well as two letters addressed to your Majesty by the Emperor of Russia & Buonaparté.

With respect to these last two letters Mr. Canning has most humbly to intreat your Majesty's forgiveness if he has done wrong: but not being accompanied with copies, Mr. Canning, after some hesitation, felt it to be his duty to open them.

The French messenger was charged with the accompanying letters to her Majesty the Queen, & to their Royal Highnesses the Princesses Augusta & Elizabeth, which were delivered to him by the Duke of Weimar. (13948–9)

[*The King's reply, Windsor Castle, 22 Oct.*] The communications from Erfurth which Mr Canning has forwarded to the King are what his Majesty expected them to be when informed of the arrival of the messengers, nor are the contents calculated to alter his opinion of the motives. The proposal of the uti possidetis as a basis is that which gave rise to so much quibble on the part of the French Government in the last negociation, and the circumstances are so materially altered by Buonaparte's subsequent usurpations in various quarters. Upon the whole the King considers that the restoration of the Royal families of Spain and Portugal to their just rights and authority, and the entire independence and integrity of their kingdoms as a previous measure, should be declared the only condition upon which his Majesty can pay any attention to the present very general and loose proposal, as it is the only principle which can prove satisfactory to this country. The King trusts his Ministers will see the subject in the same light, and will take full time to consider of the answer to be given to proposals so insidious, and which are probably only intended to produce paragraphs in the Moniteur.[2] (13950)

[*From Canning, Bulstrode, 22 Oct.*] Mr. Canning most humbly acquaints your Majesty that, feeling all the importance of taking full time for your Majesty's confidential servants to consider of the answer to be returned to the overtures from Erfurth, & feeling also the impropriety of allowing the French & Russian messengers to remain here without ascertaining distinctly that an equal admission would be given to English messengers in France, he thought it right to send back the two messengers early this morning. As the messengers required receipts for the delivery of the dispatches with which they were charged, Mr. Canning wrote a few lines to Mr. Champagny & to the Russian Ambassador at Paris, merely acknowledging the receipt of the communications from Erfurth & intimating that the answers would be sent by an English messenger.

Mr. Canning has felt it his duty to defer bringing this important subject under consideration until a full attendance of your Majesty's confidential servants can

[1] The French Foreign Minister since 1807.

[2] These proposals for a peace settlement from the two Emperors at Erfurt, dated 12 Oct., were rejected by the British Government on the 28th.

be procured, for which purpose he has sent notice to all those of them who are absent from town: & he apprehends therefore that he may not be enabled to submit to your Majesty the humble opinion and advice of your Majesty's servants before Tuesday or Wednesday. (13951–2)

[*The King's reply, Windsor Castle, 23 Oct.*] The King entirely approves of Mr Canning's having sent back the Russian and French messengers with the letters of which he has submitted the copies. His Majesty strongly recommends that on a subject of so much importance full time should be taken to consider and that no decision should be hastily adopted. (13952)

[*From Canning, Foreign Office, 24 Oct.*] Mr. Canning humbly submits to your Majesty the copies of the credential letter of Mr. Brinkmann, & of the re-credential letter of Mr. Adlerberg: & humbly to request to receive your Majesty's pleasure for presenting Mr. Brinkmann to your Majesty, & introducing Mr. Adlerberg for his audience of leave on Wednesday. Mr. Canning has also humbly to request to know if your Majesty would be graciously pleased to allow the Marquis of Douglas on his return from the Continent to pay his duty to your Majesty on Wednesday. (13953)

[*The King's reply, Windsor Castle, 25 Oct.*] The King approves of Mr Canning's appointing Messrs de Brinckman & d'Adlerberg & the Marquis of Douglas to attend at the Queen's Palace tomorrow. (13954)

[*From Canning, Foreign Office, 25 Oct.*] Mr. Canning humbly apprehends that your Majesty will be graciously pleased to forgive his not being enabled humbly to lay before your Majesty tonight the result of the deliberations of your Majesty's confidential servants upon the overtures from Erfurth: the substance of which he will, with your Majesty's gracious permission, state to your Majesty tomorrow. (13955)

3744   THE DUKE OF PORTLAND *to the* KING

[*Burlington House, Tuesday, 25 Oct. 1808.*] The Duke of Portland most humbly begs leave to lay before your Majesty for your Majesty's royal signature the accompanying warrant for a moiety of the pension of six hundred pounds per annum which your Majesty has been graciously pleased to grant to the Earl of Portmore.[1] (13956)

3745   *Letters from* VISCOUNT CASTLEREAGH *to the* KING, *and the reply*

[*St. James's Square, 26 Oct. 1808.*] Lord Castlereagh begs leave humbly to acquaint your Majesty with reference to that part of Sir D. Baird's letter which relates to money, that as the troops were subsisted previous to their sailing for

---

[1] Lord Glenbervie described him in 1809 as 'a miserable, starved skeleton'. (*Journals*, II, 33.)

two months, and as it was expected that the Paymaster-Genl. of the Army would immediately arrive at Corunna from Portugal, it was not deem'd necessary to send with this corps a separate military chest, there being reason to suppose that drafts on the Treasury could be liquidated at Corunna to an extent sufficient to carry on the service till the actual arrival of the Paymaster-General from the Tagus. As there may be some delay in his communications with Sir D. Baird's corps, in consequence of the determination taken to move the troops by land from Lisbon, a supply of dollars has been this day order'd to be forwarded to Corunna for the separate use of the troops to be landed at that place. (13957–8)

[*From Castlereagh, Downing Street, 27 Oct.*] Your Majesty's confidential servants having taken into their consideration the proceedings which it may be most adviseable for your Majesty to institute for the purpose of investigating the late armistice and Convention concluded in Portugal, are humbly of opinion that a court of enquiry is upon the whole better adapted to the nature of this case than a court martial.

Should your Majesty be graciously pleased to approve of this their humble suggestion, Lord Castlereagh submits for your Majesty's consideration the draft of a warrant which has been prepared by your Majesty's Judge Advocate, which is framed with a view not only to open to the investigation of the Court the entire [*sic*] of the case, but to make it their duty to pronounce fully a judgment upon the whole of it.

A letter to his Royal Highness the Commander-in-Chief is also submitted for your Majesty's approbation. (13959–60)

[*The King's reply, Windsor Castle, 28 Oct.*] The King approves of the warrant for instituting an enquiry into the late armistice and Convention concluded in Portugal which Lord Castlereagh has submitted, as also of the letter to the Duke of York in regard to it. (13960)

3746   *Letters from* GEORGE CANNING *to the* KING, *and the replies*

[*Foreign Office, 27 Oct. 1808.*] Mr. Canning most humbly submits for your Majesty's royal approbation the drafts of the answers which, after full deliberation, it has appeared to your Majesty's confidential servants most adviseable to return, in the first instance, to the overtures received from Erfurth: as also the draft of a dispatch to Mr Frere in which it is proposed to inclose copies of this correspondence to be communicated to the Central Government of Spain. (13961)

[*The King's reply, Windsor Castle, 28 Oct.*] The King approves most thoroughly of the answers which Mr Canning has prepared to the communications from Erfurth and of the letter to Mr Frere. In the latter, however, it has occurred to his Majesty that in two different places France is named before Russia, and he therefore suggests whether in a dispatch which may be shown to the Spanish Government the names of the Emperor of Russia and his Ministers should not stand first;

Russia being a Government acknowledged by his Majesty, while that now existing in France is not. (13962)

[*From Canning, Foreign Office, 28 Oct.*] Mr. Canning humbly presumes to lay before your Majesty a second time the draft of the official Note written in answer to the overtures from Erfurth, having made some slight changes in the latter part of it which he humbly hopes your Majesty will not disapprove. The alterations which your Majesty condescended to point out in the draft to Mr Frere have of course been adopted.

Mr. Canning has this day received from Admiral Apodaca[1] his Letter of Credence as Chargé d'Affaires from the Central Government of Spain; & humbly requests to receive your Majesty's commands as to the presentation of Admiral Apodaca to your Majesty in that character on Wednesday. (13963)

[*The King's reply, Windsor Castle, 29 Oct.*] The King approves of the alterations in the official Note in answer to the overtures from Erfurth which Mr Canning has submitted, as they have certainly rendered the concluding parts more explicit.

H.M. will receive Admiral Apodaca on Wednesday next as Chargé d'Affaires from the Central Government of Spain. (13964)

3747   *Letters from* LORD ELDON *to the* KING, *and the reply*

[*Bedford Square, 28 Oct. 1808.*] The Lord Chancellor, offering his most humble duty to your Majesty, has the honor to communicate to your Majesty that Charles Flower,[2] Esq, Alderman of the City of London, has been chosen Lord Mayor for the ensuing year, and the Lord Chancellor takes leave to enquire whether your Majesty thinks proper to sanction that choice by your Majesty's royal approbation of it. The Lord Chancellor believes himself to be justified in stating that this gentleman is a good Magistrate and a loyal subject. (13965)

[*The King's reply, Windsor Castle, 29 Oct.*] In consequence of the Chancellor's letter, the King readily sanctions the choice which the City of London has made of Alderman Flower as Lord Mayor for the ensuing year. (13965)

[*From Lord Eldon, Bedford Square, 29 Oct.*] The Lord Chancellor has the honour, after offering his most humble duty to your Majesty, to transmit a Commission for proroguing the Parliament to receive your Majesty's Royal Sign Manual, if your Majesty shall graciously so think fit.

The Lord Chancellor further humbly begs leave to apologise to your Majesty for his absence from the Queen's House on Wednesday last, at which he fully intended to have personally offered his most humble duty to your Majesty. He is happy that the circumstances which disappointed that intention did not prevent his being personally among your Majesty's confidential servants before the answer to Russia & France was finally considered. (13966)

[1] Admiral Don Juan Ruiz de Apodaca (1770–1835).
[2] Alderman of Cornhill since 1801. Created Baronet, Dec. 1809 (*d.* 1834).

[*Foreign Office, 30 Oct. 1808.*] Mr. Canning most humbly submits for your Majesty's royal approbation the name of Mr. Merry for the appointment of your Majesty's Envoy Extraordinary & Minister Plenipotentiary to the Court of Stockholm: and that of Mr Augustus Foster,[1] who is at present absent on leave from his post as Secretary of Legation in America,[2] as Secretary of Legation to Mr. Merry's Mission. He requests your Majesty's gracious pleasure, as to the presentation of Mr. Merry & Mr. Foster to your Majesty on Wednesday next. (13967)

[*The King's reply, Windsor Castle, 31 Oct.*] The King acquiesces in Mr Canning's recommendation of Mr Merry for the appointment of Minister at the Court of Stockholm & of Mr. Foster for that of Secretary of Legation, and H.M. will receive both these gentlemen on Wednesday next at the Queen's Palace. (13968)

[*From Canning, Foreign Office, 1 Nov.*] Mr. Canning humbly lays before your Majesty a very extraordinary Note received yesterday from the Chevalier de Souza, & submits at the same time for your Majesty's royal approbation the draft of an answer proposed, in the first instance, to be returned to it. He submits also a note from the Prince Castelcicala, with the draft of an answer. (13969)

[*The King's reply, Windsor Castle, 2 Nov.*] The King approves of the answer which Mr Canning proposes in the first instance to return to the extraordinary Note from the Chevalier de Souza, whose object it evidently is to get all the power into his own hands. (13969)

3749   LORD HAWKESBURY *to the* KING

[*Charles Street, 2 Nov. 1808.*] Lord Hawkesbury begs leave most humbly to submit to your Majesty the warrant appointing Commissioners to enquire into the administration of justice in Scotland, for your Majesty's royal signature. (13970)

3750   GEORGE CANNING *to the* KING

[*Bruton Street, 4 Nov. 1808, 11.30 a.m.*] Mr Canning deems it his duty humbly to submit to your Majesty the accompanying letters from Count Romanzow & Mr. Champagny immediately upon their arrival, although they contain nothing

---

[1] Sir Augustus John Foster (1780–1848), diplomatist. Secretary of Legation, 1808–10, and Chargé d'Affaires at Stockholm, 1809–10; Minister to the U.S.A., 1811–12; Minister to Denmark, 1814–24, and to Sardinia, 1825–40. M.P. for Cockermouth, 1812–16. Knighted, 1825. Baronetcy, 30 Sept. 1831. His father was John Foster, M.P. [I.], and his mother, Lady Elizabeth Foster, later (1809) Duchess of Devonshire. But according to the *chronique scandaleuse* he was related to the Royal Family. Canning, however, wrote (22 April 1809): 'Mr. Canning had learnt from Comte d' Antraigues that Baron d'Armfeldt conceives himself to be father of Augustus Foster.' (Bagot, *Canning and his Friends*, I, 281, 302.)

[2] This appointment is not noticed in *British Diplomatic Representatives, 1789–1852.*

more than the acknowledgement of the receipt of those despatched from hence by the messenger Shawe[1] on Friday last.

The only intelligence brought by the messenger is that Buonaparte left Rambouillet on the morning of the 30th, as it was supposed, for Spain.[2] (13971)

3751 LORD CHARLES SPENCER *to the* KING

[*4 Nov. 1808.*] When I last presumed to petition your Majesty for an appointment of Groom of the Bedchamber for my eldest son,[3] I understood there was at that time a vacancy, which I afterwards learnt was not so; but now that there is an actual vacancy by the appointment of General Harcourt to the office of Master of the Robes,[4] I venture to renew my petition, trusting in your Majesty's gracious goodness towards me that I shall be forgiven if from my anxiety to have my son in your Majesty's service I should have too frequently troubled your Majesty with my request.

Should your Majesty be pleased to grant this petition, though it is scarcely possible to add to my gratitude, it will be a great addition to my happiness. (13972–3)

3752 VISCOUNT CASTLEREAGH *to the* KING,[5] *and the reply*

[*Downing Street, 7 Nov. 1808.*] Lord Castlereagh presumes humbly to submit to your Majesty a letter he has received from Sir Hew Dalrymple, together with the answer which appeared to him proper to be returned thereto. Lord Castlereagh trusts it is unnecessary to assure your Majesty of his total ignorance of the paragraph alluded to, but it did not appear to Lord Castlereagh that he could give that assurance in terms to Sir Hew Dalrymple without establishing a precedent which would expose your Majesty's service to the inconvenience of having questions put at the option of any individual to your Majesty's Ministers at any time and on any subject upon no better grounds than Sir Hew Dalrymple has proceeded upon in the present instance, to which if they hesitated to give a direct answer, the most unjust and injurious inference might be drawn. (13976–7)

[1] John Schaw (the spelling in the Red Book).

[2] Taylor replied to this note at 5 p.m. that day: 'The King has honored me with his commands to acknowledge the receipt of your letter and the accompanying letters from Count Romanzow and Mr. Champagny. I take this opportunity of acquainting you that I shewed Princess Elizabeth your letter relative to the packet for the Dss. of Wurtemberg, and that the Queen and the Princesses expressed themselves very sensible of your obliging attention to their wishes.' (Harewood MSS.)

[3] In 1806 he had asked for the Bedchamber for himself. See No. 2989. John Spencer was Receiver-General of the Land Tax for Oxfordshire from 1804 to 1831. In 1790 he married his cousin Lady Elizabeth Spencer, daughter of George, Duke of Marlborough. His was not a very happy family. His father and mother had long been separated, and at the age of 78 Lord Charles was forced to retire to the Continent to escape imprisonment for debt. His son was a worthless, vicious character, later (in 1815) scandalising society by committing incest with his daughters.

Lord Charles Spencer appears in the Red Book for 1808 for the first time as a Lord of the Bedchamber (salary, £1000 a year).

[4] General Harcourt held this office from 1808 to 1809, then becoming Master of the Horse to the Queen.   [5] Not in Castlereagh's own hand.

[The King's reply, Windsor Castle, 8 Nov.] The King has received Lord Castle-reagh's letter and the accompanying correspondence with Sir Hew Dalrymple, from which it is very clear that Lord Castlereagh could not furnish the copies of letters which were never received. (13977)

3753 LORD HAWKESBURY *to the* KING, *and the reply*

[London, 7 Nov. 1808.] Lord Hawkesbury begs leave most humbly to lay before your Majesty the letter which he has received from the Earl of Coventry in consequence of the communication which Lord Hawkesbury made to him by your Majesty's command, expressing your Majesty's gracious approbation of his Lordship's services as Lord Lieutenant of the county of Worcester, and informing him of your intention to appoint Lord Deerhurst[1] to succeed him.

Lord Hawkesbury begs at the same time to inform your Majesty that in consequence of the notification of your Majesty's pleasure to the Duke of Portland, he has acquainted your Majesty's confidential servants that it is not your Majesty's intention to hold a Levée before Wednesday the 16th instant. (13978)

[The King's reply, Windsor Castle, 8 Nov.] The King acknowledges the receipt of Lord Hawkesbury's letter and that inclosed from Lord Coventry, and his Majesty is glad that the communication made to Lord Coventry has afforded him satisfaction. (13979)

3754 MISS[2] ARIANA MARGARET EGERTON *to the* KING

[Windsor, 8 Nov. 1808.] Your Majesty's goodness to me is so deeply impressed upon my mind, and has been so entirely my support and comfort in all the difficulties and distress which I have been subjected to by the pecuniary circumstances of those nearest and dearest to me, that I humbly venture to persuade myself that your Majesty will pardon me for presuming, in remembrance of the communication which your Majesty most graciously condescended to make to me of your Majesty's having signified your pleasure to your Majesty's Lord Chamberlain, the Earl of Dartmouth, that my nephew Mr. Master should at a proper time be appointed a gentleman usher, to express my most humble and anxious hope that the promotion of Colonel Capel[3] may be considered by your Majesty as a proper opportunity for my nephew's receiving this great mark of your Majesty's royal favour.

Sensible as I am that the happiness of my life is entirely owing to your Majesty, and that it wholly depends upon the continuance of your Majesty's protection, I tremble at the apprehension of incurring your Majesty's displeasure by the step

---

[1] George William Coventry, 7th Earl of Coventry (1758–1831), styled Viscount Deerhurst until he succeeded his father on 3 Sept. 1809. Lord Lieutenant of Worcestershire, Nov. 1808 until his death.

[2] Mrs. by courtesy.

[3] Thomas Edward Capel (1770–1855), a son of the 4th Earl of Essex. Colonel, 1803; Major-General, 1814; General, 1846. On 6 Feb. 1809 he was presented at the Levée following his appointment as a Groom of the Bedchamber.

I am now taking, but I so much more dread the possibility of appearing forget-full or unmindfull of the benefits which your Majesty was pleased to intimate your intention of conferring upon my nephew Mr. Master, that that consideration has superseded the fear of being thought importunate by your Majesty.

I most earnestly implore your Majesty's favourable construction of the motives of my conduct, and your Majesty's indulgent acceptance of the reasons which I most humbly offer for it.[1] (13984–5)

3755 LORD MULGRAVE *to the* KING, *and the reply*

[*Admiralty, 8 Nov. 1808.*] Lord Mulgrave has the honour humbly to report to your Majesty that the Duke of Clarence, at a conference appointed by his Royal Highness, required of Lord Mulgrave as an act of official duty to lay before your Majesty the offer of his Royal Highness to serve in the command of your Majesty's Fleet in the Mediterranean seas. Although it has not been the practice of the person presiding at the Board of Admiralty to lay before your Majesty all the customary proffers of service made by the Admirals of your Majesty's Navy, Lord Mulgrave deems it incumbent upon him not to hesitate in obeying the demand of a Prince of your Majesty's Royal family. As the measure of carrying into effect the intention of his Royal Highness would involve considerations of delicacy and of high importance, Lord Mulgrave humbly begs your Majesty's permission to consult with your Majesty's other confidential servants before he presumes to submit any opinion to your Majesty's judgment. (13982)

[*The King's reply, Windsor Castle, 9 Nov.*] The King has received Lord Mulgrave's letter respecting the offer of service made by the Duke of Clarence, and his Majesty considers his mode of proceeding upon the subject to be the most proper. (13983)

3756 VISCOUNT CASTLEREAGH *to the* KING, *and the reply*

[*Downing St., 8 Nov. 1808.*] Mr. Joliffe having declined to proceed to Surinam to take upon himself the Government of that Colony, Lord Castlereagh begs leave humbly to recommend to your Majesty Mr Charles Bentinck as a proper person to be entrusted with that situation. Mr. Bentinck is prepared to go out immediately should your Majesty be graciously pleased to confer upon him this trust.[2] (13980)

[1] Col. Taylor wrote to Lord Dartmouth on the 8th: 'In consequence of Col. Capel's promotion to the situation of a Gentleman of the Bedchamber, I am honored with the King's command to remind your Lordship of the intention which he expressed three years ago that Mr. Master should at a favorable opportunity be appointed to the situation of Gentleman Usher.' (13985)

[2] Lord Malmesbury wrote in his diary: 'It was through the Duke of Portland that, in October 1808, I learnt the first intimation of Austria's disposition to go to war with France. It came to him through Charles Bentinck, who had it from his brother, Monsieur de Rhoon.' (*Diaries and Corresp.*, IV, 408.)

According to the Red Book (1810) Major-General Sir Charles Green remained Governor of Surinam. Henry Bentinck was Governor of Demerara and Essequibo.

[*The King's reply, Windsor Castle, 10 Nov.*] The King acquiesces in Lord Castle-reagh's recommendation of Mr Charles Bentinck for the Government of Surinam. (13981)

3757 THE DUKE OF PORTLAND *to the* KING

[*Bulstrode, Friday, 11 Nov. 1808.*] The Duke of Portland humbly begs leave to submit to your Majesty for your Majesty's royal signature warrants for the pensions which your Majesty was some time since graciously pleased to grant to the following persons, namely, to the Earl of Erroll[1] in consideration of the in-adequacy of his fortune to his high rank & more particularly in compensation of the fees belonging to his high office of Hereditary Constable of Scotland which were lost at the time of the Union; to Mrs Rose,[2] with survivorship to her two daughters & the survivor of them, to Mr Maclaurin & to Susan Smollet, spinster, to each of whom your Majesty was pleased to grant an annual allowance of £100 at the instance of your Majesty's Lord Advocate.[3] (13986)

3758 VISCOUNT CASTLEREAGH *to the* KING, *and the reply*

[*Downing Street, 13 Nov. 1808.*] Lord Castlereagh begs leave humbly to submit to your Majesty the accompanying drafts to Sir John Moore which have been prepared upon conference with his Royal Highness the Commander-in-Chief, and have since been consider'd by your Majesty's confidential servants. (13987)

[*The King's reply, Windsor Castle, 14 Nov.*] The King approves of the instructions which Lord Castlereagh has prepared for Sir John Moore. (13987)

3759 GEORGE CANNING *to the* KING, *and the reply*

[*Foreign Office, 15 Nov. 1808.*] Mr. Canning most humbly submits to your Majesty whether your Majesty would be graciously pleased to allow that Mr John Villiers, whose name Mr. Canning has most humbly submitted to your Majesty for a Special Mission to Portugal, should be presented to your Majesty, on that appointment, at the Queen's Palace tomorrow.[4]

[1] William, 17th Earl of Erroll [S.] (1772–1819), succeeded his brother in the peerage, 14 June 1798. Representative Peer, 1806–7 and 1818–19. On 15 Feb. 1809 the Dowager Countess was given a pension of £100 a year.

[2] Mrs. Mary Rose was still receiving a pension of £97 a year in 1830, dating from 1808. So was Susan Smollet.

[3] Archibald Colquhoun (*d.* 1820). M.P. for the Elgin Burghs, 1807–10; for Dumbartonshire, 1810–20. Lord Advocate, 1807–16; Lord Clerk Register, 1816–20.

[4] Francis Jackson wrote on the 8th: 'This is an appointment that excites no small surprise and merriment even amongst the friends of the new Minister, and it seems to be not at all understood what could have occasioned it. Villiers is a man turned of fifty who has all his life been doing nothing: a mere courtier, famous for telling interminably long stories. Somebody was saying the other day that V.'s Mission must be a very short one, for that he would in fact be *obliged* soon to return, upon which Lord Bathurst observed that it could hardly be very short, as they must allow him to stay abroad long enough to tell one story.' (*Diaries of George Jackson*, II, 302.)

Mr. Canning has also humbly to request to know your Majesty's pleasure whether Admiral Apodaca, the Spanish Chargé d'Affaires, may be allowed to present to your Majesty tomorrow General Jacome & Mr. Sangro, the two Deputies from Andalusia & Galicia, previous to their returning to Spain. The Asturian Deputies are already gone. (13988)

[*The King's reply, Windsor Castle, 16 Nov.*] The King approves of Mr. Canning's appointing Mr. John Villiers to attend at the Queen's Palace this day, as also Admiral Apodaca with General Jacome & Mr. Sangro. (13989)

3760   THE DUKE OF PORTLAND *to the* KING,[1] *and the reply*

[*Burlington House, Tuesday, 15 Nov. 1808.*] The Duke of Portland humbly begs leave to acquaint your Majesty that the valuable living of Leverington in the county of Cambridge and in the patronage of the Bishop of Ely, having become vacant during the vacancy of the See,[2] is now at the disposal of your Majesty; and the Duke of Portland having fully satisfied himself of the very great gratification which the presentation of this benefice would afford to the Duke of Rutland, whose dutifull attachment to your Majesty was exemplarily manifested on a late occasion,[3] feels it to be his duty to lay this circumstance with all humility before your Majesty, and to submit to your Majesty the name of the Dean of Bristol[4] as a person worthy in all respects to be presented to it, and on whom your Majesty's conferring such a mark of your royal favour would impress the Duke of Rutland with the most lively and lasting sense of devotion. In consideration therefore of the uncertainty of the time during which your Majesty possesses the right of disposing of benefices under this predicament, and that that right determines at the moment at which the restitution of the temporalties of the See takes place, the Duke of Portland has presumed to desire Lord Hawkesbury forthwith to lay before your Majesty for your royal signature a proper instrument for the presentation of the Dean of Bristol to the Rectory of Leverington. (13991-2)

[*The King's reply, Windsor Castle, 16 Nov.*] The King acquiesces in the Duke of Portland's proposal that the living of Leverington should be conferred upon the Dean of Bristol. (13992)

    [1] Not in the Duke's own hand.
    [2] James Yorke, Bishop of Ely since 1781, had died, 26 Aug. 1808. His successor, Dr Thomas Dampier (1748–1812), who had been Bishop of Rochester since 1802, was nominated on 10 Sept. and confirmed on 22 Nov.
    [3] Does this refer to the sacrifice which the Duke had made the previous June in abandoning his recommendation of Dr Sparke for appointment as Bishop of Bristol? See No. 3673 n. He was always ready to put his votes in the Commons at the disposal of Ministers, and they were anxious to draw him into politics. In 1809 Ministers would have been glad to support his candidature for the Chancellorship of Cambridge University in the event of a vacancy.
    [4] Dr Bowyer Edward Sparke (c. 1759–1836). Tutor to the Duke of Rutland; Vicar of Scalford, Leics., 1800–5; Rector of Redmile, 1800–9; Vicar of St. Augustine-the-Less, Bristol, 1803–10; Dean of Bristol, 1803–9; Bishop of Chester, 1810; of Ely, 1812–36.

[*Admiralty, 15 Nov. 1808.*] Lord Mulgrave has the honour humbly to report to your Majesty that, under the sanction of your Majesty's gracious approval, he has consulted your Majesty's confidential servants upon the offer of service of his Royal Highness the Duke of Clarence. They are fully sensible of the impulse of zeal for your Majesty's service, which has dictated the proposal of his Royal Highness, but after the most attentive deliberation they are humbly of opinion that it would not be expedient to give effect to the offer of his Royal Highness, and they have authorized Lord Mulgrave to submit such, their humble advice, for your Majesty's judgment. (13990)

[*The King's reply, Windsor Castle, 16 Nov.*] The King has received Lord Mulgrave's letter and his Majesty is satisfied that in the communication to the Duke of Clarence [of] the opinion of his Cabinet that his offer of service cannot be accepted, he will be assured that the zeal which prompted him to make it is duly appreciated. (13991)

[*From Lord Mulgrave, Admiralty, 16 Nov.*] Lord Mulgrave has the honour humbly to submit for your Majesty's gracious consideration the draft of a letter to his Royal Highness the Duke of Clarence, which Lord Mulgrave has endeavoured to frame in conformity to the intimation of your Majesty's pleasure signified to him this morning. (13993)

[*The King's reply, Windsor Castle, 17 Nov.*] The King approves of the letter which Lord Mulgrave has prepared in reply to the Duke of Clarence's offer of service. (13993)

3762 GEORGE CANNING *to the* KING

[*Foreign Office, 23 Nov. 1808.*] Mr. Canning humbly submits for your Majesty's royal approbation the draft of a letter from your Majesty to the Prince Regent of Portugal, the copy of which letter Mr. Canning would humbly propose, if approved by your Majesty, to give to Mr J. Villiers as his Letter of Credence to the Regency at Lisbon. (13995)

3763 VISCOUNT CASTLEREAGH *to the* KING,[1] *and a reply*

[*St. James's Square, 23 Nov. [1808].*] Lord Castlereagh humbly begs leave to recommend to your Majesty Mr. Burton,[2] brother to the Earl of Conyngham,[3] to

---

[1] Castlereagh's next letter to the King seems to be missing from the Archives.

[2] Francis Nathaniel Burton (1766–1832). M.P. for Co. Clare, 1801–8. The new writ, following the resignation of his seat by taking the office of Escheator of Munster, was issued on 4 July 1808, and Augustine Fitzgerald was elected on 9 Aug.

[3] Lord Conyngham had recently (7 April) asked the Duke of Richmond for an Irish Marquessate. 'All my wishes would then be gratified and I should ever consider myself bound by gratitude as well as inclination to support by every means in my power the present Administration.' In Aug. 1807 he had asked Sir Arthur Wellesley for a U.K. peerage, 'but on Sir Arthur's expressing a doubt as to being

succeed Sir Robert Milnes in the Lieut.-Government of Lower Canada, your Majesty having been pleased to confer a pension on Sir R. Milnes on retiring from that situation.[1] (13994)

able to manage it, I mentioned that if an Irish Marquisate could be obtained with less difficulty, I should conceive it equally a proof of Government's willingness to oblige me, and remain perfectly satisfied.' (Wellington MSS.) 'Conyngham I have a personal regard for, but I think him unsteady as a politician. He might easily be led by the Prince,' the Duke of Richmond wrote, 19 Feb. 1808.

[1] Sir Robert Milnes' demands created much embarrassment and difficulty. Castlereagh wrote to Perceval (? 31 Oct., the letter being dated merely 'Monday'): 'I send you a letter from Sir R. Milnes. It is impossible for me after Col. Burton has given up his seat for the county of Clare to delay his appointment to the Lt.-Government of Lower Canada. He accepted the Chiltern Hundreds [sic] upon my assurance that Sir R. Milnes's arrangement would be completed in a few days, there being much reason then to fear that if the vacancy had been made when Parliament was not sitting, that an opponent might have been chosen for Clare. I gave him that assurance upon the Duke of Portland's authority, his Grace having received a letter from Sir R. Milnes or Lady Milnes, I forget which, from which he read me a paragraph stating their acquiescence in the arrangement in progress. I now understand there is some new difficulty, but I am sure the Duke of Portland will feel that after the repeated assurances given to Col. B. that all was arranged, and after he has sacrificed his parliamentary situation upon the faith of such assurances, that the office should not be withheld from him, till *surveys are* made, and a *township in Canada divided*.' (Perceval MSS.)

Milnes's letter of 29 Oct. was addressed to Castlereagh's Under-Secretary of State, Edward Cooke: 'I had the honour of receiving your letter of the 24th last night at Welbeck in answer to which I have only to say that I never have had the most distant idea of giving in my resignation of the Lt.-Government of Lower Canada, until Government has actually secured to me the retirement which has been promised me in lieu of my situation, & until the patent for my pension of £1000 net pr. annm. & that for Lady Milnes at my death of £600 net pr. annm. are actually sign'd by Government, as well as the grant of a township in Lower Canada *surveyed* & *subdivided*. I had the honour in a letter dated the 9th of July to submit to Lord Castlereagh my determination on this subject, & as I have not since that time received any official communication from his Lordship, I have no reason to think the arrangement you allude to is in greater forwardness than it was when I left town. I must therefore beg of you to submit to Lord Castlereagh that having held situations of high trust & confidence in his Lordship['s] Department from January 1795 & most faithfully discharged the duty of those situations, I claim at his Lordship's hand that justice which I am sure I may rely upon, & by which I feel myself entitled to retain the full possession of my Lt.-Government until I shall officially give in my resignation, which will be whenever the provision promised me has been finally completed & until which I shall be ready to do the duty of the situation whenever I am call'd upon.' (*Ibid.*)

Sir Arthur Wellesley wrote to Perceval from London on 10 June 1808: 'When the Government was formed last year Lord Castlereagh authorised me to assure Mr. Burton, the member for the County of Clare and the brother of Lord Conyngham, that he should be appointed the Lieutenant-Governor of Canada; and I had many discussions with the Duke of Portland respecting the mode of providing for Sir Robert Mills [sic] the present Lieutenant-Governor. At length it was settled that Sir Robert should have a pension of £400 per annum on the pension list of England; and £500 per annum on that of Ireland, as a compensation for his services, that he should vacate his office, and that Mr. Burton should be appointed to it as soon as the pensions could be granted, which was not before the 25th of March of this year.

'The Government have had the attendance and support of Mr. Burton, and of Mr. Montgomery, brought in by Lord Conyngham, for Donegal, and of Sir Edward O'Brien, the other member for the County of Clare, through the good offices of Mr. Burton and Lord Conyngham throughout this session; and he now presses that I should perform the engagement made to him; vizt. that he should be appointed Lieut.-Governor of Canada. The only difficulty in the arrangement is that of the pension here; upon which the Duke of Portland has desired me more than once to speak to you; but I have delayed to trouble you upon it, as I saw the multiplicity of business in which you was engaged; but as I shall probably soon be obliged to go, and as I am anxious not to leave the Government labouring under the imputation of a breach of faith I shall be obliged to you, if you will make such arrangements to give Sir Robert Mills his pension, as that Mr. Burton may be appointed to his office, and may vacate his seat before the close of the season.

'There will be no difficulty in giving Sir Robert his pension in Ireland, as it was provided for in the distribution of pensions which I laid before the King's Ministers last year; and the Lord Lieutenant and Lord Hawkesbury have consented to it.' (Wellington MSS.)

[*From the King, Windsor Castle, 25 Nov.*] The King approves of the instructions which Lord Castlereagh has prepared for Sir John Moore & Sir D. Baird under the unfortunate circumstances reported by the latter. The reports received hitherto are so loose that it is impossible to form any judgement, but his Majesty conceives it not impossible that the Spanish corps defeated is that which was collecting upon Burgos from Madrid & from Estremadura. (13996)

3764 THE REV. WILLIAM COOKSON *to the* KING

[*Binfield, 26 Nov.* [*1808*].] Having been already honoured with so many marks of your Majesty's undeserved favour, it is not without the greatest reluctance that I bring myself to prefer the present application to your Majesty. The object to which I aspire is the vacant Deanery of Salisbury. To exchange my Canonry of Windsor for that preferment might eventually prove highly advantageous to my family, as on account of the extensive patronage annexed to it, it might afford me the means of providing for one or more of my sons, should they, which is most probable, embrace the clerical profession. To which reason may I be permitted to add that several parishes in the immediate vicinity of my usual residence at Binfield being exempt from episcopal visitation are not only in the patronage but subject to the peculiar jurisdiction of the Dean?

Having made your Majesty acquainted with some of the reasons which induce me to lay this sollicitation at your Majesty's feet I trust that I shall at least obtain your Majesty's forgiveness for the presumption.[1] (13997–8)

[1] The application was unsuccessful: Dr Charles Talbot succeeded Dr John Ekins as Dean of Salisbury. The Duke of Cumberland wrote to Eldon in 1809 (the letter is undated): 'My old tutor Dr. Cookson, the clergyman you gave the Living of Benfield, a man of the highest respectability, called on me this morning and recalled to my recollection what had passed upon two former occasions with respect to himself, namely, that when the Deanery of Rochester was vacant by the nomination of that bright luminary of the Church, Dr. Goodenough, to his Bishopric [of Carlisle, 20 Jan. 1808] *he* was mentioned by his Majesty to the Duke of Portland for that situation, but Dr. Busby, the Duke of Richmond's secretary, got it last year when the Dean of Sarum died (I forget his name). His Majesty sent Cookson word through the Bishop of Sarum, *Fisher*, that he had not forgot Cookson but that the Duke of Portland was *so pressing* that he had waived his request. *Now*, as Dr. Powis is either dead or in the act of dying, he came to me on the subject. I recommended him to go forthwith to London to call on Perceval if he would see him then, to state *all* this verbally, otherwise to leave a letter saying he would remain in town till he could fix a time to see him, as there were many things he could not put to paper. By that I meant the King's name, and if Mr. Perceval would speak to me I could with the greatest truth assure him that I had heard his Majesty declare nobody was more entitled to a Deanery than Cookson. If you should write to Perceval in three days you may mention *this* as having heard from me. Besides, Cookson would vacate naturally the Canonry of Windsor *which*, I believe, being given to young Stopford would secure the Duke of Buccleuch's interest, and I understood some time back from the family of the Montagues that his Grace was sore on that subject.' (Eldon MSS.) Dr Cookson applied for the Deanery of Canterbury in 1809, but Perceval wrote to Eldon on 14 Oct. of that year: 'I think I can satisfy you I did right in telling him that in declining to mention his name to his Majesty upon this occasion, I was influenced by motives perfectly consistent with the respect which I believed to be due to his character and pretensions. The truth is that though I believe him to be a very respectable and deserving man, and if I had appointed him it would really have been upon the ground of his merit, yet that would not have been supposed to be the reason, and instead of having the fair credit for such an appointment, it would have been ascribed though not to improper yet certainly to less worthy motives.' (Eldon MSS.) See No. 3996.

3765 GEORGE CANNING *to the* KING, *and the reply*

[*28 Nov. 1808.*] Mr. Canning most humbly submits for your Majesty's royal approbation the drafts of instructions proposed to be given to Mr. Villiers for the conduct of his mission to Portugal. (13999)

[*The King's reply, Windsor Castle, 29 Nov.*] The King approves of the instructions which Mr Canning has prepared for Mr Villiers. (13999)

3766 THE DUKE OF PORTLAND *to the* KING,[1] *and the reply*

[*Bulstrode, Monday, 28 Nov. 1808.*] Sensible as the Duke of Portland must acknowledge himself to be of the impropriety of his presuming to lay before your Majesty the representation to which he now ventures to sollicit your Majesty's attention, the sense of duty which impells him to it is too powerfull to be resisted; and trusting that it will appear to your Majesty that he could not be urged to it by any inferior or other motive, he cannot but hope, whatever may be the result of his representation, that he shall obtain your Majesty's forgiveness.

The accident which your Majesty providentially escaped last Wednesday evening as your Majesty was returning from the Queen's Palace to Windsor Castle, has given rise to so much alarm and such apprehensions for the safety of your Majesty, that the Duke of Portland must beg leave to assure your Majesty that it is not more his wish than that of the rest of your Majesty's confidential servants, and of all your dutifull and loyal subjects, that your Majesty would condescend to spare yourself the trouble of coming to town, at least during the continuance of the short days and the uncertainty of the weather during this season of the year, which, if your Majesty would be graciously pleased to permit them, every one of your Majesty's confidential servants would be happy to render unnecessary by attending your Majesty at Windsor. But if your Majesty should deem it improper to indulge their anxious wishes in this respect, they would humbly beg leave to hope that your Majesty would condescend to give orders that another carriage should follow, in case any accident similar to that which happened last Wednesday should again take place, an event which but for her Majesty's being fortunately within a very short distance of your Majesty when it happened, might have detained your Majesty for a considerable time, exposed you to the inclemency of the night air, and subjected your Majesty to a greater variety of inconveniences than can easily be enumerated. For these and many other reasons, the Duke of Portland, at the unanimous instance of all your Majesty's confidential servants who were in town, as well as on his own behalf, most anxiously and earnestly implores your Majesty to have the goodness to receive this humble and dutifull representation with your usual favour; and that your Majesty will graciously condescend to attribute the Duke of Portland's conduct to the only motives which could have suggested it, his dutifull attachment

[1] Not in the Duke's own hand.

to your Majesty and his anxious wishes for the preservation of your Majesty's health.[1] (14000–2)

[*The King's reply, Windsor Castle, 29 Nov.*] The King is sensible of the motives which have dictated the Duke of Portland's letter to him, but his Majesty will go to town tomorrow as usual. The accident which occurred on Wednesday last was very immaterial, although these circumstances are always magnified beyond necessity, and his Majesty has every reason to be satisfied with the safety which has attended all his journies. (14003)

3767 *Letters from* VISCOUNT CASTLEREAGH *to the* KING, *and the reply*

[*St. James's Sq., 1 Dec. 1808.*] In addition to the official dispatches Lord Castlereagh presumes to submit to your Majesty an extract from a private letter from his brother B. Genl. Stewart dated on the 10th at Merida in Estremadura giving an account of the progress so far of the cavalry on their march into Spain. (14008)

[*From Castlereagh, Downing Street, 2 Dec.*] Your Majesty's confidential servants having deliberated on the intelligence received from Lt. Genl. Sir D. Baird, including his letter to Admiral de Courcey of the 23rd ult, are humbly of opinion that the measures in progress for embarking the cavalry should be proceeded in with the utmost despatch, and that the whole should be assembled at Falmouth, there to await your Majesty's further orders. They further beg leave humbly to recommend to your Majesty that the 5000 infantry now under orders for foreign service should be order'd to embark and proceed to Falmouth subject to such instructions as to their future destination as the progress of affairs in Spain and Portugal may point out. (14009)

[*The King's reply, Windsor Castle, 3 Dec.*] The King approves of the proposal submitted by Lord Castlereagh that the cavalry and the infantry under orders should be embarked and assembled at Falmouth, as it is specified that their departure from thence must depend upon the further accounts which may be received from Spain. (14010)

3768 *Letters from* GEORGE CANNING *to the* KING, *and the replies*

[*6 Dec. 1808.*] Mr. Canning humbly lays before your Majesty two Notes, from Count Nicholas Romanzow & Mr. Champagny, which were received this evening between six & seven o'clock by a Russian & French messenger from Paris. The hour of their arrival being so late, & the contents of the notes not being, in substance, very different from what might be expected, Mr Canning humbly

[2] At Turnham Green one of the leading horses on which the postilion was riding, fell, and threw him, but the carriage did not overturn. The Queen's carriage came up soon afterwards and took the King to Windsor.

conceived that he should best consult your Majesty's convenience in reserving them to be sent in the usual course of communication to your Majesty.

Mr. Canning most humbly submits at the same time for your Majesty's royal approbation the draft of the answer proposed to be returned to the communication received from Vienna. (14012–3)

[*The King's reply, Windsor Castle, 7 Dec.*] The King approves of Mr. Canning's not having sent the Notes from Messrs. de Romanzow & Champagny at an unusual and late hour, altho' the communication is satisfactory to his Majesty as bringing at once to issue the subject to which it relates. The answer which Mr. Canning has prepared to the communication from Vienna appears to the King perfectly proper. (14013)

[*From Canning, 8 Dec.*] Mr Canning humbly submits for your Majesty's royal consideration the drafts of the answer which, if approved by your Majesty, it is proposed to return to the letters received the day before yesterday from Paris. Mr. Canning takes the liberty of laying the letters themselves before your Majesty a second time, in order that your Majesty may have them under your Majesty's consideration, together with the proposed answers. (14018)

[*The King's reply, Windsor Castle, 9 Dec.*] The King approves of the answer which Mr. Canning has prepared to the letters received from Mr. Champagny and M. de Romanzow on the 6th instant.[1] (14019)

3769   VISCOUNT CASTLEREAGH *to the* KING,[2] *and the reply*

[*St. James's Square, 8 Dec. 1808.*] Your Majesty's confidential servants having taken into their consideration the dispatches this day received from Lieutt.-Generals Sir John Moore and Sir David Baird, are humbly of opinion that the requisition for tonnage to receive 2000 horses at Vigo should be immediately complied with, and that for this purpose the heavy brigade of cavalry should be disembarked at Portsmouth.

They humbly beg leave further to recommend to your Majesty that the 14th Light Dragoons now embarked at Falmouth, and the 600 horses for the service of the Artillery should be ordered to the Tagus. The artillery horses are considered indispensible to render the brigades left in Portugal moveable, and it is considered that an additional regiment of dragoons may not only be of much use in Portugal but will serve to demonstrate to the Spanish nation that in retiring the British army into Portugal your Majesty has not relinquished the hope of being enabled to support their exertions (if they shall continue to be made) against the common enemy.

[1] These diplomatic exchanges continued those arising out of the Erfurt meeting of the two Emperors in October. Whereas Champagny insisted that the Spanish insurgents should not be represented at a peace conference, Canning declared that such refusal must be regarded as precluding such negotiations.
[2] Not in Castlereagh's own hand.

They humbly conceive that it may be the more necessary to mark this determination in the arrangement now to be made, as the sending the empty transports
to Vigo, although intended to carry forward a part of the cavalry now in Gallicia
into Portugal might, if unaccompanied by any measure of reinforcement, create
an impression in Spain that the immediate return of the British army was decided
on. (14016–7)

[*The King's reply, Windsor Castle, 9 Dec.*] Under the state of things in Spain
which has been reported by Lieut.-General Sir John Moore and Sir David Baird,
the King must approve of the arrangements proposed by his confidential servants
for sending immediately to Vigo a further supply of horse transports, while his
Majesty equally acquiesces in the propriety of the principle upon which they have
submitted that the 14th Dragoons and the artillery horses should be sent to the
Tagus. (14020)

3770   LORD HAWKESBURY *to the* KING, *and the reply*

[*London, 9 Dec. 1808.*] Lord Hawkesbury begs leave most humbly to submit to
your Majesty that it has occur'd to your Majesty's confidential servants that very
considerable objections may be made to Monday as the day now fixed for the
meeting of Parliament. Lord Hawkesbury understands that it has been quite
unusual for Parliament to meet on a Monday for the dispatch of business and
various inconveniencies would arise from it both with respect to the usual custom
of reading your Majesty's Speech to the members of your Majesty's Privy Council
the day preceding, as well as with regard to the necessity under which it might
place many persons to travel on the Sunday. The day was originally fixed in
consequence of the objection to meeting on Tuesday, as the Report of the Address
must in that case have been delay'd till the day after her Majesty's birthday.
Under all these circumstances Lord Hawkesbury humbly submits it to your
Majesty as the opinion of of [*sic*] your Majesty's confidential servants that it
would be most adviseable that the meeting of Parliament should be defer'd till
Thursday the 19th of January and that a new Proclamation should be prepared for
that purpose. (14021–2)

[*The King's reply, Windsor Castle, 10 Dec.*] The King approves of the meeting of
Parliament being postponed to Thursday the 19th of Jany. next for the reasons
stated in Lord Hawkesbury's letter. The objections to Monday being so strong,
his Majesty is surprized that they did not occur previous to that day being fixed
upon and the Proclamation issued. (14022)

3771   *Letters from* GEORGE CANNING *to the* KING, *and the replies*

[*Foreign Office, 14 Dec. 1808.*] Mr. Canning humbly submits for your Majesty's
royal consideration the draft of a Declaration, which, if approved by your Majesty,
it is proposed to issue in your Majesty's name on the termination of the

intercourse arising out of the overtures from Erfurth. Mr. Canning most humbly entreats your Majesty's indulgence for his presuming to submit this paper in a printed form; humbly assuring your Majesty that this has been done only to avoid delay, & that the paper is not the less liable to any corrections or alterations which your Majesty may be graciously pleased to direct.[1] (14023)

[*The King's reply, Windsor Castle, 15 Dec.*] The King has read and approves of the Declaration submitted by Mr. Canning as perfectly proper in itself and well timed. (14024)

[*From Canning, Foreign Office, 15 Dec.*] Mr. Canning humbly submits for your Majesty's royal signature the instrument of Full Powers to Mr. Merry for enabling him to sign the Commercial Convention with Sweden which Mr. Thornton was employed to negotiate, but which his Swedish Majesty would not allow that gentleman to sign. (14025)

[*From Canning, Foreign Office, 16 Dec.*] Mr. Canning humbly lays before your Majesty the copy of Adml. Apodaca's Letter of Credence to your Majesty as Envoy Extraordinary & Minister Plenipotentiary from his Catholick Majesty: & humbly requests your Majesty's gracious pleasure for receiving Admiral Apodaca in that character to an audience of your Majesty on Wednesday next. (14026)

[*The King's reply, Windsor Castle, 17 Dec.*] The King approves of Mr Canning's appointing Admiral Apodaca to an audience on Wednesday next. (14026)

3772   LORD HAWKESBURY *to the* KING, *and the reply*

[*London, 17 Dec. 1808.*] I trust that I shall meet with your Majesty's forgiveness in addressing your Majesty for the purpose of informing you that my beloved father departed this life at six o'clock this morning after an illness of several days, during which we have the satisfaction of believing that he never suffer'd a moment's pain. I feel I owe it to his memory to add that to the last period of his life he never ceased to express the deep sense which he entertained of the many favours which he and his family had received from your Majesty, and to pray that the blessing of God might ever attend your Majesty. (14027)

[*The King's reply, Windsor Castle, 18 Dec.*] The King trusts it is unnecessary for him to assure Lord Hawkesbury of the sincere concern with which he learnt the death of Lord Liverpool. His Majesty having known and experienced, during a period of 48 years, his integrity and fidelity in the able discharge of his duty, must regret his loss on that account, no less than he condoles with Lord Hawkesbury upon an event so nearly affecting him. (14028)

[1] The official correspondence relating to the negotiations with Russia and France, received from Erfurt, is in *Parl. Deb.*, XII, 93–103; and the King's Declaration relative to these overtures is *ibid.*, 103–5, dated 15 Dec. 1808.

[*19 Dec. 1808.*] Mr. Canning humbly submits for your Majesty's royal signature the instrument of Full Powers to Mr. Adair for concluding & signing a Treaty of Peace between your Majesty & the Court of Vienna.[1] He submits also the draft of Full Powers to Mr Canning for signing a Treaty of Peace between your Majesty & Spain with Admiral Apodaca who has received Full Powers from his Government for that purpose.[2] And he submits for your Majesty's royal consideration the draft of a letter from your Majesty to the King of Abyssinia, in answer to one received by your Majesty from that Sovereign through Lord Valentia,[3] in the year 1807. (14029)

[*From Canning, Foreign Office, 22 Dec.*] Mr. Canning most humbly submits for your Majesty's royal consideration the draft of a dispatch which, if approved by your Majesty, it is proposed to send to Mr. Merry in answer to the dispatch received from that Minister yesterday. He submits at the same time for your Majesty's royal signature Mr. Merry's Letters of Recall, which it will be necessary to send with the dispatch, in the event of your Majesty's being graciously pleased to approve the draft. Mr. Canning proposes to accompany this dispatch with a private letter (in cypher) intimating to Mr. Merry for his consolation the gracious indulgence which your Majesty condescended to express yesterday with respect to the conduct which he had found himself compelled to observe under circumstances of so extraordinary & difficult a nature. (14030–1)

[*The King's reply, Windsor Castle, 23 Dec.*] The King entirely approves of the dispatch which Mr Canning has prepared for Mr. Merry. (14031)

[1] Adair, the Minister to Austria, had left Vienna in March 1808 and was appointed Plenipotentiary to Turkey in May 1808. He signed the Treaty with Turkey, 5 Jan. 1809. Lady Holland had written to Grey on 27 May, with reference to the debate on the Catholic Petition: 'I hardly know whether I was pleased or not at hearing that it was such a lucky thing for him [Adair] that he had not taken his seat, so could not vote upon this important question, because by that *fortunate* circumstance Mr. Canning was enabled to serve him by offering him the appointment to Turkey. I was told that Mr. Canning was a man of a very liberal mind, quite adverse to all party feelings and desirous of employing talents wherever he found them, and finding none to equal Adair's, was willing, if consistent with what was due to his own friends, to employ him, but if he voted, that would be impracticable.' (Howick MSS.) Lady Holland wondered whether Adair would be acting quite fairly, if he continued to hold the seat which he owed to the Duke of Bedford, and again carried off a vote. She thought Canning was eager to gain Lord Morpeth ('of which he has not the most distant chance'), and that that eagerness accounted for his generous offer to Adair. Adair would have seriously annoyed his Whig friends had he not offered to vacate his seat at Camelford. The Duke of Bedford felt unable to accept the offer (which was made at Lord Holland's suggestion), as he did not feel sufficiently secure at Camelford to risk a by-election at that time. The Treaty with Austria is referred to in the King's Message to the House of Commons on 25 May 1809. (*Parl. Deb.*, XIV, 696.)

[2] This 'Treaty of Peace, Friendship and Alliance', signed in London on 14 Jan. 1809, is in *Parl. Deb.*, XIII, 809.

[3] Viscount Valentia (1770–1844), so styled, 1793–1816, succeeded his father (1744–1816) as 2nd Earl of Mountnorris [I.]. M.P. for Yarmouth (Isle of Wight), 1808–10.

[*Downing Street, 23 Dec. 1808.*] Under the present circumstances of the war and amount of your Majesty's disposeable force employed in operations on the Continent, your Majesty's confidential servants consider it their indispensible duty humbly to recommend to your Majesty to call the attention of Parliament immediately on its meeting to the adoption of such measures for increasing the Regular Army as may enable your Majesty adequately to sustain the contest abroad without thereby unduly exposing the security of your Majesty's dominions at home.

It also appearing of the utmost importance that a British corps should be in readiness in the Tagus to proceed to Cadiz at the shortest notice, in case circumstances should render the Spaniards desirous of receiving the aid of British troops for the security of that place, and that it is highly desireable that the amount of force now under the orders of Sir John Moore, and upon which his arrangements have probably been already framed, should not be broken in upon for this object, however important in itself, your Majesty's confidential servants are therefore induced humbly to recommend that the 5000 infantry now under orders should forthwith proceed to the Tagus.

The accompanying instructions are submitted in execution of this purpose, should the measure itself be honoured with your Majesty's gracious approbation. Lord Castlereagh also presumes to submit to your Majesty a memorandum explanatory of the principles upon which it appears that your Majesty's Regular Army may be most speedily and effectually augmented at the present moment. Your Majesty's confidential servants are fully aware of the magnitude of the exertion which your Majesty's subjects are thus called upon to make, but they humbly conceive that it is not more than commensurate with the exigency of the crisis for which your Majesty's Government consider themselves bound in duty to your Majesty to make every exertion to provide. (14032–4)

[*The King's reply, Windsor Castle, 24 Dec.*] The King has received the memorandum from his confidential servants transmitted by Lord Castlereagh with the drafts of dispatches to Sir John Cradock & Sir John Moore, and a memorandum of the military force and of the measures proposed to augment it; all which under the present very extraordinary circumstances H.M. cannot but sanction. (14035)

3775 THE DUKE OF PORTLAND *to the* KING, *and the reply*

[*Bulstrode, Saturday, 24 Dec. 1808, 9 p.m.*] The Duke of Portland most humbly begs leave to acquaint your Majesty that he has this morning received a letter from the Bishop of Durham[2] by which it appears that in consequence of the joint opinion of the Bishop's two Chancellors, Sir Samuel Romilly[3] & Mr. Bernard,[4]

---

[1] Not in Castlereagh's own hand. The draft is in *Castlereagh Corresp.*, VIII, 193, wrongly dated Jan. 1809.   [2] Dr. Shute Barrington.

[3] For Romilly's appointment to this judicial office in 1805, see his *Memoirs*, II, 109–14.

[4] Sir Thomas Bernard (1750–1818), the philanthropist and promoter of many charitable foundations for the relief of the poor. Chancellor of the Diocese of Durham, 1801. Succeeded his brother as 3rd Baronet, 16 Aug. 1809.

he relinquishes all claim to the Stall in the Church of Durham vacant by the translation of the Bishop of Ely;[1] but that on the ground of the same opinion he considers himself intitled to the nomination to the Mastership of Sherborne Hospital unless Sir Samuel Romilly & Mr. Bernard should be convinced by the arguments of your Majesty's Law servants that the opinion they (Sir Samuel Romilly & Mr Bernard) have given is unfounded, a question which may remain undecided for a long time. Considering therefore the period during which the Prebend has been vacant, & that the Bishop of Durham has renounced, by the letter which is herewith submitted to your Majesty, all his pretentions to it, the Duke of Portland, in gratefull remembrance of the very gracious manner in which your Majesty has repeatedly condescended to listen to his recommendation of his nephew, Mr Anchytel Grey,[2] the youngest son of the Earl of Stamford,[3] for a similar mark of your Majesty's royal favor, once more ventures with all humility to express his hope that your Majesty may continue to think Mr Grey not unworthy of the vacant Stall. (14036–7)

[*The King's reply, Windsor Castle, 25 Dec.*] The King is glad that the renunciation of the Bishop of Durham of the claim which he had advanced, admits of his Majesty's early compliance with the Duke of Portland's application in favor of Mr. Grey for the vacant Prebendary.

The King has learnt from the Archbishop of Canterbury that Bishop Stillingfleet's[4] ecclesiastical tracts contain a speech which is very much to the point in question, and in which the right of the Crown to nominations arising from removal is decidedly maintained.

H.M. trusts that the Duke of Portland will endeavor to bring to early issue the question which regards the Mastership of Sherborne Hospital. (14037)

3776 GEORGE CANNING *to the* KING

[*Hinckley, 26 Dec. 1808.*] Mr. Canning most humbly presumes to recommend Mr. Jeffrey, (Member for Poole) as a fit person to be appointed your Majesty's Consul General in Portugal. And he most humbly submits for your Majesty's royal signature the Commission appointing Mr Jeffrey to this office, if your Majesty shall be graciously pleased to approve his nomination.[5] (14038)

    [1] Thomas Dampier had just been translated from Rochester to Ely.
    [2] Anchitel Grey (1774–1833).
    [3] George Harry, 5th Earl of Stamford (1737–1819). Styled Lord Grey from 1739 to 1768, when he succeeded his father. M.P. for Staffordshire, 1761–8. Created Earl of Warrington, 22 April 1796. In 1763 he married Lady Henrietta Bentinck (1737–1827), second daughter of William, 2nd Duke of Portland.
    [4] Edward Stillingfleet (1635–99), Bishop of Worcester, 1689–99.
    [5] John Jeffery was appointed Consul-General in Portugal, Canning writing to him to that effect on 31 Dec. 1808. (*H. of C. J.*, LXIV, 23.) The Speaker wrote (11 Jan. 1809): 'Perceval and Canning talked with me about Jeffery's vacating his seat for Poole upon his being appointed Consul-General, to his son, and Perceval seemed to think that the case of Ambassadors stood at least upon a principle now inapplicable, and could not now be extended to the case of Consuls, even independently of the analogous case of the Conservator of Scotch Privileges in the Netherlands, on which I relied as an exclusion of such persons, or as vacating the seat.' (Colchester, II, 163.) On 14 Feb. 1809 Benjamin Lester Lester

[*Admiralty, 2 Jan. 1809.*] Lord Mulgrave has the honour to report to your Majesty the death of that zealous and distinguished officer Lord Gardner, on Saturday the 31st of December[1] at Bath; the commission of Major-General of your Majesty's Marine forces has become vacant by that event. Lord Mulgrave begs your Majesty's permission to submit the name of Vice-Admiral Lord Collingwood for your Majesty's gracious consideration in consequence of his unremitting zeal and distinguish'd exertion in your Majesty's service, as a proper person to succeed the late Admiral Lord Gardner. (14044)

[*The King's reply, Windsor Castle, 3 Jan.*] The King has learnt with great concern from Lord Mulgrave the death of so worthy a man and distinguished an officer as Lord Gardner. His Majesty conceives that nothing can be more proper than that Lord Collingwood should succeed Lord Gardner as Major-General of Marines. (14045)

3778 SIR HENRY STRACHEY *to the* KING

[*Board of Green Cloth, 3 Jan. 1809.*] Sir Henry Strachey is under the necessity of troubling your Majesty in consequence of a letter which he has received from Mr. Sicard,[2] Maitre d'hotel to her Royal Highness the Princess of Wales, informing him that her Royal Highness now resides occasionally in Kensington Palace, and therefore he requests Sir Henry Strachey will order the gardener there to supply her Royal Highness with vegetables and fruit during such residence. Sir Henry Strachey is most humbly anxious to receive your Majesty's pleasure hereupon.[3] (14046)

was elected member for Poole at the by-election by a majority of 28 votes over his opponent John Blackburn, who polled 28.

For some time Jeffery had been anxious to secure public employment, and on 21 March 1807, when the Portland Ministry was being formed, he had written to George Rose: 'I trust that my past conduct in Parliament will justify my writing to you in the present situation of public affairs. Having relinquished all commercial concerns I am quite at liberty and do not scruple to say I am anxious to have some share in public business if the nature of the arrangement now on the tapis will admit of it. Having gone thus far in intimating my wishes to you, I trust I shall stand excused in pointing out the Admiralty, Treasury or Ordnance as situations most congenial to my inclinations....I have taken the liberty of writing on the same subject to Mr. Canning.' Replying on the 24th, Rose said that he had not then been mixing in the distribution of offices. 'I never spoke to the Duke of Portland in my life till 3 days ago, and thus did not utter one word to him about the pretensions of myself or of any other individual.' It was impossible, he added, to attend to all the fair claims which would probably be made. (National Library of Scotland, Melville Papers, 3795/167–9.)

[1] The date usually given is 1 Jan. 1809.

[2] John Jacob Sicard, a native of Anspach and a naturalised Englishman. Before he entered the service of the Princess of Wales as cook, in 1799 or 1800, he had been Lord Stafford's cook. Later, he was appointed her *maître d' hotel*.

[3] Docketed, 'Answered 5th Jany. Approved by H.My.'

3779 LORD MULGRAVE *to the* KING, *and the reply*

[*Admiralty, 3 Jan. 1809.*] Lord Mulgrave has the honour to transmit to your Majesty a dispatch this day received from Rear-Admiral Sir Richard Keats, and humbly submits to your Majesty the expediency of directing the Rear-Admiral (upon the grounds stated in his dispatch) to return to Yarmouth. (14047)

[*The King's reply, Windsor Castle, 4 Jan.*] The King is sensible of the unpleasant & doubtful situation of Sir Richard Keat[s]'s squadron, but as its being ordered to return to Yarmouth as suggested by Lord Mulgrave must have a decided influence upon the relations between this country & Sweden, his Majesty considers that it would be adviseable to take the opinion of Cabinet upon the question. (14048)

3780 *Letters from* GEORGE CANNING *to the* KING, *and the reply*

[*Foreign Office, 4 Jan. 1808 [1809].*] Mr. Canning humbly transmits to your Majesty a letter from the King of Sweden delivered to him (together with its copy) by Mr. de Brinkman. (Harewood MSS.)

[*From Canning, Foreign Office, 6 Jan.*] Mr. Canning most humbly submits for your Majesty's royal consideration the draft of a letter from your Majesty in answer to that recently received by your Majesty from the King of Sweden. (14049)

[*The King's reply, Windsor Castle, 7 Jan.*] The King approves of the letter to the King of Sweden of which Mr Canning has submitted the draft. (14049)

3781 *Letters from* VISCOUNT CASTLEREAGH *to the* KING, *and the reply*

[*Downing Street, 8 Jan. 1809.*] Lord Castlereagh in submitting his humble request that your Majesty would be graciously pleased to confer the Government of Fort Charles in the Island of Jamaica, vacated by the death of Genl. Edwd. Smith,[1] on Brigr.-Genl. Charles Stewart, hopes his attachment to his brother may not have induced him to intrude this request improperly on your Majesty's gracious favor and indulgence. (14050)

[*The King's reply, Windsor Castle, 9 Jan.*] The King approves of Lord Castlereagh's recommendation of Brigr.-General Charles Stewart for the vacant Government[2] of Charles Fort in Jamaica.[3] (14050)

[1] Major-General, 1782; Lieutenant-General, 1796; General, 1801.

[2] Non-resident. He held this sinecure (worth a clear £1200 a year) until 1822, when, angered by the appointment of Canning as Foreign Secretary in succession to his half-brother, Castlereagh, he threw up his various appointments and severed his connection with the Government.

[3] At the Levée on the 11th the Speaker found the King apparently in 'remarkably good health and countenance'. He 'talked to me about long speeches, long sittings, and public and private business with his usual cheerfulness'. (Colchester, II, 162.)

[*From Castlereagh, Downing St., 11 Jan.*] Your Majesty's confidential servants being of opinion that no time should be lost in bringing the Spanish Govt. to a declaration whether they will accept the co-operation of your Majesty's army in the south of Spain, admitting a British force into Cadiz, humbly recommend to your Majesty that the force under M.-Genl. Sherbrooke[1] should proceed direct to Cadiz for this purpose, proceeding on to Gibraltar in case Mr. Frere should notify to the Major-General that their services have been declined by the Central Government. (14051)

[*The King's reply, Queen's Palace, 12 Jan.*] The King approves of the proposal submitted by his confidential servants thro Lord Castlereagh that M.-General Sherbroke's [*sic*] corps should proceed direct to Cadiz to ascertain whether, in the event of a co-operation in the south, the army will be admitted to the use of that place. (14052)

3782   THE EARL OF LIVERPOOL *to the* KING, *and the reply*

[*London, 12 Jan. 1809.*] Lord Liverpool begs leave most humbly to inform your Majesty that upon a communication this day with the Lord Chancellor on the subject of the Recorder's Report, his Lordship is under the necessity of consulting the Judges on one of the cases on which there is some legal doubt, and as the preparatory business necessary for the meeting of Parliament will occupy a considerable portion of the time of your Majesty's confidential servants for the next few days, it is submitted to your Majesty whether the Recorder's Report may not be adjourned without inconvenience till Wednesday the 25 instant. (14053)

[*The King's reply, Queen's Palace, 13 Jan.*] The King does not object to Lord Hawkesbury's desiring the Recorder to postpone his Report to the week after next. (14053)

3783   GEORGE CANNING *to the* KING, *and the reply*

[*Foreign Office, 12 Jan. 1809.*] Mr. Canning humbly submits for your Majesty's royal consideration the draft of a treaty between your Majesty & his Catholick Majesty, which, if graciously approved by your Majesty, Mr. Canning would sign with Admiral Apodaca tomorrow, to be transmitted by the messenger to Mr. Frere. (14054)

[*The King's reply, Queen's Palace, 13 Jan.*] The King approves of the treaty which Mr. Canning has prepared for conclusion between his Majesty and his Catholic Majesty. (14055)

---

[1] Sir John Coape Sherbrooke (1764–1830). Ensign, 1780; Lieutenant, 1781; Major, 1793; Lieutenant-Colonel, 1794; Colonel, 1798; Major-General, 1805; Lieutenant-General, 1811; General, 1825. K.B., 1809 (after Talavera); G.C.B., 1815. Lieutenant-Governor of Nova Scotia, 1811; Captain-General and Governor-in-Chief of Canada, 1816–18.

[*Worcestershire, 13 Jan. 1809.*] With the deepest sense of obligation for your Majesty's goodness to me, which I ever bear most gratefully in my mind, I beg with all humility and respect again to intrude myself on your Majesty's notice. Should it be your Majesty's pleasure to make an advancement in your Peerage, I hope you will not think me too presuming in taking the liberty of assuring your Majesty that the greatest favor I could ever possibly receive from your Majesty's hands would be the conferring upon me the dignity of an Earl.[2] In venturing to make this petition to your Majesty, I feel it my duty to state that if your Majesty should be graciously pleased to take it into your consideration, my fortune, now forty thousand pounds per annum and still an encreasing one, would enable me to support in an adequate manner that rank which for the benefit of my family I am humbly solliciting your Majesty to obtain. The attachment and devotion of myself and family to your Majesty's person has alone emboldened me to lay this request at your Majesty's feet. (14056–7)

3785 VISCOUNT CASTLEREAGH *to the* KING, *and the reply*

[*St. James's Square, 17 Jan. 1809.*] Your Majesty's confidential servants having taken into their consideration the proceedings of the Board of General Officers directed by your Majesty to enquire into the armistice and Convention lately concluded in Portugal, they beg leave humbly to submit for your Majesty's gracious approbation the accompanying declaration of your Majesty's sentiments, to be communicated to his Royal Highness the Commander-in-Chief, upon the whole of those proceedings. Lord Castlereagh has taken the liberty of laying before your Majesty the dispatch alluded to in this paper, which your Majesty commanded to be address'd to Lt.-Genl. Sir Hew Dalrymple on the 17th of last September, upon ye receipt of the Definitive Convention in this country.[3] (14058–9)

[*The King's reply, Queen's Palace, 18 Jan.*] The King approves of the communication proposed by his confidential servants to be made to Lieut.-General Sir Hew Dalrymple which Lord Castlereagh has submitted to his Majesty. (14059)

[1] See No. 3180.

[2] He had started to be presuming in this way even before 23 July 1786, when he would have been satisfied with the revival of the title of 'Lord Beauchamp of Powick in the person of my father'. Writing to Pitt that day he had said: 'I am very sensible of the importance of the request I make, but your having obligingly allowed me leave to renew my petition on any new creation of peers, induces me to hope you will be favourable to my application, as I well know your generosity is equal to your power, and you had rather dispose of honours than receive any yourself, though they are so justly your due.' (Chatham Papers, 153.)

He made further applications on 13 June and 22 June 1790, on 12 Aug. 1794, on 23 May 1796, and on 8 and 27 Sept. 1797.

[3] Tierney attended one of the meetings of the Court of Inquiry at Chelsea, and 'came away quite disgusted with the manner in which the business was conducted. Wellesley and Burrard were placed upon the floor to examine one another! Wellesley's tone and deportment I thought very offensive. Poor Burrard made a sad figure...I never saw so dull a man in my life. Dalrymple sat quite snug and unconcerned, much in the manner of little Jack Horner.' (Howick MSS. To Grey, 15 Dec. 1808.)

[*Charles Street, 17 Jan. 1809.*] Lord Liverpool begs leave most humbly to submit to your Majesty the draft of the Speech[1] which it is proposed should be made by the Lords Commissioners by your Majesty's command to the two Houses of Parliament at the opening of the Session. Lord Liverpool thinks it necessary only to detain your Majesty, by noticing the paragraph respecting the Portuguese Convention, which Lord Liverpool has marked. As this paragraph is essentially connected with the paper which Lord Castlereagh will submit to your Majesty this evening, it may possibly be judged expedient according to your Majesty's determination upon this paper to make some alteration in this particular paragraph of the Speech. (14060)

[*The King's reply, Queen's Palace, 18 Jan.*] The King returns to Lord Liverpool the draft of the Speech which his Majesty approves, and he has signified to Lord Castlereagh his concurrence in the communication which is proposed to be made to Lieut.-General Sir Hew Dalrymple, and referred to in Lord Liverpool's letter. (14061)

---

[1] *Parl. Deb.*, XII, 1–4 (19 Jan.). See also Colchester, II, 164 (19 Jan.), for the last-minute changes in the King's Speech. 'The Speech was varied from the draft of yesterday in its expressions of the King's disapprobation of the Convention. It was stated *not* as a disapprobation of its *character* and *stipulations* generally, but as *of some* of the Articles.'

Perceval gave the customary Eve of the Session dinner at his house to official friends and supporters. Canning rather ostentatiously, perhaps, jealous maybe of Perceval's superior position as Leader of the House, was as usual absent, but Perceval wrote to him at 1.30 a.m. after the meeting (the letter is incorrectly dated the 20th): 'I called upon you just now in the hopes of catching you before you went to bed to inform you what impression our Speech has made upon our House of Co. friends—because the feeling of disapprobation and dissatisfaction was so general that we ought all to be fully apprized of it. Chs. Yorke approves heartily of all our Speech, except the Convention Article, with which he was very sorry that it would not be possible for him to concur. Rose disliked it much, & Long, Attorney-General & Solr.-Genl. expressed not only their own sentiments but what they collected to be the opinion of nearly the whole room. The Speaker told one of them that he never knew such a *firebrand* flung into the House of Commons as that passage would prove. They all, however, seemed to have no objection to the King's paper to Sir Hugh Dalrymple—but concluded, and I confess I think truly, that our Speech goes much further than that paper. They say that the passage running in the past tense is nothing, the King expresses his sentiment *now*. He cannot mean to tell his Parliament *now* merely what he felt three months ago, and not what he feels *now*—for what purpose could that be? It will be characterized as most hard by our officers—and then they ask, what Address are we to present upon this? Can the House of Commons, who know nothing of this subject, except that we have appointed a Court which we deemed competent to enquire into it, & that Court have approved (they may have approved wrongly & foolishly, & when the House examines the proceedings they might find it so) but can they be called upon, uninformed as they are, to pronounce an opinion to the effect expressed in the Speech? This is a strong part of their objection. They would think the Speech much amended if it went to express only what our paper to Dalrymple expresses, and they would be glad of an alteration which should regret "the termination of the campaign by an Armistice & Convention to some of the Articles of which his Majesty had felt himself obliged to express his formal disapprobation." Hawkesbury feels great doubts of the possibility of altering the Speech now. I confess if you could be brought to concur in the alteration that, such is my feeling collected from the opinions of our friends, that I should strongly recommend the alteration, however late, & however awkward [*sic*]. Let me hear from you as soon as you can.' (Chatham Papers, 368.)

[*Downg. St., Thursday, 19 Jan. 1809, 11.30 p.m.*] Mr. Perceval has the satisfaction to acquaint your Majesty that the Address to the Lord Commissioner's [*sic*] Speech has been carried without any division and after no very long debate. The Address was moved by Mr Frederick Robinson, Lord Grantham's brother, who distinguished himself by a very able speech, which was received in the House with very good effect;[1] he was well seconded by Mr. Lushington.[2] Mr. Ponsonby began the debate on the other side, was disposed to find great fault with the measures of yr. Majesty's Government with regard to Sweden, Spain, Portugal and America, but meaning to bring these several subjects under discussion by distinct Motions, he would not press them then, nor propose any Amendment to the Address. Lord Castlereagh replied to Mr Ponsonby, Mr Whitbread to Lord Castlereagh, & Mr Canning to Mr Whitbread. Lord Castlereagh & Mr Canning put the various points upon such good ground that Mr Perceval did not feel it necessary to follow Mr Tierney who spoke after Mr Canning. A few other very short speeches terminated the debate which was over by about a ¼ p. eleven o'clock.[3] (14062–3)

1 Robinson wrote to Lord Hardwicke (to whom he was related—his mother being the daughter of the second Earl of Hardwicke) on 2 Jan.: 'The uniform kindness which I have experienced from you gives you a just claim to be informed of everything which relates to me. I think it right therefore to let you know that I have acceded to a request from Perceval to move the Address upon the meeting of Parliament. Altho' I fear that this step may possibly not meet with your entire approbation, yet I trust it will experience the same indulgence which you have hitherto extended to the part which I have taken in Parliament.' (Add. MSS. 35648, f. 1.)

2 Stephen Rumbold Lushington (1776–1868), M.P. for Rye, 1807–12; for Canterbury, 1812–30 and 1835–7. He had been in the service of the East India Company, 1790–1807. Joint Secretary of the Treasury, 1814–27; Governor of Madras, 1827–32. In Nov. 1809 he would have liked an Under-Secretaryship of State, and he asked Wellesley to recommend him for office. 'Mr. Perceval is, I know, very kindly disposed towards me, for his request to me in the last Session to second the Address to the Throne was his own spontaneous act, and he has recently assured me of the continuance of his good opinion and confidence.' (Add. MSS. 37309, f. 303.)

3 *Parl. Deb.*, XII, 30–91; Colchester, II, 164. Tierney thought it had been a dull debate, 'though I think Ponsonby made a good speech. There were not more than 250 Members in the House.' (Howick MSS.) Whitbread had an Amendment ready for production when he attended a meeting of Opposition members (about 44 of them) at George Ponsonby's house on the night of the 18th, but he kept it in his pocket. Tierney was confident that not more than ten members in the room would have voted for it. (Howick MSS. Tierney to Grey, 19 Jan. 1809.) Whitbread explained to Lord Grey on the 29th: 'I was glad you thought the debate on the first day of the Session went off tolerably well. It is unlucky that Lord Grenville & Ponsonby should have taken the line they did about sending troops to Spain, & also about the expedition to Portugal; of the propriety of both those steps I agree with you. Had I done what I judged right at the beginning of the Session I should have moved a detailed Amendment containing my opinions on the conduct of the Ministers during the recess. Many persons were desirous it should be done & I still think it would have been the wisest thing to do, but as Ponsonby & others were of a contrary opinion I gave up my intention. I confess I should always yield my opinions with less reluctance if I thought Ponsonby had any opinion of his own, but I can see no trace of it, either in general plans or in particular actions.' (Howick MSS.)

The Members present at the party meeting at Ponsonby's were as follows: James Abercromby, William Adam, Emanuel Felix Agar, Sir John Anstruther, Alexander Baring, Thomas Baring, Augustus Cavendish Bradshaw, John Calcraft, James Somers Cocks, Harvey Christian Combe, Thomas Creevey, Charles Dundas, William Elliot, General Fitzpatrick, William Frankland, William Henry Fremantle, Lord Gower, Robert Greenhill, Thomas Grenville, Henry Arthur Herbert, George Hibbert, William Howard, Joseph Jekyll, Thomas Knox, John Leach, James Macdonald, Montagu James Mathew, Sir Thomas Miller, Sir William Milner, Lord Milton, Lord Morpeth, Lord Ossulston, Lord Henry Petty,

[*The King's reply, Queen's Palace, 20 Jan.*] The King has received with pleasure the satisfactory report which Mr. Perceval has been enabled to make of last night's proceedings in the House of Commons. His Majesty desires that Mr Perceval will convey his intimation to Lord Stopford[1] that he should attend at Windsor on Monday next at two o'clock with the Address, and that Mr Perceval will prepare the answer to it & forward it with the official papers on Monday morning at furthest. (14063)

3788   *Letters from the* EARL OF LIVERPOOL *to the* KING, *and the replies*

[*Charles Street, 19 Jan., 11.30 p.m.* [*1809*].] Lord Liverpool begs leave most humbly to submit to your Majesty the Minutes of the House of Lords of this day and at the same time to inform your Majesty that though no Amendment was proposed to the Address, intimations were given of an intention on the part of the Lords in opposition to bring forward several Motions, particularly with respect to the relations of this country with Spain and with the United States of America. Lord Grenville and Lord Moira differ'd so far in their opinion respecting Spain that Lord Grenville profess'd to object to any army having been sent into Spain. Lord Moira was of opinion that your Majesty's army should have been sent into that country but that its exertions in the first instance ought to have been directed towards the Pyrrenees.

Lord Liverpool begs leave to submit to your Majesty the answer to the Address of the House of Lords for your Majesty's gracious approbation. (14064–5)

[*From the King, Queen's Palace, 19* [*? 20*] *Jan.*] The King desires that Lord Liverpool will prepare the answer to the Address from the Lords and will send it to his Majesty with the official papers tomorrow morning, his Majesty having given notice to Lord Dartmouth to attend here with the Address soon after ten. (14072)

[*From the King, Queen's Palace, 20 Jan.*] The King acknowledges the receipt of Lord Liverpool's satisfactory report of the proceedings in the House of Lords last night. (14065)

[*From Lord Liverpool, Charles Street, 20 Jan.*] Lord Liverpool begs leave most humbly to submit to your Majesty, the letter which he has received from Sir John Nicholl, your Majesty's Advocate, informing him that the Archbishop of Canterbury had appointed him to the judicial offices[2] held by Sir William Wynne under the See of Canterbury, and which Sir William Wynne had thought proper to

Sir Arthur Piggott, George Ponsonby, Lord Porchester, Sir Samuel Romilly, Lord William Russell, Richard Sharp, George Tierney, George Granville Venables Vernon, John William Ward, Charles Callis Western, Samuel Whitbread, and probably one or two others. (Howick MSS.)

    [1] Treasurer of the Household. See No. 3792.

    [2] Principal of the Arches Court of Canterbury; Master, Keeper or Commissary of the Prerogative Court of Canterbury; Commissary of the Deaneries of the Arches of London, Shoreham and Croydon. For Sir William Scott's views on acceptance or rejection of these offices, and his brother's advice, see Twiss, *Eldon,* II, 66–7.

resign. By this appointment the office of King's Advocate becomes vacant, and Lord Liverpool requests your Majesty's permission in accepting Sir John Nicholl's resignation, to be allowed to signify to him your Majesty's gracious approbation of his able and honourable conduct for a period of more than ten years during which he has held the situation of King's Advocate.

As the office of King's Advocate is one of the greatest publick importance and should be filled by the person best qualified to discharge the duties of it without any consideration of private favour, Lord Liverpool has written to Sir William Scott to request to have his opinion as to the different pretensions of those who may become candidates for it, and his judgement as to the person most proper to be recommended to your Majesty to succeed Sir John Nicholl, and Lord Liverpool will lose no time in laying before your Majesty the result of this communication for your Majesty's determination. (14073–4)

[*The King's reply, Windsor Castle, 21 Jan.*] The King accepts of Sir John Nicholl's resignation of the office of King's Advocate and desires that Lord Liverpool will convey to him his Majesty's entire approbation of the able and honorable manner in which he has invariably discharged the laborious and important duties of that situation. The King also highly approves of the steps Lord Liverpool has taken towards the selection of a fit person to succeed to Sir John Nicholl. (14074)

3789   LORD MULGRAVE *to the* KING, *and the reply*

[*Admiralty, 20 Jan. 1809.*] Lord Mulgrave has the honour most humbly to submit to your Majesty the appointment of Admiral Sir Roger Curtis to succeed Admiral Montague[1] in the command of the port at Portsmouth, the latter officer having remained near six years in that command. (14075)

[*The King's reply, Windsor Castle, 21 Jan.*] The King acquiesces in Lord Mulgrave's recommendation of Sir Roger Curtis to succeed Admiral Montague in the command of the port at Portsmouth. (14075)

3790   THE EARL OF LIVERPOOL *to the* KING, *and the reply*

[*Charles Street, 21 Jan. 1809.*] Lord Liverpool begs leave most humbly to inform your Majesty that upon communication with Sir William Scott it appears that Dr Christopher Robinson[2] is upon the whole the most proper person to recommend to your Majesty for the office of Advocate General. There are several Advocates senior to Dr. Robinson, but those amongst them who are best qualified for the situation would not, as Lord Liverpool is informed, accept of it. Dr. Robinson has been for some years the reporter of the cases in the High Court of

---

[1] Sir George Montagu.

[2] Sir Christopher Robinson (1766–1833), M.P. for Callington, 1818–20; Knighted 6 Feb. 1809 and appointed King's Advocate (gazetted, 14 Feb.). Succeeded Lord Stowell as Chancellor of the Diocese of London and Judge of the Consistory Court, 1821; Judge of the High Court of Admiralty, 1828–33.

Admiralty and his reports bear the highest character not only in this country but on the Continent of Europe. Lord Liverpool believes he can therefore safely venture to recommend to your Majesty Dr Robinson as Sir John Nicholl's successor. (14080)

[*The King's reply, Windsor Castle, 22 Jan.*] From Lord Liverpool's report the King is satisfied that Doctor Robinson, whom Sir William Scott recommends, is the fittest person to fill the office of Advocate General in succession to Sir John Nicholl, and his Majesty approves of his appointment. (14081)

3791   *Letters from* VISCOUNT CASTLEREAGH *to the* KING, *and the replies*

[*St James's Square, 21 Jan. 1809.*] Lord Castlereagh having brought the dispatch received from Lt.-Genl. Sir John Moore under the consideration of your Majesty's confidential servants, they beg leave humbly to recommend to your Majesty that the orders sent to Sir J. Moore with respect to the disposal of his army in the event of his re-embarcation from Gallicia, should be render'd so far discretionary as to leave it to that officer to decide, according to the state and condition of his troops, whether they can with advantage to your Majesty's service be immediately employ'd in execution of those orders, or must return home to be refitted and prepared for service.¹ (14078)

[*The King's reply, Windsor Castle, 22 Jan.*] The King considers the instructions which are proposed in Lord Castlereagh's letter to be sent to Sir John Moore in regard to the disposal of his army as best suited to the circumstances under which it is placed. (14079)

[*From Castlereagh, St. James's Square, 22 Jan.*] Lord Castlereagh humbly submits to your Majesty the substance of intelligence received from Lord Paget who reach'd town this evening at 9 o'clock. Genl. Hope's dispatch was forwarded by a gun-brig not yet arrived. Lord Castlereagh, in laying before your Majesty this unofficial report of the heavy loss your Majesty's service has sustain'd in the fall of so brave and distinguish'd an officer as Sir John Moore, has to assure your Majesty, upon Lord Paget's authority, that the conduct of your Majesty's troops in action was most exemplary and such as to uphold in the highest degree the reputation of your Majesty's arms.² (14082–3)

¹ In his dispatch of the 13th from Corunna, Moore stated that he had effected his retreat to the coast with the loss of only part of his baggage; that the rearguard had repeatedly repulsed the enemy, and that he hoped to re-embark his army without much loss, as the transports which he had sent for from Vigo were entering Corunna. (Colchester, *Diary and Corresp.*, II, 164; *Castlereagh Corresp.*, VII, 26.)

² Superior French forces had compelled Moore to abandon his campaign in north-west Spain and to beat a hurried retreat to the coast, pursued initially by Napoleon himself, then, after 1 Jan., by Ney and Soult. The embarkation began at Corunna on 13 Jan.; the French, under Soult, attacked on the 16th, suffering a severe repulse. Moore was mortally wounded in the battle, and General Hope, who took over the command, completed the embarkation without further molestation next day.

[*The King's reply, Windsor Castle, 23 Jan.*] Although the King is relieved from great uneasiness by the report sent by Lord Castlereagh of the successful re-embarkation of his army at Corunna, under circumstances so trying, in which the gallantry of the troops has again been so conspicuous, his Majesty cannot in sufficient terms express the concern with which he has learnt the death of Sir John Moore, whose character his M. has always considered as highly respectable and such as must render him a very serious national loss. (14083)

3792   *Letters from* SPENCER PERCEVAL *to the* KING, *and the reply*

[*Downg. St., Sunday evg., 22 Jan. 1809.*] Mr Perceval transmits to your Majesty the answer to the Address of the Ho. of Commons. Mr Perceval has acquainted Lord Stopfort [*sic*] with your Majesty's commands, who will accordingly attend your Majesty with the Address. (14084)

[*The King's reply, Windsor Castle, 23 Jan.*] The King has received from Mr Perceval the answer to the Address of the House of Commons which his Majesty approves. (14085)

[*From Perceval, Downg. St., 23 Jan.*] Mr Perceval regrets to report to your Majesty that there were but 39 members assembled in the Ho. of Commons this day and therefore that there was no House to proceed to the business which was appointed.[1] (14086)

3793   LORD MULGRAVE *to the* KING, *and the reply*

[*Admiralty, 23 Jan. 1809, 10 a.m.*] Lord Mulgrave humbly hopes that the importance of the intelligence which he has the honour to transmit to your Majesty may plead his excuse for sending it at an unusual time. (14089)

[*Lieut.-Colonel Taylor's reply, Windsor Castle, 23 Jan.*] I am honored with the King's commands to return his thanks to your Lordship for the early communication of the intelligence received from Admiral Young, which his Majesty considers extremely material as removing all apprehension which remained for the safety of the troops on board the transports. (14090)

3794   *Letters from the* DUKE OF PORTLAND *to the* KING,[2] *and the reply*

[*Burlington House, Monday, 23 Jan. 1809.*] Sir John Nicholl, late your Majesty's Advocate General, having been appointed by the Archbishop of Canterbury to the office of Dean of the Arches, is no longer capable of continuing his practice

---

[1] 'A most extraordinary circumstance,' commented Whitbread, writing to Lord Grey on the 29th with reference to the 26th. (Howick MSS.) The minimum number needed for a House was forty. In a House of Commons of 658 Members, there were similar adjournments this Session on 26 Jan., 21 April, 15 and 17 May, 13 and 14 June.   [2] Not in the Duke's own hand.

at the Bar, but it is considered by the Lord President of the Council, the Master of the Rolls, and Sir William Scott, who are unremitting in their attendance on prize causes and plantation appeals, that he might render essential service to your Majesty and to the publick by being placed by your Majesty in such a situation as would enable him to give his assistance in the decision of the causes which come before them. The Duke of Portland therefore most humbly submits for your Majesty's superior wisdom the propriety of appointing Sir John Nicholl to be a member of your Majesty's Privy Council, by which he would be intitled to attend both those Boards; and the Duke of Portland has been assured that, in that case, Sir John Nicholl would consider it to be his indispensible duty punctually to attend both these Boards. (14087–8)

[*The King's reply, Windsor Castle, 24 Jan.*] The King approves of the Duke of Portland's proposal that Sir John Nicholl should be called to the Privy Council where his attendance may become very useful, and his Majesty desires that he may take the oaths tomorrow.

The King has learnt with great pleasure that Lord William Bentinck has had an opportunity of distinguishing himself so much,[1] and his Majesty flatters himself that both[2] the Duke of Portland's other sons are quite well. (14095)

[*From the Duke of Portland, Burlington House, Tuesday, 24 Jan., 5 p.m.*] Impressed with the most lively sense of your Majesty's great condescension and goodness the Duke of Portland most humbly requests your Majesty's permission to express to your Majesty those sentiments of gratitude which he can never cease to feel for the most gracious terms in which your Majesty has condescended to notice the manner in which his son Lord William Bentinck performed his duty on the 16th instt. before Corunna, & to recollect that the Duke of Portland had two other sons employed in that part of your Majesty's army. And he trusts your Majesty will forgive his presumption on the present occasion for venturing to state the summit of his hope that it may be the constant endeavour & the greatest object of the ambition of those two young men to render themselves worthy of that notice by which your Majesty has been graciously pleased to distinguish the services of their brother. (14096)

[1] In Aug. 1808 he had been appointed to the Staff of the army under Sir Harry Burrard in Portugal. He had joined Moore's army and had commanded a brigade at the battle of Corunna.

[2] The Duke's eldest son, the Marquess of Titchfield, was not in the army. The King was referring, first, to the disreputable Lord William Charles Augustus Cavendish Bentinck (1780–1826), whose first wife, Georgiana Augusta Frederica Seymour (*d.* 1813), chose to believe that she was the Prince of Wales's daughter (though Lord Cholmondeley too claimed the doubtful distinction of being her father). Lord Charles was M.P. for Ashburton, 1807–12, and was appointed Treasurer of the (Prince Regent's) Household in 1812, and served in the army until he retired in April 1811 (Ensign, 1796; Lieutenant, 1798; Captain, 1798; Major, 1802; Lieutenant-Colonel, 1802).

The second son referred to was Lord Frederick Cavendish Bentinck (1781–1828), Captain, 1799; Lieutenant-Colonel, 1804; Colonel, 1813; Major-General, 1819.

[*St. James's Square, Tuesday morning, 2 a.m.* [*24 Jan. 1809*].] Lord Castlereagh has the satisfaction of humbly submitting to your Majesty the accompanying dispatches, communicating the meritorious services and the safe re-embarcation of your Majesty's army from Corunna. The Honble. Capt. Gordon left the whole fleet at sea on the 18th all well, with a fair wind, steering for the Channel. Your Majesty will observe that Sir D. Baird's dispatch is sign'd by his own hand, and the report of his prospect of recovery is favorable.[1] Sir John Moore lived to be inform'd of the fate of the day, and seem'd only apprehensive, from the degree of strength he retain'd, that being assured of this fact, the close of his life might be unnecessarily protracted. Lord Castlereagh humbly hopes your Majesty will approve of proposing to the House of Commons to address your Majesty to direct a monument to be erected to the memory of this distinguished and meritorious officer. (14092–3)

[*The King's reply, Windsor Castle, 24 Jan.*] The King has received very sincere satisfaction from Lord Castlereagh's communication of the dispatches of Sir David Baird and Lieut.-General Hope, which assure him of the safe removal of the army from Corunna after services so meritorious and so gallant, and he rejoyces that the report of the state of Sir David Baird's wound is so favorable.

His Majesty highly approves of its being proposed to Parliament to address him to direct a monument to be erected to the memory of Sir John Moore, the sense of whose valuable and distinguished services cannot be too strongly marked.

The King has read with admiration the dispatch of Lieut.-General Hope in which, while he so ably describes the operations of the army and does justice to the gallant conduct of officers and men, he shews so much modesty in the mention of himself, although his firmness, resources & ability must have so essentially contributed to the successful issue of so arduous a service. His Majesty therefore trusts that every part of his letter will be published, in justice to him, to the army and to the exertions which it will prove to the world to have been made in support of the Spaniards while there was any prospect of their continuing the contest. (14094)

[*From Castlereagh, Downing Street, 25 Jan.*] Lord Castlereagh in submitting to your Majesty Lieutt.-General Hope's letter and a report from Captn. Bowen, Agent for Transports, on the embarkation of the troops at Corunna, begs permission humbly to observe that any inconvenience that arose from the empty store and forage ships not having been supplied with provisions did not result from there not having been with the army a due proportion of victuallers, but from a distribution not having been previously made into these ships, which are seldom used for the reception of troops.

A large fleet of empty transports with some additional victuallers sailed from Portsmouth on the 14th for Corunna.

[1] In the battle of Corunna his left arm was broken by a cannon-ball, and was amputated on board a transport.

Lord Castlereagh hopes your Majesty will pardon his entering into this detail, but he is anxious your Majesty should be persuaded that whilst your Majesty's troops have been engaged in their late arduous and trying services, there have been no exertions omitted on the part of your Majesty's servants in contributing to their comforts, and in keeping them largely provided with every article of supply from home which could be made available, according to the nature of the service in which the army was engaged.[1] (14099–100)

[*The King's reply, Windsor Castle, 26 Jan.*] The King has received Lord Castlereagh's letter and is perfectly satisfied that there has not been any want of exertion in providing for the wants and accomodation of the troops, and that if there has prevailed any deficiency of arrangement at the moment of embarkation it is solely attributable to the circumstances of extraordinary difficulty under which so arduous a service has been executed, with so much credit to all those concerned. (14100)

3796 LORD MULGRAVE *to the* KING, *and the reply*
[*Admiralty, 25 Jan. 1809.*] Lord Mulgrave has the honour humbly to submit to your Majesty the expediency of detaching without delay, from the ships of war returned from Corunna or such others as may be fit for sea a sufficient number of ships to complete the naval force at Lisbon & Cadiz respectively to six sail of the line. The great advantage derived at the embarkation of the army at Corunna from a numerous squadron of line of battle ships has strongly impressed Lord Mulgrave's mind with the important services which may possibly result from a similar force at Lisbon. The ships proposed for Cadiz are with a view to facilitate the equipment of the French & Spanish ships of war at present in that port, and to provide against any attempt of the Brest squadron to assail the harbour of Cadiz. Lord Mulgrave proposes, if it should meet with your Majesty's gracious approbation, that, in the event of the enemy directing his principal operations against the south of Spain, a detachment should be made from Lisbon to complete the force under Rear-Admiral Purvis to ten sail of the line. (14097–8)

[*The King's reply, Windsor Castle, 26 Jan.*] The King entirely approves of the arrangements which are proposed in Lord Mulgrave's letter for completing the naval force at Lisbon and Cadiz so as to render it adequate to the services which may be required. (14098)

3797 SPENCER PERCEVAL *to the* KING, *and the reply*
[*Downg. Str., 25 Jan. 1809.*] Mr Perceval acquaints your Majesty that Lord Castlereagh made his several Motions relating to the army in Spain & Portugal this evening. His Lordship began with the Motion for a monument for General

---

[1] There are inaccurate and sometimes undated versions of Castlereagh's letters in the *Castlereagh Corresp.*

Sir John Moore.[1] He expatiated at great length and with great effect upon his various merits as an officer and a man and carried along with him completely the feelings of the House in deploring his loss. The vote was extremely well received, and passed *nemine contradicente*—as did also the votes of thanks to the officers & men for their conduct at the battle of Corunna. Votes of thanks were also passed to Admiral de Courcey & Sr. Saml. Hood and the officers of the Navy for the effective assistance which they gave in the embarkation of the troops.

These Motions having been disposed of his Lordship proceeded to move the thanks of the House to Sr Arthur Wellesley for his conduct in the two engagements in Portugal. This Motion, having been opposed by Lord Folkestone, produced more of a debate, in which, however, every gentleman who spoke except Lord Folkestone concurred most heartily in the vote which was proposed, and spoke in the highest possible terms of Sr. A. Wellesley. Mr. Whitbread moved an Amendment to include the name of Sr Harry Burrard in the Vote, as Commander-in-Chief, but after its being explained that Sr. Harry Burrard had himself in his own dispatch disclaimed all merit either in the dispatch of the Army or in the execution of the achievements of the day—that he had made Sr. A. Wellesley report to him the course of proceedings on that day and transmitted home that report, not as an account of his own conduct but as the act of Sr. A. Wellesley, and thereby evidently laid the ground for the distinction in this case— that it would be impossible to thank Sr. Harry Burrard but for what he did— which, under the circumstances indeed was very generous, meritorious & forbearing, but was not that sort of conduct which could justify a vote of thanks of the Ho. of Commons; & that to thank him for not having taken the command of the army would not be felt by him as a compliment, and might be turned by his enemies into an insult. Upon this explanation Mr Whitbread withdrew his Motion of Amendment, and the Vote passed, not indeed nemine contradicente, because Ld. Folkestone adhered to the expression of his dissent; but his Lordship was the single person who did so. Then followed the votes to the other officers & men.

After this Lord Castlereagh brought in his Bill for augmenting the army, and after a short conversation from Mr. Tierney, Lord Milton, Mr Calcraft, Mr Herbert,[2] Mr Perceval and one or two more, in which the topics of future discussion were rather opened than dwelt upon, the House was taken by surprise by a division

[1] The monument was to be erected in St. Paul's.

[2] Henry Arthur Herbert (c. 1756–1821), M.P. for East Grinstead, 1782–86, as a supporter of Pitt; for Co. Kerry, 1806–12; for Tralee, 1812–13. On 6 Sept. 1789 he reminded Pitt of a promise he had made to him in 1785, on the recommendation of the Duke of Dorset, of an Irish Barony. (Chatham Papers, 144.) He had voted for Brand's Motion on 9 April 1807 and with the Whigs on many other occasions, but in 1810 he was rightly considered by the Opposition to be only a 'doubtful'. The Duke of Richmond wrote to his new Chief Secretary, R. S. Dundas, from Dublin on 10 May: 'I find Mr. Herbert, member for Kerry, is very angry with me. He has I understand voted on every question but the Duke of York's against Government and then written to me to give a very good living at Kenmare to his friend. I of course sent him a formal sort of letter in answer. The father of his friend (First Commr. of the Account Office) came to me yesterday to explain that he had pressed Mr. Herbert as much as possible to support Government, that Lord Westmorland & Castlereagh had done so also but that they could only get him to stay away on the Motion relative to Ld. Castlereagh. He added in confidence that Mr. Herbert said he hoped I should not drive him into opposition.... You will find many attempts to bully, and if we give way we shall be held very cheap.' (Melville MSS.)

being called for by Lord Milton against the introduction of the Bill. As the members had gone away thinking there would be no opposition in this stage of the business the numbers were but small, but the majority was very sufficient, the numbers being 25 against the Bill and about seventy for it.[1] (14101–2)

[*The King's reply, Windsor Castle, 26 Jan.*] The King acknowledges the receipt of Mr Perceval's report of last night's proceedings in the House of Commons and his Majesty is glad to learn that although some of the Members had left the House previous to Lord Milton's Motion, the numbers remaining were sufficient to carry the first reading of the Bill for augmenting the army. (14104)

3798 *Letters from* GEORGE CANNING *to the* KING, *and the reply*

[*Foreign Office, 26 Jan. 1809.*] Mr. Canning humbly lays before your Majesty a letter from the Prince Regent of Portugal to your Majesty, which has been delivered to him today by the Portuguese Minister[2]. (14105)

[*From Canning, Foreign Office, 28 Jan.*] Mr. Canning most humbly submits for your Majesty's royal consideration the draft of a letter to the Lords Commissioners of the Admiralty, prepared in consequence of the letter from the Prince Regent to your Majesty on the subject of Sir Sidney Smith.[3] (14106)

[*The King's reply, Windsor Castle, 29 Jan.*] The King approves of the letter to the Lords Commissioners of the Admiralty which Mr. Canning has prepared. (14106)

[1] *Parl. Deb.* XII, 138–67. The numbers were 77 *v.* 26. This incident well illustrates the disarray into which the Opposition had fallen. Tierney explained the matter in a letter to Lord Grey on 1 Feb.: 'On the Motion for leave to bring in a Bill for increasing the Regular Force by drafting from the Militia, I took occasion to say that I would on that night give no opposition to the measure but that I protested against putting another army, however raised, into the hands of Ministers until they had accounted for their conduct in the last campaign. I stated this very shortly, and professedly only with a view to lay in my claim to a more ample discussion on a future day. Ponsonby and Whitbread were gone away, and we had but about 25 on our side of the House. A division was insisted upon by some on the back benches in spite of all Petty and I could say, and, before we and some others could make our escape into Bellamy's the door was locked and we could get no further than the passage. There our Tellers came to look for us, and, having been present when the question was put, we were obliged to vote in the House, that is, against giving leave to bring in the Bill. The consequence was that as soon as the House was resumed Petty felt himself obliged to declare that he had been made to vote against his inclinations, and I, Calcraft, and others did the same!' (Howick MSS.)

[2] De Souza.

[3] In Feb. 1808 he had been appointed to the command of the South American station, but, following a bitter quarrel with Lord Strangford, the British Minister to the Prince Regent of Portugal resident in Brazil, he was recalled in the summer of 1809. See Bagot, *Canning and his Friends*, I, 289.

[*Downg. Str., 27 Jan. 1809.*] Mr. Perceval humbly acquaints your Majesty that Mr Wardle[1] brought on, this evening, in the House of Commons, the Motion against his Royal Highness the Duke of York.[2] Mr Wardle stated three or four different cases, specifying them by the names of the persons concerned, and by the dates when they occurred, in which commissions in the army had been procured by means of money paid to some woman, whom he stated to have been living at the time with his Royal Highness, and by whose means such commissions had been procured, and these facts, Mr Wardle pledged himself to bring home directly to his Royal Highness. Mr Perceval should acquaint your Majesty that immediately upon notice of this Motion having been given by Mr Wardle, Mr Perceval felt it his duty to give the earliest intelligence of it to his Royal Highness, thro' Col. Gordon;[3] and that Mr. Perceval received his Royal Highness's commands to court on the part of H.R. Highness any enquiry (the most public would be the most acceptable to his Royal Highness) that the forms and proceedings of Parliament would admit of. That this wish of his Royal Highness was at once most honorable to his Royal Highness's feelings, and most useful to the vindication of his character from the vile insinuations which these charges brought against him, was the unanimous opinion of everyone whom Mr Perceval could consult upon this occasion; and accordingly when Mr Wardle sat down, Sr. James Pulteney[4] rose, and after expressing his Royal Highness's wishes to this effect, and after stating the reasons upon which he felt confident that the charges would be found totally groundless, as far at least as his Royal Highness was concerned, he concurred in the propriety of the Motion for a Committee to enquire into his Royal Highness's conduct in respect to the sale of Commissions. Sr. James Pulteney bore full testimony to the great services that H.R. Highness had performed to your Majesty's Army since his R. Highness had been in the chief command of it. Mr Charles Yorke & Lieut.-Genl. Sr. Arthur Wellesley followed in the same sense, and Sr Arthur Wellesley in particular availed himself of this opportunity to speak of the high order, discipline and military efficiency which distinguished the army which he had commanded in Portugal, and ascribed to the Duke of York his due merit in sending it so complete upon that service. Mr York[e] and Mr Wilberforce rather thought that the enquiry should be prosecuted before a Commission appointed by Act of Parliament for that express purpose, but Mr. Perceval has the satisfaction of thinking that what Mr Adam,

[1] Gwyllym Lloyd Wardle (*c.* 1762–1833), M.P. for Okehampton, 1807–12. Earlier, he had been a Colonel, or Lieutenant-Colonel, in Sir Watkin Williams Wynn's volunteer troop of dragoons, and he was said to have fought at Vinegar Hill against the Irish rebels in 1798.

[2] The Duke was accused of corrupt practices, one of his former mistresses, Mrs Mary Anne Clarke, having been allowed, it was alleged, to traffic in army commissions and promotions.

[3] Sir James Willoughby Gordon (1772–1851). Ensign, 1783; Lieutenant, 1789; Captain, 1795; Major, 1797; Lieutenant-Colonel, 1801; Colonel, 1810; Assistant Quartermaster-General in the Southern District, 1802; Military Secretary to the Commander-in-Chief, 1804–9; Commissary-General, 1809–11; Quartermaster-General of the Army in the Peninsula, 1811–12; Quartermaster-General at the Horse Guards, 1812–51; Major-General, 1813; Baronetcy, 3 Oct. 1818; M.P. for Launceston, 1829–31; Lieutenant-General and G.C.H., 1825; G.C.B., 1831; General, 1841.

[4] The Secretary at War.

Mr Secretary Canning, Lord Castlereagh, & Mr Perceval said upon that subject reconciled Mr York as it did the House in general to the opinion that the enquiry should be prosecuted before a Committee of the whole House, at the Bar. This proceeding, Mr Perceval is fully aware, may be attended with no small inconvenience to the public business, but he humbly submits to your Majesty, and he trusts your Majesty will think, that so serious a charge against so illustrious a personage so near to your Majesty, could not with propriety have been sent to any other enquiry than that which was the most public and the most solemn; had any Select Committee been appointed for this enquiry, tho' constituted of the most honorable persons which the House of Commons could produce, yet the revilers of his Royal Highness would have asserted that the Committee had been packed for the purpose of smothering fair enquiry, and it would therefore have afforded no prospect of that satisfactory result which Mr Perceval so anxiously wishes for and so confidently expects. Mr Perceval trusts that upon a subject so important in every possible view of it, and so interesting to the honor of your Majesty's Royal Family and to your Majesty's own feelings, your Majesty will excuse him for having given so full a statement of the course of the proceedings which was adopted in the House of Commons. And considering the numberless base, anonymous charges & insinuations which have been for some time, in a manner frequently too guarded to be reached by law, and too general to be distinctly disproved in fact, brought before the public, in libellous prints, against his Royal Highness, Mr Perceval thinks he may be justified in congratulating your Majesty that his Royal Highness will now have an opportunity (which no one can more anxiously wish for than his Royal Highness) of disproving in the face of Parliament and of the public those slanders which the enemies of his Royal Highness and of your Majesty's Royal Family have brought before the world. Of Mr Wardle Mr Perceval can say nothing; he is intitled to be considered as acting upon public grounds, and it is possible he may have been imposed upon by his R. Highness's enemies to believe what he has undertaken to prove; but Mr Perceval looks forward with confidence to an early day on which he may have the happiness of informing your Majesty that this enquiry has terminated to the perfect honor of his Royal Highness, & the discomfiture and disgrace of his enemies.

Lord Folkstone, Sr. F. Burdett and Mr Whitbread took part in the debate, but Mr Perceval would be wanting in justice to them if he did not state to your Majesty that they spoke with due respect of his Royal Highness & expressed their confident trust that the charges would prove unfounded.

Monday being the 30th of Jany.[1] Mr Perceval acquaints your Majesty that the House has adjourned till Tuesday—and Wednesday is appointed for the first sitting of the Committee of Enquiry.[2] (14107-9)

[1] During this period the House never met for business on this day, the anniversary of the execution of King Charles the Martyr.

[2] Tierney wrote to Grey on 1 Feb.: 'Mr. Wardle, without the slightest communication with anybody but Whitbread, who says he advised him to postpone the business, brings on a Motion against the Duke of York personally. As far as I can see, he will not be able to fix the charge of corrupt conduct on the Duke, though he will damage him considerably in public estimation; but think what a situation we are all placed in unless the accusation can be fully substantiated!' (Howick MSS.) Writing to Grey

[*The King's reply, Windsor Castle, 28 Jan.*] The King entirely approves of the course which Mr Perceval followed in last night's proceedings in the House of Commons, and altho' an enquiry into Mr Wardle's charges before a Committee of the whole House may be attended with some inconvenience to public business, his Majesty trusts that the Duke of York will be able so clearly and positively to refute those charges, that the enquiry will not be productive of much delay, while his Majesty decidedly concurs in the propriety of the Duke of York's wish to court the most public and the fullest investigation. (14109)

3800   THE KING *to* VISCOUNT CASTLEREAGH

[*Windsor Castle, 29 Jan. 1809.*] The King approves of the instructions from Lord Castlereagh to Sir John Cradock, but it has occurred to his Majesty that some specific direction should be given for the disposal of the cavalry in the event of the troops from Portugal removing to Gibraltar & not to Cadiz. (14110)

3801   THE EARL OF CHATHAM *to the* KING, *and the reply*

[*Hill Street, 29 Jan. 1809.*] Lord Chatham had hoped it wou'd have been in his power long before this to have attended your Majesty, but being still confined to the house, he humbly begs permission to trespass upon your Majesty's indulgence with a short statement he had prepared of the circumstances attending the equipment (as far as the Ordnance Department is concerned) of the corps under the orders of Lt.-Genl. Sir Arthur Wellesley. Tho' Lord Chatham believes that he has at different times stated most of the points to your Majesty, yet he is anxious to bring the subject at one view before your Majesty in consequence of the partial manner in which it has been treated before the Court of Enquiry, and the observations to which that has necessarily given rise, and Lord Chatham feels it more particularly his duty humbly to submit the accompanying paper to your Majesty, as it may, in the event of the discussions in Parliament, on a consideration of the proceedings of the Court of Enquiry, leading to any question upon the Ordnance preparation, become necessary for him to give (shou'd papers be called for by the House) a detailed explanation of all the circumstances of the case. (14111)

[*Enclosure, dated 23 Jan.*]
Upon the question of the Ordnance equipment which accompanied the expedition to Portugal under the command of Lt.-Genl. Sir Arthur Wellesley, and with respect to which much misconception has arisen in consequence of the partial manner, in which this subject was treated before the Court of Enquiry, the facts are as hereafter detailed.

on the 29th, Whitbread commented: 'I have no doubt there is a great deal of bad work going forward, but I dare say he [Wardle] will not be able to prove it and will therefore come to disgrace. I represented to him all the perils of his situation but he was determined to persevere.' (Howick MSS.)

Before stating them, it may be right to notice the points most dwelt upon before the Court. They are three.

1st. The insufficiency of the draft horses for the artillery.

2ly. The want of heavy ordnance and ammunition and of heavy guns on travelling carriages.

3ly. The calibres of the heavy brigades of the field train, being only *nine po[unde]rs*.

It might perhaps be enough to say that the equipment never was thought of or intended for the service of Portugal, but was fitted out for a particular and secret service, under a signification of your Majesty's pleasure to that effect, according to the express requisition of Lt.-Genl. Sir Arthur Wellesley.

But to enter more fully into the details of this question. It shou'd be remarked that Sir Arthur Wellesley had (previous to any actual appointment to command) been long destined for this remote service, to which it was understood he had for a very considerable time directed his attention and researches. Accordingly, upon the expedition to South America being determined on, and his being appointed to the command of it, he made a requisition for such an equipment as was judged necessary for this object, and I have no reason to suppose it was not well adapted to the service for which it was destined. It consisted of three divisions from this country, together with an additional ordnance equipment with three companies of artillery, which were to join him, with the troops from Halifax and from Madeira. Two distinct objects were in view, which will account for the different periods at which the divisions were to sail.

The first, which was collected at Cork, with the troops, consisted of the companies of artillery, the field brigades, arms, ammunition stores, the engineers and engineer stores, &c. &c. &c. &c., and was intended to proceed in the course of the month of June off Cadiz and Gibraltar, where some further arrangements for the expedition were to be made.

It was distinctly understood (and the signification of your Majesty's pleasure as well as Sir Arthur Wellesley's requisition shew it) that no horses were to accompany the expedition, but an ample detachment of gunner drivers was thought essential, and they accordingly embarked with the companies of artillery.

When Sir Arthur Wellesley's destination was suddenly changed, and he received orders thro' the Secretary of State to proceed immediately, with the force assembled at Cork, to the coast of Portugal, he, having his gunner drivers with him, thought it better to take the commissariat horses from Ireland, thinking them adequate to ye service, rather than to make a requisition for artillery horses from hence, which were in perfect readiness, and stationed to ye westward; and when I suggested afterwards whether it might not be expedient to send them, I was given to understand that the state of the transport tonnage wou'd not permit it. Why the 300 horses embarked at Portsmouth with three brigades of artillery attached to Brigr.-Genls. Acland[1] and Anstruther's corps, did not proceed with

[1] Sir Wroth Palmer Acland (1770–1816). Ensign, 1787; Lieutenant, 1790; Captain, 1791; Major, 1795; Lieutenant-Colonel, 1795; Colonel, 1803; Major-General, 1810; Lieutenant-General, 1814. K.C.B., 1815.

them, but followed with Sir Harry Burrard, I do not know. They were in perfect readiness at the place of embarkation desired by the Secretary of State (Portsmouth) before the troops embarked in the Downs.

The second part, which consisted of heavy mortars, howrs., platforms, and ammunition for *ship guns*, were to sail on ye *1st of July*, and follow Sir Arthur Wellesley off Cadiz.

The third part of this equipment was exactly the same as that enumerated in the second, with the addition of four *24*prs. on travelling carriages, and was appointed to follow Sir Arthur Wellesley to a named rendezvous on the *1st of September*.

But neither of these equipments had the smallest reference to any service (if there was any) in contemplation in Europe, for on ye 14th of June, Sir Arthur Wellesley writes to me to say that, as under present circumstances the first object of his expedition (meaning the siege of Monte Video) might probably not be undertaken, he suggested that there need be no hurry in embarking the heavy ordnance and ammunition ordered for the 1st of July, thereby clearly shewing that any embarkation desired of heavy ordnance and ammunition was not considered by him as having any reference to any service then in contemplation in Europe.

This ordnance &c &c &c however being ready, as well as the transports, the Secretary of State desired they shou'd be embarked, and they sailed from the river on ye 3rd of July, and afterwards proceeded with the convoy to the coast of Portugal.

As to the third point, that there were no heavier guns than *nine prs.* with the field train, the fact is that *twelve prs.* had been destined for the heavy brigade, but at Sir Arthur Wellesley's express desire, the *9 prs.* were sent. They are a new gun of a very improved construction.

From the foregoing statement, I trust it will appear that there is no ground for any imputation on the Ordnance as an executive Department. Into matters of opinion which wou'd rather refer to me personally than to the Department, this paper does not profess to enter, nor is it necessary. Your Majesty is fully acquainted with my sentiments, they having been from time to time as it was my duty to do, most humbly submitted to your Majesty. (14113–16)

[*The King's reply, Windsor Castle, 30 Jan.*] The King has received Lord Chatham's letter and the accompanying statement, which his Majesty has read attentively and which appears to him a very fair and clear exposition of the circumstances which Lord Chatham has stated from time to time. (14112)

3802   THE DUKE OF PORTLAND *to the* KING,[1] *and the reply*

[*Burlington House, Monday, 30 Jan. 1809.*] The sanction which your Majesty has usually condescended to bestow on the proceedings of the two Houses of your Parliament on such events as have appeared to them of sufficient importance

---

[1] Not in the Duke's own hand.

to intitle to their thanks the officers of your Majesty's Army and Navy who have had the honour and good fortune of having been instrumental to their accomplishment, is held in too much reverence by your Majesty's confidential servants to suffer them to omit making their humble representations to your Majesty in consequence of the notice which has been taken by your Parliament of the distinguished conduct and exemplary valour which have been displayed by the Commanders-in-Chief, and General and other Officers in Portugal and Spain, and more especially in the battles of Vimiera and Corunna. It is therefore at the unanimous request of your Majesty's confidential servants that the Duke of Portland most humbly begs leave to lay at your Majesty's feet their most dutifull recommendations of Lieutenant-General Sir David Baird, Lieutenant-General Hope, and Major-General Spencer, as persons who have rendered themselves worthy of being admitted to the honourable Order of the Bath. And as this mark of your Majesty's royal favour is necessarily restricted within very narrow limits, it is most humbly submitted to your Majesty's consideration, to resort to the same means to which your Majesty has heretofore had recourse upon similar occasions, and to order medals to be struck in commemoration of the actions of Vimiera and Corunna for the purpose of being distributed to and worn by the General and other Officers, under the same regulations and restrictions as have been repeatedly sanctioned by your Majesty. But as, by confining the distribution of the medals to the two occasions of Vimiera and Corunna, the very brilliant services of the cavalry would seem to pass unnoticed, and as it might be doubtfull whether even the General Officers under whose command their reputation had been acquired, would in strictness be intitled to that mark of distinction, it is humbly hoped that your Majesty may not deem it improper to order a medal to be struck in commemoration of the affair of Benevente, and in honour of the cavalry, which it is to be observed was in fact the only description of your Majesty's forces in Spain that had any opportunity of distinguishing itself prior to the action before Corunna.

There now only remains one other circumstance connected with the present subject which the Duke of Portland is anxious to be permitted to bring under the consideration of your Majesty, and that is, the embarassment and distress to which he has reason to believe Sir John Moore's mother and sister will be reduced by the melancholy event of his death. The Duke of Portland has been informed that the principal part of Mrs Moore's subsistence was composed of the allowance she received from her sons, of which much the largest share was supplied by Sir John, whose private fortune would not allow of his providing for her after his death. But as it happens that Major Stanhope, who lost his life on the same day that your Majesty was deprived of the services of Sir John Moore, had a pension upon the Civil List of £600 pr annm. it has occurred to the Duke of Portland that if your Majesty should think proper to appropriate the whole or a part of that pension to the use of Sir John Moore's mother and sister, it would afford such a provision for them as would obviate the apprehensions that they must necessarily be under upon their own account, in aggravation of the affliction they must feel for the loss of so near and dear a relation. (14117–21)

[The King's reply, Windsor Castle, 31 Jan.] The King entirely approves of the Duke of Portland's proposals that the Order of the Bath should be conferred upon Lieut.-Generals Sir David Baird & Hope and upon Major-General Spencer,[1] and that medals should be distributed to the troops which have been engaged in Spain and Portugal in commemoration & reward of their gallant services. His Majesty also approves of the Duke of Portland's proposal that the whole of the pension which was enjoyed by the late Major Stanhope should be conferred upon the mother and sister of the late Sir John Moore. (14122)

3803   THE KING *to the* EARL OF LIVERPOOL, *and the reply*

[Windsor Castle, 31 Jan. 1809.] The King acquaints Lord Liverpool that, from the great rise of the waters in this neighbourhood, there has been no passage for a carriage from hence to London since Friday last, in consequence of which it will not be in his power to go to London tomorrow, but as the waters appear now to be falling, his Majesty trusts that he shall be able to find a good passage by Friday, when he will go to town. Should the journey however continue then impracticable, his Majesty will not fail to acquaint Lord Liverpool, who may be assured that as far as it depends upon him no business shall be put off. (14125)

[Lord Liverpool's reply, 31 Jan.] Lord Liverpool begs leave most humbly to inform your Majesty that in obedience to your Majesty's commands, he has directed notes to be sent out to put off the Privy Council summoned for to-morrow. Lord Liverpool will wait your Majesty's further orders for Friday, but he trusts that he may be allowed to express a hope that your Majesty will not think of coming to town on that day unless it shall have been first ascertained that the road between London and Windsor may be passed over in a carriage without either difficulty or inconvenience. (14126)

3804   *Letters from* SPENCER PERCEVAL *to the* KING, *and the replies*

[Downg. St., 31 Jan. 1809.] Mr. Perceval acquaints your Majesty that a debate has taken place this evening upon the late overture & negotiation for peace. Mr. Canning moved an Address to your Majesty approving of the course which was pursued upon that occasion, and expressing the determination of the House to support your Majesty in the war. Mr. Whitbread moved an Amendment condemning the manner in which this overture was met by requiring that Spain should be admitted as a party to the negotiation, and amongst other things expressing a desire that your Majesty would lose no opportunity of entering into negotiations for peace. This Amendment was opposed by Mr. Ponsonby, Lord Henry Petty, Lord Porchester and generally by the Opposition, so that there appeared little occasion for your Majesty's servants to take part in the debate.

---

[1] Sir Arthur Wellesley had written to Castlereagh on 14 Nov. 1808: 'It is said that Spencer would not like to accept any mark of the King's favour at present, but I am convinced that I shall be able to prevail with him.' (*Castlereagh Corresp.* VII, 13.)

Sr. F. Burdett, indeed, opposed the Address but he opposed the Amendment also, and desponding of the cause of Spain and indeed of the country, was prepared to support nothing but an Address for a total change of men & measures. Mr. Canning replied, and the House agreed to his Address without any division.

Mr. Wardle moved for the attendance of some witnesses, and proposed going into one of the charges against H.R.H. the D. of York tomorrow.[1] (14127–8)

[*The King's reply, Windsor Castle, 1 Feb.*] The King acknowledges the receipt of Mr Perceval's report of the proceedings in the House of Commons last night. (14128)

[*From Perceval, Thursday morng., 2.30 [2 Feb. 1809].*] Mr. Perceval acquaints your Majesty that he is just returned from the House of Commons where he has been engaged since 5 o'clock yesterday afternoon till this time in the investigation of one of Mr. Wardle's charges against H.R.H. the Duke of York. That charge in substance was that an exchange between a Lieut.-Col. Knight[2] & Lt.-Col. Brook,[3] was expedited by means of a promise from Col. Brook's brother to Mrs Clarke that he would give her £200 if she would manage to accelerate it, that she informed his R. Highness that such were the terms upon which her influence was engaged to be exerted. That H.R.H. did therefore consent to accelerate it, that she did in consequence receive the £200, & that after having received it she acquainted him that she had done so. This case was attempted by Mr. Wardle to be supported by the evidence of Dr Thynn,[4] of Col. Knight's brother, and of Mrs. Clarke. Dr. Thynn & Col. Knight's brother proved that this sum of £200 was engaged to be given Mrs Clarke for this service, & that when the exchange was gazetted the money was paid to her—and of the fact so far, Mr Perceval does not think there is any reason to doubt. But that his R. Highness was in any degree

[1] *Parl. Deb.*, XII, 210–40. Tierney wrote to Lord Grey on 1 Feb. on the subject of this debate: 'On Saturday Whitbread called on me, and told me he was determined to move an Amendment to the Address on the papers relative to the Erfurt negotiation, and that a copy of it would be sent to Ponsonby that evening. He himself left town that day and returned on Monday night. Yesterday morning he saw Petty and Ponsonby, who urged him as much as possible to give up his scheme—but in vain, and the result was that we were made to exhibit a public proof of the little concert there is amongst us by one leading person deliberately moving what two others had deliberately opposed! Under all these circumstances, can you be surprised if I feel disgusted and indisposed to look forward with anything like confidence or even hope to our future proceedings? Nothing, I do assure you, but a knowledge of the difficulties in which you are personally involved, a sense of the peculiar delicacy of your situation with respect to Whitbread, and an apprehension that what I do may in some degree, in his estimation, affect you, prevents my taking a very decided line.

'Canning last night made a very good speech in moving the Address, and with less than usual of Canning in it, but the best performance of the evening was Burdett's. He spoke with more effect than I have heard anyone do for some time back, and delivered some truths in a manner that made them not only felt but acknowledged by the whole House. Canning in his reply tried to raise a cry about dangerous and alarming doctrines, but completely failed in the attempt.' (Howick MSS.)

[2] Henry Raleigh Knight (*d.* 1836). Lieutenant-Colonel, 1802; Colonel, 1811; Major-General, 1814; Lieutenant-General, 1830. This episode, then, did not prove detrimental to his career. His brother Robert said that he had served 23 years in the army and had been in every battle since 1793. (*Parl. Deb.*, XII, 272.)

[3] William Brooke (*d.* 1843). Cornet, 1793; Lieutenant, 1793; Major, 1794; Lieutenant-Colonel, 1800; Colonel, 1810; Major-General, 1813; General, 1841.

[4] Andrew Thynne, M.D., who had attended Mary Anne Clarke for seven years.

acquainted with the transaction or influenced by it, tho attempted to be proved by Mrs. Grant [*sic*], Mr. Perceval has the satisfaction to acquaint your Majesty that he does not think there is the slightest colour of credible evidence to prove. Mrs. Clarke was directly contradicted in a most material circumstance by Mr. Knight, Mr. Knight having distinctly stated that after this transaction took place Mrs Clarke desired him to be particularly cautious of mentioning it, because she would not on any account have it come to the ears of his Highness. This she flatly contradicted. She was also contradicted in other circumstances but her whole carriage was so extremely impudent, not to say audacious, that Mr. Perceval does not believe that any member in the House could fail to see that she did not deserve any credit. Against the charge Mr Adam was examined who explained some circumstances very satisfactorily, especially the grounds upon which the connexion between her & his R.H. broke off,[1] namely upon Mr. Adam having discovered that she was engaged in transactions in which she was obtaining money upon his R.H.'s credit. Mr. Wardle underwent a long examination, by which considerable contradiction was shewn in the evidence of Mrs. Clarke, and finally Col. Gordon was called who proved the grounds on which the exchange was recommended, and Mr. Perceval is convinced shewed to the House that there was a degree of accuracy prevailing in his R.H.'s Office which could hardly be parallelled, certainly not exceeded, in any Office, and Col. Gordon by reference to his papers was enabled to speak confidently that the exchange took place in the ordinary course upon the recommendation of General Norton,[2] the Col. of the Regt. into which Col. Knight was to exchange, and upon the report which he himself had made to his R. Highness upon that subject, and therefore that there was no room for the interference of Mrs. Clarke's influence. The enquiry however at his charge is not yet finally closed—& it is adjourned till Friday, when the remainder of this charge will be gone thro' and Coll. Wardle will proceed upon another. Mr Perceval cannot close this report without stating to your Majesty, what he does with infinite satisfaction, that if Col. Wardle should not be able to make anything appear stronger or more credible in his other charges than he has done in this, that he will completely fail in his attack against H.R.Hss. and that however unpleasant, it must be at all times & under any circumstances to have brought under public examination & notice a private connexion of the nature of that which subsisted between H.R.H. & Mrs Clarke, yet the charge of that connexion having in any degree influenced H.R.H.'s conduct and advice to your Majesty as Commander-in-Chief will appear to be wholly without any foundation in fact, to originate in the malice probably of Mrs. Clarke, but certainly of some enemy of H.R. Highness.[3] (14132–4)

[1] In May 1806. The Duke thought it his duty, said Adam, to give her an annuity of £400 a year, payable, however, only during satisfactory behaviour; consequently he refused to enter into a bond. Adam did not know whether the allowance had been paid. Mrs Clarke alleged (19 June 1808) that the Duke owed her £500 (col. 331), and she threatened to publish the story of their relationship, and also fifty or sixty of his letters to her, unless the arrears were paid forthwith and the annuity secured by bond.   [2] John Chapple Norton (1746–1818).

[3] *Parl. Deb.*, XII, 264–311. Mrs Clarke appeared in the House, it was suggested, dressed as if she had been going to an evening party—in a light-blue silk gown and coat edged with white fur, and carrying a white muff. In size she was rather small and not particularly well made. She had lively blue

[The King's reply, Windsor Castle, 2 Feb.] The King is much pleased to learn from Mr Perceval that the proceedings in the House of Commons upon Mr. Wardle's first charge have proved so satisfactory, and, however his Majesty may deplore the unfortunate connexion which has produced an enquiry which in many respects must be so unpleasant to the Duke of York, he has never doubted that, in the discharge of his duty, the Duke of York would at no time allow himself to be influenced by any motive or circumstance which would not bear the strictest scrutiny. (14135)

3805   THE KING *to* LORD LIVERPOOL, *and the reply*

[Windsor Castle, 2 Feb. 1809.] The King acquaints Lord Liverpool that having caused the passage by Eton to the main road to be examined his Majesty has ascertained it to continue impracticable for a carriage, by which he is under the necessity of again putting off his journey to London. The waters are now subsiding, though very slowly, and the King hopes that before Monday next there will be no material impediment. Should a safe passage be established, his Majesty will not fail to give Lord Liverpool notice on Sunday of his determination to go to London on the following day. (14131)

[Lord Liverpool's reply, London, 2 Feb.] Lord Liverpool begs leave most humbly to inform your Majesty that in obedience to your Majesty's commands he has given directions that the Privy Council and Recorder's Report appointed for tomorrow should be put off till your Majesty's further pleasure is known. (14130)

3806   SPENCER PERCEVAL *to the* KING, *and the reply*

[3 Feb. 1809.] Mr. Perceval acquaints your Majesty that the House of Commons has proceeded this evening with Mr Wardle's charges—some further evidence was given upon the charge respecting Col. Knight's exchange, which was the subject of the former evening's enquiry. It had this singular circumstance connected with it. Mrs. Clarke had said that she had not seen Mr. Wardle last Tuesday at her house, at any part of that day, & she was convinced she had not, because she was not at home at any part of the day. Mr. Wardle had so far contradicted her as to say he had called upon her in the evening of that day and seen her at her own house for a few minutes. He gave notice yesterday that he would wish to be examined again, as he had recollected himself, and that he had seen her in the morning. Upon his re-examination it came out that he had called upon her *twice* on that morning, and had seen her both times. To explain and account for this

eyes, but her features were not considered handsome. Her nose was rather short, and turning up; teeth indifferent—but her appearance was vivacious, her manners fascinating.

Lord Temple wrote to W. H. Fremantle on 29 Jan.: 'I am sorry beyond measure for all that is passing relative to the Duke of York. These are not times for such discussions, even if the facts charged were truer than I believe them to be. I *know* (as least I believe so) one case in which the Duke dismissed a man from the service for having offered Mrs. Clarke a bribe to get him an exchange to avoid going to the West Indies. I have sent a note of it to Gen. Grenville.' (Fremantle MSS.)

contradiction to his former testimony he said it was owing to a mistake between Monday and Tuesday—and that what he had said as to the Tuesday he was misled to say by thinking it applied to what he had done upon the Monday; namely, that he had indeed called upon her, & not finding her at home had waited for her for some time but had not seen her. After this explanation he was then asked whether he did see her on the Monday, and it turned out that he had seen her on the *Monday* also. So that he got into a double contradiction and left both his own and Mrs. Clarke's evidence in a much worse state than it was before.

After some further evidence on this case was gone through he then proceeded to his charge respecting the rapid promotion of Capt. *Maling*[1] but upon this charge Mr Perceval has the satisfaction of stating to your Majesty that he has really nothing to report, only that the charge came litterally to nothing. It appeared that the original Comsn. of Mr. Maling was given upon the recommendation of the Col. of the Regiment into which he entered;[2] that he had his promotion fairly according to your Majesty's Regulations, that he was a man in every way perfectly qualified to obtain it, and an officer of very high estimation in the Army with those under whom he served. As to *this* charge therefore there is not remaining the slightest possibility of reflection upon H.R.H. the Comr.-in-Chief—and it only gave an excellent opportunity to Col. Gordon in his evidence to shew how much this very subject of promotion in your Majesty's Army was improved by the Regulations introduced into the service by his Royal Highness the Duke of York himself. Mr Perceval trusts he shall be able to send your Majesty as satisfactory an account of the proceedings on Tuesday, when the House is to enter further into the enquiry.[3] (14142–3)

[*The King's reply, Windsor Castle, 4 Feb.*] The King has received great satisfaction from Mr. Perceval's report of the further proceedings in the enquiry into Mr Wardle's charges against the Duke of York. (14144)

3807   *Letters from* GEORGE CANNING *to the* KING, *and the replies*

[*Foreign Office, 3 Feb. 1809.*] Mr. Canning most humbly presumes to submit for your Majesty's royal approbation the name of Mr Oakeley,[4] late your Majesty's Secretary of Legation at Stockholm, to succeed Mr Foster as Secretary of Legation in America.[5]

Mr. Canning at the same time submits for your Majesty's royal signature a Full Power to Mr. Erskine to be used in case of any arrangement between your Majesty & the Government of the United States, either in respect to the affair of

[1] John Maling. Ensign, 1805; Lieutenant, 1806; Captain, Sept. 1808.
[2] Lieutenant-General Sir John Doyle, Colonel of the 87th Foot.
[3] *Parl. Deb.*, XII, 326–64.
[4] Sir Charles Oakeley (1778–1829). Chargé d'Affaires, 1801–2, and Secretary of Legation, 1801–4, to Bavaria; Secretary of Legation, 1807–8, and Chargé d'Affaires, 1808, at Stockholm. Succeeded his father as 2nd Baronet, 7 Sept. 1826.
[5] Foster's appointment is not mentioned in *British Diplomatic Representatives, 1789–1852*. Augustus John Foster was Secretary of Legation at Stockholm from Nov. 1808 until June 1810.

the Chesapeake, or any other of the points in discussion between the two Governments. (14136)

[*The King's reply, Windsor Castle, 4 Feb.*] The King approves of Mr Canning's recommendation of Mr Oakeley to succeed Mr Foster as Secretary of Legation in America.[1] (14137)

[*From Canning, Foreign Office, 4 Feb.*] Mr. Canning most humbly submits to your Majesty the draft of a letter which he proposes (if not disapproved by your Majesty) to address to Prince Castelcicala for the purpose of conveying to the knowledge of the Emperor of Russia, through the Duke of Serra Capriola the letter from Mr. Champagny to Buonaparte which was intercepted in Spain.

The time which has been requisite for perfecting the *facsimile* of this letter (which seemed necessary to establish its authenticity) prevented Mr. Canning from sooner laying it before your Majesty—and it is only within these two days that he has been able to find a certain & secure communication to St. Petersburgh.

Mr. Canning most humbly presumes to transmit to your Majesty two copies of the *facsimile*; conceiving that your Majesty might perhaps condescend to preserve so curious a document. (14138–9)

[*The King's reply, Windsor Castle, 5 Feb.*] The King approves of the letter which Mr Canning proposes to send to Prince Castelcicala with the *facsimile* of Mr. Champagny's letter, the two copies of which his Majesty has kept. (14139)

3808 THE EARL OF LIVERPOOL *to the* KING

[*London, 7 Feb. 1809.*] Lord Liverpool begs leave most humbly to lay before your Majesty the Minutes of the House of Lords of this day. Lord Grosvenor[2] opened the business in a very long but very vapid speech and was well answered by the Duke of Montrose. The Motion was supported by Lord Grenville, Lord Erskine and Lord Moira. Lord Harrowby spoke at the conclusion of the debate and very ably. There was no division. Lord Grenville has decidedly fixed upon Tuesday for bringing on his Motion respecting the Orders-in-Council.[3] (14145)

3809 SPENCER PERCEVAL *to the* KING, *and the reply*

[*Downg. St., Wedny. morng.,* [*8 Feb. 1809*].] Mr. Perceval acquaints your Majesty that the proceedings upon the enquiry into the conduct of his Royal Highness the Duke of York were resumed in the Ho. of Commons yesterday evening, and were continued till ½ p. one this morning. Some time was taken up in examining some witnesses to parts of the preceding charge, the result of whose testimony certainly left the enquiry upon that charge in a light to be full as satis-

---

[1] The appointment is not listed in *British Diplomatic Representatives, 1789–1852.*
[2] Lord Belgrave (see No. 644) had succeeded his father as 2nd Earl Grosvenor on 5 Aug. 1802.
[3] *Parl. Deb.,* XII, 378–91.

factory for H.R.Hss. as it was before. When their examination was concluded Mr Wardle proceeded to his enquiry respecting Col. French's levy,[1] and the examination and cross-examination of two of his witnesses, a Mr. Corri[2] and a Mr. Dowler[3] took up so much time, that the Comee. were obliged to leave this case not near finished. From what had fallen from these witnesses and particularly from Mr. Dowler it was felt to be very desireable that Mrs. Clarke should be examined before the Committee broke up, and she was therefore called in. But she represented herself to be so extremely fatigued and exhausted by waiting so long that she was utterly incapable of undergoing an examination. And after some consideration it was determined that it would be better (altho but little credit was given to the statements she made of her fatigue) to incur the inconvenience of an adjournment previous to her examination rather than to take a step which might have the appearance of proceeding with harshness against the witness, and proceeding when she might have the opportunity of excusing any defects in her testimony by the state of fatigue which she had alledged; the Comee. therefore adjourned before Mr. Wardle had nearly closed his case and consequently before it was possible to go into that satisfactory statement which a reference to the official documents will enable his Royal Highness the D. of York to give on the whole of the transactions concerned with this levy. But notwithstanding that situation in which the case was left Mr Perceval is happy to state that he sees no reason to apprehend that it will produce any other impression than what has been made by the former parts of the enquiry.[4] (14150–1)

[*The King's reply, Windsor Castle, 8 Feb.*] The King acknowledges the receipt of Mr Perceval's report of the proceedings in the House of Commons last night upon Mr Wardle's third charge. (14151)

[1] William Fry French. The Colonel had obtained a letter of service enabling him to raise recruits and pay them bounties. Mrs Clarke, through whom the negotiations for the letter of service were carried on, was given £850 for her assistance. He had been promoted Captain in the 48th Foot in Sept. 1804.

[2] Dominigo Corri, a music master, who acted as Mrs Clarke's agent or go-between.

[3] William Dowler, the son of a wine merchant, had just returned from Lisbon with dispatches, and had recently been put in charge of the accounts department of the Commissariat in Lisbon. Mrs Clarke had procured for him the office of Assistant Commissary of Stores and Provisions in 1805 on payment to her, initially, of £1,000, 'and at other times other sums to a very considerable amount'.

[4] *Parl. Deb.*, xii, 391–438. Sir Arthur Wellesley's report of the proceedings was gloomier than Perceval's. He wrote to the Duke of Richmond on the 8th: 'We had a terrible night last night in the House of Commons. It appeared that Mrs. Clarke had received 1350 pounds from Col. French to facilitate the grant of the King's letter for his Levy; and 1000 pounds from Mr. Dowler to make him a Commissary. Besides this the evidence of Ludowick, the Duke's footman, on a point respecting the cashing of a banknote for Mrs. Clarke, on which point the Duke himself had examined him before he appeared in the House, was contradicted by a respectable looking man by the name of Peirson who had been Mrs. Clarke's butler. It appeared that Dowler gave Mrs. Clarke a thousand pounds to be made an Assistant Commissary: that she recommended him to the Duke of York & the Duke to Mr. Pitt and he was appointed in 1805; having made no application to any other person for the appointment. Huskisson & Bourne, the Secretaries of the Treasury of the day, could give no account of his appointment. The impression from last night's examination is very much against the Duke.' (Richmond MSS. 58/52.)

3810 VISCOUNT CASTLEREAGH *to the* KING, *and the reply*

[*St. James's Sq., 8 Feb. 1809.*] Lord Castlereagh begs leave humbly to acquaint your Majesty that he has received from Spain three boxes address'd to your Majesty containing books of which the Bishop of Leon solicited your Majesty's acceptance some time since. The boxes have been detain'd for a length of time at Gihon [*sic*]. Lord Castlereagh humbly requests to receive your Majesty's commands with respect to their disposal. (14148)

[*The King's reply, Windsor Castle, 9 Feb.*] The King desires that Lord Castlereagh will order the books which have arrived from Spain to be sent to his Majesty's Library in London. (14149)

3811 THE DUKE OF PORTLAND *to the* KING, *and the reply*

[*Burlington House, Thursday, 9 Feb. 1809.*] The Duke of Portland humbly conceives it to be his duty to lay before your Majesty without delay a letter which he has received this morning from her Royal Highness the Duchess of Brunswick in consequence of the unaltered unfortunate situation of the Princes her sons—& he trusts that he shall not be deemed too presumptuous by your Majesty for stating that the sum your Majesty was graciously pleased about this time last year to order to be issued for the use of their Serene Highnesses Prince George & Prince Augustus of Brunswick was £2000 to each, & that on a subsequent representation of the Duke of Brunswick-Oels to your Majesty of the distressed state of his Serene Highness's pecuniary affairs your Majesty was farther pleased to order the sum of £2000 to be advanced as a temporary provision for his Serene Highness. (14152)

[*The King's reply, Windsor Castle, 10 Feb.*] As it appears from the Duchess of Brunswick's representation to the Duke of Portland that the circumstances under which a temporary provision was made last year for the Princes of Brunswick & the Duke of Brunswick-Oels continue the same, the King approves of its being renewed at this period. (14153)

3812 *Letters from* SPENCER PERCEVAL *to the* KING, *and the replies*

[*Downg. St., Friday morng.* [*10 Feb. 1809*].] Mr. Perceval acquaints your Majesty that the House has been engaged in the enquiry upon the charge against H.R.H. the Duke of York till 4 o'clock this morning. Mrs. Clarke has been again examined, & has told a most extravagant & incredible story, and her credit has again been materially impeached. The case has been spun out to great length, and is not yet concluded. In the course of the evidence a great deal of proof has been laid before the Committee of persons obtaining money for the purpose of obtaining promotion in the Army and places of profit of different descriptions, but nothing has appeared to bring any part of such transactions home either to H.R.H. the D of York or any other person in official situation.[1] (14154)

[1] *Parl. Deb.*, XII, 439–504 (9 Feb.).

[*The King's reply, Windsor Castle, 10 Feb.*] The King has received Mr Perceval's report of the proceedings in the House of Commons last night which appear to his Majesty perfectly satisfactory as far as they regard the charges brought against the Duke of York & other individuals in official situations. (14155)

[*From Perceval, Downg. St., 10 [11] Feb.*] Mr. Perceval acquaints your Majesty that the House of Commons proceeded again upon the charges against the Duke of York till near three o'clock this morning. The charge concerning Col. French's levy was concluded and Major Toning's[1] case was also gone thro'. Mrs Clarke again exposed herself by testimony which could not gain credit, and Mr Perceval thinks that the impression of the House upon the enquiry of last night & this morning has been very much to the prejudice of the accusers. Mr Perceval hopes that on Monday the evidence will be closed.[2] (14156)

[*The King's reply, Windsor Castle, 11 Feb.*] The King acknowledges the receipt of Mr Perceval's report of what passed last night in the House of Commons and his Majesty is glad to hear that the impression on the House continues the same. (14157)

3813   LORD ELDON *to the* KING

[*13 Feb. 1809.*] The Lord Chancellor, offering his most humble duty to your Majesty, has the honour to transmit a Commission for passing the Bill for dissolving the marriage of Lord Boringdon tomorrow, to receive your Majesty's Royal Sign Manual if your Majesty shall graciously so think fit.[3] (14158)

  [1] George Augustus Tonyn. Captain, 1795; Major, 1804. In 1804, it was said, he had served in the army 23 years. He was the son of General Tonyn, who died in 1804 (General, 1798). His name is wrongly given as Jenyn in Colchester, *Diary and Corresp.*, II, 166.
  [2] *Parl. Deb.*, XII, 505–57 (10 Feb.).
  [3] Canning's friend Lord Boringdon had married, 20 June 1804, Lady Augusta Fane (1786–1871), second daughter of John, 10th Earl of Westmorland. On 18 May 1808 she eloped from her husband's London house, and Sir Arthur Paget, with whom the Duchess of Rutland had earlier been in love, was subsequently cited as co-respondent in a divorce suit. Boringdon was awarded £10,000 damages, with costs, in an action of *crim. con.* Lady Bessborough described her as 'a good-humoured girl' who did not 'seem to have much in her'. 'He stipulated before they came [i.e. to visit the Duchess of Devonshire in 1805] that they should sleep in separate rooms, saying if it was inconvenient they could return at night.' (*Corresp. of Lord Granville Leveson-Gower*, II, 57.) On 16 Feb. 1809 she married Paget at Heckfield, Hants. She had one child, Viscount Boringdon (1806–17), by her first husband. It has been suggested that Mrs Henry Wood founded *East Lynne* on the tragic story of the boy's death and his mother's return to him during his last days.
  On 23 Aug. 1809 Boringdon married Frances, daughter of Thomas Talbot. She died in 1857, aged 76. He had had two sons previous to his first marriage, one of whom was Augustus Granville Stapleton (1800–80), well known as Canning's private secretary and biographer. He made ample financial provision for them.
  Canning commented, in a letter to Mrs Canning, 7 April 1810: 'Boringdon talks of his present wife and her *predecessor* just as one would of a new butler.' (Harewood MSS.)

[*Foreign Office, 13 Feb. 1809.*] Mr. Canning, humbly conceiving that it might be advantageous that some person accredited by your Majesty to the Emperor of Austria should be stationed at Malta, under the present circumstances, prepared to proceed by way of Trieste to Vienna either upon invitation from the Austrian Government, or in the event of war actually breaking out between Austria & France, but that this person should not be (in the first instance) one of any high ostensible character, or one whose departure from this country would be liable to much notice—Mr Canning most humbly submits to your Majesty the name of Mr. Benjamin Bathurst,[1] late your Majesty's Chargé d'affaires & Minister Plenipotentiary *ad interim* at Stockholm, & formerly Secretary of Legation at Vienna [*sic*], for this Mission—which, if your Majesty shall be graciously pleased to approve, Mr Canning will humbly submit tomorrow the instructions which he has prepared for Mr Bathurst, & the Letter of Credence to be eventually delivered by him from your Majesty to the Emperor of Austria.

Mr Canning has learnt today from what he conceives to be good authority—that Buonaparte has returned to Paris,[2] & that the war with Austria is considered as certain. It is also said that Buonaparte has determined to repeal, or modify, his Decrees affecting American commerce. (14161–2)

[*The King's reply, Windsor Castle, 14 Feb.*] The King approves of Mr Canning's recommendation of Mr. Bathurst for the mission to Vienna, under the circumstances referred to in his letter. (14164)

3815 *Letters from* SPENCER PERCEVAL *to the* KING, *and the replies*

[*Downg. St., Tuesday morng., 3 a.m., 14 Feb. 1809.*] Mr. Perceval acquaints your Majesty that the House has been again engaged with Col. Wardle's charges against H.R.H. the Duke of York, and has sat till near 3 o'clock this morning. Two letters from H.R.Highness to Mrs Clarke have been produced which Mr Perceval is grieved to say have undoubtedly made an unfavorable impression. The general style & language of them is expressive of great affection for Mrs Clarke, in terms little calculated to meet the public eye[3]—but the parts which have been most felt in them were the notices which H.R.H. takes in each of them of two applications which appear to have been made to his R.Hss. by Mrs Clarke. The one of them in favor of Genl. Clavering,[4] and the other of Dr

---

[1] Third son of Dr Henry Bathurst (1744–1837), Bishop of Norwich, 1805–37. Secretary of Legation, 1805–8, and Chargé d'Affaires, 1807, at Stockholm; Extraordinary Mission to Vienna, 1809, arriving there on 26 April and retiring to Buda, where he remained until Oct., being then forced to leave following the signing of the Treaty of Schönbrunn (14 Oct.) which provided for the severing of diplomatic relations between Great Britain and Austria. Bathurst was murdered near Hamburg whilst on his way home (1784–1809).

[2] From Spain, where he had been pursuing Moore's army.

[3] 'My sweetest, my darling love,' etc.

[4] He was only a Brigadier-General. Colonel, 1802; Brigadier-General, 1804. The House, far from accepting his evidence (on 10 February), found him guilty of prevarication, and on 24 March ordered him to be committed to Newgate.

O'Mara[1]—Dr O'Mara is an Irish clergyman of whom the Archbishop of Tuam,[2] whose letter in his commendation was produced, appears to have had a very high opinion, and his R. Highness, in a letter from Weymouth to Mrs Clarke talks of an application which she made to his R. Highness to endeavour to procure for Dr O'Mara the honor of preaching before yr. Majesty, which his Royal Highness says he will endeavour to procure. As to Genl. Clavering the letter mentions that the General is mistaken in supposing that there are any new Regiments to be raised, as it was only intended to raise 2d Battalions, so that she may tell him that she is sure her application cannot succeed, or to that effect. In these letters your Majesty will be glad to find that there is not the slightest trace of anything that looks like corruption or that exhibits any appearance of H.R. Highness's knowing that Mrs. Clarke was to derive any pecuniary advantage from the recommendations, but H.R.H.'s friends have been much disappointed in finding by them, what they did not believe on any former evidence, that his R.H. permitted Mrs. Clarke to mention such subjects to him at all. Independent of these letters the general course of the evidence was by no means unfavorable. Mrs. Clarke's credit was still further shaken, as well as that of Mr Dowler, whose testimony bore with some weight upon the case. There was, however, at the close of the examination this morning, evidence given by Mrs. Clarke of a Commsn. having been obtained by her for a person of the name of Saml. Carter, who had used to wait as a sort of foot boy behind the chairs of his Royal Highness and Mrs Clarke at dinner & supper. But as there has been no opportunity of making any enquiries as yet into the last-mentioned fact, Mr Perceval hopes that some explanation may be capable of being given which may remove the impression which this case is calculated to make.[3] (14159–60)

[*The King's reply, Windsor Castle, 14 Feb.*] The King has received Mr Perceval's report of last night's proceedings in the House of Commons, & his Majesty trusts that before the evidence closes the points referred to in it will be satisfactorily explained. (14163)

[*From Perceval, Downg. St., Wednesday morng.* [*15 Feb.*].] Mr. Perceval acquaints your Majesty that the Committee upon the enquiry into the conduct of H.R.Hss. the D of York was engaged in that enquiry till about one o'clock this morning. Nothing of very material importance appeared in the course of this last sitting, certainly nothing to encrease any unfavorable impression. The charge relative to Col. Shaw[4] has failed entirely of establishing anything to the prejudice

---

[1] O'Meara. Mrs Clarke stated that she never received any suggestions regarding ecclesiastical promotions involving money payments, but that Dr O'Meara, who wanted to be a Bishop, did apply to her in 1805. (*Parl. Deb.*, XII, 473 [9 Feb.].)

[2] William Beresford (1743–1819), brother of the 1st Marquess of Waterford. Bishop of Dromore, 1780; of Ossory, 1782–94; Archbishop of Tuam, 1794–1819. Created Baron Decies [I.], 21 Dec. 1812. He married the 1st Earl of Clare's sister Elizabeth and they had sixteen children.

[3] *Parl. Deb.*, XII, 558–612.

[4] J. Shaw, of the 40th Foot. In 1806 he had been in the army about 23 years (*Parl. Deb.*, XII, 619), and in that year, being then a Major, he was appointed Deputy Barrack Master General at the Cape, with the rank of Lieutenant-Colonel.

of H.R.Highness as well as the charge which was brought forward by Lord Folkstone relative to the resignation of a Capt. Turner.

The commission which was granted to Samuel Carter, which Mr Perceval mentioned to your Majesty in his report of yesterday, appears to have been solicited three years before by a Col. Sutton,[1] certainly before his R. Highness was acquainted with Mrs Clarke; but there are no means of denying that he was in the service of Mrs Clarke during the time that his Royal Highness was connected with her, and that he was appointed to his commission from her service.

Some material contradiction was brought forward against Mrs. Clarke, and Mr Perceval hopes that the Committee may close its enquiries tomorrow, altho upon that point he cannot be certain.[2] (14165)

[*The King's reply, Windsor Castle, 15 Feb. 1809*] The King acknowledges the receipt of Mr Perceval's report of last night's proceedings in the House of Commons. (14166)

[*From Perceval, 16 Feb.*] Mr Perceval acquaints your Majesty that the Committee upon the charges against his R. Highness the D of York, broke up this morning at about $\frac{1}{2}$ p. one o'clock. The proceedings began by the examination of certain letters which had been delivered into the House the day before by a person[3] in whose house they had been left by Mrs Clark [*sic*]. They had been referred to a Select Committee to inspect them, and produce such as had any reference to these charges. There were produced three from Genl. Clavering; three from Baroness Nollekin, and three or four from a person of the name of Elderton.[4] One of the letters from General Clavering was explaining a plan of enlistment from the militia which he wished to have submitted to the Duke of York by Mrs Clarke, and in the execution of which plan he proposed to be employed himself; and there was evidently the letter which led to that to Mrs Clarke from his R. Highness the D. of York, in which his R.H. mentions the name of General Clavering and states that he is mistaken in supposing that there are any new regiments to be raised. The third letter was one of no consequence. Those from the Baroness Nollekin were soliciting Mrs. Clarke's influence with his R.Hss. to obtain a pension for her, but upon these it did not appear that anything had been done by H.R.H. the D of York. The letters of Elderton respected an application for a Paymastership which he wished to procure thro' the influence of H.R.Hss., and connected with this Mrs. Clarke stated that H.R.H. had told her that he had

---

[1] Thomas Sutton, a Lieutenant, in 1801, in the Royal Artillery, and, it was said, at one time Mrs Clarke's inseparable friend. Samuel Carter was a fifteen-year-old orphan when Sutton first addressed the Commander-in-Chief on his behalf, on 7 Dec. 1801. He was given an Ensigncy in 1804. (*Parl Deb.*, XII, 628.)

[2] *Parl. Deb., ibid.*, cols. 612–51.

[3] William Nicholls, in whose house at Hampstead Mrs Clarke lived for some months in 1807–8, representing herself sometimes as a married woman, sometimes as a widow.

[4] H. Elderton. Mrs Clarke alleged that she had procured for him a paymastership in the 22nd Light Dragoons. (*Parl. Deb.*, XII, 667.) His son, Charles Elderton, was appointed to a cadetship in the Madras infantry, Jan. 1805, and Mrs Clarke was asked to use her influence with the Duke of York to get him transferred into the cavalry.

applied to Mr Greenwood in his favor to procure him a recommendation for a Paymastership—and that he had procured it at last tho' with some difficulty as Mr Greenwood was Mr Elderton's enemy. This was by no means *distinctly confirmed* by Mr Greenwood, but it did appear upon Mr Greenwood's evidence that his R. Highness *did mention Elderton's name to him* as a person on whose behalf an application for a Paymastership would be made to him, that in consequence of that he made enquiries into his character, that at first he thought so well of him from these enquiries that he recommended him for the Paymastership of Sr. R. Abercromby's regiment, but hearing afterwards something to his prejudice he wrote again to Sr. R. Abercromby that the appointment might not take place; and that upon the application of someone else, however, notwithstanding Mr Greenwood's second letter to Sr R. Abercromby, he was appointed Paymaster. The circumstances of this case, tho it is not an appointment under the patronage of H.R.H. as Commander-in-Chief, yet coupled with the letter of H.R. Highness to Mrs Clarke, in which he mentions the name of Genl. Clavering, was evidently felt by the House as confirming so far Mrs Clarke's testimony, as she states that she was permitted by his Royal Highness to obtain from him the exercise of his influence in favor of persons on whose behalf she applied to H.R.H. for preferment, and Mr Perceval cannot disguise from your Majesty that it has therefore made an unfavorable impression. The other parts of the enquiry of this evening were marked with nothing very particular, certainly with nothing which was of a nature to raise any unfavorable opinion upon the case. Lord Folkstone has still a new case to bring before the Comee. tomorrow, when Mr Perceval anxiously hopes that the evidence upon this distressing investigation will be brought to a close.[1] (14167–9)

[*The King's reply, Windsor Castle, 16 Feb.*] The King acknowledges the receipt of Mr Perceval's report of last night's proceedings in the House of Commons & his Majesty sincerely hopes that the examination may be closed this night. (14170)

[*From Perceval, Downg. Str., 17 Feb.*] Mr Perceval acquaints your Majesty that the Committee of Enquiry into the conduct of H.R.H. the Duke of York have proceeded in their examination till near four o'clock this morning. Their proceeding commenced by the examination of a new charge of Lord Folkstone's. The charge supposed that H.R.H., being anxious to procure a large sum of money (£40,000) upon an annuity, had with a view to induce the moneylender to lend it him more readily, exerted his influence to get him a place under Government. It appeared that there was a negotiation for such a loan in the year 1804 with a Mr Kennet,[2] and that Col. Taylor had at the direction of H.R. Highness applied for two or three places for him but that he did not succeed. Col. Taylor's evidence however shewed that there was no ground for supposing that the

---

[1] *Parl. Deb.*, XII, 658–702.
[2] Robert Kennett had been a Bond Street upholsterer who twice went bankrupt and subsequently lived in Lincoln's Inn Fields as 'a toothache curer' 'by smelling a bottle'. He had been prosecuted on a charge of conspiring to cheat his creditors, and, being found guilty, was put in the pillory.

promise of H.R. Hss.' influence in obtaining a place was ever used as an inducement of the kind, but that Col. Taylor himself, upon the application of the moneylender, had in consequence of Sir Horace Man's[1] recommendation prevailed upon
the Duke to make the applications; and that afterwards, finding reason to think
ill of the man, his R. Highness directed that no further applications should be
made for him, and no place was obtained and no loan was ultimately procured—
and upon the whole Mr Perceval has the satisfaction to think that this case did
not make any bad impression upon the House. There might have been good
ground of form to have resisted the going into the enquiry upon this charge, as
it was not a case in which H.R.H. was charged with having abused his authority
as Commander-in-Chief, but Mr Perceval and your Majesty's other confidential
servants were of opinion that much more prejudice would be done to H.R.H. by
appearing to shrink from it than by entering into it, and Mr Perceval is convinced
by the event that it would have been so, and that the examination has done away
the impression which the statement and the refusal of examination would certainly
have made. After this Mr Wardle & Lord Folkstone had no more witnesses to
call. Mr Perceval then by the direction of H.R.Hss. brought before the Committee
a circumstance relating to the charge in Major Tonyn's case, which had come to
Mr Adam's & Mr Perceval's knowledge—namely, a clear suppression of evidence
by a witness who had been examined in a very unpleasant particular. The witness
Capt. Sandon had told Col. Hamilton[2] that in order to prove to Major Tonyn
that Mrs Clarke had the influence which she pretended to have over H.R.Hss. he
had produced to him a note which he had received from Mrs Clarke purporting
to be a note from his R. Hss. to Mrs Clarke upon the subject of Major Tonyn's
business. In shewing this to Col. Hamilton he had mentioned that he could
destroy the note, & Col. Hamilton desired that he would not think of doing so.
Col. Hamilton informed Mr Adam of this, and having got a copy of the note was
sent by Mr Adam to Mr Perceval; they concurred in thinking that Col. Hamilton
should again enjoin Capt. Sandon to preserve the paper. Capt. Sandon told Col.
Hamilton that he *had destroyed it*. Mr Adam acquainted H.R.Hss. with the circumstance, who upon the statement had no recollection whatever of such a note,
and had the most confident conviction that it was a forgery. Upon this Mr Adam &
Mr Perceval and your Majesty's servants in the Ho. of Commons, including the
Aty. & Solr.-General, thought it not only wrong & improper in principle, but
impolitic also in the highest degree to suffer this matter to remain a secret, and
it was determined that after waiting to hear the story of the witnesses upon it
and at the close of the proceedings it should be stated to the Comee. and the
witnesses re-examined to it. Capt. Sandon most expressly denied ever having
had such a note from Mrs Clarke, or ever having shewn it to Major Tonyn, but
at last after a great deal of prevarication he confessed that he had had such a note,
but that it was mislaid. The House upon his prevarication, committed him to the

[1] Sir Horace Mann (1744–1814) succeeded his uncle, Sir Horace, as 2nd Baronet on 6 Nov. 1786.
M.P. for Maidstone, 1774–84; for Sandwich, 1790–1807. Knighted, 10 June 1772, to act as proxy for
his uncle at the installation of the Bath.

[2] Digby Hamilton. Lieutenant-Colonel, 1799; Colonel, 1803.

custody of the Serjeant, and after his committal he came forward, prayed to be heard again by the Comee. and stated that the note was in existence and that he could bring it—and accordingly he was sent for it in custody of the Serjeant. In the meantime Mrs Clarke was examined to the same point. She denied ever having had such a note from the Duke, or ever having given it to Capt. Sandon. This she did in the most positive manner. Capt. Sandon after this returned with the note. It was produced; Mrs Clarke was called in, and upon being shewn the note she still persisted in having no recollection of the circumstance but said that she supposed she must have given it him, as it was the handwriting of H.R. Highness. In this state the proceeding of the Committee closed. Col. Gordon was not in the House, and as the question is a most anxious & nice one upon the fact of the handwriting, it appeared to Mr Perceval to be much better to have that examination by daylight and by the best witnesses which could be procured, and who had the most knowledge of H.R.Hss.' handwriting. The Committee therefore have adjourned till tomorrow—when it is intended to call Col. Gordon and as many witnesses as can be collected who are best acquainted with his R. Hss.' handwriting to examine the paper. Mr Perceval cannot disguise from your Majesty that this question is of the utmost importance, and the issue of it will have the greatest weight upon the whole case. Capt. Sandon's conduct is most unaccountable. If he really thought it his R. Hss. handwriting and kept it back, it should seem that he must have done it, tho' contrary to the advice of H. R. Hss.' friends, yet with a view to serving him—and in that case there is no accounting for his not having actually destroyed it as he said he had. But the saying he had destroyed it, & yet keeping it safe, seems rather as if he meant to make use of it at some future time, and either by making a merit of such conduct or by threatening to disclose it, to make some advantage of H.R.Hs. If on the contrary it is a forgery & he knew it was so, there is abundant reason for keeping it back, but then the same reason would, as it seems, have led him to destroy it. The fact of his not having destroyed it, however, Mr. Perceval submits to your Majesty evinces more than anything the policy of having disclosed the fact. For had it been concealed, & H.R.Highness the Duke's examination had been closed ever so much to his honor, Capt. Sandon would have had it at any time in his power to have brought it forward & have disgraced all those who were parties to the concealment, & have inevitably involved his R. Highness in their own disgrace. Delicate however in the extreme as this question has been Mr Perceval did not act without the best advice he could procure, and the Lord Chancellor particularly was kind enough to give him his opinion, which entirely concurred with his own—namely, that in point of public duty it was impossible that we should be the silent depositary of this secret; and that if we could have reconciled such a concealment to our duty we could not have reconciled it to policy. There were some more papers produced from Capt. Sandon's house which may lead to some more information. But Mr Perceval confidently hopes that he shall not again disappoint your Majesty when he expresses his expectation that the evidence will be closed this day.[1]
(14178–81)

[1] *Parl. Deb.*, XII, 704–71.

[*The King's reply, Windsor Castle, 17 Feb.*] The King has received Mr Perceval's report of what passed in the House of Commons last night, and he admits the propriety of the reasons which have influenced his conduct and that of those who have concurred with him in the proceedings relative to the note pretended to have been written by the Duke of York to Mrs Clarke. His Majesty has understood that the Duke of York persists in his positive denial of ever having written that note, and in his assertion that it must be a forgery, and that he is prepared to make a formal declaration to that effect if it should be considered adviseable. The King is satisfied that the Duke of York would never state such conviction if he did not feel it scrupulously, and his Majesty trusts that the consequent declaration would have due weight. (14182)

3816 LORD ELDON *to the* KING

[*Friday, 17 Feb. 1809.*] The Lord Chancellor, offering his most humble duty to your Majesty, has the honour to transmit a paper to your Majesty, to receive yr. Majesty's Royal Sign Manual as an authority for adding the name of Mr Clarke, one of your Majesty's Council, in the Commission for the Midland Circuit, if your Majesty shall graciously so please. (14177)

3817 THE EARL OF LIVERPOOL *to the* KING, *and the reply*

[*Charles Street, 17 Feb. 1809.*] Lord Liverpool begs leave most humbly to lay before your Majesty the Minutes of the House of Lords of this night. The debate was open'd by Lord Grenville in a very long speech which was most ably and satisfactorily answer'd by Earl Bathurst. Lord Liverpool finds that it was the general impression that the debate went off very favourably and creditably to your Majesty's Government.[1] (14171)

[*The King's reply, Windsor Castle, 18 Feb.*] The King acknowledges the receipt of Lord Liverpool's report of the proceedings in the House of Lords last night which appear to have been very satisfactory. (14171)

3818 SPENCER PERCEVAL *to the* KING, *and the reply*

[*Saturday, 17 [18] Feb. 1809.*] Mr Perceval acquaints your Majesty that the Committee upon the charges against his Royal Highness the Duke of York proceeded yesterday afternoon in their enquiries. They called witnesses conversant in the handwriting of his R. Hss. to speak to the letters which had been produced as written by H.R.Hss. The two letters which Mr Perceval acquainted your Majesty were produced some days ago dated the one from Sandgate, & the other from Weymouth, in which mention was made of General Clavering & of

---

[1] *Parl. Deb.*, XII, 771–803. The debate was on Lord Grenville's Motion to address the King to repeal the Orders-in-Council as injurious to British trade, especially with the United States, which, alarmed at the dangers to which neutral commerce was exposed, had laid an embargo on American trade to this country.

Doctor O'Mara, were proved by Colonel Gordon, General Brownrig, General Alex. Hope[1] & Mr Adam to be his Royal Highness's handwriting in a manner to remove all possible doubt with respect to them. But with respect to the important note respecting Major Tonnyn's business, tho' they all spoke of its bearing a great resemblance to his Royal Highnesses handwriting, yet they could not say that they believed it to be his. The quantity of writing was so small that they could not speak positively to it one way or the other. Yet considering the grounds of their doubt, Mr Perceval is apprehensive that if it should ultimately rest upon the direct evidence which has been given upon that point, the House would think it amounted to that degree of proof which would induce them to believe it was authentic. Mr Perceval cannot forbear observing that no man could well be placed in a more delicate or distressing situation than Col. Gordon, called to speak to the authenticity of a small scrap of writing which he had never seen before, in a case in which too probably the honor & character of the person to whom his duty & his affections attach him most strongly, depended almost entirely upon his testimony if he had been obliged by the force of truth to have given his clear & positive evidence against him—and Mr Perceval is sure that it is not more than due to Col. Gordon to state to your Majesty that it was impossible for any man to conduct himself more manfully nor more correctly; he has indeed during the whole of this examination exhibited himself in the most distinguished manner, as a man of excellent understanding, accuracy, perspicuity and judgement; but on this most trying occasion he excelled most particularly, for tho' the doubt with which he spoke to H.R.H.'s handwriting to that note might have been suspected to arise from his inclination rather than his judgment, yet he spoke so correctly and gave such good reasons for the opinion which he expressed, that Mr Perceval is confident that the general impression of the House was that he did not speak from his wishes but from the best of his judgement. In the course of the evening the paper was inspected by several members of the House and amongst others by Mr Beresford, who has observed, and convinced many other gentlemen that there is a great & striking dissimilitude between the formation of several of the letters in this important note, and that of those in the writing which is clearly proved to have been his Royal Highness's; for this purpose it has been thought necessary to cause these papers in the course of tomorrow & Monday morning to be inspected by persons from the Bank & from the Post Office who are conversant in handwriting; and if upon their inspection it should so appear to them as to enable them to give their evidence that they do not believe it to be the same handwriting, it will be attended with the most beneficial result, and for this object therefore Mr Perceval persuades himself that however much your Majesty wished that the enquiry should be closed this evening, yet your Majesty will be reconciled to its being adjourned till Monday. Exclusive of this reason, however, there was another which would have rendered such an adjournment

[1] Sir Alexander Hope (1769–1837), M.P. for the Dumfries burghs, 1796–1800; for Linlithgowshire, 1800–34. Second son of John, 2nd Earl of Hopetoun. Ensign, 1786; Lieutenant, 1788; Major, and Lieutenant-Colonel, 1794; Lieutenant-Governor of Edinburgh Castle, 1798; Brigadier-General, 1807; Major-General, 1808; Lieutenant-General, 1813; General, 1830. K.B., 1813; G.C.B., 1815.

necessary. The papers which were brought from Capt. Sandon's lodgings were read to the Committee; they consisted of a great many (not less then 40) letters & notes from Mrs Clarke to Capt. Sandon, proving a long & continued intercourse between them in this nefarious traffic of procuring commissions. Mr Perceval cannot disguise from your Majesty that there are many circumstances in these letters which have made a very considerable and deep impression upon the House, for tho' they do not contain any of H.R.H.'s handwriting, yet they contain such allusions from day to day of military promotions reported as coming from his R. Hss. himself and difficult to be procured from any other quarter as to bear strong internal marks of probability that they were derived from H.R.H.; at the same time there are others which express such a solicitude for secrecy on the part of Mrs Clarke as to give great appearance of her being afraid that her conduct might be discovered by H.R.Hss. These papers contain allusion to so many facts & names that it was thought highly necessary that they should be deliberately looked at, and that opportunity should be given for considering whether materials might not be collected out of them which might greatly affect the testimony of Mrs Clarke & the probability of the charge. The interval till Monday next will be employed for this purpose. And Mr Perceval has this satisfaction at least of stating to your Majesty that but for these two considerations the Committee would have closed this morning, Mr Wardle & Ld. Folkstone having stated that they had no more evidence to call. A considerable impression had been made in many minds from the statement of Mrs Clarke that H.R.Hss. only allowed her one thousand pounds a year, with a few occasional payments which being so far short of what must have been wanted for the expences of her establishment led to the inference that H.R.H. must have known that she derived her money from some other means: to obviate this impression H.R.Hss. had a statement prepared of such expences and payments as he had any means of retracing, and authorised Mr Perceval to make it to the House, and Mr Perceval has the happiness to believe that such statement has materially diminished the extent at least of the unfavorable impression made by this part of the case. The House rose a little before two o'clock this morning.[1] (14183–6)

[*The King's reply, Windsor Castle, 18 Feb.*] The King acknowledges the receipt of Mr Perceval's report of last night's proceedings in the House of Commons, and his Majesty approves of the reasons assigned for adjourning the enquiry until Monday. His Majesty is still persuaded that the Duke of York is correct in his declaration that the note in question is a forgery, and his Majesty cannot disguise from Mr Perceval his opinion of the cruelty of the Duke of York's case; his character made to rest upon the opinion which may be given upon the alledged authenticity of a scrap of paper, found in the hands of a witness whose veracity has been impeached, & pretended to have been addressed to and received from another witness, as little deserving of credit & who has admitted that she has been in the practice of imitating handwriting & particularly that of the Duke of York. (14187)

[1] *Parl. Deb.*, XII, 813–40.

[*Burlington House, Sunday, 19 Feb. 1809.*] Your Majesty having graciously condescended, on the promotion of Dr. Walker King[1] to the Bishoprick of Rochester, to signify to the Duke of Portland your royal pleasure to confer on Dr. William Carey, Head Master of Westminster School, the Prebend of Westminster which would become vacant by that event; in consequence of your Majesty's having received the Bishop of Rochester's homage on Wednesday last, the Duke of Portland most humbly conceives it to be his duty to lay before your Majesty the necessary warrant for carrying into effect your Majesty's gracious intentions in favor of Dr. Carey. (14188)

3820   LORD ELDON *to the* KING, *and the reply*

[*Sunday, 19 Feb. 1809.*] I should not have failed in person to offer to your Majesty my humble duty on this day, if the proceedings in the House of Commons had reached their conclusion, or if in their present state I could have ventured to represent to your Majesty with confidence the probable result of them.

Since I have had the honour of seeing your Majesty every evening's proceedings have furnished matter for new enquiries; and the hope which is now entertained that the next sitting of the House will, at least, conclude the examination, is not more confidently entertained than that expectation was which supposed that all examination would have been finished some nights ago. Till it is entirely finished, till the whole of the evidence can be considered together, it would be rash to venture to state an opinion upon the result. I am, however, desirous to assure your Majesty that I have felt, and must continue to feel, during these proceedings all the extreme anxiety which, in a matter of such infinite importance, ought to press upon the mind of a servant bound to your Majesty as I am by every consideration which duty & gratitude can suggest.

When I last had the honour of seeing your Majesty I expressed my humble opinion that the evidence then before the House did not establish any charge of corruption against the Duke of York, or any privity on his part of the corruption of others, which, as to others, is unfortunately most fully proved. I still think that the evidence does not establish such charges. But there is a question now before the House upon the fact whether a letter, necessarily & unavoidably produced, is of the handwriting of the Duke. If this letter was not written by him, & is proved not to have been written by him, I should entertain a confident hope of a favorable conclusion; if the letter shall be proved of his handwriting, or, if that matter shall be left in doubt, I cannot conceal from your Majesty that, from all I can learn (and whatever may be the true opinion as to the inference to be finally drawn from the whole evidence taken together) there is some reason to apprehend that it is not unlikely that the House should think that the case is of a nature to render it extremely difficult to shut out further enquiry. I understand

[1] Prebendary of Peterborough, 1794; Canon of Wells, 1796; Prebendary of Canterbury, 1803, and of Westminster, 1827. Bishop of Rochester, 1809–27. (*c.* 1752–1827.)

also that on Friday evening some other letters were produced which are of material consequence and which lead to unfavorable conclusions, if the particular letter before alluded to shall be believed to be genuine, but which can have little effect if that letter is not believed to be genuine.

Upon another point, viz., whether Mrs Clarke had an undue influence upon the Duke's mind in his conduct as to military appointments, abstracted altogether from pecuniary matters, he asserts most solemnly that she had not. The impression as to that, upon the House & the public, I am grieved to state to your Majesty, is very different: and this woman has so actively, so artfully and apparently so successfully interfered in military appointments, that I fear few will be brought to believe that she had not great influence respecting them; & this seems to be believed to have been actually the fact even by those who are not unwilling to believe that the Duke was not aware that he was acting under any such influence. This opinion has unfortunately gained great strength by an alledged fact that an ensigncy was given to a young man of the name of Carter, who is represented to have been at the time of that appointment a menial servant of Mrs Clarke's. The Duke of York gives a very different character to his situation with Mrs Clarke, but it is among the misfortunes of this case that testimony as to the fact can only be had from Mrs Clarke herself, or others as abandoned as herself who lived in her family.

It will be most obvious to your Majesty that the general nature of the transactions growing out of a connection with this worthless woman, will create in the public mind, together with a great deal of just feeling, a great deal of prejudice inflamed by malice. I ought not to conceal from your Majesty that the case is represented to me as having made an impression upon the House of Commons more unfavorable than may appear to be just to those who can collect its nature only from reading what is printed, and who have not been present during the proceedings. This impression necessarily creates much difficulty in determining what steps are the most prudent to be adopted. The circumstances & incidents which have had a tendency to create that impression, can be explained only by those under whose observation they have actually fallen, and your Majesty will receive full explanation upon them from Mr Percival.

I presume that tomorrow the question upon the genuineness of the letter will be decided, and of that decision your Majesty will receive immediate information.

I humbly trust that your Majesty will not think I have mistaken my duty in making this statement to your Majesty. The matter to which it relates is of infinite consequence: the state of uncertainty in which it rests deeply affects and oppresses me, and, if I am led by my feelings into unintentional error, your Majesty's gracious goodness will pardon me.

Permit me, Sire, to conclude with very humble & heartfelt assurances that I am, with the highest sense of duty, & with the warmest devotion & gratitude [etc.]. (14189–91)

[*The King's reply, Windsor Castle, 20 Feb.*] The King acknowledges the receipt of the Lord Chancellor's letter and is sensible of the motives which have prompted him to submit so candid a statement to his Majesty in regard to the distressing business which has engaged the attention of the House of Commons of late. The King heartily concurs with the Chancellor in deploring that the Duke of York should ever have formed any connection with so abandoned a woman as Mrs. Clarke, but his Majesty never will allow himself to doubt for one moment the Duke of York's perfect integrity & his conscientious attention to his public duty, or to believe that in the discharge of it he has ever submitted to undue influence, and his Majesty thinks that this opinion ought to be established when the character of those men is considered who have held responsible situations under the Duke of York. Upon the whole the King cannot refrain from noticing the great hardship & injustice of suffering the character of any man, the accusations against whom are supported by such evidence as that which has been produced, to be made dependant upon the opinion which may be given on a scrap of paper which could not be called a forgery, if the imitation were not very exact. (14192)

3821 *Letters from* SPENCER PERCEVAL *to the* KING, *and the replies*

[*Downg. St., 4 o'clock, Tuesday morg., 21 Feb. 1809.*] Mr Perceval acquaints your Majesty that the Committee upon the enquiry into the charges against H.R. Highness the Duke of York sat this morning till three o'clock; much time having been consumed in incidental debate upon questions on evidence. The witnesses from the Post Office and the Bank were examined first to their judgement whether the writing of the note about Tonyn's business was the writing of the same hand as wrote the two letters of his Royal Highness from Sandgate & Weymouth. *Two* witnesses from the Post Office said they thought it was. The *first* witness from the Bank thought it was not, the *second* from the Bank thought it clearly was, and a *third* witness belonging to the Bank thought so also, but had a little doubt about it because he observed that there was some of the writing of Mrs. Clarke which he thought resembled the note. Mr Perceval however laments extremely to say that the balance of this evidence was in favor of the authenticity of the note, and that as far as he can collect the impression of the House is very strong that it is his Royal Highness's handwriting, altho' his Royal Highness so completely forgets it. When this evidence was closed, General Clavering got Sir Ralph Milbank to move that he might be called in again to explain some of his former evidence. He was admitted, and in the course of his further examination he confessed that he had had more communication with Mrs Clarke upon the subject of his military promotion than he had stated before, and amongst other things that he had offered to give her £1000 for a regiment, which, however, he could not procure. He made so bad an appearance that the House was going to commit him, and notice has been given that a Motion shall be made for his committal at a future day. The extent to which he confessed his intercourse with Mrs Clarke on the subject of promotion, and the manner in which he represented himself as applying to her for information upon military subjects which he could not get at the Office of the Comr-in-Chief or the Secretary at War, has undoubtedly strengthened the opinion of Mrs Clarke's communications with his Royal Highness upon military matters.

The proceedings would have closed this morning but that Mrs Clarke, whose presence was necessary for the proof of the letter which his Royal Highness wrote upon his breaking off his connection with her, and which it is thought material to produce; was unable to attend as was certified by her physician, on account of her being ill. For the purpose of procuring that evidence and also of examining a gentleman who is to prove that one of her servants who has given much evidence respecting the expences of her family, has been guilty of gross falsehood in his testimony, the Committee is appointed to sit again on Wednesday when Mr. Perceval trusts Mrs Clarke will be able to attend, and the Committee will close its labours in little more than an hour or so—and as the evidence will be printing in the meantime Mr Perceval trusts that this interruption will not postpone the ultimate decision.

Upon the whole Mr Perceval would not do his duty by your Majesty if he did not state that the impression is at present very much against his Royal Highness. The establishment, as it is generally considered, of the handwriting of the note of which your Majesty has heard so much, gives such a colour to the story and to the asserted influence of Mrs Clarke in matters of military promotion, in a case where money was actually paid, that Mr Perceval entertains considerable doubt whether it will be possible to prevail upon the House of Commons to forego some further proceeding by way of trial, or else to prevent their presenting an Address to your Majesty affecting his R. H.'s situation at the head of the Army.

Mr Perceval is confident that if justice is done to his Royal Highness there is no evidence which ought to convince any fair and unbiassed mind that his Royal Highness knew anything of Mrs. Clarke's nefarious practices. But the general prejudice which is exerted by the unworthy & unfortunate connexion with so base a woman, and the extent to which she profited by the semblance of influence which that connexion appeared to give her, have so roused the minds of the House of Commons & of the publick upon the subject that it will be extremely difficult indeed to obtain a fair hearing for argument, or a due attention to the many circumstances, for there are many, which must be urged on his R. Hss.'s behalf.[1] (14193-5)

[*The King's reply, Windsor Castle, 21 Feb.*] The King acknowledges the receipt of Mr Perceval's report of the proceedings in the House of Commons last night, and although his Majesty must lament that any circumstances attending this distressing enquiry should have produced a doubtful impression, his Majesty derives much relief from Mr Perceval's opinion that if justice is done to the Duke of York there is no evidence which ought to convince any fair and unbiassed mind that the Duke of York knew anything of Mrs. Clarke's nefarious practices. (14196)

[1] *Parl. Deb.*, XII, 844-97.

[*From Perceval, Downing Street, Tuesd.* [*sic*] *morg.* [*Wednesday, 22 Feb.*].] 'That the Convention concluded at Cintra on the 30th of Augt. 1808 and the Maritime Convention concluded off the Tagus on the 3d of September 1808 appear to this House to have disappointed the hopes and expectations of the country.

'That the causes and circumstances which immediately led to the conclusion of those Conventions appear to this House in a great measure to have arisen from the misconduct and neglect of his Majesty's Ministers.'

Mr Perceval acquaints your Majesty that Lord Henry Petty moved the above Resolutions yesterday evening, the first of which was met by the previous question, and the second by a direct negative.

The Motion was supported and opposed by the following gentlemen:

For the Motion: Ld Henry Petty, General Tarlton, Mr Windham, Mr Whitbread, Col. Hutchinson, Mr Bathurst, Ld Henry Petty.

Against it: Ld Castlereagh, Sir Arthur Wellesley, Mr Perceval, Mr Canning, Mr Yorke, Mr R. Ward.

Ld. Percy spoke also, saying that he should vote for the first Motion, but not for the second. The debate was very long; the House was not up till near six o'clock and the Opposition divided very strong. For the quest., 152; against it, 203. And upon this division Ld. H. Petty declined moving his second Resolution.[1]
(14197)

[*From Perceval, Thursday morng., 3 a.m.* [*23 Feb. 1809*].] Mr. Perceval has the satisfaction to acquaint your Majesty that the Committee of Enquiry into the charges against H.R.H. the Duke of York is at length closed. The course of examination this day has upon the whole been favorable, the letter which H.R.H.

[1] *Parl. Deb.*, XII, 897–974 (21 Feb.). The numbers should be 153 *v.* 203. (*H. of C. J.*, LXIV, 71.) 'We made an excellent division,' commented Tierney who, because of leg trouble, was unable to stand up to support Lord Henry. (Howick MSS. To Grey, 25 Feb.). Before the debate, Tierney had written, 'We have 147 certain supporters at hand for Petty['s] and Ponsonby's Motions.' (Howick MSS. To Grey, 10 Feb.) 'If you are correct in your numbers,' Grey replied on the 17th, 'Ministers must be hard run on both Petty's and Ponsonby's questions, for it is hardly to be supposed that the same events which have produced so good an attendance on our side should not have slackened theirs. But even supposing them beaten, what is to come of it? There is such a maze of difficulties that I cannot at all see my way through them, even if events were placed at my own command.' (Tierney MSS.)

W. H. Fremantle had expected a minority of at least 150, excluding the Duke of Northumberland's members. Many of the Government's friends, he said, had gone out of town to avoid voting; 'and we shall have some rats' (Buckingham, *Court and Cabinets*, IV, 320.) He wrote to Lord Grenville on the 22nd: 'We had a most famous division last night, as you will see by the papers, nothing could be better than Lord Henry Petty's speech, and nothing could be worse than the defence of Ministers; with respect to Lord Castlereagh, he literally was unintelligible and the whole of Wellesley's argument and language, which was infinitely the best, was a condemnation of the Ministers; and Canning's speech was a reproof both to Ministers and Generals. No one made out any defence whatever for the want of cavalry, for the change of Generals or for the total want of all general instructions, and the argument was completely on our side and was most manfully maintained. A great number of our friends were wanting. I am just come from Tierney with whom and Lord Temple I have been over the list, and we have sent to those whom there is any chance of getting in time for Ponsonby's Motion.... The Doctor's people and the Duke of Northumberland were with us, the latter not meaning it, if the division had been taken on the second Resolution—Sir John Sebright, Tarleton and I think three or four more, whose names I can't recollect, were with us. A great number of their friends went away, particularly Canning's friends. Only one of the Duke of Rutland's members voted, the rest remained at Belvoir. We had four and twenty County members. I am afraid we shall not make so good a division on Friday. I hope we shall have as many, but I fear they will make great exertions to get more.' (Fortescue MSS.)

sent to Mrs Clark upon the occasion of his separation from her was read in evidence, and is undoubtedly creditable to H.R.H. and such as ought to have great weight in satisfying impartial minds that H.R.Hss. could not think that Mrs. Clarke was acquainted with any circumstances which she could divulge to his prejudice or he would not have discarded her in such a manner. Evidence was also addressed to discredit one of the witnesses of Mrs. Clark, and of Mrs Clark herself, which was very successful. Upon the conclusion of this evidence, Mr York[e] called upon the General Officers who was in the House [*sic*]: General Norton, Fitzpatrick, Sr. J. Pulteney & Sr Arthur Wellesley & General Grosvenor who bore ample testimony to the benefit which the Army has derived under his Royal Highness's command. And with this evidence the enquiry closed. But notwithstanding this Mr Perceval is sorry to say that he should inexcusably deceive your Majesty if he did not add that he apprehends the prejudice against his Royal Highness arising out of the circumstances which Mr Perceval has already mentioned to your Majesty still remains.[1]

As the evidence taken before the Committee will not be printed & delivered before Monday next it appeared to Mr Perceval impossible to accelerate the consideration of it by appointing an earlier day than next Thursday—and accordingly the House has appointed that day for that purpose. (14198)

[*The King's reply, Windsor Castle, 23 Feb.*] The King acknowledges the receipt of Mr. Perceval's report of the satisfactory proceedings in the House of Commons last night. His Majesty has also received his report of the debate & division on the preceding night. (14199)

[*From Perceval, Downing Street, 23 Feb.*] Mr Perceval acquaints your Majesty that the Speaker read from the Chair this day a letter[2] from his Royal Highness the Duke of York, of which Mr Perceval humbly presents to your Majesty the inclosed copy.

[1] *Parl. Deb.*, XII, 978–1032.
[2] *Parl. Deb.*, XII, 1032, dated the 23rd, protesting his innocence, and expressing the hope that the House would not adopt any proceeding prejudicial to his honour, upon the evidence that had been heard. 'But if…the House…can think my innocence questionable, I claim of their justice that I shall not be condemned without trial.' 'The letter,' wrote Abbot, 'was very much shorter and less explicit than the original draft which I had seen in Perceval's hands.' (Colchester, *Diary and Corresp.*, II, 168.) Perceval had shown him the draft on the 20th—'1. Denying…all participation or connivance in the corrupt practices, &c.; 2. Avowing with the deepest regret and humiliation the habits which had exposed his honour to the artifices of the most degraded characters; 3. Relying on his integrity and his services in raising and maintaining the efficiency of the army, and desiring to be set clear of the charges by the judgment of the House of Commons upon a view of the evidence, or to be put on his trial before his Peers….His last mistress (Mrs. Carey) is dismissed. The draft of this paper has not yet been shown, but, if approved of by all concerned, it must be submitted to the King before it can be produced.' Tierney was highly critical of the Duke's letter: it was 'one of the most foolish productions which has ever appeared, and the concluding paragraph is so indecent an attack on the privileges of the House of Commons that it cannot be passed over.' (Howick MSS. To Grey, 27 Feb.). The *Courier* informed the public on the 23rd: 'We cannot but feel pleasure in stating that H.R.H. the Duke of York, from deference to public opinion, has put an end to the intercourse that has subsisted for a considerable time between himself and a lady of the name of Cary—that the establishment she had at Fulham has been given up—that the house is to be sold or let immediately, and that the lady has retired into the country.'

Mr Perceval trusts that your Majesty will not think Mr. Perceval proceeding beyond the line of his official duty in stating to your Majesty that Mr Perceval would not presume of himself alone to advise his R. Hss. the Duke of York in a point of such extreme difficulty and delicacy, and therefore desired not only the assistance of the Lord Chancellor but also of your Majesty's other confidential servants; and it was not till after a very full and deliberate examination for some hours in Cabinet this morning of every sentence in the letter, and approbation of its contents in all its parts, that Mr Perceval submitted to his Royal Highness the few alterations which appear in it from the draft as first proposed by his Royal Highness. (14202)

[*The King's reply, Windsor Castle, 24 Feb.*] The letter from the Duke of York to the Speaker of which Mr. Perceval has sent a copy to the King appears to his Majesty highly proper and such as ought to be satisfactory to the House of Commons. (14203)

3822   VISCOUNT CASTLEREAGH *to the* KING, *and the reply*
[*St James's Sq., 23 Feb. 1809.*] The intelligence this day received from Mr. Frere that the Spanish Government has declined to accept the services of your Majesty's troops at Cadiz, has induced your Majesty's confidential servants humbly to submit to your Majesty the accompanying instruction to M. Genl. Sherbrooke (14200)

[*The King's reply, Windsor Castle, 24 Feb.*] The King approves of the instruction for M. General Sherbroke [*sic*] which Lord Castlereagh has submitted in consequence of the last dispatches from Mr. Frere. (14201)

3823   GEORGE CANNING *to the* KING, *and the reply*
[*Foreign Office, 25 Feb. 1809.*] Mr. Canning most humbly submits for your Majesty's royal consideration the draft of a letter from your Majesty to the Prince Regent of Portugal in answer to that received by your Majesty from H.R.H. on the subjects of the late transactions in Portugal & of the conduct of Sir Sidney Smith.[1] (14208)

[*The King's reply, Windsor Castle, 26 Feb.*] The King approves of the letter to the Prince Regent of Portugal of which Mr Canning has submitted the draft. (14209)

[1] In Feb. 1808 Rear-Admiral Sir Sidney Smith had been sent out to Rio de Janeiro to take charge of the South American station, but a quarrel between him and Lord Strangford, the British Minister to the Portuguese Court in Brazil, led to his recall in the summer of 1809.

[*25 Feb. 1809.*] Mr. Perceval acquaints your Majesty that Mr Whitbread made some observations on the letter of H.R.H. the D. of York yesterday eveng. He endeavoured to represent it as an attack upon the privileges of the House, as impeaching the validity of any proceeding in this House in respect of the defective manner in which evidence was taken at our Bar. Mr Perceval replied to him and took the opportunity of explaining the object of the letter, shewing, as was very easy, that it was impossible to give that interpretation to it which had been given to it by Mr Whitbread. The explanation was well received, and with a few observations from Ld. Hy. Petty that conversation ended.

The House then proceeded to consider a Motion which was made by Mr Ponsonby—'That it was indispensably necessary to enquire into the causes and events of the late campaign in Spain.'

Lord Castlereagh answered Mr Ponsonby in a very full and able exposure of the whole of the proceedings in Spain. Mr Tierney followed him, and after Mr Tierney, a young member, a Mr Goulburn,[1] made a speech of very good promise against the Motion. He was followed by Mr Canning—who made one of the best, most eloquent and commanding speeches that was ever heard. An event occurred in the midst of his speech which occasioned considerable confusion in the House. The theatre of Drury Lane unfortunately had taken fire, and the immense blaze of light from the conflagration shone in at the windows of the House, as strongly as if it had been in the Speaker's garden—and many members from curiosity went to look at it, and a most tremendous and splendid sight it was, illuminating as it did the river, the bridge, Lambeth Palace and all the surrounding buildings.[2] This interruption was inconvenient, but it did not materially disturb Mr Canning, whose speech had a very great effect on the House. An attempt was then made to adjourn the debate by Mr Eliott[3] upon the ground of this fire, which however was too ridiculous to be seriously entertained by the House. The Motion was therefore after a short conversation withdrawn, and the debate went on. Mr Windham & Lord Percy spoke for the Motion—Mr Bragg Bathurst against the Motion as premature rather than as thinking enquiry unnecessary. Mr Ponsonby replied and the House went to a division at three o'clock. The Ayes 127, the Noes 220.[4] (14210)

---

[1] Henry Goulburn (1784–1856), M.P. for Horsham, 1808–12; for St Germans, 1812–18; for West Looe, 1818–26; for Armagh, 1826–31; for Cambridge University, 1831–56. Under-Secretary of State, Home Department, Feb. 1810; for War and the Colonies, Aug. 1812; Irish Secretary, Dec. 1821–April 1827; Chancellor of the Exchequer, Jan. 1828–Nov. 1830; Home Secretary, Dec. 1834–April 1835; Chancellor of the Exchequer, Sept. 1841–June 1846.

[2] The light was so strong, said the Speaker, that persons at Fulham could see the hour by their watches in the open air at midnight. (Colchester, *Diary and Corresp.*, II, 168.) 'I cannot make out how Sheridan stands about Drury Lane', wrote Tierney on the 25th, 'but I rather believe £40,000 was insured. He stayed in the House of Commons the greater part of the time while the fire was burning, and appeared to me to be in a sort of stupid despair. Poor fellow. It is a hard blow on him and a still harder one on Tom.' (Howick MSS.) Moira wrote on 17 March 1809: 'The Prince gave Tom Sheridan £1000 to relieve him in the difficulties entailed by the burning of Drury Lane.' (*Hastings MSS.*, III, 271).

[3] According to the *Parliamentary Debates* Lord Temple suggested the propriety of adjourning the debate, the adjournment being moved by General Mathew and seconded by H. A. Herbert. (XII, 1105.)

[4] The division was less favourable for the Opposition than the one on Lord Henry Petty's Motion

[*The King's reply, Windsor Castle, 25 Feb.*] The King acknowledges the receipt of Mr Perceval's report of the debate and division in the House of Commons last night, which is very satisfactory. His Majesty entirely acquiesces in opinion as to the absurdity of adjourning the debate on account of the fire at Drury Lane Theatre, however melancholy the event. (14211)

[*From Perceval, 28 Feb.*] Mr Perceval feels it to be his indispensable duty to inform your Majesty that he is more and more convinced that the impression which has been made against his R.H. the D. of York by the public exposure of the unfortunate and unworthy connexion which H.R.H. had permitted himself to form with Mrs. Clarke is so strong that tho' Mr Perceval cannot bring himself to believe that the Ho. of Co. can be guilty of the injustice of coming to any resolution expressive of their opinion that the charges are proved against his R.H., yet Mr Perceval apprehends that it will be extremely difficult indeed to prevent the House from coming to some Address to your Majesty with the view of removing his R.H. from his present situation. Such an Address Mr Perceval begs leave humbly to assure your Majesty that Mr Perceval and his colleagues will feel it to be their duty to do everything in their power to prevent the House from adopting, but Mr Perceval would fail of his duty to your Majesty if he did not state that from all he can collect of the sentiments of the Ho. of Co. and of the public, the current of opinion seems strongly in favor of such an Address. The language held by many members of Parlt. is that it has appear'd that at least the Army were imposed upon to think that a worthless woman had an influence in the advancing or retarding the promotions of officers in the Army, and that she exercised this influence for money, and that the suspicion will be too likely to remain of the probable existence of hereafter [*sic*] of a similar influence over H.R.H. in some other person, and that if the Ho. of Co. should overlook these circumstances, they will be disgraced in the eyes of their constituents, that Addresses and Petitions will be prest upon them and upon your Majesty from all quarters, and that the pretence for a reform in Parliament will be greatly encreased by an instance in which the Ho. of Co. shall act in such direct opposition to the feelings and opinions of their constituents.

Mr Perceval is so strongly impressed with an opinion of the prevalence of these sentiments, that he is quite satisfied that the attempt to prevent an Address for the removal of H.R.H. without doing something which may in some degree at least fall in with these sentiments, will be utterly impossible to succeed.

Under this impression Mr Perceval has drawn up two Resolutions to be adopted by the House and presented to your Majesty with an Address, a draft of which he has likewise prepared; and these he thinks it just possible that the House might be prevailed upon to adopt as the substitutes for an Address of removal. Mr Perceval has presumed humbly to submit these Resolutions and Address to your

on the 21st, even though, as Tierney informed Grey, 'We...[were] joined by several who were not with us on the first night.' But, he added, 'Government appear to have as many difficulties at least as we have in mustering their strength. 220, after bringing up everything they could lay their hands on, is but a sorry show on a question directly affecting Ministers.' (Howick MSS.)

Majesty for the purpose of his being authorised, if your Majesty should think fit, to bring the same before your Majesty's confidential servants for them to consider the propriety of endeavouring to substitute such Resolutions and Address in the place of an Address of removal. Mr. Perceval hopes that an expression of strong regret on the part of the Ho. of Co. at the existence of such a connexion, and of the fatal consequences which would ensue from the existence of a similar connexion, may [be] felt by the House as sufficient to satisfy their feelings both in expressing their opinion upon what is passed, and in guarding against the danger of the recurrence of similar mischief in future. But in expressing this hope Mr Perceval does not feel justified in expressing it with any confidence. (14214–5)

[*From Perceval, Downing Street, Tuesday evg., 28 Feb. 1809.*] Mr Perceval acquaints your Majesty that Lord Folkstone moved in the Ho. of Co. this evening that the House should be called over on Wednesday sev'nnight for the purpose of securing a full attendance upon the discussion which is to take place on that day upon the subject of the enquiry into the conduct of H.R.H. the Duke of York. The delay of the printer in getting forward the evidence which had been received before the Committee, had rendered it impossible to enter into that discussion on Thursday next as was originally intended, and the other business of the House precluded the appointment of any intermediate day for that purpose. Mr Perceval did not think it adviseable to oppose this Motion, for tho' he would not have proposed a call of the House himself (as it is always an obnoxious measure) yet when it was proposed he felt it imprudent to resist it, and indeed he rather inclines to think that it may be advantageous to the decision itself, as Mr Perceval is of opinion that there may be many persons who would if they could shrink from the decision, who will nevertheless not be prevailed upon by any fear of their constituents to take any step of violence against H.R.H. upon such evidence as the House has before it.

After this Motion was disposed of Mr Wms. Wynn gave notice of his intention of bringing under the consideration of the House, after the discussion upon the enquiry was closed, the letter of his R. H. the D of York, as an attack upon the privileges of this House. He stated that he would not bring on this Motion before that discussion, lest it should prejudice the discussion upon the main question. Mr Perceval urged as strongly as he could the unfairness of such a proceeding; that if there was anything objectionable in that letter, which Mr Perceval denied, that it would be but fair by H.R.H. that such subject should be discussed and disposed of before the main question came to be considered, that H.R.H. might not go to that question under any prejudice arising from the statement that he had attacked the privileges of the Ho. of Co. and endeavoured to assume a princely privilege which would not be tolerated in a common subject. That the assertion that he had so attacked the privileges of the House raised a prejudice against him which a discussion would allay; as that discussion would prove that there was not the slightest ground or pretence for the objection stated to the letter. Mr Perceval therefore pressed Mr. Wynn as much as he could out of justice to the D. of York, to bring on this question of privilege upon the letter previous to the other question upon the general merits of the enquiry, but Mr. Perceval could not prevail, and Mr. W. Wynn gave his notice for Monday sev'nnight.

The House then proceeded to other business of no interest, and rose about seven o'clock.[1] (14216–7)

[*The King's reply, Queen's Palace, 1 March.*] The King is perfectly satisfied that Mr Perceval has fairly stated what he conceives to be the impression made upon the House of Commons by the circumstances which have been brought before it, connected with the enquiry into the conduct of the Duke of York in his situation of Commander-in-Chief, but H.M. never can persuade himself that upon such evidence as has been produced, the House of Commons can be guilty of the injustice of coming to any Resolution expressive of its opinion that the charges are proved, or that, under the conviction and a declaration that the charges are not proved, an Address for the removal of the Duke of York from his office would not be successfully resisted.

However desireable it appears to the King not only for the sake of the Duke of York, of whose innocence he is convinced, but also from considerations deeply affecting the interests of the Crown and the State, that such an Address should be counteracted, H.M. cannot conceal from Mr Perceval that he does not consider that the alternative by which it is proposed to guard against it is calculated to insure the general object in view, altho' he is sensible that Mr Perceval's suggestions are the result of his attachment to his Majesty and of his anxiety for the general welfare of his family.

The King has attentively read and considered the proposed Resolutions and Address, and they appear to him to convey a censure upon past conduct, and an admonition or rather a threat for the future in terms so strong as to establish a stigma under which he conceives it to be impossible that any man could hold a public situation consistently with his honor, or to which the Duke of York could submit without setting aside what is due to his own character and situation and to the dynasty and interests of the Crown. Although the King continues of opinion that the only circumstances upon which the House of Commons is called upon to decide are those affecting conduct in public & responsible situations, and that the admission of extraneous matter as a ground of decision and censure would be not less unusual than generally objectionable; still if it should be deemed necessary to notice thus formally transactions of a private nature which no person can deplore more sincerely than his Majesty, he conceives that it should be done in terms more mild and more general, and that expressions of regret should be substituted for those of censure, and one of confidence as to future conduct for the admonition or reproof now proposed. The King therefore is desirous that Mr Perceval should consider the matter maturely and endeavor to frame such Resolutions as shall be less distressing to the feelings of the Duke of York before he brings them to the consideration of his colleagues.

The King has lost no time in answering Mr Perceval, but his opinions have not been given upon a hasty view of his communications, still less of the distressing

[1] *Parl. Deb.*, XII, 1136–41.

subject which has so long and almost exclusively occupied his thought. His attention has not been confined to the interests of the Duke of York, but his Majesty considers those of his Crown and of the State deeply involved in the issue of this question, and he therefore must feel most anxious that these should be secured by a system of conduct so firm and dignified, as shall induce his loyal subjects at this critical period with confidence to join his Government in resisting encroachments which would be encouraged by anything that could be construed into apprehension or concession.[1] (14222–3)

3825   GEORGE CANNING *to the* KING *and the reply*

[*Bruton Street, Tuesday night, 28 Feb. 1809.*] Mr Canning humbly lays before your Majesty the translation of a Note received this day from Don Pedro Cevallos, the Ambassador Extraordinary from Spain,[2] the object of which is to entreat your Majesty's acceptance of the Collar of the Order of the Golden Fleece. Upon receipt of this Note Mr Canning thought it his duty previously to submitting it to your Majesty to endeavour to ascertain whether any of your Majesty's royal predecessors had ever accepted foreign Orders. And he most humbly presumes to transmit herewith a letter from Sir Isaac Heard, (in answer to an inquiry made through Mr. Hammond) by which it appears that King Edward the 6th is the last Sovereign of England who is recorded as having accepted any foreign Order.

Mr Canning most humbly intreats your Majesty's pardon for the haste & possibly the incorrectness with which this inquiry has been made & answered. But as your Majesty is to receive Don Pedro Cevallos tomorrow & as the offer of the Collar may possibly make part of the Ambassador's Address, Mr Canning

[1] Writing to the Duke of Richmond on 1 March, Lord Bathurst thus summarised the course of events, and commented: 'Previous to Mr Wardle's Motion coming on, there was a meeting of the principal House of Commons' Members of Administration at Perceval's. At this meeting Adam, & Gordon, the Duke's Secretary, attended. They were confident of the strength of their cause, and gave it as their opinion that nothing should be attempted to prevent the Inquiry. All the friends of the Duke of York, and he more than any of them, stated everywhere that it was an opportunity which has been long looked for & by which his character would be fully justified. The two first days were indeed most favourable—the third less so—but the House continued well disposed until his letters to Mrs. Clarke were read—this gave the first unpleasant impression—the advancement of Captain Sutton's boy completed it. The disposition now is most unfavourable, the disposition of the country still worse. There is, I am afraid, a greater cry against him than there was against Lord Melville. The Duke's letter to the Speaker has I think upon the whole had a good effect; it has made many acknowledge that some decision should be given on the truth of the charges, or more properly speaking, it enables the Government to press that question: and I believe there would be no doubt of our being able to carry that resolution if it was either followed or preceded by the Duke's resignation. But I am afraid there is not much hope of being able to resist a Motion for his removal if no resignation is to take place. The Opposition have play'd the game which might be expected from them. They at first were for the Duke—when the tide began to change, they changed—and now they are decided against him, intimating at the same time that Government ought to have prevented the whole business: and ready to accuse them of desertion, if they advise the Duke to retire. There is no disposition in the Duke to do this, and as little in the King to recommend him to do so. Neither thinks that such a question will be carried, and there is nothing left for us but to try our strength in the way the most likely to succeed. An intire acquittal would run so counter to the feelings of the whole country that it could not be listen'd to.' (Richmond MSS.)

[2] The Ambassador had arrived at Portsmouth on the 13th in the 74-gun *Algeciras*, Captain Apodaca.

felt it incumbent upon him to state the matter with the best information which he could obtain upon it to your Majesty tonight, not doubting that your Majesty will be enabled from your Majesty's own knowledge to correct any error, if there be any, in the suggestions now submitted for your Majesty's royal consideration.

It will not escape your Majesty that, supposing the precedents to have been otherwise, there might yet be a question as to the power of a Provisional Government to confer an Order of Knighthood which may perhaps be considered as (of all others) most peculiarly an act of individual sovereignty. (14212–3)

[*The King's reply, Queen's Palace, 1 March.*] The King has received Mr. Canning's letter and the accompanying papers, and it is his Majesty's intention to acquaint M. de Cevallos that, being at the head of the Orders in his own Kingdoms, his Majesty had invariably declined accepting of foreign Orders, and that, however sensible of the feelings under which that of the Golden Fleece is now offered, he could not depart from an established principle. (14221)

3826   THE EARL OF LIVERPOOL *to the* KING
[*Charles Street, 1 March 1809.*] Lord Liverpool begs leave most humbly to submit to your Majesty the letter from Mr Graham to Mr Beckett which Lord Liverpool mentioned to your Majesty this morning as containing the result of the examinations respecting the late fire in Drury Lane Theatre. (14224)

[*Enclosure*]

[*Aaron Graham to John Beckett, Tuesday, 28 Feb. (Copy).*] I should have done myself the honor of anticipating your note by sending you one last night if I had been able to hold my pen, but so many people pressed themselves upon me in the course of the day that shortly after dinner I was obliged to go to bed incapable of writing or attending to anything in the shape of business. I have examined I believe everyone capable of giving the least information respecting the burning of Drury Lane Theatre—and I am perfectly satisfied it was the effect of accident resulting from great carelessness. It has been clearly proved both from the inside and the outside of the building that the fire began in the upper coffee room where the plumbers had been at work till past four o'clock in the afternoon of Friday, and from the stove in which they made a fire to heat their iron, there can be no doubt the mischief proceeded. Several times this season I find the coffee-house keeper has been alarmed by the appearance of things even during the hours of representation, and more than once extraordinary means have been resorted to to put out the fire. In the original plan no preparation was made for a fireplace in that room, and from the quantity of timber all round above and below the stove I can believe that some of it may have been charring for months and that the fire made by the plumbers (which must necessarily have been a fierce one) lighted some of the hidden parts which crept on till it found its way into the air and then burst forth. As to the stories in the papers of a woman in a straw bonnet and the flames coming up from the Egyptian Hall, they are the fabrication of a Mr Kent, a collector of news for the papers who has several times given me a great deal of trouble to enquire into supposed murders and other accidents which could never be traced farther than to his report.

I should have been more particular in my description but my fingers have several times failed me in getting on to this length and I have been upwards of two hours about it. (14225–6)

3827 GEORGE CANNING *to the* KING, *and the reply*

[*Foreign Office, 2 March 1809.*] Mr Canning humbly lays before your Majesty a letter from the Prince Regent of Portugal to your Majesty, the object of which is to propose to your Majesty the raising of the Missions of the two Courts from the rank of Envoy Extraordinary & Minister Plenipotentiary to that of Ambassador. This letter was received here (as Mr Canning believes) some weeks ago but was not delivered to him by the Chevr. de Souza till long after its receipt. The same subject is referred to in one of Lord Strangford's despatches, and Mr Canning has most humbly to intreat your Majesty's forgiveness for not having sooner requested to receive your Majesty's pleasure upon it.

He has now humbly to submit to your Majesty a draft of a despatch to Lord Strangford in which Mr Canning states (subject to your Majesty's approbation) what he collected to be your Majesty's general sentiments upon the subject when a proposal of a similar nature was lately submitted to your Majesty on the part of the King of the Two Sicilies.

Mr Canning has not prepared the draft of any answer to the Prince Regent's letter, humbly conceiving that if your Majesty should determine not to accede to the proposal at the present moment, it might be more agreeable to your Majesty that the reasons for declining to do so should be stated through your Majesty's Minister at Rio de Janeiro, rather than directly by a letter from your Majesty.

Mr. Canning humbly submits at the same time a draft (alike subject to your Majesty's approbation) conveying your Majesty's permission to Lord Strangford & Mr. Hill to accept the Order proposed to be conferred upon them by the Prince Regent. Your Majesty's permission was in a former instance withheld until it should be ascertained whether the Prince Regent had thrown aside the Insignia of the French Legion of Honour. (14230–1)

[*The King's reply, Queen's Palace, 3 March.*] The King approves of the dispatches which Mr Canning has prepared for Lord Strangford in reference to the several points mentioned in his letter.[1] (14232)

<hr/>

[1] Lieutenant-Colonel Taylor wrote to Canning from Windsor on the 5th: 'You will I hope forgive my troubling you with a few lines at this moment to convey to you some information which has reached me accidentally. The circumstance may possibly be known to you or may appear generally immaterial, but at all events if you should think proper to notice it I shall be obliged to you not to quote me, as I am anxious not to be named, which is my motive for addressing you instead of writing to Lord Liverpool.

'While I was in London last week I happened to meet a person who is well acquainted with Mr. Clifford, the lawyer, and who told me that he (Mr. Clifford) has been employed as a principal agent

[*Downg. Str., Thursday evng., 2 March 1809.*] Mr Perceval humbly submits to your Majesty the two Resolutions intended to be proposed upon the subject of the enquiry into the conduct of H.R.H. the D of York, altered as Mr Perceval humbly hopes in a manner comfortable to the view which your Majesty was graciously pleased to present to Mr Perceval upon this subject. Your Majesty will find in the margin of the draft of these Resolutions the expressions of H.R. Hss.'s letter, which Mr Perceval has introduced into the Resolutions, and which Mr. Perceval has underlined for the convenience of your Majesty's more easy reference to the same. Mr Perceval acquaints your Majesty that the general nature of these Resolutions has been fully discussed by yr. Maj.'s confidential servants, since Mr. Perceval last received yr. Majesty's commands upon this subject. But Mr. Perceval has foreborne to bring them in their precise form before your Majesty's confidential servants until, after having been submitted to your Majesty's reconsideration, he might have your Majesty's permission for so doing. When your Majesty shall be graciously pleased to return them, Mr Perceval will lose no time in bringing them under the final consideration of the Cabinet. (14227)

[*The King's reply, Queen's Palace, 3 March.*] The King has received Mr. Perceval's letter and the accompanying Resolutions proposed upon the subject of the enquiry into the conduct of the Duke of York as now altered, and his Majesty approves of Mr Perceval's bringing them before his colleagues in their present shape, with only one alteration which has occurred to the King, as tending to

of a committee composed of Lord Folkstone, Mr. Wardle and (I think he said) Sir Francis Burdett, to find out grounds of accusation against the Duke of York, other branches of the Royal family & against various Departments under Government. That nothing can exceed the violence of Mr. Clifford's language, that he talks of the destruction of the House of Brunswick and of a revolution as events which are preparing & must take place, and he hinted that active measures were pursuing. This person also told me that Mr. Clifford is much given to drinking and easily thrown off his guard from his natural violence. I promised this person not to name him, as he is determined not to come forward, & if what I have said appears to you at all material or can be turned to any purpose, I am certain that you will have the goodness to use it generally without hinting at the quarter whence you receive it.

'It has occurred to me that it might be possible to bring something positively home to Mr. Clifford by employing some intelligent individual whose connections & habits would not expose him to suspicion to cultivate the society and acquaintance of Mr. Clifford and under pretence of communicating or procuring information for him to lead him by degrees to commit himself and his employers. I must however further observe that I was told that these miscreants are very well served by their spies who are posted near the Public Offices and watch every person going in & out.

'Two other observations have also been made to me which may perhaps be deserving of attention. The one regards the late very great increase of itinerant Jews who are supposed to be either themselves active agents, or persons thus disguised. The other regards the latitude given to French prisoners of war and the abuse which is made of the indulgence, their intercourse with the lower classes, and the suspicion which has arisen that they have been endeavoring to influence the minds of the Irish soldiers who are chiefly Catholics. Whether these remarks are just might easily be ascertained by the Police, if its attention were called to the circumstance.' (Harewood MSS.) The letter is endorsed by Canning, 'Disposed of.'

Henry Clifford (1768–1813) was the son of the Hon. Thomas Clifford, of Tixall, Staffs., and a Catholic. 'Impatience of the unjust disabilities under which his sect labours had reconciled him to violent opinions in politics; and unrestrained habits of intemperance had inflamed the malignity of a disposition not originally amiable, without impairing the very acute perceptions and strong intellect with which Nature had endowed him.' (Lord Holland, *Further Memoirs*, p. 56.)

soften the second Resolution, by substituting for the words '*that altho*'' which his M. has underlined in pencil the word *while* & by the omission of the word *yet* in a subsequent part of the Resolution, also underlined in pencil. (14237)

[*From Perceval, Downg. St., Friday evg., 3 March.*] Mr. Perceval acquaints your Majesty that in pursuance of your Majesty's commands he submitted to your Majesty's confidential servants this day the Resolutions as returned to him by your Majesty this morning. And Mr. Perceval has humbly to represent to your Majesty that your Majesty's servants gave to them that deliberate consideration which the nature of the subject and its importance so justly demanded—and after that consideration it appeared to them that it would be fit to submit to your Majesty the propriety of recasting the second Resolution, leaving the first as it was before, in the manner in which Mr Perceval herewith transmits it for your Majesty's approbation, namely, that it would be better to turn the second Resolution into the form of an Address to your Majesty, preserving the substance of the Resolution in every material part except so far as it points to the future conduct of H.R. Highness—as to which your My.'s servants humbly submit to your Majesty that the words of the Resolution as before submitted to your Majesty by Mr. Perceval were by their particularity more harsh than they are in the altered form in which they are now presented to your Majesty.

Mr Perceval transmits to your Majesty at the same time the Resolutions in their former shape that your Majesty may be enabled by the comparison the better to judge of the propriety of the alteration which is thus humbly submitted to your Majesty. (14233–4)

[*The King's reply, Windsor Castle, 4 March.*] The King approves of the proposed Resolution and Address submitted by Mr Perceval after having undergone the consideration of his colleagues, and his Majesty concurs in the opinion conveyed in Mr. Perceval's letter, that the words of the Resolution and Address have been rendered more mild by the alterations without weakening the material parts. (14238)

[*From Perceval, Tuesday morng., 6 o'clock a.m.* [*7 March*].] Mr Perceval acquaints your Majesty that Mr Whitbread made a Motion for an Address to your Majesty for the purpose of making some conciliatory overtures to America. The debate was very long tho the speakers were few. Mr Whitbread was followed by Mr. Stephen, Mr Stephen by Mr Baring.[1] Mr Rose[2] followed Mr Baring. Mr Grattan spoke next and Mr Canning followed Mr Grattan, and Ld Henry Petty closed the debate. Mr Stephen and Mr Canning both made very able speeches, and placed the conduct of yr. Majesty's Government with regard to America on a very satisfactory point of view.

[1] Alexander Baring, Lord Ashburton (1774–1848), second son of Sir Francis Baring. M.P. for Taunton, 1806–26; for Callington, 1826–31; for Thetford, 1831–2; for North Essex, 1832–5. Master of the Mint and President of the Board of Trade, 1834–5. Peerage, 10 April 1835. Special Mission to the U.S.A., 1842. For many years head of the great merchant banking house of Baring Brothers.
[2] George Rose. His son also spoke in this debate.

The House had been full in the course of the evening, but many members had gone home before the division—which was for the ayes, 145; for the noes, 83; majority, 62. (14239)

[*The King's reply, Windsor Castle, 7 March, 1 p.m.*] The King acknowledges the receipt of Mr Perceval's report of last night's proceedings in the House of Commons,[1] which his Majesty could not do earlier, as it arrived after he had gone out riding. (14239)

[*From Perceval, Downing Street, 7 March.*] Mr Perceval has again to trouble your Majesty with a copy of the Resolution and Address which it is intended to propose in the Ho. of Commons tomorrow. The alterations which yr. Majesty's confidential servants have thought adviseable upon the reconsideration which their great natural anxiety upon this subject has led them to give to it, are, as far as the Address is concerned, as Mr Perceval conceives, so purely verbal that they would hardly have justified Mr Perceval in troubling your Majesty with a reperusal of it, but as the Resolution of acquittal has been altered by the omission of one whole member of the sentence, and by the alteration of a material phrase in another, Mr Perceval has thought it his duty humbly to submit it again for your Majesty's approbation, as being in the judgement of your Maj.'s confidential servants in language more Parliamentary and appropriate to the constitutional function of the Ho. of Commons than it was before. Mr Perceval has on the margin of the draft inserted the words of the Resolution as it stood before.

Altho' your Majesty's confidential servants did not think it right to take the advice of his R. Hss. the Duke of York as to the line which it was proper for them to take in the House of Commons, yet they conceived it to be no more than a mark of proper attention to his Royal Highness to apprize his R. Highness of the measure which it was proposed to take—and therefore Mr Perceval sent to H.R.H. this evening a copy of the draft of this Resolution and Address as it is now submitted to your Majesty, informing his Royal Highness at the same time that with the exception of some verbal alterations the sense and substance of them had been approved by your Majesty. (14240-1)

[*The King's reply, Windsor Castle, 8 March.*] The King has received Mr Perceval's letter and the inclosed copy of the Resolution and Address, in which his Majesty regrets that Parliamentary forms should have pointed out the necessity of any alteration, as the Resolution appeared to him perfectly proper as it stood previously. (14241)

[*From Perceval, Downg. St., 4 o'clock Thursday morg.* [*9 March 1809*].] Mr Perceval acquaints your Majesty that the House has proceeded on Mr Wardle's Motion upon the Report from the Comee. to enquire into the conduct of H.R.H.

[1] *Parl. Deb.*, XII, 1159-1210 (6 March). 'On Whitbread's Motion', Tierney had written to Grey (25 Feb.), 'I fear we shall come off but badly, for our friends, being under no control, cannot be kept in town a single day beyond their pleasure.'

the Duke of York. Mr Wardle after a long speech concluded with moving an Address to yr. Majesty of which Mr Perceval encloses for yr. Majesty a copy. Mr Perceval had intended to have taken up the debate immediately, but having understood that Mr Burton saw the subject in the same light as Mr Perceval and that he was desirous of speaking, Mr Perceval thought it desireable to take advantage of Mr Burton's respectable character, his great experience and his judicial situation,[1] to make the first impression upon the House, and therefore gave way to him—and he is happy that he did so, as Mr Burton made a very excellent and impressive speech. He was followed by Mr Kirwan,[2] who was answered by Mr Perceval. Mr. Perceval was obliged to go into very great length,[3] for it is not one case but ten or twelve cases, each of which require to be observed upon—and Mr Perceval was so fatigued that the House indulgently called for an adjournment before Mr Perceval had nearly finished his speech. Mr Perceval however would not yield to that call till he had fully explained the course which he should recommend to be taken—and read the Resolutions & Address which he meant to conclude with moving.

Your Majesty will perceive that in addition to the Resolution and Address which your Majesty had been graciously pleased to approve that Mr Perceval with the advice of his friends in the House of Commons has thought it proper to move an introductory Resolution—of which Mr Perceval sends to your Majesty a copy—and as this introductory Resolution is only to propose a Resolution on which, if the House divides, Mr Perceval is confident it will be supported by a very great majority indeed—and as it will not occasion the slightest alteration in the Resolution and Address previously settled, Mr. Perceval has no apprehension that your Majesty will not be graciously pleased to approve of it, upon these considerations, tho' it was not submitted to your Majesty because it did not seem to be adviseable till the debate was some way advanced.

Mr Perceval has great satisfaction in informing yr. Majesty that he thinks the debate as far as it has gone has had a most happy effect in making a very favorable impression in the House, and Mr. Perceval feels now quite confident of carrying the acquitting Resolution by a very great majority—and tho he will not run the risk of disappointing your Majesty with speaking too confidently upon the result of the other Motion for Mr Perceval's Address, yet he certainly thinks there is a better prospect of it than he could hope for when he had the honor of seeing your Majesty.

If your Majesty will be graciously pleased to direct Col. Taylor to return the copy of the first Resolution which Mr. Perceval incloses Mr Perceval will take care to return to your Majesty another copy of it tomorrow.[4] (14243–4)

[1] Francis Burton (c. 1744–1832), M.P. for Heytesbury, 1780–4; for New Woodstock, 1784–90, and for Oxford, 1790–1812, was Second Justice of Chester, 1788–1817. He spoke for 2¾ hours.

[2] Curwen, who spoke for half an hour.

[3] He spoke for three hours, beginning at 11.45 p.m.

[4] *Parl. Deb.*, XIII, 3–114; Colchester, II, 171–2. W. H. Fremantle described the debate in a letter to Lord Grenville written in two parts, the first at 9.30 p.m. on the 8th: 'Wardle has been speaking from 6 till half past 8 o'clock; he went into the examination of every case, and argued upon the corruption being proved in them all: he did it very ill and very heavily but was heard with great attention and concluded by moving an Address stating that "Various corrupt practices and abuses having been

[The King's reply, Windsor Castle, 9 March.] The King has received great comfort from Mr Perceval's very satisfactory report of last night's debate in the House of Commons, and his Majesty entirely approves of the introductory Resolution and the principle on which it was moved, as not interfering with anything which is contained in the others. The King desires Mr Perceval will be assured how truly sensible he is of his very zealous exertions upon this anxious occasion. (14248)

3829   THE DUKE OF PORTLAND *to the* KING

[Burlington House, Thursday, 9 March 1809, 1 p.m.] It occurs to the Duke of Portland to be so very improbable that Mr Perceval's report of the proceedings of yesterday in the House of Commons should do justice to himself that the Duke of Portland is induced to hope that your Majesty will forgive his presumption, in venturing at so undue an hour as the present to lay before your Majesty a note[1]

said to prevail in the Army, the Commons, having examined the proof of such abuses by the evidence of witnesses at the Bar, have found them to be substantiated, and which they are under the necessity of stating to his Majesty with the utmost concern and astonishment, that they are restrained by personal motives from entering into a detail of these transactions which would only be wounding the feelings of his Majesty—that they have proceeded with all due deliberation into these enquiries." It then goes on by stating "That if an opinion prevailed in the land forces that promotion could be gained without merit and by corrupt influence it would wound the feelings of the army, that such abuses as have appeared could not have existed without the knowledge of the Commander-in-Chief, and if they could it would not warrant the conclusion that the army should be left in his hands, and therefore they are of opinion he ought to be deprived of his command." This is the general tenor of the Address and nearly the words. It is well drawn up, but we understand Perceval is to move an Amendment negativing the whole of the conclusions—Burton is now speaking, the Welsh Judge. He followed Wardle, but I do not understand he moves the Amendment. The business cannot end tonight, the call of the House is adjourned till tomorrow. Burton is likely to continue an hour longer and therefore I shall not delay this. Upwards of 400 members and the House still very full. I think the complexion much in favour of the Duke. I shall send a note in the morning.' (Fortescue MSS.)

The second note was written at 3.30 a.m. on the 9th: 'Burton made a very bad speech, and a very improper one as a Judge, extracting and omitting evidence which best suited his arguments, and laying down very improper doctrines. Curwen answered him with great animation and effect and certainly created a much stronger impression than I should have expected from a person supporting the Address. This speech called up Perceval at about 11 o'clock—who began by stating that the charge having been originally for corrupt practices of the Duke of York, it ought to be met by a direct condemnation or acquittal which the Address did not admit of, and therefore he should move as a first Resolution that the Duke of York had no knowledge or connivance in the corruption—that if this Resolution was negatived he must go to trial; if admitted, that it would then be for the House to judge of the proper course to be pursued. He then in support of this Resolution went on to discredit the whole of Mrs. Clarke's evidence, and argued I think with much ability and effect throughout the whole of his speech. At half past 2 o'clock he appeared so much exhausted that an adjournment was proposed, which after some little discussion was agreed to, upon Perceval announcing what would be his view of the subject when he concludes his speech tomorrow, which is this—1st, a Resolution upon which a judgement must be given by the House that no personal corruption or criminal connivance has existed; 2nd, that there are no grounds for charging the Duke of York with personal corruption or connivance; 3dly, an Address to his Majesty containing these Resolutions with the decision of the House upon them and followed by the opinion of the House from the assurances which have been made by the Duke of York, of his regret at the connection which he had formed, and a sort of declaration from the House that he will behave better in future and follow the virtuous example of his royal father. I could not get hold of this Address, but Ponsonby had it and Charles Wynn has copied it, and therefore I give you what I picked up, partly read by Perceval, partly said, but this Address was ill received and I should think would not be carried. Perceval never spoke so well in his life and undoubtedly he made a very strong impression.' (Fortescue MSS.)

[1] Missing.

which he has just received from Mr Charles Long. The opinion which your Majesty has been graciously pleased to express of Mr Long's fairness & of the correctness of his judgement encourages the Duke of Portland to beleive that that gentleman's thoughts may not be unacceptable to your Majesty & may in some degree contribute to your Majesty's satisfaction—motives which the Duke of Portland trusts will dispose your Majesty to forgive this intrusion at so unusual a time of day.[1] (14249)

3830 LORD ELDON *to the* KING

[*10 March 1809.*] The Lord Chancellor, offering his very humble duty to your Majesty has the honour to transmit a Commission for passing Bills on Monday to receive your Majesty's Royal Sign Manual if your Majesty shall graciously so think fit.

The Lord Chancellor has reason to believe that Mr Perceval's very able speech has made a strong & favorable impression: Mr Burton's the Lord Chancellor also believes to have been highly useful. Upon the question relative to corruption or privity to it or connivance at it, the Chancellor confidently hopes that the decision will affirm the Duke of York's conduct to have afforded no ground of charge, but the Chancellor cannot venture, after seeing in last night's debate that so many Motions are intended to be made by different members, to express, as yet, to your Majesty any confident opinion as to what may be the result of the proceedings of the House in any other view of this very important subject. (14250)

3831 GEORGE CANNING *to the* KING, *and the reply*

[*Foreign Office, 10 March 1809.*] Mr Canning humbly lays before your Majesty a letter from Count Stadion delivered to him this day by an Austrian officer who left Vienna on the 30th of January & arrived here by way of Heligoland. Mr Canning has desired the officer to reduce into writing the propositions with which he is charged; which are in the substance the same with those which have been already received here, & to which an answer from your Majesty has been transmitted through Count Hardenberg.

A Prussian officer is also arrived whom Mr Canning is to see tomorrow, & whom he understands to be charged, not by the Prussian Cabinet but (as he states) by several persons of rank and influence in the Prussian States who are

[1] Sir Arthur Wellesley wrote to the Duke of Richmond on the 12th: 'We have had three days' debates upon the Duke of York's concerns. Perceval made I think the best speech I ever heard in Parliament; but the impression is very strong against the Duke, not on the score of corruption, or on the knowledge or even connivance or suspicion of corruption, but on the score of imprudence, & submission to the influence of Mrs. Clarke. I think that Bankes' Motion will be carried. If it is not it is probable that something equally strong in a different shape will be carried, & this will force him out of office. If this should be the case I think that Lord Harrington will succeed him. I have urged this arrangement really thinking it the best: and that you should have the command of the army in Ireland.' (Richmond MSS. 60/267.)

prepared & determined to take advantage of the commencement of the war between Austria & France, & have concerted measures for a general rising throughout Westphalia & Lower Saxony. Both these gentlemen appear to agree in the opinion that some blow must already have been struck by Austria, though they have no certain knowledge of such an event. The Austrian Army is described as being in the highest state of preparation. The French Army was understood to be assembling near Erfurth.

General Wallmoden is the person mentioned in Ct. Stadion's letter as being to be sent with full powers to England. He had actually left Vienna to proceed to Trieste at the time of the officer's departure. (14251–2)

[*The King's reply, Windsor Castle, 11 March.*] The King acknowledges the receipt of Mr Canning's letter relative to the arrival of Lieut. Wagner and the communications made by him and the Prussian officer, also mentioned in his letter. (14252)

3832 *Letters from* SPENCER PERCEVAL *to the* KING, *and the replies*

[*Dng. St., Friday, 4 a.m.* [*10 March 1809*].] Mr Perceval acquaints your Majesty that the adjourned debate on Mr Wardle's Motion was resumed about half past five o'clock, and Mr Perceval finished his speech. Mr Bragg Bathurst followed Mr Perceval. He argued in support of the Resolution acquitting H.R.H. of the corruption, but he objected to the Address and instead of that Address would propose a Resolution in which he was desirous of introducing the passage from the Address as intended to be moved by Mr Perceval which expresses the satisfaction and approbation of the House at the conduct of H.R.H., as Commander-in-Chief, with the addition of the words of which your Majesty will receive a copy, professing, however, that he did not mean to follow this up with any Address for removal. Mr Whitbread followed Mr Bathurst in a very long speech, with considerable impression, in which he declared himself convinced that his R.Hss. must have known that these corrupt practices were carried on, and that he was willing to support Mr. Wardle's Address. The Attorney-General replied to Mr Whitbread, and successfully exposed many of Mr Whitbread's arguments, and Mr. Perceval still thinks that the two first Resolutions moved by Mr Perceval will be carried by a considerable majority; altho' upon the conclusion of the Attorney-General's speech, when the House was too fatigued to admit of the prolongation of the debate, Mr Bankes got up and gave notice of his intention of moving another Amendment in which he means to introduce a negative upon the *corruption* or *corrupt participation*, but not to go the length of denying *connivance or knowledge* of its existence and to couple this with a censure, the object of which will be to convey the opinion of the House, whether to be presented in the state of an Address or not to your Majesty does not seem quite to be determined, tho he rather expressed himself, if I rightly understood him, as if he probably should not proceed to move an Address. What other Amendments may be to be moved by others Mr Perceval cannot yet anticipate, but he has been given to understand that this Amendment of Mr Bankes is to comprehend the sentiments of Mr Wilberforce, Ld Henry Petty & Mr Ponsonby. The manner in which these ideas were received by the House, tho they do not shake Mr Perceval's expectation of carrying the vote of acquittal in the most comprehensive & satisfactory terms, will still have the effect probably of diminishing the numbers of the majority, and also lead Mr Perceval still to entertain the apprehension that some Address for removal, or some censure so strong as may produce the removal, may possibly be carried by the House, in preference to the Address or Resolution to be moved by Mr. Perceval.

The number of persons still remaining to speak is so great that Mr Perceval can hardly hope to be able to come to a vote upon this question even this day. Mr Perceval sends his Majesty a copy of the first Resolution which he has moved.[1] (14253–4)

[*The King's reply, Windsor Castle, 10 March.*] The King has received Mr Perceval's letter stating what passed in the House of Commons last night, and he is aware that, under the uncertainty which so many different Motions must produce, it is difficult to form any judgement as to the result of the discussion. From what his Majesty has heard he is confident that Mr Perceval's speech will have produced a great effect. (14254)

[*From Perceval, Downg. Str., 11 March 1809.*] Mr Perceval acquaints your Majesty that Mr Bankes began the debate yesterday evening and moved an Amendment to Mr Perceval's Amendment for the purpose of introducing an Address a copy of which Mr Perceval herewith transmits to your Majesty. Mr Yorke followed Mr Bankes with a very able & useful speech most heartily &

[1] *Parl. Deb.*, XIII, 114–265. Fremantle described the first part of the debate in a letter to Lord Grenville at 8.30 p.m. on the 9th: 'Perceval spoke for two hours. His arguments on the remaining cases were not so ably produced as those of last night; he concluded however with great effect, appealing to the House for judgement on his conduct as a Minister throughout the whole transaction, and stating that in a case of so much difficulty and even danger, he still felt confident that the mode in which it had been conducted at the Bar of the House was infinitely preferable to any other. In this sentiment he was not seconded by any part of the House. Upon his concluding several got up, among others Whitbread, Lord Folkestone and Bragge-Bathurst; the latter was named by the Speaker, and he began at 8 o'clock by observing that he had taken a view of the subject perfectly different from either Wardle or Perceval and which he should state. This view was grounded upon the distinct consideration of influence and actual corruption, and it became the House to pass some decision upon the former if they found it existed—that if Perceval's second Resolution passed there was no use in the first—that he thought it not necessary to address the Crown at all upon the subject, but if the influence was proved to the extent which he thought it proved, it would be sufficient for the House to pass a Resolution to that effect which would necessarily remove the Duke from command. His speech was heard with very great attention and he spoke it with great feeling and effect. He was particularly cheered by the House when he said that the House expected more than what was contained in "the delusory Address of the Chancellor of the Exchequer." I think it hardly possible this Address can be carried; their own friends object to it. Bathurst has just concluded half past nine by proposing to adopt Perceval's second Resolution and then to leave out the Address and move the following Resolution: "That this House has observed with the deepest regret, that in consequence of a connection the most immoral and unbecoming a communication on official subjects and an interference in the distribution of military appointments and promotions have been allowed to exist which could not but tend to discredit the official administration of his Royal Highness the Commander-in-Chief and to give colour and effect, as they have actually done, to transactions the most criminal and disgraceful—" Whitbread is now up.' (Fortescue MSS.)

zealously in support of the line of conduct recommended to the House by Mr Perceval's Amendment. Mr Leach[1] followed Mr York on the same side and with very great ability. Lord Folkstone followed Mr Leach and took up the question with great violence, discussing various parts of it with very considerable force, but as he concluded by thinking *Mrs Clarke as credible a witness as ever appeared*, your Majesty may judge of the prejudiced state of his mind. Mr Adam made a very good speech in answer to Ld Folkstone, and Mr Wm. Smith closed the debate when, at ¼ before 4 o'clock, the House adjourned till Monday. Your Majesty will observe in Mr Bankes's Amendment that the absence of corruption and participation is directly affirmed, altho an implication of suspicion or knowledge is very unwarrantably and objectionably introduced, it is also open to much of the objection which was stated & felt to Mr Wardle's original Address, so much so that Mr Perceval ventures to hope that it may be very successfully opposed to the extent at least of introducing Mr Perceval's two first Resolutions before the House. But Mr Perceval is sorry to be obliged to say that there still continues to be a very strong opinion prevalent in the House upon the idea that even tho' official criminality be negatived yet there is something behind in the other circumstances of the case arising from the connexion with Mrs Clarke which will make the question of Address for removal a very difficult matter to resist, and which because the moral impropriety of that connexion is not more pointedly censured in the Address proposed by Mr Perceval (as objectionable in itself independent of the consequences which have followed it) makes that Address of Mr Perceval's by no means so well received by the House as his two Resolutions.

Mr Perceval hopes he will be able to report to your Majesty on Monday the numbers upon a division. But considering the number of persons who still remain ready to speak exclusive of the Solicitor-General, & yr. Maj.'s two Secretaries of State, Mr Perceval feels by no means confident that the debate will be closed on that day.[2] (14256)

[1] Sir John Leach (1760–1834), M.P. for Seaford, 1806–16. K.C., 1807. Chancellor of the Duchy of Cornwall, 1816; Chief Justice of Chester, Aug. 1817; Vice-Chancellor of England, 1818, and knighted, Jan. 1818; Master of the Rolls, 1827. Leach was an Opposition member, though not yet specifically connected with Carlton House. He had supported the 'Talents', and Lord Grenville wrote to Erskine, the Lord Chancellor, on 9 Jan. 1807: 'I have reason to believe that Mr. Leach is desirous of obtaining a silk gown. Your Lordship will be better able to judge than I am how far his professional pretensions entitle him to it and whether it would be attended with any inconveniencies, and I have therefore taken the liberty to recommend the subject to your consideration and at the same time to express my wish that if practicable the measure may be adopted.' (Fortescue MSS.)

[2] *Parl. Deb.*, XIII, 269–358. The effect of Bankes's Amendment, wrote the Speaker, 'was to retain so much of Mr. Wardle's Motion as kept it in the form of an Address, proposing afterwards to negative the corruption, but in consequence of the *immoral* conduct of the Duke, and the *influence* given by his name to the corrupt practices of others, &., *that he ought not any longer to be Commander-in-Chief*. In this course of proceeding the Grenvilles and Wilberforce concurred.' William Smith spoke for the Duke on the question of corruption, and against him on the question of removal. (Colchester, II, 172.)

Robert Ward wrote to Lord Lonsdale on the 11th: 'Perceval's Amendment will, I think, not only not be carried, but if persisted in, will leave us in an irrespactable minority [*sic*]. Long ago several County members waited upon Lord Wellesley and informed him they could not vote for the Duke, and though Perceval's admirable speech … has turned some few (among them Blackburne of Lancashire), I think upon the whole the decided opinion of our best friends is against us. I have seen a list of full twenty of our staunchest friends who will vote either for Bankes' or Bathurst's Amendments, among them Cartwright and Goulburn, so that I perceive nothing but defeat unless the Duke resigns.

[*The King's reply, Windsor Castle, 11 March.*] The King acknowledges the receipt of Mr Perceval's letter, from which his Majesty is led to hope that last night's proceedings may be considered upon the whole more favorable. Whatever may be the result the King is satisfied that a perseverance in the firm line of conduct which has been adopted will prove most generally beneficial. (14257)

[*From Perceval, Downg. St., Tuesday morg., 14 March* [*1809*].] Mr Perceval acquaints your Majesty that the House of Commons has been sitting again till three o'clock this morning on the debate upon the enquiry into the conduct of his Royal Highness the Duke of York. In which debate the following speakers spoke in the following order. Sir James Pulteney, Sr Fran. Burdett, the Master of the Rolls, Sr Saml. Romilly, Mr Smith[1] the Solicitor to the East Ind. Company, & the Solicitor-General. The Master of the Rolls & the Solicitor-General made very able and impressive speeches. Sr. Saml. Romilly spoke against the Duke. Mr Smith thought we should not proceed to any Address or adopt any other course than that of impeachment. Nothing occurred in the course of the debate to lead Mr Perceval to take any other view of the subject than what he last represented to your Majesty; that in his opinion the Resolution of acquittal will be carried, but that it will be extremely difficult to prevent a Resolution of censure or an Address of removal—for notwithstanding the arguments for acquittal seem to make their way they do not seem to diminish the impression which unfortunately has been taken up, upon the general subject as connected with Mrs Clarke.[2] (14260)

[*The King's reply, Windsor Castle, 14 March.*] The King acknowledges the receipt of Mr Perceval's report, from which his Majesty has learnt with satisfaction that the Master of the Rolls and the Solicitor-General have spoken so ably and impressively. (14261)

[*From Perceval, 15 March.*] Mr Perceval acquaints your Majesty that the debate upon the Report of the enquiry into the conduct of H.R.Hss. the Duke of York continued till about ¼ p. 3 o'clock. It was begun by Mr C. Wms. Wynn, who spoke against his R. Hss. and was followed by Mr Croker who made a most excellent speech examining many particulars of the evidence with great force,

---

This I understand he was, even the night before last, prepared to do, upon condition however that his acquittal of corruption was carried; and this last, altho' the opinion I think of a very great majority, will not be allowed to pass as a naked proposition, unalloyed by such observations as were contained in the Amendment, unless upon an understood condition that the Duke shall resign. The difficulty therefore is to come to this understanding in a *public* way, which I own appears to be impossible. I should think the debate not much above half over; certainly Opposition speculate upon its producing a change, tho' as Tierney told me, they themselves have no chance of coming in. I asked if he could not join his old friend the Doctor; he said he had outlived his friendship.' (Lonsdale MSS.)

[1] Henry Smith, M.P. for Calne, 1807–12, Lord Lansdowne's pocket borough. 'Mr. Smith, we believe, is Clerk to one of the great City Companies, and Solicitor to the Hon. East India Company.' (J. Wilson, *Biographical Index to the House of Commons* [1808], p. 105.) One of his sons, too, was an Attorney, the other a wine merchant. (Lord Dudley's *Letters to 'Ivy'*, ed. Romilly, p. 175.) Little else is known about him. He rarely voted with the Opposition, and in 1810 was listed as a supporter of Administration.

[2] *Parl. Deb.*, XIII, 359–420.

and bringing fresh light to shew the falsehood of the accusations against H.R.H., but he concluded with thinking him to a degree culpable in suffering her to have communication with him upon military matters. Mr Martin[1] spoke next against H.R.H. Mr Rose answered him; Mr Wortley followed very strongly in favor of His R. Hss. as did Mr Chas Long. Mr Coke of Norfolk spoke with great earnestness against the Duke to the full extent of charging him with corruption. Mr Windham followed Mr Coke, and Mr Perceval has great satisfaction in bearing his testimony to your Majesty in favor of the very honorable & liberal manner in which Mr Windham spoke upon the subject. With much of that ingenuity and ability that almost always distinguish him, he did away many of the arguments & supposed presumptions which had appeared to weigh upon several persons, and acquitted his Royal Highness most entirely in his opinion of all corruption, participation or criminal connivance. He however concluded that he thought, all things considered, that it would be necessary that H.R.Hss. should not retain his station at the head of the Army; that he should be sorry that the House should be obliged to come to any Address upon that subject, and if it should be necessary was anxious that it should be expressed in the terms the most delicate and the least offensive to the feelings both of his Royal Highness and of your Majesty. Lord Castlereagh spoke next to Mr Windham, and urged many topics very forcibly and effectively against the injustice of proceeding upon such evidence and in such a case to drive either by Address or by Resolution from the command of the Army a person who had served your Majesty so long & so ably, and had done such essential service to the Army. The debate was then closed by a speech from Mr Calcraft against H.R.H. when the House became too impatient to hear any more—and it therefore adjourned the debate till this day, when Mr Perceval trusts the House will come to some decision; whether it will go further than decide upon the question of form which Mr Bankes's Motion introduces, Mr Perceval cannot undertake to say, but at all events he conceives that the debate upon the merits will be so much exhausted, that the following questions will be disposed of at one sitting more.

Mr Perceval regrets extremely to be obliged in duty to state to your Majesty that altho' the debate has upon the whole been most satisfactory and convincing upon the subject of the criminal charge, yet the sentiment expressed by Mr. Windham of the necessity that H.R.H. should retire, at least for a time, is so general & has been so little broken in upon by the proof of his R. H's innocence that Mr Perceval does not think it will be possible to resist a vote to that effect, and that it is therefore a subject of most anxious consideration in what manner that sentiment on the part of the Ho. of Commons had best be met with a view to the return of H.R.Hss. at the earliest possible opportunity to the same situation —and Mr Perceval cannot but humbly state to your Majesty that the most prevalent opinion as far as he can collect it amongst those whom Mr Perceval believes to be most anxious for his R.H.'s restoration to the command of the Army, in the event of his retiring, seems to be that an Address to your Majesty for his

[1] Henry Martin (1763–1839), M.P. for Kinsale, 1806–18. A barrister and staunch Opposition member. Brought in by Lord De Clifford.

removal would create a sort of bar to his R.H.'s return, which would not exist in the same or in anything like the same degree were his R.Hss. to announce his intention of retiring with your Majesty's approbation as soon as the vote upon his acquittal may have passed. That it may then be well stated that H.R.H. would not think of shrinking from his situation, at a time when it might be considered as shrinking from a charge, but when once he had been cleared by the opinion of the Ho. of Commons, his R. Hss. then thought that upon the whole he could, for the time at least, best serve your Majesty by retiring from his office than by continuing to hold it.

Mr Perceval entreats your Majesty not to understand him to be presuming singly to intrude this opinion upon your Majesty as his humble advice upon this great question, but merely humbly to suggest for your Majesty's consideration a point which it is certainly more than probable that in the distempered & inflamed state of the opinion of the Ho. of Co. on this subject it may be necessary for your Majesty to decide.[1] (14262–3)

[*The King's reply, Windsor Castle, 15 March.*] The King is glad to learn from Mr Perceval's report that Mr Windham took so honorable and liberal a part in last night's debate and that his sentiments were so ably delivered. In regard to what remains to be done in this distressing business, his Majesty considers the unconditional acquittal of the Duke of York to be the most material object.[2] (14264)

[*From Perceval, Downg. St., Thursday morg., 6.30, 16 March [1809].*] Mr Perceval acquaints your Majesty that the adjourned debate upon the enquiry lasted this morning till near 6 o'clock. The speakers were Lord Milton, Ld. Stanley, Sr. T. Turton, Ld. Temple, Mr Wilberforce & Mr Ponsonby against his R. H. imputing to him different degrees of blame and shades of offence. On the other side Mr Leycester, Mr Ryder, the Ld. Advocate and Mr Canning—all of whom spoke very usefully and with good effect. But Mr. Canning, who spoke after Mr Wilberforce, and who had purposely reserved himself to be able to answer any speech which might appear likely to produce the greatest effect, spoke at very great length, and with even more than his usual ability. His speech was impressive and

---

[1] *Parl. Deb.*, XIII, 423–538.

[2] The Duke of Richmond, the Lord Lieutenant of Ireland, wrote to Lord Bathurst on the 19th: 'I understood the Duke of York's friends were anxious the business should come on as it did. They were ignorant of the letters, & he never suspected they would have been brought forward. I must own I think the transaction very disgraceful to the House. They had no business to listen to such witnesses nor even to such charges. The former would have been turn'd out of any Court of Law. The latter were not of magnitude enough or at least not sufficient in number to bring before such an Assembly as the House of Commons ought to be, against the Duke of York after nearly 20 years' service as Commander-in-Chief. The majority was greater than I expected on both divisions but yet the cry of the country is I understand so strong that I am convinced his Royal Highness should retire. Probably the division after the debate on Friday will be something like that on Bankes' Motion. I can't expect it to be better, and Govt. will run a great risk if the Duke does not resign after such a division. I am extremely sorry for it as I really believe no man to be so proper for the situation, tho' I certainly on most occasions have a great objection to the Royal Family being employed.' (Richmond MSS. 61/331.)

useful in a very high degree, and the firmness and manliness with which he spoke upon the dangerous effects which might be produced by these proceedings were extremely creditable to himself & to your Majesty's Government and were well received by the House.

The House divided about 5 o'clock upon Mr Bankes's Amendment to the Amendment of Mr Perceval, the effect of which was to determine the course of proceeding which should be pursued, viz. whether by an Address, in the first instance, or by Resolutions. The idea of determining to address your Majesty before it was determined by the House what the nature of H.R.Hss.' conduct was or what should be said in the Address appeared to Mr. Perceval to be so absurd that he hoped by taking advantage of that state of the question to be able to bring the first question upon this subject to a favorable vote—and the result was that upon the division there were 293[1] for Resolutions and for

Mr Bankes' proposition for an Address $\dfrac{199}{84}$

In this division there certainly were some, tho' Mr Perceval hopes but a few, who will vote against the Resolution of acquittal; but there were many who will vote for the removal of his R.H., whilst on the other hand there were also several who will vote for the acquittal, but none, as Mr Perceval apprehends, who will not vote for his removal. The House having disposed of Mr Bankes's Amendment, then proceeded to vote upon Mr Wardle's original Address, which was negatived by a very large majority viz.

against Mr W.'s Address	364
for it	123
giving a majority of	241

From this last vote Mr Perceval is sorry to be obliged to state that no conclusion whatever can be formed one way or the other except that all those, or at least almost all those who voted in the minority must be considered as decided votes against his R.H. in all the stages of the proceeding. Mr Perceval wished to have gone on to the acquitting Resolution, but it was near 6 o'clock, debate was threatened, and adjournment was moved. It was in vain to attempt to resist that Motion at such a time, and the debate was therefore adjourned till tomorrow. Your Majesty will therefore be graciously pleased to observe that a day is interposed in the course of the proceedings, in which interval Mr Perceval humbly submits to your Majesty that it may be expedient that your Majesty's confidential servants should, if your Majesty should think proper, take into consideration the propriety of advising your Majesty upon the question whether H.R.H. the D. of York should, in the event of his obtaining (what Mr Perceval confidently looks to) an unconditional acquittal, authorise any person in the House of Commons to state that he had determined that no consideration should lead him to shrink from his situation while the enquiry was going on, but that when he had been acquitted,

[1] The number should be 294. (*H. of C. J.*, LXIV, 143.)

collecting from what the impression was which was created by the enquiry and the discussion, that it would be more desireable for your Maj.'s service that he should retire.[1] (14267–8)

[*The King's reply, Windsor Castle, 16 March, 1 p.m.*] The King has learnt with great satisfaction from Mr Perceval's report of last night's proceedings in the House of Commons that the Addresses of Mr Bankes and Mr Wardle have been negatived by so respectable a majority, and that Mr Canning had an opportunity of delivering his sentiments with so much credit to himself and so much advantage to the question.

His Majesty is perfectly convinced that, in offering any suggestion in regard to the question of resignation, Mr Perceval is actuated solely by motives of attachment to himself and zeal for the Duke of York's interests, but his Majesty continues of opinion that the acquittal ought to be unconditional, and that it will be more consistent with the Duke of York's honor and his future interests that it should not be preceded by anything like a compromise or even a hint at compromise. The King is satisfied that the Duke of York will feel disposed upon this point to shew every attention to the opinions of his Majesty's Ministers and to the arguments by which those opinions may be supported, and his Majesty, sensible as he is that the Duke of York is influenced by the truest attachment for him, must feel the more unwilling to fetter by any previous opinion of his own a decision in which he must be guided by his feelings, and of which his Majesty will not destroy the merit by his interposition. (14269)

[*From Perceval, Downg. St., 16 March, Thursday evg.*] Mr Perceval acquaints your Majesty that he laid your Majesty's gracious letter to him of this day before your Majesty's confidential servants; when after the most attentive consideration of all the very delicate and distressing circumstances connected with the present proceedings in Parliament they thought it most expedient to meet the discussion of the question of guilt without previously submitting to your Majesty any opinion upon the subject of H.R.H.'s continuance in the office of Commander-in-Chief, and to endeavour to leave the state of the debate upon that subject after a division upon that point tomorrow in such a situation as to enable them to resume the consideration of that subject on Saturday. (14265)

[*The King's reply, Windsor Castle, 17 March.*] The King acknowledges the receipt of Mr. Perceval's letter, from which his Majesty is glad to find that the question of resignation remains as it has appeared to him that it should rest. (14266)

3833   THE DUKE OF PORTLAND *to the* KING, *and the reply*

[*Burlington House, Thursday, 16 March 1809.*] Your Majesty having been graciously pleased to direct your royal approbation to be signified to the Duke of Portland

[1] *Parl. Deb.*, XIII, 540–639.

for having presumed to submit to your Majesty the report of the proceedings of the House of Commons on Wednesday the 8th inst., the day on which that House began to investigate the conduct of his Royal Highness the Duke of York, which had been made to the Duke of Portland by Mr Charles Long, and having at the same time condescended to express the opinion your Majesty had most graciously formed of the soundness of that gentleman's judgement; the Duke of Portland most humbly requests your Majesty's permission to lay at your Majesty's feet another report,[1] which he received this afternoon from Mr Long, of yesterday's proceedings in the House of Commons. (14270)

[*The King's reply, Windsor Castle, 17 March.*] The King acknowledges the receipt of the Duke of Portland's letter enclosing Mr Long's report and opinion upon the divisions in the House of Commons yesterday morning. (14271)

3834 SPENCER PERCEVAL *to the* KING, *and the reply*

[*Downg. St., 17 [18] March 1809.*] Mr. Perceval acquaints your Majesty that the debate upon the Report from the Comee. of Enquiry was renewed about 6 o'clock yesterday evening. In consequence of the House having negatived the two Addresses on the last day of its sitting upon this subject, for the purpose of proceeding by way of Resolution instead of by Address the first Resolution intended to be moved by Mr. Perceval became unnecessary; and as there was some objection taken to the wording of the Resolution itself, Mr Perceval proposed to withdraw it. Upon this a long debate arose in which the persons whose names stand in the first list of the accompanying paper, spoke in the order in which they stand—not confining themselves indeed to that mere question but proceeding to discuss in part the general question. The debate lasted till near 9 o'clock when it was agreed that the Resolution should be withdrawn. Mr Perceval then proposed his second Resolution upon the innocence of his Royal Highness—and a new debate arose which continued till about $\frac{1}{2}$ p 3 o'clock this morning.

Sir Thomas Turton moved an Amendment to it for the purpose of converting it from a negative proposition that there were *no* grounds for the House charging his Royal Highness, into an affirmative that there were grounds for charging his R. Hss. with knowledge of the corruption which has been disclosed in the testimony heard at the Bar. The 2d list of names in the paper before referred to will give your Majesty the names of the persons who spoke in this debate. Your Majesty will not imagine that there would be much novelty in the debate upon a subject which has been so completely discussed. A division was called for on Sr. Thomas Turton's Amendment—which was to leave out the words of Mr Perceval's Resolution for the purpose of inserting his own. And there were for Mr Perceval's Resolution as it stood originally $\left.\begin{array}{c} 334 \\ 135 \end{array}\right\}$ 469

For Sr. T. Turton's Amendment

199

[1] Missing.

The House then divided upon Mr Perceval's Resolution itself (after Sr T. Turton's Amendment was disposed of) when the division was,

$$
\left.\begin{array}{lr}
\text{for the Resolution} & 278 \\
\text{against it} & 196
\end{array}\right\} 474
$$

$$\underline{82}$$

The difference in the numbers of these two divisions which seems so extraordinary Mr Perceval is at a loss to reconcile to any principle of common sense or fair reasoning—because it might have been reasonably expected that those who had refused to assent to Sr T. T.'s Amendment, which said there were grounds for charging his R.H. with knowledge, &c. &c., would have affirmed Mr Perceval's Resolutions which negatived corruption & connivance. But Mr Windham, Ld H. Petty, Mr Tierney, Mr Wilberforce, Mr Thornton and many others chose to imagine that they saw a distinction, and that in negativing connivance they would have negatived the only reasonable grounds for proceeding to the ulterior vote, of blame or for removal. At the rising of the House Mr Bathurst declared that he should on Monday at all events move his Resolution, which the Opposition was very desirous of pushing forward at the close of the debate. They were however obliged to abandon that idea and adjourn the question till Monday. Before that time your Majesty's confidential servants will have taken into consideration and have submitted to your Majesty their humble opinion upon the subject of the continuance of H.R.H. in his present situation, against which Mr Perceval regrets to be obliged to state that several members who voted for Mr Perceval's Resolution this day, declared their intention of voting when that question should be put.[1] (14272–3)

On the first Resolution: Mr. Perceval, Mr. Tierney, Mr. Bathurst, Sr. Js. Montgomery, Mr. Cartwright, Sr. Js. Hall,[2] Mr. Lockhart,[3] Mr. Aldn. Curtis, Ld. W. Russel, Mr. M. Fitzgerald, General Ferguson,[4] Ld. Hy. Petty, Mr. Cripps.[5]

On the Resolution of Requittal: Mr. Perceval, Mr. Lyttleton, Sr. Thos. Turton, Mr. Hawkins Brown, Mr. Herbert, Mr. Brand, Mr. Dickinson, Mr. Fuller, Ld. A. Hamilton, Ld. Morpeth, Mr. Portman,[6] Mr. Banks, Mr. Hibbert, Mr. Ellison,

[1] *Parl. Deb.*, XIII, 646–709 (17 March); Colchester, II, 173–4.

[2] Sir James Hall (1761–1832), M.P. for St. Michael, 1807–12; more interested in science and architecture than politics. President of the Royal Society of Edinburgh. Succeeded his father as 4th Baronet, 3 July 1776. Voted with the Opposition (in Feb. 1793 he had expressed his opposition to the war).

[3] John Ingram Lockhart (1765–1835), M.P. for Oxford, 1807–18 and 1820–30. A barrister on the Oxford Circuit. He occasionally voted with the Whigs, but in 1810 they reckoned him as only a 'hopeful'.

[4] Sir Ronald Craufurd Ferguson (1773–1841), Whig M.P. for the Dysart burghs, 1806–30; for Nottingham, 1830–41. Ensign, 1790; Captain, 1793; Lieutenant-Colonel, 1794; Colonel, 1800; Brigadier-General, 1804; Major-General, 1808; Lieutenant-General, 1813; General, 1830. K.C.B., 1815; G.C.B., 1831.

[5] Joseph Cripps (1765–1847), M.P. for Cirencester, 1806–12 and 1818–41. It is said that one of his electioneering devices was to get the local baker to produce loaves of bread stamped with the words 'Cripps for ever', and after that long service in Parliament the slogan seemed justified. A banker, an East India proprietor and a Colonel of Volunteers. He generally voted with the Tories.

[6] Edward Berkeley Portman (1771–1823), M.P. for Boroughbridge, 1802–6; for Dorset, 1806–23 (coming in for the county in 1806 on the Government interest). He acted in Parliament as an independent country gentleman, giving the various Governments, in general, his support.

Sr. C. M. Burrell,[1] Mr. Home Sumner, Mr. Wilberforce, Mr. Lushington, Ld. Hy. Petty, The Solicitor General of Scotland,[2] Mr. Chs. Dundas, Mr. Perceval, Mr. Whitbread, Mr. Secretary at War, Mr. Canning, Sr. Arthur Wellesley.[3]

1 Divn. Ayes 334 ⎫ 469   2 Divn. Ayes 278 ⎫ 474
         Noes 135 ⎭   Noes 196 ⎭
              199   82   (14274)

[*The King's reply, Windsor Castle, 18 March.*] The King acknowledges the receipt of Mr Perceval's report of last night's proceedings in the House of Commons from the result of which, considering the prejudice which has prevailed to so unaccountable a degree, his Majesty derives great satisfaction. (14275)

3835   THE COUNTESS WALDEGRAVE[4] *to the* KING

[*Berkeley Square, 18 March 1809.*] I trust your Majesty will pardon the great liberty I take in addressing you. I feel encouraged to do so, having heard from many of your Majesty's gracious condescension in expressing your concern at the last severe affliction with which it has pleased the Almighty to visit me. In the year 1789 I lost my Lord, & was left with six children. Your Majesty then most condescendingly sent me your gracious promise of protection, & the assurance that my children should never want a father while you lived. In the course of these 20 years I have never intruded myself upon your Majesty with any request in their behalf. Your Majesty knows full well the repeated and unexpected melancholy events which have occurred to bereave me of my children, and that I have only two sons remaining! I had three till lately! My Edward was a most gallant & promising officer and served in Spain with honour to himself & usefulness in his profession. Will your Majesty pardon me if I mention that he had only obtained the rank of Lieutenant in his Regiment the 7th L.D. & was disappointed in the purchase of a troop a short time before his embarkation? I was anxious to obtain one for him, but, upon his receiving the intimation that his regiment was likely to go to Spain, he wrote to desire that I would stop my exertions as, if he got a troop, he should as junior captain remain at home. He went & after escaping all the perils of that harassing campaign, was wrecked upon his native shore.[5]

At the same time that Edward sailed for Spain, William,[6] my youngest son,

---

[1] Sir Charles Merrik Burrell (1774–1862), M.P. for Shoreham, 1806–62. Succeeded his father as 3rd Baronet, 20 Jan. 1796. He opposed Catholic emancipation and generally supported the various Tory Governments.

[2] David Boyle, Lord Boyle (1772–1853), M.P. for Ayrshire, 1807–11. Solicitor-General for Scotland, 1807–11; Lord Justice Clerk, 1811; Lord President of the Court of Session, 1841–52.

[3] There are differences between these lists and the list of speakers in *Parl. Deb.*

[4] The 4th Earl Waldegrave (1751–89) married, 5 May 1782, his cousin, Elizabeth Laura (1760–1816), daughter of his paternal uncle, 2nd Earl Waldegrave, by Maria, natural daughter of Sir Edward Walpole. At the time of the marriage her mother was Duchess of Gloucester, the King's sister-in-law.

[5] Edward William Waldegrave (1787–1809), the third son, was lost in a transport off Falmouth, on his return from Spain, 22 Jan. 1809.

[6] William, 8th Earl Waldegrave (1788–1859). Lieutenant, July 1806; Commander, Dec. 1809; Captain, March 1811; Rear Admiral, 1846; Vice-Admiral, 1858. In 1812 he married Whitbread's daughter Elizabeth. Whig M.P. for Bedford, 1815–18.

who is a Lieutenant in the Navy, sailed for the Mediterranean upon a promise of Lord Mulgrave's of promotion to the rank of Commander. He has now been with Lord Collingwood some months, is not promoted & writes me word has no expectation of it, and I should despair of it without your Majesty's gracious interference. I understand there are several sloops now vacant upon that station. My poor boy, of course, is in constant expectation of receiving letters notifying his promotion, and when he does hear from home he will only learn that he continues a Lieutenant & that his next brother has perished in the service of his country! I was in hopes that Lord Mulgrave would have felt upon such an aweful circumstance as that, anxious and eager to give that comfort & consolation to a mother, which her son's promotion would have afforded her.

I can assure your Majesty that much as I love my children, I never should wish to see them promoted were they not equal to fulfil the duties of their stations. My son William is a young man of uncommon ability in his profession—those he has served with will give him the highest of characters! Sir John Gore who educated him, has repeatedly said that he possessed all the qualities which would constitute a good man and a brilliant officer. Captn Prowse,[1] with whom he served his time as Lieutenant on board the Sirius, always speaks of him in such terms as are truely grateful to a parent to hear. Lord Collingwood has very lately written in his praise to Lord Radstock.

William was a midshipman on board the Medusa (when it took the Governor-General to India in 1805). The late Lord Cornwallis in the last letter which I ever recd. from him, which was written when he was upon his march to join the Army, speaks thus of him: 'I have the satisfaction to assure you that William is a most promising youth, and that it is the opinion not only of his superior officers but likewise of his cotemporaries, that he will make a distinguished figure in his profession.'

May I presume to intreat your Majesty graciously to interpose in my son's favour that he may be made a Commander? Both his cousins Granville Walde-grave[2] & George Seymour[3] were Post Captains at his age, & altho' he has served his full time remains a Lieutenant, he who is not inferior to either of them in abilities.

My eldest son Lord Waldegrave[4] after serving with much credit on the Staff in Sicily and Egypt is now a Major in the 72d Foot. (14284–7)

[1] William Prowse (c. 1752–1826). Lieutenant, 1782; Commander, 1796; Captain, 1797; Rear-Admiral, 1821. C.B., 1815.

[2] Granville George Waldegrave (1786–1857). Lieutenant, 1804; Commander, 1806; Captain, 1807. Succeeded his father, the Admiral, as 2nd Baron Radstock, 20 Aug. 1825. The Admiral was the younger brother of the 4th Earl Waldegrave.

[3] Sir George Francis Seymour (1787–1870), eldest son of Vice-Admiral Lord Hugh Seymour (1759–1801), who was the fifth son of the 1st Marquess of Hertford. Lieutenant, 1804; Commander, Jan. 1806; Captain, July 1806; Rear-Admiral, 1841; Admiral, 1857. C.B., 1815; K.C.H., 1831; G.C.H., 1834; a Lord of the Admiralty, 1841–4; G.C.B., 1860.

[4] John James, 6th Earl Waldegrave (1785–1835), his mother's eldest surviving son, his brother George, the 5th Earl (1784–94), having been accidentally drowned whilst bathing in the Thames, 29 June 1794. Ensign, 1802; Lieutenant, 1804; Captain, 1805; Major, Oct. 1808; Lieutenant-Colonel, 1812. A Lord of the Bedchamber, 1830–31.

[*Windsor Castle, 18 March 1809.*] The King acquaints Mr Perceval that the Duke of York has been with his Majesty this morning, and has tendered to him his resignation of the office of Commander-in-Chief in a letter of which the King transmits a copy inclosed, and which letter his Majesty authorizes Mr Perceval to communicate to the House of Commons, acquainting the House at the same time that the King has with great reluctance accepted of the Duke of York's resignation.

The King cannot forbear adding upon this occasion that he must ever regret any circumstances which have deprived him of the services of the Duke of York in a situation in which his able, zealous and impartial conduct during so many years have secured to him his Majesty's entire approbation; and have appeared to him not less conspicuous than his strict integrity, all tending to confirm the King's sincere affection for the Duke of York & to convince him of the benefits which have resulted to the King and to the country from his honorable administration of the Army, nor can his Majesty omit expressing the admiration with which he has witnessed the forbearance and the temper shewn by the Duke of York under circumstances so painful & so trying. (14277)

[*The Duke of York to the King, Stable Yard, 18 March (Enclosure).*] The House of Commons having, after a most attentive and laborious investigation of the merits of certain allegations preferred against me, passed a Resolution declaratory of my innocence, I may now approach your Majesty and may venture to tender to you my resignation of the Chief Command of your Majesty's Army, as I can no longer be suspected of acting from any apprehension of the result nor be accused of having shrunk from the full extent of an enquiry which, painfull as it has been, I trust I shall appear, even to those who have been disposed to condemn my conduct, to have met with that patience and firmness which can arise only from a conscious feeling of innocence.

While I humbly presume to hope that your Majesty will be graciously pleased to acquiesce in the step which I am induced to take upon due consideration of every circumstance which attached to it, I am anxious to assure your Majesty that I am deeply impressed with and sincerely gratefull for the warm support which upon this occasion, so important to my character and to my interests, I have experienced from your Majesty and from your Government, and that I am firmly convinced that a continuance of such support and countenance would not have been withheld from me if I had felt that I could reconcile it to my honor and to my future satisfaction not to retire from a situation in which my conscience assures me that I have not been undeserving of that approbation which must always prove a comfort to my wounded feelings.

The motive which influences me arises from the truest sense of duty and the warmest attachment to your Majesty, from which I have never departed, and which your Majesty has, if possible, confirmed by the affectionate and paternal solicitude which you have shewn for my honor and my welfare upon this distressing occasion. To you, Sir, as a most kind and indulgent parent, as a gracious Sovereign I owe everything, and this feeling alone would have prompted me to forego all considerations of personal interest in the determination which I have taken. It would not become me to say that I shall not quit with[out] sincere regret a situation in which your Majesty's confidence and partiality had placed me, and the duties of which it has been my anxious study and my pride during fourteen years to discharge with integrity and fidelity; whether I may be allowed to add with advantage to your Majesty's service, your Majesty is best able to decide. (14278–9)

[*Perceval's reply, 18 March.*] Your Majesty's gracious letter reached Mr Perceval at the moment when your Maj.'s confidential servants were all assembled at his Grace the D. of Portland's for the purpose of taking into consideration the result of last night's proceedings in the Ho. of Commons. Mr Perceval hopes he may be permitted to express to your Majy. in the names of himself and of all his colleagues the strong feelings of admiration with which they are impressed by a determination and conduct on the part of H.R.H. the D. of York at once so honorable & dignified in itself and so full of affection and duty to your Majesty.

Mr Perceval humbly presumes to add that tho' it would have been with the most painful feelings of anxiety and reluctance that your Maj.'s confidential servants would have come to the consideration of any advice to be tendered to your Majy. on a subject so peculiarly distressing, yet it may possibly be some satisfaction to your Majy. to learn that, while your Maj.'s confidential servants sincerely condole with your Majy. in the temporary loss of his R.H. the Duke of York's services in a station of which he executed the important duties with so much satisfaction to yr Majty. and so much advantage to the public, it is nevertheless their unanimous opinion that the step which H.R.H. has now voluntarily taken cannot fail to produce universally an impression the most honorable to H.R.Highness's character & feelings.

Mr Perceval humbly begs leave to express in the names of all your Maj.'s servants the gratitude with which they feel the kind & gracious manner in which H.R.H. has been pleased to acknowledge their humble but zealous efforts in his support, humbly assuring your Majy. that in everything which has been done by them on this trying and difficult occasion, they have been guided to the best of their judgement by the truest considerations of duty to your Majesty and of affectionate solicitude for the interests of H. Royal Highness.

Mr Perceval will not fail in obeying your Majesty's commands by communicating H.R.H.'s resignation to the Ho. of Co. on Monday next, to read the letter of H.R.H. and to express the reluctance with which your Majesty accepted that resignation.[1] (14282–3)

[*From the King, Windsor Castle, 19 March.*] The King acknowledges the receipt of Mr Perceval's letter of yesterday, from which he has learnt with great satisfaction that the conduct of the Duke of York is viewed by his Majesty's confidential servants in the same light in which it has struck him.[2] (14288)

[1] See *Parl. Deb.*, XIII, 712. Perceval read to the House merely excerpts. The Duke's letter of the 18th to Perceval is in Colchester, II, 176.

[2] The Duke of Kent commented, in a letter to his friend Colonel Charles Stevenson, 26 March: 'With respect to the late resignation, you may depend upon it as a fact, notwithstanding anything you

[*Windsor Castle, 18 March 1809.*] The King acquaints the Duke of Portland that he has this day reluctantly accepted the resignation of the Duke of York, which has been conveyed to his Majesty in a letter of which he has sent the copy to Mr. Perceval, and which he will of course communicate to his colleagues.

Under these painful circumstances his Majesty's attention has been directed to the necessary arrangements for the future administration of the Army, and after consulting the Army List, the King has satisfied himself that General Sir David Dundas is, of all those whose names have occurred to him, the fittest person to be entrusted with the chief temporary command both from habits of business, respectability of character, and from the disposition which his Majesty is convinced that he will feel to attend strictly to the maintenance of that system and those regulations which, under the direction of the Duke of York, have proved so beneficial to the Service.[1] It does not appear to his Majesty that any change will be required in the constitution of the Commander-in-Chief's Office, or in the various official establishments connected with it.[2] (14276)

[*The Duke of Portland's reply, Burlington House, Saturday, 18 March.*] The Duke of Portland most humbly begs leave with the deepest sense of gratitude to acknowledge your Majesty's most gracious condescension in acquainting him with your Majesty's having this day reluctantly accepted the resignation of the Duke of York which had been conveyed to your Majesty in a letter from his Royal Highness of which your Majesty had sent the copy to Mr Perceval, which, conformably to your Majesty's expectation, he immediately communicated to his colleagues who were assembled at the D. of Portland's house.

The Duke of Portland is so unable to do justice to the effect which that

may hear to the contrary in the world, that it was wholly my brother's spontaneous act, and that he was altogether induced to take that step from the most honorable of motives, that of not exposing his father & the Government to a predicament that would have been replete with difficulties.' (46387–90)

[1] The phrasing is important. The King did not seek advice from his Ministers. The appointment was his, not theirs, and the Duke of Kent's letter of 26 March to Colonel Stevenson is ample corroboration: 'You may equally be assured that the appointment of Sir David Dundas was made by my father of *himself*, without consulting Ministers.' The Duke added, 'I will candidly tell you that it would have been very repugnant to my own feelings to have been named my brother's successor *in the first* instance, especially after being so long professionally upon bad terms with him.' He went on: 'At the same time, however, I have no scruple in saying that, some time hence, if, upon trial it should prove that a person of higher rank than Sir David Dundas ought to be at the head of the Army, and his Majesty is pleased to think of me, I shall not feel the same backwardness to undertake the charge, altho' I shall ever consider it a most arduous one. As to my father putting one of my younger brothers at the head of the Army, I think I know him to be too just a man ever to think of so doing, but were *that* to be the case it would be my duty to submit to his decision without murmuring, and to console myself with the gratifying reflection that I had never done anything to *merit* being pass'd by.' (46387–90)

[2] The Duke of York wrote to the Duke of Richmond on 5 April: 'During the 14 years that I held that situation I can safely say that it was ever my most anxious desire and study to promote to the utmost of my abilities the good of his Majesty's service and the interests of the Army. Accused as I have been of the most infamous and atrocious crimes, I owed it to my own character boldly to meet the investigation. After that was closed & the falsehood of every charge most completely proved before those very persons who had admitted the evidence produced in support of them, I thought it equally my duty to his Majesty to retire from a situation when I had been so unjustly assailed by every attack which malice and rancour could devise, and which had succeeded in raising such a popular cry against me.' (Bathurst MSS.)

communication produced, that he trusts your Majesty will forgive him for declining to say more upon it than that every sentiment which the most heartfelt gratitude, the most sincere admiration & the most dutifull attachment to your Majesty could suggest was expressed by every means which could give it utterance; nor were the most fervent prayers omitted, or declarations forgot to be made that no exertion should be wanting to undeceive the publick, to expose to them the enormity of the proceedings into which they have run headlong & to bring them to a due sense of justice & that respect for Government which the laws require.

The Duke of Portland observes your Majesty's commands with respect to the appointment of General Sr. David Dundas to the chief temporary command of your Majesty's Army. He has no doubt of the fitness of your Majesty's choice, & cannot presume to suppose, as it has not occurred to your Majesty, that any change can be required in the constitution of the Commander-in-Chief's Office, or in the various official establishments connected with it. (14280–1)

[*From the King, Windsor Castle, 19 March.*] The King acknowledges the receipt of the Duke of Portland's letter, of which the contents are very satisfactory to his Majesty. (14281)

3838   THE DUKE OF SUSSEX *to the* KING

[*Up. Lodge, Windsor, 19 March 1809.*] The warmth and sincerity with which I have enter'd into and constantly combated the cause of my brother the Duke of York from its first beginning will I trust be a guarantee to your Majesty that my actions have been solely guided by my attachment and duty towards your sacred person, by my devotion to the welfare of the State, as likewise by my most sincere affection towards my brother. With such sentiments may I hope that your Majesty will graciously listen to these lines, preferring this mode of communication to an audience, from a knowledge that the agitation my feelings would undergo at such an interview would most probably impede my explaining myself as clearly as I could wish and as I consider it my duty, as your Majesty's son, as a Peer of the Realm, and as one of your Privy Counsellors, to do on the present important situation of affairs.

Yesterday the Duke of York communicated to me that your Majesty had been graciously pleased to accept of his resignation as Commander-in-Chief of your Forces, which place he had faithfully filled for the last sixteen years of his life. Convinced as I feel of my brother's innocence, I am fully satisfied that his attachment to your person has prompted him after the maturest consideration to take this step. It therefore does not become me to argue the circumstance although I as deeply lament that your Majesty should be deprived of the services of so zealous a servant as I deplore any necessity for making such a tender on his part. Accustomed since a long time to watch with the most scrupulous attention all popular clamours from a knowledge of their serious consequences & baneful effects, I have considered the persecution of the Duke of York from its earliest stage as a continuation of a long plann'd conspiracy against the whole Royal Family which has been most successfully prepared by numerous scurrilous, infamous, and inflamatory pamphlets and libels which have been sufferd to polute the walls of London & the shops of various booksellers in the country & metropolis, thus becoming a most profitable trade to their nefarious authors, without calling down upon their heads till very lately condign punishment. Impress'd with the justice and importance of this remark I hold it my duty to implore your Majesty's attention to the serious consequences which such a measure as the resignation of the Duke of York may entail with it, were the command of the Army of this country to be placed in the hands of any other subject except those of one of your sons.

Various Administrations have wished to impress upon the public mind that none of the Royal Family ought to fill places of responsability in the State. Whilst I deny the justice & see the fallacy of such a proposition, and which is most clearly proved so by the present investigation, I maintain that such doctrine is injurious to your Majesty's interests, to the welfare of the State, and most fatally prejudicial to the honor & consequence of your Family. Was your Majesty to be deprived in this way of the services of those of your Family in whom you are pleased to place your trust, it would be shackling your power and rendering any contest which might arise afterwards between you and your Ministers more disadvantageous for yourself and more easy for them to overcome, while it would convey to the public the sanction of your Majesty and come out in the most plausible manner that none of your sons were capable of filling any public situation: besides in my humble opinion the power of a King of England is nothing without his having his Army in his own hands, and that Army under the command of one of his sons, which consideration becomes daily more important should it be thought at any time advisable hereafter to incorporate the Army of the East India Company with our present establishment. This subject has weighed so seriously on my mind that I have held it my most imperative duty to lay these ideas of mine at your Majesty's feet, and I do hope the liberty I have taken will be attributed as little to intrusion and presumption on the one part as to self interest on the other. Nothing but the common welfare of the family could make me thus state my sentiments as in my situation I can have no pretensions to any military employment whatsoever.

With every wish for your Majesty's welfare and happiness, with the most fervent prayer that your Majesty may speedily and gloriously overcome your present severe trials & difficulties I have the honor [etc.]. (48294–5)

3839 *Letters from the* DUKE OF PORTLAND *to the* KING, *and the replies*

[*Burlington House, Sunday, 19 March 1809.*] Considerable doubts having occurred to the Duke of Portland with regard to the extent of your Majesty's intentions respecting the communication to be made to General Sir David Dundas, under the painfull circumstances of the present moment, of the arrangement which it is in your Majesty's contemplation to make for the future administration of the Army—the Duke of Portland has wholly abstained from taking any step whatever for the purpose of apprizing Sir David Dundas of the probability of his being intrusted by your Majesty with the chief temporary command; the D. of Portland deeming it to be more consistent with his sense of his duty to lay this circumstance of his conduct before your Majesty & to wait for the farther signification of your Majesty's commands. (14289)

[*The King's reply, Windsor Castle, 20 March.*] The King has received the Duke of Portland's letter, in consequence of which his Majesty authorizes him to acquaint General Sir David Dundas that, from the impression which the King has received of the respectability of his character, of his long habits of business, and of his steady and zealous attachment to the Duke of York, which would not only lead him to maintain the present system and regulations but also to consider the Duke of York's interests, whenever circumstances shall admit of his resuming the administration of the Army, his Majesty has determined to confer upon him the situation of Commander-in-Chief of his Army, with the same authority and upon the same principles on which the Duke of York has held it. (14290)

[*From the Duke of Portland, Burlington House, Monday, 20 March.*] The Duke of Portland humbly begs leave to acquaint your Majesty that on the receipt of your Majesty's commands he immediately communicated them to General Sir David Dundas whom he had previously desired to call upon him.

The General, upon being informed of your Majesty's orders to him to assume the chief temporary command of your Majesty's Army, hesitated no longer to express his entire devotion to your Majesty's will, than while he requested the Duke of Portland to lay him with all humility at your Majesty's feet & to accompany his assurances of the absolute resignation of himself to your Majesty's pleasure with those of his gratitude to your Majesty for your gracious acceptance of his services. He concluded by requesting to be permitted to pay his duty to your Majesty on next Wednesday or the first day on which your Majesty will come to the Queen's Palace or elsewhere, & intimated a wish that it might not be deemed improper by your Majesty for him to have a seat at the Council Board in virtue of the employment with which it is your Majesty's pleasure to intrust him.

The Duke of Portland has taken upon himself without waiting for your Majesty's further commands to assure Lord Castlereagh of your Majesty's intentions to confer the chief temporary command of your Army on Genl. Sir David Dundas, on the supposition that the necessary instrument for that purpose would be to be prepared in his Office. (14292-3)

[*The King's reply, Windsor Castle, 21 March.*] The King approves of General Sir David Dundas attending at the Queen's Palace tomorrow, and of his being admitted to a seat at the Privy Council in consequence of his appointment to the chief command. His Majesty also approves of the Duke of Portland having notified that appointment to Lord Castlereagh, but as his is the Colonial Department, the Commission in this instance should be made out by the Secretary for the Home Department.

The King further acquaints the Duke of Portland that the Duke of York, desirous of avoiding anything that can tend to inflame the minds of the troops, has requested that the Complimentary Order which is usually issued when officers retire from high commands may be dispensed with on the present occasion. (14301)

[*From the Duke of Portland, Burlington House, Tuesday, 21 March.*] The Duke of Portland most humbly begs leave to acquaint your Majesty that in pursuance of your Majesty's commands he gave immediate notice to the Earl of Liverpool that General Sir David Dundas's commission should be made out at his Office—neither did the Duke of Portland lose a moment in making known to the rest of your Majesty's confidential servants the communication which your Majesty had most graciously condescended to make to him of the additional proofs which your Majesty had received of his Royal Highness the Duke of York's sollicitude & dutifull attachment to your Majesty in the great foresight & forbearance his Royal Highness has manifested in desiring that the Complimentary Order which is usually issued when officers retire from high commands may be dispensed with upon the present occasion in order to avoid anything that can tend to inflame the minds of the troops—a circumstance which the Duke of Portland presumes to hope must e'er long force the most malevolent & perverse to do his Royal Highness that justice which they have so pertinaciously endeavoured to withhold from him, & must endear his Royal Highness more & more to all your Majesty's most loyal & dutifull subjects. (14299–300)

3840 LORD MULGRAVE *to the* KING, *and the reply*

[*Admiralty, 20 March 1809.*] Lord Mulgrave has the honour to report to your Majesty that Capt. Hope, on the ground of family considerations, has tendered the resignation of his seat at the Board of Admiralty. Lord Mulgrave humbly begs leave to recommend Capt. Moorsom[1] to your Majesty's gracious consideration as perfectly qualified to discharge the duties of a Commissioner of the Admiralty. Capt. Moorsom is an officer of service & of science, who was brought into the Navy and instructed in his profession by the late Lord Mulgrave. (14291)

[*The King's reply, Windsor Castle, 21 March.*] The King acquiesces in Lord Mulgrave's recommendation of Captain Moorsom to succeed Captain Hope at the Board of Admiralty. (14291)

3841 SPENCER PERCEVAL *to the* KING, *and the reply*

[*Downg. St., 20 March 1809, Monday, 11 p.m.*] Mr Perceval acquaints your Majesty that he informed the House of Commons this evening that his Royal Highness the Duke of York had tendered his resignation to your Majesty, & that

[1] Sir Robert Moorsom (1760–1835), M.P. for Queenborough, 1812–20. Lieutenant, 1784; Captain, 1790; Rear-Admiral, 1810; Vice-Admiral, 1814. A Lord of the Admiralty, 1809–10. Surveyor-General of the Ordnance, July 1810–20.

your Majesty had with great reluctance accepted it. Mr Perceval then proceeded to state that he was concerned that the motives which had led his Royal Highness to take this step (which was his own spontaneous act, without any advice from your Majesty's servants) were so honorable to himself that they could not but prove satisfactory to the House, and for that reason that Mr. Perceval would distinctly state them in the manner in which his Royal Highness had expressed them to your Majesty at the time when he tendered his resignation. Mr Perceval then read his Royal Highness's letter to your Majesty, putting the words of it in the third person as what his Royal Highness stated. Mr Perceval however omitted to state to the House the middle paragraph in the letter in which his Royal Highness thanks your Majesty for the support which he had received from your Majesty, and in which he is graciously pleased to express his thanks also for the support which he had received from yr. Maj.'s Government. Mr Perceval apprehended that that paragraph would have been open to much criticism & it might have been turned to the prejudice of his R. Hss., as if he ascribed his acquittal rather to the support of Government than to his own innocence; and it might have been turned to the prejudice of the Government as if we had influenced otherwise than by our individual exertions, in this case of a judicial nature. Mr Perceval however had the precaution to acquaint his Royal Highness of his intention to omit noticing this paragraph, and his R. Hss. entirely concurred in the propriety of so doing. Having concluded this statement Mr. Perceval expressed a hope that the communication would induce Mr. Bathurst not to persevere in his Motion. Mr Bathurst however thought it necessary to persevere and he made the Motion a copy of which Mr Perceval sent to your Majesty some days ago. Lord Althorpe[1] moved an Amendment to that Motion, to leave out the whole of it for the purpose of introducing the following—

That 'His Royal Highness the Duke of York having resigned the command of the Army, this House does not think it necessary NOW to proceed any further in the consideration of the minutes of evidence taken before the Committee who were appointed to investigate the conduct of his Royal Highness the Duke of York as far as they relate to his Royal Highness.'

Mr Perceval would have wished to have got rid of both these Motions, and to have terminated the proceedings with the vote of acquittal of last Friday, but as far as he could collect the temper of the House he could not have done so. Both Mr Bathurst & the rest of the Opposition would have united upon that point,

[1] John Charles Spencer, 3rd Earl Spencer (1782–1845), styled Viscount Althorp from 31 Oct. 1783, when his grandfather died, to 10 Nov. 1834, when he succeeded his father as 3rd Earl. Whig M.P. for Okehampton, 1804–6; for Northamptonshire, 1806–32; for South Northamptonshire, 1832–4. A Lord of the Treasury, 1806–7; Chancellor of the Exchequer, 1830–4. It was Althorp's maiden speech, and his friends were well satisfied with his performance. George Ponsonby wrote to his father on the 21st: 'I never heard anything better done, and it was universally so felt by the House.' (Althorp MSS.) Tierney commented, on the 27th, 'He spoke without any affectation or appearance of study, with great fluency, remarkable clearness, good manner and very correct language.' (*Ibid.*) And Charles Wynn wrote, on the 21st: 'From the visible alarm he was under before he rose, I was not without apprehension for him, but from the moment he began, he appeared to have complete self-possession, and the manner in which he replied to many parts of Bragge-Bathurst's speech shewed a power of debating which will, I trust, encourage him to proceed in the same course. His matter and manner were equally good.' (*Ibid.*)

together with many country gentlemen who, having voted with his Royal Highness on the antecedent votes, wished to mark upon the Journals of the House the reasons which induced them to forbear proceeding any further. Mr Perceval therefore opposed Mr. Bathurst's Motion and supported the Motion of Mr Cartwright to amend Ld. Althorpe's Amendment by leaving out the word *now*; an Amendment which from the course of the debate was much more material than from the mere perusal of the Motion your Majesty might be led to imagine. For Lord Althorpe had distinctly stated that he had introduced that word for this purpose: viz., to express the opinion that if *at any future* time his R. Hss. should *ever* be restored to his situation it would *then* become necessary, tho' it was not so *now*, as his R. Hss. had just resigned. Upon the ground afforded by this interpretation of the intended effect of the word *now*, Mr Perceval supported the Amendment proposed by Mr Cartwright. The debate went into no great length; and upon the Motion for leaving out the words of Mr Bathurst's Motion, it was negatived without a division, and on Ld. Althorpe's Motion the Amendment of Mr Cartwright was carried by 235 to 112, majority 123, and then Lord Althorpe's Motion without the word now was carried, which merely declares that the House does not think it necessary to proceed any further in consequence of H.R.Hss.'s resignation. This certainly may be said to imply that but for that resignation they would have proceeded further tho' to what point does not appear; there is, however, this advantage gained by the Motion which might not have arisen from disposing of the question in any other way, namely, that it does completely dispose of the business and declares an opinion of the House that they will not proceed further; whereas if nothing had been said it might have been open upon some future day to have revived a discussion upon it. And as Lord Folkstone has proposed to take the Report into an early consideration after the holidays, altho he does not mean it with any view to H.R.H. the D. of York but with a view to examine how far measures might be taken to trace and to punish the instances of corrupt traffic which the evidence discloses, yet if the Resolution of the House had not precluded it, we could not be certain that reflection in the recess might not have led to bring forward some other Resolution.

Mr Perceval gave notice of intending to move for leave to bring in a Bill for preventing the abuses in the brokerage & sale of offices which had been disclosed in this examination.[1] (14294–7)

[*The King's reply, Windsor Castle, 21 March.*] The King has received with great satisfaction Mr Perceval's report of last night's proceedings in the House of Commons, which, under all the distressing circumstances connected with the discussion appear to his Majesty to have been as favorable as could reasonably have been expected.

In justice to the Duke of York, the King acquaints Mr Perceval that he has desired Sir David Dundas to abstain from recommending upon this occasion the notification of his resignation to the troops in a Complimentary Order as has

---

[1] *Parl. Deb.*, XIII, 712–45; Colchester, *Diary and Correspondence*, II, 176. Bathurst's was a Motion of censure upon the immoral connection and influence.

been the general custom when officers retire from an high command; the Duke of York being anxious that no step should be taken which could tend to inflame the minds of the troops, whose attachment to him has already been manifested by partial expressions of their feelings.[1] (14298)

3842   MRS. JOHN MOORE[2] *to the* KING

[*Brook Farm, Cobham, 24 March 1809.*] From the constant protection and distinguished marks of favor with which your Majesty was graciously pleased to honour my late son Lieutenant-General Sir John Moore, it is natural for me to look up to your Majesty for protection to his memory and to save his mother's feelings from a most cruel mortification. Under the present circumstances your Majesty I trust will not deem it intrusive if I presume to submit to your Majesty a sketch of Sir John Moore's military services.

In the year 1779, when in America with the rank of ensign only, his conduct in the first action in which he was engaged[3] drew upon him the praises of his Commanding Officer.

In 1793 & 4 during the campaign in Corsica, when he was second in command, he stormed two fortresses and was wounded in the head. For his conduct at that period he was rewarded by the distinguished praises of his General, the late Sir Charles Stuart. In 1795 & 6 he served with distinction in the West Indies, under the late General Sir Ralph Abercromby—he commanded the attack of the French out-works of the Morne-Fortuné[e] at St. Lucia, in which he was victorious; and had the good fortune soon after to repel with great loss to the enemy a furious attack on his advanced posts. The day following that attack the Castle capitulated. He was then left by Sir Ralph Abercromby, as Governor and Commander of the forces to reduce the remainder of the island—a most arduous service, which he was fortunate enough to accomplish—altho, in consequence of his great fatigues and exertions, he was twice brought to the brink of the grave by the yellow fever. At a subsequent period his conduct in Ireland attracted the conspicuous notice and gained him the friendship of the late Marquiss Cornwallis. With a small force he defeated six thousand rebels, took the town of Wexford and saved some hundreds of your Majesty's subjects from the massacre to which they were destined on the evening of the same day. He here received a slight wound. In the expedition to Holland Sir Ralph Abercromby gave him the direction of the landing and he was one of the first that leapt on shore. Soon after, the French and Dutch army attacked the British lines, but were defeated. On this occasion my son had the honor to command the left wing and received a third wound. In the victory of Alkmaer, gained by his Royal Highness the Duke of York, my son commanded the advanced guard, bore down everything in his front, and, tho'

[1] Sir David Dundas kissed hands as Commander-in-Chief on the 22nd.
[2] John Moore, M.D. (1729–1802), physician and man of letters, married in 1757 Jane Simson, daughter of the Professor of Divinity in the University of Glasgow. They had one daughter and five sons. She died on 25 March 1820.
[3] In the war of American Independence, on the Penobscot river.

shot through the thigh, continued advancing, driving the enemy before him 'till he was shot through the face, beat senseless to the ground and carried off the field.

Soon after his recovery from these wounds he accompanied Sir Ralph Abercromby to Egypt who gave him the command of the Reserve. This corps was the first employed in the memorable landing on that coast; and it was again distinguished in the action of the 14th of March. In that of the 21st Sir Ralph Abercromby placed the Reserve on his right wing, where he foresaw that General Menou would make his principal attack. After sustaining repeated charges of infantry and cavalry, my son received a fifth wound whilst driving back the French with great slaughter. It was on this occasion that Sir Ralph Abercromby terminated a glorious life.

Soon after my son's return from Egypt your Majesty was pleased to honour him with the command of that part of the coast most threatened with invasion.

He was much consulted upon all military measures during Mr. Pitt's last Administration. He was employed in Sicily & succeeded to the chief command in the Mediterranean, from whence he was no sooner returned than he was sent on an expedition to Sweden: and, immediately after his return, was ordered to Portugal: and, upon the recal of Sir Hew Dalrymple your Majesty was pleased to honor him with the command in chief of the army sent into Spain. Unfortunately, before he could reach the scene of action the Spanish armies were routed and dispersed. Thus left with his small army to contend against the immense force which the enemy had brought into Spain; by a bold but hazardous movement, made at the instance of your Majesty's Ambassador[1] resident with the Central Junta, he caused a signal diversion, which completely succeeded in relieving the south of Spain from the immediate pressure of the enemy, by drawing the whole force of the French armies led by Bonaparte against the brave but comparatively small British force. The circumstances of the able and glorious retreat of your Majesty's army, crowned by the memorable victory of Corunna, are too recent to require a recapitulation. There my son terminated his zealous & honorable career by a death he had always aspired to—his last moments cheered by the sound of victory—his last prayer for his country's welfare—his last hope that his country would do him justice.

The favor & protection which your Majesty deigned to shew my son when living, assures his mother that your Majesty will protect his fame after death—and it must therefore have been totally without your Majesty's knowledge that an intimation was made to me of an intention to reward the above services by a pension on your Majesty's Civil List of £600 a year, producing little more *nett* than two-thirds of that sum, on my eldest surviving son & his family, in whose favor I and my other children have waved all pretensions we might be deemed to possess to any share of such provision as might be graciously intended by your Majesty on this occasion. But your Majesty, I humbly trust, will condescend to make an allowance for the deep mortification of a mother, on being apprized of a proposal so ill suited, as she ventures to think it will appear to your Majesty, to the services and reputation of a man to whose memory your Majesty has deigned

[1] John Hookham Frere.

(245)

to recommend to Parliament that a statue should be erected—whose death has been publickly deplored as a national loss—and whose life has been held up by his Royal Highness the Commander-in-Chief as a bright example to your Majesty's army.

Humbly entreating your Majesty's forgiveness for this appeal of an anxious mother to a benevolent Sovereign, I am, with the utmost veneration, and submission [etc.].[1] (14302–7)

3843 LORD ELDON *to the* KING

[*25 March 1809.*] The Lord Chancellor, offering his very humble duty to your Majesty, has the honor to represent that there is at present a vacancy in the office of Attorney-General in the counties of Carmarthen, Pembroke & Cardigan, & he humbly begs leave to recommend to your Majesty, as a proper person to fill that office (which, tho' not in any degree lucrative, it is important to your Majesty's service should be well filled), Mr Touchet, who is the senior English barrister attending that Welch circuit. If your Majesty should be graciously pleased to make this appointment, the Chancellor submits to your Majesty the accompanying warrant to receive yr Majesty's Royal Sign Manual. (14308)

3844 *Letters from* VISCOUNT CASTLEREAGH *to the* KING, *and the reply*

[*Downing St., 26 March 1809.*] Your Majesty's confidential servants having had under their consideration the amount of force (in infantry amounting to about 18,000 men) which will be assembled in Portugal upon the arrival of M. Genl. Hill's[2] corps from Cork, and the return of M. Gen. Sherbrooke's, and M. Genl. McKenzie's[3] from Cadiz, are humbly of opinion that it may be expedient to order 3 Regts. of cavalry, for which the necessary tonnage is prepared, to proceed immediately to the Tagus from hence.

They further beg leave humbly to propose to your Majesty that Sir John Cradock should be appointed to succeed Sir Hew Dalrymple in the command at Gibraltar, and that the chief command in Portugal should be entrusted to Sir Arthur Wellesley.[4]

[1] On 8 May Lord Morpeth complained in Parliament that the female part of Moore's family had not been properly provided for. Perceval said, in reply to a question, that it was the Government's intention to make provision for them, but that, when approached on the subject, they expressed a wish that any provision intended for them might be transferred to a male branch of the family; consequently, Ministers intended to recommend that provision be made for Moore's brother James. (*Parl. Deb.*, XIV, 408–9.) See No. 3884.

[2] Rowland, 1st Viscount Hill (1772–1842). Entered the Army, 1790; Lieutenant-Colonel, 1794; Colonel, 1800; Major-General, 1805; Lieutenant-General, 1812; General, 1825. K.B., 1812; G.C.B., 1815; M.P. for Shrewsbury, 1812–14. Created Baron Hill, 17 May 1814; General Commanding-in-Chief, 1828–42. Created Viscount, 1842.

[3] John Randoll MacKenzie (*c.* 1763–1809), M.P. for the Tain Burghs, 1806–8; for Sutherlandshire, 1808–9. Lieutenant-Colonel, 1794; Colonel, 1801; Major-General, 1808; Governor and Commandant of Alderney. Killed at battle of Talavera. He had served for many years in India, returning home about 1801. In 1809 he commanded the containing force left by Wellesley on his advance to Oporto.

[4] For Cradock's appointment, see also *Castlereagh Corresp.*, VII, 45. A force of 10,000 men had been left in Lisbon by Sir John Moore under Cradock (or Caradoc). Though he was superseded in the

In submitting the latter appointment for your Majesty's approbation, your Majesty's servants have not been unmindful of the inconvenience that might arise in case of any considerable increase of this force, from Sir Arthur Wellesley being so young a Lt.-General, but as any material increase of the army in Portugal cannot be at present look'd to as probable either from the state of the regts at home or the immediate circumstances of the war, they humbly conceive that your Majesty's service (without prejudice to the claims of the distinguish'd officers in your Majesty's army who are his seniors in rank) may have the benefit of Sir Arthur Wellesley's being employ'd where he has had the good fortune to be successful, and that it will remain open for your Majesty's future consideration to make a different arrangement of the command if under all the circumstances it shall appear to your Majesty proper to confide it to a General Officer of higher rank. (14309–10)

[*From Castlereagh, St James's Sq., 26 March.*] The accompanying dispatches having been received from Lisbon and Cadiz since Lord Castlereagh's note of this date was prepared to be submitted to your Majesty—however much he must regret that so small a corps as M. Genl. McKenzie's should have been directed to so distant and so uncertain a service, Lord Castlereagh is induced to hope your Majesty may consider it as an additional motive for sending an officer of rank to Gibraltar, who by his superintending authority may confine the support to be given to the Spaniards within the limits which your Majesty's instructions have prescribed. (14312)

[*The King's reply, Windsor Castle, 27 March.*] The King acquiesces in Lord Castlereagh's proposal that three regiments of cavalry should proceed to Portugal in addition to the force already there; and that upon the removal of Sir John Cradock to the Government of Gibraltar, Lieut.-Genl. Sir Arthur Wellesley should succeed to the command of the troops in Portugal. In agreeing however to so young a Lieut.-General holding so distinguished a command, while his seniors remain unemployed, his Majesty must desire that Lord Castlereagh will keep in view that if the corps in Portugal should be further increased hereafter, the claims of senior officers cannot with justice be set aside.[1] (14313)

command in Portugal by Wellesley, his proposed appointment as Lieutenant-Governor of Gibraltar did not take effect; he felt severely the disappointment at the new arrangements, and obtained leave to return home. (*Castlereagh Corresp.*, VII, 74.) Major-General Colin Campbell succeeded General Henry Edward Fox as Lieutenant-Governor. The Duke of Kent wrote to Lieutenant-Colonel Robert Wright, 28 April 1809: 'As the good General [Drummond] will communicate to you all I know in regard to Sir J. Craddock's appointment to the command of the Garrison, it will be unnecessary for me to repeat it here. If he should, however, accept of it, which is rather doubted, I think I will answer for your finding yourself to the full as comfortable as with your present General, for it is impossible for anyone to be more gentlemanlike, or personally more attach'd to me than he is, in consequence of our having served together in the same Brigade during the campaign of 1794.' (46391–4)

The Duke wrote again to Wright on 13 June: 'Ere this, I conclude, my old friend Sir John Craddock has join'd you, with whom I am confident you will go on as pleasantly as possible, but I fear his stay with you will be short, as he has express'd his wish not to be left upon the Rock. I lament this much, for the sake of all my friends who would never have wanted any other recommendation with him than to make themselves known as such.' (46395–7)

[1] On the 29th Sir Arthur Wellesley vacated his seat in Parliament (Newport, Isle of Wight). His brother Henry had written to him from Treasury Chambers on 11 Jan., 'Sir Henry Holmes has written

[*Sunday, 26 March 1809.*] Mr. Canning humbly conceiving that the intelligence received from Sweden (though perhaps not altogether unexpected) is of a nature not to be kept back from your Majesty for a whole day, has humbly thought it his duty to transmit to your Majesty at this unusual hour the most important of the dispatches received this morning from Mr. Merry. (14311)

[*From Canning, Foreign Office, 28 March.*] Mr Canning humbly acquaints your Majesty of the arrival of General Count Walmoden from Vienna with the letter from Count Stadion to Mr. Canning which Mr. Canning herewith humbly lays before your Majesty. Count Walmoden's papers are detained on board the vessel in which he arrived at Portsmouth, but will probably be sent up by tomorrow's or Thursday's posts. (14314)

[*The King's reply, Windsor Castle, 29 March.*] The King acknowledges the receipt of Mr Canning's letter transmitting that received from Count Stadion by General Wallmoden. (14315)

3846   SIR HENRY STRACHEY *to the* KING, *and the reply*

[*Board of Green Cloth, 29 March 1809.*] Sir Henry Strachey is sorry to be under the necessity of troubling your Majesty with the enclosed letter which he has received from Mr. Aiton, your Majesty's gardener at Kensington, together with a letter to that gentleman from Mr. Sicard, the Steward of her Royal Highness the Princess of Wales.

It appears from Mr. Aiton's letter that, in his opinion, the sale of the elm trees (3 or 4 in number) which he says must be removed if the proposed alteration should take place, will defray the expences of the alteration, but, although the alteration, as desired, seems very material to the convenience of her Royal Highness, yet as it relates to a part of the Royal Garden, Sir Henry Strachey presumes it to be his duty to submit the matter to your Majesty's consideration and decision. (14316)

[*The King's reply, 30 March.*] The King does not object to the proposal for widening the carriage approach in the garden, and approves of Sir H. Strachey's reference for his My.'s sanction. (14317)

3847   GEORGE CANNING *to the* KING, *and the reply*

[*Foreign Office, 1 Apr. 1809.*] Mr. Canning humbly lays before your Majesty a note delivered to him by Mr. Brinkmann, together with the draft of an answer

to Long to express his hope that you will vacate your seat early in the Session. I have desired Long to say in reply that it will be extremely inconvenient to the public service if you should be compelled to vacate, and that the Duke of Portland hopes he will allow you to continue in another year upon paying at the rate you have hitherto paid for the seat.' (Wellington MSS.)

to it which Mr. Canning has prepared, & most humbly submits for your Majesty's royal consideration. (14320)

[*The King's reply, Windsor Castle, 2 April.*] The King approves of the answer which Mr Canning has prepared to M. de Brinkman's note of the 29th March. (14321)

3848 LORD MULGRAVE *to the* KING, *and the reply*

[*Admiralty, 1 April 1809.*] Lord Mulgrave has the honour to transmit to your Majesty dispatches received this day from Rear-Admiral Sir Richard Keats by which it appears that the Admiral has conducted himself with his usual zeal & discretion under circumstances of some difficulty.[1] (14322)

[*The King's reply, Windsor Castle, 2 April.*] The King concurs with Lord Mulgrave in his opinion of the zeal and discretion with which Sir R. Keats has acted under the late circumstances of difficulty in Sweden. (14322)

3849 THE EARL OF LIVERPOOL *to the* KING, *and the reply*

[*London, 3 April 1809.*] Lord Liverpool begs leave most humbly to lay before your Majesty the annual returns of offenders committed to the different gaols in England and Wales.

Lord Liverpool begs leave at the same time to submit to your Majesty a letter which he has received from the Earl of Effingham,[2] and to request your Majesty's commands as to the answer which is to be returned to his Lordship's application. (14323)

[*The King's reply, Windsor Castle, 4 April.*] The King acquaints Lord Liverpool that, under the circumstances which are represented in Lord Effingham's letter, his Majesty will not object to his driving through the Horse Guards. (14324)

3850 *Letters from* VISCOUNT CASTLEREAGH *to the* KING, *and the reply*

[*St. James's Square, 7 April 1809.*] Lord Castlereagh in submitting for your Majesty's approbation Sir Arthur Wellesley's instructions, in the present state of the campaign in Portugal and the peculiar circumstances of the command, hopes your Majesty will not disapprove of his humbly soliciting your Majesty's permission to order that officer to proceed immediately on service, without having previously had it in his power to pay his duty to your Majesty.[3] (14327)

[1] Keats with his squadron had remained in the Great Belt after facilitating the escape of 10,000 Spanish troops from service under Napoleon, and had narrowly escaped being ice-bound during the following winter.

[2] Richard Howard, 4th Earl of Effingham (1748–1816) succeeded his brother, 19 Nov. 1791. Secretary and Comptroller of the Queen's Household, 1784–1814; Treasurer of the Queen's Household, 1814–16.

[3] The draft of this letter, in *Castlereagh Corresp.*, VII, 51, is dated the 8th.

[*From Castlereagh, St. James's Sq., 7 April 1809.*] M. Genl. Nightingall's[1] health having for some time precluded his departure for New South Wales, Lord Castlereagh in the present state of the Colony is humbly of opinion that your Majesty's service will be best consulted by detaching the 73rd Regt. under Lt. Col. McQuarrie's[2] command immediately to that situation, leaving the Major-General to follow as soon as his health will permit, and in order that the necessary measures for restoring regular authority within the Settlement may be forthwith adopted, Lord Castlereagh begs leave humbly to recommend that the Lt. Government should be entrusted to Lt. Col. McQuarrie whilst his Regt. continues to be employ'd in N.S. Wales.[3] (14328)

[*The King's reply, Windsor Castle, 9 April.*] The King approves of Lord Castlereagh's proposal that Sir Arthur Wellesley should proceed immediately to Portugal. His Majesty also acquiesces in the propriety of detaching without further delay the 73d Regiment to New South Wales under the command of Lt Colonel McQuarrie, and of entrusting the Lieut.-Government to that officer. (14329)

3851   THE DUKE OF PORTLAND *to the* KING, *and the reply*

[*Bulstrode, Sunday, 9 April 1809.*] Lieut.-General Sir David Baird & the two other General Officers whose services in Spain & Portugal your Majesty has graciously determined to reward by bestowing on them the Order of the Bath have applied to the D. of Portland to be informed of the time at which your Majesty may have pleased to intimate any intention of investing them with the Ensigns of that most honorable Order, and as the D. of Portland has reason to believe that this inquiry has been suggested to them or at least to two of them by the impaired state of their health, he presumes with great humility to express his hope that your Majesty will condescend to forgive this importunity, & to direct that your royal pleasure may be signified to him respecting it. (14331)

[*The King's reply, Windsor Castle, 10 April.*] As some days will be required to collect the persons whose attendance will be necessary when the officers mentioned in the Duke of Portland's letter are invested with the Order of the Bath, the King thinks that it will be most adviseable to fix upon Wednesday sen'night for the ceremony. (14332)

[1] Sir Miles Nightingall (1768–1829). Entered the Army, 1787; Captain, 1794; Colonel, 1803; Major-General, 1810; Lieutenant-General, 1814. He was only a Brigadier-General in 1809. K.C.B., 1815. M.P. for Eye, 1820–9. In Dec. 1808 he had been nominated Governor and Commander-in-Chief in New South Wales.

[2] Lachlan Macquarie (*d.* 1824). Entered the Army, 1777; Lieutenant, 1781; Major, 1796; Lieutenant-Colonel, 1800; Colonel, 1810; Major-General, 1813. Governor of New South Wales, 1809–21.

[3] The draft of this letter is in *Castlereagh Corresp.*, VIII, 200, where it is dated the 8th.

3852 VISCOUNT CASTLEREAGH *to the* KING

[*Stanmore, 10 April* [*1809*].] Lord Castlereagh has the honor humbly to acquaint your Majesty that a message by telegraph from Plymouth announcing the surrender of Martinique was received this day at two o'clock. The official dispatches have not yet arrived in town. (14333)

3853 THE DUKE OF PORTLAND *to the* KING, *and the reply*

[*Burlington House, Friday, 14 April 1809.*] The Duke of Portland most humbly begs leave to submit to the gracious consideration of your Majesty the eminent service of Lieutt.General Beckwith[1] in the capture of the Island of Martinico & the fitness of his receiving a similar mark of your Majesty's royal favor to that which your Majesty has been graciously pleased to signify your intention to confer on Lieutt.-Generals Sir David Baird & John Hope & Major-General Spencer for their services in Spain & Portugal—and a vacancy having taken place in the Transport Board by the death of Captn. Towry, late one of the Commissioners, the Duke of Portland ventures with all humility to propose to your Majesty's superior judgement Capt. Boyle,[2] the brother of the Earl of Cork,[3] to be his successor who, upon the fullest inquiry which the Duke of Portland has been able to make, appears to be perfectly well qualified to perform the duties of that office. (14335)

[*The King's reply, Windsor Castle, 15 April.*] The King acquiesces in the Duke of Portland's proposal that Lieut.-General Beckwith should receive the Order of the Bath. His Majesty also approves of his recommendation of Captain Boyle, who is personally known to his Majesty, for the vacant Commissionership of the Transport Board. (14336)

3854 LORD MULGRAVE *to the* KING, *and the reply*

[*Admiralty, 15 April 1809.*] Lord Mulgrave has the honour to transmit to your Majesty a dispatch relating the capture of a French frigate of 44 guns by Capt. Seymour,[4] commanding your Majesty's ship Amethyst; under the circumstance of a disproportion of force, similar to that which so recently distinguished the capture of La Thetis, by the same officer. (14337)

[1] Sir George Beckwith (1753–1823). Ensign, 1771; Lieutenant, 1775; Lieutenant-Colonel, 1790; Colonel, 1795; Major-General, 1798; Lieutenant-General, 1805. Governor of Bermuda, 1797; of St Vincent, 1804; of Barbados, 1808. K.B., 1 May 1809. General, 1814.

[2] Sir Courtenay Boyle (1769–1844). Lieutenant, 1790; Captain, 1797; Vice-Admiral, 1821. K.C.H., 1832.

[3] Edmund, 8th Earl of Cork (1767–1856). Entered the Army, 1785; Major, 1793; Colonel, 1798; A.D.C. to the King, 1798–1805; Major-General, 1805; Lieutenant-General, 1811; General, 1825. K.P., 1835.

[4] Sir Michael Seymour (1768–1834). Lieutenant, 1790; Captain, 1800; Rear-Admiral, 1832. Created Baronet, 6 May 1809. K.C.B., 1815.

[The King's reply, Windsor Castle, 16 April.] The King has received with great satisfaction Lord Mulgrave's report of the capture of La Niemen French frigate by the Amethyst, and his Majesty is glad that Captain Seymour has had a second opportunity of distinguishing himself so much. (14337)

3855   THE EARL OF LIVERPOOL *to the* KING, *and the reply*

[London, 17 April 1809.] Lord Liverpool begs leave most humbly to inform your Majesty that the Recorder's Report may be put off without inconvenience till Wednesday the 26th instant, and that there is no other publick business which renders it necessary for your Majesty to come to town for a Levée or Council this week (14338).

[The King's reply, Windsor Castle, 18 April.] The King is glad to learn from Lord Liverpool that there is no particular public business which requires his presence in London tomorrow, as his Majesty has for some days had a very heavy cold, which, although certainly going off, will be better for his remaining at home. His Majesty therefore approves of the Recorder making his Report on Wednesday the 26th, and he desires that the Knights of the Bath may be summoned for the Investiture of the new Knights for the same day at two o'clock. (14338)

3856   THE DUKE OF PORTLAND *to the* KING, *and the reply*

[Burlington House, Monday, 17 April 1809.] It is with sincere concern that the Duke of Portland humbly requests your Majesty's permission to lay before your Majesty the answer he has received from Lord Harrowby to the gracious offer of the Presidency of the Board of Commissioners for the Affairs of India which your Majesty commanded the D. of Portland to make to him,[1] by which Ld. Harrowby desires him to make the most favorable representation to your Majesty of the sincerest gratitude that he has always felt for your Majesty's gracious acceptance of his former endeavours in your Majesty's service, a sentiment which

---

[1] Portland wrote to Harrowby on the 12th: 'It is with infinite satisfaction I obey the commands which I have just received from the King to express to your Lordship his Majesty's wishes for your assistance and advice in the capacity of one of his Majesty's confidential servants, and for that purpose to desire your acceptance of the Presidency of the Board of Commission for the Affairs of India which is become vacant by the appointment of Mr. Dundas to be Chief Secretary to the Lord Lieutenant of Ireland. I trust it must be unnecessary to trouble you with many arguments to convince you of the pleasure with which my colleagues will learn your assent to this proposal, but I must not omit to inform you of the conduct of our excellent friend Lord Bathurst, who, upon my acquainting him with my intention of submitting your Lordship's name to the King as the most desirable for the office in question, instantly requested that he might be permitted to give you the option of his Presidency of the Committee of Trade upon a notion of that office being more eligible to you than the Board of Control. Indeed, my dear Lord, I do not say more than I feel myself fully warranted in assuring you that there is not one of us who would not most readily have acted [?] as our friend Ld. Bathurst to ensure us the advantage of your counsels—and I will only add that when I made the King acquainted with Ld. Bathurst's request, his Majesty ordered me to return his thanks to Ld. Bathurst and declared himself sincerely obliged to whomever it might be who contributed to procure him your Lordship's assistance.' (Harrowby MSS.)

would necessarily urge him to pay the most implicit obedience to your Majesty's commands, did not the state of his health remind him that such an exertion would only prevent him from rendering that occasional service in Parliament which he has been able to perform from time to time & wholly disappoint those expectations which your Majesty's great goodness & condescension may have induced your Majesty to form, & therefore to lay his humble but anxious hopes at your Majesty's feet that he may be excused by your Majesty from undertaking the employment proposed to him.[1] Such being the case, the person who upon the fullest consideration appears to be best qualified & intitled to be submitted to your Majesty is Mr. Charles Yorke who has the good fortune to be too well known to your Majesty to make it necessary to enter into the particulars of his former conduct, or rather not to render anything the D. of Portland might say respecting him injudicious & superfluous. What Mr. Yorke's inclinations may be with respect to the business of the Board of Controll the D. of Portland is not enabled to inform your Majesty, but his attachment & devotion to your Majesty are so well approved & known, his attention & diligence in the discharge of the official duties of every employment in which your Majesty has been pleased to place him, have been so fully & satisfactorily tried, & his zeal, integrity, disinterestedness, ability & firmness have been so conspicuous upon all occasions that the D. of Portland cannot entertain any apprehension of Mr. Yorke's shrinking from

[1] Perceval had written to Harrowby on the 10th: 'As probably tomorrow's post will bring you a letter from the Duke of Portland upon a subject on which I feel very anxiously, I must just prepare you for it by a line from myself. Sr. Arthur Wellesley's post in Ireland is to be filled by Dundas—whereby the Presidency of the Board of Control becomes vacant. It is as you may easily conceive, or at least as everybody but you would easily conceive, strongly wished by the D. of Portland and our colleagues that we could see you in that office and amongst us in the Cabinet. I think I hear you exclaim, "Poh! Stuff! I could as well in my state of health think of being First Lord of the Admiralty or any of the most laborious offices in the State," and it is with the view of guarding the D. of Portland from receiving an answer from you under such first impression, that I am guilty of almost a breach of confidence in writing to you upon this subject before him. But he thinks he should mention it to the King before he authoritatively writes to you upon it, and as I am convinced there is not in his Maj.'s dominions a man whom the King would wish more to see in his Governt. than yourself I do not feel the necessity of this reserve—and I write accordingly. What I wish you to consider before you determine upon this subject is the very peculiar nature of the office, that it is particularly suited to an invalid because you may chuse your own time for doing anything. Dundas & (Ld. Melville, I believe, but certainly Dundas) spent his summer in Scotland, so might you in Staffordshire, except so far as your Cabinet duties might require your presence in London. Do therefore give us a fair chance of your cool & deliberate opinion.' (Harrowby MSS.)

Bathurst wrote to Harrowby on the 12th: 'Since I have been in office I do not know of any event which has given me so much satisfaction as that of which I was informed on my arrival in London yesterday—viz., that circumstances had occurred which had enabled the Duke of Portland to offer to you a Cabinet situation. It is one which from the state of things both at home and in India has become of great importance. Perhaps it may not be generally thought so, and it is certainly not one, equal to what everything but the actual state of your health would require should be offer'd to you, but I cannot let the Duke of Portland's letter go without expressing my anxiety that you should give a favourable answer. If the situation which I hold should for any reason be consider'd as one of higher rank, I hope I need not say how unbecoming I should feel it, were I to delay for an instant to offer an exchange. If for any other reasons, either your habits or your health (in which I include the little anxiety which attaches to my office) you should prefer mine, I trust you will have no scruple to tell me so. The affairs of India would certainly terrify me, but that would be amply compensated if the exchange made the difference of your being or not being one of the Administration. In all what I write I hope you will see nothing but my earnest desire that you should become part of the Government, and whatever faults I have I do not think I can be justly charged with complimentary professions.' (Harrowby MSS.)

any undertaking in which it shall be your Majesty's pleasure to call upon him to engage, & in this opinion the Duke of Portland has the satisfaction of finding that Mr. Perceval intirely concurs. (14339–41)

[*The King's reply, Windsor Castle, 18 April.*] The King acknowledges the receipt of the Duke of Portland's letter from which he learns with concern that Lord Harrowby's state of health continues such as must deprive his Majesty of his valuable services in an official situation, at the same time that he is well convinced that his Government will always receive from Lord Harrowby the utmost support which zeal and attachment can give. Under this circumstance, the King thinks that the Duke of Portland cannot recommend a person more eligible in every respect than Mr Yorke for the Presidency of the Board of Controul, and his Majesty sincerely hopes that he will not feel any difficulty to undertake the office. (1441)

3857 SPENCER PERCEVAL *to the* KING, *and the reply*

[*Downg. St., Tuesday, 18 April 1809.*] Mr Perceval acquaints your Majesty that the House of Commons has this evening gone thro the Militia Completion Bill in the Committee without any material opposition.

Mr Perceval has to lament that he omitted to acquaint your Majesty yesterday with the event of Lord Folkstone's Motion. The House rose at so much earlier an hour than is usual upon any subject of interest, and Mr Perceval upon his return home having engaged in other business, it really escaped his recollection that he had a duty to perform to your Majesty to acquaint your Majesty of one of the most interesting & important debates which has taken place for some time. Lord Folkstone proposed to refer to the consideration of a Select Committee the general enquiry into various corrupt abuses in all the Departments of Government. This was objected to upon several important grounds but most particularly upon the impropriety of setting on foot an enquiry, not upon any special case upon the statement of which a presumptive ground of enquiry might be raised, but upon an assumed general presumption implying a distrust & suspicion that the whole frame of your Majesty's Government was radically corrupt, not as applicable merely to your Majesty's present servants, but to any other servants at any time who have been employed in your Majesty's service. The debate that took place upon the question is the first which has occurred in which there has appeared any strong mark of a disposition on the part of the Opposition to take fright at the lengths which Lord Folkstone and those who act with him are disposed to go. Lord Henry Petty, Mr Tierney, Sr. John Anstruther, Mr Ponsonby & Mr Brand all spoke against the Motion, and there were but 30 members out of upwards of 200 who were found to vote for this Motion. Sr Francis Burdett was not present, whether owing to illness or not Mr Perceval cannot say, but Mr Perceval has to regret that Lord Althorp went with the minority.

Mr Perceval cannot forbear congratulating your Majesty upon the good spirit & disposition which were manifested in the House upon this occasion, which he cannot but regard as a proof that the good sense of the House of Commons will still be found, notwithstanding the manner in which the enquiry into the conduct of H.R.H. the Duke of York was unhappily pursued by many, sufficient to resist the impulse which may be attempted to be given to the public feeling at the present moment.[1] (14342)

[*The King's reply, Windsor Castle, 19 April.*] The King rejoyces to find from Mr Perceval's report that the proceedings in the House of Commons on Monday night last have appeared to him so satisfactory and such as to afford hopes that the House of Commons begins to see the necessity of opposing a more decided check to the mischievous lengths to which some individuals are disposed to go. (14343)

3858 GEORGE CANNING *to the* KING, *and the reply*

[*Foreign Office, 18 Apr. 1809.*] Mr. Canning most humbly submits for your Majesty's royal consideration the draft of the answer which (if approved by your Majesty) it is proposed to return to Count Walmoden's note of the 1st of April. He submits at the same time the draft of a proposed answer to a note of Don Pedro Cevallos requiring a loan for Spain of 10 or 20 millions sterling which note he humbly lays before your Majesty. (14344)

[*The King's reply, Windsor Castle, 19 April.*] The King approves of the answers to Count Walmoden & to Don Pedro Cevallos which Mr Canning has submitted. (14345)

3859 THE KING *to the* DUCHESS OF BRUNSWICK

[*Windsor Castle, 19 April 1809.*] I have much pleasure in paying immediate attention to the wish expressed in your kind letter of the 17th that I should nominate a trustee for you in the room of the late Lord Liverpool, and I do not think I can recommend any more fit person than the Lord Chancellor whose respectable character is so well known to you that I am persuaded you will approve of him. (16785)

---

[1] *Parl. Deb.*, XIV, 48–68 (17 April). The numbers were 178 to 30. And XIV, 91–3 (18 April). Whitbread supported the Motion, the only leading member of Opposition to do so. (Colchester, *Diary and Corresp.*, II, 178.) The Duke of Portland appealed to the Duke of Rutland on 12 April for support against Folkestone's Motion: 'Lord Folkestone having given notice of his intention to move on next Monday for the appointment of a Standing Committee to enquire into the abuses which have arisen or may arise in the disposal of the patronage of the Crown, or in other words to assume the actual disposal of that patronage, I have to entreat your Grace's good offices with such of your friends as may be at Belvoir Castle or within your reach to induce them to attend the House of Commons on next Monday the 17th instant when this extraordinary Motion is to be made to them.' (Rutland MSS.)

[*Foreign Office, 19 April 1809.*] Mr. Canning in humbly submitting to your Majesty the accompanying drafts of despatches to Mr. Frere, most humbly begs leave to state to your Majesty that it was his intention to have taken your Majesty's especial commands this day with respect to the despatch which relates to the correspondence between Mr. Frere & Sir John Moore, before he should presume to submit that despatch for your Majesty's royal consideration—humbly assuring your Majesty that he has endeavoured to treat the subject of that despatch according to the best of his judgement without favour or partiality, & humbly entreating, if he shall in anything have mis-stated your Majesty's sentiments upon it, that your Majesty will graciously permit him to make such alterations in the draft or such additions to it as your Majesty may be pleased to approve.[1] (14349–50)

[*The King's reply, Windsor Castle, 20 April.*] The King has read with great attention the draft of Mr. Canning's letter to Mr. Frere respecting the correspondence between him and the late Sir John Moore, and it appears to his Majesty so perfectly proper and fair that he can only express his unqualified approbation without desiring that any addition or omission should take place. (14350)

[*From Canning, Foreign Office, 20 Apr.*] Mr. Canning most humbly submits for your Majesty's royal approbation the draft of the Convention for a loan of six hundred thousand pounds to the Prince Regent of Portugal, which has been so long in negotiation with the Portuguese Minister. (14354)

[*The King's reply, Windsor Castle, 21 April.*] The King approves the draft of the Convention for a loan of six hundred thousand pounds to the Prince Regent of Portugal which Mr Canning has submitted. (14354)

3861 THE DUKE OF PORTLAND *to the* KING, *and the reply*

[*Burlington House, Thursday, 20 April 1809.*] The Duke of Portland humbly begs leave to acquaint your Majesty that knowing the friendship & intimacy which subsisted between Mr. Perceval & Mr. Yorke, he took the liberty, in consequence of the permission he had received from your Majesty, to employ the former of those gentlemen to inform himself of the sentiments of the latter in case it should be your Majesty's pleasure to appoint him to the Presidency of the Board of Controll. Mr. Perceval had an interview yesterday with Mr. Yorke, & reports that nothing could be more proper or respectfull than the manner in which Mr Yorke treated the possibility of such an offer being made to him. After having assured Mr. Perceval of his readiness to take any situation in which it was thought that he would render any real service to your Majesty, he expressed a wish that it might be considered whether there were not several persons who

---

[1] See *Parl. Deb.,* XIV, 400–5, for Frere's dispatch to Canning, 24 Nov. 1808, in which he referred to Moore's complaint of the inattention and negligence which his army had experienced from the Spanish Government; together with other official papers relating to Spain.

would discharge the duties of the office in question with much greater ability than he possessed, for he could not but feel that he was not qualified either by previous habits or pursuits to fill it, nor had he any inclination to turn his mind to that course of study which was necessary to render him worthy of it. He then very frankly added that if it was true that the Secretary of War[1] had obtained your Majesty's leave to retire at the conclusion of the Session he should very much prefer that situation to the other, & should your Majesty condescend in that case to accede to Mr. Yorke's wish, which with the utmost deference the D. of Portland would incline to hope your Majesty would not deem unreasonable on the part of Mr Yorke or disadvantageous to your Majesty's service, the D. of Portland most humbly presumes that your Majesty would be so gracious as not to insist on Mr. Yorke's prior acceptance of the Presidency of the India Board & his thereby incurring the expense of two elections in the space of three or four months; & should this be your Majesty's determination your Majesty will probably command the D. of Portland to submit some other person as a proper successor to Mr. Dundas for your Majesty's consideration, for which he must acknowledge that he is not at present sufficiently prepared.[2]

The brilliant services of Captn. Seymore in the late capture he made of *La Niemen* have suggested to your Majesty's confidential servants most humbly to submit to your Majesty the additional title he has acquired to some new mark of your Majesty's royal favor & approbation, & it seems the general opinion of the first characters in the naval line that the Baronetage would be a mark of distinction which would be highly gratifying to Captn. Seymore & afford great satisfaction to the Service in general. (14351–3)

[*The King's reply, Windsor Castle, 21 April.*] The King entirely approves of the communication which the Duke of Portland made to Mr. Yorke and of the arrangement proposed in his letter, his Majesty being well assured of the advantage

[1] He meant the Secretary at War (Sir James Pulteney). The office, said Lord Liverpool, needed a thorough reform, and no one would be so competent as Yorke to put it in order. (Richmond MSS. 71/1390.)

[2] Lord Harrowby succeeded Robert Dundas as President of the India Board on 17 July. See No. 3913 n. Dundas, who became Irish Secretary on 13 April, wrote to Lord Liverpool on the 6th: 'I have received your Lordship's letter and have only to repeat what I mentioned to you today, that though undoubtedly the change of situation which you propose to me is neither very agreeable nor personally convenient, I do not feel myself at liberty on those considerations only to withhold any assistance which I can afford and which his Majesty's Government may think that I can render to them in any other Department. Under these circumstances therefore your Lordship will of course consider yourself as at liberty to communicate my determination to the Duke of Portland and the Duke of Richmond, but I must beg at the same time to express my doubts as to the propriety of the selection which you have made of a successor to Sir Arthur Wellesley. As it may possibly be convenient for you that some days at least should elapse before this measure is announced, in order that the necessary arrangements in the India Board may be completed, I shall take no steps towards my own re-election or give any further notice of the circumstance till I am authorised by your Lordship.' (Add. MSS. 38571, f. 134.)

The Duke of Richmond had earlier expressed a wish for the appointment of Huskisson, who would readily have accepted it, but he was told that it was essential that he should remain in his laborious situation at the Treasury. (Richmond MSS.; Add. MSS. 38737, f. 309.) The Duke wrote to Huskisson on 9 April: 'Nothing would have given me more pleasure than to have had you here, but it is both your business and mine to do what is considered as best for the public good. Pitt taught us those principles and we are not likely either of us to forget them.' (Add. MSS. 38243, f. 104; 38737, f. 309; Richmond MSS. 71/1391.)

which will result from Mr. Yorke's zealous and able services in any situation which may suit his inclinations and habits, and the Duke of Portland will consider of a proper person for the Presidency of the Board of Controul.[1] His Majesty also approves of Captain Seymore receiving a Baronetage in reward of his distinguished conduct upon too [*sic*] late occasions. (14353)

3862   LORD MULGRAVE *to the* KING

[*Admiralty, 21 April 1809.*] Lord Mulgrave begs your Majesty's permission humbly to offer his dutifull congratulations on the splendid success of the attack on the enemy's fleet in Basque Roads, four line-of-battle ships have been destroyed & the other seven are on shore in different parts of the Charante. This victory has been achieved with the loss only of one lieutenant, one gunner & eight men killed, two lieutenants & thirty-five wounded. Sir Harry Burrard has brought the dispatches. Lord Mulgrave humbly hopes that the importance of the event may plead as an excuse for sending a messenger at an unusual time.[2] (14355)

3863   *Letters from* GEORGE CANNING *to the* KING, *and the reply*

[*Foreign Office, 21 Apr. 1809.*] Mr. Canning humbly submits for your Majesty's royal signature the instruments of full powers enabling him to conclude & sign with Count Walmoden a Treaty of Amity between your Majesty & the Emperor of Austria. He submits at the same [time] a second letter to Count Walmoden, inclosing the plan of an operation of finance for aiding the credit of the Austrian Government, which plan has been drawn up at the Treasury, & which Count Walmoden undertakes to carry with him for the consideration of the Court of Vienna. Count Walmoden proposes to leave England as soon as the Treaty (the draft of which Mr. Canning will most humbly submit for your Majesty's royal consideration tomorrow) shall have been signed. (14356)

[1] Yorke refused office because he felt that he could not afford a breach with his brother Lord Hardwicke, who was in opposition. Hardwicke would have allowed him to accept the offer had it been part of a wider reconstruction of the Administration on the basis of a union of parties. Hardwicke wrote to him on the 25th: 'I could never wish to see you appointed to office for the purpose of bolstering up the present Ministry, & could only see it with satisfaction under an Administration of more strength & efficiency, & more likely to be permanent. These have been my invariable sentiments in all our conversations, & I am not aware of having ever contradicted them, much less of having pledged myself to come over to the present headless & weak Ministry if you were appointed to a place... The circumstances of the moment require and offer a fair opening for an union of parties, of men like yourself with a power themselves to effect it. If such an union takes place, I shall be again united with you and we shall be embarked in the same bottom. But if you are satisfied with being told that it is difficult & impracticable, & therefore come into office with the addition possibly of the Marq. of W[ellesley] &c, to keep together the present Ministry, it must operate as a separation in politics more complete than that which has existed between us since the end of March 1807, with the exception of a few days of agreement on the dissolution of Parliament. I am not without a feeling for the public; but on this subject, I feel much more for my private affections & regards, & care for little else. Nothing of this sort will alter those feelings, but if you have made up your mind to accept office at all events, I shall feel much better satisfied not to be consulted upon the subject, for I cannot and will not be made a party to it.' (Add. MSS. 35394, f. 33.)

[2] See No. 3865.

[*The King's reply, Windsor Castle, 22 April.*] The King approves the letter to Count Walmoden which Mr. Canning has submitted and the accompanying plan of an operation of finance for aiding the credit of the Austrian Government. (14357)

[*From Canning, Foreign Office, 21 Apr., 1 p.m.*] Mr. Canning thinks it his duty to lose no time in humbly laying before your Majesty the accompanying despatch just received from Mr. Horne:[1] humbly trusting that the importance of the intelligence will excuse him to your Majesty for presuming to break in upon your Majesty at an unusual hour. (14358)

3864   THE EARL OF LIVERPOOL *to the* KING, *and the reply*

[*Charles Street, Saturday morning, 7 a.m.* [*22 April 1809*].] Lord Liverpool begs leave most humbly to submit to your Majesty the Minutes of the House of Lords, and to inform your Majesty that the result of the debate appears to have been very satisfactory.[2] (14359)

[*The King's reply, Windsor Castle, 22 April, 1 p.m.*] The King is glad to learn from Lord Liverpool's report that the result of last night's debate in the House of Lords was satisfactory, at the same time that his Majesty cannot but be surprized that, upon such a question, the numbers of the minority should have been so considerable. It appears to the King that little encouragement is held out to the production of papers, as, altho it has of late been carried to a greater extent than was ever known at any former period, it has not secured Government against the complaints of witholding information. (14359)

3865   THE DUKE OF PORTLAND *to the* KING, *and the reply*

[*Burlington House, Sunday, 23 April 1809.*] The various manners in which Lord Cochrane[3] distinguished himself in the course of the late glorious event in Basque Roads, by the arrangement & direction of the fire vessels, the making the Calcutta, a two-deck ship, strike her colours to his frigate, and the vigorous & gallant attack he is stated to have made upon the enemy's line-of-battle ships which were on shore, have induced the Duke of Portland, with the utmost deference to your

---

[1] Or Horn: an Agent employed by the British Government in obtaining information. See *Letters of George IV*, I, 380 n.

[2] *Parl. Deb.*, XIV, 121–72 (debate on Grey's Motion criticising the Government's conduct of the war in the Peninsula, accusing Ministers of rashness and mismanagement). The numbers were 145 to 92.

[3] Thomas Cochrane, 10th Earl of Dundonald (1775–1860), styled Lord Cochrane until 1 July 1831, when he succeeded his father. Lieutenant, 1796; Commander, 1800; Captain, 1801; Rear-Admiral, 1832; Vice-Admiral, 1841. M.P. for Honiton, 1806–7; for Westminster, 1807–18. His drawing attention to naval abuses whilst in Parliament gave offence to the Admiralty and hindered his promotion, but his attack on the French fleet in the Basque Roads earned him a K.B. In 1814 he was convicted, along with his uncle, on a charge of fraudulently raising Stock Exchange prices by spreading rumours of Napoleon's death, and he was fined and imprisoned. He commanded the Chilean Navy, 1817, and contributed to the independence of Chile and Peru.

Majesty's superior judgement, to submit Ld. Cochrane's services to your Majesty's most gracious consideration & most dutifully to lay at your Majesty's feet the humble hope & opinion of your Majesty's confidential servants that your Majesty may deign to consider Lord Cochrane worthy of the honor of being admitted into the Order of the Bath—by which the Duke of Portland has reason to believe that the profession generally will be highly gratified as well as Lord Cochrane, & that he will deem his services most amply compensated by this mark of your Majesty's royal favor & ever hold it in most gratefull remembrance. (14365–6)

[*The King's reply, Windsor Castle, 24 April.*] Although it has not been usual to confer the Order of the Bath upon a *Captain* in the Navy (Lord St Vincent's being the only instance which has occurred) Lord Cochrane's personal rank may give a colour to it, and the King will therefore not object to the Duke of Portland's proposal that he should receive that honor. Lord Cochrane should therefore be desired to attend with the other officers on Wednesday next at the Queen's Palace & notice should be given to the proper person to bring an additional Ribband. (14366)

3866   *Letters from* GEORGE CANNING *to the* KING, *and the replies*

[*Foreign Office, 23 Apr. 1809.*] Mr. Canning humbly takes the liberty of troubling your Majesty again with the draft of the Treaty between your Majesty & the Emperor of Austria, having admitted into it some alterations suggested by Count Walmoden, to which Count Walmoden attached great importance, and which appeared to Mr. Canning in no degree prejudicial to your Majesty's interests. Mr. Canning sends the draft as originally submitted to your Majesty with the alterations in the margin. Count Walmoden has also desired the addition of a separate Article, stipulating that the Treaty shall be kept secret until the exchange of the ratifications. (14363)

[*The King's reply, Windsor Castle, 24 April.*] The King approves of Mr Canning's introducing into the Treaty between his Majesty & the Emperor of Austria such alterations as, without being material, may render it more satisfactory to Count Walmoden. (14364)

[*From Canning, Foreign Office, 24 Apr.*] Mr. Canning humbly lays before your Majesty the substance of the demands received from Mr. Kleist, the person employed here to state the determination of the people of Westphalia & other parts of the north of Germany to rise against the French, in the event of the commencement of an Austrian war, with the answers which it is proposed, if approved by your Majesty, to give to them. Count Walmoden is personally acquainted with Mr. Kleist, & proposes to return with him to the Baltick, conceiving that Mr. Kleist will be enabled to facilitate his passage by way of Colberg & Berlin to Vienna.[1] (14369)

[1] Thomas Grenville wrote to his brother on 7 April: 'Kleist, the son of the Magdeburg general, is come here as a private agent to Canning from several leading men in Prussia and in Saxony to ask for

[*The King's reply, Windsor Castle, 25 April.*] The King approves of the answers which Mr. Canning proposes should be returned to the demands which have been brought forward by Mr. Kleist. (14370)

3867   *Letters from* SPENCER PERCEVAL *to the* KING, *and the reply*

[*Downg. St., Monday, 24 April 1809.*] Mr. Perceval acquaints your Majesty that Lord Porchester moved this evening for leave to bring in a Bill to prevent the granting of offices in reversion. Your Majesty will recollect that an Act passed in the last Session to suspend till the first six weeks of the next Session of Parliament after the present, your Majesty's power of so granting them. Mr Perceval therefore objected to entertaining the Bill at the present time. A debate followed; Mr Bankes, Lord Henry Petty, Mr Tierney, Mr Whitbread and Mr Ponsonby supported Lord Porchester, and Mr Canning supported Mr Perceval.

The House divided, for the Bill 106, against it 121, and it was therefore rejected by the small majority of 15.

But as your Majesty will recollect the feeling which was excited on this Bill in the last Session of Parliament, perhaps it will not appear extraordinary, however much it may be regretted, that so small a number of the friends of Governt. attended.[1] (14371)

[*The King's reply, Windsor Castle, 25 April.*] Considering what passed last year in regard to offices in reversion, the King is not surprized that Lord Porchester's Motion should not have been rejected by a greater majority, although his Majesty joins with Mr Perceval in regretting that it should have been so small. (14371)

[*From Perceval, Downing Street, 27 [26] April, Wed. morng., 4.15 a.m.*] Mr. Perceval acquaints your Majesty that Lord Archibald Hamilton brought forward his Motion against Lord Castlereagh yesterday eveng. in the Ho of Commons, founded upon the evidence which had been taken before the Committee which had been appointed to take into consideration the abuses in the disposal of East India patronage. He opened his case, and Lord Castlereagh, having been heard in his defence, retired. Lord Archibald then moved the three Resolutions, which Mr. Perceval herewith encloses. Lord Binning[2] spoke in defence of Lord Castlereagh, and moved the Orders of the Day. The transaction which was alluded to

arms to assist a general insurrection in the north of Germany, but I do not believe that the King of Prussia is any party to this mission.' (*Dropmore Papers*, IX, 292.)

   [1] *Parl. Deb.*, XIV, 191–203.
   [2] Thomas Hamilton, 9th Earl of Haddington [S.] (1780–1858), styled Lord Binning from 1795, when his grandfather, the 7th, Earl died, until 17 March 1828, when his father died. Tory M.P. for St. Germans, 1802–6; for Cockermouth, Jan.–April 1807; for Callington, 1807–12; for St. Michael, 1814–18; for Rochester, 1818–26; for Yarmouth (Isle of Wight), 1826–7. A Commissioner of the India Board, July–Nov. 1809, and 1814–22; Lord Lieutenant of Ireland, 1834–5; First Lord of the Admiralty, 1841–6; Lord Privy Seal, Jan.–July 1846. Created Baron Melros [U.K.], 24 July 1827, by the influence of his friend Canning. K.T., 1853. His India Board Commissionership was unpaid, but he did not mind that: 'as no sort of expense is attached to it, and there would, I presume, be no necessity for my attendance in London during the recess of Parliament'. (Harrowby MSS. To Harrowby, 7 July 1809.)

was one which rested merely in intention and had not been accomplished, and as the Resolutions which were moved by Lord Archibald would have conveyed so strong a Parliamentary censure as might have rendered it impossible for Lord Castlereagh to preserve his situation in your Majesty's service, the punishment appeared to be so disproportionate to the offence, which, whatever was its Parliamentary character, cast no moral imputation upon Lord Castlereagh, that his Lordship contended that the offence not being attempted to be justified the House was under no necessity of noticing it, and therefore that it was right to pass to other business.

The debate then proceeded in the following order—

For Lord A.'s Motion	For Lord Binning's
1 Mr Williams Wynn	
	2 Mr. Croker
3 Mr Wm. Smith	
	4 Mr. Manners Sutton[1]
5 Mr Grattan	
	6 Mr Perceval
7 Mr Ponsonby	

Mr Bankes followed Mr Ponsonby. He strongly objected to Lord Archibald's Motion as being much severer than the case called for, but at the same time he was apprehensive that the Motion for the Orders of the Day would be misconceived out of the House, and he therefore preferred a Resolution which might express the duty of Parliament upon such cases when they came before it, but adverting to the uncompleted intention in this case might give that as a reason for not expressing any censure or reprehension upon it—that he could not vote for the original Resolution because it would probably have the effect of removing Lord Castlereagh, whereas such a Motion as he proposed would rather imply that such a step was not thought necessary by the House. This suggestion was well received by many persons in the House, and many who would have voted for the Orders of the Day rather than have adopted the Resolution of Lord Archibald would have opposed them for the purpose of adopting Mr Bankes's suggestion. Sr. F. Burdett followed Mr Bankes, opposing his suggested Amendment. Mr Windham followed Sir Francis and tho he agreed, as it seemed, very much with Mr Bankes, yet he went away before the division. Mr Lascelles also spoke recommending some such measure as was proposed by Mr Bankes, Mr Whitbread followed Mr Lascelles in support of the original Motion, and Mr Canning answered Mr Whitbread. Upon the best consideration which Mr Canning & Mr Perceval and others could give to the temper & feeling of the House they thought it adviseable to fall into Mr Bankes's suggestion, as it was quite clear they would have more votes upon it than for the Orders of the Day, and therefore Mr Canning proposed the Resolution which Mr Perceval incloses for your Majesty's perusal. Mr Tierney

---

[1] Charles Manners-Sutton, 1st Viscount Canterbury (1780–1845). M.P. for Scarborough, 1806–32; for Cambridge University, 1832–5. Speaker of the House of Commons, June 1817–Dec. 1834. Peerage, 10 March 1835.

spoke against it, Sr. Chs. Price for it, and Lord Porchester against it. The Orders of the Day were therefore negatived without a division—and upon Mr Canning's Amendment the House divided—

For that Amendt.	216
For the orig. Motion	167
	49

There was another division upon another Amendment in which the numbers were the same against Lord Castlereagh and two less for him.

Mr Perceval humbly submits to your Majesty that upon the whole the Resolution which was carried was in effect to the full as satisfactory as the Orders of the Day, and that considering the nature of the question and the temper of the times, he cannot say that the majority was less than he expected.[1] (14372–4)

---

[1] *Parl. Deb.*, XIV, 203–56 (25 April). In 1805, when he was President of the Board of Control, Castlereagh had placed a writership in the East India Company's service at the disposal of Lord Clancarty to facilitate his getting a seat in Parliament. See the Report of the Select Committee on East India patronage in *Parl. Deb.*, XIII, Appx. No. IV, cxxv. Lord Bathurst explained the matter to the Duke of Richmond on 1 March: 'Lord Castlereagh has got into a foolish scrape which will soon become the subject of much talk; and, in the frame [?] in which the country now is, it may lead to unpleasant consequences—his general unpopularity (I know not why) will aggravate them. In the year 1805 when he was made Secy. of State & lost his re-election, a person came to offer him a seat in England which he rejected, but refer'd the person to Lord Clancarty, who was looking out for one. After some conversation in which the price which was to be paid to the member who was to vacate was discussed, the man said that his friend would not have money, but wished to have his son made a writer in the East Indies. On this being told to Lord Castlereagh he told Lord Clancarty that as head of the Board of Control he had one or two to give away, and would dispose of one to this gentleman, provided his son was properly qualified. On this being reported to the agent & his being pressed to name the individual, he declined doing so, & after a little while said he would give three thousand pounds for the writership; on which Lord Clancarty turned him out of the room. The man turns out to be one of the agents who are going about trafficking offices: & before a Committee appointed to examine into the disposition of writerships (in consequence of something which came out in evidence during the Duke's inquiry) he has made some mention of this transaction, which has obliged both Lord Castlereagh & Lord Clancarty to give the true account. Now there is nothing more in this than what it is known is frequently done to get a seat in Parliament.' (Richmond MSS. 70/1358.) The Duke replied on the 19th: 'With respect to Ld. Castlereagh's scrape, in common times it would be nothing, but in times when such fellows as Sir F. Burdett, Mr. Wardle, Ld. Folkstone (who from his situation in life is worse) &c. &c. can make a cry in the House and be helped in their plans by those detestable Saints, I fear it may be serious. Lord Castlereagh is very unpopular & if Opposition can make anything like a case, depend on it he will also be obliged to resign.' (*Ibid.* 61/331.) Castlereagh himself thought that, upon the whole, the debate had been satisfactory. He wrote to his brother on 27 April: 'The debate was bitterly urged on the constitutional, but not on personal grounds, and the Party drew forth all their strength, making Temple and others disgrace themselves by a breach of their promises, most unnecessarily and voluntarily made. The desponding tone of our friends—the constitutional scruples of the country gentlemen, and the shabby desire some felt to ride home on a Minister for their unpopular votes on the Duke's question, led them to hope for a victory. You will observe that they had a weighty division, but as they did not venture to declare in the debate that removal was their object, but some on the contrary said, in order to catch votes, that they only wish'd strongly to censure the act itself, I don't think these members had much effect, the majority being secure. The temper of the House was favorable, and the feeling with me; they were unaffectedly embarrassed with the case, and wish'd to save both themselves and me. I am glad it has been brought fully into discussion as it has been thereby fully sifted, and on all sides was treated as a mere breach of Parliamentary Law, proceding from no bad or dishonorable motive. Grattan was particularly gentleman-like, Windham defending it too roundly, but very useful. The former voted against, the latter did not vote. Whitbread and Tierney very violent, but from none any personal imputation. I am upon the whole well pleased that the Order of the Day was not persever'd in. The Resolution is an adjudication

[*The King's reply, Windsor Castle, 26 April.*] The King acknowledges the receipt of Mr Perceval's letter and he agrees with him that the result of last night's debate upon Lord Archibald Hamilton's Motion has been as satisfactory as could be expected under the embarassing circumstances connected with it. His Majesty entirely approves the line of conduct which Mr Perceval took upon this occasion. (14374)

3868   *Letters from* GEORGE CANNING *to the* KING, *and the reply*

[*Foreign Office, 28 April 1809.*] Mr. Canning humbly submits for your Majesty's royal signature Letters of Credence to Mr. Adair as your Majesty's Ambassador to the Porte: & the Commission appointing Mr. Stratford Canning[1] Secry of Embassy.

Your Majesty's gracious approbation of Mr. Frere's appointment to this Embassy having been obtained by Mr. Canning before any discussion had taken place upon the subject of Mr. Frere's correspondence with Genl. Sir John Moore, Mr. Canning does not think himself at liberty to avail himself of your Majesty's goodness in this respect while there is any danger of such an appointment being in any degree prejudicial to your Majesty's service. Mr. Canning hopes that this

of the question—the other course might have led to a revival of the question. It will also satisfy the country better than an evasion of the merits. I declined to defend the principle, that I might not encourage future abuse, and after stripping the case of all its aggravations left it as a simple case of influence to the House.' (Londonderry MSS.) To another (unknown) correspondent, he wrote (the letter is undated): 'With respect to the Opposition generally, I have nothing to complain of. They availed themselves of a political advantage. They pushed it to the utmost, but in the mode of doing so, they did not attempt to give an untrue or illiberal colouring to the case. Having got into the scrape I cannot regret that the whole has been sifted to the bottom. I am perfectly satisfied with the result, and although there were perhaps two or three votes in the division which surprised me, I can truly say that yours was the only one which gave me the smallest pain.' (*Ibid.*)

Writing to the Duke of Rutland on 20 April the Duke of Portland said that the Opposition was endeavouring to remove Castlereagh from office if not to expel him from the House of Commons. 'However unfortunate one must acknowledge the want of caution on the part of Lord Castlereagh, as it is impossible to impute his conduct to any bad motive, and if it is a crime is one, that, though not in the same way (probably from want of the means rather than from a sense of the impropriety of employing them) few people who have taken a part in Parliamentary politics, might not and *would* not have committed, I trust your Grace will have no objection in exerting your powerful influence in the House of Commons to prevent either of the measures above stated from taking place and that you will have the goodness for that purpose of acquainting your friends with your wishes that they should support any proposition which may be made by Mr. Perceval for averting the censure which will be moved against Lord Castlereagh and preventing his removal from the King's service, an event which at this moment would be attended with the most injurious consequences to the interests of the public.'

Thomas Grenville wrote to Lord Spencer on the 28th: 'All is here at sixes and sevens; half the Government wanted Castlereagh out, and Wellesley most especially wanted it inasmuch as he was the destined successor if the Irish Lord should be forced out, and so eager were the friends of Wellesley to accomplish this, that his three members all voted against Castlereagh, and Canning made a most feeble and washy speech of a few minutes only. The consequence is the small majority that you saw.... Their own friends begin to exclaim loudly against their insufficiency, and Cartwright is reported to me to be among the loudest on this topic.' (Althorp MSS.)

[1] Stratford Canning, Viscount Stratford de Redcliffe (1786–1880), Canning's cousin. Précis-writer in the Foreign Office, 1807; Second Secretary of the Mission to Copenhagen, 1807; Secretary of Embassy at Constantinople, 1809–12, and Minister Plenipotentiary there, 1810–12; Minister to Switzerland, 1814–19; to the U.S.A., 1820–3; Ambassador to Turkey, 1826–7, and 1842–58. M.P. for Old Sarum, 1828–30; for Stockbridge, 1831–2; for King's Lynn, 1835–42. G.C.B., 1829. Peerage, 1852.

would not turn out to be the case: but still, as it seems advisable to send out the ratification as soon as possible, and as there will be another opportunity of sending to Constantinople when the presents which ought to accompany the ratification are ready (the delay in preparing which has been the cause of the delay in sending the ratifications) Mr. Canning feels it his duty humbly to submit for your Majesty's royal approbation the appointment of Mr. Adair in the first instance: humbly intreating your Majesty's gracious permission to submit at a future opportunity the name of Mr. Frere, if Mr. Adair shall continue to wish to return home & if the issue of the discussions respecting Mr. Frere shall be as favourable as Mr. Canning ventures to hope it will be.[1]

Mr. Canning, at the same time, thinks it his duty most humbly to submit to your Majesty the expediency of appointing a Minister to Spain, where, whatever may be the merits of Mr. Frere's conduct, the report of the discussions upon it in this country may possibly tend to diminish his credit & authority in the management of your Majesty's interests with the Spanish Govt., and having already humbly submitted to your Majesty the advantages which might probably be derived, in the present state of that Government, from the mission of a person of high rank & with the highest diplomatick character, Mr. Canning humbly trusts that your Majesty may be graciously pleased not to disapprove of the nomination of Lord Wellesley to be your Majesty's Ambassador Extraordinary & Minister Plenipotentiary at Seville. (14377–9)

[*From Canning, Foreign Office, 28 April (Copy)*.] Mr. Canning humbly submits for your Majesty's Royal signature the instrument of your Majesty's ratification of the Separate & Secret Articles of the Treaty with the Porte. Mr. Canning has most humbly to solicit your Majesty's gracious forgiveness for thus a second time troubling your Majesty on this subject. But in the former instrument of ratification was inadvertently included an additional Secret Article signed by Mr. Adair *sub spe rati*, which engaged for a sum of £300,000 to be paid by your Majesty to the Ottoman Porte without specifying distinctly in the body of the Article what unquestionably was Mr. Adair's intent in signing it, that this assistance is promised eventually upon war breaking out between Turkey and France. This Article, upon consideration, it is humbly submitted that your Majesty might decline to ratify in its present shape, giving, however, to Mr. Adair full authority to promise such assistance in your Majesty's name, in the event of war actually taking place.

The former ratification Mr. Canning will send to the Lord Chancellor to be cancelled (having taken his Lordship's opinion upon the practicability of that proceeding) when the present ratification has the Great Seal affixed to it. (Harewood MSS.)

[1] Adair had negotiated and signed a peace treaty with Turkey on 5 Jan., the Sultan being impressed by the danger to which he was seemingly exposed in consequence of the partition plans concerted between Napoleon and the Tsar at Erfurt in Oct. 1808.

[*The King's reply, Windsor Castle, 29 April.*] The King will not object to Mr. Frere's nomination to the Embassy at Constantinople, as recommended by Mr. Canning, if circumstances should hereafter admit of it, but his Majesty is persuaded that Mr. Canning must feel how much the cry of the public is against Mr. Frere at this moment.[1] The King acquiesces in the proposed appointment of Lord Wellesley to the Embassy at Seville. (14379)

3869 SPENCER PERCEVAL *to the* KING, *and the reply*

[*Downg. St., Monday night, 12 o'clock* [*1 May 1809*].] Mr. Perceval acquaints your Majesty that Mr. Ord[2] (Member for Morpeth) brought the Fourth Report of the Committee of Public Expenditure before the House this evening, and submitted the five first [*sic*] Resolutions which stand upon the paper which Mr. Perceval herewith incloses, as containing his view of that Report: the two first criminating your Majesty's Governments in succession since the first appointment of the Dutch Comssn. in 1795, and the three following directed against the Comssioners [*sic*] themselves. It appeared undoubtedly by the Report that those Commissioners had greatly misconducted themselves in not following the directions of the Act of Parliament under which they were appointed, by neglecting to pay the money which they received from the Dutch-captured property into the Bank, and by putting it out to interest for their own benefit, but the Committee had upon the whole view of the case not advised any criminal proceeding against them, but only that their accounts should be audited & that instead of the great profits which they had made & retained for themselves they should not receive more than 5 pr. ct. on the net proceeds of the property under their management. It appeared also that yr. Majesty's Government had omitted to prescribe the rate of commission which they should receive, and had omitted also to call upon them for their accounts. It appeared however to Mr Perceval that there was no such blame on the part of your Majesty's Government as should call for so marked a censure as was implied & conveyed by the two first Resolutions, and that as the present Treasury had upon the receipt of the Report of the Commee. directed the accounts to be audited, as that Report recommended, there was no sufficient reason for the House to proceed to do anything, or at least that it had better wait for the result of the enquiry before the auditors before it came to any resolution against the Comssrs. Mr. Perceval therefore proposed the previous question to the first Resolution, meaning to have followed it up with the same Motion upon the others. A debate of some length followed, and many gentlemen on both sides

---

[1] Lady Hester Stanhope, who, it was believed, was to have married Sir John Moore, wrote to George Rose on 13 Sept.: 'Frere is certainly disgraced for ever. His birth was always, in my opinion, a sufficient reason against sending him Ambassador to the proudest nation in the world. Nobody who knows him can deny he has talents, but conceit and indolence prevent their being turned to account; and since his conduct towards General Moore, I shall never be able to endure the sight of him.' (Rose, *Diaries and Corresp.*, II, 344.) Frere was greatly blamed for the advice he had given Moore to advance on Madrid, at a time when Napoleon's vastly superior forces were preparing to crush him. See the correspondence between Frere and Moore in *Parl. Deb.*, XIV, 3–14, 291.

[2] William Ord (1781–1855), Whig M.P. for Morpeth, 1802–32; for Newcastle-upon-Tyne, 1835–52.

of the House expressed themselves with great strength against the Commssers., and Mr Thornton, who was the Chairman of the Committee, stated that he thought the third Resolution much too strong, but would wish to substitute one which Mr Perceval has also inclosed for your Majesty's perusal. But the previous question was first to be disposed of, and the division was: for Mr Ord's Resolun. 77, against it 102.

Mr. Thornton then moved his Resolution, which as it expressed the real state of the case Mr Perceval thought it was best to adopt. It was by Opposition wished to amend that Motion by introducing the word *neglect* as applied to yr. Majesty's former Govt. under Mr. Pitt, instead of the word *omission*. Mr. Thornton himself yielded to this Amendment, but it was resisted on the part of Mr. Perceval and the House divided, for the word *omission* 98, for the Amendt. 78.

Mr. Perceval then moved that there should be laid before the House the direction of the Treasury with respect to these accounts—and then the House adjourned.

Mr Martin has put off his Motion upon the Third Report from the same Comee. respecting offices & pensions till next Monday. And Lord Temple his Motion upon the campaign in Spain till tomorrow week.[1] (14380–2)

[*The King's reply, Windsor Castle, 2 May.*] The King acknowledges the receipt of Mr Perceval's report of the proceedings in the House of Commons upon the Resolutions moved by Mr. Ord, in reference to the conduct of the Dutch Commissioners, and his M. entirely approves of the manner in which they were met by Mr Perceval. The King does not remember who the Dutch Commssioners are, but he regrets that any individuals should have conducted themselves with so much impropriety. (14382)

3870   VISCOUNT CASTLEREAGH *to the* KING, *and the reply*

[*St James's Sq., 2 May 1809.*] Lord Castlereagh proposes with your Majesty's permission to appoint the Honble. Mr. Robinson Under-Secretary of State for the Colonial Department in the room of B. General Stewart[2] who has resign'd, and humbly requests your Majesty's leave to present Mr. Robinson to your Majesty on his appointment tomorrow if your Majesty should be pleased to approve thereof. (14388)

[*The King's reply, Queen's Palace, 3 May.*] The King approves of Lord Castlereagh's proposal to appoint Mr. Robinson, Under-Secretary of State for the Colonial Department in the room of B. General Stewart, and he may be desired to attend here this day to be presented. (14388)

[1] *Parl. Deb.*, XIV, 291–325. The Commissioners were James Craufurd, John Brickwood, Allen Chatfield, Alexander Baxter, and John Bowles, appointed in 1795 to dispose of the cargoes of Dutch ships detained in or brought into British ports. For Henry Martin's Motion see No. 3873; for Lord Temple's, No. 3876.

[2] Castlereagh's half-brother.

[*Foreign Office, 2 May 1809.*] Mr. Canning humbly lays before your Majesty a letter which he has this day received from his S.H. the Elector of Hesse by a person who left Vienna the beginning of April. This letter inclosed one addressed to your Majesty, which, as it is without a copy, Mr. Canning does not presume to transmit to your Majesty without your Majesty's special commands to that effect. Mr. Canning also humbly lays before your Majesty a letter received by him at the same time from the D. of Brunswick-Oels. (14385)

[*From Canning, Foreign Office, 2 May.*] Mr. Canning humbly solicits your Majesty's gracious commands with respect to the presentation of Lord Wellesley to your Majesty tomorrow on his appointment to the Embassy to Spain;[1] & of Lord William Bentinck on his Mission to the Austrian army. (14386)

[*The King's reply, Queen's Palace, 3 May.*] The King approves of Mr. Canning's desiring Lord Wellesley & Lord William Bentinck to attend here this day for the purpose of being presented on their respective Missions. H.M. also desires that Mr. Canning will bring with him the private letter from the Elector of Hesse. (14386)

[*From Canning, Foreign Office, 3 May.*] Mr. Canning humbly submits for your Majesty's royal signature two copies of a Message from your Majesty to the House of Lords & House of Commons[2] respecting the loan to H.R.H. the Prince Regent of Portugal, which your Majesty by the late Convention has undertaken to recommend to Parliament to guarantee. (14389)

3872 LORD MULGRAVE *to the* KING, *and the reply*

[*Admiralty, 4 May 1809.*] Lord Mulgrave has the honour to submit to your Majesty the minutes and sentence of a court martial held on board your Majesty's ship Royal Sovereign in Port Mahon harbour, Minorca, on the 21st of March 1809, for the trial of John May, private marine, on a charge of mutinous conduct towards his officer, & for striking Joseph Petty, serjeant of the guard. The Court have found the prisoner guilty of the charge and have sentenced him to suffer death. Vice-Admiral Lord Collingwood has, however, respited the execution of the sentence till your Majesty's pleasure shall be signified. The Vice-Admiral, in a letter addressed to the Secretary of the Board of Admiralty, had stated circumstances of mitigation arising from the general good character of the culprit; his absence of sound mind from a state of excessive intoxication which deprived him of all consciousness of the nature of his offence; & the increased confusion of his

---

[1] Soon afterwards Canning received a letter from Lady Wellesley informing him that her husband intended to take one of his mistresses, Mrs. Leslie, with him, to Spain. The Government laid an embargo on this part of the Marquess's baggage, and Canning said that his interview with him on this subject passed off very well.

[2] See *Parl. Deb.*, XIV, 408 (8 May). The loan was one of £600,000, and the Convention provided that the loan should be serviced from the revenues of the island of Madeira.

intellects in consequence of blows which he had received from the musquet of the centry whose post he had endeavoured to pass. Influenced by these considerations the Vice-Admiral has recommended John May as a fit object for the interposition of your Majesty's gracious clemency: the Commander-in-Chief on the station where the offence was committed, whose peculiar duty it is to watch over the due maintainance of discipline in your Majesty's fleet committed to his charge, being of opinion that the awful example of execution is not necessary on this occasion, Lord Mulgrave feels it his duty humbly to submit to your Majesty's gracious consideration the recommendation of Vice-Admiral Lord Collingwood. (14394-5)

[*The King's reply, Queen's Palace, 5 May.*] The King has received Lord Mulgrave's letter and the accompanying proceedings of a court martial held for the trial of John May, a private marine. However heinous the offence for which he was sentenced to death, his Majesty considers the recommendation of Lord Collingwood sufficient ground for extending his mercy to the prisoner. (14395)

3873   *Letters from* SPENCER PERCEVAL *to the* KING, *and the replies*

[*4 May 1809.*] Mr. Perceval acquaints your Majesty that the Motion which he has the honor to enclose was made in the House of Commons by Mr. Curwen. In opening the Motion he referred to the temper of the times, and considered that the measure which he was proposing would have the effect of conciliating and satisfying all the discontent which connects itself with the subject of Parliamentary reform. His mode of effecting this object, as far as he explained it, was by requiring an oath of Members before they take their seats that they had given no money to procure them, that penalties should be inflicted upon persons selling seats, and that the penalties of bribery should be extended to acts of giving money after the elections are over, as well as before. The detail of his measure he did not describe more precisely. He disclaimed any idea of intending what he called Parliamentary reform, but contended that these regulations were only giving more effect to existing law. Mr Windham opposed the Bill because he said it was the first step towards a reform, and he made a very able speech upon the subject. Lord Folkstone followed Mr Windham, speaking for the Bill. Mr Perceval followed Lord Folkstone. Tho he was much more disposed to concur with Mr Windham in his view of the subject than with those who supported Mr Curwen, yet he thought that a Bill professing so fairly in its title ought not to be rejected by the House till upon being seen in its details objections might be more easily & distinctly pointed out to it. Mr Perceval took the opportunity of expressing himself as strongly as he could against the delusions & artifices which are now practicing upon the public upon topics connected with Parliamentary reform, endeavouring to shew how the people were imposed upon by false assertions in point of fact & false impressions of every kind—which observations were well received by the House. Mr. Perceval guarded himself against being supposed to be pledged in any degree to support the Bill or of admitting its necessity or the practicability of its execution by giving his consent to its introduction; giving that consent merely upon the ground of wishing to see & examine the Bill in its detail—the detail of the Bill appearing to Mr. Perceval as that which would most develop its objections. Mr Ponsonby supported the introduction of the Bill, and gave his approbation distinctly to the principle of it. Mr Hawkins Brown opposed it—Mr Brag Bathurst supported it and entered strongly into the necessity in his view of adopting the measure—professing that he did not see it as a measure of reform but merely of regulation. Mr W. Smith spoke for it and Mr Curwen replied—when leave was given to bring in the Bill. Mr Perceval concludes his report to your Majesty upon this subject with observing that the temper of the House seemed to be very good against reform, but he is rather apprehensive that this proposal, termed a regulation, but certainly leading too nearly to reform, will have a support which, if the details of the Bill are what Mr Perceval expects them to be, in his opinion it ought not to have—but Mr Perceval has no apprehension that he shall not be able to prevail upon the House to reject it if it shall contain the objectionable provisions which he anticipates; altho he thinks the Opposition generally, including Lord Sidmouth's friends, will support it, and at all events Mr Perceval is satisfied that the opposition to be given to it will come with much better effect when it is applied to the Bill after it has been seen in its details.[1] (14390–2)

[*The King's reply, Queen's Palace, 5 May.*] The King acknowledges the receipt of Mr Perceval's report of last night's proceedings, and his Majesty entirely admits the propriety of the principle upon which Mr Perceval has preferred to make his opposition to Mr Curwen's Bill when the details of it can be discussed. (14392)

[*From Perceval, Friday, 4 [5] May [1809], 11.30 p.m.*] Mr Perceval acquaints your Majesty that Mr Madocks[2] made a Motion this evening in the Ho of Co. of which he had given notice in these terms: 'for a Committee to enquire into the conduct of Ministers in procuring returns of Members to Parliament.' He began by stating modestly his own inability, and enlarging upon the great importance of the charge which he was about to make. He then referred to the Journals for the proceedings of the House against two persons of the name of Shepherd who in the year 1700 were expelled for bribery. The Journals were read and it appeared that a charge to that effect having been made, the House appointed a day for taking it into consideration.[3] He then stated that he should follow the course of that precedent, and therefore he charged the Rt. Hble. Spr. Perceval of having been guilty, thro Mr Henry Wellesley, of corrupt practices in obtaining returns of

---

[1] *Parl. Deb.*, XIV, 353–80 (4 May). 'Of the Ministers', wrote the Speaker, 'for the Bill are Lord Liverpool, Lord Harrowby, Long, Yorke, Huskisson and the Attorney-General. Against it—Rose, Perceval, Lord Arden and Lord Castlereagh. Disposed towards it, but not declared, Canning.' (Colchester, II, 187.)

[2] William Alexander Madocks (1773–1828), Whig M.P. for Boston, 1802–20; for Chippenham, 1820–6. A parliamentary reformer, he first obtained a seat in the Commons by giving the Boston voters ten guineas each for a plumper and five guineas for a single vote.

[3] The Clerk of the House read the entries in the *Commons' Journal*, dated 13 and 15 Feb. and 18 March 1700. Samuel Shepherd, one of the two accused Members, had been committed to the Tower.

Members to Parliament—and also charged Ld. Visc. Castlereagh of the same. He then moved that those charges should be heard at the Bar of the House on a day which he named—and sat down. His speech had at least one merit in it. Your Majesty will perceive that it was not a long one, for it contained no more than Mr Perceval has above stated to your Majesty. Mr Perceval said that he could not pretend to state what rules might have governed the proceedings of the House in the year 1700 on subjects of this nature—but that from any experience which he had had in it, courtesy at least, if nothing else, generally secured to any Member who was personally to be accused, the notice of the Motion which was intended to be made against him—but that he had not had either publicly or privately the most distant intimation of the proceeding which Mr Madocks had brought forward—that to a charge so entirely vague and indeterminate, of the object of which he had not the slightest intimation, he could not possibly enter into any defence; he could only make his bow to the Chair, and leave it to the justice of the House to determine what course should be taken upon it—and he withdrew. A debate followed of some little length, of which Mr Perceval cannot tell your Majesty the particulars, as he was not present. Sir John Anstruther began it, how-ever, as Mr Perceval understood, & reprobated the cause [*sic*] of proceeding. Mr Bathurst did the same, and, adverting to some late meetings for Parliamentary reform, commented with [such] severity upon them as called up Mr Biddulph & Mr Whitbread in their defence—Mr Whitbread saying he should certainly support the Motion. Mr Canning, perceiving that Mr Madocks was disposed to withdraw the Motion, protested against the withdrawal and contended that it must be brought to a decisive vote. Mr Sturges Bourne spoke and Mr C. Yorke, and Mr Gooch,[1] who in the course of what he said, and he spoke, Mr Perceval under-stands, with great effect, adverted to the meetings in which votes of thanks were given to Mr Wardle—and he said whatever might be the effect of the enquiry what Mr Wardle had moved [*sic*] he should as soon think of thanking Mrs *Clarke* for her *chastity* as Mr. *Wardle* for his *patriotism*. The question was at last put and negatived without a division. Mr Madocks then proposed to bring forward the charges in a specific shape, and after some conversation as to the day he decided to bring them forward on Thursday next. What they are, or to what boroughs they allude or to what transactions in which Mr Wellesley may or may not with more or less caution [have] made use of Mr Perceval's name, Mr Perceval is unable to state to your Majesty, but as there do unquestionably sometimes occur instances in which more communication is had upon such subjects by the Secy. of the Treasury (under the authority doubtless of the Chr. of the Exchequer or the First Lord) than what it would be desireable to make the subject of public dis-cussion in Parliament, Mr Perceval must wait, not without some anxiety, till he hears the nature & extent of the statement which may be made against himself and Lord Castlereagh. After this business was disposed of Sr. O. Moseley[2] moved for

[1] Sir Thomas Sherlock Gooch (1767–1851), M.P. for Suffolk, 1806–30. Succeeded his father as 5th Baronet, 1826. An opponent of Catholic emancipation; generally supported Administration; a leading representative of the agricultural interest.
[2] Sir Oswald Mosley (1785–1871), M.P. for Portarlington, 1806–7; for Winchelsea, 1807–12; for Midhurst, 1817–18; for North Staffordshire, 1832–7. Succeeded his grandfather as 2nd Baronet, 29

a Comee. to enquire into the transaction relative to the grant of a lease to Col. Gordon of some ground near Chelsea. There had been some papers laid before the House on that subject, and the Chelsea Board had gone into an enquiry into it, which they transmitted to the Treasury yesterday. Mr Perceval therefore resisted the Committee and at least desired the House to wait till they might have before them the result of that enquiry. This however after some debate was pressed to a division and the House divided, against the Motion 170, for it 73.[1] (14396–8)

[*The King's reply, Windsor Castle, 6 May.*] The King acknowledges the receipt of Mr Perceval's report of the manner in which Mr Maddock's Motion was received last night in the House of Commons which has appeared to his Majesty very satisfactory. The King is not surprized that the very illiberal & unfair attacks which are now made should be more or less unpleasant to all those concerned, but his M. is perfectly convinced that no man can meet them with a clearer conscience than Mr Perceval, and that, if the proceedings of every successive Government during General Elections were to be strictly scrutinized, not any would afford less ground for attack than those of the present Administration. (14399)

[*From Perceval, 8 May 1809.*] Mr. Perceval acquaints your Majesty that Mr Martin brought forward his Motion on the Report from the Committee of Finance. He opened several Resolutions which he intended to propose in a Committee of the Whole House on this day sevnnight. He did it with great moderation and without any attempt at exciting popular feeling & clamour upon the subject. Mr Perceval rather supposes that Lord Grenville has had some influence in reducing the strength of the Resolutions which Mr Martin might otherwise have moved. The

Sept. 1798 (his father having died in 1789 at the age of 28). He thought of offering himself for Lancaster in 1806 but was too late in coming to a decision. He was defeated at Stafford in 1807. He was reckoned an Opposition man, but in 1807 his politics had seemed doubtful to Lord Darlington, who contemplated bringing him in for Winchelsea, his nomination borough (*vice* Sir Frederick Fletcher Vane, who vacated the seat). Mosley certainly had had Lord Grenville's goodwill in 1806–7. Lord Darlington wrote to Lord Howick on 14 June 1807: 'May I request the favor of your Lordship to inform me by a line as soon as possible, whether Sir Oswell Mozley's [*sic*] vote & general line of politicks were consider'd as friendly to the late Administration in the last Parliament? I beg leave to assure your Lordship that it is not from idle curiosity that I am induced to be anxious for the information I desire, & hope you will excuse this liberty.' (Howick MSS.)

[1] *Parl. Deb.*, xiv., 380–400; Colchester, ii, 181–2. The Speaker wrote on the 14th: 'Called on Yorke ...upon Curwen's Bill for preventing sale of seats in Parliament; and upon Lord Harrowby, both of whom were strongly inclined to agree with me upon the principle of the Bill and its main provisions, but neither liking the proposed test of an oath.' (*Ibid.*, ii, 186.)

Robert Dundas, the new Irish Secretary, wrote to the Duke of Richmond on 4 May: 'Your Grace will observe by our Parliamentary proceedings that Motions on questions of every description are every day brought forward, particularly in the House of Commons, and that the persevering activity of our opponents is more conspicuous than the zeal of our friends. Questions carried by a small majority, as has frequently happened lately, give encouragement to a repetition of the attack, and there is no effectual mode of counteracting this system but increased vigour in our resistance. My new Irish friends have lately been very lukewarm in their attendance & support, but I should hope they will now be more alert. It is of material importance that all those who are now absent should if possible be sent over, as a demonstration of that nature is the most effectual mode of stopping any further measures of hostility. Several members I believe went over to attend the Assizes in Ireland, and a few are come back, but there are others who have not made their appearance, and who might possibly be prevailed upon to come over.' (Melville MSS. and Richmond MSS. 168.)

principal part of them respect regulations in the manner of granting certain allowances and pensions which are not under the regulations of Mr Burke's Act,[1] and are granted in the nature of superannuations upon the establishment of several Departments of your Majesty's Government; and these seem to Mr. Perceval wholly unexceptionable. They require these allowances to be comprized in separate estimates distinct from the establishments of the Departments—& that an account of any new ones should be laid before Parliament with the grounds on which they are granted. Besides this he proposes that the allowances to Foreign Ministers, which have encreased extremely of late years, should be put under regulation, and limited with reference to the service which those Ministers may have performed. These regulations Mr Perceval conceives instead of embarrassing will ease your Majesty's service, and in no degree abridge your Majesty's means of rewarding and providing for your servants.

The Resolution to which it will be most necessary to attend & to resist is one that aims at the abolition of sinecure places, but this he opened with considerable qualification, admitting the necessity either of keeping many of them, or of substituting something else in their room.

Mr. Thornton followed him, and he expressed himself more strongly upon the subject of sinecure places. Mr. Perceval gave Mr. Martin credit for the manner in which he brought forward the business, expressed his concurrence with him upon several of his Resolutions, but reserved for the future discussion the entering into detail upon their respective merits. Lord Henry Petty supported Mr. Martin, and maintained the necessity either of sinecures or some other provision for persons who had been employed in your Maj.'s service, and were thought by your Majesty deserving of your favor. Mr. Rose expressed his approbation of several of the Resolutions—but Mr. Creevy,[2] Mr. Biddulph & Mr. Moore[3] were by no means satisfied that they went far enough.

In the course therefore of the next discussion there will probably be a good deal of difference of opinion upon some points, but except as to the abolition of sinecures there does not appear at present to be any point upon which there is likely to be any serious difficulty as upon the other points the Opposition in general will not be likely to support Mr Creevy & Mr Biddulph.[4] (14459–60)

[*The King's reply, Windsor Castle, 9 May.*] The King is glad to find from Mr. Perceval's report that Mr Martin's Motion and the discussion connected with it were not marked by any great degree of violence. His Majesty however cannot but view with a jealous eye any proposals coming from such a quarter which have

---

[1] Burke's Economical Reform Act of 1782. His Bill had proposed to reduce the pension list to £60,000 a year, but, said Martin, the limit had later been increased to £95,000.

[2] Thomas Creevey (1768–1838), Whig M.P. for Thetford, 1802–6 and 1807–18; for Appleby, 1820–6; for Downton, 1831–2. Supposed to be the natural son of Charles William, 1st Earl of Sefton. Secretary to the Board of Control in the 'Talents' Ministry, 1806–7; Treasurer of the Ordnance, 1830–4; Treasurer of Greenwich Hospital, 1834–8.

[3] Peter Moore (1753–1828), Whig M.P. for Coventry, 1803–26.

[4] *Parl. Deb.*, XIV, 409–32; Colchester, II, 184.

a tendency, however distant, to encroach upon his powers, and he must trust to Mr. Perceval's discretion and discrimination not to admit any innovation, under the plea of correcting abuse, which might have that effect. (14400)

3874 LORD MULGRAVE *to the* KING, *and the reply*

[*Admiralty, 9 May 1809.*] Lord Mulgrave has the honour to submit to your Majesty the proceedings and sentence of a court martial, held at the Cape for the trial of ten mutineers on board your Majesty's ship Nereide, who had, at St. Mary's in Madagascar, refused to weigh the anchor except on condition of proceeding to the Cape, with the view of exhibiting charges against their Captain: they were all found guilty, & sentenced to suffer death. William Wilkinson has been executed at the Cape, and the remaining nine have been recommended by the Court as objects of your Majesty's gracious clemency. It appears in evidence on the trial that no act of violence was committed nor any mark of personal disrespect to their officers manifested by any of the culprits; Lord Mulgrave, therefore, humbly submits to your Majesty's favourable consideration the recommendation of the court martial. (14401)

[*The King's reply, Windsor Castle, 10 May.*] In consequence of the recommendation of the court martial, whose proceedings have been submitted to the King by Lord Mulgrave, his Majesty consents to extend his mercy to the nine mutineers of the Nereide who were sentenced to suffer death. (14402)

3875 HENRY SEDLEY *to the* KING

[*Nuttall Temple,*[1] *10 May 1809.*] Your Majesty's goodness to me for nearly forty years encourages me to hope that you will not be displeased at my taking this way to lay before your Majesty my wishes to succeed Lord Harcourt, in the office of Master of your Robes.[2] (14406)

3876 *Letters from* SPENCER PERCEVAL *to the* KING, *and the replies*

[*Wedny. morng., 10 May 1809.*] Mr Perceval acquaints your Majesty that Lord Temple moved yesterday eveng. several Resolutions censuring your Majesty's Government for their conduct in the Spanish campaign. The subject has been so much observed upon that there was but little novelty in the debate, and Mr Perceval has little worth reporting to your Majesty but the names of the speakers & the numbers on the division. Lord Castlereagh answered Ld. Temple, Mr Ponsonby Ld Castlereagh; Mr Canning followed Mr Ponsonby; Mr Tierney spoke next. Mr Perceval followed, & Ld Henry Petty & Mr Whitbread concluded the

---

[1] Near Nottingham. Sir Charles Sedley, 2nd Bart. (? 1721–78) of Nuttall (or Nuthall), had been M.P. for Nottingham, 1747–54.

[2] General Harcourt resigned his office on succeeding his brother as 3rd Earl Harcourt (20 April). Sedley succeeded him.

debate at a ¼ p. 4 o'clock—when the House divided—for the Resolutions, Ayes 111, Noes 230. Mr Perceval encloses a copy of Lord Temple's Resolutions.[1] (14403)

[*The King's reply, Windsor Castle, 10 May.*] The King acknowledges the receipt of Mr Perceval's report of last night's proceedings in the House of Commons from which his Majesty is glad to learn that the division was so satisfactory. (14403)

[*From Perceval, 12 May.*] Mr. Perceval acquaints your Majesty that Mr Madocks made his charge, according to his notice, against Lord Castlereagh & Mr. Perceval. He confined it he said at that time to their conduct with respect to the election for Cashell, but he should on some other day move for enquiries relative to Rye, Hastings & Queenboro'. The statement he made was that Lord Castlereagh had made an engagement or bargain with Mr Quintin Dick[2] that he should come in for Cashel and that Mr Perceval was privy to it & Mr. H. Wellesley a party—and that after having gone to Lord Castlereagh to communicate to him the vote which he intended to give on the enquiry into the conduct of his Royal Highness, after consultation with Mr. Perceval Lord Castlereagh told him that he should resign his seat. Mr. Madocks opened this charge with very little effect. Mr. Perceval was then heard. He said in substance that he had great doubt what course he should take upon this charge; that if it were an ordinary case of a charge brought against Lord C. & himself for punishing an act in violation of the honor of the House of Commons, which beginning with them was to end with them also, he would have had no hesitation in meeting that statement by contradicting what was false & explaining what was incorrect in it, and then shewing that he had done nothing which any law of Parliament or Resolution of the House could prohibit —but that as it was evident from Mr Madock's speech & his previous conduct that his object was not to bring to justice an offence but to pave the way to Parliamentary reform, and that this was only the first step in the system & plan of accusations which was to be followed evidently by many more—that it was therefore material not for himself only but for those who might be the objects of further prosecution not to set a precedent from which it might be inferred that the

1 *Parl. Deb.*, XIV, 439–82.
2 Quintin Dick (c. 1777–1858), M.P. for Dunleer [I.], Jan.–Dec. 1800; for West Looe, 1803–6; for Cashel, 1807–March 1809; for Orford, 1826–30; for Maldon, 1830–47; for Aylesbury, 1848–52. Apparently it was the dispute about the proportion of the price of the seat to be returned to Dick which induced Dick to tell his story very freely, and in this way Madocks got hold of it. Castlereagh wrote to Sir Arthur Wellesley from London on 7 May 1807: 'Hitherto elections have gone very well indeed here. I believe Long wrote to you yesterday relative to Dick's coming into Parliament for one of the Irish seats at the nomination of Government. Before I gave him a firm answer, he had been in treaty with some agent here who stated himself authorised to dispose of Tralee and had concluded a bargain for it for £5000. I rather suspect this agent has misled him, as Tralee was amongst the seats on Long's list. I think it right to apprise you of this, and should recommend, if Tralee is really at your disposal, not to return Dick for it, but to have him chosen for some other place, that he may not mistake that he owes his seat to Government. He voted with us in opposition and we have therefore no right to be suspicious, but it is better there should be no doubt as to the quarter from whence the seat is derived.' (Wellington MSS.)

person who did not deny or satisfactorily explain any circumstance which might be stated as a charge against him should be presumed to be guilty. Protesting therefore against any conclusion being drawn to his prejudice by his present conduct, which he trusted would not be thought wanting in respect to the House of Commons if he contented himself with no other denial than what might be in the nature of a plea of not guilty, till he knew whether the charge was adopted by the House of Commons—confident that if it should be so adopted he should be able, as he unquestionably would be desirous of explaining satisfactorily to the House, & satisfactorily to his own honor whatever might be conceived as the matter of charge against him—and then left the House. Lord Castlereagh followed to the same effect and left the House also. Mr Perceval is of course unable to give your Majesty a report of what has passed in the debate since he left the House. He can only generally say that Mr. Cartwright, & Sr. Charles Mordaunt[1] took the lead, and, considering it as the first step to reform, determined to resist it. Sr. J. Anstruther, Mr Giddy,[2] Mr Tierney, Mr Bathurst & Lord Milton took the same objection to Parliamentary reform, with some shades of difference as to the manner in which the Motion should be received. On the other hand Mr Biddulph, Sr Francis Burdett & Mr Whitbread supported the Motion to the utmost. But all the reports which Mr Perceval has as yet received report the temper & state of the House to be most satisfactory. It is now 12 o'clock when Mr Perceval is writing to your Majesty, and he will conclude his report of the further proceedings when he has recd. intelligence of the remainder.

½ p. 2 o'clock. Mr Perceval continues his report to your Majesty. Mr Windham & Mr Canning have spoken against the Motion; Lord A. Hamilton, Mr Wilber-force, Mr. Hutchinson and Mr Peter Moore for it.

The House divided, for the Motion 85, and against it 310.[3] (14407–9)

---

[1] Sir Charles Mordaunt (1771–1823) was M.P. for Warwickshire, 1804–20. Succeeded his father as 8th Baronet, Nov. 1806. He generally voted with Ministers, but his attitude became uncertain in 1810 and the Opposition then listed him as a 'doubtful'—from their point of view.

[2] Davies Giddy (1767–1839), M.P. for Helston, 1804–6; for Bodmin, 1806–32.

[3] *Parl. Deb.*, XIV, 486–527; Colchester, II, 182. Madocks alleged that Dick had bought his seat for Cashel through the agency of Henry Wellesley, the Joint Secretary of the Treasury and with the knowl-edge and consent of Perceval; that on the Mary Anne Clarke business Dick had been told by Castlereagh that he must either vote with the Government or resign his seat; and that Dick, determined to vote according to his conscience, vacated his seat. Madocks also showed how Hastings, a Treasury borough, was managed for the Government by Milward, the Mayor, and his son; how Rye was similarly managed by Thomas Lamb; how Queenborough was under the joint patronage of the Ordnance and the Ad-miralty. But, as Grey remarked, all this had been common Treasury practice throughout the eighteenth century, and in other times no man of liberal spirit would have raised such a matter. 'But now a new code of political morality and honour has been adopted, and everything that can tend to throw discredit on the general system of government.' (Howick MSS.) 'Opposition', said Grey in another letter to his wife, 'was split in pieces—some voting with the Ministers, some for the Motion, and some going away without voting. Amongst the first were your uncle, Ld. George Cavendish, Ld. Morpeth and some others. Amongst the last, Tierney, Ld. Henry Petty, Calcraft, &c. The effect of this on the Party is very bad, and ultimately I fear it will prove so for the country...The Ministers feel themselves stronger and are encouraged to go on. The change in their tone and spirits within the last five days is very remarkable...Tierney...is now in a state of flat despondency...Instead of going to the Opera last night I went to the House of Commons. I heard only three or four speeches. One was your uncle's. It was not bad, but neither was it what is required by his situation. Windham spoke beautifully, though in his general doctrines on the subject of Parliamentary Reform I differ with him.' (Howick MSS.) The Whig Party remained divided on this subject right down to 1830, and the problem of Party unity

[*The King's reply, Windsor Castle, 12 May.*] The King highly approves the firm and manly course which Mr. Perceval took in the debate last night in regard to Mr. Maddock's Motion, and his Majesty sincerely rejoyces that the sentiments of so great a majority of the House of Commons have been so decidedly given against the Motion & the further purpose connected with it. (14409)

3877 LORD MULGRAVE *to the* KING, *and the reply*

[*Admiralty, 12 May 1809.*] Lord Mulgrave begs permission to submit to your Majesty the annexed extracts of records relating to the rewards established by the custom of the Navy for such officers and seamen as shall distinguish themselves in the desperate enterprize of fire-ship attacks, together with an extract of an Order-in-Council extending similar rewards to Lieutenants borne in fireships. Lord Mulgrave humbly submits to your Majesty that by a comparison of the conduct of Capt. Wooldridge[1] of the Mediator with that of the officers mentioned in the records of the Admiralty, the services & enterprize of the former appear to have even surpassed those of his predecessors. Capt. Wooldridge had determined not to quit his ship till he should have placed her in contact with that of the French Admiral. Capt. Wooldridge with this view had placed the seamen of the Mediator in the boat provided for their escape, the Captain continuing in the ship with his Lieutenant & the gunner after he had set fire to her; he continued steering her himself towards the enemy after the foremast had been for ten minutes in flames, & the main mast had taken fire; but a sudden explosion of powder blew Capt. Wooldridge & his two gallant associates into the sea, at the time that he had every reason to hope for the accomplishment of his heroick purpose. The gunner perished; but the Capt. & Lieutenant were taken up, the former much scorched. Lord Mulgrave humbly submits to your Majesty that Capt. Wooldridge is deserving of the Gold Chain & Medal, and begs your Majesty's permission to revive the ancient practice of the Navy by the distribution of rewards to Capt. Wooldridge & to such other officers and seamen as may appear to have deserved that high distinction in the brilliant & successful enterprize in Basque Roads. (14410-11)

was solved in some measure by treating the question as an 'open one', just as Catholic emancipation was so treated by the Tory Party. Grey, consequently, was excessively pessimistic in saying: 'The Party is in fact dissolved, and I am convinced it is the best way openly to declare that it is so, as affording the only chance of re-uniting a set of men who may be able to pull better together, but at all events to relieve those who stand nominally at the head of the Party from all embarrassment and responsibility of that situation whilst they are unable to control or to direct its inferior members.' (*Ibid.*, 13 May.)

Sir Arthur Wellesley did not yet know the Christian name of the future Prime Minister, to be his colleague for many years. When still Irish Secretary he wrote to Sir Charles Saxton, the Under-Secretary of State (Civil Department) in Dublin, on 25 March: 'I have moved for a new writ for the city of Cashell in the room of Mr. Quintin Dick; and I shall be obliged to you if you will let Mr. Pennefather [patron of Cashel] know that the person who I wish should be returned is Mr. Peel. I will let you know his Christian name by express tomorrow. We wish to have him returned by the meeting of Parlt. after the Recess.' (State Paper Office, Dublin Castle, 539/290/6/82.) He wrote again to Saxton on 10 April, from Portsmouth: 'In answer to your letter of the 4th I have to say that I never heard of the issue of a sum of 100 guineas to Mr. Pennefather upon the change of the Member for Cashell, and that no such claim was made at the time the arrangement was made that Govt. should have the nomination to the borough.' (*Ibid.*, 539/290/6/90; *Wellington Supplementary Despatches* [*Ireland*], pp. 619, 646.)

[1] William Woolridge. Lieutenant, 1794; Captain, 1807.

[*The King's reply, Windsor Castle, 13 May.*] The King entirely approves of Lord Mulgrave's proposal that the ancient practice of the Navy should be revived by the distribution of rewards to Captain Wooldridge who so greatly distinguished himself in the late enterprize in Basque Roads, and to such other officers & seamen as may appear to have deserved them. (14411)

3878 *Letters from* GEORGE CANNING *to the* KING, *and the replies*

[*House of Commons, Friday morning, 12 May, 2.30 [1809].*] Mr. Canning, in the absence of Mr Perceval, thinks it his duty most humbly to acquaint your Majesty that the Motion of Mr. Maddox is happily disposed of by a division of 310 to 85. The course of the debate was as follows. After Mr. Maddox had spoken Mr. Perceval shortly submitted himself to the judgement of the House[1] & withdrew, & Lord Castlereagh followed. Mr. Maddox then moved that 'the charge against Mr Perceval & Lord Castlereagh be heard at the Bar of this House.' Lord Milton moved as an Amendment that it be 'referred to a Select Committee.' Mr Cartwright opposed the Motion *in toto* on the ground of its being intended to lead to Parliamentary reform. Mr Curwen & Mr Biddulph supported it. Sir Charles Mordaunt opposed it. Sir Francis Burdett supported. Mr Davies Giddy opposed. Mr Tierney took a middle line, & proposed an Amendment to refer to examination only so much of the charge as related to the advice given to Mr. Quintin Dick to *resign* his seat: omitting the part which related to the purchase of the seat. Mr Whitbread answered Mr Tierney with a violent speech in favour of Parliamentary reform. Mr. Bragge Bathurst answered Mr Whitbread. Mr. Ponsonby followed Mr Tierney's line. Lord Folkestone answered Mr Ponsonby. Mr. Windham spoke strongly and ably against Parliamentary reform. Lord Archibald Hamilton for it. Mr Wilberforce for the enquiry. Mr. Canning in support of Mr. Cartwright's opposition to it. Col. Hutchinson & Mr. Peter Moore (as far as could be collected) for it. The division took place on the main question, the Amendments of Lord Milton & Mr. Tierney having been previously negatived without division. Included is a copy of Mr. Maddox's Motion. (14412–3)[2]

[1] 'In a most proper and manly manner,' said R. S. Dundas, writing to the Duke of Richmond on the 12th. (Richmond MSS.)

[2] *Parl. Deb.*, XIV, 486–527 (11 May). R. S. Dundas wrote to the Duke of Richmond on the 12th, commenting on the division: 'This is rather a damper upon Jacobinism.' He added: 'Lord Gower, Grattan, Wilberforce, and Charles Grant, were among the minority; Ponsonby, Windham, Sir J. Anstruther, Sir John Newport and Parnell in the majority. Lord Henry Petty and Tierney & Adam did not vote on the main question. Lord Temple, Wm. Elliot and the two Wynn's went away about an hour before the division.' (Richmond MSS.) Castlereagh wrote to his brother on the 12th about the debate ('my second impeachment'): 'I thought that it might not have come to *my* turn during the present Session to be again accused, but I was mistaken. I had however a companion, and you will observe that the House disposed of the question with a high hand. We required some decisive vote to commit our friends against the Reformers, and none could more opportunely have arisen. Perceval and I could have no difficulty in explaining the transaction so as to have taken from it all real awkwardness. We did not think it right, however, to make a bad precedent by a premature defence, and as the House dismiss'd the complaint by a majority of nearly 4 to 1 upon the simple statement, the vote may be considered as the more decisive against the Reformers. The Old Opposition were as usual shabby, not coming forward boldly to crush the attempt. Windham was the only decided person—Ponsonby,

[The King's reply, Windsor Castle, 12 May.] The King has received great satisfaction from the report which Mr. Canning has made of the proceedings in the House of Commons last night during Mr. Perceval's absence from the House. (14413)

[From Canning, Foreign Office, 13 May.] The inclosed letters from Mr. Horne & Mr. Nicholas[1] containing accounts more satisfactory than have yet been received of the operations of the Austrian armies, Mr. Canning humbly hopes that your Majesty may be graciously pleased to forgive his intruding upon your Majesty at an unusual hour. Mr. Canning felt it the rather his duty to do so, as Mr. Nicholas's letter, & a German paper to which he refers, contains an account of the death of the Duke of Brunswick-Lunenburgh-Bevern. (14415)

[From Colonel Taylor, Windsor, 13 May.] The King has honored me with his commands to acknowledge the receipt of your letter of this day and to return you his thanks for the early communication of the accompanying intelligence, which appears upon the whole far more satisfactory than there was reason to expect from the general nature of the reports previously received. (Harewood MSS.)

3879   THE KING *to the* DUCHESS OF BRUNSWICK

[Windsor Castle, 14 May 1809.] I acknowledge with many thanks the receipt of your letter of yesterday informing me of the death of the Duke of Bevern, which I shall consider as the official notice of that event and order the mourning accordingly. I am also obliged to you for the communication of the Duke of Brunswick's letter, and I have much pleasure in acquainting you that from the intelligence which I received yesterday from Germany, the general state of affairs appears

not succeeding in getting out of the House altogether, voted with the majority. His speech was useful, but unnecessarily *gross* in its admissions... Tierney... made a very good speech, but tried towards the end of it to give the charge a malicious turn against me. Petty, Tierney, Temple, etc. went away but in general the Party voted against, in which they were join'd by Wilberforce and the Saints. Nothing could be better than the tone of the House. The country gentlemen consider'd it as a *revolutionary* and not a personal vote, and having exhausted their scruples upon my former question (on which several voted against) they were ready and determined to negative this, whatever might be the statement made by Madocks, considering that the fate of half the House and all the public men in it would by the admission of such an enquiry be placed in Burdett's hands.

'This question and that of the preceding Tuesday on the campaign in Spain, on which we divided 230–111, have put our friends in great heart, and given the Government much more weight than they have yet had. The battle was last night waged for us without the necessity of a single ministerial speech except a short one from Canning at the close of the debate. The Opposition were firing into each other's ranks in every direction—Tierney at Burdett, Whitbread at Tierney—Bragge at Whitbread and Folkestone at Windham—nothing could indicate more division on their part, or determined union on ours than this debate did. It was the more satisfactory, coming after some very weak divisions on our side, which gave the Opposition so strong a notion that our friends were grown indifferent that Lord Grey was sent for back from Northumberland. The express call'd him up in consequence of our only shewing a majority of 25 on some enquiry question, and he found us at the head of two divisions in which we had 119 and 225 majority. We now begin to look to terminating the Session with a higher hand than we expected. Perceval thinks the business may be out of the House of Commons soon after the Birthday.' (Londonderry MSS.)

[1] The British representative in Heligoland.

more satisfactory than there had been reason to hope from the previous accounts. P.S.—As to your own mourning, you will of course use your discretion in regard to the nature & period of it. (16786)

3880   LORD MULGRAVE to the KING

[*Admiralty, 16 May 1809.*] Lord Mulgrave has the honour to transmit to your Majesty dispatches from Rear-Admiral Sir Alexander Cochrane giving intelligence of the arrival of the L'Orient squadron of three sail of the line & two frigates at the anchorage of the Saints near Guadaloupe; and holding out the most satisfactory expectation of the capture of the enemy's ships, subject only to the possible contingency of unfavourable circumstances of weather. (14416)

3881   THE DUKE OF PORTLAND to the KING, and the reply

[*Burlington House, Thursday, 18 May 1809.*] In obedience to your Majesty's commands the Duke of Portland acquainted the Bishop of Bangor[1] with the inclination your Majesty had graciously condescended to express, to translate him to the See of London; in answer to which communication the Duke of Portland has received a letter from the Bishop so descriptive of his submission to your Majesty & of his gratitude for this mark of your Majesty's favorable opinion of him that the Duke of Portland cannot, in justice to the Bishop, but request your Majesty's permission to lay it at your Majesty's feet. (14417)

[*The King's reply, Windsor Castle, 19 May.*] The King acknowledges the receipt of the Duke of Portland's letter & returns him his thanks for the communication of that addressed to him by the Bishop of Bangor. (14418)

3882   SPENCER PERCEVAL to the KING, and the reply

[*Downg. Street, Friday, 19 May [1809].*] Mr. Perceval acquaints your Majesty that Mr. Parnell[2] brought forward this evening in the Ho. of Commons a Motion for leave to bring in a Bill to enable the clergy to lease their tythes to their parishioners in Ireland for 21 years. This measure introducing an alteration into the state of the law respecting tythes, and not appearing to Mr. Perceval to be likely under any modifications which Mr Parnell had suggested to be capable of being usefully adopted, he thought it better to oppose its introduction in the first instance—and after a debate of some length, in which there appeared more disposition to entertain at a future Session a proposition for the alteration of the

---

[1] John Randolph; translated to London, 9 August.
[2] Sir Henry Brooke Parnell, 1st Baron Congleton (1776–1842). Second son of Sir John Parnell, 2nd Baronet [I.]. Succeeded as Baronet, 30 July 1812. M.P. for Maryborough, 1797–1800, in the last Irish Parliament; for Queen's County, April–June 1802; for Portarlington, July–Dec. 1802; for Queen's County, 1806–32; for Dundee, 1833–41. A Lord of the Treasury [I.], 1806–7; Secretary at War, 1831–2; Treasurer of the Navy, 1835–6; Paymaster-General, 1835–41. Created Peer, 18 Aug. 1841.

law of tythes, especially amongst the Irish members, than what could be wished (altho they pretty generally concurred in thinking it not adviseable to introduce it in this Session), the House divided, when there were against bringing in the Bill, 132,[1] for the Bill, 62.

The House then proceeded upon Mr. Curwen's Bill when a debate arose upon the Speaker's leaving the Chair, in which, after Mr. Cockburn[2] had spoke against the principle of the Bill, Sir Watkin Wms. Wynn for it, and Mr Geo. Johnstone against it, Lord Milton moved to adjourn the debate till Thursday next—and it appearing clear that the debate would not be finished in the course of that sitting the House agreed to the adjournment. (14419)

[*The King's reply, Windsor Castle, 20 May.*] The King is glad to find from Mr Perceval's report that Mr. Parnell's Motion relative to the leasing of tythes in Ireland for 21 years was successfully resisted, and his Majesty is well assured that his Government, sensible as it must be of the tendency of such proposals, will carefully watch the proceedings of those disposed to encourage them and will endeavour to prevent their gaining ground. (14420)

3883   GEORGE CANNING *to the* KING, *and the reply*

[*Foreign Office, 20 May 1809.*] Mr. Canning, in pursuance of your Majesty's gracious permission has directed it to be notified to the Foreign Ministers that your Majesty will be pleased to receive them at the Queen's Palace on Wednesday: on which day Don Pedro Cevallos might with your Majesty's permission, have his Audience of Leave of your Majesty. (14421)

[*The King's reply, Windsor Castle, 21 May.*] The King approves of Mr Canning's proposal that Don Pedro Cevallos should have his Audience of Leave on Wednesday next. (14421)

3884   THE DUKE OF PORTLAND *to the* KING,[3] *and the reply*

[*Bulstrode, Sunday, 21 May 1809.*] The late Lieutenant-General Moore's mother and sister having positively declined, in favour of one of their brothers, who is a surgeon with a very large family, to avail themselves of the pension of six hundred pounds a year which your Majesty had been graciously pleased to confer on them; that circumstance created such a sensation in the House of Commons, that your Majesty's confidential servants there deemed it highly inexpedient, if not

---

[1] The number should be 137. (Colchester, II, 187.) And see Perceval's letter to the Speaker, 23 May. (*Ibid.*, II, 188.)

[2] Nicholas William Ridley-Colborne, Baron Colborne (1779–1854), second son of Sir Matthew White Ridley, 2nd Baronet. Took name of Colborne after that of Ridley, in compliance with the will of his mother's brother, William Colborne, June 1803; Whig M.P. for Bletchingley, 1805–6; for Malmesbury, 1806–7; for Appleby, 1807–12; for Thetford, 1818–26; for Horsham, 1827–32; for Wells, 1834–7. Peerage, 15 May 1839.

[3] Not in the Duke's own hand.

impracticable, to resist its effects. They have accordingly desired the Duke of Portland most dutifully to lay their humble opinions before your Majesty, that it would be highly adviseable for your Majesty to consent to the transfer of Mrs. Moore's intended pension to her son the surgeon, and, notwithstanding the very reduced state of the Pension Fund, to permit it to be increased from six hundred to one thousand pounds per annum, agreeably to the expectations of the House of Commons.[1] (14422–3)

[*The King's reply, Windsor Castle, 22 May.*] The King, in consideration of what is expressed by the Duke of Portland, will not object to the augmentation of the pension proposed to be given to Mr. James Moore, at the same time that the Duke of Portland will readily conceive that, after all that has passed lately upon that subject, his Majesty cannot confer it very willingly. (14423)

3885   LORD MULGRAVE *to the* KING, *and the reply*

[*Admiralty, 22 May 1809.*] Lord Mulgrave has the honour to transmit to your Majesty a dispatch from Vice-Admiral Sir Alexander Cochrane announcing the capture of a ship of the enemy of 74 guns by your Majesty's ship Pompée after a severe action. The captured ship was one of the L'Orient squadron; the other two line-of-battle ships of the enemy, with two frigates, have escaped for the moment. (14424)

[*The King's reply, Windsor Castle, 23 May.*] The King acknowledges the receipt of Lord Mulgrave's letter, enclosing Sir Alexander Cochrane's dispatch which details proceedings very honorable to those concerned in the capture of the French ships which had escaped from the Saints & the capture of one of them. (14424)

3886   *Letters from* SPENCER PERCEVAL *to the* KING, *and the reply*

[*Downg. St., 24 May 1809.*] Mr. Perceval humbly submits for your Majesty's approbation the accompanying Messages to the House of Lords & Commons— which, if your Majesty should be graciously pleased to approve and sign them, Mr. Perceval proposes to make the foundation for a vote of credit for 3,000,000.[2] (14425)

---

[1] The matter is only briefly referred to in *Parl. Deb.*, XIV, 408–9 (8 May). See *Dropmore Papers*, IX, 293. The family accused Ministers of lack of generosity and gratitude. 'I certainly wish them and their £1000 damned for such paltry and miserable conduct,' wrote Graham Moore. (*Creevey's Life and Times*, p. 44.)

[2] *Parl. Deb.*, XIV, 696 (25 May). Though the Treaty of Alliance restoring friendly relations with the Emperor contained no stipulation for financial assistance, the Government proposed to furnish aid both to the Emperor and, as hitherto, to the peoples of Spain and Portugal in their struggle for freedom. No specific sum was mentioned in the Message to the Commons that day. The King's Message respecting a Vote of Credit for £3,000,000 was debated in the Lords on the 26th. (*Ibid.*, 711–13.)

[From Perceval, Downg. St., 24 May.] Mr Perceval acquaints your Majesty that Col. Shipley[1] moved this evening in the House of Commons for the papers referred to in the accompanying paper relative to Lord Burghersh's promotion.[2] Lord Castlereagh opposed the production of them; he contended that nothing could be more inconvenient or more to be deprecated than for the House of Commons to interfere in any question relative to the promotions in your Majesty's army, & that the House would not do so except in some extremely strong case; that in the case in question, tho the promotion had taken place subsequent to the late Order,[3] yet it had been in consequence of a promise communicated to Lord Burghersh in your Majesty's name, and that it was therefore with reference to that promise that it ought to be viewed. Lord Temple, Col. Hutchinson, Lord Henry Petty, Lord Newark, Meyrick [*sic*] spoke for the papers and Mr Perceval opposed their production. The House divided and there were for the Motion 71, against it 67, so that the papers were ordered. Great dissatisfaction appeared in the House, Mr Perceval is sorry to say, upon this subject.[4] (14426)

[The King's reply, Windsor Castle, 25 May.] The King acknowledges the receipt of Mr. Perceval's report of the division upon Colonel Shipley's Motion relative to the promotion of Lord Burghersh which his Majesty has learnt with regret. (14426)

3887   *Letters from* VISCOUNT CASTLEREAGH *to the* KING, *and the reply*

[St. James's Sq., 24 May 1809.] Lord Castlereagh humbly submits to your Majesty a memorandum which Captain Stanhope[5] received from Lt.-Col. Bathurst[6] on the morning of the 14th as he was leaving Oporto, which although written in

---

   [1] William Shipley (*c.* 1778–1820), Whig M.P. for St. Mawes, 1807; and 1812–13; for Flint, 1807–12. He was connected by marriage with the Grenvilles, his wife, Charlotte, being a daughter of Sir Watkin Williams Wynn, 4th Baronet, and the granddaughter of George Grenville, the Prime Minister.

   [2] John Fane, 11th Earl of Westmorland (1784–1859), styled Lord Burghersh until 15 Dec. 1841, when he succeeded his father. M.P. for Lyme Regis, 1806–16. Ensign, 1803; Lieutenant, 1804; Captain, 1805; Assistant Adjutant-General in Sicily and Egypt, 1806–7, and in Portugal, 1808; Extra A.D.C. to Sir Arthur Wellesley, in Portugal and Spain, 1809; Lieutenant-Colonel, 1811; Major-General, 1825; Lieutenant-General, 1838; General, 1854. Minister at Florence, 1814–30; at Berlin, 1841–51; Ambassador at Vienna, 1851–5.

   Shipley complained of Lord Burghersh's excessively rapid promotion in defiance of Army Regulations (no officer was to be made a field officer until he had served nine years, nor a Lieutenant-Colonel for two years after becoming a Major). On 4 May Burghersh had been appointed to a Majority, and a few days later made a Lieutenant-Colonel, with the result that he passed over the heads of 600 officers, many of whom were in the army before he was born. Castlereagh, in reply, defended the King's right to dispense with Regulations in order to reward exceptional zeal, activity and enterprise. Burghersh had laid aside 'all the soft and seducing allurements of pleasure at home' to devote himself to the service of his country abroad. For the outcome, see Nos. 3893–4.

   [3] Dated 20 March 1809. It extended from six years to nine the period of service between the gazetting of an officer and his becoming a field officer.

   [4] *Parl. Deb.*, XIV, 670–7. The numbers should be 72 *v.* 67. (*H. of C. J.*, LXIV, 341.)

   [5] Major Stanhope's brother.

   [6] Sir James Bathurst (d. 1850). Major, 1803; Lieutenant-Colonel, 1805; Colonel, 1813; Major-General, 1819; Lieutenant-General, 1837. K.C.B., 1831.

a hurry will serve to explain the movements of the enemy after the action of the 12th.[1]

Sir Arthur Wellesley moved on the 14th towards Braga.[2] It appears that a letter from Lt.-Col. Doyle had apprized Sir Arthur Wellesley of the French division which was on march from Arragon by Burgos to reinforce Soult, and he will have been enabled to regulate his measures accordingly. The German Regt. of Lt. Dragoons had arrived and were order'd to disembark at Mondego.

Lord Castlereagh also transmits for your Majesty's information the report of a reconnaissance made by Capt. Mellish[3] on the 13th.

Lt.-Genl. Paget's[4] arm was amputated after the action; he was otherwise well and likely to recover favorably. (14429–30)

[*The King's reply, Windsor Castle, 25 May.*] The King acknowledges the receipt of Lord Castlereagh's letter and the accompanying communications relative to the operations of Sir Arthur Wellesley's army in Portugal which appear generally satisfactory, and highly to the credit of those engaged in them. His Majesty sincerely regrets the severe wound which Lieut.-General Paget has received, but hopes that the accounts which have been received of his doing well will be fully confirmed. (14430)

[*From Castlereagh, Downing Street, 25 May.*] Your Majesty's confidential servants upon a full consideration of the efforts making by the enemy to reinforce their army in Gallicia by a corps of from 12 to 15,000 men detach'd from Arragon (via Burgos) for that purpose; and the critical situation in which the British army may be placed in Portugal, if it should be threaten'd by a force of equal strength with itself on each of its flanks, beg leave humbly to submit for your Majesty's consideration the expediency of reinforcing Sir Arthur Wellesley to the extent of 5000 infantry, exclusive of the Light Brigade now under orders for Portugal.

Your Majesty's servants humbly conceive that a corps of this extent may be

[1] Sir Arthur Wellesley had been sent out to supersede Sir John Cradock, who was appointed to the command of Gibraltar, and his strength, with the arrival of reinforcements, amounted to about 30,000 men. See No. 3844. On 12 May Wellesley forced the passage of the Douro and drove Soult from Oporto, which he had captured on 29 March.

[2] In pursuit of Soult's retreating army.

[3] Captain Mellish was Assistant Adjutant-General in Wellesley's army.

[4] Sir Edward Paget (1775–1849), one of Lord Anglesey's brothers. Entered the army, 1792; Major, 1793; Lieutenant-Colonel, 1794; Colonel, 1798; Major-General, 1805; Lieutenant-General, 1811 (local rank, 1809); General, 1825. Governor of Ceylon, 1821–3. G.C.B., 1812; M.P. for Carnarvon, 1796–1806; for Milborne Port, 1810–20. He had commanded the reserve at Corunna, and he lost his right arm in the action on 12 May. The Duke of Kent mistakenly believed that he was to be sent to Gibraltar. The Duke wrote to his friend Colonel Robert Wright, 5 Sept.: 'I am truly concerned that it did not suit my old friend Sir John Craddock to remain in the command at Gibraltar, for I agree with you entirely in opinion that there never was a man better cut out for it, from his mild and conciliatory measures, as well as for his good sense and judgement. At present General Paget is named to succeed him & Major General Fraser, the one-legged one who is famous for his defence of Goree, to be under him. The Paget family in general are remarkable for their hauteur, at least such is the character of the 3 elder brothers, but I believe Edward, the one now destined to be my locum tenens at Gibraltar, is different from the rest, & that besides being a thorough good soldier, he is a perfect gentleman. I am not, however, on any terms of intimacy with him.' (46401–4)

drawn from the Regts. now station'd in Ireland, and the Islands of Jersey and Guernsey, without improperly reducing their respective garisons—and without breaking in upon the large disposeable force at present in Gt. Britain, so as to interfere with the execution of any service to which it might be in your Majesty's contemplation to apply it.

They are induced the rather to recommend this arrangement for your Majesty's sanction, as in whatever proportion it may operate to render the position of the British army secure in Portugal, it will enable Sir Arthur Wellesley to place at the disposal of your Majesty's Government a considerable proportion, if not the whole, of the transport tonnage which is now detain'd at a heavy expence in the Tagus, and without the assistance of which, Lord Castlereagh apprehends it will be extremely difficult in the present state of the commercial marine of the country to provide the means of rendering any considerable proportion of the force at home moveable in the course of this campaign. (14431-2)

[*The King's reply*, *Windsor Castle*, *26 May*.] The King acquiesces in the arrangement which is proposed by Lord Castlereagh for sending a further reinforcement to the army assembled in Portugal under Sir Arthur Wellesley of 5000 infantry. (14432)

3888   *Letters from* SPENCER PERCEVAL *to the* KING, *and the reply*

[*25 May 1809*.] Mr Perceval humbly submits to your Majesty's Majesty's [*sic*] perusal and consideration a return of the number of livings in England and Wales under £150 pr. anm., which has recently been obtained from the Archbishops & Bishops by your Majesty's commands in pursuance of an Address which was presented to your Majesty by the House of Lords in the last Session of Parliament. That return is not complete, as the four Dioceses of St David, Ely, Norwich & Rochester are not included in it. But upon the best estimate which can be made of the number of small livings in those Dioceses, it is conjectured that they will amount to nearly one-third of the number which is contained in the present return. Adding therefore to that number one third, it would appear that there are upwards of 4000 livings in England & Wales under £150 pr annum; about 2000 under 100, and not less than 1160 under £50 pr anm.

Your Majesty will be graciously pleased to observe that it is entirely impossible for the clergyman who derives such small emoluments from his preferment either to reside himself upon his living or to provide a curate with a sufficient salary to maintain that decent appearance amongst his parishioners which is essential to secure him from the contempt to which extreme poverty is so likely to expose him, and altho the deficiency of the provision for the poorer clergy has been generally known before, yet Mr. Perceval submits to your Majesty that when so authentic a document brings this fact under the immediate knowledge of your Majesty and your Parliament your Majesty may be graciously pleased to think it a proper opportunity for distinctly calling the attention of your Parliament to the subject.

Any proposition for the effective remedy and removal of so extensive an evil could not, even if it were already well digested and had been approved by your Majesty, be submitted with any propriety to Parliament at so advanced a period of the Session. But when your Majesty is informed that it would require an annual grant of not less than 100,000 pr an. for *four* years to raise all the livings in England & Wales to no more than between 50 & 60 pr. anm. and that upon the same calculation it would require *25* years to raise them by the same means to £100 pr anm. and about 35 years or upwards to raise them to £150, Mr. Perceval ventures to submit to your Majesty whether your Majesty would not be graciously pleased to authorise him to propose that Parliament should in this Session vote a sum of one hundred thousand pounds, as that sum cannot in any view be excessive, and Mr. Perceval would be disposed with your Majesty's permission to profess [*sic*] to Parliament that your Majesty's servants would during the recess consider of some plan by which a grant to a similar extent might be secured for the same object, accompanied with such regulations as to the residence either of the incumbent or his curate with a sufficient provision and also for the building & repairing dilapidated glebe houses, as might appear to be reasonable.

To the extent of making this grant in the present year Mr Perceval has the satisfaction to acquaint your Majesty that the Archbishop of Canterbury and the Lord Chancellor have been apprized of the idea, and that they heartily concur in the propriety of it.

If your Majesty should be graciously pleased to approve of this suggestion, Mr Perceval conceives that the best mode of directing the attention of Parliament to the subject will be by a Message from your Majesty, and for that purpose Mr Perceval has prepared a Message which he submits for your Majesty's approbation & signature.[1]

Your Majesty will be graciously pleased to observe that the variation between the Message intended for the House of Lords and that for the House of Commons arises from the fact of the return of the number of small livings being already before the House of Lords in pursuance of an Address from that House to your Majesty. (14435–7)

[*From Perceval, 25 May.*] Mr. Perceval regrets to have again to report to your Majesty the decision upon another question in the House of Commons in which your Majesty's servants in vain endeavoured to prevail upon the House to adopt what appeared to them the proper course.

Your Majesty will be graciously pleased to recollect that in the last Session of Parliament Major Palmer had excited a great interest in the House of Commons

---

[1] 'His Majesty having directed returns to be made and certified by the Archbishops and Bishops of England and Wales, of the number of Livings under the value of £150 per annum, and perceiving from those returns that, notwithstanding the operation of the Act passed in the second and third years of her Majesty Queen Anne, for the making more effectual her Majesty's gracious intentions for the augmentation of the maintenance of the poor clergy by enabling her Majesty to grant in perpetuity the revenues of the First Fruits and Tenths, the maintenance belonging to the clergy in divers parts of the kingdom is still mean and insufficient, his Majesty has directed an abstract of those returns, as far as the same have been completed, to be laid before the House of Commons; and if the House of Commons can find any proper method of enabling his Majesty to accelerate the operation of the said Act, it will be a great advantage to the public and very acceptable to his Majesty.' (*Parl. Deb.*, XIV, 715 [26 May].)

upon the subject of his father's claims in regard to the Post Office, and had prevailed upon the House to vote a large sum of money for him which was sent up to the House of Lords in a Bill which was lost in that House.[1]

This evening he moved an Address to your Majesty a copy of which Mr Perceval transmits to your Majesty, in order that your Majesty might give directions that the claim should be brought to a decision in a Court of Law. Your Majesty's Attorney & Solicitor-General, Mr Stephen, Mr Perceval & Mr Canning endeavoured to shew the absurdity of this course of proceeding, but Mr Palmer had interested so many persons in his favor that upon a division there were 127 for it and against it 123.[2] (14433)

[*The King's reply, Windsor Castle, 26 May.*] The King laments to find from Mr Perceval's report of the division upon Mr Palmer's Motion that so large a proportion of the House of Commons may be influenced by private solicitation upon a public question.

His Majesty has signed the Messages to both Houses and entirely approves of the steps which Mr Perceval recommends should be taken for the relief of the poorer clergy in England & Wales. (14433)

3889   LORD MULGRAVE *to the* KING, *and the reply*

[*Admiralty, 25 May 1809.*] Lord Mulgrave has the honour to transmit the minutes of the court martial held at Portsmouth for the trial of Rear-Admiral Harvey, humbly presuming that it may be your Majesty's pleasure to be informed of the proceedings upon which an officer of so high a rank in the Navy has been dismissed from your Majesty's service.[3] (14438)

[*The King's reply, Windsor Castle, 27 May.*] The King returns to Lord Mulgrave the minutes of the court martial held for the trial of Rear-Admiral Harvey which his Majesty received from him yesterday. (14438)

3890   SPENCER PERCEVAL *to the* KING, *and the reply*

[*Downg. St., 27 May 1809.*] Mr Perceval acquaints your Majesty that the House of Commons has been engaged till near three o'clock this morning upon the question that the Speaker should leave the Chair on Mr. Curwen's Bill. Sir Francis Burdett made a very violent speech in which he opposed the Bill as doing nothing that could be useful as nothing in his opinion but a radical reform could be so. He was very ably replied to by Mr Windham and his arguments & conduct very roughly handled by him and Mr Tierney. Mr Windham however opposed

[1] See No. 3671.
[2] *Parl. Deb.*, XIV, 696–711.
[3] Harvey was court-martialled for having publicly expressed his anger at the appointment of Lord Cochrane to a special command at sea. He was reinstated in his rank and seniority in March 1810, in consideration of his long and meritorious services, but was never again employed.

the Bill as well as Sir Francis, but upon very different grounds, Sir Francis apprehending that it would prevent reform, and Mr. Windham that it might lead to it. In general, except these two and Mr Madocks, the House were desirous that the Bill should go into a Committee. The debate in general was very satisfactory as shewing a strong sense in the House against any reform of Parliament, and those who supported the Bill supported it as only an additional provision against bribery. The Bill itself in its present form is given up by everybody, but it seems to be a pretty general opinion that if it can be cut down, which Mr. Perceval rather thinks it may, to a mere provision to prevent the sale of a seat for a sum of money, as an act of bribery, and to vacate the seat so procured, submitting the trial of the question to a Committee of the House of Commons, that it would be adviseable so to pass it. But as it cannot be seen till it comes out of the Committee what the Bill may be Mr Perceval has distinctly reserved giving any decided opinion upon it till he sees it after the amendments which may be introduced into it.

The House did not at last divide upon the qu. but it was too late to go into the Committee.[1] (14439–40)

[*The King's reply, Windsor Castle, 27 May.*] The King is glad to find from Mr Perceval's report of what passed in the House of Commons last night that the generality of the members are disposed to view the present attempt at a reform of Parliament in the proper light. (14440)

3891   GEORGE CANNING *to the* KING, *and the reply*

[*Foreign Office, 27 May 1809.*] Mr. Canning most humbly acquaints your Majesty that having received from Mr. Brinkmann in a conference this day an official notification of the abdication and deposition of the King of Sweden, he has thought it right, in reply to a question put to him by Mr. Brinkmann, to intimate to him that his publick character must be considered as at an end; & to advise his not presenting himself at Court on your Majesty's birthday. This event having been known only through Mr Foster on Wednesday last, Mr Canning did not then interpose to prevent Mr Brinkmann from paying his respects to your Majesty on that day. Mr Brinkmann's communication having been only verbal Mr. Canning has thought it his duty to endeavour to obtain a repetition of it in writing.[2] (14441–2)

---

[1] *Parl. Deb.*, XIV, 717–84. Burdett 'was loudly and indignantly called to order for saying that "since the sale of seats in this House was openly avowed, it was no longer to be called the Commons House of Parliament"'. (Colchester, II, 193.) 'Burdett got badgered to your heart's content last night by everybody,' Tierney wrote to Grey. (Howick MSS.)

[2] Augustus Foster, whom Canning had sent on a mission to Sweden, informed the Foreign Office that the Queen of Sweden had expressed a strong inclination to be allowed to live in England with her husband, England being the only country where they could be away from Napoleon's influence. The Swedish Diet was prepared to make him an allowance, and he expected no pecuniary aid from Great Britain. The application was hardly welcomed by Canning, who replied that an asylum alone could be granted and that his residence in or anywhere near London would be highly inconvenient. The ex-King came to England in Nov. 1810.

3892   THE DUKE OF PORTLAND *to the* KING[1], *and the reply*

[*Burlington House*, *Sunday*, *28 May 1809*.] The Duke of Portland most humbly
begs leave to represent to your Majesty that the peculiarity of the circumstances
out of which the war with Denmark arose having led to various applications on
the part of your Majesty's subjects trading to that country for indemnification
for the losses they have sustained, either by the direct confiscation of their property
by the Danes or by the payment of the debts due to them from Danish subjects
being withheld, or by means of other causes which have been ascribed to the
Danish war; it has been a subject of very anxious deliberation between the Chancellor of the Exchequer and Mr. Secretary Canning, assisted by your Majesty's
Advocate, whether at all, or to what extent, it may be proper to recommend to
your Majesty to comply with the prayer of those applications—and, upon the
best consideration given to it by those gentlemen, they have not been able to lay
down any principle upon which they can venture to advise such a step to be taken
which would not be liable to the most solid objection, either as countenancing
claims which have never yet been admitted, or suggesting and holding out encouragement to the enemy to commence the war by the confiscation of the
property of your Majesty's subjects, and the sequestration of the debts which
might be due to them.

These considerations however having led the gentlemen above-mentioned to
be of opinion that it could not be recommended to your Majesty, consistently
with the interests of your people, to admit the claims of the sufferers, they deemed
it no less material to guard the decision which your Majesty may be advised to
come to, against any suspicion of being influenced by any other motive than that
of promoting the attainment of some great publick and national object; and in
this view it would be that they wish most humbly to submit to your Majesty that
the excess beyond what your Majesty may be graciously pleased to direct to
be paid to the captors of this property should be applied in ease of some national
expence, and none has occurred so appropriate to them, or so little objectionable
as the purchase from the captors of the ships which were captured at Copenhagen,
a very large proportion of the value of which has been granted by your Majesty
to the captors.

This measure having been fully discussed and concurred in by the parties to
the deliberations respecting it, warrants were directed by the Chancellor of the
Exchequer to be prepared for your Majesty's royal signature, provided, on the
statement of the proceedings to your Majesty, it should be so fortunate as to be
approved by your Majesty—and here it is necessary for the Duke of Portland,
in compliance with the most anxious request of the Chancellor of the Exchequer,
and in consideration of the multiplicity and pressure of the business which he
has to go through, and his necessary and long and late attendances in the House

---

[1] Not in the Duke's own hand.

of Commons, most humbly to intreat your Majesty to forgive the inadvertence he has committed in suffering the warrants to be submitted to your Majesty, prior to the foregoing statement being laid before your Majesty, and to permit him and the Duke of Portland to express their humble but anxious hope that the measure herewith most humbly recommended to your Majesty will meet with your Majesty's sanction and confirmation of it. (14443–6)

[*The King's reply, Windsor Castle, 29 May.*] The King approves of the grounds upon which the Duke of Portland has recommended that the excess beyond what may be paid to the captors of Danish property should be applied to the purchase of the ships which were captured at Copenhagen. (14447)

3893   THE EARL OF WESTMORLAND *to the* KING, *and the reply*

[*29 May [1809].*] The situation which has arisen upon your Majesty's gracious favor to Lord Burghersh makes me feel it a duty in his name & mine to make my humble request to your Majesty to withold the promotion, the Commissions not being yet signed.

   Painful as this request is to my feelings, as I must confess my pride has been that Lord Burghersh had by his zeal & spirit in the profession shewn himself deserving of your Majesty's distinction of him, yet most unhappy shd. I be if any interest or wish of me or my family shod. at these alarming times produce questions & discussions either affecting the right & prerogatives of your Majesty or embarrassing to your Government.

   In humbly therefore solliciting your Majesty to stop the grant of this inestimable favor, permit me in his name & mine to make our most respectful & heartfelt thanks for this special mark of your kindness, & that as we shall by our gratitude shew our due sense, so I trust by our dutiful & zealous attachment to your Majesty deserve a continuance of your gracious protection. (14448–9)

[*The King's reply, Windsor Castle, 30 May.*] The King acknowledges the receipt of Lord Westmorland's letter and his Majesty is sensible of the motives which induce Lord Westmorland to decline availing himself of his intentions in favor of his son Lord Burghersh. (14453)

3894   THE EARL OF LIVERPOOL *to the* KING, *and the reply*

[*London, 29 May 1809.*] Lord Westmorland having express'd his intention, in consequence of the irritation produced in the publick mind by the discussion of the question respecting Lord Burghersh's promotion, to solicit your Majesty not to allow the promotion to be compleated, Lord Liverpool begs leave most humbly to communicate to your Majesty the opinion of your confidential servants that your Majesty would be graciously pleased to comply with the request which has been so handsomely made by Lord Westmorland.

When the Motion was made for the papers relative to this transaction in the House of Commons on Wednesday last, the explanation given on the occasion by Lord Castlereagh and Mr Perceval rested upon the point that this departure from the new Regulations lately issued by your Majesty's direction, arose in consequence of your Majesty having been graciously pleased previously to promise that Lord Burghersh should have the rank of Lieutenant-Colonel in the Army as soon as he had compleated the six years service required by the former Regulations; and which they understood had been compleated in the month of March last; Lord Burghersh's first commission having been dated in March 1803. The correctness of this statement was disputed by those who made the Motion for the papers in the House of Commons, and the Gazette was produced, to prove that Lord Burghersh had not been gazetted as an Ensign till the month of Decr. 1803, and that even under the former Regulations therefore the promotion could not be justified.

Upon inquiry, it turns out that your Majesty's pleasure with respect to Lord Burghersh's first commission was not taken till the month of Decr. 1803, but that the commission was ante-dated from the March preceeding. The Lord Chancellor is strongly inclined to entertain an opinion that antedating any original commission where no service can have been performed, and giving it validity for any period, antecedent to that at which your Majesty's approbation of the appointment was signified, is in itself illegal, and though there are numerous cases in which this practice may have prevailed, it has not hitherto been noticed, but there can be no doubt of its becoming a most prominent topick of discussion in any future debate which may take place on this subject, and it is humbly submitted to your Majesty that it is most desireable to avoid such a discussion, especially at this time, not only with reference to this particular case, but to many other past transactions.

Lord Liverpool begs leave to inform your Majesty that neither the commission for the Majority nor that for the Lieutenant-Colonel have yet been prepared, and he therefore requests (in conformity to Lord Westmorland's application) to receive your Majesty's gracious pleasure that no further progress should be made in compleating these commissions, and that the usual article should be inserted in the Gazette. (14450–2)

[*The King's reply, Windsor Castle, 30 May.*] In consequence of what is represented in Lord Liverpool's letter, the King approves of his suggestion that the late promotions of Lord Burghersh to a Majority & Lieut.-Colonelcy should be declared not to have taken place.[1] (14452)

[1] This was referred to in the Commons by Lieutenant-Colonel Shipley who, on 1 June, congratulated the country on the victory which had been gained over the Administration. (*Parl. Deb.*, XIV, 833.) Tierney heard that the affair had annoyed the King, who, he said, was 'quite outrageous against Lord Westmorland.' (To Grey, 27 May. [Howick MSS.].)

Lieutenant-Colonel Taylor had written to Colonel J. W. Gordon, Military Secretary to the Commander-in-Chief, on 13 April: 'I am honoured with the King's commands to transmit to you for the information and guidance of General Sir David Dundas the enclosed copy of a letter written by his Majesty's direction to H.R.H. the Duke of York relative to Lord Burghersh's claim to promotion by

19-2

[*Downing Street, 1 June 1809.*] Mr Perceval acquaints your Majesty that he proposed this evening in the House of Commons the encrease in the salaries of the Judges of England & Wales, which your Majesty was graciously pleased to approve. Mr Perceval proposed £1000 pr anm. to the Chief Baron & the Puisné Judges, and three hundred a year upon the Welch Judges. The House received the proposition with great satisfaction, and Mr Williams Wynn having moved £500 instead of £300, and Mr Horner[1] proposed £400 which last sum was adopted.

The House then proceeded to Mr Curwen's Bill, and resolved itself into a Committee. The Speaker made a very able and impressive speech upon the subject, agreeing in the principle of the Bill, tho' he objected to Mr Curwen's provisions. Mr Perceval proposed an Amendment confining the provisions of the Bill to the bribery of persons whether they have votes at the election or not, in order to procure a return, & vacating the seat of the person so elected, and inflicting as a penalty upon the person receiving the gift the forfeiture of the sum given, and £500 besides. These Amendments were received upon an agreement that the Bill should be reprinted and the further consideration of it is postponed till next Tuesday.[2] (14461)

3896 *Letters from* GEORGE CANNING *to the* KING, *and the replies*

[*Foreign Office, 2 June 1809.*] Mr. Canning most humbly requests your Majesty's gracious commands as to the answer to be returned to the offer by the Supreme Junta of 4000 merino sheep as a present to your Majesty. (14462)

[*The King's reply, Queen's Palace, 3 June.*] The King desires Mr Canning will assure Don Pedro Cevallos that he is very sensible of the attention of the Supreme Junta in offering a present of 4000 sheep, but that his Majesty has already so large a stock as not to require further supply, for the accomodation of which he has not indeed the means to provide. Independent of this the last sent from the Asturias were so improperly crowded on board the transports as to occasion very great mortality and, to provide conveniently for the conveyance of so large an additional number, ships must be sent which are required for other pressing services. Upon the same grounds the King thinks it would be adviseable to decline equally the offer of the horses at this moment. (14462)

purchase, in consequence of the promise made to Lord Westmorland previous to the establishment of the late Regulation.' The following was enclosed: 'Period required for an officer to serve before he could obtain promotion prior to the late Regulations. Two years in the Service before an officer can obtain the rank of Captain. Six years in the Service before an officer can obtain the rank of Major.' (Blair Adam MSS.)

[1] Francis Horner (1778–1817), Whig M.P. for St. Ives, 1806–7; for Wendover, 1807–12; for St. Mawes, 1813–17. A well-known economist.

[2] *Parl. Deb.*, XIV, 833–51. See also P.R.O. 30/9/15 for Perceval's long and interesting letter to the Speaker, 23 May, in which he discussed the Speaker's proposed amendments to the Bill and indicated the extent to which he agreed with them.

[*From Canning, Foreign Office, 3 June.*] Mr. Canning most humbly submits to your Majesty whether, as Mr. Henry Wellesley's private affairs[1] do not allow of his accompanying the Marquis Wellesley to Spain, in the first instance, as Secretary to the Embassy, your Majesty would be graciously pleased to approve of the appointment of Mr. Bartholomew Frere to that situation until such time as Mr. Wellesley may be enabled to repair to Seville.

Mr Canning most humbly submits a draft to Mr. Frere, to this effect, for your Majesty's gracious consideration. (14463)

[*The King's reply, Queen's Palace, 4 June.*] The King acquiesces in Mr. Canning's proposal that Mr Bartholomew Frere should receive the temporary appointment of Secretary of Embassy to the Spanish Government.[2] (14464)

3897   THE KING *to* PRINCESS AMELIA

[*Queen's Palace, 5 June 1809.*] I thank you sincerely for the very kind letter which I received from you yesterday and I am truly sensible of the warmth of your affection for me and of the manner in which you express yourself on the occasion of my birthday. I need not tell you how much I regret your absence, particularly as it is occasioned by illness, but I derive some comfort from the assurance that, although the weather has unfortunately not been favourable to you, you have, upon the whole, felt better since I left Windsor, and I trust your progress will keep pace with the anxious wishes of [etc.].[3] (Add. Georgian 14/82.)

3898   *Letters from* VISCOUNT CASTLEREAGH *to the* KING, *and the reply*

[*Downing Str., 5 June 1809.*] Lord Castlereagh begs leave humbly to recommend to your Majesty the Honle. M. General Broderick to be entrusted with the

---

[1] He was overwhelmed by domestic misfortune. His wife, Lady Charlotte (1781–1853), daughter of the 1st Earl Cadogan, had recently run off with Lord Paget (later Marquess of Anglesey), and in 1810 he obtained a divorce. Paget then married her, and found her dearer to him by £24,000 (plus costs) after an action against him for *crim. con.* Robert Ward wrote to Lord Lonsdale on 8 March: 'Lady Charlotte Wellesley seems to have been the utter victim of her seducer, after resisting him long and sincerely; she has even often retained Sir Arthur Wellesley near her in public for the express purpose of avoiding Lord P.'s importunities. She has written to Arbuthnot, W.'s friend, to say she knows she has consigned herself to perdition and unhappiness for life but was irresistibly driven to it by what she could not avoid. Lord P. has written in a similar way to his father, adding he had sought death frequently in Spain, to avoid this misfortune and that the greatest benefit that could now befall him wd. be to have his brains blown out. Wellesley is like one distracted.' (Lonsdale MSS.) He wrote again, three days later: 'I was correct I find in what I stated respecting the elopement, and Ld. Uxbridge, half heart-broken, has written, Pole tells me, in these words to Ly. Charlotte, "Madam, I implore you as an old and dying man, to restore to his father a son; to a disconsolate wife, her husband, and to unprotected children, their father, Uxbridge." Ly. Charlotte resents this as a letter that would not have been written to a housemaid, and Lord P. is profligate enough to intimate to his father that he joins in that resentment. The times seem indeed to be out of joint.' (*Ibid.*)

[2] Bartholomew Frere was Secretary of Legation to Spain, 1808–9, Secretary of Embassy, 1809, and Minister *ad interim* at Seville and Cadiz from Lord Wellesley's departure in Nov. 1809 until Henry Wellesley's arrival as Minister in Feb. 1810.

[3] Princess Amelia wrote from Windsor. In August she was sent to Weymouth in the vain hope that her health would benefit from the sea air.

Government of the Island of Martinique, and that the M. General may at the same time be placed on your Majesty's Staff in the West Indies, the better to unite the civil and military authority within the island. (14465)

[*From Castlereagh, Downing St., 5 June.*] Your Majesty having been graciously pleased to appoint Lt.-Genl. Morrison[1] to be Commander of your Majesty's forces in Jamaica, Lord Castlereagh humbly submits to your Majesty that Genl. Morrison should receive the appointment of Lt.-Governor of the Island, so that upon the death or resignation of the Duke of Manchester the Government may devolve upon him until your Majesty's further pleasure is declared. (14466)

[*The King's reply, Queen's Palace, 6 June.*] The King acquiesces in Lord Castlereagh's proposal that Lieut.-General Morrison should receive the appointment of Lieut.-Governor in the Island of Jamaica, and that M. General Brodrick should be entrusted with the Government of the Island of Martinique, uniting the civil & military authority. (14467)

3899   THE KING *to* LORD ELDON

[*Queen's Palace, 6 June 1809.*] The King, knowing how much the Lord Chancellor's time is engaged in the important duties of his office, has felt unwilling to require his attendance on any extraordinary day, but as his Majesty is desirous of speaking to him before he leaves town, he trusts that the Chancellor will be able to come here tomorrow. (14468)

3900   SPENCER PERCEVAL *to the* KING

[*Downg. St., 7 June 1809.*] Mr Perceval acquaints your Majesty that he moved in the Comee. of Supply this evening the vote for one hundred thousand pounds for the poor clergy, and that the same was extremely well received by the House.[2]

The House went thro Mr Curwen's Bill in the Committee, and reported with the Amendment which Mr Perceval proposed, and it is to be taken into further consideration on Friday next.[3] (14469)

3901   *Letters from* GEORGE CANNING *to the* KING, *and the replies*

[*Foreign Office, 8 June 1809, 3.30 p.m.*] Mr. Canning humbly trusts that your Majesty will graciously forgive his intruding upon your Majesty at an unusual hour with the accounts received from Heligoland & from Mr Horne at Brunn,

---

[1] Edward Morrison (*c.* 1759–1843), Lieutenant-Colonel, 1790; Colonel, 1795; Major-General, 1797; Lieutenant-General, 1805; General, 1814.

[2] The proposal originated with Lord Harrowby, who, on 14 May, wrote the Speaker, 'communicated to me his proposition to Perceval for a grant of £100,000 to augment (this year) all small Livings below £50 a year, on which there were resident clergymen; as part of a plan to be pursued progressively if the Church could be brought in another year to co-operate'. (Colchester, II, 187.)

[3] *Parl. Deb.*, XIV, 920–8.

of the victory obtained by the Archduke Charles on the 21st & 22d May.[1]
Mr. Canning sends with these accounts the French bulletin of the same affair.
(14470)

[*Col. Taylor's reply, Windsor, 8 June, 8.30 p.m.*] I am honored with the King's
commands to acknowledge the receipt of your letter and to return you his thanks
for the early communication of the accompanying intelligence which his Majesty
received with very great pleasure, & which even exceeds the hopes which he had
formed from the accounts given in the French bulletin. His Majesty trusts that
this signal advantage will prove the prelude of further success.

I cannot conclude without congratulating you most heartily upon these aus-
picious events. The King having read the abstract of the 10th bulletin in the
English papers did not order me to read the original French, but upon looking it
over I find the former so loose & incorrect that, if you can spare the Moniteur
tomorrow, I shall be obliged to you to return it that I may read it to the King, as
I trust his Majesty will find it interesting. I have not ventured to keep it, conceiving you might want it. (Harewood MSS.)

[*From Canning, Foreign Office, 9 June.*] Mr Canning humbly acquaints your
Majesty that the Baron de Heerdt accompanied by M. de Fagel has this day
waited upon Mr. Canning & brought him a letter from the Prince of Orange to
Baron de Heerdt, of which Mr. Canning humbly submits a copy.

Mr. Canning also humbly acquaints your Majesty that the Hanoverian officer
whom Mr. Canning sent back with Mr. Kleist, to ascertain the real state of the
insurrections in the north of Germany is returned this day with accounts highly
favourable; particularly as they concur with what is stated in the Prince of Orange's
letter as to the disposition of the King of Prussia.

Count Walmoden, who went in company with this officer & Mr. Kleist,
landed near Colberg on the 17th of May & proceeded on his journey to the Archduke's headquarters. (14471-2)

[*The King's reply, Windsor Castle, 10 June.*] The King acknowledges the receipt
of Mr. Canning's letter and the accompanying communications from Mr. de
Heerdt and Major Kleist. (14472)

3902   *Letters from* SPENCER PERCEVAL *to the* KING, *and the reply*

[*Downg. St., 12 June 1809.*] Mr. Perceval humbly submits to your Majesty
for your Majesty's signature two commissions for appointing Sr. Allan Chambré[2]
and Sir Geo. Wood the Justices of Assize for your Majesty's County Palatine

---

[1] The Archduke had been defeated by Napoleon at Eckmühl on 22 April, and the battle of Aspern-
Essling on 21-22 May was indecisive, both sides sustaining heavy losses.

[2] Sir Alan Chambré (1739-1823), Recorder of Lancaster, 1796; Serjeant-at-law, 1799; Baron of the
Exchequer, 1799; Justice of the Common Pleas, 1800-15.

of Lancaster; and also a warrant for the payment of £2000 to your Majesty's Privy Purse by the Receiver of your Majesty's revenues of the Duchy of Lancaster. (14473)

[*From Perceval, Downg. St., 12 June.*] Mr. Perceval acquaints your Majesty that Mr. Curwen's Bill with Mr. Perceval's Amendments passed this evening after a debate in which Mr. Windham, Sir F. Burdett and the former opponents of the Bill continued their opposition to it; & Mr Tierney and many of the Opposition who supported it before Mr Perceval's Amendments were introduced into it, opposed it also. The House divided for the Third Reading, Ayes 98, Noes 83; then on the Motion for the passing of the Bill, Ayes 97,[1] Noes 85.

After this Lord Folkstone moved a new title to the Bill in the following terms: 'A Bill for better preventing the sale of seats in Parliament for money, and for securing the monopoly of the same to the Treasury by the means of patronage.'

Upon this the House divided, Ayes 28, Noes 133.[2] So the Bill passed with the original title.[3] (14474)

[*The King's reply, Windsor Castle, 13 June.*] The King acknowledges the receipt of Mr Perceval's report of the debate and division in the House of Commons last night from which his Majesty has learnt with pleasure that the majority upon Lord Folkstone's Motion was so respectable. (14474)

3903 *Letters from* GEORGE CANNING *to the* KING, *and the replies*

[*Foreign Office, 13 June 1809.*] Mr. Canning, in laying before your Majesty the accompanying note from the Spanish Ambassador, humbly requests to receive your Majesty's gracious commands whether he may encourage Don Pedro Cevallos to hope that your Majesty at some future time might be graciously pleased to accept a limited number of merino sheep; & also a few of the horses, when the means of transport can be conveniently afforded. (14475)

[*The King's reply, Windsor Castle, 14 June.*] The King desires Mr. Canning will persist in declining the offer of the merino sheep conveyed in Don Pedro Cevallos's note, his Majesty really not having room for them and being actually under the necessity of hiring ground for those last received. In regard to the horses, Don Pedro Cevallos may be told that at a future more convenient opportunity his Majesty will accept a few. (14476)

[1] Wrongly given as 96 in Colchester, II, 197.
[2] Wrongly given as 134 in Colchester, *ibid*.
[3] *Parl. Deb.*, XIV, 990–1015. Perceval's Amendments had made the Bill largely ineffective. Romilly wrote: 'When the Bill was first brought in, the Ministers were hostile to it but had not the courage to oppose it openly; and after the Speaker had in the Committee made a speech of very great effect in favour of the Bill, they found it indispensably necessary, in order to save their reputation with the public, that some such Bill should be passed. They have, however, struck out the clause which required an oath of the member, and which annexed the penalties of perjury to the taking such an oath falsely, and every other clause that could make the Bill effectual...I could have no hesitation in voting against it.' (Romilly, *Memoirs*, II, 286–7.)

[*From Canning, Bruton Street, Wednesday night, 14 June.*] Mr. Canning humbly lays before your Majesty a letter addressed to him by H.S.H. the Prince of Orange. Mr. Canning conceives this letter to be the 'Despatches' which he humbly mentioned to your Majesty this morning as being announced in the Post Office return. (14477)

[*From Canning, Foreign Office, 15 June.*] Mr. Canning most humbly requests to receive your Majesty's gracious pleasure with respect to the permission solicited by H.S.H. the young Prince of Orange[1] to be allowed to pay his respects to your Majesty & the Royal Family. (14480)

[*The King's reply, Windsor Castle, 16 June.*] The King will acquaint Mr Canning tomorrow when his Majesty and the Queen can receive the young Prince of Orange. (14480)

[*From the King, Windsor Castle, 17 June.*] The King desires Mr. Canning will acquaint the young Prince of Orange that his Majesty will be glad to see him at the Queen's Palace on Tuesday next at three o'clock. (Harewood MSS.)

3904 SPENCER PERCEVAL *to the* KING, *and the reply*

[*Downing Street, 15 June* [*1809*].] Mr Perceval acquaints your Majesty that Sir Francis Burdett brought forward his Motion respecting Parliamentary reform this evening. His Motion was that the House would early in the next Session of Parliament take into consideration the state of the representation of the people. His speech was in every respect very moderate; it made no impression at all. His project of reform was to give the right of voting to every man who paid to the poor rates, the Church rate, and to the direct taxes of the State, to divide the country into separate districts in proportion to the population & to let each district return one Member, and to have annual Parliaments. Mr Perceval contented himself with saying a very few words against this Motion, perceiving that nothing could more tend to give consequence to the Motion than answering it at much length. Mr Madocks supported Sr Francis, Mr Robert Williams[2] opposed him, as also did Mr Barham; Mr Hanbury-Tracey[3] supported Sr Francis also. The House then divided against Sr Francis' Motion 74 to 15.

The House then proceeded to Lord Erskine's Bill for preventing cruelty to animals, and the House refused to go into the Committee and got rid of the Bill

[1] Later King William II. See No. 1196. He had just arrived from the Continent: 'said to come for education, and as a future husband for the Princess Charlotte of Wales,' wrote the Speaker (Colchester, II, 198). He seemed to be the only match for her in the existing state of Europe, thought Lord Glenbervie; but, he added, 'her mother cannot bear the idea. She has hardly taken any notice of him, and she detests his grandmother, whose ambition and love of governing she is afraid of if her grandson should become the Princess's husband.' (*Glenbervie Diaries*, II, 20.)
[2] Robert Williams (1735–1814), Tory M.P. for Dorchester, 1807–12.
[3] Charles Hanbury-Tracy, 1st Baron Sudeley (1778–1858), Whig M.P. for Tewkesbury, 1807–12, 1832–37. Peerage, 12 July 1838.

by putting it off for three months by 37 to 27. The House then adjourned till Monday.[1] (12966–7)

[*The King's reply, Windsor Castle, 16 June.*] The King is glad to learn from Mr Perceval's report that Sir Francis Burdett's Motion for a Reform in Parliament was so easily disposed of last night, and his Majesty was not surprized to know that Lord Erskine's Bill has been got rid of. (12967)

3905   VISCOUNT CASTLEREAGH *to the* KING, *and the reply*

[*St. James's Square, 15 June 1809.*] Lord Castlereagh begs leave to acquaint your Majesty that your Majesty's confidential servants, having consider'd the information which has been collected relative to an operation against the enemy's naval resources in the Scheldt, are humbly of opinion that, by employing an adequate force of not less than 35,000 men, the attempt may be made with every prospect of success, provided the practicability of a landing in force at Sandfleet can be assured. Till this point can be further investigated they are desirous to postpone receiving your Majesty's final commands upon the measure, requesting in the meantime your Majesty's permission to proceed with as much expedition and secrecy as possible with all the preliminary arrangements which, when completed, will render the troops equally applicable to any other service.

Your Majesty's servants are desirous of humbly submitting to your Majesty that the conduct of the proposed expedition should be entrusted to the Earl of Chatham.

Lord Castlereagh lays before your Majesty the Report received from B. Genl. Decken relative to the state of affairs in the North of Germany.[2] (14478–9)

[*The King's reply, Windsor Castle, 16 June.*] The King approves of Lord Castlereagh's proposal that the preparations for an expedition to the amount stated should be made with as much secrecy and promptitude as possible, and that Lord Chatham should be entrusted with the command of it. (14479)

3905 A   GEORGE CANNING *to the* KING, *and the reply*

[*Foreign Office, 17 June 1809.*] Mr. Canning most humbly submits for your Majesty's gracious consideration the draft of a letter from your Majesty to the Emperor of Austria, intended, if approved by your Majesty, as a credential for Lord William Bentinck. (14489)

[*The King's reply, Windsor Castle, 18 June.*] The King approves the letter to the Emperor of Austria which Mr. Canning has proposed as a credential for Lord William Bentinck, with the introduction of the word *récemment* after ' *Victoires signalées & brillantes qu'ont*' which has occurred to his Majesty as appropriate under present circumstances. (14489)

[1] *Parl. Deb.*, XIV, 1041–71. Windham took the lead in opposing Erskine's Bill, which had passed the Lords without difficulty. See Romilly's *Memoirs*, II, 287–8.
[2] A slightly different draft, dated the 14th, is in *Castlereagh Corresp.*, VI, 275.

[*Burlington House, 18 June 1809.*] The anxious desire which the Duke of Portland felt to obtain the advantage of Mr. Yorke's talents and good qualities for the service of your Majesty, occasioned the Duke of Portland to try every means and to give every facility that consideration or the interposition of friends could interpose in preventing the unjust interdict imposed upon him by his brother Lord Hardwicke, & which the refinement of Mr. Yorke's feelings makes him deem himself obliged to submit to.[1] But as no hope remains of any alteration of sentiment on the part of the Earl of Hardwicke, the Duke of Portland has found himself obliged to have recourse to the authority your Majesty was pleased to give him of sounding Lord Granville Leveson Gower, who will be most

[1] Lord Hardwicke wrote to his brother on 4 June: 'Having understood from Lord Clive that the decision which you have made is principally founded upon the personal feeling which I entertain upon the subject, & upon an idea that I should consider your acceptance of office as an act of personal unkindness, I think it better for your sake as well as for my own to explain distinctly what I have hitherto meant to convey, and what I really thought you had clearly understood. Considering the question of your acceptance of office at this moment upon private grounds only, and so far as concerns ourselves & family, I have been desirous that you should act in the manner best suited to your own inclination, provided that I should not be involved in the consequences of such a decision by supporting your re-election for the County of Cambridge. That I should very deeply lament & regret it upon many public & private grounds, I cannot deny; but you should never hear from me either now or hereafter a word of reproach on any ground of family sacrifice. I meant to convey this in our conversation some days ago, when I stated my readiness to waive any credit which may belong to Cambridgeshire continuing to be represented by one of my family; & I meant to add also that it appeared to me the only way of reconciling the honourable maintenance of my own opinions with the gratification of your wishes at the present moment. At the same time I cannot be so self denying or so insincere as not to say that I shall certainly feel much happier if upon the whole you think it right to adhere to your determination; though I should not wish the sacrifice to be made solely upon account of my opinions, and at all events not upon the supposition of any personal feeling of unkindness.' (Bodleian MSS.)

Yorke replied, next day: 'I found your note on my return from St. James's which I cannot but consider as kindly intended towards me; & so far as it is a great consolation to me under my present circumstances. But, however I may feel the situation in which I have been placed, I cannot hesitate as to the line of conduct which it is proper for me to pursue on this occasion, & I shall accordingly delay no longer to communicate my resolution to decline the honourable offer which has been made to me of returning into his Majesty's service....I cannot think of taking any step by means of which the County would suddenly be abandoned, for a time at least, without resource; & there is no sacrifice of my personal views & interests which I can consider as too great for me to make when put into competition with your happiness, & with the perfect maintenance of our hitherto uninterrupted friendship & cordiality.' (*Ibid.*)

Consequently, Yorke wrote to the Duke of Portland on the 6th: 'I am much concerned to be obliged to acquaint Y. Grace that I find myself placed in such an unpleasant and embarrassing position with respect to my re-election & other circumstances which might attend my acceptance of office at this conjuncture, that I am under the necessity of requesting permission to decline the honourable offer which Y.G. has been pleased to propose to me, of returning into H.M.'s service, an offer which under more favourable circumstances would have been a matter of great pride & satisfaction to me. But I must always continue to retain a very high sense of obligation to Y.G. & to my other friends for the attention & kindness which has been shewn me on this occasion. I venture to hope that Y.G. will have the goodness to take a proper opportunity of laying before H.M. together with my most humble duty, the expression of my deep regret in being thus disappointed in having the honour of again serving H.M. I have no protector but his Majesty, to whom I have ever accustomed myself to look up, on earth; and I never can expect nor do I desire to meet with any other. I have heretofore had the high honour of serving H.M. in responsible employments in times of much difficulty & demanding considerable exertion; & however low I ought to estimate my abilities, I hope that I may rely a little on the qualities of zeal, diligence & loyalty, in which I trust I never have been & never will be found wanting. I had the unhappiness at a very early age to lose my father, also in his Majesty's Service, in the prime of his life, & with the Great Seal of Great Britain in his hands; which was an irreparable

gratefully ready to undertake to execute the duties of either of the offices of Secretary at War or of that of President of the Board of Comptroll; and as there is reason to beleive that nothing but the absolute necessity of your Majesty's service would dispose Lord Castlereagh to go back to his former seat at the Board of Controull, and as it has been suggested that in the person of Sir John Anstruther, lately Chief Justice in Bengal, a most particularly well qualified and well informed President would be met with, the Duke of Portland most humbly requests your Majesty's permission to signify to Lord Granville Leveson your Majesty's pleasure to confer upon him the office of Secretary at War,[1] and to take the proper means of making himself acquainted with Sir John Anstruther's sentiments respecting the Presidency of the Board of Comptroll in order that they may be laid before your Majesty in sufficient time to admit of his writ being moved before the prorogation of Parliament takes place, in case it shall be your Majesty's pleasure to accept his services.[2] (14490–1)

[*The King's reply, Windsor Castle, 19 June.*] The King must ever regret that Lord Hardwicke's opposition should deprive him of the services of Mr. Yorke, and under that circumstance his Majesty approves of the Duke of Portland's signifying to Lord Granville Leveson his intention of conferring upon him the office of

misfortune to all his family, but perhaps in many respects, more particularly so, to myself. I fear that I must consider what has passed on the present occasion, as amounting almost to an interdict from public life; at any rate as a most material (tho' indispensable) sacrifice of those honourable prospects to which the time I have spent in the public service has fairly entitled me to look; & which my private fortunes do not by any means entitle me to disregard. Situated as I am, I hope I may presume to request Y.G.'s favourable recommendation of me to H.M.'s gracious consideration for such moderate provision as, under all the circumstances of the case, H.M.'s condescending goodness may deem one of his former servants not wholly undeserving of.' (*Ibid.*)

Lord Hardwicke wrote again to his brother, on the 7th: 'I certainly feel much gratified by your letter and the determination you have taken. At the same time I regret much that you should have been brought by any circumstances into the situation of making what I shall always consider as a sacrifice to your personal kindness & affection to me. The regret I feel is much increased by the idea that independendently of other considerations, your personal convenience is in some degree affected by it; and this leads me to mention what I have for some time wished to state in the most confidential manner, that so soon as my Gloucestershire affairs are brought to a close, I propose to place at your disposal five thousand pounds of the money which I shall then receive. To satisfy any scruple you may entertain upon the subject, I will only add that though my wish and intention is that at all events you should consider this as your own, yet if you chose hereafter, supposing future circumstances should make it convenient, you might bequeath it to any surviving branch of my family, after yourself & Mrs. C. Yorke. I shall be personally much gratified if this arrangement, which has been long in my mind, should be attended with any present convenience, & I will only add that whenever the affair connected with this transfer of my property is settled (as I trust it will in a few weeks) I shall be in a situation to admit of it without the least inconvenience.' (*Ibid.*)

Yorke replied, the same day: 'I cannot delay returning you my best thanks for your affectionate and considerate attention to my concerns, manifested in the obliging offer you have made. But as I am not in immediate want of any pecuniary assistance, the matter shall if you please stand over for further consideration, for I am extremely loath to be a further burthen to you or to trespass more upon your goodness than is absolutely necessary, which I trust will not be the case.' (*Ibid.*)

[1] Lord Sidmouth, who, no doubt, disliked Granville Leveson as one of Canning's closest friends, suggested that 'he was so devoted to piquet...that it was necessary to find him some other employment to save him from ruin'. (Sidmouth MSS. To Bragge-Bathurst, 7 July 1809.)

[2] Canning wrote to Bathurst on 28 June: 'Anstruther has recanted his refusal of the India Board. He commissioned Wellesley to tell me two or three days ago.' (*Bathurst Papers*, p. 96.)

Secretary at War, and of his sounding Sir John Anstruther in regard to the situation of President of the Board of Controul.[1] (14492)

3907 GEORGE CANNING *to the* KING, *and the reply*

[*Foreign Office, 20 June 1809.*] Mr. Canning humbly submits to your Majesty that the Chevalier de Souza requests permission to present to your Majesty at the Queen's Palace tomorrow M. Ferras, one of the Deputies who came here from Oporto, & who is now about to return there. (14493)

[*The King's reply, Queen's Palace, 21 June.*] The King approves of Mr. Canning desiring the Chevalier de Souza to bring Mr Ferras here this day. (14493)

3908 THE EARL OF LIVERPOOL *to the* KING, *and the reply*

[*Charles Street, 20 June 1809.*] Lord Liverpool begs leave most humbly to submit to your Majesty the draft of the Speech proposed to be made by command of your Majesty, by the Lords Commissioners, on the prorogation of Parliament. Lord Liverpool has directed that the usual summonses may be issued for a Privy Council to be held at the Queen's Palace tomorrow at two o'clock for the purpose, with your Majesty's approbation, of reading the Speech in Council previous to the Prorogation. (14495)

[1] Dundas, the new Irish Secretary, had been performing the duties of President of the Board of Control until his successor could be appointed. One reason for the delay in nominating a new President is given in Portland's letter to Perceval, 18 May: 'I am sure that Lord Granville Leveson will accept the Presidency of the Board of Control, but I am no less sure that Canning and he will expect that he should have a seat at the Cabinet, and it is that circumstance which has prevented my proceeding further in it. Sir James Pulteney I am to see tomorrow...

'[P.S.] I have a particular reason for wishing you not to say anything to Canning upon Lord Granville Leveson's expectation of being of the Cabinet.' (Perceval MSS.)

Tierney wrote to Grey on 7 July, and Charles Long was evidently his informant: 'I wrote to you first that Lord G.L. was in the Cabinet, and then that C.L. assured me he was not. The fact is that he is, but that he got there in a way quite new. Not one of the Ministers knew they had a colleague till they were informed of the King's pleasure by a circular note from the Duke of Portland. This sounds so incredible that I would not venture to state it if I was not sure of it. The Chancellor was in a fury when he received the notification, and swore he would speak his mind roundly to the King on Wednesday but whether he did or not I cannot tell, as I carefully avoided seeking for information, and what I have told you came to me and not I to it. You will easily conceive what a precious meeting a Cabinet dinner must be under the circumstances I have related, and how difficult, I had almost said how impossible, it must be for things to go on long on such a footing.' (Howick MSS.)

Tierney was surprised at Granville Leveson's acceptance. 'I should have thought that he would not have liked that kind of office, and I must suppose he has only taken it as a stepping-stone to something more to his mind.' (*Ibid.*, 18 June.) 'The appointment,' wrote Thomas Grenville, 'gives great scandal from Granville having sat up thirty-six hours a week ago to lose £20,000 at *piquet*, which does not teach John Bull to form great expectations of his diligence and activity in office.' (*Dropmore Papers*, IX, 311.) Lord Melville commented: 'It is an appointment called for by no public occasion, and when that is the case, such extra Cabinet appointments, selected from the political partisans of particular Ministers, always carry with them the semblance of cabal and political intrigue among Ministers, each contending to strengthen his own importance in the Cabinet. The appointment of Lord G. Leveson to a seat in the Cabinet cannot...receive any other construction than as an addition to the weight of Mr. Canning, who has already either too much or too little.' (Lonsdale MSS.)

[The King's reply, Queen's Palace, 21 June.] The King approves of the Speech which has been prepared and submitted by Lord Liverpool and of his having summoned a Privy Council to be held here this day.[1] (14495)

3909   LORD ELDON *to the* KING

[Tuesday, 20 June 1809.] The Lord Chancellor, offering his most humble duty to your Majesty, has the honour to transmit two Commissions, one for passing the Local Militia Bill, the other for proroguing the Parliament tomorrow, to receive your Majesty's Royal Sign Manual, if your Majesty shall graciously so please. The Lord Chancellor has presumed to send the Commission for proroguing the Parliament, tho' the Order-in-Council for that purpose has not yet been made, as he thought it would give your Majesty less trouble than the signing it after the Council. The Lord Chancellor proposes humbly to offer his duty to your Majesty tomorrow in person, & will take your Majesty's further pleasure on the Prince's paper. (14494)

3910   VISCOUNT CASTLEREAGH *to the* KING, *and the reply*

[Downing Street, 21 June 1809.] Lord Castlereagh has to submit humbly to your Majesty the report of the Board of Admiralty on the practicability of effecting a landing in force within the Scheldt, between Sandfliet and Lillo. Under the sanction of this opinion upon the principal point which had been reserved for investigation, your Majesty's confidential servants, not disguising from themselves the general difficulties of the enterprize but deeply impress'd with its importance, feel it their duty humbly to recommend to your Majesty that the operation should be undertaken.

Lord Castlereagh would humbly propose to your Majesty that the regts. most remote from the points of embarcation should be immediately put in motion. It is intended to embark at Portsmouth, in the ships of the line, about 17,000 men, a proportion of which force will be moved from the Eastern District in order the better to mask the operation as destined to the westward, and as the troops from Essex will require 14 days from their march and embarcation, it is presumed that the embarcation and equipment of the whole force, including ordnance, stores, &c. so far as it depends on tonnage now at home, may be completed within that period, counting from Monday next.

The principal part of the equipment which depends on the return of ships from foreign service is the transport of a proportion of the horses. As a fleet was under orders to sail from Lisbon on the 5th of this month, Lord Castlereagh presumes to hope that no delay will be ultimately occasion'd by this deficiency of means, which his utmost exertions have not been able to remove.[2] (14498–9)

[1] The Speech of the Lords Commissioners which closed the Session on the 21st is in *Parl. Deb.*, XIV, 1161.

[2] The differently phrased draft of this letter is in *Castlereagh Corresp.*, VI, 281.

[*The King's reply, Queen's Palace, 22 June.*] The King acquiesces in the proposal of his confidential servants submitted by Lord Castlereagh that the operation to the Scheldt should be undertaken, although his Majesty could have wished that the information upon which the practicability has been finally decided had not been so imperfect. (14499)

3911   LORD MULGRAVE *to the* KING, *and the reply*

[*Admiralty, 22 June 1809.*] Your Majesty having been graciously pleased to approve the proposed expedition to the Scheldt, Lord Mulgrave humbly submits to your Majesty Rear-Admiral Sir Richard Strahan [*sic*], (at present commanding the squadron stationed off the Scheldt) as an officer qualified by his zeal, enterprize & professional talents to conduct the naval branch of the important service which is by your Majesty's command to be proceeded upon.

Lord Mulgrave humbly submits to your Majesty a statement of the naval means provided for the attack of the enemy, and for the conveyance of troops.

Ships of the line (of which nine will be reserved for battle)	30
Frigates	17
Sloops	40
Bomb vessels	5
Armed en flute	5
Gun brigs	29
Cutters & small vessels	31
Gun boats	78
Total armed vessels	235
Flat boats	100 (14500)

[*The King's reply, Queen's Palace, 23 June.*] The King entirely approves of Lord Mulgrave's recommendation of Rear-Admiral Sir Richard Strachan for the conduct of the naval branch of the proposed expedition to the Scheldt. (14501)

3912   *Letters from* GEORGE CANNING *to the* KING, *and the replies*

[*Foreign Office, 24 June 1809.*] Mr Canning in humbly laying before your Majesty the note transmitted to him this day by Mr. Brinkmann with the copy of his new credentials, & of the Duke of Sudermania's letter to your Majesty, thinks it his duty humbly to state to your Majesty that he has avoided giving Mr. Brinkmann any ground to infer what will be your Majesty's decision as to the acknowledgement of the new Government until, after full consultation with your Majesty's confidential servants, he shall have received your Majesty's gracious commands upon that subject.[1] (14502)

1 Failure in his war with Russia, involving the loss of Finland, compelled Gustavus IV to abdicate under pressure from the army (29 March). On 10 May the Estates of Sweden accepted this action and called the Duke of Sudermania to the throne, with the title of Charles XIII. For him *see* No. 399.

[*The King's reply, Windsor Castle, 25 June.*] The King entirely approves the caution which Mr. Canning has observed in his communication with Mr. de Brinckman as to the acknowledgement of the new Government of Sweden. The question is one of so serious an import that his Majesty thinks it ought to be very maturely considered before any decision is taken. (14503)

[*From Canning, Foreign Office, 25 June, 5 p.m.*] Mr. Canning humbly hopes that your Majesty will graciously forgive his presuming to break in upon your Majesty at an unusual hour with despatches which do *not* contain any decisive intelligence. But the rumours which are afloat throughout the town, & the arrival of the messenger who brings these despatches Mr Canning apprehended might reach your Majesty, & perhaps create some uneasiness & anxiety in your Majesty's mind, unless your Majesty were at the same time apprized of the real extent of the intelligence received.

The messenger who brought these despatches reports that he passed through the Emperor's Headquarters at Wolkersdorff on the 5th. The Archduke Charles's army was concentrated between Wolkersdorff & the Morawa & Buonaparte's on the opposite side of the Danube not far from Presburg. He had once attempted to cross the river, & had been repulsed in a partial action by a General *Reditzky*.[1] A great battle was expected every day.

The loss of Buonaparte in the battle of Aspern is stated in a private letter of Mr Bathurst's to Mr Hammond at nearly the half of his whole army—or not much less than 50,000. It is said that there are 20,000 wounded French in the suburbs of Vienna.

Mr. Canning thinks it his duty to add that the messenger affirms that a merchant at Colberg (where the messenger embarked) assured him, at the moment of his embarkation, that intelligence had just been received of a revolution at St Petersburgh. The name of the merchant is well known as a man of character.

Mr Canning intreats your Majesty's pardon for troubling your Majesty with these reports, but he thought it right that as your Majesty might hear them otherwise, your Majesty should know on what authority they rest. (14504–5)

[*The King's reply, Windsor Castle, 26 June.*] The King has this morning received Mr. Canning's letter and the accompanying dispatches, and his Majesty is sensible of his attention in writing yesterday evening under the impression that the reports afloat might have reached him, which, however, was not the case. (14506)

3913 *Letters from the* DUKE OF PORTLAND *to the* KING, *and the replies*

[*Burlington House, Monday, 26 June 1809.*] The Duke of Portland humbly requests your Majesty's permission for the Dean of Bristol,[2] who has been ac-

---

[1] Count Radetzsky, the Austrian Field Marshal (1766–1858), best known for his command of the Austrian army in Lombardy during the 1848 Revolution.

[2] Bowyer Edward Sparke. See No. 3760. Romilly alleged that this dignitary of the Church was raised to the Bench partly for his sermon in July 1807 in which, in addition to criticisms of the dismissed 'Talents', he had given the King the chief credit for the abolition of the slave trade. (*Memoirs*, II, 298.)

quainted with your Majesty's most gracious intentions to promote him to the See of Chester, to have the honor of kissing your Majesty's hands for that preferment on Wednesday next. (14507)

[*The King's reply, Windsor Castle, 27 June.*] The King approves of the Duke of Portland's desiring the Dean of Bristol to attend. (14507)

[*From the Duke of Portland,*[1] *Burlington House, Sunday, 2 July.*] The very liberal motives which are happily known to your Majesty to have induced Lord Harrowby to offer himself to your Majesty's service, have brought back to the Duke of Portland's recollection an intimation that he understands was made to him several years ago that your Majesty would not be disinclined to raise his father[2] to the rank of an Earl in order to place Lord Harrowby in the House of Lords.

The reasons for its not taking place are not correctly known to the Duke of Portland. He is much inclined to believe that upon consideration it was found Lord Harrowby's services would be more essential to your Majesty by his continuance in the House of Commons than by his removal to the other House—but as the House of Lords is now the only place in which Lord Harrowby's talents can be displayed, it has occurred to the Duke of Portland, and has met with the concurrence of those of your Majesty's confidential servants to whom he has thought himself at liberty to communicate the reasons for Lord Harrowby's offer, that it could not but be highly gratifying to him and very advantageous to your Majesty's service, that the offer of an Earldom should be now made to Lord Harrowby, with liberty to avail himself of it in such manner as should be most agreeable to him.

The Duke of Portland therefore presumes to recommend to your Majesty with all humility that he should receive your Majesty's commands to ascertain Lord Harrowby's wishes with respect to an advancement in the Peerage. (14508-9)

[*The King's reply, Windsor Castle, 3 July.*] The King entirely approves of the Duke of Portland's ascertaining Lord Harrowby's wishes with respect to an advancement in the Peerage, which cannot, in his Majesty's opinion, be better applied.[3] (14509)

3914 LORD BORINGDON *to the* KING

[*Portman Square, 3 July 1809.*] The uniform condescension with which your Majesty has ever deigned to notice me & my family emboldens me at this time most humbly to prefer to your Majesty the expression of my earnest prayer that

---

[1] Not in the Duke's own hand.

[2] Nathaniel Ryder, 1st Baron Harrowby (1735–1803), M.P. for Tiverton, 1756–76; Peerage, 20 May 1776.

[3] On 19 July Lord Harrowby was created Earl of Harrowby. On 28 June Portland had written to Harrowby: 'I can most sincerely assure your Lordship that I hardly ever went into the Closet with so much pleasure as I did today, having been authorized by our excellent friend Ld. Bathurst to request his Majesty that, if it was his wish, you would accept the Presidency of the Board of Control, and to state the reasons which induced you at this moment to return into his Majesty's service. It would be

your Majesty might be graciously pleased to advance me to the rank of Earl in the Peerage of the United Kingdom.

Your Majesty's gracious communication made to my guardians[1] thro' Lord Aylesbury in 1789, the year in which your Majesty honoured with your presence the western parts of your kingdom (when your Majesty was condescendingly pleased to direct Lord Aylesbury to enquire whether there was any particular manner in which I was desirous that your Majesty's consideration might be testified to me, & when my guardians on my behalf declined availing themselves of such marks of your Majesty's royal condescension) can never be recollected by me but with sentiments of the most profound gratitude to your Majesty: & I may possibly be permitted to express my regret at the conduct of those who acted on my behalf, since it was afterwards intimated to me that the communication which your Majesty was pleased to direct had pointed at the advance which I now humbly solicit, & the elevation to the rank of Earl of the three other Peers (Lds. Fortescue,[2] Digby[3] & Edgcumbe[4]) who had that summer the honour to receive your Majesty's commands was cited to me in support of the correctness of that intimation.

Your Majesty may perhaps also graciously be induced to pardon my stating that with the exception of the last Administration, I have now uniformly for above 16 years given my zealous support in Parliament to your Majesty's Government—that during that time I have always yielded to those more eager for office than myself, & that between myself & the youngest Earl there is not any Peer who is situated in similar circumstances.

In adverting to these topicks which I have thus presumed to bring under your Majesty's gracious observation, I am most anxious that your Majesty should not conceive that I have done so with any view to establish a claim or pretension to that mark of grace & favour which I have ventured to solicit. I have adverted to them altogether under the hope that your Majesty might graciously be pleased to consider them as some small, tho' I am aware inadequate, justification of my presumption in having thus obtruded myself upon your Majesty's notice.

extremely difficult for me to give your Lordship a just idea of the impression the information made upon his Majesty. He explained that it was most excellent, that it was the handsomest conduct he had ever known, and commanded me to return you his particular thanks for it; and I will only add that there is not one of *our* colleagues, for so I hope I may now call them, to whom I have mentioned this event, whose sentiments upon the occasion are not in perfect unison with those of his Majesty. It did not occur to me at the moment that I had some time since heard that it would not be disagreeable to your Lordship to be advanced to the dignity of an Earl, or I certainly would have mentioned it to the King. But if my information is well founded, I will immediately propose it to his Majesty, who I am sure will be happy in the opportunity of testifying his sense of your conduct.' (Harrowby MSS.) Harrowby replied the same day, accepting the offer. (P.R.O., Granville Papers. Portland to Canning, 28 June.)

[1] He was only fifteen when his father, the 1st Baron Boringdon, died (27 April 1788).

[2] Hugh Fortescue of Castle Hill, Devon (1753–1841), who succeeded his father as 3rd Baron Fortescue on 10 July 1785, was created Earl Fortescue on 1 Sept. 1789.

[3] Henry Digby of Minterne House, Cerne Abbas, Dorset (1731–93), who succeeded his brother as 7th Baron Digby [I.] in 1757, and who was created Baron Digby [G.B.] on 13 Aug. 1765, became an Earl [G.B.] on 1 Nov. 1790.

[4] George Edgcumbe (1720–95), of Mount Edgcumbe, Devon, who succeeded his brother as 3rd Baron Edgcumbe on 10 May 1761, and who was created Viscount Mount Edgcumbe on 5 March 1781, was created Earl of Mount Edgcumbe on 31 Aug. 1789.

Should your Majesty have it in your royal contemplation at *any* period graciously to yield to the prayer with which I have presumed to approach your Majesty, your Majesty's paternal goodness will perhaps pardon my observing that there never could be any period at which such mark of your Majesty's benevolent condescension could, for reasons of a private & personal nature, be so peculiarly valuable to me as at the present moment.[1] (14510–11)

3915 GEORGE CANNING *to the* KING, *and the reply*

[*Foreign Office, 4 July 1809.*] Mr. Canning humbly submits to your Majesty's consideration the draft of instructions to Mr. Jackson:[2] and humbly requests your Majesty's gracious permission that Mr. Jackson may take leave of your Majesty tomorrow. (14512)

---

[1] Docketed, 'Receipt acknowledged 4th July.' Boringdon had to wait until 1815 for his Earldom, which he owed to his friend Canning.

'The King is quite prepared to give it,' wrote Canning on 9 Aug. Had it then materialised it would have been the first Earldom in English history to be given as a consolation to a man who had recently been the victim of a heartless seducer, or, perhaps one should say, as a wedding present—for Boringdon, on 23 Aug., found new happiness in a second marriage, to Frances, daughter of Thomas Talbot, of Gonville, Norfolk. 'She is *not* pretty,' said his friend Canning, 'but I think pleasing enough. I could not think whom she was like till Knobbs [the King] told me today that he heard she was more like a sort of a Lady Grenville than anybody else—and so I think she is—not so pretty perhaps as Ly. G. sometimes looks—& certainly not so shy—not immodest either—but quick & *smartish* (if she were quite at her ease) & likely to do for him very well.' The King's views on matrimony as then reported by Canning are not without interest: 'Kn. says, "I hope it will do—but I don't know how it is, there are some people to whom marriage seems to be the *natural state* & others to whom it is strange & unnatural. Now I don't know why, but Lord B. always strikes me as one of the latter sort, yet he is very good-natured, very good. I hope he will be happy"—in short, talking very kindly but very comically about him.' (Harewood MSS. To Mrs. Canning, 9 Aug.)

Canning described the outcome of his friend's application in another letter to his wife (11 Aug.), and, in one of his concluding remarks, said, 'No, the new Ly. B. is not the least like my own love—not the least.'

'1st...as to Ld. B.'s Earldom. I did not get him the promise. He wrote himself to Knobbs: reminding Kn. of an offer which had been made to him many years ago, when Kn. was at Saltram (which offer was then refused by his guardians—or not understood)—& saying that it would be peculiarly acceptable to him now. *I* would *not* apply in the first instance to the old D. [Portland] because it was not right just now to ask anything as a personal favour, or to appear to take advantage of the fear of disobliging me to gain what might be considered perhaps as an unreasonable object. B. was very sensible of these difficulties & did not at all press me. Besides, I told him that if the old D. applied for *him* I knew he must apply for many others. *He* could not as Minister enter into *his* (B's) claims "as a cuckold" to be preferred to others—though the K. might, as matter of personal favour. Upon this too B. was perfectly reasonable. His expedient therefore to save both me & the old D. was to write himself. He did so—& then sent through me a copy of his letter to Kn.—to the old D. The report which Taylor & G. Villiers gave, the one of the K.'s manner of receiving the letter, the other of his general conversation about the intended marriage, & some things reported through his sister from Princess Sophia led B. to be quite confident that the K. would himself speak to the D. of P. & that the thing would therefore be done as matter of special personal favour. However week after week passed, without Knobbs saying a word—& the old D. of course said not a word on his part. At last, on Wed. at my request the old D. did speak—but (as I had always told B. he must) spoke of others at the same time. The result was as unfavourable as might be. I confess I had not very much liked the way in which Kn. talked to me about the marriage—but his remark to the old D. was still more contradictory to all that Boringd. had been taught to expect: "I think it's quite enough to make her a *Lady*—without making her a Countess at once," said old Kn., & the old D., I dare say, was of the same opinion.' (Harewood MSS.)

George Villiers was a Groom of the Bedchamber, and his wife, Theresa, was Lord Boringdon's sister.

[2] Francis James Jackson had just been appointed Minister to the U.S.A.

[*The King's reply, Windsor Castle, 5 July.*] The King approves of the instructions for Mr. Jackson which Mr. Canning has submitted and of his desiring him to attend at the Queen's Palace this day.[1] (14512)

3916 THE DUKE OF PORTLAND *to the* KING,[2] *and the reply*

[*Burlington House, Thursday, 6 July 1809.*] The Duke of Portland most humbly begs leave to acquaint your Majesty that in consequence of the intimation which your Majesty condescended to give him on Wednesday the 28th of June, that it was determined that the Hereditary Prince of Orange was to finish his studies at the University of Oxford, the Duke of Portland gave the Vice-Chancellor[3] of that University and the Dean of Christ Church[4] notice of the intended measure, and desired them to contribute to the utmost of their power every assistance and facility towards its perfect accomplishment.

At the particular desire of the Hereditary Prince of Orange, the Duke of Portland repeated his wish to the Vice-Chancellor and the Dean, and in consequence of it those gentlemen had frequent and long conversations with Mr. Fagel and Major de Constant, the persons to whose care the superintendance of the Prince's education was entrusted, and after much thought and deliberation, the outlines of a plan for it have been drawn up which are contained in the accompanying paper which the Duke of Portland begs leave with all humility to submit to the inspection of your Majesty.

In presuming to lay this paper before your Majesty, the Duke of Portland feels himself called upon, in justice to those gentlemen who had a share in the drawing it up, or who are willing to take a part in giving it effect, humbly to represent to your Majesty that if they shall appear to have exceeded the bounds which their situations prescribed for them, or to have assumed a decisive tone to

---

[1] Canning wrote to Taylor at 4 p.m. on the 6th: 'The accompanying dispatches relate to a subject on which the King naturally feels so much interest that I have thought it right to put it in your power to read them to his Majesty immediately; leaving it, however, to your discretion, according to the time and circumstances of the messenger's arrival, whether you will communicate them to his Majesty this evening or wait 'till the usual hour. I do not write a letter to the King, as, if you should see reason for not hastening the communication, it is unnecessary to give his Majesty any trouble upon the subject.' (Harewood MSS.)

Taylor replied at 8.30 that evening: 'The messenger came in perfect time to admit of my submitting your letter and the accompanying papers to the King without disturbing him in any degree, & his Majesty has honored me with his commands to thank you for the early communication of what is so interesting to him. Also to acquaint you that although the King regrets that the insurrection in Hanover should break out prematurely & without the means of effectually supporting it, and therefore had approved of Count Munster's endeavors to repress the zeal of its promoters, as there is now reason to apprehend that it has begun, his Majesty is convinced that no time will be lost or exertion spared in affording from hence every aid in regard to supplies which can conveniently be given, and his Majesty entirely approves of your instructions to Mr. Nicholas.' (Harewood MSS.)

[2] Not in the Duke's own hand.

[3] John Parsons, D.D. (1761–1819). Master of Balliol, 1798–1819; Vice-Chancellor, 1807–10; Dean of Bristol, 1810; Bishop of Peterborough, 1813–19.

[4] Cyril Jackson. Resigning in October, he was succeeded by Charles Henry Hall, D.D. (1763–1827), Dean of Christ Church, 1809–24; Dean of Durham, 1824–7. Perceval wrote to Eldon on 14 Oct.: 'I understood Dr. Hall to be a very unequal successor to the present Dean, but that there was really no person who could well be considered as a competitor with him.' (Eldon MSS.)

which in any respect they may seem not to have been intitled, it is wholly to be attributed to the anxiety with which the Duke of Portland is but too well aware he may have expressed himself in desiring them to give their ideas upon a subject of so much delicacy and importance, so novel to them in its most essential circumstances, and upon which he urged them to give their sentiments without any reserve.

It is further necessary that he should represent to your Majesty his full and unreserved concurrence in the opinion which is herewith submitted to your Majesty of the talents, acquirements, and character of Dr. Howley,[1] and the Duke of Portland's full conviction that no other consideration but that of rendering the best service to your Majesty which the circumstances of his situation will permit, would have induced that gentleman to have undertaken so arduous and delicate a task as he appears disposed to attempt.

The whole however must depend upon the sanction of your Majesty, without which the Duke of Portland has no hesitation in assuring your Majesty that no consideration whatever would induce the gentlemen who had any share in the preparation of this plan, to consent to carry it into effect. (14513–6)

[*The King's reply, Windsor Castle, 7 July.*] The King entirely approves of the arrangement which has been submitted by the Duke of Portland for the education & residence of the Hereditary Prince of Orange at Oxford, and his Majesty authorizes him to give effect to it, being sensible that, both in his capacity of Chancellor of the University and of Minister the Duke of Portland is the person who should take the lead upon this occasion. The King cannot have the smallest objection to Doctor Howley's being addressed in his name respecting his acceptance of the task which he has so liberally expressed his readiness to undertake. (14517)

3917 LORD MULGRAVE *to the* KING, *and the reply*

[*Admiralty, 8 July 1809.*] Lord Mulgrave humbly submits to your Majesty the minutes & sentence of a court martial held for the trial of Benjamin Grimshaw and John Scott, for a breach of the 29th Article of War; they were found guilty & condemned to suffer death; but in consideration of the nature of the evidence upon which the conviction was founded, the president of the court martial, at the suggestion of the court, submitted the propriety of supplicating your Majesty to commute the punishment of death for such other as your Majesty should deem meet. Lord Mulgrave, impressed with the importance of checking the progress of so detestable a crime in your Majesty's Navy, has referred the recommendation of the court martial to your Majesty's Attorney & Solicitor-General & to the Council to the Admiralty, for a legal opinion upon the nature of the evidence on which the suggestion of the court martial is grounded; and the legal authorities having given their opinion that this is a fit case for recommending the criminals

---

[1] William Howley (1766–1848), Canon of Christ Church, Oxford, 1804; Regius Professor of Divinity at Oxford, 1809–13; Bishop of London, 1813–28; Archbishop of Canterbury, 1828–48.

to your Majesty's royal mercy for a remission of the capital punishment to which they are sentenced, Lord Mulgrave most humbly submits to your Majesty's gracious consideration the substitution of transportation for life instead of the sentence of death. (14518–9)

[*The King's reply, Windsor Castle, 9 July.*] The King approves of the reference which Lord Mulgrave was induced to make in the cases of Benjamin Grimshaw & John Scott previous to his submitting the recommendation of the court martial in their favor, and in consequence of what is stated in Lord Mulgrave's letter, his Majesty acquiesces in a commutation of the sentence of death to transportation for life. (14519)

3918   GEORGE CANNING *to the* KING, *and the reply*

[*Foreign Office, 10 July 1809.*] Mr. Canning, in humbly laying before your Majesty a note received this day from Baron Heerdt, humbly requests to receive your Majesty's gracious commands as to the permission which Baron Heerdt solicits to be allowed to pay his respects to your Majesty before his departure from this country. (14520)

[*The King's reply, Windsor Castle, 11 July.*] The King approves of Mr. Canning's desiring the Baron de Heerdt to attend at the Queen's Palace on Wednesday next. (14520)

3919   THE EARL OF LIVERPOOL *to the* KING

[*Charles Street, 11 July 1809.*] It was with the utmost pain and regret that Lord Liverpool was for the first time informed some days ago of the embarrassment in which your Majesty's Government was involved, in consequence of communications which have been passing between the Duke of Portland and Mr. Canning. Lord Liverpool has never received from the Duke of Portland any communication whatever upon this subject. Lord Liverpool feels that he has some right to complain of this want of confidence on the part of his Grace, upon a transaction so deeply interesting to the character and existence of your Majesty's Government, and affecting in a greater or less degree the feelings and situation of all your Majesty's confidential servants. Whilst the subject was still matter of discussion and there were hopes that by secresy and management the crisis might be prevented Lord Liverpool had no right to expect that the personal confidence should have been extended to him: but he does think he had a claim to a communication from the Duke of Portland and an opportunity of delivering his opinion before his Grace's determination was finally taken, and his word irretrevably pledged that Lord Castlereagh should at all events be removed from the War Department.

Lord Liverpool believes most sincerely that he is actuated by an equal feeling of fairness and justice towards both the individuals involved in this discussion, and if any difference of opinion had arisen in the Cabinet between them on any important publick question, and it had been necessary in consequence of this difference of opinion for your Majesty to determine which of them should quit your Majesty's service, Lord Liverpool has no difficulty in stating that with every feeling of regard, affection, and esteem for Lord Castlereagh, he is of opinion that Mr. Canning is under the present circumstances a more important and essential member of the Government than Lord Castlereagh, and that if it was therefore a question between them as individuals the decision on publick grounds must be made in favour of Mr. Canning. But this proceeding has not originated in any such manner; an objection is taken by Mr. Canning to Lord Castlereagh as Minister of the Military Department of the State on no ground to which Lord Liverpool, as far as he is acquainted with it, could subscribe. Lord Castlereagh is not removed, as Mr. Canning desired, previous to the commencement of the military operations of the year; he is suffer'd to remain in office to prepare and digest all the military arrangements of the campaign, and amongst others the most extensive and perhaps important expedition, which ever sailed from the ports of your Majesty's dominions, and the time is chosen at which the troops are embarked, and the wind is fair for the expedition to sail, under the immediate and official responsibility of Lord Castlereagh, to inform him that he is not to be permitted to continue any longer Minister for the War Department, and this is to be done without any other arrangement being proposed to him which can be expected in the slightest degree to reconcile so harsh a proceeding to his feelings. Lord Liverpool is satisfied that your Majesty will forgive him for stating that he never could contemplate such conduct towards any individual without considering it as an act of manifest cruelty and injustice.

Lord Liverpool is most fully aware that the resignation of Mr Canning, followed at this time by the events which would necessarily follow it, would lead in a very short space of time if not immediately to the dissolution of the present Administration, and with a view of preventing a catastrophe which might be so repugnant to your Majesty's feelings, and so prejudicial, as Lord Liverpool conscientiously believes, at this moment to the publick service, Lord Liverpool most humbly requests that your Majesty would accept of his office of Secretary of State for the Home Department for the purpose of obviating in the least unsatisfactory manner the difficulties which at this time exist in your Majesty's Government.

This office might be offer'd to Lord Castlereagh together with a Peerage and the conduct of the business of Government in the House of Lords, with the understanding likewise that the correspondence relative to the expedition which is about to sail, and which has been arranged under his auspices, might still be left in his hands. It might be represented to Lord Castlereagh that it was thought desireable to introduce Marquis Wellesley into the Government, as an addition of strength and efficiency to it, and that the office which Lord Castlereagh held was consider'd to be the one to which his talents and experience were most applicable. Lord Liverpool believes that [? such][1] an arrangement but such [an] arrangement alone would prevent at [this] time the dissolution of your Majesty's Administration.

[1] Paper torn.

Lord Liverpool must beg your Majesty's permission to be allowed to add that there are considerations which would in this case certainly determine Lord Liverpool at this time, and under the present circumstances not to accept of any other office in your Majesty's Government nor to remain a member of the Cabinet, but Lord Liverpool trusts that your Majesty will do him the credit to believe that he is determined as long as the Government is really and in fact your Majesty's Government, and that the persons who now compose it hold their situations, to give it as effectual support as far as is within his power, and to exert himself as [? vigorously][1] in its defence and justification in the House of Lords as if he held the most important and responsible situation [? in it].[1]

Lord Liverpool has not [? sent][1] any communication to the Duke of Portland on the subject of this letter. Your Majesty will make whatever use of it your Majesty may think proper. Lord Liverpool begs only to observe that for obvious reasons no communication should be made to Lord Castlereagh till your Majesty has accepted Lord Liverpool's resignation.[2] (14521–4)

3920   THE EARL OF WESTMORLAND *to the* KING, *and the reply*

[*London, 12 July 1809.*] Having received from Ld Burghersh at Lisbon, where he had been some time before he was acquainted with his disappointment, a letter desiring me to make his humble duty to your Majesty, I cannot better convey his sentiments than by laying before your Majesty the terms in which he has expressed himself to me—humbly hoping that your Majesty will excuse the frame of a sentence which was only intended for my perusal & will graciously receive Ld. Burghersh's dutiful acknowledgements on this distressing occasion.[3] (14525)

[*The King's reply, Windsor Castle, 13 July.*] The King returns his thanks to Lord Westmorland for the communication of Lord Burghersh's letter, which, in his Majesty's opinion, contains sentiments becoming him both as the eldest son of a Peer and a soldier. (14526)

3921   GEORGE CANNING *to the* KING, *and the reply*

[*Foreign Office, 15 July 1809.*] Mr Canning has humbly to intreat your Majesty's pardon for having omitted to take your Majesty's pleasure on Wednesday whether he should prepare a draft of an answer from your Majesty to the letter received by your Majesty from the Prince of Orange. As, however, Baron de Heerdt has fixed his departure for the beginning of the next week, Mr. Canning presumes humbly to submit to your Majesty the draft of such a letter, only requesting your

[1] Paper torn.
[2] The King did not reply to this letter.
[3] Westmorland enclosed the following extract from his son's letter. It is undated: 'I wd beg you to express to his Majesty from me, how sincerely I feel myself obliged for his kind intentions towards me, & that altho I have received a great disappointment, yet that nothing will abate my zeal for his Mjy.'s service or make me forget that the first law a soldier shd chearfully obey, is to serve, where he is ordered, without mentioning whether the rank or the service is or is not agreeable to him.' (14527)

Majesty's gracious indulgence if it should not be such as your Majesty may be graciously pleased to approve. (14528)

[*The King's reply, Windsor Castle, 16 July.*] The King approves of the letter to the Prince of Orange of which Mr. Canning has submitted the draft. (14529)

3922   LORD MULGRAVE *to the* KING, *and the reply*
[*Admiralty, 15 July 1809.*] Lord Mulgrave humbly begs leave to lay before your Majesty the draft of instructions prepared for Rear-Admiral Sir Richard Strachan, whose appointment to command the naval force assembled for the attack of the enemy in the Scheldt your Majesty has been graciously pleased to sanction with your Majesty's royal approbation. (14530)

[*The King's reply, Windsor Castle, 16 July.*] The King approves of the instructions which Lord Mulgrave has submitted for Rear-Admiral Sir Richard Strachan. (14530)

3923   *Letters from* VISCOUNT CASTLEREAGH *to the* KING *and the replies*
[*St. James's Square, 15 July* [*1809*].] Lord Castlereagh, in submitting to your Majesty the accompanying instructions and Minute of Cabinet, begs leave humbly to acquaint your Majesty that it is hoped the force embarking at Portsmouth will be enabled to sail on Tuesday next, and that the armament which is to assemble in the Downs will be collected and in readiness to proceed by the time the Fleet from Portsmouth arrives. The remainder of the cavalry transports have arrived from Lisbon, and being complete in forage, were enabled to proceed on to Rams-gate without the delay of coming into harbour at Portsmouth.
   The number of sail, when the whole is assembled, will amount, as nearly as can be calculated, to 616, of which 352 will be transports and 264 ships of war.
   Having completed as far as depends on him all the arrangements in town, Lord Castlereagh proposes with your Majesty's permission, to absent himself for a few days with a view of meeting Lord Chatham on the coast and of accelerating as much as possible the departure of the expedition.[1] (14531–2)

[*Enclosure*]
[*Cabinet Minute, 14 July, Burlington House.*]
Present: The Lord Chancellor, the Lord President, the Lord Privy Seal, the Duke of Portland, the Earl of Chatham, the Earl Bathurst, the Earl of Liverpool, the Earl of Harrowby, the Lord G. Leveson, the Lord Mulgrave, Mr. Canning, Mr. Perceval, & Viscount Castlereagh.
   It was determin'd humbly to advise his Majesty that the expedition now under orders should be directed to proceed forthwith to its destination, and that the

---

[1] The draft of this letter is in *Castlereagh Corresp.*, VI, 283. The King's Instructions to Lord Chatham, dated the 16th, are *ibid.*, VI, 285–6.

accompanying instructions for the conduct thereof should be submitted for his Majesty's Royal approbation and signature. (14533)

[*The King's reply, Windsor Castle, 16 July.*] The King approves of the instructions which Lord Castlereagh has submitted for Lord Chatham, and his Majesty is glad to hear that the preparations for the proposed expedition are so nearly completed. His Majesty cannot object to Lord Castlereagh's absenting himself for a few days for the purpose mentioned in his letter. (14532)

[*From Castlereagh, Downing Street, 17 July.*] Lord Castlereagh begs leave to submit to your Majesty the substance of the reports this day received from the several points of embarcation, by which your Majesty will perceive that the whole force, with the exception of the cavalry, which is to embark at Ramsgate, will be on board tonight and that the service has been carried on without any accident occurring hitherto.

Lord Castlereagh humbly submits for your Majesty's consideration the instructions which have been framed for the guidance of your Majesty's commanders with respect to the supply of the Army on the proposed service, and he trusts your Majesty will not consider that the rights of war, *in an enemy's territory*, have been push'd beyond the necessity of the case, regard being had to the very limited amount of specie that can be sent with the Army, and the present unfavorable state of the exchange with the Continent, which is at the present moment so much depress'd that the Dutch ducat, which is intrinsically worth and is issued to the troops at nine shillings and sixpence, costs the Treasury when purchased by a Bill upon England thirteen shillings and four pence.[1] (14534–5)

[*The King's reply, Windsor Castle, 18 July.*] The King approves of the instructions which have been submitted by Lord Castlereagh for the guidance of the military and naval commanders of the proposed expedition, in regard to the removal of stores and the supply of the Army, as the necessity of the measure is obvious to his Majesty. (14535)

3924   *Letters from* GEORGE CANNING *to the* KING, *and the reply*

[*Foreign Office, 18 July 1809.*] Mr. Canning, at the request of the Chevalier de Souza, humbly solicits your Majesty's gracious permission for M. de Souza's presenting to your Majesty at the Levée tomorrow Mr. Quinn, the Portuguese Chargé d'Affaires at the Court of Palermo, who was prevented by indisposition from attending your Majesty when your Majesty last received the Foreign Ministers at the Levée. (14536)

[*From Canning, Bruton Street, Tuesday night, 18 July.*] Mr. Canning humbly reports to your Majesty the intelligence received this day from the Admiralty of the arrival at Portsmouth of 1,500 merino sheep, part of the present destined for your Majesty by the Supreme Junta, which had been embarked before your

---

[1] For the draft, see *Castlereagh Corresp.*, VI, 286.

Majesty's desire to decline that present was made known in Spain. Mr. Canning trusts that the notification has arrived there in time to prevent any farther embarkation. (14537)

[*The King's reply, Windsor Castle, 19 July*.] The King approves of Mr. Canning's desiring the Chevalier de Souza to bring Mr. Quinn to the Queen's Palace this day. His M. is much embarassed by the arrival of the sheep from Cadiz as he has not any ground at present for them, and cannot make any arrangements for bringing them up by land. The King therefore desires that Mr. Canning will communicate to the Admiralty his wish that the sheep should be sent from Portsmouth by sea up the river to Deptford, as the transports will not be immediately required, the embarkations being completed, and in the meantime H.M. will endeavor to provide for their disposal on shore. Should a few more die from remaining on board it will be immaterial.[1] (14538)

3925   *Letters from the* DUKE OF PORTLAND *to the* KING, *and the reply*

[*Burlington House, Thursday, 20 July 1809*.] The Duke of Portland most humbly submits the accompanying warrant for £1,000 for the purpose of enabling her Royal Highness the Princess Charlotte to go to and reside at Bognor in obedience to your Majesty's commands, for your Majesty's Royal signature. (14539)

[*From the Duke of Portland, Burlington House, Friday, 21 July*.] The Duke of Portland humbly conceiving that it may not be displeasing to your Majesty that he should take the earliest opportunity of laying before your Majesty the result of what has passed between Mr. Canning and him in consequence of the commands which the Duke of Portland received from your Majesty on Wednesday last, most humbly acquaints your Majesty that in answer to a letter which he wrote on the subsequent day to Mr. Canning for the purpose of letting him know that your Majesty did not think proper to authorize such a communication to be made to Lord Wellesley as Mr. Canning had desired might be submitted to your Majesty,[2]

[1] Taylor wrote to Canning from Windsor on the 19th: 'The King having ordered the bearer Mr. Snart to make arrangements for landing the sheep at Deptford &c. I trouble you with this letter at his desire to request you will have the goodness to furnish him with the necessary authority if he should have occasion to apply to you.' (Harewood MSS.) The letter is endorsed, 'July 20. Letter to Ld. Mulgrave given to Mr. Snart.'

Canning referred to these sheep in a letter to his wife, 9 Aug.: 'The only other publick business that Kn. & I had to talk about today besides Bor.'s marriage (we did not talk about the Earldom) was the new flock of Spanish sheep that is coming over as a present to Kn: for him to distribute among his agricultural subjects. He told me to write to Sir Joseph Banks to say that he must come & superintend the distribution—& then asked how Charles Ellis's flock went on—& said "He must have some—" & when I said that I had divided mine between Charles & Ld. T[itchfield] he added—O! & Ld. T. to be sure must have as many as he likes.' And Canning wrote again to his wife on the 11th: 'Next for the sheep. It is not too late. I think I can undertake for a flock of 50—if that will satisfy my own love —without setting aside either Ld. T. or Charles Ellis—& if I give Charles some more—my own love's flock can be taken in at Claremount till she has a farm to put them on, herself. I am to settle every thing with Sir Joseph Banks, and shall certainly take the liberty of taking care of my own love among the first.' (Harewood MSS.)

[2] Canning's proposal was that his friend Wellesley should succeed Castlereagh as Secretary of State for War and the Colonies, and that he should be told about it before he left England (which he

the Duke of Portland this morning received a letter from that gentleman in which, after apologizing at great length for having presumed to submit such a proposition to your Majesty, he concludes by saying that 'He acquiesces implicitly in your Majesty's commands, with the deepest impression of your Majesty's most gracious condescension and persevering goodness'. (14540)

[*The King's reply, Windsor Castle, 22 July.*] The King acknowledges the receipt of the Duke of Portland's communication of yesterday which is very satisfactory to his Majesty. (14541)

3926 *Letters from* LORD MULGRAVE *to the* KING, *and the replies*

[*Admiralty, 21 July 1809.*] Lord Mulgrave has the honour to report to your Majesty that printed papers, purporting to be the 25th and 26th bulletins of the French Army, were picked up at sea by your Majesty's ship Peruvian; they are dated on the 8th and 9th of July at Wolkersdorff and convey the melancholly intelligence of the defeat of the Archduke Charles in two successive actions. The first on the 5th inst. (the French having passed the Danube on the night of the 4th) took place at Enzersdorff and terminated in the occupation by the enemy of the entrenched camps at Esling & Gross Aspern; the battle of Wagram on the 6th inst. was commenced at the break of day and concluded at ten o'clock by the retreat of the Austrians towards Bohemia, who are stated by the French account to have thereby abandoned Moravia & Hungary. Generals Masséna and Marmont[1] had been detach'd in pursuit of the Austrian Army, but it does not appear that any further impression had been made on the Army of the Archduke up to the 9th July, as the capture of 900 men only of the rearguard on that day is stated. The bulletin states the loss of the Austrians to amount to 40 pieces of cannon, 20,000 prisoners, from three to four hundred officers, and a considerable number of Generals; the latter however are not named. The French account represents the retreat as a route [*sic*] and that 12,000 wounded had fallen into their hands; their own loss is represented as incredibly small. With every allowance for evident exaggeration in the assertion that the Austrian Army in loss & desertion must

did, shortly before the 25th) for Seville in the capacity of Ambassador Extraordinary to the Spanish Junta. He arrived at Seville on 11 Aug. Though Canning accepted the King's decision in favour of silence, he assured Wellesley, just before he left London, 'that it was positively determined to make the proposed arrangement for the War Department.' Canning wrote to his wife on the 25th: 'Yes, dearest love, I think all is well settled upon the whole. Poor old Kn. has behaved most perfectly throughout. It is true that he does not like W. at all—but there is nothing dishonest in that, for he has *always* told *me* so; & now he has expressed to the D. something like my own love's opinion that "he wonders I should like that arrangement, he is afraid I shall get tired of it." I shall tell him tomorrow—what is true, that it was not my proposal—but that when one [was] proposed I could not contend for the other—for *his*—without appearing to *claw* at power for myself &c. I am going, by my own offer to dine with the poor old D. I thought it right to be kind to him after so much hard, perhaps a *little* harsh —discussion, but indeed it would have been highly imprudent—it would have ruined all—to have written less positively & peremptorily.' (Harewood MSS.)

  [1] Marshal Marmont (1774–1852). Duke of Ragusa, 1805; Marshal of France after Wagram, 1809; succeeded Masséna in Portugal, 1811.

be reduced below 60,000 men, which the bulletin affirms, there can be no doubt that the result of an obstinate conflict of two days has been most disastrous to Austria & pregnant with the most serious consequences. (14542–3)

[*The King's reply, Windsor Castle, 22 July.*] The King has learnt with the deepest concern the intelligence contained in the French bulletins which Lord Mulgrave has conveyed to his Majesty. (14542–3)

[*From Lord Mulgrave, Admiralty, 24 July.*] Lord Mulgrave humbly submits the enclosed intelligence to your Majesty's perusal, although founded on rumour alone and with no official authority to support it, but the aspect of probability which it bears has induced Lord Mulgrave to hope that your Majesty may be pleased to pardon the communication of an unofficial report which tends to mitigate the uneasy impression of the French bulletins.[1] (14544)

[1] Taylor wrote to Canning from Windsor on 25 July at 7 p.m.: 'I lost no time in reading to the King the intelligence from Heligoland and Brünn which you have sent, and his Majesty has ordered me to return you many thanks for your attention in forwarding what, under all circumstances, appears to him so much more satisfactory than there was reason to hope. The only thing which puzzles me is the rapid advance of the French to Znaym. If however the Archduke John or General Chasteler should have defeated the French at [? *Stuptweissenburg*] & follow up their advantage by an advance to Vienna, Buonaparte may find himself in a very awkward situation.' (Harewood MSS.)

Taylor wrote to Canning on the 28th: 'I have sent to the King your letter and the enclosed intelligence from Brunn & Vienna which, under all circumstances, appears to his Majesty very extraordinary, but (he agrees with you) too good to be true. Indeed, if so decisive a battle had been fought on the 11th some notice would have been taken of it in the bulletins of the 12th and *14*th, and such an armistice could not possibly have been concluded.' (Harewood MSS.)

Taylor wrote again to Canning on the 28th: 'I have upon one or two occasions ventured to trouble you with a few observations which have always been kindly received, and this encourages me to intrude upon you what has occurred to me at the present anxious moment, not from any idea that what I mention would, if discovery of attention have been forgotten or overlooked, but rather with a view to ease my mind of what has borne heavy upon it since the disastrous intelligence from the Danube. I fear that we must consider the armistice as the forerunner of a peace by which the Spaniards will lose every ally excepting ourselves, and every hope of further diversion in their favor on the continent, and I conclude that we shall consider ourselves bound to support them to the utmost of our means while they maintain the struggle against France. Our force in the Peninsula is respectable, and when the expedition to the Scheldt has ended, whether successful or not, we may probably be able to spare a reinforcement to Spain of 10 or 12,000 men without losing sight of our security here or in Ireland, which indeed cannot be threatened for some time to come. Nothing, however, which we can send to the Peninsula will be able to keep the field in the long run against the very superior numbers eventually brought against us. We must allow for great wear and tear upon such a service, and experience has proved how little we can rely on the co-operation of the Spaniards for regular enterprizes in the field. We ought not therefore to make a step forward without considering the probability of an early retreat, and without securing a place of refuge which we may either maintain against superior forces, or whence we may embark without too great risk when defence becomes hopeless or useless. Unless the Spaniards will admit us into Cadiz, Lisbon appears the only point on which we can calculate, & it seems to me that the utmost exertion and expedition should be used in placing that town and the neighbouring positions, the principal passes of the Tagus &c., in the best possible state of defence. I believe that some precautions were taken by Sir John Cradock & some works raised, but they were upon a contracted scale in proportion to his small force, & more intended to check any temporary interruption to embarkation than to offer lengthened resistance to a superior force. It also appears from the requisition recently sent by Sir A. Wellesley at the desire of General Beresford that the defences of Lisbon and its outworks are in a bad state, miserably deficient in heavy ordnance and ammunition, and that there are no entrenching tools in store. Had the war in Germany continued this requisition would not have demanded early attention, but, as matters now stand, it becomes urgent, and I submit whether steps should not be immediately taken for supplying what is required to place Lisbon in a state of defence and whether engineers with artificers & possibly

[*From Lord Mulgrave, Admiralty, 24 July.*] Lord Mulgrave has been desired by Vice-Admiral Sir Edward Pellew to mention at a proper opportunity to your Majesty that the Vice-Admiral has brought from India a Royal tiger, perfectly white (the second of that description that has ever been seen in India) in the humble hope that your Majesty, in consideration of the extraordinary rarity of the animal, may graciously condescend to receive him as an humble tribute of duty from Sir Edward Pellew. (14545)

[*The King's reply, Windsor Castle, 25 July.*] The King returns his thanks to Lord Mulgrave for sending him the intelligence received from Rotterdam, and his Majesty desires that Lord Mulgrave will assure Sir Edward Pellew that he is sensible of his attention in bringing from India for him the white tyger which may be sent to the Tower. (14544)

3927   VISCOUNT CASTLEREAGH *to the* KING, *and the reply*

[*Dover Castle, 29 July* [*1809*], *2 p.m.*] Lord Castlereagh begs leave humbly to acquaint your Majesty that Admiral Otway sail'd this morning (with the division of the Fleet destined for the attack of the Island of Walcheren) from the Downs. Want of pilots for some of his ships prevented his moving, in obedience to his orders from Sir R. Strachan, with the two divisions which sail'd yesterday. The

a detachment of the Staff Corps should not be sent out to superintend the repairs of & additions to the works on which the garrison and the inhabitants should be employed. If this is done before there is an actual necessity for retreat, our army, being certain of an ultimate refuge, will act with more confidence in the field and will not be forced to detach a part or to hasten the retreat of the whole in order to prepare for its security when the crisis approaches, and when hurry may render such preparation very inadequate. Another very essential object is to avoid any separation or detachment which would prevent the whole force from uniting at Lisbon. Perhaps it may be material to place a good garrison in Elvas which is tenable and may occupy a part of the enemy's force, but Oporto and other places which are not tenable for any time, and from which retreat is precarious, might be left to the protection of our good friends the Portugueze.

I have only dwelt upon the importance of Lisbon, on the supposition that the Spaniards will persist in their refusal to admit us into Cadiz, but there is no doubt that, of the two, the latter is in every respect far preferable as a point of support & refuge, & perhaps this would be the moment to renew the proposal and to hold out to the Spaniards the prospect of additional efforts which might eventually procure to them at least the Province of Andalusia, provided they will enable us to make them, by affording that protection which we have a right to claim, while their refusal must oblige us to adopt the alternative of looking to Lisbon for a place of refuge, to confine our efforts to its defence, thus abandoning the south of Spain to its own resources, & of course not risking any more troops where so little disposition is shown to provide for their security under the chances of war. Even in the event of the Spaniards agreeing to receive us into Cadiz, the preservation of Lisbon should not be wholly lost sight of, but the preparations for it would be naturally upon a more limited scale, nor would it be advise-able to reduce the main force in any essential degree in order to provide a garrison for Lisbon which, unless protected by an army, can at best be defended for only a short time. We might, however, cal-culate upon a certain proportion of the Portugueze troops & add to them a small number of British to encourage them, & in all cases the maintenance of Lisbon would operate as a diversion for our army in the south of Spain. The general hospital and principal depot being also established there, the con-valescents would afford an addition to the garrison.

I beg you will not trouble yourself with answering this letter, and that you will forgive my taking up so much of your time with remarks which are probably very superfluous. As an excuse for entering into matters which do not concern me, I can only state that the subject is military and that this has always been my hobby horse.' (Harewood MSS.)

wind is so fair and the breeze now sufficiently strong to enable the whole force, with the exception of the reserve under the Earl of Rosselyn, to reach the rendez-vous before night. The reserve will proceed tomorrow. Lord Castlereagh submits to your Majesty a statement from the Transport Board of the equipment and force of the expedition, and proposes to return to his duty in town tomorrow morning.[1] (14547)

[*The King's reply, Windsor Castle, 30 July.*] The King acknowledges the receipt of Lord Castlereagh's letter and the accompanying statement from the Transport Board of the equipment and force of the expedition. His Majesty rejoices that the wind has continued so favorable since the first division sailed. (14548)

3928 LORD MULGRAVE *to the* KING, *and the reply*

[*Admiralty, 1 Aug. 1809.*] Lord Mulgrave has the honour to transmit to your Majesty dispatches from Vice-Admiral Sir James Saumarez containing the detail of a brilliant and successful attack in boats against a very superior force of the Russian flotilla, calculated to impress on the sailors of that country a just sense of the gallantry & enterprize of the officers and seamen of your Majesty's Navy.[2] (14553)

[*The King's reply, Windsor Castle, 2 Aug.*] The King entirely concurs in the sentiments which Lord Mulgrave's letter expresses in regard to the gallant attack made by the boats of the ships detached under Captain Martin[3] upon a part of the Russian flotilla in Perkola[4] Sound, at the same time that his Majesty laments the loss of so distinguished an officer as Lieutenant Hawkey and of the other valuable men who fell with him upon this occasion. (14553)

3929 PRINCESS AMELIA *to the* KING

[*Thursday night, 3 Aug. 1809.*] Much as it greives me to touch on anything un-pleasant to you, yet I feel more equal to doing it by writing than speaking, & after the affection you have shewn me, & more especially of late, I feel I shall be excused the liberty of addressing to you this letter.

After you left me today I saw Sir Francis Milman & Dr. Pope,[5] who assured me they were satisfied with the amendment they found in me, but they were of opinion there was great tenderness remaining on my lungs, & that being so much weakened I required strengthening, as a cold or any inflamation might

[1] For the draft of this letter, see *Castlereagh Corresp.*, VI, 297.

[2] Saumarez was still in command of the fleet which had been sent into the Baltic to support the Swedes against the Danes and the Russians. The action took place on 7 July. The Russian flotilla was convoying a number of vessels laden with provisions and ammunition for the Russian army in Finland. Six of the eight gunboats were captured, and one was sunk. The ships engaged were *Implacable, Bellero-phon, Melpomene* and *Prometheus.*   [3] Thomas Byam Martin, Captain of the *Implacable.*

[4] Contemporaries sometimes spelt it Pencola or Percola.

[5] A Quaker physician of Staines who, with unjustified optimism, was confident of his ability to restore her to health and strength.

prove of great consequence. They therefore were of opinion it was necessary I should go to the sea & that the warm baths & mild air of Weymouth would be of essential service & and better enable me to bear the winter. Under three weeks I shall not be able to move from hence but then it is their wish I should. You, my dearest father, may conceive how much I lament this but after Dr. Pope & Sir Francis have spoken so to *me* I could say nothing. My wish is to get *well*, & God knows I long to feel I am no longer a plague to my family. Hitherto I have submitted to everything & though a separation from all I love here is the most painful of all, yet I will not refuse doing anything which is likely to procure me health & enable me to return here well.

I have one request to make which if you grant would be a particular comfort to me; it is that Miny might go *with me*. I know she would be so very good to do it if she has leave & her good heart would feel pleasure in doing such a kind thing by me.

I hope I shall have the happiness of seeing you tomorrow. I will not take up more of your time upon this subject, but I cannot conclude without expressing my heartful gratitude for your tenderness to me & assure *you* that these feelings can end but with the existence of, my dearest papa [etc.]. (Add. Georgian 14/86)

3930   THE DUKE OF PORTLAND *to the* KING, *and the reply*

[*Burlington House, Monday, 6 [7] Aug. 1809.*] Considering the expectations which your Majesty will probably have formed that Lord Camden would undertake to convey to Lord Castlereagh the communication with which your Majesty had directed that he should be made acquainted; the Duke of Portland feels it to be his duty to inform your Majesty that in the course of the last week Ld. Camden repeatedly called upon him & endeavoured by every argument he could adduce to convince the Duke of Portland of the disadvantages to which the measure would be exposed by his being entrusted with the management of it; and if he did not succeed in bringing over the D. of Portland to his opinion in that respect, the D. of Portland cannot & ought not to conceal from your Majesty that Ld. Camden's reluctance appeared to be so great that the Duke of Portland did not think it right or usefull to urge him to get the better of it; & rather preferred the means of representing these circumstances to your Majesty, most humbly recommending it to your Majesty to indulge Lord Camden's wishes, which are *now*, as far as the Duke of Portland is capable of forming any judgement, the only means by which Lord Camden's influence & good offices appear likely to be exerted with effect. This then being the case, no other less objectionable mode of making the communication in question to Ld. Castlereagh suggests itself to the Duke of Portland than that of his being the immediate channel of your Majesty's commands & for that purpose he requests that your Majesty's pleasure may be signified to him both as to the time & manner of doing it. He would most humbly submit to your Majesty that some advantage may accrue from the communication being made prior to the final issue of the expedition, & though it is thought by many that the most fortunate moment at which it could be made would be *that* of complete success, as the reverse would render the measure all but impracticable (to those at least who are of opinion that nothing has been omitted, neglected, or overlooked in the Department over which Lord Castlereagh presides, of which your Majesty will permit the D. of P. to say that he is most fully convinced & satisfied) your Majesty will graciously condescend, I hope, to forbear from deferring the intimation to Ld. Castlereagh, & not require the Duke of Portland to subject himself to the risk of carrying your Majesty's orders into effect at so inauspicious a moment as that of failure—a moment which the D. of Portland most humbly begs leave to observe further would be one at which if such a removal should happen to take place, it would be impossible for Ld. Castlereagh to remain in your Majesty's service with advantage to your Majesty or credit to himself. All these circumstances therefore considered, the D. of Portland humbly presumes to hope that your Majesty will graciously condescend to accept this anxious request as a testimony of his dutifull attachment to your Majesty & a sollicitous regard to carry your commands into effect in such a manner as may appear to your Majesty most consistent with your Majesty's gracious intentions. (14556–8)

[*The King's reply, Windsor Castle, 7 Aug.*] The King has received the Duke of Portland's letter from which he clearly understands that Lord Camden declines being the channel of any communication to Lord Castlereagh. Under the circumstances it must rest with the Duke of Portland to consider of the best means and of the proper time to make a communication of which his Majesty has from the first felt the embarassment and the difficulty, and in which, as he has very reluctantly acquiesced, his Majesty cannot be expected to become a principal. The Duke of Portland must be aware that many of his colleagues are adverse to the measure & that it has been pressed forward much earlier than they had expected, and the King therefore conceives that the Duke of Portland should consult very fully with them upon the subject before he proceeds further in it. Whatever may be decided, H.M. is persuaded that every endeavor will be used to render so unpleasant a step as little distressing as possible to Lord Castlereagh. (14558)

3931   *Letters from* GEORGE CANNING *to the* KING, *and the replies*

[*11 Aug. 1809.*] Mr Canning humbly acquaints your Majesty that having received the accompanying despatches from Mr. Nicholas so late this evening that he could not venture to trouble your Majesty with them, & the Heligoland mail setting out tonight, he thought it his duty after communicating with Lord Mulgrave to write to Mr Nicholas the letter of which he humbly submits a copy. Lord Mulgrave is taking measures for providing the means of transporting the Duke of Brunswick's corps to whatever destination your Majesty may, upon consideration, think proper to assign to them. Upon this point Mr. Canning hopes to be able to collect, & humbly to lay before your Majesty the opinion of your Majesty's confidential servants tomorrow.[1] (14561)

[1] The Duke arrived in England a few days later (see No. 3933), as Lord Glenbervie said, 'after a retreat from the heart of Germany with a corps of about 2,000 men.... This retreat, as well as his spirited

[*The King's reply, Windsor Castle, 12 Aug.*] The King approves of the steps which Mr Canning has taken in consequence of the communications from Mr. Nicholas relative to the arrival of the Duke of Brunswick's corps at Elsfleith on the Weser. (14562)

[*From Canning, Foreign Office, 12 Aug.*] Mr. Canning humbly submits to your Majesty the draft of a dispatch to Mr. Nicholas, prepared after consultation with such of your Majesty's confidential servants as are in town; which dispatch, if approved by your Majesty, will be forwarded to Heligoland by Colonel Dornberg[1] tomorrow. (14563)

[*The King's reply, Windsor Castle, 13 Aug.*] The King approves of Mr Canning's dispatch to Mr. Nicholas respecting the corps of the Duke of Brunswick-Oels. (14564)

[*From Canning, 13 Aug.*] Mr. Canning thinks it his duty humbly to transmit to your Majesty the copy of a letter from Count Wessenburg, the Austrian Minister at Berlin, to Count Waldstein (the original of which has been communicated to Mr. Canning by Prince Starhemberg) although he does not venture to indulge in all the favourable inferences which Prince Starhemberg is inclined to draw from it. (14565)

[*The King's reply, Windsor Castle, 14 Aug.*] The King acknowledges Mr. Canning's communication of Count Wessenburg's letter to Count Waldstein which does not appear to his Majesty very encouraging as it was written previous to Count Wessenburg's knowledge of the armistice.[2] (14566)

3932 VISCOUNT CASTLEREAGH *to the* KING

[*Downing Street, 14 Aug. 1809.*] Lord Castlereagh cannot delay till the morning submitting to your Majesty the accompanying dispatches from Lt.-Genl. Sir Arthur Wellesley.

The force of the enemy is stated in all the private accounts not to have been less than 45,000 men, and as the whole effort was directed against your Majesty's troops, the glory of the defeat is entirely attributable to their steadiness and bravery.

Lord Castlereagh deeply laments the severe loss which he has to lay before

exertions in the earlier part of the year with his little army, has been much celebrated, and he has been talked of as another Xenophon.' (*Glenbervie Journals*, II, 24.)

Castlereagh believed that the Duke would probably wish to proceed to Walcheren with his Corps, which was to be taken into British pay. (*Castlereagh Corresp.*, VI, 303.)

[1] Castlereagh referred to Colonel Dubourg [*sic*] as the officer sent by the Duke to signify to the British Government his desire to place himself and his corps under Lord Chatham's orders; and the Colonel was ordered to communicate to the Duke the King's pleasure. (*Castlereagh Corresp.*, VI, 303.)

[2] An armistice on 12 July, a few days after the battle of Wagram, ended Austria's war with France.

your Majesty, but he has the satisfaction to learn from Lord Fitzroy Somerset,[1] that a large proportion of the wounded are but slightly injured.

Sir A. Wellesley was himself struck in the shoulder by a spent ball from the enemy's tiralleurs towards the close of the action. (14567–8)

3933   *Letters from* GEORGE CANNING *to the* KING, *and a reply*

[*14 Aug. 1809.*] Mr. Canning most humbly acquaints your Majesty that, upon receiving the letter which he humbly submits to your Majesty from the Duke of Brunswick-Oels, he has thought it right to send down his private secretary to Harwich (as the most probable place for his Serene Highness's landing), to conduct his Serene Highness up to town. (14569)

[*The King's reply, Windsor Castle, 15 Aug.*] The King entirely approves of Mr. Canning's having sent his private secretary to Harwich to meet the Duke of Brunswick-Oels & to conduct him to London.[2] (14570)

[*From Canning, Foreign Office, 15 Aug., 1 p.m.*] Mr. Canning thinks it his duty to lose no time in humbly acquainting your Majesty of the arrival of H.S.H. the Duke of Brunswick-Oels who reached London this morning. His Serene Highness expresses great desire to be allowed an opportunity of paying his duty to your Majesty. His Serene Highness, upon learning from Mr Canning that he could not expect to be enabled to report to H.S.H. your Majesty's gracious pleasure in this respect before tomorrow morning, has resolved to proceed immediately to the house of H.R.H. the Dutchess of Brunswick, to whom Mr Canning had notified H.S.H.'s arrival.

The Duke of Brunswick appears in perfect health. (14571)

3934   *Letters from the* DUKE OF PORTLAND *to the* KING, *and the reply*

[*Bulstrode, Tuesday, 15 Aug. 1809.*] The Duke of Portland most humbly begs leave to offer to your Majesty the tribute of his gratefull & unbounded admiration of the extraordinary achievement performed by your Majesty's troops under the command of Sir Arthur Wellesley & to express his earnest hope & prayer that it may be attended with all the favorable effects which it is intitled to, & which it is calculated to produce. (14572)

[1] Lord Fitzroy James Henry Somerset, 1st Baron Raglan (1788–1855), youngest son of Henry, 5th Duke of Beaufort. Entered the Army, 1804; Lieutenant, 1805; Captain, 1808; Major, 1811; Lieutenant-Colonel, 1812; Colonel and A.D.C. to the Prince Regent, 1815; Major-General, 1825; Lieutenant-General, 1838; General, 1854; Field-Marshal, 1854. A.D.C. and Military Secretary to Wellington during the Peninsula War (appointed Jan. 1811). K.C.B., 1815; G.C.B., 1847. M.P. for Truro, 1818–20 and 1826–9. Secretary to the Master-General of the Ordnance, 1819–27; Military Secretary to the Commander-in-Chief, 1827–52; Master-General of the Ordnance, 1852–5. Peerage, Oct. 1852. British Commander-in-Chief in the Crimea, 1854–5.

Wellesley's dispatches described the battle of Talavera (27–8 July) and the defeat of the French under Victor, both sides sustaining heavy casualties in desperate fighting.

[2] The Duke arrived at the Clarendon Hotel in London on the 15th.

[*From the Duke of Portland, Bulstrode, Tuesday, 15 Aug.*] The Duke of Portland most humbly requests your Majesty's permission to lay his most dutifull & gratefull thanks at your Majesty's feet for the great goodness & indulgence which your Majesty has condescended to shew him on occasion of his present indisposition from which he can venture to assure your Majesty that he is already sufficiently recovered to be able to execute any commands your Majesty may think proper to lay upon him but at the same time he cannot but acknowledge that he shall not be sorry to avail himself of your Majesty's indulgence for the remainder of this week unless your Majesty shall deem his return to town necessary or desireable in any respect.[1] (14573)

[*The King's reply, Windsor Castle, 16 Aug.*] The King has learnt with sincere satisfaction from the Duke of Portland's letter that he is so much recovered, but his Majesty trusts that he will not think of moving from Bulstrode for some days, as he must be sensible that the first moments of re-establishment are not those suited to exertion. The King concurs with the Duke of Portland in the sentiments which he expresses on the conduct of his gallant Army in Spain, but deeply laments that success, however glorious, has been so dearly bought. (14574)

3935 VISCOUNT CASTLEREAGH *to the* KING, *and the reply*

[*Downing Street, 17 Aug. 1809.*] The splendid services of your Majesty's Army in Spain has induced your Majesty's confidential servants humbly to submit to your Majesty the propriety of a general order being issued by your Majesty's Commander-in-Chief to the Army, signifying the sense which your Majesty is graciously pleased to entertain of the conduct of your troops in Spain upon the late occasion. They also beg leave to submit to your Majesty that the commanders of Corps should receive the same distinction which your Majesty was pleased to signify your intention of conferring in the instances of the actions of Vimiera and Corunna. (14575)

[*The King's reply, Windsor Castle, 18 Aug.*] The King approves of Lord Castlereagh's proposal that a general order should be issued to the Army on the occasion of the late victory in Spain, and that medals should be conferred on the commanding officers of corps engaged on the 27th & 28th of July. (14576)

[1] On Friday the 11th the Duke had an epileptic seizure whilst on his way from London to Bulstrode. The King was so strongly impressed with the serious consequences of this attack, though the Duke temporarily and rather unexpectedly recovered, that he began seriously to think of replacing him. (Chatham Papers. Camden to Chatham, 17 Aug.) According to W. H. Fremantle the Duke's illness was described to the King only as a fainting fit, yet, he added, 'nothing can equal the gloom it has created at Windsor, and adding this difficulty to the sensations created by the complete failure of the expedition, it has, I believe, at last made the King feel that something must immediately be done to satisfy the public mind, and to secure himself. . . I fully believe he will endeavour to support this wretched and desperate Government by offering the Treasury to Lord Harrowby or Bathurst. That either of these men will be mad enough to accept it under the present circumstances I cannot possibly believe. The present temper of the King is gloomy to a degree, and I know him to be in a state of the greatest distress of mind, but not irritable in the slightest manner.' (Buckingham, *Court and Cabinets of George III*, IV, 349.)

3936　GEORGE CANNING *to the* KING, *and the reply*

[*Foreign Office, 17 Aug. 1809.*] Mr. Canning, in humbly submitting to your Majesty a draft which he has prepared of a despatch to Lord Amherst,[1] in consequence of despatches received this day from that Minister, & herewith laid before your Majesty, begs permission humbly to state to your Majesty that he had not troubled your Majesty with the letter from the Duke of Orleans to which Lord Amherst's despatch refers; that letter being marked *confidential* & being of a nature, in Mr. Canning's opinion, rather to be left without any answer whatever than to be made matter of official correspondence.

Mr. Canning is now under the necessity of troubling your Majesty with the Duke of Orleans's letter, & he humbly submits to your Majesty at the same time the draft of an answer which he has prepared to it. (14577–8)

[*The King's reply, Windsor Castle, 18 Aug.*] The King approves of the answer which Mr. Canning proposes to return to the Duke of Orleans's letter & of that which he has prepared for Lord Amherst. (14578)

3937　LORD MULGRAVE *to the* KING, *and the reply*

[*Admiralty, 17 Aug. 1809.*] Lord Mulgrave has the honour most humbly to report to your Majesty that in obedience to your Majesty's commands notice has been given to Capt. Sir Harry Neale to take the command of your Majesty's yatch for the accommodation of her Royal Highness the Princess Amelia; the seamen of the Royal Sovereign having volunteer'd their services were permitted to join the expedition to the Scheldt, but orders have been sent for their immediate return; and in the interim tried & steady seamen will be sent on board of the yatch.

The Nereus of 32 guns 18 lbs. commanded by Capt. Heywood[2] and the Narcissus of 32 guns 18 lbs. commanded by the Honble. Capt. Aylmer[3] have been ordered to Weymouth for the security of her Royal Highness the Princess Amelia. (14579)

[*The King's reply, Windsor Castle, 18 Aug.*] The King acquaints Lord Mulgrave that the arrangements which he has made in consequence of the Princess Amelia's intended residence at Weymouth are perfectly satisfactory to his Majesty. (14580)

3938　THE DUKE OF PORTLAND *to the* KING,[4] *and the reply*

[*Bulstrode, Friday, 18 Aug. 1809.*] The Viscount Castlereagh having informed the Duke of Portland of the commands he had received from your Majesty to signify to the officers and privates composing your Majesty's Army under the command of Sir Arthur Wellesley, your most gracious approbation and acceptance

---

[1] Minister at Palermo.　　　[2] Peter Heywood (1773–1831). Lieutenant, 1795; Captain, 1803.
[3] Frederick Whitworth William Aylmer (1777–1858). Lieutenant, 1796; Captain, 1805; Rear-Admiral, 1837; Vice-Admiral, 1848; Admiral, 1854. Succeeded his brother as 6th Baron Aylmer [I.], 23 Feb. 1850. C.B., 1816; K.C.B., 1855.　　　[4] Not in the Duke's own hand.

of their services in the signal victory obtained by them over the French at Talavera, and that your Majesty had been pleased to order medals to be struck in commemoration of that most glorious event, and presented to the officers commanding corps on that occasion, the Duke of Portland most humbly submits to your Majesty's superior judgement the propriety of conferring upon Sir Arthur Wellesley himself that eminent mark of honour by which your Majesty has been used to distinguish the Commanders-in-Chief of your forces upon occasions of a similar nature, and as, notwithstanding the many acts of military skill and prowess which have signalized your Majesty's glorious reign, a parallell to the event of Talavera will not readily occur, the Duke of Portland presumes to hope that your Majesty may not deem it too great a reward to raise Sir Arthur Wellesley not only to the rank of the Peerage but to the dignity of a Viscount in the first instance—a suggestion which upon reflection may not appear so unreasonable when his services at Vimiera[1] and in the passage of the Douro[2] are taken into the scale, for neither of which he ever received any consideration whatever—and the Duke of Portland ventures to flatter himself that he shall not be deemed too presumptuous by your Majesty in submitting to your Majesty's gracious consideration the eminent services of Lieutenant-General Sherbrooke, as intitling him to the honourable distinction of a supernumerary Ribbon of the Order of the Bath. (14581–3)

[*The King's reply, Windsor Castle, 19 Aug.*] The King entirely approves of the Duke of Portland's proposal that Sir Arthur Wellesley should be raised to the dignity of a Viscount & that Lieut.-General Sherbroke should receive a supernumerary Ribband of the Order of the Bath. (14583)

3939 VISCOUNT CASTLEREAGH to the KING, and the reply

[*19 Aug. 1809.*] Lord Castlereagh has the satisfaction of laying before your Majesty the accompanying dispatches from Lt.-Genl. the Earl of Chatham notifying the surrender of the fortress of Flushing to your Majesty's arms on the 16th inst. (14585)

[*The King's reply, Windsor Castle, 20 Aug.*] The King has received with great satisfaction Lord Castlereagh's communication of Lord Chatham's dispatches containing the account of the surrender of Flushing, in consequence of exertions so honorable to those employed on the occasion, and which his Majesty observes with pleasure have not been attended with any serious loss to his Army & Navy. (14585)

3940 GEORGE CANNING to the KING, and the reply

[*19 Aug. 1809 (Copy).*] Mr. Canning humbly trusts that your Majesty will forgive his troubling your Majesty at an unusual hour with intelligence so important as that contained in the accompanying dispatches from Mr. Horne. (Harewood MSS.)

[1] 21 Aug. 1808.   [2] 12 May 1809.

[*Col. Taylor's reply, Windsor, 19 Aug.*] The King has honored me with his commands to thank you for the communication of the intelligence from Mr. Horne & Mr. Nicholas which his Majesty considers extremely interesting & important and which he trusts will be fully confirmed. (Harewood MSS.)

3941   *Letters from* LORD MULGRAVE *to the* KING, *and the replies*

[*19 Aug. 1809.*] Lord Mulgrave has the honour to transmit to your Majesty the dispatches of Rear-Admiral Sir Richard Strahan with enclosures, detailing the naval operations against the town of Flushing, together with the terms of capitulation & surrender of that fortress. Lord Mulgrave humbly begs leave to point out to your Majesty's gracious notice the cordial emulation of the Navy with your Majesty's land forces in the display of dutiful zeal for your Majesty's service; in which Rear-Admirals Strahan and Lord Gardner & the officers & men acting under their orders have manifested the customary & characteristick skill & enterprize of your Majesty's Navy. (14586)

[*The King's reply, Windsor Castle, 20 Aug.*] The King has received with great satisfaction Lord Mulgrave's letter with the accompanying dispatches from Rear-Admiral Sir R. Strachan, and showing the whole course of the arduous service in the Scheldt. His Majesty has viewed with great pleasure the cordial emulation which has distinguished the joint services of his Army & Navy. (14587)

[*From Lord Mulgrave, Admiralty, 27 Aug.*] Lord Mulgrave has the honour to transmit to your Majesty the proceedings & sentence of a naval court martial held at Rio Janiero by which Luke Mighton was condemned to death for mutinous behaviour and striking Lt. William Edwards his superior officer: the members of the court martial & the Commander-in-Chief on that station have severally recommended Luke Mighton to your Majesty's mercy under such united recommendation, and considering that the arrival of the criminal in this country precludes the effect of example upon those who were serving where the crime was committed, if the law should here take its course, Lord Mulgrave feels that he cannot do otherwise than most humbly submit to your Majesty's gracious consideration to acquiesce in the recommendation of Rear-Admiral Sir Sidney Smith & of the court martial, by extending to Luke Mighton your Majesty's most gracious pardon. (14589)

[*The King's reply, Windsor Castle, 29 Aug.*] In consideration of what is stated in Lord Mulgrave's letter and the recommendation of the court martial in the case of Luke Mighton, the King consents to the proposed extension of his pardon to him. (14590)

3942   THE KING *to the* DUCHESS OF BRUNSWICK

[*Windsor Castle, 27 Aug. 1809.*] I am glad to learn from your kind letter that you approve of the intention of bringing your grandchildren to this country, & I should conceive that it will rest with you to determine upon the number of persons who shall accompany them. I was very happy to learn from Count Munster this day that you are perfectly well. (16788)

3943 PRINCESS MARY *to the* KING, *and the reply*

[*Hartford Bridge, 28 Aug.* [*1809*].] My heart was so full this morning when we parted I could not express half what I felt & how deeply I feel all your kindness to me. Believe me I am grateful & hope in God I shall ever deserve all your goodness.

Our dearest Amelia has performed her journey far beyond my hopes & expectations, the last half hour before we arrived at Hartford Bridge she was a good deal fatigued & I think has done full as *much* today as she ought in her delicate state. She has been much relieved by tears & is now perfectly composed laying down on the couch & has ordered her dinner to be ready at half passed three o'clock. Pope is not yet come; I shall send his opinion if possible by the post as it will be more satisfactory to hearing he is [more] satisfied than I even am. Indeed her recovery has been so great within these last 10 days that I own I am full of hope I may have the happiness to bring her home much *restored* to health if not quite so, & that alone can reward us for all we have suffered & must be bearing untill we all meet again. Nothing but seeing what Amelia suffers at the idea of leaving her family could have induced *me* to *agree* to such a *trial* as the leaving you all, but when I reflected how much more shocking it would have been for her, *ill* as she is, to have been obliged to *submit* to go from home without one of her family, I felt I was blessed with health & was so much more able to stand such a trial than her that it was a duty to try to elevate [*sic*] her distress by sharing her sorrows & doing all I could to make up for all the misery she has endured from want of health for the last six months, & I trust in God all our anxiety may now be turned into joy. Dr. Pope is not yet arrived. (Add. Georgian 12/34)

[*The King's reply, Windsor Castle, 29 Aug.*] I have received very sincere pleasure from your kind letter of yesterday evening and the satisfactory report which you were enabled to make of your first day's journey, & I anxiously hope that your accounts will continue equally favorable and promising & that my dear Amelia's progress will realize our most sanguine expectations. I am fully sensible of the dutiful and affectionate motives by which you are influenced upon this & every occasion and too much alive to the warm attachment which you have always shewn towards me, not to feel deeply affected by your absence, to which a conviction of the comfort which your attendance on Amelia must afford to her could alone have reconciled me. I need not add that your conduct in this instance has, if possible, endeared you still further to [etc.]. (Add. Georgian 12/35)

[*Hartford Bridge, 28 Aug. 1809.*] Feeling myself refreshed from laying down I cannot resist taking up my pen to inform you, my beloved father, that we reached this place near three o'clock & I think as well as I could expect, though a good deal tired, & the last few miles I felt more pain in my side. Everything is very comfortable here & the carriage I found remarkably easy & the coachmen drove a very steady pace.

Once more allow me to express my thanks for your *never ceasing* but *increasing kindness* to me, & my prayer is I ever may prove worthy of it. All I felt at leaving Windsor I will not attempt to say anything about, but assure you my heart is left behind & my gratitude can end but with my existence. Dearest Miny is all goodness and is very well, as also Ly. George.[1]

May every blessing attend you, my dearest papa, is my constant prayer; pray give my duty to dear mama & I hope she will excuse my writing to her till tomorrow. (Add. Georgian 14/89)

[*The King's reply, Windsor Castle, 29 Aug.*] I will not delay thanking you for your kind and welcome letter of yesterday which has afforded me the greatest satisfaction and, from the improvement which had lately taken place in your health and the manner in which you have borne the first day's journey, I flatter myself that your progress at Weymouth will keep pace with my anxious wishes. Persuaded as I am of your sincere attachment, I am sensible of what you must have felt at parting from me, & you will believe that nothing but a conviction of its being necessary to the restoration of your health could have induced me to consent to the absence of yourself & dear Mary, who have ever been such a comfort to [etc.]. (Add. Georgian 14/90)

3945 THE DUKE OF NEWCASTLE *to the* KING

[*Ramsgate, 28 Aug. 1809.*] With the utmost defference I venture to address your Majesty and trust that with your usual condescention your Majesty will be graciously pleased to attend to the petition I have to lay before you and allow me humbly to beg that in the case of the Government of the Royal Military College becoming vacant, Genl. Craufurd[2] may be appointed to succeed the Earl Harcourt.[3]

Presuming upon your Majesty's goodness and gracious disposition towards me, I am emboldened thus humbly to address to you, Sire, my earnest wishes for Genl. Craufurd's success, and hope I may be allowed to express the high sense

[1] The widow of Lord George Murray (1761–1803), Bishop of St. David's. Anne Charlotte Murray (1765–1844), whom he married on 18 Dec. 1780, was the daughter of Lieutenant-General Francis Grant, M.P. (1717–81). She and the Marchioness of Ely were Ladies of the Bedchamber to the elder Princesses. In 1804 the King had thought of her as Governess to Princess Charlotte, and George Rose gave him a very favourable account of her. (Rose, *Diaries and Corresp.*, II, 186, 188.)

[2] The Duke's mother (1760–1834), who was widowed on 18 May 1795, had married Lieutenant-General Sir Charles Gregan Craufurd (*d.* 1821) on 7 Feb. 1800.

[3] Major-General Alexander Hope succeeded Lord Harcourt as Governor in 1811.

I should entertain of the favor which would be conferred upon me by his being appointed, on a vacancy, to succeed Earl Harcourt as Governor of the Royal Military College.[1] (14591–2)

3946 GEORGE CANNING to the KING, and the reply

[*Foreign Office, 29 Aug. 1809.*] Mr. Canning humbly requests your Majesty's gracious permission to present Lord Walpole[2] (who brought the last despatches from the Austrian Headquarters) to your Majesty at the Levée tomorrow. (14593)

[*The King's reply, Windsor Castle, 30 Aug.*] The King approves of Mr. Canning's appointing Lord Walpole at the Queen's Palace this day. (14593)

3947 PRINCESS MARY to the KING, and the reply

[*Weymouth, 31 Aug. [1809].*] I must begin by returning you my most grateful thanks for the very gracious letter I had the honour of receiving at Andover & which I delayed expressing the pleasure & happiness it gave me untill I could give you the joyfull intelligence that our dear Amelia was safely arrived at this place, & considering all circumstances has borne the journey better than could be expected in her very delicate state of health, and Dr. Pope, who saw her half an hour after we got to Weymouth, found her less fatigued & better than he expected. We left Woodgate Inn[3] this morning at 9 o'clock & got to Blandford soon after 11 when Amelia was so faint & unwell that we rested near half an hour, when we proceded to General Garth's, who received us with the greatest kindness, & nothing could exceed his attention & wish that Amelia should find everything comfortable at his house, and everything I must say was quite perfection; all in the most compleat order, & just as one would expect to find his house. I am sorry to add he looks very ill & is still very lame & appeared in his large cloth shoes, & I fear must have fatigued himself with all the trouble he gave himself, as he would hobble up & downstairs much oftener than necessary & would not let anybody attend at breakfast but himself. The house[4] is quite an old-fashion[ed] mansion; it stands

---

[1] The Duke of Newcastle was a 'King's Friend'. He had supported the 'Talents' and he supported the Portland Ministry. He wrote to Lord Grenville from Clumber on 2 April 1807: 'It is a matter of great regret to me that the country is deprived of your Lordship's able direction of affairs, which is much to be lamented at this important period. With respect to the subject which is the object of your Lordship's letter the only answer I can make is, that it is my intention to remain with the King. My duty and inclination require this under the present circumstances—and I am sure your Lordship will be the last to condemn the motive which will preclude the possibility of my having the honour of continuing to act in concert with you.' (Fortescue MSS.)

[2] Horatio, Lord Walpole (1783–1858), styled Lord Walpole from 24 Feb. 1809, when his grandfather, the 1st Earl of Orford, died, until 15 June 1822, when he succeeded his father as 3rd Earl. M.P for King's Lynn, 1809–22. Attaché at Petersburg, 1806, and at Madrid, 1808; a Lord of the Admiralty, 1811–12; Secretary of Embassy at Petersburg, 1812–15, and Minister *ad interim*, 1813–15; a Commissioner for India, 1818–22.

[3] Four miles north of Cranborne.

[4] Ilsington, in the village of Puddletown (or Piddletown), three miles from Dorchester. The General rented it from the Earl of Orford.

in a courtyard & the approach up to it is under an old avenue of fir trees. You come into an emence [*sic*] old large hall, up a very large staircase which brings one into the most delightful, comfortable long library I ever saw, which has three windows & one in with [*sic*]¹a long kind of recess with a balcony, which is quite charming, & this room is the General's constant living-room, summer & winter. His bedroom is next to it, which is likewise a very large good room. Below I saw a very good dancing [?]² room & a drawing room, all equal large rooms, very lofty & well proportioned. The General was very much overcome at seeing Amelia & from being so unwell himself I beged he would *recover* himself before he went upstairs to her, during which time Amelia recovered & we got all very cheerful at breakfast, so much so that Amelia was quite comfortable before we set off on our journey again. We left the General about half past three & got home by a quarter after 5 o'clock. From Dorchester Amelia was very much overcome indeed, but greatly relieved with tears. The first coming into this house here no less affected us all as every place put us in mind of you all.

Sir Harry Neal met us at the door & helped to take Amelia out of the carriage. We drove as you desired into the courtyard & took Amelia at once into the room that is now her bedroom, which she finds very comfortable. All her own things she found all placed just as she likes. The little couch arrived & looks very nice in that room. Dr. Pope likes her appartment very much; thinks *your room* will be a very charming room for her to eat in & is quite delighted with the place. General Garth has made every arrangement you desired & thought of *everything* for our comfort, not even forgeting to leave asses milk ready if Dr. Pope found it necessary; he has secured good milk & butter for our breakfast & *fruit* of all sorts, in particular, grapes for Amelia: indeed he has forgot nothing & thought of everything. He intends to be with us tomorrow by dinner. I beged him not to hurry himself as I was sure you never could wish him to make himself ill by over exertion. Sir H. Neal finds No. 4 very comfortable; Lady Neal³ comes early in the next week. This house is very clean & nice & we found all in good order. The place appears very full but I can give you no account of it yet. I will not add all I felt in coming into the house as my heart was so full it was with dificulty I could keep my feelings from Amelia, who, poor soul, was so dreadfully overcome herself that she required every attention from us all. I shall add how she passed the night before I put up this. With duty to the Q. & love to my sisters.

[P.S.] Sepr. the 1st. Amelia has had but an indiferent night; a good deal of pain in her side which Pope says is more owing to fatigue than anything else, but as he will write his own opinion I will add no more today. I shall write to the Q. tomorrow. (Add. Georgian 12/36)

[*The King's reply, Windsor Castle, 2 Sept.*] I lose no time in thanking you for your kind & interesting letter with the account which you have given me of your

---

¹ 'With' is written over another word. The Princess obviously meant 'within'.

² Not 'dressing' room and apparently not 'dining' room. The writing is very indistinct.

³ Sir Harry Burrard (1765–1840) married Grace Elizabeth (*c.* 1773–1855), daughter and coheiress of Robert (or Richard) Neale of Shaw House, Wiltshire, on 15 April, 1795, and he took the additional surname of Neale.

proceedings since you wrote from Hartford Bridge, and of your safe arrival at Weymouth which has relieved me from much anxiety. Much as I regret that dear Amelia has suffered so much from the fatigue of her journey, I had not dared to flatter myself that in her weak state she would have supported it better, but I trust that after a few days quiet & rest and when the first agitation of her feelings, which are so natural, has subsided, the improvement in her health & spirits will reward her for the exertion she has made & afford you every comfort & satisfaction which your affection & attention to her so well merit.

I was well assured that you would experience every possible attention from General Garth & am very sensible of the trouble he has taken. I only hope that his indisposition will not be increased by the exertions he has made. (Add. Georgian 12/37)

3948   VISCOUNT CASTLEREAGH *to the* KING, *and the reply*

[*Downing Street, 2 Sept. 1809.*] Lord Castlereagh having brought the dispatch of the Earl of Chatham under the consideration of your Majesty's confidential servants, it has appear'd to them that, under the circumstances stated, it only remains for them humbly to recommend to your Majesty that the Army, with the exception of the force requisite for the security of Walcheren, should be order'd to return to England. They have not deem'd it adviseable, under the circumstances stated, with respect to the health of the troops, to suggest any further operations in that quarter beyond those contain'd in your Majesty's original instructions, as the enemy's naval force in the Meuse does not appear to them of sufficient magnitude to justify them in recommending protracted operations at this season in an unhealthy climate for the chance of effecting their destruction. (14594–5)

[*The King's reply, Windsor Castle, 3 Sept.*] The King entirely concurs in the opinion of his confidential servants which Lord Castlereagh has submitted for his Majesty's approbation, and sanctions the instructions prepared in conformity to it for Lord Chatham.[1] (14595)

3949   PRINCESS AMELIA *to the* KING, *and the reply*

[*Saturday, 2 Sept. 1809.*] Had dear Miny not written to you I would not have delayed so long writing to you to inform you of our arrival at this place, & to

---

[1] 'I look upon the Antwerp expedition as being wholly at an end,' the Duke of Cumberland had written to Eldon on 25 Aug.; and he then urged the dispatch of an expedition to North Germany where the people would welcome a liberating army. He again spoke bitterly of Ministers for ignoring his own claims to a military command: 'The time is now come to break through that narrow and vile policy which has seemed to reign in our Cabinet that the King's sons are to be held out to the country not as useful members but merely as burthens to the people...I feel ashamed of my situation; I appear debased in my own eyes, and yet I feel I *could be of service to my country if my country would allow me.*' (Eldon MSS.) He had this comment to make when a Military Government (Portsmouth) became vacant by the death of Sir William Augustus Pitt on 29 Dec. 1809: 'Some time ago I was informed that *I* was to have that Government. Now the Devil take me if I would ask for that or any other thing, but I shall be *curious* if it is *offered me.*' (*Ibid.*)

tell you how very comfortable in every respect I find the house. Most thankful was I to feel myself arrived at this place & under my dear father's own *roof*, but I cannot express all the sensations I felt at coming here.

I was very much fatigued with my journey & the pain in my side and fatigue I still feel considerable, & Doctor Pope thinks it will be some days before I recover [from] it. Doctor Pope's arrival was a great comfort to me; he applied leeches to my side gen[erall]y & the whole side is very much inflamed. He left me this morng. much better satisfied & indeed had he not been he would have staid longer, but he returns in a fortnight & will then stay longer. Dr. Pope has left every written direction with Mr. Beaver,[1] with whom he has had a great deal of conversation & he is to hear from him every other day.

I must now tell you, my dear father, & how am I to say what I want & feel for you *increase* my affection & gratitude to you every day. Long has it been out of my power to express what my heart feels for your affection which I really find every hour more, for here you have planned & thought of everything which would make me comfortable. I find it in something new every day.

My rooms are very comfortable & I like to think of you so much; everything recalls former times & I like your knowing everything about us & that we *are* under your roof & not in any strange place.

Dr. Pope has forbid my walking upstairs at present & your footmen carry me very well; the carriage I found very easy. We found Sr. Harry[2] here; he is very well & all good nature as well as Gl. Garth. Miny tells me Sir Harry told her a new constructed vessel of some gentleman's with four masts tried to sail round the yacht, but the yacht completely beat it.

I have not moved out of my room yet except just to dine in your dressing room & have been quite quiet & alone & dear Miny has sat reading with me. I have beged her to ask Sr. H. & Gl. Garth all the particulars of the improvements of this place which I will enclose to one of my sisters. There is a great deal of company here, but the houses, tho' occupied, are let by *floors* chiefly, & three & four families occupy one house.

I believe the yacht & only one frigate is come in; the sea is very rough today & wind very high.

God bless you, my dear papa, & excuse this long dull letter, but I wished to give you an account of myself, knowing how kind you are on this subject. (Add. Georgian 14/91)

[*The King's reply, Windsor Castle, 4 Sept.*] Your kind letter of the 2d. has given me great pleasure as it contains upon the whole a more favorable account of your health & in addition to what I learnt from Doctor Pope last night confirms me in the hope that I shall now have the comfort of receiving assurances of your dayly progress. I am sensible that some days rest will be required to remove the effects of a fatiguing journey and I trust that with these the pain will also subside, and that you will then be enabled to derive the utmost benefit from the change of air & gentle exercise, but I am confident that you will feel the necessity of keeping in

---

[1] Or Beavor, the local apothecary.　　　　　　[2] Neale.

other respects as quiet as you can & not attempting any over exertion. I am very glad that you have found the house and all the arrangements comfortable as it has been my anxious desire that nothing should be wanting which could in any degree tend to your ease & satisfaction.

I must not omit thanking you for the very excellent pair of Salisbury scissors which you have sent me and I remain [etc.]. (Add. Georgian 14/92)

3950 PRINCESS MARY *to the* KING, *and the reply*

[*5 Sept.* [*1809*].] I have the happiness of informing you dearest Amelia this morning, with Beavor's consent, was carried from her own room into a bathing machine that G. Garth and Sir H. Neal contrived to be placed just opposite Number 4 and was drawn out into the sea as if she was going to bathe. Sir H. Neal had the arrangement of making the inside comfortable & nothing ever answered so well. It is the machine they call yours. By taking off the side benches it enabled Sir H. to place one of the couches belonging to the yacht on one side which Amelia lay upon & gave place for two little small chairs which Lady George & me sat upon & did not keep the air from her. Sir H. contrived a green canvass window that takes on & off to be placed before the door of the machine towards the sea so that when placed in this window draws up & down just as is convenient or pleasant to Amelia so that it keeps off all draft & the great glare of the sea. We remained near a quarter of an hour; she was rather faint as the motion of the sea rather affected her; in consequence we returned home, I trust sooner than we shall another day. Sir H. thought of every convenience ever contrived, a small table for her; therefore I flatter myself if this mild weather lasts she may enjoy herself in breathing the sea air without any fatigue & untill she is stronger may answer better than a boxed-in carriage. This machine puts me in mind of our dear old baby house at Kew. I wish I could say Amelia finds any diference as to the pain in her side, which certainly has been increased by the journey & which some degree of pain brought on from the fatigue helps to have made worse since we left Windsor. As she has never been out of the house till today & indeed has hardly been out of her bed we can be no judge of what affect this mild air may have in restoring her & a few days going out constantly may cause a great change for the better as she has by no means recovered [from] the journey. Yet it requires some days still before any decided opinion can be formed one way or the other. It appears to me as if Bevor perfectly understood her complaint; he is very attentive & when once one gets over his dreadful manner he certainly talks most sensably & may add comfortably as to her recovery with care, but calls her 'a *hot house plant*'. G. Garth had some dificulty in procuring an ass and when Mr. Weld heard of it he sent two over this morning which we are to keep as long as is necessary. We have not seen the Welds yet as they are only just come into this part of the world. The Grosvenors, Framptons & Lord Ilchester have all called to enquire. Yesterday I thought Amelia better all day than I have ever seen her since we arrived at this place. I was therefore disapointed this morning to hear she had had but an indiferent night, which of course makes her languid today.

I am perfectly ashamed to have wrote as far & not yet returned you my most greatful [sic] thanks for your kind letter I received two days ago; deeply do I feel every word contained in it & I pray God our joint prayers may be heard as to the restoration of dear Amelia's health.

I have always forgot to name in any of my letters what a very good affect [sic] your figure was cut out in the rock on horseback. Sir H. Neal went to see it the other morning & draged [sic] his horse up the rock to measure the size of the hat, which in length measures fourteen yards, & of course the rest is all in proportion. G. Garth says nothing but a sailor or a madman ever would have draged a horse up that hill.

I am happy to add since writing the above Amelia has made a better dinner than she has done since we arrived at this place.

Sept. the 6. I am most happy to be able to say dear Amelia since three o'clock has had a great deal of good quiet sleep & Mr. Bevor assures me she has less pain today. (Add. Georgian 12/38.)

[*The King's reply, Windsor Castle, 7 Sept.*] Your kind letters afford me too much interest and comfort to allow me to delay thanking you for that which I have received this morning. Although the continued debility of dear Amelia & the pain which she suffers give me the most concern, I have been cheered by the concluding part of your letter of the 5th & the postscript of the 6th which are certainly calculated to encourage better hopes. The means contrived by Sir Harry Neale to make Amelia to breath[e] the sea air appears to have been very well imagined but as the exertion still seems to be too great for her actual strength it has occurred to me that she might receive equal benefit with less fatigue from being moved to the field adjoining the Lodge, where a tent might be placed & might admit any quantity of air that may suit her, & I am persuaded that there will be no difficulty in procuring an officer's marque of convenient dimensions at Weymouth. (Add. Georgian 12/40)

3951 GEORGE CANNING *to the* KING, *and the reply*

[*Foreign Office, 8 Sept. 1809.*] Mr. Canning most humbly submits to your Majesty whether, Mr. Villiers having earnestly solicited to be recalled from Portugal, your Majesty would be graciously pleased to approve of the nomination of Mr. Henry Wellesley to succeed Mr. Villiers in that Mission.[1] (14596)

[*The King's reply, Windsor Castle, 9 Sept.*] The King entirely approves of Mr Canning's proposal that Mr. Henry Wellesley should succeed Mr. Villiers in the Mission to Portugal.[2] (14596)

[1] Canning had been most anxious that Villiers should stay on. 'But', he said (5 Aug.), 'I do not disguise from myself that there are some unpleasantnesses in his situation (as well as mine) which as I cannot at present remedy to his mind (or to my own) I have no right to make his compliance with my recommendation such a *point* of duty as to be sure of his consenting to remain.' (Bagot, *Canning and his Friends*, I, 317.)

[2] Taylor wrote to Canning from Windsor on the 4th: 'The King has ordered me to thank you for the copy of the Pope's correspondence which his Majesty will keep, and I am to look it through & state

[*St James's Square, 8 Sep. 1809.*] The Duke of Portland having inform'd Lord Castlereagh this morning of the circumstances in which your Majesty's Government has been for a considerable time placed, avails himself of the first occasion of humbly entreating your Majesty that his retiring from office may not be consider'd as the smallest impediment to any arrangement which may be deem'd for the advantage of your Majesty's service. In submitting this request to your Majesty at the present moment, Lord Castlereagh trusts your Majesty will be graciously disposed to believe that he is alone actuated by a dutiful sense of what is due to your Majesty's service, the interests of which, he is humbly, but most anxiously solicitous should be consulted, without any reference to considerations personal to himself.[1] (14597–8)

[*The King's reply, Windsor Castle, 9 Sept.*] The King acknowledges the receipt of Lord Castlereagh's letter, and his Majesty desires he will be assured that he is perfectly convinced of his zeal and of his ready disposition to come into any arrangement which, under present circumstances, may be conducive to the general interests of his Government. (14598)

3953 LORD ELDON *to the* KING, *and the reply*

[*Saturday, 9 Sept. 1809.*] The Lord Chancellor has the honour to inform your Majesty that in obedience to the commands communicated by the Earl of Liverpool, he came to town last night. He has since had a conversation with Lord Liverpool and Mr Percival, in the course of which he has learnt that some communication is likely to be made from Mr Canning through the Duke of Portland to your Majesty: and it has occurred to the Lord Chancellor, who is ignorant of the nature of that communication, which your Majesty may probably receive this day or tomorrow, that, after informing your Majesty that he has come to town, it may, on some accounts, be expedient to forbear personally waiting upon your Majesty at this moment unless he should receive your Majesty's commands so to do, before that communication has been made. (14599–600)

[*The King's reply, Windsor Castle, 10 Sept.*] The King acquaints the Lord Chancellor that he has not received any communication from Mr. Canning thro' the

the general purport to him. The despatches from Lord Wellesley are so extremely voluminous that the King has been pleased to order me to keep them back until tomorrow & to take the heads for his information, as also the contents of the Malta mail.' (Harewood MSS.)

Taylor wrote again on the 10th: 'The Spanish shepherds are at the Queen's Palace and at Kensington, and in consequence of your letter and the enclosure (herewith returned) Mr. Snart has desired Mr. Guiswell [Giesewell], one of the King's Pages at the Queen's Palace, to receive & convey any directions which you may be desirous of giving to them.' (*Ibid.*)

[1] The Duke had resigned the Premiership on the 6th at the Levée. On the evening of the 7th Castlereagh pressed Camden so strongly to explain why Canning had not attended the Cabinet meeting earlier in the day that Camden reluctantly revealed the whole story of the concealment. The Duke remained nominally in office until, as he told Chatham on the 8th, 'his Majesty shall have satisfied himself in the selection of the person who is to be my successor'. (Chatham Papers, 368.)

Duke of Portland, but as his Majesty understood that the latter would remain in London as yesterday, he concludes that the Lord Chancellor will have seen him. The King therefore approves of his not coming here until made acquainted with the nature of the communication in question, & if in the meantime his Majesty should receive it, he will not fail to apprize the Lord Chancellor of its contents. (14600)

3954   PRINCESS MARY *to the* KING, *and the reply*

[*9 Sept.* [*1809*].] I hasten to return you my most greatful [*sic*] thanks for the kind letter I received yesterday & to inform you that I lost no time in communicating to General Garth your orders concerning a tent being placed in the field adjoining the Lodge & which General Garth said could be done with the greatest ease. Upon Mr. Beavor's coming in the evening I named the tent to him; he is of opinion that at present it had better be postponed as we have had so much rain lately that he fears the damp, & 2ly, the breeze from the backwater is not so *pure* or so efficacious as the air from the *sea side*, but G. Garth will have the tent ready that we can pitch it any day that it may be wanted. The great object is air without draft, as the smallest breath of wind brings on cough.

I am happy in being able to tell you that dear Amelia has past a very *comfortable* night, the best she has had since we came to Weymouth, & we lay *great stress* on this *quiet* night as it is the first since the journey that has been passed without *moaning* in her *sleep*. Beavor is very decided in his opinion, though we have gained nothing yet, that notwithstanding that no material ground has been lost & that when once the fatigues of the journey are over he sees no reason at present to doubt the good affects [*sic*] the sea air may produce. I hope as this day promises well she may get out by & bye.

Lady Neal arrived the day before yesterday. Ld Crewe [?] came in his yacht from Southampton Tuesday evening; it appears a very small vessel. I looked at your books yesterday, found them all in perfect order & as dry as possible.

[P.S.] I forgot to say the outward inflammation in the side which was produced by the leeches is going off sensibly. (Add. Georgian 12/41)

[*The King's reply, Windsor Castle, 10 Sept.*] Your kind letter of yesterday has proved very satisfactory to me as it conveys a more comfortable account than any yet received of dear Amelia, and confirms my hopes that as she recovers [from] the effects of the journey, her health will also improve. I intirely approve of what has been done in consequence of my suggestion of the use of a tent, and I admit the propriety of Mr. Beavor's objections, of the nature of which those on the spot must naturally be the best judges. (Add. Georgian 12/42)

3955   PRINCESS AMELIA *to the* KING, *and the reply*

[*Weymouth, Sunday, 10 Sept. 1809.*] I have delayed some days writing to you as Miny informed you how I was going on & I felt anxious to have something new today. My night on Friday was certainly the best I have had, last night was not so good for my sleep was disturbed, but I got out about noon on the sands; in your carriage the air revived me & though the motion increased the pain in my side a little it was not to any violent degree & Beavor thought the carriage a good thing as it was a little exercise. I feel very anxious my setons should discharge for certainly since that has ceased the pain has increased in my side, which proves how right Doctor Pope has been & is in his wish to continue them. I think he will return here about the end of the week.

Dear Dolly arrived yesy. evening soon after five; you will easily believe, my dear papa, his arrival was a great joy to us & how anxious we were to make every enquiry about all those we love at Windsor. Thank God his accounts are so good, & he gratified me much by repeating the kind anxiety you express about me. As I hope I am now recovering [from] the effects of the journey, I flatter myself I shall soon find benefit from this air. Ly. Neale arrived on Thursday looking remarkably well; she and Sir Harry are all gratitude for your goodness to them & having lodged them so comfortably. Captain Heywood is going away; Sir Harry had a letter yesy. to say he was to be replaced by the Dryad,[1] Captain Galway,[2] an Irishman, & who was a Lieut. to Lord Nelson. Dear Miny I think is looking remarkably well & the sea bathing agrees as well as ever with her.

Miny desires her affectionate duty to you & desires me to inform you *from her* that there are several of the Barouche Driving Club here & that she thinks your *carriage* with the *six horses* looks *quite* as well & *better* on the sands than they do.

Mr. C. Buxton, Mr. Methuen[3] & Ld. Clinton[4] are all here. There is one gentleman here who I met yesy. on the sands & did surprise me; who he is I don't know, but he is very rich & pays regularly, but rides a great deal & has the reins of his horse covered with shells picked up off the beach & flourishes when on horseback with blowing an immense horn. I *trust* he *will* never do it when we are out. I saw it in his hand & have heard it, tho' not yesy. He plagues the tradespeople by riding up their steps into their shops but as he does no mischief they cannot prevent it.

I will not take up more of your time, my dearest papa, than to beg you will be assured absence if possible increases my affection for you. (Add. Georgian 14/93)

[*The King's reply, Windsor Castle, 11 Sept.*] I am certain that I need not assure you that I have received great comfort from your kind letter of yesterday which appears to me upon the whole as satisfactory as I could expect, while you continue to feel the effects of the journey. Your being able to bear the exercise of the carriage is one step gained & although I sincerely wish it had been unattended by

[1] A 36-gun ship.

[2] Edward Galway (sometimes spelt Galwey) (*d.* 1844). Lieutenant, 1793; Commander, 1798; Rear-Admiral, 1837. Nelson's Lieutenant in the *Vanguard* at the Battle of the Nile. Commanded the *Dryad* frigate in the Walcheren expedition.

[3] Probably a member of the well-known Wiltshire family; possibly Paul Cobb Methuen (1752–1816), M.P. for Great Bedwin, 1781–4, who asked Perceval on 27 Oct. to recommend him for a peerage.

[4] Robert Cotton St. John, 18th Lord Clinton (1787–1832). Entered the Army, 1803. A.D.C. to Wellington in the Peninsular War. Colonel, 1825. A Lord of the Bedchamber, 1827–32.

pain in the side, I trust that may be ascribed in great measure to the causes which you mention & that I shall soon have the happiness of hearing that it is entirely removed. The good accounts you have given me of dear Miny have afforded me great pleasure. (Add. Georgian 14/94)

3956 PRINCESS MARY *to the* KING, *and the reply*

[*12 Sept.* [*1809*].] I put off thanking you for your kind letter by the post this morning as I had a faint hope than [*sic*] as the day was both mild and warm that Beavor would let Amelia go out in the boat, & therefore as I wanted to give you the first inteligence of this joyful event & felt sure it must make a letter from me more welcome, I took the liberty of defferring writing till I could say that my hopes had been realised. We are just returned home after having been out better than half an hour in your beautiful boat & I am most happy to add Amelia bore the motion of the boat in every respect *better* than I ventured to hope. She complained of being rather giddy & faint, but was not *sick at all* & finds the motion of the boat much easer [*sic*] & pleasanter to her side than that of a carriage. She certainly coughed a great deal but I flatter myself not quite as much as she does in a carriage. We did not go quite so far as the yacht but near enough to see her in great perfection, & I cannot help flattering myself we may get on board her sooner than I expected some days ago if Amelia goes on gradually recovering the journey as she has done these last three days. Sir H. Neal had intended to row out further, but upon finding Amelia unequal to anything but smooth water we kept as much within the harbour as possible. She is rather fatigued & now laying down to recover herself. The only thing that must be altered is that Amelia another day must not walk up the steps of the pier as even these 7 steps brought on so much cough that such an *irritation* must be guarded against as it take off the good affects of the sea air & that the row had produced before. She was a good deal overcome at first, finding herself in your boat & indeed I believe our feels where [*sic*] very *mutual* on this subject. Sir H. & Lady Neal, Lady George Murray & myself only went with Amelia; G. Garth went yesterday home to receive Dolly today who is gone to shoot at his place, but they return tomorrow.

As I can *with* great *truth* say Amelia is begining to recover [from] the affects of the journey, I trust I may be able soon to add *we are gaining ground*, the first step *towards* it being accomplished.

Sepr. the 13th. I am thankful to be able to add dear Amelia has had between five & six hours quiet sleep. I wish I could say she appeared more refreshed by so much sleep or that she complained less of her side, but I think it a great *point gained* the good nights returning. (Add. Georgian 12/43)

[*The King's reply, Windsor Castle, 14 Sept.*] The assurances which your kind letter of the 12th & yesterday conveys of dear Amelia's progress are extremely satisfactory to me, and although it cannot keep pace with my anxious wishes, it is as great as, under all circumstances and the very severe effects of the journey, I could reasonably expect. I had attached great importance to your getting out in the boat, conceiving that the motion would be more easy than that of the carriage, and I sincerely rejoice that the first trial has answered so well. (Add. Georgian 12/44)

3957   GEORGE CANNING *to the* DUKE OF PORTLAND[1]

[*Bulstrode, Tuesday morning, 12 Sept. 1809.*] *Private & confidential.* According to my promise I will state to your Grace, without disguise or reservation, my opinions with respect to the arrangement to be made upon your Grace's retirement from office.

You will do me the justice to remember that when I reminded your Grace last week of Lord Wellesley's intended succession to the War Department[2] I knew not that your Grace had any thought of retiring.

In my conversation with your Grace on Wednesday I first learned that your determination was taken. In the same conversation I likewise learned that, independently of your Grace's resignation, the execution of the intended arrangement would be accompanied with difficulties of which I had never before been apprized. To others, indeed, your Grace's resignation appeared to smooth these difficulties; to me it created new ones, and I therefore at once requested your Grace to put wholly out of your consideration &, if necessary, formally to withdraw any claim of mine for the performance of his My.'s gracious promise with respect to the War Department. Humbly and gratefully as I acknowledged his Majesty's extraordinary goodness and condescension, I could not honestly be party to the arrangement being carried into effect under circumstances which might deprive it of all its benefit and after your Grace's resignation had superceded all questions of merely partial arrangement.

Perceval had indeed already required of me, and had at length by dint of friendly importunity and of a frankness and confidence on his part which I felt it impossible to resist, extorted from me a disclosure of what my sentiments *would* be on the *contingency* of your Grace's retirement, a disclosure which I should have thought more likely to retard that contingency than to hasten it.

What I then stated to Perceval hypothetically I can have no objection now to repeat to your Grace.

I think then that it would be idle to attempt to carry on the Government by merely filling up your Grace's situation—filling up your *office*, I should rather say, for there belong to your Grace's personal situation in that office circumstances which, in addressing myself to your Grace I will not particularize, but which render your Grace's holding of the First Lordship of the Treasury a very different thing indeed, both in public impression & with regard to the King's service, & to your colleagues, from that of any other man in whom your Grace's successor might be to be found or to be made.

I think that an Administration of Departments with an elective head is not calculated for the well carrying on of the King's Government in these times.

[1] Copy, in Taylor's hand.
[2] See No. 3925.

I think that *a* Minister, & that Minister in the House of Commons, is essentially necessary to that object.

I have not pretended to disguise from myself or from Perceval (who admits the principle of these opinions) how directly and personally they affect himself and me. We have discussed the subject together, however delicate & embarrassing, with perfect good humour (as I am sure your Grace will have heard from him) and as nearly as possible as if we had been talking of a third person. The easiest arrangement, on this principle, would be the devolution of your Grace's office on Perceval. I should see this arrangement without the smallest disatisfaction or regret. I trust indeed that neither your Grace nor his Majesty would think the worse of me if I avow those ordinary feelings of human nature which would preclude my remaining in office under such a change as this arrangement would necessarily produce in my situation; but I should carry out of office with me the most sincere and undiminished goodwill towards Perceval, and I shall retain equally, as in office, the most lively sentiments of gratitude and of affectionate veneration towards his Majesty. For myself I have already said to Perceval with unaffected truth that I could neither expect nor desire his consent to act with me in office in the House of Commons in a relative situation, the reverse of that in which we have hitherto stood towards each other.

It is not for me to presume to suggest any other alternative. But of this I am entirely convinced, that the situation to which I have referred, either in Perceval's hands or in mine, or in those of any third person whom his Majesty might select to honour with his confidence, would be better for the public service & better *especially* for every part of that service in which the authority of the Crown is concerned than a Government of compromise, or uncertain preponderancy & of divided responsibility. Upon this point I am confident your Grace would find a prevailing opinion among persons who are the most conversant with the business of the House of Commons and who witnessed the difficulties and embarrassments of the last Session. Nay, I am confident that Perceval himself is so fully impressed with the truth of the principle that, with all his desire to keep things as they are & to avoid any change either in my situation or his own, he will find it absolutely necessary if the Government of compromise shall take place, to stipulate for such an accession of power to his present office as (though it will not in my opinion be sufficient to enable him to carry on the management of the House of Commons with the energy which the times require) would, in effect, produce to a great degree a change (which he wishes to avoid) in *our* relative situation.

I have thus spoken to your Grace with perfect frankness. I hope that what I have been obliged to say incidentally with reference to myself will not be misinterpreted by your Grace or by his Majesty. I thought that the affectation of pretending not to see how far I was myself necessarily concerned in these questions would have been as foolish as insincere. There are occasions which justify explicit declarations of opinion, even at the risque of being misinterpreted, and this appears to me, if ever there were one, to be an occasion which calls for such a declaration. But having made it, I can most conscientiously assure your Grace that amongst the alternatives which I have stated, far from preferring that which motives of personal ambition might be supposed to recommend to my preference, my sincere wish is to be enabled to retire, at the same time with your Grace, with his Majesty's gracious approbation.[1] (14601–3)

3958 LORD ELDON *to the* KING, *and the reply*

[*Tuesday, 12 Sept. 1809.*] The Lord Chancellor, offering his most humble duty to your Majesty, begs leave to mention that he apprehends, as the funeral of his sister-in-law Lady Scott[2] has not yet taken place, there may be a doubt whether he can, with propriety, attend at your Majesty's public Levée tomorrow. He proposes, however, to be at the Queen's House before your Majesty's Levée, that he may be able to receive any commands which it may be your Majesty's pleasure to mention. When the Chancellor saw the Duke of Portland, his Grace mentioned that he had received Mr. Canning's communication, but did not inform the Chancellor of any of its contents. (14604)

[*The King's reply, Windsor Castle, 13 Sept.*] The King will be glad to see the Lord Chancellor at the Queen's Palace this day before the Levée. His Majesty is as much in the dark as the Chancellor as to the nature of any late communication from Mr. Canning to the Duke of Portland, the latter not having noticed it to him. (14604)

3959 GENERAL SIR DAVID DUNDAS *to* LIEUTENANT-GENERAL ROBERT BROWNRIGG

[*13 Sept. 1809 (Copy).*] The King desired me to recommend to General Brownrigg to advise Lord Chatham that as he acted under the signed orders of the King, he should send a special report to his Majesty of the reasons which, during the siege of Flushing & towards the end of it, prevented the men of war from going up the Scheldt, and there undertaking a combined operation of the troops and Navy against the enemy on the mainland, and that he should communicate a copy of this report to the Cabinet.[3] (14605)

3960 *Canning's Memorandum of an Audience with the King on 13 Sept. 1809*[4]

[*14 Sept. 1809.*] After having received his Majesty's commands on all the points of business connected with my Department on which I had occasion to trouble him, I waited a few minutes to see whether his Majesty would begin with me on

---

[1] *Endorsement by Lieut.-Col. H. Taylor:* 'In obedience to his Majesty's commands I certify that this is a full and correct copy of the original letter delivered to the King by the Duke of Portland and returned to him by his Majesty.'

[2] Sir William Scott married, 7 April 1781, Anna Maria, daughter of John Bagnall of Erleigh Court, near Reading. She died on 4 Sept. 1809.

[3] Chatham's Narrative, however, was not communicated to the Cabinet.

[4] There is no copy of this Memorandum in the Royal Archives, but it is included here because it is of first-rate importance for an understanding of the political crisis which now faced the King.

the subject of my letter[1] to the Duke of Portland, which (as I had just learned from the Duke) the King made him read over to him twice, and then took it, saying he must keep it to consider. Finding that the King did not begin with me, I began with saying that, having been apprised by the Duke of Portland of what had passed between the Duke and his Majesty, I had the less occasion to take up much of his Majesty's time, but that on a subject so important and at a moment so critical I felt it a duty to lay my opinions fully before his Majesty, and that I relied upon his Majesty's great goodness and condescension to hear me with the indulgence which he had before shown me on similar occasions. The King made a sign of encouragement to me to go on and put himself in his most patient and listening attitude. I proceeded:

'There are two points upon which most especially I am anxious to set myself right with your Majesty, if your Majesty can have any doubts upon them; the first, that I have not underrated the extraordinary and gracious condescension which your Majesty showed in consenting to a partial change in the Government, and the second, that I have not sought the opportunity of disclosing the opinions which have been just now communicated to your Majesty by the Duke of Portland, that it was my firm intention, tho' I should have acted upon them when the occasion arose, not to disclose them, but that they were extorted from me by Perceval's repeated friendly importunity.

'With respect to the new arrangement in the War Department, Sir, it is certainly true that I did on Saturday sennight write to the Duke of Portland to remind him that the period for executing that arrangement was come, but I did not then know of the Duke of Portland's intention to resign. I do not believe that he had then resolved upon it. When I saw him on Wednesday he told me of it. I immediately requested his Grace to take no step whatever with respect to the partial arrangements, and as this was before he had seen your Majesty, and I know he had not written to your Majesty on the subject, I hoped that no step had been taken upon it. If any has, it has not been from my fault, or for want of my endeavours to prevent it.

'The Duke of Portland's resignation made a new case in which it would have been unfair in the highest degree to bind your Majesty to the literal execution of a promise made under circumstances which had no reference to that event.'

The King interrupted me with expressions of perfect concurrence: 'To be sure it did—certainly—quite a new case.'[2] 'I have confessed, Sir, that it was not my intention that your Majesty should ever know the opinions contained in the letter which has this day been sent to you by the Duke of Portland upon the subject of the state of the Government after his resignation. I have long foreseen

[1] No. 3957.
[2] Note written alongside this section: 'Letter to the Duke of Portland; he suppressed this passage. The King mentioned it to the Duke of Portland this day. The Duke expressed his surprise at it, and denied having made such a communication. This I had from the Duke of Portland before I went to the King. The obvious policy of this representation by Castlereagh and of his hurried resignation was to put me in the wrong with the King who, if Castlereagh's retirement had been in consequence of the Duke of Portland's communication and that communication in consequence of my demand, would have had a right to say that after having received a part of the price of my stay in office, I refused without new terms to fulfil my part of the contract.'

that whenever he resigned I should go with him because I saw that (in my judgment at least) it would be impossible to replace him and I felt the hazard and ridicule of anything so presumptuous as what might be construed into a putting forward of myself. I intended to retire, therefore, on the simple ground that my connection was with the Duke of Portland and that I should go with him, which, even if the world had not believed to be the true reason, they would have no right to question.

'Perceval destroyed this plan of mine by engaging me in a discussion in which he at length obtained from me an avowal of my real opinions, such as your Majesty has heard them today, and that avowal having been once made, I have felt it my duty that what anyone else knows of my opinion should be known also distinctly and without reserve by your Majesty.

'The circumstances of the time, Sir, are such that your Majesty ought to know everything, every view and opinion of any of your servants.'

The King interrupted here with strong expressions of concurrence: 'Yes, I ought to know everything, nothing should be kept back from me.' 'You are very right; you have done right,' &c.

'Sir, your Majesty shall see to the very bottom of my heart upon this subject. There is nothing but what I wish your Majesty thoroughly to understand. It will be for your Majesty afterwards to form your determination. I do think then, Sir, that the times require more strength and more unity in the Government than can be had by substituting anyone in the room of the Duke of Portland. I think the Government cannot go on well without a Minister in the House of Commons.

'In the first place nothing like a substitute *can* be found for the Duke of Portland. He is not one of a species, he is an individual, the last of his species—there is nothing like him to be found. His rank, his age, his relation of friendship with your Majesty, the prescriptive veneration which he enjoys from having been so many years of his life at the head of political parties, so that almost every man in public life has at one time or other looked up to him. Then the sacrifice which he is known to have made on taking office two years ago and in continuing to serve your Majesty under such infirmities, all these things give to the Duke of Portland a character which cannot be found or made in any other individual. And an individual less respected and less distinguished—merely holding the office of First Lord of the Treasury would not keep the Government together as he has done.[1]

'I am aware at the same time, perfectly aware, Sir, that it is impossible to ask him to go on.'

'So impossible', said the King, 'I could not reconcile it to my conscience to do so. You know that two or three months ago when he offered to resign I put it off and begged him to try a little longer, but now, when he came to me, I could only say that [it] must be as he wished, that I could not as an honest man press him to go on any longer.'

[1] Note written alongside: 'The King here entered into a warm and vehement panegyric upon the Duke of Portland, his honesty, his disinterestedness, his affectionate attachment to him, &c.'

'Sir, your Majesty could do no otherwise. The last attack has certainly made a great difference in him. Before that I own I did not see why, wishing to go on as I believe he did, he might not have continued another year or two years, as well as he has gone through the two last. I knew, Sir, that he had tendered his resignation at the time to which your Majesty alludes, and your Majesty had declined it. But I confess I thought that he acquiesced in that refusal very cheerfully. Your Majesty will know I had advised (upon his asking my opinion), I advised at Easter the tender of the resignation which he soon afterwards made. I should never have done so again: first, because I thought your Majesty averse to parting with him, and second, because I no longer saw any way to any arrangement for replacing him. At that time your Majesty may remember that I *had* thought that a person *might* be found—not one who would *fill* the Duke of Portland's place, but one who would have some qualities at least to recommend him to it. Perhaps I was mistaken, but whether that be so is no great matter, for now that person is certainly not available, not to mention that the times are considerably changed.' 'Yes, I remember you mentioned Lord Chatham,' said the King.

'Sir, your Majesty condescends to ask me whom your Majesty *could* fix upon if the Duke of Portland retired. I answered that I had always *supposed*, tho' I scarcely knew whether on good grounds, that your Majesty had looked to Lord Chatham for that succession; and that I thought there were circumstances in your Majesty's known kindness and partiality for Lord Chatham and your confidence in him in his being Mr. Pitt's brother, in his having been associated by your Majesty with the Duke of Portland in the formation of the Administration, which might lead to his being placed at the head of it with less jealousy and with more effective control than any other person. I did not disguise my opinion of Lord Chatham's defects, but some of those very defects perhaps might be said to point him out for the first place rather than a subordinate one. He is too *big* for a Department in a Government so constituted as this. His office is, I dare say, admirably carried on, but it is an office of great expenditure and under no check or control. The Treasury, *as it is*, cannot cope with the Ordnance under Lord Chatham. Where there is great power there ought to be responsibility, and where there is the responsibility *there* should be the power, so that on this ground I thought Lord Chatham might be better placed at the head of the Treasury than where he is. But this, Sir, is only what I then thought. The whole was founded on a supposition of your Majesty's being pre-disposed in his favour, which I think I found was not the case. I have no reason to believe that Lord Chatham looked to it.' The King said, 'No, certainly not: I believe he never had a thought of it. I don't believe he would take it.' 'And I again give your Majesty my honour, as I did before, that I never hinted a syllable either of my own opinions or of my conversation with your Majesty to Lord Chatham. Whatever those opinions were I am afraid they are good for nothing now. Late events make it utterly impossible that Lord Chatham should be placed at the head of the Government. Your Majesty will do me the justice to see, however, that I had no want of good-will towards Lord Chatham had he been the object of your Majesty's choice, and that at that time at least I had no notion of putting forward myself. Lord Chatham being out of the question, I see nobody else that is equal in any degree, or could be made so, to the Duke of Portland's situation: therefore I should have avoided ever again recommending his retirement because I would not be accessory to creating a difficulty for which I could not suggest any remedy. That difficulty has however arisen: your Majesty knows from the Duke of Portland what my opinions are as to the only mode in which the Government can beneficially be framed. It is for your Majesty to judge whether you approve the principle of placing your chief confidence in any one man at the head of your Administration in the House of Commons. I am intimately persuaded that in these times nothing else can give even the chance of a strong Government. I do not presume to say that even this arrangement will secure your Majesty against disappointment, but I think it is the only chance. If approving the principle your Majesty's choice should fall upon Perceval, I do assure your Majesty I shall see that arrangement without the smallest discontent, with the most entire and perfect goodwill towards Perceval. He having this from me, and I venture to affirm he believes it, and tho' in that case I shall continue to beg your Majesty's permission to retire, I shall do so only in the same way as when one officer in your Majesty's army cannot serve under another, which implies no sort of personal hostility or unkindness.'

'No, to be sure,' said the King.

'Just so, Sir, I should feel with respect to Perceval. We are placed by accidents and circumstances not of our own choice in a situation towards each other in which neither can serve under the other either creditably to himself or with advantage to your Majesty's service. Supposing, I mean, your Majesty to adopt that principle upon which alone a Government can, as I am now taking for granted, be formed with any chance of being found equal to the crisis. One therefore must give way. I am ready to give way: out of office, Sir, I shall, I trust, still be enabled to render your Majesty some service in the House of Commons and to prove to your Majesty the deep impression which your Majesty's goodness has made upon my heart. I would not however be misunderstood by your Majesty. I do not mean (and I know your Majesty's way of thinking well enough to be assured that you would in your own mind think the worse of me and despise me if I did mean) to profess that I would *always support in Parliament the Government* in which your Majesty might please to place your confidence. No public man can honestly take such a pledge, and your Majesty I am sure [would] consider all such professions as worth nothing. It is impossible that any man out of Government should not be liable to see faults in the conduct of Administration, even to differ with them upon points upon which they may, or may not, have reasons which he cannot know. I certainly shall not go out with a disposition to seek occasions for finding such faults, but if I see them I must act according to my honest judgment. But what I do mean to say is that in all that whole class of questions which goes to the foundation of things, to the frame of the Constitution and Government, to the just rights and necessary prerogatives of your Majesty's Crown, your Majesty will have an anxious and determined supporter, out of office, at whatever risk of personal unpopularity, as if I were still in your Majesty's service.'

'That is all you can or ought to say,' said his Majesty. 'It is very fair and handsome and proper. I like it better than if you said more,' or words to that effect.[1]

I proceeded: 'I must further beg your Majesty to allow me to assure you that I have not the slightest intention of connecting myself with any man or any set of men now in opposition to your Majesty's Government; upon my honour with not one man of that description of any class have I had the remotest communication. Nor do I at present intend it. I am not speaking of my whole life to come, Sir, that would be as foolish a pledge as the other, Sir, which I have disclaimed of constant support to Government, but I mean distinctly and solemnly to assure your Majesty that no such motive or speculation has any the smallest influence upon my present conduct: that it is founded purely and simply on the grounds of principles which I honestly avow to your Majesty.

'And this leads me to add, Sir, that if, which I do not pretend to think wholly improbable, if your new Government should not stand, [and] your Majesty should be obliged to form another, you will have in me, Sir, and the few who may be with me (what we may be *worth* in that respect your Majesty is to judge), but your Majesty may have the option in me and others of one *chance*, between your Government and Opposition.

'In saying this, Sir, I am reminded of one point which I should be extremely concerned to have omitted. When I admit the possibility of your new Government not standing, do not let your Majesty believe that it is *therefore* and on account of the difficulties of the times that I wish to fly from it. I am sure your Majesty cannot suspect me of this, for I need not remind your Majesty that the last time that your Majesty condescended to allow me to speak to you upon these subjects I then entreated your Majesty to let me go out while affairs were bright and prosperous and when I thought and stated to your Majesty that the hopes of a satisfactory issue to the campaign and perhaps to the war were more encouraging than at any former period. I foresaw that if the question (not the question of the *general* arrangement, which was not then in contemplation, but that of the partial arrangement) should come to an issue under circumstances less favourable, I should be liable to the imputation of shrinking from difficulties;[2] I presumed to warn your Majesty of this danger and your Majesty is graciously pleased to remember it.' (His Majesty gave signs of assent.) 'But, Sir, I can perhaps avoid this imputation in some degree at least with your Majesty by what I am now to say. I entreat your Majesty's pardon for the apparent presumption of speaking of myself, but I must not leave it unsaid—that if your Majesty's choice of a Minister should fall on me, fearful and tremendous as I know and feel the responsibility to be—I would obey your Majesty and undertake it. Do not misapprehend me, Sir: I do not *seek* it, but *I would obey* your Majesty's commands, and it is necessary to a full statement of the subject that you should know this.

[1] But Castlereagh's Under-Secretary, Edward Cooke, thought this 'the most insolent proposition that was ever obtruded upon a Monarch by a presumptuous subject. To tell the Sovereign, forsooth, that he would never act under any Minister of his Majesty's appointment, but that if his Majesty chose Mr Perceval he should, to show his attachment, give him his independent support.' (Londonderry MSS. To Charles Stewart, 21 Sept. 1809.)
[2] That is, if he resigned.

'Sir, in this case, the improbable case of your Majesty's choice falling upon me, it is necessary that I should say what would be my views and feelings about Perceval. I could not and would not bear, if *he* could consent to it, his serving in the House of Commons with me and under me. At one time for a moment he talked to me of this as possible as if he might be Secretary of State and I in the other situation. I told him at once as I now repeat to your Majesty, that it was utterly impossible. He *could* not, ought not, to bring his own feelings to bear [on] this—if he could his friends could not, and if they did, *I* could not bear it. This I hope, Sir, will satisfy your Majesty of the truth of what the Duke of Portland has told your Majesty, that Perceval and I have discussed this matter as if it were the concern of a third person.

'Yes,' said the King, 'the Duke of Portland told me so.'

'My feelings towards Portland, Sir, are as friendly as towards any man in the world, and I believe the same of his towards me. He is too honest to affect them if they were not so.'

'He is as honest a man as ever lived,' said the King.

'Sir, he is not only so, but a most honourable, upright and able servant of your Majesty. My wish for Perceval, Sir, in the case which I am now supposing (*only* supposing it that I may leave nothing unsaid) would be that with high rank, high office, and the most ample provision that your Majesty could make for him, he should continue to act with me as a colleague in your Majesty's Government. I do not presume to suggest this as proper or right for your Majesty to agree to; the whole subject and the principle of it is yet for your Majesty to consider. I have only presumed to state the different ways, in one or other of which the principle, if admitted, would be to be applied.

'Sir, the result of the whole is that in my opinion your Majesty, to make a Government equal to the times must put your affairs into the hands of a Minister in the House of Commons. There the battle is to be fought and there the power of deciding and acting must be. The Government cannot in my opinion be carried on by deputy in the House of Commons. This being the principle it so happens that Perceval and I stand to each other in a situation which does not allow of either being Minister and the other remaining where he is; and that from no fault of either—from no illwill, but from the given circumstances.

'If your Majesty (it is the last time I will put the supposition) should put your command upon me, I have stated what I should wish to endeavour to effect with respect to Perceval. If, as is much more natural, your Majesty's choice falls upon *him*, *I* have in the nature of things no retreat but *out of office*. But out of office I trust your Majesty will believe me I should still be zealous and active in my best service to your Majesty. But I venture confidently to state to your Majesty that either of us *alone* with such help as we could get (though that help in either case would not be as good as what each lost in the other) yet would be better able to carry on your Majesty's service than both together, circumstanced as we now are. Nay, Sir, if your Government wants help, as perhaps it may, not from Opposition but from such stray strength as might be to be had, either of us alone could get that help to your Majesty better than both together. Sir, I have only to add that in Perceval's case, so far from taking your Majesty's preference amiss, I have nothing to blame in it. I only ask of your Majesty and I hope may conclude from the kind and gracious manner in which your Majesty has listened to me, that your Majesty will not consider my retreat as any want of duty to your Majesty; I hope that I have explained myself in a way to satisfy to your Majesty that —'

'Your explanation is perfectly clear and fair—you have laid everything before me. It is a most important question; I am of course sorry that it is come to this, but must consider of the whole'—King.

'Of course, Sir, I do not think of pressing your Majesty for a decision now.'

'No, to be sure, that would be impossible. I must think it all over.'[1]

'I have only to hope, Sir, that if I said anything amiss, anything not satisfactory, or still worse, anything that could be imagined to be undutiful or disrespectful to your Majesty, your Majesty will pardon it, or allow me to correct it, and will attribute it only to the extreme difficulty and embarrassment in speaking on such a subject, especially in speaking of oneself.'

'You have said nothing amiss, nothing but what is perfectly proper.'

'I have nothing more to say, Sir; I am concerned to have troubled your Majesty so long, but I have felt that I was discharging a duty to your Majesty in leaving nothing undisguised.'

'You have done quite right.'

And so the audience ended. I write this memorandum this 14th day of September within twenty-four hours after the audience. I am confident in many parts of the very phrases, in almost all parts of the connection and arrangement and throughout the whole of the substance of what passed, and I think I have not omitted anything material. The King was very gracious and perfectly calm and clear. My impression is that he will let me go, but without displeasure.[2] (Harewood MSS.)

[1] See No. 3962 for his instructions that day to Perceval.

[2] Perceval saw the King on 19 Sept., and wrote an account of the audience to Lord Liverpool that day. The draft differs slightly from the letter which Liverpool received. The long passage enclosed in square brackets is omitted from one copy.

'As you desired me to give you a line upon my return from Windsor, I sit down for that purpose. But in the first place I must state that not arriving here till past 4 o'clock, I found the summons to the Cabinet at ½ p. 3 which as I could not possibly attend 'till past 5 o'clock, I am obliged to neglect. As the King kept me for full an hour and half, and as his conversation was very precise, distinct and continued, it is impossible to attempt giving you any full idea of it. Many points indeed I shall hardly notice, what he said of Lord Chatham, who he says is hurt, and adds *with reason* and what I observed upon that will keep. But he began with it—upon quitting that subject he said *but now* to our business— and then he told me he must give me an account of Canning's conversation which he called the most extraordinary he ever heard. He went through it with wonderful accuracy, I will endeavour at another time to give you the particulars. All that is now important is that in the King's impression, and in mine also from his relation of it, it was very little different from his letter except that it was more explicit & more strong—and except that he distinctly stated to the King as his opinion that the Duke of Portland's health was such that it was not possible he should retain his situation. The points in which he was more precise were that the Minister, who must in these times be necessarily in the House of Commons, must also necessarily have *complete authority* over all other Departments; that at this time, H.M. had no choice for such Minister on either side or in any Party, but between me and him; that he should not be at all surprised nor at all dissatisfied if H.M. should prefer me; that it would be much the most natural & most easy thing; it would scarce require a new patent; it would only require the insertion of one new name into the old one; but that if he had stated his Majesty would honour him with his commands, he would not hesitate to undertake it; [that he would not indeed think of undertaking it with me in the House of Commons, as Secretary of State; he could not bear the idea of offering me

[*Weymouth, 14 Sept. 1809.*] I have a most kind letter to thank you for; I hope I need not say the pleasure I feel at every mark of your affection & how grateful I am to you for your constant thought of me. Yesy. was so bad a day it was quite

such an indignity, but that I might take a situation as high in the House of Lords as might be suitable for me (and here I did not quite understand whether it was only that he would be glad to find such situation for me or that he would not undertake it unless I consented to such an arrangement; but I conceive it must have been the former, and only that he strongly preferred the latter)—that when he had pressed Lord Wellesley in the Cabinet he had not approved of the D.'s resignation—that he had long thought the Government much too weak, and intimated that sufficient stand had not been made in the House of Commons on questions in the last Session—that he conceived Lord Wellesley's coming into it would have strengthened it; that however there was in the Duke of Portland's name and character something, he hardly knew what to call it, that enabled him to be at the head of the Treasury without doing Treasury business, and at the head of the Government without going into either House of Parliament, that would not be endured in anyone else. That he had hoped the Duke of Portland might have lasted perhaps a couple of years longer, and that in the meantime one might have been seeing what might be done. That he had at one time thought of Lord Chatham, that he had thought the King leaned to him. The King told him that he was sure there was nothing Lord Chatham would dislike so much, and that for himself he had never thought of it. This was the substance of the conversation as well as I can recollect it, given with wonderful precision and clearness. He concluded by remarking that in short it was for all practical purposes the same as his letter, and that he afterwards stated that he condemned the Administration after Mr. Pitt's death for giving up; that he was not in the Cabinet at the time, but that he should have advised *standing*. I said it was very easy to condemn past councils in which one was not a party, and that I did not recollect having heard that to have been his opinion before, and should not have suspected it if I had not heard it. That it was easy also to intimate that sufficient resistance had not been given in the House of Commons, but I certainly did not consider him as having objected at the time and to have urged more resistance. That on the contrary I could distinctly recollect instances in which he would have recommended less.]

'"Not," said the King, "that he would consider of it, that he would advise with others, as you or any other person would have said, but he was fully prepared to undertake it—" "Now," continued his Majesty, "I do not believe, if he was to be the Minister, that there is any one of you who would continue with him, and he does not seem at all to think of that." I told him I had no authority to say or means of knowing that none of his present servants would continue. I thought some certainly would not, but I could not pretend to speak for any one but myself. I told him that when I had penned the passage in the Minute in which it was said that his Majesty might collect from Mr. C.'s letter that he would undertake it, I had been almost afraid that I might have drawn an inference beyond what might have been intended. "Oh, no," he said, "he stated it to me most distinctly, and said that the Ministers who retired when Mr. Pitt died, had done in his opinion very unwisely, that he was not then in the Cabinet, but that he should [have] advised otherwise—I said I had never heard before that he had thought so, but I could not pretend to say what his opinion was at that time, but if he had not said that he would have advised their continuance, I should rather have suspected the contrary to be his opinion. These are I think the most material points in the K.'s narrative of Canning's conversation. The comment and observation upon it I have no time for now, nor for many other particulars which I could state but for want of time.

'The account of this narrative and the observations upon it being over, he then proceeded to the subject of the Minute of Cabinet. He said he would consider of it very maturely, could not deliver any opinion then. I assured him I had not expected one, I only thought he might wish to see me, and converse upon various points of it. He was very glad I had come, he said, was glad to talk to me upon it, that he should talk to the Ld. Chr. & Lord Liverpool & others upon it tomorrow. He knew indeed that they could not represent it in any other view than had been done in the paper, but it was a decision *for life*, everything was at stake, and he must not come to that decision without the maturest consideration—that he did not know how to make up his mind to it. He seemed disappointed at the [word omitted] leading to a communication both with Ld. Grey & *Ld. Grenville*; the latter evidently formed, as we anticipated, the great objection. He could do nothing towards it, he said, till he was satisfied upon one point (the Cathc. quesn.). When he was advised last to send to Mr. Pitt by the Ld. Chr., he had required to know expressly from Mr. Pitt that he would not bring forward that question—that he had the most direct assurance from Mr. Pitt in writing, he knew he had his letter, he had been looking for it—(he then digressed into an account of his papers—He was arranging them all regularly—that up

impossible for me to stir even had I not taken my callomel. Today I fear it will be equally impossible, for the rain & wind is considerable. My side continues very much the same, the damp weather has affected me a little as I cough more & have more tenderness upon my chest, but Beavor, who has just been here, thinks it entirely owing to the weather & of no *material consequence* tho' he finds me with more fever. I find my cough is certainly excited with less exertion; I have had about four hours sleep in the course of the night. I am very glad Pope comes tomorrow; his absence will enable him to judge better of my progress.

to 1802 they were quite perfect—& from the commencement of the late Administration to August last, and that from that period he could turn to any paper in a minute)—but he said he should find Mr. Pitt's paper—it was an express assurance—& further, he said when he saw Mr. Pitt, he not only confirmed the assurance but added that he would not only not bring it forward, but that for private reasons of his own, he would oppose it whoever brought it forward. This he says he voluntarily said to him, it was more than he expected, it surprised him, it appeared to be an expression of his own opinion, that he might have paid him (the King) the compliment of supposing that the determination was taken out of compliment to him, but he stated it to be for private reasons of his own. He must, he said, have a similar assurance now; that this was a point he could not give up in honour, no more, he said, could I —that I as well as he had both given our opinions upon that point solemnly to the country, that we could not give them up. I agreed that we could not give them up, that his servants were unanimous in their opinion that he must be protected against that question—that it was with that view and upon that principle that they had humbly given his Majesty the opinion which that paper contained—that they thought, under the circumstances of the times, that it was the most effectual, if not the only effectual means of protecting him. That if Lord Grey & Lord Grle. consented to form a Govt. with us, who were known to have such decided opinions upon that subject, they must come into that Government with a perfect knowledge that that measure could never be a measure of that Government, that this would necessarily be *implied* from the very formation of the Govt. It must be *expressed*, he said, or he could not be satisfied. I stated that it did not appear to me possible to expect that Lds. G. & G. could as men of honour, consent, after all that had been said upon this subject, to have even the question put to them to require an express declaration upon this. "Then," said he, "I am driven to the wall, and would be deserted." I assured his Majesty again that the object of his present servants was to protect him, they would not desert him—that the opinion we had submitted to his Majesty was, as we thought, the best mode of protecting him—that if we made an ineffectual attempt to form an Administration alone, we should be overthrown and would not be able to stand between him and the wall. "Then," said he (rather hastily but very collectedly & firmly) "they should take the Government to themselves, he would have nothing to do with it, they should not have his name." "Oh! Sir," said I, "what an extremity your Majesty is contemplating! What would become of your Majesty's country?" "No country had a right to expect a man should give up his own honour—his honour was in his own keeping; if his country deserted him he could not help it." I again assured his Majesty that deserting him was the last thing they ever thought of. But we conceived that the combined Govert. which we had an idea of forming was to be formed by his Majesty's present servants and with such a proportion of them that, having a full share in the efficient offices, we should, by refusing at any time, as we should refuse, to concur in any measure of that description be enabled to put a stop to it, by bringing the Govt. to an end—that they would feel this, and that they therefore would naturally not think of attempting it. He then asked what reason we had for thinking they would form such a Govt. I said that we could not fully, without making an overture to them, have found their real sentiments, but that we had reason, from various conversations of their friends, to think it probable they would not generally object, tho undoubtedly we could not tell in what manner they would expect it to be made. He asked what these conversations were. I told him—Ld. H. P[etty]'s to Ld. Euston—Ld. Grey to Col. Gordon; Ld. G. Cavendish to Ld. W. Bentinck. But then, he said, what is to be done if they refuse? I said we had not omitted to think of that, but that the manner of their refusing, and the grounds on which they refused might be so various, and it would depend so much upon them, that there was no possibility beforehand of distinctly saying what would in that event be to be done 'till the event occurred. Then he asked how it was to be done. I suggested the letter to both, at once, stating his M.'s commands that they should communicate with us and that we should jointly consider on the formation of a Govt. and that we had his commands also to acquaint them that if they wished to see his Majy. first, that his Majy. would see them. That would be very hard upon him, he said, he had no means of letting the world know what might pass, they might tell their own story. The last time he had the good fortune

Adolphus returned yesy. for dinner; he appears very much pleased with his visit to Gl. Garth, both as to his civilities & to the house & place.

Nothing ever was so kind as dear Miny in every respect. I sit entirely in your room to the sea. When I work, read & write Miny is so good to sit with me; I find quiet very necessary & if I wish for anybody I ask them in for a little while after dinner, but I prefer being quite quiet.

Mr. Radber's [?; not Godber] Ball was on Tuesday & was tolerably attended. The Dowr. Ly. Harewood[1] & Miss Cope[2] arrived yesy. at the hotel; as yet they can procure no house.

Knowing, my dear papa, your partiality for the St. Fiorenzo & its *crew*, I must tell you how pleased Sr. Harry is to find that Mr. Garson[3] [*sic*], the Master of the Topaz frigate who is so well spoken of in a late action, was Quarter Master to him in the St. Fiorenzo during the mutiny[4] & from his good conduct on that occasion Sir Harry[5] got him promoted.

Miny desires her affte. duty; dear Adolphus is very well. I am very glad he is here for he is a comfort to Miny & I feel her kindness to me is such that she deserves everything that could give her pleasure.

to have it in writing, that would not do; he could not see them, but he knew from us what they were prepared to do; that he was the worst person in the whole world to settle any point with them; he was sure he should quarrel with them at the first setting out. I said that certainly would not answer any purpose; that it was certainly an important consideration that his Majesty might think of, but that we had considered that it would be better to offer them the alternative. Then he asked whether I thought I alone should communicate with them, or I and anyone else, I said that as there were to be two of them, I thought it preferable that there should be someone joined with me. He agreed in this and suggested the Chancellor, as the person. I explained the Chancellor's objection, from the various instances of personal conflict in which he had been engaged with them. "What," says he, impatiently, "do you think I could be advised to form a Govt. without the Chancellor?" "By no means," I said. I thought that the present Chancellor must be one of the Govt.—that your Lordship must form another, that I considered this as indispensable. He then seemed to be satisfied as to the reason for not joining the Chancellor with me, & canvassed the question whether it should be you or Lord Bathurst, or who else, and this as well as other questions were left open for our further consideration. Much more passed which I may possibly in part recollect tho' I am not certain that I shall, but I think I have given you enough to shew the temper of mind in which I found him, and that at last his mind was led to consider the proposition with more reference to the detail of it than he would have done if he had insurmountable objections to the whole. He concluded, however, with saying that he could not yet form any opinion —that he must take time to think of it. He thanked me for coming down to him, and for giving him, as he expressed it, that opportunity of *thinking aloud* upon it.

'Upon the whole I never knew him in any conversation which I have had the honour of having with him, so collected, so distinct, or anything like so methodical in the view which he took of the different parts of the subjects on which he conversed. I much doubt whether you will think my account gives you a fair representation of it in these particulars, but I have been writing as fast as my pen could move, and I fear you will have some trouble in deciphering it. You may read it to any of our colleagues you please, & I will thank you to send it to the Chancellor for his information before he sees the K. tomorrow.' (Perceval MSS.)

[1] Edwin Lascelles (1713–95), who was created Baron Harewood on 9 July 1790, married, as his second wife, on 31 March 1770, Jane (*c.* 1732–1813), daughter of William Coleman and widow of Sir John Fleming, 1st Baronet.

[2] She may have been related to Sir John Cope, Bart., of Bramhill Park, Hants. Mary, daughter of Sir Robert Jenkinson, married Sir Jonathan Cope, she being the aunt of the 1st Earl of Liverpool, whose second son, later third Earl of Liverpool, was named Charles Cecil Cope Jenkinson.

[3] Could this be Richard Matson? Lieutenant, 1794; Commander, Sept. 1797; Captain, March 1799; Rear-Admiral, 1825; *d.* 1848. There was no one of the name of Garson in the Navy List at this time. F. A. J. Griffiths commanded *Topaze* about this time (Royal Kalendar, 1810).

[4] In 1797. The *St. Fiorenzo* refused to join the mutineers.   [5] Neale.

I will not take up more of your time, my dearest papa, then to beg you will believe me [etc.]. (Add Georgian 14/95.)

[*The King's reply, Windsor Castle, 15 Sept.*] I have learnt with very sincere regret from your kind letter of yesterday that you suffer from the change of weather and that the effects of it should have produced any interruption in the progress which I had learnt with so much satisfaction that you were making. I could not flatter myself that, delicate as you are at present, any encrease of cold and damp would not affect you in some degree, but I trust that the effect will be only momentary & that I shall have the comfort of learning that Doctor Pope has found upon the whole a material improvement. I can easily conceive what a comfort you must receive from dear Mary's endearing attentions, and I highly approve of your keeping youself so quiet. I am very glad that Sir Harry Neale's protegé Mr. Garson [*sic*] has distinguished himself in the Topaze; I perfectly recollect him in the St. Fiorenzo. (Add. Georgian 14/96)

3962   SPENCER PERCEVAL *to the* KING, *and the reply*

[*Friday 15 Sept. 1809.*] Mr. Perceval is sensible how anxious your Majesty must be to hear what progress he has made in executing the commands with which your Majesty entrusted him last Wednesday.[1]

Mr. Perceval has not yet been able to collect any opinion which he can present to your Majesty, Lord Harrowby has not been in town in this interval, and the Lord Chancellor has been obliged to go into Berkshire to attend the funeral of his brother's wife, and will not return till Sunday. Mr Perceval therefore at present much fears that it will be impossible for him to communicate to your Majesty any decisive opinion before he pays his duty to your Majesty on Wednesday next. (14606)

[*The King's reply, Windsor Castle, 16 Sept.*] The King is satisfied with the reasons which Mr Perceval assigns for not having as yet been able to proceed in the matter upon which his Majesty spoke to him on Wednesday last, and he desires that Mr. Perceval will be assured that his Majesty attaches more importance to a mature consideration of what should be done than to any despatch in the execution. (14607)

3963   VISCOUNT CASTLEREAGH *to the* KING, *and the reply*

[*Stanmore Park, 15 Sept. 1809.*] Lord Castlereagh humbly submits to your Majesty's confirmation the appointment of Lt.-Col. Hamilton to the

---

[1] The King had instructed Perceval on the 13th, not to form a Government but to consult the remaining Cabinet Ministers about Canning's letter of the 12th to the Duke of Portland. As Perceval told the Speaker, the King, before commissioning anyone to take the Treasury, would naturally 'wish to know what person was likely to keep all together'. (Colchester, II, 204.) For the ministerial conversations, lasting many hours, on the 14th, see Twiss, *Eldon*, II, 93.

Lt.-Government of Heligoland, the duties of which he has performed for the last two years. Also of Major Maxwell to the Government of Senegal, the conquest of which Colony he has recently made.

Lord Castlereagh also submits for your Majesty's royal signature a warrant appointing Mr Robert Wood harbour master at Malta.[1] (14608)

[*The King's reply, Windsor Castle, 16 Sept.*] The King approves of the appointments of Lt.-Col. Hamilton & Major Maxwell which Lord Castlereagh has submitted. (14609)

3964 PRINCESS MARY *to the* KING, *and the reply*

[*17 Sept.* [*1809*].] I have many thanks to return you for your kind letter & hasten to inform you that Amelia went on board the yacht yesterday about 12 o'clock. Nothing could be better arranged or more comfortable; she went up in the chair & as Sir H. Neal & Capin. [*sic*] Spence never let the chair go, Amelia was not so much alarmed as she would have been otherwise. She lay on the couch all the time, very composed & quiet, but not at all sick, though we had a good deal of sea at times, more than I can remember being out in before. When the motion of the yacht was more than Amelia could stand on account of the pain in her side, Dr. Pope advised her coming home which most fortunately Sir H. Neal was able to do almost immediately. On leaving the yacht Amelia fainted & did not recover till we landed, but for all that Dr. Pope assures me it went off better than he expected. After laying down for half an hour on her return home she recovered the fatigue & really after dinner appeared to me almost cheerful. The seaton in the side has begun to discharge, which *pleased* Dr. Pope very much last night, as he says *all* depends upon the seaton acting perfectly; however, Amelia does not find much if any relief from the discharge yet, as the shootings still continue the same. The cough did not appear worse to me on board the yacht; she certainly coughs more than she did when she first came & I think now finds great comfort in siting [*sic*] *quiet* all day & not *speaking*. Dr. Pope is not inclined to give any very decided opinion as yet, in fact yesterday was *quite a day* of *trial*; therefore we cannot judge. After church we are to go in the boat & take a row that he may see what affect that has.

The Prince arrived Saturday night; in consequence of his carriage breaking down at Andover he came much later than he intended. He is very kind & anxious not to put us out of our way & realy wishes to be directed to do what is right & kind by everybody. I do not know how long he intends staying.

We only went on board Lady George, Sir H. Neal, Dr. Pope & myself, & for

---

[1] Though Castlereagh had resigned on the 8th he continued, according to custom, to transact official business until the appointment of his successor.

Eldon wrote to Lady Eldon on the 15th: 'We have been closeted again today, that is, each of us as the King places any confidence in, for hours. Our opinions, for we have very different opinions, are about to be laid before the King. Would to God what relates to myself was settled one way or the other. If I stay in office, the moment that was settled, I should be able to fix instantly when we shall see each other.' (Eldon MSS.)

fear Amelia might be sick we made Gaskin[1] & Byerly go with us. To the no small amusement of Sir H. Neal & the ship's company, the Dr. was *very unwell,* so giddy he could not stand, never having been on board a ship in his life, not even in a boat. His surprise & *remarks* amused us all *not a little.* I was quite well, to my great joy, & able to assist my Byerly who was very bad indeed.

[P.S.] Amelia has had between 4 & 5 hours sleep, which I think a good thing considering all the tortures Pope put her into last night & the night before. (Add. Georgian 12/45.)

[*The King's reply, Windsor Castle, 18 Sept.*] I have received your kind letter of yesterday and cannot delay thanking you for your continued attention in communicating to me all that regards the state of dear Amelia, in whose progress I feel so deeply interested. It was impossible not to apprehend that she would suffer very much from her first attempt to go out in the yacht, nor am I surprized that the motion should have for the moment increased the pain in her side, and produced faintness, but as Doctor Pope attached so much importance to the trial, I rejoyce that it has been made and I trust that the general effects of it & of a repetition of these excursions will answer his expectations & realize our anxious hopes. I am very glad that you, my dearest Mary, suffered no inconvenience from the motion of the ship. (Add. Georgian 12/46)

3965   PRINCESS AMELIA *to the* KING, *and the reply*

[*Monday, 17 [18] Sept. 1809.*] Many thanks for your last dear letter. I went out yesy. for an hour in your delightful large boat. I was faintish a little when we got into any swell, but I bore it better than the day before. Dr. Pope does not leave us till tomorrow. He has found it necessary to enlarge the seatons & did it effectually last evening by putting in the larger silks: of course it was very painful & I have not had a good night, but he finds me as well as he could expect considering all this morng. & he thinks when they begin to act I shall find relief to my *side* as well as on my chest. You will hear more particulars from Pope than I can write & I feel very anxious for him to see you & acquaint you thoroughly how I am, knowing the kind & tender affection you have for me & the interest you take in my health. I believe the opinion I gave of myself when I last wrote you will find to be a very just one. Nothing can be kinder than both the Prince & Adolphus; they both feel thoroughly my situation & the cause of my being here & are so good [as] to be *no* gêne or trouble & to wish we should in every respect pursue the plan we adopted on coming here.

It is a singular thing that tho' I am not sea sick, the moment the vessel pitches

---

[1] Miss Mary Anne Gaskoin (*c.* 1779–1811), one of the Wardrobe Maids to the Princesses. Miss J. Byerley was another. The death of *Mrs.* Byerley, who for many years attended Princess Augusta, was announced in Feb. 1830, at the age of 84.

Miss Gaskoin died in Feb. 1811, aged 31, and in one of his lucid intervals the King directed that she should be buried in St. George's Chapel 'as near as might be to her Royal mistress'. He himself composed the inscription for the mural tablet at the entrance to the cloisters, which was placed there 'in testimony of his grateful sense of the faithful service and attachment of an amiable young woman to his beloved daughter'.

at all it makes me very qualmish & appears to increase the pain in the side & as if it *dragged* from where I find the pain, but the tenderness extends entirely round the right side.

Miny saw yesy. Ld. Rivers & Mrs. Morton Pitt[1] & Mr. Drax Grosvenor.

The yacht looks quite different to what it did when you were here; the only two on board who you remember is Portius [*sic*] & Henderson. The midshipmen are a nephew of Mrs. Banks's,[2] young Woodley, & George Burrard,[3] son to the General. The chair I went up in was very easy & Sr. Harry was so good to have it held steady all the way, both coming up & down.

I will not take up more time now than to express my warmest attachment & gratitude for all your kindness & to beg you will believe me [etc.]. (Add. Georgian 14/97)

[*The King's reply, Windsor Castle, 19 Sept.*] I have received your kind letter of yesterday and am truly grateful to you for entering so fully & candidly into the state of your health and the effects which you feel from the course recommended to you. From what you state, & Doctor Pope's reports, I flatter myself that there has been some amendment since you have recovered[4] the first consequences of the journey and that you will derive more decided benefit from a perseverance in the system which you are now pursuing than you have as yet been able to receive. Of my affection for you & my anxiety for your welfare you are too well assured not to believe how sincerely I grieve that you should continue to suffer so much from the pain in the side & be forced to submit to remedies so painful & distressing, while you bear them with a degree of patience & resignation which cannot be sufficiently commended. That your progress may henceforth reward you for all you have undergone is the sincere & anxious prayer of [etc.]. (Add. Georgian 14/98)

3966 SPENCER PERCEVAL *to the* KING

[*Downing Str., 18 Sept. 1809.*] Mr Perceval returns to your Majesty Mr Canning's letter to the Duke of Portland, which in obedience to your Majesty's commands he has submitted to the consideration of the Lord Chancellor, the Lord President, the Privy Seal, the Earl of [*sic*] Bathurst, Earl of Liverpool & Earl of Harrowby, to whom Mr. Perceval also, in obedience to yr. Maj.'s commands submitted the consideration of the present state of your Majesty's Administration for the purpose of their submitting to your Majesty their humble advice upon that subject.

Mr. Perceval informed Lord Chatham of the meeting at his house upon this subject which his Lordship declined attending, by a letter which Mr Perceval incloses for your Majesty's perusal.

---

[1] William Morton Pitt (1754–1836) married in 1782, Margaret (*d.* 6 Nov. 1818), daughter of John Gambier, Governor of the Bahamas.

[2] Henry Bankes (1756–1834), M.P., of Kingston Lacy, Dorset, married, in 1784, Frances, daughter of William Woodley, M.P. (1728–93). See No. 3994.

[3] John Burrard, Lieut. R.N. (*d.* 1809). Son of Sir Harry Burrard (1755–1813). See No. 3994.

[4] It was then customary to omit 'from' after 'recover'.

Mr Perceval does not imagine that it will be possible for your Majesty to form any opinion upon the enclosed Minute but after some time for considering it. But imagining that your Majesty may possibly require some explanation of that Minute, after having read it, Mr Perceval proposes to be at Windsor tomorrow by twelve o'clock to be ready to attend your Majesty if your Majesty should be disposed to command his attendance.[1] (14610)

[*Enclosure*]

[*Cabinet Minute, at the house of the Chancellor of the Exchequer, Downing Street, 18 Sept.*]

Present: The Lord Chancellor, the Lord President of the Council, the Lord Privy Seal, the Earl Bathurst, the Earl of Liverpool, the Earl of Harrowby, and the Chancellor of the Exchequer.[2]

Your Majesty's confidential servants above-named have, in obedience to your Majesty's commands, taken into their most serious consideration the present state of the administration of your Majesty's Government in consequence of the intended resignations of the Duke of Portland, Lord Castlereagh and Mr. Canning, which they have reason to apprehend will be followed by that of Lord Granville Leveson-Gower.

They have directed their attention in the first instance to the consideration of the question how far it would be practicable for the remainder of your Majesty's servants, after so important a defalcation of strength, to carry on the Executive Government of the country with advantage to your Majesty without additional strength from any other quarter, by any new arrangement of the offices of Government amongst themselves and those who are connected with them.

They have examined this question with reference to the state of both Houses of Parliament.

In the House of Lords the persons in opposition to your Majesty's servants form at present a most formidable party, consisting of not less than 110 or 112 members of that House.[3] The events which are about to happen can scarcely fail

---

[1] This explains why the King sent no written reply to Perceval's letter.

[2] Mulgrave was *not* mentioned as being present as stated in Walpole's *Perceval*, ii, 7–21 (the draft is different from the Archive copy). The Cabinet met at 4 p.m.

[3] The following 'State' of the House of Lords in April 1807 is in the Welbeck MSS. The list would not have been substantially different in 1809.

Government

Dukes: York, Kent, Cumberland, Cambridge, Atholl, Beaufort, Buccleuch, Gordon, Montrose, Portland, Queensberry, Rutland, Richmond, Newcastle, Marlborough, Leeds.

Marquesses: Abercorn, Bath, Hertford, Salisbury, Townshend, Ely, Thomond, Sligo, Waterford, Wellesley, Drogheda, Donegal, Cornwallis, Lansdowne.

Earls: Ashburnham, Ailesbury, Aberdeen, Aylesford, Bathurst, Bridgwater, Camden, Chichester, Cardigan, Chatham, Chesterfield, Coventry, Craven, Dartmouth, Digby, Effingham, Egremont, Galloway, Glasgow, Harcourt, Harrington, Macclesfield, Malmesbury, Morton, Mt. Edgcumbe, Northampton, Onslow, Normanton, Pembroke, Pomfret, Manvers, Lonsdale, Powis, Poulett, Romney, Sandwich, Stamford, Strathmore, Talbot, Uxbridge, Westmorland, Wilton, Winchilsea, Courtown, O'Neill, Erne, Longford, Roden, Westmeath, Shannon, Londonderry, Conyngham, Elgin, Dorchester, Harborough, Mansfield, Bandon, Abergavenny, Portsmouth, Cassillis, Glandore, Rosse, Limerick, Charleville, Liverpool.

in some degree to add to their number, and to diminish proportionably that of the persons who support your Majesty's administration. But this addition of strength on the one hand, or diminution of it on the other, would probably not be considerable, and though it is impossible to say that your Maj.'s Administration in the House of Lords would be as strong as would be desireable, under all the circumstances of the present times, they would nevertheless be sufficiently strong (if the question were confined to that House alone) to afford your Majesty's present servants a reasonable expectation that they could carry on your Majesty's Government without the necessity of looking to any addition of strength from other quarters.

The state of the House of Commons is far more unfavorable. Your Majesty must have been aware of the difficulties which occurred in the conduct of the business of Government in that House during the last Session of Parliament, and that the strength of Government did scarcely, at any time, appear more than equal, and on some occasions not sufficient, to oppose the difficulties to which they were exposed. There can be no reason to believe that these difficulties will be less considerable in the next Session of Parliament, especially when your

Viscounts: Bridport, Courtenay, Curzon, Falmouth, Hood, Sydney, Wentworth, Midleton, St. Asaph, Grimstone, Gage, Melville, Northland, Carleton, Longueville, Sackville, Torrington.
Bishops: Canterbury, Tuam, London, Durham, Winchester, Ely, Hereford, Lichfield, Salisbury, Bath & Wells, Norwich, Peterborough, Exeter, Bristol, Chichester, Chester, Rochester, Derry, Meath.
Barons: Amherst, Arden, Bagot, Barham, Bayning, Berwick, Bolton, Boringdon, Boston, Hood, Cathcart, Caher, Dorchester, Douglas, Dynevor, Eldon, Eliot, Grantham, Gwydir, Harewood, Harrowby, Hawkesbury, Kenyon, Le Despencer, Mulgrave, Montagu, Northwick, Redesdale, Ribblesdale, Rivers, Rous, Rolle, Seaforth, Selsey, St. Helens, Somerville, Southampton, Vernon, Walsingham, Willoughby de Broke, Beauchamp, Sherborne, Wodehouse, Sheffield, de Dunstanville, Bradford, Carteret, Gardner, Scarsdale, Suffield.

Opposition

Dukes: Clarence, Gloucester, Argyll, Devonshire, Grafton, Norfolk, St. Albans, Somerset.
Marquesses: Winchester, Buckingham, Bute, Headfort, Stafford.
Earls: Albemarle, Berkeley, Carlisle, Carnarvon, Cowper, Essex, Darlington, Derby, Fortescue, Suffolk, Guilford, Bristol, Leicester, Breadalbane, Oxford, St Vincent, Spencer, Stair, Stanhope, Cholmondeley, Tankerville, Thanet, Bessborough, Carysfort, Darnley, Fife, Fitzwilliam, Moira, Clanricarde, Lucan, Orford, Selkirk, Lauderdale, Grosvenor, Erroll, Jersey, Northesk, Peterborough, Grey, Rosslyn, Landaff, Leven.
Viscounts: Maynard, Anson, Bolingbroke.
Bishops: St. Asaph, Landaff, Oxford, Lincoln.
Barons: Crewe, Braybrooke, Carrington, Glastonbury, Ponsonby, Cawdor, Dundas, Foley, Grantley, Grenville, Holland, King, Montfort, St. John, Stawell, Yarborough, Elphinstone, Kinnaird, Granard, Reay, Minto, Ashburton, Audley, Auckland, Keith, Somers.

Doubtful

Dukes: Sussex, Northumberland, Hamilton, Manchester.
Earls: Clarendon, Eglintoun, Ferrers, Portsmouth, Radnor, Rochford, Scarbrough, Ormonde, Upper Ossory, Nelson, Cassillis, Egmont, Enniskillen, Balcarres, Moray, Shaftesbury, Warwick, Wicklow, Donoughmore, Darlington, Hardwicke.
Viscounts: Dudley, Duncan.
Barons: de Clifford, Forbes, Byron, Monson, Saye & Sele, Callan, Delaval, Rodney, Collingwood, Gardner, Brownlow, Carteret, Ducie, Heathfield, Lilford, Lyttelton, G. Middleton [*sic*], Scarsdale, Blandford, Bulkeley.
Sidmouths: Buckinghamshire, Sidmouth, Ellenborough, B. St. David's, Gloucester.
Bishops: Carlisle, Bangor.

Majesty shall consider not only the disappointments which have attended the exertions of your Majesty's arms in the course of the present year, but also the new taxes which the necessities of the country will require to be imposed. And the loss of the active support of two such members of the Government as Lord Castlereagh, Mr. Canning & Lord G. L. Gower[1] and of those who may personally adhere to them, cannot fail to place your Majesty's servants in the House of Commons in a most critical situation, such as no new arrangement of the offices of your Majesty's Government, amongst themselves, appears likely adequately to remedy.

Your Majesty's servants have been anxious, therefore, to consider whether it was probable that any addition of strength could be obtained to your Government from individuals not at present connected with it.

With this view they have endeavoured to ascertain whether, in any contingency, there was a probability of being able to persuade the Speaker of the House of Commons to accept of a political situation, but the communication which has been made to him has led to a very candid but decisive explanation on his part in which he states that he has long determined never to quit his present situation as long as the House of Commons will accept of his services, and as his health enables him to discharge the duties of it.[2]

Your Majesty's servants feel it material to add that they understand that the same obstructions on the part of Lord Hardwicke which prevented Mr. Yorke from accepting office some months ago are likely to operate with equal force at

[1] An afterthought—hence 'two'. Writing to his friend Boringdon from the War Office on 17 Oct., Granville Leveson thus described what passed at his Audience the previous Wednesday, the 11th: 'I began my audience by saying that Mr. Perceval had of course communicated to his Majesty the tender I had made of my resignation; that I hoped his Majesty was satisfied that in this step I was influenced by no want of attachment to his Majesty's person to whom I was bound by every tie of gratitude not only for the kindness with which H.M. had ever treated me but also for that which he had never ceased manifesting both to my father & mother; that I had taken office under the hope, in consequence of the intimate friendship & confidence that subsisted between Mr. Canning & myself, of being of some service in the councils of his Majesty, & of pursuing that harmony amongst the members of it which was on every account so desireable for the good of his Majesty's service; that Mr. Canning having quitted his situation, I felt it incumbent on me, the object with which I had entered the Govt. no longer existing, to offer most humbly my resignation. After some personal civility to me, & also expressions of regard to my father, followed by assurances of his regret at my not remaining in office, & adding oddly enough that he should have liked to have had one of my father's family in office, he said, "but did you do all you could to preserve harmony?" I answered that I had certainly approved & advised Mr. Canning to agree to the various delays which had taken place in the changes which he had thought requisite in H.M. Government, & that I had hoped by so doing that an amicable arrangement might have taken place with respect to Ld. Castlereagh; that I could not but regret the manner in which Ld. Camden had executed, or rather neglected to execute that task which was assigned to him, & which had led to that disunion & violence which had nearly ended fatally to Mr. Canning. After some conversation about the duel, & about duelling in general, he acknowledged that Canning could not do otherwise than accept Castlereagh's challenge. This is, as far as I can recollect, the substance of what passed. I know of no news—a circulation box has this instant been brought to me, but I have given up my Cabinet key & attend no Cabinets—so I am not the wiser for the sight of the red box.' (Morley MSS.)

[2] Perceval's letter of the 12th asking him if he could be induced to accept the office of Secretary of State, is in Colchester, II, 204, and Abbot's reply at 8 a.m. on the 13th follows. Though Abbot was offered only a Secretaryship of State the offer is a further illustration of the tendency during this period to ask the Speaker to help the politicians out of exceptionally difficult situations. See Vol. III, Introduction, p. xx.

the present moment. Lord Wellesley's absence in Spain prevents yr. Maj.'s servants from ascertaining his sentiments.[1]

Your Maj.'s servants are at present in doubt what line Lord Melville & his friends will be disposed to take under the present circumstances: to ascertain this point most expeditiously Mr. Dundas has been sent for from Ireland, and it was at one time a serious question with your Majesty's servants whether they should offer any opinion to your Majesty upon this subject before they had had an opportunity of collecting from him his sentiments & those of his friends. But in the interval they have found reason to apprehend that Mr. Canning's resignation would diminish the strength of your Maj.'s Govt. to an extent so much beyond what they expected that they think even upon the supposition that Lord Melville's friends would cordially support them it would be misleading your Majesty to recommend the formation of a Government from among themselves.[2]

They have ascertained that Mr. Sturgess Bourne and Mr. Huskisson are so connected with Mr. Canning that they desire to retire with him.[3] They have too much reason to apprehend that Mr. Rose will adopt the same resolution;[4] Mr. Long also has given notice of his intention to resign,[5] and your Majesty will not fail to perceive how much more serious the loss of the support of those gentlemen

---

[1] Tierney wrote to Grey on the 14th: 'The Wellesleys are but in bad odour just now, and I do not believe the King will let the Marquis into the Cabinet, partly from personal dislike, and partly because he is an adherent of Canning's.' (Howick MSS.)

[2] Canning's friends in the House of Commons in the autumn of 1809 or the beginning of 1810 were as follows: Barrington Pope Blachford, William Sturges-Bourne, Colonel George Canning (his cousin, later Lord Garvagh), John Dent, Charles Rose Ellis, George Bellas Greenough, William Huskisson, Hylton Jolliffe, Robert Holt Leigh, Lord Granville Leveson-Gower and Edward Bootle Wilbraham. Lord Binning joined the group in March 1810.

Writing to Mrs. Canning on 15 Nov. Canning referred to 'Mr. Jolliffe (a raff), who wants to swear allegiance'. (Harewood MSS.)

[3] Sturges-Bourne's explanation of his personal position in his letter of 17 Sept. is in Rose, *Diaries and Corresp.*, II, 349, though there are some errors of transcription (for example, 'I hate the rumour [rancour] of party.' He told Rose, 'I owe to him [Canning] my first introduction to Mr. Pitt, Parliament and public life,' but it is interesting to note that he deleted 'first'. 'And', he added, 'have been attached by long, intimate [not 'intimacy'] and, generally, confidential friendship.'

[4] Canning showed Rose the correspondence between him and his Cabinet colleagues, and Rose then reluctantly decided that he could be no party to breaking up the Government merely because Canning had failed to obtain the Premiership, when Perceval, his competitor, was prepared to acquiesce in Canning's nominating a third person. It was on 19 Sept. that Rose told Canning that he should not resign. (Rose, *Diaries and Corresp.*, II, 353, 369 ff., 378.)

[5] Charles Long's decision was sensibly influenced by the views of his patron Lord Lonsdale, who had brought him into Parliament. He wrote to the Earl on 14 Sept.: 'It is impossible not to agree with him [Canning] in the objection to that tone of concession which Perceval held in the House of Commons last Session, which really let down the dignity of the Government and made the tenure of office irksome in the extreme.' (Lonsdale MSS.) And again, on the 15th: 'I saw Lord Camden after I wrote to you yesterday; he meant to write to you today and you have probably heard from him very fully upon the subject on which I have written. Mr. Perceval has been kind enough to say that he does not call upon me at present for any decision, and I wish not to come to any till I have seen or heard from you fully. Had I been obliged to decide it must have been (what I hope you will not disapprove) to relinquish my office. I am very anxious to see a strong Government and to support it out of office; such a one cannot now be formed without some junction, though I understand Canning thinks that either himself or Perceval separately might form a much stronger one than the Duke. I wish most anxiously you were in town.' (*Ibid.*)

George Rose wrote on 3 Oct.: 'Mr. Long saw Mr. Perceval today and agreed to remain in office. What has induced him to this change of resolution I know not; possibly the declared opinion of Lord Lonsdale who brings him into Parliament.' (*Diaries and Corresp.*, II, 401.) And see No. 3992.

will be in impression upon others than merely from their own numerical weight. Their characters for efficiency as men of business justly give great consideration to them—long & steadily as they have been connected in Government with Mr. Pitt and his friends—and particularly acquainted as they are known to be with the state of the House of Commons, their retirement will be considered as indicating a well-informed opinion of an almost total disunion of Mr. Pitt's old connexions and of the want of strength in your Maj.'s Administration, and it is to be feared that it will be followed to a considerable extent & will guide the judgement and conduct of others.

Your Maj.'s servants therefore cannot forbear from adding that the formation of a Government without the assistance of some strength from the persons now opposed to them, which they had considered, independent of the resignation of those gentlemen, as very difficult, is, from that circumstance, rendered infinitely more so, if not impossible.

Your Majesty's servants cannot here omit calling to your Majesty's notice that, tho' they conceive it to be next to impossible for them to form a Government without assistance from their opponents, your Majesty may collect from Mr. Canning's letter to the Duke of Portland (which your Majesty desired Mr. Perceval to lay before them) that he conceives a Government might be formed under him. The expediency therefore of your Majesty's sending to Mr. Canning and requiring him to use his endeavours for that purpose is one of the considerations on which your Majesty will have to determine. Your Majesty's servants however ought not to disguise from your Majesty that in their apprehension Mr. Canning's attempt to form a Government without external assistance would be attended with difficulties as many, and of a similar nature, to those which they have described as attendant upon an attempt by themselves.

Under these circumstances the question arises whether any, & what additional assistance can be procured from those who at present are usually opposed to your Majesty's servants.

Your Majesty's servants have adverted, in the first place, to the persons connected with Lord Sidmouth. But the object of recurring to any external assistance is to obtain additional & effective strength. The numbers of this party are but small,[1] and it appears evident that so strong a prejudice has been created in the minds of many persons who support your Majesty's Administration at present against Lord Sidmouth & his friends in consequence of the part taken by them in the last year of Mr. Pitt's Administration that there is every reason to believe that more friends would probably be lost by an attempt to connect Lord Sidmouth with the Government than would be gained by the numbers which he would be able to bring with him.[2]

[1] See the list in 4138 n.

[2] Canning told the Speaker that Bragge Bathurst and Vansittart were very useful persons in the House of Commons, and the efficient members of the 'Doctrinal' party. 'Sidmouth he understood not to be desirous of keeping any party about him, and that he had so declared.' Abbot replied to Canning, 'I said that I had seen him but once since Parliament met, and that was six weeks ago, and did not know what his sentiments now were, but he certainly had formerly desired his friends not to consider him as the head of any party, but to act for themselves.' (*Colchester*, II, 185–6.)

It remains therefore to consider the expediency of applying to the Earl Grey or to Lord Grenville, or to both. From every information your Maj.'s servants have been able to collect, they are satisfied that it would not be possible to procure the assistance of one of these noble Lords without the other, and even if the separate assistance of either could have been obtained, yet the nature of the present times and the exigencies of your Majesty's service indisputably require as strong a Government as can be formed. And considering the loss of strength which the resignation of Lord Castlereagh[1] & Mr. Canning, and the other persons above-mentioned will occasion (encreased also as it must in a degree be expected to be by the effect of an application to any persons now opposed to the Administration) nothing short of the united strength of both can effectually counterbalance that loss. Your Majesty's servants therefore feel it to be their duty to state to your Majesty after anxiously, repeatedly & maturely weighing all the foregoing considerations and every part of the important question submitted to them by your Majesty, that in their humble opinion it would be most expedient that your Majesty's confidential servants should be commanded to make a direct communication to Lord Grey & Lord Grenville with a view to their uniting with them in forming an extended & combined administration.[2] (14611–15)

[1] See No. 4138 n. for a list of his friends in the House of Commons.

[2] See Eldon's comments in Twiss, *Eldon*, II, 94, 96. The King replied verbally, to Perceval, the following day. Eldon wrote on the 20th: 'Perceval was with the King yesterday.... He would not give his consent: he took time to consider of it. I think he will finally consent to the proposition being made.' (Twiss, *Eldon*, II, 97.) Tierney heard from J. C. Herries, Perceval's private secretary, on the 19th about the projected invitation to Lords Grey and Grenville. From his other, his 'military' friend (Colonel Gordon) he received other information about resignations and the threatened duel between Castlereagh and Canning.

Tierney wrote to Grey on 13 Sept.: 'The present Administration is at an end. This afternoon the Duke of Portland and Castlereagh have resigned, and no successor is named to either of their places. The Chancellor, Perceval, and Lord Liverpool have unequivocally declared that you and Lord Grenville must be sent for immediately. I mean declared this at a meeting they had last night. The object in the first instance will be to offer you and Lord Grenville six or seven seats in the Cabinet, but, as I should suppose the Chancellor cannot expect that this offer will be accepted I look upon the whole game as up with Ministers. Canning is considered as out, though he has not formally tendered his resignation. You will probably receive some intimation of all this by tonight's mail if not a direct message from the King, but whether you do or not you may rely on all I have written, as I have it from Gordon, to whom Perceval's private secretary has just communicated it, adding that he understood Perceval was to state the whole matter to the King after the Levée from which he was not returned when I left the Horse Guards.' (Howick MSS.)

Tierney wrote on the 14th: 'What I told you some time ago about Lord G.L.G.'s seat in the Cabinet laid the foundation of all that had happened, and set the whole Cabinet by the ears. There has been nothing but ill blood from that hour to this, and the failure of our expeditions, and the increased illness of the Duke of Portland, has increased the ferment. Matters at last came to such a pass that the King directed the Chancellor to be sent for, and he arrived in town last Saturday or Monday. Canning it appears has plainly and without disguise set up for himself. He has declared his determination to resign unless the Duke of Portland's successor is in the House of Commons, and he has not disguised the meaning of this to be, unless he himself is made Minister. This Perceval and Lord Eldon strenuously resist, and they have the King on their side. Perceval made a statement of their difficulties to him yesterday; the Chancellor is to see him on Monday as he returns from Lady Scott's funeral, and on Wednesday something is to be settled. The Chancellor told the Duke of C[umberland] how high an opinion he had of you, and how ready he should be to act with you. In the meantime everything is at a stand, and at the Public Offices they consider the Administration as at an end, a state of affairs at all times bad, but at the present moment particularly mischievous. Our friend is particularly desirous that you should turn a deaf ear to any communications but a direct message from the King, and I have assured him he need be under no misapprehensions on this head from what I know of your sentiments.' (*Ibid.*)

[*Windsor Castle, 19 Sept. 1809.*] Lieut.-Colonel Taylor having submitted to the King Lord Chatham's letter,[1] his Majesty hastens to assure him that he shall be glad to receive him tomorrow at the Queen's Palace, and that he feels perfectly sensible that, in the general line of conduct which Lord Chatham has pursued, he has always been guided by the utmost zeal for his service, and in his late decision by a just consideration of the difficulties which occurred and of the preservation of his troops under the probable effects of a most destructive climate & season.[2] (14616)

Tierney wrote again on the 15th: 'I sent you this morning a short note I had just received from Gordon. The upshot of all I have heard in the last few days (and I have seen others as well as the two persons you know of whose information goes for something, though it may not be equal in point of authority) the upshot seems to be that if the Ministers were anything but what they are, they would go out of themselves, and if the country was anything but what it is, it would turn them out, but that such is the nature of the one, and the other that the Government will be allowed to hang together until so torn asunder by internal divisions as to be absolutely incapable of maintaining itself. How far distant that day may be is the only question. According to all appearances it should be near at hand, and such is the general opinion out of doors, a circumstance which frequently tends to produce the result foretold. That you will before two months are over be sent for I am much disposed to believe, but whether you will receive a message from the King or a proposition from some of his Ministers is not so clear. I should hope, if for either, for the last, because the decided manner in which all idea of a junction with the Chancellor or any of his adherents might be rejected would either prevent a communication from a higher quarter altogether, or bring it in a plain and intelligible shape. When the Chancellor talks of your joining him I cannot think he is serious. He must be aware of the numberless objections to such a step, and my speculation is that he is only anxious to try whatever the King desires without having any expectation that it can succeed. He has not forgotten the reproaches he met with from his master for having advised the surrender of the Government upon the death of Mr Pitt, and he will this time endeavour to convince him that he does not walk off from panic but from the impossibility of staying where he is. What proofs of this impossibility the King may require remains to be seen, but I have no doubt he will have recourse to many manœuvres before he gives in, that is, before he agrees to any Administration which he cannot call *his own*.' (Howick MSS.)

[1] Missing. But we know from Perceval's memorandum of his interview with the King that Chatham desired to know whether he might come to the Levée.

[2] Lord Rosslyn saw Chatham on the 18th, and wrote, that day, to Grey: 'Lord Chatham has not seen the Ministers, either in or out, and did not yesterday, and will not attend any of their meetings. I believe him to be quite confident that he stands as well with the King as ever, and, as I suspect, better than any other person.' (Howick MSS.) He wrote again, on the 20th: 'Lord Chatham was most graciously received by the King, but he has not received any official answer to his last dispatch, or any formal approbation of his conduct through the Ministers.' (*Ibid.*) Eldon commented, on Chatham's refusal to attend Cabinet meetings: 'As an officer coming from an expedition with his conduct not formally expressed to have been approved, he cannot.' (Twiss, *Eldon*, II, 96.)

Perceval's notes (undated, but after 20 Sept.) of an interview with the King on the 19th contain some references by the King to Chatham: 'After some observations on the state of his blindness he expressed his feeling strongly upon the situation in which he was placed, and the pain which he had received from the duel. He then observed that he perceived Lord Chatham was arrived. I said 'yes', and referred to the communication which I had had with him. He said he perceived Lord Chatham was much hurt. He had had a letter from him desiring to know whether he might come to the Levée and that he had answered by all means, and added, he saw no reason why he should not come. He repeated that he was hurt, and indeed he said with great reason, for he had seen Lord Castlereagh's letter which was the coldest thing imaginable, that it did not even say that he was persuaded he had done his duty. I said that Lord Chatham had really left us so much in the dark as to material points that no judgment or opinion could, as I conceived, be given. And adopting what I had conceived to be his own word, I said there were material chasms that required to be filled up. His Majesty said that Lord Chatham had written opinions from the General officers under him (I think he said all his Staff) before the expedition sailed, that it could not succeed. I said I conceived that Lord Chatham himself hardly could have been of that opinion or he would not have undertaken it. He said that he felt that as an officer he was to

[*Downing Street, 19 Sept. 1809.*] Lord Castlereagh having used his best endeavors to inform himself from the Earl of Chatham and other officers lately return'd from the Scheldt, of the actual situation of your Majesty's troops in the island of Walcheren and of the circumstances connected with the occupation of that island, deems it his duty humbly to represent to your Majesty that an early decision upon the expediency and practicability of keeping that island appears to him to be of essential importance to your Majesty's service.

In the very peculiar situation Lord Castlereagh at present stands in your Majesty's Councils (the nature and extent of which was wholly unknown to Lord Castlereagh when he last presumed to address your Majesty on that subject) your Majesty will be graciously pleased to consider how very incompetent he must feel himself to form and submit for the consideration of your Majesty's confidential servants an opinion upon a question of so much importance, and upon which it is so desireable that those who may be entrusted prospectively with the conduct of your Majesty's affairs may find themselves in a situation to exercise an unfetter'd judgment.

Lord Castlereagh humbly begs leave to assure your Majesty that he will continue to employ his most diligent endeavors to provide for the health and comfort of the troops. (14617–18)

[*The King's reply, Windsor Castle, 20 Sept.*] The King returns his thanks to Lord Castlereagh for his letter, and the representation which it contains in regard to the situation of his troops in Walcheren and the circumstances connected with the occupation of that island, which his Majesty will take into his early consideration. The King is very sensible of the propriety of the motives which have led Lord Castlereagh under the extraordinary circumstances in which he is placed to make this representation. (14618)

3969 LORD MULGRAVE *to the* KING, *and the reply*

[*Admiralty, 21 Sept. 1809.*] Lord Mulgrave has just learned that his name does not appear upon the Minute of Cabinet which was transmitted to your Majesty, & humbly begs your Majesty's permission to have his name inserted in that instru-

---

undertake it, as he was employed, that he told him himself that he thought it very hazardous, but that he would do his best. I said that as to its being hazardous no one I believed ever supposed that it was sure of success, but that it was thought worth running the hazard for, on account of the importance of the object—but that as to Lord Chatham's opinion his Majesty would recollect that Lord Chatham was one of his Majesty's servants who concurred in the opinion that it was expedient to undertake it. He said he must acknowledge that was the worst of Lord Chatham. He was present at Cabinets, did not dissent from councils at the time but found fault with them afterwards. I said it was not fair by those with whom he appeared to concur. He told me upon the subject of the failure of the expedition that Sir David Dundas asked him whether he had ever seen the paper which he drew up and gave to Lord Castlereagh upon the subject of the expedition. The King had not seen it, and Sir David said he would shew it him that his Majesty might see what he had thought and said of it—that he had felt when the Cabinet had decided in favor of it, that it was his duty to find the army and collect the force.' (Herries MSS.)

ment, having coincided with your Majesty's other servants in the opinions therein expressed.[1]

Lord Mulgrave humbly hopes for your Majesty's gracious indulgence upon the communication of a private letter[2] received this morning from Lord Lonsdale, as the sentiments & feelings of Lord Lonsdale are such as Lord Mulgrave is persuaded will be highly satisfactory to your Majesty.

Lord Lonsdale arrived this evening in London prepared to give every assistance in his power to any arrangement which may be for the advantage of your Majesty's service.[3] (14655)

[*The King's reply*, *Windsor Castle*, *22 Sept.*] The King acknowledges the receipt of Lord Mulgrave's letter of yesterday and will not fail to have his name inserted in the Minute of Cabinet of the 18th inst. His Majesty thanks Lord Mulgrave for the communication of the letter from Lord Lonsdale which is extremely handsome & satisfactory & fully confirms the opinion which the King has always entertained of Lord Lonsdale's zealous attachment. (14656)

3970   THE DUKE OF PORTLAND *to the* KING,[4] *and the reply*

[*Burlington House, Friday, 22 Sept. 1809.*] The Duke of Portland most humbly begs leave to represent to your Majesty that of the three only civilians who have offered themselves or have been in contemplation as qualified to supply the vacant office of Regius Professor of Civil Law in the University of Oxford, Dr. Phillimore[5] is considered by those whom the Duke of Portland has consulted upon the occasion, and particularly by the Vice-Chancellor[6] and some of the most respectable Heads of Houses, to be the most proper person to be submitted to your Majesty for that appointment; and as the ensuing Term commences so early as the 10th of next month, the Duke of Portland begs leave to recommend Dr Phillimore for your Majesty's selection, and to request your Majesty's permission to direct Dr. Phillimore to prepare himself for that appointment.

[1] This paragraph was added to the Cabinet Minute (No. 3966) on 22 Sept. in Taylor's hand and signed and dated by him the 22nd. (14615.) Eldon wrote on the 19th: 'After sitting together till one o'clock this morning, we got the length of drawing out an opinion to be offered to the King (if Mulgrave could be got out of bed) this morning.' (Twiss, *Eldon*, II, 96.) There was a Cabinet dinner on the 21st at the Duke of Portland's, though the Duke had resigned. (Rose, *Diaries and Corresp.*, II, 388.)

[2] Missing. Tierney wrote to Grey on the 23rd: 'Lord G. Cavendish called upon me yesterday in Grafton Street, and desired that I would tell you that he had just had a good deal of conversation with Lord Lonsdale, who certainly supports Canning. He speaks highly of you, but seems to be sore because you and Lord Grenville would not enter into a negotiation with Canning when it was offered to you *before* our dissolution of Parliament. I do not remember to have heard of any proposition made at that time.' (Howick MSS.)

[3] Lord Lonsdale had travelled from Lowther in two days on hearing of the break-up of the Government. 'He coincided completely in my view of matters,' wrote George Rose on the 21st. (*Diaries and Corresp.*, II, 385.)

[4] Not in the Duke's own hand.

[5] Joseph Phillimore (1775–1855), M.P. for St. Mawes, 1817–26; for Yarmouth (Isle of Wight), 1826–30. Regius Professor of Civil Law at Oxford, 1809–55. Commissioner of the Board of Control, Feb. 1822–Jan. 1828. He was then a Grenvillite.

[6] John Parsons.

Your Majesty, at various times at which the Duke of Portland has had occasion to submit the subject to your Majesty, having appeared to approve of his ideas for an improvement in the management of that part of the property of the Crown which is under the care of the Surveyor-General of Woods and Forests, and the Surveyor of Crown lands respectively, by an union of those offices, and by forming a Board consisting of three Commissioners as recommended in the year 1793 by the Commissioners appointed by the House of Commons for that purpose, he now avails himself of the vacancy of the latter office by the death of Mr Fordyce, humbly to suggest to your Majesty the propriety of carrying that measure into effect; and the Duke of Portland accordingly most humbly begs leave to recommend that Lord Glenbervie should be placed at the head of the Commission, with his present salary of £2000 per annum, together with the use of the official house occupied by Mr Fordyce, and that the two Junior Commissioners should each have an annual salary of £1000 net; and the Duke of Portland would, with the utmost deference to your Majesty's inclinations, humbly propose that those situations should be filled by Mr. George Villiers[1] and Mr. Adams,[2] the first of whom has too long had the advantage of performing his services immediately under your Majesty's own eye to suffer the Duke of Portland to presume to do more than express his anxious hope that this suggestion may be so fortunate as to meet the approbation of your Majesty. As for Mr. Adams, the Duke of Portland no less earnestly hopes that the ability, the diligence, and the integrity by which Mr. Adams's conduct has been uniformly distinguished for a space of little less than twenty years, will be admitted by your Majesty as a sufficient justification of the Duke of Portland's request in his favour. Mr. Adams was first introduced into your Majesty's service in the office of Secretary of State for the Home Department. He was afterwards Private Secretary to the late Mr. Pitt during the whole of his last Administration, and has acted in the same capacity with the Duke of Portland ever since your Majesty placed him at the head of the Treasury.[3]

The extreme anxiety expressed yesterday by Mr. Canning that your Majesty might be correctly informed of all the circumstances which occasioned the un-

[1] George Villiers (1759–1827), M.P. for Warwick, 1792–1802, the younger brother of Thomas and John Charles, 2nd and 3rd Earls of Clarendon respectively. Paymaster of Marines, 1792; Paymaster and Inspector of Marines, 1803–Jan. 1810; Ranger of Cranborne Chase, 1807–27. He was also a Groom of the Bedchamber for many years. For his disgrace in 1810 see No. 4063. Lord Glenbervie was thoroughly annoyed with Perceval in Dec. 1809 for having consented to the proposed nomination of Villiers 'to be one of my colleagues in the projected Board for managing the Woods and Lands of the Crown. I know personally that he feels and is vexed at the intriguing, selfish, meddling, mischief-making qualities of Villiers, who by his own teizing, and the *illecebrae* of his wife has gained a great ascendancy over the royal mind, and has teized his Majesty and the Duke of Portland for that appointment, hoping thereby to smooth the way for his many jobs at Cranborne Lodge and his domineering authority over the Parks and Forest of Windsor.' (Glenbervie MS. Journal, 19 Dec. 1809.)

[2] William Dacres Adams.

[3] The Duke's draft of this letter (in the Wm. Dacres Adams MSS.) adds the following at this point: 'And should your Majesty condescend to acquiesce in this proposal, Mr. Adams will be a gainer only in point of rank, as he will be under the necessity of resigning the situation he holds in the Secretary of State's Office, which is very nearly equal in point of emolument to that which the Duke of Portland solicits for him.' Adams was then Senior Clerk at the Home Office. He and Henry Dawkins became the Junior Commissioners (date of patent, 31 July 1810.) Adams wrote to Lord Liverpool on 30 Sept. saying that the new Board could not be constituted without the authority of Parliament. (W. D. Adams MSS.)

fortunate transaction which took place that morning at Wimbledon between him and Lord Castlereagh, induced the Duke of Portland to consent to ask your Majesty's leave to lay before your Majesty copies of Lord Castlereagh's letter to Mr. Canning[1] and of Mr. Canning's reply;[2] but when the copies arrived, the Duke of Portland was too much disordered to admit of his making use of his pen, and he was, however reluctantly, under the unavoidable necessity of relinquishing his intention, and was unable to give Mr. Canning notice of it. At the usual time

[1] Castlereagh's challenge, 19 Sept. (14669–72).

[2] (14673.) Both letters subsequently appeared in the newspapers. Charles Ellis's efforts to avert the duel are described in his Minute 'taken at Henry Wellesley's immediately after his conversation with Lord Yarmouth on Wednesday night, 20 Sept.': 'I stated to Lord Yarmouth that Lord Castlereagh's letter was such as to put it out of Mr. Canning's power to offer any explanation. That I had no authority from him to do more than to settle with Lord Yarmouth the time and place of meeting, with a strict injunction not to allow of any delay beyond tomorrow morning at an early hour; but that I felt it my duty to state to Lord Yarmouth that I had been informed by Mr. Canning confidentially, at the moment, of every step which he took in this business, and that it did not at any time occur to me that Lord Castlereagh had, in any step which Mr. Canning took, cause for offence, nor, upon recollection, did I now think that Lord Castlereagh had a case which could justify the step he had taken. That I stated this without Mr. Canning's knowledge (in confirmation of which I referred to Mr. Henry Wellesley, who had been present during the whole time while I was at Brompton) but that as Lord Yarmouth had expressed a desire for an explanation of any misunderstandings or misrepresentations (which were alluded to in Mr. Canning's letter) I would state to him the course of the transaction, according to my recollection of it, which was:

'That the arrangement of a change in the War Department did not originate in a demand on the part of Mr. Canning, but was the consequence of the expression of his dissatisfaction at the general state of the Government, and of his tendering, upon that ground, his resignation. In this arrangement, which was proposed as a means of strengthening the Government, he acquiesced, and consented to continue in office.

'The time of carrying it into execution was not left at his option, nor was it of his choice. It had been in contemplation to execute it at the close of the Session, but it was postponed till the issue of the expedition, at the desire of some of Lord Castlereagh's friends, notwithstanding Mr. Canning's having pointed out and warned them against the possibility of the result of the expedition being such as to render the execution of the arrangement at that time still more unpleasant to Lord Castlereagh's feelings.

'That it was urged by Lord Castlereagh's friends, as an argument in favour of that postponement, that the interval might be employed in breaking the arrangement to Lord Castlereagh; and that Mr. Canning did not know that the interval had not been so employed.

'That when Mr. Canning, having reminded the Duke of Portland that the time was come for carrying the proposed arrangement into effect, learnt that some new difficulties would attend the execution of it, he immediately withdrew his claim, before it was possible for any step to be taken, and tendered his own resignation.

'That this arrangement was throughout treated by Lord Castlereagh's friends as an amicable one, and one which need not lead to his retirement from the Administration.

'That I made this statement, not in the expectation of its producing any alteration in Lord Castlereagh's determination; that this mode of reasoning on the facts stated in his letter was such as almost to preclude any such hope—but because I felt it right to give Lord Yarmouth the opportunity of laying before Lord Castlereagh a correct statement of the facts of the transaction, which was the ground of his quarrel; that Lord Yarmouth might if he chose, report as much as he thought fit of our conversation to Lord Castlereagh, and that if he conceived Lord Castlereagh to be under any misapprehension, I would, upon his putting any questions to me as to any of the facts of the transaction, return him an answer, after a reference to Mr. Canning. It would then be for Lord Castlereagh to make any overture in explanation which he might be disposed to do; but that Lord Castlereagh's letter rendered any such overture on Mr. Canning's part impossible.

'Lord Yarmouth desired me to wait till he had reported our conversation to Lord Castlereagh, and returned saying, that what he had stated had produced no alteration in Lord Castlereagh's feelings.

'My conversation with Lord Yarmouth was very desultory, and comprehended several other points, but this is, to the best of my recollection, an abstract of that part of it, which was in explanation of the transactions which Lord Castlereagh had made the ground of his challenge.' (Carlisle MSS.)

therefore of the messenger's return from Windsor, on Mr. Canning's not hearing from the Duke of Portland whether your Majesty had condescended to admit the letters above-mentioned to have been read to your Majesty, his anxiety became irresistible. He wrote again to the Duke of Portland, most earnestly and anxiously pressing him to submit the letters in question to your Majesty's perusal, 'feeling it', as he states it, 'a duty to let your Majesty see that he had not forgotten what he owed to his situation in your Majesty's service and the publick appearance and example; but that he could not, without absolute discredit have acted otherwise than he did.'

The Duke of Portland has now laid before your Majesty without disguise the motives for his having presumed to offer these papers to your Majesty's persual, and trusts that your Majesty will condescend to admit them as a sufficient apology for the step he has taken. (14663–8)

[*The King's reply, Windsor Castle, 23 Sept.*] The King has received the Duke of Portland's letter and entirely approves of his recommendation of Doctor Phillimore to supply the vacant office of Regius Professor of Civil Law at Oxford, and of the arrangement which he has proposed for the union of the two offices of Surveyor General of Woods & Forests and the Surveyor of Crown Lands, his Majesty also approving of the suggested appointment of Lord Glenbervie, Mr. George Villiers & Mr. Adams.

The King returns to the Duke of Portland the originals of the letters which passed between Lord Castlereagh & Mr. Canning which produced the late unfortunate meeting, and the Duke must be sensible that as it is his My.'s duty not to countenance in any manner such transactions, it must be equally his wish to abstain upon this occasion from replying to Mr. Canning's letter, or from any comment except an expression of the sincere concern with which he must ever view this event.[1] (14675)

[1] Castlereagh had resigned on the 8th: the duel was fought at 6 a.m. on 21 September on Putney Heath, so he did not act without due deliberation. Tierney knew before the 19th that Castlereagh contemplated fighting. The Duke of York's friend, Colonel J. W. Gordon, had been consulted and had given it as his opinion that nothing had passed which would justify a personal *rencontre*. (Howick MSS. Tierney to Grey, 19 Sept.) Charles Ellis was Canning's second, and Lord Yarmouth acted for Castlereagh. Canning received a bullet in the thigh, and was carried back to Gloucester Lodge, where he was confined for about ten days. Charles Ellis told his friend Lord Binning on 2 Oct.: 'The wound, as it happens, was a very good wound, as wounds go, but an inch more to the right it would have killed him.' 'Portland', he went on, 'undoubtedly was, by the line of conduct which he enjoined, the cause of the duel.' He had 'distinctly engaged to take upon himself all the responsibility, if at any time blame should be imputed to Canning for the concealment. Canning has been fighting the poor old Duke's duel, or Lord Camden's, or that of any of the different friends of Castlereagh who insisted on the concealment rather than his own.' (Haddington MSS.)

Canning wrote a very moving letter to his wife who was with her children at Hinckley, in the belief that it might well be the last she would receive from him. Like the Duke of Portland, earlier, he had public money temporarily in his possession, according to the practice of the time. It was dated Foreign Office, 20 Sept. 'The poor old Duke's procrastination & Lord Camden's malice or mismanagement have led to the consequences which the inclosed correspondence will shew you. If anything happens to me, dearest love, be comforted with the assurance that I could do no otherwise than I have done; & that the publication which I leave in charge to Charles Bagot of all that has passed between me & the Duke of Portland since Easter, will clear my fame to the world; & I hope give to my own best & dearest love the consolation of seeing my memory held in honour. I am conscious of having acted for what I thought best for my country; with *no more* mixture of selfish motives than the impatience of misconduct in others & of discredit to one's self, & the anxious & confident hope of being able to do good, & the desire of being placed in a situation to do it, naturally & laudably inspire. God bless my own best & dearest love! A better & a dearer never did God give to man. But yet, my own beloved Joan, do you know, I derive some comfort from reflecting upon the sort of *widowhood* in which you have been living for the last two or three years. I think—I *hope*—you will feel my loss less than if we had been in habits of constant & uninterrupted society. I wish, to be sure, that I had been able to execute my intention of coming down to you last week—but even that perhaps is better as it is.

Gloucester Lodge, Wednesday night, 20 Sept. Now, dearest love, while Charles Ellis is gone to settle with Lord Yarmouth the time & place of our meeting tomorrow, I resume the letter which I was obliged to break off this morning. I should have liked to see my poor little George. He is a good little boy—& an extraordinary one, I think. His feelings are too sensitive for publick life even if (which God grant!) his health should admit of his being anything else than a sedentary scholar. He may be a scholar I hope —& it will be for his happiness to be so, if his lameness continues—but lame or not, do not breed him a statesman. He would feel, & fret, & lament, & hate, & despise—as much as his father: & those sentiments altogether make existence troublesome—& the opportunity of doing good—& the means, are comparatively so few—that the chance of success is not worth the anxiety of the contest. If George can imbibe a strong taste for reading & (what Hinckley will have contributed to produce) moderation of wants & desires, he will have enough to live a quiet life—without ambition—& so he may be happy —& in a moderate degree useful. I could almost wish him to be a clergyman: but not unless he wished it too.

'I know not what to say of William. I am afraid he is unamiable. But then he certainly is not loved like his brother & sister: & it is sometimes hard to say in such cases which is cause & which effect. George's health & Harriet's exquisite delightfulness have *perhaps* been in his way; & may *perhaps* have made him selfish & singular. I know my own dearest love's good sense too well to think that she wants any warning upon this subject: but let her be sure, before she decides on William's character that kind —distinguishingly kind—treatment might not change his nature altogether. I leave his lot, as well as that of his brother & sister cheerfully & confidently in my own beloved's hands. What shall I say of dear, dear, little Toddles? Let her think of papa—as if he were only absent—& love him always—as she appeared to do when last I saw her—George will conceive what death is—but neither of the others need ever know a pang upon my account.

'Almighty God bless them all!

'Now, best of loves, I must come to a less delightful subject—that of money. But I have not much to say upon it & I hope nothing embarrassing. I leave my affairs (such as they are) I hope in no great disorder. I have in my hands £8800 belonging to Alienation Office. This must be paid instantly. £6000 of it is in Exchequer Bills in Drummond's custody. About £800 in Drummond's hands—and my quarter's salary & dividends due the 10th Oct. will produce nearly £2000—add to which my Cousin Henry owes me £800. But it is so very important that this sum should be paid immediately that no suspicion should attach upon me as a defaulter of a shilling—that I shall request Charle Ellis to advance £2000 for the purpose—giving him as a security three diamond snuff boxes—or rather I should say one snuff box & two pictures set in diamonds—which are together worth more (as I believe)—& my own love will redeem them as soon as the quarter's salary & dividends are paid. These diamonds are I hope enough or more than enough to set against my bill to Rundle & Bridge—for which indeed the plate itself is answerable. And that is the only considerable bill that I have against me—nothing beside that indeed except the current bills of housekeeping (since July 1) & of annual bills—(tax &c, &c) since Jan. 1 1809.

'I owe Dent £4000, Lord Limerick owes me £8000. There is a surplus of £4000. My books & furniture & *wine* especially &c cannot be less than £3000 more—or say only £2000. But then I would not have my own love have occasion to part with [*sic*]. I borrowed of her £8000—I leave Brompton as its representative. There is therefore I hope at least £4000—or perhaps near £5000 ready money. I leave her all. But out of this I earnestly request her to give to my mother £2000—*or*, which I should like better, to allow her £300 a year (which is less than the income of my Irish estate) during her life. But then she must secure this £300 or make a Will, leaving my mother the £2000 in case my own dearest love should die before her. But this will hardly be—my mother is past 60.

'I take this precaution about my poor mother because though while I live the pension to her daughters is, under my direction, applied in part to her use, I cannot trust to its always being so when I am gone. I have added a codicil to my Will in my own hand making this request to my own love in behalf of my mother. I do not make it an absolute *bequest*, because I owe my own love *all*. But I am sure it will be as effectual as if I did so.

'The rest of my Will is very simple—& leaves *all* to my own love: making her & Lord Titchfield my Executors & joint guardians of my children.

[*Gloucester Lodge*,[1] *22 Sept. 1809.*] Mr. Canning in most humbly laying before your Majesty the accompanying letter from Lord Castlereagh, & the copy of the answer returned to it (which the Duke of Portland, as Mr. Canning understands, was prevented by indisposition from forwarding to your Majesty last night)— humbly entreats your Majesty not to suppose that he presumes to appeal to your Majesty for a judgement in his favour on a subject personal to himself: but he does think it his duty to endeavour to excuse himself to your Majesty for his part in a transaction of which he is aware how greatly & how justly your Majesty must disapprove, by shewing to your Majesty how little option was left to him as to engaging in it, or rather how impossible it was for him to decline doing so. (14674)

3972 PRINCESS MARY *to the* KING, *and the reply*

[*22 Sept.* [*1809*].] Having nothing very new to say & as I felt confident you would hear all particulars from Dr. Pope, I put off thanking you for your last letter till today in hope of being able to communicate a more satisfactory account than the last I had the honour of sending, & so far I may venture to assert that the seatons are begining to *act*, not enough yet to relieve the *inward darting* & *shooting* pains, but sufficiently to make us hope that in a few days she may find some benefit & from all the *tortures* she has submitted to go through *for* the *blessing* of *returning health*. Since Pope left us I think she has continued very much the same, never complaining but when the shooting pain in the side obliged her to ask for something such as salts or lavender water, &c. We have not been out in the boat since Monday as the wind has been very high & the sea very rough; we have gone out every day in the carriage on the sands; the motion of the carriage certainly affects her very much, the smallest jolt brings on violent pain & with all the care possible that cannot be always avoided. Her cheerfulness is quite wonderful & [she is] constantly employed reading or working all day, but lays on the couch as she does not sit up as well as she did before she left Windsor, & the moving only across the room brings on cough. At times she looks much better than at others & a degree of languor prevails at times that is painful to witness; then again at others she appears so very cheerful that it is quite

'And now, my own best, & dearest, & most beloved love, I think I have said nearly all that it is necessary to say.

'There would be no end to taking leave & of saying how dearly I have loved you. I hope I have made you sensible of this, dearest, dearest, Joan. I hope I have been good & kind & affectionate towards you. I hope I have made you happy. If you have been a happy wife—& if I leave you a happy mother & a *proud* widow, I am content. Adieu. Adieu.' (Harewood MSS.)

On the question of appropriating public money temporarily to private purposes see *Parl. Deb.*, IX, lxvii ff. After this disclosure concerning the Pay Office, the Treasury Board decided on the necessary reforms & circularised the Departments concerned. (P.R.O. T.29/91/453–8; *Parl. Deb.*, x, 184 [28 Jan. 1808].)

[1] Built by Maria, Duchess of Gloucester and called Oxford Lodge. After her death there in 1807, her daughter, Princess Sophia of Gloucester, re-named it Gloucester Lodge. Canning had bought it some weeks earlier than the date of his letter. The house was pulled down in 1850, and its name perpetuated in Gloucester Road.

surprising to see how she enters into all that is passing. Last night she went into the warm bath which fatigued her a great deal, but I was happy to say she has had between 4 & five hours sleep in the night & is now geting up. Beavor does appear satisfied with the appearance of *things* today & therefore I hope in God we may soon begin to gain some ground.

Mrs. Drax[1] came over yesterday to see us; she found Amelia not looking so well as when she saw her at Windsor, but better than she expected considering how ill she has been since the journey.

[P.S.] Dolly went over to Lord Ilchester's yesterday & returns tomorrow; he is all kindness & attention to Amelia & reads a great deal to her which I think amuses her & keeps up her attention.[2] (Add. Georgian 12/47)

[*The King's reply, Windsor Castle, 23 Sept.*] The kind letter which I received from you this morning appears to me to convey upon the whole a less unsatisfactory account of the state of dear Amelia, and I had also been in some degree relieved by the general observations & assurances given to me by Doctor Pope when here on Thursday last, but I have still to lament that the slow progress which she makes is subject to such interruptions and to the absolute necessity of resorting to remedies which, in their momentary effect, are so distressing and must so greatly increase the pain & sufferings to which she submits with so much fortitude & resignation. (Add. Georgian 12/48)

3973   LORD MULGRAVE *to the* KING, *and the reply*

[*Admiralty, 23 Sept. 1809.*] Lord Mulgrave has the honour to transmit to your Majesty the proceedings and sentence of a naval court martial held at Sheerness for the trial of John Black, a private marine, charg'd with the commission of an unnatural crime of which he has been convicted and condemned to suffer death, upon evidence so direct and conclusive as to leave no alternative but to submit humbly to your Majesty that the law should take its course. (14676)

[1] The Draxes were a Dorset family. Edward Drax (*c.* 1726–91), of Charborough, near Wimborne Minster, was M.P. for Wareham, 1755–61. Richard Grosvenor (1762–1819), of Swell Court, Somerset, and M.P. for various constituencies after 1786, married (11 March 1788) Sarah Frances, daughter and heiress of Edward Drax, and took the names of Erle Drax before Grosvenor.

[2] The King's long letter to Perceval, 22 Sept. (14660–2), authorising him to make overtures to Lords Grey and Grenville, is in Walpole's *Perceval*, ii, 27–30. The following corrections are needed: p. 27, line 15, delete 'in'; p. 28, para. 2, line 10, read 'principles'; p. 29, line 12, read 'and private'; next para., line 5, read 'to his country'; line 8, read 'every pressure'; line 9, read, 'should from that moment'; p. 30, lines 10–11, read 'equally feels'. See also Twiss, *Eldon*, ii, 98, and Rose, *Diaries and Corresp.*, ii, 394, for comments on it. In the last paragraph the King paid a handsome tribute to the Duke of Portland, to whom Perceval wrote on the 24th: 'Your Grace will, I am sure, permit me to say that I have had great pleasure in copying, for the purpose of sending to your Grace, a paragraph in a letter from his Majesty to myself of the 22d inst. in which his Majesty expresses in such just and feeling terms the sense he entertains of your Grace's services. A testimony more honorable and more truly deserved by the servant to whom it was given, or more sincerely felt by the master who pronounced it, was never, I believe, delivered by a grateful King to his retiring Minister.' (Perceval MSS.)

[The King's reply, Windsor Castle, 24 Sept.] In consequence of the proceedings of the court martial on John Black, & what is stated in the accompanying letter from Lord Mulgrave, the King is under the painful necessity of confirming the sentence by which he is adjudged to suffer death. (14676)

3974 PRINCESS AMELIA *to the* KING, *and the reply*

[Weymouth, 24 Sept. 1809.] Having nothing new to communicate, I postponed troubling you with a letter but no longer can delay expressing my gratitude for your last most dear letter. The affection expressed in it was quite a *cordial* to my *heart* & I cannot tell you all I feel for you, my dear papa. I write as I feel, & forget perhaps I am writing to the King, but thank God you are my dear papa & that I never can forget, & as such I ever must speak to you.

I have had a better night than the preceeding one & I think my rest is generally better after the warm bath. I do not feel any material alteration in my side; I am afraid the discharge is not sufficient to relieve me & the greatest relief I find is for a short time after the effect of the calomel.

The weather continues very boisterous & since Tuesday it has been impossible to get out upon the sea. I have drove on the sands. Adolphus returned yesterday from Lord Ilchester's; he met the Pauletts[1] there; not Ly. Paulett for she is ill & I understand the end of Octr. they go to town, for Lady Sophia is to be married early in Novr.[2]

Nothing ever was more kind than dear Adolphus giving up all his pleasant parties to remain with us; he is remarkably well & in very good spirits as well as dear Miny.

I hope the weather at Windsor admits of your getting your ride.

I will not trespass longer, my dear papa, than to beg you will believe me [etc.]. (Add. Georgian 14/100)

[The King's reply, Windsor Castle, 25 Sept.] I had suffered great uneasiness since the receipt of the letters from Weymouth yesterday morning, from which I had reason to fear that your progress had been interrupted and the pain in the side increased since Doctor Pope left Weymouth. I had therefore very anxiously expected the arrival of this day's post & I thank God that the kind and affectionate letter which I have received from my dearest Amelia is calculated in some degree to relieve me. The weather is certainly very much against you & has hitherto operated against your receiving the benefit which was hoped for from change of air and a residence near the sea, but I am looking forward with better hopes to the month of October which is in general fine. I am very glad to hear that you derive so much comfort from Adolphus's kind attentions to you. (Add. Georgian 14/101)

[1] The Pouletts. The 4th Earl Poulett (1756–1819) married, 22 July 1782, Sophia (*d.* Jan. 1811), daughter of Admiral Sir Charles Pocock.

[2] On 18 Nov. 1809 Lady Sophia Poulett (1785–1859), daughter of the 4th Earl Poulett, married Henry, Viscount Barnard (1788–1864), so styled from 8 Sept. 1792, when his father succeeded to the title of Earl of Darlington, until 29 Jan. 1833, when his father was created Duke of Cleveland. Henceforth he was styled Earl of Darlington until 29 Jan. 1842, when he succeeded his father as 2nd Duke.

[*Whitehall, 26 Sept. 1809.*] Lord Liverpool begs leave most humbly to acquaint your Majesty that as there appears to be a general disposition to celebrate the 25 of October next, the day on which your Majesty commences the 50th year of your reign, with more than usual solemnity, it has occur'd to his Grace the Archbishop of Canterbury that it might be proper that there should be a special prayer for the occasion, and if your Majesty shall be pleased graciously to approve this suggestion, the Order-in-Council for such a prayer might be taken tomorrow; and the Archbishop would lose no time in adopting the necessary measures for circulating it in the accustomed manner through all parts of the United Kingdom. (14677)

[*The King's reply, Windsor Castle, 27 Sept.*] The King acquaints Lord Liverpool that if the suggestion of the Archbishop of Canterbury that a special prayer should be ordered for the 25th of October next should be adopted by Council, his Majesty will not object to the measure.[1] (14678, and Add. MS. 38564, fo. 94)

3976 PRINCESS MARY *to the* KING, *and the reply*

[*27 Sept.* [*1809*].] I am happy to inform you that for the last three days Amelia's cough certainly has been less frequent, which I think is owing to the seaton on the chest begining to act. I wish I could add the pain in the side was in any way relieved; the inward pains are much the same & untill the seaton will perform its duty we can not expect any change for the better, for with all the care and attention and the number of things tried, the seaton in the side does not appear to advance as kindly as the one in the chest. Beavor is satisfied though that she is by degrees deriving benefit from the course of medecine she is now under, & he has found her with less pain these last two evenings. We went out in the boat yesterday for near three quarters of an hour & Amelia was full as well as we could expect, a little faint but not much fatigued after, & coughed very little but when we met the wind, which always brings on cough. She has had better nights this last week but certainly not refreshed after a good night and as she complains that in her sleep she dreams she is in pain the not feeling the better after her sleep is accounted for. She certainly looks better more days than others & never complains but when she cannot help it.

My anxiety to give you an account of Amelia must plead my excuse for not having thanked you before for the kind letter I received some days ago & which, as all your letters do, gave me great pleasure. We expected the Pauletts yesterday but they are not arrived yet. (Add. Georgian 12/51)

[1] Thomas Grenville wrote to his brother on 3 Oct.: 'Lord Liverpool is now the great favourite at Windsor. Last week the King dictated a letter to him in which were these words, which were repeated afterwards by Lord Liverpool, "You are my eyes, and I know I can trust you that I shall not be imposed upon."' (*Dropmore Papers*, IX, 333.) There is no copy of such a letter in the Archives and none in the Liverpool Papers in the B.M.

[*The King's reply, Windsor Castle, 28 Sept.*] I was fearful that dear Amelia would be disturbed by the high wind which has blown these last two days and therefore was less surprized than concerned that the account conveyed in your affectionate letter of yesterday is not so satisfactory as those which had been received on the two preceding days. I am however inclined to hope from the cough being lessened and the pulse being free from fever that a gradual amendment is taking place, and I shall be most anxious to hear that the seaton in the side has taken as good effect as that in the chest & has succeeded in relieving dear Amelia from the pain which I grieve to think she continues to suffer. (Add. Georgian 12/52)

3977   THE DUKE OF PORTLAND *to the* KING, *and the reply*

[*Burlington House, Wednesday, 27 Sept. 1809.*] The Duke of Portland humbly begs leave to acquaint your Majesty that he was desired by Mr Canning to inform your Majesty that he had received an intimation that the Duke of Brunswick had it in contemplation to take the first opportunity of returning to the Continent. The motives which may have suggested this step to his S. Hss. or the particular object for which it was to be taken had not come to Mr Canning's knowledge, neither did the information he had received of the Duke of Brunswick's intention appear sufficiently authenticated to be fully relied upon; yet so much so as to lead him to consider it to be his duty to desire the D. of Portland to lay it before your Majesty when he attended your Majesty today at the Queen's Palace, & which the D. of P. should have done had not the repeated marks of your Majesty's great goodness & condescension so occupied his thoughts that he must acknowledge that this subject as well as some others escaped his recollection. (14679)

[*The King's reply, Windsor Castle, 28 Sept.*] The King acknowledges the receipt of the Duke of Portland's letter which conveys the first intimation his Majesty had received of any intention on the part of the Duke of Brunswick to return to the Continent.[1] (14680)

3978   *Letters from* SPENCER PERCEVAL *to the* KING, *and the replies*

[*Earl Camden's, Arlington St., 27 Sept. 1809, 9.30 p.m.*] Mr. Perceval has just received a letter from Lord Grenville, whereof the following is a literal copy which Mr. Perceval takes the liberty of sending to yr. Majesty.

---

[1] 'The Duke', wrote Glenbervie (18 Nov. 1809), 'seems on the best terms with his mother and sister, but the Ministers are clearly shy of him, and the Prince of Wales's attentions to him are entirely fallen. He had been but once invited to Frogmore and the King has shown great unwillingness to see him. All the Royal Family except himself and his sister and mother (except Princess Amelia and Princess Mary who were at Weymouth, were invited to the festival given by the Queen on the day of the Jubilee, and of late he complains that the Prince has entirely changed his behaviour to him.' (*Glenbervie Journals*, II, 25.)

On 7 Oct. the newspapers announced that the Duke had been appointed a Lieutenant-General in the British Army.

Sir, I have the honor to acknowledge your letter of the 23d inst. and understanding it as an official signification of his Majesty's pleasure for my attendance in town, I shall lose no time in repairing thither in humble obedience to his Majesty's commands.

I must beg leave to defer untill my arrival all observations on the other matters to which that letter refers. (14681)

[*The King's reply*, *Windsor Castle*, *28 Sept.*] The King acknowledges the receipt of Mr. Perceval's letter with the transcription of that which he had received from Lord Grenville.[1] (14682)

[*From Perceval*, *Downg. St.*, *28 Sept.*] Mr. Perceval acquaints your Majesty that he has just received the inclosed letter[2] from Lord Grey. Mr. Perceval has in consequence summoned a meeting of yr. Maj.'s servants, the results of which Mr. Perceval will transmit to your Majesty by this night's messenger.

Mr. Perceval humbly conceives that it will not be thought adviseable to take any steps under the present circumstances, till Mr Perceval shall hear again from Lord Grenville. (14683)

[*From Perceval*, *28 Sept.*] Mr. Perceval humbly acquaints your Majesty that he has laid the letters of Lords Grey & Grenville before those of your Majesty's confidential servants who are acting with him, and that they were unanimously of opinion that it would be highly imprudent to take any step or to advise your Majesty to take any till Lord Grenville should arrive in town and acquaint them with his arrival—and that what should be done in that case would depend upon the nature of Lord Grenville's communication. (14686)

[*The King's reply*, *Windsor Castle*, *29 Sept.*] The King has received Mr. Perceval's letter and his Majesty entirely acquiesces in the propriety of his confidential servants taking no step and offering no opinion while they continue ignorant of the manner in which Lord Grenville may act, or until Mr. Perceval receives a further communication from him. (14687)

[*From Perceval*, *Downg. St.*, *29 Sept.*] Mr. Perceval has the honor of transmitting to your Majesty the letter which he this morning received from Lord Grenville together with a copy of his reply both to Lord Grey & Ld. Grenville.[3]

Mr. Perceval communicated Lord Grenville's answer immediately upon the receipt of it to those of your Majesty's servants with whom he is acting, and it is

---

[1] The correspondence between Perceval on the one hand, and Lords Grey and Grenville on the other, 23–29 Sept., was published in the newspapers on 11 Oct. There are copies in the Archives. See also Walpole's *Perceval*, ii, 31–2.

Eldon wrote to Lady Eldon on 25 Sept.: 'I think Grey and Grenville can never be such idiots as to think of junction...I am sure they will never act with me. And if this proposal goes off we must patch up a Ministry that will die in the first week of Parliament.' (Eldon MSS.)

[2] Dated 26 Sept. (14684–5)   [3] All dated the 29th (14689, 14690–2)

upon full communication with them, and with their unanimous concurrence that he has framed the answer, which he has sent to his Lordship.

Mr. Perceval conceives the communication between him & Lord Grenville to be now closed, but as it is just possible that his Lordship may return a further answer, Mr. Perceval has requested his colleagues to meet again at his house tomorrow at two o'clock, where they will be assembled for the purpose of considering such further answer if it should arrive, and also to receive your Majesty's further commands. (14688)

[*The King's reply, Windsor Castle, 30 Sept.*] The King has received Mr. Perceval's letter with that from Lord Grenville & the copies of the answers returned by him to both Lord Grey's & Lord Grenville's.

The King entirely agrees with Mr. Perceval that the communication with Lord Grenville must now be considered as closed, at least his Majesty cannot authorize any farther in his name; although the result of the proposal made has not disappointed his first expectations of the liberality with which it would be met.

Lord Grenville speaks of his junction with the present Government as of a dereliction of principle. He states that his objections apply to the principle of the Government itself, and to the circumstances which attended its formation. It is impossible to misconceive such a declaration after what passed upon that occasion. It is avowing the intention of bringing forward the Catholic question whenever he shall have the means of so doing, and the question is therefore whether the Sovereign shall be guilty of a dereliction of principles to which he has steadily adhered during fifty years, to which he is bound by his Coronation Oath, or whether Lord Grenville shall abandon a principle which he has contracted at option and assumed within these few years. His Majesty need hardly declare what is and ever shall be his decision upon this question.

It appears very clear to the King from the similarity of expression in the concluding part of the first paragraph in Lord Grenville's letter that he had seen Lord Grey's answer before he wrote to Mr. Perceval himself, and such being the result of the proposals made to these Lords, his Majesty conceives that nothing remains to be done, but for his servants to endeavor to secure assistance in other quarters.[1] (14693)

[1] Tierney wrote to Grey on 6 Oct. ('our friend' is evidently Lieutenant-Colonel J. W. Gordon, and his 'companion' evidently the King): 'I did not see our friend before today, and from him I can give you very satisfactory information. He had a long ride the other day and more conversation than usual, his companion being particularly communicative. Your letter was talked over, and the great man's expression was: "I wish he had come, considering it was a communication from myself, or at any rate that he had pleaded ill health as an apology for not coming. It would have looked more respectful." Our friend said that he had seen your letter, and he was certain that nothing was more contrary to your nature than to give H.M. offence, or to shew any want of respect. He was asked how he knew this, to which he answered that he had heard you say the kindness and condescension you experienced in your different official audiences had made an impression upon you which would never be effaced. The other then replied, "For my own part I agree with you in thinking he did not wish to offend. I am satisfied no disrespect was intended." The whole of his manner in speaking of you was perfectly gracious and I have endeavoured to give you word for word what was reported to me. Our friend believes both your letter and Grenville's to have been read to the King, but, if not, proper steps are taken that they shall be. If you were here I could entertain you much with the rest of the conversation during the ride

[*Gloucester Lodge, 29 Sept. 1809 (Copy).*] *Private & confidential.* I am confident that I do not deceive myself in supposing that you will feel some degree of interest on my account in the subject of the inclosed paper. Nothing can be more difficult than the dilemma in which I am placed by the result of the late meeting between Lord C. and me. It was utterly impossible (as I am sure you will agree with me) to answer Lord C.'s letter in detail. The consequence is that that letter, which Lord C.'s friends have no scruple in communicating, remains, though not un-contradicted, for I state it to be full of misapprehensions and misrepresentations, yet without any distinct explanation of the points misapprehended or misrepresented. If I acquiesce in this state of things, I run the risque of being considered as having given just cause for the challenge. If I speak, I *know* there are those who flatter themselves that I shall incur the displeasure of the King, by disclosing the interior transactions of his Government. In this difficulty, I would fain hope that the statement contained in the inclosed paper will be found as unobjectionable as any statement on such a subject could be. It discloses no facts but what Lord C.'s letter has already made notorious, and I am sure it will be felt by all who know the real course of the transaction, that I have *much* understated my own case in order to avoid any, the remotest, allusion to his Majesty's name. I hope that if ever this statement should come to his Majesty's knowledge, he will not think that I have transgressed the limits of duty and reverence to him, in communicating to my friends this justification of my conduct. But, at whatever hazard, I confess I could not bear to lie under the imputation of a dark & treacherous intrigue when I am conscious of having acted throughout with the utmost openness, & of having been myself the victim of the unfortunate (though I am sure well-intended) dilatoriness of others.

I inclose to you in addition to the statement, the copy of a letter of mine to the D. of P[ortland] & of his Grace's answer which are referred to in it. (Harewood MSS.)

[*Lieut.-Colonel Taylor's reply, Windsor, 30 Sept.*] I lose no time in acknowledging the receipt of your letter of yesterday and of the enclosures, and in assuring you that you do me justice in being convinced of the sincere interest which I feel on your account, as also that it was not without the truest regret that I learnt the late unfortunate event in which you were concerned.

Being persuaded that, in sending me your statement and the accompanying

---

but it is a great deal too long for a letter. Honourable mention was made of me, especially in the finance line. Canning, though he has taken extraordinary pains, as well as extraordinary means, to set himself right with his master, has in no degree succeeded. Westmorland was abused pretty handsomely: great dislike shewn to the Wellesleys—but the Marquis admitted to be a clever man. The Duke of Portland was voted too bad; Castlereagh completely scouted; and Perceval's conduct pronounced to have been angelic.

'Our friend is very desirous that you should write a letter to the King (under cover to Colonel Taylor) stating your uneasiness at having been informed that your conduct in not coming to town upon Perceval's summons had been attributed to want of respect, &c., &c., and I am strongly inclined to agree with him. It would be sure to be well received not only by the person to whom addressed but by all those who regret the line you took. If you see this in the same light no time should be lost.' (Howick MSS.)

papers your object was that they should be submitted to the King, I did not hesitate in requesting his Majesty's permission to send them to him as well as your letter, which I considered to be written with the same view. His Majesty made no further remarks upon their contents than those previously conveyed to the Duke of Portland in reply to his Grace's letter transmitting the correspondence between yourself & Lord Castlereagh, namely, that his Majesty must confine himself to an expression of his sincere concern on the subject of what had passed. The King added that he was very glad to hear that you were doing well. It may perhaps be satisfactory to you to know that the King has not received any communications upon the subject in question excepting those which had been made to his Majesty by your desire.

I sincerely hope that you will very soon recover from every effect of your wound and be relieved from confinement. (Harewood MSS.)

3980 VISCOUNT CASTLEREAGH *to the* KING

[*Stanmore, 1 Oct. 1809.*] A letter[1] from Mr. Secretary Canning to the Duke of Portland, dated the 24th March last, having as Lord Castlereagh understands been laid before your Majesty previous to your Majesty's pleasure being received in June last for Lord Castlereagh's removal from the War Department, Lord Castlereagh feels it due to himself, before he retires from your Majesty's service, humbly to submit to your Majesty a few observations upon that letter, which was for the first time communicated to Lord Castlereagh on the 22nd ult.

Lord Castlereagh humbly conceives it is the first instance in your Majesty's service, in which the person entrusted with your Majesty's confidence, and to whose protection is consequently confided the honor and character of your Majesty's other servants, has consider'd himself at liberty to communicate to your Majesty a reasoned paper from a colleague in office, reflecting on the conduct of another Department of the Government, with a view of obtaining your Majesty's consent to remove the person administering that Department from his situation, without having previously communicated to that person the existence or nature of such a complaint, and with the purpose of further concealing both the complaint and the decision upon it for an indefinite period, whilst the individual thus affected was permitted in ignorance of what awaited him to involve himself in new and greater official responsibilities.

Lord Castlereagh considers it unnecessary to press this subject further upon the justice of your Majesty's mind, his object is (although late) humbly to call your Majesty's attention to the solidity of the grounds upon which this proceeding has been taken, and to leave it with your Majesty's wisdom to judge of the propriety of the advice which has been tender'd to your Majesty in this instance.

It is satisfactory to Lord Castlereagh to observe that no part of the representation alluded to proceeds upon the assumption of any want of exertion in the person entrusted by your Majesty with the conduct of the war. Nothing is said to impeach the extent of means employ'd, the energy with which they have been

[1] Walpole's *Perceval*, I, 347–50.

call'd forth, the objects to which they have been directed, or the selection which has been submitted for your Majesty's approbation of officers to command your Majesty's armies in the field. On none of these leading points has any complaint been founded—the whole rests upon three grounds of dissatisfaction, 1st with the line taken on the Convention of Cintra—2nd with the language held upon the conduct of the late campaign in Spain, and 3ly upon the delay interposed in the course of the spring in strengthening Portugal.

With respect to the first point, Lord Castlereagh humbly trusts your Majesty will be of opinion that whatever were the demerits of that Convention, that the honor of your Majesty's Councils was sufficiently vindicated in the eyes of Europe and the world with respect to any violation of the rights of other nations which the officers framing that instrument may inadvertently have committed, by the immediate recall of the Commander-in-Chief, by the immediate and express signification of your Majesty's disapprobation of the Articles affecting the rights and interests of your Majesty's Allies, and by the solemn enquiry subsequently instituted by your Majesty's command into the whole of that transaction, and into the conduct of the officers concern'd.

With respect to the second point, namely, the conduct of the campaign in Spain, although perhaps not at the time as much impress'd by the reports received from Sir J. Moore with respect to the general want of means and disposition in the Spanish authorities to give effect and support to the movement of your Majesty's troops as he now is, from subsequent experience and concurrent testimony, [he] could never bring himself to feel that there was anything either in the military conduct or representations of that officer to his Government which ought, whilst living, to deprive him of the confidence of those who concur'd in the propriety of entrusting to him that command, or which, after death, should induce them to withhold from his memory that tribute of respect and veneration to which his long and honorable services as an officer seem'd so justly to entitle him. Nothing has since occur'd to shake the propriety of that sentiment in Lord Castlereagh's mind; indeed, the experience of the present campaign, and the uniform course of information received from Lord Wellington, has tended indisputably to establish the truth of Sir J. Moore's opinions, and to prove how much it becomes your Majesty's servants in judging upon military affairs to be extremely cautious in forming conclusions, either upon their own sanguine conceptions taken up at a distance, or upon the reports which your Majesty's diplomatick servants may transmit home, in opposition to the deliberate and professional judgment form'd on the spot by the officers placed by your Majesty in the command of your armies.

To the third point, that is, that there was the smallest hesitation or delay in reinforcing Portugal, Lord Castlereagh can only oppose the most distinct denial. The most strenuous exertions were uninterruptedly made from the time of the return of the troops from Corunna to forward every battalion of infantry at home in a state for service to that country. The only delay which Lord Castlereagh conceives can be intended to be refer'd to in this remark is the sending out Lord Wellington to assume the command.

Upon this subject, however high his sense is of Lord Wellington's military talents and services, Lord Castlereagh did certainly not disguise from your Majesty at the time that he felt it a painful act of publick duty to recommend that Sir J. Cradock, whose conduct had met with your Majesty's approbation, should be superseded by an officer so much his junior in rank; but however painful it certainly was, Lord Castlereagh['s] declared determination to his colleagues was that he should humbly offer that advice to your Majesty so soon as he could be satisfied that the British army was likely to retain a footing in Portugal. The events of the former year when the command of the troops pass'd in such rapid succession through the hands of three different Commanders, did not appear to Lord Castlereagh to suggest the expediency of making a new appointment under circumstances professionally embarrassing, whilst it yet remain'd uncertain, whether Soult's army, after the fall of Oporto, had not been in sufficient strength to advance upon Lisbon, and to compel Sir J. Cradock, whose preparations were made for such an event, to evacuate Portugal.

Such is the nature of the representations upon which Lord Castlereagh's removal from the Colonial and War Department has beeen submitted to your Majesty. Lord Castlereagh does not find in them anything further to remark upon, other than the general charge of a disposition *to compromise* on his part, instead of to meet difficulties boldly as they occur'd—exemplified by the course adopted being that of endeavoring to protect those concern'd in the Convention of Cintra, and in the conduct of the campaign in Spain, instead of throwing upon them the blame from which the Government at home was consider'd as exempt.

If an earnest desire to protect the fame and character of officers, exposing their reputations as well as their lives in your Majesty's service: if not sacrificing them either to the temporary convenience of Government, to the impressions of a colleague naturally influenced by the judgment of those in who he specially confides, or to the popular delusion of the moment, can be denominated *compromise*, Lord Castlereagh cannot wish to exculpate himself from the imputation. He never can cease to reflect with satisfaction that in the course of the many arduous services, to the execution of which it has been his lot, under your Majesty's orders, to summon officers, that he never yet has abandon'd one of them in a manner, of the justice of which, they felt themselves entitled to complain—he cannot persuade himself that it would either have been consistent with justice or for the advantage of your Majesty's service that Sir J. Moore, (had his life been happily spared to your Majesty) or that Lord Wellington should have been disgraced by your Majesty's Government: nor can Lord Castlereagh in looking back at the different views taken by Mr. Secretary Canning and himself of the transactions in question (differences which he never imagined had survived the moment when they were honestly discuss'd and decided on in your Majesty's Councils) reproach himself with the part he has taken, or wish, if it were yet in his power, to alter any part of his past conduct.

So far as his intended removal can be supposed to rest upon any publick grounds, Lord Castlereagh may be permitted to regret that a proposition for entrusting to the Marquis Wellesley the conduct of the war, should have been entertain'd so far back as the Easter Recess, and actually decided on previous to the rising of Parliament, and yet that the entire campaign, including that in Spain, the most extensively important in itself that has ever been carried on by your Majesty's arms, should in its execution have been entrusted (Lord Wellesley being on the spot) not to the person thus designated as preferably entitled to your Majesty's confidence, but to the individual whose dismissal had been decided on, and that whilst that noble Lord's superior talents were to remain dormant till the season of activity and exertion was gone by, Lord Castlereagh was destined, whatever might be the issue of the contest, to be disgraced, and in the event of failure left to defend his publick conduct under the weight of a dismissal which, however long decided on, on other grounds, must necessarily in the view of Parliament and of the publick be consider'd as originating in that failure.

It is painful to Lord Castlereagh to feel himself obliged to approach your Majesty on this subject as he now does. He is fully aware that it is through the individual at the head of your Majesty's Councils that your Majesty's other confidential servants should alone humbly submit on matters not purely departmental their sentiments to your Majesty, but your Majesty will graciously be disposed to admit that it is impossible for Lord Castlereagh, wounded as his feelings deeply are, to avail himself of a channel through which representations to the prejudice of his publick conduct have been allowed to reach your Majesty without any opportunity being allowed to him to meet and to refute them.

After having served your Majesty for ten years, whether usefully or not, it is for your Majesty alone to judge, but undoubtedly with a disinterested and anxious zeal for your Majesty's interests and happiness, your Majesty will not be surprized, nor as Lord Castlereagh trusts condemn, the feelings of regret and disappointment with which he now retires from your Majesty's service. If Lord Castlereagh has at any time been enabled to render your Majesty any publick service, he is confident that your Majesty will be graciously disposed to render him more than justice in reflecting upon the times and circumstances under which he has acted; humbly hoping that your Majesty's accustom'd goodness will induce your Majesty under the circumstances to pardon this too long intrusion, Lord Castlereagh trusts your Majesty will not consider it unbecoming that he should feel no small solicitude to be assured that whatever consent your Majesty may have been advised to yield to the transactions of which Lord Castlereagh considers himself entitled most deeply to complain, that such consent has not been yielded by your Majesty under an impression on your Majesty's part, that Lord Castlereagh has ever fail'd in his duty to your Majesty, or that his conduct in office has call'd for a publick mark of your Majesty's disapprobation.[1] (14696–703)

3981   LORD ELDON to the KING

[*Sunday morning*, [*1 Oct. 1809*].] The Lord Chancellor, offering his very humble duty to your Majesty, has the honor to inform your Majesty that he has

[1] See No. 3986 for the King's reply on the 3rd.

brought from town a Minute of Cabinet:[1] & humbly requests permission to deliver it to your Majesty at such time as your Majesty may be pleased to appoint. (14704)

[*2 Oct. 1809.*] Many thanks for your last dear letter. Yesy. was a most beautiful day & after Church I went out in your boat for an *hour*; it was very smooth & very *easy* & I own the *first day* I *ever* was *glad* to have been out. To give you an idea how easy the motion was, I had been suffering great pain in the morng. from having my side causticked, & therefore being able to say, what with that & the inward pain, the boat was easy is a proof what a fine day we had. I went into the warm bath last night and have had a good deal of sleep. The calomel is certainly, I hope, taking effect, but as yet the pain in my side continues very much as it was. Dr. Pope comes Thursday & tho' I may not find *such* an *amendment* in my own feelings, I hope he may find me better. The medicine gives me sickness & naucea at my stomach, but no relief with it, & Pope talks of an emetic if that continues. Stomach & bile are sad plagues.

Dear Miny, Dolly, Sr. H. & Ly. Neale & Gl. Garth went out with us yesy. I cannot say how grateful I feel to you in allowing the dear Neales to be here. Ly. Neale is a great comfort & so quiet; I have known her now fourteen years & she has ever been the *same* in her kindness to *me*; they really are attached from *affection* & not from any *interested motives*.

Miny is very much pleased with Mr. Gorton's[2] preaching; his pronunciation she says is always bad but his sermons are very good; on Sundays here they give two sermons, one at morng. service & the other at six in the evening, & the warm bath is never used on a Sunday after twelve o'clock, nor the rooms opened.

Ly. G. Murray has got a cold, Miny has therefore sent over for Mrs. Drax. Adolphus goes to day to Lord Pawlett's for one night and then to Mr. Sandford's, a gentleman he knew at Hannover, & where he is to meet Gl. Linzingen.[3] He returns here the middle or end of the week.

[1] Walpole's *Perceval*, II, 33–4 (30 Sept.). (14695.) Eldon wrote, on the 2nd, to Lady Eldon: 'I told you in a little note, on Saturday, that I was obliged to go to Windsor. I was compelled to do it, and therefore I could not help myself. I was called up in the night, so as to set off exactly at 3 o'clock in the morning, and I was with the King from seven till a little after eight.... The general result is that we stay in, making such arrangements, without junction, as we can—standing of course till Parliament meets, and then standing or falling as that body will please to deal with us. I think we had better have resigned, but *that* the King would not hear of for a moment. I think going on, with the certainty of being turned out, would be better than junction: at least to me it is more acceptable, and if we are turned out, as we shall be, I shall have the satisfaction of remembering that I declined being a negotiator for junction, and have stood, throughout, the servant of no man or men but the King.' (Twiss, *Eldon*, II, 102.)

[2] The Rev. William Gorton (c. 1766–1830). Rector of Chickerell, 1795, and Vicar of Sherborne, Dorset, 1811–30.

[3] Charles von Linsingen (1742–1830) .See No. 172, where he is mentioned without a note. A member of one of the oldest Hanoverian families, he had been a member of Prince Ernest's household as his military instructor when the Prince was pursuing his studies in Germany. In the early 'nineties he was a Captain in the 9th or Queen's Light Dragoons, in Hanover. In 1804 he was in England, commanding a Brigade of Hanoverian Cavalry, and eventually he was put in command of the King's German Legion, with the rank of Lieutenant-General.

God bless you, my beloved papa, I hope you will have fine weather for your rides. (Add. Georgian 14/107)

[*The King's reply*, *Windsor Castle, 3 Oct.*] I have to thank you for a very kind letter and one which has given me great comfort as it certainly affords more encouragement than any I have yet received from you, to hope that you yourself begin to feel in some degree the amendment which has been observed by others, and I consider what you say of the difference you found in the effect of your last excursion in the boat and any preceding to be a very favorable symptom. Doctor Pope was with me yesterday and I anxiously hope that he will not be disappointed in his expectations of being able to send me a very satisfactory report after he has been with you. I am very happy that you find such a comfort in the attendance of Sir Harry & Lady Neale; knowing your partiality to them it afforded me great pleasure that circumstances admitted of his being absent from other duties upon this occasion. (Add. Georgian 14/108)

3983   PRINCESS MARY *to the* KING, *and the reply*

[*2 Oct.* [*1809*].] I have a most kind letter to thank you for, received two days ago. I am happy in being able to continue assuring you dear Amelia's cough is less frequent when the weather is mild & that she does not feel any wind then upon her. What fever she now has Mr. Beavor attributes more to the affects of the medicine she is taken [*sic*] than anything else. I wish I could add the pain in the side was in any way relieved; I fear as to that her sufferings are much the same & untill the seaton will act properly we cannot expect much change for the better. The warm bath certainly agrees & Amelia herself says she feels more comfortable after the bath; though it fatigues her very much she can remain in longer than she did 10 days ago. We went out in the boat yesterday for an hour; she was faint & low but not more so than I have seen her before. She assured us the sea air rather revived her. General Garth, who had not seen Amelia since the last time we went out in the boat, was struck with Amelia looking better & he as well as Sir H. Neal thought she got into the boat stronger. Her nights upon the whole are better in some respect as she sleeps more, but she complains of constantly dreaming she is in pain & as she often moans in her sleep I fear the side is the cause of that uneasy sleep; the consequence of that is that she never is refreshed after her sleep.

I had the pleasure of seeing Lady Reed[1] last night on the walk; she made very particular enquiries after you; she has been very ill & is come to this place for change of air & has taken a house for two months. She is grown dreadfully old since I have seen her & has great dificulty in walking at all.

Capin. [*sic*] Vashon[2] in the Thalia arrived the night before last; he is the oddest looking little man I ever saw, much shorter than Col. Newdigate with a face nearly as long, if not longer, than his *own body*; he has a very *nice* pretty looking wife with him. Capin. Towers[3] arrived in the Isis yesterday: I have not

[1] Lady Reid.   [2] James Giles Vashon. Lieutenant, 1794.
[3] ? John Tower. Lieutenant, 1797; Captain, 1804.

happened to meet him yet in the walk, but I understand from Sir H. Neal he is a very sensable good officer.

[P.S.] Beavor has just been with us; he assures me her pulse is stronger; he does not attach the same consequence as to the discharge of the *seatons* as Pope does.

Lady George having been unwell with a cold I hope you will not disaprove my having sent for Mrs. Drax to come for a few days which will enable Lady George to take care of herself. (Add. Georgian 12/54)

[*The King's reply, Windsor Castle, 3 Oct. 1809.*] The accounts which your kind letter conveys & those which dear Amelia herself sends me, appear to me more satisfactory and such as confirm my anxious hopes that a gradual amendment is taking place. What you observe however in regard to the pain in the side still gives me great concern and I shall be impatient to learn after Doctor Pope's arrival at Weymouth that he has been able to find some more effectual means of relieving it than have been hitherto adopted. I entirely approve of your having sent for Mrs. Drax to relieve Lady George Murray during her indisposition. Your description of Captain Vashon entertained me not a little. (Add. Georgian 12/55)

3984   THE DUKE OF PORTLAND *to the* KING,[1] *and the reply*

[*Burlington House, Monday, 2 Oct. 1809.*] As it is understood that the Bishop of Chester[2] will be ready to do homage to your Majesty on Wednesday next for the See of Bangor, the Duke of Portland most humbly begs leave to ask your Majesty's gracious permission for Mr Gerald Wellesley[3] to kiss your Majesty's hands on the same day for the Canon Residentiaryship of St. Paul's which will become vacant by the Bishop's translation; and to resign his Prebend of Westminster, to which your Majesty has condescended to allow the Duke of Portland to recommend his nephew Mr. William Bentinck to succeed.[4] (14705)

[*The King's reply, Windsor Castle, 3 Oct.*] The King approves of the Duke of Portland's desiring the Bishop of Chester and Mr. Gerald Wellesley to attend at the Queen's Palace tomorrow for the purposes mentioned in his letter. (14706)

----

1 Not in the Duke's own hand.

2 Henry William Majendie.

3 Gerald Valerian Wellesley, D.D. (1770–1848), one of Wellington's brothers. On 2 June 1802 he married Emily Mary (*d.* 1839), daughter of the 1st Earl Cadogan. Her misconduct ruined his professional career. They separated in or about 1821, but he forbore to divorce her, and his forbearance caused Lord Liverpool, the Prime Minister, to veto his promotion to the Irish Bench in 1826, on the ground that no clergyman living apart from his wife should be made a Bishop.

4 Lord Eldon wrote to Perceval on 15 Oct.: 'I had a letter from the Duke of Portland in which he tells me Wellesley's canonry cannot take place unless I will first make him a Prebend of St. Paul's, which Majendie vacates at the same time. I answered by saying I would certainly enable his Majesty's gracious intention towards Wellesley to be carried into effect.' (Perceval MSS.)

[*Windsor Castle, 2 Oct. 1809.*[1]] The Chancellor having delivered to the King yesterday the Minute of the Cabinet Council held at the house of Mr. Perceval on the preceding day, and having also stated to his Majesty that his confidential servants were unanimous in their opinions that the individual who shall succeed to the situation of First Lord of the Treasury should, for the advantage of his service, be a member of the House of Commons, the King, after due consideration of what is submitted in the Minute, and of what the Chancellor has represented verbally, cannot hesitate in conveying to his confidential servants, through Mr. Perceval, his entire concurrence in their sentiments.

Mr. Perceval's conduct has so fully confirmed the impression which the King had early received of his zeal, his abilities, and of the honourable principles by which he is invariably actuated, that his Majesty cannot pause in the choice of the person to whom he should intrust a situation at all times most important, but particularly so under the present arduous circumstances; and his Majesty trusts that the warm and zealous attachment which Mr. Perceval has manifested towards him upon former trying occasions, will now ensure to his Majesty his acceptance of an office in which he may rest assured that he will possess his Majesty's entire confidence.

Mr. Perceval will observe that, situated as he now is, he will not step into that office as a new person, that he rises to it by no unusual or unprecedented progression, that the duties of the two offices are closely connected, and that his appointment will not even require that he should vacate his seat in Parliament.

The King has seen with no small degree of satisfaction in the conduct of his confidential servants, their determination to make every exertion in their power for the advantage of his service, and in support of the course which his Majesty follows from a thorough conviction that it is correct and such as can alone be reconciled to what he owes to himself and to the country.

His Majesty has, he trusts, given sufficient proof that, in his adherence to that course, he has not been swayed by prejudice or even by the recollection of past occurrences, grating to his feelings and naturally calculated to produce strong and lasting impressions; but that he has been guided solely by principles which, if he could abandon, he could also forget that he is the guardian of a free Constitution.

The King must repeat that he does not attempt to conceal from himself the difficulties which must be encountered, but he assures his confidential servants that he will not shrink from any which his duty bids him to encounter, and that they shall never fail to experience from him the countenance and encouragement, the firm and declared support to which they are entitled from their attachment and devotion to a just cause which, with the powerful aid of Providence, he trusts he shall be able to maintain. They will find him equally disposed to concur in such measures as they shall recommend for adding or securing strength to his Government.

The King has, in a former letter to Mr. Perceval, expressed his reliance upon the attachment and loyalty of his people; and it is natural that he should at this

[1] There is an inaccurate version of this letter in Walpole's *Perceval*, II, 35, and it is also wrongly dated.

moment advert to the importance of strengthening or securing those feelings by such means as can with propriety be adopted towards convincing the country at large that his Majesty's proceedings have been directed with a view to its peace and tranquillity; and that he has not hesitated to sacrifice his personal feelings to the object of reconciling those political differences which deprive it of the advantage of a more extensive combination of its abilities.

The King is confident that at least no pains will be spared by his confidential servants to counteract the effect which might result from the misrepresentation of the circumstances which have taken place, a full exposure of which, if it were possible, would but serve his Majesty's cause and future interests. He trusts that the country would then admit how weak is the ground on which Lord Grenville maintains principles assumed in opposition to a leading feature of that Constitution which, as a Peer and a servant of the public, it was his duty to support, when compared with those on which his Majesty adheres to principles which he feels that he is bound to consider as no less sacred than he does every right which is secured to his people by the conditions under which he succeeded to the throne.[1] (14707–8)

[*From Perceval, Downg. St. 2 Oct.*] Mr. Perceval has received your Majesty's most gracious letter, and communicated it to your Majesty's confidential servants. Mr Perceval is entirely unable adequately to express to your Majesty the dutiful & grateful sense which he entertains of your Majesty's most gracious & indulgent estimate of his services. Mr. Perceval would indeed feel happy in the obedience which he shall pay to your Majesty's gracious commands if he thought that his exertions & services could merit such an opinion. Mr. Perceval can only say that he will not be wanting in exertion, in industry, in zeal & in duty—but in talent & power he feels his great defects for such a station in such arduous times. (14711)

[*The King's reply, Windsor Castle, 3 Oct.*] The King cannot acknowledge the receipt of Mr. Perceval's letter of yesterday without repeating to him that the sentiments conveyed in his reply to the Minute of the 30th are those which his M. has long received, and which he is confident will be confirmed by the whole tenor of Mr. Perceval's future conduct. (14712)

[*From Perceval, Downg. St., 3 Oct.*] Mr. Perceval humbly submits to your Majesty that he should have your Majesty's gracious permission & commands to offer to Mr. Dundas the Seals of the Office of Secretary of State which are now held by Lord Castlereagh. Mr Dundas will return from Ireland in time, should your Majesty approve of his appointment, to present himself to your Majesty at the Levée on Wednesday sevnnight.[2]

Mr. Perceval has received a note from Mr. Canning informing him that his

---

[1] Perceval kissed hands as First Lord of the Treasury on 4 Oct.

[2] Lord Bathurst wrote to the Lord Lieutenant of Ireland, the Duke of Richmond, on 30 Sept.: 'I think it will end in Perceval being placed at the head, and Robert Dundas to be Secretary of State for the War Department. You will lose a good Secretary. Would you have any objection to Pole?' (Richmond MSS. 72/1517.)

wound is so far recovered that he would be able without much inconvenience to attend at the Levée tomorrow to deliver up the seals of his office, to which Mr. Perceval has ventured to reply, that as no public inconvenience would be incurred by Mr Canning's keeping the seals till the Wednesday following, he hoped he would not risk any personal inconvenience by coming out too soon, but that if he should prefer waiting upon your Majesty tomorrow your Majesty should be apprized of his intention.

Mr. Perceval humbly requests that your Majesty would cause a copy of Mr Canning's letter to the D. of Portland to be sent to Mr. Perceval. (14717)

[*The King's reply, Windsor Castle, 4 Oct.*] The King approves of Mr. Perceval's recommendation of Mr Dundas for the office of Secretary of State for the Colonial Department. His Majesty will be prepared to receive Mr Canning if he should come to the Queen's Palace this day, but he approves of what has been written to him by Mr. Perceval on the subject. The King has ordered a copy to be made of Mr. Canning's letter to the Duke of Portland which will be sent to Mr. Perceval in the course of the day. (14718)

[*George Canning to Spencer Perceval, Gloucester Lodge, Monday night, 2 Oct. (Enclosure).*] I return the correspondence with Lords Grey & Grenville with many thanks for the communication of it. If I have done wrong in keeping copies of it, let me know & I give you my word I will destroy the copies.

I am glad to find that the principle which I took the liberty of stating, with respect to the formation of a new Government, is so fully admitted, after so full a deliberation as it appears to be, by 'the devolution of the Duke of Portland's office' upon you. I venture to hope that the nonsense & the calumnies which I have seen for the last week in the ministerial papers directed against me upon this subject must now subside. I have at least the King's sanction for the advice which I humbly presumed to offer.

I am sure you will be glad to hear that I am so far recovered from the effects of my wound that my surgeon assures me that I shall be able with very little inconvenience to attend the Levée on Wednesday. I shall therefore be ready to deliver the Seals into his Majesty's hands on that day, if you have the goodness to let me know that his Majesty will be pleased then to receive them. (14725)

3986   THE KING *to* VISCOUNT CASTLEREAGH

[*Windsor Castle, 3 Oct. 1809.*] The King has received Lord Castlereagh's letter of the 1st instant and, before H.M. enters into transactions of which he must ever lament the occurrence and the consequences, he thinks it necessary to assure Lord Castlereagh thst he readily admits that, situated as he is, he could not with propriety have made his representation to the King in any other than the direct mode which he has adopted.

The King does not recollect any communication to him of Mr. Canning's letter of the 24th March last, to which Lord Castlereagh refers, nor has want of zeal or of efficiency on the part of Lord Castlereagh in the execution of the duties of his Department ever been urged to H.M. as a ground for the arrangement which was suggested. The Duke of Portland stated verbally to the King in May last that difficulties had arisen from Mr. Canning's representation that the duties of the Foreign & the Colonial Departments clashed, and that, unless some arrangement could be made for the removal of Lord Castlereagh, he had reason to believe that Mr. Canning would resign his situation in the Government. This was the reason assigned to his Majesty, and in June Lord Wellesley's name was first submitted to him as the eventual successor to Lord Castlereagh, the continuance of whose services as a member of the Government it was hoped would be secured by some further arrangement. It was not intended that the communication to Lord Castlereagh of what was in agitation should have been subject to the delay which progressively took place from circumstances into which the King does not think it necessary to enter.

The King has no hesitation in assuring Lord Castlereagh that he has, at all times, been satisfied with the zeal and assiduity with which he has discharged the duties of the various situations which he has filled, and with the exertions which, under every difficulty, he has made for the support of his Majesty's & the country's interests. His Majesty must ever approve the principle which shall secure the support & protection of Government to officers exposing their reputations as well as their lives in his service, when their characters & conduct are attacked and aspersed upon loose and insufficient grounds, without adverting to embarassments & local difficulties of which those on the spot can alone form an adequate judgement. His Majesty has never been inclined to admit that Lord Castlereagh was wanting in zeal or exertion in providing for the reinforcement of his Army in Portugal: on the contrary, Lord Castlereagh must remember that the King was not disposed to question the correctness of the representations made by the late Sir John Moore which subsequent experience has too fully confirmed, and although he was induced to yield to the advice of his confidential servants, he never could look with satisfaction to the prospect of another British Army being committed in Spain under the possible recurrence of the same difficulties.

It was also this impression which prompted the King to acquiesce in the appointment of so young a Lieut.-General as Lord Wellington to the command of the troops in Portugal, as he hoped that this consideration would operate with others against any considerable augmentation of that Army, altho' that augmentation has been since gradually produced by events not then foreseen. In making this observation the King is far from meaning to reflect upon Lord Wellington, of whose zealous services & abilities he had the most favorable opinion, and whose subsequent conduct has proved him deserving of the confidence reposed in him: but as Lord Castlereagh has laid so much stress on this point, his Majesty has considered it due to himself & to Lord Castlereagh to shew clearly that he had never entertained an idea that there had been any neglect on his part in providing for that service.[1] (14713–4, and, with trifling differences, Perceval MSS. [copy].)

[1] Writing to his half-brother on 16 Oct., Castlereagh described the King's letter in these terms: 'On Wednesday last I resigned the Seals, having a few days before laid before the King a full exposé of my sentiments and grievances, disposing I hope satisfactorily of the three points on which Canning

[*Weymouth, Friday evening, 6 Oct. 1809.*] Knowing the kind & tender anxiety you have about me I cannot let this day pass without writing to you, first to thank you for your last kind letter & to inform you that Doctor Pope arrived yesterday. He was decidedly of opinion that a greater discharge must be obtained from the side & in consequence he has made *issues* but *has* not taken away the seaton. Do not, my dear papa, think it has been done with any instrument, for it was only putting in the peas in addition to the silk & therefore it was less painful than if he had been obliged to use a lancet. I am sorry to *say* Dr. Pope *confirms* my feels that the side is *no better* & the tenderness to the feel as great as when he was *last here*. I rejoice he is come as I am sure it requires great attention & watching, & that the seat of my illness is in the side. Many changes have taken place which require constantly being attended to & Dr. Pope certainly will remain till Monday. The cough is better. You will hear many particulars from him when he returns & which will be more satisfactory to hear from him than me, as well as that he will be better able to give you his opinion, but all he sees confirms his opinion the disorder is deep seated in the side.

The weather is stormy but I went out for half an hour on the sands. Ly. Reid is here & Miny has seen her; by all accounts she is very much altered. As to anything amusing, I must leave that to dear Miny to inform you of, for I am in no *way fit* for *anything* & I feel the kindness of all to *me* & which encourages me to write to *you*, my beloved father, as I feel nothing but your affection for me could make so dull a letter in any way acceptable, but I feel very anxious *you should know everything about me*, & let me assure you that the greatest *comfort* I can experience is the affection I ever meet with from you. God grant I may soon have the happiness of seeing you & believe me [etc.]. (Add. Georgian 14/111)

[*The King's reply, Windsor Castle, 8 Oct.*] I have received your kind letter of the 6th & cannot describe to you how much I feel distressed at the thoughts of all you have undergone and are still suffering. Your situation is ever present to my mind, and you cannot give me too much credit for the warmest affection, and the most anxious solicitude for your recovery. I look forward with impatience to every succeeding report and am now indulging hopes which, I trust in God, will not be disappointed, that the account which I shall receive tomorrow will assure me that the effects of the issue and the other remedies to which you submit with so much resignation have answered Doctor Pope's most sanguine expectations and that they afford a fair prospect of relief from the severe pain in the side. Anxious as I shall be to see him on his return, I shall rejoyce in his continuing as long as he can with my dearest Amelia, whose comfort is now the first object of [etc.]. (Add. Georgian 14/113)

in his letter of the 24th March rested his claims for my removal. The King's answer is very full, and as far as it could be made, after having yielded the point himself, perfectly satisfactory—very full of regret, very complimentary on my services—admits how justly I was entitled to complain, and negatives all Canning's propositions. In conversation he was still more explicit; in short, he said, it was proposed to him and agreed to, upon no one ground, except the apprehension of breaking up the Government by Canning's secession in the House of Commons.' (Londonderry MSS.)

[*Weymouth, 6 Oct.* [*1809*].] I think it may be a satisfaction to you to hear from me today as I can assure you Amelia has gone through with her usual fortitude the making the issue in her side, which, as she has given you the account how it has been done, I will not trouble you with a repetition of. It has left her both sick & low, therefore I hope if she has wrote out of spirits you will not forget it was almost immediately after all she suffered that she sat down to write to you, for believe me she is full as *well* as we have any right to expect after so much pain: and I pray God her fortitude and resignation may be rewarded in time by the blessing of returning health. Dr. Pope is very decided we never can expect the *side to* be any *better* untill a proper discharge is produced. The cough he finds better but in all other respects I fear we are just *as we were*, as the side remains very tender to the *touch* as well as the constant *inward* pain which never leaves her night nor day. We went out for half an hour on the sands but as the side was very sore we could not remain longer. Dr. Pope has promised to stay on till Monday, when, if he is not quite satisfied with the appearance of *things*, he *will* not leave us *then*. Dr. Pope, upon looking at the side this evening, is very well satisfied with the discharge that has been already produced by the peas, but does not expect Amelia to have a good night as he thinks she may suffer much pain from the side. I shall add tomorrow morning the accounts of the night.

Dolly returns to us tomorrow; he writes me word he has enjoyed his party much at Mr. Sanford's[1] as it is quite an old German party all met together again; G. Lensingen [*sic*], Decken & Moller. He passed one day at Lord Paulett's which he says is a very fine house[2] & comfortable, at the same time nothing ever was so kind as both Lord & Lady Paulett had been to him.

Give me leave to return you thanks for your kind letter received some days ago.

Octr. the 7th. Amelia has passed a very indiferent night from pain & is very uncomfortable today under the influence of a strong dose of calomel, & as she complains so of the side Dr. Pope talks of bleeding her to see the state of her blood. (Add. Georgian 12/57)

[*The King's reply, Windsor Castle, 8 Oct.*] I am truely sensible of your kind & affectionate attention in cautioning me against receiving too deep an impression from the manner in which poor Amelia might possibly describe her feelings & sufferings. Her letter is certainly very melancholy and I am willing to attribute this in some measure to weakness & depression of spirits, the natural consequences of all she has to undergo, but I fear that I cannot flatter myself that, severe as have been the remedies applied, any material effect has as yet been produced by them, and I must ever lament that she should have been advised to undertake a journey to which her strength was by no means equal & the effects of which have evidently thrown her back to so great a degree. (Add. Georgian 12/58)

[1] Sandford in 3982 and 3993.
[2] Hinton St. George, near Crewkerne, Somerset.

[*Downg. St., 7 Oct. 1809.*] Mr. Perceval humbly acquaints your Majesty that Lord Chatham was not able to see Lord Sidmouth till the day before yesterday and the report his Lordship made to Mr. Perceval yesterday was very far from favorable as to Lord Sidmouth's disposition to give any encouragement to Mr. Bathurst or any of his friends to form a part of the Administration, more especially if Lord Sidmouth himself was not to take office. It did however appear to Mr Perceval to be so important if possible to obtain Mr Bathurst's assistance that Mr Perceval has this day written to Lord Sidmouth very fully upon the subject, explaining to his Lordship very frankly not only that there was no office at present vacant which would suit his Lordship but also that Mr Perceval could not feel himself justified in risquing the effect which might be produced upon many persons to whom he now looked for support, after Lord Sidmouth's forming part at present of the Government. Mr. Perceval felt it a matter of great delicacy to explain this to Ld Sidmouth, but hopes he has succeeded in doing it in a manner that will not be offensive to him—and upon these grounds and also upon consideration of Lord Grenville's objection to the *principle* of the present Governmt. and the consequences of that objection he has still some hopes that he may prevail upon him to give yr. Maj.'s Governt. the assistance of his friend Mr. Bathurst in office.

Upon Lord Bathurst's taking the office of Secretary of State for Foreign Affairs,[1] as your Majesty was graciously pleased to approve pro tempore while

---

[1] Bathurst accepted the Foreign Secretaryship very reluctantly, and he was delighted to be relieved of his burden when Wellesley returned from Spain. Richard Ryder remarked (3 Jan. 1810): '[He] drinks his wine with double zest since he left the Foreign Office.'

Charles Yorke had previously refused the Foreign Secretaryship, the Secretaryship at War, and the Chancellorship of the Exchequer. He wrote to his brother, Lord Hardwicke, on 4 October at 2.30 p.m.: 'I have just seen Perceval. He gave me half an hour before he went to the Queen's House to kiss hands ...Perceval was of course anxious to know how you felt about what had passed; & I related to him as much of our conversation yesterday as I thought proper & necessary; & particularly dwelt upon your great regret at the failure of an attempt to unite Lord Grenville & *himself* in an Administration, which if formed, you thought would have been able to do real service, & would have had your confidence. It would be superfluous to detail the pros & cons about *my* accepting office; because I told him fairly that as Dundas had succeeded Ld. Castlereagh, the *only* office in which I thought I could be of any use (& the possession of which would enable me with any degree of weight or satisfaction, to fight the battle of this forlorn hope) having been disposed of, there remained no other event, on which I could for a moment bestow a thought, under the present circumstances; & I explained to him particularly why I felt that I *could* not with credit take the *War Office under Dundas*, who was my junior in H.M.'s service, & to whom I could not in any degree acknowledge myself to be inferior; altho' had events been more propitious some time past, I should not have objected to hold it under Castlereagh, who was my *senior* in the service, &c. He admitted the distinction, which indeed is obvious enough, tho it appeared to have escaped him. I told him however that he might rely on such support as I could give him in *Parliament*; a line of conduct which I was happy to think, you did not disapprove of in my person; tho' you still continued to have your own opinion as to what had passed in the *late* (& partly *present*) Government, &c. The Foreign Office was tendered to me as well as others, but not so strongly pressed as the Chancellorship of the Exchequer; but I could not entertain the idea for a moment. In truth, it will become a mere office of detail & subordination under a First Lord of the Treasury in the House of Commons; & details, too, of an irksome & unpleasant description just now, besides being such as I do not very well understand. Upon the whole I feel myself much relieved from a painful anxiety arising from a sense of public duty & feeling towards our good old King, & heartily thank Mr. Dundas Saunders for having stepped over my head on this occasion.' (Add. MSS. 35394, fo. 55.) He was of course mistaken about the War Secretaryship.

Lord Wellesley's disposition was consulted, Lord Harrowby will accept of Lord Bathurst's present office, and Mr Perceval with your Majesty's gracious approbation will offer the Presidentship of the Board of Control to Sir John Anstruther.

Mr Perceval does not feel himself obliged to wait for Lord Sidmouth's approbation before he should apply to Mr Vansittart, altho he had much rather have had it, as it would probably have secured its success. Mr Perceval therefore writes to Mr Vansittart today, and sends to him a mutual friend to talk over the matter with him tomorrow. Mr Vansittart is unfortunately in Devonshire, and it will therefore necessarily be some time before he can send his answer. But there will be no inconvenience felt in the meanwhile.[1]

The Secretaryship at War cannot be settled till Mr Bathurst's determination is known. (14719–20)

[*The King's reply, Windsor Castle, 8 Oct.*] The King entirely approves the steps which Mr. Perceval has taken towards obtaining the general support of Lord Sidmouth[2] and securing the assistance of Mr. Bathurst and Mr. Vansittart. Upon these occasions, as indeed in every transaction, his Majesty is satisfied that a fair, straightforward course is that which must ultimately prove most beneficial, but he is well aware of the delicacy which attached to the communication which Mr. Perceval has made to Lords Melville & Sidmouth.

The King approves of Mr. Perceval's offering the Presidentship of the Board of Controul to Sir John Anstruther.[3] (Add. Georgian 2/14, and Perceval MSS., with trifling differences)

3990   PRINCESS AMELIA *to the* KING, *and the reply*

[*Weymouth, Sunday morning, 8 Oct. 1809.*] Though I am sure Dr. Pope will send you a report I think it will be agreable to you to have a few lines from myself to tell you that he thought it proper to bleed me yesy. & I certainly feel my head relieved by it, & Dr. Pope finds my pulse better this morng., but the

[1] Vansittart declined taking the Exchequer unless Sidmouth formed part of the Administration. See, too, Rose, *Diaries and Corresp.*, II, 407. Sidmouth wrote to his brother Hiley on the 16th: 'It has been a great source of satisfaction to me, as it has proved to others the impregnable firmness of my friends. *Vansittart* has behaved very nobly.' (Sidmouth MSS.) And he wrote to the Earl of Buckinghamshire on the 18th, with reference to his reply to Perceval's offer: '*Vansittart*...cuts with a smooth and well-set razor.' (*Ibid.*)

[2] On 21 September Rosslyn had written to Grey: 'Lord Sidmouth has advanced his return to town four days, which in his family excites much surprise, but he has not been sent for and perhaps is now sitting in the Windsor uniform with his sword by his side, in painful and anxious expectation.' (Howick MSS.)

[3] Perceval wrote to his brother, Lord Arden, 2 Nov.: 'To Sir J. Anstruther I did some time ago at the first formation of this Administration offer the Board of Control, which he declined upon grounds which would extend to any other offers. Whether upon Lord Wellesley's return, if his Lordship should come amongst us, Sir J. might see things differently, may be doubtful.' (Perceval MSS.) Lord Glenbervie wrote from Bath on 7 Jan. 1810: 'Sir John says both Perceval & Lord Wellesley have written to him, requesting that he would support the present Ministry, but that he has declined. He thinks, or says he thinks, that Ld. Wellesley will bring little or no accession in numbers to Perceval, that Canning is not likely, &, after what has passed, cannot be expected, to take any office under Perceval but that, notwithstanding this weakness, the present Administration will go on if the King live[s], who is their powerful, but only, support.' (Glenbervie MS. Journal.)

side continues the same. I hope you will forgive my adding more at present &
believe me [etc.]

[P.S.] Dr. Pope means to be at Windsor on Tuesday eveng. & in *a mistake* he
has mentioned tomorrow eveng. in his letr. to Col. Taylor. (Add. Georgian
14/114)

[*The King's reply, Windsor Castle, 9 Oct.*] Although I wrote to you yesterday, I
cannot deny myself the satisfaction of thanking you for the few kind lines which
I received from you this morning and assuring you how happy I am to hear from
Doctor Pope's & dear Mary's reports, dated subsequently to yours, that you had
been relieved by the bleeding and that the discharge from the side had answered
Doctor Pope's expectations. I entirely approve of his staying with you a day
later than he had intended & I hope that he will be able in consequence to bring
me a more satisfactory account of you. (Add. Georgian 14/115)

3991 *Letters from* PRINCESS MARY *to the* KING, *and the replies*

[*8 Oct.* [*1809*].] I take the liberty of troubling you again today with a few lines
to say that our dear Amelia is certainly better for the bleeding yesterday & does
not appear at all *weaker* for all she suffered & went through yesterday. The
dressing of the issues was a sad trial; I never remember her in all this long illness
suffering more pain, but, thank God, Dr. Pope today is satisfied with the discharge
it has produced & desires me to say he wrote his letter to Col. Taylor before he
had dressed the side this morning & as I was writing to you did not open his
letter to add how *much* pleased he is with the appearance of the issue, as he did
not like to deprive me [of] the happiness of informing you of this pleasing inteligence. Dr. Pope likewise wished me to add that he shall be at Windsor for
certain Tuesday evening, not tomorrow, as he has promised Amelia to stay &
dress her side before he goes, which will make him set out an hour or two latter
[*sic*] than he first intended. The inward pain in the side is as yet just the same & the
night has been but indiferent. (Add. Georgian 12/59)

[*The King's reply, Windsor Castle, 9 Oct.*] Your kind letter of yesterday and what
Doctor Pope desired you to say after he had closed his report have indeed proved
a great comfort to me, & have tended in some measure to relieve me from the
painful uneasiness which those received yesterday had occasioned. It is satisfactory to know that the bleeding has produced relief & that the discharge from
the side has answered Doctor Pope's wishes. I sincerely pray that its early effect
may be the abatement of the violent pain which poor Amelia suffers. (Add.
Georgian 12/61)

[*From Princess Mary, Weymouth, 9 Oct.*] I am happy to be able to say that dear
Amelia passed a much more comfortable day yesterday than the day before & Dr.
Pope is *satisfied* the bleeding has relieved her very much. The side is just the same,
& as she has wrote her own account that Dr. Pope may lay it before you & the

Queen as well as Sir F. Milman, I shall not enter into *particulars* in this letter as it is *so clear* that I can say no more than that *I believe* the more you talk over her complaints with Dr. Pope, the more you will find her statement just. The paper was wrote by herself & then she showed it Dr. Pope who beged he might have it to give Sir F. Milman. She certainly has had a better night but complains of her chest being more *tender* today as the wind is very cold.

I had the pleasure of seeing Miss Scot[1] yesterday, the Chancellor's daughter, who was most anxious in her enquiries after you. (Add. Georgian 12/62)

[*The King's reply, Windsor Castle, 10 Oct.*] The letters which I have this day received from you and dear Amelia appear to me to afford hopes that Doctor Pope has not been disappointed in his expectations of affording her some relief, although it is impossible that I should not regret that the course pursued has tended so little as yet to reduce the pain in the side. I am very thankful to you both for your attention in writing to me on a subject so near my heart and each day tends to endear you more to me, if possible. I was glad to hear that Adolphus had so much enjoyed his party in Somersetshire. (Add. Georgian 12/63)

3992 SPENCER PERCEVAL *to the* KING, *and the reply*

[*Downing St., 9 Oct. 1809.*] Mr. Perceval acquaints your Majesty that he has heard from Lord Sidmouth in answer to his letter of Saturday.[2] Lord Sidmouth takes in perfect good part the frankness of Mr. Perceval's communication respecting the difficulties that prevented Mr. Perceval from suggesting to Lord Sidmouth himself the acceptance of any office; but his Lordship gives Mr Perceval to understand that Mr Bathurst under no circumstances would accept office without his Lordship; and that as things stand at present, from some idea that Lord Grenville might possibly explain the meaning of his expressions in his second letter to Mr Perceval as not applying to the Catholic Question, his Lordship seems to think that a union with Lords Grey & Grenville is not yet impracticable, and therefore on that ground would decline office himself at this moment. If he finds that no such explanation is given of these expressions, he will give your Majesty's present Government every possible support. He desires to leave Mr Vansittart to his own discretion. Mr Bathurst being therefore entirely out of the question Mr Perceval would with your Majesty's approbation offer the office of Secretary at War to Mr. Long. There are many qualities and much official knowledge in Mr. Long which would be very serviceable in putting that office on a good footing, but Mr Perceval cannot disguise from your Majesty, that he fears Mr Long will decline it, in which event Mr Perceval thinks if your Majesty should approve, that provided Lord Wm. Bentinck could manage to come into Parliament, that he could not do better than propose his Lordship to your Majesty for that situation.

[1] Elizabeth Scott (*d.* 1862). In 1817 she married George Stanley Repton (*d.* 1858).
[2] Sidmouth's letter to Perceval, dated the 7th, is in Walpole's *Perceval*, II, 44–5 (line 5 should read 'it is written'; and the P.S. should read 'Mr Vansittart').

Lord Castlereagh has desired to know whether it would be agreeable to your Majesty to receive the seals of office from him on Wednesday. Mr Perceval has replied that he expects Mr Dundas to be returned from Ireland by that day, in which case it will be perfectly convenient, but if the east wind or any other cause should prevent him Mr Perceval will acquaint Lord Castlereagh.

Mr Perceval encloses the letter from Mr Canning which he mentioned to your Majesty the other day. (14723–4)

[*The King's reply, Windsor Castle, 10 Oct.*] The King returns Mr Perceval his thanks for his statement of the result of the communication with Lord Sidmouth from which his Majesty is sorry to perceive that Lord Sidmouth is more influenced by private feelings than by his concern for the welfare & interests of the public cause.

The King approves of Mr Perceval's offering the situation of Secretary at War to Mr Long, and in the event of his declining it, to Lord William Bentinck. The King will also be prepared to receive the Seals from Lord Castlereagh tomorrow if Mr Perceval shall desire him to attend. (14724)

3993 PRINCESS AMELIA *to the* KING, *and the reply*

[*Weymouth, 9 Oct. 1809.*] I make no apology for troubling you so soon again with a letter, but having written to you in such haste yesterday morng. I think you will be glad to hear again from me, as I can assure you the bleeding has relieved me, tho' I cannot say I find any difference in my side. However, the side discharges & I do hope I may return about the time first mentioned. I think I need not say how I long to see you again. It will be likewise a great satisfaction to me to be nearer to Pope & I own I wish for anything I think most likely to promote my recovery.

You will hear every particular from him & I have written down my own feelings exactly that he may shew it to Milman, which he wished me to do, & Pope approved of my having done it. It will also enable him to enter more fully into all your kindness may wish you to enquire, as it is the exact account I give *him* without his questioning me on the subject.

The weather is very much against me for as long as the east wind continues I am not able to go upon the sea, which is a much easier motion than the carriage.

Pope has promised to return soon. I have had since two o'clock some good sleep. Adolphus returned on Saty., much pleased with his tour into Somersetshire & the loyalty shewn everywhere. He was particularly delighted with his party at Mr. Sandford's as it was the exact same *sett* they had at Hannover eleven years ago. We were very happy to see him return to us; the roads he says were dreadfull. I will now conclude, begging you to believe me [etc.]. (Add. Georgian 14/116)

[The King's reply, Windsor Castle, 10 Oct.] It has afforded me great comfort to hear from your kind letter of yesterday that you are yourself sensible of the general relief produced by the bleeding and I trust that I shall shortly have the happiness of hearing that the discharge from the side has had a similar effect on that part. I am aware how much the prevalence of the east wind & the cold which attends it must be against you & sincerely regret it, as I do every impediment to your amendment which is the constant and anxious subject of my thoughts. You have done perfectly right in stating fully & candidly to Doctor Pope all you feel & I shall be impatient to hear his sentiments. (Add. Georgian 14/117)

3994   *Letters from* PRINCESS MARY *to the* KING, *and the replies*

[10 Oct. [1809].] I take the liberty of returning you my most greatful thanks for the gracious letter I received yesterday & am happy to have it in my power to assure you Amelia passed a tolerable day yesterday, the pain in the side much the same; the cough certainly continues less & Beavor found her with no great degree of fever last night. She has passed a tolerable night & I may add Beavor assures me he finds her pulse much less hurried than he expected this morning, which I am sure you will rejoice at when I inform you that she has been much shocked this morning by being told a most melancholy circumstance which happened last night & which we did contrive to keep from her till today, which was that Mr. Burrard was unfortunately lost in towing in your barge. He was sent from the yacht with Mr. Woodley & six seamen to bring the barge into harbour & when they got up to the barge Woodley & 4 seamen jumped in & Burrard & the two other seamen remained in the small boat. In trying to put up the sails unfortunately the boat upset, the two seamen [were] saved but poor John Burrard was drowned. You may judge of the distress & misery this has caused to poor Sir H. & Lady Neal who loved him quite as their child & indeed he was so fine a boy everybody liked him. Sir H. & Lady Neal wished if it was possible to keep it from Amelia but as Lady Neal had promised to pass the evening with Amelia it was dificult to find an excuse for her not coming. However, Lady Neal wrote a note & said she was unwell, *which Amelia would not believe.* However, we told her nothing of it till this morning when Amelia wrote a note to Lady Neal & beged for God sake to learn what had happened by her not seeing her last night, which obliged Lady Neal to write the truth. Sir [Harry] Neal sent off an express to poor Sir H. Burrard last night, who is truly to be pitied. The storm is still very great but they assure me the shiping [*sic*] is in no danger. (Add. Georgian 12/64)

[The King's reply, Windsor Castle, 11 Oct.] I cannot leave this place without first thanking you for your very kind letter of yesterday. Your report of dear Amelia is more satisfactory than I could have expected under the impression which must have been made upon her by the shocking accident which has happened. I pity poor Sir Harry Burrard from my heart and can easily conceive what Sir Harry & Lady Neale must feel upon this truly melancholy event & how distressing it must have been to you all.

I saw Doctor Pope yesterday; he entered very fully into dear Amelia's situation & I trust that what passed will be satisfactory to her. (Add. Georgian 12/65)

[*From Princess Mary, 11 Oct.*] I have to return you many thanks for a most kind letter received yesterday; how very good you are to answer me so immediately.

I am most thankful to have it in my power of assuring you Amelia certainly is *not the worse* for the dreadful melancholy and afflicting event that I told you in my yesterday's letter had taken place the night before concerning the loss of poor John Burrard. She passed yesterday very much as usual, the pain in the side just the same; some degree of fever came on last night but not more than she has often had since we have been at Weymouth. I persuaded her to keep in her bedroom all day that she might not look at the sea in the dreadful stormy state it was in all day & as they expected the body of the poor young man to be washed on shore every moment people were placed in diferent places to be ready to receive it, therefore it made it very necessary to keep in the back part of the house, which was just as quiet as if we had been a hundred miles off from any storm. Amelia saw both Sir [Harry] & Lady Neal yesterday by my advice to have it over as soon as possible & as she was much relieved by tears I rejoice she saw them so immediately. Many circumstances belonging to this unfortunate event makes it very painful to poor Sir H. Neal, for he did not belong any more to the yacht & was going on board Lord William Stuart's[1] ship. Sir H. Neal intended sending the poor boy round in the cutter, but poor Lady Burrard wrote to Sr. H. Neal to beg for God sake he would not send him in so small a vessel for fear of *accident*, which has [*sic*] delayed this poor boy's going, & to compleat everything he volunteered going in the boat to fetch the barge as the other little *mid* who was to have gone with Woodley was sea sick, & in consequence poor John offered to go for him. Sir H. Neal's own distress, his tenderness for fear the blow should be too much for Lady Neal (who loved this boy just as much as he did) & his misery at being obliged to write to the poor father &, lastly, his fear that Amelia should be told it before yesterday morning, are the diferent situations I saw Sir H. Neal suffering under, & *in all*, his fine, upright, manly character manifested itself in the strongest manner.

The yacht was brought safe into harbour this morning about half passed 8 o'clock & I never saw it look more beautiful in my life than when it came in. We passed a day of great anxiety yesterday as it was in a most alarming situation at times, but, thank God, she has weathered it *nobly* & is now safe, and our good & worthy Sir H. Neal quite [at] ease & happy, not to add *proud*, that the yacht stood such a storm. Mr. Drax says, as well as Mr. Beavor, that they never remember such a storm before in the Bay, it is very bad still, but all the other shiping they assure me is quite safe.

Amelia has had a great deal of good sleep & Beavor is satisfied with the pulse; this morning she has rather more cough owing to the cold wind which is very

[1] Lord William Stuart (1778–1814), sixth son of John, 4th Earl and (1796) 1st Marquess of Bute. Lieutenant, 1797; Captain, 1799.

sharp today. Edward came to breakfast yesterday & made us most happy by the good accounts he brings from Windsor. (Add. Georgian 12/66.)

[*The King's reply, Windsor Castle, 12 Oct.*] I have again to thank you for a very kind letter & for your attention in writing to me so fully respecting dear Amelia at a moment when it was natural I should feel particularly anxious to know that she had not suffered from her feelings in consequence of the melancholy & distressing event which I learnt yesterday, and I thank God that, in this respect, your letters are so satisfactory. Sir H. Neale's conduct upon this sad occasion has been such as I should have expected from the opinion which the experience of many years has given me of his character, & it must confirm the regard which I feel for him. Poor Sir H. Burrard had not, I was told, received the distressing intelligence at four o'clock yesterday afternoon & I dread the effect which the loss of so promising a boy must have upon him & Lady Burrard whose feelings have lately been subject to trials so severe.[1] The storm must have been dreadful by your accounts and I am glad that Sir Harry Neale is relieved from all uneasiness respecting the yacht, the continuance of which in harbour I cannot but approve.

[P.S.] I am happy to hear that Lieut. Money shewed so much judgement in the late storm. (Add. Georgian 12/67)

3995 PRINCESS AMELIA *to the* KING, *and the reply*

[*Weymouth, Wednesday, 11 Oct. 1809.*] How can I express my thanks for the most kind and affectionate letters I have had from you? Believe me, under every circumstance the greatest comfort & delight I can have is your tender affection, & much as I have to lament in my illness & long confinement, your kindness is ever a cordial to my heart & I trust in that Providence who knows what is best for us he will restore me to health in time, & I feel truly grateful for the many blessings I enjoy, amongst the first the affection of my beloved father.

I know your dear good heart will have felt much for the melancholy event that has taken place here in the loss of poor John Burrard, a most fine & excellent boy. He promised to be everything the parents cld. wish; how I feel for poor Sr. Harry & Ly. Burrard. Sr. H. & Ly. Neale are deeply afflicted but they both shine much at this moment;[2] they had quite adopted him as their own child, therefore the blow is very deep. However, I think when they hear from the parents their minds will be more relieved, for everything was done that was possible to save the poor young man, tho' alas!, without success. Even in this *trial* I must say how much affection & kindness Sr. H. & dear Ly. Neale have shewn for they wished to prevent my knowing it & to avoid my being distressed with any part of it. I never saw anything so tremendously awfull as the storm, & the inhabitants

---

[1] They lost their eldest son Paul (1790–1809), of the 1st Foot Guards, on 21 Jan., when he died of a wound received at Corunna, whilst acting as A.D.C. to Sir John Moore. Four years later a third son was killed at San Sebastian.

[2] Meaning, presumably, that they both showed up very well at that trying time.

don't recollect such a one hardly. It is now even coming on more. The tide comes into Ryall's shop: the esplanade opposite Harveys has given way & the surf is quite over into the road.

Ly. Neale is just come in to inform me the yacht is, *thank God*, come in safe into harbor & Sir Harry begs, as I am writing to you, my dear papa, I will inform you from him had he not got her in she wld. in the course of a very few hours have been drove on the shore. Her cabals [*sic*], tho' good, were cut away nearly by the pebbles, & as the weather is so boisterous he wishes to have your leave to keep her in the harbour. The ship is not materially damaged, but the outside gilding is very much washed away. Lieut. Money has behaved with great activity & judgment, & Sir Harry feels most thankful she is *safe* in harbour, but really is too much flurried to write. Ly. Neale says his anxiety about the yacht has, *now all is safe*, been fortunate, as it has to a degree taken his thoughts from the melancholy event that has occurred.

I have had some good sleep in the night; my side feels very much the shame [*sic*] & this wind has given me a good deal of headake. Thank God you have been spared seeing the sea in this sad state. It certainly is one of the most striking & awfull things that can be seen. Sir Harry assures us the frigates are safe.

I will not take up more of your time, my dear papa, than to return you again my grateful thanks for your dear letters & to assure you of the love of [etc.].

[P.S.] Great praise is due, Sr. H. says, to two shore boats who went out to save those that were upset with poor Burrard; the rest they saved. The sea at that time was not equal to what it is now. (Add. Georgian 14/120)

[*The King's reply, Windsor Castle, 12 Oct.*] Knowing how much you would be affected by the sad event so peculiarly distressing to your friends, Sir Harry & Lady Neale, independently of your own general feelings on the subject, I had been very apprehensive that the shock would prove injurious to your health & I have therefore been much relieved by the contents of yours & dear Mary's kind letters which allow me to hope that however severely you have felt on this truly melancholy occasion, your health has not been affected in the proportion which I had feared. Every circumstance which you mention in regard to poor John Burrard must add to the distress of his parents & of Sir Harry & Lady Neale, whose conduct upon this trying occasion has been consistent with his manly & amiable character & with the kind attentions which you have invariably experienced from both & for which I feel very thankful to them. (Add. Georgian 14/121.)

3996 SPENCER PERCEVAL *to the* KING, *and the reply*

[*Downg. St., 12 Oct. 1809.*] Mr Perceval humbly acquaints your Majesty that he has seen his Grace the Duke of Portland since he last saw your Majesty—that his Grace was something better, and being desirous to do anything which could in any degree mark his anxiety to support in the most effectual manner your Majesty's present Government he has accepted the offer which your Majesty was graciously pleased to empower Mr Perceval to make, that he should continue in the Cabinet.[1]

Upon mentioning to his Grace the appointment of Dr. Andrews[2] to the Deanery of Canterbury, his Grace expressed a very strong wish that the Deanery of Bristol should be given to Dr Parsons, the present Master of Baliol College, and as Mr Perceval understands upon information upon which he can fully rely, that Dr. Parsons is a very learned man, and a most respected character at Oxford, and as this Deanery may have been considered in some degree as vacant almost before his Grace had quitted the Treasury, he submits to your Majesty that it is not likely he shall be able to present a person more fit to be appointed, and therefore humbly recommends him to your Majesty for that situation.

Mr. Perceval has received an answer from Lord Melville which he has the honour to enclose.

Mr. Perceval has seen Lord W. Bentinck, and his Lordship is under some uncertainty whether he can get into Parliament, and wishes also to consult Lord Titchfield before he finally determines to accept the office of Secretary at War. His Lordship has promised Mr Perceval his answer on Saturday. Mr Perceval has had another letter from Mr Vansittart, and entertains now very little hope of his accepting the office of Chr. of the Exchequer, but he desires to withold his final answer till he shall have heard from Lord Sidmouth. (14726–7)

[*Enclosure*]

[*Viscount Melville to Spencer Perceval, Arniston, 8 Oct.*] I return you my cordial and unfeigned thanks for the candor of the statements contained in your letter[3] of the 5th inst. which I have this moment received. I have experienced so little of a similar spirit for these three years past, [that] I put a greater value upon it when it makes its appearance. If it be any satisfaction to you to know, I can assure you with great truth that a return to office would not have afforded any personal gratification to me. I hazard nothing in making this distinct assertion, because there are more than one among your colleagues to whom I have had occasion to make the same communication repeatedly in the course of these last three years. At the same time, I have never disguised from any person that if, by resuming my official habits, I could have gratified any wish of his Majesty, or rendered any essential service to my country, I should not have felt myself at liberty to entertain a moment's hesitation.

It would be an idle waste of your time, and I am sure you will not expect me to enter into any minute discussion of the topicks treated of in your letter. I would

[1] Perceval had written to the Duke on 2 Oct.: 'I have one favor to ask of your Grace, and that is that you would permit me to mention your Grace to his Majesty as not unwilling to continue in the Cabinet after your retirement from office. Upon this point I know not what arguments I can use which can have so much avail with your Grace, as the assurance that it will be of great use in my opinion to his Majesty's service, by proving that your Grace will afford your countenance to the new Government.' (Perceval MSS.)

[2] Dr. Gerard Andrewes (1750–1825), Dean of Canterbury, 1809–25. Lord Eldon wrote to Perceval, 15 Oct.: 'Dr. Andrewes' promotion is quite right.' (Perceval MSS.)

[3] See *Memoirs of R. Plumer-Ward*, I, 255–63. Perceval said that the King was desirous of making him an Earl.

not act with a candor corresponding with yours if I was to admit that the reasoning on which you found your conclusion was either true in fact or wise in policy, but it will be a very great consolation to me if this shall be the last concession you shall find it necessary to make to the description of people whose feelings in the present instance you have thought it expedient to consult. I have industriously avoided any such discussions, but with the impressions you feel and the opinions you entertain, you would have ill discharged the duties you have undertaken to discharge, if you had followed any other course with regard to me than that which you have adopted.

I trust you will lay me at the feet of his Majesty with every expression of duty, and while I decline the additional honours intended for me, I am nevertheless deeply sensible of the condescending goodness with which his Majesty is graciously pleased to recollect the services of an old & faithful servant.[1] (14721–2)

[*The King's reply, Windsor Castle, 13 Oct.*] The King acknowledges the receipt of Mr Perceval's letter from which he is glad to learn that the Duke of Portland is willing to continue in the Cabinet.

His Majesty highly approves of Mr Perceval's recommendation for the Deanery of Bristol of Doctor Parsons of whose character and extensive information the King had, for some years past, heard the most favorable mention. Lord Melville's letter appears to his Majesty a very proper one. (14727)

3997   *Letters from* PRINCESS MARY *to the* KING, *and the replies*

[*12 Oct.* [*1809*].] I have another most kind letter to thank you for & have the comfort of assuring you our beloved Amelia certainly is *not the worse* for all the *horrors* of the last three days as she has been most wonderfully supported under so much distress & as the storm is begining to go off I pray God in a few hours more we may have calm weather again. The prospect of returning towards home has cheered her much & your kind consideration her greatest comfort & support under all her sufferings. I flatter myself the bed carriage may answer. She appears perfectly satisfied & greatful for your thinking so much of her comfort and I pray God her patience, resignation & fortitude may be rewarded in time by returning health. I am sure no *patient* can give her physicians so fair a trial as she has, as her *exertion* both in mind & body for the sake of health is a lesson for both young & old. She passed a very tolerable day yesterday; the side continues just the same. The discharge is not enough to procure the relief necessary to subdue the pain. The cough was rather worse all day, the wind being so very cold. The first part of the night she had a good deal of pain but since two o'clock she has had some good sleep, but complains of her head feeling oppressed today & feeling un-[re]freshed. Sir H. & Lady Neal are much more composed today & hope to hear something of Sir H. & Lady Burrard today. The body is not found yet. (Add. Georgian 12/68)

[1]   The letter is in *Plumer-Ward*, I, 264–6, with some variations from the above.

[The King's reply, Windsor Castle, 13 Oct.] I am happy to find from your kind letter that dear Amelia derives so much comfort from the prospect of returning here, and I need not assure you that if I had consulted only my own wish to have you both with me again I should not have hesitated in agreeing to the proposals that she should return to Windsor, but as she suffered so much from the journey to Weymouth, it was natural that I should dread the recurrence of the same effects. I trust however that from the additional precautions which may be taken, those may be obviated and Doctor Pope assures me that he sees no objection to her residence in her own apartment here, which is very satisfactory to me, for, altho' I shall never suffer my own comfort & inclinations to interfere where the health of any of you is at stake, I cannot deny that any separation from you is painful to me. (Add. Georgian 12/69)

[From Princess Mary, 13 Oct.] How can I express how deeply I feel your kindness in writing me such constant, kind & aff. letters. I am desired by both Sir H. & Lady Neal to express how greatful they feel for the share you take in their present affliction. Sir H. Neal received a letter yesterday from poor Sir H. Burrard full of expressions of kindness towards them & humble submition to the will of Heaven, just such a letter as you would expect to come from so respectable a man as Sir H. Burrard.

Our dear Amelia, I am sorry to say, passed a very indiferent day yesterday, much pain in the side & a great degree of languor & oppression in the head distressed her much. She went into the warm bath in the evening by Mr. Beavor's desire, which for fear of cold (as the bath has no fireplace) we had prevented her doing ever since this cold wind, but as Beavor made such a point of it she did bath & was very cold in the bath & felt chilled coming out. However, Beavor says he found her with so much fever last night the chill may have been more from the fever coming on than any cold: at all events she is to go no more into that bath & we have got a slipper bath which will answer as well. She has not had a good night but Beavor finds her with less fever today. This cold sharp wind is really against her; Beavor says he never remembers it so cold at Weymouth before.

I saw old Pontins [?] yesterday; what with the loss of John Burrard & the anxiety he was in about the yacht, the poor old man has been really shook & cryed like a child when I spoke to him. (Add. Georgian 12/70)

[The King's reply, Windsor Castle, 14 Oct.] I sincerely regret that you should not have been enabled to send me a more comfortable account of poor Amelia than that which your kind letter of yesterday conveys, and I fear that she must be very much affected by the cold weather which has set in with unusual sharpness so early in the season. What you say of poor Sir Harry Burrard proves not only the excellence of his character but also the blessing of a religious mind, which, under the most severe trials, must ever enable even those whose feelings are most acute to submit with that firmness & due resignation to the decrees of Providence which you will never observe in those who do not seek consolation in the same source. (Add. Georgian 12/71)

[*From Princess Mary, 14 Oct.*] Your truly affte. kind letter gave me the greatest pleasure & I am most happy to be able to assure you that Amelia passed a better day yesterday than the day before, being less languid. The pain in the side is just the same; towards evening she had a good deal of pain, but had some quiet sleep in the night. Beavor does not find her free from fever today which makes her feel uncomfortable.

Sir H. Neal asked me to express how greatful he feels your generous mention of him in your letters to Amelia & me & will take the first opportunity of communicating to Sir H. Burrard the feeling manner in which you have condescended to name him. (Add. Georgian 12/72)

[*The King's reply, Windsor Castle, 15 Oct.*] Although your kind letter of yesterday contains an account somewhat more satisfactory of poor Amelia, I am much concerned to find that the fever still hangs upon her & that there is no abatement of the pain in the side. As the weather has been more moderate these last two or three days, I hope she may not have been so much affected by it. (Add. Georgian 12/73)

[*From Princess Mary, 15 Oct.*] Again I have to express my most greatful thanks for another most kind letter received by the post yesterday. I am sorry to say Amelia passed a very indiferent day from pain in the side, some degree of fever & languor very distressing to herself. She went into the warm bath which always agrees with her & insures a quiet night, after which she certainly had & had some sleep [*sic*], but is unrefreshed this morning, complains of feeling very uncomfortable & much oppressed. Beavor, who has just been with her, says it is in consequence of the medicine she feels so oppressed this morning & that when she has been out in the carriage he flatters himself she will feel better. Amelia desires me to say she shall write, if possible, by tomorrow's post but from having been so unwell these last three days we persuaded her not to write as sometimes the writing brings on pain in the side. (Add. Georgian 12/74)

[*From Princess Mary, Sunday evening* [*15 Oct. 1809*].] As it was not in my power to send you a comfortable account of Amelia by this morning's post, I take the liberty of troubling you with these few lines by Edward to say that Amelia has been rather better towards evening, has been out in the carriage for more than half an hour & it went off better than I expected as to the pain in the side, but the cough came on very much during the time she was out. I shall have the honour of writing as usual by the post tomorrow. (Add. Georgian 12/75)

[*The King's reply, Windsor Castle, 15 Oct.*] I am glad to learn from your kind letter of yesterday that the weather was considered sufficiently mild to admit of dear Amelia going out in the carriage, and I trust I shall have the comfort of hearing that she derived benefit from the airing. Pray assure her that I should feel very much distressed in the idea that she should at any time suffer from her attention in writing to me & that while I shall lament the cause of her not writing,

26-2

I shall feel very desirous that she should not on my account exert herself in any manner which can give her the smallest additional pain or uneasiness, that I shall trust to you for the information which I am so anxious to receive from Weymouth. (Add. Georgian 12/76)

[*From Princess Mary, 16 Oct.*] I take up my pen with great pleasure this morning as I can have the comfort of saying dear Amelia, after having been in the warm bath last night (which went off very well) had a great deal of quiet sleep & Beavor found her pulse *better* for the bath. This morning Beavor finds her free from fever and she thinks herself more comfortable. The pains in the side disturbed her sleep often in the night but between whiles she rested with more ease to herself than she has done for some nights past.

I have to thank you for a kind letter received yesterday which gave me the usual pleasure I ever experience when you are so gracious as to write to me.

[P.S.] Amelia hopes to be able to write herself by the post tomorrow. (Add. Georgian 12/77)

[*The King's reply, Windsor Castle, 17 Oct.*] I have to thank you for the kind letter which Edward brought me from you and was very glad to hear from it that dear Amelia had borne the airing in the carriage better than you expected. The accounts received this morning are also more satisfactory than they have been of late, & the continuance of the south west wind leads me to hope that she will be able to persevere in going out. (Add. Georgian 12/78.)

3998 SPENCER PERCEVAL *to the* KING, *and the reply*

[*Downg. St., 16 Oct. 1809.*] Mr. Perceval has this day received the final answer of Mr. Vansittart declining to accept the office which with his Maj.'s approbation Mr. Perceval had offered to him.

Mr. Perceval regrets extremely to have to state to your Majesty that Mr. Dundas upon his arrival from Ireland has found two letters from his father, in a very different tone from those which Mr. Perceval reported to your Majesty before. In these letters Lord Melville dissuades his son in the strongest manner from accepting any new office under the new arrangement, representing to him that possibly his (Lord Melville's) friends will not be disposed to support the Govt. without Lord Melville forms a part of it—Mr. Dundas feels under this injunction from his father, which he has received with the deepest regret, that he must pause till he hears from his father again before he takes any further step toward the possession of the office of Secretary of State. But he has written to his father, and is not without hope that upon his explanation & statement his father will see that it is impossible to execute what appears to be his father's purpose as well as his own, of supporting your Majesty at this moment unless he accepts that office. In the meanwhile, your Majesty will perceive how much this embarrasses the formation of your Majesty's Governt. For it seems too important an object to obtain Mr. Dundas's official support not to make it preferable to wait till Lord Melville's answer is received, rather than by filling up the office in any other manner (which would be attended with great difficulty) to deprive your Majesty of the chance of his services.[1]

Mr. Perceval with your Majesty's leave will endeavour to procure the assistance of Lord Palmerston & Mr. Milnes in efficient situations; in the difficulty in which he feels himself placed he thinks of offering to their consideration the offices of Secretary at War (which Lord W. Bentinck has declined to accept) and also the Chancellorship of the Exchequer.[2]

Mr. Perceval is determined that nothing shall be wanting on his part to discharge his duty to your Majesty, but he cannot forbear stating to your Majesty that he feels the difficulties, considerable as they were at first, to be encreasing & not diminishing before him. (14728–9)

[*The King's reply, Windsor Castle, 17 Oct.*] The King has not learnt without serious concern from Mr Perceval that doubts have arisen as to Lord Melville's

[1] 'Government', wrote Dundas to the Duke of Richmond (29 Sept.), 'have but one line to follow. They must stand by the King and fight the battle manfully, and the country will probably support them.' (Melville MSS.) The Duke regretted the loss of his Chief Secretary, and said that Dundas was fit for any situation. 'An excellent man of business,' was Lord Liverpool's description of him. 'We want him in a situation in which we can have the advantage of his exertions as a parliamentary speaker.' Hiley Addington credited him with sound judgment, great prudence and indefatigable industry, but thought that as a speaker he was 'nothing'—and indeed his subsequent record lacked distinction. But Dundas found himself awkwardly situated. His father raised difficulties. Earlier in the year Melville had expressed the hope that he might be offered a place again, though, he admitted, 'if any proposition ever comes, it is most probable it will be so late as to render the acceptance of it undignified and of course impossible'. Financial difficulties could be overcome if he were again in office. Perceval explained to him regretfully that he could not invite him to take office because such an invitation would give offence to 'certain descriptions of persons in the House of Commons' (by that he meant, as Charles Long said, the country gentlemen, who had thrown him out of public life in 1805). Perceval was also afraid of an avalanche of Addresses from the country protesting against an appointment, so he tried to mollify him by offering him an Earldom as a mark of the King's approbation of his past services. But Dundas discovered some objections to such advancement in the peerage. He himself would be unable to afford the higher dignity in the event of his father's death. And, too, he thought the time inopportune: it would create a wrong impression in the public mind as to the motives which actuated both of them in supporting the Government. But Dundas wrote again to Perceval, the next day, saying that if his father did accept the King's offer, his own objections must not be considered as insuperable: he would not stand in the way of his father's advancement. In the meantime his father had told him (writing on 2 Oct.) that it was impossible to advise him to accept office without knowing who were to be his colleagues and what situations they were to fill. He wrote again to his son on 8 Oct. after receiving Perceval's letter offering the Earldom: 'You must...consider what is best both for your private and political character, never forgetting that you are connected with a great and powerful interest which has long wished, and that, too, very recently, for my return to office, as essential to their having any confidence in the Administration, even at a period when it was stronger than it is likely now to be. I cannot take it upon me to predict what may be their feelings on the present occasion.... In the new arrangement of the Government I would much rather, for many reasons, see you again at the head of the Board of Control, than with the Seals of the War Department. It may perhaps occur to yourself that the same feeling against the appearance of a compromise which induces me to refuse an advance in the rank of peerage, should operate with you to avoid, if you can, an advance in the progress of your ambition at the present moment.' (Lonsdale MSS.)

[2] For these offers see Palmerston's letters in Bulwer's *Palmerston*, i, 90–104, and *Life of Lord Houghton*, i, 15. He thought that Milnes would decline the Exchequer 'unless his ambition got the better of his partiality to Canning and his aversion to Perceval....Though a man of very brilliant talents, I should much doubt his steadiness.' Perceval wished to divide his two offices of First Lord of the Treasury and Chancellor of the Exchequer 'in order to have more leisure for the general business of Government'. (*Memoirs of R. Plumer-Ward*, i, 271.)

support and Mr. Robt. Dundas's taking office, from the inconsistency between the former's declarations to Mr. Perceval and his letters to his son. His Majesty fully expected that, after what had passed, Mr. Vansittart would decline the situation offered to him. Under these circumstances the King acquiesces entirely in what Mr. Perceval has submitted in regard to Mr Dundas, and must leave it to him to make such arrangements for filling up the other offices as shall appear to him most adviseable. His Majesty is fully aware of the extent of the present difficulties & laments that they should have encreased; but his Majesty has drawn his line, and no prospect of embarassment or opposition shall induce him to shrink from it. (14730)

3999   THE DUKE OF BRUNSWICK-OELS *to the* KING

[*Londre, ce 17 d'Oct. 1809.*] Les ordres que Votre Majesté a eu la grace de faire donner pour le voyage de mes enfans, m'a rendû le bonheur d'être réunie à eux: ils sont heureusement arrivé & je ne connois de dévoir plus cher, que de démander à Votre Majesté la permission d'oser les lui prèsenter.

Les divèrs malheurs[1] qui ont poursuivée ma famille dèpuis plusieurs années priver injustement de toute notre fortune; me feroit prévoir un triste avenir: si je n'osois mêttre hardiment entre les mains de Votre Majesté le sort de mes enfans & le mien.

Veulliés en décider Sire et vous convaincre que je tacherai de me rendre digne de la haute protection, dont Votre Majesté m'honore.

C'est avec les sentiments de l'hommage très-résptueux que je suis Sire [etc.]. (14731)

4000   PRINCESS AMELIA *to the* KING, *and the reply*

[*Weymouth, 17 Oct. 1809.*] I am quite ashamed when I think, my dearest papa, how long it is since I have written to you, but Miny was so good to explain that I was very unwell & not equal to writing. Having past a better day yesy. I cannot resist troubling you with a few lines today as I could not bear to put off any longer thanking you for your dear letter. The weather is much improved; both yesy. & today are quite mild, which suits me. My night has not been good but I *feel* my head heavy & oppressed, but I hope it will go off by & bye. The side continues very much the same & the discharge of the seatons are very uncertain, sometimes more & sometimes very little.

Sir Harry & Lady Neale are, I am happy to say, certainly much better; they yesterday came down into the drawing room again. If the body is not found by Wedy. I much fear it is buried in the sand, as near where he sunk there is a hole of sand. I wish this may not be the cause as I most heartily pray he may be found & buried as I think it would be such a comfort to his family.

[1] His father had been mortally wounded in 1806; his eldest brother Charles had died on 20 September 1806, and his two remaining brothers were mentally deficient and had consequently been compelled to renounce their rights to the succession on their father's death.

You will, I trust, excuse my saying more at present, my dearest papa, & will you give my duty to the Queen? I will have the honor of thanking her for her letters soon. Accept, my dearest papa, the heartfelt & grateful prayers for your health & happiness. (Add. Georgian 14/122)

[*The King's reply, Windsor Castle, 18 Oct.*] I had great pleasure in receiving your kind letter as it leads me to hope that, being more equal to exertion you may have experienced some improvement in your general health, but I must repeat the desire, conveyed thro' dear Mary, that you will not at any time think of writing unless you can do it with perfect ease & convenience. I sincerely hope you may be able to take every advantage of the weather while it continues more mild. (Add. Georgian 14/123)

4001   *Letters from the* KING *to* PRINCESS MARY, *and the replies*

[*Windsor Castle, 18 Oct. 1809.*] I have this moment received your kind letter of the 16th, which conveys a very comfortable account of dear Amelia & proves the benefit which she receives from the warm bath. That which I have received from you of yesterday is less satisfactory, from which I must apprehend there had been some return of fever. (Add. Georgian 12/79)

[*From Princess Mary, 18 Oct.*] I have to thank you for two kind letters both received yesterday by the post. As Amelia wrote herself yesterday & I had nothing new to say I would not trouble you untill today with a letter.

Yesterday was a very indiferent day with Amelia, much languor & pain at times in the side. She went into the warm bath last night; Beavor found her with some degree of fever which I am sorry to say continued all night, therefore she has had but very little sleep & much disturbed with the pain in the side as the inward shootings have been very acute at times, & added to the dull heavy pain she never is without night & day as well as the shootings she has complained of at *times* every now & then; this last three or four days she has felt a throbing pain which I have not named before because Beavor has thought it of no consequence & assured me it was more owing to the *medicine* working about her than anything else, and as she had not felt this new pain yesterday (or at least did not complain of it) I flattered myself it might go off, but now that she has suffered from it again I think it my duty to inform you of it; to that pain we do not wish to *conceal* any thing from you [*sic*], though Beavor again & again this morning *declares* he sees no reason for being alarmed at this new symptom. I wish it was in my power to send you a more satisfactory account of our beloved patient. We took a drive yesterday for almost three quarters of an hour which I flattered myself revived her as the air was mild, & I trust we may be able to do the same today. She is as ready to do anything recomended by many of restoring her health that, however painful or disagreable, she submits cheerfully to whatever is prepared & her mind appears to me to *strengthen* every day & her fortitude & resignation quite wonderful. (Add. Georgian 12/80)

[*The King's reply*, *Windsor Castle*, *19 Oct.*] Although the account contained in your kind letter of yesterday has both grieved and disappointed me, I feel thankful to you for not disguising from me anything that regards the state of poor Amelia, whose sufferings I lament no less sincerely than I admire the fortitude and patience with which she bears them. I had flattered myself that she had been in some measure relieved from the violence of the pain in the side, but your last account has destroyed my hopes in this respect, & when I consider her present state & how little she is equal to even the exertion of a short airing, it is impossible that I should not view with uneasiness the approaching journey, however satisfied I may be that no precautions will be wanting to render it as little fatiguing as possible. To your continued attentions dear Amelia owes much and they have not been lost upon [etc.]. (Add. Georgian 12/81)

[*From Princess Mary*, *19 Oct.*] Our dear Amelia passed but an indiferent day yesterday but towards evening was more comfortable though Beavor found her with some fever & fullness of pulse. She has not had a good night from pain in the side, & the throbing and pulsation came on after the shooting pain at diferent times in the course of yesterday & in the night, for all that Beavor finds her *better* today & the pulse less full, therefore he hopes the fever is subsiding.

Two 74 came in yesterday; the Achille[s], Sir R. King,[1] and the Illustrious, Capin. Broughton;[2] I understand they put in for provisions.

Amelia took a drive yesterday for an hour & that certainly went off better than it often does. The weather being so mild is much in her favour & it appears now as if it would last.

I beg leave to return you many thanks for your kind letter. (Add. Georgian 12/82)

[*The King's reply*, *Windsor Castle*, *20 Oct.*] Your kind letter of yesterday appears to me upon the whole more satisfactory than that of the preceding day in regard to the state of dear Amelia, as the feverish tendency appears to have decreased and as she was able to bear the airing better and for a greater length of time. I have desired Sophia to write to you respecting the arrangements to be made for your return from Weymouth & those which regard dear Amelia's accomodation here. She may either reside in her own apartments in the Castle or in the house that was Doctor Heberden's which Doctor Pope has seen, & as he has not started any objection to either I wish her to consult exclusively her own inclination, my object being that her comfort should be considered in whatever is settled on the subject. (Add. Georgian 12/83)

[*From Princess Mary*, *20 Oct.*] Many thanks for a most kind letter I received yesterday by the post, & for another this moment received by Frederick.

---

[1] Sir Richard King (1774–1834), succeeded his father, Admiral Sir Richard King, as 2nd Baronet, 27 Nov. 1806. Entered the Navy, 1788; Lieutenant, 1791; Captain, 1794; Rear-Admiral, 1812; Vice-Admiral, 1821. K.C.B., 1815. Commander-in-Chief in the East Indies, 1816–20; at the Nore 1833–4.

[2] William Robert Broughton (1762–1821). Lieutenant, 1782; Captain, 1797.

I am grieved to say Amelia passed a sad day yesterday of pain in the side &
fever, which fever lasted all night & in consequence she has had very little sleep,
but appears much as usual today. I shall have the honour of entering into more
particulars tomorrow. (Add. Georgian 12/84)

[*The King's reply, Windsor Castle, 21 Oct.*] I was much grieved to learn from your
kind letter of yesterday that poor Amelia had suffered in an increased degree from
pain in the side & that her rest had been disturbed by the recurrence of fever. I
trust in God that I may have the comfort of receiving tomorrow accounts less
painful than have been those of the last three or four days. (Add. Georgian
12/85)

4002   *Letters from* SPENCER PERCEVAL *to the* KING, *and the replies*

[*Downing St., 20 Oct. 1809.*] Mr. Perceval acquaints your Majesty that he has
not yet had any answer from Mr. Milnes; and till he hears from him, and till Mr.
Dundas hears from Lord Melville, Mr Perceval is obliged to postpone any further
proceeding in the arrangement of your Majesty's Government.

   Mr. Perceval informs your Majesty that the warrant which your Majesty signed
the other day for paying into your Majesty's Privy Purse the sum of six thousand
pounds from the surplus revenue of Gibraltar will have the counter-signatures of
the Lords of the Treasury to it by Monday next. And Mr. Perceval humbly trusts
that your Majesty will forgive him if, without presuming to offer to your Majesty
any advice upon the subject, he conceives it to be his duty to bring under your
Majesty's notice the fact that the contribution towards some fund either for the
relief of poor prisoners for debt, or some such purpose of general charity, upon
the celebration of the approaching anniversary of your Majesty's accession, is
almost universal thro'out the country. Whether under these circumstances your
Majesty would think it right to manifest your Majesty's gracious & benevolent
feelings in a similar manner it is not for Mr. Perceval to presume to state—but
Mr Perceval would have had to reproach himself most deeply if such should be
your Majesty's feelings had he not apprized your Majesty of this fact, the univer-
sality of which your Majesty might not otherwise have known—and the occasion
of notifying to your Majesty the above payment to your Majesty's Privy Purse,
some portion of which your Majesty might think of so applying, suggested to
Mr Perceval that the present is the most appropriate period for making the communication. (14733-4)

[*The King's reply, Windsor Castle, 21 Oct.*] The King acknowledges the receipt
of Mr. Perceval's letter of yesterday & he acquiesces in the proposal conveyed
therein that a portion of the six thousand pounds to be paid into the Privy Purse
from the surplus revenue of Gibraltar should be appropriated to the relief of poor
prisoners. The King desires that Mr. Perceval will use his discretion in regard to
the amount to be reserved for the above purpose from the sum to be paid into the
Privy Purse. (14734)

[*From Perceval, Downg. St., 21 Oct.*] Mr Perceval acquaints your Majesty that Mr Milnes has come up to town at the request of Mr Perceval, and after having a very long conversation in Downing Street with Mr Perceval has desired to take a day to think of Mr Perceval's offer. Mr Perceval will certainly have his answer by Monday at latest. Mr Perceval greatly apprehends it will not be favorable—but is by no means certain.

Mr Perceval humbly submits to your Majesty that three thousand pounds will be a proper sum for your Majesty to appropriate to the purpose of the relief of poor prisoners. Mr Perceval humbly informs your Majesty that the payment of the whole six thousand pound under the warrant already signed by your Majesty must in the first instance be paid into your Majesty's Privy Purse; and that it will be for your Majesty, if your Majesty shall be graciously pleased so to do, to direct the payment of £3000 to be made from the Privy Purse to the Committee of Bankers & Merchants of London who are collecting a subscription for the relief of poor prisoners for debt, or if your Majesty would direct the Privy Purse to pay that sum into Mr Perceval's hands Mr Perceval would humbly & gratefully charge himself with transmitting it in yr. Majesty's name & by yr. Maj.'s authority into the proper fund. (14737–8)

[*The King's reply, Windsor Castle, 22 Oct.*] The King acknowledges the receipt of Mr Perceval's communication of what has passed with Mr Milnes. His Majesty concurs in Mr. Perceval's proposal that three thousand pounds should be the sum appropriated for the relief of poor prisoners, & he will direct the Privy Purse to pay it, as soon as received, into Mr. Perceval's hands to be by him conveyed to the proper fund. (14738)

4003 LORD MULGRAVE *to the* KING, *and the reply*

[*Admiralty, 21 Oct. 1809.*] Lord Mulgrave most humbly represents to your Majesty that in consequence of the naval promotion which has been sanctioned by your Majesty's gracious approval; two vacancies of Colonel of Marines will arise by the advancement of Capt. Boyles[1] and Sir Thomas Williams[2] to the rank of Rear-Admirals; Lord Mulgrave humbly submits to your Majesty's gracious consideration that Capt. Sir Charles Hamilton[3] and Capt. the Honble Henry Curzon,[4] both officers of reputation, and actually engaged in the active duties of their profession, are the next in seniority to those who have already been appointed Colonels of Marines; Lord Mulgrave therefore most humbly recommends

[1] Charles Boyles (*d.* 1816). Lieutenant, 1777; Captain, 1790; Rear-Admiral, 25 Oct. 1809; Vice-Admiral, 1814.

[2] Sir Thomas Williams (*c.* 1762–1841). Lieutenant, 1779; Captain, 1790; Rear-Admiral, 25 Oct. 1809; Vice-Admiral, 1814; Admiral, 1830. Knighted, 1796. G.C.B., 1831.

[3] Sir Charles Hamilton (1767–1849), succeeded his father as 2nd Baronet, 24 Jan. 1784. Entered the Navy, 1776; Captain, 1790; Rear-Admiral, 31 July 1810; Vice-Admiral, 1814; Admiral, 1830. K.C.B., 1833. M.P. for St. Germans, February–June 1790; for Dungannon, 1801–2 and 1803–6; for Honiton, 1807–12.

[4] Henry Curzon (*d.* 1846). Lieutenant, 1783; Captain, 1790; Rear-Admiral, 1810; Vice-Admiral, 1814.

those officers to your Majesty's favour, as well on account of their professional merits as on the principle which your Majesty has been graciously pleased to permit, of conferring the benefit of promotion on the present occasion, on the sole ground of seniority of service without afflicting any individuals with the exclusion, which by the regulation of ordinary promotions might attach upon them. (14735)

[*The King's reply, Windsor Castle, 22 Oct.*] The King entirely approves of Lord Mulgrave's recommendation of Captain Sir Charles Hamilton & Captain Curzon for the appointment of Colonels of Marines on the vacancies which will result from the intended promotion. (14736)

4004 PRINCESS AMELIA *to the* KING, *and the reply*

[*Weymouth, Saturday, 21 Oct. 1809.*] I have many thanks to return you for a most kind letter I recieved yesy. & that affection you have always shewn me & expressed in your dear letters encourages me to lay open to you what I really feel.

Nothing can give me more pleasure then the idea of seeing *you*, & believe me no fancy of mind induced me to name one place more than another, for all Pope told me was that I was to return homewards, but certainly I was led to think the Castle would not do from being too elevated & my rooms to the eastward. Dr. Pope slightly named Kew which I was very willing to come into as I believe the chief object was to keep me quiet, as I feel how necessary that is, & the illness & medcines I have and am taking are of a nature to enervate very much, which makes me feel often more unwell some parts of the day than another & quite unequal to exertion or society on that account. I enter into the propriety of my not being at the Castle, for my object is to be where I may have the comfort of seeing you, but I am not able to bear the constant visits at the Castle wch. I should be liable to & which it would not be *proper* or *possible* for me to decline. I trust this statement will not lead you, my dearest papa, to think me *selfish* or *ill-tempered*; most earnestly do I watch and pray God I may not possess these qualities in addition to what I suffer, & feeling the burden I must be to my family & friends. I am therefore sure you will forgive my stating all this to *you* & you will now be so good to decide whatever you think is most likely for my being quiet if I am able to move.

I have had a long conversation with dear Frederick who will be so good to tell you many things which by letter I cannot enter into.

I hope the contents of this will *remain wholly* to *yourself* for I am sure your affectionate heart will understand what my feelings are whereas others[1] might construe them into *selfishness* or *ill temper*.

The great comfort I have experienced from the society of my dearest Miny whose kindness I cannot ever do justice to, but which I know you fully appreciate, induces me to hope that I shall still have the blessing of having her wherever I

---

[1] She probably meant the Queen.

may be. I may with truth say she has greatly supported me & many a day have I been able only to see her & dear Dolly. I fear there is still much to be done, for my side continues very indifferent and I should think the calomel must be further pushed. All I wish is to get well, & finding from the already tried effects of this medcine it is the only thing that seems to touch the real complaint, I cannot but wish for its continuance if it will cure me, & which could not be used to any greater degree till I was under Doctor Pope's own eye.

I was out yesterday on the sea; it was a very mild day. Frederick's arrival gave us great pleasure. (Add. Georgian 14/124)

(*Copy*)

[*The King's reply, Windsor Castle, 22 Oct.*] I thank you sincerely for your kind letter of yesterday & for the candid & affectionate manner in which you have entered into your feelings & wishes, which I assure you appear to me not less mild than reasonable. God forbid that I should ever have thought even of attributing to you any selfish motive or any that could not be positively reconciled to your affection for me: far from it, I have ever given you the greatest credit, though not more than you deserve, for the temper & resignation with which you submit to your sufferings & confinement, & I have admitted to the fullest extent your claim to whatever might promote your ease & comfort. These have been and must continue the objects nearest my heart, and they shall be exclusively attended to in any future arrangement, either with regard to your quiet residence here, dear Mary's continuance with you, or the facility of Doctor Pope's regular attendance, of which I fully admit the necessity & propriety. I have been cheered by the accounts received this day, which are certainly more satisfactory than any which had reached me for some days past, and I venture to hope that from the arrangements made for your return, the journey will be free from those effects which attended the last & which occasioned such serious & just grief to me. To have my dearest Amelia near me will be a great comfort, but you shall never be disturbed by any unreasonable wish to interrupt that quiet so essential to your recovery or by any expectation of exertions beyond your strength. (Add. Georgian 14/125)

4005   *Letters from* PRINCESS MARY *to the* KING, *and the replies*

[*21 Oct. 1809.*] I am happy to say our dear Amelia has had more sleep in the night, passed a better day yesterday & we went in the boat for an hour which went off better than I have seen it yet. Some fever came on in the evening & Beavor finds the pulse full today but does not appear disheartened. She was much roused by seeing Frederick but the joy caused some fever; however it has given her so much pleasure that I cannot say how glad I am he came down to see her.[1] (Add. Georgian 12/86)

---

[1] Perhaps this letter, unlike the next, was intended as one which the Queen could read.

[*From Princess Mary, 21 Oct.*] I am most happy to be able to say Amelia passed a better day yesterday; Frederick's coming *roused her much* & gave us both much pleasure. She was in the boat for near an hour & certainly it went off better than any day yet as she was less faint & less fatigued. Some fever came on towards evening but she has had a better night; feels languid today & some oppression in the head & Beavor finds the pulse full, however does not appear at all disheartened about her & desired her, the weather being so mild, to go on the sea again today, in particular as it answered so well yesterday. The great thing is air without fatigue & the motion of the boat is so easy that it does not bring on the pain in the side as the carriage does.

I think it my duty to assure you Amelia is ready to do anything or *submit* to any pain or inconvenience for the sake of promoting the recovery of her health. Her only grief is all the trouble & distress she causes you & her chief & only object is to consider your feelings as much as possible. Her *great* wish for being near home was for the sake of *seeing you* every now & then; she never proposed returning to any one place in particular but I tell you fairly, *set* her face against Frogmore from the first. When Dr. Pope came to Weymouth the last time he told her she could not return to the Castle, therefore from the first she made up her mind to the impossibility of returning to her own appartment. He then hinted slightly to Frogmore & Kew, at the same time desired Amelia not to name any place of residence in her letters to Windsor as he did not wish that to be talked of till he had seen Sir F. Milman & that only has caused her silence as well as mine from the fear of making mischief between these two gentlemen, well aware they *did not* agree. I assure you Amelia has no wish for any one particular place, her only *object* is to get well & she thinks if more under Pope's *own* eye he may be able then to persue the calomel in larger doses which he would not venture to do if he was not near enough to watch the progress of the calomel, as it will require constant care & attention. The affect I have witnessed of the increased doses of calomel Pope has given her when he has been at Weymouth which makes me feel how likely in the long run it is to answer & procure a cure. It is particularly painful to find that Sir F. M. & Dr. Pope do not agree on the subject of the calomel, and indeed this illness has proved to me how little they can judge what may happen, for else I am sure so long a journey never would have been advised by any medical man as the affects of it we never have recovered & was it not with the idea of being near a skilfull person to watch the progress of the calomel (if that system is the one to be followed up) I should dread another journey in her very precarious state. Added to that I cannot disown to you, painful as it is to me to be obliged to say so, that innervated as Amelia is from the length of the illness, any *hardness* or a sharp *word* goes very deep with her, & if she is so situated as to be liable to have those comeing in & out she cannot with any propriety *refuse* to see, I cannot answer for the *consequences* at present, having seen what the effect was before she came *here* & even how some letters since we are at Weymouth have vexed her. I am the last person that have any right to complain myself, as nothing can be kinder or more affe. than all the letters wrote to me, but upon one subject, which is *my being absent* from home & makeing myself so necessary to

Amelia, which is not thought right & considered as *selfish* of *Amelia*. If that is ever said to Amelia you must perfectly understand it will half *kill her* who really, poor soul, never thinks of herself & only wishes to give us all as little trouble as possible, and I am sure you will give me the credit to believe that nothing but nursing a sister in so suffering a state could ever make me wish to be absent one moment from home & from all I love & value so much, but as she has ever expressed so much pleasure in my being with her, don't you think it would be *horrid* of me was I to wish to leave her at such a moment? I am told my health *will* suffer; I assure you I never was in better health in all my life & I am sure Heaven always gives one strength to go through trials. I get out every day for an hour & a half, am in bed before 11 & up at 7 every morning and out before breakfast. Pray excuse this scrawl. (Add. Georgian 12/87)

[*The King's reply, Windsor Castle, 22 Oct.*] I have received both your kind letters of yesterday and thank you for having stated fully and candidly your ideas and wishes in regard to the arrangements which may be most conducive to dear Amelia's comfort on her return from Weymouth. It has ever been my anxious desire to come into any which can in any degree relieve her from uneasiness or embarassment & promote the restoration of her health, & being now aware of the real object in view, nothing shall be wanting on my part to facilitate it, either with regard to her quiet undisturbed residence or to your constant stay with her and it shall be equally my study not to commit either of you in any way. The report which you have sent me & that received from Frederick are upon the whole more comfortable & satisfactory & I sincerely hope that the system now persued may have every effect which is expected from it, while I readily admit the necessity of Doctor Pope's more constant attendance. That you, my dearest Mary, do not suffer in your health from your unwearied & affectionate attentions to my poor suffering Amelia is no small consolation upon this occasion to [etc.]. (Add. Georgian 12/88)

[*From Princess Mary, 23 Oct.*] Your kind & most affe. letter caused both Amelia & me the greatest pleasure & she has desired me to express her gratitude in the strongest terms for your kind consideration about her going home, which she trust[s] may be attended with as few dificulties as possible considering the suffering state she is laboring under. She begs me to add that she shall be satisfied with whatever arrangement you may think proper to make, & if *objections* had not been originally *started* against the Castle she never should have made any *dificulties* herself further than feeling that if the Castle may prove too cold by & by it would be most *cruel* & painful to her feelings to be obliged to move again.

As I have answered Sophia fully I must refer you to her on the subject of the journey. Amelia passed a very indiferent day yesterday, much pain in the side & increase of inward pain & great deal of fever we went though for half an hour in the boat; it did not go off well as she felt so very uncomfortable. She has had a bad night but Beavor finds her with less fever today. (Add. Georgian 12/89)

[*The King's reply, Windsor Castle, 23 Oct.*] I have been very much concerned that you were unable to send me yesterday the favorable report of dear Amelia for which I had been led to hope from the general nature of that which I received yesterday, and I lament most sincerely the recurrence of the pain to the degree which I must apprehend from what you say. My letters will have, I trust, convinced you & dear Amelia of my readiness to concur in any arrangement which may but ensure her comfort, and as you leave the decision to me I have spoken to the Queen who will see Doctor Pope this day & desire him to state fairly whether he does or does not object to a residence in the Castle. If he should decide for that in preference to the house that was Doctor Heberden's & poor Amelia's removal should nevertheless prove necessary thereafter, I have taken care to have it understood that you are not to be separated from her, & indeed I must add that I have found every disposition to meet my wishes in this respect. (Add. Georgian 12/90)

[*From Princess Mary, 23 Oct.*] I am most thankful to be able to send you rather a better account of our poor dear Amelia as she passed a more comfortable day yesterday with less fever; the pain in the side I am sorry to add continues very severe at times. Beavor found her with little or no fever last night; he desired her to be kept perfectly quiet all day yesterday & would not let her go out of the house. She has had more sleep in the night but not comfortable sleep, but appears less low this morning than she was yesterday.

[P.S.] Since I wrote the above Mr. Beavor has found it necessary to bleed Amelia. Her pulse is quieter since & she feels her head relieved. (Add. Georgian 12/91)

[*The King's reply, Windsor Castle, 24 Oct. 1809.*] After the comfortable report received yesterday your kind letter conveyed no small degree of satisfaction to me as dear Amelia appears to have been more free from pain & fever since you wrote on the 22d, and to have received further relief from the bleeding. Doctor Pope will not be at Weymouth until Monday & therefore you cannot commence your journey until Tuesday. We have arranged that you shall sleep at General Garth's on that night, at Woodgate's Inn on Wednesday, Andover Thursday night, Hartford Bridge on Friday night & reach Windsor on Saturday. You will proceed at once to the house that was Doctor Heberden's, which I have ordered to be prepared for yours & dear Amelia's reception & where I trust she will find the rooms perfectly warm and well aired. I am satisfied that this is the best arrangement which could have been made & that her residence there will prove more quiet and, under all circumstances, more comfortable than it could have been in any other house. I am certain that I need not repeat that nothing shall be wanting on my part which can tend to her satisfaction.

P.S. I have received the Prince of Wales's carriage which shall be sent down with horses in good time. (Add. Georgian 12/92)

(415)

[*Whitehall, 23 Oct. 1809.*] Lord Liverpool begs leave most humbly to submit to your Majesty for your royal signature the Proclamation for granting a general pardon to the seamen and marines who may have deserted from your Majesty's service. Lord Liverpool begs to add that it is thought most adviseable that this Proclamation should bear date from the 18th instant, the last day on which your Majesty held a Privy Council, and it will be added with your Majesty's approbation to the list of Council business for that day.

Lord Liverpool takes this opportunity of transmitting to your Majesty a letter which he has received from Dr Cyril Jackson, in consequence of a letter which Lord Liverpool wrote to him in obedience to your Majesty's commands on his resignation of the Deanery of Christ Church. (14741)

[*The King's reply, Windsor Castle, 24 Oct.*] The King has signed the Proclamation submitted by Lord Liverpool and his Majesty approves of its being added to the list of Council business of the 28th inst. His Majesty has received satisfaction from the perusal of Doctor Jackson's letter. (14742)

4007 *Letters from* SPENCER PERCEVAL *to the* KING, *and the replies*

[*23 Oct. 1809.*] Mr Perceval humbly acquaints your Majesty that Mr. Milnes has after much deliberation at length determined to decline both the offices which Mr Perceval offered to him. But Mr. Milnes was extremely anxious that Mr Perceval should in communicating this to your Majesty, assure your Majesty of his anxious desire to support yr. Maj.'s Govt. at the present juncture, and that in truth his reason for ultimately refusing to give his official assistance was that he had so little experience in the Ho. of Commons that he distrusted his own abilities, and feared that he might do more harm than good. He assured Mr Perceval that he should give constant & steady attention to business in the next Session, and if upon further trial of himself he acquired greater confidence and there then could be made an opening for him he would not decline to avail himself of it.[1]

Mr Perceval next applied to Mr Rose, who seems much to dread the change of his situation and to apprehend that at his time of life to embark in such an office as that of Chr. of the Exchequer might expose himself and the Govt. to some

[1] See Bulwer's *Palmerston*, I, 101. Canning described Milnes as one of the two most promising of the young men in the House of Commons (J. W. Ward being the other). Milnes had told Perceval that he could give no answer until he had seen Canning—which he did on the 21st. As Canning said, these offers proved the distress to which Perceval was reduced. Lord Bathurst, incidentally, thought Milnes 'too volatile' for the War Office, 'which requires great sobriety of conduct', and he had hoped that Lord William Bentinck would be appointed. 'We want some men of rank among us, unless Ryder would accept that office, which would give general satisfaction.' (Perceval MSS. Bathurst to Perceval, 8 Oct.) Milnes, said Perceval, declined the two offices in the most friendly way, 'upon a feeling of modesty that I could not overcome, but with the express determination of constant attendance and exertion in the House during the next Session, and if he succeeds to his own satisfaction in his exertions, he will then, should there be an opening for him, have no objection to accept office. He desired me to tell the King that his refusal was so far from proceeding from any indisposition to support his Government that his fear of disappointing us and doing us harm was his great objection.' (Perceval MSS. To Lord Arden, 24 Oct.)

ridicule. Mr Perceval, however, desired that he would not finally determine against this proposition without further consideration, and he has consented to think of it till tomorrow.[1]

Mr Dundas has not received any answer from Lord Melville, tho he expected it this morning. Mr Perceval hopes to hear tomorrow.

Lord Palmerston is willing to accept the office of Secy. at War but will leave it open till tomorrow lest, from Mr Rose's acceptance of the Chancellorship of the Exchequer, upon Mr Rose's office at the Navy Office being vacated, it should be more convenient to Mr Perceval's arrangements that his Lordship should succeed to Mr Rose's office. (14739–40)

[*The King's reply, Windsor Castle, 24 Oct.*] The King acknowledges the receipt of Mr Perceval's letter, and his Majesty gives credit to Mr Milnes for the propriety of his motives & feelings in declining the situation which Mr Perceval had been authorized to offer to him. (14740)

[*From Perceval, Ealing, 24 Oct.*] Mr Perceval regrets to state to your Majesty that Mr Dundas has heard from his father, and in consequence cannot accept any office in your Majesty's Government at present.[2] Mr Dundas continues to express the same sentiments of kindness and the same good wishes as before. Mr Perceval has sent again to Mr Yorke, who would have accepted the office of Secretary of State for the Colonies if Mr Perceval had not considered it as occupied by Mr Dundas. It is much to be apprehended that since that time Lord Hardwick has prevailed upon him to refuse any office whatever, but Mr Perceval thought that it was well worth twenty-four hours delay to take the chance, small as it is, of thus obtaining Mr Yorke's services.[3]

[1] Perceval told Palmerston that the King objected to Rose's being appointed Chancellor of the Exchequer on the ground of his being Clerk of the Parliament, 'an office he thought inconsistent with the other'. (Bulwer's *Palmerston*, I, 99.) See Rose, *Diaries and Corresp.*, II, 412–15, for a full account of his views; and *Memoirs of R. Plumer-Ward*, I, 274.

[2] 'I am sorry for the part Lord Melville has taken,' Charles Long wrote to Lord Lonsdale on 25 October. 'I should have thought it would have been more advisable for him to have taken a decided part this session, his son being in high Office, and it must have led to his obtaining Office with less difficulty another year. At the same time I think upon the whole, considering the difficulties, I should have been rather for making him the offer now than displeasing him, though I am fully aware there are many persons who think it would not do, and I cannot think we should be under the present circumstances strong enough to get rid of the resolution of the House of Commons with which he could not I imagine consistently hold Office. Upon this subject however I feel less sanguinely than I think you do. Personally my wishes would be for the employment of Lord Melville, but if I were called upon to decide this question I should wish to know with a view to the effects of his appointment to office the opinions of several persons in the House of Commons with whose sentiments I am at present wholly unacquainted.' (Lonsdale MSS.)

Perceval wrote to his brother, Lord Arden, on the 24th: 'Dundas has received his letter from his father today, and he feels himself obliged to refuse all office, and so ends Lord Melville's determination to support the King at this time. This certainly is a most distressing and embarrassing circumstance. Had not Dundas accepted the office of Sec. of State for the Colonies, Yorke would have accepted it. But now I fear it will not do to send to him, and to let him know that the office is vacant and that his acceptance of it would be a most happy circumstance. This failing, which I conceive to be almost certain, I see nothing that remains but to prevail upon Lord Liverpool to take that office & to get Ryder to go to the Home Department.' (Perceval MSS.)

[3] Yorke wrote to his brother, Lord Hardwicke, on the 25th: 'I think it proper to inform you that late last night a messenger from Perceval brought me a letter notifying that old Melville had insisted

Mr Rose declines accepting the office of Chancr. of the Exchequer, as also does Mr. Long.[1] Mr Perceval therefore conceives that he must abandon all idea of prevailing upon anyone at present to accept that office, but must proceed to fill up the vacant commissions at the Treasury without parting with that office himself. Mr Perceval will, however, keep in his view the idea of that arrangement as one which he conceives would be of great convenience to your Majesty's service, and will recur to it if any favorable opportunity should offer itself—and in the meantime Mr Perceval will decline receiving the salary of it.

Lord Palmerston will accept the office of Secretary at War, and Mr Perceval will with your Majesty's approbation give directions for making out his Lordship's appointment.

Mr Perceval feels great concern in acquainting your Majesty that he heard this day from Dr. Jackson (the late Dean of Christ Church) that there were no hopes of the Duke of Portland's surviving many days.

Mr Perceval has had a communication both with Dr. Jackson & the Bp. of London[2] upon the subject of the Professorship of Divinity in Oxford—and Dr. Jackson seems to think it not quite hopeless to prevail upon Dr. Howley to reconsider his refusal of it. Mr. Perceval has requested Dr Jackson to undertake the attempt of persuading Dr Howley to accept it and this Dr Jackson has obligingly promised to do.[3] (14743–4)

[*The King's reply, Windsor Castle, 25 Oct.*] The King is much concerned to learn from Mr Perceval that Lord Melville's continued opposition prevents Mr Dundas from accepting office at this moment. His Majesty is well assured of his good inclination & will make no comments on the conduct of his father. His M. approves of Mr Perceval's renewed application to Mr Yorke, but is too well aware of Lord Hardwicke's hostile disposition to feel sanguine as to the result. He also approves of Mr Perceval's intentions in regard to the office of Chancellor of the Exchequer, & his Majesty is very sensible of the zeal & perseverance which he manifests & by which he so strongly evinces his attachment. Lord Palmerston's appointment as Secretary at War may be made out.

upon Saunders Dundas giving up all idea, not only of the *War Department*, but of any other office under the present Ministry; & that consequently *that* office was open for my acceptance, if I chose, expressing at the same time his fears that he must understand my last letter as a complete answer to any question which he could now put to me with regard to *any* office; but that his duty would not suffer him to pass by the, *just possible*, opportunity of obtaining me for the King's service, &c. &c. To this I immediately returned an answer by the messenger, referring to my last communication with him (which was subsequent to our correspondence of the 5th, 7th & 8th inst.) & acquainting him that upon the principle I had laid down for myself not to accept of any office at this conjuncture without *your* concurrence, I was under the necessity of declining the offer that had been made me.' (Add. MSS. 35394, fo. 57.)

[1] Charles Long wrote to Lord Lonsdale on 1 Nov.: 'I did not take it [the Chancellorship of the Exchequer] because I have never felt either disposed or fit for a Cabinet Office and it would be to degrade the office to take it on any other terms. The office I should have liked the best because I really think I could render some public service in it was that of Secretary at War: Perceval offered me that also, but upon the whole I told him I had rather remain where I was, though certainly if it had been at all conducive to his general arrangements I would not have refused to make the exchange.' (Lonsdale MSS.)   [2] John Randolph.

[3] Dr Howley accepted the Professorship.

The King has learnt with deep concern the very precarious state of the poor Duke of Portland which Doctor Jackson's account to Mr Perceval now confirms. His Majesty hopes that Doctor Jackson will succeed in persuading Doctor Howly to accept the Professorship of Divinity in Oxford. (14747)

4008   PRINCESS AMELIA *to the* KING, *and the reply*

[*Weymouth, Tuesday evening, 24 Oct. 1809.*] What words can ever sufficiently express or how can I ever prove the feelings of my heart both of love & gratitude for your very kind & great consideration of me in every respect? It is utterly impossible for me to say anything, for I feel *really brim full.* I am quite delighted at your choice of Dr. Heberden's home & above all in your kindness about my dearest Miny. Your affection, my dear father, is everything to me & enables me to bear anything, & pray God soon may restore me to health.

I have taken the liberty of begging dear Frederick to deliver you a message from me & he will also be able to enter into many particulars which in a letter I cannot. I look forward with great joy to seeing you, dear dear papa; what a happy moment it will be to me. The bleeding has, I assure you, relieved me generally but not my side.

This letter you will receive on a day[1] so justly dear to all that I cannot but express my sorrow at not being able to see you, but beg I may say, though I can't make fine speeches, that no one will pray more *fervently* for you & that God may bless you as you deserve. I can't love you better one day than another. (Add. Georgian 14/126)

[*The King's reply, Windsor Castle, 25 Oct.*] Frederick brought me your very kind & affectionate letter, from which and what he said to me I am extremely pleased to find that the arrangements which have been finally made for your future residence are so satisfactory to you. I pray God that you may be able to bear the journey well, and that when you are comfortably settled here & have the advantage of Doctor Pope's constant attendance & advice, your progress will be equal to my anxious wishes. Mr. Bevor appears to have judged very right in bleeding you as your account as well as others assure me that it has afforded relief to you.

I cannot close this letter without thanking you, my dearest Amelia, for the very kind & endearing expressions of your affection for me, and without assuring you that no one can regret your absence or lament the cause more sincerely than I do. You have upon all occasions given me the strongest proofs of your warm & steady attachment, & it is no small comfort to me to believe that my dearest Amelia is convinced that the same feeling towards her exists in the strongest degree in the breast of [etc.]. (Add. Georgian 14/128)

[1] The 25th was the anniversary day of the King's accession to the throne.

[*24 Oct.* [*1809*].] How can I ever express to you, my dearest papa, my gratitude for the kind & affe. letter I received yesterday and for your entering so compleately into my feelings concerning our poor Amelia. I trust I ever shall deserve the affcn. I ever have experienced from you; believe me it is my first object in live [*sic*] to study to act so as to meet with your approbation, and it has been a great relief to my mind to *explain things* in such a way that you *now* understand *my situation* in regard to Amelia. I have beged Frederick to tell you one or two things, if he has a good opportunity tomorrow, not worth troubling you with in a letter, but which will give you a still stronger idea of what very *unpleasat situations* we may be drawn into if *I* am not constantly on my *guard*.[1]

Amelia was better all day for having been bleed [*sic*]. Beavor made her keep in bed till quite evening when she had her bed made; she had some degree of fever again towards night but the pulse less full than in the morning. The blood was very much inflamed, much more so than when Pope bleed her the last time he was at Weymouth, but her mind was so much relieved by your kind letter that she got quite composed and in comfortable spirits after the post came in. She has not had a good night, very little sleep & that much disturbed with the pain in her side. However, Beavor finds her better today but desired her not to get up.

As you will receive this on the 25 I cannot help expressing my sorrow at being deprived the pleasure & happiness of seeing you on the anniversary of a day so dear to this country as well as to all your family, & to assure you that among the many that will humbly offer up their prayer for your preservation no one will do it with more fervency than [&c.]. (Add. Georgian 12/93)

[*The King's reply, Windsor Castle, 25 Oct.*] I have to thank you for a very kind letter which has been very satisfactory to me, as it confirms the reports previously received of the relief which dear Amelia has derived from the bleeding and at the same time assures me that the arrangements finally made for her residence here have removed all uneasiness which she naturally felt on that score. I am very grateful to you, my dearest Mary, for the truely kind and affectionate manner in which you have expressed your wishes for my welfare. Your conduct thro' life has amply proved how much my satisfaction & comfort have been your object, and every act of yours has tended yet more to endear you to me, none more than the tender care & attention which you have bestowed on a beloved suffering sister, and the chearfulness with which you have devoted yourself to her service. These are circumstances which must ever secure to you my cordial approbation & attachment, and, independently of the general sentiments which they inspire to all around you, you will find a reward in your own enviable feelings. (Add. Georgian 12/94)

[*From Princess Mary, 25 Oct.*] It is impossible to express how greatful I feel for the kind letter received yesterday & by which I rejoice to find Dr. Heberden's

---

[1] It seems unlikely that this can be a veiled reference to Princess Amelia's attachment to General Fitzroy, for, so far as we know, the King was not then aware of it—though the Queen was.

house is decided upon as I really think in every point of view it is by far the best situation for her & I feel most happy in being permited to remain on with her and the being near you all again, & the comfort of feeling you will be so near her that you will hear all day how things are going on & that I can apply & ask your advice & obey your orders upon every trifling circumstance that may arrise in the course of the day, will be the greatest relief and comfort to me, & I am sure as great a satisfaction to herself who feels much pleasure at the thoughts of seeing *you*. As Frederick will have told you how she passed yesterday I have not much more to say but that she went into the warm bath after he left us, which went off tolerably, but from fatigue & perhaps being a little weakened from the fever she has had for some days past, she was inclined to be very low and faint. Beavor gave her some wine & water which revived her, but brought on a good deal of cough. She had some fever in the night & passed an unquiet night in consequence. When I told Beavor last night that Pope was to be down with us the 30 & that the plan was that Amelia should begin the journey the next day, he said in her present state he feared it would be impossible to have her so soon & is now writing to Dr. Pope to explain his reasons, but hopes by next Monday week she may be enough recovered from the affects of this fever to enable her to leave Weymouth. The side is just the same. The mind has been so much relieved this last two days from your kind letters & for entering so into her very precarious state of health & sufferings that I assure you your letters act like *magic* upon her & calm & revive her for hours after. I rejoice we have so fine a day.

[P.S.] Beavor has just been with her, finds the pulse better today & gives her leave to get up about two o'clock. (Add. Georgian 12/95)

[*The King's reply, Windsor Castle, 26 Oct.*] I have received your kind letter of yesterday and should be very sorry by anything I have said or proposed to hasten the period of dear Amelia's leaving Weymouth before the journey is considered perfectly safe & elegible by those who, being on the spot, must be the best judges. I shall therefore readily subscribe to whatever delay may be considered necessary, but I trust that this will not prevent Doctor Pope from going to Weymouth as he had intended. I sincerely wish it had been in your power to send me a more satisfactory account of poor Amelia. (Add. Georgian 12/96)

4010   *Letters from* SPENCER PERCEVAL *to the* KING, *and the replies*

Downg. St., 25 Oct. 1809.] Mr Perceval humbly lays before your Majesty the letter which he received from Mr Yorke. (14745)

[*Enclosure*]
[*Charles Yorke to Spencer Perceval, Tuesday, 24 Oct. (Copy in Taylor's hand.)*] You very naturally concluded, after my last letter with its enclosures, that you can receive only one answer to the communication which has just reached me. If I thought that there could exist any, the smallest chance of any alteration or even hesitation in my brother's sentiments upon this occasion, I would send your

letter over to Wimpole[1] & wait for an answer from thence before I returned my own. But as I am perfectly convinced that no such chance exists, nothing remains for me but to decline the proposal you have now made. I cannot do so without reluctance & grief, because it is most painful to my feelings to find myself obliged to forego the endeavor to assist a friend whom I regard & the master whom I venerate in circumstances so critical & embarassing.

One ought to be amazed at nothing in such times as these; but still this turn of Lord Melville's does appear amazing. What can have caused it? But it is in vain to speculate.

This is but a bad way of celebrating the Jubilee, & of commencing the 50th year of the reign of our good King. (14746)

[*The King's reply, Windsor Castle, 26 Oct.*] The King returns Mr Yorke's letter to Mr Perceval, and while H.M. gives to Mr Yorke the credit for attachment & zeal in his service to which his conduct has ever entitled him, he cannot but lament that upon such an occasion & when such are the sentiments, such implicit deference should be paid to the dictates of a brother. H.M. is desirous that in his endeavors to fill up so important an office as that which Mr Yorke has declined, Mr Perceval should not consider it necessary to hasten the arrangement as the inconvenience which may result from a choice to be hereafter regretted, would prove much greater than that now arising from delay. (14745)

[*From Perceval, Ealing, 26 Oct.* [*1809*].] Mr. Perceval has the satisfaction to acquaint your Majesty that Mr. Dundas has this morning received another letter from Lord Melville, which Mr. Dundas conceives leaves him at liberty to give your Majesty's Government his official support.

Mr. Perceval collects that Lord Melville's near relations and friends in Scotland have by no means concurred in the view which Lord Melville took of Mr. Perceval's apprehensions of your Majesty's taking Lord Melville into your Maj.'s service at the present moment, but on the contrary seemed to think that whether those apprehensions were just or not, there was so much probability of their being realized as not to make it reasonable for Lord Melville & his friends to wish that Mr. Dundas should withold any support he could give to your Maj.'s Govermt. at the present time; and under the impression of this opinion Mr Perceval collects that Lord Melville has desired his son to act upon his own discretion entirely, and to consider Lord M.'s letters, dissuading him from taking office, as never having been written. Upon the receipt of this letter from his father, Mr. Dundas immediately apprized Mr Perceval of his being ready to take any office which your Majesty might assign to him, but he stated so strongly to Mr Perceval that he conceived it would be much more easy to him to reconcile his father completely to what he did, if he went back to the Board of Control, than if he took the higher office of Secretary of State, that Mr Perceval, feeling that Mr Dundas himself had acted thro'out most honorably & frankly, and that in this last as well as in every other representation he was entitled to every consideration, has undertaken to

[1] Lord Hardwicke's seat in Cambridgeshire, near Royston.

recommend to your Majesty that he should be permitted to return to the Board of Control. Mr Perceval was led originally to recommended [*sic*] Mr Dundas to the office of Secy. of State not only because he thought he would discharge the duties of that office with great ability, but because Mr Perceval imagined that it would be agreeable to Lord Melville & his friends to see Mr Dundas in that elevated situation, but now that Mr Perceval finds that Mr Dundas himself thinks the other situation is more likely to conciliate the acquiescence of Lord Melville than the office of Secretary of State, Mr Perceval submits to your Majesty that it would be desireable that your Majesty should approve of his returning to the office of President of the Board of Control.[1]

Under the difficulty which Mr Perceval feels of finding any person not now in office to fill the station of Secry. of State for the Colonies, he has no doubt that Lord Liverpool may from his great devotion & zeal for your Maj.'s service be prevailed upon to take that office,[2] and in that case Mr Perceval would recommend Mr Ryder to succeed Lord Liverpool as Secretary of State for the Home Department if your Majesty should approve of this arrangement. Mr Perceval has no doubt that Mr Ryder is eminently qualified for that situation, but he regrets to think that this change will remove him from the office which he now fills so well of your Majesty's Judge Advocate. Mr Perceval has thought that it would be desireable to endeavour to procure Mr Manners Sutton, the Archbishop of Canterbury's son, as Mr Ryder's successor, but he is not without his apprehensions that Mr M. Sutton will decline quitting his profession—in which event Mr Perceval knows not where to look for a successor to Mr Ryder but in Mr. Wallace.[3]

Mr Perceval has this day written to the D. of Northumberland, who is at Clifton near Bristol, offering a seat at the Treasury to Lord Percy[4]—and has thro' Lord Mulgrave offered Lord Palmerston's seat at the Board of Admiralty to Lord Lowther. Mr Perceval has seen Lord Lowther who very properly declines giving any answer till he has heard from his father, to whom he has written.[5]

[1] Dundas wrote to W. W. Pole on 26 Oct.: 'I have received today a letter from the North, in very kind and affectionate terms, recalling what had been already written, and leaving me at full liberty to act as I may think right and proper. I find also that all my friends in that part of the world approve entirely of the course I had pursued. As it seemed to be my father's wish that I should return to the Board of Control, and as I really think that for the next six or eight months, at least, I can be of more use there than in any other situation, I shall probably land again in that office. Perceval wishes me to be in the Cabinet, but has consented to postpone that question till my father comes to town. We shall all go on heartily together now and perhaps what has happened may not have been useless.' (National Library of Ireland MSS.)

[2] 'Lord Liverpool is to have the War Department, much against his inclination,' wrote Dundas on the 28th, 'and Ryder is to succeed him in the Home Department. Perceval insists upon having at least two Cabinet Ministers besides himself in the House of Commons, and as Ryder's health and his being liable to frequent and severe attacks rendered him wholly unequal to the War Department, there was no other way of arranging it.' (Melville MSS.) See also Bulwer's *Palmerston*, I, 104.

[3] For Wallace's dissatisfaction with his position at this time, see the long account in *Plumer-Ward*, I, 289–94. His name is there omitted but the reference is undoubtedly to him.

[4] *The Corresp. of George, Prince of Wales*, VI, 482. Palmerston said on 18 Oct. that Lord Mulgrave had offered Lord Percy a seat at the Admiralty Board (Bulwer, I, 100); and on the 27th that Lord Percy had refused it. (*Ibid.*, I, 105.)

[5] Lord Lowther wrote to his father on the 26th: 'It is now five o'clock, so I can say little upon the subject I am about to write to you. Lord Mulgrave has sent to offer me Palmerston's situation as one of the Lords of the Admiralty. Whether I am to accept of that situation I am entirely open to be guided

Mr Perceval humbly acquaints your Majesty that he has thought that your Majesty's bounty to the poor debtors should be distributed in fair proportion in the three parts of your United Kingdom. He has therefore given two thousand pounds in yr. Maj.'s name and by yr. Maj.'s authority to the Society in England established for the relief of such debtors;—he is sending £2000 to the Ld. Lieut. of Ireland to be distributed for the relief of similar objects, and will with your

by you and I should like, as soon as you can, if you would give me your advice what steps to take. I feel some very strong objections to be confined to London, but at the same time it would open to me the necessary forms of business, which at some time I shall probably have to transact. I will write to Lord Mulgrave saying that I should not like to give an answer until I hear from you.' (Lonsdale MSS.)

Lord Lowther wrote again on the 31st, from Newmarket, where he was enjoying 'good sport': 'Tomorrow I expect to hear from you, and my anxiety with respect to a seat at the Admiralty will be at an end. Upon consideration, if you assent, I shall accept Lord Mulgrave's offer, as it will be the means of getting an insight into the general management of the affairs of this country.' (Ibid.)

He wrote again to his father on 3 Nov. from Newmarket: 'I fully weighed all you said to me with respect to a seat at the Admiralty before I sent an answer to Lord Mulgrave. I have enclosed a copy of my letter to him, in which you will see I have made a stipulation with respect to the Walcheren question. If he accepts my proposal I shall immediately go to London, since I have considered deliberately upon the offer made me. The only strong objection or reluctance I feel in acceding to Lord Mulgrave's proposal is the attendance in Parliament, which, if I find too irksome on account of my health I shall have an excuse sufficiently good to request *Lord Mulgrave* to look for some one to supply my place. Though the tenor of your letter appears rather adverse to my accepting the situation, and chiefly upon the ground of the Walcheren question, which will be clearly understood by Lord Mulgrave before it is finally settled; a Lord of the Admiralty is far from a desirable situation, yet if I have a wish at any future period to accept an office having once held an office it will necessarily give me a precedence over those who for the next few years will be joining the Government, and also in any future arrangement. It also occurred to me that as I have no particular engagement or anything to occupy me for the next few months, that I could not employ myself better than obtaining a general insight into the management of the affairs of this country, and particularly into our great national defence, the Navy. Though a Civil Lord of the Admiralty has but little to do, yet I understand he may have opportunities of enquiring and learning the general routine of business and of acquiring a general information of the management of every Department of the State. I also thought if I bluntly refused the offer now I should not perhaps be able to obtain it when I should wish it. I also conceived it would shew the world I was interested in politics, a consideration far from *trifling in these days.*' (Ibid.)

Lowther wrote to Lord Mulgrave: 'I have this day received an answer to the letter which I sent to my father upon the subject of your offer to me of a seat at the Admiralty. In my letter to him I stated some objections which I felt to the availing myself of your offer, in consequence of my sentiments with respect to the Walcheren expedition; conceiving that my support would be looked for in all questions I had some hesitation in accepting a situation which would in some degree compel me to act in a manner repugnant to my feelings. Could you waive my support on this question, a question which I cannot accord with Ministers, however zealous I may otherwise be to support them, I shall be proud to accept the situation and act in a manner which both my father and myself conceive proper in such an event.'

Perceval's letter to Lord Chatham, 5 Nov., completes the story: 'I trouble you with this line upon a subject as I feel it of great delicacy and on which I certainly will take no step but as you shall direct me. Lord Lowther having shewn a great deal of zeal in our cause, Ld. Mulgrave & myself agreed in thinking that it was desirable to offer him a situation at the Board of Admiralty. That offer was made and this day the post has brought his answer of which the enclosed is an extract. You may naturally feel how embarrassing it is to me to think of introducing any person into an office under a sort of understanding that he shall not be expected to take any part, which I conceive to be the meaning of his letter, upon a subject so material as this in question. And I have determined that I will not consent to it unless you shall give me leave. The case is not without its difficulty either way. If he does not take the office, it will no doubt be known why he does not, and when any question does come on he will probably, if not in office, take an active part against us upon it, whereas if he accepts office, we shall have the advantage of his name & support in all other questions, and I conceive we shall prevail upon him at least to stay away upon that question. As the thing is suspended till I hear from you, of course you will let me hear from you as soon as you can.' (Chatham Papers, 368.)

Maj.'s approbation direct a warrant to be prepared for authorizing the Barons of the Exchequer in Scotland to apply a similar sum for similar purposes from yr. Majesty's civil revenue in Scotland. (14750–2)

[*The King's reply, Windsor Castle, 27 Oct.*] The King has learnt with great pleasure from Mr Perceval that the difficulties which had occurred on the part of Lord Melville to Mr Dundas's taking office are at length removed, and his Majesty approves of his returning to the Board of Controul, sensible as he is that he shall have in any situation the active and zealous support of a man who has acted so honorably and frankly. In regard to the proposal submitted by Mr Perceval for filling the Colonial Department, it appears to the King that as the Home Department suits Lord Liverpool so well & is so ably filled by him, as it is the first in rank & therefore desirable on that account to be held by him, it would be more consistent with Lord Liverpool's situation & wishes not to remove him from it, while on the other hand H.M. thinks that Mr Ryder's appointment to the Colonial Department may be more eligible on various accounts. He has had opportunities of acquiring a certain insight into Army business, of making himself known to great advantage to officers, and the Department itself, not requiring so much regular confinement, would be better suited to his health. The King knows the full value of Mr Ryder's services & therefore feels that it will be difficult to supply any situation from which he retires; his M., however, conceives the arrangement proposed by Mr Perceval to be the fittest, either in regard to Mr Manners-Sutton or subsequently Mr. Wallace. His M. also approves of the offer made to Lord Percy and Lord Lowther.

The King entirely acquiesces in the proposed distribution of the bounty to the poor debtors. (14752–3)

4011   EARL BATHURST[1] *to the* KING, *and the reply*

[*Foreign Office, 26 Oct. 1809.*] Lord Bathurst, conceiving the observations & intelligence contain'd in the private letter[2] of Mr Gentz may be interesting to your Majesty, humbly submits them to your Majesty. (14754)

[*The King's reply, Windsor Castle, 27 Oct.*] The King, having had an unusual quantity of business this morning, has kept back the letter from Mr Gentz sent by Lord Bathurst for perusal at a more leisure moment. (14754)

4012   *Letters from* PRINCESS MARY *to the* KING, *and the replies*

[*26 Oct.* [*1809*].] Many thanks for your kind letter received yesterday containing your orders about our journey which of course will be most punctually obeyed. G. Garth says he can lodge us all very well & appears quite delighted at the thoughts of his house being made use of by Amelia & I believe intends going

---

[1] Foreign Secretary until Lord Wellesley's return from Spain.
[2] See *Bathurst Papers*, pp. 119–26, dated 29 Sept. and received 26 Oct.

home tomorrow to make all his arrangements that we may find everything comfortable. All things considered I feel certain Dr. Heberden's house is by far the best place for Amelia & I make no doubt she will like the appartment preparing for her very much. As to myself, I am certain I shall be satisfied with whatever room you may think proper to place me in. My only object is to be a comfort & of use to her & when she can spare me I never can be so happy as in the Castle with all of you who I look forwards to see again with a pleasure no words can discribe.

She passed a very tolerable day yesterday; got up about 4 o'clock & sat up till 9: she had not much fever but certainly was not without it. The pain in the side was much the same, but considering that the *day* overcame *her very much* and all circumstances considered, she really passed a better day than I ventured to hope might be the case. Everything was kept perfectly quiet on her account & the state of agitation she was in upon first seeing me & Dolly yesterday morning proved how necessary it was to prevent her hearing any of the rejoicings. She has had but a very indiferent night as a good deal of fever came on in the night, but Beavor finds her with less again this morning & hopes to keep it off by extreme quiet & has desired her not to think of geting up before one o'clock. (Add. Georgian 12/97)

[*The King's reply, Windsor Castle, 27 Oct.*] The account conveyed in the kind letter which I have received from you this morning is upon the whole more satisfactory than those preceding it, and I hope that dear Amelia will be able to undertake the journey about the period mentioned in your letter of the 25th, though I wish it to be understood that I should very much regret its taking place even then if the delay of a few days should be considered beneficial to her. Every attention appears to have been paid to the quiet so essential to her in her present state and I am sensible of the feelings of those who concurred in it. You will, I trust, be comfortably lodged in Doctor Heberden's house and you cannot rejoice more in the prospect of being again with us than does [etc.]. (Add. Georgian 12/98)

[*From Princess Mary, 27 Oct.*] I have again to thank you for a most affe. kind letter received yesterday, every word of which has gone deep into my heart.

Amelia had a good deal of fever off & on yesterday, got up about one o'clock & went to bed after the warm bath about 9 o'clock. Beavor found her better than he expected last night. She has passed a quiet night but is languid this morning. However, Beavor finds her pulse better than he has found it for some days past. Beavor continues very *decided* in his opinion that Amelia will not be able to leave Weymouth so soon as next Tuesday & I believe has wrote his reasons to Dr. Pope, which I suppose the Dr. will explain to you.

William arrived last night about 9 o'clock in high spirits. The Ball last night went off very well, it was very full. Dolly got home about half past two o'clock.

[P.S.] Lady Neal is very ill with an inflammation in her lungs. (Add. Georgian 12/99)

[*The King's reply, Windsor Castle, 28 Oct.*] I was very glad to learn from your kind letter of yesterday that dear Amelia had enjoyed better rest the preceding night and that you considered her state upon the whole more satisfactory. Doctor Pope will go to Weymouth on Monday next, at which I rejoyce, as I am convinced that his attendance is gratifying to Amelia. I have stated very positively to him and must repeat it to you, that I do not wish the period of her departure from Weymouth to be hastened. I have no doubt from what you say that the 6th of November is as early as it ought to take place, but if it should prove in any degree desirable to postpone it further, it must be done. (Add. Georgian 12/100)

4013 LORD ELDON *to the* KING, *and the reply*

[*27 Oct. 1809.*] The Lord Chancellor, offering his very humble duty to your Majesty, has the honour to send a Commission for proroguing the Parliament, to receive your Majesty's Royal Sign Manual if your Majesty shall graciously so please.

The Lord Chancellor takes leave also to inform your Majesty that the City of London humbly solicits your Majesty's gracious approbation of their choice of Mr Alderman Smith[1] to be their Lord Mayor, a gentleman whom the Lord Chancellor believes to have served the office of Sheriff with great propriety. (14755)

[*The King's reply, Windsor Castle, 28 Oct.*] The King desires that the Lord Chancellor will communicate to the City of London his Majesty's approbation of their choice of Mr Alderman Smith to be their Lord Mayor for the ensuing year. (14755)

4014 SPENCER PERCEVAL *to the* KING, *and the reply*

[*Downg. St., 28 Oct. 1809.*] Mr Perceval humbly acquaints your Majesty that Mr Manners Sutton is desirous, before he finally determines upon the proposition submitted to him, to have some conversation with the Chancellor, but he has promised me his answer on Monday, and Mr Perceval has great hopes that he will accept the office of Judge Advocate.

With respect to the arrangement of the two Secretary of State's offices between Lord Liverpool & Mr Ryder—Lord Liverpool will write to your Majesty this evening what his Lordship's feelings are upon that subject.

Mr Perceval has great pleasure in acquainting your Majesty that Dr Jackson has prevailed upon Dr Howley to accept the professorship of Divinity in Oxford, and Mr Perceval believes Dr Howley proposes to kiss your Majesty's hand, if your Majesty should be pleased to permit him, on Wednesday next. (14756)

[1] Thomas Smith, who had been elected Alderman of Farringdon Ward Within in 1802.

[*The King's reply, Windsor Castle, 29 Oct.*] The King is glad to learn from Mr Perceval that he entertains hopes that Mr Manners Sutton will accept the office of Judge Advocate.

Lord Liverpool has written very fully to H.M. respecting the arrangement of the two Secretary of State's offices, & has expressed his readiness to take that of the Colonial Department in order to obviate the difficulties in the way of Mr Ryder's coming forward, from the state of his health; that being the case, his M. cannot have any objection to the proposed exchange, which proves Lord Liverpool's zeal & readiness to give every aid in his power.

The King will receive Doctor Howly on Wednesday next. (14757)

4015 *Letters from the* EARL OF LIVERPOOL *to the* KING, *and the replies*

[*London, 28 Octr. 1809.*] Mr Percival having communicated to Lord Liverpool the letter which your Majesty was graciously pleased to write to him on the subject of the proposed change in the Departments of Secretary of State, Lord Liverpool trusts your Majesty will allow him to express the grateful sense which he must ever entertain of the approbation which your Majesty has been so good as to signify of his conduct in the office which he now has the honour of holding. Lord Liverpool has been very far from desirous to exchange it for either of the other Departments of Secretary of State nor would the idea have been suggested to him by Mr Percival if all efforts to obtain strength to your Majesty's Govt. from external quarters had not at this time faded and if Mr. Dundas had not felt himself under the necessity of declining the situation of Secretary of State for the Colonies.

Under these circumstances Lord Liverpool entirely concur'd with Mr Percival that the most creditable and efficient arrangement of your Majesty's Govt. would be that your Majesty should give the seals of Secy. of State to Mr Ryder, but the state of Mr Ryder's health has induced him to decline the office of Colonial Secretary of State, as the business of that office, though not more important than that of the Home Department, is of a much more anxious nature, and such as he is fearful, when combined with constant attendance in the House of Commons, he might feel himself so unable in point of strength to execute, that he might by the attempt render himself in a short space of time incapable of serving your Majesty altogether.

It is from a conviction of the difficulties in which your Majesty's Government is at this time placed, that Lord Liverpool has offer'd to make the proposed exchange, which under other circumstances would appear to him as far from desireable, but which may afford considerable facilities to the arrangements necessary for compleating your Majesty's Government at the present moment. (14758-9)

[*The King's reply, Windsor Castle, 29 Oct.*] The King is very sensible of the zealous motives which induce Lord Liverpool so readily to make his own inclinations subservient to an arrangement of offices which may secure the advantage of Mr Ryder's services as a Secretary of State, & under the circumstances which

Lord Liverpool has represented, the King cannot hesitate in sanctioning what has been proposed. (14759)

[*From Lord Liverpool, Whitehall, 28 Oct.*] Lord Liverpool begs leave most humbly to inform your Majesty that at a meeting of your Majesty's confidential servants yesterday they desired to have a formal report from the Admiralty on the expediency of retaining the island of Walcheren as a naval station. The indication of their opinion on the papers already before them was that in the event of peace having been concluded between Austria and France it would not be expedient to advise your Majesty to retain the island, but they did not wish to come to a formal and decisive opinion on this subject without having a regular report from the navy and without more consideration.

As it appeared to them, however, of the utmost importance in the event of the evacuation of the island, that the basin of Flushing and the other naval resources of the island should if possible be destroy'd, they thought no time ought to be lost at this period of the year in taking preparatory measures for that purpose, and as the retention of the island during the winter or the occupation of it even for a time might in the present disabled state of the garrison require some reinforcement, they were of opinion that it was adviseable that all the sick should be removed from the island as soon as possible, and that a detachment of four or five thousand men should be kept on the coast of Kent and Essex in order that they might be sent to Walcheren in case of necessity.

Lord Liverpool has understood from the Commander-in-Chief that a force to this amount may be provided without much inconvenience, and he therefore wrote to Lieut.-Genl. Don the letter of which the draft is submitted to your Majesty. The object of this letter is only to make such arrangements as may render all delay unnecessary when the definitive decision, whatever it may be, shall be taken.

Lord Liverpool has the honour likewise of submitting to your Majesty the report of Messrs Whitbie and Rennie[1] on the practicability of destroying the works at Walcheren. (14760-1)

[*The King's reply, Windsor Castle, 29 Oct.*] The King entirely concurs in the opinions which Lord Liverpool has submitted in regard to the island of Walcheren, & approves of the instructions to be given in consequence to Lieut.-General Don. His Majesty only hopes that the measures recommended for the destruction of the naval works may prove practicable & that no additional force may be required for the execution. No time has however been lost by Sir David Dundas in submitting an arrangement of that force as a measure of precaution. (14761)

---

[1] John Rennie, the civil engineer (1761–1821).

[*28 Oct.* [*1809*].] I am thankful to be able to say dear Amelia passed a better day yesterday than she has done for the last week; got up about one o'clock & did not express a wish to retire to bed till near 9 o'clock. She was rather more languid towards evening, but cheerful, & Beavor found her pulse rather less full. She has had some sleep in the night, from 12 till three very quiet sleep, after that was much disturbed with the pain in her side; she appears unrefreshed & languid this morning.

I have to thank you for a very kind letter received yesterday by which I rejoice to find that you wish Dr. Pope not to delay his visit to Weymouth; therefore I trust we shall see him Monday at all events & then he will be the best judge *when we may* set out with safety. I believe it will be a great satisfaction to Beavor as well as to myself, the arrival of Dr. Pope.

[P.S.] Beavor has just been with Amelia; he finds her full as well as yesterday. (Add. Georgian 12/101)

[*29 Oct.*] Your kind letter of yesterday made me very happy. Our dearest Amelia passed a very tolerable day with little fever; got up about three & returned to bed about 9 after having been in the warm bath which went off very well. She has had a very restless night with a great return of fever the first part of it & much pain in the side, but Beavor finds her with little or no fever this morning.

The Prince's carriage arrived yesterday at 4 o'clock; Beavor fully intended her going out in it today but the weather is so damp & foggy it is quite [out] of the question.

G. Garth returned yesterday after having made every arrangement at his house to receive us & says he can lodge us all very comfortably & appears delighted with the thoughts of seeing us again at his house. Lady Neal, I am happy to say, is better today; she was very alarmingly ill the day before yesterday with a compleat inflammation on her lungs. I have not seen her as she has been in bed these 4 days. (Add. Georgian 12/102)

4017 PRINCESS AMELIA *to the* KING, *and the reply*

[*Weymouth, 29 Oct. 1809.*] Having nothing very new to say I did not trouble you with any letter; indeed I cannot say there is any very material alteration since I last had the pleasure of writing. The fever is certainly decreased but the side continues very obstinate. This last week Mr. Beavor has thought it right to keep me entirely on potatoes & turnips & to postpone the calomel. I am very glad Doctor Pope intends coming on Tuesday as he can then judge better than from any written account, but I am sure he will approve of Beavor, which he has done in his letters.

I must now, my dear papa, thank you for the carriage which arrived yesy. evening between four & five.

Dear Lady Neale is rather better to day but has been excessively ill & Miny tells me Sir Harry has been very much alarmed.

I have had an indifferent night & I feel very billious which I hope will plead an excuse for the stupidity of my letters, but I could not resist sending you, my ever dearest papa, a few lines to recall myself to your recollection & to report what I never cease feeling, but *feel* more every hour of my life, how dearly I love you & how grateful I am for your kindness. (Add. Georgian 14/130)

[*The King's reply, Windsor Castle, 30 Oct.*] I do not delay thanking you for your very affectionate letter, from which I have learnt with great pleasure that the fever has decreased and that you have not suffered from the unfavourable weather. I wish most sincerely that you had been enabled to tell me that the pain in the side had equally subsided, but I trust that a perseverance in the course at present pursued will afford me that comfort, and I shall await with no small anxiety the report which Doctor Pope will make on his arrival at Weymouth. I had heard from dear Mary that poor Lady Neale had been seriously unwell, and it gave me great concern, not only on her's and Sir Harry's account, but also from knowing your attachment to her and the uneasiness you would feel. I have therefore received additional satisfaction from learning this morning that she was better. (Add. Georgian 14/131)

4018   SPENCER PERCEVAL *to the* KING, *and the reply*

[*Ealing, 30 Oct. 1809, Monday evg.*] Mr Perceval has the satisfaction to acquaint your Majesty that Mr Manners-Sutton will accept the office of yr. Maj.'s Judge Advocate. Mr Perceval humbly apprizes your Majy. that Mr. M. Sutton intends, in the event of his quitting yr. Maj.'s service in that office, to return to the profession of the Law. Some doubt occurred if your Majesty should think it necessary that he should be a Privy Councellor, whether he could with propriety return to the Bar. In England there are no recent instances, if there are any, of a Privy Councellor's practicing at the Bar; but in Ireland they are very common, and upon communication with the Atty & Solr. General he has satisfied himself that there can be no objection to a Privy Councellor's so practicing. Mr. Sutton therefore wishes to submit it entirely to your Majesty's pleasure whether he should or should not be sworn of yr. Maj.'s Privy Council on the occasion of his having the honor of being appointed to this office.

His Grace the Duke of Portland has informed Mr Perceval that when his Grace took your Maj.'s pleasure upon the advancement of Mr Wellesley to the Canonry of St. Paul's, he obtained your Majesty's approbation to the appointment of Mr Jones, his Grace's domestic Chaplain, to the living of West Ham, which Mr Wellesley was to vacate. Mr Perceval therefore with your Maj.'s approbation will give directions for executing this appointment. His Grace also mentioned that he had some time since laid before your Majy. the cases of Lady Athlone,[1] & Lady

[1] Frederick Christiaan Reinhart van Reede, 5th Earl of Athlone [I.] (1743–1808), married, 1765, his cousin Anna Elisabeth Christina (1745–1819), daughter of Maximilian, Baron van Tuyll van Serooskerken. She was the Dowager Countess. On 1 Aug. 1800 the Irish House of Lords gave him a pension on account of his poverty. His son, the 6th Earl (1766–1810), who died insane, married, as his second wife, 11 Nov. 1800, Maria (c. 1770–1851), daughter of Sir John Eden, 4th Baronet. She married, 30 Oct. 1821, Vice-Admiral Sir William Johnstone Hope (d. 1831).

Lavington,[1] and had obtained yr. Maj.'s consent that as soon as the Pension list would admit of it, they should be placed upon it, the one for £200, & the other £300—and as the Pension list will now just admit of it, his Grace has expressed his anxious wish that your Majesty's gracious purpose to these ladies should now be accomplished. And altho' Mr Perceval humbly submits to your Majy. that it is of great inconvenience to your Maj.'s service that the means of granting pensions should ever be so reduced as the granting these pensions will now reduce them, still, as he believes that the distressed state of these ladies does very much require such assistance, and as they have been encouraged to expect it, Mr Perceval ventures humbly to recommend the granting of them.

The Lord Mayor of London has prest Mr Perceval to recommend him to your Majesty for the honor of a Baronetage—and considering not only that he has gone thro his Mayoralty with becoming spirit, and great good intention, but also that the Jubilee of your Majesty's accession (which will occasion his attendance upon your Majesty with an Address from the City on Wednesday week), has happened in his year, Mr Perceval conceives, if yr. Majesty shall be graciously pleased to approve, that this honor may with great propriety be conferred upon him.

Mr Perceval has the satisfaction to inform your Majesty that the D. of Portland, having resolved again to submit to the operation of cutting for the stone, had undergone that operation before Mr Perceval left town this afternoon, and that as far as Mr Perceval could learn, there were no symptoms attending the operation which were unfavorable, and Mr Perceval therefore hopes that his Grace may be relieved from the excruciating sufferings which he has endured so long.[2] (14762–3)

[*The King's reply, Windsor Castle, 31 Oct.*] The King is glad to learn from Mr Perceval that Mr Manners Sutton accepts the office of Judge Advocate, & his

[1] Sir Ralph Payne (1739–1807), who had been one of the Prince of Wales's friends, and who was created Baron Lavington [I.], 1 Oct. 1795, married, 1 Sept. 1767, Frances Lambertina Christiana Charlotte Harriet Theresa, sister of Rudolph, Baron Kolbel, and daughter of Henry, Baron Kolbel, of the Holy Roman Empire, a General in the Emperor's service. She died at Hampton Court Palace on 2 May 1830, at a great age.

[2] Canning wrote to his wife on Monday night, 30 Oct.: 'Planta brings word that the old Duke has undergone another operation and is quite brisk again.' (Harewood MSS.) By the time Canning wrote that, the Duke was dead. Wm. Dacres Adams wrote to his friend T. P. Courtenay on the 31st: 'The operation was successfully performed—and a very large and pointed stone taken from him—sufficient to account for all that he has endured. Everybody then left the house, in order that it might be kept as quiet as possible—and we were in the fullest hope that he was doing well. But nature was exhausted with the effort, and he died, not as the newspapers say in a fit—but calmly, without a struggle—and in his perfect senses...Perhaps I am a singular instance of a man having been P. Secy. to two Prime Ministers—but certainly of having had the misfortune to lose them both by death—while in possession of the office.' (Wm. Dacres Adams MSS.)

The new Duke of Portland's letter of 4 Nov. to his father's private secretary, W. Dacres Adams, seems to point to still another example of a Minister making temporary use of public funds for his private purposes: 'Last night I received your letter of the 2d. If you see Arbuthnot, pray tell him that the money shall be replaced as soon as I come to town, or sooner if he desires it, and will let me know where he wishes that it should be paid. Of course I knew nothing about it. With regard to the £200 it will be necessary to explain whether Arbuthnot advanced the money, or whether it was a part of the Sec[ret] Serv[ice] money. But I suppose it will be quite time enough to enter into this explanation when I am in town on Tuesday sennight.' (Wm. Dacres Adams MSS.)

Majesty, being desirous that he should hold it upon as respectable a footing as his predecessors, cannot object to his being sworn of the Privy Council, if Mr Perceval does not apprehend any difficulty from it. His Majesty acquiesces in the appointment of Mr Jones to the living of West Ham, & in the grant of the proposed pensions to Lady Athlone and Lady Lavington. The King also consents to the Lord Mayor's wishes to be advanced to a Baronetcy.[1] Previous to the perusal of Mr Perceval's letter, his Majesty had learnt with deep concern the death of the poor Duke of Portland, which altho it may be considered a blessing, in such a state of suffering, must nevertheless be a subject of sincere grief to those who did justice to his worthy & respectable character. (14763)

4019   PRINCESS MARY *to the* KING, *and the replies*

[*30 Oct.* [*1809*].] Your kind letter as usual gave me great pleasure. I am happy to say Amelia passed a very tolerable day yesterday, less pain & inclined to be cheerful; she did not get up till late as Beavor advised her laying in bed longer than usual having had so late a night. Towards evening fever came on again and grieved am I to add she has passed a sad night with very sharp pains in her side & much fever, in consequence she is very uncomfortable this morning & appears languid & fatigued. I fear the weather is so unfavourable she will not be able to get out again today as it is very damp & foggy. I own I look forwards with great joy to Pope's arrival tomorrow as I think the pain in the side rather if anything gains *upon her* & this fever lurking about her I should suppose must require care & attention. (Add. Georgian 12/106)

[*From the King, Windsor Castle, 30 Oct.*] Your kind letters are always a great comfort to me and it has been very satisfactory to me to learn from that which I received this morning that dear Amelia has not been affected by the damp & foggy weather as I feared she would be. I am well aware that it would not be adviseable for her to venture out while it prevails, but whenever the weather does admit of her taking an airing, I shall be very anxious to hear that the Prince of Wales' carriage is really so easy as comparatively to lessen my apprehensions of the effects of the journey.

I am very glad to hear that Lady Neale is better & I sincerely hope that she may soon be entirely re-established. I have felt cordially for poor Sir Harry under this additional cause of uneasiness after the severe blow so lately experienced. (Add. Georgian 12/103)

[*From the King, Windsor Castle, 31 Oct.*] I have received both your kind letters and I regret most sincerely that the last does not convey so favorable an account as I had been led to hope for from the contents of the first dated. I grieve to learn that the pain in the side returned with so much violence & produced so uncomfortable a night to poor Amelia, but I trust that, upon the whole, Doctor

[1] Charles Flower was created a Baronet, 4 Nov. 1809.

Pope will not find that she has lost ground since he was last at Weymouth and I hope that his personal attendance may enable him to recommend some effectual means of relief. (Add. Georgian 12/107)

4020 THE EARL OF LIVERPOOL *to the* KING, *and the reply*

[*London, 31 Oct. 1809.*] Lord Liverpool most humbly submits to your Majesty copies of the Addresses which are to be presented tomorrow by the City of London and the two Universities, and the answers which with your Majesty's approbation it is proposed to return to them. (14764)

[*The King's reply, Windsor Castle, 1 Nov.*] The King approves of the answers which Lord Liverpool has prepared to be prepared this day to the Addresses from the City of London and the Universities of Oxford and Cambridge [*sic*]. (14764)

4021 *Letters from* PRINCESS MARY *to the* KING, *and the replies*

[*31 Oct.* [*1809*].] I am happy to have it in my power to say that dear Amelia has had a great deal of good quiet sleep in the night, much pain in the side at times but this has been the best night she has had for the last 10 days. Beavor finds her with not much fever today & has given her leave to go out between 12 & one. Yesterday, notwithstanding the bad night she had the night before, she really passed a more comfortable day than she has done for the last week, very cheerful, though often complaining of pain, yet able to employ herself. I cannot help hoping Dr. Pope may find her better than he expects to *find her* but as she changes so in the 24 hours I am afraid of flattering you to[o] much. I trust I shall be able by tomorrow's post to say when Dr. Pope thinks we may begin our journey; the *uncertainty* cannot worry you more at Windsor than it does us at Weymouth but I feel now Dr. Pope will not wish to put it off longer than necessary.
[P.S.] Poor Lady Neal was very ill yesterday; they put her on leeches & blisters behind her ears. I fear she will be a long time recovering so severe an illness. Sir H.'s attentions to her are beyond everything I ever heard of in my life. (Add. Georgian 12/108)

[*The King's reply, Windsor Castle, 1 Nov.*] I have received great pleasure from your kind letter of yesterday which certainly contained a better account of dear Amelia than had reached me for some time past. I shall be anxious to learn how the trial of the bed carriage answers and still more so to receive Doctor Pope's first report.
I am very much concerned to hear that poor Lady Neale has had so severe a return of her illness; that Sir Harry's attentions would be most kind I am well persuaded. (Add. Georgian 12/109)

[*From Princess Mary, 1 Nov.*] Many thanks for your kind letter received yesterday by Dr. Pope & who arrived between three & 4 o'clock. Amelia went out in the Prince of Wales' carriage and found it eas[i]er than any carriage she has been in since her illness; however the motion certainly brought on some increase of pain in the side. She remained out not quite three quarters of an hour and considering how ill she has been since the last time she went out the drive went off tolerably, very faint & low but less fatigued when she came home than I ventured to hope.

Dr. Pope found her full as well as he expected from the accounts he had received from Beavor & gives us hopes we may begin our journey on Friday. She was very unwell last night with a compleat indigestion caused by something disagreeing with her stomach which she eat at dinner. Dr. Pope wished her stomach to be relieved and with much dificulty, which brought on great pain in the side, at last it was effected. She has had a very indiferent night as the side and lungs have been much *strained* & fatigued by all that happened early in the evening & of course have much increased the shooting pains in the side which prevented all sleep. Dr. Pope finds her pulse better than he could expect this morning considering all she suffered last night, but desired her to remain in bed the best part of today; however the Dr. still says he thinks we should be able to leave Weymouth Friday.

[P.S.] Poor Lady Neal was very ill all day yesterday; they put her on leeches again last night & Dr. Pope is to see her today. I fear she is as ill *now* as she was 8 years ago & poor dear Sir H. in very great distress about her. (Add. Georgian 12/110)

[*The King's reply, Windsor Castle, 2 Nov.*] The assurance conveyed in your kind letter of yesterday that Doctor Pope had found dear Amelia quite as well as he expected would have proved more satisfactory to me if I had not learnt at the same time that she had suffered so much in consequence of having eaten what disagreed with her. I grieve to think how painful must have been the exertion, and I trust that this will be carefully guarded against in future. I am glad that Doctor Pope thinks she may with safety begin her journey tomorrow & it will be a real comfort to me to know her settled quietly here & to be relieved from all apprehension of the effects of the journies which have been so prejudicial to her. (Add. Georgian 12/111)

4022   *Letters from* PRINCESS AMELIA *to the* KING, *and the reply*

[*Weymouth, Wednesday,* [*1 Nov. 1809*].] It is quite impossible for me, my beloved papa, to let the post go without a few lines to return you many thanks for your dear letter thro' Dr. Pope & to say with what pleasure I think that this day week I shall be with you.

Dr. Pope will write a particular account of me. From having been so dreadfully sick I feel a good deal fatigued and strained & I own I was very glad the Dr. was here when it happened as I should have been sorry to have felt my side so much affected by it without knowing the cause. I am sure you will be very sorry to hear how very ill dear Ly. Neale is. Poor Sr. Harry is miserable; his attentions are very great to her. He has taken a house for her into which, as soon as she can be moved with safety, he intends taking her to.

I will not take up more of your time but may I beg you will give my duty to the Queen and I will answer her if I am able in the course of the day.

I tried the carriage yesy.; it has a very easy motion but I feel everything affect my side. (Add. Georgian 14/132)

[*The King's reply, Windsor Castle, 2 Nov.*] I have learnt with great concern from your very kind letter of yesterday that you had suffered so much from having eaten something that disagreed with you & that the means unavoidably taken to relieve you should have brought on an increase of the pain already so severe. I shall feel great anxiety during the progress of your journey, for although the motion of the bed carriage may be comparatively easy, I am aware how much you must feel any at present. It is however satisfactory to know that Doctor Pope considers you able to bear the exertion & that, upon the whole, he has found you full as well as he expected.

I regret most sincerely poor Lady Neale's illness & that Sir Harry should experience so much uneasiness. It grieves me not less on your account, knowing your attachment for her which her attentions to you so justly claim. (Add. Georgian 14/133)

[*From Princess Amelia, 2 Nov.*] I cannot leave this place without returning you thanks for the many comforts you have given me during my stay here; tho' I feel I am *now returning* to my *greatest*, that of being near you & able to thank God to see you, it is impossible to feel more then I do the kindness of EVERY BODY to me. The idea of returning gives me *courage* & I assure you I will abide intirely by the doctor's directions & I hope to give as little trouble as possible.

Dear Ly. Neale is I trust a little better tho' still very ill. Sr. Harry is firmly of opinion that Dr. Pope has saved her life. Had the bleeding & discipline been defered I fear it must have been fatal. She has been bled five times & had on six blisters. The friendship & kindness of Sr. Harry & Ly. Neale have ever been the same to me & most deeply do I feel it.

My night has been but very indifferent & tho' I lament I *own* all the *trouble* I have given to your dear self & others by this journey has not answered, yet everything has been *tried* that was recommended, which must ever be a comfort & for which I am truly grateful, & I trust with the blessing of God yet to be supported & restored to health, an event I anxiously wish & pray for, & nothing on my part *shall* be wanted to obtain that first of blessings. (Add. Georgian 14/134)

[*The King's reply, Windsor Castle, 4 Nov.*] I thank you sincerely for your very affectionate letter and must assure you of the credit which I give you, not only for the patience & resignation which you have invariably shewn under most severe suffering, but also for the resolution with which you have undertaken a journey which I grieve to think must be so painful. The accounts received this morning of your safe arrival at General Garth's have been a great relief to my mind & I anxiously pray that your further progress may prove comparatively easy from the precautions taken.

[P.S.] I am very glad to hear from the Duke of Clarence that poor Lady Neale is so much better. (Add. Georgian 14/136)

[*Foreign Office, 2 Nov. 1809.*] Lord Bathurst most humbly requests your Majesty's pleasure on the contents of two dispatches from Lord Amherst which have been already submitted for your Majesty's consideration. Lord Bathurst had intended to have presented them to your Majesty yesterday at the Levée but the late hour to which it was protracted by the Addresses induced Lord Bathurst not to detain your Majesty longer in London. (14765)

[*The King's reply, Windsor Castle, 3 Nov.*] The King acquaints Lord Bathurst that he does not think that the provision which the Duke of Orleans has hitherto received from this country can with propriety be withheld in the event of his marriage with the Princess of Sicily, at the same time that his Majesty considers this alliance to be very ill-judged under circumstances where both parties must be so destitute of adequate support.[1] (14765)

4024 *Letters from* PRINCESS MARY *to the* KING, *and the replies*

[*2 Nov.* [*1809*].] Many thanks for your kind letter. Amelia was out for three quarters of an hour yesterday; we ment to go as far as Upway[2] but she suffered so much pain in the side that we turned home about half way between Weymouth & that place & stoped 4 times to recover herself in going out & comeing home. The early part of the day she was languid & fatigued from the bad night she had had, but towards evening got cheerful. The issues in the side Dr. Pope has thought proper to dry up, but put her strings into the seatons which, though it gave much pain, the inward pain in the side is so much *greater* that I do not think the seaton in the side gives her much trouble but when dressing. She has had more sleep than the night before, though much disturbed with pain in the side at diferent times.

Dr. Pope is very decided we shall be able to leave this [place] tomorrow & as he goes all the way *with us* I hope in God we may be able to *get on* as Lady George as well as myself shall certainly do *nothing* without his *orders*; we then can have nothing to reproach ourselves with, & God in Heaven grant I may have the comfort of sending you good accounts on the road.

Lady Neal was very ill yesterday. Dr. Pope when he first saw her thought her *very ill* indeed & bleed her but last night her breathing was relieved & she has had some sleep.

[1] On 25 Nov. the Duke of Orleans married Maria Amelia (1782–1866), daughter of Ferdinand IV, King of Naples. The Duke of Kent wrote, 5 Sept. 1809: 'My last letters from the Duke of Orleans were from Cagliari on the eve of his embarkation for Palermo, where he was induced to repair from hearing that his friend Prince Leopold was going to embark as a volunteer with the Sicilian troops attached to Sir John Stuart, arising from an anxious desire to see a little service with him, but I apprehend this expedition must have been over before he got there...I conclude it is settled between her [Mademoiselle d'Orleans] and her mother to make Malta their place of residence, which I always was of opinion they would prefer to England. In *that* case I am apt to think the Duke will not much longer protract his return to England, when he finds he cannot get into active employ by remaining in the Mediterranean.' (46401–4)
[2] About four miles north of Weymouth, on the Dorchester road.

[P.S.] Sir H. Neal has just been with me in great distress as he fears it will be quite impossible to move Lady Neal for a great length of time. He is looking out for a house but at present can hear of none; he therefore hopes he may have leave to remain in N. 4 till he can move her with safety. If you will be so kind as to order a letter to be wrote to him on the subject it would be a great relief to his mind as we shall be gone before any answer can come to this. (Add. Georgian 12/112)

[*From Princess Mary, 2 Nov.*] We went out again this morning in the carriage & I think it went off much as it did yesterday, only she was so *determined* to go as far as she could for the sake of *prepareing* for the journey that we went as far as where the road turns off to Upway. We had much dificulty to arrange & make the pillows and cushions easy as the side required more support & as the pain increased it became more necessary; in consequence when we got home I made Dr. Pope get into the carriage & drive round the courtyard & then as far as the turnpike & back again with her first that he might be a judge what she does suffer in the carriage, and 2ly in hopes that he might, from being more used to sick people than Lady George & myself, assist us in makeing her lay more comfortable in the carriage. At last, after many very fruitless trials, which of course fatigued her much, Sir H. Neal was sent for by Dr. Pope to see if he could not contrive a cot for her so to hang on in the carriage and swing backwards & forwards. Sir H. I trust has succeeded as Amelia thinks the one that came this evening may answer. Pope does not allow he is *at all* disheartened & still says we are to set out tomorrow. Amelia herself is not at all discouraged & assured me unasked (as you may believe) that she *thought* she should have both strength and resolution to perform the journey & that nothing should make her give up the going on but if Pope found it necessary, & then of course she should look upon it as her duty so to do.

I write this over night for fear of not having time tomorrow before I go to enter into all these particulars, & I wished you to know that Lady George as well as myself have done all in our power to try to *make* her as comfortable as we can & have nothing to reproach ourselves with *now* that Dr. Pope has seen the full extent of her sufferings in the carriage, which I am certain no one can have an idea of but those that witness them, as Lady George & me have done ever since the journey down to Weymouth. She has lived upon nothing but arrowroot for the last two days to keep her cool for the journey and the seatons hardly tuched to prevent all *irritation* whatsoever. I therefore hope in God as Pope will be with us all the way that under his directions all may turn out better than I now venture to hope.

Poor Lady Neal continues very ill; was bleed again today & Dr. Pope appears uneasy about her but makes the best of it to Amelia. As to our respectable & amiable Sir H. Neal, he can hardly hold up his *head today* & is quite worn down with fatigue & anxiety.

I have to thank you for a kind letter received today & now I will take my leave for tonight, but not before I beg you to believe me [etc.].

[P.S.] The warm bath went off well & she appeared comfortable & composed after, so I hope to have a good report to send tomorrow. (Add. Georgian 12/113)

[*The King's reply, Windsor Castle, 3 Nov.*] The account which your kind letter of yesterday contains of poor Amelia's attempt to reach Upway and the pain which attended it has naturally increased my dread of the effects of the journey and has also added to my surprize that Doctor Pope should persist in the intention. My anxiety will continue very great indeed until this sad journey is over, and I lament also that which you, my dearest Mary, will undergo on this distressing occasion. I have desired that Sir Harry Neale may be acquainted that I wish him to inhabit No. 4 during his stay at Weymouth, which I sincerely hope may be shortened by poor Lady Neale's amendment. He was assured by yesterday's post of my best thanks for their kind attentions to yourself & dear Amelia. (Add. Georgian 12/114)

[*From Princess Mary, 3 Nov.* [*1809*].] Our dear Amelia has had a very indiferent night with much pain in her side but Dr. Pope finds her much as usual today; she appears *quite* ready to do anything the Dr. thinks proper, therefore is geting up to set off by 12 o'clock. The *sun shines* upon us so I hope in God we shall be supported & our dearest Amelia suffer less than my *own anxiety* will allow me to hope at present.

Lady Neal is rather if any thing better today.

As Venables is ill I have ventured to take upon myself to desire Brackle [?] to go with us as we cannot well be at the inns without some man-servant. Dolly is kind enough to go all the way with us & William will go as far as G. Garth's, dine with us & then set off for Windsor. (Add. Georgian 12/115)

[*From Princess Mary, Wednesday, 3 Nov.*] I write to say we are arrived at G. Garth's. Considering all things I really think I may say it has not gone off *worse* than I expected, very much as our usual drives have been ever since we have been at Weymouth, only from going further she of course got more faint. We stoped very often as the cot was not as easy as was hoped it would be, but Dr. Pope thinks he can make it better tomorrow. I can say no more now. (Add. Georgian 12/116)

[*The King's reply, Windsor Castle, 4 Nov.*] The post brought me your kind letter of yesterday from Weymouth, soon after which I had the comfort of receiving your kind note by the Duke of Clarence's servant, acquainting me that poor Amelia had reached General Garth's & that the journey had really gone off as well as you expected. The information has proved the greatest relief to me as I dreaded the nature of the account which I might receive, nor can I yet say that I am free from serious uneasiness. I entirely approve of every step you took towards rendering the carriage more easy and of your having called Sir H. Neale to your assistance, & I hope that the alterations to be made in the cot will contribute to poor Amelia's ease & relief from pain. I also approve of your having ordered Brackele [*sic*] to attend you in the absence of Venables. I feel most sincerely for poor Sir H. Neale's present distress and from all you say I must fear that his situation is very precarious. (Add. Georgian 12/117)

(439)

[*Charles Street, 3 Nov. 1809.*] Lord Liverpool begs leave most humbly to submit to your Majesty the draft of a dispatch to Lieut.-Genl. Don, which with your Majesty's approbation it is proposed to send to Flushing tomorrow. (14766)

[*The King's reply, Windsor Castle, 4 Nov.*] The King entirely approves of the instructions to Lieut.-General Don which Lord Liverpool has submitted. (14766)

4026   SPENCER PERCEVAL *to the* KING, *and the reply*

[*Ealing, 3 Nov. 1809.*] Mr. Perceval acquaints your Majesty that Mr. Dundas has consented, if your Majesty should think proper, to take a seat in the Cabinet, notwithstanding Lord Melville appears to have preferred his declining it—and Mr. Perceval, conceiving that it will be of great importance that Mr. Dundas should be in the Cabinet, both with regard to the assistance to be derived from his advice and with regard to his efficiency in the House of Commons, humbly recommends to your Majesty that he should be permitted by yr. Majesty to be one of yr. Maj.'s confidential servants.

Lord Harrowby, who has relinquished his seat as President of the Board of Control, altho he intended to avail himself of your Maj.'s gracious permission to succeed Ld. Bathurst at the Mint and as President of the Committee of Council for Trade,[1] has found his health so much impaired by the business he has had to transact at the Board of Control, that he humbly hopes your Majesty will be pleased to excuse his declining to accept Lord Bathurst's former office—and Mr Perceval is so fully convinced that Lord Harrowby's health is unequal to the discharge of any official business, that he trusts your Majesty will permit his Lordship to continue in the Cabinet without office. For unless an opportunity should occur of placing him in an office with little or nothing to do, it will be impossible your Majesty should be able to have the advantage of his excellent judgement in your Maj.'s Councils, except he held a seat in the Cabinet without an office.

Mr. Perceval encloses the letter which he has received from the Society for the Relief of Prisoners for Debt, returning the grateful acknowledgements of that Society for your Majesty's gracious donation. (14715–16)

[*The King's reply, Windsor Castle, 4 Nov.*] The King entirely approves of Mr Dundas being admitted to a seat in the Cabinet as recommended by Mr Perceval. His Majesty regrets very much that Lord Harrowby's state of health should render him unequal to an office of business, but will feel the full value of his continuance in the Cabinet without an office. (14716)

---

[1] 'Lord Harrowby reluctantly declined, from positive necessity, the Presidency of the Board of Trade; the whole labour, therefore, must unavoidably fall upon me,' wrote George Rose on 16 Oct. (*Diaries and Corresp.*, II, 410.)

[*4 Nov.* [*1809*].] Though Dr. Pope has made his own report, yet I cannot help first thanking you for the kind letter I received yesterday & to say that our dear Amelia has passed a better night than we could expect considering the fatigues of yesterday, but Dr. Pope says *we* are to leave this at 11 o'clock, the pulse being very *tolerable*. Nothing can be more comfortable than we have found this house; the General gave us a famous dinner & very good beds & is all attention. (Add. Georgian 12/118)

[*From Princess Mary*, [*4 Nov.*].] We arrived at Woodgates Inn half past 5 o'clock. The cot did better today owing to Sir H. Neal's kind[ness] in coming over early this morning to G. Garth's & arranging it, otherwise she [would] have suffered much pain & fainted often.

[P.S.] I have not time to write to the Q. My love to all. (Add. Georgian 12/119)

[*The King's reply, Windsor Castle, 5 Nov.*] I have to thank you for two kind letters received this morning from which I have learnt with great satisfaction that poor Amelia had passed a better night than could have been expected after a day of such painful exertion. Your attention in writing subsequently to your arrival at Woodgates Inn has not been lost upon me and to know that dear Amelia had got so far upon her journey is a great comfort, although I cannot deny that her arrival here will alone relieve me from the constant anxiety which I feel.

I am glad that the cot has been made more easy and am not indifferent to Sir Harry Neal's kind attention in riding over to General Garth's, nor to the care shewn by the latter in providing for your accomodation. (Add. Georgian 12/120)

4028 SPENCER PERCEVAL *to the* KING, *and the reply*

[*4 Nov. 1809.*] Mr. Perceval transmits for your Majesty's perusal a letter from Lord Wellesley, to Mr Wellesley Pole together with a paper which accompanied it, and which Mr Perceval has received from Mr Pole.[1] Mr Perceval however

---

[1] Lord Wellesley's letter to Perceval accepting the Foreign Secretaryship, is in Walpole's *Perceval*, II, 41. Lord Wellesley's private and confidential letter to his brother, Wellesley-Pole, dated Seville, 8 Oct., is in *Wellesley Papers*, II, 263. Wellesley-Pole himself wrote to Perceval on 30 Oct. from Dublin Castle: 'I send you a packet I have just received from Lord Wellesley. The contents have given me a pleasure which I cannot express, but which I am sure you can well understand to be unbounded—that of knowing that a most respected and beloved brother has taken the line, and manifested the principles I approve from the very bottom of my heart—thoroughly, and to the utmost extremity would I have supported you, even if my dear Wellesley had been against us—but as it is, I shall have the supreme happiness of according with my brother in politics, and of thereby strengthening the attachment I have uniformly borne him from my cradle. You will perceive how Lord Wellesley feels your conduct towards him, and you will recollect that when he wrote he did not know half your kindness. That he will accept the offer convey'd to him by Sydenham there can be no doubt. As he is so anxious that the King should be apprized of his conduct throughout this business, I should be glad (if you see no objection) to have such of the papers laid before his Majesty as you may judge to be proper for his perusal—the whole of the statement which Wellesley has sent to Canning would perhaps be sufficient; but if you think all that I transmit should be seen by the King, I beg you to lay them before him. Every line that Wellesley has written on the subject is creditable to him as a man of honor, as an attach'd friend to the King, and as a true patriot.

'I beg of you to shew Wellesley's packet specially to my friend Lord Mulgrave, to Lord Bathurst,

cannot transmit it without humbly informing your Majesty that Lord Wellesley is under a misconception with respect to what had passed with Mr Perceval upon the subject of Ld. Wellesley's appointment as First Lord of the Treasury. Mr Perceval never presumed, as he trusts your Majesty will give him full credit that he could not presume to make a proposal for any person to hold that or any situation in your Majesty's Government without having been authorised so to do by your Majesty, and it is also equally incorrect to suppose that the rest of his colleagues had consented to any such proposal.

Mr Perceval did certainly in conversation with Mr Canning both before and after his resignation, with the earnest desire, which he always felt of endeavoring to keep yr. Majesty's confidential servants together, press Mr Canning to consider whether there was not some third person, a member of the House of Lords, whom Mr Canning might be reconciled to see in the situation of the D. of Portland and with whom Mr Perceval would be ready to continue to act as Chancellor of the Exchequer if your Majesty should approve of the appointment—and Mr Perceval did certainly upon such occasions, suggest the names of Ld Harrowby, Ld. Bathurst, Ld Liverpool & Ld Wellesley as persons with whom he would so consent to act—as well as desiring Mr Canning to consider, if he had objections to them, whether there was any other person, who could occur to him & to whom he would not object—but Mr Perceval did not make this as an authorised proposal, nor had he consulted even his colleagues upon it, but only proposed the question for Mr Canning's consideration—impressed undoubtedly with the opinion that his colleagues would have been disposed probably to acquiesce in any fit person who should be approved by yr. Majesty & who could reconcile Mr Canning to remain in his office. Mr Perceval has thought it necessary to accompany these papers with this explanation, & laments very much that Ld Wellesley should have had this circumstance conveyed to him so erroneously. (14767–8)

[*Enclosure*] (*Copy*)

During the course of the last spring and summer, confidential communications passed between Mr Canning and Lord Wellesley with respect to the state of his Majesty's Government and to the conduct of the war.

Lord Wellesley declared his disapprobation of the conduct of the war, which appeared to him to be defective from want of system in the plan, and of vigour & alacrity in the execution. He attributed these defects to the want of a due portion of practical experience and acknowledged efficiency for the management of military affairs, in the Cabinet, as well as to the want of a sufficient degree of concert and unity of action in all the Departments of the Government. Mr Canning repeatedly expressed nearly the same sentiments and stated his intention to urge the necessity of strengthening his Majesty's Councils and of improving the management of military affairs; and he added his determination to resign if he

Lord Liverpool, and to Dundas—but probably you may think it desirable that all the Cabinet should see it. When you have done with the packet be so good as to send it to Mrs. Pole at Blackheath.' (Perceval MSS.)

should be disappointed in his endeavours to accomplish these necessary improvements.

In the course of these discussions Mr Canning stated his desire to introduce Lord Wellesley into the Cabinet, and particularly with a share of the management of the war, whenever an arrangement could be made for that purpose.

Lord Wellesley stated (as he has uniformly declared since he has thought himself at liberty to enter his Majesty's Councils) that he was ready to serve his Majesty in any situation to which he might be called by his Majesty, being persuaded that his Majesty would never command him to accept any situation inferior to his just pretensions, and to the scale of his public services. In the course of these conversations the probability of Mr Canning's resignation was repeatedly discussed with reference to his failure in the proposed plan of strengthening the Government. Lord Wellesley, without any necessity or any previous engagements of any description, always declared on those occasions that if Mr Canning should resign in consequence of such a failure, Lord Wellesley would decline any part in a Government which might be formed to the exclusion of Mr Canning under such circumstances.

In considering the various contingencies which might arise, and the several arrangements of office which might be proposed, Lord Wellesley has often stated to Mr. Canning that he would cheerfully serve his Majesty in the Cabinet if Mr Canning should be placed in the situation of First Lord of the Treasury, under the supposition that the public service required the selection of a person for that situation from the members of the House of Commons. Lord Wellesley however never considered the principle to have been established in theory or practice as a positive rule to restrain his Majesty's choice of a person for the office of First Lord of the Treasury.

When the Embassy to Spain was first proposed to Lord Wellesley it appeared probable that Spain might become the theatre of a most important scene, and it was understood at that time to be Mr Canning's wish that the Embassy to Spain should ultimately lead to Lord Wellesley's introduction into the Cabinet with the views and for the purposes already stated.

Although the intentions of the Government with regard to operations in Spain did not ultimately coincide with Lord Wellesley's expectations, wishes or opinions, he thought himself bound by his duty towards his Majesty not to decline the Embassy after having formally accepted that high trust, and accordingly, at Mr Canning's particular desire, although much against his own inclination, he proceeded to Spain.

In the course of these discussions it was more particularly stated by Mr Canning to Lord Wellesley that an arrangement was in contemplation for vacating the Seals held by Lord Castlereagh, and for calling Lord Wellesley to that situation. Lord Wellesley signified his readiness to serve his Majesty in that capacity whenever he might be called upon; he never expressed any indisposition to act with Lord Castlereagh nor with any other member of the Cabinet.

Lord Wellesley immediately before his departure from London understood from Mr Canning that it was positively determined to make the proposed arrangement for the War Department and to place Lord Castlereagh in the situation of Lord President of the Council or of Lord Privy Seal as soon as the expedition to the Scheldt should be terminated, whatever might be the success of the expedition.

Lord Wellesley always understood that the proposed arrangement was known to Lord Castlereagh's most intimate friends, and that Mr Canning's wishes and intentions were that it should be known to Lord Castlereagh from[1]   Lord Wellesley   Mr Canning never entertained any idea of concealing the transaction.

Lord Wellesley left England expecting that the arrangement would be made within the probable period of his continuance in Spain. But his particular anxiety was directed to the object of stipulating for an early return from Spain whatever might be the state of his Majesty's Councils at home; and in his last conversation with Mr Canning he expressly desired it to be understood that a period of two months must be the limit of his Embassy. He understood it to be Mr Canning's intention to resign if the proposed arrangement for strengthening the Government should be frustrated. He always deprecated Mr Canning's resignation under any circumstances, and in the various conversations which passed, Lord Wellesley frequently stated his opinion that circumstances might arise which might require Mr Canning's continuance in office although he should be disappointed in the proposed arrangement respecting the Military Department. Lord Wellesley desired that in such a case Mr Canning would consider his Majesty's service alone and not Lord Wellesley's pretensions, and that Mr Canning would deem himself to be under no other obligation to Lord Wellesley than that of liberating Lord Wellesley in the most distinct manner from any engagement of any description either towards Mr Canning or towards his Majesty's Ministers. On the other hand Lord Wellesley expressly desired that if Mr Canning should resign Lord Wellesley might be favored with the earliest notification of his Majesty's permission to return to England.

The resignation of Mr Canning would in any event have been considered by Lord Wellesley as a serious calamity to his Majesty's service and to the public interests.

When Lord Wellesley quitted England he did not contemplate any event which was likely to occasion Mr Canning's resignation, excepting his failure in the proposed plan of strengthening the King's Government and of improving the conduct of the war. In the event of Mr Canning's resignation on such grounds Lord Wellesley certainly would have declined any share in the Government.

It now appears that resignations actually occurred in his Majesty's Councils previously to Mr Canning's resignation, which admitted of the proposed arrangements for strengthening the Government and of improving the Military Department; that these resignations had been accompanied by the retirement of the Duke of Portland; that Mr Perceval and Mr Canning could not satisfactorily adjust their respective claims to the Duke of Portland's office, but that Mr Perceval had proposed Lord Wellesley for that office, to which arrangement all Mr Perceval's friends had acceded, and no dissent had been expressed by any of his Majesty's

---

[1] The last line of page 5 of the MS. has been cut away.

Ministers; that Mr Canning being of opinion that the office of First Lord of the Treasury must be occupied by a commoner, and that his own claims to that situation could not be postponed to those of Mr Perceval, had resigned his Majesty's service.

In this situation Mr Canning, with great kindness and attention, has obtained for Lord Wellesley his Majesty's gracious leave of absence from his post, with the condition that his Majesty's indulgence shall not be used under circumstances in which Lord Wellesley's quitting Spain might be prejudicial to his Majesty's service. Lord Wellesley has received this permission with a deep sense of gratitude for his Majesty's indulgent consideration. Under the impression of this sentiment, and with the anxious solicitude for the critical state of his Majesty's service, Lord Wellesley declares that although he has for some time past considered that his early return to England might be advantageous to his Majesty's affairs in Spain, he will use every degree of exertion in exercising the discretionary powers which his Majesty has been pleased to entrust to him. The actual condition of his Majesty's Councils will afford a reason for delaying rather than hastening his departure.

Lord Wellesley is anxious that his Majesty should be assured on all occasions of his most dutiful and strenuous support. Lord Wellesley also declares that he is entirely free from any engagement which might restrain him in the execution of any commands with which his Majesty may be pleased to honor him.

Lord Wellesley would have declined any part in a Government which should have been formed to the exclusion of Mr Canning if Mr Canning had resigned in consequence of the disappointment of his endeavours to strengthen his Majesty's Government and to extend the basis on which it was formed.

Lord Wellesley would have acted most cheerfully with Mr Canning in any situation to which his Majesty might have called Mr Canning, and the intelligence of Mr Canning's retirement is to Lord Wellesley a subject of the utmost regret and of the most serious apprehension.

Lord Wellesley however is neither pledged nor prepared to insist on the appointment of a member of the House of Commons or of any particular person to the situation of First Lord of the Treasury as a condition indispensable to the prosperity of his Majesty's service, although he entertains the highest respect for Mr Canning's talents and virtues, and the most affectionate regard for his interests & honor. (14769–74)

[*The King's reply*, *Windsor Castle*, *5 Nov.*] The King has received Mr Perceval's letter, transmitting those written by Lord Wellesley to Mr Wellesley Pole, & his M. is perfectly satisfied that what had passed between Mr Perceval & Mr Canning in regard to the contingency of Lord Wellesley's appointment as First Lord of the Treasury has been wholly misconceived by the latter, and that the explanation which Mr Perceval has thought it necessary to give upon that point is a fair & correct statement of communications which confirm the liberality & moderation with which he has invariably acted.

His Majesty conceives from the tenor of Lord Wellesley's letters & particularly the contents of the private letter that he has no intention of accepting office, & his

Majesty is so well satisfied with Lord Bathurst in his present Department that he cannot hesitate in saying he should regret any arrangement[s]¹ tending to his removal from it. The King cannot help expressing his surprize that Mr Canning's memory should have been so imperfect in regard to what passed between him & Lord Wellesley, Mr Canning having positively declared to his Majesty when he gave up the seals of his office that he had not made the most distant communication to Lord Wellesley of any intended arrangement which provided for his appointment to the Colonial Department.

The King will be glad to receive copies of Lord Wellesley's communications or will get them copied here, if sent for that purpose. He returns them to Mr Perceval at present, as they may be wanted. (14775, and Perceval MSS.)

4029 *Letters from* PRINCESS MARY *to the* KING, *and the reply*

[*Salisbury, 5 Nov.* [*1809*].] We arrived at this place a quarter before two o'clock, having left Woodgate Inn at 11 o'clock. Dr. Pope says all things considered she is full as *well as he expected* & as he must be a far better judge than Lady George and myself I pray God this journey may not do *her as much* harm as the one in August. She has suffered dreadfully with pain in the side & constant faintings but the Dr. says in about an hour we shall be able to get on to Andover. She is now laying down on a very comfortable couch in a quiet room & appears recovering a little from all she has suffered for the last two hours. She passed but a very indiferent night, from fatigue & pain got little or no sleep, but got up *determined* if Dr. Pope wished it to get on as far as she could on the journey. Her fortitude and resignation is beyond what I can say, as I feel *certain* no one but herself could have *resolution* to go on so many days running suffering such *tortures* on a journey.

I have to thank you for a most kind letter received yesterday. (Add. Georgian 12/121)

[*The King's reply, Windsor Castle, 6 Nov.*] I have received your kind letter dated from Salisbury during the stop you were forced to make on account of poor Amelia's very great sufferings on the road, and fully impressed as I am with the extent of what she bears with so much resolution I should have been alarmed at the thoughts of your being forced to continue at Salisbury if I had not, at the same time, learnt your safe arrival at Andover. I feel more hurt than I can describe when I consider how truely painful must be the exertions of so many successive hours & days, and poor Amelia's situation is ever present to my thoughts. I cannot sufficiently admire the fortitude which she shows & which I am convinced can only be produced by a sense of duty for the reward of which, in the complete restoration of her health, I trust in the powerful aid of the Almighty. (Add. Georgian 12/122)

[*From Princess Mary, Hartford Bridge, Monday, 6 Nov., 6 p.m.*] We arrived at this place about a quarter of an hour ago & I am thankful to say this day's journey

¹ 'Arrangement' in Perceval MSS.

has gone off full as well as yesterday's, *certainly not worse*, though much fatigued & a great deal of pain at times & faintings, yet I assure you all things considered *I think* she has got on much better than I expected. (Add. Georgian 12/123)

4030 PRINCESS AMELIA *to the* KING

[*Andover, Monday morning*, [*6 Nov. 1809*].] I will not leave Andover without writing you a few lines as I think it will be a greater satisfaction to *you* to hear from myself I have borne the journey as well as I cld. expect in my suffering state. It has certainly increased the pain in my side but I think really it has been quite as well as I had any right to *expect*. Thank God in little more than 24 hours I shall be at home. My night has been rather better; I have had about two hours sleep.

Excuse my adding more, my beloved father, but I tryed to tell you this myself & to thank you for your last dear letter.

I have just had a better account of dear Ly. Neale; I do hope the worst is over. (Add. Georgian 14/137)

4031 PRINCESS MARY *to the* KING

[*Harford Bridge, Tuesday morning, 7 Nov.* [*1809*].] I must thank you before I leave this place for your kind letter which I received this morning & likewise for another I got yesterday before I left Andover & which in my hurry last night I am ashamed to think I forgot to express my gratitude for & which I am sure nothing but my wish to send off the express with all hast[e] prevented my thanking you for, as no one *feels* all your kindness more deeply than I do. I am happy to say Dr. Pope finds Amelia full as well as he could *expect* after so much fatigue & she is all anxiety to get to Windsor as soon as she can, when I shall lose no time in coming up immediately to the Castle. (Add. Georgian 12/124)

4032 *Letters from* SPENCER PERCEVAL *to the* KING, *and the replies*

[*Downg. St., 7 Nov. 1809*.] Mr Perceval herewith transmits to your Majesty a copy of Lord Wellesley's statement, Mr Perceval conceiving that it was that paper and not the confidential letter to Mr Pole of which your Majesty wished to be furnished with a copy. Mr Perceval had not read these papers with the impression which your Majesty has received from them, and he perceives Mr Pole draws a different conclusion from the perusal of them, as he conceives Lord Wellesley will certainly accept the office which has been offered to him.

Mr Perceval regrets very much the embarrassment which has occurred in the canvas for the election of Chancellor at Oxford, by the Duke of Beaufort having been prevailed upon at length to stand, after having declined it before, and by declining it induced the Lord Chancellor to declare himself a candidate. Between the two unless the matter can be well arranged & settled Mr Perceval fears Lord Grenville will have but too good a chance of succeeding. But he hopes previous to the election a communication may take place between the Ld. Chancellor's & the D. of Beaufort's friends, and upon an examination of their respective strengths the person of the two who appears to have the least chance might endeavour to transfer as far as he can the votes of his friends to the other as the best means of preventing Lord Grenville from having the triumph of succeeding just at this moment, after the recent publication of his obnoxious opinions in a place where those opinions should meet with every discountenance.[1] (14776–7)

[*The King's reply, Windsor Castle, 7 Nov.*] The King has received Mr Perceval's letter and the copy of Lord Wellesley's statement which is the paper that his Majesty desired to have.

The King regrets equally with Mr Perceval the embarassment which has arisen in the election of the Chancellor at Oxford, from the Duke of Beaufort's proceeding, and his Majesty's feelings as to the possibility of Lord Grenville's success are not less strong than Mr Perceval's.[2] (14777)

[*From Perceval, Downing Street, 11 Nov.*] Mr Perceval humbly acquaints your Majy that he has ascertained that his Grace the Duke of Portland does not desire to succeed his father as Lord Lieut. of the Co. of Nottingham.[3] Mr Perceval therefore, if your Majesty should so please, will acquaint his Grace the Duke of Newcastle of your Maj.'s gracious intention to grant the Lord Lieutenancy to his Grace. (14780)

[*The King's reply, Windsor Castle, 12 Nov.*] The King approves of Mr Perceval's acquainting the Duke of Newcastle that his Majesty intends to confer upon him the Lord Lieutenancy of the County of Nottingham. (14780)

[*From Perceval, Downing St., 13 Nov.* [*1809*].] Mr. Perceval acquaints your Majesty that Lord Desart[4] has declined accepting the Office of one of the Lords of the

---

[1] Grenville had re-stated his views on the Catholic question in a printed letter to Dr. Hodson, Principal of Brasenose College, Oxford. Dated 2 Nov., it was intended for private circulation amongst the Oxford voters whilst he was campaigning for the Chancellorship of the University. His letter is in *Dropmore Papers*, IX, 359–62.

[2] Lord Bathurst's letter to the King (Foreign Office, 10 Nov. [14778–9]) on the subject of financial assistance to the Tyrolese who were continuing to fight for freedom, is in *Bathurst Papers*, p. 131. The King's brief reply on the 11th (14779) is on p. 132.

[3] The Duke was already Lord Lieutenant of Middlesex.

[4] John Otway, 2nd Earl of Desart [I.] (1788–1820). Styled Viscount Castle-Cuffe from 4 Dec. 1793, when his father, the 3rd Baron Desart [I.], was given an Earldom, until he succeeded his father as 2nd Earl, 9 Aug. 1804. Tory M.P. for Bossiney, 1808–17; a Lord of the Treasury, Dec. 1809–June 1810. The Duke of Richmond described him (2 Nov.) as 'a very promising young man, who I have every reason to suppose steady with us. He is cousin to Lord Sligo. An appointment might perhaps bring him forward.' (Richmond MSS. 72/1508.) The Duke had earlier recommended his appointment as a Lord of the Treasury in Ireland, but the U.K. Treasury offer superseded it. (*Ibid.*, 71/1374.) The Duke wrote to Perceval on 23 Nov. from Phoenix Park: 'Lord Desart has just been with me to explain the motives on which he refused your offer of belonging to the English Treasury. He states that he does not know what his abilities are, that if he accepted particular situations his friends might be disappointed and he still more, that if he accepted others he might possibly find himself superior to them and therefore he wished to support the present Administration out of office. Since he received your letter Mr. Denis Browne has shewn him what he received from you by which it appears that you are anxious to have

Treasury. His Lordship declines it in civil terms, and with such expressions of good wishes as to induce Mr Perceval to hope that his Lordship's refusal is not owing to any disinclination to your Maj.'s present Government. Mr Perceval thinks it not impossible that some difficulty with respect to his re-election might have deterred his Lordship from vacating his seat. Mr Perceval would recommend, if your Majesty pleases, that Mr Snowdon Barne,[1] a very steady supporter of your Majesty's Government, should be appointed to the Treasury, Mr Perceval has reason to believe that Mr Barne will accept that situation. But there will still remain another seat at the Treasury not filled up.

Mr Perceval takes the liberty of transmitting to your Majesty the letter which he has received from his Grace the D. of Portland upon the subject of the Lord Lieutenancy of Nottingham, as it will shew your Majesty how satisfactorily the proposed appointment of the D. of Newcastle to that situation will be received by the Duke of Portland. (14781)

[*The King's reply, Windsor Castle, 14 Nov.*] The King has received Mr Perceval's letter and is satisfied that Lord Desart has not declined the seat from any unfavorable disposition, but from the office not suiting him. His Majesty approves of Mr Perceval's proposal that Mr Snowden Barne should be appointed to the Treasury.

The King thinks that nothing can be more satisfactory than the Duke of Portland's letter in respect to the appointment of the Duke of Newcastle to the Lieutenancy of Nottingham. (14782)

[*From Perceval, Downg. St., 17 Nov.*] Mr. Perceval has the honor to transmit to your Majesty a letter which he has received from the Duke of Brunswick— and upon the subject of which he will, with your Majesty's permission, take your Majesty's pleasure when he next pays his duty to your Majesty. Mr Perceval in the meantime merely acquaints the Duke of Brunswick that he has laid his letter before your Majesty.

Mr Perceval has humbly to entreat your Majesty's forgiveness for a mistake which he committed in executing the wishes of his Grace the late Duke of Portland with respect to one of the pensions on which Mr Perceval took your Majesty's pleasure the other day, Mr Perceval having mentioned the name of Lady Athlone, instead of her daughter Lady Jemima Bentinck,[2] in favor of whom his Grace had undertaken to solicit that pension. Mr Perceval has however discovered his mistake in time to avoid the inconvenience which would have occurred from this

him in office. He appears very anxious to assist Govt. as far as possible, and circumstanced as we are he desires me to say that if you think it would be useful he will waive his objection and take the situation you offered him if it is not disposed of. The impression on my mind is that Lord Desart looks higher. He certainly is a young man of much learning and considerable talent but I am not certain that he does not overrate himself. At the same time it is very possible that he does not.' (Richmond MSS. 72/1490.)

[1] Snowdon Barne (1756–1825), M.P. for Dunwich, 1796–1812. A Lord of the Treasury, 1809–12; Commissioner of Customs, 1812–23.

[2] John Charles Bentinck (1763–1833), a Count of the Empire, great-grandson of William, 1st Earl of Portland, married Lord Athlone's daughter (1767–1839) in 1785.

mistake having been communicated to Lady Athlone, and if your Majesty shall be graciously so pleased, he will take care that it shall be carried into effect in favor of Lady Jemima Bentinck. (14783)

[*The King's reply, Windsor Castle, 18 Nov.*] The King returns the Duke of Brunswick's letter to Mr Perceval, and his Majesty will be glad if Mr Perceval will consider whether any arrangement can be made for affording to the Duke & his children such assistance as may be necessary, observing however that whatever is done can only be considered as a temporary resource which the circumstances under which they are placed may warrant.

The King approves of Lady Jemima Bentinck's name being substituted for Lady Athlone's in the proposed grant of a pension. (14784)

[*From Perceval, Downg St., 20 Nov.*] Mr Perceval transmits to your Majesty for your Majesty's signature the warrant for his salary as First Commissioner of the Treasury, to which rank in the Commission he has now succeeded by the death of the Duke of Portland before the issuing of a new Commission. Mr Perceval wishes this warrant, if your Majesty pleases, to receive your Majesty's signature before the passing of the new Commission, as some persons, (and Lord Redesdale among the number) entertain some doubt, notwithstanding the precedent in Lord North's time, whether it may not be necessary for Mr Perceval to be re-elected upon his accepting the office under the new Commission with an enlarged salary[1]—and Mr Perceval thinks it may remove some part of the force of their objections if, before the passing of the new Commission, he is in possession of all the advantages of the office of First Commissioner.

Mr Perceval with your Majesty's approbation would propose that Lord Brook[2] should be offered the remaining seat at the Treasury. (14785)

[*The King's reply, Windsor Castle, 21 Nov.*] The King approves of the grounds on which Mr Perceval has submitted the warrant for his salary as First Commissioner of the Treasury, and he trusts that the necessity of a re-election will be obviated. His Majesty also approves of Lord Brook as a very proper person to fill the remaining seat at the Treasury. (14786)

4033   EARL BATHURST *to the* KING, *and the reply*

[*Foreign Office, 20 Nov. 1809.*] Lord Bathurst most humbly submits to your Majesty a letter addressed to your Majesty. It was delivered to Lord Bathurst by a merchant who had directions to give it into the hands of Lord Bathurst and said it came from Koningberg [*sic*]. (14787)

---

[1] Lord North, already Chancellor of the Exchequer, did not seek re-election for Banbury in Jan. 1770 when the King appointed him First Lord of the Treasury. Nor did Perceval resign his seat for Northampton.

[2] Henry Richard Greville (1779–1853), styled Lord Brooke from 2 May 1786, when his elder brother George died, until 2 May 1816, when he succeeded his father as 3rd Earl Brooke and Earl of Warwick. Tory M.P. for Warwick, 1802–16. K.T., 10 May 1827; a Lord of the Bedchamber, 1828–30. He did not become a Lord of the Treasury.

[*The King's reply, Windsor Castle, 21 Nov.*] The King returns to Lord Bathurst the letter received from Königsberg which conveys the notification from the King of Prussia of the birth of a son.[1] (14787)

4034 SPENCER PERCEVAL *to the* KING, *and the reply*

[*Downing St., 23 Nov. 1809.*] Mr Perceval transmits to your Majesty the copies of the letters which passed between the Atty.-Genl and his Royal Highness the Duke of Kent upon the subject of Mrs Clarke's affidavit. The motion for the new trial against Col. Wardle came on this morning and the Court refused the new trial without requiring the Atty.-Genl to produce the affidavit to which the above letters referred.

Mr Perceval also sends to your Majesty the letter[2] which he received this day from the Marquis Wellesley, by which your Majesty will perceive that Lord Wellesley accepts without reserve or hesitation the office which your Majesty graciously permitted Mr Perceval to offer to him, and Mr Perceval cannot but add that he conceives the Marquis's acceptance of that office will have a very considerable effect in strengthening your Majesty's Government.[3] Mr Perceval understands by other letters which have been received from Lord Wellesley that his Lordship expected to sail on the 8th of this month. (14788)

[*The King's reply, Windsor Castle, 24 Nov.*] The King acknowledges the receipt of Mr Perceval's letter enclosing copies of the correspondence between the Duke of Kent and the Attorney General; also a letter from Lord Wellesley, conveying his acceptance of the office of Secretary of State for the Foreign Department. H.M. is glad to learn that Mr Perceval conceives that Lord Wellesley's acceptance of that office will have the effect of strengthening his Government. (14789)

[*Sir Vicary Gibbs to the Duke of Kent, Russell Square, 19 Nov. (Enclosure).*] I take the liberty of troubling your Royal Highness with an account of some proceedings which are likely to be brought forward in the Court of King's Bench, and which, when they had come to my knowledge, I thought it not fit that your Royal Highness should be left unacquainted with them.

Col. Wardle has applied to the Court for a new trial in the action in which Mr Wright obtained a verdict against him,[4] and to repel this application Mrs Clarke has made an affidavit in which she states that Col. Wardle represented to her that your Royal Highness had been ill used by the Duke of York, that it was the wish of him (Col. Wardle) to serve your Royal Highness, which he

[1] Prince Albert (1809–72), born 4 October.
[2] Dated Seville, 30 Oct. (14796–7). See Walpole's *Perceval*, II, 41–2, *Bathurst Papers*, p. 130, and Rose, *Diaries and Corresp.*, II, 432.
[3] Richard Ryder wrote to the Duke of Richmond on the 23rd: 'Your Grace will share with us in the sincere pleasure we receive in the prospect of Lord Wellesley's union with us. If Pole had not been prepared for this event, I should have sent your Grace over a straight waistcoat to guard against the effects of his ecstasies.' (Richmond MSS. 72/1521.)
[4] Francis Wright, an upholsterer, brought an action against him on 3 July for furnishing Mrs Clarke's house, and he was cast in a large sum of money.

conceived he should do by getting the Duke of York turned out of his office of Commander-in-Chief, in which case he had no doubt but your Royal Highness would get his situation; that your Royal Highness was acquainted with his, Col Wardle's, interference, and that if she did not give credit to his assertions he would bring her such a letter from your Royal Highness's private secretary[1] as would leave no doubt in her mind of their knowledge of what she was required to do.

Mrs Clarke adds that she said she would consider of it, and when she saw the letter she should be better satisfied upon the subject—that Col. Wardle afterwards sent her a letter from Major Dodd to him, which she exhibits, and in which Major Dodd expresses himself strongly in favor of what he calls the great cause, evidently meaning the enquiry into the conduct of the Duke of York, says that from what Col. Wardle mentioned of a certain female he had no hesitation in believing that her co-operation would be more material than that of any other human being and concluded with observing that she may have an opportunity of redressing her own wrongs, & by serving a generous public most effectually benefit herself.

I consider this, as far as it regards your Royal Highness, to be one of the numerous misrepresentations which have been circulated by designing men for the purpose of raising a prejudice against several branches of the Royal Family, and therefore I have felt it my duty to communicate it to your Royal Highness, but as Mr Wright cannot be prevented from using any facts by which he may suppose that his case is strengthened, and as I trust they are as little likely to be turned to any mischievous purpose under my management as under that of any other Counsel into whose hands they might fall, I have thought it on every account adviseable to retain the conduct of the cause myself, in doing which I hope I shall meet with your Royal Highness's approbation. (14790–1)

[*The Duke of Kent to Sir Vicary Gibbs, Castle Hill Lodge, near Great Ealing, Tuesday, 21 Nov., 7 a.m. (Enclosure No. 2, Copy).*] The Duke of Kent returns his best acknowledgments to the Attorney-General for his polite letter of the 19th this instant received by express, and the attention he has so obligingly shewn him in communicating the purport of Mrs Clarke's affidavit, as also that of a letter from Capt. Dodd to Mr Wardle which Mrs Clarke exhibits. From the manner in which the Attorney-General expresses his opinion as to the purport of the affidavit alluded to, it may appear unnecessary for the Duke of Kent to do more than express his thanks for the liberality with which he considers the matter; but having it much at heart that the Attorney-General as one of his Majesty's servants should be confirmed in his opinion by the clearest proofs, he judges it right to transmit to him the original of a paper signed by Capt. Dodd himself and witnessed by the Earl of Harrington[2] and Col. Vesey,[3] which contains certain questions put by the Duke to the Captain and answered by that officer so far back as the month of July last, upon that officer having retired from his House-

[1] Captain Thomas Dodd.
[2] Colonel of the 1st Life Guards and Gold Stick.
[3] He was now one of the Duke's Grooms of the Bedchamber. Lieutenant-Colonel, 1798; Colonel, 1808; Major-General, 1811; died 1812.

hold, in the presence of the two respectable witnesses above named, as that paper will prove by Capt Dodd's own declaration that he (the Duke of Kent) not only never encouraged directly or indirectly any attack on the Duke of York, nor ever had any knowledge of Col. Wardle, Mrs Clarke or their proceedings, but also that he invariably expressed his disapprobation of the whole business from the first of its being known to him (which he can solemnly declare was only from the public prints). The Attorney-General will further observe, on the perusal of this paper, that Capt. Dodd positively denies ever having at any time so expressed himself in word or in writing to Col. Wardle, Mrs Clarke, or anyone else, as to give them reason to conceive that the Duke of Kent would countenance those concerned in attacking his brother; nay more, that the Capt. on the contrary asserts he had uniformly declared that the Duke of Kent would have a very different feeling.

The Attorney-General being furnished with these facts, will afterwards be the best judge how far it will be in his power in the course of the trial which is about to take place to do justice to the Duke of Kent, whose character has already been so cruelly misrepresented in the public prints, particularly in the National Register,[1] and is likely to be still more injured when the affidavit in question is made public, unless the falsity of the fact therein stated, as far as regards him, can be established by the production of the proof which the paper herewith inclosed affords: but if the impression which that affidavit is likely to produce be not removed, the Duke cannot help feeling that his will be a case of very great hardship.

The Duke of Kent having committed the inclosure in confidence to the Attorney-General, requests the favor of him to return it (after taking a copy of it, if he thinks proper) at his earliest convenience, and that he will not think him indiscreet in requesting that the Attorney-General's letter and his answer to it may be communicated as early as possible to the Duke of York. (14792–3)

[*Sir Vicary Gibbs to the Duke of Kent, Lincolns Inn, 21 Nov. (Enclosure No. 3, Copy*).] I had the honor of receiving your Royal Highness's letter this morning, with an inclosure containing the questions put to Capt Dodd, and his answers to them, which afford the most convincing proof, if any were wanted, not only that your Royal Highness never authorized him to promote or countenance the late proceedings against the Duke of York, but that you always expressed a strong disapprobation of them.[2]

I have availed myself of the liberty which your Royal Highness allows me of

[1] The *National Register* was started on 3 Jan. 1808. The last number noticed in *The Times Handlist of English and Welsh Newspapers* is dated 12 May 1823.

[2] The Duke had publicly denied having had anything to do with the attacks on his brother, the Duke of York, but his denial was not universally believed—hence the questions put to his private secretary, Captain Dodd, in July. The Duke's statement was made in the House of Lords on 7 Feb. 1809: 'He believed that certain insinuations had gone abroad whereby the public were led to suppose dissension now existed between himself and his Royal brother whose conduct was under inquiry. Whatever credit had been given to such reports, they were unfounded and untrue, and he was happy in making the declaration that no professional dispute had been entertained, nor did there exist any such schism as had been alluded to in the Royal family. So far was he from thinking that there was anything improper in the conduct of his Royal brother, he was fully persuaded that all the charges made against him were false.' (*Parl. Deb.*, XII, 378.)

taking a copy of this paper, understanding that I have your Royal Highness's permission to use the communication which you have done me the honor of making to me, as occasion may require, for the purpose of shewing that if any persons have presumed to introduce your Royal Highness's name into this transaction, it has been done without your authority or knowledge.

I have also in obedience to your Royal Highness's suggestion sent to the Duke of York a copy of my letter to your Royal Highness, and of the answer which you did me the honor of sending to me. I did not add a copy of the questions put to Capt Dodd and his answers, because I take it for granted that the Duke of York has already seen the original which I have now the honor of returning to your Royal Highness. (14794–5)

[*Enclosure*]

[*Questions put to Capt. Dodd by the Duke of Kent, and his answers. Kensington Palace, 27 July 1809.*]

Q. Have I either directly or indirectly sanctioned, advised or encouraged any attack upon the Duke of York, to your knowledge?

A. Never.

Q. Have I had to your knowledge, any acquaintance or communication with Col. Wardel, or any of the persons concerned in bringing forward the investigation respecting the Duke of York's conduct, which took place in Parliament last winter, either direct or indirect?

A. I feel confident that your Royal Highness has no such knowledge or acquaintance.

Q. Have I to your knowledge, ever had any acquaintance with or knowledge of Mrs Clarke, or any communication with her direct or indirect, upon the subject above mentioned, or any other?

A. I am confident your Royal Highness never had.

Q. Have I ever expressed to you any sentiment which could induce you to believe that I approved of what was brought forward in Parliament against the Duke of York, or of any proceeding that would tend to his obloquy or disgrace?

A. Never. I have heard your Royl. Highness lament the business, viva voce, & you made the same communication to me in writing.

Q. Have you ever to your recollection, expressed yourself either by word or in writing, either to Colonel Wardle or Mrs. Clarke, or to any other person connected with the investigation on the Duke of York's conduct, in any way that could give them reason to suppose that I approved of the measure or would countenance those concerned in bringing it forward?

A. Never, but I have on the contrary expressed myself that your Royal Highness would have a very different feeling.

Q. What were my expressions upon the subject of the pamphlets which appeared, passing censure on the conduct of the Duke of York & other members of my family, and holding up my character to praise, and what have been the

(454)

sentiments which I have uniformly expressed on similar publications whether in the newspapers or elsewhere?

A. I have invariably heard your Royal Highness regret that any person should attempt to do justice to your own character at the expence of that of the Duke of York or of any other member of your Family.

Q. During the ten years you have been my Private Secretary,[1] when in the most confidential moments I have given vent to my wounded feelings on professional subjects, did you ever hear me express myself inimical to the Duke of York or that I entertained an expectation of raising myself by his fall?

A. Never. On the contrary I have frequently heard your Royl. Highness express yourself very differently.

The above questions written in Col. Vesey's hand, were dictated by me in presence of Lord Harrington.

(Signed) Edward
Harrington
J. A. Vesey[2]   (46399–400)

[1] In April 1810 the Duke said that Dodd had voluntarily resigned his employment eight months earlier.

[2] Lieutenant-General Sir Thomas Trigge wrote on 13 Dec.: 'I was on Monday above fourteen hours in Westminster Hall, as I wished much to hear the trial between Wardle and Mrs Clarke...Had the circumstances which appeared on this trial, of W. having given Mrs Clarke £100, £20 and £500 previous to the inquiry by Parliament, it would certainly have saved the D. of York.' (*Hastings MSS.*, III, 275.) Brougham, writing to Lord Grey on 12 Dec., had this to say of the Court proceedings: 'The result of Wardle (of which I never had a doubt) is very satisfactory in many respects. He was puffed up by most unmerited popularity and made the worst use of his sudden influence. The present Ministry owe their continuance in place more to him than to anybody. He is in truth not a right, straightforward man—he shuffled yesterday—though his cross-examination did not materially damage him. But the case failed and even without Stokes evidence the verdict would have been against him—although he had all the benefits of a leaning towards him and presumptions in his favour, which usually belong to defendants. In fact it was he who was tried rather than Mrs. C. and the Wrights—and so everybody felt. Lord Ellenborough was very violent and injured the side he (I must say) espoused. His charge was very good, however. Gibbs not very good, but very blunt—for he fairly told Wardle that he had neither honour nor honesty and that he was not to be believed on his oath. All description however falls short of Alley's speech—which I dare to say the papers will call able, energetic, etc. The Court was convulsed with laughter during nine-tenths of it. It was worse in the serious part than Sylvester Daggerwood, and the blunders were beyond Mrs. Malaprop.' (Brougham MSS.)

'There can be no doubt,' said Lord Lauderdale, writing to Grey on 17 July, 'that if Major Dodd had been examined he must have most deeply implicated the Duke of Kent in all the preparatory proceedings against his brother.' (Howick MSS.)

Dodd's connection with Mrs Clarke damaged his professional prospects. The Duke of Kent wrote to his friend Lieutenant-Colonel Robert Wright on 8 Oct. 1809, with reference to Major-General Colin Campbell, 'your future Commandant': 'Altho' *he* would wish to retain you in the situation of Secretary, I fear *that* will very soon be at an end, Lord Castlereagh having in the most unhandsome and illiberal manner as one of his last acts before he quitted office, when he found, I presume, that no proof of criminality could be adduced against Capt. Dodd, or that there was any ground for his removal, contrived to get the situation altered by a Treasury Minute from a military one, as it always had been heretofore considered, to a civil one, thus placing it on the same footing as the Secretaryships in all his Majesty's Colonies, the patronage to which he was thereby enabled to assert as Colonial Secretary of State, and to confer the nomination on Col. Rutherford, late of the Engineers, who I hear is preparing to go out; but all this I only know by a side wind, altho' you may depend upon it as being the case, not one word of communication having been made to me by any Department upon the subject. In short, there never was any man worse used on the occasion than Captain Dodd has been except myself, for the injustice to him is only to be equall'd by the gross illiberality that has been shewn to me: but I fear Dodd's connection with Colonel Wardle and Mrs. Clarke, which I deeply lamented from the hour I first knew

(455)

[*Foreign Office, 24 Nov. 1809.*] Lord Bathurst most humbly submits to your Majesty Mr Frere's re-credentials which Admiral Apodaca has transmitted to Lord Bathurst in order to be presented to your Majesty. Admiral Apodaca had previously given to Lord Bathurst a copy, and had required an Audience of your

of it, has been the occasion of bringing this business to this termination, as but for that I do not think that Ministers would have dared to commit so flagrant an act of injustice as turning him out of his place without ever informing him of what he is accused of, or giving him the opportunity of defending himself, while every step was taken to collect the evidence of his enemies against him.' (46407–10)

The Duke wrote to Wright on 21 Oct.: 'Upon the subject of Dodd I cannot tell you *all* I have gone thro', for to this hour I am as warmly attach'd to him as ever, and indeed I firmly believe that that personal sentiment never can alter while I live, as it is grounded upon my conviction that, notwithstanding the appearance of his connection with Col. W—e and Mrs. C—e, he is not guilty of having ever abetted the attack upon my brother which no man in the country would disapprove of more than myself, and that nothing can be ascribed to him but the imprudence, *when in my family*, of keeping up habits of intimacy with those who were actually employ'd in working his ruin, an imprudence arising from his own unsuspicious nature. As to the separation being only a *temporary* one I wish I could bring myself to think, that *that* could be the case, but from what has since pass'd in confidential communication between him & Mr. Parker, who writes this, and has for some years past been his assistant as my Private Secretary, I fear his resolution is bent upon retirement, and that no consideration would induce him, notwithstanding his unshaken regard for me to resume his former situation; but be that as it may, untill such time as it is proved clear as the day, that he *has* been an active instrument in the hands of those who conducted the attacks on my brother, (in which case I must reprobate his conduct, as he was fully apprized of my sentiments being diametrically averse to it), my friendship for and opinion of him (except in respect to his imprudence, as regarding myself) will remain unmoved.' (46413–18)

The Duke wrote again, on 11 Dec. 1809: 'I have now before me your letters of the 10th and 20th ulto., the former received on the 3d, and the latter on the 8th inst. I can easily judge, from my own feelings, what you must have experienced at learning the cruelly unjust supercession of our friend Dodd in the Secretaryship by the joint act of Mr. Perceval and Lord Castlereagh, which was aggravated if possible by the mean dirty subterfuge they had recourse to of changing the nature of the place, from Secretary to the Governor to Civil Secretary to the Government, the motive of which is self-evident, for they dared not address me on the subject, who they knew well had the exclusive right to the patronage; indeed I never should have receivd any positive information upon the subject if Colonel Rutherford had not been advised by a mutual friend of his and mine (Sir Thomas Dyer) to wait on me as a matter of decorum, when the new Secretary candidly told me that Mr. Perceval had of his own accord sent for him and offer'd him the place, of which he was altogether ignorant, and consequently he never could have taken a single step to obtain it, which I think proves more strongly than any thing else, the wantonness and villainy of their conduct: in fact they were put to a nonplus when they found that, notwithstanding all their illegal and inquisitorial proceedings against Dodd, they could not substantiate their accusations, which that jealous and revengeful man Sir Hew had laid to his charge, and not daring openly to avow that they owed him a grudge for his apparent intimacy with Col. Wardle, and on which ground alone in fact they were determined to make him smart, they had recourse to that truly petty fogging subterfuge of altering the nature of the commission to oust him. God knows how I feel upon the subject, for I am in my soul convinced that Dodd is perfectly innocent on both points, as knowing my sentiments so fully as he did, it is morally impossible that he ever would have join'd in any measure to degrade a member of my Family, and therefore, altho I am unavoidably silent now, I live in hope that a time will yet come, when I shall be able to confound his enemies, and restore his character to that state of estimation in which it ever stood before with every one who knew him, and which I am sure he never has done anything to forfeit. When I say this, I don't mean that I can approve of his continued intimacy with Colonel Wardle after the public line that gentleman took in Parliament against my brother, for as belonging to my family and knowing the professional difference that had subsisted between my brother and me, he ought to have been aware that such a line of conduct, at such a time, must inevitably throw suspicion and call down the shaft of calumny upon *me*, but I believe he is more than punished for his culpable imprudence in that respect, by the knowledge he has of all the affliction it has occasioned me, and the severe attacks we have both, in consequence, experienced from the vile pens of hireling scribblers, who delight in nothing so much as spreading far and wide the seeds of mischief and confusion.' (46425–9)

Majesty, in order to deliver the original to your Majesty. This Lord Bathurst declined doing until he had ascertain'd whether it was customary, and having after inquiry informed Admiral Apodaca that such was not the practice of this Court, the Admiral has transmitted the original to Lord Bathurst. (14798)

[*The King's reply, Windsor Castle, 24 Nov.*] The King has received Lord Bathurst's letter and returns Mr Frere's re-credential. Mr. Perceval having communicated Lord Wellesley's acceptance of the office of Secretary of State for the Foreign Department, his Majesty cannot forbear upon this occasion from assuring Lord Bathurst of the satisfaction which he has received from the able and regular manner in which he has conducted the business of that Department, and that, whatever is the result of a general arrangement, his M. cannot expect that the office in question can be filled more to his advantage than at present. (14798)

[*From Lord Bathurst, Foreign Office, 24 Nov.*] Lord Bathurst most humbly and gratefully acknowledges your Majesty's gracious acceptance of his earnest endeavours to discharge the duties of the office which your Majesty was pleased to confide to him until Lord Wellesley's answer was receiv'd.

Lord Bathurst is too well aware of his own insufficiency to attribute your Majesty's condescending expressions of approbation of his conduct to anything but your Majesty's known indulgence to your servants; and to the repeated instances of favour & protection which your Majesty has been graciously pleased to shew to three generations of Lord Bathurst's family.[1] (14799)

4036   GEORGE CANNING *to* LIEUT.-COLONEL TAYLOR, *and the reply*

[*Gloucester Lodge, 24 Nov. 1809 (Copy).*] In a packet which will (I hope) accompany this letter, but which if not ready today will certainly be forwarded to you tomorrow, you will receive a printed copy of a letter to Lord Camden containing a vindication of my character from the gross misrepresentations which have been published against me respecting the transaction which led to my meeting with Lord Castlereagh.[2] In another cover, franked by myself, I send a copy of a

[1] Lord Bathurst's father, the 2nd Earl (1714–94) had been Lord Chancellor, 1771–8, and Lord President of the Council, 1779–82. Lord Bathurst's grandfather, the 1st Earl (1684–1775), after being Captain of the Band of Pensioners (1742–4), was given a pension of £2,000 a year on the Irish revenues soon after the King's accession, and was given an Earldom in 1772 (having been a Baron since 1712).

[2] The printed letter had been subject to constant revision. 'I never worked so hard at anything,' Canning told his wife on the 24th.

On the 13th he had written to Mrs. Canning: 'Lord William has been here today—& I have shewn him his father's letters, & read the whole letter to Ld. C[amden] through to him from beginning to end—and he has assured me that he is quite satisfied that I treat his father in the kindest manner, that I am perfectly justified in publishing—that in my case he should probably do the same—that he cannot help feeling deep sorrow at the necessity of the publication—but he only feels sorrow & no blame—but thankfulness to me.

'It appears that he & Ld. T[itchfield] have a difference of opinion about the alternative that Ld. Wm. suggested in the prefatory letter—and so I have proposed to print both versions.

'Ld. T. comes up tomorrow. I shall have a complete copy to shew him on Wednesday morning. I hope it will be out on Thursday—this week certainly.' (Harewood MSS.)

He wrote again, on the 15th: 'Here is a provoking thing! Lord Chuckle very ill—so ill as to keep

private letter to Lord Camden with which I accompany the packet, and which (of course is not) and is not intended to be printed [*sic*].

When I took leave of his Majesty in delivering up the seals on the 11th of October, I humbly submitted to his Majesty my apprehension, from the course of violent and intemperate abuse then begun to be poured out upon me, that I might be compelled to assert my reputation as an honest man by a simple detail of the circumstances of the transaction as they took place. This I felt to be all that could be necessary to do myself right, and for this I humbly implored his Majesty's gracious permission, promising and really determining not to have recourse to the use of that permission unless it should become indispensably necessary. The publication of Lord Castlereagh's letter alone would not (I think it would not) have appeared to me to constitute this case of indispensable necessity. The outrageous paragraphs and letters in the newspapers certainly would not, but a statement with Lord Camden's name and authority, implying, if not imputing something like direct falsehood to me, could not be passed over by me in silence without appearing to acquiesce in that imputation. I trust nevertheless that, though under the influence certainly of very strong feelings, I have not employed towards Lord Camden one harsh or disrespectful word, nor have said or left to be inferred, anything that could be supposed to cast any suspicion upon his motives, or that can create any reasonable uneasiness in his mind. I really am willing to believe that he may not have intended any harm, though he did much.

I have been, of course, most anxious to save the Duke of Portland, and I am led to hope that I have not failed of my object in this respect, as both Lord William Bentinck and the present Duke of Portland have had the whole of what relates to their father submitted to them; have compared it (particularly the Duke of Portland) with the original correspondence, and have done me the justice to express themselves not only satisfied, but justified by the manner in which I have avoided everything that could create an unpleasant feeling in their minds. The fact, to be sure, that the silence was injoined by the Duke of Portland could not be suppressed, and ought not in justice to others. But I hope it is so guarded and qualified as to imply no higher degree of blame, at the most, than that of an unfortunate, though well intentioned, error.

Not less has been my anxiety to abstain from transgressing the limits of discretion, in disclosing any circumstances of a political nature. I trust and believe no disclosure is made that can be of the smallest prejudice, and none which Lord Castlereagh's letter did not call for, and which will not go to relieve *every* person concerned in the transaction from those imputations of *intrigue*; which though *he* lays them upon *me* alone, could not but extend, *if true*, to *all* who were parties to it.

Above all things I hope that I have succeeded in so making use of his Majesty's name (where a direct reference to his authority could not be altogether avoided) as to present his Majesty's conduct in this affair in the light in which I have always

his room—& to be attended by Sir Wr. Farquhar four times a day. So says *Morng. Chron.*, & *Morn. Post* too, Ross tells me. I believe he shams. I am now going to walk to town to call on Ld. T[itchfield]. I shall leave a complete copy—just as it is to stand, to shew to him tomorrow.' (*Ibid.*)

viewed and gratefully represented it, as one continued course of kindness, impartiality, and direct *straight forwardness*, with respect to all parties concerned.

I shall be obliged to you if you will return me, at your leisure, the *manuscript* letter to Lord Camden. (Harewood MSS.)

[*Lieut.-Colonel Taylor's reply, Windsor, 26 Nov.*] I received yesterday your letter of the 24th instant, the printed copy of your letter to Lord Camden and the copy of a private letter to Lord Camden accompanying the former, but not intended to be printed, and I have this day had the honor of submitting the whole to the King.

You have had opportunities of learning how sincerely the King has lamented every circumstance connected with the subject of your publication, and the events which have led to this and other publications. You are equally aware from various communications how carefully his Majesty has abstained from the expression of any opinion, or indeed of any observation beyond that of the concern which the circumstances in question have caused to him. You will therefore not be surprized that, upon this occasion, I have not been authorized to convey to you any opinion or observation upon the contents of the papers submitted to his Majesty as far as they refer immediately to those circumstances. But the King has expressed himself sensible of the desire which you have shewn to be cautious in the use of his name, and in the disclosure of any circumstance of a political nature, not less than of the wish which you have felt to avoid everything that could create an unpleasant feeling in the minds of the late Duke of Portland's family, and, in your letter to Lord Camden, any word which might appear harsh or disrespectful towards his Lordship.

I return the manuscript letter to Lord Camden. (*Ibid.*)

4037   *Letters from* SPENCER PERCEVAL *to the* KING, *and the replies*

[*Downing Street, 25 Nov. 1809.*] Mr Perceval acquaints your Majesty that he this day received a letter from the Duke of Richmond informing him that Lord Desart, upon understanding that it was considered that it would be useful to your Majesty's service that he should accept the office of a Lord of the Treasury, that he would waive his objection and accept it if it was not yet disposed of. Mr Perceval has therefore answered that he thinks it would be useful, and with your Majesty's approbation he will now give directions for the issuing of the new Commission, the Board being complete.[1]

Mr Perceval has been much pressed to mention to your Majesty an application

---

[1] Perceval wrote to the Duke of Richmond, the Lord Lieutenant of Ireland, on the 25th: 'I can have no hesitation after my last letter to Mr D. Browne to authorise your Grace to state to Lord Desart that I do feel that his name, character & talents will make him a great accession to us at the present moment, and that therefore, as the seat at the Treasury has been kept open for him, I will direct his name to be inserted in the new Commission, according to his permission, & I will write a line to him myself to this effect. I shall be perfectly satisfied with anything your Grace arranges about Mr Fitzgerald's seat at the Board of Privy Council—as I enter entirely into all the observations which you make upon that subject.' (Richmond MSS. 72/1515.)

which has as he understands been made to your Majesty on behalf of the grandsons of the late Marquis of Thomond, who, having survived their father, are deprived of the rank by curtesy, which they would have derived from him if he had not died before the title descended upon him. The object therefore of this application is that your Majesty should be graciously pleased to grant to them, Capt. Edward, & Capt. James O'Bryen, and to their two sisters patents of precedence as the sons & daughters of a Marquis.[1]

Mr Perceval has had a letter upon this subject from the Chancellor of Ireland, stating that yr. Maj.'s Attorney-General Mr Saurin, whom the Chancellor represents as a most excellent officer, has married one of these sisters, and is very much interested in the success of this application. The only other sister is a Mrs Hoare, the wife of a gentleman of property in the county of Cork. Mr Perceval, having understood that your Majesty does not in general approve of granting such patents of precedence, has felt some difficulty in submitting this subject to your Majesty, but believing the family to be very respectable and very anxious upon this subject, he has at length been prevailed upon to take your Majesty's pleasure upon it. (14800–1)

[*The King's reply, Windsor Castle, 26 Nov.*] The King approves of Mr Perceval's ordering the new Commission to be issued for the Board of Treasury with the insertion of Lord Desart's name as one of the Commissioners. From Mr Perceval's representation of the respectability of the parties (relatives of the late Marquis of Thomond) applying for patents of precedence as the sons & daughters of a Marquis, the King will not withhold his compliance, although he is very desirous that these claims should in general be met with great caution. His M. must observe that the Captains O'Brien must be the nephews & not the grandsons of the late Marquis of Thomond. (14801)

[*From Perceval, Downg. St., 26 Nov. 1809.*] Mr Perceval humbly acknowledges to your Majesty that it was his mistake in calling the Capt. O'Bryens the grandsons of the late Marquis of Thomond. Upon reference to their statements he finds that they are, as your Majesty states, his nephews, but that their father was specifically introduced into the entail of the Peerage, so that had their father survived the late Marquis, the title would have descended upon him.

By the Admiralty telegraph of this day it appears that Lord Wellesley is arrived at Portsmouth.[2] (14802)

[1] Their father, Edward O'Brien [or O'Bryen] (*d.* 1801) was the younger brother of Murrough O'Brien (1726–1808), who was created Marquess of Thomond in 1800. Lord James O'Bryen (*c.* 1768–1855) was in the Navy: Lieutenant, 1790; Captain, 1799; Rear-Admiral, 1825; Vice-Admiral, 1837; Admiral, 1847. On 21 Aug. 1846 he succeeded his brother William as 3rd Marquess of Thomond. His brother Lord Edward (*d.* 1824) was also in the Navy (Lieutenant, 1793; Captain, 1802). Their sister Mary (*d.* 1840) married, first, Sir Richard Cox, Baronet; and second, William Saurin. Their sister Harriet (*c.* 1775–1851) married, 17 April 1800, Sir Joseph Wallis Hoare, 3rd Baronet (1775–1852).
[2] After a fifteen-day passage from Cadiz (Rose, *Diaries and Corresp.*, II, 433). He arrived in London on Tuesday the 28th, from Sussex. Rose said that the King did not come to town for the Levée as usual on Wednesday the 29th, and the Marquess could not therefore kiss hands for the Seals until 6 December. (*Ibid.*, II, 434.)

[*From Perceval, Downg St., 28 Nov.*] Mr Perceval acquaints your Majesty that he has received a letter from her Royal Highness the Duchess of Brunswick, in which noticing the approaching return of the period at which your Majesty had been graciously pleased to direct the payment of the sum of two thousand pounds to her R. Highness's two sons the Princess [*sic*] George & Augustus of Brunswick who reside in Holstein,[1] for the purpose of providing for their subsistance so long as the unfortunate circumstances of their situation should continue, her Royal Highness desires that Mr Perceval would bring before your Majesty her humble supplication that your Majesty would be graciously pleased to grant the same favour to them for the ensuing year. Mr Perceval has accordingly undertaken to bring this request before your Majesty. Mr Perceval does not immediately recollect the manner in which this assistance was afforded before, but believes that it was issued out of the Secret Service money of the Secretary of State for Foreign Affairs, and if your Majesty should be graciously pleased to continue this payment, which in all probability is as much wanted now as it was when last it was granted, Mr Perceval will acquaint himself more particularly with the manner in which it was issued before.

Mr Perceval has thought it necessary before he could take your Majesty's pleasure finally with regard to the amount of allowance which your Majesty might be disposed to bestow upon his Serene Highness the D. of Brunswick, to endeavour to learn whether his Serene Highness has been so fortunate as to rescue any part of his former fortunes from the continent; and for that purpose has addressed to his Serene Highness a letter, of which he presumes to enclose a copy to your Majesty in the hope that your Majesty may think that he has made that enquiry in a proper and respectful manner to his Serene Highness.[2]

Mr Perceval further acquaints your Majesty that Lord Wellesley arrived in town this afternoon, and finding that your Majesty will not come to town till tomorrow sevnnight, his Lordship is desirous of receiving your Majesty's commands whether he should pay his duty to your Majesty at Windsor or wait till your Majesty next comes to town, being anxious to pay his duty to your Majesty in the manner which may be most respectful and agreeable to your Majesty. (14803-4)

[*The King's reply, Windsor Castle, 29 Nov.*] The King has received Mr Perceval's letter and he is sensible of the necessity of continuing the assistance which had been given to the two Princes of Brunswick residing in Holstein, which his Majesty perfectly recollects having been heretofore issued out of the Secret Service money of the Foreign Department. The King also approves of Mr Perceval's letter to the Duke of Brunswick.

As the King is willing to allow Lord Wellesley time to recover from the fatigues of his voyage and to make his arrangements in London, his Majesty will not require his attendance here, but will defer seeing him until this day sen-night at the Queen's Palace. (14804)

[1] The two sons had recently visited their father, arriving from Harwich on 14 Oct., at his house in Clarges Street, Piccadilly.

[2] According to the *Nuremberg Gazette* the Prussian King had sequestrated all the estates and dominions of the Duke of Brunswick-Oels.

[*Whitehall, 29 Nov. 1809.*] Mr Ryder humbly submits to your Majesty's consideration the names of two gentlemen of Ireland whom his Grace the Lord Lieutenant has strongly recommended in former communications which his Grace has made to Mr Ryder as well as in the letter which Mr Ryder has now the honor of enclosing to your Majesty, as proper persons to be honoured with the title of Baronet.

Mr Alexander[1] is the father of the Corporation of Dublin and Mr Stamer[2] founds his request for this distinction upon the occasion of his having presented an Address from the City of Dublin upon the Jubilee in his public character as Lord Mayor of that city: and the Duke of Richmond informs Mr Ryder that they are both from character and fortune not undeserving this mark of your Majesty's royal favor.

Under these circumstances Mr Ryder humbly submits to your Majesty that it might be desirable to comply with the recommendation of the Lord Lieutenant.[3] (14805)

[*The King's reply, Windsor Castle, 30 Nov.*] The King acquiesces in Mr Ryder's recommendation of Mr Alexander of Dublin & Mr Stamer also of that city for the dignity of Baronet, in consideration of the circumstances by which their applications are supported. (14806)

---

[1] William Alexander, Lieutenant-Colonel of the Royal Dublin Militia (1743–*c.* 1820).

[2] William Stamer (1765–1838), Lord Mayor of Dublin, 1809–10, and 1819–20.

[3] The Duke of Richmond wrote to Ryder from Dublin on 2 Nov.: 'Lord Rosse accepts the Post Office and seems much pleased at the offer. An Address from the Lord Mayor & Corporation of Dublin was presented to me today for his Majesty and will be immediately officially sent to you. Previous to its being brought into the Presence Chamber I desired Pole to offer Knighthood to the Lord Mayor & the two Sheriffs. The Lord Mayor refused it, saying that he hoped, as his Majesty had honor'd the Lord Mayor of London with creating him a Baronet, he hoped to have the same honor. I was aware this was likely and had prepared Pole to answer it. He said Knighthood was the only honor a Lord Lieutenant can give and that tho' he was sure I should wish to shew every mark of attention to his Lordship and the City that I could not promise to procure what was not in my gift. The Sheriffs also refus'd unless the Lord Mayor had a promise to be made a Baronet. They all three desired Pole to speak to me again to know how far I would go. The present Lord Mayor (Stamer) is a wine merchant of some property. That species of merchant is considered higher than most particularly in Ireland, as you will suppose. I was certain the City would be disappointed if this wish was not complied with and still more so if no Knight was made. I therefore desired Pole to say that I would recommend it to be done, but that as I knew there was strong objections to encreasing that dignity I could by no means answer for success. In consequence of this message the Sheriffs accepted Knighthood. So the thing stands at present, and I am convinced it will be a popular measure to accede to what I am certain is the wish of the Corporation & City. If however, the Lord Mayor is created a Baronet I dont see how it is possible to avoid the same dignity to Alderman Alexander, the Father and leader of the Corporation. He was at the head of the old Police and made no opposition to the new one. For this he deserves credit. He is related to the Earl of Caledon, and in many respects a proper person. I did recommend him strongly a short time ago but there then seemed to be a great objection to making but very few. I am inclined to think that objection was chiefly in the Duke of Portland but am not certain.' (Richmond MSS. 72/1507.)

[*Foreign Office, 29 Nov. 1809.*] Lord Bathurst most humbly submits to your Majesty a note verbal which Lord Bathurst proposes to deliver to Prince Castelcicala tomorrow.

Lord Bathurst is desirous that your Majesty should be informed of the state in which he leaves the question arising from Lord Amherst's proposal of the three Articles to the Sicilian Treaty. (14807)

[*The King's reply, Windsor Castle, 30 Nov.*] The King approves of Lord Bathurst's note to Prince Castelcicala as being suited to present circumstances, and he trusts that the points in discussion will be thoroughly considered before the final decision is made. Prince Castelcicala's proposals should be received with great caution as it may be his object to excite false impressions here, at the same time that the demands of this Government should not be carried to unreasonable lengths. (14807)

[*From Lord Bathurst, Foreign Office, 29 Nov.*] Lord Bathurst most humbly submits to your Majesty the draft of a dispatch granting to Mr Villiers your Majesty's permission to return to England.[1] Lord Wellesley's arrival in London will most probably prevent any great length of time elapsing before Mr Villiers's successor will be able to depart from hence for Portugal; and it appears by the private as well as by the public letters of Mr Villiers that he is anxious to be able to return. (14808)

[*The King's reply, Windsor Castle, 30 [Nov.] Dec.*] The King approves of the letter to Mr Villiers which Lord Bathurst has submitted. (14808)

4040   LORD ELDON *to the* KING

[*Saturday, 2 Dec. 1809.*] The Lord Chancellor, with every sentiment of humble duty, has the honor to send a Commission for proroguing the Parliament, and an immediate warrant for appointing the Duke of Newcastle Custos Rotulorum for Nottinghamshire, to receive your Majesty's Royal Sign Manual if your Majesty shall graciously so please.

The Lord Chancellor's friends at Oxford remain confident: the Chancellor himself thinks that he cannot be beat without difficulty, but he does not think that the result can be confidently foretold. (14812)

4041   *Letters from* SPENCER PERCEVAL *to the* KING, *and the replies*

[*Downg. St., 2 Dec. 1809.*] Mr Perceval transmits for your Majesty's perusal, Lord Wellesley's answer to Mr Perceval's letter acquainting his Lordship with your Majesty's gracious concurrence in Mr Perecval's humble recommendation

[1] Charles Stuart succeeded him as Minister at Lisbon on 12 Feb. 1810.

that your Majesty should be pleased to confer the late Duke of Portland's Garter upon Lord Wellesley. Mr Perceval trusts that your Majesty will think that he would not be doing justly by Lord Wellesley if he witheld from your Majesty the expressions of his Lordship's gratitude upon this occasion.[1] (14813)

[1] Perceval first thought of offering the Garter to the Duke of Richmond, to whom he wrote on 30 Oct.: 'The very uncertain state of the Duke of Portland's health, makes it desireable, that I should be prepared, in the event of his death, how to advise his Majy. with regard to the disposition to be made of his Grace's Garter. There is no person whose services to the King, or whose good disposition towards the present Government, appears to me to give him so good a claim to it, as your Grace. I wish therefore, before any steps may be taken upon this subject, to know your Grace's sentiments with regard to it; and particularly under the circumstances in which it may come to be considered. I have not had a syllable of communication with the King upon this subject. I therefore do not know, from his Majesty, what his views may be with regard to it; but I understand from those who have been acquainted with them, on former occasions, that he may have so far given the Earl of Aylesford reason to expect the next vacant Garter, that his Majesty may hardly feel himself at liberty to bestow it upon anyone else. To what extent therefore his Majesty may be pledged I cannot tell, but if he is completely so any more proper or useful application of it would be attempted in vain. Your Grace will therefore understand what follows as subject to the contingency of his Majesty's being at liberty to admit of this honor being conferred in the manner best suited to the character & interests of his Government. In that event, then, I have no difficulty in saying that if your Grace should wish to succeed to the D. of Portland's Garter, as far as depends upon me it shall certainly be yours. And I only wish to submit to your Grace's consideration what I conceive will be the case, upon the D. of Portland's death, with respect to one probable competitor with your Grace for it, and I will leave it to your Grace to determine how far that circumstance should influence your decision. The Duke of Newcastle has already applied to the King, requesting to succeed the D. of Portland, as Lord Lieut. of the County of Nottingham. Connected as we have been with the D. of Portland, and related as our Administration still continues to be with his Grace's, if Lord Titchfield should wish to succeed his father in the Lieutenancy and should be disposed to support the Government (which I have some reason to suppose will be the case) I could not feel myself at liberty much less should I be inclined, to do otherwise than recommend that he should so succeed. This would not fail to occasion great disappointment to the D. of Newcastle, and unless the effect of that disappointment could be cured by some other mark of the King's favor, I fear his Grace, whose Parliamentary influence is very considerable, would be disinclined to give us his assistance. The Garter, I conceive, would be such a favor as would reconcile him to the disappointment, and if your Grace's claims did not stand in the way, or were to be waived by your Grace, I should think it prudent to keep it in such a state as to be at liberty to offer it to him. Having thus stated to your Grace the whole of what I feel upon this point, I repeat, that subject to what the King may have engaged with regard to it, your Grace shall decide between yourself & the D. of Newcastle. (Richmond MSS. 72/1502.)

Then, Lord Bathurst wrote to the Duke of Richmond on 6 Nov.: 'I have this moment receiv'd your letter. The promise of the King to Ld. Aylesford is supposed to have been made at the time of his recovery from his last illness in 1804, when he made similar promises to Lords Dartmouth & Winchilsea. These two first have been performed, and it was apprehended that he would renew his instances in favour of Lord Aylesford on this occasion, as he had done to a certain degree when the two last Ribbons were disposed of. In the audience which Perceval had last Wednesday the King did not come out with it, and it is hoped that he will see the prudence of not insisting upon it now. The death of the Duke of Portland is too recent to have heard yet from Lord Titchfield; but his wishes on the subject of the Lord Lieutenancy of Nottingham must be known soon: and I should have waited until something had been known, if Perceval had not this moment come into me to tell me of an unexpected difficulty in the whole business. Arbuthnot has just put into his hands a correspondence between Lord Wellesley & the Duke of Portland, the one pressing for & the other engaging to procure if possible a promise from the King of the first vacant Ribbon. It appears that this had been proposed to the King, who declined making any positive engagement, but in the account the Duke gave of this transaction, he represented the King as having said everything except a direct promise. Perceval has beg'd I would lose no time in putting you in full possession of this, of which he was until this day perfectly ignorant, but he thought that in your conversations with Pole you should be aware of this claim....I think there is a difference between Lord Wellesley accepting office & having the Ribbon at the same time; and Lord Wellesley asking it as a reward for past service when he supported Government without office—but he is so great a card at the present moment, and *so aware of it*, that I know not what to say....The King on Wednesday said something in reference to Lord Wellesley's claims...

(464)

[*The King's reply, Windsor Castle, 3 Dec.*] The King acknowledges the receipt of Mr Perceval's letter, inclosing one from Lord Wellesley, which H.M. returns. (14813)

[*From Perceval, Downg. St., 5 Dec. 1809.*] Mr Perceval humbly solicits your Majesty's gracious consideration to a paper upon the state of the finances of your Majesty's kingdom, which Mr Perceval thought it his duty to prepare and circulate for the information of his colleagues a little before the close of the D. of Portland's Administration. From this paper your Majesty will perceive how serious a duty is imposed upon your Majesty's servants to endeavour to reduce the expences of the War in every department of your Majesty's Government within as narrow limits as good faith to yr. Majesty's Allies and the security of your Majesty's dominions will allow.

Mr Perceval transmits to your Majesty the papers which he has received from his Serene Highness the Duke of Brunswick. (14814)

[*The King's reply, Windsor Castle, 6 Dec.*] The King has received Mr Perceval's paper upon the state of the finances which his Majesty will return as soon as he

but nothing distinct. (Entre nous—Lord Wellesley is no favourite with his Majesty.)' (*Ibid.,* 70/1349.)

Finally, the Duke of Richmond wrote to Lord Bathurst on 4 Dec.: 'Mr. Perceval informs me that after my concurrence in any arrangement that might be thought useful to Govt. abt. the Garter he has thought it best to recommend Ld. Wellesley...Ld. Wellesley founds his claims on their having been admitted by Mr. Pitt, Ld. Grenville & the D. of Portland. Nobody is more ready to acknowledge Ld. Wellesley's abilities than I am and his services in India. He received a step in the Peerage which it rather appears Mr. Pitt thought sufficient as he did not recommend him to his Majesty for the Garter when he had an opportunity, and I must own I think if Ld. Wellesley's claim on Mr. Pitt is allowed, that it wd. have been more proper to have given him the Garter Ld. Lonsdale had (who gained two steps in the Peerage at the same time) than that now vacant. The plea of Ld. Grenville admitting his claim is most extraordinary. Ld. Wellesley certainly wd. not have taken the Garter from an Administration he was not willing to support, and I conceive a person who was ready to act with that Administration has no particular claim to the favor of his Majesty or the present Administration. The third claim is the correspondence with the D. of Portland. The Duke was of too mild a disposition to say No, and if Mr. Perceval means to fulfill all the half promises of his predecessor he will find but little patronage for himself. For instance, I know of strong hopes being given to three Irish Peers that they shd. succeed to the next vacant Representative Peerage. I believe this correspondence was not long ago, and if so I must own I am surprised the D. of Portland shd. not have considered me as he invariably acknowledged more merit to my administration in this country than I claimed. You will recollect the state in which Ireland was represented to be when I accepted the situation of Lord Lieutenant. You will also remember the weight I took off the mind of the D. of Portland by that acceptance, and that at the very time Ld. Wellesley was making his claim Ireland was more quiet than it had been for years. You will do me the justice to say I never mentioned my claim 'till Mr. Perceval wrote to me and will I trust not think I have now said too much.

'I believe there is little doubt I might have secured the first vacancy if I had made it a sine qua non of the acceptance to the office I hold. Do not suppose I am out of humour. Govt. will find me as anxious as ever to support them and I assure you I regret the Ribbon much more on their account and that of my old friend Ld. Wellesley than on my own.

'The world will never be persuaded that the Garter was not the price Govt. offered and he accepted for his taking office; it will make him extremely unpopular, and consequently it will hurt Govert. People in general will think he can carry what he pleases and indeed it will be difficult to prevail on him not to join in this opinion. I have now done with this subject. I shall never ask for the Garter, and to say the truth, tho' I shd. accept it from an Administration I lookd. up to, it can never give me the same satisfaction it wd. have done in this instance.' (*Ibid.,* 72/1513.)

shall have been able to consider it more fully. The King has long seen with concern the encreased expences of the War & had felt the necessity of reducing them as far as may be consistent with the security of the country, from a conviction that they could not be borne much longer at this rate, and that a peace would, under present circumstances & those which may be looked forward to for some ensuing years, be destructive to this country. (14815)

[*From Perceval, Downing St., 7 Dec.*] Mr Perceval acquaints your Majesty that he has received a communication from the Duke of Richmond this day in which his Grace suggests the propriety of recommending the Marquis of Sligo[1] to your Majesty for the Order of St. Patrick, which will be vacated by the Marquis Wellesley's resignation of that Order upon accepting the Order of the Garter. Mr Perceval concurs entirely with the Duke of Richmond in the propriety of this recommendation, if your Majesty should be pleased to approve it.

Mr. Perceval omitted to mention to your Majesty when he received your Majesty's commands upon the appointment of Dr Goodall to the Provostship of Eton College, the circumstance of Dr Goodall's being in possession of a Canonry of Windsor; Mr Perceval understands that Dr Davies resigned his Canonry upon being appointed to the Provostship, and Mr Perceval is not aware of any circumstance which should make it necessary or expedient to make such a difference in favor of Dr Goodall as to leave him in the possession of both. Mr Perceval therefore has witheld from Doctor Goodall the notification of the appointment this day, that he might be able to receive your Majesty's commands as to the propriety of signifying to Dr Goodall that it would be expected that he should resign his Canonry of Windsor. (14816–17)

[*The King's reply, Windsor Castle, 8 Dec.*] The King acquiesces in the recommendation of the Duke of Richmond which Mr Perceval has conveyed with the expression of his own concurrence that the Marquis of Sligo should receive the Order of St Patrick whenever the season shall admit of Lord Wellesley's previous investment with the Order of the Garter.

In regard to Doctor Goodall's being expected to resign the Canonry of Windsor upon his succeeding to the Provostship of Eton College, H.M. observes that, altho' Doctor Davies took that step, his predecessor, Doctor Barnard,[2] retained the Canonry with the Provostship. The King however does not object to the proposed communication to Doctor Goodall, who may then make his option.

The King returns Mr Perceval's paper on finance & has only to repeat that he shall approve of any practicable reduction of expenditure which may be consistent with the general interests & security of the State. (14817)

[1] Howe Peter, 2nd Marquess of Sligo (1788–1845), succeeded his father, 2 Jan. 1809. Styled Viscount Westport until 1800, and Earl of Altamont from 29 Dec. 1800, when his father was created Marquess, until his father's death. K.P., 24 March 1810; Governor-General of Jamaica, 1833–6.

[2] Edward Barnard (1717–81), Headmaster of Eton, 1754; Provost, 1765–81; Canon of Windsor, 1760–81.

[*From Perceval, Downg. St., 9 Dec.*] Mr Perceval acquaints your Majesty that the Marquis of Sligo has very gratefully accepted the intimation made to him by Mr Perceval of your Majesty's gracious intention towards his Lordship of conferring upon him the Order of St. Patrick when the Marquis of Wellesley shall have been invested with the Order of the Garter.

Mr. Perceval has seen Dr Goodall since Mr Perceval received your Majesty's pleasure with regard to the Canonry of Windsor. Dr Goodall has made so strong a representation to Mr Perceval of the situation of the Provostship, of the necessary expences attendant upon the due and proper support of that situation, to which circumstances Mr Perceval was a stranger before, that however desireable he felt it, from other considerations, that the Canonry of Windsor should have been vacated, yet he must admit the reasonableness of Dr Goodall's representation, and would therefore with your Majesty's permission submit to your Majesty that Dr Goodall should be allowed to retain the Canonry with the Provostship. And Mr Perceval has the less reluctance in bringing this question again under your Majesty's consideration, because he rather collected from your Majesty's note that some doubt might be entertained as to the reasonableness of the precedent which he had referred to in the case of Dr Davies. (14818)

[*The King's reply, Windsor Castle, 10 Dec.*] The King has received with satisfaction Mr Perceval's intimation of his concurrence in the desire which Doctor Goodall has expressed to retain the Canonry of Windsor with the Provostship, & his M. is sensible of the liberal motives which have produced Mr Perceval's recommendation to this effect. The King was aware that the necessary expences attending the situation of Provost were considered as requiring the aid in question, particularly when the value of the situation is referred to which he relinquishes, nor was it thought handsome that Doctor Davies should have been called upon to give up the Canonry. (14819)

4042   *Letters from the* MARQUESS WELLESLEY *to the* KING, *and the reply*

[*Foreign Office, 11 Dec. 1809, Monday, 11 p.m.*] The Marquess Wellesley submits to your Majesty the expediency of sending to Spain without delay a person properly qualified to take charge of the affairs of that Mission, and therefore proposes that the Honorable Henry Wellesley be appointed your Majesty's Envoy Extraordinary & Minister Plenipotentiary in Spain. He requests your Majesty's gracious commands on this appointment. (14820)

[*From Lord Wellesley, Foreign Office, 11 Dec., Monday, 11 p.m.*] The Marquess Wellesley has the honor to submit for your Majesty's royal signature an answer from your Majesty to the letter received from the King of Prussia on the birth of a Prince. By reference to the books of the Office it appears that the letter received from the King of Prussia is similar to the last letter[1] addressed by the King of

---

[1] Frederick William II's youngest son, Prince William (1783–1851), was born on 3 July 1783.

Prussia to your Majesty on a similar occasion during the existence of peace. The answer now submitted for your Majesty's signature is therefore drawn in the same terms as your Majesty's answer on that occasion. (14821)

[*From Lord Wellesley, Foreign Office, 11 Dec., Monday, 11 p.m.*] The Marquess Wellesley has the honor to inform your Majesty that an Austrian messenger arrived yesterday evening with a flag of truce from Calais, bringing dispatches to Prince Stahremberg. Prince Stahremberg this morning informed the Marquess Wellesley that this messenger brings his recall; he also stated that he had received an official copy of the Treaty of Peace[1] between France & Austria. Although these communications from Prince Stahremberg are not formal, it appeared to be proper to submit them to your Majesty without delay. To these are added a private note from Prince Stahremberg enclosing the Treaty and the copy of a private letter addressed by Prince Stahremberg to his Sovereign. The Marquess Wellesley hopes that your Majesty will approve his conduct in submitting these papers to your Majesty's consideration.[2] (14822)

[*From Lord Wellesley,*[3] *Foreign Office, 11 Dec., 11 p.m.*] The Marquess Wellesley has the honor to inform your Majesty that an Envoy Extraordinary and Minister Plenipotentiary from the King of Persia arrived in London on Tuesday evening, December the fourth.[4] The Earl Bathurst had paid the judicious and extra-ordinary attention of sending his Lordship's private secretary Mr. Vaughan,[5] and another gentleman acquainted with the Persian language to meet the Persian Minister at the distance of forty miles from London. A house had also been prepared for his reception in Mansfield Street, Portland Place; and in every respect, unusual marks of consideration had been manifested towards him. It appeared, however, that some dissatisfaction existed in the mind of the Persian Minister, who had expected to be received with those ceremonies unusally observed in oriental Courts, and particularly with military honors.

The Marquess Wellesley trusts that he shall obtain your Majesty's royal approbation in the appointment which he thought it his duty to make of a person intimately conversant with the Persian language and customs to attend the Persian Minister immediately upon his arrival in London. This appointment is conformable to the established usages of Persia, and is deemed indispensable to the due observance of the rites of hospitality. The officer of this description

---

[1] The Treaty of Schönbrunn, 14 October. Austria ceded to Napoleon, for the Princes of the Confederation of the Rhine, Salzburg, Berchtesgaden and a large part of Upper Austria; to Napoleon, for his own use, Trieste, Carinthia, Croatia and Dalmatia; to Saxony, the whole of western Galicia; and part of eastern Galicia to Russia. She adhered to the Continental System, paid an indemnity, and agreed to reduce her army to 150,000 men.
[2] Wellesley, then, started off as Foreign Secretary with a great flourish, writing or dictating four letters at 11 p.m. Long before he resigned the Foreign Secretaryship he could hardly be induced to put pen to paper and Ministers abroad were left without instructions. The reason for this shortcoming is sufficiently well known.   [3] Not in Wellesley's own hand.   [4] He meant the 5th.
[5] Sir Charles Richard Vaughan (1774–1849), Lord Bathurst's private secretary, 1809; Secretary of Legation in Spain, 1810–11; Secretary of Embassy, 1811–20, and Minister there *ad interim*, 1815–16; Secretary of Embassy in Paris, April 1820; Minister to Switzerland, 1823–5, and to the U.S.A., 1825–35; Knighted, 1833.

appointed to attend all Foreign Ministers in Persia is styled *Mehmandar*. The Marquess Wellesley accordingly named Sir Gore Ouseley,[1] Baronet, to attend the Persian Minister in that capacity. The reports of Sir Gore Ouseley are transmitted for your Majesty's information.

It appears that Sir Harford Jones[2] (your Majesty's Envoy Extraordinary to Persia) was received in that country with honors superior to those due to his rank by the established usages of that country; and it is evident that those honors were paid from an anxious desire to cultivate a close intimacy of alliance with your Majesty. It seemed therefore to be advisable that a reciprocal disposition should be manifested on the part of your Majesty's Government to such an extent as might not be inconsistent with the established usages of this Court, or injurious to your Majesty's dignity. Under these impressions, the Marquess Wellesley has this day visited the Persian Minister, although that attention cannot be claimed by any European Minister below the rank of Ambassador.

With the same view, the Marquess Wellesley humbly submits to your Majesty the expediency of granting a Public Entrance to the Persian Minister; and, considering the extraordinary attention paid to Sir Harford Jones in Persia, and the great efforts which the French Government has made to alienate the King of Persia from your Majesty, it would appear to be highly desirable that the ceremony should be distinguished by every convenient degree of splendour. This mark of attention will be peculiarly acceptable to the Court of Persia; and as the Minister is a personage of high birth (being nearly connected with those who have held the most distinguished situations in that country, & allied to the female branches of the Royal Family) this testimony of your Majesty's consideration would probably produce the most favorable impression in Persia.

At the interview which the Marquess Wellesley had with the Persian Minister this day, he appeared to be reconciled to his reception, but to be extremely anxious for an early opportunity of presenting to your Majesty the letters from the King of Persia. The Persian Minister is also charged with letters from the Queen of Persia to her Majesty, which he is very desirous of presenting.

The Marquess Wellesley requests your Majesty to honor him with your royal commands respecting the time at which your Majesty may be pleased to receive the Persian Minister, and respecting the Public Entrance of that Minister. (14823–8)

[*The King's reply, Windsor Castle, 12 Dec.*] In consequence of the representation made by Marquis Wellesley, the King will not object to the Persian Minister making a Public Entrance, but as these Oriental ceremonies are little suited to the simplicity of European Courts & inconsistent with the general practice of this country, the King desires that care may be taken that the adoption of them upon this occasion be not drawn into a precedent. In the present state of his sight, his

---

[1] Sir Gore Ouseley (1770–1844), created Baronet, 24 Sept. 1808. Ambassador to Persia, 1811–14. G.C.H., 1831. Appointed, Dec. 1809, to the office of *mihmandár* to Mirza Abul-Hasán, the Persian Ambassador visiting England, who returned home with Ouseley in July 1810.

[2] Sir Harford Jones (1764–1847), in the service of the East India Company in his early years. Created Baronet, 22 Aug. 1807; Envoy to Persia, 1809–11 (though appointed in June 1807, he arrived at Tehran only in Feb. 1809). Took the additional name of Brydges in 1826.

Majesty can receive the Persian Minister at the Queen's Palace only, & Wednesday sennight may be the day fixed for his Audience if then prepared for it. The Queen cannot receive him until January, when she goes to London. The appointment of Sir Gore Ouseley to attend the Persian Minister appears necessary & therefore very proper.

The King approves of Marquis Wellesley's having submitted to him the communications from Prince Starhemberg, also of his recommendation of Mr Henry Wellesley for the mission to Spain. (14829)

4043   THE DUKE OF BRUNSWICK *to the* KING, *and the reply*

[*Londre, ce 12 Dec. 1809.*] Votre Majesté a eû la grace de me faire savoir par son Ministre Monsieur Percéval ses intentions de bienveillance qui décide de mon sort et de celui de mes enfans.

Veulliés, Sire, agréer mes très humble rémercimens d'avoir fixé mes révènues à sept milles livres par an, et soyés convaincue que je tâcherai de me rendre digne de ces marques de haute protection.

Je saisies avec empressement cette occasion pour supplier Votre Majesté d'agréer mes sentimens, du plus profond dévouement, et de l'hommage très réspêctueux avec les quels je suis, Sire [etc.]. (14830)

[*The King's reply, Windsor Castle, le 13 Dec.*] J'ai bien reçu hier la lettre que vous m'avez addressé par le canal de Mr Perceval & je m'empresse de vous assurer combien j'ai étè charmé d'avoir pu marquer l'interêt que m'inspire votre sort & celui de vos enfans, en contribuant aux avantages d'un asyle que les malheurs qu'éprouve le continent vous ont fait chercher dans ce pays. (14831)

4044   THE EARL OF LIVERPOOL *to the* KING, *and the reply*

[*Charles Street, 13 Dec. 1809.*] Lord Liverpool begs leave most humbly to submit to your Majesty the draft of a dispatch which it is proposed with your Majesty's approbation to send to Lord Wellington in answer to his letter on the defence of Portugal.

Lord Liverpool has felt it his duty at the same time to send to your Majesty the letter of Lord Wellington to which this draft is an answer, in order that your Majesty may have an opportunity of again considering the whole subject. (14832)

[*The King's reply, Windsor Castle, 14 Dec.*] The King entirely approves of the dispatch to Lord Wellington submitted by Lord Liverpool which appears to his Majesty very clear and explicit. (14832)

4045   LORD ELDON *to the* KING, *and the reply*

[*15 Dec. 1809.*] The Lord Chancellor, offering his most humble duty to your Majesty, is apprised that your Majesty has learnt the issue of the Oxford contest by the messenger placed at Oxford by Lord Liverpool and the Chancellor.[1] The Lord Chancellor cannot but deeply regret that this contest has not been brought to a more fortunate termination: and if this contest could have been rendered successful, if carried on by one candidate only against Lord Grenville, and that candidate not Lord Eldon, the Lord Chancellor can never cease to lament that the Duke of Beaufort did not stand alone through the contest. The Chancellor, upon much painful reflection upon this subject, cannot convince himself that he could possibly have avoided taking the part which he has adopted, either in allowing himself originally to be named a candidate, which was unavoidable, or in continuing to be a candidate till the close of the poll. After his friends had been numerously engaged, it does not appear to him that he could with honour or with advantage to the general cause retire, unless his friends had thought it proper, voluntarily, to transfer their support to another candidate. The Chancellor had no personal view in this contest, and he earnestly hopes that his Majesty does not disapprove the conduct which, acting to the best of his judgement & upon public grounds only, he has pursued.

In the result of the contest, supported as the Chancellor has been by a great body of most respectable persons, the Chancellor feels no painful personal disappointment. In examining that result upon general & the most important grounds, the Chancellor's apprehensions are somewhat softened by the fact that the majority of Lord Grenville above Lord Eldon only is small & the fact that the opinion of the University ought to be collected, not by looking only at the numbers who polled for Lord Eldon, but at those also who voted for the Duke of Beaufort, and by circumstances which grew out of the fact that both the Chancellor & the Duke of Beaufort were candidates, which were thought perhaps unavoidable, but which might not have been deemed clearly so, upon a more just & firmer view of the subject. (14833–4)

[*The King's reply, Windsor Castle, 16 Dec.*] The King has received the Chancellor's letter and sincerely concurs with him in lamenting the issue of the contest at Oxford both on public grounds & from motives personal to the Chancellor. His Majesty desires the Chancellor will feel assured that he has approved his conduct throughout the whole course of this business, as well by allowing himself to be named a candidate, and as continuing so to the close of the poll; his Majesty being very sensible that he could not with honour or with advantage to the general cause retire after his friends had been engaged to support his well-founded pretensions.[2] (14835)

[1] The voting (13 and 14 Dec.) for the Chancellorship of the University was as follows: Grenville, 406; Eldon, 393; Beaufort, 238. Eldon wrote to his brother on 6 Jan. 1810: 'Charles Long [Paymaster-General] canvassed throughout for Beaufort. He says, I hear, he did not know I was the Government candidate.' (Eldon MSS.) And, again, in an undated letter: 'A Bishop tells me that the Princess [of Wales] got Lord Grenville 17 votes.' (*Ibid.*) And, in Dec. 1809 (postmark, 30 Dec.): 'If Old England does not rue the day that Oxford elected Grenville I am greatly mistaken. As to the *clergy* who voted for him it is quite scandalous. The triumph it is among the Dissenters, Methodists, etc. to see *them* so act, I am told, is inconceivable.' (*Ibid.*)
[2] Eldon described this as 'a very handsome letter', adding, 'Some about him behaved sadly in misleading themselves and the Duke of Beaufort.' (Twiss, *Eldon*, II, 113.) Eldon had written to the King

[*Foreign Office, 17 Dec. 1809, Sunday, 10 p.m.*] The Marquess Wellesley has the honor to submit to your Majesty an official Note received this day from Prince Starhemberg, requesting passports for himself and his suite, and also desiring a flag of truce for the return of the Austrian messenger lately arrived from Paris. It is proposed, with your Majesty's gracious approbation, to grant Prince Stahremberg's requests. A private note from Prince Stahremberg is also submitted to your Majesty's notice. The Marquess Wellesley proposes to submit for your Majesty's approbation some observations on the late Treaty of Peace between Austria & France to accompany the official answer to Prince Stahremberg. (14836)

[*From Lord Wellesley, Foreign Office, 17 Dec., Sunday, 10 p.m.*] The Marquess Wellesley has the honor to acquaint your Majesty that it has been found impracticable to make the necessary preparations for the Public Entrance of the Persian Envoy previously to Wednesday next. On similar occasions it has not been unusual to grant a private Audience previously to the ceremony of a Public Entrance; and as the Persian Envoy is most anxious to have the honor of presenting his Letters of Credence to your Majesty at the earliest moment, it is humbly proposed that he should be admitted to that honor on Wednesday next in the accustomed mode, and that the ceremonial of his Public Entrance should be postponed to a more distant day. (14837)

to ascertain, as he said, 'whether any part of my conduct could justify the Oxford reports that I had not his support, or that he was hurt that I did not give way to Beaufort.' (*Ibid.*, II, III.) 'My object', he said in another letter (postmark, 21 Dec.) 'was to have the means of setting myself right, not only with myself but others, and I can't see why the King's letter should not be communicated—not *published*, but communicated. I have myself shown it to different persons. I let him know my whole mind yesterday, and I solemnly declare to you that I would have resigned at my audience if it had not been from personal feelings about him...' (Eldon MSS. To his brother.) In another undated letter to his brother, Eldon again considered the idea of resigning: 'I agree with you that the late transaction has unmasked many enemies. Has it exhibited any friends? I mean among political men? I know of none. And this, as to my business, is truly important. You ask me what part I mean to take among the contending factions. *Holding my office* I can, with no honour, act against even those who, being unmasked, are my enemies. This creates no difficulty because I could resign it. The difficulty is furnished by the very peculiar situation in which I stand *at this moment* to the King. He and all his and all also that hate me and many that do not, will, if I go, attribute all that will infallibly happen of what is mortifying to him, whether I go or stay, to me. If I go, to whom can I go? Whether I go now or at the fortnight, or a month hence, when all will go? Nobody will receive me if I were disposed to offer myself to anybody—but I have no such disposition. These men have used me ill, but so have all others living who have gone before them. And I am weary—years—declining health—two raps on the head in twelve months, more serious than is supposed, I verily believe—the reflections of the last month—the conviction that there is no comfort in the company of any of these people—all lead me to what I think alone becomes me—retirement—that I may settle my accounts before I go hence...Retirement, it is true, may open to other men, who may be wished to be therein, the situation I hold. But that must always be the case, and I cannot live in misery and insecurity on *that account*. I must either go now or with the Administration a few weeks hence. The circumstances between the King and myself make it *at this instant* very delicate and difficult. Whenever it is, the step is final. I abuse others about the Oxford election: others attribute the failure entirely to myself in not canvassing as other candidates did.' (Eldon MSS.) Eldon, then, as always, found it difficult to make up his mind whether to stay or go (on one occasion he could not even decide to have his hair cut until Lady Eldon returned home and made up his mind for him).

[*From Lord Wellesley, Foreign Office, 17 Dec., Sunday, 10 p.m.*] The Marquess Wellesley has the honor to acquaint your Majesty that Mr Erskine, your Majesty's late Minister in America, having expressed his desire to be presented to your Majesty at the next Levée, it has not been thought necessary to refuse him the honor of being presented to your Majesty in the ordinary manner by your Majesty's Secretary of State for Foreign Affairs; but it has been fully explained that although Mr Erskine could not justly be denied access to your Majesty's presence, he is not to infer from that indulgence any diminution of the disapprobation which has been signifyed to him respecting various circumstances in his conduct in America, of which he proposes to offer further explanation.

With this reserve, Lord Wellesley hopes to meet your Majesty's gracious approbation in presenting Mr Erskine to your Majesty in the ordinary manner on Wednesday next. (14838)

[*From Lord Wellesley, Foreign Office, 17 Dec., Sunday, 10 p.m.*] The Marquess Wellesley submits to your Majesty's gracious consideration the expediency of appointing Mr Henry Wellesley to be of your Majesty's Privy Council previously to his departure for Spain. The peculiar circumstances of that country in the present crisis appear to require that the person charged with your Majesty's credentials should possess every advantage which can give additional weight to his representations.

It is humbly proposed that Mr Wellesley should be presented to your Majesty on Wednesday next and should take leave on the same day, and that, with your Majesty's gracious permission, he should at that time be sworn of your Majesty's Privy Council.

The Marquess Wellesley further proposes to your Majesty that Mr Charles Edward[1] Vaughan be appointed Secretary of Legation in Spain. Mr Vaughan has been for some time private secretary to Lord Bathurst, & is well acquainted with the language, manners & customs of Spain, having visited most parts of that country. (14839–40)

[*The King's reply, Windsor Castle, 18 Dec.*] The King has received Lord Wellesley's letters & approves of a compliance with Prince Starhemberg's requests. His Majesty also acquiesces in Mr Henry Wellesley's being appointed of the Privy Council and sworn in on Wednesday next, when the Persian Envoy may be admitted to a private Audience, & when Mr Erskine may be presented to his Majesty with the reserve properly pointed out by Lord Wellesley.

The King also sanctions the appointment of Mr Charles Vaughan as Secretary of Legation in Spain. (14841)

[1] Should be Richard.

[*London, 18 Dec. 1809.*] Mr Ryder has the honor of transmitting to your Majesty a copy of the Address of the Common Council to be presented to your Majesty at the Levée on Wednesday next. It was not communicated to Mr Ryder till this afternoon. Your Majesty's servants have since met to consult upon the answer which they might think it expedient humbly to propose for your Majesty's decision as proper to be given by your Majesty to the Address, but they separated without coming to any conclusion, and are to meet again tomorrow for the purpose of resuming the consideration of the same subject. Mr Ryder understands from good authority that the exertions of the friends of your Majesty's Government in the City have succeeded in moulding the Address into a shape much less objectionable than that in which it was originally proposed and carried at the first meeting of the Common Council. But though the amendments thus introduced into it have rendered it far less offensive in its terms, they have rather encreased than diminished the difficulty of answering it.[1] (14842)

[*The King's reply, Windsor Castle, 19 Dec.*] The King has read the proposed Address from the City, transmitted by Mr Ryder, which appears to him even in its present shape very objectionable and unnecessary. His Majesty conceives that a short dry answer would be the fittest to return to it. (14843)

[*From Richard Ryder, London, 19 Dec.*] Mr Ryder has the honor of transmitting to your Majesty a copy of the answer to the Address of the Common Council which your Majesty's servants have, under all the difficulties of the case and after much deliberation, agreed upon, and humbly submit to your Majesty's consideration. The meeting was attended by all your Majesty's confidential servants, excepting the Earl of Chatham, who desired to retire, considering the question under discussion to be more or less connected with his own conduct. The last paragraph has been introduced to stifle further Addresses by pointing out that although your Majesty has seen no reason to institute a military enquiry, there is no indisposition on the part of your Majesty's Government to produce such information as may be satisfactory. (14846)

[*The King's reply, Windsor Castle, 20 Dec.*] The answer to the Address of the Common Council which Mr Ryder has submitted appears to his Majesty perfectly proper. (14847)

4048 SPENCER PERCEVAL *to the* KING, *and the reply*

[*Downing St., 19 Dec. 1809.*] Mr Perceval humbly acquaints your Majesty that Lord Sheffield has for a long time been very anxious to be admitted into

---

[1] This Address, asking for a rigid, impartial and general enquiry into the expeditions to the Peninsula and to Holland was taken to St. James's by the Lord Mayor and Sheriffs, who, however, 'were not only prevented from delivering the same to the King at the Levée, but also denied a personal audience of his Majesty...Such right was never before questioned or denied, and they were thereby prevented from laying their just complaints and grievances before their Sovereign.' (*Parl. Deb.*, xv, 601.)

your Majesty's most honorable Privy Council—and he has particularly pressed it with the view of assisting at the Committee of Council for Trade.[1] While it was uncertain who would be the President of that Committee I declined mentioning his Lordship's name to your Majesty because I concluded it not desireable to introduce a new member into that Committee without communicating with its President. Upon Lord Bathurst's returning to that Comttee. Ld. Sheffield has renewed his application, and renewed it thro' Ld. Bathurst himself—and in submitting Lord Sheffield's name to your Majesty to be made a Privy Counsellor, if your Majesty should be so graciously pleased, I mention it not only with the concurrence but at the desire of Lord Bathurst. (14844)

[*The King's reply, Windsor Castle, 20 Dec.*] The King has received Mr Perceval's letter and his Majesty will not object to Lord Sheffield's admission to the Privy Council, with a view to his assisting at the Committee of Council for Trade. (14845)

4049 PRINCESS AMELIA *to the* KING, *and the reply*

[*22 Dec. 1809.*] I hope you will forgive the liberty I take in addressing a letter to you, but I am now so easily flurried & agitated that I do not like to trust myself to speak to you lest I should distress you, & as your kind & daily visits are the greatest comforts of my life I cannot bear to risk your suffering by them.

I cannot disguise from myself that I have not gained any ground since my return from Weyth., nor has anything yet tried done me essential good. I have strove hard to think I decieve myself, but I find it is not so & the evil is still there. In consequence of Dr. Pope's conference with the physicians & their present plan, I have determined, without naming it to Dr. Pope or any of my family except Adolphus, to communicate to you my earnest wishes for further advice. I feel it a duty to preserve that life God has given me & I hope I have not proved unworthy of all the blessings I enjoy, but I feel it is impossible for me to submit to any further operation without the assurance of its being absolutely necessary, & in closing the seatons I consider it a *risk* & *also* as *leading* by the doctors' own avowal to the chance of the necessity of their being reopened, which is still more confirmed by a conversation I have had again with Dr. Pope this eveng., in whom I place *so much confidence & to whom* I *asked* fairly whether he thought it was necessary to heal them. He answered me by *saying* that they all agreed the seatons

---

[1] Lord Sheffield had long coveted this distinction. Lord Auckland had written to Lord Grenville, then Prime Minister, on 11 Feb. 1806: 'Lord Sheffield means to apply to you to place him in the Privy Council, and afterwards at the Board of Trade....But though he is friendly, honourable, well-informed and sedulous, you know well that those qualities alone are not sufficient to facilitate the business of a Board which is in danger of being overwhelmed by the variety of applications crowding into it.' (*Dropmore Papers*, VIII, 29.) Sheffield himself wrote to the Duke of Richmond, the Lord Lieutenant of Ireland, on 11 March 1808: 'I was quite tired of the repeated factious and party [?] declamations of Lord Grenville and his adherents, between whom and Sir Francis Burdett it is not easy to discover any very material difference, therefore I availed myself of the advantage of leaving my proxy with a friend of Government.' (Richmond MSS. 69/1246.)

had been of great use tho' they *decided* they were to be healed, but that he, Dr. Pope, thought one was *necessary*, & if I cld. have one made *forwarder*, then closing these would be desirable. Under these circumstances, my beloved father, I think, cannot wonder & will not object, I hope, to my having wished for more advice that such steps may not be taken without as much certainty as human beings can have that it really is necessary. I therefore venture to lay my case before you & implore as my last resource that I may see Dr. Bailley[1] who is so good an anatomist, which in my *intricate* case I think would be of good benefit, & Sir Henry Halford, who is your Majesty's physician.

The greatest scruple I have in making this application to you is the additional expence, for I feel every day more with deep regret the great burthen I have so long been to you & I am so unwilling to trespass further on your parental kindness & generosity that I cannot help adding I *feel quite equal* to incuring this fresh expence myself.

I should wish much to be allowed to see these two doctors *unprejudiced* & that they should hear *from myself* without any communication with any of the four others till they have heard my own story.

In the midst of all my sufferings I still feel it a duty to try to preserve life, & it would be a great satisfaction to me to feel nothing had been left undone that could promote a chance of my recovery, & therefore, my dearest father, I trust to your goodness, of which I have such daily proof, to grant this request. (Add. Georgian 14/145)

[*The King's reply, Windsor Castle, 23 Dec.*] I have received your affectionate letter and will not defer until this afternoon assuring you that I readily acquiesce in the wish which it conveys and that I entirely admit the propriety of the feeling under which it was written. Under a continuation of suffering which no one can more deeply lament than I do, and under the impression that you have not received the benefit which you might have expected from the advice to which recourse has as yet been had, the desire to consult others at a moment when additional torture is suggested appears to me both natural and reasonable, and I should have been wanting in the warm affection which I feel for you & in the anxiety with which I must ever wish to promote whatever can tend to your comfort & relief, if I had hesitated a moment in agreeing to it. When I see you this afternoon I will talk over with you the steps to be taken, but in the meantime I must assure you that I never can allow that you should be subjected to any expence upon this occasion. (Add. Georgian 14/146)

4050 LORD MULGRAVE *to the* KING, *and the reply*

[*Admiralty, 22 Dec. 1809.*] Lord Mulgrave has the painful duty of submitting humbly to your Majesty the case of James Nehemiah Taylour, late surgeon of your Majesty's ship Jamaica, tried before a naval court martial assembled on

---

[1] Matthew Baillie (1761–1823), physician to St George's Hospital, 1787–99; physician extraordinary to the King.

board your Majesty's ship Gladiator on the 11th & 12th days of the present month on a charge of the perpetration of the unnatural and detestable crime expressed in the 29th Article of War, and condemned to suffer death. The fact was proved by the concurrent testimony of three witnesses, but the prisoner having urgently called the attention of the Court to a question of law set forth in his defence, Lord Mulgrave deemed it his duty to have recourse to the opinion of your Majesty's Law Officers & of the Council for the Admiralty, and he has the honour humbly to report to your Majesty that their opinion fully confirms the legality of the sentence. Under this decision of the point of law and the proof of the crime being thus established upon the most distinct & conclusive circumstances, Lord Mulgrave most humbly submits to your Majesty that there does not appear any ground of mitigation or doubt that might claim the interposition of your Majesty's clemency to arrest the course of the law.

Lord Mulgrave has further humbly to submit to your Majesty, the case of Pierre Francois, seaman, who was condemned to suffer death, together with William Coates, boatswain and five others, for mutiny on board your Majesty's ship on the Halifax station in the month of July last. The boatswain and five others were executed at Halifax in pursuance of their sentence, but Vice-Admiral Sir John Borlase Warren has respited the execution of Pierre Francois 'as being a most miserable and ignorant wretch, & thereby an object for mercy'. Lord Mulgrave most humbly submits to your Majesty's gracious consideration this recommendation for mercy, upon the ground of the defective intellect of the culprit. (14848–9)

[*The King's reply, Windsor Castle, 23 Dec.*] The detestable crime committed by James Nehemiah Taylour, so clearly proved, and the circumstances which Lord Mulgrave has stated, do not appear to the King to warrant any hesitation in the confirmation of the sentence of death passed upon him.

His Majesty acquiesces in the recommendation of Sir John Warren that the sentence of death passed on Pierre Francois should be remitted. (14849)

4051   *Letters from the* EARL OF LIVERPOOL *to the* KING, *and the reply*

[*Downing Street, 23 Dec. 1809.*] Lord Liverpool begs leave most humbly to recommend to your Majesty Rear-Admiral Sir Richard Keats to be successor to Sir Alexander Ball as Civil Commissioner at Malta.

Lord Liverpool has been induced to select Sir Rich. Keats for this situation as he knows no person more likely to discharge the important duties of it with advantage to your Majesty, and with satisfaction to the inhabitants, at the same time that the state of his health prevents his being employed at present in more active service. (14850)

[*From Lord Liverpool, Downing Street, 23 Dec.*] Lord Liverpool begs leave most humbly to lay before your Majesty a letter which he has just received from the Earl of Chatham on the occasion of the City Address and your Majesty's answer.

(477)

Lord Liverpool would be glad with your Majesty's permission to communicate this letter to your Majesty's confidential servants.[1] (14851)

[*The King's reply, Windsor Castle, 24 Dec.*] The King acquiesces in Lord Liverpool's wish to communicate Lord Chatham's letter to his confidential servants. His Majesty highly approves of Sir Richard Keats as the successor to the late Sir Alexander Ball as Civil Commissioner at Malta. (14851)

[1] Lord Liverpool wrote to Chatham on the 30th (Chatham's letter of the 22nd is not in the Archives): 'According to your Lordship's desire I have laid your letter of the 22d inst. before the King, and I have since communicated it with his Majesty's permission to those of his Majesty's confidential servants who were in town. After having made this communication, I am desirous, in answering your letter, to say that if your Lordship means that in the event of an enquiry either military or parliamentary being judged expedient respecting the expedition to the Scheldt, on publick grounds, you were anxious that no consideration of a nature personal to yourself should enduce his Majesty's Government to resist it, but that in such case you were ready to submit your conduct to the fullest and strictest investigation, it is nothing more than what we have always understood to be your Lordship's feeling, and indeed what we might be assured must, under all the circumstances, have been that feeling. But if your Lordship's meaning is (whether on publick or private considerations) that it would be the duty of his Majesty's Government to assent to any Motion which may be made in Parliament for enquiry, or that you would feel it your own duty to express by yourself in the House of Lords, or through some person authorized for that purpose in the House of Commons, your desire that such enquiry should take place, I am confident your Lordship will see how important it is that his Majesty's Government should not be acting under any uncertainty or misapprehension of your Lordship's views and intentions upon this subject. I cannot conclude without adverting to that part of your letter, in which you express your regret that Parliament should not have met at an earlier period after your arrival in England. I am sure you will excuse me for observing that I was not aware of any intimation having ever been made by you, that it was your wish, that Parliament should have been assembled at an earlier period.' (Chatham Papers, 368.)

Chatham replied on 31 Dec.: 'I received your letter yesterday evening on the subject of one which I had addressed to you on ye 22d. ulto., as Secretary of State for the Colonial and War Department, and you must excuse me, if I cannot admit any letter from you as an official answer to mine, unless written by the King's command. I certainly did not expect to receive any, unless it shou'd have been his Majesty's pleasure that a military investigation shou'd take place into my conduct. Perhaps, when I wrote to you, and which I felt it my duty as a military [man] to do in order that some authentick document shou'd exist of my entire readiness to meet ye enquiry demanded upon me, it wou'd have been more correct if I had stopped there, the other part which alluded to a Parliamentary proceeding being rather one on which I might with more propriety have taken some occasion of of [*sic*] offering to H. Majesty whatever might appear to me to be necessary when I had the honor of attending his commands. But you will, I think, at ye same time, agree with me that as the King's answer did not confine itself to the enquiry asked for by ye Address of the City of London, but went further and directly pointed to a proceeding in Parliament, it was not unnatural that I shou'd not be wholly silent on that point. With regard to the line which it may be proper for his Majesty's Government to take in Parliament on the subject of the expedition to the Scheld, it must, as I conceive, somewhat depend on circumstances, but whenever that question is brought under the consideration of the King's servants, I shall be happy to discuss it with my colleagues at the Cabinet, or individually with any of them who may be so disposed, and I shall be always glad to converse with you on this or any other subject you may wish. I will only add that you must have very much misunderstood me if you supposed that by any expression of regret that the interval shou'd happen to be so long between my return to England and the meeting of Parliament I meant in any shape to complain of it—so far from it, I can assure you, that it never once entered my mind to wish, much less to intimate any desire, that on the ground of considerations personal to myself, Parliament shou'd have been called together an hour sooner, than under a view of all circumstances was deemed most conducive to ye good of H. Majesty's service.' (*Ibid.*)

Richard Ryder saw this letter next day, and commented, in a letter to his brother (1 Jan. 1810): 'It is satisfactory as to his opinion of the delay of the meeting, but as to the other point it leaves us as much in the dark as ever. It seems to me to make it necessary to have a Cabinet soon to take this most important point into consideration, and to learn his real sentiments....There is no notion yet

4052 RICHARD RYDER *to the* KING, *and the reply*

[*London, 23 Dec. 1809.*] Mr Ryder has the honor of humbly submitting to your Majesty that he finds, upon communicating with your Majesty's confidential servants, that there is no publick business depending of a nature to require your Majesty's presence in London on Wednesday next. (14852)

[*The King's reply, Windsor Castle, 24 Dec.*] In consequence of Mr Ryder's communication the King will not go to London on Wednesday next. (14852)

4053 THE MARQUESS WELLESLEY *to the* KING

[*Foreign Office, 25 Dec. 1809, 5 p.m.*] The Marquess Wellesley has the honor to transmit to your Majesty the original letter from the King of Persia to your Majesty. It is a very beautiful & curious manuscript. An attested copy is retained in this Office. A translation of the letter has already been submitted to your Majesty. (14853)

4054 THE VERY REVEREND EDWARD LEGGE *to the* KING

[*Deanery, Windsor, 2 Jan. 1910.*] It is with reluctance proportioned only to the sentiments of dutiful respect and gratitude with which my heart is filled that I presume to approach your Majesty on [the] occasion of the vacancy which has of late been frequently reported to me to be likely to take place in the See of Llandaff:[1] a reluctance which nothing could have enabled me to overcome but that due regard for my own estimation in the world, without which I should deem myself unworthy of your Majesty's notice and protection.

It is, in fact, your Majesty's gracious condescension and expressions of unmerited goodness towards me (combined with the services in which it has been my pride to be employed about your Majesty's person) which have, of late, on every similar occasion, excited a very general expectation that I should be raised to the situation to which my predecessors have for so many years past uniformly attained. Thus it is that conjecture in every shape has been as frequently set to

of a Cabinet though Ld. W[ellesley] said last week he must have one today for his brother's instructions, who sets out this morning.' (Harrowby MSS.)

Finally, Lord Liverpool wrote to Lord Chatham on 2 Jan. 1810: 'I entirely agree with you, that it could not be competent to me to write an official answer to your letter, conveying to you any determination of Government upon the subject to which it relates, except by the King's command. But the object of my letter, as you will see, upon referring to it, was not to intimate any determination or even opinion upon any part of the transaction which had led to your communication, but solely to desire explanation upon some points on which it appeared to be necessary, in consequence of that letter, that some explanation should take place before it was possible for the King's Government to decide on the course which it might be most expedient for his Majesty's service that they should adopt in Parliament, upon the agitation of any question relative to the expedition to the Scheldt. I admit that this explanation may take place in some respects more conveniently by personal communication than in any other manner, and I am only anxious in conjunction with those of my colleagues with whom I have communicated upon the occasion, that the whole subject should be thoroughly consider'd and discuss'd, and the line to be taken upon it as far as is practicable definitively settled before the meeting of Parliament.' (Chatham Papers, 368)

[1] Richard Watson (1737–1816) was Bishop of Llandaff, 1782–1816.

work in order to account for the postponement of my claims, & that objects have consequently received a value in my estimation which they would otherwise never have possessed, & to which I should otherwise never have presumed to aspire.

In this predicament it is to your Majesty alone that, unconnected as I am with anyone in power, I can have recourse. Whatever may be your Majesty's pleasure upon this occasion, I beg to assure your Majesty that I shall bow with implicit deference and submission to your Majesty's decision; and whatever my lot may be I shall have obtained the satisfaction of feeling that it has received your Majesty's sanction, & consequently must be the best & most proper for myself. (14859–60)

4055   *Letters from the* MARQUESS WELLESLEY *to the* KING, *and the reply*

[*Foreign Office, 5 Jan. 1810.*] Lord Wellesley has the honor to submit to your Majesty his humble recommendation of Mr Charles Stuart (who has distinguished himself in several diplomatic situations) to succeed Mr Villiers as your Majesty's Envoy Extraordinary & Minister Plenipotentiary at Lisbon. (14861)

[*From Lord Wellesley, Foreign Office, 5 Jan.*] Lord Wellesley has the honor to submit to your Majesty the draft of a dispatch to your Majesty's Minister at Lisbon which has been approved by your Majesty's servants,[1] & which Lord Wellesley hopes may meet your Majesty's gracious approbation. (14862)

[*The King's reply, Windsor Castle, 6 Jan.*] The King entirely approves the instructions to Mr Villiers which Lord Wellesley has submitted. His Majesty also sanctions the appointment to the mission at Lisbon of Mr Charles Stuart, whose conduct upon former occasions has proved him a sensible young man. (14862)

4056   SPENCER PERCEVAL *to the* KING, *and the reply*

[*Downg. St., 6 Jan. 1810.*] Mr Perceval returns your Majesty the letter from the Dean of Windsor to your Majesty upon the subject of the next vacant Bishoprick. Mr Perceval has received several applications upon the same subject on behalf of the Dean of Windsor since he has had the honor of being in his present

---

[1] Ryder wrote to his brother Lord Harrowby on the 4th: 'There is no news of any kind. Perceval and Ld. Liv[erpoo]l are to have a conference with Ld. C[hatham] tomorrow. I suggested it was better to confine it to those two, as he would be more likely to speak out to them than if more were present. This previous to a Cabinet. Ld. Wellesley has talked of one all the week for the instructions to his brother, but I hear no more of it.' (Harrowby MSS.)

Ryder wrote again, on 5 Jan.: 'We have at last had a Cabinet for Ld. Wellesley's instructions to Villiers, and Ld. Liverpool's to Ld. Wellington. It was not attended by Ld. Chatham who is very unwell, but who has had a long talk with Ld. Liverpool, from which I can collect nothing in the cursory account I have had of it, except that he will have another with Perceval. It is plain that he never will and I think can't be expected to pledge himself as to any line in the House of Commons till the time comes, and he knows what is said agst. him. He says that he had disregarded former charges till the Address of the City—that then the charge appeared to wear a more serious appearance and to require some recorded testimony on his part of his desire to meet enquiry. Whether he will withdraw the present letter [i.e. to the King] and write another, leaving out what he admits to be exceptionable, I do not rightly understand.' (*Ibid.*)

office, and fully apprized as he is of the great respectability of the Dean of Windsor's character, he should have had no hesitation in promising either to the Dean himself or to the Earl of Dartmouth[1] that he would recommend the Dean to your Majesty upon a vacancy occurring on the Bench of Bishops, if he had not inherited from the D. of Portland the experience of the extreme embarrassment occasioned to your Majesty's service by promises made at any distance from the time when they are to be carried into execution; at which time circumstances wholly unexpected at the period of making the promise may render the performance of it greatly inconvenient. Mr Perceval, however, is ready to consider this case as forming an exception if your Majesty should think right that it should be so; and will with your Majesty's approbation communicate your Majesty's intention to the Dean of Windsor. Mr Perceval, however, has to observe (what encreases the objection he has felt) that the Bp. of Landaff from the last accounts Mr Perceval has received of the state of his health is very much recovered.

Mr Perceval has received an application on behalf of the Revd. Mr Gibson,[2] the Rector of the living of Fyfield, which he humbly conceives your Majesty would be disposed to comply with. Mr Gibson some years ago accepted a perpetual curacy which he did not apprehend would vacate his living of Fyfield, but the perpetual curacy having been augmented by Queen Ann's Bounty occasioned in law a vacancy of the living which he held before. The vacancy, however, was not observed till from length of time the presentation to the living has lapsed to your Majesty. The patroness of the living (Miss Tylney Long[3]) is desirous that Mr Gibson should be restored to it, and under these circumstances joins with Mr Gibson in praying a presentation from the Crown, and if your Majesty should be graciously pleased to approve it, Mr Perceval will direct it accordingly. (14863–4)

[*The King's reply*, *Windsor Castle, 7 Jan.*] The King is as unwilling as Mr Perceval possibly can be to make promises of any description, and sees the inconvenience of such a practice very forcibly. In the case of the Dean of Windsor, his Majesty does not wish to encourage an exception, nor does he consider any answer to his letter necessary. It is only required to recollect that the application has been made.

The King approves of the Revd. Mr. Gibson being presented to the living of Fyfield. (14865)

[1] The Earl of Dartmouth, who died on 10 Nov. 1810, was the Dean's brother.
[2] Robert Gibson (*c.* 1765–1840), Vicar of Newland, Glos., 1797–1803; Rector of Fyfield, Essex, 1803.
[3] Catherine (1789–1825), sister and coheiress of Sir James Tylney-Long, 8th and last Baronet (who died on 14 Sept. 1805 at the age of 11), and daughter of Sir James Tylney-Long, 7th Baronet. She was reputed to be worth £40,000 a year, and for that reason the Duke of Clarence was prepared cheerfully to sever his connection with Mrs. Jordan and to marry 'the dear, lovely angel', 'the lovely and fascinating Catherine'. In vain, however, did the Duke pay his suit to this bewitching young lady with all the ardour of an English tar: she married (14 March 1812) William Wellesley-Pole (1788–1857), afterwards (1845) 4th Earl of Mornington, who squandered her vast fortune and broke her heart.

[*London, 8 Jan. 1810.*] Lord Liverpool has the greatest concern in being under the necessity of informing your Majesty that it appears by letters which have been received this day from Govr. Maitland from Ceylon, that the discontent which had long subsisted in the Company's Army under the Presidencies of Madras and Bombay had broken out into a mutiny, and in some instances even into what must be termed rebellion. The Govt of Madras were adopting the most vigorous measures for repressing it, and the most compleat confidence was placed in your Majesty's troops. A large detachment was marching from Madras for Hydrabad, which was one of the principal stations of the mutineers. Lord Minto[1] was expected at Madras; the Army in Bengal had not manifested any symptom of disaffection.

The dispatches are very long. Lord Liverpool has directed an abstract to be made of them which shall be sent to your Majesty tomorrow. (14866)

[*The King's reply, Windsor Castle, 9 Jan.*] The King has learnt with very serious concern from Lord Liverpool's letter that the discontent which has so long prevailed in the Company's Army in the Presidencies of Madras & Bombay has at length broken out into mutiny & rebellion. It is, however, satisfactory to his Majesty to know that his own troops had continued steady to their duty under such circumstances. (14867)

4058 *Letters from the* MARQUESS WELLESLEY *to the* KING, *and a reply*

[*Foreign Office, 9 Jan. 1810.*] Lord Wellesley has the honor to submit to your Majesty a letter received from Mr Pinkney relative to the conduct of Mr Jackson, the proceedings, & request of the American Government.[2] (14868)

[*From Lord Wellesley, Foreign Office, 9 Jan.*] Lord Wellesley has the honor to submit to your Majesty the draft of a letter to Mr Villiers, containing a particular expression of approbation of his services & conduct in Portugal. Lord Wellesley possessed the means of ascertaining that the conduct of Mr Villiers had obtained general respect & good will in Portugal.

A draft is also submitted to your Majesty of Credentials for Mr Stuart; these Credentials are conformable to those given to Mr Villiers. (14869)

[*The King's reply, Windsor Castle, 10 Jan.*] The King approves Lord Wellesley's letter to Mr Villiers and the draft of Credentials for Mr Stewart, and his Majesty has read Mr Pinkney's letter. (14870)

[1] Sir Gilbert Elliot, who had become Lord Minto on 20 Oct. 1797 (Earl of Minto, 24 Feb. 1813), was Governor-General of Bengal, 1806–13.

[2] The United States Government suspended intercourse with Francis James Jackson, the British Minister, on 15 Nov. 1809 and he withdrew from Washington, first to Philadelphia and then to New York. He sailed for home on 16 Sept. 1810.

[*War Office, 11 Jan. 1810.*] The Secretary at War begs leave to request that if the King can spare the report of the Commissioners of Military Inquiry on the offices of the Adjutant-General & Quarter Master General, his Majesty will be pleased to allow it to be sent to the War Office for Lord Palmerston's perusal. (14871)

4060 THE EARL OF LIVERPOOL *to the* KING, *and the reply*

[*London, 12 Jan. 1810.*] Lord Liverpool begs leave most humbly to submit to your Majesty the arrangement by which it is proposed to reinforce the garrison of the Cape of Good Hope, in consequence of the corps which have been detached from that Settlement to India, upon the intelligence being received by the Governor of the mutinous disposition which had appear'd in the Company's army under the Presidentcies of Madras and Bombay. Lord Liverpool begs leave at the same time to lay before your Majesty a letter which he has received from the Earl of Chatham to be substituted for the one which has been already submitted to your Majesty and which does not appear liable to any of the objections which had occur'd to the former letter. (14872)

[*The King's reply, Windsor Castle, 13 Jan.*] The King approves of the arrangements proposed by Lord Liverpool for the reinforcement of the Cape of Good Hope, and the relief of the Regiments to proceed from Gibraltar. His Majesty concurs in opinion with Lord Liverpool that Lord Chatham's letter, as now altered, is not liable to objection & it appears to him both manly & proper. (14872)

4061 RICHARD RYDER *to the* KING, *and the reply*

[*London, 13 Jan. 1810.*] Mr Ryder has the honor of informing your Majesty that the Sheriffs of London waited on him by appointment on Thursday last and read to him a copy of one of the Resolutions passed at a Common Hall on the 9th Jany: 'That the Sheriff attended by Mr. Remembrancer do forthwith wait upon his Majesty, and deliver into his Majesty's hands in the name of the Lord Mayor, Aldermen & Livery of London a fair copy of the Resolutions agreed to this day signed by the Town Clerk.' They insisted in the course of a desultory conversation upon the different modes of presenting Addresses to your Majesty, on the right of the Sheriffs to have the honor of an Audience of your Majesty when deputed by the Livery as well as by the Common Counsel and they cited the precedents of 1797 & 1800 which appear to relate to Addresses of the Livery only and not of the Livery & Common Council in support of the usage on which they rested the claim.

Mr Ryder did not think it his duty to allow their claim to the extent to which they urged it; but to avoid all misapprehension upon the subject of their application to him, he desired them to put it in writing, and added that he would return an answer in the same manner.

They accordingly wrote the letter which Mr Ryder has now the honor of enclosing to your Majesty as well as the answer which your Majesty's confidential servants who met today upon the subject have agreed upon as proper to be submitted to your Majesty's consideration and to be forwarded to the Sheriffs if it should meet with your Majesty's gracious approbation.

As the Lord Chancellor was not sufficiently recovered to attend the Cabinet, Mr Ryder had an interview with him at his own house, and his Lordship concurs in opinion with those of your Majesty's confidential servants who are now in London.

That the Sheriffs of London when deputed by the Livery have in some instances been permitted the honor of an Audience appears to be clear from an extract of the proceedings of Common Halls in 1800 with which Mr Ryder has been furnished, and which he has now the honor of enclosing to your Majesty. But whether exclusive of that precedent and another in 1797 of a similar nature, there have been any and what other instances of the same kind Mr Ryder has not been able to ascertain, or how far the Sheriffs are warranted in the assertion they made to him and which was confirmed by the City Remembrancer, that the Sheriffs had never been refused an Audience: but it should seem that there is no principle upon which the Sheriffs of London, when deputed by the Livery, can claim that privilege which might not equally apply to every other class and description of your Majesty's subjects.

Mr Ryder humbly submits to your Majesty the propriety of marking in the answer the distinct characters of the Sheriffs, when deputed by the Common Council, a body who have an acknowledged legal existence, and when deputed by the Livery, who are not, as Mr Ryder is informed, recognized by the Charter as a Corporation, in order to obviate as far as may be any misconstruction of the answer, as if your Majesty's servants had advised your Majesty to take a measure which would have the effect of depriving the body corporate of the City of their just rights. (14873–5)

[*The King's reply, Windsor Castle, 14 Jan.*] The King acknowledges the receipt of Mr Ryder's letter enclosing the communication from the Sheriffs of London and the answer proposed to be returned. H.M. entirely approves of what has been done upon this occasion, also of the answer in question, to which he has only thought it necessary to add a few words (written in pencil) which assign more directly his reasons for discontinuing the public Levées. (14875)

4062   THE MARQUESS WELLESLEY *to the* KING

[*Foreign Office, 13 Jan. 1810.*] Lord Wellesley has the honor to submit to your Majesty a draft of general instructions to Mr Henry Wellesley, your Majesty's Envoy Extraordinary & Minister Plenipotentiary in Spain. (14876)

4063   SPENCER PERCEVAL *to the* KING, *and the reply*

[*Downg. St., 15 Jan. 1810.*] Mr Perceval has humbly to acquaint your Majesty that Mr Geo. Villiers has resigned his situation as Paymaster of the

Marines, and Mr Perceval hopes that your Majesty will excuse Mr Perceval's not having acquainted your Majesty with this event immediately as it occurred, when he states to your Majesty his reason for witholding the information for a few days. Mr Perceval thought (and he has been since confirmed by Mr Villiers himself that he was right in that opinion) that Mr Villiers would be desirous of acquainting your Majesty with the circumstance himself, and of being the first to apprize your Majesty of it. For that reason Mr Perceval has abstained from mentioning it till he could feel assured that Mr Villiers must have been able to obtain an opportunity of mentioning it. It is much to be lamented that Mr Villiers had for many years entrusted the management of his office with too unstinted a confidence to his chief clerk. The accounts were till very lately many years in arrear and unaudited; considerable exertions have been made lately to bring them up. They have now been audited up to the year 1804 inclusive. The balance against Mr Villiers on the audit of that year is about £280,000. Mr Perceval had heard that this was the state of the account as it appeared upon that audit, and that reports were circulating upon the subject to such an extent as to make it impossible to hope that it would not become the subject of Parliamentary observation. Mr Perceval therefore sent to Mr Villiers in the hopes of being able to receive some explanation from him which might give a satisfactory account of the accounts and enable Mr Perceval to repel any attack which might be made in Parliament upon Mr Villiers or his Office. Mr Perceval, however, found that tho' there was no reason to impute to Mr Villiers anything but too negligent a confidence in his clerk, yet that there was no such good account to be given as could be deemed satisfactory, and tho' there may be some reason to hope, at least Mr Villiers sanguinely expects, that the balance since 1804 is much diminished, yet there can be no doubt that there is a very considerable sum due from Mr. Villiers. Mr Perceval therefore recommended to Mr Villiers that he should consider what sums of money he could collect, or what securities he could deliver over to the Navy Office, to set against such balance. But after some days taken to consider of it Mr Villiers thought upon the whole that it would be best that he should surrender his office, and offer to make over in trust for the public to secure this balance all his property.[1]

This step he having deliberately determined to take after communication with his brother-in-law Lord Boringdon,[2] Mr Perceval could not certainly think of dissuading him from taking it. Mr Perceval has communicated with Lord Mulgrave upon the subject of the office. They have agreed that it should be put upon a

[1] Lady Erroll wrote to her future husband, J. H. Frere, who was still in Spain, from Hampton Court Palace on 7 March: 'Poor George Villiers never quits his bed. He is at his brother's, Lord Clarendon's, who will pay part of the money, but the sum is so enormous that he can't pay all without ruining himself; poor Mrs Villiers wretched with eight helpless children. It is a shocking affair, and all the family are indeed much to be pitied.' (Frere MSS.) Canning wrote to Mrs. Canning on 20 Jan.: 'A very bad story indeed...I know not what to think of it. Be that as it may, never was anything more unfortunate for the country and for Government—for the cause of all Governments, I mean, than this blow-up, at this particular moment. It really seems as if all sorts of evils had been accumulated for this opening of Parliament—yet I cannot believe in the overthrow of the Administration, though I find others do.' (Harewood MSS.)

[2] Lord Boringdon's sister Theresa married George Villiers, brother of John Charles, Earl of Clarendon, in April 1798.

new footing; that the balances should not be suffered to remain in the Pay-master's hands, and that measures should be taken to prevent such a case occurring in future. Before, however, such an arrangement can be finally & satisfactorily settled it is necessary for the public service that a new officer should be appointed to carry on the current business, and Lord Mulgrave having in concert with Mr Perceval thought that his brother Genl. Phipps[1] would be very properly ap-pointed to that office, that appointment will if your Majesty pleases be made by the Admiralty as soon as possible, subject to such arrangement as may be found proper when time has been taken to consider of it. (14878–80)

[*The King's reply, Queen's Palace, 16 Jan.*] The King has received Mr Perceval's letter, and entirely concurs in the propriety of his proceeding in respect to Mr Villiers, attention to the interests of the public being the first duty upon these occasions. His Majesty also approves of his recommendation of Lieut.-General Phipps to succeed Mr Villiers as Paymaster of Marines. (14880)

4064 LORD MULGRAVE *to the* KING, *and the reply*

[*Admiralty, 15 Jan. 1810.*] Lord Mulgrave having received from Mr Percival an intimation of his intention to lay before your Majesty the circumstances which have led to Mr Villiers's resignation of the office of Paymaster of the Royal Marines, Lord Mulgrave abstains from giving your Majesty the trouble of a repetition of those details. He humbly submits to your Majesty's gracious con-sideration the proposed appointment by the Board of Admiralty of the Honour-able Edmund Phipps to succeed the Honourable George Villiers as Paymaster and Inspector of the Corps of Royal Marines. The imprest for the current payment of the Marines being at this time due, the immediate appointment of a Paymaster is indispensably necessary for your Majesty's service. (14881)

[*The King's reply, Queen's Palace, 16 Jan.*] The King approves of Lord Mul-grave's recommendation of Lieut.-General Phipps for the Paymastercy [*sic*] of the Marines in the room of Mr Villiers. (14882)

4065 *Letters from* PRINCESS MARY *to the* KING, *and the reply*

[*Monday night, 15 Jan.* [*1810*].] I am most happy in being able to say dear Sophia has continued very much better all day, was able to dine with us & assures me she feels very comfortable this evening. As to dear Amelia, this has not been quite so good a day as yesterday as the cold weather affects her very much, & notwith-standing all the care that is taken it is dificult to prevent her geting more cold. Her

---

[1] Edmund Phipps (1760–1837), M.P. for Scarborough, 1794–1818, 1820–32; for Queenborough, 1818–20. Lieutenant, 1780; A.D.C. to the Lord Lieutenant of Ireland, 1784–7; Lieutenant-Colonel, 1793; Colonel, 1796; Major-General, 1801; Lieutenant-General, 1808; General, 1819. Secretary to the Master-General of the Ordnance, 1811–12; Clerk of the Deliveries of the Ordnance, 1812–23; Pay-master of the Marines, 1810–11; Under-Secretary of the Ordnance, 1811.

head has been much stuffed today, partly from a fresh cold & partly from a slight degree of erysipelas that has come out about the head & eyes which has caused more headach this evening. However, Dr. Pope did not allow Amelia was at all *worse*, only not so well as yesterday, but has not found it necessary to alter anything.

I shall add tomorrow morning how she has passed the night.

Tuesday morning. Amelia has had three hours sleep & very little cough. Sophia has had a good night & has got leave to come & see Amelia this morning. (Add. Georgian 12/130)

[*The King's reply, Queen's Palace, 16 Jan.*] Although I shall have the satisfaction of seeing you tomorrow I cannot suffer the groom to return to Windsor without thanking you for your kind letter & for the report which it contains of my dearest Sophia & Amelia, respecting whom I must feel so anxious, particularly when absent from them. (Add. Georgian 12/131)

[*From Princess Mary, Tuesday night,* [*? 16 or 23 Jan. 1810*].] I must beg leave to return you my most greatful thanks for your kind letter received this evening. Amelia has passed but an indiferent day as she has sufferd much from pain in her head caused by the erysipelas which has come out a good deal more about the face & eyes & made her feel very dull & heavy. Dr. Pope desired Amelia not to get up for fear of more cold & even in bed she has suffered so dreadfully from the weather that I am sure it was the only proper place for her to be in today. As Amelia has complained of much heat about the head this evening Dr. Pope ordered a blister to be put on her back which he hopes will *draw* the erysipelas from the head. Dr. Pope has promised to come by nine o'clock tomorrow that I may be able to bring you his opinion of her.

Wednesday. Amelia has had two hours sleep. The blister has drawn very much which of course prevented her having her usual sleep. (Add. Georgian 12/132)

4066 PRINCESS AMELIA *to the* KING, *and the reply*

[*Windsor, Monday night* [*15 Jan. 1810*].] How very very kind & good you are to wish to hear of me & to desire an account may be sent up. I cannot help writing you a few lines for it is a very long day to me as I have not my dear visit from you & to which I always look forwards with such delight: one day of the four is over & I am very glad. I have got a little more cold in my head & Dr. Pope thinks a little tendency to *erysipolis* which has increased my headake. I got up between five & six, the day being so cold dear Sophia did not come out for fear of taking cold, but dear Miny gives me a good account of her. Dear Miny is just returned to the Castle to tea. I will not take up more of your time than to beg you will believe me [etc.]. (Add. Georgian 14/150)

[*The King's reply, Queen's Palace, 16 Jan.*] I thank you very much for your kind attention in writing to me and for expressing so affectionately your wish for my return to Windsor in which I need hardly assure you that I cordially join. I am much concerned to hear that you suffer from your cold and from the weather, but from dearest Mary's report of this morning I may flatter myself that the eresypilis will not materially affect your progress and that when I have the comfort of seeing you again on Friday you will be able to give me a more satisfactory account of yourself. (Add. Georgian 14/151)

4067 THE MARQUESS WELLESLEY *to the* KING, *and the reply*

[*Foreign Office, 16 Jan. 1810.*] The Marquess Wellesley has the honor to submit to your Majesty a note from Prince Stahremberg, a part of which is particularly addressed to your Majesty's gracious consideration. Orders have been given according to Prince Stahremberg's request for the dispatch of his baggage & suite, & he will take his departure at the close of this week. (14883)

[*The King's reply, Queen's Palace, 17 Jan.*] The King acknowledges the receipt of Lord Wellesley's letter transmitting one from Prince Starhemberg from which H.M. learns that he will quit England at the close of this week. (14883)

4068 PRINCESS AMELIA *to the* KING, *and the reply*

[*Wednesday evening.* [*17 Jan. 1810*].] Your dear kind & affte. letter made me very happy & I am not a little rejoiced to think that within forty eight hours I shall see you. I was very sorry to see the snow, but hope the weather will not materially affect the road till after Friday. I am very happy dear Sophia is not to go to Court as I dreaded both the fatigue & cold for her. My dear sisters have given you so full an account of me that I have little to say. The blister has drawn very much & I hope has relieved my head a little, for tho' I feel more pain & heat tonight Dr. Pope thinks it less inflamed.

I will not add more than to say how happy I shall be to see you all return. (Add. Georgian 14/152)

[*The King's reply, Queen's Palace, 18 Jan.*] I hasten to thank you for your affectionate letter of yesterday & to express the satisfaction with which I have learnt that you have been in some degree relieved by the blister. I am looking forward with impatience to the comfort of seeing you tomorrow and you need not apprehend that any increase of snow will deprive me of it. (Add. Georgian 14/153)

4069 SPENCER PERCEVAL *to the* KING, *and the reply*

[*Downg. St., 18 Jan. 1810.*] Mr Perceval having just received a comparative account of the exports & imports from and into Great Britain in the three quarters of the last three years ending on the 10 of October, conceives them to exhibit an encrease in the commerce of your Majesty's Kingdom at once so surprising and satisfactory, that Mr Perceval thinks it his duty to lay them before your Majesty. Mr Perceval has only troubled your Majesty in detail with those articles in which the encrease is the most striking.[1] (14884)

[*The King's reply, Queen's Palace, 19 Jan.*] The King has received with great satisfaction the favorable report which Mr Perceval is enabled to make of the amount of exports and imports from and into Great Britain in the last year, & his Majesty considers the encrease of the commerce within that year is very surprizing. (14884)

4070   RICHARD RYDER *to the* KING, *and the reply*

[*Whitehall, 19 Jan. 1810.*] Mr Ryder has the honor of transmitting to your Majesty a Petition which he has received from Majr. Cartwright,[2] and of submitting to your Majesty the answer which Mr Ryder proposes to return to the letter with which it was accompanied, in case it should meet with your Majesty's gracious approbation. Mr. Ryder humbly submits to your Majesty that the object he has in view in the answer is to prove that your Majesty has heard Majr. Cartwright's Petition, and Mr Ryder hopes that this assurance may obviate the necessity of his giving your Majesty any additional trouble upon this subject. (14887)

[*The King's reply, Windsor Castle, 20 Jan.*] The King entirely approves of Mr Ryder's answer to the letter of Major Cartwright whose Petition has been read to him. His Majesty conceives that the impertinent attempts of such individuals as Major Cartwright cannot be too positively checked. (14888)

4071   SPENCER PERCEVAL *to the* KING, *and the reply*

[*Downg. St., 20 Jan. 1810.*] Mr Perceval humbly represents to your Majesty that in consequence of his having understood from his Grace the Archbp. of Canterbury that it was your Majesty's wish that the two Houses of Parlt. should attend Divine Service on the 30th of Jany.[3] Mr Perceval took care that the two Houses should meet on that day in the last two years, and that he should appoint a sermon to be preached before them. But Mr Perceval thinks it his duty to submit to your Majesty's consideration that the attendance of the two Houses of Parliament on these occasions, as well as upon the same occasion in the preceding year 1807, was very discreditably thin, as there were not above three or four Members exclusive of the Speaker in St. Margaret's, nor above as many Lords besides the Chancellor at the Abbey. Mr Perceval cannot hope that the attendance will be greater on the approaching anniversary; and he therefore ventures humbly

---

[1] The annual figures for these years are in *English Historical Documents, 1783–1832*, ed. A. Aspinall and E. A. Smith, pp. 550–1.

[2] John Cartwright (1740–1824), one of the leaders of the Radical movement in the country. Major of Militia, 1775–90.

[3] The anniversary of the execution of Charles I.

to doubt whether it is not upon the whole better that the two Houses of Parliament should adjourn over that day than that they should express collectively a determination to observe it, & should individually so entirely neglect it. Mr Perceval solicits your Majesty's pleasure upon this subject, having undertaken to convey your Majesty's wishes upon it to his Grace the Abp. of Canterbury.[1] (14889)

[*The King's reply, Windsor Castle, 20 Jan.*] The King regrets to learn from Mr Perceval that the attendance of the two Houses of Parliament on the 30th of January at Divine Service should have been of late years so thin, but as that day has been fixed by Act of Parliament for the purpose, H.M. would feel unwilling to prescribe anything which might be considered as encouraging the too prevalent wish to introduce changes & innovations. He must also observe that the late Lord Thurlow, altho sensible of the defective attendance, was of opinion that as the Order resulted from an Act of Parliament it would not be adviseable to dispense with it. The King, however, leaves the question open for the consideration & opinion of Mr Perceval, upon further consultation with the Archbishop of Canterbury. (14890)

4072   *Letters from* RICHARD RYDER *to the* KING, *and the replies*

[*London, 20 Jan. 1810.*] Mr. Ryder has the honor of transmitting to your Majesty the report made to him by Mr Dundas of the intelligence received today from Bombay for the purpose of being laid before your Majesty. (14891)

[*The King's reply, Windsor Castle, 21 Jan.*] The King has had great satisfaction in receiving from Mr Ryder the report made to him by Mr Dundas of the intelligence received from Bombay which is much more favorable than his Majesty had expected. (14891)

[*From Richard Ryder, London, 21 Jan.*] Mr Ryder humbly submits to the King the draft of the Speech[2] which your Majesty's confidential servants have agreed upon, as fit to be proposed for your Majesty's consideration. (14892)

---

[1] See also Colchester, II, 225.

[2] *Parl. Deb.*, XV, 1–3 (23 Jan.). The Speech was read by the Lord Chancellor, the Session being opened by Commission, the Commissioners being the Archbishop of Canterbury, the Lord Chancellor, Lord Camden, Lord Aylesford and Lord Dartmouth.

Ryder wrote to his brother, Lord Harrowby, on 4 Jan.: 'I hope you will have found time to correct the first copy of the Speech. It was from the cursory perusal of it generally good in idea and principle but too long and in some points faulty in style. Liverpool has given another edition, I think, worse.' (Harrowby MSS.)

Perceval wrote to Lord Chatham on 16 Jan.: 'Lord Liverpool tells me you disapprove much of the draft of the King's Speech as it has been circulated. I trust you will therefore be able to attend the Cabinet upon it which will be held at two o'clock today. I shall be very glad to find it possible to adopt any suggestions which may render it more acceptable to you. I only beg that you will keep in mind these things—the awkwardness of refusing or declining to *echo* in the Address the sentiments distinctly expressed in the Speech; the acknowledged impropriety at all times & on all occasions of calling upon Parliament to pledge itself to the approbation of any measure on which they have not before them the

[*The King's reply, Windsor Castle, 22 Jan.*] The King has received Mr Ryder's letter, enclosing the draft of the Speech, and his Majesty approves the firmness and the fairness which it evinces and considers what is said as being in general well suited to the present times. (14893)

[*From Richard Ryder, Whitehall, 23 Jan., 3 p.m.*] Mr. Ryder has the honor of submitting to your Majesty the copy of a letter from the Chairman of the East India Company to Mr Dundas enclosing the copy of a letter from Lord Minto, which Mr Ryder has likewise the honor of laying before your Majesty. Mr. Ryder has this moment received them and thinks it his duty to lose no time in humbly submitting to your Majesty this gratifying and authentic confirmation of the important intelligence received from India a few days ago. (14901)

[*Enclosure*]

[*Charles Grant to Robert Dundas, Russell Square, 23 Jan., past eleven a.m. (Copy).*] It is with great satisfaction that I hasten to communicate to you a copy of a letter received this morning from the Governor-General of Bengal dated at Fort St. George the 15 of September 1809 announcing the suppression of the revolt among the officers of the Madras Army. This letter came by express from Falmouth & seems to be the only dispatch yet received from the Ganges. (14902)

4073 THE EARL OF LIVERPOOL *to the* KING, *and the reply*

[*London, 24 Jan.* [*1810*], *3.30 a.m.*] Lord Liverpool begs leave most humbly to submit to your Majesty the Minutes of the House of Lords. Lord Grimston[1] made an excellent speech in seconding the Address. The debate went off upon the whole very satisfactorily and the division was as good as was expected. Lord Grenville and Lord Grey made very violent speeches and Lord Liverpool regrets to be under the necessity of stating to your Majesty that there is too much reason to expect that there will be many long debates.[2] (14905)

information which may be thought necessary to form their judgement; and the impossibility on the present occasion of getting the Parliament to express approbation of the Walcheren expedition, either in its plan or its execution, without some information being had. This difficulty may indeed all be parried if it should be thought right in the King's Speech to say that the King had given directions that such papers should be laid before Parliament as would enable them to form their opinion. Then the course of Parliament is clear; they will thank the King for having given such direction and assure him that they will take the papers into consideration without delay. To this course of proceeding I know of no objection but that it is unprecedented—but the inclination of my mind is that it is the best way out of our difficulties. I wish you to bear this in your mind before the Cabinet, and let us know what you think of it when we meet.' (Chatham Papers, 368.)

[1] James Walter, Viscount Grimston [I.] (1775–1845), succeeded his father as 4th Viscount Grimston, 30 Dec. 1808, having previously (3 Dec. 1808) succeeded his maternal cousin as 10th Lord Forrester [S.]. He was Tory M.P. for St. Albans, 1802–8. Created Earl of Verulam, 24 Nov. 1815. A Lord of the Bedchamber, Jan.–April 1835. On 11 Aug. 1807 he married Lady Charlotte Jenkinson, only daughter of the 1st Earl of Liverpool. He was in the House of Lords from Dec. 1808 because his father had a G.B. peerage too (title, Baron Verulam [1790]).

[2] *Parl. Deb.*, xv, 1–37. The numbers were 144 *v.* 92. 'The debate on the side of the Ministers was miserable,' wrote Lord Grey. 'Grenville was as usual most powerful...Our division in the House of

[*The King's reply, Windsor Castle, 24 Jan.*] The King has learnt with satisfaction from Lord Liverpool's letter that the division in the House of Lords has been as good as was expected. Altho' his Majesty cannot but be amazed at the violence of Lord Grenville and at the indecent wording of the Amendment, he trusts that such conduct will carry its own antidote with it, will open the eyes of the public and induce the supporters of Government to stand up very firmly in opposition to the mischief which it betrays. (14905)

4074   *Letters from* SPENCER PERCEVAL *to the* KING, *and the replies*

[*Downg. St., 24 Jan. 1810.*] Mr Perceval acquaints your Majesty that Lord Bernard[1] moved an Address as near as could be an eccho [*sic*] to the Speech of the Lords Commissioners, and was very ably seconded by Mr Peele.[2] Mr Peele has a very great character for talent and he fully maintained it upon this occasion. The Amendment was moved by Lord Gower[3] and seconded by Mr Ward (Ld.

Lords was not bad, though not so good as it might have been if some of our friends had not been absent, and that fool the Doctor had not taken the objection of prejudging, which was just suited for the meridian of fools like himself.' (Howick MSS.) The minority of 92, suggested Lady Holland, 'would formerly have broken up any Administration'. (*Journal*, II, 253.)

Canning wrote to Mrs. Canning on the 25th: 'No, dearest love, I am not out of spirits—nor unwell. But I confess I see my way less than ever I did. Here is Wellesley's note. But as to what he may wish or intend—he must first take care of himself. His not speaking on Tuesday has sunk him in the opinion of all the world. Grey...is determined to goad him again the next opportunity (perhaps to-night or to-morrow), and Ld. Gren. to lie by to answer him. If he stand that trial, well—but if not—if he really has not the talent or the nerves to debate, there is an end of him. His very colleagues will begin to hold him cheap. The King, who hates him, will crow over his failure, and he must be contented for the rest of his life to hold his office upon sufferance, without domineering or looking higher. I hear but a bad account, besides, of his conduct in his office. He does little or nothing (they say), sees nobody, and answers no letters. But then, to be sure, that is easily said—and I make allowances, which other people perhaps do not, for the desperately distracting things which the Government must have had to perplex them for the last six weeks. However, be that as it may, if he cannot take his part, and a splendid part, in Parliament, he is gone—and I grieve for that, because, be he good or bad, he is the only one—there is nothing but him wherewith to make up an Administration between the present, and the Grey and Grenv[ille]. All this is very puzzling, and gives room for reflection, but it does not make me low-spirited, I assure my own love—because I feel sure that somehow or other, sometime or other, things will come right as to *me* individually—though I certainly do not now see how. Character and prudence must do everything. I sometimes doubt whether if Lord Chat[ham] be saved (as perhaps he may be by the indecision of the Ministers, on the one hand, and the desire of Opposition on the other to throw the blame on Ministers rather than on him)—it may not still be possible to make him available as a 1st Ld. of the Treasury. But all is obscure and uncertain at present. Opposition are disappointed—I think more than they need be.' (Harewood MSS.)

¹ James, Viscount Bernard (1785–1856), so styled from 29 Aug. 1800, when his father, Lord Bandon [I.], was created Earl of Bandon [I.], until 26 Nov. 1830, when, by his father's death, he became 2nd Earl of Bandon. Tory M.P. for Youghal, 1806–7 and 1818–20; for Co. Cork, 1807–18; for Bandon, 1820–6, and Aug.–Nov. 1830. Irish Representative Peer, 1835–56.

² Afterwards Prime Minister (1788–1850). M.P. for Cashel, 1809–12; for Chippenham, 1812–17; for Oxford University, 1817–29; for Westbury, 1829–30; for Tamworth, 1830–50. Succeeded his father as 2nd Baronet, 3 May 1830. Under-Secretary of State for War and the Colonies, June 1810; Irish Secretary, Aug. 1812–18; Home Secretary, Jan. 1822–April 1827, and Jan. 1828–Nov. 1830; Prime Minister, Dec. 1834–April 1835, and Aug. 1841–June 1846. Peel, said Creevey, 'made a capital figure for a first speech'. (*Creevey Papers*, p. 122 [1906].)

³ George Granville, Earl Gower (1786–1861). Styled Lord Strathnaver until 1803; Earl Gower from 26 Oct. 1803, when his father succeeded as 2nd Marquess of Stafford; and Marquess of Stafford from 28 Jan. 1833, when his father was created Duke of Sutherland, until 19 July 1833, when by his father's

Dudley's[1] son). The Amendment proposed to omit all that part of the Address which respected the expedition to Walcheren, and expressed the indignation and regret of the House at the failures of the late campaign—and professed a determination to enquire in the most effective manner, and take such proceedings in consequence as may be proper. Mr Perceval will send the Amendment to your Majesty to-morrow but he humbly requests your Majesty's pardon for his forgetfulness in having left the House without a copy of it.

Mr Herbert followed Mr Ward against the Amendment, Mr Lamb for it—Mr Bragge Bathurst also against the Amendment, upon the ground of its being criminatory before enquiry, but he clearly would have voted for the Amendment had it merely pledged the House to enquiry. Mr Ponsonby followed Mr Bathurst, Lord Castlereagh against the Amendment, Genl Tarleton for it, Mr Canning against. Mr Whitbread for. Mr Perceval followed Mr Whitbread, Mr Tierney followed, & Mr Wharton[2] concluded the debate & a division was called for at about $\frac{1}{2}$ p. 4 o'clock.

> The numbers were for the Amendt.   167
> For the original Address   264[3]

Mr Perceval cannot help apprehending that the size of this majority is in some degree owing to the intemperate nature of the Amendment—as Lord Sidmouth's friends[4] were comprehended in that majority and some others who would have voted against the Address as Mr Perceval believes, had the Amendment been merely been [sic] for an enquiry.[5] (14909)

death he became 2nd Duke. M.P. for St. Mawes, 1808–12; for Newcastle-under-Lyme, 1812–15; for Staffordshire, 1815–20. Summoned to Parliament, v.p. in his father's Barony as Baron Gower, 22 Nov. 1826.

[1] William, 3rd Viscount Dudley and Ward (1750–1823), succeeded his half-brother in the peerage on 10 Oct. 1788. Tory M.P. for Worcester, 1780–8.

[2] Charles Long had written to Lord Lonsdale on 1 Nov. 1809: 'Wharton is to be the Secretary of the Treasury. I think he will do well in many respects, but he must work hard to make himself master of finance, for the Treasury is not just now strong in that point.' (Lonsdale MSS.)

[3] The number should be 263 (H. of C. J., LXV, 6). The Speaker had the number correct (Colchester, II, 230).

[4] The Opposition reckoned the following as members of the Sidmouth party in 1810: Charles Adams, J. H. Addington, Alexander Allan, Charles Bragge-Bathurst, Henry Bowyer, T. G. Estcourt, Davies Giddy and Benjamin Hobhouse.

[5] Parl. Deb., XV, 38–105. 'If we have a good attendance I think it probable we shall beat them at once,' Grey had told Fitzwilliam on 6 Jan. (Fitzwilliam MSS.) The division, he said, was infinitely worse than he had expected. 'Our numbers were lower, and theirs very much higher than our previous calculation.' He added, 'This gives no real and efficient strength to the Government, and serves to depreciate the character of the Parliament in the opinion of the people.' (Howick MSS.) In another letter (26 Jan.) Grey said that Ponsonby had spoken 'better than usual, and appeared to have raised himself quite appreciably in the estimation of the Party'. (Ibid.) Ponsonby, said the Speaker on the 20th, had been reinstated in the nominal lead of the Opposition, but that Tierney was the efficient man on that side. (Colchester, II, 225.) Lord Moira wrote on the 23rd: 'Tierney swears that the Opposition will have a majority. Government folks assert that they will have three-score majority at least. Both sides appear to me to form their calculation upon the numbers likely to be not forthcoming on each list respectively...and I should think Ministers have better means of computing justly on that point than we have.' And next day he wrote: 'A majority of 96 in the House of Commons, when the question urged was the strongest ever advanced against a Ministry, gives the men now in office a new lease, if the country at large can tolerate this continuance. There were many absentees on the part of Opposition, while the Ministerialists had been well whipped-in. Several persons, also, reckoned in the muster

[*The King's reply, Windsor Castle, 24 Jan.*] The King considers Mr Perceval's report of last night's proceedings in the House of Commons as very satisfactory, and the division, under all circumstances, good, allowing even for the contingency which Mr Perceval has so fairly stated. His Majesty observes the same violence on the part of Opposition in both Houses, and he trusts that it will tend to defeat generally its mischievous intention, by inducing the more moderate of that party to withhold their concurrence & by acting as an additional stimulus to the friends of Government in their resistance to proceedings so intemperate & avowed in terms so indecent. (14910)

[*From Perceval, Downg. St., 24 Jan. 1810.*] Mr Perceval acquaints your Majesty that there were but 39 members assembled at 4 o'clock this day in the House of Commons & therefore the House was lost. Mr Perceval laments this event as it will prevent your Majesty from receiving the Address of the Ho. of Co. tomorrow, but he trusts it will be attended with no other inconvenience—as Mr Perceval will take care that it shall be properly presented to your Majesty at Windsor.

Mr Perceval finding that the Amendment in the Lords was the same as in the Ho. of Commons, and that Lord Liverpool had furnished your Majesty with an account of it, Mr Perceval forbears giving your Majesty the trouble of receiving the copy which he otherwise would have sent. (14911)

roll of the former, most unaccountably turned tail. The most material defection was that of the Sidmouth party.' (*Hastings MSS.*, III, 277.)

Castlereagh, said Creevey, spoke from under the Gallery, two rows behind Canning, who evidently came down from the back benches to make his speech. 'He was at least two feet separated from the Treasury Bench.' (*Creevey Papers*, pp. 122–3.)

The Government's strength, said Creevey, was composed of five parties—the Government, Castlereagh's, Canning's, Sidmouth's, and the Saints. (*Ibid.*) 'And possibly some others,' said Perceval, after mentioning these various groups, 'who would have voted for a more temperate Amendment, seeking only for inquiry, and not prejudicing it by a criminatory introduction.' (Add. MSS. 37295, fo. 219.) See also Lady Holland's *Journal*, II, 253.

Canning wrote to Mrs. Canning on the 24th: 'The division last night was much more favourable to the Ministers than Cacodemon had been taught to expect. But tho' the Opposition had infinitely over-rated their numbers, yet they have to thank themselves for the division having fallen *so much* below their calculation. Ld. Gren[ville] with his usual violence framed the Amendment so as to disgust many who would naturally have supported it—even the Addingtons went with Govt. in both Houses. The Amendment was just as much an attack upon me as upon the remaining Ministers—upon Castlgh. more. I intended, when I went down, to speak early. But I altered my determination to let Castgh. go before me, that I might take care of anything from him that required an answer from me. He said nothing of that sort however; and his speech was a very good one (which my own love will say is so much the worse). Mine was a very *brilliant* one—but not very long, not above an hour—a great deal I kept back for the great day that we are to have on Friday. I said that I should *probably* vote for Walcheren inquiry. I advised Ministers not to give an inquiry into *Spain*, and said I would support them in resisting it—but if they chose to give way I of course could not help it. Lastly about Castgh and myself. I said, in observing upon Ward's allusion to that business, that I had determined, however called upon or provoked, never to utter one word in that House upon that subject. I do not think that I shall go down to-day. I have said my say—and they may do without my vote to-night....I dare say there is no report of my speech in papers—but I hope it is taken in shorthand.' (Harewood MSS.)

He referred to this debate in another letter to Mrs. Canning on the 25th: 'Perceval's speech, to be sure, was very very bad—very very poor—and low—and my chief endeavour—and the chief merit of mine perhaps was the tone of it—which I think they must have felt to be better suited to a situation of difficulty. I never saw a more dispirited Lobby, even though the division was beyond their expectations. But from this division—deduct the Addingtons—the Cast[lerea]ghs and me—giving us only 10 each on an average—and the majority for *Ministers* would shrink below 40.' (Harewood MSS.)

[*The King's reply, Windsor Castle, 25 Jan.*] The King approves of Mr Perceval's sending the Address to Windsor, as the non-attendance of a sufficient number of Members at the regular hour on the second day of the Session precludes its being presented this day. His Majesty has indirectly learnt with satisfaction that the Opposition have been much disappointed by the first divisions, and he trusts that the persevering firmness of his Government and the exertions of its friends will continue to check their mischievous attempts. He also hopes that the House in general will be at length so disgusted with the coarse & indecent language held by some of its members, as to adopt some steps towards maintaining its dignity. (14912)

[*From Perceval, Downg. St., 25 Jan.*] Mr Perceval acquaints your Majesty that the House of Commons went thro the Report upon the Address this evening. Sir F. Burdett made a violent speech which was very well answered by Mr Yorke. Sir John Sebright[1] followed Mr Yorke, expressed himself strongly against the conduct of Government for the expedition to Walcheren and Spain, and professed his determination to oppose the Government upon the conviction of its inability to serve your Majesty. Mr Whitbread proposed an Amendment which Mr Perceval encloses, and which was negatived on a division of 96[2] to 54. Mr Tierney then moved another Amendment to express the necessity of having at this time an 'efficient and united Government'—which was negatived by 100 to 52. The House had been much fuller in the course of the evening but gentlemen on both sides had gone away, not expecting a division.[3]

The Earl of Liverpool having communicated to Mr Perceval that your Majesty had been graciously pleased to dispense with the personal attendance of a Privy Counsellor with the Address, Mr Perceval will take care that it shall be forwarded to your Majesty, and that your Majesty's answer shall also be forwarded by the messenger of tomorrow night. (14914)

[*The King's reply, Windsor Castle, 26 Jan.*] The proceedings in the House of Commons last night & the divisions, as reported by Mr Perceval, appear to H.M. very satisfactory, considering the numbers in the House. Mr Ryder has sent to the King the draft of the answer to the Address which, if it meets with Mr Perceval's concurrence, may be sent tomorrow morning with the Address by the messenger, & his Majesty will return the answer to be delivered by Mr Perceval to the Privy Councillor who is to present it to the House. (14915)

[1] Sir John Saunders Sebright, 7th Baronet, (1767–1846), M.P. for Hertfordshire, 1807–34. The Opposition in 1810 considered him as a 'hopeful'. He professed to be independent of party. 'I...shall always consider myself at liberty to act as I may think proper,' he wrote to Lord Spencer in April 1807. 'I have not nor will I ever ask the support of any Administration lest it should be considered as a pledge of my future conduct.' (Althorp MSS.) He succeeded his father as Baronet, 23 Feb. 1794.
[2] The number should be 95.
[3] *Parl. Deb.*, xv, 114–30.

[*Whitehall, 25 Jan. 1810.*] Mr. Ryder has the honor of humbly submitting to your Majesty's consideration the draft of an answer proposed to be returned by your Majesty to the Address of the House of Commons. (14913)

[*The King's reply, Windsor Castle, 26 Jan.*] The King returns the draft of the answer to the Address transmitted by Mr Ryder, which his Majesty considers very proper. (14913)

4076 *Letters from* SPENCER PERCEVAL *to the* KING, *and the replies*

[*Downg. St., 26 Jan. 1810.*] Mr Perceval has great pain in informing your Majesty that there is great reason to believe that Mr Eden, Lord Auckland's son, is dead.[1] He has not been heard of now for many days and great apprehensions are entertained of his having made away with himself; altho the cause of such an act cannot be traced to any circumstance whatever. Your Majesty is aware that Mr Eden is one of the Tellers of the Exchequer and in the event of Mr Eden's death being ascertained the convenience of the public service will require that the office should be filled up as soon as possible. Mr Perceval cannot but humbly submit to your Majesty that this occasion would afford a most favorable opportunity for marking your Majesty's gracious approbation of the services and fidelity of one of your Majesty's most valuable subjects; Mr Perceval means Mr Charles Yorke. A more disinterested and manly support has not been given to your Majesty's Government at any time by any one than by him. Mr Perceval ought to acquaint your Majesty that he has received applications from Lord Cornwallis & from Lord Chichester for this office, but without any disparagement to the merits & claims of either of those noble Lords Mr Perceval cannot but think (and he trusts his old private friendship for Mr Yorke does not mislead him to that opinion) that especially considering the present time and the situation of yr. Majesty's Government, that Mr Yorke's services peculiarly deserve such a mark of your Majesty's approbation, and that it would be peculiarly useful that they should have it. Mr Perceval, however, conceives that it must depend upon this; whether Lord Hardwick will consent to return him again to Parliament, as it

---

[1] William Frederick Elliot Eden (see No. 2857 n) was drowned in the Thames. The following advertisement appeared in some of the London newspapers on 18 Jan., and was several times repeated:

PUBLIC OFFICE, BOW STREET
MISSING   Jan. 23, 1810

Whereas a young gentleman in good health and spirits, after having occupied himself in his ordinary businesses through the day, walked out from his house in Westminster, at eight o'clock in the evening of Friday last, and told his servants that he should return about nine o'clock; and where as he has not since been heard of.

This is to give notice, that any Person or Persons who will bring any intelligence respecting him, so as to relieve his family from their extreme alarm and distress, shall be very liberally rewarded, by application to Mr. Stafford, Chief Clerk at the above Office.

He is 26 years of age, about five feet ten inches in height, of a fair complexion, thin, and rather pale. He had put on a brown great coat previously to going out. His other clothes were a blue coat, a striped waistcoat, blue pantaloons, and short boots.

would undoubtedly much defeat Mr Perceval's view of public utility in this appointment, if it should deprive the Ho. of Co. of so valuable a Member.[1] (14917–18)

[*The King's reply, Windsor Castle, 28 Jan.*] The King had learnt with great concern the melancholy event which vacates one of the Tellerships of the Exchequer. In communicating to Mr Perceval his approbation of his recommendation of Mr Yorke for that situation, his M. cannot in sufficient terms express his sense of the liberality & public spirit which Mr Perceval shews upon this occasion, where an opportunity occurred of making a handsome provision for one of his own numerous family, & where indeed it had already occurred to H.M. to have proposed such an arrangement to him. The King has no hesitation in saying that few men would be capable of so disinterested an act, & such being the case, H.M. could not have received a proposal more satisfactory to himself than that which enables him to mark his approbation of the faithful services of Mr Yorke & the manly support which he has received from him in times of the greatest difficulty & embarassment. He trusts that Lord Hardwicke will not go the length of endeavoring to preclude his brother from the enjoyment of so valuable an office, but if he should, his M. conceives that Mr Yorke owes it to himself to accept the office & that he should endeavor to find another seat independent of Lord Hardwicke's interference.[2] (14918)

[1] This statement shows how few were the seats now at the disposal of the Treasury.
Palmerston wrote, 27 Feb.: 'I cannot help thinking, on the whole, that it is almost a pity he [Yorke] has taken it [the Tellership] as he stood so high as an independent character; and the other day in the House, having said that he should support every and any Government during the life of the present King, he added, in answer to a taunting cheer from the Opposition, that he did it from independent conviction of what was right, and that he had nothing *to hope* or fear from any set of Ministers. On the other hand, he is a very fit man for any mark of favour, and is, moreover, very poor. At all events it is a great instance of self-denial and disinterestedness on the part of Perceval that, with his large family, he did not give it to his son. It certainly would have made an outcry, but there is not a man, I am persuaded, on the Opposition side who would not have taken it under the same circumstances.' (Bulwer's *Palmerston*, I, 117.)
[2] Charles Yorke accepted this valuable sinecure and made himself independent of his brother (who followed the fortunes of Lord Grenville) by resigning his seat for Cambridgeshire and coming in for the Eliot family's borough of St Germans on 27 April, *vice* Sir Joseph Sydney Yorke, his brother, who then remained out of Parliament until 1812.
On 27 Jan. Yorke told his brother about the Tellership and the condition attached to the offer, and expressed the hope that he might be able to retain his seat 'through your friendship and affection'. (Bodleian MSS. English Letters, c. 60, fo. 56.) On that day Hardwicke wrote to congratulate him, and anxiously hoped 'that you may meet with as little unpleasant trouble in Cambridgeshire as may be expected'. (*Ibid.*, fo. 76.) He wrote at greater length on the 28th: 'The offer which has been made to you of the Tellership of the Exchequer brings forward the question of your re-election for Cambridgeshire in a shape which is undoubtedly less repugnant to my feelings than if the seat had been vacated by your acceptance of a Cabinet office; and without adverting to past occurrences or discussions I have no hesitation in saying that I do not feel myself called upon to object to it. With every degree of true & affectionate friendship for you, and of brotherly interest in your happiness & welfare, this is as much as, consistently with what is due to myself, I can say upon this occasion. With respect however to the offer being unaccompanied by any condition except that of your retaining a seat in Parliament, it seems to me that everything is implied in that condition which can pass between one gentleman & another: at the same time I must say that as far as you are concerned Perceval has acted a friendly part, being already as much assured of your support & adherence as he can possibly be after your acceptance of this favour. On my part, in consenting in this direct manner to be thus neutralised in point of

[*From Perceval, Sat. morn., 2 o'clock, 27 Jan. 1810.*] Mr Perceval humbly acquaints your Majesty that Lord Porchester moved in the House of Commons yesterday evening 'That the House should resolve itself into a Committee of the Whole House to consider of the policy & conduct of the expedition to the Scheldt.' He was seconded by Mr Quin[1]—and Mr Croker[2] moved the previous question, upon the ground that it was most unreasonable and absurd, when papers and information upon this subject had been promised in the Speech from the Throne, which were expected to be laid next Monday, that it should precipitately determine not only for an enquiry but also for an enquiry by a Comee. of the Whole House before the Members had seen the papers which were to be produced, and could judge of the necessity of any further information, and of the manner in which it should be required. The speakers who followed, spoke in the following order:

For Lord Folkstone's [*sic*] Motion: For the previous quest.:

Mr B. Bathurst

Mr Fuller

Mr Perceval

Parliamentary connection, I desire no other condition than to be left at full liberty to give my opinions at any time, and in any place and form, that may appear proper & expedient.' (*Ibid.*)

Yorke wrote to Hardwicke on the 29th: 'What has happened to me has been entirely *unsolicited* & in a manner *unthought* of, certainly *unexpected* by me. You say truly indeed that Perceval has acted a most friendly part towards me. He has indeed; & I must add that few men would have been capable of an action so noble & disinterested, when he might with the most perfect justice & propriety have requested of the King to bestow it upon one of his numerous offspring, or even upon *himself*, in exchange for the Dutchy at present held by him on a *precarious* tenure, tho' his only provision, & as a means of strengthening the Administration, by advising the bestowal of it, upon some person who was likely to form an accession to the Cabinet. But he recommended *me* for it, because he thought something was due to me as his friend, & perhaps as a public man; & I am persuaded you will be pleased to learn that the King accepted of that recommendation in a manner both grateful & honourable to my feelings.' (Add. MSS. 35394, fo. 69.)

Canning, who was not in easy financial circumstances out of office, told Mrs. Canning (27 Feb.) 'how provoking it is that young Eden's Tellership should have fallen just now and gone to Yorke—who would have had no pretension to it in comparison with me, if I had been in office—while *it* would have made me quite easy, in pecuniary concerns, for life'. (Harewood MSS.)

[1] Windham Henry Wyndham-Quin, 2nd Earl of Dunraven [I.] (1782–1850). Whig M.P. for Co. Limerick, 1806–20. Took the additional surname of Wyndham in 1815, after his wife Caroline (*d.* 1870) had inherited the estates of her father, Thomas Wyndham. Styled Viscount Adare from 5th Feb. 1822, when his father, the 1st Baron Adare [I.], was created Earl of Dunraven [I.], until 24 Aug. 1824, when, on his father's death, he became 2nd Earl. Irish Representative Peer, 1839–50.

[2] Croker had been Secretary of the Admiralty since the formation of the Perceval Ministry. He transformed the character of the office. A keen politician, he was now occupying a place which had never hitherto been subject to party changes, and henceforth its holder went out on a change of Government (the Second Secretary, a civil servant, remained). George Rose thought the appointment a very undesirable one. 'He is an honourable man, I believe, and certainly has talents, but there is a something belonging to him that makes me much regret the selection.' (*Diaries and Corresp.*, II, 408.) Lord Grey said the appointment was 'certainly one of the most scandalous that ever was made'. (Brougham MSS.) Vansittart was almost as critical, telling Lord Sidmouth on 4 Nov. 1809 that the Court, on whose influence Ministers so much depended, would probably drive them into some 'glaring jobs, by which they will be degraded and disgraced'. He went on: 'The appointments of Croker at the Admiralty and Manners Sutton as Judge Advocate are a pretty good specimen of this sort of influence, and I know not which of them is most disgraceful and most mischievous. Indeed, the disposal of important offices such as these, upon such motives and in such a manner, deserves much severer condemnation than mere pecuniary jobs however gross, because the injury to the public is beyond comparison greater.' (Sidmouth MSS.)

For Lord Folkstone's [*sic*] Motion: For the previous quest.: (*cont.*)

Mr Windham
Mr Ponsonby

Mr Stephen

Sr Sam Romilly

Mr Leslie Forster[4]

Sr. Geo. Warrender[1]

Mr H. Smith

Genl. Grosvenor
Sr. Home Popham
Col. Eyre[2]
Mr Wilberforce

Sol. Gen. of Scotland

Sr. W. Curtis

Mr Home Sumner

Mr Martin[3]
Mr W. Smith
Mr Tierney
Ld. Newark
Mr Lockhart

Mr Gooch
Mr Canning

Mr Patteson[5] moved an adjournment of the debate. Mr Sumner supported that Motion, which both Mr Ponsonby & Mr Perceval opposed. The adjournment was negatived without a division.

The question then, 'that the question should be then put' was put from the Chair. The House divided

Ayes 195
Noes 186
───────
9

Mr Perceval has no doubt that your Majesty will be surprised to find that so many of the friends of Governt. should have voted against your Majesty's serts.

---

[1] Sir George Warrender (1782–1849), M.P. for the Haddington burghs, 1807–12; for Truro, 1812–18; for Sandwich, 1818–26; for Westbury, 1826–30; for Honiton, 1830–2. Succeeded his father as 4th Baronet, 14 June 1799. A Lord of the Admiralty, 1812–22; a Commissioner of the Board of Control, 1822–8. In 1810 he was in opposition, but joined the Government as a placeman in 1812. Later, he was a Canningite. His friends styled him Sir George Provender, on account of his good dinners.

[2] Anthony Hardolph Eyre (1757–1836), M.P. for Nottinghamshire, 1803–12. He had supported the Addington Ministry, and had been labelled a 'doubtful' Addingtonian in 1805, whilst in 1810 the Whigs referred to him as one of their 'doubtfuls'. He was, in fact, an independent country gentleman.

[3] Henry Martin (1763–1839), Whig M.P. for Kinsale, 1806–18.

[4] John Leslie Foster (*c.* 1781–1842), Tory M.P. for Dublin University, 1807–12; for Yarmouth (Isle of Wight), 1816–18; for Armagh, 1818–20; for Louth, 1824–30. Advocate-General [I.], 1816; Counsel to the Commissioners of Revenue [I.], 1818–28. Baron of the Court of Exchequer [I.], July 1830; Judge of the Court of Common Pleas [I.], 1842.

[5] John Patterson (1755–1833), M.P. for Minehead, 1802–6; for Norwich, 1806–12; an Alderman and brewer of Norwich. He had supported Pitt's Government and he supported Perceval.

upon such a question, where all the reasoning was so much in favor of the Motion which they supported. It shews however how strong a feeling there is in the country for an enquiry into the expedition. It would be far from proper in Mr Perceval to disguise from your Majesty that it has [made] a very unfavorable impression against your Majesty's servants that they should upon any considerable question be found in a minority; and perhaps the more clearly they are right, the more unfavorable impression of their strength is made by it. Mr Perceval, however, trusts that it will not impair their means upon general questions of Govt. of serving your Majesty with advantage to the country.[1] (14919–20)

[*The King's reply, Windsor Castle, 27 Jan.*] The King has learnt from Mr Perceval the result of last night's debate with more regret than surprize as he has long been sensible of the unfavorable impression generally produced by the expedition to the Scheldt. Upon a question where the reasoning was so much in favor of Government his Majesty considers that Mr Perceval acted very properly in opposing the Motion, altho' with a doubtful prospect; and he laments that those friends of Government who joined against it last night do not see more clearly the mischief which they are encouraging by even a partial support given to the Opposition. The King trusts, however, that they will act more consistently upon questions more generally affecting the security of Government, & he is convinced that Mr Perceval will cordially join with him in a determination to meet with firmness the dangerous attempts now making.[2] (14920)

---

[1] *Parl. Deb.*, xv, 161–207. Creevey wrote: 'Canning was in the minority with Perceval; Castlereagh in the majority with us. He sat aloof with four friends, and these five, instead of going out, decided the question in our favour. Had they gone out we should have been beat by *one*!' (*Creevey Papers*, p. 124.) 'Wilberforce', wrote Lady Holland, 'behaved in the most flagrant but sanctified manner. He deserted his friend Perceval at the critical pinch.' (*Journal*, II, 253.) Ponsonby, said Grey, 'by the testimony of everybody, made a most admirable speech'. (Howick MSS.)

Admiral Harvey and Thomas Carter also spoke in favour of Lord Folkestone's Motion; and Henry Lascelles against it. After giving the division and the list of speakers, W. H. Fremantle wrote to Lord Grenville: 'The defeat was unexpected, as you may well imagine when I tell you that Arbuthnot lost a guinea to me upon a bet that they had fifty majority. Ponsonby distinguished himself particularly and made the best speech I have ever heard from him since he has been Leader. Canning wretched, opposing it upon the ground of it being more parliamentary in case the papers should prove any guilt for the enquiry to proceed by King's Message, as the guilt might rest upon the officers and in that case it ought to proceed by a military tribunal. The ground that Perceval took was the obvious one that until the papers were produced the forming a Committee for enquiry was premature and promised the papers on Monday and to be printed on Tuesday, therefore it could only be the delay of two days. He spoke with more confidence than he did on Tuesday but was not applauded by the House. You may well imagine the effect of this division in the House; nothing could appear more defeated and fallen than Perceval. Lord Porchester moved for the House to form itself into a Committee on Friday next. Lord Castlereagh did not speak and voted with the majority: he has judged infinitely wiser than Canning. Romilly's was a very able speech, but those which had most effect in the House were the few words from Grosvenor and Sir Home Popham, which in the name of the army and having called for enquiry and therefore left the resistance on the Ministers alone, and Wilberforce as usual gave the finishing stroke to his friends in distress. The debate was animated and good, and the cry of the House throughout with us in the strongest manner. Although this will probably not drive them out, yet it will shake them most severely and I much doubt if they will be able to continue to procure attendance. We had many who did not attend—the two Foleys, Sir John Hippisley, the Dundass's and one or two more whom I forget.' (Fortescue MSS.)

[2] Canning commented on the debate, in a letter to his wife on the 27th: 'My own love need not be alarmed at the Govt. majorities or reckon upon the humility of Opposition any longer—for last night

[*From Perceval, Downg. St., 30 Jan. 1810.*] Mr Perceval acquaints your Majesty
that he has satisfied himself that the Bp. of Winchester[1] will have no objection
to appoint Dr. Knott[2] to the Prebend of Winchester should your Majesty be

the question of inquiry by a Committee of the Whole House (which I disapprove) was carried *against*
Govt. by a majority of 9—195 to 186. So there they are for the rest of the Session with a business upon
their hands which must distract and worry them day after day—*if* after such a vote they can stand—
which *I* think they can, after a manner—submitting to constant indignities and occasional defeats—
but the impression, as may be supposed, is otherwise. My own love will collect that I did not vote
against them. She will perhaps wish I had. The question is one of very doubtful policy perhaps, but
I am pretty sure I did right. First—on the first day of the Session I *said* I would wait for the papers
promised in the King's Speech before I pronounced for inquiry. Secondly—I am decidedly adverse
to an inquiry by a Committee of the Whole House into military matters. Thirdly, I mean to oppose
inquiry into Spain—and if I had voted plump *for* this, that would have been more difficult to resist.
Fourthly, if there is a culprit among Ministers (independent of Ld. Chat[ham]) it is Cast[lerea]gh, and
I thought it might look as if I was in a hurry to put *him* upon his trial—which would have been con-
trasted hereafter with my resistance to the Spanish inquiry in which I am as much concerned as he.
Fifthly, I did not like the appearance of courting Opposition—who have done anything but court *me*.
Sixthly, if the Government are turned out by this effort, it is better that I should not have been instrumental to it. I should have gained nothing with Opposition. If *they* come in, *I* must be in opposition,
and the Pittites whom I must then look to lead—deposing Perceval—would follow me much less
willingly if I had actually joined the Grenvilles to turn them out. But do not let my own love suppose
that because I voted with Govt. I therefore spoke in support of them. No—no—no. My speech was
framed after the model of Wilberforce—that sort of admonitory friendship that does more mischief
than the most direct hostility—and I laid the ground for a directly hostile vote the *next* time that the
question should be agitated—if it had not been carried now. I took occasion to refer to it to remind the
House of my difference of opinion with my colleagues upon the Convention of Cintra—and to speak
of that transaction as it deserved. I blamed Perceval's conduct in not having had the papers ready—and
that of the Govt. in not having instituted a military inquiry by the authority of the Crown previous to
the meeting of Parliament, so as to have had the result to communicate to Parlt. as in the case of Cintra
—instead of throwing the inquiry into so loose and inconvenient a shape as was now inevitable. I said
that though I waited for the papers, according to my original pledge, I could not conceive it possible
that the papers would preclude the necessity of inquiry—though they might point the objects of it.
I spoke only to explain my vote, not to argue, and I flatter myself no Saint in the House ever supported
more inconveniently. Accordingly, Wilberforce and Bankes (though they voted the other way) gave
me great praise for the line which I had taken—for my forbearance towards the Govt., and so did the
Speaker—and upon the whole I am satisfied I was right, tho' it cost me some anxiety to decide what I
should do. Castgh. did not speak—but voted with Opposition. We calculate that about *five* voted
with him. I had *five* also in the House—Leveson, C. Ellis, Sturges, Mr. Taylor and my cousin. Dent
was not there: Huskisson is gone back to Eartham. Holt Leigh is not come up yet, and Jolliffe, who
has not yet positively made his profession to *me*, but I know intends it, was not in the House. With
him I am *ten* sure. And I think Adm[ira]l Harvey means to swear allegiance too—for he asked me last
night what line I meant to take—and when I told him, got up and took it before me. I do not think
Castgh. *has* ten, though his friends say more—some twenty—but I saw Harbord (who is one of his
nearest friends) voting with us in the Lobby. Govt. certainly have no majority upon which they can
reckon with confidence. On the first night with all their exertions they could bring but 263—and
Opposition had 167, without the Addingtons. They are from 7 to 10, and my 10, and Cast[lereagh]'s 10
together, if shifted from one side to the other, make a difference of 60—and reduce the majority of
the first night to under 40. With this they could not go on. Last night I did not quit them—but the
Saints did—and there were altogether about 50 members *less* in the House than on the first night—all
deducted from the Govt. side as it appears—for they divided 77 fewer than before—of which Castgh.
was 5 or 6—the Add[ington]ns 6 or 7—the Saints and stragglers the remainder of the 27.' (Harewood
MSS.)

¹ Dr. Brownlow North.
² George Frederick Nott, D.D. (*c.* 1767–1841), who had been Sub-Preceptor to Princess Charlotte;
the son of the Rev. Samuel Nott (*d.* 1793), Vicar of Blandford and one of the King's Chaplains. He
was presented to the perpetual Curacy of Stoke Canon, Devon, by the Dean and Chapter of Exeter, in
1807; became a Prebendary of Winchester, 1810, and in 1812 was presented by All Souls, of which he
was a Fellow, to the Rectory of Harrietsham, which he held with that of Woodchurch. See *Glenbervie*

graciously pleased to appoint Dr. Garnett, now a Prebendary of that Cathedral, to the Deanery of Exeter. Mr Perceval therefore humbly recommends Dr Garnett[1] for that Deanery. Mr Perceval also conceives that the vacant Canonry of Christ Church should be filled without further delay, and would submit to your Majesty one of the late Chaplains[2] of the Ho. of Co. who has been recommended to your Majesty by an Address from that House for that Canonry.

Mr Perceval also humbly submits to your Majesty the Revd. Mr. Saml. Sharpe[3] to be appointed to the living of Wakefield, which he has served as curate to the late incumbent with great character & credit, as it is reported to Mr Perceval by Lord Harewood[4] & Lord Lonsdale; that living being now vacant by the death of Dr. Monkhouse. (14921)

[*The King's reply, Windsor Castle, 31 Jan.*] The King approves of Mr Perceval's recommendation of Doctor Garnett for the Deanery of Exeter, as it is understood that the Bishop of Winchester will appoint Doctor Knott to the Prebend of Winchester. H.M. also sanctions the nomination of one of the late Chaplains of the House of Commons to the Canonry of Christ Church, & that of the Revd. Mr Sharpe to the living of Wakefield. (14922)

[*From Perceval, Downg. St., 31 Jan. 1810.*] Mr Perceval regrets to be obliged to repeat to your Majesty the progress of business in the House of Commons this evening. Mr Bankes proposed his Bill for making perpetual the Act for preventing your Majesty from granting offices in reversion. He was seconded by Mr H. Thornton. Mr Perceval opposed Mr Bankes's Motion by proposing an Amend-

Journals, II, 26. Perceval wrote to Eldon on 14 Oct. 1809: 'As to the Canonry the King mentioned Dr. Nott for it. I have my doubts whether Christ Church is just the situation for him, but his Majesty said he was to hear from you upon this subject and therefore it was expressly taken ad referendum. Would not a less conspicuous situation do better?' (Eldon MSS.)

[1] John Garnett (*d.* 1813).
[2] The Rev. Frederick Barnes. See *H. of C. J.*, LXII, 833, 840 (8 and 13 Aug. 1807). The King replied that he would bestow some preferment.
[3] Vicar of Wakefield, 1810–55. The date of his death seems to be unknown. He was 18 in October 1791.
[4] Edward Lascelles (1740–1820) was created Baron Harewood, 18 June 1796, and Earl of Harewood, 7 Sept. 1812. Lord Harewood had recently again renewed his application for an advancement in the peerage, writing to Lord Liverpool on 2 Oct. 1809: 'I very reluctantly intrude upon your Lordship at this time, when I know you must be fully occupied with business of the utmost importance. But I cannot refrain from troubling your Lordship with a few lines to remind you of the request which I made a considerable time ago respecting promotion in the Peerage. I have twice written to the Duke of Portland upon the subject without having had an answer to either of my letters. Your Lordship may very well recollect what passed upon the occasion of my making the request—which I could not but conceive amounted to a promise that it should be laid before the King—with every good wish and exertion to obtain his consent. Indeed I was afterwards inform'd that his Majesty had been graciously pleased to say he had no objection to it. Under these circumstances I cannot but feel that I have been very much slighted by not having had this favor granted to me. As I look upon the Duke of Portland to have resigned his situation in the Administration, I have thought it proper & respectful to your Lordship to address this letter to you, and I shall be much obliged to your Lordship if you will do me [the] favor to renew my request to his Majesty.' (Add. MSS. 38243, fo. 165.)

On 7 Dec. he renewed his application, this time to Perceval (Add. MSS. 38244, fo. 77), and was informed that the Duke of Portland had entered into an embarrassing number of engagements of this kind. (Add. MSS. 38244, fo. 135. To Perceval, 28 Dec. 1809.)

He was M.P. for Northallerton, 1761–74, and 1790–6.

ment for suspending the power of granting reversions for a limited time. The question, as Mr. Perceval had before mentioned to your Majesty, was one upon which the friends of Government were most disinclined to give their attendance, whilst the members on the other side flocked to the question with great eagerness; and Mr Perceval saw with certainty that if he pressed the question to a division that he should have been beat by at least two to one. He therefore thought it best after having stated and argued his objection, to decline pressing it to a division.

Mr Bankes then proceeded to move the Committee of Finance. He proposed to leave out several names which were upon the Comee. last year, and to recast it. Mr Perceval wished to re-establish it as it was last year, with the addition of six more names. The question was taken upon the first new name which Mr Bankes proposed, which was Mr Sturgess Bourne, a name perfectly unexceptionable in every respect except that he had not been upon the Comee. of the former year. Mr Perceval therefore proposed Mr Hawkins Brown who was on the Comee. last year instead of Mr Bourne, and the House divided: Ayes for Mr S. Bourne 107, Noes 98.

The next division was upon the name of Mr Cavendish[1] instead of whom Mr Perceval proposed Mr Leycester. The House divided for Mr Cavendish: Ayes 108, Noes 103.

The third division was upon the name of Mr Aldn Combe instead of whom Mr Perceval proposed Mr Dennis Brown.[2] The House divided for Mr Alderman Comb: Ayes 117, Noes 104.

Mr Perceval finding that by these repeated divisions he was only harrassing his friends without advancing any object, declined dividing the House any further —and Mr Bankes therefore carried his Committee just as he named it.

Mr Perceval knows not to what to ascribe the fate of these questions but to the dislike which was entertained to the idea of opposing Mr Bankes's Bill for abolishing reversions; this dislike kept people who were generally friendly to the Government away from the House for that question, and with all the exertion which could be made they could not be brought down to the House in the course of the evening. The House rose about 10 o'clock.[3] (14923–4)

[1] William Cavendish (1783–1812), M.P. for Knaresborough, 1804; for Aylesbury, 1804–6; for Derby, 1806–12. He was the eldest son of Lord George Augustus Henry Cavendish (1754–1834), who was created Earl of Burlington, 10 Sept. 1831. Lord George was the youngest brother of William, 5th Duke of Devonshire (1748–1811).

[2] Denis Browne (? 1760–1828), second son of Peter, 2nd Earl of Altamont [I.]. M.P. for Co. Mayo, 1782–1800 [I.]; 1801–18; for Kilkenny City, 1820–6. A supporter of Government and of the Catholic question.

[3] *Parl. Deb.*, xv, 251–65. Comparatively unimportant though the questions were on which the Government was defeated, Grey nevertheless considered them decisive as proofs of the defection of the House of Commons. 'In other times an Administration would not have attempted to go on an hour after such events, and I think even these Ministers must immediately strike.' (Howick MSS. 1 Feb.) In the battle between Leycester and Cavendish there was a most curious mis-counting of numbers. Creevey wrote: 'I saw the tellers count wrong by 3. I called to have the House told again, and again I saw them make the same mistake. I shewed it to General Tarleton, who became furious; and the Speaker called him and me to order in the most boisterous manner. It ended in the House being counted a third time, and the tellers were sent out into the galleries to be more certain. In going they picked up young Peel, the seconder of the Address, in concealment, who, being brought in, voted for Cavendish. They then counted the House again, and they counted right, making 3 more than before, and with Peel

[*The King's reply, Windsor Castle, 1 Feb.*] The King regrets the unfavorable divisions as reported by Mr Perceval last night, but his M. considers that Mr Perceval has acted perfectly right in stating his objection to Mr Banke's Bill, altho' he could not press the question to a division, as, by such proceeding he has left it to the House of Lords to follow the course which they shall think proper, without being influenced by any concession in the Commons. (14924)

[*From Perceval, Downg. St., 1 Feb.*] Mr Perceval acquaints your Majesty that he moved this day the Thanks of the House to Lord Wellington for the victory at Talavera. Lord Milton moved the Amendment which Mr Perceval transmits herewith. Lord Castlereagh made an excellent speech in defence of Lord Wellington's conduct in the campaign in Spain which had a very powerful effect on the House. Mr. Windham & Mr Canning and General Crawfurd, Mr Lyttleton and Sir Thos. Turton spoke on the same side. Mr Vernon,[1] the A. Bp. of Yorke's [*sic*] son, spoke for the Amendment—it was his first speech and was certainly a very promising one. Mr Whitbread, Genl. Tarleton, Mr Ponsonby & Lord Folkstone spoke also for the Amendment—but there was no division. Indeed, if there had been one the numbers against the Motion would have been exceedingly few.[2] (14925)

making the majority of 4. Otherwise we had been equal, and the Speaker would have decided the thing undoubtedly against us.' (*Creevey Papers*, p. 126.)

Canning was not in the House. (Harewood MSS. To Mrs. Canning, 1 Feb.). Charles Long, writing to Lord Lonsdale on 5 Feb. thus explained the Government defeats: 'We have not managed things well since we met; if we had we should not have been in a minority. How could Perceval think it possible that we could resist enquiry into the Walcheren expedition? It was quite impossible, and he should have made up his mind to it. Again, the folly of opposing the Reversion Bill lost us the Committee of Finance, for our friends were invited *for the Reversion Bill only*, and as it had twice passed, refused to come down to oppose it, the consequence of which was that when the next business (the appointment of the Finance Committee) came in we were in a minority and beat upon every name: but all this is bad management, not want of strength. Upon both points I had given my opinion, but in vain, and the only way I can account for what was done is that Perceval was hampered by his Cabinet and that he considered them rather than the House of Commons.' (Lonsdale MSS.) Lord Morpeth, who arrived in the House only in time for the last division, wrote, after the House rose: 'This is not perhaps at all a decisive trial of strength, as the House was not full, but it is a disagreeable question for Government to lose, & the consequence is that a very vigilant & scrutinizing Committee will commence its functions without loss of time. Some Ministerial people must have made a short turn, & the great remissness in attendance upon such a question is a bad symptom for the duration of the Govt. They will however have a favourable day tomorrow, if our friends are ill-judged enough to divide against the thanks to Ld. Wellington. It is not certainly wished, but control is nearly impossible.' (Castle Howard MSS.)

Robert Ward agreed with Charles Long that the defeats were due to 'sheer mismanagement and irresolution'. He added, writing to Lord Lonsdale on 3 Feb. 'In regard to our friends it must be confessed there is far too much indifference to any trouble in our defence...in the way of attendance, to make it ...probable we can carry anything with vigour. Many professed friends are already gone out of town; more prefer their dinner to attendance, though the fate of the Ministry depends upon it.' (Lonsdale MSS.) Five days later, however, Ward told Lonsdale that the ranks of the Opposition were being similarly depleted. 'Our opponents...complain bitterly of their own friends deserting their posts, particularly of Coke, for preferring shooting to killing the Ministry.' (*Ibid.*)

1 George Granville Venables Vernon [afterwards Harcourt] (1785–1861), M.P. for Lichfield, 1806–31; for Oxfordshire, 1831–61.

2 *Parl. Deb.*, xv, 277–302. The letter must have been written in the early hours of the 2nd. In the Lords, Grey, Grenville and Lauderdale opposed the thanks to Wellington, and the two last entered a Protest to the vote. (xv, 108, 140, 152; Lord Holland, *Further Memoirs of the Whig Party*, p. 47.)

Canning wrote to his wife on the 2nd: 'The thanks to Lord Wellington were voted last night after

[*The King's reply, Windsor Castle, 2 Feb.*] The King is glad to learn from Mr Perceval that his Motion passed without a division in the House of Lords [*sic*] last night. (14925)

[*From Perceval, Downg. St., 3* [2] *Feb. 1810.*] Mr Perceval acquaints your Majesty that the House resolved itself this evening into the Committee to enquire into the policy & conduct of the expedition to Walcheren. Lord Porchester began by calling the Commander-in-Chief, Sr. Dd. Dundas, and after a few questions his Lordship proceeded to enquire into what passed upon an occasion of Sr D. Dundas's attending a meeting of your Majesty's confidential servants. Mr Perceval, after communication with the Attorney & Solr. General, doubted whether it was fitting for the House to proceed to enquire from a Privy Counsellor of what passed at a Council, as the witness as well as the other Counsellors were all sworn to secrecy. A considerable debate ensued; the question was considered as a very important one, and in order to avoid coming to a determination upon it without sufficient time to enquire & examine into it, it was ultimately determined to adjourn the Committee—and the Committee broke up. When the House was resumed Lord Porchester proceeded to move for the appointment of a Secret Committee to examine evidence of a secret nature as to information which might have been had relative to the state of the enemies force in the neighbourhood of Antwerp, and his Lordp. was proceeding immediately to name that Committee. This Mr Perceval opposed, not that he did not approve of a Secret Comee. for such part of the enquiry, but because it was taking the House by surprise as to the persons of whom it was to consist, and he insisted that notice was necessary. The Speaker gave it as his opinion that notice was necessary and with great reluctance the Motion was given up. It is intended to resume the consideration of this subject on Monday.[1] (14927–8)

a long debate without a division. I spoke at near two in the morning, merely because I did not choose the question to go by without my having said something—and especially as I think the debate of last night and the division upon it may save us a discussion of the Spanish campaign—or at least save us a Committee upon it—to which I am by no means inclined. The sooner we can get out of the questions in which I am involved with the Govt. into a new score, the better. My own love will be very angry with Castgh. for having spoken very well again, but so he certainly did—il faut avouer. Being turned out has certainly done him a world of good—both given him speech and obtained him a hearing. I have no reason to be dissatisfied with the House. On the contrary—though there had been a tumult of half an hour before I got up, and Ponsonby who preceded me was scarcely heard, the noise subsided instantly upon my getting up, and during my speech everything was hushed, to the dropping of a pin —the clamour reviving again as soon as I sat down. But *yet* I cannot disguise from myself that pity works for Castgh. and that many well disposed people look upon me with a sort of a half-reproachful eye, as the cause of the ruin of the Govt. "When will you speak from your right place again?", is a question which is put to me ten times in the course of a night—and put exactly as if the putters were satisfied that it even *now* depended upon myself to answer it. When we get to *new* questions in the House, that will clear up a little—but that cannot be till the inquiry is disposed of—and *that* cannot be disposed of, I imagine, much before Easter. I doubted a good while what I should do upon the Inquiry —whether attend it all through diligently, and examine the witnesses—or abstain from attendance altogether as being a matter in which I am concerned as a defendant—or attend, but take no part. I rather think I have decided for the last. Charles [Ellis] and Leveson would not hear of the second—and the first I cannot make up my mind to think right. To-day the Committee begins.' (Harewood MSS.)

[1] *Parl. Deb.*, xv, 305–9 (2 Feb.). Grey thought Perceval's objection a foolish one. The proceedings of the Committee of Inquiry are set out in full in the Appendix to that vol. pp. i ff. and in vol. xvi.

[*The King's reply, Windsor Castle, 3 Feb.*] The King acknowledges the receipt of Mr Perceval's report of last night's proceedings in the House of Commons, and H.M. highly approves of his strenuously resisting a pretension so indecent & unwarrantable as that advanced by Lord Porchester in regard to questioning a Privy Councillor as to what passed at a Council, which he is bound by oath not to reveal. (14928)

[*From Perceval, Downg. St., 4 Feb.*] Mr Perceval humbly acquaints your Majesty that, in consequence of the doubt which has been raised as to the propriety of the Commander-in-Chief's answering to any question which might be put to him with regard to what passed upon the occasion of his attending the Cabinet or a Council held relative to an expedition to the Scheldt, the Commander-in-Chief has requested Mr Perceval to obtain your Majesty's pleasure upon this subject.

The Commander-in-Chief represented to Mr Perceval that it had not occurred to him to suppose that there was anything in his oath as a Privy Counsellor which should bind him to refuse to communicate in the examination before the House of Commons what passed on an occasion of his attending the Cabinet—not in his character as a Privy Counsellor to give advice upon any subject which might be before the Council, but merely to give to your Majesty's confidential servants that information which they might require from him as Commander-in-Chief with regard to the state of the Army; and that he had therefore not hesitated upon his examination before the House of Commons to answer the questions which had been put to him; but that understanding that some doubts were entertained whether in strictness his oath as a Privy Counsellor did not extend to require the concealment on his part of what had passed on that occasion, he was desirous of receiving the sanction of your Majesty's consent, if your Majesty should be pleased to give it, to his answering any such question.

The importance of this subject has appeared to Mr Perceval to be such that he has brought it under the consideration of your Majesty's confidential servants both yesterday and today, and upon full deliberation this day of all your Majesty's confidential servants (except Lord Wellesley and Mr Ryder who were obliged to be absent on account of indisposition) they are of opinion, by reference to what

Canning wrote to his wife at 5.30 p.m. on the 3rd: 'I do not pretend to say that there is *no* danger of the policy being attacked in *debate*, but I do not think it will be condemned by a vote; the failure in the execution is too obvious for that. Besides, about the policy I had no choice—I *am* responsible—and it was therefore handsomer to claim my responsibility. I hope my own love will approve of what I did last night...I am satisfied that my conduct since the beginning of this Session has been marked by most *unusual prudence*, and it has been more successful than if it had been more bustling and brilliant and obtrusive. It has disappointed both Opposition and Ministry, I believe—who would both have been glad to see me committed in altercation with Castlereagh and in direct hostility with Govt.—the first for obvious reasons, common to both—the second because Opposition would be glad to see me cut off by my own act from a junction with Perceval (do not be afraid, dearest love, I have no thoughts of it), and because P. would be happy to have to say to the K[ing] and to his friends in the H. of C. who pester him with questions—that I had made it impossible for any proposal to be made to me. *He* would rather go out than make any proposal to me. I believe that his part of the Cabinet, Bath[urst], Har[rowby] &c would rather give up to Lord Grenv[ille] than be saved by me. But not so Wellesley—and hence divisions—if I am rightly informed...' (Harewood MSS.)

has passed in Parliament on former occasions—on occasion of the impeachment of the Earl of Strafford;[1] of the Partition Treaty[2]—and of the enquiry into the war in Spain in 1810–11[3] [*sic*] that your Majesty's consent has been considered at once necessary and sufficient to authorise the disclosure of such matters which have passed in Council, as your Majesty may consent to have disclosed. That there is great reason to doubt whether the oath of a Privy Counsellor does authorise a person, tho a Privy Counsellor, who may have attended a Cabinet or Committee of your Majesty's Council, not in his character as a Privy Counsellor but as an executive officer to give information to such Cabinet or Committee, to refuse disclosing what may have passed upon the occasion of such attendance. And that at all events there can be no objection, either in law or good policy, which should prevent the Commander-in-Chief from communicating (if your Majesty should be graciously pleased to consent to his communicating) whatever may have passed upon such an occasion. And Mr Perceval is therefore authorised to submit to your Majesty as the humble advice of your Majesty's confidential servants, that your Majesty should be graciously pleased to give your Majesty's consent to the Commander-in-Chief to state whatever he may recollect to have passed on that occasion. Mr Perceval will communicate, if your Majesty should think fit, your Majesty's pleasure to the Commander-in-Chief upon this subject. (14929–30)

[*The King's reply, Windsor Castle, 5 Feb.*] In consequence of the opinion of the Cabinet conveyed in Mr Perceval's letter that Sir David Dundas is not bound by anything in his oath as a Privy Counsellor to decline answering the questions which may be put to him as to what he stated when he attended the Cabinet to give information upon certain military points, his Majesty will not withhold his sanction to his stating what then passed, being confident that Sir D. Dundas will take care himself to draw the proper line in regard to what should or should not be disclosed. (14931)

[*From Perceval, Downg. St., Monday night, 5 Feb. 1810.*] Mr Perceval acquaints your Majesty that a Secret Committee was appointed this evening by the House of Commons to receive such evidence and secret intelligence as it might not be adviseable to examine in public. Lord Porchester had intended to compose the Committee of a decided majority of Opposition Members, which Mr Perceval resisted, and the House divided upon Sir John Sebright being proposed, instead of whom Mr Perceval moved for Mr Yorke—and Mr Perceval carried the question by 196 to 128—after which they did not divide again—and Mr Perceval encloses for your Majesty's inspection the names of the Comee. which were appointed.[4] The House then resolved itself into the Committee on the Enquiry, & upon Sir

---

[1] Sir Thomas Wentworth, 1st Earl of Strafford, Charles I's famous Minister (1593–1641).

[2] The Second Partition Treaty of 1699 which assigned Spain, the Netherlands and the Spanish colonies to the Archduke Charles of Austria, and the Spanish possessions in Italy to France. The Tories in Parliament threatened with impeachment William III's Whig Ministers who had negotiated the Treaty.   [3] He meant 1710–11.

[4] Lord Porchester, Bragge-Bathurst, F. J. Robinson, Admiral Markham, General Ferguson, Wilberforce, Sturges-Bourne, Charles Yorke, Captain Beresford, D. Giddy and General Craufurd. (14934)

D. Dundas being called in Mr Perceval stated the distinction which he felt between the case of the Commander-in-Chief attending the Privy Council in his office as Commander-in-Chief to give information to the Privy Council, and that of a Privy Counsellor attending as one of the Counsel to deliberate upon what is going on—and strongly stating that he still retained his opinion upon the general question respecting the examination of a Privy Counsellor, waived pressing his objection against the examination of the Commander-in-Chief.

Mr Perceval conceives that he has left the general question less prejudiced by so doing than it would have been had he attempted to raise it in this case, or than if he had brought forward to the House your Majesty's consent to the examination—which consent, however, he delivered to Sr. D. Dundas for his satisfaction—and Mr Perceval can assure your Majesty that there was nothing which the Commander-in-Chief had to say which was at all beyond the limits of your Majesty's permission. Having gone thro his examination Lord Porchester proceeded to call Sir Lucas Pepys who was examined as to the deceases of Walcheren & the sickness in the army, and with his examination the Committee closed. It sits again tomorrow.[1] (14932–3)

[*The King's reply, Windsor Castle, 6 Feb.*] The King has learnt with pleasure from Mr Perceval that Lord Porchester's attempt to compose the Secret Committee of a majority of Opposition Members was successfully resisted, and that the question, on the examination of Sir D. Dundas, has been left in a more satisfactory manner than had been apprehended. (14933)

[*From Perceval, Downg. St., 6 Feb.*] Mr Perceval acquaints your Majesty that Mr Sheridan moved this evening that it be referred to the Comee. of Privileges to consider of the Standing Order relative to the exclusion of strangers.[2] Mr Windham opposed the Motion in his best style and after a debate of some length in which Lord Folkstone and Sr Frs. Burdett & Mr Tierney spoke for the Motion, and Mr Yorke against it the House divided *166* against the Motion, and *80* for it.[3]

The House then resolved into the Comee. of Enquiry and examined the Surgeon-General Mr Keate, & the Inspector General of Hospitals Mr Knight, and then adjourned. The Comee. is to sit again on Thursday next.

Mr Perceval transmits to your Majesty for yr. Majesty's approbation and signature (if your Majesty should be graciously pleased to approve them) two Messages to the House of Lords & Commons[4] for the purpose of carrying into

[1] *Parl. Deb.*, xv, 314–20.

[2] On 1 Feb. Charles Yorke gave notice that he should enforce the Standing Order for the exclusion of strangers during the inquiry into the conduct of the Walcheren expedition. (*Parl. Deb.*, xv, 269.) He had had no wish to prevent publicity, but was anxious to prevent newspaper misrepresentations before the publication of the Minutes.

[3] *Parl. Deb.*, xv, 323–45. Sheridan, though a zealous advocate of the freedom of the press, did not suggest the abandonment of the Standing Order. He wished it to be modified so that its exercise should depend, not upon the caprice or pleasure of a single Member, but on the decision of the House.

[4] The King's Message to the Commons is in *Parl. Deb.*, xv, 355 (8 Feb.). The House was invited to bestow on Wellington and the two next succeeding Viscounts a net annuity of £2,000, as a reward for his victory at Talavera on 28 July 1809.

effect your Majesty's gracious purpose towards Lord Wellington, which Mr Perceval understands from Lord Castlereagh that your Majesty was pleased to express upon the application of his Grace the late Duke of Portland, at the time when the title was conferred on him. (14935)

[*The King's reply, Queen's Palace, 7 Feb.*] The King acknowledges the receipt of Mr Perceval's report of what passed in the House of Commons last night & his Majesty returns the Messages which he has signed. (14936)

4077   *Letters from* PRINCESS MARY *to the* KING, *and the reply*

[*Tuesday night* [*6 Feb. 1810*].] I hope I may say Amelia has not passed a worse day than yesterday though Dr. Pope was anxious she should give up the idea of any more cold meat dinners, yet Amelia with her usual resolution determined to try it one day more, therefore had cold chicken again today & got up & lay on the couch in hopes that being out of bed might make the dinner go off better, but the spasm came on just the same & lasted full as long as yesterday, but is now perfectly easy again, & in consequence of having received Sir Henry Halford's most *positive* & *decided* orders that no more solid food is to be thought of, she has ordered chicken panada for to name which is what the phyans. advise, as well as beef tea or arrowroot. The pain in the side has been rather worse today but neither Dr. Pope or Batiscombe[1] found the pulse very quick this evening. She was out of bed about an hour, much fatigued but I thought more comfortable for having had the bed made.

Wednesday morning. I am happy to inform you that Amelia has had her three hours sleep & untill five o'clock passed a quieter night than she has done for some time, but since five o'clock she has been restless. She says she feels much the same today but admits she was less heated than usual in the night. Mr. Dundas found Amelia rather if anything better than the last time he saw her. (Add. Georgian 12/133)

[*The King's reply, Queen's Palace, 7 Feb.*] I am very glad to hear from your kind letter, just received, that dear Amelia has passed a more quiet night and was less heated. I also rejoyce that the idea of making her take solid meat is given up & that chicken panada is to be substituted, which I hope will not disagree with her. (Add. Georgian 12/134)

[*From Princess Mary, Wednesday night, 7 Feb.*] I have many thanks to return you for your kind letter & am most thankful to be able to assure you that Amelia has passed a better day in every respect than I have seen her God knows when: though much pain at times in the side, yet she thinks herself relieved from the operation of the medicines. Chicken panada was the dinner & did not disagree; a very small quantity was taken but it brought on no spasm. She has been up for

[1] Robert Battiscombe, the Windsor apothecary (salary, £160 a year).

an hour and lay on the couch, & indeed, all things considered, I feel very certain Amelia is *a little better* today.

Thursday morning. I am happy to say dear Amelia has had better than three hours sleep & *two hours at once*, and Mrs. Davenport[1] who sat up says it is one of the quietest nights Amelia has had for some time past. (Add. Georgian 12/135)

[*The King's reply, Queen's Palace, 8 Feb.*] Your kind letter received this day afforded me more comfort than any report concerning dear Amelia which had been made to me for a considerable time past, & I observe with great pleasure that the hopes expressed yesterday that she had been relieved by the medicine are confirmed by the subsequent assurance that her rest had been so much better than usual. The Queen desires me to add that she has not time to write to you before she goes to St. James's, but that she proposes to see Amelia tomorrow on her return to Windsor. (Add. Georgian 12/136)

4078   PRINCESS AMELIA *to the* KING, *and the reply*

[*Wednesday night [7 Feb. 1810].*] As I had nothing new to say of myself, my beloved & dear papa, I would not trouble you with a letter this morng. All I could say I hope you know & now repeat how sorry I am to be deprived the pleasure of seeing you & with what delight I look forwards to Friday. The doctors here forbid the meat being persevered with, for which I am very thankfull, & have recommended chicken panada, thin beef tea & arrowroot with orange as a substitute. The panada I tried today & it did not oppress me like the meat, & I assure you I have not forgot my gruel or orange juice. The calomel has relieved me by its effect. I am now lying on the couch. I get up about seven for my tea & I hope it will give me a better night. I will not take up more of your time than to repeat how I am feasting on the thoughts of seeing you Friday. (Add. Georgian 14/159)

[*The King's reply, Queen's Palace, 8 Feb.*] I am truly sensible of your affectionate attention in writing to me & not less pleased to have received both from yourself and dear Mary a more comfortable account of you. I also rejoice that the last change of diet has answered my hopes that it would not disagree with you as did the solid meat, and I shall be impatient to receive a further confirmation tomorrow of what is so essential to my comfort.

The Queen has desired me to say that she has not time to thank you for your letter before she goes to St. James', but that she will call upon you tomorrow in her return to Windsor. (Add. Georgian 14/160)

4079   *Letters from the* MARQUESS WELLESLEY *to the* KING, *and the reply*

[*Foreign Office, 8 Feb. 1810.*] Lord Wellesley has the honor to submit to your Majesty a copy of a communication received late last night from an agent of the

---

[1] The 'necessary woman' in the Princesses' establishment.

Dutch Government. The verbal explanations received from the same person tend to prove that this communication is not made without the connivance of France, & that it is intended to open the way to a negotiation for a general peace. (14937)

[*The King's reply, Queen's Palace, 9 Feb.*] The King acknowledges the receipt of Lord Wellesley's letter transmitting the very extraordinary overture made by the Dutch Government. It appears a strange pretension from a country having no claim whatever on this, that England should subscribe to a bad peace in order to benefit that country, or should, with a view to its partial relief, alter her system under the precarious expectation that France will annull its useless Decrees when concessions shall have been made by England. (14937)

[*From Lord Wellesley, Foreign Office, 9 Feb.*] Lord Wellesley has the honor to submit to your Majesty a letter from his Sicilian Majesty on the subject of the marriage of the Duke of Orleans; a letter to her Majesty on the same subject; a letter from the Supreme Central Junta of Spain in the name of King Ferdinand the 7th, acknowledging the recredentials of your Majesty's late Ambassador to Spain.[1] (14939)

4080 SPENCER PERCEVAL *to the* KING, *and the reply*

[*Downing St., 9 Feb.* [*1810*], *Friday morng.*] Mr Perceval acquaints your Majesty that the Comee. of Enquiry sat from six o'clock yesterday evening till $\frac{1}{4}$ p. 1 o'clock this morning; it was wholly engaged in the examination of Sir Thos. Trigg, Genl. Calvert, Col. Gordon[2] and Sir Home Popham.[3]

Mr Perceval forwards to your Majesty herewith a warrant for your Majesty's signature for transferring thirty thousand pound[s] from the Civil List of Scotland in aid of your Majesty's Civil List in England; if your Majesty should think fit to approve of such transfer there will remain on the account of your Majesty's Civil List in Scotland [*sic*]. (14938)

[*The King's reply, Queen's Palace, 9 Feb.*] The King acknowledges the receipt of Mr Perceval's report of last night's proceedings in the House of Commons, and his Majesty returns the warrant which he has signed. (14938)

---

[1] Wellesley himself. The recredentials were dated 29 Dec. 1809.

[2] Colonel Gordon had become Commissary General in 1809. He wrote to his friend Tierney on 29 Sept. 1809: 'On Monday I move to my office in Great George Street. Be careful in marking *private* on the cover of your notes and put them under cover—To the Secretary of the Commander-in-Chief, London.' (Tierney MSS.)

[3] Canning wrote to Mrs. Canning on 8 Feb.: 'Ld. Grey thinks that Opposition are mismanaging the inquiry; and he is right. *My* opinion is that it will do no mischief—except to Lord Chatham—and that the Government will stand *tel qu'il est*. I think it was lucky for the Govt. to be beaten upon the motion for the Committee. I would have saved them from it if I could—not out of kindness—motion upon motion would have followed—and upon them they would have been discredited and beaten *at last*. But this vote has satisfied qualmish consciences. The inquiry is no more Perceval's business than mine, and just so much as Cast[lerea]gh's—and so two months will be lost—which would have been employed in constant attacks upon the *Govt.* And nothing will come of it—except a Court Martial, *perhaps*, upon Ld. C[hatham]. So, I am not sanguine, dearest love, of any good result this year—and I cannot be in opposition till next.' (Harewood MSS.)

4081 THE MARQUESS WELLESLEY *to the* KING, *and the reply*

[*Foreign Office, 11 Feb. 1810.*] Lord Wellesley has the honor to submit for your Majesty's gracious approbation the draft of a communication which it is proposed to make to the agent of the Dutch Government, lately arrived with the overture from Holland. It does not appear advisable to return any official or formal reply to this proposal; & it is therefore intended, with your Majesty's sanction, that the answer should appear to be nothing more than a note of a verbal communication from your Majesty's principal Secretary of State for Foreign Affairs, without his signature. The Dutch Agent will be permitted to take a copy of the paper, & another will be retained in the Foreign Office. Lord Wellesley proposes to advise M. Labouchere[1] to return to Holland without delay; but as he is naturalised in this country, it will not be easy to compel his departure. His continuance here is certainly not desirable.

The draft of the proposed Note and the intended course of proceeding have been approved by your Majesty's confidential servants. Lord Wellesley humbly hopes to receive the notification of your Majesty's gracious approbation. (14940–1)

[*The King's reply, Windsor Castle, 12 Feb.*] The King returns to Lord Wellesley the draft of the communication to Mr. Labouchere, the sentiments of which his Majesty entirely approves, as he also does the clear & concise manner in which they are conveyed. (14941)

4082 SPENCER PERCEVAL *to the* KING, *and the reply*

[*Downg. St., 12 Feb. 1810.*] Mr Perceval acquaints your Majesty that in consequence of the death of Lady Chs. Fitzroy[2] (Lord Castlereagh's sister) it has been agreed to put off the further prosecution of the Enquiry till Thursday next. (14942)

[*The King's reply, Windsor Castle, 13 Feb.*] The King has learnt with much concern from Mr Perceval that the adjournment of the Enquiry until Thursday next is occasioned by the death of Lady Charles Fitzroy. (14942)

4083 THE MARQUESS WELLESLEY *to the* KING, *and the reply*

[*Foreign Office, 13 Feb. 1810.*] Lord Wellesley has the honor to acquaint your Majesty that a person of the name of Fagan is arrived from Paris by the way of Ostend with the purpose of ascertaining the views of your Majesty's Government respecting peace with France. This person bears no regular credentials nor even

---

[1] Peter Caesar Labouchere (*d.* 1839 in his 68th year). A Dutch banker who, in 1796, had married Dorothy Elizabeth, third daughter of the London banker Sir Francis Baring (1740–1810). Henry Labouchere, Baron Taunton (1798–1869), was his elder son. Napoleon hoped that the prospect of annexing Holland to France might intimidate England into making peace.

[2] Lady Frances Anne Stewart (1777–1810) married Lord Charles Fitzroy (1764–1829) as his second wife, on 10 March 1799. She died on 9 February. Lord Charles was M.P. for Bury St. Edmunds, 1787–96, 1802–18, and was the second surviving son of the 3rd Duke of Grafton.

any written certificate; nor does he pretend to be authorized in any way by the French Minister for Foreign Affairs; he represents himself to be employed by the French Ministers, Maret,[1] and Fouchet,[2] with the supposed connivance of Bonaparte, to learn whether your Majesty's Government is disposed to receive propositions of peace from France. The first overtures from M. Fagan were received this morning by Mr Smith,[3] Under-Secretary of State; Lord Wellesley has seen Mr Fagan this evening, & will have the honor of submitting to your Majesty, with all practicable expedition, a detailed view of that agent's communications. In the meanwhile Mr Smith's report is transmitted to your Majesty.

Lord Wellesley conceives it to be his duty to add his humble opinion that no other reply can be given to this overture than that already given under your Majesty's sanction, to M. Labouchere. With this view, it may appear to be sufficient to inform Mr Fagan that your Majesty's sentiments with regard to peace with France are already known & require no further explanation. (14943–4)

[*The King's reply, Windsor Castle, 14 Feb.*] Lord Wellesley appears disposed to treat the indirect proposals received from Holland & those brought more recently by Mr Fagan so entirely upon the only principle in which the King can concur, that his M. has merely to encourage him to persevere in that course. (14944)

4084   SPENCER PERCEVAL *to the* KING

[*Downg. St., 15 Feb. 1810.*] Mr Perceval acquaints your Majesty that the Enquiry proceeded yesterday evening and Sr. Rd. Strachan & Lord Gardener[4] were examined. The House adjourned about ½ p. one o'clock this morning.[5] (14945)

4085   ROBERT BOWYER[6] *to the* KING

[*80 Pall Mall, 16 Feb. 1810.*] May it please your Majesty, the kind attentions which I have repeatedly been honored with from your Majesty, demand & will ever receive my most grateful & dutiful acknowledgments. Having just completed a most beautifully embellished volume of poems (which have been written expressly for the occasion) on the abolition of the slave trade, a measure which must have so much accorded with those feelings of humanity & kindness which have ever been so conspicuous in your Majesty's disposition, I would most humbly flatter myself with the hope that your Majesty will deign to accept a copy of this

---

1 Hughes Bernard Maret, Duc de Bassano and Secretary of State for Foreign Affairs, 1811.

2 Joseph Fouché, Duc d'Otranto (1763–1820), was Napoleon's Minister of Police. Unknown to the Emperor, he sent Fagan to London to negotiate unofficially for peace. At the end of May Napoleon heard of this secret intrigue, and Fouché was dismissed.

3 Charles Culling Smith (*d.* 1853), Under-Secretary of State for Foreign Affairs, Dec. 1809–Feb. 1812. He was Lord Wellesley's brother-in-law, having married Lady Anne Wellesley (whose first husband, Henry Fitzroy, had died in 1794). She died in Dec. 1844. Lord Glenbervie, who loved to retail scandal, alleged that Culling Smith had been 'long supposed to be, *au dernier point*, in the good graces of the Duchess of York'—Lady Anne being one of the Duchess's Ladies of the Bedchamber. (*Glenbervie Journals*, I, 363.)   4 Gardner.

5 So the letter really should have been dated the 16th. For the examination see *Parl. Deb.*, xv, Appx., pp. ccxxxix–cclxx.   6 The painter and book illustrator (1758–1834).

my new publication which with the utmost respect & gratitude I would beg leave
to lay at your Majesty's feet, rejoicing at the same time in the opportunity it
affords me of assuring your Majesty of the unfeigned attachment & regard with
which I would humbly beg leave to subscribe myself [etc.]. (14946)

4086   THE EARL OF ARRAN[1] to the KING

[*Dover St., 17 Feb. 1810.*] Emboldened by your Majesty's gracious notice during
a period of 14 years, I venture to tresspass on your time for a few minutes, relying
on your Majesty's experienced goodness to pardon the intrusion, and that if in
my mode of addressing yr. Majesty there is any seeming want of respect, it can
arise from no other cause than a want of knowing the proper form.

About four years ago, when your Majesty was so gracious to admit me to an
Audience, I named my having, from my first setting out in life, decided on attach-
ing myself to your Majesty, & supporting those whom I considered as your most
faithful servants. Unfortunately my father[2] (tho' a most loyal subject & firmly
attached to yr. Majesty's person & House) differed with me in the way of shewing
it; the consequence was my not being brought into Parliament again by him—and
I told yr. Majesty how shamefully the party my father supported, with almost
unexampled steadiness, treated him when they came into your Majesty's Councils.
Again, at the solicitation of my friends, I came into Parliament for a county my
ancestors had represented for more than a century, but certainly under the immediate influence of my brother-in-law, Lord Abercorn.[3] We differed on a
question relative to yr. Majesty, a coolness has ever since subsisted between us,
& as I mentioned to your Majesty on the dissolution of that Parliament, I declined
offering myself again for the county, resolved never to come in under the influence
of any man.

Had I been able to pay my duty, since I became the head of my family, to your
Majesty I should, with yr. gracious permission, have stated in person what I am
now obliged to write.

In December last I wrote to Mr Perceval, stating that having uniformly supported those with whom he acted (& whom I considered as yr. Majesty's most
attach'd servants) whilst I was in Parliament, I trusted he wou'd have no objection
to lay my humble duty at yr. Majesty's feet, and solicit for me some mark of your
gracious approbation, telling him that I did not for myself want a place, as my
means are, tho' not very great, sufficient, with prudence, to mentain that rank
yr. Majesty has been pleased to raise my family to; but that either a Representative
or a British Peerage wou'd be the most gratifying mark of yr. favor & approbation, mentioning that my father had left me a large young family with little or

---

[1] Arthur Saunders, 3rd Earl of Arran [I.] (1761–1837). Tory M.P. for Baltimore, 1783–90; for Co.
Donegal, 1801–6. Succeeded his father, 8 Oct. 1809; earlier, from 1773, he had been styled Viscount
Sudley.

[2] Arthur Saunders, 2nd Earl of Arran (1734–1809), succeeded his father, 17 April 1773. M.P. for
Donegal, 1759–60, 1768–73; for Co. Wexford, 1761–68. K.P., 5 Feb. 1783.

[3] John James, 1st Marquess of Abercorn (1756–1818), married (3 April 1800), as his third wife,
Lady Anne Hatton (1763–1827), widow of Henry Hatton and daughter of the 2nd Earl of Arran.

nothing;[1] & requesting some preferment for a brother in the Church,[2] and I ventured to say, I hoped, if he did lay my request before yr. Majesty, that you wou'd not be indisposed to gratify me, at some convenient opportunity. In answer, he said he wou'd enquire if there was any prospect of meeting my wishes for my brother, but that as to either the Representative or the British Peerage, he could not, from *existing engagements*, give me any encouragement. I shou'd have said I mentioned that by my not having a family, there might be less objections to my getting a Peerage than in other cases. In asking this I can truly affirm I have no ambition for myself, my only object being to have the means of enforcing my claims for the the [sic] advancement of my young brothers. There is a widow with a very small jointure & seven children, by my father's last marriage, *unprovided* for except by the professions the boys are in; two in the Army & two in the Navy, and I own I am at a loss to find a reason why Mr Perceval refuses to entertain *my* request, & prefers that of others *untried*, who have not either more power, or a larger stake in the country than I have; I mean my Lord Thomond.[3]

Sire, having intruded so long in stating my situation, I once more lay myself at yr. Majesty's feet, praying yr forgiveness, & I will only add my greatest ambition is a continuance of that gracious notice I have experienced from yr. Majesty & your family, nor is there any place I cou'd wish to have but one which, from my misfortune of being lame I am unfit for, that of belonging to your Majesty's family, as it wou'd have been the most gratifying circumstance to me to be about the person of one I so truly revere. With the most fervent prayers for every blessing an all-wise & just God can bestow on your Majesty, & your august family I remain [etc.]. (14947–51)

4087   SPENCER PERCEVAL *to the* KING, *and the reply*

[*Downg. St., 17 Feb. 1810.*] Mr Perceval acquaints your Majesty that he moved in the Committee of the House of Commons yesterday evening to vote for Lord Wellington's pension according to your Majesty's Message. The debate went to considerable length. Mr Howard,[4] Lord Carlisle's son, Mr Calcraft, Mr

---

[1] His father had six children by his first wife, three by his second, and seven by his third, Elizabeth (*d.* 1829), daughter of Richard Underwood, of Dublin.

[2] His brother, the Rev. George Gore (1774–1844), became Dean of Killala.

[3] William, 2nd Marquess of Thomond (*c.* 1765–1846). In the Army, 1790–1800. P.C. [I.], Jan. 1809; K.P., Nov. 1809; Representative Peer [I.], 1816–46. *Cr.* Baron Tadcaster [U.K.], 3 July 1826. On 10 Feb. 1808 he had succeeded his uncle, the 1st Marquess, under the special remainder. The Duke of Richmond wrote to Perceval on 10 Jan.: 'I enclose a letter I have this morning received from Lord Thomond, his statement is just but he has omitted one circumstance which I have understood to be the case namely that Mr. Pitt had intended to have recommended to his Majesty to put his name in the entail of the late Marquis's English Peerage. I have known Lord Thomond intimately for many years and can fairly say there cannot be a more respectable man. He has some weight in the County Cork and very considerable weight in Clare. His relation Sir Edwd. O'Brien was in opposition to the present Ministers when we came in but through his influence has now joined us heartily. I am aware of your objection to encrease the peerage and perfectly agree with you in the principle. It is for you to judge whether in Lord Thomond's case a bad precedent would be made.' (Richmond MSS. 72/1499, and Add. MSS. 38244, fo. 177.)

[4] William Howard (1781–1843), second son of the 5th Earl of Carlisle. M.P. for Morpeth, 1806–26, 1830–2; for Sutherland, 1837–40.

Lyttleton, Lord Milton, Sr Francis Burdett, Lord Archibald Hamilton, Mr Whitbread and Mr Windham opposed it. Mr. F. Robinson, General Craufurd, General Loftus, Mr Fuller, Mr Wilberforce, Lord Desart and Mr Canning supported it. Lord Desart spoke for the first time, and Mr Perceval thinks that when his Lordship gets a little used to the House that he will speak with very great effect.[1]

The Comee divided for the Motion, 213; against it, 106. (14952)

[1] *Parl. Deb.*, xv, 440–67. The minority is erroneously given as 206 in Colchester, II, 234. Canning, writing to his wife on the 17th, had this to say about the debate: 'I told my own love yesterday that I was going down to the House of Commons to vote and not to speak. But lo! at twelve o'clock, or thereabouts, after Windham had spoken against the pension, tho' very gentlemanlikely, and nobody (as I thought) had spoken well for it—what should I do but get up and make such a speech as quite surprized my own self, and seemed to carry the whole House with it? Charles, who has been fastidious and dissatisfied this year—the first day, because I did not speak long and early—and the next, because I spoke short and late—professes himself completely satisfied now, and ranks the speech of last night next to great Spanish speech of last year. I protest I had no more notion when I went down, of saying one word than I had of the particular words and things which I did say. I believe Bootle was the first cause of my speaking, for he called me out about eleven while the debate was going mortal dully, and told me that people who sat about him, country gentlemen and Government discontented voters, were wondering whether I would speak, to lend them a lift, and hoping that I would. So I went back to my place and began ruminating, and Windham's speech determined me. But I was not the least hostile to Windh. His speech did not deserve it. His distinctions were very rational and just, between this vote and the thanks—but he afforded me the better opportunity for discussion, without angry difference—and I called him once (almost by a slip) my Rt. Honble. friend. Morning Chron., I see, does not give much of speech, though it praises it—and Windham it leaves out altogether. It leaves out also a part of Mr. Calcraft's speech, which I had occasion to answer. Mr. C[alcraft] said that this pension and honours to Ld. Welln. arose from a contest between me and Perceval for Wellesley's support—in which *I* had been beaten by Perceval through means of these bribes to W[ellesle]y's brother. I answered that I at least could not be influenced in my vote by those considerations—even according to C[alcraf]t's own shewing that I had nothing to gain by it, and that I certainly had nothing to *pay for* by it. As to the honours I thought it right to confirm Robinson's statement that Castgh. had been the chief mover of them. If there was blame in giving them, I claimed my share of it—if there was merit, I left it all to Castgh. (He was not present, owing to his sister's death.) Now the truth is, there *is* blame and great blame, generally felt, for the *double* peerage—and I was not sorry to get *handsomely* out of my share in it, by this claiming and disclaiming.

'I think this is all that is worth telling my own love except that Morpeth was in a pleasant sort of a passion (as Granville reported) at my having described the House of Peers as 'a stagnant lake of collected honour, requiring to be occasionally refreshed and augmented by infusions from new springs of merit bursting forth from all the different sources of eminence and glory'—or something to that effect. Morpeth did not approve of the disparagement of hereditary stagnation. The use of speech last night, dearest love, was to shew how a debate on such subjects ought to be concluded, on the ministerial side of the House—and to leave people with an impression of confidence and spirit, which no preceding part of the debate had given them—and so it has done its work.' (Harewood MSS.)

Wellesley-Pole, writing to the Duke of Richmond, had these comments: 'We had as you will see by the papers a very triumphant day yesterday on Arthur's pension; the debate was most flattering to him, and there was a most beautiful panegyric from Wyndham on him, which I have not seen in any of the papers—tho he voted against us he was Arthur's strongest advocate; Robinson spoke remarkably well—Lord Desart made his debut. He was very nervous, but I think his speech gives promise of some talent; if I were to criticise him which would not be fair, for he evidently did not possess himself, I should say that the speech contained nothing but a string of set sentences upon the general question, and that he made no observation upon any thing that fell in debate. He spoke in too low a tone of voice, and in a hurried manner—but these defects I think he will correct. The question was made completely a party one and the greatest exertions were used by Opposition for a full attendance. Sir J. Anstruther and Banks voted against us—Wilberforce for us. Numbers 106–213—the majority you will perceive was a good one. But Opposition getting 106 persons to vote with them on such a question is a strong proof of their strength and discipline.' (Richmond MSS. 73/1718.)

[*The King's reply, Windsor Castle, 17 Feb.*] The King has learnt with much satisfaction from Mr Perceval the favourable result of last night's proceedings in the House of Commons. (14952)

4088 THE EARL OF LIVERPOOL *to the* KING, *and the reply*

[*London, 18 Feb. 1810.*] Lord Liverpool begs leave most humbly to submit to your Majesty that as it appears by Mr Frere's last dispatches that Major-Genl. Campbell[1] has detached from Gibraltar 1000 men for the garrison of Cadiz, and as it is probable that Lord Wellington has detached from the army in Portugal for the same purpose, in consequence of the instruction of the 3d of April 1809, your Majesty's confidential servants are of opinion that it may be proper to send some officer of sufficient rank from this country to command the said force, and as Major-Genl. Graham[2] is personally acquainted with Genl. Castanos, and has already been at Cadiz, they venture to submit his name to your Majesty for this command. (14953)

[*The King's reply, Windsor Castle, 19 Feb.*] The King entirely concurs in the opinion conveyed by Lord Liverpool that an officer of sufficient rank should be sent to command the force which may be assembled at Cadiz, and H.M. considers the choice made of M. General Graham for that duty as extremely proper. (14953)

4089 SPENCER PERCEVAL *to the* KING, *and the reply*

[*Downg. St., 19 Feb. 1810.*] Mr Perceval acquaints your Majesty that Lord Cochrane moved for some papers from the Court of Admiralty, in moving for which his Lordship expressed himself with great acrimony & severity against that Court. The Court was most ably defended by Sr J. Nicholl & Mr Stephen, and the debate ended very satisfactorily, such papers only being produced as in Sr. W. Scott's opinion would give more weight to the defence than it would have had without their production.

The House then proceeded to the Enquiry. Lord Folkstone took notice of Lord Chatham's narrative which had been laid upon the table. His Lordship, Mr Tierney, Mr Ponsonby and Mr Wms. Wynn contended that the delivery of that paper to yr. Majesty, instead of being delivered thro' your Majesty's Secretary of State, was so irregular & unconstitutional that the House should not have received the paper. Mr Perceval, Mr Ryder & Mr Dundas contended against that objection as most unfounded—and after a long and eager debate on the part of the Opposition the debate ended by calling on the Speaker to give his [opinion] whether it was consistent with Parliamentary form to receive a paper which had been so

---

[1] Colin Campbell (1754–1814). Ensign, 1771; Lieutenant, 1774; Major, 1783; Lieutenant-Colonel, 1795; Colonel, 1798; Major-General, 1805; Lieutenant-General, 1811; Lieutenant-Governor of Gibraltar, 1810–14.

[2] Thomas Graham, Lord Lynedoch (1748–1843). Lieutenant-Colonel, 1794; Colonel, 1795; Major-General, 1809; Lieutenant-General, July 1810; General, 1821. K.B., Feb. 1812; peerage, 17 May 1814. M.P. for Perthshire, 1794–1807.

presented. The Speaker had no doubt that it was so—and the paper was referred to the Committee. It was read, and the impression it made was certainly, tho not intended by Lord Chatham, that it was meant as an attack upon the Admiral [*sic*]. The Comee. examined Admiral Sr. R. Keats and sat till near three o'clock.[1] (14954)

[*The King's reply, Windsor Castle, 20 Feb.*] The King is glad to learn from Mr Perceval's report that Lord Cochrane's intemperate Motion was so well met last night & that the objection started to the admission of Lord Chatham's report was overruled by the reference to the Speaker. (14955)

4090 RICHARD RYDER *to the* KING, *and the reply*

[*Whitehall, 20 Feb. 1810.*] Mr Ryder has the honor of laying before the King a letter he has received from the High Bailiff of Westminster,[2] and a copy of his answer. Mr Ryder had so lately received your Majesty's commands upon a similar subject that he did not think it necessary to submit the draft of the answer to your Majesty previously to the sending it to the High Bailiff. (14956)

[*The King's reply, Windsor Castle, 21 Feb.*] The King entirely approves of the answer Mr Ryder has returned to the communication from the High Bailiff of Westminster. (14946)

4091 *Letters from* SPENCER PERCEVAL *to the* KING, *and the replies*

[*21 Feb. 1810.*] Mr Perceval acquaints your Majesty that a printer[3] was brought to the Bar of the House of Commons yesterday evening on the Motion of Mr Yorke for reflecting upon the proceedings of the House in clearing the Gallery. He expressed his sorrow and gave up the name of the author, John Gale Jones.[4] The House committed him to the Serjt. at Arms, meaning to discharge him tomorrow, having ordered J. G. Jones to attend who is likely to be more severely [punished].

[1] *Parl. Deb.*, xv, 469–93. The letter must have been written early in the morning of the 20th. Lord Morpeth wrote, on the 20th: 'Ld. Chatham's narrative was produced yesterday, & a most extraordinary production it proved to be, with scarce any reserve or disguise imputing the whole failure of the expedition to the conduct of Sr. R. Strachan & the Navy, from the period at [which] they were [*sic*] first appeared off the enemy's coast, to that at which he thought it necessary to discontinue all farther operations. The sensation produced in the House was considerable. By the step he has thus taken he will prejudice the House of Commons against him; he will, I think, grievously offend the Navy, & disgust the public. There was a debate of some length in consequence. Tierney did not menager Ld. C. Perceval's two colle[a]gues in the Cabinet make but a moderate figure. The examination of Sr. R. Keates did not begin till 12 o'clock. I was too tired to stay.' (Castle Howard MSS.)

[2] Arthur Morris.

[3] John Dean, who said that he had been employed by John Gale Jones to print what the Speaker described as 'a scandalous and libellous handbill' reflecting on the proceedings of the House; and that he was unaware of its contents until the whole impression had been thrown off. (*Parl. Deb.*, xv, 496.)

[4] An apothecary, and Radical agitator, who had already, in 1798, been imprisoned for sedition. (1769–1838.)

The House then proceeded to the Enquiry and examined Lord Huntley, and Sir Wm. Erskine.[1] The Comee. then adjourned at ½ p. one this morning.[2] (14957)

[*The King's reply, Windsor Castle, 21 Feb.*] The King acknowledges the receipt of Mr Perceval's report of what passed in the House of Commons last night. (14958)

[*From Perceval, Downg. St., 22 Feb.*] Mr Perceval acquaints your Majesty that the House of Commons sent J. Gale Jones to Newgate yesterday evng. for a breach of the privileges of the House in commenting upon its proceedings, and discharged the printer who had published the comment.

The House then went into the Committee on the Enquiry, and examined Genl. Sr. J. Hope and the Earl of Rosslyn. It had been agreed that the House should proceed to other business at ten o'clock. The Committee therefore went no further with the Enquiry. But Mr Tierney wishing that the Enquiry should have precedence of other business again this day moved that the Chairman should be directed to move that the Committee should sit at 4 o'clock this afternoon. Other business which pressed in point of time, namely the renewal of the Distillery Restriction Bill, stood appointed for today; Mr Perceval therefore opposed Mr. Tierney's Motion and the Committee divided 53 against the Motion, & 52 for it. When the House was resumed the Motion was repeated, and, some more persons of the Opposition having come in, the Motion was carried in the House by 55 to 53. The friends of Governt. had left the House and this question was therefore thus carried against it by surprise. Mr Perceval however trusts that he shall be able to set this right again when the House meets this day.[3] (14959)

[*From Perceval, Downing St., 22 Feb.*] Mr Perceval herewith transmits to your Majesty the copy of a new arrangement for your Majesty's Commissariat Establishment, which has been proposed by the present Commissary-General Col. Gordon, and which your Majesty's Treasury will give directions to be carried into execution, if the arrangement should meet with your Majesty's approbation. (14961)

[*The King's reply, Windsor Castle, 22 Feb.*] The King acknowledges the receipt of Mr Perceval's report of the proceedings in the House of Commons last night & his Majesty returns the proposal for a new arrangement of the Commissariat upon which he has marked his approval. (14960)

[1] Sir William Erskine (1770–1813) succeeded his father as 2nd Baronet, 19 March 1795. Lieutenant-Colonel, 1794; Colonel, 1801; Major-General, 1808. M.P. for Fifeshire, 1796–1806.

[2] *Parl. Deb.*, xv, 495–500.

[3] *Parl. Deb.*, xv, 500–3. The printer escaped severe punishment on the ground that he readily revealed the name of the author of the libel, that he had shown contrition for his offence, that he was an honest and industrious man with a family and not in affluent circumstances, and that the MS. was printed by his workmen without his personal knowledge.

The 'other business' referred to was not reported, the Gallery having been cleared.

[*London, 22 Feb. 1810.*] Lord Liverpool begs leave most humbly to submit to your Majesty the Minutes of the House of Lords, and to inform your Majesty that there has been a very good debate upon the Address respecting Portugal. Lord Wellesley moved the Address very well, and Lord Harrowby made a most excellent speech towards the close of the debate. The Marquis of Landsdowne spoke for the first time and with considerable ability,[1] Lord Sidmouth and Lord Buckinghamshire supported the Address. The division was less favourable than it ought to have been owing to several Peers who had no proxies being accidentally absent.[2] (14962)

[*The King's reply, Windsor Castle, 23 Feb.*] The King acknowledges the receipt of Lord Liverpool's report on the proceedings in the House of Lords last night. (14962)

4093 *Letters from* SPENCER PERCEVAL *to the* KING, *and the replies*

[*Downg. St., 23 Feb.* [*1810*].] Mr Perceval acquaints your Majesty that the House met yesterday afternoon at 4 o'clock and Lord Porchester moved that the Order of the Day for the House resolving itself into the Comittee of Enquiry at 4 o'clock should then be read. This was opposed by Mr Wharton; a short debate ensued and the House divided for Lord Porchester's Motion *136*, against it *180*. As Lord Sidmouth's friends voted with the Opposition upon this question, and Mr. Canning's[3] with the exception of Lord Binning (but in the absence of Mr.

[1] Lord Henry Petty's half-brother (who, incidentally, chose to spell his name Lansdown), the second Marquess, had died on 15 Nov. 1809. J. W. Ward thought that his inheritance might be worth at least £26,000 a year. (*Letters to Ivy*, p. 87.) But it was by no means certain that Lord Henry had become 3rd Marquess on 15 Nov. His brother's wife, one of the most vulgar women ever to wear a coronet, disliked him intensely. On 9 Dec. Lord Rosslyn wrote to Grey: 'I regret there should be any obstacles to your wishes respecting the Camelford seat, though I hear that Lady Lansdowne's malice is likely to keep Lord Henry in the House of Commons for some months longer.' (Howick MSS.). On 5 Dec. Tierney wrote to Grey: 'Lady Lansdowne has as yet given no answer whether she is with child or not, and she has by law seven months allowed her for the declaration. My own opinion is that she will be silent to the last moment on purpose to annoy Petty, and give the finishing stroke to the malignity of her deceased Lord.' (*Ibid.*)

[2] *Parl. Deb.*, xv, 505–36. On the 16th the King sent a message to both Houses of Parliament saying that he had authorized pecuniary advances to be made to Portugal and increased military assistance was to be given—up to 30,000 troops in all. (*Ibid.*, col. 440.)

[3] See No. 3966 n for the list of Canning's friends. Early in 1810 William Taylor and Lord Binning became definite members of his 'connexion', and Colonel Canning, who had already been considered an adherent, pledged himself much more definitely.

Canning wrote to Mrs. Canning on 25 Jan. 1810: 'This morning George Canning is with me reading the Cast[lerea]gh correspondence. He is quite right. He took me aside in the H. of Coms. on Tuesday, to say that he was glad of this opportunity to make his profession to me of intire and constant attachment—that it had always been his intention and disposition, that he had made some advances which, from various reasons, I had not encouraged—that he had not liked to press upon me in office—but that now he could have no greater pleasure than in professing to me out of office his desire and determination to follow me. I told him, what is very true, that I received his declaration with the greatest possible delight—that I had always rather avoided the subject of personal politicks with him because, situated as I was in the Govnt. and as he was with regard to Castlgh., I could not court his attachment to myself without entering into explanations into which, while I was a member of the Govt., I did not think myself at liberty to enter. I now wished him to be fully acquainted with every particular—

Canning himself) voted on the same side, and as Lord Castlereagh's friends were absent, Mr. Perceval thinks the numbers as favorable as he expected under such circumstances.

The House then proceeded upon the Distillery Bill; and there was a division upon the question of extending the restriction of distilling from grain to Ireland —on which there was a division—64[1] for extending it to Ireland and 110 against it.

The House then proceeded to the examination of Lord Chatham. His Lordship was called in about ½ p. 9 o'clock & continued under examination till about ½ p. 2 this morning. His Lordship went thro his examination with great good sense and clearness. The only part of it the substance of which Mr Perceval thinks it necessary particularly to report to your Majesty, respects the narrative delivered to your Majesty on the 14th inst. His Lordship was asked how it happened to be dated on the 14 of Oct. To which he answered that the 14 Oct. was the time when it was composed, that the subsequent alterations were merely verbal, that he had reasons for not delivering it sooner, that he did not know but that he might be called upon to answer upon some enquiry and did not like to bring forward his case before he could ascertain whether he should do so or not. Besides that he had heard that Sr. R. Strachan had been called upon for a report and he wished that they should come forth together,—that this was delivered to your Majesty on the 14th of this month, and on the same day to the Secretary of State. He was asked whether he had delivered any other report, paper or memorandum to your Majesty on the same subject, to which his Lordship answered that he had already said that he had delivered his official report to your Majesty on the 14th, and that he must decline giving any other answer. The question was repeated several times, and his Lordship persisted in declining to answer it. He was asked whether he declined answering it on the ground of his Privy Counsellor's oath; and he said generally that he declined answering it. Mr Whitbread seemed at first to imagine

and accordingly here he is, reading while I write, and repeating his professions at every turn. I told him too that I had heard that Castgh. reckoned upon him—and *that* had deterred me from courting him. My Edinbgh. correspondent, Mr. Taylor, was in the House, and renewed his vows—or rather explained the meaning of his letter to be a vow of allegiance. He was ready to vote as I pleased—and so he had told Huskisson before.' (Harewood MSS.)

On 27 Jan. Canning wrote: 'Binning has not made any positive profession yet, but I think he means to do so. He has been indoctrinated by Huskisson. Scroggs [Sturges Bourne], who used to be shilly shally, is now stout—and does not mind old Rose, to whom, indeed, he owes no obligation—for he *does*, I find, pay G. Rose's expenses at Southampton (taking the chance of what they may be) with an engagement too to give up Ch[rist]ch[urch] to G. Rose if he fails there. I really think the obligation is on old Rose's side, but I dare say old Rogue does not think so.' (*Ibid.*)

Finally, Canning wrote to Mrs. Canning on 3 March: 'Binning called upon me to-day to make his profession of faith and following, reserving only the question about Lord Chatham against whom he cannot vote for private reasons, Lady Binning being Lady C[hatham]'s intimate friend, I believe connection. For the rest he vows to follow me, in or out, implicitly. This is very satisfactory. From what little G[eorge] C[anning] said to Aunt Fanny I have *some* hopes of *Lord Francis Spencer*. This could be a *great*, great card—as he has great influence with all the Marlborough votes. Today I am going to dine with D[og] Dent, where are to be all the Senate, and *Sheridan*.' (*Ibid.*)

Tierney had written to Grey on 4 Oct. 1809: 'It is pretended that Canning will carry with him a great many, but I cannot make out above twelve, and I suspect his little Cabinet reckon upon some who have no idea of standing by him. Twelve, however, is a great number to be taken from so scanty a muster as Government made last year.' (Howick MSS.)

[1] The number is given as 68 in *Parl. Deb.*, xv, 552. It cannot be checked from the *Journals* as can the earlier division.

that some means might be adopted for compelling an answer, but he got corrected, and found that as a Peer, he could not be subject to any compulsion. When his Lordship had retired Mr Whitbread gave notice that he should move this day for an Address to your Majesty that yr. Majesty should be graciously pleased to lay before this House any paper which may have been delivered to your Majesty by Lord Chatham on this subject. Mr Perceval has thought that this question is one on which he should desire the assistance of his colleagues as to the course which should be taken with regard to it—and he has therefore directed a Cabinet to be summoned upon it at two o'clock this afternoon. (14967–8)

[*The King's reply, Windsor Castle, 23 Feb.*] The divisions in the House of Commons last night as reported to the King by Mr Perceval, appear to his Majesty, under all circumstances, satisfactory.

The King has not in his possession any report from Lord Chatham, that intended for him having been sent by Lord Liverpool to the House of Commons. (14968)

[*From Perceval, Downg. St., Friday night, 23 Feb. [1810].*] Mr Perceval acquaints your Majesty that Mr Whitbread's Motion for an Address to your Majesty that your Majesty would be graciously pleased to direct that there be laid before the House a copy of any memorandum, narrative or paper which had been delivered to your Majesty by the Earl of Chatham relative to the expedition to the Scheldt, came on this evening. It had been determined by your Majesty's confidential servants that the Address should be resisted. Mr Ryder therefore opposed the Motion of Mr Whitbread; Mr Ponsonby followed Mr Ryder, and Mr. Perceval Mr. Ponsonby. Mr Tierney replied to Mr. Perceval. Sir Home Popham spoke next for the Motion, Mr Robt. Ward[1] against it. Sir Saml. Romilly replied to Mr. Ward. The Attorney-General followed. Mr Bragg[e] Bathurst and Mr Canning both spoke for the Address and the Sol.-General against it. Mr Whitbread's reply then concluded the debate. The numbers were for the Address 177[2] and against it 171 only.[3]

[1] Ward was still a Lord of the Admiralty. In 1809 he had declined Perceval's offer to transfer him to the Treasury (which would have been a slight promotion). Some people thought that in declining the offer, he had let slip opportunities of 'looking to higher things'. (Lonsdale MSS.) 'I have, however,' he said, 'I fear, so little ambition as to confine my greatest wish to any respectable object in which I might be useful and which at the same time would take me out of the uncomfortable situation of a pensioner.' (*Ibid.*) [2] The number should be 178.

[3] Canning, writing to his wife, had some important comments on the debate: 'I told my own love this morning that I should probably support Govt. by my vote, on the Chatham Papers, though my speech would be unpalatable to them. My own naughty dear will be glad, I am afraid, to hear that my vote and speech went the same way, and that they both together produced a division in which the Ministers were beaten—178 to 171. Even without my speech, my numbers evidently turned the scale—for if my 'little Senate' had voted with Ministry they would have had a majority of eleven

from	178	to	171
deduct	9	add	9
	169		180
			169
			11

But I verily believe speech did a great deal more—and was what my own love wished to hear of an

Mr Perceval laments extremely the loss of this question, but he is in duty bound to state to your Majesty that the prejudice excited by Lord Chatham's Narrative, and all the circumstances connected with it is so great that Mr Perceval much fears the loss of this question will not be the only inconvenience that paper will produce.

Mr Perceval has directed a meeting of your Majesty's confidential servants to be called tomorrow for the purpose of considering what advice they should submit to your Majesty upon the mode of meeting this most embarassing question.[1] (14970)

[*From Perceval, Downing Street, 23* [*? 24*] *Feb.*] Mr. Perceval humbly takes leave to acquaint your Majesty that your Majesty's confidential servants met this day to consider what advice they should humbly offer to your Majesty upon the subject of the Address which was carried last night in the House of Commons. Mr. Perceval thought it his duty to lay before them your Majesty's letter to Mr. Perceval of this morning. The embarrassment which Mr. Perceval conceives to exist upon the subject arises out of the certainty he feels that, if your Majesty's answer to the House of Commons should only state that your Majesty had no such paper as their Address desired to have produced, and that no other communication should be made to the House upon the subject, the strongest impression would be made that there had been another paper presented to your Majesty, and also, however contrary it would be to the fact, that such paper had been removed from your Majesty's custody or destroyed since the Motion made in the House of Commons, and for the purpose of preventing the production of it to the House, while your Majesty's servants would be suspected of having unworthily

'effective speech' against them. For in the division were multitudes of persons who do not usually vote with Opposition—many county members—many quiet friends of Govt. and good Pittites, who, I *think*, voted under cover of my speech. I spoke so slow and temperately, leaning upon my stick (leg is not the worse for it) that I rather hope it is possible my speech may be better reported than usual. What will they do upon such a defeat? *I* put the question wholly on *their* misconduct of the business of the Inquiry—the House, and even their followers felt this strongly. But what will they do now? Resign? No, not they—stick fast, and call in the Grenvilles or Greys or Doctors or Castlereaghs, or anybody to keep me out. I do not know whether Castgh. voted with them or went away. The Doctors were against them...Binning will vote with us next time. They are—1, I; 2, Leveson; 3, C. Ellis; 4, Huskisson; 5, G. Canning; 6, D. Dent; 7, H. Leigh; 8, Sturges; 9, Jolliffe. Bootle went away.' (Harewood MSS.)

Wellesley-Pole wrote to the Duke of Richmond on the 24th: 'You will perceive by the news papers that we were beat last night in the House of Commons 178 to 171—the majority was composed of Opposition, the Saints, Canning's party, and Ld. Sidmouth's—Castlereagh and his friends left the House—The question was a very unpleasant one for us, and the combination was evidently made to give Perceval a hint that he could not carry on the Government without additional strength. The proceedings of Lord Chatham have essentially weaken'd Administration, for the general feeling is, and it has been express'd to me by several Irish members, that Perceval by suffering Lord Chatham to communicate his narrative &c to the King without apprizing the Cabinet, has proved that he does not possess that control over his colleagues which a Prime Minister ought to have, and which our party wish for and expect. I apprized Perceval this morning of the feeling of the House on our side, as I thought it proper he should be aware of it: my own opinion is that we shall be pushed upon several questions before the close of the Enquiry and that the issue of any is doubtful. But Perceval feels very stout, and is not apprehensive of the necessity of any decision on our situation 'till the result of the enquiry is known.' (Richmond MSS. 73/1715.)

[1] The King's brief reply (14971) on the 24th is in Walpole's *Perceval*, II, 74. His reply to the Address would be very simple: '*The King has no paper.*'

advised the withdrawal of such paper for that purpose, and Mr. Perceval has no hesitation in saying that he fears that it would be impossible, in the present state and temper of the House of Commons, to prevent the House from presenting another Address to your Majesty to desire to know whether Lord Chatham had not presented to your Majesty another paper relating to the expedition to the Scheldt, and to entreat your Majesty that your Majesty would acquaint the House who advised your Majesty that it should be withdrawn or destroyed.

That such an Address should be obviated if possible Mr. Perceval has no difficulty in stating to be his opinion, but in what manner to advise your Majesty best for the purpose of obviating it admits of considerable doubt. Your Majesty's confidential servants separated without having come to any decided opinion upon it, and they have determined to meet again tomorrow to consider it further. Mr. Perceval deeply regrets to be obliged to say that this unfortunate subject has occasioned more prejudice to the character of your Majesty's Administration, has more encreased the opinion of a want of communication, concert and confidence amongst them, and will do more to endanger their stability than any other circumstance which has arisen out of the Walcheren expedition. (14972–3)

[*The King's reply, Windsor Castle, 25 Feb.*] In consequence of the letter which the King has received from Mr. Perceval this morning, his Majesty readily furnishes him with all the information he can give on the subject of Lord Chatham's paper, of which he may make such use as he shall think adviseable. The King received Lord Chatham's Report on the 15th of January, and in consequence of a wish expressed by Lord Chatham on the 7th inst. to make a few verbal alterations, his M. returned it to him on the 10th inst. The Report, as altered, was delivered to the Secretary of State on the 14th February, and his M. has not kept any copy or Minute of either, nor has he received at any time any other paper on the subject.[1] (14973)

[*From Perceval, Downg. St., 25 Feb.*] Mr Perceval acquaints your Majesty that your Majesty's confidential servants met this day, and that Mr Perceval laid before them your Majesty's most gracious communication of this morning. Your Majesty's servants are so anxious to know in what manner they may best meet the further enquiry which they apprehend likely to be made respecting the interval in which the Report as first delivered to yr. Majesty continued in your Majesty's hands that Mr Perceval has determined to pay his humble duty to your Majesty at Windsor tomorrow before ten o'clock, if your Majesty will be graciously pleased to receive him at that time. (14977)

4094 *Letters from the* KING *to the* MARQUESS WELLESLEY, *and the reply*

[*Windsor Castle, 25 Feb. 1810.*] The King acquaints Lord Wellesley that he has ordered a Chapter of the Garter to be held here on Saturday the 3d of March, and

---

[1] These letters, without dates, are in Walpole's *Perceval*, II, 75–6, but as the drafts are different in eleven places from the letters actually sent, they are here reproduced.

his Majesty desires that Lord Wellesley will attend here on that day at two o'clock for the purpose of being elected and invested. (14976)

[*Lord Wellesley's reply, Foreign Office, 25 Feb.*] Lord Wellesley has received with the most respectful sentiments of gratitude your Majesty's gracious commands directing him to attend a Chapter of the Garter at two o'clock on Saturday the 3d of March at Windsor Castle for the purpose of being elected & invested under your Majesty's countenance & favor. He humbly requests your Majesty to accept his most dutiful acknowledgments of the great and distinguished protection with which your Majesty has been pleased to mark his anxious & zealous wishes for the prosperity of your Majesty's service; and he cannot omit this occasion of submitting to your Majesty his unfeigned sense of your Majesty's benevolent goodness towards every branch of his family.

The high honor by which your Majesty is now graciously pleased to signify your royal approbation of his services, cannot fail to inspire him with additional confidence in the execution of your Majesty's commands.

Lord Wellesley solicits the honor of your Majesty's directions with respect to the Order of St. Patrick, of which he was constituted a Knight Companion on the 17th of March 1783 by your Majesty's original Institution.

He requests that your Majesty will be graciously pleased to appoint the time when he shall resign the Insignia of that Order into your Majesty's hands. (14974-5)

[*From the King, Windsor Castle, 26 Feb.*] The King has received Lord Wellesley's letter and acquaints him that, when he attends here on Saturday next at two o'clock, H.M. will receive him previous to holding the Chapter of the Garter, that he may resign the Insignia of the Order of St Patrick into H.My.'s hands. (14975)

4095   RICHARD RYDER *to the* KING, *and the reply*

[*Whitehall, 26 Feb. 1810.*] Mr Ryder has the honor of humbly submitting to your Majesty the opinion of your Majesty's confidential servants that it might be desirable for your Majesty to come to town, as your Majesty proposed to do, some day this week. And Mr Ryder begs leave humbly to suggest to your Majesty that if Thursday next should not prove in any degree inconvenient to your Majesty for that purpose, it might in their opinion be the day the most advantageous for the public business. (14978)

[*The King's reply, Windsor Castle, 27 Feb.*] In consequence of Mr Ryder's letter, the King will go to town on Thursday next. (14979)

4096   THE EARL OF LIVERPOOL *to the* KING, *and the reply*

[*London, 26 Feb. 1810.*] Lord Liverpool begs leave most humbly to submit to your Majesty the Minutes of the House of Lords, and has the greatest satisfaction in stating that the Lord Chancellor made on the occasion one of the finest speeches ever heard, to which no answer was attempted to be made.[1] (14980)

[*The King's reply, Windsor Castle, 27 Feb.*] The King has received much satisfaction from Lord Liverpool's favorable report of what passed in the House of Lords last night. (14980)

4097   THE QUEEN *to* LADY ELIOT[2]

[*27 Feb. 1810.*] My dearest Lady Ely, I cannot possibly feast upon Lrd. Ely's bounty without being desirous of returning him thanks for his attention in thinking of me, & I shall be much obliged to you if you will be kind enough to say everything civil upon the subject. I do admire the taste of the pye besides its goodness for there was nothing forgot to make it look Royal as both Crown, the Arms & my name were introduced in the pastry. What could he do more—pour la future, & should there prove to be such a one in idea, I shall keep this galanterie a secret for fear of creating mischief & I cannot fear yr. prudence.

I do long to hear that you found poor Mr Elliott at yr. return to London in good health. I do not inquire after his spirits, nothing but time can mend that, and his excellent principles will lead him to be carefull of himself for the sake of his dear children, whose loveliness must not only endear them to him, but must make him wish to live for their happiness & comfort in life.[3]

I beg to be remembered to Mrs. Bonfoy. I have thought a good deal of the smell of paint in her apartment, & tho I do know that she will not occupy it at present, yet the smell is so penetrating that it spreads over the whole house. Happy shall I be to hear that she has not been incomoded by it.

News you will of course not expect from this place where one day is passed like another. The best news I can tell is that dear Amelia has had five hours sleep last night, which is an essential amendment, & that the physicians were more chearing about her on Fryday last. Thank God we are at least not worth [*sic*]. And now, my dear Ldy E[l]y, I will relieve you of this dull epistle. If you have any news it will be charitable to share them with yr. sincere friend. (St. Germans MSS.)

4098   SPENCER PERCEVAL *to the* KING, *and the reply*

[*Downg. St.*, *27 Feb.* [*1810*].] Mr Perceval humbly acquaints your Majesty that he delivered yesterday evening yr. Maj.'s answer to the Address from the Ho. of Co. in the following words.

[1] The debate was on the Offices in Reversion Bill. There was a majority against the second reading of 39 (106 to 67). (*Parl. Deb.*, xv, 587–600.)
[2] Lord Eliot married, as his first wife (9 Sept. 1790), Caroline (1765–1818), daughter of Charles Yorke, Lord Chancellor, 1770.
[3] William Eliot (1767–1845) succeeded his brother John, 2nd Lord Eliot (created Earl of St. Germans, 28 Nov. 1815), on 17 Nov. 1823. His second wife, Letitia, daughter of Sir William A'Court, died, 20 Jan. 1810, in childbed.

The Earl of Chatham having requested his Majesty to permit him to present his report to his Majesty and having also requested that his Majy. would not communicate it for the present, his Majy. received it on the 15th of January last, and kept it till the 10th of this month, when, in consequence of a wish having been expressed by the Earl of Chatham on the 7th inst. to make some alterations in it, his Majy. returned it to the Earl of Chatham. The report as altered was again tendered to his Majesty by the Earl of Chatham on the 14th inst. when his Majesty directed it to be delivered to the Secretary of State. His Majesty has not kept any copy or minute of the report as delivered at either of these times nor has he had at any time any other report, memorandum, narrative or paper submitted to him by the Earl of Chatham relating to the late expedition to the Scheldt.

When Mr Perceval had delivered this answer Mr Whitbread in a very dictatorial tone desired to put a question to Mr Perceval, which was what Privy Counsellor it was that took your Majesty's pleasure upon this Address and answer. Mr Perceval sat silent. Mr Whitbread got up again and repeated his question with some expression of impatience & surprise at not having an answer given to him. Mr Perceval observed that he knew not by what authority Mr Whitbread asked any question; if the House put any question to him, he said he would be ready to give an answer, but to a question put in so threatening a tone by an individual Member he felt no inclination to give any answer. Mr Whitbread replied that he had no intention of using any threatening tone, he disclaimed any idea of it, he wished to ask the question, as the answer to it might save the trouble of a Motion. Mr Perceval then said that it was not from any disinclination that he felt to communicate to the House who had taken yr. Maj.'s pleasure upon this subject that he had declined answering at first—for he had no difficulty in saying that he had himself taken your Majesty's pleasure & been honoured with your commands upon it. The conversation then ended with some absurd statement from Mr Tierney that it would have been proper for some Privy Counsellor, who voted for the Address, to have carried it to your Majesty. This absurdity the Speaker put at rest.

The House then read Lord Wellington's Pension Bill a 2d time; a short debate ensued and a division—for the Bill 106, against it 36.

Lord Palmerston then opened the Army Estimates, which he did in a very able and perspicuous manner, giving very great satisfaction to his friends and extorting commendation from his adversaries. The debate lasted till about 2 o'clock when the Resolutions were carried without a division.[1] (14983–4)

[*The King's reply, Windsor Castle, 27 Feb.*] The King has received Mr Perceval's report and entirely approves of the course which he adopted in delivering his answer to the House of Commons, & in checking Mr Whitbread's intemperance. His Majesty is pleased to hear that Lord Palmerston acquitted himself so well. (14985)

[1] *Parl. Deb.*, xv, 600–33.

4099 *Letters from the* MARQUESS WELLESLEY *to the* KING, *and the reply*

[*Foreign Office, 28 Feb. 1810.*] Lord Wellesley will have the honor to obey your Majesty's commands on Saturday next previously to the Chapter of the Garter, & will not fail to attend at Windsor Castle for the purpose of delivering the Insignia of the Order of St Patrick into your Majesty's hands. (14986)

[*From Lord Wellesley, Foreign Office, 28 Feb.*] Lord Wellesley has the honor to acquaint your Majesty that Mr Villiers, your Majesty's late Minister at the Court of Portugal, arrived in London this day. (14987)

[*From Lord Wellesley, Foreign Office, 28 Feb.*] Lord Wellesley has the honor to acquaint your Majesty that he proposes with your Majesty's gracious permission to present tomorrow Mr Wellesley recently arrived from Spain, & Mr Holmes,[1] a Member of the House of Commons who is going to Portugal. (14988)

[*The King's reply, Windsor Castle, 29 Feb. [sic] [1 March].*] The King has received Lord Wellesley's letter & acquaints him that he may present the gentlemen therein named to his Majesty at the Queen's Palace this day. (14988)

4100 *Letters from* SPENCER PERCEVAL *to the* KING, *and the replies*

[*Downg. St., 28 Feb. 1810.*] Mr Perceval acquaints your Majesty that the Enquiry proceeded yesterday evening, and Lord Chatham's examination was closed, and afterwards Sr. Eyre Coote was examined. During Ld. Chatham's examination an incident occurred which Mr Perceval never witnessed before. Mr Fuller, one of the Members for Sussex, who Mr Perceval imagines to have been drunk, behaved with so much violence & intemperance that the Committee was broke up, the House resumed, and Mr Fuller ordered into custody of the Serjeant-at-Arms.[2] He would not leave the House, tho ordered by the Speaker to withdraw, and it was not till the Serjt.-at-Arms had got the assistance of several messengers of the House that he could be removed, and then not without force.[3]

---

[1] There were two Members named Holmes in the Commons at this time. William Holmes (*c.* 1778–1851) sat for Grampound, but the reference must be to Leonard Thomas Worsley-Holmes (1787–1825), who was elected for Newport (Isle of Wight) on 7 April 1809, *vice* Sir Arthur Wellesley. He was, in fact, presented at the Levée on 1 March on his coming of age and on account of his going abroad. (*The Times,* 2 March 1810.)

[2] Francis John Colman. On 10 April 1811 he asked the Speaker whether he could return to the army. (Colchester, II, 324.) He did so, later, and died in Portugal in Dec. 1811.

[3] 'Blast Fuller' had been drinking to excess, and, entering the Chamber, he put gross and absurd questions to Lord Chatham in such a style that no one took the slightest notice of him. He protested loudly that his questions had just as much right to be attended to as those of the Prime Minister. 'God damn me, Sir,' he roared, 'I have as much right to be heard as any man who is paid for filling the place he holds!' The Speaker was hurriedly sent for, and, on his arrival, ordered the inebriated gentleman into the custody of the Serjeant-at-Arms. Soon afterwards Mr Fuller overpowered his jailers and re-entered the Chamber. He kicked over the chair placed for the accommodation of the witnesses, and forced the startled Earl of Chatham to beat a hurried retreat. Shouting at the top of his voice he shook his fist at the Speaker, referring to him as 'the insignificant little fellow in the wig!' It took five men to overpower him and remove him from the scene of his appalling misbehaviour. Members thought he was very lucky in not being sent to Newgate or the Tower. Two days later he was released from custody

Mr Perceval believes that Lord Folkstone does not mean to call above one or two more witnesses. Mr Perceval takes this opportunity of transmitting to your Majesty the copy of the Address from the Ho. of Commons which he humbly asks his Majesty's forgiveness for having omitted to send before. (14989)

[*The King's reply, Windsor Castle, 28 Feb.*] The King acknowledges the receipt of Mr Perceval's letter of this day and of the copy of the Address from the House of Commons. His M. has learnt with serious concern that such an incident as that to which the conduct of Mr Fuller gave rise should have occurred in the House of Commons. (14989)

[*From Perceval, Downg. St., 1 March.*] Mr Perceval acquaints your Majesty that Lord Porchester has declined calling any more evidence on the Enquiry. Sr. Home Popham means to call a few witnesses & Ld. Castlereagh does also, but the Enquiry is not likely to last much longer.

Mr Whitbread gave notice of his intention of moving tomorrow some Resolutions upon the subject of Ld. Chatham's communication of his narrative to your Majesty, and his desire that it should be not communicated for the present. This Motion Mr Perceval apprehends it will be extremely difficult to prevail upon the House to resist. (14990)

[*The King's reply, Windsor Castle, 2 March.*] The King acknowledges the receipt of Mr Perceval's report of the proceedings in the House of Commons last night. (14990)

4101   THE EARL OF LIVERPOOL *to the* KING, *and the reply*

[*Friday, 12 o'clock [2 March 1810].*] Lord Liverpool begs leave to submit to your Majesty the Minutes of the House of Lords and to acquaint your Majesty that the debate has gone off upon the whole as well as could possibly have been expected on so disagreable a subject.[1] (14991)

[*The King's reply, Windsor Castle, 3 March.*] The King acknowledges the receipt of Lord Liverpool's letter enclosing the Minutes of the House of Lords. (14991)

after he had humbly apologised to the House and received a severe reprimand from the Speaker. He was not re-elected by his Sussex constituents in 1812 and never again sat in the House of Commons.

1 On the 2nd there was a long debate on the Scheldt expedition. The Government had a majority of 46 (136 to 90). (*Parl. Deb.*, XVI, 1–2*.) Lord Camden had written appealingly to Lord Lonsdale on 27 Feb.: 'I do not know whether you will hear from anyone else on the subject of attending the House of Lords on Friday next—but I venture to write to you to inform you that your presence will be very useful and indeed most essential.... The Motion is meant of course as one to shake the Government to its foundation & it is very material to its credit to have as good a division as we can. I shall also be very glad you are in London for a day or two to converse with some of us on the state of things, which I think (confidentially) cannot continue as they are. If I did not really think your presence material I would not write to you in this manner.' (Lonsdale MSS.)

[*Downg. St.*, *2 March 1810.*] Mr Perceval acquaints your Majesty that Mr Whitbread moved this day his Resolutions against the Earl of Chatham, the effect of which was first to resolve the fact that his Lordship had, after having requested yr. Majesty to permit him to present his narrative, and after having requested that it might not be communicated for the present, presented it to yr. Majesty—&c., and next to resolve that such conduct was unconstitutional.

These Resolutions were in part formed upon Lord Chatham's evidence which had been delivered on Tuesday, and which was not printed till this afternoon, and Mr Whitbread had, in giving notice of his intended Motion, stated that he would not bring it forward if the evidence was not printed last night. Mr Perceval, therefore, in objecting to the Motion objected particularly to the unseemliness & injustice of calling upon the House to form its judgement upon evidence which they had not had time to examine, and he proposed that the debate should be adjourned till Monday. Mr Perceval went a little into the question, and the line he took was to say that he could not defend Lord Chatham's conduct as correct, but that, allowance being made for the situation in which his Lordship stood, his conduct did not deserve to be characterised with the epithets which the Motion & the mover's speech ascribed to it, and that being thoroughly convinced that it was not ascribable to the motives to which it was attributed, he should think it his duty when the Motion came on on Monday to meet it by the previous question. Mr Brand followed Mr Perceval in support of Mr Whitbread. Mr Bragg Bathurst supported the adjournment, but expressed his opinion that he could not vote for the previous question, thinking that some censure must be passed on the noble Lord. Mr Whitbread fell into the idea of adjournment, finding that Mr Bathurst would not divide with him, and the House was therefore up by an early hour.

Mr Perceval cannot undertake for what may be the event of this unfortunate business. Mr P. hopes to be able to avert a Parliamentary censure from Ld Chatham, but acts upon the impression that, even if he should fail in the attempt, that it will be more to the credit of your Majesty's servants to be beat in an attempt to defend their colleague, tho' in an instance in which he has not acted in concert with them, as he has failed thro an error rather than from any improper motive, than to avoid a defeat by joining in the attack against him.[1] (14994–5)

[1] *Parl. Deb.*, XVI, 3*–2**. Perceval's speech, said Wellesley-Pole, was very 'manly and good'. He added, 'We shall, I think, certainly be beat on Monday. Beresford has been with Perceval to say that he and his friends will go any length with Government, but they cannot support Lord Chatham. Several others, I believe, are of the same way of thinking.' Lord Chatham, I conceive, must go out and I see no prospect of our standing. However, nobody seems to know what is to be done. That we cannot carry on the Government as we are, I think is quite clear.' (Richmond MSS. 73/1712.) The House rose about 8 p.m.

Perceval wrote to Lord Chatham on the 4th: 'I was in expectation of seeing you to day at the Cabinet, & I should have endeavoured to procure a meeting with you by appointment. You are aware of the line which I took in the Ho. of Co. on Friday last; it succeeded to the extent of putting off the discussion, and gave me the opportunity of making known to our friends, that while on the one hand I did not mean to justify you in delivering your narrative to the King with the request that it should not be communicated for the present, so on the other I could not consent to ascribe to such delivery any of that motive or character which our adversaries endeavour to impute to it; and therefore that

[*The King's reply, Windsor Castle, 3 March.*] The King has received Mr Perceval's report of what occurred in the House of Commons last night, and his Majesty entirely approves of the principle upon which Mr Perceval has determined to resist Mr Whitbread's Motions respecting Lord Chatham. (14995)

4103 THE KING OF THE SANDWICH ISLANDS *to the* KING

[*Island Woahoo, 3 March 1810.*] Sir, Having had no good opportunity of writing to you since Captn. Vancouver[1] left here has been the means of my silence. Captn. Vancouver inform'd me you would send me a small vessel; am sorry to say I have not yet receiv'd one. Am sorry to hear your being at war with so many Powers and I so far off cannot assist you. Should any of the Powers which you are at war with molest me I shall expect your protection, and beg you will order your ships of war & privateers not to capture any vessel whilst laying at anchor in our harbours, as I would thank you to make ours a neutral port as I have not the means of defence. I am in particular need of some bunting, having no English colours; also some brass guns to defend the islands in case of attack from your enemies. I have built a few small vessels with an intent to trade on the north west of America with tarro root the produce of these islands, for fur skins, but am told by the white men here I canot send them to sea without a register, in consequence of which beg you will send me a form of a register & seal with my name on it. Being very poor at these islands, anything which you may think

I should recommend it to the House to pass it by with the previous question. With this impression known to be felt by me, we shall meet the question in the Ho. of Commons tomorrow, and I believe that this is the most advantageous manner in which the question can be met. I wish it may succeed; but I have too much reason to fear that we shall be beat. I have heard today and yesterday of several who will keep away, and not support us—Lascelles, & the Master of the Rolls are two, who think the House of Commons cannot pass over the subject by the previous question. These are authorities of great weight. Still I feel most strongly that, if the Ho. of Co. should pronounce any judgement against this proceeding of yours, more especially if they characterize it as unconstitutional, it will be impossible that the King's service can go on, particularly in our state of weakness, with the weight of such a vote against any one of his servants; and therefore it is absolutely necessary to endeavour to resist it. This I shall do to the best of my power. But I should not think I acted fairly by you if I did not thus fully apprize you of the view which I take of this unfortunate business. I cannot conclude this note without assuring you how deeply I lament all the untoward circumstances which this unfortunate narrative has brought upon us all, and more particularly upon you.' (Chatham Papers, 368.)

Perceval wrote again to Chatham, probably on the 6th (the letter is undated): 'Towards the close of the night yesterday in the H. of Commons, I learnt from Arbuthnot, that Whitbread had asked him, "whether Lord Chatham was still Master Genl. of the Ordnance?" to which Arbuthnot answered that you were;—upon this Whitbread responded, "Well," said he, "I shall wait a day or two, and then I shall put the same question in another place"—meaning as Arbuthnot collected, that he should put the question in the H. of Commons, and upon the answer, if to the same effect as that which Arbuthnot gave, bring the question again before the House: I thought you ought to be apprized of this fact as it may make an important ingredient in the judgement which you may form as to what it will be proper for you to do—it being evident from this circumstance that the question will not be left at rest, but be brought forward again. I have directed the Messenger to wait for your answer, being ready to come up to you if you would wish to speak to me, indeed I should be particularly desirous of seeing you before I go in to the King. I enclose you a note from Long with a list of the members who voted against us, and who generally vote with us. *I will thank you to return it.*' (Chatham Papers, 368.)

[1] George Vancouver, the explorer (1758–98). Lieutenant, R.N., 1780; Commander, 1790; Captain, 1794. He was in the South Seas at the end of 1791. Vancouver, the island, which he circumnavigated, is named after him.

useful to me I beg you will send by the earliest opportunity. My best respects to you & your Queen & all your family wishing you health, happiness & a long prosperous reign and am Sir, your Majesty's most devoted friend & servant, Tamaahmaah.

P.S. My removal from Owytru to this island was in consequence of their having put to death Mr Brown & Mr Gordon, Masters (of the Jackall & Prince lua boo [?] two of your merchant vessels). I have sent by Mr Jno Clark Spence, Commander of the ship Duke of Portland, a feather'd cloak & beg your acceptance. (14996)

4104 RICHARD RYDER *to the* KING, *and the reply*

[*Whitehall, 5 March 1810.*] Mr Ryder has the honor of humbly submitting to your Majesty a request which has been made to him by Adml. Sir William Sidney Smith that he might be admitted to the honor of an Audience on the next Levée day. Mr Ryder thought it right to mention this circumstance to Lord Mulgrave, who informed him that he saw no objection to his laying Sir Sidney Smith's request before your Majesty. (14997)

[*The King's reply, Windsor Castle, 6 March.*] The King desires Mr Ryder will acquaint Sir Sidney Smith that his Majesty will admit him to an Audience tomorrow at the Queen's Palace.¹ (14997)

¹ Sir Sidney Smith's objects at this time are mentioned in two letters he wrote to Perceval. On 3 Jan. (marked 'private, but not confidential as to communication with colleagues'): 'With the utmost confidence in your justice and liberality & with a full conviction of your kind disposition towards me for which as such I am duly & equally well disposed towards you personally, I submit the enclosed ostensible letter to your perusal before you see the *King today* as H.M. first Minister, & consequently the channel through which his favour ought naturally to flow. I did hope that the government of Malta being a place of trust to which I may venture to say the public voice call'd the man who knows the politics of the Levant & Africa the best, would have drawn me in an honourable manner from the retirement into which I have been forced by the effect of the intrigue of a foreign Court, fomented by those who it might have been expected would not have allow'd an officer of rank to be in any degree the victim of his obedience to precise instructions without a previous reference to him; the disposal of the Government of Malta to a junior officer has shewn me the little expectation I ought to encourage of suitable employment. I shall therefore confine my views *at present* having my official *justification in my possession* to the obtaining such a distinguished mark of the King's favour as shall preclude my any longer *appearing* degraded in the eyes of those who cannot know the fair claim I have to *reward* till parliament by calling for secret instructions & correspondence may allow me to bring forward not only my unequivocal justification but the proof of my having in conformity to Lord Castlereagh's ample authorisation prevented the resources of Spanish America being thrown into the scale against us. I have borne much injustice with patience as long as the country's *future interests* did not suffer by my silence—I have forborne to arm the eloquence of any of those who have requested me so to do as long as I had hopes of my being no longer held up as a warning to all officers rather to allow the worst evils to the country than to step forward & prevent them without looking for support or waiting for inadequate means. I act conscientiously, but I cannot in conscience support a defective system under which such discouragement as I labour under is allow'd to subsist & to damage zeal & energy.' (Add. MSS. 38244, fo. 157.)

And he wrote on the 10th: 'I am duly sensible of the promtitude and kindness of your frank reply to my letter of the 3d instt. & I cannot but admit that it is conclusive as to my application for an *Irish Peerage*, but I appeal to your justice and candour whether with admitted claims to *some* public proof of approbation beyond the general acknowledgement of the merits of my various public services being highly esteem[e]d, I may not fairly expect an immediate recognition of those claims by *some* mark of the royal favour. I have already said in my former letter that I consider the recovery of Egypt for His

[*Downg. St., Tuesday morg., 6 March [1810].*] Mr Perceval acquaints your Majesty that the adjourned debate on Mr Whitbread's Motion came on yesterday evening. General Crawfurd began the debate against Mr Whitbread's Motion and the principal speakers on the same side with him were Mr Stephen, Mr Bankes, Mr Owen,[1] Mr Perceval, Genl. Loftus, Genl. Grosvenor and the Solicitor General; on the other side Lord Temple, Lord Folkstone, Mr Windham, Mr Canning, Lord Castlereagh, Mr Ponsonby & Mr Whitbread. The previous question having been moved it was carried against your Majesty's servants by 221 to 188.

Upon the first Resolution of Mr Whitbread being carried, Mr Canning proposed an Amendment to his second Resolution. Mr Whitbread withdrew his second Resolution for the purpose of admitting of Mr Canning's Amendment. Mr Perceval transmits to your Majesty on another paper all the Resolutions. Mr Canning's Resolution was then carried without a division. Mr Whitbread then moved that the two Resolutions which had been carried should be laid before your Majesty. To this Mr Perceval objected, and as his objection was supported by Mr Canning, Mr Bathurst & Mr Wilberforce, Mr Whitbread withdrew this last Motion. Mr Perceval has transmitted to Lord Chatham a statement of these events.[2] (14998)

Majesty's Ally according to my instructions as H.M. Minister Plenipotentiary (having been sent to Turkey expressly *for that purpose* & not merely to sign H.M. accession to the Russian Treaty of alliance which my brother was authorised to sign before I arrived) as entitling me to the same reward that a younger field officer in H.M. service (Lord Hutchinson) received for the attainment of the same object with greater means than I had at my disposal yet notwithstanding with greater sacrifices than I found it necessary to make. The delay occasion'd by the error in the political judgement of Mr. Pitt so far from being an admissible reason for withholding a reward now only increases the sense I cannot but feel of the injustice that has been & is done me. You will perceive in my letter to Lord Mulgrave of this day (the contents of which will no doubt be communicated to you & the exact copy of which I beg leave to submit to your perusal) that I have indicated the vacant Red Ribbon as a mark of favour which would in my estimation remove the ill impression given by my sudden recall under humiliating circumstances from my command in the Southern Hemisphere. Should that be promised it must be in his Majesty's power to give me the remaining portion of the reward above alluded to as given to Lord Hutchinson for a similar service to that performed by me, a service atchieved after all by my collateral aid: I mean an *English Peerage* to which it is generally consider'd I am as much entitled as any public servant who has received one since the beginning of the revolutionary war in 1793 and on this I appeal to the Court Calendar on your table. To any other man than yourself I should feel it necessary to apologise for this second appeal to you but my conviction of your liberality & love of justice makes me consider it unnecessary & I beg you to be assured of the sincere regard & esteem with which I am [etc.].' (Add. MSS. 38244, fo. 175.)

    [1] Sir John Owen (*c.* 1776–1861), Tory M.P. for Pembroke, 1809–12 and 1841–61; for Pembrokeshire, 1812–41. Created Baronet, 12 Jan. 1813. Changed his name from Lord to Owen, 23 Aug. 1809, after inheriting property of his distant cousin, Sir Hugh Owen, 6th Baronet (1782–1809). An anti-Catholic, he followed Peel in 1829. An anti-Reformer, he voted for the Whig Reform Bill from July 1831 onwards. His election contests ruined him.
    [2] *Parl. Deb.*, xvi, 2**–12*. This, one of the most crucial debates of the Session, is highlighted in the correspondence of the politicians. First, Canning wrote to his wife at 5 a.m. on the 6th: 'Huzza—huzza—huzza—my own love *will* be satisfied I think with the transactions of to-night. Imprimis—Govt. was beaten by 33—188 to 221. Secondly, I beat them. *More* voted with me, I am confident, than would have turned the question. 3dly, in declaring my resolution to vote against the previous question (moved by Govt.) *for* Whitbread's first Resolution, I declared at the same time that I could not vote for Whitbread's second Resolution, which was a criminatory and penal one, and would therefore move an amendment to it—substituting one much milder. This the House received so well that Whitbread thought it better to withdraw his second Resolution than to fight it, and *mine* was carried without

opposition. So after beating Govt. on the first, I beat him on the second. But this was not all. After the division, Ryder proposed to amend *my* Resolution by inserting in it words still softer, and praising Ld. Chat[ham]. The House shewed great repugnance to this, and I got up and entreated him to with-draw his Motion—which he did. Then Whitbread moved to lay the Resolutions before the King (as in Ld. Melville's case). I said I would oppose this, as I thought enough had been done, and Whitbread gave up *this* Motion. So that in four alternate cases I carried the House with me, for and against Govt. and for and against Whitbread—and though Lord Chatham's friends were excessively angry with me at first for not supporting the previous question, I believe they left the House at last fully convinced that I had done all that could be done for him—and had saved and protected him when the Govt. *could* not. He must go out, I suppose—and how the Govt. is to go on after such a defeat I do not see. Who will take the Ordnance or any other responsible office under Perceval, after so many specimens of his inability to carry the House of Commons with him? Bootle voted with me—so we were eleven clear and sure, beside at least six or seven occasional conformists. During the debate I received a message through George [his cousin] from Lord Francis Spencer, the substance of which was that he wished to attach himself to *me*—that of all the publick men in the House of Commons he thought me the fittest to form and lead a Government—that he would co-operate with all those who were attached to me in forcing me into that situation—that he wished to carry his father's influence with him, and for that purpose intended to have a full explanation with his father, and then to speak to his father's friends in Parliament—who are three in number—and would do this in the course of a day or two—that he had better not vote with me till this had been done—that in the meantime he should be most happy if I would speak to him—he had an awkwardness in beginning with me—that, to be quite fair and explicit, he had only to add that in professing *general* following he was of course to be understood liberally, and not as bound to *every* question that could possibly occur—though there was none but the Walcheren business on which he desired specially to reserve himself—and that his object being truly and honestly to see a good and strong Govt. in the country, while he would exert his best efforts to help me to form one, and would infinitely prefer me to any other leader, yet that if from my own choice or any unforeseen circumstances I were not to form a part of a Govt. otherwise unexceptionable, he should not be bound to go with me into systematick opposition...I liked the frankness and particularity of this profession better than if it had been more general and unqualified...Charles Moore is one of his members. Young Eden (who is returned, not like his brother to follow his own fancies—but to act with Ld. F.) is another. What more? O—Lord Huntly stopped me going into the House, and said, "Well, when do you come into play again?" I—"never". "O, by G—, but you must—and remember—I am *yours*"...I ought not to omit that Castgh. made a poorish figure, voted as I did on the previous question, but with *three* followers—and professed his readiness to vote with Whitbread for his second Resolution—which I made Whitbread give up...Lord Grey, Ld. Lansdowne, Harrowby, Bathurst and Mulgrave and the Duke of Cumberland were under the Gallery and witnessed the battle.' (Harewood MSS.)

He wrote again, later that day: 'Perhaps I was wrong when I said in my letter of this morning that I could have turned the first division. I doubt it. I could have deducted **22** from the majority of **33** certainly: myself—Leveson—Huskisson—Sturges—C. Ellis—G. Canning, D[og] Dent, Holt Leigh, Joliffe, W. Taylor and Bootle—**11**—which telling both ways is **22**, but that would have left a majority of eleven against Government—and I doubt whether my speech would have gained six—though perhaps it might. Even the however so poor a majority as at best Govt. could have had would have been equivalent to a defeat. The question would have been renewed, probably to-day in some other shape—and Ld. Chat[ham] would still have been worried out of office, and probably by a much harsher process. ...I have had my interview with Ld. Francis Spencer. It was very satisfactory. He says he is sure of his father's sentiments. I think however he will be a leetle difficult to manage now & then—but it is a great card.' (*Ibid.*)

Charles Long, writing to Lord Lonsdale on the 7th, remarked: 'The Prince, who, it was understood, was to be neuter, sent his Members to vote against Lord Chatham on Monday, and there were near forty of those who usually vote with us, in the majority.' (Lonsdale MSS.)

Wellesley-Pole wrote to the Duke of Richmond on the 7th: 'I was...not prepared for many things that happen'd—such as Wynn & Temple feeling the necessity of performing their *duty so very much* at variance with their inclination, by speaking violently as well as voting against the brother of the great aggrandizer and benefactor of their family—such as Mr Canning being impell'd also to speak against the brother of his creator, and becoming at last the mover of the question that sets his sun for

[*Tuesday night, 10.30 p.m.* [*6 March 1810*].] Amelia has had a good deal of pain in her head today but after the affect of the medicine she felt much relieved. We had a visit from Mr. Dundas who I am happy to say found her better in every respect than when he saw her Saturday, the pulse quieter & less fever. She got up before 7 o'clock & lay on the couch till near 10; as the weather is so cold Dr. Pope desired her not to venture out into the next room, therefore she has not been out

ever, forgetting, I suppose, for the moment in his zeal for the good of his country—the seat in Parliament—the sinecure place—the pensions for the Miss Hunns—the office of the Treasurer of the Navy, and the office of the Secretaryship of State &c &c &c which he had attained through the protection and partiality of Mr. Pitt—such as Lord Castlereagh's finding it indispensable *distinctly* to take the very worst view of Ld. Chatham's case that was put to the House in the course of the debate—notwithstanding all his enthusiasm for Mr. Pitt's memory, and all the favors & honors conferr'd upon him and his family through his kindness—these things certainly in some degree surprized me, and gave rise to many melancholy reflections upon human nature. The cry against Lord Chatham is very great, and I think the Resolution of the House must put him out of office immediately. I understand, however, that he is of a different opinion, and that yesterday the Cabinet had not decided whether he should be forced to resign. In the meantime I *know* that Mulgrave gave Perceval notice yesterday that if Lord Chatham was not out of office today, he, Mulgrave, wd. resign at the Levée, and he has prepared a letter for the King explanatory of his reasons. What has been determined I know not—the Cabinet I believe sat early this morning, in order to enable Mulgrave to determine how he should act at the Levée. You must perceive by what I have already said that matters are come as nearly as possible to a crisis, and in this state of things I do not believe that any negociation for strengthening ourselves is actually on foot. It is said that Canning is most anxious to come back to us on any terms, this I do not know, but I believe it—of others I hear little or nothing. It is quite evident, that altho the Talents believe we are beaten, and in a manner dissolved, they do not expect to come in themselves, and the House of Commons is in such a state, that I cannot form to myself the hope that any man could carry on a Government with it, with either credit to himself or advantage to the country. I think there must be a very convulsive crash speedily, but what sort of order may arise out of the confusion I have not sagacity sufficient to determine—I believe that Ministers will have a vote of censure carried against them on the Walcheren question—the great difficulty of justifying themselves without bearing heavy upon the Commanders will I fear ultimately prove ruinous to them. Lord Chatham at present stands clear of all blame on the evidence and if nothing more turns up, he will appear to have done his duty and the censure will fall upon the undertaking, and upon the delay of evacuating. The King I hear is very stout, and has no thoughts of submitting to the Talents. An Amendment was proposed to Mr. Canning's Motion by Ryder, expressive of the opinion of the House that Lord Chatham had not been actuated by improper motives, but the temper of the House was such that the Amendment was withdrawn, and the most that could be obtained was—that it should not appear upon the Journals, and that the motion shd. not be carried to the foot of the Throne....Sturges Bourne did not vote—Huskisson voted against us—Binning left the House—so did the Pagets. Of our Irish troops, Shaw and Archdall voted against us—the Beresfords had some doubts, but they *all* voted with us. I could not prevent Sir Ed. O'Brien (who has uniformly voted with us) from going to Ireland. I hope all our other members will remain...' (Richmond MSS. 73/1710.)

Perceval commented, in a letter to the Lord Lieutenant on the 8th: 'The course of events in Parliament is such as must distress your Grace and every friend of his Majesty's present Govt. Undeniably it is sufficiently distressing and irksome to me. The divided state of parties at the present moment hardly offers any prospects in any hands of a strong Government—and the peculiarly awkward nature of the question which Lord Chatham's communication of his report to the King gave rise to, embarrassed us more than anything else. It appeared to me, however much we might have to complain of Lord Chatham, yet, if we had resented his conduct by *requiring* his retirement, while the Walcheren Enquiry was pending, our conduct would be open to just criticism, as ungenerous, and directed by the policy of sacrificing him the better to escape ourselves: we therefore determined to stand the brunt of a discussion upon his conduct, which we could not defend, but which we could not concur in reprobating in the manner in which our adversaries described it. By a union of almost all the floating strength of the House against us, by the indisposition of many of our friends to meet the question, and by the determination of no small number of them even to vote against us upon it, we lost the question upon which we divided.' (Richmond MSS. 66/883.)

of the bedroom today. When Batiscombe came to see her at six o'clock he told me he had not for days found her pulse so quiet. Within this hour some degree of fever is come on again which must be expected towards night after so long an illness.

Wednesday, 8 o'clock. Amelia's first sleep was from half past 12 till three and then from 4 till six and she is now asleep. (Add. Georgian 12/137)

[*The King's reply, Queen's Palace, 7 March*.] I lose no time in thanking you for your kind letter and in expressing the satisfaction which I have received from your mention of what Mr. Dundas & Battiscombe said to you yesterday respecting dear Amelia & from her having passed so good a night. (Add. Georgian 12/138)

[*From Princess Mary, Wednesday night* [*7 March*].] I return you my most greatful thanks for the letter received this evening by the return of the groom. I am happy to be able to say that Amelia has passed a very tolerable day barring the pain & oppression in the head which at times distressed her very much, therefore Dr. Pope thought proper to apply leeches which have relieved her as they bleed very well. She went into the warm bath this evening & when Dr. Pope came at 9 o'clock found the pulse *very* quiet & little or no heat about her. She is to take her medicine again to night.

Thursday morning, 8 o'clock. I am happy to be able to say dear Amelia went to sleep at 12 o'clock and did not wake till 4, then went to sleep again at 5 and slept another hour. (Add. Georgian 12/139)

[*The King's reply, Queen's Palace, 8 March*.] I have received your kind letter, the contents of which are very comfortable & I need hardly assure you of the satisfaction which I derive from your being enabled to send me reports of dear Amelia which I must flatter myself are progressively favorable. (Add. Georgian 12/140)

4107 PRINCESS AMELIA *to the* KING, *and the reply*

[*Wednesday evening* [*7 March 1810*].] I put off writing to you till this evening that I might tell you the effect of six leeches Sir Henry Halford ordered to be applied to my head, finding the cold application had not relieved me. They have bled very much & the tightness over the eyes I think lessened, tho' I still feel great weight & oppression at the back of the head. I have since been in the warm bath. This has certainly been a tolerable day. Tonight I take my medcine [*sic*] again.

I shall count anxiously the hours till we meet, my dearest father. I was grieved yesy. was such a bad day for your journey and hope none of you have caught cold. I felt relieved from the medicine yesy. & it proves it does good as I always get better nights after it.

I am glad Mrs. Howe[1] is better but am sorry to hear from my sisters how indifferent Gooly[2] is.

I will now conclude, begging you to believe me ever. . .(Add. Georgian 14/161)

[1] Mrs Caroline Howe. See No. 1082.
[2] Miss Martha Carolina Goldsworthy ('Goully'), sister of Colonel Philip Goldsworthy, Equerry to the King. She had been Sub-Governess to the Princesses. See Fanny Burney's *Diary*.

[*The King's reply, Queen's Palace, 8 March.*] I return you many thanks for your very affectionate letter which upon the whole has been very satisfactory to me, and dear Mary's has given me the additional comfort of knowing that you have passed a good night. I anxiously hope that on my return to Windsor tomorrow I may be greeted by reports not less favorable & I am looking forward with pleasure to that moment. The Queen & your sisters are well. (Add. Georgian 14/162)

4108 LORD MULGRAVE *to the* KING, *and the reply*

[*Admiralty, 7 March 1810.*] Lord Mulgrave has the honour most humbly to submit to your Majesty a letter addressed to the Secretary of the Admiralty by Rear-Admiral Sir Richard Strachan, together with its enclosure entitled 'Observations on the Earl of Chatham's statement of his proceedings dated 15th October 1809 and presented to the King on the 14th of February 1810'. These papers bear date the 5th of March; they were sent last night to the Secretary of the Admiralty, and were this day officially read at the Admiralty Board. (15002)

[*The King's reply, Queen's Palace, 8 March.*] The King has received Lord Mulgrave's letter enclosing one from Sir Richard Strachan to the Secretary of the Admiralty together with a paper of observations which his Majesty will return as soon as he has finished the perusal of them. (15002)

4109 *Letters from* SPENCER PERCEVAL *to the* KING, *and the replies*

[*Downg. St., 8 March 1810.*] Mr Perceval acquaints your Majesty that the House went into the Enquiry again this evening, and examined Gen. Don and two or three other witnesses. Mr Perceval thinks that it will not last many days longer. It proceeds again upon that subject on Monday.

Lord Chatham acquainted Mr Perceval yesterday evening that your Majesty had most graciously accepted his resignation of his office.[1] Mr Perceval has been

---

[1] On the 7th Chatham informed Perceval that the King had accepted his resignation. Perceval at once replied: 'I do most sincerely regret that any circumstances should have occurred which should have rendered this step expedient either with a view to yourself or to his Majesty's service; but as you have taken the determination I have no difficulty in saying that in my opinion you have acted not less usefully for his Majy.'s service than nicely & honorably for yourself, in retiring at this moment from yr. office. I am sensible that his Maj.'s service will experience great loss by your retirement; but in the temper of the House, upon the subject of the late discussions, nothing could be well more embarrassing than the repeated revival of them with which we should unquestionably have been harassed. As to yourself your retirement will extinguish the feelings that are hostile to you and ampler justice will be done to your conduct in the expedition against which conduct there has not been a syllable hitherto adduced. And Sir R. Strachan's paper, a copy of which I trust I shall be able to send you either this evening or tomorrow morning, will, if I do not much mistake, do less injury to you than to him.' (Hoare MSS.)

Perceval wrote to the Lord Lieutenant of Ireland on the 8th: 'His retirement will relieve us from a great weight of prejudice which his late conduct had excited, but it cannot be disguised that the loss of such a question in the H. of C. unsettles the minds of many supporters, and makes our future stability more questionable. What that stability may be, or what may be the means of strengthening it, we can have no satisfactory means of ascertaining till the enquiry upon the Walcheren expedition has come to its close. At present, and with this question hanging over us, we cannot either with any proper feeling

anxiously considering whom he should recommend to your Majesty as Lord Chatham's successor. He conceives it to be very desireable to avoid making an offer of such a situation to anyone who may not please to accept it. With that view he has endeavoured to find out circuitously whether it would be acceptable to the Earl of Pembroke, to whom [*sic*] if Mr Perceval should find that he would accept it, he would venture to submit to your Majesty as, upon the whole, the most advantageous appointment, if your Majesty should be graciously pleased to approve of it.[1] (15003)

[*The King's reply, Queen's Palace, 9 March.*] The King has received Mr Perceval's letter & his Majesty has no hesitation in stating that the choice of the Earl of Pembroke as successor to Lord Chatham in the Ordnance appears to him as proper as any that could be made. His M. however doubts, from the dislike which Lord Pembroke has always shewn to engage in business, whether he will accept of the offer which his M. now sanctions. (15004)

[*From Perceval,* [*9 March*].] Mr Perceval acquaints your Majesty that your Majesty's Message relative to the Portuguese troops was taken into consideration this day and a Resolution proposed by Mr Perceval for granting to your Majesty £980,000 for their maintenance. It was opposed by Mr Curwen, Mr Fitzgerald, Sr. J. Newport, Mr Bankes, Mr Whitbread & Mr Tierney, and supported by Mr Leslie Foster, Mr Montagu, Ld Desart, Capt. Parker,[2] Mr Jacob[3] & Mr Huskisson

for ourselves, or any reasonable expectation of success expect that any person not now involved with us in party connexion should be invited to embrace our fortunes at this moment, and this consideration not a little embarrasses me with regard to the appointment of a successor to Ld. Chatham. It is material, if possible, to avoid having an offer of that sort rejected, which I am endeavouring to avoid, but I do not as yet so see my way to effect it as to enable me to tell your Grace to whom the appointment will be offered.... There can be no doubt that if the House of Commons withdraws its confidence and addresses the King for our removal, that no man amongst us can think of attempting to retain our situations, but I do not expect that the House will go to any such length. The difficult question which we may have to decide, may be in case the House should cast some censure upon our Walcheren expedition or impede our public measures. In any other times and under any other circumstances, I have no doubt it would be our duty to retire upon such *hints*; but our situation is extremely peculiar in this respect. By so doing we should be surrendering the King; it would be an act in some degree of choice and not of necessity, and we should be answerable for the consequences which such an event might produce. That these consequences would be most serious for us I very greatly apprehend, and therefore, as far as I am at present advised, think that they ought not to be risked, if they can be avoided.' (Richmond MSS. 66/883.)

[1] Perceval asked Lord Bathurst to make the enquiry, and Bathurst wrote to Lord Pembroke on the 8th: 'Lord Chatham resigned yesterday and Mr. Perceval has this morning asked me if I thought you would accept the Ordnance. I declined giving any opinion, but I desired he would give me leave to write to you a confidential letter in order to discover your sentiments. In the present situation of public affairs you may possibly object to being in the Cabinet. There is no necessity for the Master-General to belong to the Cabinet, but of course I need not add that Mr. P. would be very glad if you chose to be one of that number. This will therefore be left entirely to your choice. If you are disinclined to accepting, I hope you will not take any notice of this letter to anybody, as in case of your declining it will probably be offered to some officer senior to you in rank, and he might be hurt if he knew that the offer had been made to a junior officer.' (Wilton House MSS.)

[2] Sir Peter Parker (*c.* 1785–1814), M.P. for Wexford, 1810–11. Lieutenant, 1801; Commander, 1804; Captain, 1805. Succeeded his grandfather, Vice-Admiral Sir Peter Parker, as 2nd Baronet, 21 Dec. 1811 (his father, Vice-Admiral Christopher Parker, having predeceased him). The Opposition referred to him in 1810 as a 'doubtful'.

[3] William Jacob (*c.* 1762–1851), Tory M.P. for Westbury, 1806–7; for Rye, 1808–12.

and Mr Bathurst. The Committee divided about ½ p. one—upon a Motion of Mr. Tierney's that the Chairman should leave the Chair, when there were for Mr Tierney's Motion 142, against it 204. (15009)

[*The King's reply, Windsor Castle, 10 March.*] The King acknowledges the receipt of Mr Perceval's report of the proceedings in the House of Commons last night.[1] (15009)

4110   *Letters from the* MARQUESS WELLESLEY *to the* KING, *and the reply*

[*Foreign Office, 9 March 1810.*] Lord Wellesley has the honor to submit to your Majesty that as Sir Harford Jones cannot continue in Persia it is desirable to appoint a Minister at that Court without delay. It appears to be proper, for the purpose of obviating the recurrence of past inconveniences, that the Minister at the Court of Persia should be entirely under the authority of the Crown, & for this object it will be necessary that he should not only be appointed but paid by the Crown, that he may not be subject to the interference of the East India Company or of their servants, who have lately impeded Sir Harford Jones in the discharge of his duty, & even refused to furnish him with the requisite supplies of money. It is an anxious object of pride with the King of Persia that the Mission to his Court should proceed directly from your Majesty, and that the diplomatic character of your Minister in Persia should not be inferior to that of your Majesty's Minister at Constantinople. It appears to be wise policy to gratify the King of

---

[1] *Parl. Deb.*, XVI, 15**–11****. Lord Lowther wrote to his father on the 10th: 'All the *flying Parties* voted with us... Only with a majority of sixty it evidently shows our force is much dwindling, though I think that we lose a vast number of votes by having no one who can collect them. Arbuthnot is perfectly *useless*. He is not acquainted with one-third of the House and sits perfectly idle, although no exertions could have gained a majority for Ministers on Lord Chatham['s] question, as every member came voluntarily to the House. But on all other questions when members conceive that Ministers will be in [a] considerable majority [they] leave the House and so leave us in so small majorities, which causes our members to dwindle on other accounts. I begin to fear we *cannot last*. If we do, some improvement must be made on gathering our members to the House, or *not letting them leave it previous to divisions*.' (Lonsdale MSS.)

Canning wrote to Mrs. Canning on the 10th: 'I am vexed with myself, dearest love, excessively vexed—for not having spoken last night. I never was more determined to speak, but Huskisson having been alluded to by all the speakers on the other side, on account of his economical and bullion opinions, I gave way to him, and he made just speech enough (beside the bullion part) to make it awkward for me to get up after him, without some opponent intervening—and the Opposition, who had seen me *up*, did not choose to intervene. This morning I am provoked with myself for suffering this delicacy to prevent me from speaking—though I am not sorry to have put Huskn. forward—for *if I* have a Govt. to make, or mend, he is my best material, and it would be well if I could get him high enough in the opinion of the House to be Chancr. of the Exchqr. and take care of the House in my absence. I told all my Senate last night that Huskn. had done so well, and put our votes so much on the right ground that I did not think it necessary to follow him. But I am heartily vexed in my own mind that I did not—for I *should have* made a *very fine* speech, I can tell my own love. But it was two o'clock in the morning—and the House jaded—and the debate the dullest that I had almost ever heard. But I wish I had shewn them the difference. However I dare say there will be no want of opportunities to speak. No—I cannot think that they will be contented with that one change. Nor do I much think that even *it* will be made now. I *rather* think they will leave the Ordnance open for the present. The Board and the L[ieutenan]t Gen[era]l carry on the business perfectly well without a Master Genl. and that *after* the enquiry if they remain in—they will make other arrangements—and bring in—Castlereagh.' (Harewood MSS.)

Persia in this respect; the difference of expense will not be considerable as the charges of any British Minister in Persia must be nearly the same, whatever may be his diplomatic character. Lord Wellesley therefore humbly submits to your Majesty the propriety of appointing Sir Gore Ouseley to be your Majesty's Ambassador to the King of Persia, with the same diplomatic character now held by Mr Adair at Constantinople. Sir Gore Ouseley is peculiarly qualified for the station, & Lord Wellesley proposes that he should accompany the Persian Envoy now in London on his return to Persia; which event it is hoped may take place in the course of a few weeks after the departure of the dispatch now preparing for Persia. (15006–7)

[*From Lord Wellesley, Foreign Office, 9 March.*] Lord Wellesley has the honor to submit to your Majesty the copy of a Patent of Honor from the King of Persia to Sir Harford Jones, for which your Majesty's royal sanction is humbly solicited. He also submits to your Majesty a note from M. de Sousa, requesting your Majesty's confirmation of certain gratuities & honors granted by the Prince Regent of Portugal to your Majesty's officers & forces employed at Cayenne. (15005)

[*The King's reply, Windsor Castle, 10 March.*] The King approves of Lord Wellesley's recommendation of Sir Gore Ouseley for a direct Mission from his Majesty to the Court of Persia with a diplomatic character, not inferior to that of his Minister at Constantinople. The King also acquiesces in Sir Harford Jones's wish to avail himself of the Patent of Honor conferred upon him by the King of Persia, & his Majesty confirms the gratuities & honors granted by the Prince Regent of Portugal to the officers & men employed in the reduction of Cayenne. (15005)

4111 LORD MULGRAVE *to the* KING, *and the reply*

[*Admiralty, 10 March 1810.*] Lord Mulgrave has the honour humbly to submit to your Majesty that a private letter which he has received from Vice-Admiral Lord Collingwood gives so unfavourable an account of the state of health of that zealous and distinguish'd officer as to render it necessary without delay to appoint an Admiral to succeed him in the important command of the Medeterranean station. Lord Mulgrave cannot hope in the person of any successor to supply the long experience and peculiar qualification of Lord Collingwood for that command; but in humbly submitting for your Majesty's decision the appointment of Admiral Sir Charles Cotton, Lord Mulgrave feels confident that the most unremitting attention and the most anxious zeal for your Majesty's service would be exerted by that officer if it should be your Majesty's pleasure that the command in the Medeterranean should be entrusted to him.

Lord Mulgrave having received an intimation that it is the intention of Mr Eliab Harvey to present an humble petition to your Majesty in Council, praying his restoration to the rank of Rear-Admiral of which he was deprived by the sentence of a naval court martial,[1] Lord Mulgrave begs leave most humbly to represent to your Majesty that Admiral Lord Gambier, against whom the offence was personally committed, has expressed his wish that the case of Mr Harvey may be favourably considered by your Majesty; and that the naval officers at the Board of Admiralty are unanimously of opinion that the discipline of your Majesty's Navy would suffer no injury from the success of Mr Harvey's petition if the justice and propriety of the sentence of the cour[t] martial should be fully asserted in the report which it would be for the Admiralty to make upon your Majesty's gracious reference from the Council; and if the favourable grounds of that report should rest entirely upon the distinguish'd gallantry of Mr Harvey's conduct in the Battle of Trafalgar; under these impressions Lord Mulgrave humbly hopes that your Majesty may not disapprove of his making no objection to the presentation of Mr Harvey's petition to your Majesty in Council. (15010–11)

[*The King's reply, Windsor Castle, 11 March.*] The King entirely approves of Lord Mulgrave's recommendation of Admiral Sir Charles Cotton to succeed to the command of the naval forces in the Mediterranean upon the return of Lord Collingwood whose ill state of health his Majesty has learnt with much concern. Under the circumstances respecting Mr Eliab Harvey's petition which Lord Mulgrave has stated, H.M. can see no objection to its being received by the Privy Council. (15011)

4112   SPENCER PERCEVAL *to the* KING, *and the reply*

[*Downg. St., 12 March 1810.*] Mr Perceval acquaints your Majesty that Sr Francis Burdet brought on his Motion this day for the discharge of Mr Gale Jones. The House rejected his Motion by a majority of 153[2] to 14. The debate lasted so long that it was not convenient to go on with the Enquiry. It proceeded to receive the report upon the Portuguese subsidiary vote. The examination is appointed to go on tomorrow. Lord Porchester has given notice that next Monday sevnnight he will bring forward some Motion upon that Enquiry.

Mr Perceval regrets to acquaint your Majesty that Lord Pembroke has, as your Majesty expected, declined the offer which yr. Majesty has sanctioned Mr Perceval in making.[3] The constitution of the Board of Ordnance not requiring absolutely an immediate appointment, Mr Perceval will submit to your Majesty what occurs to him upon that subject next on Wednesday next. (15012)

---

[1] See No. 3889.
[2] The majority is wrongly given as 152 in Colchester, II, 238.
[3] Lord Pembroke wrote to Bathurst on the 9th: 'It is the utmost I can do to comply with your request by sending a very short answer by return of post.... In no situation of public affairs should I ever covet a seat in the Cabinet, and tho' the situation of Master-General of the Ordnance is the only one which it has ever occurred to me I might possibly be able to fill with any degree of credit (not that I ever sought or ever shall seek that or any other public situation), yet for various reasons I can have no hesitation in declining Mr. P.'s offer. In return for it I beg you will express to him from me what I should attempt to express were I not so unwell as I happen to be at this moment.' (Wilton House MSS.) Perceval wrote to him on the 12th, saying that the King had expressed doubts whether he would accept, 'from the dislike which your Lordship had always shown to engage in public business'. (*Ibid.*)

[The King's reply, Windsor Castle, 13 March.] The King has received Mr Perceval's letter and is sorry to find that his idea was well grounded that Lord Pembroke would decline the offer made to him. H.M. will be open to receive on Wednesday next whatever Mr Perceval may propose on the subject of the Ordnance, respecting which it certainly is not necessary to come to any immediate determination, his M. having known the Master-Generalship open for years. (15012)

4113   *Letters from the* MARQUESS WELLESLEY *to the* KING, *and the reply*

[Foreign Office, 13 March 1810.] Lord Wellesley has the honor to submit to your Majesty the propriety of appointing Mr James Morier[1] to be Secretary to your Majesty's Embassy in Persia. Mr James Morier was Private Secretary to Sir Harford Jones,[2] & discharged the duty of Secretary of Legation in Persia; he accompanied the Persian Envoy to this country, & now resides with him. If your Majesty should be graciously pleased to approve this appointment, Lord Wellesley proposes to have the honor of presenting Mr Morier with Sir Gore Ouseley to your Majesty at the Levée tomorrow.[3] (15013)

[From Lord Wellesley, Foreign Office, 13 March.] Lord Wellesley has the honor to submit to your Majesty the draft of an answer to Mr Pinkney on the subject of the late dissentions between the American Government & Mr Jackson. Several conferences have been held between Mr Pinkney & Lord Wellesley respecting those transactions, & in the peculiar circumstances of the case & under the great heat & animosity which existed between the contending parties, Lord Wellesley thought it advisable to delay his formal reply to Mr Pinkney untill the lapse of time & the change of events might have allayed the violence of the ferment which

[1] James Justinian Morier (*c.* 1780–1849), diplomatist and traveller. Secretary of Embassy at Tehran, 1811–15; Chargé d' Affaires there, 1814, and Minister *ad interim*, 1814–15.
[2] The British Envoy at Tehran, 1809–11.
[3] On the 13th Wellesley wrote to an unknown correspondent about the desirability of seeking additional strength for the carrying on of the Government, and the desirability of comprehending, if practicable, the three main groups of Mr. Pitt's friends then out of office: Canning's, Castlereagh's and Sidmouth's. Personal sacrifices would be needed: he himself was ready either to remain without office, and not in the Cabinet, or to become President of the Council or to take any other post. (*Wellesley Papers*, II, 5.) Canning wrote to Mrs. Canning on the 12th: 'I really believe the prevailing *wish* in the House of Commons and in the publick, is in favour of my return to the Foreign Office, and what I confess pleases me (and will please my own love still more) is that Wellesley's Premiership is never mentioned except as a mean, for *that end*. On the other hand, it is, I believe, equally certain that Wellesley has not taken a single step, nor uttered, *to any purpose*, a single word on the subject of such a change (to his *alentours* he talks of it, and they to all their acquaintance—but to the K[ing] or to his colleagues —not)—and that Perceval would seek any help in any quarter rather than come to me on my terms. It *is* certain that he did offer Castlereagh the Admiralty. I have heard that in a way which makes it impossible to doubt of its truth. George told it me last night of his own certain knowledge. He added that Castlereagh had declined the offer. It is natural enough that Perceval should prefer Castgh. to me—because Castgh. would leave him precisely where he is—and though the choice would be a declaration of war against me, yet in the very helpless state in which he stands in the House of Coms. without one single soul to help him in debate (for Saunders is dumb, and R. Ryder worse than if he were so) the accession even of Castgh. who has spoken better than he ever did before this Session, would be a help in debate. What it would be in character and following I do not know. I think Castgh. has but four.' (Harewood MSS.)

had been excited by causes of no real substance or importance. In preparing the reply to Mr Pinkney Lord Wellesley has endeavoured to avoid all topics of acrimonious discussion, to render justice to Mr Jackson's honest zeal for your Majesty's service, & to conciliate the Government of America, without any compromise of the dignity of your Majesty's Government. (15015–16)

[*The King's reply, Windsor Castle, 14 March.*] The King approves of Lord Wellesley's answer to Mr Pinkney on the subject of the late differences between the American Government & Mr Jackson. His Majesty also sanctions the appointment of Mr James Morier as Secretary of Embassy in Persia, and he & Sir Gore Ouseley may be presented this day at the Queen's Palace.[1] (15016)

4114 THE EARL OF LIVERPOOL *to the* KING, *and the reply*

[*London, 13 March 1810.*] Lord Liverpool begs leave most humbly to submit to your Majesty the draft of a dispatch to the Duke of Manchester in consequence of the differences which have lately arisen between the Government and the Assembly of Jamaica.[2] (15014)

[*The King's reply, Windsor Castle, 14 March.*] The King approves of the instructions which Lord Liverpool has prepared for the Duke of Manchester on the subject of the late differences with the House of Assembly in Jamaica. (15014)

4115 LORD MULGRAVE *to the* KING, *and the reply*

[*Admiralty, 19 March 1810.*] Lord Mulgrave has the honour to submit to your Majesty the minutes of a court martial held at Yarmouth for the trial of Denis Mahony seaman on board your Majesty's ship Desirée for striking a boatswain's mate; of which he was convicted & condemned to suffer death. By subsequent enquiry it has been satisfactorily proved that the unfortunate man is a lunatick, in consequence of which Lord Mulgrave presumes most humbly to recommend the said Denis Mahony as a fit object for your Majesty's royal mercy. (15017)

[1] Wellesley was still striving to get his friend Canning back into the Cabinet. Canning wrote to Mrs Canning on the 17th: 'Just as I had sent off my other letter of to-day Charles Bagot came to tell me that Arbuthnot had sent to desire to see him this morning—and had told him in confidence (but meaning that he should tell me) that Wellesley was hard at work—and *running true to me*—that he had written to Perceval a strong representation on the state of the Government, insisting upon the necessity of a change—and offering to give up his own office, and *to take any other*, the Presidency of the Council for instance, to make way for my return—that Perceval had answered this letter in a very mild tone, acquiescing in the general statements, but requesting him to take back his letter, and generalize what he says about office, leaving out Presidency of the Council as he should wish to make use of his letter, and not to bind him to *that* offer: that Wellesley has accordingly has accordingly [*sic*] taken back his letter, and *re*-written it, more strong than before—that he and Perceval are to meet today or tomorrow —and in short that changes are in agitation.' (Harewood MSS.)

[2] The House of Assembly of Jamaica, in consequence of an alleged infringement of the Constitution of the island, had resolved not to grant any supplies after 1 May 1810 for the support of the military establishment. In consequence, the Duke of Manchester, the Governor, dissolved the Assembly.

[*The King's reply, Windsor Castle, 20 March.*] In consequence of the circumstance stated in Lord Mulgrave's letter respecting Denis Mahony, the King cannot hesitate in agreeing to a remission of the sentence of death passed upon him. (15018)

4116 *Letters from* SPENCER PERCEVAL *to the* KING, *and the replies*

[*Downg. St., 20 March 1810.*] Mr Perceval acquaints your Majesty that Mr Martin brought under the consideration of a Committee of the Ho. of Co. yesterday evening his Resolutions upon the 3d Report of the Committee of Finance— when Mr Bankes proposed an Amendment to one of the Resolutions, which went to the abolition of all sinecures and the substitution of a limited right to grant pensions instead. Mr Perceval opposed this Amendment, and after some time consumed in the debate of it, it was agreed that more time should be taken for considering it, as the House did not expect that it should be brought forward. Mr Perceval did not object to the postponement, and it was therefore put off till tomorrow fortnight. Mr Perceval has the satisfaction of thinking that his opposition to it seemed to be well received by the House. (15019)

[*The King's reply, Windsor Castle, 20 March.*] The King is glad to learn from Mr Perceval's report of what passed in the House of Commons last night, that his opposition to Mr Banks's [*sic*] Amendment (for the abolition of all sinecures &c) was well received by the House. (15020)

[*From Perceval, Downg. St., 20 March.*] Mr Perceval acquaints your Majesty that Mr Bankes brought in his Bill respecting the granting of offices in reversion this evening, under a new title; the measure however was in effect the same. The title was 'for altering the mode of granting offices.' Mr Perceval recommended as before that the Bill should be brought in merely for a limited time, and would have proposed an Amendment to the title of the Bill to that effect; but as he perceived he should have been in a minority upon the question, he contented himself with giving notice that in the Committee upon the Bill he would move to amend it in that manner. He doubts however extremely whether he can prevail upon a sufficient number of members to attend upon this Bill to enable him to carry his Amendment. (15021)

[*The King's reply, Windsor Castle, 21 March.*] The King is sorry to learn from Mr Perceval that he apprehends that he shall not be able in the Committee to carry his Amendment to the title of Mr Banke[s]'s Bill respecting offices in reversion. (15021)

4117 THE KING *to* SIR DAVID DUNDAS

[*Windsor Castle, 21 March 1810.*] Upon consideration of what Sir David Dundas has submitted respecting the Memorial of Lieut.-General St. John,[1] the King is

---

[1] Frederick St. John (1765–1844). M.P. for Oxford, 1818–20. Younger brother of George Richard, 3rd Viscount Bolingbroke (1761–1824). Lieutenant-Colonel, 1791; Colonel, 1795; Major-General, 1798; Lieutenant-General, 1805; General, 1814.

of opinion that it will be more expedient to re-assemble such members of the former Board as can be collected without inconvenience, thus relieving the Commander-in-Chief & the Judge Advocate General from a responsibility which might prove embarassing, altho' their opinion should be exactly that which shall be given by the Board. (15022)

4118   SPENCER PERCEVAL *to the* KING, *and the reply*

[*Downg. St., 23 March 1810.*] Mr Perceval acquaints your Majesty that the Estimate for the Staff of the Army was brought on in the Committee of Supply this evening. When the Army Estimates were before the House on a preceding evening, such great objection was taken in the House to the amount of the Staff that Mr Perceval thought it prudent to withdraw that Estimate, and upon consultation with the Commander-in-Chief some reduction was made in it—one Lieut.-General & one Major-General in Scotland, one Major-General in the London District, one Lieut.-General in the Eastern; the Severn & the Midland District were reduced; and with these reductions the vote was proposed this evening. Objection was still made to it—and a Motion was made by Mr Tierney to reduce the vote so as to strike off the two Generals in the Home District, his R. Highness the D of Cambridge and Lord Heathfield.[1] This Mr Perceval opposed. Mr Tierney was supported by Mr Wardle, Mr Whitbread & Mr Huskisson & Mr Moore, and was opposed by General Hope, Mr Perceval, Lord Palmerston and Capt. Parker. The Committee divided for Mr Tierney's Amendment 61, for the original Motion 99. (15023)

[*The King's reply, Windsor Castle, 24 March.*] The King has received with satisfaction Mr Perceval's report of the division in the House of Commons last night upon Mr Tierney's amendment to the Estimate for the Staff.[2] (15024)

4119   LORD MULGRAVE *to the* KING, *and the reply*

[*Admiralty, 26 March 1810.*] Lord Mulgrave has the honour most humbly to submit to your Majesty that your Majesty's confidential servants entertain an hope from recent communications that the Government of France may be induced to accede to the interesting and important measure of a general exchange of prisoners upon the following concessions: 1st, the exchange of your Majesty's civil subjects who were detained in France upon the commencement of hostilities, against prisoners taken from the enemy in the due course of ligitimate warfare; and secondly the admission of the interpretation applied by the French Government to the conditions of surrender of the prisoners captured at St Domingo. Your Majesty's confidential servants are most humbly of opinion that an exchange of

---

[1] Francis Augustus, 2nd Lord Heathfield (1750–1813), succeeded his father, 6 July 1790. Lieutenant-Colonel, 1779; Major-General, 1793; Lieutenant-General, 1799; General, 1808. A Lord of the Bedchamber, 1812–13.

[2] *Parl. Deb.*, XVI, 40–5.

prisoners on these conditions, if it should receive your Majesty's most gracious approbation, would be advantageous & desirable; Lord Mulgrave therefore humbly submits to your Majesty's pleasure the appointment of a Commissioner to treat (with Commissioners to be appointed by the French Government) at Morlaix, for an exchange of prisoners.

If your Majesty should be graciously pleased to sanction the adoption of this measure by the signification of your Majesty's pleasure, Lord Mulgrave would most humbly beg leave to submit Mr Colin Alexander Mackenzie as a person fully qualified to discharge with advantage to your Majesty's service, the duties of Commissioner for the exchange of prisoners; that gentleman having conducted himself with great zeal & judgment during his residence at Portsmouth as Commissioner for carrying into effect the conditions of the surrender of the Russian squadron in the Tagus, under the Convention of Cintra. (15025–6)

[*The King's reply, Windsor Castle, 27 March.*] The King has received Lord Mulgrave's letter, and, considering the sufferings of many of his subjects from so long a detention in France, his Majesty is induced upon a principle of humanity to sanction the measures proposed by his confidential servants for a general exchange of prisoners. His Majesty concludes that Mr McKenzie is a person upon whose discretion full reliance may be placed. (15026)

4120   *Letters from* SPENCER PERCEVAL *to the* KING, *and the reply*

[*Downg. St., 27 March 1810.*] Mr Perceval acquaints your Majesty that the living of Aberffraw in Anglesea has become vacant; and Lord Uxbridge having recommended the Revd. Mr Evan Lloyd[1] as a very proper person for that living, Mr Perceval humbly submits to your Majesty's gracious approbation the propriety of appointing Mr Lloyd accordingly. Mr Perceval understands that he is a very respectable clergyman and what is no inconsiderable qualification for a living in Anglesea, that he understands the Welsh language. (15027)

[*From Perceval, Downg. St., 27 March.*] Mr Perceval acquaints your Majesty that Mr Lethbridge,[2] after asking Sr. F. Burdett whether he was the author of a letter signed by his name which appeared in Cobbett's paper[3] of last Saturday and having received Sr. F. Burdett's answer acknowledging the letter, announced his intention of bringing a complaint against Sr. Francis, on the ground of that letter as a gross insult on the House, and a high breach of its privileges. After this notice had occasioned some short conversation Lord Porchester brought on his Motion

---

[1] Rector of Llangyfelach, Glam., 1805–41; Perpetual Curate of Penmynydd, Anglesey, 1808; Rector of Aberffraw, Anglesey, 1810; Rector of Llangelynin, Merioneth, 1838 (*d.?* 1843).

[2] Sir Thomas Buckler Lethbridge (1778–1849), M.P. for Somerset, 1806–12, 1820–30, succeeded his father as 2nd Baronet in 1815. The Opposition classed him as a 'doubtful' in 1810. An independent country gentleman, he usually supported Ministers. He was popularly known as Leatherbreeches.

[3] William Cobbett (1763–1835), the Radical journalist and politician, started his *Weekly Political Register* as an independent Tory organ in 1802. By 1806 he had taken the popular side. Burdett's letter of 23 March is in *Parl. Deb.*, XVI, 137. Burdett was denying the right of the House of Commons to imprison the people of England.

upon the expedition to the Scheldt; he spoke for about 4 hours and concluded with moving several Resolutions of fact—a long string of them, both upon the subject of the policy of the expedition, and upon the detention [*sic*] of Walcheren.

Mr Perceval trusts your Majesty will permit him to send your Majesty the Resolutions of fact tomorrow, and he now sends to your Majesty the Resolutions of *opinion*; the two first of them relate to the policy & conduct of the expedition, and the last to the detention of Walcheren.

Lord Castlereagh followed Lord Porchester and made an excellent and very impressive speech with very great effect.[1] Mr Ponsonby replied to Ld. Castlereagh but after having spoken about $\frac{1}{2}$ an hour finding the House very inattentive and clamorous for an adjournment he proposed to adjourn the debate which was accordingly adjourned.[2] (15028)

[*The King's reply, Windsor Castle, 27 March.*] The King acknowledges the receipt of Mr Perceval's report of the proceedings in the House of Commons last night. (15028)

4121 *Letters from the* MARQUESS WELLESLEY *to the* KING, *and the reply*

[*Foreign, Office 27 March 1810.*] Lord Wellesley has the honor to transmit to your Majesty the original & translation of a letter from the Grand Vizier to your Majesty, accompanying presents from the Sultan to your Majesty. A list of the presents is annexed; and the presents will be forwarded to the Queen's Palace tomorrow morning. (15030)

[*From Lord Wellesley, Foreign Office, 27 March.*] Lord Wellesley has the honor to submit to your Majesty the request of the Persian Envoy to be permitted to pay his respects to your Majesty at the Levée to morrow, as he was prevented by

[1] Even Canning admitted that he had made 'a prodigiously good speech'. (Harewood MSS. To Mrs. Canning, 28 March.)

[2] Writing to Lord Grenville at 2.30 a.m. on the 27th, W. H. Fremantle had this to say about part of the night's debate: 'Lord Castlereagh continued till half past one o'clock, and throughout was extremely dull and weak in his defence. He went through the evidence, built much upon the small expense which had attended it; said that the undertaking had commenced from the best and most satisfactory information of the enemies' force and quoted as one instance the Army List procured from Catalonia (adverted to in the Second Report) which he styled a most perfect official document. He then attacked Sir William Erskine's evidence most violently, and after touching upon most of the other points, concluded with an apparent most animated address to the House upon the subject of the risk incurred by the attempt, saying that all our former victories and naval and military achievements had been undertaken with considerable risk, and went back to the capture of Quebec under Wolfe and finished by the battle of Vimeira as uniform instances of success attending risk. In no part of his speech was he much applauded; in the latter part, Perceval gave the token but it was not caught with much effect. Ponsonby began a reply to him and as far as it went with considerable effect and ability. He broke off at half past 2 o'clock and adjourned the debate. Lord Castlereagh did not touch upon the second question of the examination. I am glad to find the Addingtons do not object to our first Motion and support both of them. I think very well of the division though their whip has been most powerful. I could not make out more than 400 members during the whole night. They must bring two hundred and fifty to beat us. All the Belvoir people are come, also Cartwright, and I fear the Portlands vote against us, but yet we shall be most powerful in our numbers.' (Fortescue MSS.)

indisposition from having that honor on Wednesday last. Lord Wellesley also requests your Majesty's gracious permission to present to your Majesty tomorrow Lord Jocelyn,[1] eldest son of the Earl of Roden, lately returned from Spain. (15031)

[*The King's reply, Windsor Castle, 28 March.*] The King has received Lord Wellesley's letter and his Majesty will receive the Persian Envoy at the Queen's Palace this day, when Lord Jocelyn may also be presented. (15032)

4122   *Letters from* SPENCER PERCEVAL *to the* KING, *and the replies*

[*Downg. St., 28 March 1810, Wed. mong.*] Mr Perceval acquaints your Majesty that the House of Commons was occupied some time yesterday evening upon Mr Lethbridge's Motion against Sr. Fr. Burdett. The letter complained of was very long, it was read thro' by the Clerk, and took up near two hours in reading. Sir Francis Burdett was then heard, and said little, expressing his opinion that it contained no breach of the privileges of the House. He then retired—and Mr Lethbridge proposed his Motion, that the paper contained a libel against the House. Mr Ponsonby moved to adjourn the debate till this day sev'nnight on the ground of the publication being so long that the House could not be competent to judge upon it by once hearing it read. Mr Perceval agreed for the same reason to an adjournment, but objected to such a question being delayed more than one day, and therefore proposed an Amendment to Mr Ponsonby's Motion, by changing this day sevnnight, to tomorrow. Mr Whitbread opposed Mr Perceval's Amendment and suggested Friday next instead. Mr Perceval persevered in his Amendment and the House divided:

For Mr Ponsonby's Motion 146, for Mr Perceval's Amendment 190.[2]

Mr Giddy then opposed the Motion for adjournment altogether, preferring to have the discussion come on immediately—when the House divided again:

For the adjournmt. till tomorrow 211, against it 138.[3]

The debate then was resumed by Mr Ponsonby on the Walcheren expedition. Mr Ponsonby was followed by General Crawfurd who went much at large into the subject and made a very good and useful speech. He concluded by moving an Amendment with a copy of which Mr Perceval will furnish your Majesty tomorrow. Mr Herbert followed Genl. Crawfurd on the same side, and Sir James Hall answered Mr Herbert—and the debate of the night concluded by a speech from Mr Marryat[4] in favor of Genl. Crawfurd's Amendment, when the House

---

[1] Robert, 3rd Earl of Roden (1788–1870), styled Viscount Jocelyn from 21 June 1797, when his grandfather, the 1st Earl, died, until 29 June 1820, when his father died. Tory M.P. for Co. Louth, 1806–7 and 1810–20. Treasurer of the Household, May–July 1812, and Vice-Chamberlain, July 1812–21. Auditor-General of the Exchequer [I.], 1820–2. Created Baron Clanbrassill [U.K.], 17 July 1821. K.P., 1821; a Lord of the Bedchamber, 1828–31.

[2] The number is wrongly given as 196 in *Parl. Deb.*, XVI, 194.

[3] The number is wrongly given as 134 in Colchester, II, 242.

[4] Joseph Marryat (1757–1824), M.P. for Horsham, 1808–12; for Sandwich, 1812–24. He was classed as a Government supporter in 1810. He was a representative in Parliament of the shipping interest. His second son, Captain Frederick (1792–1848), was the novelist.

adjourned, the debate upon this question being intended to come on after the discussion on Sr. F. Burdett's business, if there should be time for it.

Mr Perceval transmits to yr. Majesty a copy of Lord Porchester's Resolutions.[1] (15033–4)

[*The King's reply, Windsor Castle, 28 March.*] The King has received Mr Perceval's report of last night's proceedings in the House of Commons, which appears to have been satisfactory, and his Majesty considers it to have been good policy on the part of Mr Perceval to have pressed his Amendment on Mr Ponsonby's Motion to a division. The King approves of Mr Lloyd being presented to the living of Aberffraw in Anglesea. (15034)

[*From Perceval, Downg. St., 28 March.*] Mr Perceval acquaints your Majesty that the House of Commons proceeded this day with the debate on Sir Francis Burdett's letter. Mr Brand moved an adjournment, which was supported by Mr Whitbread & opposed by Mr Owen, Sir Saml. Romilly answered Mr Owen, Mr Perceval followed Sir S. Romilly, Mr Windham was also for the adjournment— as were Mr Wilberforce, Mr Adam and also the Master of the Rolls. Mr Perceval thought that when the Master of the Rolls took the line of considering that more time should be given, it was necessary not so much for the sake of the House as for the public out of doors who might be induced to believe that what the Master of the Rolls thought should be delayed was intemperately & passionately brought forward if it had been pressed on at that time. Mr Perceval laments the necessity under which he felt himself placed of yielding to his adjournment as he believes the real reason with too many for wishing to delay the question was the fear of meeting it—the fear of Sr. F. Burdett & his followers—a sentiment which Mr Perceval begs to assure your Majesty had not the slightest influence upon him.[2]

[1] W. H. Fremantle sent Lord Grenville an account of the debate at 11 p.m. on the 27th: 'The discussions till 10 o'clock were occupied with Sir F. Burdett; questions of order arose whether he should withdraw or not previous to the Motion to be made by Lethbridge. The first Motion goes to condemn his letter and his arguments as inserted in Cobbett's Register as an attack upon the privileges and dignity of the House, and the second goes to criminate him as the author of this publication. A debate then took place as to the time when it should be taken into consideration. Perceval proposed tomorrow, Whitbread Friday. A division took place at 9 o'clock. We had 146 against 190. A second division took place on a proposition of Davies Giddy that the question should immediately be taken into consideration—on this we had 138 against 211—so that it now stands for tomorrow. It is understood that the intention of Government is to send Sir F. Burdett to the Tower—but there is no doubt that the whole of this is a concerted project to turn the attention of the public from this question to another and to involve us in difficulties, which it undoubtedly will do. Ponsonby has just finished a very able speech, but to a thin House, and Crawford is now hammering away with about a hundred members to attend to him. We believe that he will move Perceval's Resolutions. I see no difference in the House. I think we have only found two additional members appear to-night and one is Charles Moore whom [*sic*] I am afraid will not vote. I don't see the prospect of finishing the first question.' (Fortescue MSS.)

[2] *Parl. Deb.*, XVI, 257–305. W. H. Fremantle described the debate in a letter to Lord Grenville at 11 p.m. on the 28th: 'The question of adjournment on the motion respecting Sir F. Burdett was moved by Brand, and a long debate has ensued upon it. Mr. Owen, Croker and Perceval as yet on one side, Whitbread, Lord Folkestone, Windham and at this moment Adam on the other. When I call them on the other, I mean merely as to the question of adjournment, for Windham and Adam are strong in their opinion as to the libel. Sir Samuel Romilly has made (in my opinion) a most indiscreet and injudicious speech, arguing against the libel, admitting a doubt in his mind to exist upon it, but not in

The Walcheren debate will come on tomorrow and Mr Perceval transmits to your Majesty a copy of Genl. Crawfurd's Amendments.

Mr Perceval has the satisfaction also of sending to your Majesty an abstract of the annual account of the exports and imports of the last three years, by which your Majesty will be pleased to see the prodigious encrease of trade in the last year, and its excess not only above the most abundant year of war, but even of peace.[1] (15035)

[*The King's reply, Windsor Castle, 29 March.*] The King is satisfied that Mr Perceval, under the circumstances which he has reported, acted right in finally yielding to the adjournment of the debate upon Sir Francis Burdett's letter, and his Majesty is not less convinced that no sentiment of fear from violence out of doors can influence him, but he cannot forbear expressing his surprize at the line taken by the Master of the Rolls upon this occasion.

The King has received with great satisfaction the reports of the exports & imports, the encrease of which in the last year is really very astonishing. (15036)

[*From Perceval, Downg. St., 29 [30] March 1810.*] Mr Perceval acquaints your Majesty that the adjourned debate on the Walcheren expedition was resumed

any way satisfying the House as to the validity of such a doubt. Perceval took exactly the line which you argued this morning, taking it upon the letter and arguing it upon the grounds of an appeal on the part of Sir F. Burdett to his constituents to resist the powers of the House of Commons. The feeling of the House is most strongly against us and I am quite persuaded we have lost most considerably indeed by the line which has been adopted in the public estimation. It is a shabby attempt to screen the individual and shrink from our duty, and I own I am quite disgusted at it. As to the Walcheren question it is quite laid aside. This subject will occupy at least this night and I should not wonder if the main question upon it should be adjourned till tomorrow. Sir Sidney Yorke got up to reply to some allusions of Whitbread about his brother, and most illiberally alluded to his being a brewer of bad porter. Whitbread behaved with most extraordinary good judgement and calmness and good humour and recommended himself greatly to all parts of the House by it. The Speaker was most unjust and partial in not noticing it. I should not stay the event of this debate if it lasts beyond 12. I am quite out of sorts by the turn it has taken and quite disgusted with the want of judgement and courage in those who denominate themselves as belonging to the Opposition.' (Fortescue MSS.)

He wrote again, at 1 a.m. on the 29th: 'To my most extreme surprise and gratification, the debate took a turn after I wrote to you most favourable. Bragge Bathurst and Wilberforce supported the adjournment the former making a small Amendment by prefacing the original question of adjournment with the statement of the grounds on which the adjournment was voted, namely the important business then before the House. This was resisted by Dundas, and the debate was closed by the Master of the Rolls who made a most able and very impressive speech in favour of the adjournment. Perceval followed, more mortified and stung than you can conceive, relinquishing the Motion; he lost his temper completely upon our triumph and very angry and violent words passed on the part of Ponsonby, Tierney and him: the two former glorying in the triumph, and upbraiding him with having given way not to their suggestions, but to the rebuke of his own friends and from the fear of being left in a minority. Nothing could be more mortifying or more humiliating to the Government than the close of this debate, and I really think we are most fortunately out of the dilemma for a time at least. I hope it may have some effect on our future division, but I fear their numbers increase; we know of 530 members having been in the House, and they boast most extremely indeed, and say we are deceiving ourselves in our promises. I still think we must have 240 to vote.' (*Ibid.*)

1	Exports (declared values)	Imports (official values)
1807	£37,245,877	£26,734,425
1808	£37,275,102	£26,795,540
1809	£47,371,393	£31,750,557

yesterday afternoon. Genl. Tarleton began the debate, Mr Rose replied to him, Lord Pollington to Mr Rose, and Mr Fitzgerald, one of the Lords of yr. Majesty's Treasury in Ireland, spoke next very sensibly and well. Mr. Grattan followed next; Mr Canning then spoke. The important part of his speech respected the detention [*sic*] of Walcheren. He only objects to General Crawfurd's Amendment in bringing forward the situation of Austria as one of the considerations which weighed upon the question of its detention, but as to negativing the Resolution of censure, and concurring in a vote of acquittal, he is quite prepared to support your Majesty's present servants. Mr Whitbread answered Mr Canning. He attacked him very strongly upon the subject of his conduct to Lord Castlereagh, but upon the whole he did not make in any degree a powerful speech and made very little impression upon the House. Capt. Parker in a few words followed Mr Whitbread and the House adjourned about 2 o'clock.[1]

Mr Perceval has the satisfaction to assure your Majesty that as far as he can judge the debate has been extremely satisfactory and that the effect of the discussion has been to remove much false impression which was entertained upon the subject before it was discussed—so much so that Mr Perceval anticipates with great confidence a favorable conclusion—and he hopes it may be concluded tomorrow.[2] (15047–8)

[1] *Parl. Deb.*, XVI, 306–72. W. H. Fremantle wrote to Lord Grenville at 2 a.m. on the 30th: 'Canning finished at 12 having made an exceeding bad speech and with no effect whatever or support in the House. He finished by announcing his intention of opposing both the Resolutions moved by Lord Porchester, but he could not agree to the second Resolution moved by General Craufurd. Whitbread replied, and I really think most ably and with great effect; he spoke till 2, and most particularly attacked Canning for his conduct towards his colleagues and the public during the time when this expedition was in progress and at the moment of its termination. Nothing could be stronger than his language and I think he carried the House with him. Canning did not enter much into the evidence or the detail of the subject, but dealt in general arguments and opinions. The division will certainly take place tomorrow. Canning's intention to oppose our second Resolution will make a difference, and I fear will save them. We have most diligently scrutinised the list today and we make of persons whom we have seen in the House at different times, including pairs, 289 for them, 252 for us, on our Resolutions. With respect to Craufurd's Resolutions I am sure it will make a most material difference. I have not an idea that they will be carried. I am afraid Wilberforce will move an Amendment to them. Of the 541 persons whom we have seen perhaps 30 may not vote at all, but we have taken them supposing the whole vote. Captain Parker said a few words, Sir Thomas Turton then got up and the House adjourned.' (Fortescue MSS.)

[2] At the request of Lord Grenville, James Loch, William Adam's nephew, made the following calculations on the 21st as to the probable voting on the Walcheren question: 'One way each Party is 221. The most unfavourable way (which is supposing 481) to vote gives them 31 of a majority. My own opinion is that if nothing happens in the House to make some of their people shy, they will carry it by about 7, certainly not, I think, by 16.
'The House is accounted for thus:

Administration	253
Opposition	234
Hopeful doubtful	29
Doubtful	90
Absent	51
Speaker	1
	658

Carlton House uncommonly active. And Yarmouth and Tyrwhitt pressing for permission to vote. I cannot help thinking they perceive something like a change, or they would not be so kind. I was [with] Taylor till two this morning with Tyrwhitt making out a list for Carlton House.' (Blair Adam MSS.)

[*The King's reply, Windsor Castle, 30 March.*] The King acknowledges the receipt of Mr Perceval's report of the debate last night & his Majesty has very great pleasure in finding that Mr Perceval anticipates with so much confidence a favorable conclusion of it. (15048)

4123   THE KING *to the* DUCHESS OF BRUNSWICK

[*Windsor Castle, 31 March 1810.*] I entirely approve of your intention, communicated in the kind letter which I received from you yesterday, of going into mourning for the Abbess of Gundersheim & of conforming to the new rule. I am truely happy to learn that you are so well & very thankful to you for your kind enquiries respecting my dear Amelia who, I flatter myself, has not lost ground upon the whole, although her progress has been checked for some days past. (16791)

4124   *Letters from* SPENCER PERCEVAL *to the* KING, *and the reply*

[*Downg. St., 1 April [31 March] 1810, Saturday morng., 7.30.*] Mr Perceval humbly acquaints your Majesty that he is this moment returned from the House of Commons. The debate on the Walcheren expedition was resumed yesterday evening, when the speakers were Sr. Thomas Turton, Sr. F. Burdett, Mr Bathurst, Mr Windham, Mr Tierney, Gen. Loftus, Mr Peele, Mr Perceval, Mr Dundas, Sr Ho. Popham.

Mr Bathurst took a decided line against the expedition in all its parts. At 4 o'clock this morning the House came to a division and has continued dividing ever since. There were two divisions on General Crawfurd's first Amendment which Mr Perceval transmitted to your Majesty the other day. On the first, for leaving out the words of Lord Porchester's Motion, the numbers were: Ayes 275, Noes 227.

The next for inserting Genl. Crawfurd's: Ayes 272, Noes 232.

There were also two divisions on the second Resolution which was so much altered since it was first sent to your Majesty that Mr Perceval troubles your Majesty with another copy.

For leaving out Ld Porchester's words, 275; for insert, 224.

For inserting General Crawfurd's: Ayes 253,[1] Noes 232.

On the last division Mr Perceval believes that there were some of his friends that went away from fatigue & impatience, but there were some who voted for

---

[1] The number is wrongly given as 255 in *Parl. Deb.*, XVI, 422. W. H. Fremantle wrote to Grenville, probably towards the end of March (the letter is dated merely 'Saturday'): 'We have gone most accurately over the lists of the House of Commons on the Walcheren question and make our numbers as follows:

		Government	228	Opposition, exclusive of Castleh.,	
		Doubtful, including Castleh.,		Cang., & Saints .	238
		Canng. & Saints . .	28	Doubtful	31
			256		269
					256
					13

This is what we make our majority—and I really don't think it is overrated.' (Fortescue MSS.)

the Opposition—amongst whom were two or three of Mr Canning's friends. Mr Canning proposed an Amendment which Mr Perceval has inserted in the margin of Lord Porchester's Resolution.

The object of Mr Canning's Amendment was this, that as he does not think Walcheren should have been given up at all, he wished to have a Resolution so worded as might not express any opinion upon the propriety of the evacuation, but only in favor of the long time that was taken to deliberate upon it. Mr Perceval thought that accepting such an Amendment, with such an explanation of its meaning was in fact very nearly admitting an implied censure for the evacuation —and therefore he did not consent to it.[1] (15049–50)

---

[1] *Parl. Deb.*, XVI, 388–422 (30 March). Robert Ward wrote to Lord Lonsdale on the 31st: 'Upon the whole, very few of our friends left us for the Opposition, though some certainly stayed away. On the contrary, many voted with us who were considered doubtful, if not adverse. There was great fear at one time that the Rutland party would desert us, having all said on Friday at Boodle's that they would leave town yesterday to join the hunt. I was commissioned to represent this to Perceval, who took measures...to keep them. Fane of Oxfordshire voted against us all through; so did Patten; Gascoigne on the first question, and, strange to say, *with* us on the last. Opposition were much out in their calculations upon the retention question...The severity of the censure also contributed to defeat itself, as it brought the thing to a complete issue between Ministers and the Grenvilles, there being no alternative. This I know, operated with several. The phenomenon of the evening was Milnes, who has for ever forfeited all reputation for consistency...He...attended the meeting that was to decide upon our course...He shirked the question on Lord Porchester's Motion, and voted against General Crawfurd's Amendment....Bathurst, so far from supporting, was bitter against, and Canning, though certainly, from the line he took, he was of the greatest use, yet marred the grace, at least, of his assistance, by giving almost a *solitary* vote upon the last and greatest question on the second Amendment, and allowing Huskisson and Dent to go away, and Lord Granville Leveson, Binning and Ellis actually to vote against us.' (Lonsdale MSS.)

Wellesley-Pole sent the Duke of Richmond on the 31st this account of the divisions: 'Ryder tells me he has sent you an account of our proceedings in the House of Commons last night, but he gave you an erroneous statement respecting the manner in which the parties voted on the last question. Canning voted with us—but Ld. Granville Leveson, Lord Binning & Dent against us. Huskisson went away; Sturges Bourne voted with us. Castlereagh and all his friends except Harbord, who staid away, voted with us throughout. Upon the whole we got through better than I expected. Upon the last division several of our friends left the House, as they did not choose to vote an acquittal respecting the evacuation. The Irish members voted in some instances strangely. Genl. Archdall was against us on the second question and with us on all the others—Shaw against us on the two first, and with us on the two last. Cooper against us on all but the last, I think, but I cannot speak with certainty, as I did not see him in the division. Opposition are much disappointed, but what has happen'd has in my opinion fully proved that our Administration cannot carry on the Government without additional strength. But I have not heard whether any steps are likely now to be taken for that purpose. As we are all now completely cleared of the embarrassment of the Scheldt expedition, the way seems to be in some measure smoothed.' (Richmond MSS. 73/1697.)

Lord Lowther wrote to his father: 'The issue of the debate last night terminated as I fully expected. Though the majority was greater than was calculated by those well acquainted with the House, all *Parties* were united in carrying the Resolutions against Lord Chatham, added to many of our warmest supporters who opposed us, and many others stayed away. All attached to Government seem to regret the manner in which Mr. Perceval tries his strength, as it must shake the confidence of all the country in him and must make our numbers dwindle considerable [*sic*]. Canning has now taken a decided part against the Government and his opposition is now I think entirely declared. In short, I do not think that last night anyone could conscientiously support the Government. All who voted with us murmured and grumbled and merely supported them on the ground of wishing to support Perceval. In point of debating, Government made but a despicable figure: indeed, they had so bad a cause to plead it would have required extraordinary ingenuity to have met *them*.' (Lonsdale MSS.)

Finally, Canning commented on the debate in a letter to his wife, 1 April: 'Exactly as I foresaw... Perceval preferred giving up his second Resolution to fighting it against mine—and adopted enough of mine to make the difference between us not wide enough to justify a division—and Opposition, whose business it certainly was not to let me play the Chatham game over again, plainly declared that they would not vote for an Amendment of mine—so that my only sure support in a division would have been very small—but larger than I had a right to reckon upon, for Wilberforce would have voted with me. As it was, however, Perceval, having struck out of his Resolution all that I had objected to in my speech—and adopted, with one exception, all the changes that I had suggested, I thought it best to say that as he had given way so far I should no longer feel a difficulty in voting for his Resolution, nor think it necessary to give the House the trouble of a division for the difference which remained between us—but that as that difference was still of a nature sufficiently important to make one wish that my Resolution should be recorded, I should move an Amendment upon his for the sake of having mine upon the Journals. The Resolution to which I originally objected put the *retention* of Walcheren on the grounds, 1st, of the probability either of the renewal of the Austrian War or of the effect which our possession of Walcheren would have upon the terms of the Austrian Peace—2dly, on the expediency of blowing up the Basin. I utterly disclaimed these grounds—neither of which I said I could consent to affirm. If evacuation was otherwise right, on account of sickness, we ought not to have lost a man for the sake of bettering the Austrian Peace—nor for the hope of renewing the war after the Tyrol was given up—and as to the blowing up of the basin I treated that as a most trumpery business—very right to be done—but not worth a single life—lost by sickness, to accomplish it. The real justification of the retention of Walcheren I stated to be that they were considering and inquiring whether it were not practicable to retain it altogether—and I confessed that if I were to say what I thought most questionable, it was whether after having kept it through the sickly season, it was right to abandon it at all. That, however, was not made a charge against Ministers by anybody, and therefore it need not be argued—but I should feel unwilling to vote for a Resolution which directly implied that the only question was as to the validity of the *temporary* causes of the retention—and not as to the possibility of keeping the island and its value if it could be kept. My Amendment therefore went to say that "considering the importance of the island of Walcheren as a position commanding the entrance of the principal naval station of the enemy, no censure could justly attach to Ministers for not having decided, without the most anxious inquiry and deliberation, to advise the evacuation of a conquest so important to the interests of this country." Perceval agreed to omit Austria and Basin—in short the whole of the Resolution first moved so far as I objected to it—and to adopt all my suggestion, except that instead of the words "*without the most anxious inquiry and deliberation*" he insisted upon putting "*at an earlier period*". I objected to this as implying, or being capable of being construed to imply that *at* that period the evacuation was clearly right. Wilberforce objected to it as implying that *before* that period it was *impossible*, whereas *my* words, as Wilberforce observed, implied neither the one nor the other—but only affirmed that it was right to deliberate before evacuating, and that the necessity of deliberating was the cause of the delay. If people had been determined to divide, this distinction would have afforded ground enough for a division. But it was not one upon which one could force a division with advantage. Accordingly I contented myself with moving mine, to shew the difference, and Wilberforce seconded it—but at the same time that I said *I* would vote for Perceval's, in consideration of his adoption of my suggestions—I could not answer for other persons doing so—and I set all my friends free. The result was that, beside myself, only Sturges voted with Ministers in the last division. Huskn. and D[og] Dent—and I believe Holt Leigh did not vote at all. Charles and Granville and Binning were going away—but finding the door locked, came back and voted *against* Govt., as did also W. Taylor and Blachford and Jolliffe and my cousin. We therefore made the *difference* of 17 votes to them on the last division; 14—by the 7 who voted against, and 3 by the 3 who went away. Wilberforce also voted against them—and a great many of Perceval's friends were very angry at his not adopting my Resolution altogether instead of his own. I do not think I *could* do more than this. I think there would have been something very ungenerous—and so [I] felt and represented, in turning round against the Govt. the moment that I was myself cleared by the first vote on the policy—not to mention that in my conscience I *do* believe the distracted state of the Govt. might have something to do with the delay and mismanagement of the evacuation. As it is, I have done quite fairly by them—and though Opposition are furious against me for not having turned against on the last question, they would have abused me ten times more if I had done so—while all the friends of Govt. that I happened to converse with expressed to me great gratitude for my support—Steven for instance—and Croker did so in very strong terms. They abuse me probably behind my back, in terms much stronger. Now as to the general result. First, it is pretty important that the question is carried on the part in which I am concerned. I never had any serious doubt that it would be so as to that point. But I confess I was surprised that the second question

been raised upon the subject of them, appear to his Majesty satisfactory. The King rejoyces that Mr Perceval has disposed of a question which has produced so much anxiety & fatigue to the Administration. (15050)

[*From Perceval, Downg. St., 2 April 1810.*] Mr Perceval acquaints your Majesty that the House of Commons met this afternoon and proceeded with some ordinary business but there was nothing passed of interest or information enough to be reported to your Majesty.

Mr Martin's Resolutions upon the Report of the Comee. of Finance will come on tomorrow evening; and the encrease of the pensions on your Majesty's Civil List in Scotland is one of the subjects which will come under discussion. This pension list has nearly doubled in no very great distance of time; and Mr Perceval humbly submits to your Majesty that it would be adviseable that Mr Perceval might have your Majesty's sanction to say that he should be authorised by your Majesty to recommend that the grants of pensions on the Civil List of Scotland should be restrained to some limited annual sum till the pension list was reduced to a given amount—this would be a measure in strict conformity to what has been already done both in England & Ireland; and it will as Mr Perceval trusts forestall an attempt to address your Majesty upon this subject.[1] (15052)

[*The King's reply, Windsor Castle, 3 April.*] The King entirely approves of Mr Perceval's proposal that he should recommend in his Majesty's name that the grants of pensions on the Civil List of Scotland should be restrained to some limited annual sum, till the pension [list] shall be reduced to a given amount. (15053)

was carried with so much ease. I did think that upon that there would have been a nearer division. So did Opposition, but they reckoned upon me and Castgh. too—and if we had turned agt. Govt. they would certainly have been beaten, for thus it was. They had 53 or 51 (I am not sure which) on the last question but one—and only 21 on the last. The difference 30. Of that 30 mine were 17. If *I* had gone myself and taken my whole body, this 17 would have been 24—for I and Sturges, who voted with Govt., should have made the difference of 4—and the three who went away and staying and voting against would have been 3 more. The remainder of the 30 must be accidental goers-over or goers-away. They would be the same in either supposition. Take therefore 13 for them, put me down 24 and add for Castgh.'s 5–10, which would be the effect of their transfer—and there would have been 47 to deduct from 53. Then consider that if I had voted against I should also have *spoken* against—speculators or converts—only 3—and there would have been an end of the majority—and 3 I might have converted. Indeed *Swann* (Charles's Swim Swann) told Huskisson that he and Mr. Lowndes, the member for Buckinghamshire, were determined to vote with me. But what would have been the effect of success? Either that the Govt. would nevertheless have determined to stay in—saying that the Walcheren question was a question *by itself*, and then the effect would have been nothing—for as to the Resolution of *censure*, as moved by Opposition, *that could* not have been carried, I believe—an amendment would —or if they went out and were considered as unuseable for a new Govt., what could have been done? Wellesley and I alone could not form a Govt., and the addition of Castgh. would only have embarrassed instead of helping. Opposition must have had the game in their own hands, and once *in* I have no belief that they would be easily got out again. Upon the whole, therefore, I believe it is best as it is. Whether the event, *such* as it is, will lead to anything, is more than I can tell. I know nothing more of what passed between the K[ing] and W[ellesley], except indeed that the K. said *nothing* more than that he was sorry things were so bad.' (Harewood MSS.)

[1] The debate on the 3rd is not reported in the *Parl. Deb.*, but Speaker Abbot wrote on the 3rd: 'Debate on the Motions of Martin, Bankes and Perceval respecting reforms of office, according to Third Report of Committee on Public Expenditure.' (Colchester, II, 245.)

[*Foreign Office, 3 April 1810.*] Lord Wellesley has the honor to submit to your Majesty the request of Sir Charles Cockerell, Baronet,[1] to be presented to your Majesty at the Levée tomorrow upon his advancement to that honor. (15054)

[*The King's reply, Windsor Castle, 4 April.*] The King desires that Lord Wellesley will appoint Sir Charles Cockerell at the usual hour this day. (15054)

4126   *Letters from* SPENCER PERCEVAL *to the* KING, *and the replies*

[*Downg. St., Wed. morg., 3 March* [*sic*] [*4 April*] *1810.*][2] Mr Perceval acquaints your Majesty that Sr F. Burdett brought before the House yesterday evening the subject of a court martial against Capt. Lake,[3] and moved that it should be referred to a Committee. The case was a very bad one. Capt. Lake had landed one of his crew[4] on an uninhabited island in the West Indies, and left him there alone. Capt. Lake had been tried & convicted & sentenced to be dismissed from yr. Maj.'s service. Mr Perceval objected to the appointment of the Committee as there was no probability of any advantage arising from it, and as the Committee could do nothing upon the subject. But as there was some doubt whether the sailor was still alive, upon the suggestion of Mr Whitbread that an Address should be presented to your Majesty that your Majesty would be graciously pleased to direct that a search should be made on the island as to any trace which might be found of him, the House agreed in such Address unanimously.[5]

The House then proceeded to the consideration of Mr Martin's Finance Resolutions when Mr Bankes moved his Amendment for the abolition of all sinecures. A long and desultory debate took place upon it and about ½ p. one o'clock the Opposition called for an adjournment; this Mr Perceval resisted and the House divided for the adjournment 37, against it 68. The debate was then resumed till about 3 o'clock when upon a renewed call for an adjournment, Mr Perceval found it impossible effectually [to] prevent it, and the House accordingly adjourned, without having come to any vote upon any of the Resolutions.[6] (15055–6)

[1] Sir Charles Cockerell (1755–1837), merchant and banker. M.P. for Tregony, 1802–6; for Lostwithiel, 1807; for Bletchingley, 1809–12; for Seaford, 1816–18; for Evesham, 1819–30, 1831–7. The Treasury labelled him a 'doubtful' Addingtonian in 1804 and again in 1805; in 1810 the Opposition described him as a Government supporter. In 1830 the Wellington Ministry listed him as 'a friend'. Created Baronet, Sept. 1809.   [2] A very curious misdating.
[3] Warwick Lake (1781–1848); succeeded his brother Francis Gerard as 3rd Viscount Lake on 12 May 1836. See No. 3607.   [4] Robert Jeffery. The island was Sombrero.
[5] *Parl. Deb.*, XVI, 426–49. The later debate is not reported.
[6] Canning wrote to his wife on the 7th: 'I forgot to tell my own love—and the newspapers will not have told her how on Tuesday night I made a speech upon sinecures—expounding my doctrines upon them—which are different from Perceval's as well as from Bankes's—and how good a speech it was— so good that Boringd[on] told me yesterday that Tierney had said to him that it was without any exception the best speech on that subject that he had ever heard in Parliament. But it was between two and three o'clock in the morning—and so nothing of it was reported. I suppose the subject will come on and that I shall have an opportunity of speaking the substance of it again next week. I want to settle that question, *out* of Govt., for *in* I should differ with the Cabinet upon it. If I can get Bankes to compromise with me together we can force Perceval.' (Harewood MSS.)

[*The King's reply, Windsor Castle, 4 April.*] The King acknowledges the receipt of Mr Perceval's report of last night's proceedings in the House of Commons. (15056)

[*From Perceval, 6 April.*] Mr Perceval acquaints your Majesty that the adjourned debate on Sir F. Burdett's paper was resumed this evening. Lord Ossulston[1] began it, and was answered by Sr John Anstruther. There followed Lord Folkston, who moved to adjourn the question for six months and the debate proceeded in the following order:

For the previous question	For original Motion
Sir Sam Romilly	Lord Binning
Mr Whitbread	Mr Stephen
Mr Ponsonby	Mr Adam
Mr Grattan	Mr Canning
Genl. Mathew	Mr Perceval
Ld Forbes[2]	Mr Windham
Mr Hutchinson	Ld Jocelyn
Mr Curwen	Ld W. Russel
Mr Foley	Mr Wms. Wynne
Mr Sherridan	Mr Herbert
Mr Tierney	Ld Geo. Grenville[3]
Mr Portman	Sr. R. Salisbury[4]
Mr Lockhart	Mr. Sol. Gen. of Scotland
Lord Porchester	Capt. Parker
	The Attorney General
Mr Lyttleton	
	Mr. W. Pole
Sr. J. Newport	Mr. Wilberforce
Ld. Morpeth	Sr J. Orde
Mr Ponsonby	Sr Js. Shaw
	Mr Johnston
	Mr Perceval
Ayes 80	Sr. C. Price

Noes 271
Ayes 80
Maj. 191

---

[1] Charles Augustus, 5th Earl of Tankerville (1776–1859), styled Lord Ossulston from 27 Oct. 1767, when his grandfather, the 3rd Earl, died, until 10 Dec. 1822, when his father, the 4th Earl, died. Whig M.P. for Steyning, 1803–6; for Knaresborough, 1806–18; for Berwick, 1820–2. Treasurer of the Household, 1806–7.

[2] George John, Viscount Forbes (1785–1836), so styled until his death. He was the eldest son of George, 6th Earl of Granard [I.] (1760–1837), who was given a U.K. peerage as Baron Granard, 24 Feb. 1806. Whig M.P. for Co. Longford, 1806–32 and 1833–6. He was still in opposition in 1813 but by 1817 he had become a Government supporter.

[3] George Nugent-Grenville, Lord Nugent [I.] (1789–1850), second son of George, Marquess of Buckingham. His mother (*d.* 1812), the daughter of the 1st Earl Nugent [I.], was created Baroness Nugent [I.], 26 Dec. 1800, with a special remainder to her second son, Lord George Nugent; and to her peerage he succeeded, 16 March 1812. Whig M.P. for Buckingham, 1810–12; for Aylesbury, 1812–32 and 1847–50. A Lord of the Treasury, 1830–2. Lord High Commissioner to the Ionian Islands, 1832–5.

[4] Sir Robert Salusbury (1756–1817), M.P. for Monmouthshire, 1792–6; for Brecon, 1796–1812. Created Baronet, 4 May 1795. He had supported both Pitt and Addington, and in 1810 was a ministerialist.

Sir Robt. Salisbury at 10 m. p. 6 o'clock then moved that Sir F. Burdett for said offence be committed to the Tower, & that the Speaker do issue his warrant accordingly.[1]

Lord Newark seconded this Motion.

Mr Adam moved an Amendment to substitute a reprimand instead of a committal to the Tower:

For the amendment	For original Motion
Mr. Wilberforce	Mr. Windham
Mr. W. Smith	Mr Perceval
Mr Sherridan	
Mr Gooch	
152	190
	152
	38

The original question for the committal to the Tower was then carried without further division.[2] (15057–8)

[*The King's reply, Windsor Castle, 6 April 1810.*] The King is glad to learn from Mr Perceval's report of last night's debate that the House of Commons has supported its dignity in the decision upon Sir Francis Burdett's paper, but his Majesty could not help being surprized at the strange mixture of speakers upon this occasion. (15058)

[1] It was with great reluctance that Salusbury did this. Perceval had said to him (so Farington reported): 'You would be a proper person to move it, being a country gentleman, and, not always voting with us, it could not seem from ministerial influence.' Salusbury objected, saying that he was unaccustomed to addressing the House. Perceval tried to re-assure him: 'A few words will be sufficient, as we shall support you.' (*Farington Diary*, VI, 51–2.) His action endangered his life in London. His aunt shut up her house in Russell Street lest he should take refuge there; hotel-keepers refused him accommodation, fearing for their property, and Monmouthshire Radicals organised a run on his bank (at Newport and Abergavenny) in an attempt to ruin him.

[2] Canning wrote to his wife on the 7th: 'I do believe, dearest love, that had I followed your suggestion and interfered to prevent the Tower being carried, I *should* have prevented it, and by so doing should have done a great good. But at the same time I should have been exposed to endless misrepresentations, to the world and to the King, and should have taken upon myself a great responsibility, for the evils avoided would not then have been known—and the friends of Perceval would have represented that *he* was all stoutness and I all timidity—that all that had been said of *his* way of managing Parlt. was a calumny; that in fact *he* had always been for strong and decisive measures, and I had always impeded them, and then joined in the cry against him for weakness and concession. These considerations, and Charles's strong and decided opinion, whose opinion is generally right, and has great weight with me, prevented me from turning round, as I should otherwise have been inclined to do, at the end of the night, and voting against the Tower: but they did not prevent me from stating my opinion to many persons in the Lobby during the division, upon the impolicy of pushing the vote to that extent—and I found many, many of those who were voting, decidedly of the same opinion—and wishing that I had taken a line against Govt. which they could have followed. Peel, whom I told you I hoped to seduce, was one—who told me that he would have gone with me—and would *not* have voted *with* Govt. if *I* had not. Nothing, to be sure, could be more unwise than bringing forward the question at all—and so I said in my speech. But once brought forward it was impossible to pass it by. I wish however, that it may not be the beginning of great troubles—and I am sure, the sooner we get out of it the better.' (Harewood MSS.)

Mr Perceval feels the deepest concern in having to acquaint your Majesty with the disturbance which has taken place in London during Friday & yesterday. A considerable mob had been assembled in the course of Friday about the house of Sr. F. Burdett in Piccadilly; and they had proceeded to the length of requiring persons to pull off their hats to Sr. F. Burdett's house, and to express some wish in his favour. The precaution of having the civil and military power in readiness had been taken; the police Magistrates were in attendance at their respective Offices the whole of Thursday & Friday & Saturday with their constables, but on the Friday night between 9 & 10 o'clock the mob began to be very riotous in several places, & had committed considerable outrages before the military could reach the places where the mob were assembled. Lord Castlereagh's, Lord Chatham's, Mr Yorke's, Sr. J. Anstruther's, Mr Perceval's and other houses were attacked & the windows broken. About 12 o'clock all seemed to be quiet, but about one on Saturday morng. the disturbance broke out again. Lord Wellesley's house was attacked with great violence, and Mr Pole's; but Mr Perceval is happy to be able to state to your Majesty that as far as he had heard no lives have been lost. The mob again assembled on Saturday before Sr F. Burdett's house; the Riot Act was read, and the military has dispersed and kept them under. Some appearance of disturbance has shewn itself about Bond Street, but it was soon got under. The military have been distributed in the principal squares and in various parts of the town, and the force is so considerable that no serious mischief can well be apprehended. At this time ($\frac{1}{4}$ p. one o'clock) there is every reason to believe that the peace of the town will not be disturbed this night.

Mr Perceval however regrets to have to state to your Majesty that the Speaker's warrant has not yet been executed. The Serjeant-at-Arms omitted to execute it, which he might have done without difficulty, by some strange misconception of what his duty required of him; and Sr. F. Burdett now seems determined to resist the warrant & has barricaded his doors. Doubts are entertained by the Attorney-General whether the warrant is sufficient to justify the breaking open the outward door of Sr Francis's house; the Attorney-Genl. was therefore not able to give his opinion last night upon this question.

Sr. F. Burdett has written to the Speaker a letter[1] of which Mr Perceval encloses a copy, and which Mr Perceval imagines will satisfy the whole House of Commons of the illegality of his conduct.

Mr Perceval takes great shame to himself that it did not occur to him to write to your Majesty by the messenger of yesterday—and he feels that it is no excuse which could avail him except your Majesty's gracious indulgence will please to accept it, that the information which he could have communicated would have been at that time so dark & imperfect that your Majesty could have derived no satisfaction from it.

Mr Ryder, who is now with Mr Perceval & has been so all yesterday afternoon, has been & still is so occupied with the detailed superintendence of the necessary arrangements that Mr Perceval has undertaken to make the above communication

[1] See *Parl. Deb.*, XVI, 550 (dated the 6th).

to your Majesty which Mr Ryder would have felt it to have been his more immediate duty to have done. Mr Ryder desires Mr Perceval to add that the 10th Light Dragoons from Rumford (783 R. & E.) and the 15 Lt Drag. from Hounslow 810 R. & F. arrived in town early yesterday eveng. and he desires that Mr Perceval will enclose to your Majesty a copy of the distribution of the force which has been stationed in different quarters of the town, in the course of this night—with the names of the Magistrates who are attending upon them. (15059–62)

[*The King's reply, Windsor Castle, 8 April.*] The King has received Mr Perceval's letter and the enclosures, and sincerely laments that the violent & misguided conduct of Sir Francis Burdett should have led to transactions so disorderly & embarassing. His Majesty trusts however that by a due exertion of authority & firmness the further progress of the evil will be checked, and he conceives that there can be only one opinion as to the nature & tendency of Sir Francis Burdett's letter of the 6th inst. The King did not expect to receive any communication from Mr Perceval yesterday morning, being sensible that matters could not, when he dispatched the messenger, have proceeded to such lengths as to afford much information. His M. can easily conceive that Mr Ryder's attention is wholly engaged in the maintenance of the peace of the town & is therefore very glad that Mr Perceval undertook to write for him. (15066)

4127   *Letters from* RICHARD RYDER *to the* KING *and the replies*

[*Whitehall, 8 April 1810.*] Mr Ryder humbly submits to your Majesty that not long after he had closed the statement which he had the honor of transmitting to your Majesty yesterday morning he received information that a small party of the Guards, who, under the direction of a Magistrate, had succeeded for many hours in completely preventing the assembling of any number of people in all that part of Piccadilly adjoining to Sir Francis Burdett's house, had been removed to a greater distance by the order of the Sheriffs, who arrived there with a large party of constables, and undertook to keep the peace. Their efforts however soon proved ineffectual and the mob assembled in greater numbers than ever, and renewed their former proceedings, stopping the carriages, compelling everybody to pull off their hats before Sir F. Burdett's house, & pelting with mud those who delayed compliance. After some time the number & outrages of the mob encreased so much as to determine the two Police Magistrates and Mr Atkins[1] (one of the Sheriffs) to call in the aid of the military. Mr. Sheriff Wood[2] protested, & declared, as I am informed, to the people that he washed his hands of it. The mob were dispersed entirely and without any mischief of any kind by one Regt. of Life Guards, and since that hour, about 6½, every part of London from which I have had information has been perfectly quiet. The military have been stationed as

---

[1] John Atkins (*c.* 1760–1838), Sheriff of Middlesex and an Alderman of the City of London. M.P. for Arundel, 1802–6 and 1826–32; for London, 1812–18.

[2] Sir Matthew Wood (1768–1843). M.P. for London, 1817–43. Alderman of Cripplegate Without, 1807; Lord Mayor, 1815–16 and 1816–17. Created Baronet by Queen Victoria, 1837.

they were last night, but in reduced numbers, and there is not anywhere the slightest appearance of disturbance. The mob had in the early part of the night run up two barricadoes of bricks & materials from a house under repair between St. James's Church & the end of Piccadilly near the Haymarket, & had broken all the lamps, but very few men were found there by the military, & no attempt made to defend them against a small party of horse & foot who broke them down. Though this account may appear favorable I dare not entertain the expectation that the riots of the three last days will not be renewed tomorrow. But as the military force in and near London encreases every day, there is better ground for hoping that they may be repressed with ease.

Mr Ryder has the honor of further submitting to your Majesty that your Majesty's confidential servants are of opinion it may be desirable to issue a Proclamation on Tuesday next; and as they understand that your Majesty intends coming to town on that day, they recommend that a Council should be held on that day. (15067–8)

[*The King's reply, Windsor Castle, 9 April.*] The King is glad to learn from Mr Ryder's second report of yesterday that the mob collected in consqeuence of the interference of the Sheriffs, had been so easily dispersed and that there was no symptom of disturbance when he wrote. His Majesty will not fail to go to London tomorrow & he approves of a Council being held and a proclamation issued. (15068)

[*From Richard Ryder, Whitehall, 8 April, 3 p.m.*] Mr Ryder has the honor of humbly submitting to your Majesty that he has this moment been informed by his Royal Highness the Duke of Cambridge that H.R.H. has received no official reports, but that as far as H.R.H. can learn there has been during the night no material disturbance except in Piccadilly when two of the Life Guards and one officer were wounded, one by a shot in the cheek and the other in the thigh and with a sharp instrument, but neither of them very severely. The cavalry fired their pistols up some of the passages leading from Piccadilly, where they could not follow the mob and are understood to have wounded several of them, but it being dark at the time it has not been found possible to ascertain the extent of the mischief done. It does not however appear from the most authentic accounts hitherto received, that any lives have been lost. Mr Ryder is extremely sorry that it is not in his power to communicate to your Majesty more detailed information upon a subject of such importance. He has every reason to hope that a continuance of the same exertions on the part of the military & civil power tonight will ensure the tranquillity of the town. (15069–70)

[*Lieut.-Colonel Taylor's reply, Windsor, 8 April, 9 p.m.*] The King, not being at this time in his own apartment, has honored me with his commands to acknowledge the receipt of your letter of this afternoon, from which H.M. is glad to learn that the disturbances have not, during the preceding night, been greater than, under all circumstances, there was reason to apprehend. The King has ordered me to say that he has understood that Sir F. Burdett had rode out yesterday about one o'clock and had been seen in St. James's Park and that he cannot but be surprized that the officers of the House of Commons should have been so negligent as to suffer such an opportunity of apprehending him to escape them. (15071)

4128 THE EARL OF LIVERPOOL *to the* KING, *and the reply*

[*Whitehall, 9 April 1810.*] Lord Liverpool begs leave most humbly to inform your Majesty that with your Majesty's approbation a Privy Council will assemble at the Queen's Palace tomorrow at two o'clock. (15072)

[*The King's reply, Windsor Castle, 10 April.*] The King approves of Lord Liverpool's having ordered a Privy Council to assemble at the Queen's Palace at two o'clock this day. (15072)

4129 THE EARL OF LIVERPOOL *to* LIEUT.-COLONEL TAYLOR, *and the reply*

[*Whitehall, 9 April 1810.*] As Mr Ryder is indisposed in consequence of the fatigue which he has undergone for the last three days, I feel it to be my duty to acquaint you for his Majesty's information, that the Serjeant-at-Arms accompanied by the Civil Magistrates enter'd by force the house of Sir Francis Burdett this morning between ten and eleven o'clock, and convey'd him to the Tower where he was received by the Earl of Moira[1] about one o'clock. A considerable mob was collected in parts of the City Road and on Tower Hill, but the escort of the military was sufficient to prevent any attempt at rescue and any acts of violence. I am happy to be able to add that the most satisfactory arrangements have been made for preserving the peace of the town in the event of the mob assembling again this night and that all is now quiet. (15073)

[*Lt.-Col. Taylor's reply, Windsor Castle, 9 April, 6.30 p.m.*] I have lost no time in submitting your Lordship's letter to the King & I am honored with H. My.'s commands to return you his thanks for the information which it conveys—also to express H.My.'s satisfaction that so much at least of the present difficulty is removed, as regards the commitment of Sir F. Burdett to the Tower, & that this has been accomplished before the House of Commons again met & has been unaccompanied by any acts of violence. The King is concerned to learn that Mr Ryder's health has suffered from the late fatigue. (15074)

4130 *Letters from* SPENCER PERCEVAL *to the* KING, *and the reply*

[*9 April 1810.*] Mr Perceval acquaints your Majesty that the events of the three last days & the safe depositing of Sr F. Burdett in the Tower, had brought together a very full House of Commons. Sr. Saml. Romilly had given notice of his

---

[1] Constable of the Tower.

intention to move for the release of Mr Gale Jones from Newgate but he postponed his Motion sine die. He took that opportunity of denying the reports which had been circulated of his having been at Sr. F. Burdett's house, which he protested had never been the case. The Speaker then produced Sr. F. Burdett's letter—which Mr Perceval moved should be on the table. Mr Wynn moved that the debate on that Motion should be adjourned till tomorrow, to which Mr Perceval assented. The Serjeant was then called in to report what he had done with the warrant, and when his report was closed he underwent a very long examination, and a debate arising, Mr Windham, Mr Tierney & Sr J. Anstruther and some others attacked yr. Majesty's servants as the cause of all the disturbance which had taken place during the last four days because they had not taken upon themselves to direct the servant of the House of Commons to execute his warrant by their authority by breaking open Sr Francis' house at once—altho doubt was entertained of the legality of so executing it. Mr Ryder & Mr Dundas & the Attorney-General repelled this charge & the House was fully impressed that a stronger charge would have been made against your Maj.'s Ministers if they had done so.

Mr Perceval is happy to state to yr. Majesty that the state of London at present is reported to be quite quiet at present [*sic*]. Mr Ryder was confined by one of his very bad headaches this morning and was very unwell in the House, but it did not appear in his speech which was very spirited and good. Lord Liverpool acted for Mr Ryder today & has, as Mr Perceval supposes, reported to your Majesty the particulars of the capture of Sr. F. Burdett. (15080–1)

[*The King's reply, Windsor Castle, 10 April.*] The King acknowledges the receipt of Mr Perceval's letter, from which his Majesty is glad to hear that the House of Commons was so fully attended yesterday. He is by no means disposed to agree with Mr Windham & others that his Ministers should have taken upon themselves the forcible execution of the Speaker's warrant, or to admit the propriety of the Government acting upon these occasions, until the House of Commons had declared its inability to enforce the order. The King rejoyces that Mr Perceval is enabled to confirm the report previously received that no material disturbance prevailed in London, but H.M. is persuaded that it would not be prudent to reduce the force now assembled until every sympton of disorder shall have subsided. (15081)

[*From Perceval, Downg. St., 10 April.*] Mr Perceval acquaints your Majesty that he has been earnestly pressed by Sr. Sidney Smith to request that your Majesty would be graciously pleased to grant him your royal permission to bear as a Crest 'the Standard of the United Kingdom on a Trident from the Sea issuant'. The enclosed paper with which Sr. Sidney Smith has furnished Mr Perceval for the purpose of communicating to the Heralds' Office, your Majesty's gracious pleasure in the event of its being obtained, will explain to your Majesty the ground on which Sir Sidney applies for it—and Mr Perceval humbly takes leave to submit to your Majesty that considering the high value which Sr. S. Smith attaches to such a mark of your Maj.'s royal favour, that it is desireable if your Majesty should be graciously pleased to see it in the same light, to indulge Sr. S. Smith with the grant which he desires.[1] (15082)

4131   PRINCESS MARY *to the* KING, *and the reply*

[*Tuesday night, 11 p.m.* [*10 April 1810*].] I am most thankful to be able to say dear Amelia is much relieved by the medicine & Dr. Pope appears satisfied this evening with the pulse. I hope to have the satisfaction of hearing your stomach is better & that you got no cold going up to town this damp day. No words can say how anxious we are to receive good accounts from town & believe me ever, far or near & in every situation in life, your affte. [&.].

Wednesday morning, 8 o'clock. Amelia has had four hours sleep, two of which was very quiet comfortable sleep. (Add. Georgian 12/142)

[*The King's reply, Queen's Palace, 11 April.*] I acknowledge with many thanks the receipt of your very affectionate letter and of the account which it conveys of dear Amelia, which is very satisfactory. I can with truth reply to your kind enquiries that I feel quite well this morning, having had a good night's rest & found the benefit of a water gruel dish in which I shall persevere another day. I shall rejoyce to see you both on Friday. (Add. Georgian 12/143)

4132   *Letters from* PRINCESS AMELIA *to the* KING, *and the replies*

[*Tuesday night* [*10 April 1810*].] You will do me justice in believing how much I lament your absence & how my thoughts attend you, & how earnestly I pray for your return. I was sorry to hear your stomach was not quite right but hope it is better & I wish I could bear any pain for you & so prove my gratitude for all your kindness to me; God knows cld. I do that for you I should willingly submit. I am certain your kind heart will be glad to hear my medcine which Mary informed you I took last night has relieved me & Dr. Pope is satisfied. I will not take up more of your time than to say God bless you. (Add. Georgian 14/163)

[*The King's reply, Queen's Palace, 11 April.*] I am very happy to hear from your kind letter that you have been relieved by the medicine & that Doctor Pope is satisfied, also from dear Mary that you have had some comfortable sleep since. I am very thankful to you for your affectionate enquiries and am certain you will be glad to hear that I am perfectly well this morning after a good night's rest, & that I have restored my stomach by confining myself to your diet, the water

---

[1] Lord Liverpool wrote to Sir Sidney on the 13th: 'I received a few days ago the favour of your letter, and am sorry it is not in my power to comply with your wishes respecting the situation of Civil Commissioner at Malta. But in consequence of Sir R. Keates having intimated his intention to relinquish that situation, his Majesty has determined, on the present occasion, to unite it with the military command on the Island.' (Add. MSS. 38323, fo. 50)

gruel. I look forward with pleasure to returning to you on Friday and I am desired by the Queen to say that she will write to you tomorrow. (Add. Georgian 14/164)

[*From Princess Amelia, Wednesday evening* [*11 April*].] How truly happy your kind letter has made me as it gives me the pleasure of hearing your stomach is better & that my good friend *water gruel* has been of use to *you*. Most heartily do I rejoice at the prospect of your return on Friday. I think I feel much as usual this day. I expect Sr. H. Halford this eveng. & dear Miny will be able to add his account. His attention is very great & he enters thoroughly into my case; indeed I feel grieved I don't reward everybody for their kindness to me by advancing quicker towards recovery. (Add. Georgian 14/166)

[*The King's reply*, *Queen's Palace*, *12 April*.] Accept my best thanks for your affectionate letter and kind solicitude about me. I feel entirely recovered from the late attack in the stomach & shall certainly have the comfort of being with you tomorrow. I was glad to hear from dear Mary that Sir Henry Halford had been at Windsor yesterday & that upon the whole he expressed himself satisfied. His reports would be cheering indeed if your progress kept pace with the anxious wishes of [etc.]. (Add. Georgian 14/167)

4133   SPENCER PERCEVAL *to the* KING, *and the reply*

[*Downg. St., Wedy. morng.* [*11 April 1810*].] Mr Perceval acquaints your Majesty that upon the adjourned debate on Sr. Fr. Burdett's letter to the Speaker Mr Curwen spoke first and proposed an adjournment of it to a distant day, stating as far as the question itself was concerned, that he thought it most consistent with the dignity of the House to take no notice of the letter. But he took the opportunity of stating that altho he had voted against the commitment of Sr F. Burdett, that he now concurred in the propriety of that vote, reprobated the conduct of Sr. Francis, and stated that he thought your Majesty's present Government should be supported; and that he would give them his support. This brought up Mr Adam & Sr J. Anstruther who renewed their attack upon the alledged misconduct of your Majesty's Government. Mr Perceval defended, of course, that conduct and proposed an Amendment instead of the question of adjournment, which, for the purpose of procuring an unanimous vote, Mr Perceval altered into the shape in which it will appear to your Majesty in the copy which he encloses. Mr Whitbread & Mr Windham followed Mr Perceval, both condemning the conduct of Ministers, but both condemning also the conduct of Sr. F. Burdett. Mr Windham coupled in his censure the Speaker, who thought it necessary to explain his conduct and justify it from Mr. Windham's charge. Lord Temple, the Atty Genl., Sir Saml. Romilly, Capt. Parker, Lord Porchester, Sr J. Sebright, Mr Stephen, Mr Wms. Wynn, Lord Milton, Mr Littleton, Sr James Hall, Mr Gooch, Mr Curwen, Lord Cochran[e], Mr Bathurst, Sr C. Burrell, Mr Wilberforce & the Sol.

Genl. of Scotland[1] spoke in the order in which Mr Perceval has named them—not one single person amongst them all who did not reprobate the conduct of Sr. Fr. Burdett except Lord Cochran—and even his Lordship withdrew from the House before the division was called for, for the purpose of letting the vote pass unanimously. Mr Gooch & Sr J. Sebright both expressed their regret for the vote they had given against the commitment to the Tower, and Sir C. Burrell expressed his determination to support the Government in these anarchical times. Upon the whole Mr Perceval has the satisfaction of stating to your Majesty that the debate went off extremely well, that the embarassment Mr Perceval apprehended was got over by the Resolution which was moved and which by passing neme. contradicente he hopes will have an useful effect on the country.[2] (15083–4)

[*The King's reply, Queen's Palace, 11 April.*] The King has received Mr Perceval's report from which he is glad to learn that the House of Commons has been so unanimous in its censure of Sir Francis Burdett's conduct, and that all embarassment was got over by the very proper Resolution proposed by Mr Perceval.

As Mr Perceval has recommended a compliance with Sir Sydney Smith's request 'to bear as a crest the Standard of the United Kingdom', H.M. will not object to it although the object appears to him a ridiculous piece of vanity. The King considers that it will be necessary to issue a warrant to the Herald's Office upon the occasion. (15086)

4134 PRINCESS MARY *to the* KING, *and the reply*

[*Wednesday night [11 April 1810].*] I beg leave to return you my most greatful thanks for your kind letter which gave me very great pleasure as it contained such good accounts of yourself, & I most sincerely hope the water gruel diet will have removed every unpleasant feel in the stomach by tomorrow. I think I may venture to assure you all things considered that dear Amelia has passed a tolerable day. After her dinner she was faint, giddy & uncomfortable, but it did not last long & she got up as usual & went into the warm bath, which always does her good. In consequence of the events of the last week & Amelia's nerves being so compleately shook with the length of this illness & the affects of the strong medicines she is still under the necessity of takeing, Sir Henry Halford thought his comeing down to see her this evening would cheer her; he arrived about half an hour ago & desires me to say he does not find her *worse* than when he saw her last Friday, but the nerves require some care & attention. He likes her *countenance* better than last week & does not think she appears weaker.

With every hope to see you to morrow.

Thursday. Amelia has had in all 4 hours sleep. (Add. Georgian 12/144)

[1] As this is the last mention of Boyle, one may say that in 1811 he was appointed Lord Justice Clerk. 'Undoubtedly', said Lord Rosslyn, 'it is an appointment the most disgusting and disgraceful—from his utter incapacity—that could have taken place. It is a strong additional proof of the Prince's entire submission to the present Ministers.' (To Grey, 19 Oct. 1811. Howick MSS.)
[2] *Parl. Deb.*, XVI, 592–629.

[*The King's reply, Queen's Palace, 12 April.*] I have again to thank you for a very kind letter and I am glad to hear that dear Amelia has passed a tolerable day, all things considered. I am also sensible of Sir Henry Halford's attention in going to Windsor yesterday. I am really quite recovered from my late indisposition in the stomach and much pleased that nothing occurs to prevent my returning to you tomorrow. (Add. Georgian 12/145)

4135 SPENCER PERCEVAL *to the* KING, *and the reply*

[*Downg. St., Friday, 13 April 1810.*] Mr Perceval acquaints your Majesty that Mr Parnell brought forward yesterday evening a Motion for a Committee to enquire into the state of tythes in Ireland. He was supported by Sr. J. Newport, Mr Maurice Fitzgerald, Mr W. Fitzgerald,[1] Mr Grattan, General Mathew, Mr Herbert & Mr Wilberforce; and opposed by Mr Pole, Mr Leslie Forster, Dr Duigenan, Mr Perceval & Sr Geo Hill, and the House divided for the Committee 48, against it 69. (15088)

[*The King's reply, Windsor Castle, 14 April.*] The King has received Mr Perceval's report &, considering that the House of Commons was so thinly attended last night, his M. thinks the division upon Mr Parnell's Motion satisfactory.[2] (15088)

4136 RICHARD RYDER *to the* KING, *and the reply*

[*Whitehall, 17 April 1810, 3.15 p.m.*] Mr Ryder has the honor of informing your Majesty that the Westminster meeting has passed off without the slightest attempt to make a riot or disturbance of any kind, and that the mob have dispersed quietly. Every precaution had been taken to prevent mischief, and Mr Ryder has directed that the same precautions should be continued tonight and to the same extent to which they were carried last week, and that the picquets should not be withdrawn till it shall appear that there is no chance of similar disturbance. (15089)

[*Lieut.-Colonel Taylor's reply, Windsor, 17 April, 8 a.m.*] I am honored with the King's commands to acknowledge the receipt of your letter of this day, and to return you H.M.'s thanks for your attention in communicating the event of the Westminster meeting.

H.M. rejoyces to hear that all has passed so quietly & he highly approves the precautions which had been taken to prevent mischief, as also a perseverance in them until every possibility of disturbance shall have disappeared. (15090)

---

[1] William Vesey-Fitzgerald (c. 1783–1843); succeeded as 2nd Baron Fitzgerald, 1832. M.P. for Ennis, 1808–12, and 1813–18; for Co. Clare, 1818–28; for Newport (Cornwall), 1829–30; for Lostwithiel, Aug.–Dec. 1830; for Ennis, 1831–2. A Lord of the Treasury [I.], Dec. 1809–12, and [U.K.], 1812–16; Chancellor of the Exchequer [I.], 1812–16. Envoy to Sweden, 1820–2; Paymaster-General, 1826–8; President of the Board of Trade and Treasurer of the Navy, 1828–30. U.K. Peerage, as Baron Fitzgerald, 10 Jan. 1835. President of the Board of Control, 1841–3. The Duke of Richmond, the Lord Lieutenant of Ireland, recommended him to Richard Ryder, the Home Secretary, on 2 Nov. 1809, for the vacancy at the Treasury. 'I am told [he] is clever and not decided in politics.' (Richmond MSS. 72/1508.) Earlier, he had been a member of the Carlton House party.

[2] *Parl. Deb.*, XVI, 658–89.

4137 LORD MULGRAVE *to the* KING, *and the reply*

[*Admiralty, 17 April 1810.*] Lord Mulgrave has the melancholly duty of reporting to your Majesty the death of that zealous and distinguished officer Vice-Admiral Lord Collingwood who expired on the 7th inst. on board your Majesty's ship Ville de Paris, on his voyage from Minorca to England. (15092)

[*The King's reply, Windsor Castle, 18 April.*] The King has learnt from Lord Mulgrave with serious concern the death of so respectable and meritorious an officer as Lord Collingwood, whose zeal had upon all occasions been so conspicuous. (15092)

4138 *Letters from* SPENCER PERCEVAL *to the* KING, *and the replies*

[*Downg. St., Tuesd. morng., 17 April 1810.*] Mr Perceval acquaints your Majesty that Sir Saml. Romilly brought in his intended Motion for the release of John Gale Jones. Mr Ryder opposed it. Lord Folkstone, Sir Thomas Turton and others of the Opposition supported Sr Saml. Romilly. The Master of the Rolls, Mr Canning, Mr Wilberforce & Mr H. Addington spoke and voted for the Motion, Mr Perceval & Mr Windham and Mr Banks, and Mr Owen spoke against it. The House divided: for the Motion 112, against it 160.

Mr Perceval trusts your Majesty will conceive, considering that Mr Canning and all his friends, Mr Addington & his[1] & Mr Wilberforce also with his friends voted against the Govt., that Lord Castlereagh & his friends[2] were not in the House, and that the weight of the Master of the Rolls's authority was added to their numbers, that the majority was as great as could reasonably under such circumstances have been expected.[3] (15091)

[*The King's reply, Windsor Castle, 17 April.*] The King acknowledges the receipt of Mr Perceval's report of last night's proceedings in the House of Commons, and not only agrees that, under all circumstances noticed by Mr Perceval, the majority against Sir Samuel Romilly's Motion was as good as could be expected, but his M. considers it to be an encreasing majority. The King cannot but regret that the Master of the Rolls should carry his scruples so far as to support the Motion in question. (15091)

[1] The Commons members of the Addington group in 1810 were reckoned as follows by the Opposition calculators: Charles Adams, John Hiley Addington, Alexander Allan, Charles Bragge Bathurst, Henry Bowyer, T. G. Estcourt, Davies Giddy and Benjamin Hobhouse.

[2] Castlereagh's friends were G. P. Holford, F. J. Robinson, William Sloane, Charles William Stewart and Thomas Wood.

[3] *Parl. Deb.*, XVI, 691–726. Canning wrote to his wife on the 17th: 'I wonder whether my own love will be more surprized or amused at my speech and vote of last night. It was a piece of mischief—suggested by finding the Master of the Rolls prepared to vote against Govt. I told him I would support him if he did. The surprise of the Govt. at seeing such a combination against them was ludicrous—and it was the more provoking to them as our hypocritical candour took in Wilberforce to vote with us. But unluckily Opposition had not prepared their numbers for a division—half of my forces were absent—and the Govt. whipped in before the division so as to get what is for *them* a tolerable majority.' (Harewood MSS.)

[*From Perceval, Downg. St., 17 April.*] Mr Perceval acquaints your Majesty that Lord Cochran presented a Petition & *Remonstrance* from the Westminster meeting this day, praying that the House would release their representative and proceed to a reform in Parliament. There were some offensive and objectionable phrases in the Petition upon the effect of which the Hon. Mr. Ward thought the Petition should be rejected. Mr Creevy & Mr Whitbread supported it. Mr Perceval felt some difficulty upon the subject, but upon the whole, considering the great reluctance which the House has always shewn to reject a Petition, & when the object of it was a legitimate one, the inclination which they had always shewn to overlook if possible expressions which they have at the same time been obliged to condemn, he thought it the most prudent course to advise its acceptance, and that it should be laid on the table. Mr Ponsonby & Mr Canning concurred in the same view of the subject and the Petition was accordingly received.

Mr Whitbread stating that he had heard that Lord Chatham still continued to act as Master-General of the Ordnance, asked if it was true. Mr Perceval stated that in point of law undoubtedly his Lordship still continued till his Patent was revoked by the appointment of his successor to hold the office—but that he had ceased to communicate in Council with yr. Majesty's servants, that he had ceased to bring to your Majesty the Ordnance returns, which were now presented by the Lieut.-General,[1] and that in communications with the Secretary of State that the Lieut.-General attended Ld Liverpool, instead of Ld Chatham—that his Lordship had been naturally enough expecting from day to day that his successor would be appointed, and therefore had not taken any extra step to effectuate & complete his resignation and that till that was complete his official station & duties continued. He also stated that considering the manner in which your Majesty's servants had been occupied since the notification was made of his Lordship's resignation having been tendered to your Majesty and accepted, the House would not be surprised at the delay that had been incurred in the appointment. Mr Whitbread was by no means satisfied, and gave notice that if his Lordship's removal was not effected when he next made the enquiry he should propose some measure upon it. Mr Perceval again stated that the tender and the acceptance of the resignation, did not & could not be understood to vacate the legal appointment; that in short to his question Mr Perceval had given the answer as the case was, and it was for Mr Whitbread to form what opinion upon it he pleased.[2] (15093–4)

[*The King's reply, Windsor Castle, 18 April.*] The King has received Mr Perceval's report of what passed in the House of Commons last night, and his Majesty is sensible that Mr Perceval, being in the House, must have been the best judge of the propriety of receiving the Petition from the Westminster meeting. Mr Whitbread's conduct in regard to Lord Chatham appears to the King very captious and illiberal. (15095)

[*From Perceval [18 April].*] Mr Perceval acquaints your Majesty that Lord Ossulston asked Mr Ryder in the Ho. of Commons this evening whether he had advised

---

[1] Sir Thomas Trigge.   [2] *Parl. Deb.*, XVI, 727–36. And see Colchester, II, 264.

your Majesty to offer a reward for the apprehension of the soldier who shot the man by St James's Church in the late riots? Mr Ryder said he had not; and as far as he could as yet understand the case upon the best enquiry he had as yet been able to make, he did not think that he should. Mr Whitbread rose in great wrath upon this, and complained of his not taking the necessary means of bringing the person to trial who had been found by the Coroner's inquest guilty of murther. Mr Whitbread was called to order as there was no Motion before the House. He said he would make one. The Speaker stated that without a notice that would be unusual; he persisted, stating that however unusual he had the right, and the occasion was so important that he was justified in exercising it—& he moved that a copy of the Coroner's Inquest should be laid before the House. After some debate in which testimony was borne by many Members to the temperate forbearance of the soldiers, the House rejected his Motion without a division.

Mr Lyttleton then presented a Petition from a Captain Foskett[1] complaining that he had been very ill used by his R.H. the Duke of Cumberland, the Colonel of his Regiment, and that at length he had desired the Comr.-in-Chief under the 12 Article of War to examine his complaint & make a report of it to your Majesty, and that the Comr.-in-Chief in violation of his duty had refused to comply with his request. General Crawfurd, General Phipps, Sr. Rob. Montgomery[2] & Genl Loft[us] & Mr Lockhart were against receiving the Petition; but Mr Perceval thought that, from the words of the Article of War, above alluded to, there was colour enough for the Petition to justify the reception of it, however little the House might be disposed to do anything upon the subject of it when it was received. It was then ordered to be laid on the table, & Mr Lyttleton gave notice that he would move to have it taken into consideration on some early day after the recess.

The House adjourned till Monday sevn'night.[3] (15096–7)

[*The King's reply, Windsor Castle, 19 April.*] The King acknowledges the receipt of Mr Perceval's report from which his Majesty is glad to learn that Mr Whitbread's attempt to bring before the House a charge against the troops in consequence of any unfortunate accident arising from the late riots has been so easily disposed of. Captain Foskett's Petition, as brought forward by Mr Lyttleton, is certainly not a subject for the interference of the House of Commons, & his Majesty has no doubt that it will be found that that officer has not been treated otherwise than was justified by his general character & conduct, altho' there may not have been any positive ground for military investigation. (15097)

[1] Henry Foskett, Captain in the 15th Light Dragoons. Cornet, 1797; Lieutenant, 1798; Captain, 1803. See *Parl. Deb.*, XVI, 751–4.

[2] A slip for Sir Henry Conyngham Montgomery (1765–1830). M.P. for St. Michael, 1807; for Donegal, 1808–12; for Yarmouth (Isle of Wight), 1812–16. Created Baronet, 24 Sept. 1808.

[3] *Parl. Deb.*, XVI, 737–57 (18 April). Foskett's Petition is in cols. 751–4.

[*Admiralty, 19 April 1810.*] The appointment of Major-General of the Marines having become vacant by the death of Vice-Admiral Lord Collingwood, Lord Mulgrave begs leave most humbly to submit to your Majesty's gracious consideration Vice-Admiral Sir Richard Bickerton as an officer worthy of that mark of your Majesty's favour. Sir Richard Bickerton is an highly meritorious officer; and his able, uninterrupted and laborious exertions, as Senior Naval Commissioner of the Admiralty, have left nothing either wanting or deficient in the various, extensive, and complicated equipment which the active course of naval operations have rendered necessary for your Majesty's service. (15098)

[*The King's reply, Windsor Castle, 20 April.*] The King acknowledges the receipt of Lord Mulgrave's letter & entirely approves of his recommendation of so zealous and meritorious an officer as Sir Richard Bickerton to succeed Lord Collingwood as Major-General of Marines. His Majesty rejoyces that this promotion should have come to an officer whose first service as a midshipman he perfectly remembers being on board the yacht with him in 1773, and whose father[1] was a very respectable man. (15099)

4140 THE MARQUESS WELLESLEY *to the* KING

[*Foreign Office, 23 April 1810.*] Lord Wellesley has the honor to submit to your Majesty the draft of a letter from your Majesty to the Emperor of China with relation to the late unfortunate attempts of the Government of India against the Island of Macao.[2]

If your Majesty should be graciously pleased to approve the draft, it would be desirable that the letter should receive your royal signature as soon as may be convenient to your Majesty, as the ships for China must speedily take their departure. (15100)

4141 THE EARL OF LIVERPOOL *to the* KING, *and the reply*

[*London, 24 April 1810.*] Lord Liverpool begs leave most humbly to submit to your Majesty the drafts of his dispatches which are proposed to be sent to Lord Wellington, if they shall meet with your Majesty's most gracious approbation. (15101)

[1] Rear-Admiral Sir Richard Bickerton (1727–92). Lieutenant, 1746; Captain, 1759; Rear-Admiral, 1787.
[2] Before the flight of the Portuguese royal family to Brazil, at a time when there was reason to believe that the British would be excluded from Portuguese ports, orders were sent to the Governor-General of Bengal (which were afterwards countermanded) to seize the Portuguese settlements in the East, except Macao, which was not to be attacked without the Chinese Government's permission. The Governor-General, being informed by the supercargoes at Canton that the French were preparing to attack Macao, despatched an expedition under Admiral Drury which seized the island in spite of protests from both the Governor and the Chinese authorities at Canton. The Viceroy at Canton issued a Proclamation prohibiting all trade with the English aggressors, and hostilities followed.

[*The King's reply, Windsor Castle, 25 April.*] The instructions for Lord Wellington in the two dispatches which Lord Liverpool has submitted for the King's approval appear to his Majesty so clear that he cannot doubt this proving satisfactory to any officer to whom they might be addressed. (15101)

4142 *Letters from* SPENCER PERCEVAL *to the* KING, *and the replies*

[*Downg. St., 26 April 1810.*] Mr Perceval acquaints your Majesty that the living of Clayworth, which was vacated by the death of the late Dean of Lincoln,[1] and in respect of which it was doubted whether the presentation for this turn belonged to your Majesty or to the new Dean,[2] in the opinion of the Attorney & Solicitor-General does belong to your Majesty; and the Dean will acquiesce in that opinion. Mr Perceval therefore humbly recommends to your Majesty that it should be presented, if your Majesty should be so graciously pleased, to Mr Shepherd, a clergyman who has for many years been the tutor of Mr Henry Lascelles's children, for whom Mr Lascelles's [*sic*] is very anxious, & in whose favor he bears the most ample testimony.

Mr Perceval, before he would finally recommend to your Majesty any person to fill the office of Master-General of the Ordnance, has felt it his duty to endeavour to find out whether your Majesty's present Government could acquire any additional strength in any manner consistently with the feelings of his colleagues. He ascertained that whatever objection there might be amongst them to bringing into your Majesty's Government either Lord Sidmouth & his friends alone, without an attempt to procure the assistance of Lord Castlereagh, and Mr Canning, or to bringing in Mr Canning alone without Lord Sidmouth, yet such objection would not be felt if these several parties could be prevailed upon to cooperate on a general principle of re-assembling as much as possible of the remains of Mr Pitt's old friends and of uniting to support your Majesty in these times of difficulty. Mr Perceval therefore endeavoured to learn thro' Mr Yorke what was likely to be Lord Sidmouth's feeling upon a proposal which might be made to him upon the principle of such a general arrangement, if Mr Perceval should receive your Majesty's gracious permission to propose it. Mr Perceval found that Lord Sidmouth would not consent to be a party to so general an arrangement. By this Mr Perceval inferred that he would not consent to join with Mr Canning. And as it was felt by some of your Majesty's servants that it would neither be creditable nor serviceable to your Majesty's Governt. at the present time for Mr Canning alone to come into your Majesty's service, whilst it was also felt that it was not free from objection to receive Lord Sidmouth & his friends without at the same time making an offer to Mr Canning—as it was impossible to prevail upon Lord Sidmouth to receive any proposal which might have been made to him upon the

[1] Sir Richard Kaye, Bart. (1736–1809). Prebendary and Dean of Lincoln, 1783; Archdeacon of Nottingham, Rector of Marylebone, 1788–1809, and of Kirkby Clayworth, Notts.; Chaplain to the King, 1766; Prebendary of Southwell, 1774–80 and 1783–1809; Prebendary of Durham, 1777–84; Archdeacon of Nottingham, 1780–1809; Prebendary and Dean of Lincoln, 1783–1809. Succeeded his half-brother as 6th Bart., 27 Dec. 1789.

[2] Dr. George Gordon, earlier, Dean of Exeter (appointed March 1809).

only terms on which with common consent amongst your Majesty's servants, it could have been offered—it has been found necessary to abandon the idea, and to endeavour to keep your Majesty's present servants together with as much united strength as they can.

Mr Perceval has therefore to submit to your Majesty that the laborious duties of the Admiralty have been pressing for some time so heavily upon Lord Mulgrave's health, that he has told Mr Perceval repeatedly that it was impossible that he should be able to hold that office much longer. And Mr Perceval would therefore humbly submit to your Majesty that your Majesty should be graciously pleased to relieve his Lordship from the fatigues of that very laborious office, and to authorise Mr Perceval to offer to his Lordship the vacant office of Master-General of the Ordnance. By these means, your Majesty would still retain the benefit of his Lordship's services & his support to your Government. The difficulty of filling the office at the Admiralty is one that it would be impossible long to avoid, and Mr Perceval has only to submit to your Majesty one of two persons whom he could recommend for that important post, namely Lord Gambier or Mr Yorke. Mr Perceval should not hesitate in preferring Mr Yorke (tho he has no doubt Lord Gambier would fulfil the duties of it extremely well) if Mr Perceval did not feel some doubt whether at this moment there is not a temporary feeling of unpopularity against Mr Yorke which might make it neither so agreeable to him nor so useful to your Majesty's service to have him in that situation just at this moment, as it would be at another time.[1] But still if your Majesty would permit Mr Perceval so to do, he would at least prefer frankly communicating with Mr Yorke upon this subject, and finding out what his opinion would be upon it before he made any proposition to Lord Gambier. Mr Perceval feels that there is not any time to lose upon this point, as it will be extremely embarrassing to meet Parliament on Monday next without having filled up the office of Master-General of the Ordnance. (15102–4)

[*The King's reply*, *Windsor Castle*, *27 April*.] The King has received Mr Perceval's letter and readily acquiesces in the nomination of the Revd. Mr. Shepperd to the vacant living of Claywork [*sic*].

His Majesty concurs entirely with Mr Perceval in his view of the considerations which regard any application to Lord Sidmouth's party or to Mr Canning for the purpose of strengthening the Government. He is sensible of the propriety of

---

[1] Charles Yorke had made himself very unpopular by enforcing the Standing Order for the exclusion of strangers from the Gallery during the enquiry into the conduct and policy of the Walcheren expedition. (*Parl. Deb.*, xv, 309 [2 Feb.].) Out of doors his action was denounced as an attack on the freedom of the Press, and at the by-election caused by his acceptance of the Tellership of the Exchequer he withdrew his candidature in Cambridgeshire in March, and was forced to take refuge in Lord Eliot's borough of St. Germans (27 April; and re-elected, 25 May, after appointment as First Lord of the Admiralty). Lord Holland attributed Lord Francis Osborne's triumph in Cambridgeshire partly to his generosity to his supporters, his agents being given 'an unlimited credit on his banker'. Towards the end of March W. H. Fremantle had written to Grenville: 'It is said Yorke is to come in for Westbury, if so, he must pay money for the seat, as it is not to be had on other terms, and I should think he would not find that very easy—I don't believe he is to come in for St. Germans. No writ has been moved for the latter.' (Fortescue MSS.) The writ for the by-election at St. Germans was moved for on 16 April.

filling up the Ordnance immediately, and thinks that under every consideration of the question the removal of Lord Mulgrave to that office would be most eligible, particularly as this arrangement would open the Admiralty for Mr Yorke, the benefit of whose services should not, in his Majesty's opinion, be sacrificed to any apprehension of a temporary feeling of unpopularity so unjustly raised against him. If however Mr Perceval should see that objection in so strong a light as to induce him to persist in it, or if Mr Yorke should give way to it, the King must observe that, although he has a high opinion of Lord Gambier's honorable character and of his courage, he conceives that his appointment to the Admiralty would not be a popular one with the Navy in which his professional abilities are not held in the highest estimation; that consequently it would be very desirable, if some arrangement could be made within the Cabinet, by the transfer of one of the members of which to the Admiralty, a situation might still be opened which should offer the means of strengthening the Government. At all events, the King authorizes an immediate offer of the Ordnance to Lord Mulgrave and will sign the warrant tomorrow when it may possibly be prepared & forwarded. His M. has fairly stated the reasons which appear to him to operate against Lord Gambier's appointment, but, if Mr Perceval should, upon a further view of the subject, find it impossible to make the arrangement proposed by removing a member of the Cabinet to the Admiralty, his Majesty wishes it to be understood that he does not then object to Lord Gambier. (15105)

[*From Perceval, Downg. St., 27 April 1810.*] Mr Perceval acquaints your Majesty that after the receipt of your Majesty's note of this morning, he saw Mr Yorke, who was duly impressed by the gracious communication which Mr Perceval was authorised to make to him from your Majesty upon the subject of his succeeding Lord Mulgrave at the Admiralty. But ready as he was to obey your Majesty's commands, he so earnestly deprecated being brought into that situation at this time, if it could be avoided consistently with the good of your Majesty's service, that Mr Perceval was anxious if possible to avoid imposing upon him a duty which he so much preferred to decline. And adverting to your Majesty's weighty reasons upon the subject of Lord Gambier, and also to the idea suggested by your Majesty of endeavoring to procure from within the Cabinet a successor to Lord Mulgrave, Mr Perceval has thought himself authorised to propose the change of situation to Mr Dundas. Mr Perceval has no doubt that Mr Dundas would discharge the duties of the office of First Lord of the Admiralty extremely well, that his good sense, temper & firmness would particularly qualify him for it, if he can be prevailed upon to undertake it. His appointment may also have the effect of making Lord Melville better satisfied, and less likely to come forward with any Motions or speeches hostile to your Majesty's Governt., which if he does make them, are most likely to be directed against the management of the Admiralty. Mr Dundas has desired to have till tomorrow morning to think of this proposal, and to consult his father upon the subject of it. This Mr Perceval could not refuse, and he has therefore foreborne till tomorrow from giving directions for preparing the warrant for the appointment of Lord Mulgrave to the Ordnance, as

Mr Perceval does not think it desireable that it should be known that the place of First Lord of the Admiralty was about to be vacated until the successor might be known also. (15106-7)

[*The King's reply, Windsor Castle, 28 April.*] The King has received Mr Perceval's letter and H.M. entirely approves of his having proposed the change of situation to the Admiralty to Mr Dundas who would, he is persuaded, discharge the duties of that office with advantage to his service. (15107)

[*From Perceval, Downg. St., Saty., 28 April.*] Mr Perceval acquaints your Majesty that Mr Dundas has declined changing his situation by going to the Admiralty.[1] Mr Perceval has therefore prevailed upon Mr Yorke to take upon himself the office of First Lord of the Admiralty. Your Majesty will receive by this night's messenger the warrant for Lord Mulgrave's appointment to the Ordnance, and the warrant for the new Commissioner to the Admiralty shall be forwarded to your Majesty on Monday. (15108)

[*The King's reply, Windsor Castle, 29 April.*] The King is glad to learn from Mr Perceval that Mr Yorke will take upon himself the office of First Lord of the Admiralty and he duly appreciates the principle of zeal and attachment which has influenced his determination. His M. cannot also but consider it very desirable that his Government should give a proof of its firmness and of the conviction of its stability, by bringing forward a meritorious individual whose proceedings have ever been upright, in contempt of a clamour which has been excited upon grounds which are not maintainable. (15108)

[*From Perceval, Downg. St., 29 April.*] Mr Perceval transmits to your Majesty for your Majesty's signature a Message to both Houses of Parliament for the purpose of carrying into effect your Majesty's gracious purpose in favor of his Serene Highness the Duke of Brunswick.[2] (15109)

[*From Perceval, Downg. St., 30 April.*] Mr Perceval acquaints your Majesty that the House met pursuant to its adjournment and went thro the business which stood appointed for the day without any remarkable or interesting occurrence, with an account of which it is necessary to trouble your Majesty. (15110)

[*The King's reply, Windsor Castle, 1 May.*] The King acknowledges the receipt of Mr Perceval's report of yesterday. (15110)

[1] 'Dundas would not go to the Admiralty unless there had been an arrangement of office in view for more strength,' Perceval wrote to Wellesley on the 28th. He added, 'Dundas and his Scotch friends will not, I think, leave us immediately, but he will not be reconciled to stay long unless we can get more strength.' (*Wellesley Papers*, II, 9.)
[2] *Parl. Deb.*, XVI, 757 (30 April). The Message recommended that 'some provision' should be made for the Duke until he was able to return to his dominions—a provision 'suitable to the rank and fortune of a Prince so nearly allied to his Majesty's throne'.

[*London, 1 May 1810.*] In the year 1770 he sailed on board the Montreal frigate for the Mediterranean and continued upon that station until the year 1775 when he returned to England in the Levant frigate.

On the breaking out of the American War he embarked in the Bristol bearing Commodore Sir Peter Parker's broad-pendant, and was serving in that ship during the memorable action against Sullivan's Island, on which occasion he received his first promotion, having been appointed Acting-Lieutenant of the Bristol which was confirmed by Lord Howe. From that period to the year 1779 he was employed in America upon most important and active services connected with the Army, having been appointed to the command of an armed vessel which he was under the necessity to destroy in order to prevent her being captured by the enemy's fleet commanded by Count D'Estaing off Rhode Island. He was employed on shore during the siege of that place as Aid-de-Camp to Commodore Brisbane,[2] and finally commanded a party of seamen and marines at one of the principal advanced posts.

After his return to England he was appointed a Lieutenant of the Victory under Sir Charles Hardy,[3] and continued in that ship under different Flag Officers successively, and followed Rear-Admiral Sir Hyde Parker on board the Fortitude, being Second Lieutenant of that ship during the action on the Dogger Bank.[4]

Upon the return of the squadron to port he was promoted to the rank of Master and Commander and appointed to the command of the Tisiphone fireship then fitting out at Sheerness. In the month of December following he sailed under the orders of Rear-Admiral Kempenfelt,[5] and had the good fortune to be the first who discovered the enemy's fleet consisting of nineteen sail of the line escorting a numerous convoy from Brest, when several of the latter were captured and the object of the expedition rendered entirely abortive.[6] He was then detached from the Fleet to convey this intelligence to Vice-Admiral Sir Samuel Hood in the West Indies, and was shortly after appointed by him to the command of the Russel, which ship he commanded in the victory obtained by Sir George Rodney on the 12th of April 1782 and had a distinguished share in that action.

At the commencement of the war in 1793 he was appointed to the command of the Crescent, and in the month of October following captured the French frigate La Réunion,[7] for which service, his Majesty was pleased to confer upon him the honour of knighthood.

In the month of June in the following year, having the Druid and Eurydice under his orders, he maintained an action with the enemy's squadron, more than

---

[1] 'Received from Mr. Greville May 10, 1810, with a request from Sir James Saumarez that it should be submitted to the King.'

[2] Admiral John Brisbane (*d.* 1807). Lieutenant, 1757; Captain, 1761; Rear-Admiral, 1790; Vice-Admiral, 1794; Admiral, 1799.

[3] Sir Charles Hardy (*c.* 1714–80). Captain, 1741; Rear-Admiral, 1756; Vice-Admiral, 1759; Admiral, 1770. Knighted, 1755. M.P. for Rochester, 1764–8; for Plymouth, 1771–80. Commander-in-Chief, Channel Fleet, 1779–80.   [4] On 5 Aug. 1781.

[5] Richard Kempenfelt (1718–82). Lieutenant, 1741; Captain, 1757; Rear-Admiral, 1780. Went down with the *Royal George*.   [6] On 12 Dec. 1781.   [7] On 20 Oct. 1793.

double his force, consisting of two seventy-four's cut down, two frigates and a corvette, and succeeded in extricating the Eurydice from falling into the enemy's hands.

He soon after obtained the command of the Orion, and was under the orders of Lord Bridport in the action off L'Orient,[1] when three ships of the line were captured. The Orion was one of the first ships which brought the enemy to action.

He was soon afterwards detached from the Channel Fleet to join Admiral Sir John Jervis, now Earl St. Vincent, and had the honor to bear a distinguished part in the action of the 14th of February, 1797,[2] for which he received the strongest marks of his Lordship's approbation, and soon after was entrusted with the command of the advanced squadron off Cadiz.

In this ship he accompanied Lord Nelson off Toulon, and was second-in-command in the memorable action of the Nile in which he received a severe contusion on the side by a splinter nearly at the conclusion of the action.

Having been ordered to repair to Gibraltar with the captured ships, he soon after returned to England and a promotion of Admirals taking place, his Majesty was pleased to confer upon him one of the Colonelcies of Marines, and he was at the same time appointed to the command of the Cæsar.

During two successive winters he was entrusted with the command of the squadron employed to watch the enemy's fleet in Brest, which arduous service he performed with so much vigilance that not a single ship escaped from the port during any part of that time. Having been promoted to the rank of Rear-Admiral the 1st of January 1801, he continued in the Channel Fleet till the month of June when his Majesty was graciously pleased to create him a Baronet, and he was nominated to command a squadron appointed to watch an expedition preparing at Cadiz for the invasion of Portugal.

Soon after his arrival off that port, having obtained information that three French line of battle ships had anchored off Algeziras, he proceeded from his station to attack them, which he did on the following morning (6th July) and after a long and severe conflict in which the squadron had to contend against the enemy's formidable batteries as well as line of battle ships; his Majesty's ship Hannibal having unfortunately grounded and the enemy having succeeded in warping their ships on shore he was compelled to withdraw from the attack and repaired to Gibraltar Mole to refit the squadron, which had suffered very considerably in their masts and hulls as well as loss of men.

The enemy having been joined by a reinforcement of six sail of the line from Cadiz, the utmost exertions were used in getting the squadron in a state to engage them, and on the morning of the 12th of July, the whole force of the enemy having put to sea, the Cæsar, which had got a new main mast in only the day before, was warped out of Gibraltar Mole, and the squadron, consisting altogether of five sail of the line, proceeded in pursuit of this combined force, which, having bore up through the Straits, they came up with and attacked before midnight; when two Spanish three-deckers mounting 120 guns, each took fire and blew up, and a French seventy four was taken.

[1] On 23 June 1795.   [2] The battle off Cape St Vincent.

By this action the whole of the enemy's force in Cadiz was rendered totally useless, never having ventured out of the port during the war.

For this service his Majesty was pleased to create Sir James Saumarez a Knight of the Most Honorable Order of the Bath and the thanks of both Houses of Parliament were unanimously voted to him, and on his return to England a pension of £1200 per annum was also settled upon him by Parliament.

On the eve of the present war, he hoisted his flag at the Nore and a strong force was placed under his orders to guard against an expected invasion from the enemy. He was afterwards superseded by Lord Keith and appointed to command upon the Guernsey and Jersey station at that time threatened with an immediate attack from the ports of St. Malo and Granville.

In December 1806 he was promoted to the rank of Vice-Admiral and appointed second-in-command in the Channel Fleet under the Earl of St. Vincent. His Lordship being absent with Admiralty leave, he was employed in watching the enemy's fleet in Brest till the month of August following, when upon the appointment of Lord Gardner to the command of the Channel Fleet, he resumed his former station.

In the month of March 1808 Sir James Saumarez was appointed to the command of the fleet destined for the Baltic, upon which station he still continues with a force of twenty sail of the line exclusive of frigates and smaller vessels. (15359–63)

4144 SPENCER PERCEVAL *to the* KING, *and the reply*

[*2 May 1810.*] Mr Perceval acquaints your Majesty that Mr Bing[1] presented to the House of Commons this day the Petition of the freeholders of Middlesex. Altho Mr Perceval had supported the Motion for letting the Petition from Westminster lay on the Table, yet the it appeared to him [*sic*] that the expression and language of this Petition was so much more offensive, charging the House with having assumed a power unwarranted by the Constitution, and taking upon themselves to protest against the existence as well as the exercise of such power, that it was not possible to consent to deal with it in the same manner. He therefore opposed it; the House, not expecting it, was not full—and several persons who agreed with him in thinking it a Petition which could not be received, yet wished to adjourn the debate upon the question till tomorrow. This wish being apparently very generally felt, Mr Perceval complied with it, and the debate was so adjourned. The House then proceeded to some ordinary business and adjourned by about ½ p. 7 o'clock.[2] (15321)

[*The King's reply, Windsor Castle, 3 May.*] The King approves of Mr Perceval's having resisted the reception of the Petition presented by Mr Byng and, although he thinks that there could be no hesitation in rejecting it immediately, H.M. considers that in general these sort of questions are better disposed of on the second day, especially if the House should be thinly attended upon the first. (15322)

---

[1] George Byng. [2] *Parl. Deb.*, XVI, 780–90. A Petition for the release of Burdett.

4145   THE EARL OF LIVERPOOL *to the* KING, *and the reply*

[*London, 3 May 1810.*] Lord Liverpool begs leave most humbly to inform your Majesty that he has communicated to Sir Brent Spencer this morning the proposition which was most graciously approved by your Majesty, and that Sir Brent Spencer is willing to go out to Portugal for the purpose of being placed on the Staff of your Majesty's Army within the Peninsula immediately after Lord Wellington and Genl. Graham. (15323)

[*The King's reply, Windsor Castle, 4 May.*] The King is glad to hear from Lord Liverpool that Sir Brent Spencer agrees to go out to Portugal. (15323)

4146   LORD ELDON *to the* KING, *and the reply*

[*Thursday evg., 3 May 1810.*] The Lord Chancellor, offering his most humble duty to your Majesty, takes leave to mention that the second reading of the Reversion Bill, again sent up from the House of Commons, is to be moved in the House of Lords tomorrow. The Ld Chanr. thinks that the Motion will be negatived, though probably after more of struggle to carry it than was exerted in the case of the former Bill of this Session. The Lord Chancellor finds that it is the opinion of such of your Majesty's confidential servants as are in the House of Commons that the rejection of this Bill will be followed in that House by an Address to your Majesty, praying that no reversions may be granted—a proceeding wrong in itself, which would seem to the Lord Chancellor extremely objectionable at all times, & peculiarly so at a time when the public mind is agitated extremely, even upon points as to which the House of Commons is entirely right. It has been professed repeatedly & uniformly in both Houses by those who object to the Reversion Bill as it has hitherto been framed, that they would not oppose any Bill suspending for a limited & short period the granting of reversions, that it may be seen upon a fuller consideration, &, upon a view of the whole subject, whether it is expedient to make any change, or whether it is not, in truth, most expedient to make none. Your Majesty's servants in the House of Commons think that if the Lords sent down to the Commons a Bill of this sort, they might be able to prevent an Address being carried in the House of Commons. It seems to your Majesty's servants that it might be expedient by such a legislative measure operating for a short period to prevent at this moment a measure in the Commons having a tendency to create very inconvenient disputes between the Houses of Parliament. The Lord Chancellor, however, has thought it his duty not to proceed upon this Motion till he has learnt how far your Majesty, under all the circumstances of the case, might be pleased to permit it to be acted upon. If such should be your Majesty's pleasure, the Lord Chanr. would take upon himself the conduct of this measure that it may be rendered as unexceptionable as he can make it. If it is thought fit to adopt it, the purpose to adopt it, the Lord Chancellor humbly thinks, should be mentioned in tomorrow's debate. (15324-5)

[*The King's reply, Windsor Castle, 4 May.*] The King cannot, upon consideration of the sound reasoning contained in the Lord Chancellor's letter hesitate in sanctioning the course which he proposes to be adopted in respect to the Reversion Bill, his M. being persuaded that a temporary Bill would, in the present temper of the times, be infinitely preferable to any opposition which might produce disputes between the two Houses, besides affording time for a more full consideration of the ultimate question. (15325)

4147   *Letters from* SPENCER PERCEVAL *to the* KING, *and the replies*

[*Downg. St., Friday morg., 4 May [1810].*] Mr Perceval acquaints your Majesty that the debate upon the Middlesex Petition was resumed last night, when, after a debate in which Mr Ponsonby & the principal part of the Opposition who were present voted for the reception of the Petition, but Mr Barham, Mr Grenfell[1] & Mr Wm. Smith spoke against it;—on the part of the Govt. Mr Dundas, Mr Stephen, Mr Wilberforce, Mr Ellison spoke against. The House divided against the Petition 139—for it 58.

The House then proceeded with a debate upon three Motions upon three several charges made by Sr. J. Newport against the Irish Govt. The first respected the payment of £1000 to a Mr Croker,[2] (the father to the Secretary to the Admiralty, and an old servant in your Majesty's Customs in Ireland), which payment was charged by Sir John Newport upon the Report of the Commissioners of Enquiry in Ireland to be a great abuse. This however was so satisfactorily explained by Mr Forster[3] and Mr Croker that Sr. John Newport himself was obliged to give it up, & to ask leave to withdraw it—which was granted.

The second respected the grant of a compensation to a person who was removed from having been Treasurer to the Post Office in Ireland, who was removed from his office upon a new arrangement & reform which was made in it.[4] This Motion, after an answer to the charge, by Mr Pole, was negatived by 83, to 26. Sir John Newport would not then bring forward his other Motion, it being ½ p. one o'clock, but postponed it till Tuesday next & the House adjourned.[5] (15329–30)

[*The King's reply, Windsor Castle, 4 May.*] The King considers the report which Mr Perceval has been enabled to make of last night's proceedings in the House of Commons as extremely satisfactory, and his Majesty is further convinced of the advantage which has attended the postponement of the debate upon the Petition from Middlesex, thereby admitting of its being rejected by a respectable House. (15330)

[1] Pascoe Grenfell (1761–1838), Whig M.P. for Great Marlow, 1802–20; for Penryn, 1820–6. An anti-reformer, he changed his views on the subject of parliamentary reform in 1820, on the ground that Parliament had ignored public opinion on the restoration of Queen Caroline's name to the Liturgy. He derived a large income from his investments in the North Wales copper-mining industry.
[2] John Croker (1743–1814), for many years Surveyor-General of Customs and Excise in Ireland. In 1800 he had been appointed Surveyor-General of the Port of Dublin, salary £800 a year.
[3] John Foster.   [4] A person named Forward, who had held the office from 1800 to 1808.
[5] *Parl. Deb.*, XVI, 791–830; *Wellesley Papers*, II, 12. The numbers are wrongly given in Colchester, II, 268.

[*From Perceval, Downg. St., 4 May.*] Mr Perceval acquaints your Majesty that the Committee of the House of Commons agreed this night to a vote for granting £7000 pr anm to his Serene Highness the Duke of Brunswick in compliance with your Majesty's Message. There was no other business of any interest before the House.[1] (15331)

[*The King's reply, Windsor Castle, 6 May.*] The King acknowledges the receipt of Mr Perceval's report of last night's proceedings in the House of Commons. (15331)

4148   MRS. GEORGE VILLIERS *to* LIEUT.-COLONEL TAYLOR, *and the reply*

[*4 May 1810.*] Mr. Villiers has been so overwhelm'd with distress & unhappiness since Mr. Engall shew'd him yesterday a paper by wch. he found himself superseded in the care & management of the Home Park, that I have really been under the greatest alarm on his account, & been dreadfully perplex'd to what was best to be done. I hope you will not think me wrong in having prevail'd on him to *dictate* to me the enclos'd letter for his Majesty, wch. he was quite unequal to *writing* himself, & wch. I take the liberty of requesting (if you see no objection) that you will read to his Majesty. (15326)

[*Taylor's reply, Windsor, 5 May.*] I could not hesitate for a moment in conveying to the King the letter addressed to his M. by Mr. Villiers, which I received with your obliging note this morning, & I should have written immediately to say that I would take the earliest opportunity of presenting it if, upon enquiry, I had not found that your servant had left the Lodge. I now beg to enclose to you the answer which H.M. ordered me to write to Mr. Villiers, & I hope you will forgive my adding how truely I regret the affliction & distress which have arisen to yourself & Mr. Villiers & to your family from the late unfortunate circumstances. (15333)

4149   GEORGE VILLIERS *to the* KING, *and the reply*

[*4 May 1810.*] With every sentiment of humility and respect, I humbly presume to address your Majesty in consequence of a paper which Mr. Engall shew'd me yesterday as his authority for ceasing to transact the duties of his situation under my controul, hoping that I may be allow'd to assure your Majesty that every receipt of money from the farms has either been paid away by the bailiffs & accompted for by them, or else plac'd at your Majesty's bankers, so that had the Board of Green Cloth paid the money on the dairy account to Mr. Engall, who has sign'd the receipts for it, the transaction would have been wholly on your Majesty's service, & if Mr. Gorton, in preference to bringing the money down, had paid it into Messrs. Drummonds for the use of your Majesty, no risk of loss could have been sustain'd from the effects of an extent against me, the operation

[1] *Parl. Deb.*, XVI, 843–5.

of wch. however ceases on the 9th of this month, except in leaving Mrs. G. Villiers, myself & five children in the greatest pecuniary distress. This circumstance how-ever, I humbly presume to state to your Majesty, will not preclude the probability (according to the last calculations) of the speedy liquidation of the apparent demands against me, tho' I have judg'd it prudent for the present to decline accepting the liberal & extensive offers of security which have been made to me.

I should not have presum'd to have address'd your Majesty had not the bare idea of the possibility of having incurr'd your Majesty's displeasure been too painful for me to endure in silence, & I cannot therefore help humbly, but most earnestly, imploring your Majesty to suspend your judgment on the Report of the Finance Committee, wch. from the nature of the case is only an ex parte proceeding & wch. contains many points that admit of a favorable explanation. In this humble request to your Majesty I venture chiefly to rely on that paternal kindness & uniform consideration which it has been the pride & happiness of my life to have experienc'd for near 30 years & wch. have created sentiments of gratitude & devotion to your Majesty which can only cease with my existence & with which I beg to subscribe myself [&c.]. (15327–8)

[*Taylor's reply, Windsor, 5 May.*] I am honored with the King's commands to acknowledge the receipt of your letter of yesterday, and to acquaint you that the directions which his Majesty had given in regard to the Home Park were such as had occurred to him as indispensible under the present circumstances. H.M. directs me further to assure you that he sincerely laments the perplexed state of your affairs, and that he readily acquiesces in the wish which you have expressed that his Majesty should suspend his judgement upon the report of the Finance Committee until the general question shall have been brought to a final issue.[1] (15332)

4150   THE KING *to the* PRINCESS OF WALES

[*Windsor Castle, 5 May 1810.*] The King acknowledges the receipt of the Princess of Wales's letter[2] and he loses no time in assuring her that it had been his intention and that of the Queen to have the pleasure of seeing the Princess of Wales the next time that the Duchess of Brunswick should come to the Queen's Palace. (16792)

[1] Villiers had been appointed Ranger of Cranbourne Chase in 1807 (2601 n, where the dates 1807–27 should evidently read 1807–10). The Duke of Cumberland had then been interested in him—writing to Eldon (28 April 1807): 'I have written again this evening to the Duke of Portland, reminding him of his promise respecting George Villiers, and wish, if you have an opportunity of putting in your good offices, that you will do it, and I know that a favour when granted comes better when done im-mediately, and I believe never can be better bestowed than this one to George Villiers who has acted so handsomely to all our party.' (Eldon MSS.) He wrote again to Eldon, some time in Nov. 1807, the letter being dated merely 'Monday' (Dr Markham, the Archbishop of York, died on 3 Nov.): 'What fine things has his Grace of Portland *now* to give away—an Archbishopric, and a place at Liverpool worth £3,000. Now this latter place might do for [my] friend George Villiers, as I understand it may be done by deputy.' (*Ibid.*)

[2] The Princess wrote to the King on the 5th from Kensington Palace: 'Finding that your Majesty will be graciously pleased to pardon the great liberty I take in asking the favour of being allowed to

[*Downg. St., 7 May 1810.*] Mr Perceval acquaints your Majesty that the Speaker brought under the consideration of the House this evening the notice which he had received of the intended action of Sir Francis Burdett against him—and desiring the directions of the House as to the course which he should pursue. Mr Perceval recommended the appointment of a Comee. to consider of the subject and to report such facts as they might think proper with their opinion upon them. There was much opposition given to this course of proceeding—and the House came to two divisions upon the subject—the first upon a Motion to leave out the words requiring the Committee to report their opinion

and for retaining the words, 115; against it, 58;

against the Committee altogether, 46; for it, 116.

Mr Aldn. Combe then brought forward a Motion a copy of which Mr Perceval herewith encloses—it was supported by the three other members of the City. Mr Ryder opposed it, and after a short debate the House divided for the Motion 52; against it, 138.[1]

Mr Perceval transmits to your Majesty a letter which he has been desired to present to your Majesty from his Serene Highness the D of Brunswick. (15334)

[*The King's reply, Windsor Castle, 8 May.*] The King entirely approves the course taken by Mr Perceval, in consequence of the Speaker's notice of the intended action of Sir Francis Burdett against him, and is glad that it was adopted by so respectable a majority. H.M., altho he is satisfied with the majority upon the Motion of Mr Alderman Combe, is much surprized that it should have found even that support which it did in the House of Commons. (15334)

4152   *Letters from the* MARQUESS WELLESLEY *to the* KING, *and the reply*

[*Foreign Office, 8 May 1810.*] Lord Wellesley has the honor to acquaint your Majesty that, according to your Majesty's gracious permission he will present at the Levée tomorrow M. de Brinkmann, late Swedish Envoy, on his departure for Sweden. (15336)

[*From Lord Wellesley, Foreign Office, 8 May.*] Lord Wellesley has the honor to submit to your Majesty the expediency of appointing a person properly qualified to perform the duties of Chargé d'Affaires in America, for which purpose he proposes that Mr John Morier,[2] lately your Majesty's Consul in America, should

pay my dutiful respects to your Majesty and to the Queen, should my mother have the honor of being invited for next week. The great anxiety I feel to have that happiness, of which I have been deprived since the month of January, is my motive for intruding on your Majesty's leisure hours, and it would be to my mother as well as to myself a very serious mortification were I not allowed the honor of personally presenting on that occasion my humble homage to your Majesty and the Queen.' (42488–9.)

¹ *Parl. Deb.*, XVI, 854–69. See Colchester, II, 264, 268–76.

² John Philip Morier (1776–1853), Secretary of Legation and Chargé d' Affaires at Washington, 1810–11; Envoy to Saxony, 1816–24.

be appointed Secretary of Legation in America. If your Majesty should be graciously pleased to approve this appointment, Lord Wellesley will have the honor of presenting Mr Morier to your Majesty at the Levée to morrow. (15337–8)

[*The King's reply, Queen's Palace, 9 May.*] The King approves of Lord Wellesley's proposal that Mr John Morier should be appointed Chargé d'Affaires in America, & his Majesty will receive him and Mr de Brinkman this day. (15338)

4153 SPENCER PERCEVAL *to the* KING, *and the reply*

[*Downg. St., Tuesd. evng., 8 May 1810.*] Mr Perceval acquaints your Majesty that Sir Wm. Curtis brought up the Petition from the Livery of London & moved that it should lie on the Table. Mr Ryder opposed it upon the same ground on which the Petition from Middlesex had been refused—Mr Whitbread spoke for the Petition with great violence. Mr Wilberforce moved an adjournment till tomorrow. Several gentlemen followed next objecting to the adjournment, and Mr Perceval, after stating his sentiments against the Petition as strongly as he could, consented to the adjournment till tomorrow, as he had done upon the former Petition; and he trusts the House will mark their opinion in the same manner as they did upon that occasion.[1] (15339)

[*The King's reply, Queen's Palace, 9 May.*] The King has received Mr Perceval's letter, and his Majesty thinks that he acted with perfect propriety in agreeing to the adjournment of the debate upon the Petition from the Livery of London, as this course is consistent with that followed in respect to the Middlesex Petition & will shew that there is no desire to proceed hastily. (15339)

4154 *Letters from* PRINCESS MARY *to the* KING, *and the replies*

[*Tuesday night.* [*8 May 1810*].] I am thankful to be able to say dear Amelia's cold is not worse today & Dr. Pope does not find her more heated than yesterday, and if fever can be kept off he still flatters himself the oppression on the chest as well as bar she complains of across the lungs may be nothing of consequence; however, he says as long as the weather remains so unsettled she must be very careful of more cold, therefore would not let her get up but for to go into the warm bath. The side has been but indiferent today & her spirits low in consequence of the idea of parting with Mrs. Williams[2] tomorrow.

Wednesday. Amelia has had off & on nearly five hours sleep. The chest is very indiferent this morning & she is inclined to cough a good deal. The strong medicine was not taken last night, which may make the side more painful *now*, but Dr. Pope thought with so much cold about her it would be better to put it off till tonight, thinking it likely, by a letter he received from Sir H. Halford last night, that he may come & see Amelia this evening & *decided* about the dose

[1] *Parl. Deb.*, XVI, 885–902; Colchester, II, 274.
[2] Her old nurse, who had been staying with her.

himself as Sir Henry's expression to Pope is, 'If the chest does not get better I think I ought to come & give you some assistance, & as the Pss. is very low, perhaps a visit may cheer her'. (Add. Georgian 12/146)

[*The King's reply, Queen's Palace, 9 May.*] I return you many thanks for your kind letter from which I am glad to learn that dear Amelia is at least not worse that [*sic*] when I left Windsor, notwithstanding the cold from which she actually suffers. Sir Henry Halford's intention of going to see her this evening is an additional proof of his attention.

The Queen desires me to say that she will write to you tomorrow. (Add. Georgian 12/147.)

[*From Princess Mary, Wednesday night.* [*9 May*].] I return you many thanks, my dearest papa, for the kind letter I received this evening & I am thankful to be able to say that considering how much distressed Amelia has been all day at having parted with Mrs. Williams, this day has gone off better than I ventured to hope. Sir Henry Halford assures me he does not find Amelia materially worse, and hopes this cold may be prevented from doing any essential mischief as he finds the *pulse* able to bear some degree of lowering which the pain in the chest & bar across the lungs will make it necessary to have recourse too. He therefore has given her the strong dose this night & will see her tomorrow morning before he leaves Windsor. He laments much her having got this cold as it must be a draw-back for some days, but he is pleased to find still so much *power* of pulse as it will inable him to act without so much fear of lowering her. He will write himself the moment he gets to town to morrow. Amelia appears much cheered by Sir Henry's visit, but has had a good deal of pain in her chest this evening as well as side. I do not think she has coughed quite so much & after the warm bath certainly was more comfortable.

Thursday. Amelia got no sleep till nine o'clock from cough & pain in the side; from three till six she has had some quiet sleep, since that the cough has been *distressing*. (Add. Georgian 12/148)

[*The King's reply, Queen's Palace, 10 May.*] I have received your very kind letter containing last night's & this morning's report of dear Amelia & altho' I cannot but feel much grieved that she suffers so much from cough & pain in the side, I am willing to make every allowance for the effect of a temporary cold and for the distress which she feels at parting with Mrs. Williams.

The Queen desires me to say that she fully intended to have thanked you this day for your letters but has been prevented by head ach from writing. (Add. Georgian 12/149)

4155 PRINCESS AMELIA *to the* KING, *and the reply*

[*Wednesday night, 8 p.m.* [*9 May 1810*].] Before Sir Henry Halford arrives I take up my pen to address you these few lines as I am fully convinced from your kindness at all times to me an account from myself will be satisfactory. I still have cold & some oppression upon my chest & therefore Dr. Pope has only allowed my getting up for to go into the bath and as Sir Henry wrote to say he intended coming Dr. Pope delayed my spring medcine till tonight. I have had more shooting in the side & I am glad Sr. Henry comes as the new medcine does not quite agree with my stomach.

I was most truly sorry to lose dear Mrs. Williams & I really cannot express sufficiently how kind she has been to me & how much I feel her affection in having given up so much time to me, & your goodness in allowing her to be here & now permitting me to avail myself of Mrs. Adams's[1] kind offer in coming to replace her. Believe me, my dearest dear papa, I feel most truly grateful for the many blessings I enjoy & I trust in the goodness of the Almighty to carry me thro' this trial of such an illness & that I may ever gratefully value & remember the kindness I receive, but which no words can ever express what I feel on this subject, above all to your dear self. (Add. Georgian 14/173)

[*The King's reply, Queen's Palace, 10 May.*] Pray accept my best thanks for the affectionate letter which I have received from you this morning and for a kind attention which you are with reason convinced must always afford me satisfaction. I sincerely wish it had been in your power to acquaint me that you were free from cold and the consequent cough and oppression on the chest which must naturally produce increased pain in the side, from which I grieve that you continue to suffer. I trust however that I shall have the comfort of finding you better to-morrow & relieved by the effect of the medicine. I am not surprized that you should feel so much at parting from Mrs. Williams, whose attentions have been so kind & affectionate. (Add. Georgian 14/174)

4156 SPENCER PERCEVAL *to the* KING, *and the reply*

[*Downg. St., 9 May 1810.*] Mr Perceval has the satisfaction to acquaint your Majesty that the adjournment of the debate upon the Middlesex Petition answered every expectation which could have been formed with regard to it. Mr. Wallace began the debate against the Petition; he was answered by Sir Thos. Turton. Mr Jacob followed Sir Thomas, and made a very good and impressive speech against the factious proceedings out of which these Petitions have arisen. Sir Saml. Romilly spoke for the Petition, Mr Wms. Wynne against it, Sir J. Newport for it. Mr Peele answered Sir John in a most excellent speech; he was followed on the same side by Mr W. Elliot. Mr Wardle defended the Petition, and the debate concluded with a speech from Mr Wilberforce and Mr Ponsonby; they both were very useful speeches, tho' Mr Ponsonby thought it necessary to give his vote for the Petition. The House then divided for the Petition 36; against it, 128.[2] (15340)

---

[1] She, like Mrs. Williams, had been nurse to the Princesses.
[2] *Parl. Deb.*, XVI, 922–44. Perceval meant the Petition from the Livery of London.

[*The King's reply, Queen's Palace, 10 May.*] The King acknowledges the receipt of Mr Perceval's report of last night's proceedings in the House of Commons which have proved very satisfactory to his Majesty. (15340)

4157   *Letters from* SIR HENRY HALFORD *to the* KING

[*Thursday morning, 9* [*10*] *May* [*1810*].] As her Royal Highness, the Princess Amelia, had complain'd of pain and tightness across the chest and as the extinction of inflammation there had afforded us the best ground of hope of improvement in her Royal Highness's symptoms lately, I was anxious to ascertain the extent of this new evil and to take immediate measures for its removal. I had the satisfaction of finding the Princess on my arrival at Windsor last night in no respect essentially worse, but it was obvious that a small quantity of blood ought to be taken away from the neighbourhood of the chest, and the pulse seem'd from its strength to be fully capable of bearing it. Her Royal Highness took her medicine therefore last night and submitted with great good sense and her usual patience to the operation of cupping this morning, and I trust I am justified in assuring your Majesty that it is probable this timely recourse to the evacuation will effectually prevent a continuance of that inflammatory condition of the interior of the breast which has been so productive of distress in the earlier period of the Princess's illness.

I intreat your Majesty to believe me [etc.]. (Add. Georgian 14/175)

[*Thursday,* [*10 May*[1]].] I had the satisfaction of finding her Royal Highness the Princess Amelia in no respect worse as to her symptoms than she was on Friday last. The Princess had indeed lived under great anxiety for some few days and the effect of this was most visible in her nerves. (Add. Georgian 14/171)

4158   *The* MARQUESS WELLESLEY *to the* KING, *and the reply*

[*Foreign Office, 10 May 1810.*] Lord Wellesley has the honor to submit to your Majesty for your Majesty's gracious approbation, the draft of a letter to the Lords of the Admiralty, signifying your Majesty's pleasure, with respect to the orders to be given to the officer commanding the naval forces in the Baltic, under the actual state of our relations with Sweden. (15358)

[*The King's reply, Queen's Palace, 11 May.*] The King approves of the letter to the Lords Commissioners of the Admiralty which Lord Wellesley has submitted, in consequence of the actual state of the relations with Sweden. (15358)

4159   *Letters from* SPENCER PERCEVAL *to the* KING, *and the replies*

[*10 May 1810.*] Mr Perceval acquaints your Majesty that Mr Lyttleton made a Motion for the production of some papers from the office of the Commander-in-Chief relating to the case of Capt. Foskett. This was opposed by Mr

---
[1] Taylor's endorsement.

Abercrombie,[1] Mr Ward, General Crawfurd, Genl. Phipps, Mr Perceval, Gen. Loftus. It was supported by Mr Martin & Mr Whitbread and upon a division it was rejected by 84 to 8.[2] (15342)

[*The King's reply, Queen's Palace, 11 May.*] The King considers Mr Perceval to have acted with great propriety in resisting the production of papers from the Commander-in-Chief's office, relating to the case of Captain Foskett, and his Majesty has learnt with pleasure that the Motion was rejected by so large a majority. (15342)

[*From Perceval, Downg. St., 11 May.*] Mr Perceval acquaints your Majesty that the Committee appointed to enquire into the circumstances relative to Sir Fr. Burdett's action against the Speaker & the Serjeant made their Report yesterday afternoon.

The result of it was that the bringing the actions was a breach of privilege— that the House might if it thought fit commit the solicitor who brought them, but that if they did, that commitment would not stop the actions and it would still be necessary that the Speaker & the Serjeant should defend them, otherwise judgement might be given against them. That therefore the Committee was of opinion that the Speaker & the Serjeant should be permitted to appear and plead—and that if the House agreed in that opinion it would be proper that directions should be given for defending them.

Mr Davis Giddy, who was the Chairman upon presenting the Report, moved that the Speaker and the Serjeant should appear & plead. Lord Milton expressed himself as much alarmed for the Constitution from this mode of proceeding as also did Mr Wynn. Mr Ponsonby made a good & constitutional speech, with some things indeed which had better have been omitted, but the general view of the case was that the solicitor should have been sent to prison, but he admitted that there was a necessity for the Speaker's pleading to the action. Mr Adam agreed with him. Mr Perceval had little to say as the Opposition had concurred with the only Motion which had been made, but he endeavoured to shew how very little satisfactory or useful it would have been in this case to have committed the solicitor. It could not have stopped the action; it would only probably have led to another action—and the commitment must have expired with the Session when the action might have gone on again under the same solicitor; that there was nothing to be alarmed at in the proceeding; that the law was quite clear; that no Judge in Westminster Hall would doubt of the privilege of the Ho. of Commons or would question the proceedings of the House; but that the Court could not know what the cause was about without they were informed of it, in due course of legal pleading—that the House had no reason to suppose therefore that

---

[1] James Abercromby, 1st Baron Dunfermline (1776–1858), third son of General Sir Ralph Abercromby. Auditor to the estates of the Duke of Devonshire. Whig M.P. for Midhurst, 1807–12; for Calne, 1812–30; for Edinburgh, 1832–9. Judge Advocate General in the Canning and Goderich Ministries, 1827–8; Chief Baron of the Exchequer [S.], 1830–2; Master of the Mint, July–Dec. 1834; Speaker of the House of Commons, 1835–9. Peerage, 7 June 1839.

[2] *Parl. Deb.*, XVI, 957–66.

their privileges could be touched—but that if there should happen anything which we did not expect, no injury could take place—it would only discover that our course of vindicating our privileges might require Parliamentary regulation. Mr Wynn spoke after Mr Perceval, thinking that the solicitor should be committed. But as Mr Perceval saw that the commitment could not in this case obtain its purpose, he persevered in the line which had been agreed upon in the Committee, and which he confidently believes is the best which under the circumstances could be taken. The debate went off very well, & what Mr Perceval apprehended would have been very embarrassing, proved quite the reverse, and seemed to give general satisfaction. There was no division.[1] (15364–5)

[*The King's reply, Windsor Castle, 12 May.*] The King is glad to learn from Mr Perceval that the debate was so satisfactory last night upon the report of the Committee of Enquiry into the circumstances of Sir Francis Burdett's actions against the Speaker and the Serjeant-at-Arms, & that Mr Perceval has succeeded in putting the business into that course which he has so clearly explained to be the most adviseable. (15367)

[*From Perceval, Downg. St., 14 May 1810.*] Mr Perceval acquaints your Majesty that Mr Whitbread presented a Petition fm. Capt.[2] Cartwright upon the subject of Parliamentary reform & the late proceedings against Sir Francis Burdett. The Petition contained some very offensive expressions, and Mr Perceval opposed it. The House after a short debate divided for the Petition 31—against it 92.

The House then proceeded with a Motion from Mr Tierney for an Address to your Majesty to apply out of the droits of Admiralty a sum equal in value to the annuity intended to be granted to the D. of Brunswick. A copy of that Address Mr Perceval subjoins. Mr Perceval opposed the Address. Mr Creevy answered him, Mr Huskisson spoke also for the Address. Mr Dundas answered him, Mr Brougham[3] replied. Mr Hawkins Brown answered him, & Mr Tierney replied, when the House divided—for the Address 86, against it 103.[4] (15368)

[*From Perceval, Downg. St., 14 May.*] Mr Perceval acquaints your Majesty that the Vicarage of Kirkby Moorside is vacant, and that he would submit to your Majesty if your Majesty should be graciously so pleased, that the Revd. Joseph Coltman[5] should be appointed to it. (15370)

---

[1] *Parl. Deb.*, xvi, 969–1004; Colchester, ii, 275–6.

[2] Perceval meant *Major*. The writing is not clear, but apparently he wrote 'Mr' and then 'Capt.' over it.

[3] Henry Brougham (1778–1868), Whig M.P. for Camelford, 1810–12; for Winchelsea, 1815–30; for Knaresborough, Feb.–Aug. 1830; for Yorkshire, Aug.–Nov. 1830. Lord Chancellor in the Reform Ministry, 1830–4. Created Baron Brougham and Vaux, 22 Nov. 1830.

[4] *Parl. Deb.*, xvi, 1020–38. The Address is in col. 1033. (15369) In Aug. the Princess of Wales heard that her brother's regiment had been ordered to Portugal, and she said she wished to go with it. Canning was confident that he would not be allowed to go, and he advised her not to write to the King about it. 'I know the King would take the letter and put it into Liverpool's hand, and so the Duke would be worse off than if he began at once with office.' (Harewood MSS. Canning to Mrs Canning, 29 Aug. 1810.)

[5] Rector of Sharnford, Leics.; Rector of Hammeringham, Lincs., 1801–37; Rector of Beverley, Yorks., 1803–13. (*d. ?* 1837.)

[*The King's reply, Windsor Castle, 15 May.*] The King acknowledges the receipt of Mr Perceval's report of what passed in the House of Commons last night.

His Majesty approves of the Revd. Joseph Coltman succeeding to the Vicarage of Kirkby Moorside. (15370)

4160 SIR HENRY HALFORD to the KING

[*16 May 1810, 6.30 a.m.*] Sir Henry Halford has the happiness of informing his Majesty that the Princess Amelia, after continuing to suffer the same distressful state of constant retching and exhaustion, fell into a quiet sleep at three o'clock this morning, which lasted, with the interruption of a few minutes only, during which H.R. Highness took a little gruel, until [blank]. Sir Henry Halford cannot refrain from subjoining to this report for his Majesty's comfort the satisfactory inference which may be drawn from so perfectly quiet a condition of the Princess's frame under this sleep as to the state of her vital organs. The sleep appear'd to Mr. Batescombe and Sir Henry to be of the most tranquil and easy kind.

[P.S.] ½ past six; the Princess is still asleep. (Add. Georgian 14/177)

4161 CHARLES YORKE to the KING, *and the reply*

[*Admiralty, 16 May* [*1810*].] Mr Yorke has the honor humbly to submit to your Majesty the proceedings and sentence of a court martial on three of the crew of your Majesty's ship Naiad, who have been tried for mutiny & sentenced to death. It appeared to Lord Mulgrave, Mr Yorke's predecessor, doubtful how far this sentence was authorized by the evidence, and the opinions of your Majesty's Attorney & Solicitor-General were thereupon desired. Those opinions (in which Mr Yorke entirely concurs) represent the charge on which the sentence is founded, not to have been supported or warranted by the evidence; and Mr Yorke therefore submits for your Majesty's approval his further opinion that a full pardon should be granted to the men in question. (15372–3)

[*The King's reply, Windsor Castle, 17 May.*] The King has received Mr Yorke's letter and the accompanying proceedings and sentence of a court martial on three of the crew of the Naiad, and his Majesty cannot, in consequence of the opinion submitted by Mr Yorke on those proceedings, hesitate in granting a free pardon to the prisoners in question. (15373)

4162 *Letters from* SPENCER PERCEVAL *to the* KING, *and the replies*

[*Downg. St., 16 May 1810.*] Mr Perceval has the satisfaction to inform your Majesty that his Motion on the Budget was very well received in the House, tho' the novelty of the proceeding and the impolicy of doing anything which should have the effect of diminishing the growth of the Consolidated Fund were much questioned by Mr Huskisson & much condemned by Mr Tierney.[1] (15371)

---

[1] *Parl. Deb.*, XVI, 1043–65; Colchester, II, 276.

[*The King's reply, Windsor Castle, 17 May.*] The King acknowledges the receipt of Mr Perceval's letter from which his Majesty is glad to learn that his Motion on the Budget was so well received by the House of Commons. (15371)

[*From Perceval, [17 May].*] Mr Perceval acquaints your Majesty that the House divided upon a Motion to put off the Third Reading of the Duke of Brunswick's Annuity Bill for a week, for the purpose of giving opportunity to enquire into the state of the Droits of Admiralty Fund, when there appeared for the adjourned [*sic*] 22 and against it 51.[1] The Bill then passed upon another division where the numbers were greater but the proportion much the same.[2]

The House then went into a Committee upon Mr Martin's Resolutions upon the Third Report of the Finance Committee. And upon a Resolution moved by Mr Perceval in the following words: 'That for the purpose of economy, in addition to the useful and effective measures already taken by Parliament for the abolition & regulation of various sinecure offices & offices executed by deputy, it is expedient *to extend the like principles of abolition or regulation to such other cases as may appear to require it.*'

Upon this Mr Bankes moved to leave out the words which are underlined in the foregoing Resolutions—for the purpose of substituting these words 'after providing other & sufficient means for enabling his Majesty duly to remunerate the faithful discharge of public service in civil offices, to *abolish* all offices which have revenue without employment, and to regulate all offices which have revenue extremely disproportionate to employment, excepting such as are connected with the personal service of his Majesty or of his Royal Family, regard being had to the existing interests in any such offices so to be regulated or abolished.' Upon this Amendment a debate arose in which Mr. C. Long answered Mr Bankes & Mr Martin, who had seconded Mr Bankes, Lord Althorp replied to Mr Long, Mr W. Smith followed Lord Althorp on the same side; Mr Wharton answered Mr W. Smith, Mr Whitbread Mr Wharton. Mr Perceval followed Mr Whitbread. Lord Milton followed Mr Perceval. Mr Canning then spoke in favor of Mr Bankes's amendment and Mr Peter Moore closed the debate. The Committee then divided and the numbers for Mr Bankes Amendment were 93, and against it, 99.

The other Resolutions were then carried as Mr Perceval had moved them, and they are to be reported on Tuesday next.[3] (15374–5)

[*The King's reply, Windsor Castle, 18 May.*] The King has received Mr Perceval's report, and he is glad that he has succeeded in resisting the Amendment moved by Mr Bankes which would have given a most dangerous latitude to the Resolutions upon the Third Report of the Finance Committee. But his Majesty regrets that, upon such an occasion, the attendance of members was not greater, as he flatters himself that if the House had been more full, the dissent would have been more strongly marked to the country. (15375)

[1] The numbers are wrongly given as 20 *v.* 41 in *Parl. Deb.*, XVI, 1077. They are not given in Colchester, II, 276.

[2] The numbers were 37 *v.* 65 (correctly given in the *Debates*).

[3] *Parl. Deb.*, XVI, 1077–1104.

[*18 May 1810, 6.30 a.m.*] I regret with all my heart that it is not in my power to offer your Majesty the consolation of so good a report as I had the happiness of sending your Majesty at my last visit. The early part of the Princess Amelia's night has been very restless; the retching frequent and an expression of general uneasiness and distress frequent. Her Royal Highness dropped asleep however about two o'clock and slept almost without intermission until four. The Princess has slept again three quarters of an hour together twice in the early part of this morning and is now still disposed to sleep. Upon the whole, however, I cannot persuade myself to state to your Majesty that her Royal Highness is better. I think her weaker and I do not find that any one of the symptoms by which the Princess has been so heavily borne down lately have disappear'd. They are all to be found distressing in their turn and her Royal Highness has less power to bear up against them. (Add. Georgian 14/178)

4164 SPENCER PERCEVAL *to the* KING, *and the reply*

[*Downg. St., 19 May 1810.*] Mr Perceval acquaints your Majesty that Lord A. Hamilton moved last night to rescind the Resolution which was come to in the last Session of Parliament on the subject of Lord Castlereagh's offer to put an E. Ind. writership at the disposal of Lord Clancarty[1] to bring him into Parliament.[2] The House heard Lord Castlereagh and the Hon. Mr Ward against the Motion and Mr Ord and Lord Folkstone for it and negatived it without a division.

Mr Grattan then made his Motion upon the R. Ca. Petitions to refer them to a Committee. He laid it down broadly that unless the R. Catholics would submit to some arrangement which should secure the nomination of their Bps. from the influence of any foreign Power, their Petition could not be granted—and he stated that there was now no chance of their acquiescing in the veto,[3] but he hoped some other arrangement might be adopted. Sir J. Cox Hippisley seconded his

[1] See No. 2699. The Duke of Richmond had written to Robert Dundas on 29 Sept. 1809: 'I have a letter from Lord Clancarty desiring to resign his office if Lord Castlereagh goes out. He has been useful in the Post Office and I am sorry he quits, but I don't suppose he will go into opposition.' (Melville MSS.)

[2] See No. 3867. Ministers were naturally well disposed towards Lord Clancarty (who was Postmaster-General in Ireland), and in 1808 he was elected an Irish Representative Peer. Portland wrote to Perceval on 16 June 1808: 'I wished & indeed it was my intention when you were here on Sunday to have had some conversation with you upon Dundas's proposal, & I should be glad to defer coming to any determination respecting it till I have had an opportunity of discussing it with you & some other of our colleagues. The question turns upon the necessity of appointing Ld. Clancarty being so evident as to dispose the numerous claimants for the peerage to acquiesce in his promotion in the same manner as they would in case of the appointment of a Chancellor or of some eminent military or naval service, & upon this I cannot but be anxious to know your opinion & what may be that of the public—for unless it is so considered I fear the ill humour that would be created at home would counterbalance the advantage of the appointment.' (Perceval MSS.)

Lord Hawkesbury told the Duke of Richmond on 3 Aug. 1808 that Clancarty would certainly have the support of Government for a Representative Peerage, a vacancy having been occasioned by the death of the Earl of Clanricarde (27 July). 'He will be a very valuable acquisition to us in the House of Lords.' (Add. MSS. 38320, fo. 73.)

[3] The right of the Crown to negative the nomination of a Bishop by the Pope.

Motion in a very long speech, and the House becoming very impatient, it was moved to adjourn the debate till next Thursday—which, as there was no earlier day equally convenient, was consented to.[1] (15377)

[*The King's reply, Windsor Castle, 19 May.*] The King acknowledges the receipt of Mr Perceval's report of the proceedings in the House of Commons last night. (15378)

4165   DAVID DUNDAS'S *Bulletin*

[*12.30 p.m., Saturday, 19 May 1810.*] Her Royal Highness Princess Amelia has been quieter these last three hours than she was at any time yesterday, the retchings have been less frequent & less violent. She has taken very little food but the greater part has staid down. She complains much of the hot pain in the side, has been a little hysterical & has not slept any. (Add. Georgian 14/179)

4166   DOCTOR MATTHEW BAILLIE *to the* KING

[*Saturday morning, 6 a.m.* [*19 May 1810*].] I have very real satisfaction in informing your Majesty that the Princess Amelia has upon the whole pass'd a good night. Her Royal Highness slept a good deal between twelve & one; from one till two she was restless, occasionally retching and being once a little hysterical. From two till the present time (six o'clock) she has been in the most compos'd sleep. She took fifteen drops of laudanum thrice during the night, but one of the times it was rejected. Her Royal Highness took a little gruel and brandy which was rejected, and also at another time a little brandy & water which was retained. Her pulse was about 94, but I was not able to reckon it very accurately. (Add. Georgian 14/180)

4167   SIR HENRY HALFORD *to the* QUEEN

[*6.15 a.m.* [*20 May 1810*].] It will be a comfort to your Majesty, I trust, to be informed that the Princess Amelia has had nearly four hours sleep in the course of the night, with a diminish'd quantity of laudanum. Her Royal Highness slept nearly an hour immediately after midnight; after this she was disturbed by her bowels and became restless and uneasy until three o'clock, when she fell asleep again and continued to sleep almost entirely without interruption until six. Her Royal Highness has taken her sustenance with rather less difficulty but not without embarrassment, tho' I have this moment had the satisfaction of seeing the Princess take a small boatful with less effort than I have observed these three days. (Add. Georgian 14/181)

---

[1] *Parl. Deb.*, XVII, 10–85. Castlereagh viewed the Motion in this light: Lord Archibald's wish to expunge from the Journals the Resolutions of the House because they contained no censure upon him, meant passing an indirect censure on his conduct. The carrying of the Motion would leave the public to impute corruption to him. The Motion, said J. W. Ward, amounted to an attempt to try Castlereagh twice for the same offence.

[*21 May 1810.*] We are sorry to report to your Majesty that the Princess Amelia has not pass'd so good a night as the two preceding ones; she has not as yet had more than two hours and a half sleep but she is now (at six in the morning) asleep. About twelve o'clock at night her Royal Highness took fifteen drops of laudanum mix'd with some hot water and a similar dose of laudanum between four & five. In the early part of the night her Royal Highness took some Hock & water which was partly swallowed & partly rejected. Between three and four she took coffee cupfuls of beef tea, the greater part of which was retained. She has also had two small fluid motions during the night consisting of proper fæculent matter. The pulse of her Royal Highness was about ten o'clock last night at 77, during the night it rose to 100 and is now at 94; these varieties depend upon the irritability of her constitution and are very common in nervous habits. The Princess Amelia is still asleep at 7 o'clock. (Add. Georgian 14/182)

4169 SIR HENRY HALFORD *to the* KING

[*6.15 Tuesday morning* [*22 May 1810*].] I feel a satisfaction in being able to report to your Majesty that the Princess Amelia has passed a quieter night than the preceding one. She has now had at least three hours sleep and in the intervals has been more tranquil and composed, the quantity of laudanum taken, *in two doses*, having been only eighteen drops instead of thirty. Her Royal Highness had taken but very little nourishment in the course of the evening yesterday, nor were we successful in the early part of the night in administering more, but towards the morning, by a little management and patient attention, some beef tea has been got down and this in a way to encourage a good expectation that more may be admitted presently.

The Princess's pulse I have found more steady and slower this morning than it was yesterday evening, and H.R. Highness has had another natural effort of the bowels, so that we are perfectly at ease on that subject. (Add. Georgian 14/183)

4170 SPENCER PERCEVAL *to the* KING, *and the reply*

[*Downg. St., Tuesday morg., 22 May 1810.*] Mr Perceval acquaints your Majesty that Mr Tierney moved yesterday afternoon for an account of the droits of Admiralty and the services to which they had been granted—and as there has been so much misrepresentation and false impression upon the supposed misapplication of that Fund, Mr Perceval thought it would be adviseable to grant it —having previously satisfied himself that there were no improper payments that had been made out of it.

Connected with this subject Mr Perceval humbly takes leave to submit to your Majesty whether it would not be proper to have an estimate made of the expence which would be necessary to rebuild the part of St. James's Palace, which has been burnt down, and whether it would not be adviseable to apply part of the Droit Fund to that expence.[1]

After the above Motion of Mr Tierney had been disposed of Mr Brand moved for a Committee to enquire into the state of the representation of the people in Parliament with a view to a reform. Mr Davies Giddy opposed his Motion, and he was followed by the gentlemen whose names are here inserted and in the order in which they stand.

For the Motion	Against the Motion
	Lord Milton
Sr. J. Newport	
	Mr Sturgess Bourne
Col. Wardle	
Mr Whitbread	
	Mr Canning
Mr Tierney	
Mr. W. Smith	
Mr Ponsonby	
	Mr Wms. Wynn
	Lord Porchester

Your Majesty's servants did not find it necessary to take any part in the debate. The House divided—for the Motion 115, against it 234.[2] (15379–80)

[*The King's reply, Windsor Castle, 22 May.*] The King has received with much pleasure Mr Perceval's report of the satisfactory manner in which Mr Brand's Motion for a reform in Parliament was disposed of last night. His Majesty acquiesces in the propriety of Mr Perceval's proposal that an estimate should be made of what would be necessary to rebuild that part of St James's Palace which has been burnt down, with a view to the application of part of the Droits of Admiralty Fund to that expence. (15380)

4171   THE MARQUESS WELLESLEY *to the* KING, *and the reply*

[*Foreign Office, 22 May 1810.*] Lord Wellesley has the honor to acquaint your Majesty that the Duke of Albuquerque, Ambassador Extraordinary and

---

[1] The Speaker wrote, 21 Jan. 1809: 'Went to see the burnt front of St. James's Palace. About a third of the whole Palace, from the north-east corner next to the German Chapel, round by the south-east angle of the garden front, to the great tower in the middle of the garden front, including the King's Closet, Levée room, bedroom, &c.; and the Queen's dressing rooms and the Duke of Cambridge's apartments. The fire is supposed to have begun in an apartment belonging to one of the Queen's dressing women. One young woman was burnt; no other life lost.' (Colchester, II, 164.)

[2] *Parl. Deb.*, XVII, 123–64. The brief mention in Colchester, II, 277, is not under the correct date. W. H. Fremantle wrote to Lord Grenville on the 22nd: 'The question of reform had a much larger minority last night than I expected, more particularly as it was not by any means well supported by argument in debate. Canning made much the best speech he has made this year, and Ponsonby spoke the best in favour of the proposition. Lord Temple did not come to town for the debate, and Charles Williams, Lord George [Grenville] and myself voted against the Motion of going into a Committee. The numbers of the minority have given great courage and spirits to [the] friends of reform.' (Fortescue MSS.)

Plenipotentiary from Spain arrived this day in London. The Ambassador will not be prepared to have the honor of presenting his credentials previously to Wednesday the 30th, on which day Lord Wellesley will present him to your Majesty if your Majesty should be graciously pleased to approve that arrangement.[1] (15381)

[*The King's reply, Windsor Castle, 23 May.*] The King has received Lord Wellesley's letter and approves of the Duke of Albuquerque's presenting his credentials on Wednesday the 30th instant. His Majesty is sorry to hear that Lord Wellesley continues so much indisposed. (15382)

4172   MATTHEW BAILLIE *to the* KING

[*6.15 a.m., Wednesday* [*23 May 1810*].] We have great satisfaction in reporting to your Majesty that the Princess Amelia has pass'd upon the whole a good night. Her Royal Highness has already had nearly three hours sleep and she is now (at a quarter before six) in the most compos'd sleep. She has taken twice some cyder, half a glass at one time and a whole glass at another, all of which was retained. She has taken at two different times four teaspoonfuls of beef tea which she has retained. Her Royal Highness certainly swallows better and the thick white thick crust [*sic*] is shedding from her tongue. She has taken no opium whatever. Besides the cyder and the beef tea I ought to have mention'd that her Royal Highness has taken three desertspoonfuls of orange juice; she has also now (at six) taken four teaspoonfuls of beef tea.

Her pulse is at present 98, but she has been lately making some slight exertion. (Add. Georgian 14/184)

4173   SIR HENRY HALFORD *to the* KING

[*6.15 a.m.* [*24 May 1810*].] Altho' I have not the comfort of being able to state to your Majesty at this early hour of the morning that the Princess Amelia has passed a night of so much sleep as the preceding one, yet it is satisfactory to me to be able to assure your Majesty that nothing has occurred to diminish the value of the good report which the Princess Mary convey'd to your Majesty last night. The Princess Amelia has complain'd of her stomach a little in the night (*but has no sickness*) and cough'd frequently, but as the pulse did not exceed 84 in number and the skin was cool, it should seem that these symptoms are referable to that disturbed state of the nervous system which may be expected after so severe an attack. The measure of sleep in the course of the night amounts to nearly three hours, and her Royal Highness has taken her nourishment, the beef tea, as often as it was offer'd to her. I trust I may be able to add an account of more sleep presently when I have the honor to wait upon your Majesty. (Add. Georgian 14/185)

---

[1] The Duke, wrote Lord Grey, 'is one of the Spanish heroes, and much praised for his retreat to Cadiz. If he is a fair specimen of the rest, nobody need wonder that the Spaniards have not made a better figure. It was quite ridiculous to hear a little fellow (less than Monk Lewis) talking of the address and courage and strength required in a bull fight, and then state with an affected air, "qu'il avait fait cette folie"'. (Howick MSS.)

[*Downg. St.*, *24 May 1810*.] Mr Perceval acquaints your Majesty that some debate took place upon the bringing up of the Second Report from the Committee upon Sir Fr. Burdett's action—but nothing of particular interest. The House went thro' a good deal of ordinary business.[1] Mr Perceval submits to your Majesty the accompanying Messages[2] for the Vote of Credit. (15383)

[*The King's reply, Windsor Castle, 24 May.*] The King acknowledges the receipt of Mr Perceval's report of last night's proceedings in the House of Commons, and his Majesty has signed the Messages for the Vote of Credit. (15383)

[*From Perceval, Downing Street, 25 May.*] Mr Perceval acquaints your Majesty that Mr Tierney last night opposed the Bill for applying the excess of the Stamp Duties to the Loan of the year. He spoke upon it with great earnestness & at considerable length. Mr Rose answered him, Mr Huskisson replied to Mr Rose, and Mr Perceval to Mr Huskisson. Mr Bathurst supported the Bill, and the House divided upon it, for the Bill 117, against 53.[3] (15384)

[*The King's reply, Windsor Castle, 25 May.*] The King is glad to learn from Mr Perceval's report that the opposition of Mr Tierney and Mr Huskisson to the Loan Bill did not produce more effect upon the House of Commons. (15384)

4175   MATTHEW BAILLIE *to the* KING

[*6.30 a.m., Friday* [*25 May 1810*].] We have to report to your Majesty that the Princess Amelia has as yet had little sleep, not above an hour and a half, but she is now nearly asleep and may probably sleep for two or three hours, for she has generally slept best in the morning. Her Royal Highness however has taken more nourishment than was expected, viz., a desertspoonful of barley water, four desertspoonfuls of beef tea, a dozen and a half of grapes with four cherries, half a cup of beef tea, a little barley water and lately nearly half a cup of beef tea, all of which she has retained. She has had a little more cough than usual. Her pulse (by guess) is at present about 84, and sufficiently strong. Mr. Dundas sat up with her Royal Highness during the night. (Add. Georgian 14/186)

4176   SIR HENRY HALFORD *to the* KING

[*6.30 a.m., Saturday* [*26 May 1810*].] It is with sincere satisfaction I inform your Majesty that the Princess Amelia has passed a very comfortable night. Her Royal Highness slept without interruption for two hours and a half in the early part of the night; has slept more than an hour at once since and is now asleep. The Princess began to take nourishment again after having passed a great many hours

[1] *Parl. Deb.*, XVII, 169–75.   [2] *Ibid.*, 174 (24 May).
[3] *Parl. Deb.*, XVII, 175–9. The numbers on the division are correct. In Colchester, II, 277, they are given as 124 *v.* 57.

without it soon after I came last night, and has continued to take it in the intervals of her sleep in a very sufficient measure. It is the highest satisfaction to me to be able to state to your Majesty that her Royal Highness' pulse is stronger this morning than it has been during this late most severe attack. (Add. Georgian 14/187)

4177 SPENCER PERCEVAL *to the* KING, *and the reply*

[*Downg. St., 26 May 1810.*] Mr Perceval acquaints your Majesty that the adjourned debate upon the Ro. Ca. Petition came on in the Ho. of Commons last night, when the following persons spoke:

For referring the Petition to a Commiee.: 2 Sr J. Newport, 3 Mr Knox,[1] 5 Mr Lamb, 7 Lord Dursley,[2] 8 Gen. Mathew, 10 Mr Ponsonby, 12 Mr Whitbread, 14 Mr Herbert.

Against it: 1 Sir W. Scott, 4 Ld Castlereagh, 6 Ld Jocelyn, 9 Mr Ryder, 11 Mr Perceval, 13 Mr Canning.

The House became very unquiet about this time—it was about ½ p 3 o'clock, Col. Hutchinson moved to adjourn the question till Friday, and tho very much against the wish of the House there was no prevailing upon him to forego his Motion—and the debate was accordingly adjourned till Friday.

Mr Ponsonby took the opportunity of reading a letter from Dr Milner[3] which appeared fully to justify his having stated what he did state the last time this question was before the House relative to Dr Milner's informing him that the Ro. Ca. Bps. would consent to your Majesty's having a veto in the election of their Prelates.[4] (15385)

[*The King's reply, Windsor Castle, 26 May.*] The King acknowledges the receipt of Mr Perceval's report of the adjourned debate upon the Roman Catholic Petition, and his Majesty regrets that a question already so fully discussed, was not brought to issue last night. (15386)

4178 MATTHEW BAILLIE *to the* KING

[*Windsor, 6.30 a.m.* [*27 May 1810*].] We have the satisfaction to report to your Majesty that the Princess Amelia has pass'd upon the whole a good night. She has had rather more than three hours sleep and while awake has been generally

---

[1] Thomas Knox, 1st Earl of Ranfurly (1754–1840) Tory M.P. for Tyrone, 1806–12, having previously sat in the Irish House of Commons for Carlingford, 1776–83; for Dungannon, 1783–90; and for Co. Tyrone, 1790–7. Succeeded his father as 2nd Viscount Northland [I.], 5 Nov. 1818. Created Baron Ranfurly [U.K.], 6 July 1826; and Earl of Ranfurly [I.], 14 Sept. 1831.

[2] William Fitzhardinge Berkeley (1786–1857), styled Viscount Dursley from about 1799. He was the eldest son of Frederick Augustus, 5th Earl of Berkeley (1745–1810), by Mary Cole before their marriage. M.P. for Gloucestershire, 18 May 1810–11. On failing to prove his legitimacy (1 July 1811) —the House of Lords rejecting the story of the alleged marriage of his parents as early as 1785 and recognising the marriage celebrated on 16 May 1796—he styled himself Colonel Berkeley. He was given a peerage on 10 Sept. 1831 (title, Baron Segrave) and was created Earl Fitzhardinge on 17 Aug. 1841.

[3] John Milner (1752–1826), Bishop of Castabala (1803), and Vicar Apostolic of the western district of England. He was the leading representative of the Catholic hierarchy opposed to the veto.

[4] *Parl. Deb.*, XVII, 183–194*.

tranquill. Her Royal Highness has also taken a due proportion of nourishment, more than half a large cupfull of mutton broth, half a cupfull of beef tea, a glass of ginger wine, two nectarines, and a dozen and a half of grapes. She is now asleep and I have not as yet been able to feel her pulse. Mr. Battiscombe sat up with her Royal Highness. (Add. Georgian 14/188)

4179   SIR HENRY HALFORD *to the* KING

[*6.30 a.m., Monday* [*28 May 1810*].] It is with much satisfaction I report to your Majesty that the Princess Amelia has passed another quiet and comfortable night. Her Royal Highness has had at least four hours sleep and that with but short interruptions, during which she took her nourishment in a sufficient measure. I may add that I find the temperature of the skin what it ought to be, the pulse calm and steady and I think a little stronger than it was, but the Princess does not complain less of the pain of the side and of that internal heat which her Royal Highness has been in the habit of finding relieved by a more active state of the bowels. (Add. Georgian 14/189)

4180   MATTHEW BAILLIE *to the* KING

[*Windsor, 6.30 a.m., Tuesday, 29 May* [*1810*].] We have the satisfaction of reporting to your Majesty that the Princess Amelia has pass'd a good night. Early in the night her Royal Highness slept about three quarters of an hour, and afterwards slept nearly without interruption from two till six. She has taken also a good deal of nourishment, half a cupful of mutton broth twice, half a cupful of beef tea once, a glass of ginger wine, a small saucerfull of strawberries, a little pineapple, some orange and above a dozen of cherries. Her pulse now (at half past six) is 80. Her Royal Highness however complains a good deal of her right side and of her head. (Add. Georgian 14/190)

4181   SIR HENRY HALFORD *to the* KING

[*6.30 a.m., Wednesday* [*30 May 1810*].] It is satisfactory to me to be able to inform your Majesty that the Princess Amelia has passed another quiet and comfortable night. Her Royal Highness has had about four hours sleep and will probably get more, and has taken her mutton broth and some strawberrys with apparent satisfaction to herself. A pill was given last night without offence to the stomach at all, and the effect of this is expected with some interest to relieve a sense of weight and oppression which appeared at length so urgent as to render it necessary to give a little medicine in a cautious dose. (Add. Georgian 14/191)

4182   *Letters from* SPENCER PERCEVAL *to the* KING, *and the reply*

[*Downg. St., 30 May 1810*.] Mr Perceval acquaints your Majesty that Mr Tierney moved an Address to your Majesty on the subject of the Droits of

Admiralty whereof Mr Perceval transmits to your Majesty a copy. Mr Perceval opposed the Address, and went into an explanation of the state of the Droit Fund and of the application which had been made of it. Mr Tierney was supported in the debate by Mr Freemantle, Mr Creevy, Mr Brougham & Mr Whitbread, and was opposed by Mr Rose, Mr Long and Mr Stephen. The House divided against the Address 101, for it 78.[1] (15387)

[*From Perceval, Downg. St., 30 May.*] Mr Perceval acquaints your Majesty that he has had many representations made to him of the inadequacy of the salary of the Lord Lieut. of Ireland—that it is impossible for any person to maintain the dignity of that station without spending from ten to twenty thousand pounds a year more than the salary of the office. The salary has not been encreased since 1783 when it was made up £20,000 p. annum Irish. Mr Perceval has enquired into the expences of the D. of Richmond and finds that they have been very little short of £40,000 pr. an. since his Grace has been in Ireland. That the Duke of Bedford's expence was very little if at all short of that sum, and that preceding Lords Lieutenants have for many years past exceeded the salary of the office. Under the impression therefore that your Majesty would greatly regret that your servants in such high office should involve themselves and their families in deep distress by their serving your Majesty, Mr Perceval submits to your Majesty that it may be proper, if your Majesty should graciously so please, to acquaint Parliament with this fact, and call upon the Ho. of Commons to assist your Majesty in encreasing the salary of that office. Mr Perceval has accordingly prepared a Message for your Majesty's signature if your Majesty should think fit to approve of this measure. (15390–1)

[*The King's reply, Windsor Castle, 31 May.*] The King acknowledges the receipt of Mr Perceval's report of the result of Mr Tierney's Motion which is satisfactory. His Majesty entirely approves the grounds upon which Mr Perceval has submitted for his signature the Messages to both Houses of Parliament relative to an augmentation to the salary of the Lord Lieutenant of Ireland.[2] (15391)

4183   DOCTOR POPE *to the* KING

[*31* [*May 1810*].] Dr. Pope has the honor to report to the King that the Princess Amelia has pass'd a very indifferent night & has had about three hours sleep at times, which did not appear to be comfortable repose. (Add. Georgian 14/192)

4184   SPENCER PERCEVAL *to the* KING, *and the reply*

[*31 May 1810.*] Mr Perceval regrets extremely to have to acquaint your Majesty that Mr Bankes has carried his Resolutions for the abolition of sinecure offices, and

---

[1] *Parl. Deb.*, XVII, 211*–219*. The minority was 75, not 78.

[2] Perceval presented the King's Message to the House of Commons on 7 June. It recommended 'such an augmentation to the present allowances of the Lord Lieutenant as may appear to be sufficient for the due support of his office'. (*Parl. Deb.*, XVII, 455.)

offices executed principally by deputy. The subject had already been debated three times in the House and there was nothing new to be said upon it. Mr Bathurst, who had not been present at the former debates upon it, spoke against Mr Bankes's Resolutions. None of Lord Sidmouth's friends accompanied him. Mr Canning & his friends went, with the exception of Mr Sturgess Bourne, with Mr Bankes.

The numbers on the first division were: for Mr Bankes's Resolution 105, against it 95.

On the second they were for it 111, against it 100.

Lord Castlereagh was not in the House; such of his friends as were there voted with yr Majesty's servants.[1]

Mr Perceval rejoices to be able to state to your Majesty that from the last intelligence he has received, of his Royal Highness the D. of Cumberland, he appears to be going on as well as, considering the nature of his calamity, can be expected.[2] (15392)

[*The King's reply, Windsor Castle, 1 June.*] The King has learnt with great concern from Mr. Perceval that Mr Bankes has carried his Resolutions for the abolition of sinecure offices, and his Majesty is convinced that those who, otherwise well inclined to his Government, have voted against it upon this question, have not considered the mischievous tendency of the Resolutions. The King is sensible of Mr Perceval's attention in noticing the state of the Duke of Cumberland, whose preservation under so horrid an attempt has indeed been most providential. (15393)

4185   SIR HENRY HALFORD *to the* KING

[*6.30 a.m.* [*1 June 1810*].] I have the satisfaction of informing your Majesty that the Princess Amelia has passed a rather better night than the preceding one, having had in the whole somewhat more than three hours sleep. Her Royal Highness has taken some fruit in the course of the night, but little or no other nourishment. (Add. Georgian 14/194)

4186   PRINCESS MARY *to the* KING

[*Friday night* [*1 June 1810*].] I am happy to be able to say that since 8 o'clock this evening Amelia has taken some chicken broth & though it went much against her, yet it remained in her stomac; before that the stomac was much disordered, but after being well relieved by sickness Amelia has been better able to take what nourishment has been offered. The pain in the head as well as side has been often complained of today, but for all that Amelia has not been cupped as Dr. Pope wished to keep it off till the last moment & as she was rather faint at diferent

---

[1] *Parl. Deb.*, XVII, 227–9.
[2] During the night of 30–31 May an attempt on the Duke's life had been made whilst he was in bed in his apartments in St James's Palace, by his Italian valet, Sellis, who then committed suicide by cutting his throat with a razor.

times this evening that was another reason why he proposed puting it off till tomorrow.

I rejoice to find that Ernest keeps free from fever, I pray God it may be in your power to send us a good account tomorrow.

Saturday. Amelia has had in all about four hours sleep, for her a tolerable night, but thank God nourishment enough has been got down in the night. She is suffering a good deal from the oppression in the head. (Add. Georgian 12/152)

4187 *Letters from* RICHARD RYDER *to the* KING, *and the replies*

[*Whitehall, 1 June 1810, 6 p.m.*] Mr. Ryder has the honor of humbly submitting to your Majesty that as soon as he was informed of the horrid attempt made yesterday morning to take away the life of his Royal Highness the Duke of Cumberland he sent for Mr. Read[1] to take the depositions upon oath of all the witnesses who seemed likely to have it in their power to throw any light upon the subject. Mr. Read was employed in this business for twelve hours yesterday, and for a great part of this morning. The evidence is not all closed, but considering the importance of the case and your Majesty's feelings on such an occasion Mr. Ryder hopes that your Majesty will pardon his presuming to transmit to your Majesty the original depositions without loss of time, in preference to waiting till they could be copied and completed.

Mr. Ryder has no reason to believe, having himself attended by far the greater part of the time the examinations of the witnesses, that any material facts are likely to transpire from those witnesses, whose evidence there has not been hitherto an opportunity to take. When Mr. Ryder left St. James's an hour ago the Coroner's jury were assembled. As soon as Mr. Ryder is acquainted with the verdict, he will have the honor of submitting it to your Majesty.

Mr. Ryder has the honor of submitting to your Majesty that the Privy Council at which in addition to your Majesty's confidential servants the Lord Chief Justice of the Common Pleas[2] & the Lord Chief Baron[3] & the Atty. & Solr. General attended; and after hearing such of the depositions as had then been taken, they were of opinion that no further proceedings could be had in the present state of the evidence than such as are now pursuing, and therefore adjourned without coming to any decision.

The Lord Chief Justice of the King's Bench[4] was prevented from attending by the pressure of business in Court, having first informed Mr. Ryder that he would postpone it if his presence was thought material, which his Lordship justly thought in the present stage of this extraordinary business it would not be. (47222–3)

[*From Richard Ryder, House of Commons, Friday night, 11 o'clock, 1 June.*] Mr. Ryder has the honor of humbly submitting to your Majesty that he has this moment been informed that the Coroner's Jury have returned a verdict of felo de se, 13 out of 15, at a little after ten this evening. (47224)

---

[1] James Read, the Bow Street magistrate.
[2] Sir James Mansfield.
[3] Sir Archibald Macdonald.
[4] Lord Ellenborough.

[*The King's reply, Queen's Palace, 2 June.*] The King returns his thanks to Mr. Ryder for the communication of the verdict of the Coroner's Jury which sat at the Duke of Cumberland's apartments yesterday. (47224)

[*From the King, Queen's Palace, 2 June.*] The King acknowledges the receipt of Mr. Ryder's letter of yesterday (which, from circumstances which his M. understands, have been explained to Mr. Ryder, were not submitted to him until 12 o'clock this day) and of the depositions upon oath taken before the Coroner's Jury yesterday and the preceding day, which are returned herewith. The King is sensible of Mr. Ryder's attention in making an immediate communication of those papers, and he approves of all the steps which have been taken in reference to the horrid business. (47225)

[*From Richard Ryder, Great George Street, 2 June.*] Mr Ryder has the honor of transmitting to your Majesty some additional depositions which have been taken by Mr. Read last night and this morning. Mr. Ryder expects to receive some further evidence in the course of tomorrow. If your Majesty should be pleased to require any farther explanation on this subject and should condescend to signify your orders that Mr. Ryder should have the honor of attending your Majesty for that purpose or to intimate any other mode in which your Majesty may wish to receive such explanation, Mr. Ryder will respectfully wait your Majesty's commands. (47227)

[*The King's reply, Queen's Palace, 3 June.*] The King acknowledges the receipt of Mr. Ryder's letter and of the additional depositions which have been taken by Mr. Read, and his Majesty will be glad to receive Mr. Ryder here this day at three o'clock. The King also desires that Mr. Ryder will order a complete set of the depositions to be sent for his Majesty's use, whenever they can conveniently be copied. (47230)

4188 SPENCER PERCEVAL *to the* KING, *and the reply*

[*Downing St., 2 June 1810.*] Mr. Perceval acquaints your Majesty that the adjourned debate upon the Roman Catholic Petition came on last night, when the speakers were as follows:

For Mr Grattan's Motion:	Against it:
Mr Huskisson	Mr O'Hara[2]
Marquis of Tavistock[1]	Sr Thos. Turton

[1] The Marquess (1788–1861) was so styled from 2 March 1802, when his father succeeded as 6th Duke of Bedford, until 20 Oct. 1839, when he succeeded his father as 7th Duke. M.P. for Peterborough, 1809–12, and for Bedfordshire, 1812–32. Summoned to the House of Lords, *v.p.*, in his father's Barony of Howland, 15 Jan. 1833.

[2] Charles O'Hara (1746–1822), M.P. for Sligo County, 1801–22. Supported Pitt's Ministry. A Lord of the Treasury [I.] in the 'Talents' Ministry. Sir Arthur Wellesley, when Irish Secretary, thus referred to him: 'Mr. O' Hara in opposition, but does not attend.' He was still in opposition in 1810—and subsequently.

For Mr. Grattan's Motion:	Against it: (cont.)
Mr Talbot[1]	Mr Bernard[2]
Mr Parnell	
Sir Ralph Milbank	Mr Macnaghton[3]
Mr Barham	Capt. Parker
Mr Fitzgerald	Mr Secy Dundas
Mr Wms Wynn	Mr Sol. General
Mr John Smith	
Mr Peter Moore	
Mr Grattan	

The House divided at ½ p. three o'clock this morning:
For referring the Petition to a Committee   213
Against it   109   (15394)

[*The King's reply, Queen's Palace, 2 June.*] The King acknowledges the receipt of Mr Perceval's report of the proceedings in the House of Commons last night.[4] (15394)

4189   *Letters from the* KING *to* PRINCESS MARY, *and the replies*

[*Queen's Palace, 2 June 1810.*] The report of dear Amelia conveyed in your kind letter and that received from Doctor Pope was, upon the whole, as satisfactory as I could expect, though far from what I most anxiously wish them to be. I am glad that you have been able to make her take some nourishment and, should the cupping be resorted to, I hope that it may relieve without weakening her too much.

The accounts which I continue to receive of poor Ernest are, under all circumstances, as favorable as I could flatter myself they would be. (Add. Georgian 12/153)

[*Princess Mary's reply, Saturday night* [*2 June*].] I return you my most greatful thanks for your kind letter, my dearest papa, and am most happy to find dear Ernest still keeps free from fever.

I am thankful to have it in my power to assure you Amelia's head is certainly relieved by the cupping, & the stomach has been in a less irritable state today, having been able to take nourishment enough without being sick. She had some

---

[1] Richard Wogan Talbot (c. 1766–1849); 2nd Baron Talbot [I.]. Whig M.P. for Co. Dublin, 1807–30. He succeeded to his mother's peerage, 27 Sept. 1834. Created Baron Furnival [U.K.], 8 May 1839.

[2] Thomas Bernard (c. 1769–1834), M.P. for King's Co., 1802–32. He was the brother-in-law of Lord Dunally and of the Earl of Charleville, to whom he mainly owed his seat. He supported the Government.

[3] Edmund Alexander Macnaghten (1762–1832), M.P. for Antrim, 1801–12, 1826–30; for Orford, 1812–20 and 1820–6; one of Lord Hertford's members. A Lord of the Treasury [I.], 1813–17; [U.K.], 1819–30.

[4] *Parl. Deb.*, XVII, 235–304.

green pease for dinner which went down better than I have seen anything else (but with the help of vinegar). The pain in the side continues much the same, but her spirits are better & she assures me she feels stronger.

Mr. Dundas who came this evening is of opinion we are not loosing ground & found the pulse steady. Amelia desires her most affte. love & duty, hopes you will excuse her not writing as she does not feel equal to that exertion yet.

Sunday. Amelia had no sleep till three o'clock owing to the pain in her side; since that I understand what sleep she has had was restless. Some broth & grape juce was taken & Dr. Pope does not find her worse today. (Add. Georgian 12/154)

[*From the King, Queen's Palace, 3 June.*] Accept my best thanks for your kind letter, and for your continued attention in communicating to me every particular respecting dear Amelia. It is satisfactory to me to know that her head has been relieved by the cupping, but I am truely concerned that she still suffers so much pain in the side. Pray assure her, with my kind love, that I do not expect to hear from herself at present, and that I should regret very much her attempting the exertion of writing even a few lines. The reports of Ernest continue, thank God, satisfactory, as you will see in the inclosed letter from Mr. Phipps.[1] (Add. Georgian 12/155)

[*From Princess Mary, Sunday night* [*3 June*].] Pray receive my greatful thanks for your kind letter & for being so good as to inclose me the account of Ernest's night: I flatter myself he is going on as well as the nature of his present situation will admit of & Sir Henry Halford has made me most happy just now by assuring me the first dressing of the hand has gone off well, therefore if fever can be kept off I hope in God we may still have the blessing of seeing him restored to health.

Our dear Amelia has passed but an indiferent day as to pain in the side and inward heat, but the irritation of the stomach certainly is better than it was two days ago & enough nourishment has been got down, though with no pleasure, yet she refused nothing offered & has not been sick today. She went into the warm bath this evening & found it comfortable, but certainly is very much weaker since this last attack as the smallest exertion brings on faintness, in consequence the bath fatigued [her] and her spirits have been low and depressed more or less all day. Sir Henry's visit has as usual cheered her; he does not find her worse, but laments she suffers so from her side & that, as well as the inward heat she complains of, must be attended to. After so long an illness it is not to be wondered at that her spirits begin to suffer; it is only surprising that she has kept them as she has done, for really till this last attack I can hardly say I have seen them flag, but for a very short time, & then it has been caused more from violant pain than depression. The head, I am happy to say, is better & all circumstances

---

[1] Sir Jonathan Wathen Waller. First mentioned, without a note, in No. 1310. He was the son of Joshua Phipps, and his mother, Mary Allen, was the daughter of Thomas Waller and sister and co-heir of James Waller. He became an eminent oculist; on 1 Oct. 1812 he married Sophia Charlotte, Baroness Howe (1762–1821), the daughter of Admiral Lord Howe. He took the name of Waller only, in March 1814, in order to mark his descent from that family through his maternal grandmother. Created Baronet, 30 May 1815. K.C.H., 1827; G.C.H., 1830. Groom of the Bedchamber to William IV. (1769–1853.)

put together and compareing her situation today to what it was 10 days ago we must be thankful she is still preserved to us.

Monday morning. Accept my most sincere & heartfelt congratulations on this day & may every blessing attend you, my ever dearest papa, both in this world & the next. She has had one of her best nights, 4 hours in all & is still asleep. Sir Henry has not seen her yet. (Add. Georgian 12/156)

4190   DOCTOR POPE *to* LIEUTENANT-COLONEL TAYLOR

[*Augusta Lodge, near 8 a.m.* [*3 June 1810*].] Dr. Pope respectfully requests that Lt. Coll. Tayler will be pleas'd to acquaint the King that the Princess Amelia's head getting worse yesterday morning, it was thot. right to apply the cupping glasses, which the Princess bore well & express'd relief from & was more chearful in the evening. She has not pass'd quite so good a night as the preceeding one, had about three hours sleep, some of which was a little restless, her pulse this morning abt. 76 & 78; during the night a teacupful of broth was taken at twice & plenty of grape juice. The Princess says her head is relieved but the pain in her side remains as usual.

P.S. My friend Dundas has perus'd & approves the report. (Add. Georgian 14/195)

4191   JONATHAN WATHEN PHIPPS *to* LIEUT.-COLONEL TAYLOR

[*Carlton House, 6.30 a.m., Sunday* [*3 June 1810*].] It is with pleasure I inform you that his Royal Highness the Duke of Cumberland has slept with very little interruption from 10 o'clock last night till ½ past 3 this morning; that he has complained but little of pain & seems calm, collected & much less feverishly inclined than yesterday. From that hour to the present he has occasionally slept & lain quiet. I have told his Royal Highness of the shirt prepared by her Majesty's order & he seems pleased with the idea. His skin is cool & he has had 20 drops less of laudanum than last night. (47228)

4192   RICHARD RYDER *to the* KING, *and the reply*

[*Gt. George Street, 3 June 1810*.] Mr. Ryder has the honor of humbly submitting to your Majesty the depositions which were taken today. Mr. Ryder sent for & saw Mr. John Church, a son of the master of the two witnesses, but he appeared to have so little recollection of the circumstances to which their evidence related that it became unnecessary to take down his deposition. Mr. Ryder has directed, in obedience to your Majesty's commands, a complete set of the depositions to be prepared without delay, which he will have the honor of humbly submitting to your Majesty as soon as they are copied. (47229)

[*From the King, Queen's Palace, 4 June.*] The King has received Mr. Ryder's letter and the additional depositions taken yesterday, which appeared to his Majesty by no means unimportant. (47229)

4193 PRINCESS AMELIA *to the* KING, *and the reply*

[*3 June 1810.*] A day so dear to me as tomorrow I cannot resist attempting to address you these few lines & fully tho' warmly felt try to express & offer my most affte. & tender congratulations. May God bless us by blessing you & may this year be happier than the last.

I rejoice the accounts of poor Ernest are tolerable; that melancholy subject I will not attempt to speak upon now, but thank God for his escape. And now, my beloved father, allow me to try to express what my heart feels for the many kindness[es] you have shewn me during my last severe attack. My heart, believe me, overflows with gratitude to you & all, but I am not equal to saying more except to thank you & dearest Miny for being here with me. Alas! I fear I cannot repay her affection or make up what she sacrifices to be be [*sic*] with one who has so long been a burden to those she loves as I have been. My duty & love to all.

I expect Sir H. H—d tonight; his visits always are comforts & the kind & affte. attention I experience from him of a friend as well as physician I never can sufficiently say how much I feel & value. Thank God Wedy. I shall see you. (Add. Georgian 14/196)

[*The King's reply, Queen's Palace, 4 June.*] Sir Henry Halford has just brought me your truly kind and affectionate letter for which I cannot thank you in terms which can express all I feel. I have ever been convinced of your warm affection for me. I have derived the greatest comfort from the continued proofs received of it, and there is no object nearer my heart, no blessing for which I pray more fervently than that you may be restored to me & to your family in the full enjoyment of your health. Dear Mary's attentions to you have indeed been most kind and exemplary and they have, if possible, endeared her yet more to me. Of Sir Henry Halford's attention I am very sensible & I thank God that he has brought me such an account of you as I may consider upon the whole satisfactory. Ernest's escape has been truly providential and I have just received a very favorable report of him from Mr. Home.[1] (Add. Georgian 14/197)

4194 *The* KING *to* PRINCESS MARY, *and the reply*

[*Queen's Palace, 4 June 1810.*] I feel very thankful to you for your very kind letter and for the remarks with which you have accompanied your report respecting dear Amelia, in the justice of which I entirely concur, as I have often been surprized that her spirits have been so well kept up under the influence of a long and painful confinement, and I have admired the patience and resignation which she has shewn. It is satisfactory that Sir H. Halford does not find her worse and I

[1] Sir Everard Home (1756–1832). Serjeant-surgeon to the King, 1808. Created Baronet, 2 Jan. 1813.

sincerely rejoyce that her last night has been so good. This day's report of Ernest is still more favorable than yesterday's and I have great pleasure in inclosing it to you.

Accept my best thanks, my dearest Mary, for your affectionate wishes upon this day & be assured of the comfort which I have ever derived from your warm attachment and from that excellent conduct which has so justly endeared you to me. Pray give my kind [love] to dear Amelia & tell her that I shall certainly not fail to be with her on Wednesday evening, and that I am looking forward with great impatience to that moment. (Add. Georgian 12/157)

[*Princess Mary's reply, Monday night* [*4 June*].] Your kind letter, my dearest papa, was most greatfully received by me & I only wish to assure you it is my anxious desire and first object in life to continue to deserve your good opinion.

The accounts of dear Ernest are truly satisfactory and give every hope that his health may be restored. I had the pleasure of informing the Queen by the two o'clock coach that Amelia got up to have her bed made about one o'clock & was carried into the next room & lay on the couch for about twenty minutes, when she returned to bed much fatigued; she had her dinner up, which consisted of pease & they went down tolerably & during this day nourishment enough has been taken, but with great dislike, in particular after six o'clock this evening when Amelia has had some return of pain in her stomach and bowels, with a degree of sickness, but thank God she has kept every thing in her stomach. The pain in the side has been very distressing at times today & the inward had made her feel very uncomfortable, therefore I can not say we have passed so easy or so good a day as yesterday, but as the phyans. have told us we must expect ups & downs, I trust this will prove nothing of any very great consequence, & as she was much easer [*sic*] when I left her just now I pray God I may be able to send you a good report of the night tomorrow morning. Dr. Pope does not go as far as to call Amelia worse, only less well than yesterday. She was able to see Dolly for about 10 minutes & expressed great pleasure that the Queen & my sister had not suffered from the fatigue of the Drawing Room.

[P.S.] Do you wish that I should write to you by the groom Wednesday morning?; as the phyans. come tomorrow night & intend calling at the Queen's House as they get to town Wednesday. Perhaps that may do as well, but pray let me know what are your orders on this subject. I think I need not say how happy we are both with the thoughts of seeing you all return to morrow.

Tuesday. Amelia was very restless untill three o'clock; since that has had a good deal of sleep for her & is now asleep. (Add. Georgian 12/158)

4195   RICHARD RYDER *to the* KING, *and the reply*

[*Great George Street, 4 June 1810.*] Mr Ryder has the honor of submitting to your Majesty the correspondence that has taken place between Lord Holland and himself upon the subject of presenting the Address from the town of Nottingham to your Majesty.[1] (15395)

1 The Whig Corporation of Nottingham had chosen Lord Holland its Recorder, the office being vacant by the death of the Duke of Portland.

[*The King's reply, Queen's Palace, 5 June.*] The King returns to Mr Ryder the correspondence which has passed between him and Lord Holland, and he entirely approves of the letters written by Mr Ryder. Those produced by Lord Holland do not appear to his Majesty to shew either much ability or good sense. (15395)

4196 *Letters from* JONATHAN WATHEN PHIPPS *to* LIEUT.-COLONEL TAYLOR

[*Carlton House, Monday morning, 4 June 1810.*] It is with the utmost satisfaction that I can send you for the information of their Majesties a very good report of the night; his Royal Highness has slept with little interruption since eleven o'clock last night till this moment & is still asleep. At the different periods of awaking he has complained much of the soreness & tenderness of the numerous & different wounds & bruises, but is *free* from *every febrile symptom.*

Mr. Home is to see him at 12 o'clock, after which I will pay my duty to their Majesties with a farther account.

I cannot forbear on the opening of this *happy* day to beg you humbly to present to his Majesty the most warm & dutiful congratulations of a loyal & grateful heart. May all the various blessings *he* has diffused over *this* land be returned *tenfold* into *his own* bosom & every other blessing of a good & kind Providence be continually showered on *him* & *his* both here & hereafter. (47231)

[*Carlton House, Tuesday morning, 5 June.*] I very much regret that I cannot send the report of as good a night as I have hitherto done. His Royal Highness was seized soon after he went to bed with considerable pain in his left hand & arm, which has continued with little intermission thro' the night & in spite of 150 drops of laudanum he has had only one hour's sleep. He got up at ½ past 5 & sat in his chair where he now is & I am glad to say the pain has greatly subsided & that he still has no symptom of fever. (47232)

4197 THE KING *to* PRINCESS MARY

[*Queen's Palace, 5 June 1810.*] I am well aware that we must expect ups and downs in the state of dear Amelia, and therefore the account conveyed in the first part of the kind letter which I received from you this day has given me more concern than apprehension, and I trust from her having had some comfortable sleep in the night & from what Doctor Pope states, that she has felt more easy since. As the physicians will call here tomorrow on their return from Windsor and as I shall be with dear Amelia in the evening there cannot be any occasion for your writing by the groom tomorrow morning. I enclose to you the report respecting Ernest and I also send the money for the physicians. The Queen desires her love and rejoyces at the thoughts of seeing you tomorrow as does also [etc.]. (Add. Georgian 12/159)

[*Downg. St., 6 June 1810.*] Mr. Perceval acquaints your Majesty that the House had under its consideration last night a Petition from some freeholders of Gloucestershire complaining that Lord Dursley's seat was vacated on account of his not having sworn to any qualification upon his taking his seat, but merely represented himself to be the heir apparent of a Peer. The Petition stated circumstances of the registering of Lord Berkley's marriage & of the baptism of Lord Dursley several years before that marriage which raised at least a strong presumption against his Lordship's legitimacy. The debate turned upon the course which should be pursued with regard to it. Lord Dursley left it to the House to take what course they thought proper & withdrew. Mr Whitbread, Mr Tierney, Sir J. Anstruther, Mr Canning, Sir S. Romilly and the greatest part of the Opposition who had come down in numbers for the occasion were against doing anything with the Petition; Mr Perceval, the Solicitor General, Mr Wms Wynne, Mr Bragge Bathurst & Sr Arthur Piggot thought that it was quite inconsistent with what was due to the law upon the subject to refuse entering into the examination of the Petition; that it was indeed clearly not within the Grenville Act, and that the House therefore must proceed in it as they would have done before that Act passed; they therefore proposed referring it to the Committee of Privileges. But such was the assemblage of Lord Dursley's friends and so great was the feeling excited of the hardship of trying before so incompetent a tribunal so delicate a question as that of the legitimacy of Lord Dursley that the House divided for the rejection of the Petition 91, and against it 48[1]—and Mr Perceval cannot forbear from stating that tho' he thinks the correct and Parliamentary course was for proceeding to refer the Petition to a Committee of Privileges, yet that there was a good deal to *be felt* at least on the part of the majority, which might in some degree excuse their vote.[2] (15396–7)

[*The King's reply, Queen's Palace, 6 June.*] The King acknowledges the receipt of Mr Perceval's report of the proceedings in the House of Commons last night upon the Petition respecting Lord Dursley's election, & H.M. regrets the occurrence, as another instance of the embarassments arising from Lord Berkeley's carelessness as to establishing in due time the validity of his marriage. (15397)

4199 *Letters from* JONATHAN WATHEN PHIPPS *to*
LIEUT.-COLONEL TAYLOR

[*Carlton House, 12 p.m., Wednesday evening* [*6 June 1810*].] I this evening received your kind letter & it is with no small pleasure that I can inform you that his Royal Highness the Duke of Cumberland has past a very good day, free from any violent spasm & feeling himself much more comfortable. Sir Henry[3] & Mr. Home have seen him & are well satisfied that all is going on right. He is now fast

---

[1] The number should be 46.
[2] *Parl. Deb.*, XVII, 314–20; Colchester, II, 277–8.
[3] Halford.

asleep & has been so from ½ past 10 o'clock. I will write by the 8 o'clock stage tomorrow morning to Pss. Mary which[1] contain [sic] the account of the night.

I am so sleepy I can scarse hold my pen. (47233)

[*Carlton House, 12.30 p.m., Thursday* [*7 June*].] His Majesty will, I hope, have heard the account of his Royal Highness as far as 11 last night by the letter I sent to Pss. Mary by the 8 o'clock coach of this morning, but as we seem improving almost *every* hour I cannot resist the pleasure of sending you a line by this 3 o'clock conveyance to say that the Duke of Cumberland slept till 9 o'clock & that we got him up with much less difficulty than usual, & he seems refreshed. His wounds have been dressed without any pain & Mr. Home makes a most favorable report of them. I shall write again by the messenger. (47234)

[*10.30 Thursday evening* [*7 June*].] The day on the whole has past very well. His Royal Highness has had very little pain, has take[n] sufficient nourishment & is quietly gone to bed with every prospect of a good night. The wounds seem all in a fair progress of healing & no one unfavorable symptom has appeared. (47235)

4200   THE EARL OF LIVERPOOL *to the* KING, *and the reply*

[*Fife House, Thursday, 7 June, 2 a.m.* [*1810*].] Lord Liverpool begs leave most humbly to submit to your Majesty the Minutes of the House of Lords of this nite [sic], and has the honour at the same time of informing your Majesty that the debate as well as the division have proved as satisfactory as there could have been any reason to expect on so important [a] subject, after the repeated discussions which the question had undergone on former occasions.[2] (15398)

[*The King's reply, Windsor Castle, 7 June*.] The King is glad to learn from Lord Liverpool's report that the debate and the division in the House of Lords have proved so satisfactory, upon a question, which, however frequently discussed, should always be treated most seriously. (15398)

4201   *Letters from* SPENCER PERCEVAL *to the* KING, *and the replies*

[*Downg. St., 7 June 1810*.] Mr Perceval acquaints your Majesty that the general business of the House of Commons last night produced nothing interesting. The Lottery Bill, notwithstanding Mr Whitbread's opposition, passed the House, and the Resolution for granting £100,000 to the Governors of Queen Ann's Bounty for the poorer clergy of G. Britain and the vote of £50,000 for the same Board in Ireland passed the House, as well as the Bill for the relief of the poorer clergy in Scotland, thereby carrying into effect the recommendation in

[1] Imperfectly rubbed out.
[2] *Parl. Deb.*, XVII, 353–440. The debate was on the Roman Catholic Petition. The anti-Catholics had a majority of 86 (154 to 68).

your Majesty's Speech at the beginning of the Session. Two Petitions were presented from Berkshire by Mr C. Dundas, the one sufficiently violent, which, however, was permitted to lie upon the Table, for Parliamentary Reform—the other praying for the discharge of Sr F. Burdett & Mr Gale Jones from prison, and charging the House with having injured the whole people of England by their commitments by an assumption of arbitrary power contrary to Magna Charta. This allegation Mr Perceval considered as too offensive for the House to pass over, and therefore proposed to negative the Motion for laying it on the Table of the House—after a debate of some little length the House divided, for the Petition 36, against it 78.[1] (15401–2)

[*The King's reply, Windsor Castle, 7 June.*] The King acknowledges the receipt of Mr Perceval's report of the proceedings in the House of Commons last night, and his M. approves of Mr Perceval's having resisted the reception of the offensive Petition from the Meeting in Berkshire. (15402)

[*From Perceval, Downg. St., Friday morng., 8 June.*] Mr Perceval acquaints your Majesty that the business of the House of Commons was much delayed last night by a very long speech from Mr Littleton upon the subject of Capt. Foskett's Petition. But Mr Perceval has the satisfaction to state that he was extremely well answered by Genl. Crawfurd as was Mr Whitbread, who replied to Genl. Crawfurd, by the Judge Advocate. Mr Littleton did not chuse to divide the House, and his Resolutions were rejected.[2] (15404)

[*The King's reply, Windsor Castle, 9 June.*] The King has learnt with satisfaction from Mr Perceval the issue of the proceedings in the House of Commons in the case of Captain Foskett. (15404)

4202   JONATHAN WATHEN PHIPPS *to* LIEUT.-COLONEL TAYLOR
[*10.30 Friday evening* [*8 June 1810*].] We have past a very quiet day; his Royal Highness has been composed & free from pain, but I fear that within the last half hour the restlessness is coming on & that we shall not have a good night.
    Excuse my scrawl for I can scarsely keep my eyes open. This will be the tenth night & I have had but one night's sleep. (47236)

4203   RICHARD RYDER *to the* KING, *and the reply*
[*Whitehall, 8 June 1810.*] Mr Ryder has the honor of humbly submitting to your Majesty a copy of all the depositions in obedience to your Majesty's commands. (47237)

[*The King's reply, Windsor Castle, 9 June.*] The King acknowledges the receipt of Mr. Ryder's letter transmitting copies of the depositions. (47237)

[1] *Parl. Deb.*, XVII, 440–54.   [2] *Parl. Deb.*, XVII, 459–68. See No. 4138.

[*Fife House, 9 June 1810, 2.30 a.m.*] Lord Liverpool begs leave most humbly to submit to your Majesty the Minutes of the House of Lords—Marquis Wellesley made a most excellent speech in answer to the Marquis of Landsdowne. Lord Sidmouth spoke and voted against the Motion. There was no other circumstance in the debate of any importance which was terminated by a division which Lord Liverpool trusts that your Majesty will consider as very satisfactory.[1] (15417)

[*The King's reply, Windsor Castle, 9 June.*] The King acknowledges the receipt of Lord Liverpool's report of the debate and division in the House of Lords upon Lord Lansdowne's Motion which has given great satisfaction to his Majesty. (15417)

4205 SPENCER PERCEVAL *to the* KING, *and the reply*

[*Downg. St., 9 June 1810.*] Mr Perceval acquaints your Majesty that upon a Motion by Mr Wynn the object of which was to call to the Bar of the House of Commons the Clerk of the King's Bench to bring with him the record of the proceedings in the cause of Sr. Fr. Burdett against the Speaker, for the purpose of cancelling it by the authority of the House—the House divided against the Motion 74, for it 14.

And upon an Address to your Majesty moved by Mr Perceval upon your Majesty's Message for an encrease of salary to the D. of Richmond, which Address was to request your Majesty to make such addition to his salary not exceeding £10,000 pr. am. as your Majesty might think necessary, and to assure your Majesty that if your Majesty's Civil List in Ireland was unable to bear that additional charge the House would vote such addition to the Civil List as would be necessary, the House divided for the Address 95, against it 51. It was opposed principally upon the lateness of the time at which it was brought forward—by Mr Tighe,[2] Sr. J. Newport, Mr Martin, Mr Bankes, Mr Wilberforce, Mr D. Giddy, Mr Bathurst, Mr Parnell, Mr Tierney, Mr Grattan, & Mr Whitbread—and it was supported by Mr Fitzgerald, Mr Pole, Mr Huskisson, and Lord Desart.[3] (15421-2)

[*The King's reply, Windsor Castle, 9 June.*] The King has received Mr Perceval's report of the proceedings in the House of Commons last night which appear to have been very satisfactory. (15422)

[1] *Parl. Deb.*, XVII, 472–503. Lansdowne was criticising the Government's conduct of the war in Spain, and Lord Derby spoke of their imbecility. The Motion was defeated by 65 to 33.

[2] William Tighe (1766–1816), M.P. for Wicklow, 1806–16. 'Mr. Tighe in opposition, but does not attend,' wrote Sir Arthur Wellesley in 1807, when Irish Secretary. He was reckoned an Opposition man in 1810. The Duke of Bedford wrote to Fitzwilliam on 20 Sept. 1808: 'Tighe's state of health is so bad as to render him wholly incapable of attending his duty in Parliament.' (Fitzwilliam MSS.)

[3] *Parl. Deb.*, XVII, 513–30. The Lord Lieutenant's salary was raised from £20,000 to £30,000. Few, if any, holders of the office were able to save anything out of their princely salaries.

[*A Windsor, le 10 Juin 1810.*] La lettre que V.A.S. a bien voulu m'écrire le 9 Mai m'est parvenue hier et j'ai appris avec un plaisir bien vrai que la Princesse, son epouse, étoit heureusement accouchèe d'une fille.[1] J'accepte avec une satisfaction non moindre la proposition que V.A.S. me fait d'être parain de l'enfant nouveau né, & je profite de cette occasion pour lui renouveller les assurances de l'interêt que je prendrai toujours à la prosperité de sa Maison. (16794)

4207 THE EARL OF LIVERPOOL *to the* KING, *and the replies*

[*Fife House, 12 June 1810.*] Lord Liverpool begs leave most humbly to submit to your Majesty the draft of a dispatch to Lt.-Genl. Sir Samuel Auchmutty on the subject of an expedition to the Islands of Mauritius and Bourbon. Lord Liverpool takes the liberty of observing that the capture of these islands is become an object of great publick importance in consequence of the number of ships belonging to the East India Company which have been taken in the course of the last three years by cruizers from the above-mentioned islands. Lord Liverpool thinks it may be material to add that no part of the force destined for this expedition is intended to be drawn from Europe with the exception of a proportion of artillery, but that the remainder is proposed to be collected from India, from the Island of Ceylon and from the Cape of Good Hope. (15423)

[*The King's reply, Windsor Castle, 13 June.*] The King approves of the instructions which Lord Liverpool has prepared for Sir Samuel Auchmuty on the subject of an expedition to the Islands of Mauritius & Bourbon. His Majesty is well aware of the public importance of the object in view, and he is glad that the assembly of the troops to be employed will not produce any reduction of the force at home. (15424)

4208 *Letters from* SPENCER PERCEVAL *to the* KING, *and the reply*

[*Downg. St., 14 [13] June 1810.*] Mr Perceval acquaints your Majesty that several Petitions were presented to the House this day—one from Coventry for a Reform in Parlt., which it was not thought proper to resist being laid upon the Table of the House—one from Worcester very respectably signed, disclaiming all connexion with a Petition which had been presented a few days ago from the same city for a Reform in Parlt. This was a Petition very decidedly approving of the late proceedings in Parliament, and Mr Perceval feels it his duty to state to your Majesty that one of the principal china manufacturers from Worcester waited on Mr Perceval before the House sat to apprize him of this intended Petition, and expressed himself very anxious that if your Majesty should happen to have heard of the last Petition from Worcester, your Majesty should be informed that it by no means expressed the sentiments of the people of Worcester. The new Petition from Middlesex was then presented & opposed by Mr Perceval, Mr Wallace &

[1] The Princess of Orange gave birth to a daughter, Marianna, on 9 May. (1810–83.)

Mr Ryder, supported by Mr Byng & Mr Whitbread—but it was refused to be laid on the Table without a division. There was then presented a Petition from Sheffield, which was very offensive in its tenor and was refused to be laid on the Table on a division of 61 to 15.[1] Lord Cochran then made a Motion against the Admiralty Court which was rejected by 76 to 6.[2] (15434–5)

[*The King's reply, Windsor Castle, 14 June.*] The King acknowledges the receipt of Mr Perceval's report of the proceedings in the House of Commons last night which appear to have been very satisfactory. H.M. is convinced that, not in the City of Worcester alone but generally throughout the country, the offensive Petitions and Addresses which have been carried by clamour & violence do not express the sentiments of the larger proportion of the inhabitants, certainly not of the respectable inhabitants. (15435)

[*From Perceval, Downg. St., 15 June.*] Mr Perceval acquaints your Majesty that the Bill for granting by Exchequer Bills on loan to the E. India Company for £1,500,000 passed the House last night after some debate and a division of 51[3] to 10. The House then proceeded to the consideration of the Bill for regulating the office of Registrar in the High Court of Admiralty after the interests which are now vested in that office; and after a debate of considerable length, it passed thro the stage upon the Report without any division. The House went thro some other business and as there only remain three more Bills in their last stages to pass thro' the House Mr Perceval hopes the House will be able to adjourn for the House of Lords [*sic*] on this day and that the Parliament may be prorogued on Thursday next.[4] (15436)

[*The King's reply, Windsor Castle, 15 June.*] The King is glad to learn from Mr Perceval's letter that the business of the House of Commons proceeded so satisfactorily last night, and that there is a prospect of the House adjourning this day. (15437)

[*From Perceval, Downg. St., 15 June.*] Mr Perceval acquaints your Majesty that upon the Third Reading of the Vote of Credit Bill Mr Whitbread made a speech upon the State of the Nation & the war, which Mr Canning answered in a very brilliant and eloquent manner—and so satisfactorily that Mr Perceval did not think there was any occasion to say anything. The Bill passed without a division—the remaining business which was in the House passed without a division & the House is adjourned till Wednesday next.[5] (15438)

[*The King's reply, Windsor Castle, 16 June.*] The King is glad to learn from Mr Perceval's report that the Vote of Credit Bill passed last night without a division and that Mr Canning took so useful a course upon the occasion. (15438)

[1] The number should be 14.   [2] *Parl. Deb.*, XVII, 601–41 (13 June).
[3] The number should be 52.   [4] *Parl. Deb.*, XVII, 645–54.
[5] *Parl. Deb.*, XVII, 654–746.

[*From Perceval, Downg. St., 17 June.*] Mr Perceval acquaints your Majesty that he has received from Mr Mathias, the Under-Treasurer of her Majesty, an urgent repetition on behalf of her Majesty's Treasury for the assistance of which Mr Perceval believes that it stands so much in need. Mr Perceval humbly takes leave to transcribe a passage from that letter to the following effect.

'Twenty five thousand pounds would entirely liberate her Majesty from every demand of every tradesman, but it is impossible to pay any part of them with her present income. The importunity of some tradesmen is so great that her Majesty has personally directed me to assure you that if even so small a sum as six or seven thousand pounds could be granted to her for the present it would be a great relief & ease to her mind, & enable her to discharge some few demands which are peculiarly troublesome & irksome. In consequence of the marriage of Miss Dashwood, the late Maid of Honour, her Majesty has paid, as usual, about £1500 in gifts & presents to her on the occasion, which has been very inconvenient but could not be dispensed with.'[1]

Mr Perceval knows how desirous your Majesty is to relieve her Majesty from this state of embarrassment; and has therefore had the subject very anxiously in his mind for some time. He fears it will not be possible to give to her Majesty complete relief without having recourse to the Droits of Admiralty. This Mr Perceval regrets very much because as there has been a very jealous & invidious regard paid in Parliament of late to this Fund, Mr Perceval would be most anxious to avoid connecting her Majesty's name, if possible, with any of the angry & unpopular discussions which are likely to arise upon that subject. And upon the same principle, if he cannot hope wholly to disconnect the relief of her Majesty's embarrassments from that Fund, yet he would be desirous of diminishing the amount which may be drawn from it for that purpose as much as possible. Mr Perceval therefore feels it his humble duty to bring this subject under your Majesty's consideration, at a time when he has to acquaint your Majesty that he will have in the course of a day or two to send for your Majesty's signature a warrant upon the Receiver of Gibraltar to pay six thousand pounds to your Majesty's Privy Purse. Mr Perceval cannot presume to form any opinion upon the proper application of that sum, but he ventures humbly to submit to your Majesty's consideration how far it might be expedient for your Majesty to direct this sum to be paid to her Majesty's Treasury in relief of that immediate pressure which Mr Mathias represents as being so peculiarly urgent at the present moment. If no other means should occur to be possible for relieving the remainder of her Majesty's debts, at least the amount to be taken from that Fund will be diminished. (15442-4)

[*The King's reply, Windsor Castle, 18 June.*] The King has received Mr Perceval's letter and he feels too desirous that the Queen should be relieved from the difficulties which are therein represented, not readily to acquiesce in Mr Perceval's

---

[1] On 22 May 1810, Anna Maria Dashwood (1785–1857), daughter of Sir Henry Watkin Dashwood, 3rd Bart., of Kirtlington, Oxon., married John, Marquess of Ely (1770–1845), who succeeded his father as 2nd Marquess on 22 March 1806. Eventually she became a Lady of the Bedchamber to Queen Adelaide.

proposal that the sum to be paid into the Privy Purse by the Receiver of Gibraltar should be appropriated to that purpose in aid of any further amount to be taken from the droits of Admiralty, and which his Majesty will order accordingly. (15444)

4209 THE QUEEN *to the* KING

[*Undated* [? *June 1810*].] When your Majesty was so gracious some years ago to grant me a sum of money to pay my debts, you asked me if that was the true state of my affairs, & I said yes with a good conscience, for such it was that Lord Ailesbury stated it, but when Mathias received the money, who, I am sorry to say, was not consulted, he told me it would not pay all. The thing was done & could not be altered & after all the reductions being made by the advice of the latter, there are still some debts remaining which are very pressing. Unknown to me, owing to the intimacy between Mr. Percyvil & Mathias, the former was spoke to by him & the moment I was informed of it I wrote a letter to the Chancellor of the Exchequer desiring him not to name it as I was perfectly sensible that so many of the other branches of the family were were [*sic*] then in great distress, but as Mr. M. had spoken he had now my leave to lay before him the whole state of my affairs that he might be convinced that it was not by any foolish gratification my distress arose, & as he had formerly passed my accounts as my Solicter-General [*sic*], he would be better able to enter into it than anybody else. On Wednesday last Mathias came to inform me that M. P. [*sic*] had sent for him to say that he believed there was now a moment that he could propose to yr. Majesty a means of assisting me in a manner to pay off the most pressing demands & that he would have named it on Wednesday last had he not by my letter of last year being desired never to mention it without my informing you of it myself. If therefore yr. Majesty will, if you think fit, grant this request, Mr. P. will represent it on Wednesday if you will give him an opportunity to do so, & I shall let him know that I have informed you of it.

I have desired Elyza to read you my letter as it is out of my power to speak for myself, & tho' I have the highest oppinion of C[olonel] Taylor I thought anything between yr. M. & me was better to remain amongst ourselves.

I will not detain yr. M. any longer with such an unpleasant epistle but throw myself entirely upon yr. goodness, being convinced that you will always be just & kind to [&c.]. (36556)

4210 SPENCER PERCEVAL *to the* KING, *and the reply*

[*Downing St., 19 June 1810*.] Mr Perceval acquaints your Majesty that as he supposes your Majesty would think the appointment to the Mastership of the Household (if given as your Majesty intended it should be to a Member of Parliament) should take place before the Session is closed, he humbly submits to your Majesty that Mr Kenrick,[1] the Member for Bletchingley & the son of Dr Kenrick,

---

[1] William Kenrick (1774–1829), Tory M.P. for Bletchingley, 1806–14; Master of the Household, 1810–12. He necessarily vacated his seat and was re-elected on 28 June. His father was the Rev. Jarvis

the proprietor of that borough, would be well suited to the appointment if your Majesty should be graciously pleased to approve of it. Mr Kenrick is a lawyer and perfectly competent to discharge the duties of the situation. (15445)

[*The King's reply, Windsor Castle, 20 June.*] The King readily acquiesces in Mr Perceval's proposal that Mr Kenrick the Member for Bletchingly should succeed to the Mastership of the Household. (15446)

4211   RICHARD RYDER *to the* KING, *and the reply*

[*Whitehall, 19 June 1810.*] Mr Ryder has the honor of informing your Majesty that your Majesty's confidential servants met this morning to consider the Speech which it might be proper to deliver in your Majesty's name on the prorogation of Parliament, and he has now the honor of transmitting to your Majesty the draft which they agreed upon as proper to be humbly submitted to your Majesty's gracious consideration. (15447)

[*The King's reply, Windsor Castle, 20 June.*] The King approves of the Speech to be delivered in his name in [*sic*] the prorogation of Parliament of which Mr Ryder has submitted the draft. (15448)

4212   LORD ELDON *to the* KING

[*Wednesday, 20 June 1810.*] The Lord Chancellor, offering his humble duty to your Majesty, has the honour to transmit a Commission for passing Bills and a Commission for proroguing the Parliament to receive your Majesty's Royal Sign Manual, if your Majesty shall graciously so please. (15449)

4213   RICHARD RYDER *to the* KING, *and the reply*

[*Whitehall, Friday, 2.15 a.m., 22 June 1810.*] Mr Ryder has the honor of informing your Majesty that it had been previously arranged with the Earl of Moira that a flag should be hoisted on the shot manufactory on the Surry [*sic*] side of the Thames within view of the Tower as soon as the Speaker had left the Bar of the House of Lords. This signal was made about half past three o'clock, when Sir Francis Burdett's intention of going by water was announced, and he immediately left the Tower in company with three other persons. Two other persons were deputed by Sir Francis Burdett to inform the mob who were assembled in very great numbers on Tower Hill, of his departure. The populace appeared at first disposed to disperse in different directions: but a large proportion of them collected together towards the streets leading to the west end of the town, and moved in procession through the City, their numbers encreasing as they advanced through Newgate Street and the Strand.

Kenrick (1737–1809), Vicar of Chilham, Kent, from 1762 until his death, and the brother of the Rev. Matthew Kenrick, LL.D. (1736–1803), Rector of the Parish from 1775 until his death.

Mr Gale Jones, who had been liberated from Newgate immediately after the prorogation, joined the procession at the corner of Northumberland Street, and proceeded with it to Sir Francis Burdett's house in Piccadilly where they arrived about half past six o'clock and then he made a speech to the mob from the roof of a hackney coach and then went to his house in Somers Town.

The mob afterwards spread themselves through Piccadilly & the Haymarket, and in those streets and in those only, Mr Ryder is informed there was at one time a partial illumination during part of the evening, and several persons were taken up by the constables for breaking windows. About midnight a large detachment of the mob went up the Strand calling for lights and broke some windows in or near Catherine Street, and there several individuals were apprehended by the officers from Bow Street and the mob dispersed.

These are the only instances of outrage of which any information has yet reached Mr Ryder, and they were speedily and easily suppressed by the intervention of the civil power without the necessity of calling in the assistance of the military. Mr Ryder has the satisfaction of humbly submitting to your Majesty that the reports he has continued to receive every two hours from the Magistrates stationed in every other quarter of the town have uniformly concurred in the statement that no disposition to acts of violence had manifested itself in the several districts committed to their immediate care, and that the precautions which have been adopted have succeeded not only in repressing any such disposition but in preventing that insult to the law which must have resulted from a general and compulsory illumination. (15451–2)

[*The King's reply, Windsor Castle, 22 June.*] The King acknowledges the receipt of Mr Ryder's report of the occurrences in London yesterday, connected with the liberation of Sir Francis Burdett from the Tower, which has proved very satisfactory to his Majesty. (15453)

4214 SPENCER PERCEVAL *to the* KING, *and the reply*

[*Downg. St., 26 June 1810.*] Mr Perceval acquaints your Majesty that Mr Robt. Walpole who was so long in your Majesty's service at Lisbon,[1] has lately died and left a widow & several children in a state of absolute poverty & want. Mr Perceval has enquired into the state of the Pension List, and he finds that it is in a state which will enable him to submit to your Majesty that if your Majesty should be graciously pleased to grant Mrs Walpole a pension it may be granted to her to the extent of £800 pr anm. (15455)

[*The King's reply, Queen's Palace, 27 June.*] The King approves of Mr Perceval's proposal that a pension of eight hundred pounds per annum should be granted to Mrs Walpole. (15455)

[1] As Minister to Portugal, 1772–1800. He was the fourth son of Horatio, Lord Walpole (1678–1757), younger brother of Walpole, the Prime Minister. He died on 19 April 1810, aged 74. In 1785 he married, as his second wife, Sophia, daughter of Richard Sturt. She died in June 1829, the mother of eight sons.

4215 THE EARL OF LIVERPOOL *to the* KING, *and the reply*

[*Fife House, 26 June 1810.*] Lord Liverpool begs leave most humbly to submit to your Majesty the drafts of dispatches which it is proposed with your Majesty's gracious approbation to send to Major-Genl. Layard[1] in consequence of the events which have recently occurr'd in the province of Venezuela in South America.[2] (15456)

[*The King's reply, Queen's Palace, 27 June.*] The King has read the instructions to Major-General Layard which Lord Liverpool has submitted, and his Majesty highly approves not only the sentiments which they convey, which are worthy of this country, but also the excellent style and language in which they are expressed. (15456)

4216 PRINCESS AMELIA *to the* KING, *and the reply*

[*Tuesday* [*26 June 1810*].] I cannot help just troubling you with two lines myself to say I am moved into the other room & lying on the bed & everything is very comfortable & done with no trouble to me, though I have given much to many others. Dear Miny will give you an account of me, tho' there is little new to say. It has certainly been a languid day, but I cannot add more than kind & affte. duty & love to all. (Add. Georgian 14/198)

[*The King's reply, Queen's Palace, 27 June.*] I am truly sensible of your kind attention in giving me the comfort of hearing from yourself that you have been moved into the other room without inconvenience & without suffering from the exertion. I rejoyce in the thought that my absence from you will not be long and I hope to receive a good account when I return to you tomorrow. The Queen desires her love to you. (Add. Georgian 14/199)

4217 PRINCESS MARY *to the* KING, *and the reply*

[*Tuesday night* [*26 June 1810*].] I am most happy in being able to say that Amelia likes her change of room very much, finds the bed most comfortable and it was all very quietly done without any noise or hurry. She has passed a very tolerable day, all things considered, languid and depressed at times but inclined to be cheerful when the pain in the side & head allowed her to enjoy herself for a moment. She was up for an hour in the middle of the day & again this evening for half an hour. She has felt the great change of weather today very much, so much so as to desire to have a fire in her room, which really was necessary for it felt quite cold this evening.

[1] Anthony Lewis Layard (*d.* 1823). Major, 1791; Lieutenant-Colonel, 1795; Colonel, 1802; Major-General, 1809; Lieutenant-General, 1814.

[2] On 19 April the *cabildo* of Caracas ousted the Spanish Captain-General and organised a Junta to rule in the name of Ferdinand VII. On 5 July 1811 the King's rights were abandoned and the independence of Venezuela was proclaimed.

Wednesday morning. Amelia has had about two hours sleep in all, suffered a good deal from pains in the side & faintness and complains of a good deal of heat in her inside, but is much as usual this morning. (Add. Georgian 12/160)

[*The King's reply, Queen's Palace, 27 June.*] I return you many thanks for your kind letter and have received with pleasure the account which it conveys of dear Amelia, as it appears to me upon the whole satisfactory, particularly from her having borne so well the exertion of moving into the other room, which, thanks to your usual good management, appears to have been free from trouble to her. (Add. Georgian 12/161)

4218 DOCTOR POPE *to* LIEUT.-COLONEL TAYLOR

[*Augusta Lodge, 27th [June 1810].*] Dr. Pope respectfully requests that Lt.-Coll. Taylor will be pleas'd to inform the King that the Princess Amelia slept about two hours & an half during the night, has taken a sufft. quantity of nutriment & had one good natural evacuation. She was remov'd into the adjoining room yesterday to sleep & finds the room comfortable; the pain in the side remains as usual. (Add. Georgian 14/200)

4219 THE KING *to* CHARLES YORKE

[*Windsor Castle, 30 June 1810.*] In consequence of the recommendation of the court martial and what is stated by Mr Yorke,[1] the King consents to extend his pardon to Thomas Bayntum [*sic*]. (15457)

4220 LORD MULGRAVE *to the* KING, *and the reply*

[*London, 2 July 1810.*] Lord Mulgrave begs most humbly to submit for your Majesty's pleasure the appointment of Captain Moorsom of the Royal Navy to be Surveyor-General of the Ordnance in the place of Colonel Hadden. The desire naturally felt by Mr Yorke to have the assistance of his brother Sir Joseph Yorke at the Board of Admiralty has left Captain Moorsom at liberty to undertake the duties of Surveyor-General of the Ordnance, and the experience which Lord Mulgrave had of the great talents for business and indefatigable activity of Captain Moorsom induces him to be desirous of availing himself of those qualities in the Department which your Majesty has been graciously pleased to commit to his care. Without intending in any degree to derogate from the merits of Colonel Hadden, Lord Mulgrave does not conceal from your Majesty that being in no habits of intimacy or practice of business with any member of the Board of Ordnance, he feels that he shall more effectually promote your Majesty's service by having the assistance of a person of whose talents for business he has had recent & advantageous experience; & on whose cordial and zealous cooperation he can place an entire reliance. (15458-9)

---

[1] His letter seems to be missing.

[*The King's reply, Windsor Castle, 3 July.*] Under the circumstances which Lord Mulgrave has stated, the King acquiesces in his recommendation of Captain Moorsom of the Navy for the appointment of Surveyor-General of the Ordnance. (15459)

4221   LORD ELDON *to the* KING

[*3 July 1810.*] The Lord Chancellor, offering his most humble duty to your Majesty, has the honour to transmit a paper appointing your Majesty's Judges to go their respective Circuits, and another paper, adding Serjeants & others to the Judges upon their respective Circuits, to receive your Majesty's Sign Manual, if your Majesty shall graciously so please. (15460)

4222   THE MARQUESS WELLESLEY *to the* KING

[*Foreign Office, 3 July 1810.*] Lord Wellesley has the honor to submit to your Majesty the copies of several letters from the Queen of Naples to different persons at Vienna on the subject of the marriage of the Archduchess Maria Louisa.[1] These letters were delivered to Lord Wellesley by Prince Castelcicala at his last conference. (15461)

4223   SPENCER PERCEVAL *to the* KING, *and the reply*

[*Downg. St., 5 July 1810.*] Mr Perceval acquaints your Majesty that he has received information that her Royal Highness the Princess Charlotte of Wales is desirous of going to the seaside, and that her Royal Highness's income will not enable her to bear the expence of such an excursion without the assistance which his Majesty has been graciously pleased to grant to her Royal Highness on former similar occasions. Mr Perceval believes that the sum which his Majesty has directed on such occasions to be paid is one thousand pounds, and Mr Perceval wishes to receive his Majesty's pleasure whether he should direct a warrant to be prepared for issuing that sum to her Royal Highness's Treasurer.[2] (15462)

[*The King's reply, Windsor Castle, 6 July.*] The King approves of Mr Perceval's directing a warrant to be prepared for one thousand pounds to defray the expence of the Princess Charlotte of Wales's excursion to the seaside. (15463)

4224   *Letters from the* MARQUESS WELLESLEY *to the* KING, *and the replies*

[*Foreign Office, 6 July 1810.*] Lord Wellesley has the honor to submit the Persian Treaty of Alliance (of which your Majesty has already received a copy) for your Majesty's royal signature. He also has the honor to send the draft of a letter to the King of Persia for your Majesty's gracious approbation. (15464)

[1] Daughter of the Emperor Francis I of Austria, she married Napoleon on 2 April 1810. (1791–1847.) In 1822, the year after Napoleon's death, she married her lover, Adam Albert, Count Neipperg (1775–1829).   [2] Henry Norton Willis was the Princess's Comptroller and Paymaster.

[*The King's reply, Windsor Castle, 7 July.*] The King approves the letter to the King of Persia of which Lord Wellesley has submitted the draft, and his Majesty returns the Treaty of Alliance with his signature. (15464)

[*From Lord Wellesley, Foreign Office, 7 July.*] Lord Wellesley has the honor to submit for your Majesty's gracious approbation the draft of instructions to Sir Gore Ouseley, your Majesty's Ambassador to the King of Persia. (15465)

[*The King's reply, Windsor Castle, 8 July.*] The King approves of the instructions to Sir Gore Ouseley & Mr Morier which Lord Wellesley has submitted. (15465)

4225   CHARLES YORKE *to the* KING, *and the reply*

[*Admy., 7 July 1810.*] Mr Yorke finds himself under the necessity of laying the proceedings of the naval court martial upon the deserters from your Majesty's ship *Defiance* a second time before your Majesty, together with the opinions of the Attorney and Sollicitor-Generals & of the Council to the Admiralty upon some circumstances of their case, which has induced the Law Officers to recommend the commutation of their punishment to *transportation for life*. And Mr Yorke humbly recommends it to your Majesty to approve of this recommendation of the Crown lawyers. (15466)

[*The King's reply, Windsor Castle, 8 July.*] The King acquiesces in the recommendation of Mr Yorke, submitted in consequence of the opinions of the Crown lawyers & the Council to the Admiralty, that the sentence of death passed upon the three deserters from the Defiance should be commuted to transportation for life. (15467)

4226   *Letters from the* MARQUESS WELLESLEY *to the* KING, *and the replies*

[*Foreign Office, 9 July 1810.*] Lord Wellesley has the honor to submit to your Majesty the request of the Persian Envoy to be permitted to have his audience of leave on Wednesday next, preparatory to his departure for Persia. At the same time, with your Majesty's gracious permission, Lord Wellesley proposes to present to your Majesty Sir Gore Ouseley & the gentlemen attached to your Majesty's Embassy to the King of Persia, who will accompany the Envoy on his return to the presence of his Sovereign. (15468)

[*The King's reply, Windsor Castle, 10 July.*] The King approves of Lord Wellesley's proposal that the Persian Envoy should have his audience of leave tomorrow, and that Sir Gore Ouseley and the gentlemen attached to the Embassy to Persia should be presented upon the same occasion. (15469)

[*From Lord Wellesley, Foreign Office, 12 July.*] Lord Wellesley has the honor to submit for your Majesty's gracious approbation the draft of a dispatch to your Majesty's Minister in Spain, on the subject of the late transactions in the Province of Venezuela in South America. (15470)

4227 SPENCER PERCEVAL *to the* KING, *and the reply*

[*12 July 1810.*] Mr Perceval humbly acquaints your Majesty that upon enquiry he has satisfied himself that there is not according to former precedent any necessity that the Attorney-General of the Duchy of Lancaster should have rank as one of your Majesty's Counsel; and therefore he presumes to recommend for your Majesty's approbation William Walton, Senr. Barr. at law to succeed Mr Orde[1] in that office, Mr Orde having asked your Majesty's permission to retire from it. Mr Perceval herewith transmits for your Majesty's signature the warrant directing a Bill to be prepared for the grant of that office accordingly, if your Majesty should graciously please to approve of the appointment. Mr Walton has for many years been the Senior Counsel in the Duchy, and having been uniformly consulted in all legal & equitable questions arising in your Majesty's Duchy since Mr Perceval has had the honor of holding the office of your Majesty's Chancellor for that Duchy, Mr Perceval is enabled to speak with great confidence to Mr Walton's ability & fitness for the office.

Your Majesty's patent granting the office of Chancellor of the Duchy, authorising that officer to appoint the auditors, Mr Perceval has no occasion to trouble your Majesty for the signature of the necessary instruments for appointing Mr Bramston & Mr Mitford auditors in the places of Mr Popham and Mr. Newbolt, whose resignations Mr Perceval mentioned to your Majesty on Wednesday sevnnight.

Mr Perceval has caused a warrant to be prepared which he transmits for your Majesty's signature, for paying a retiring allowance to Mr Popham upon his quitting his office of North Auditor[2] in your Majesty's Duchy, pursuant to your Majesty's pleasure graciously expressed to Mr Perceval on this subject on last Wednesday sevnnight. The average profit of that office for the last three years having been £250 pr. anm. the warrant is prepared for that sum. Mr Perceval is sorry to repeat to your Majesty that from what he learns of the state of Mr Popham's health, it is not likely that he should continue long to enjoy this appointment.

Mr Perceval also transmits for your Majesty's signature the Commissions appointing Sr Allan Chambre, and Sr. Robt. Graham, Judges of Assize for the County Palatine of Lancaster; and also a warrant upon the Treasurer of the Duchy for the payment of the sum of £3000 into your Majesty's Privy Purse. (15471–2)

[1] John Orde.
[2] Alexander Popham is described in the Red Book simply as Auditor, but there were Auditors for the North and the South of the Duchy.

[*The King's reply, Windsor Castle, 13 July.*] The King entirely approves of the various arrangements & appointments which Mr Perceval has submitted as Chancellor for the Duchy of Lancaster, and H.M. returns the several warrants which he has signed. (15473)

4228 *Letters from the* MARQUESS WELLESLEY *to the* KING, *and the replies*

[*Foreign Office, 14 July 1810.*] Lord Wellesley has the honor to acquaint your Majesty of the arrival of Major Armstrong, one of your Majesty's Military Agents in Spain with dispatches from Mr Wellesley now forwarded to your Majesty. Major Armstrong also brought the box of medals now sent to your Majesty for your Majesty's gracious acceptance from the City of Mexico. From Major Armstrong's report it appears that the French were actively employed in completing their works before Cadiz, but had not received any reinforcement. The Duke of Orleans had not obtained any influence at Cadiz, & his departure seemed to be equally desired by the Government & the people. Lord Wellesley has the honor to inform your Majesty that Deputies from the new Government of the Province of Venezuela in South America are arrived at Portsmouth & on their way to London where, on their arrival, it is proposed to regulate such communications as may be held with them according to the principles stated in the dispatch from Lord Liverpool to Br.-Genl Layard & from Lord Wellesley at Cadiz, already submitted to your Majesty's gracious approbation. (15474-5)

[*The King's reply, Windsor Castle, 15 July.*] The King acknowledges the receipt of Lord Wellesley's letter reporting the arrival of Major Armstrong from Cadiz, & of a box of medals from the City of Mexico. H.M. approves of the principle upon which Lord Wellesley proposes to regulate his communications with the Deputies from the Province of Venezuela. (15475)

[*From Lord Wellesley, Foreign Office, 22 July.*] Lord Wellesley has the honor to submit for your Majesty's gracious approbation the draft of a dispatch to Mr Wellesley at Cadiz conveying your Majesty's commands respecting the recent applications of Spain for a loan, and the terms of a proposed regulation or convention of commerce. (15476)

[*The King's reply, Windsor Castle, 23 July.*] The King approves the dispatch which Lord Wellesley has prepared for Mr Wellesley respecting the recent applications for a loan, and the terms of a proposed convention of commerce. (15476)

[*From Lord Wellesley, Foreign Office, 26 July.*] Lord Wellesley has the honor to submit to your Majesty that it is become necessary to appoint a Consul to reside in the Island of Iceland, and he humbly recommends that Mr John Parke be appointed to that situation. (15477)

[*The King's reply, Windsor Castle, 27 July.*] The King approves of Lord Wellesley's recommendation that Mr John Parke should be named to reside as Consul in the Island of Iceland. (15477)

[*From Lord Wellesley, Foreign Office, 2 Aug.*] Lord Wellesley has the honor to submit for your Majesty's gracious approbation the draft of a dispatch to Mr Wellesley, on the subject of the French prisoners lately removed from Cadiz to England. (15478)

[*From Lord Wellesley, Foreign Office, 2 Aug.*] Lord Wellesley has the honor to submit to your Majesty for your Majesty's gracious approbation, the draft of an unofficial Memorandum proposed to be delivered to the Commissioners from the Caraccas & to the Spanish Ministers, on the subject of the Mission from the Supreme Junta at Venezuela to your Majesty. (15479)

[*The King's reply, Windsor Castle, 3 Aug.*] The King entirely approves of the communications which Lord Wellesley has prepared to be delivered to the Commissioners from the Caraccas & to the Spanish Ministers & also of his dispatch to Mr Wellesley on the subject of the French prisoners removed from Cadiz. (15479)

[*From Lord Wellesley, Foreign Office, 6 Aug.*] Lord Wellesley has the honor to acquaint your Majesty that Captain Fabian[1] of the Mutine, arrived this morning from Buenos Ayres, brings intelligence of a revolution at that place, nearly similar to the late transactions at the Caraccas. Letters have been received from the Junta of Buenos Ayres, addressed to your Majesty's Secretary of State for the Foreign Department, of the same tenor as those recently received from the Caraccas. The manuscript & printed papers from Buenos Ayres are voluminous & principally in the Spanish language: they will be forwarded to your Majesty as soon as they can be properly prepared. Lord Wellesley deems it to be his duty however to submit to your Majesty, that the general tenor of this intelligence strongly confirms the propriety of the determination which your Majesty has been pleased to take respecting the Province of Venezuela. (15480)

[*The King's reply, Windsor Castle, 7 Aug.*] The King concurs with Lord Wellesley in the observation which he makes in consequence of the communications from Captain Fabian of a revolution in Buenos Ayres. H.M. regrets that this spirit is becoming so general in South America, and agrees with Mr Jackson in the opinion that it is the policy of France to encourage it. (15481)

[*From Lord Wellesley, Foreign Office, 14 Aug.*] Lord Wellesley has the honor to acquaint your Majesty that M. de Sousa, Envoy from Portugal, has desired to present his Credentials as Ambassador Extraordinary & Plenipotentiary to your

---

[1] Charles Montagu Fabian. Lieutenant, 1795; Commander, 1802; Captain, 21 Oct. 1810. Wellesley, then, should apparently have styled him Commander.

Majesty, notwithstanding the intimation of your Majesty's intention not to return the Embassy; according to your Majesty's commands (after having in the most distinct terms declared to M. de Sousa that the Embassy could not be returned) Lord Wellesley, in obedience to your Majesty's pleasure, informed M. de Sousa that your Majesty would graciously receive his Credentials in his new character after the Levée to morrow.

Lord Wellesley, therefore, proposes, with your Majesty's permission (under the reserve already stated to M. de Sousa) to present him to your Majesty after the Levée to morrow, in the character of Ambassador Extraordinary & Plenipotentiary. (15482–3)

[*The King's reply, Windsor Castle, 15 Aug.*] The King approves of Lord Wellesley's presenting M. de Sousa this day, after the Levée in the character of Ambassador Extraordinary & Plenipotentiary, under the reserve that the Embassy will not be returned by his Majesty. (15483)

4229   *Letters from* SPENCER PERCEVAL *to the* KING, *and the reply*

[*Downg. St., 15 Aug. 1810.*] Mr Perceval acquaints your Majesty that the Vicarage of Sherborne in Dorsetshire is become vacant, and that Sir J. Johnston[1] has recommended the Revd. Wm. Gorton as a person whom he wishes very much should be presented to that Vicarage, and as Mr Perceval understands that both Sr. Wm. & Sr. James Pulteney had procured the promise of Lord Sidmouth & Mr. Pitt that they would recommend him to your Majesty for this Vicarage should it become vacant in their time, Mr Perceval thinks he cannot do less by Sr. J. Johnstone who has lately succeeded to the Pulteney property in Dorsetshire, than comply with his request. (15484)

[*The King's reply, Windsor Castle, 16 Aug.*] The King approves of Mr Perceval's recommendation of the Revd. Wm. Gorton for the Vicarage of Sherborne in Dorsetshire. His Majesty knows Mr. Gorton, whose character has always been represented to him as very respectable, but who appeared to him as indifferent a reader as ever he heard. (15485)

[*From Perceval, Downing Street, 17 Aug.*] Mr Perceval encloses for your Majesty's consideration a list of a few small pensions, together with the grounds on which he submits them for your Majesty's gracious approbation. (15486)

[*The King's reply, Windsor Castle, 18 Aug.*] The King entirely approves of the list of small pensions which Mr Perceval has submitted, the claims upon which they are grounded appearing to his Majesty very reasonable. (15486)

[1] Probably Sir John Lowther Johnstone (c. 1783–1811), 6th Baronet, M.P. for Weymouth and Melcombe Regis, 1810–11. On 18 Jan. 1804 he married Charlotte, youngest daughter of Charles Gordon. Sir William Pulteney, the 5th Baronet, was his uncle (on marrying an heiress, Miss Pulteney, Sir William had changed his name from Johnstone).

[*From Perceval, Downg. St., 24 Aug. 1810.*] Mr Perceval humbly submits to your Majesty for your gracious approbation a list of Scotch pensions which Mr Perceval presumes to recommend to yr. Majesty after much communication with Mr Dundas upon the respective merits and claims of the persons for whom the application is made. This list will exhaust the sum of £800 which is the total annual sum which your Majesty is empowered to grant in one year from the Civil List of Scotland under the late regulation. (15490)

[*The King's reply, Windsor Castle, 25 Aug.*] The King approves the list of Scotch pensions which Mr Perceval has recommended to be granted from the Civil List in Scotland. (15490)

[*'Small Pensions' (Enclosure*).] Miss Sophia Maria Byron—is the daughter of the late Admiral Byron[1]—she is represented to Mr Perceval as being in a very bad state of health and in very low circumstances; and burthened with the charge of supporting several orphan nephews and nieces. Mr Perceval humbly recommends her for a pension of one hundred & fifty pounds pr. an. £150

Mrs. Courtland—aged 65—she is the wife of Col. Courtland who is 71 years old. He is now the Barrack Master at Hailsham, and enjoys a pension from your Majesty as an American Loyalist of one hundred pounds per annum. They have had *23 children*, most of whom are represented to be still alive. The particular circumstance which has brought forward this application is, that they have recently had the charge of *13 grandchildren* brought upon them—and it is stated that a pension of one hundred pounds per annum net to Mrs Courtland would afford them great and substantial relief. Mr Perceval humbly recommends it. £100

Martinus de Vries—was a physician at Walcheren some years ago when your Majesty's forces were in that Island under Lord Mulgrave. Mr. de Vries was upon that occasion very active in affording them every assistance in his power, and when the French came there, and when they understood the service he had been of to your Majesty's subjects, they deprived him of his property & he was obliged to quit his country. He has been in England several years endeavouring to live upon the means which he brought over with him. These means are now exhausted and he is in great distress. In consideration of the service which he did to your Majesty's troops, and of the loss which he sustained in consequence, Mr Perceval presumes to recommend him to your Majesty for a pension of one hundred and fifty pounds per anm. £150

Mr Tarrant—was Senior Clerk extraordinary of the Privy Council—he has been a long time resident in the country. Upon the retirement of Sr. Stephen Cottrell Lord Camden ascertained from Mr Tarrant himself that his habits of life rendered him wholly incompetent to discharge the duties of the office of Clerk-in-Ordinary. Had the new arrangement not taken place in your Majesty's Privy Council Office reducing the number of the clerks in ordinary, and had the same indulgence been granted to Mr Tarrant which has been to some of his predecessors,

---

[1] John Byron (1723–86), second son of William, 4th Lord Byron. Captain, 1746; Rear-Admiral, 1775; Vice-Admiral, 1778. His eldest son was the father of Lord Byron, the poet.

and which therefore he might not very unreasonably have expected, he might have been enabled to make an arrangement with his brother clerks-in-ordinary, by which, leaving them to discharge his duty, he might have secured to himself an allowance of something better than two hundred pounds pr. anm. Perhaps your Majesty will be graciously pleased to think that under these circumstances, it will be little more than an act of justice to Mr. Tarrant to grant him a pension to that amount. £200

The Dowr. Lady Trimblestown[1] [sic] has already a small pension, she used also till lately to have one hundred pounds allowed to her annually out of the Concordation Fund of Ireland. This fund has been by a late regulation strictly reserved for such objects of charity as had no other income—and small as her Ladyship's income is, this regulation has deprived her of that £100 pr an., the loss of which she feels most severely. Mr Perceval would only recommend the granting to her Ladyship a pension to a similar amount. £100

Sir John Peter has formerly served your Majesty abroad as a Consul. He has been for many years a Comssr. of Exchequer Bills.[2] Upon the occasion of the last funding of Exchequer Bills, he was indiscreet enough to give some special accommodation to some of his acquaintance and friends, which, tho not so intended by him, had in fact an injurious operation upon the interests of other persons who wanted to fund theirs. It made a considerable noise at the time & required a special Act of Parliament to set it right.[3] A Committee of the Ho. of Co. was appointed to enquire into the circumstances, and altho they do not report anything against the integrity of Sr. J. Peter or impute any corrupt motive to him, yet they report very strongly against his irregularity. Mr Perceval thinks it would be highly injurious to the character of your Majesty's service to attempt to support Sr. J. Peter in his situation after such conduct, and he has therefore recommended to the Treasury to remove him. But not seeing any reason to suspect him of any corrupt motive, and believing that his removal in his advanced age & declining health will be extremely inconvenient to him, Mr Perceval ventures to recommend him to your Majesty for a pension of £300 pr. an. His salary was 400. £300

Mr Perceval would have had to add to this list the name of Capt. Grey, who served in your Majesty's army in the East Indies, and was seized there with the palsy. But having mentioned his intention at the Treasury of recommending him to your Majesty for a pension of one hundred & thirty pounds pr. anm. he was misunderstood as if your Majesty's pleasure had already been taken upon that grant—and the warrant was therefore sent down to your Majesty above a week ago and has been signed by your Majesty. £130

[1] The Trimleston peerage had been forfeited by the Jacobite 10th Earl in 1691. The so-called 12th Baron Trimlestown [I.], who died in 1779, married, as his third wife, Anne (c. 1758–1831), niece of the Rev. James Hervey, and daughter of a London merchant, William Hervey. His son Thomas (d. 1796, aged 60) recovered the title, as 13th Baron Trimleston, in 1795.

[2] From about 1794 onwards. He is listed as a K.M.H. in the Royal Kalendar for 1810. His colleagues in the Exchequer Bill Office were Joseph Planta and John Cudlipp (as they had been as far back as 1795). In 1784 John Peter, Esq., was Consul at Ostend, Nieuport and Bruges, and in the Lower Rhine Circle.

[3] On 2 June 1803 leave was given to bring in a Bill for remedying certain defects that had occurred in the issuing of certain Exchequer Bills. (H. of C. J., LVIII, 470.) It received the royal assent on 24 June. (Ibid., p. 542.)

The warrant which accompanies this paper for a pension to Mrs. Darell is only renewing a pension which having been granted for her benefit in the name of two trustees who are dead, would be lost to her if it was not re-granted. (15487-9)

[*List of Scottish pensions* (*Enclosure, 24 Aug.*).]

£200   Miss Campbell—the daughter of Sr. Ilay Campbell—late President of the Court of Sessions.

£50   Mrs. Fordyce—the mother of Major Fordyce[1] who was killed at the battle of Talavera.

£100   Mrs. Imlach, widow. Miss Mary—Jane—and Helen Fordyce—the four sisters of Major Fordyce—this family is represented to Mr. Perceval as being deprived of almost the whole means of their dependence by the death of Major Fordyce.

£60   Miss Jean & Ann Macquarrie.

£30   Miss Janet—Margaret & Ann Young, daughters of the late Revd. Dr. J. Young of Hawick.

£30   Miss Anna Munro Ross of Kindeare.

£100   Mrs Henrietta Wharton Mackenzie of Suddie, only surviving sister of Major-Genl. Randoll Mackenzie who died in Spain[2]—a very deserving officer and whose sister depended upon him.

£30   Miss Fergusson.

£100   Mrs Outram, daughter of Dr. Anderson.

£100   Mrs Stewart, wife of Mr David Steward [*sic*] of Edinburgh.
The relatives of persons deserving well of yr. Majesty for their loyalty & services. (15491)

[*From Perceval, Downg. St., 28 Aug.*] Mr Perceval acquaints your Majesty that Sir Alexr. Munro, one of the Commissioners of Customs, is lately dead[3]—and Mr Perceval humbly submits to your Majesty that Mr. Dean, one of your Majesty's Police Magistrates, who is a barrister and a man of great respectability & talent, would be properly appointed to succeed him, if your Majesty should be graciously pleased to approve of his appointment.[4] (15492)

4230   RICHARD RYDER *to the* KING, *and the reply*

[*Whitehall, 30 Aug. 1810.*] In obedience to your Majesty's Order-in-Council of the 25th of January, a copy of which Mr Ryder has the honor of enclosing to your Majesty, Mr Ryder humbly submits to your Majesty a list of the names of persons proper to be the first officers of the Corporation under the new Charter which your Majesty has been graciously pleased to grant to the borough of Malden.[5] (15493)

---

[1] Alexander Fordyce. Captain, June 1804; Major, Jan. 1805. At the time of his death he was Deputy Adjutant-General.

[2] MacKenzie was killed at the battle of Talavera, 28 July 1809. He was about 47 years of age. See No. 3844.   [3] He died on the 26th, aged 83.

[4] Richard Betenson Dean was appointed a Commissioner of Customs.

[5] Maldon had forfeited its Charter 46 years earlier for various illegal practices, and during that period the High Sheriff of Essex had acted as returning officer at parliamentary elections. The new Charter was obtained at an estimated expense of £2,500.

[*The King's reply, Windsor Castle, 31 Aug.*] The King approves of the persons whom Mr Ryder has proposed as proper to be the first officers of the Corporation under the new Charter granted to the borough of Malden. (15493)

4231   *Letters from the* MARQUESS WELLESLEY *to the* KING, *and the replies*

[*Foreign Office, 1 Sept. 1810.*] Lord Wellesley has the honor to submit to your Majesty a letter received from Mr. Pinkney together with the draft of an answer, on the occasion of the announced repeal of the Berlin & Milan Decrees by Bonaparte. Lord Wellesley has added, for your Majesty's notice, the copy of a letter, which contains a very clear view of this question. (15494)

[*The King's reply, Windsor Castle, 2 Sept.*] The King entirely approves of Lord Wellesley's answer to Mr Pinkney, which states in very clear and concise terms the only course which this Government can adopt under the circumstances. (15494)

[*From Lord Wellesley, Foreign Office, 3 Sept.*] Lord Wellesley has the honor to submit to your Majesty a note received from Prince Castelcicala on the subject of M. de Sousa's promotion to the rank of Ambassador. Lord Wellesley has added the draft of a reply to that note for your Majesty's gracious approbation. (15495)

[*From Lord Wellesley, Foreign Office, 3 Sept.*] Lord Wellesley has the honor to request your Majesty's commands upon the application of Prince Castelcicala soliciting your Majesty's gracious sanction to the honor conferred by the King of the Two Sicilies on Sir John Carr.[1] (15496)

[*From Lord Wellesley, Foreign Office, 3 Sept.*] Lord Wellesley has the honor to submit, for your Majesty's approbation, the draft of a dispatch to Mr Stuart at Lisbon, signifying your Majesty's consent to his acceptance of a seat in the Council of Regency, recently named by the Prince Regent of Portugal. (15497)

[*The King's reply, Windsor Castle, 4 Sept.*] The King entirely approves of Lord Wellesley's answer to Prince Castelcicala's letter on the subject of M. de Sousa's promotion to the rank of Ambassador. Also of the proposed dispatch to Mr. Stuart relative to his acceptance of a seat in the Council of Regency. H.M. sanctions Sir John Carr's acceptance of the honor of the Order of St. Constantine conferred upon him by the King of the Two Sicilies. (15495)

[1] Sir John Carr (1772–1832), traveller, who published popular accounts of his tours. Knighted (in Ireland by the Lord Lieutenant, the Duke of Bedford), 9 Dec. 1806.

[*Downg. St., 28 Sept. 1810.*] Mr Perceval, conceiving that your Majesty will have heard of the death of Mr Goldsmith,[1] and be desirous of knowing the cause of it as well as the effect which that melancholy & shocking event may have produced, humbly acquaints your Majesty that it is universally supposed to have been occasioned by pecuniary embarrassment. Mr Perceval has been anxiously endeavouring to ascertain the amount of the public money which may be exposed to hazard from having been in his hands, but from the impossibility of obtaining any intelligence from Mr. Goldsmith's house in the course of this day, has not been as yet able to acquire a certain knowledge of it. Your Majesty is aware that Mr Goldsmith has been for many years constantly employed under the Treasury in the sale of the Exchequer Bills which were issued for your Majesty's naval, military, and Ordnance services. On the Army account it happened fortunately that no Exchequer Bills were in his hands—but Mr Perceval is sorry to say that on account of the Navy he held Exchequer Bills to the amount of £474,000 and about £90,000 on account of the Ordnance.

Whether Mr Goldsmith had or had not applied all or any of these Bills to his own purposes Mr Perceval was not able in the course of this day to ascertain; but he apprehends that such a degree of distress as must have been necessary to have urged Mr Goldsmith to so rash an act, will in all probability be found to have tempted him to make use of the public money. In this state of things Mr Perceval has thought it necessary to give up his intention of going into Northamptonshire, in order that he may be at hand to pursue his enquiries, and to direct such steps as may be necessary to be taken upon this melancholy & disastrous occasion.

The consternation occasioned by this event in the City was very great. The Stocks fell as low as 63[2]—and the Omnium was at one time below 10 pr ct. discount. The market mended, however, before the close of the day; the 3 pr. cts. rose to about 64 & ¼ and the discount upon the loan was about 7 & ½ or 8 per cent. (15500–1)

[*The King's reply, Windsor Castle, 29 Sept.*] The King has received Mr Perceval's letter and he entirely approves of his remaining in London to endeavor to ascertain the extent of the consequences to the public which may have resulted from the melancholy death of Mr Goldsmith. H.M. hopes that the public may not suffer to a large amount, but he cannot but fear with Mr Perceval that a man who could resort to so rash and horrid an act would not hesitate to make use of the public money under extraordinary pressure. (15501)

[*From Perceval, Downing Street, 29 Sept.*] Mr Perceval acquaints your Majesty that in consequence of his further enquiries this day into the state of Mr Goldsmith's affairs he has found that Mr Goldsmith had applied to his own purposes not less than £414,000 of Exchequer Bills—and has left great demands from

---

[1] Abraham Goldsmid (c. 1756–1810), Jewish financier. His firm (Goldsmid, Son, and Eliason) made great efforts to discharge its liabilities, and by 1820 it had paid 16/6d in the pound. He shot himself that morning.   [2] From 65½.

individuals against him; but still that his property is so extensive that unless the distress which his failure may occasion should very much depress the Funds, there are reasonable hopes that neither the public nor individuals will ultimately experience much loss. Mr Perceval encloses for your Majesty's information a state of Mr Goldsmith's accounts as made out by his surviving partner; and has prevailed upon three principal bankers, Messrs. Kensington[1]—Bainbridge—and Barnet,[2] to examine his books & see whether the account is correct. Mr Perceval has had much consultation with the Governor[3] & deputy Govr[4] of the Bank whom he is to see again on Monday morning, by which time he will have received the account of the bankers and he will have to determine what steps should be taken upon this important subject. Mr Perceval inclines at present strongly to think, that it will be adviseable not to prosecute an extent, the consequence of which if prosecuted would be to bring immediately the great mass of the public securities belonging to Mr Goldsmith & his partners into the market, & by so doing greatly to depress it to the general depreciation and injury of the whole means out of which the public & individuals may ultimately hope to be paid. Indeed he hardly can foresee the extent of mischief which an improvident sale of all these securities might produce—and however great the responsibility may be which he may incur in forbearing to press for the immediate payment of the debt to the public, he feels that it will be his duty to encounter it if upon further consideration he should continue to see the subject in the light in which it strikes him at present. Your Majesty may rest assured that he will not incur this responsibility but upon the best consideration he can give to the subject, and he is persuaded your Majesty would justly think him unworthy of the confidence which your Majesty graciously reposes in him, if the dread of such responsibility should upon an occasion which may be of such extensive importance to the public interest, prevent him from taking any step which a consideration of that interest may appear to him to require. (15502–3)

[*The King's reply, Windsor Castle, 30 Sept.*] The King is sensible of Mr Perceval's attention in entering so fully into the result of his enquiries into the state of Mr Goldsmith's affairs, & his Majesty entirely approves of every step which he has taken upon this distressing occasion, and of the principle upon which he acts, being aware that a great mass of the public securities brought into the market would by depressing the funds create general & incalculable mischief. H.M. too highly appreciates Mr Perceval's character & conduct to think for a moment that the fears of responsibility, however serious, would make him shrink from the conscientious discharge of what he conceives to be his duty. (15505)

[*From Perceval, Downing St, 2 Oct.*] Mr Perceval acquaints your Majesty that the gentlemen who undertook the examination of the account of Messrs Goldsmith and Moxon's estate, have reported to Mr Perceval that they believe

---

1 The firm of Kensington, Styan and Adams, of Lombard Street.
2 Messrs. Hoare, Barnet, Hoare and Co., of Lombard Street.
3 John Whitmore (*c.* 1750–1826), M.P. for Bridgnorth, 1795–1806.
4 John Pearse (*c.* 1760–1836), M.P. for Devizes, 1818–32.

it to be nearly correct. Mr Perceval has been much engaged both yesterday and to day in communication with the Govr. and Deputy Governor of the Bank upon this subject, and having fully advised with such of his colleagues as are in town, has determined, with their full concurrence, to withold the issuing the Crown process against the estate of these parties, in the hope of obtaining more complete payment of the public debt and of rescuing the other creditors & the public credit from the injury which would be sustained from the immediate sale of all the Government securities which belonged to Mr Goldsmith's house. As this arrangement cannot be executed without the consent of the creditors, Mr Perceval has taken the means of ascertaining their sentiments, and probably by tomorrow the matter will be settled; by which time he hopes to obtain the assistance of the Bank to the more effectual management of the property. The Funds were rather better today. Consols at 65½. (15506)

[*The King's reply, Windsor Castle, 3 Oct.*] The King has received Mr Perceval's letter and his Majesty is persuaded that the judicious & liberal conduct which he has pursued in respect to the difficulties arising from Mr Goldsmith's death will secure the public from much of the embarassment & distress which must have attended a different course. (15507)

4233   THE REV. SAMUEL BARKER, JUNIOR, *to the* KING

[*Year of Jubilee, Yarmouth, Norfolk, 6 Oct. 1810.*] Deign to pardon the very great intrusion & liberty of an humble subject, but of one the most conscientiously devoted & attached to your sacred person, when he presumes with the best intention to offer for your Majesty's acceptance a few late strawberries, a fruit which he has been frequently informed is particularly grateful to his beloved & venerable Monarch. Nothing but this consideration, added to a conviction that strawberries of this sort are scarcely, if at all, to be met with at this late season, could have prevailed upon an individual like myself to have ventured to present so insignificant a gift to so mighty & so good a Prince, & the assurance of your Majesty's known condescension & benignity to the least of your faithful subjects not only removes from me apprehensions which I must otherwise feel on this occasion, but flatters me with the hope that if your Majesty should even tacitly censure my presumption, you will place the most favourable construction upon the motives by which I have been actuated.

I do not claim as a merit what is the bounden duty of all your Majesty's liege subjects when I truly assert that my little but sincere services as long as I have been a Minister of our holy church (of which your Majesty is at once the Supreme Governor as well as its glory and its brightest ornament) have ever been invariably directed to inculcate a due reverence for your sacred person, a love of your truly kingly and Christian virtues, & a cheerful obedience to your wise & happy government.

May a conviction of the justice and the rectitude of that cause, & of those principles which have induced your Majesty to persevere in so long and arduous a contest against the disturbers of the world & the usurper of thrones, ever animate every British bosom to pant for the glory and success of your Majesty's arms & to assist your Majesty with heart & hand in bringing your prudent & laudable endeavours to the desired issue.

May integrity, talents, judgement and valour ever direct your councils, your fleets and armies! May victory attend your banners, and success your designs! May every private happiness alleviate your public cares, & may infidelity & faction, bigotry & fanaticism lie prostrate at your feet!

That the same Divine Being who has so often mercifully interposed in behalf of this favoured nation, & especially in the preservation of your Majesty's invaluable life, may grant your Majesty many years to rule over us before you are summoned 'into the joy of your Lord & Saviour', is the sincere & daily prayer of [&c].¹ (15510–11)

4234 *The* MARQUESS WELLESLEY *to the* KING,² *and the reply*

[*Ramsgate, 14 Oct.*] Lord Wellesley has the honor to submit for your Majesty's approbation, the draft of an answer to the letters received from Lucien Bonaparté. Before Lord Wellesley submitted this draft to your Majesty he thought it advisable to consult the King's Advocate; who entertains no doubt with regard to the right of detaining Lucien Bonaparté as a prisoner of war. (15512)

¹ Lord Bathurst's letter to the King of 8 Oct. seems not to have been preserved, but Taylor replied to it on the 9th, from Windsor: 'I did not fail this morning to read to the King your letter of yesterday; and his Majesty has honoured me with his comments to convey to you his sincere thanks for entering so feelingly into his present distress. It had been his Majesty's intention to have written to you this morning, to say that he should not go to town tomorrow, as at a moment of such painful suspense and agitation he cannot feel equal to engaging with due attention in the business usually connected with his presence at the Queen's Palace, and also because he considers that he is performing a most important duty in endeavouring to support and comfort his family in so awful & melancholy a period, in which he has the consolation to reflect that he is rendering himself useful to them. The King has received too deep an impression of the tenderness & affection of your feeling disposition, and he is too well assured of your sincere attachment towards him & his family not to be convinced that you sympathise in an affliction, of which he laments to think you have yourself experienced the distressing weight. He is not less sensible how much your mind is guided by the strictest principles of religion & of deference to the will of Providence, & he is therefore certain that it will be satisfactory to you to know that severe & painful as is the present trial, his Majesty supports himself with becoming resignation, and is determined to meet the melancholy event with that fortitude which a confidence in the inestimable blessings of Christian faith can alone inspire; while he also feels it to be his duty to accept it for the sake of his family, & from a sense of the duties of his own situation. These feelings are not a little strengthen'd by the comfort which he has received from observing the angelic composure and pious resignation with which his beloved daughter is prepared to meet her approaching end, and the fortitude & truly Christian devotion with which she has performed the last sacred duties.' (Bathurst MSS.)

² Richard Ryder's letter to his brother Lord Harrowby, 20 Sept., helps to account for the gap in Wellesley's correspondence (the last letter was dated 3 Sept.): 'I believe I told you in a former letter that Lord Wellesley was much better since his last illness and looks more alive and active. He comes up next week. William Hamilton says it is owing to his having offered his Lordship to clear away the accumulation of boxes of official papers at Apsley House which appeared to overwhelm him. He did so and found 70 containing all the papers of all kinds since he has been in office, most of which he has never looked at. He left him with 6 out of the 70, the rest being now mostly useless.' (Harrowby MSS.) And Wellesley wrote to Perceval from Ramsgate on 9 Oct.: 'I have greatly benefitted by the fine weather, and (although I deeply lament the cause) the King's continuance at Windsor (which I have learnt from Ryder) has given me another most useful week for the establishment of my health.' (Add. MSS. 37295, fo. 415, and Perceval MSS.)

[The King's reply, Windsor Castle, 16 Oct.] The King approves of the draft of the answer which Lord Wellesley proposes to send to Lucien Buonaparte, and his Majesty is satisfied with the clear opinion given by the King's Advocate in regard to the right of detaining Lucien Buonaparte as a prisoner of war. (15512)

4235   THE EARL OF LIVERPOOL *to the* KING, *and the reply*

[London, 15 Oct. 1810.] Lord Liverpool begs leave most humbly to communicate to your Majesty dispatches which have been received from Lt.-Genl. Oakes in consequence of the arrival of Lucien Bonaparte at Malta, and at the same time the draft of an instruction which it is proposed to send to Lt.-Genl. Oakes on that subject if it shall meet with your Majesty's approbation. (15513)

[The King's reply, Windsor Castle, 16 Oct.] The King approves of the instruction which Lord Liverpool has proposed on the subject of Lucien Buonaparte for Lieut.-General Oakes, whose proceedings appear to H.M. to have been extremely proper & sensible. In the event of Lucien Buonaparte's arrival in this country the King trusts that, in the choice of a place of residence for him, the convenience of the individual will not be alone consulted, but that care will be taken to place him and his attendants where their presence cannot in any respect be prejudicial to the interests of this country, & with this view H.M. conceives that an inland town would be most eligible. It equally occurs to him that the Transport Board should not be suffered to leave him to the charge of one of their inferior agents, but that a man whose vigilance and discretion can be relied upon should be named to reside constantly in the same place & quietly to watch the proceedings of Lucien Buonaparte: that a proper person named by the police should also be directed to attend to the conduct & proceedings of the numerous suite of servants and other persons. (15514)

4236   *Letters from* CHARLES YORKE *to the* KING, *and the replies*

[Admiralty, 17 Oct. 1810.] Mr Yorke having been unable to attend your Majesty's person this day at Windsor, on account of the business at the Admiralty, presumes to transmit the latest disposition of the Fleet for this month, which he has not had an earlier opportunity of putting into your Majesty's royal hands.

Mr Yorke requests permission to take this occasion of humbly informing your Majesty that the Board of Admiralty consider it to be expedient for your Majesty's naval service at this time to order a promotion to take place among the subordinate ranks of your Majesty's Fleet to the extent of about 30 of the oldest *Commanders*, who are now actually serving afloat, to be Post Captains; and about 20 of the senior Lieutenants, now actually serving as *First* Lieutenants of effective ships of the line, to be Commanders; the Commissions to bear date on the 21st instant, being the anniversary of the battle of Trafalgar; all which is humbly submitted for your Majesty's gracious approbation.

Mr Yorke humbly presumes to express his deep concern for the present anxiety of your Majesty & the Royal Family under the distressing circumstances of the illness of H.R.H. the Princess Amelia; and Mr Yorke earnestly hopes that it may please the Almighty to preserve H.R.H.'s life & to restore her to health. (15515-5)

[*The King's reply, Windsor Castle, 18 Oct.*] The King has received Mr Yorke's letter enclosing the disposition of the Fleet for the month, and recommending that a promotion should take place in the subordinate ranks of the Fleet, to bear date on the 21st inst., of which the King approves to the extent proposed. H.M. takes this opportunity of expressing to Mr Yorke the great satisfaction with which he has observed Mr Yorke's very active and zealous conduct in his present situation, and to assure him that he had felt fully authorized to expect those meritorious exertions from the experience which his M. had had of the able manner in which he had formerly discharged his duties as Secretary at War and Secretary of State.

The King is truly sensible of the affectionate manner in which Mr Yorke has noticed the distress under which his Majesty suffers from the precarious state of his dear daughter, and he is too well convinced of Mr Yorke's sincere attachment to himself & his family not to feel assured that he will sympathize in their feelings on this melancholy occasion.[1] (15519)

[*From Charles Yorke, Admiralty, 18 Oct.*] Mr Yorke submits to your Majesty the minutes and sentence of a court martial held on James Toole, a private marine, for an unnatural crime, together with the opinion of your Majesty's Law Officers & the Counsel to the Admiralty that 'the sentence of death pronounced in this case is not sufficiently supported by the evidence adduced.' Under these circumstances Mr Yorke humbly proposes for your Majesty's gracious consideration, whether your Majesty may not be graciously pleased to extend your royal mercy to James Toole, by commuting the capital punishment for that of transportation for life. (15517)

[*The King's reply, Windsor Castle, 19 Oct.*] In consequence of what is stated in Mr Yorke's letter and the accompanying opinion of the King's Law Officers & the Counsel to the Admiralty, his Majesty acquiesces in the recommendation that the sentence of death passed upon James Toole should be commuted for that of transportation for life. (15518)

4237 THE EARL OF LIVERPOOL *to the* KING

[*24 Oct. 1810.*] Lord Liverpool begs leave most humbly to inform your Majesty that Capt. Parkinson, Adjt. Genl. to the detachment under the command of Lt. Col. Keating,[2] is arrived with the intelligence that the Isle of Bourbon had

---

[1] The Princess died on 2 November.
[2] Henry Samuel Keating. Major, 1800; Lieutenant-Colonel, 1804.

surrender'd by capitulation to your Majesty's arms on the 8th of July last, and that the loss sustained in the operation which led to this event amounted only to sixteen rank and file killed and sixty eight rank and file wounded.

Preparations were making at the island of Rodriguez for the attack of the Mauritius as soon as reinforcements arrived from India and the Cape of Good Hope, which were expected in the course of the present month, and from the information which had been received of the state of that colony, very little doubt could be entertained of success. (15520)

4238 SPENCER PERCEVAL *to the* KING, *and the reply*

[*Ealing, 24 Oct. 1810.*] Mr. Perceval humbly acquaints your Majesty that the Vicarage of St. Mary in Warwick is vacant by the death of the late Vicar. Mr Perceval has had a strong recommendation from Lord Warwick[1] and Lord Brooke for a Mr Packwood to succeed to it, and if your Majesty pleases Mr Perceval will direct the presentation to be made out accordingly.

Mr Perceval is happy to find from Lord Arden that your Majesty is graciously pleased to approve of Mr Perceval's intention of recommending the Revd. Mr. C. Morrice[2] to a living in the City of London. Mr Perceval cannot say till he sees the Lord Chancellor, whom he expects in town before the end of the week, which of the two livings in the City it will be most convenient that Mr Morrice should be presented to.

By the death of the Revd. Mr Hodgson, the large living under your Majesty's Duchy of Lancaster, called Barwick in Elmet, is become vacant, and Mr Perceval humbly hopes your Majesty will have no objection to granting permission to the Bp. of Bristol to hold it in commendam with his Bishoprick till Mr Perceval may be able to suggest some other means of adding to the Bishop's income so as to enable him to support the dignity & expence of his See which the revenue of that See itself is very unequal to support.

Mr Perceval will remember your Majesty's commands respecting a Stall in the Cathedral of Worcester for Mr Digby. (15521–2)

[*The King's reply, Windsor Castle, 26 Oct.*] The King has received Mr Perceval's letter and his My acquiesces in his recommendation of Mr Packwood for the Vicarage of St. Mary in Warwick. He is very sensible of Mr Perceval's attention in recommending his Majesty's Domestic Chaplain, the Revd. Charles Morice, to a living in the City.

The King rejoyces that Mr Perceval is not prevented by any local application from recommending his friend the Bishop of Bristol & Master of Trinity College for the large living in the Duchy of Lancaster, & he has great pleasure in confirming this nomination.

---

[1] The Earl of Warwick was also Earl Brooke. Earl Brooke (1746–1816) had been M.P. for Warwick, 1768–73, and a Lord of Trade, 1770–4. Lord Brooke was his son and successor. *See* No. 4032.

[2] The Rev. Charles Morice (c. 1744–1818), for 32 years Chaplain to the King and Queen. He was also Chaplain to the Duke of York.

His M. is very glad that Lord Arden has communicated to Mr Perceval his wishes in regard to Mr Digby.[1] (15522)

[1] This is the last letter the King dictated. The onset of his final attack of insanity is described in Lord Liverpool's letter to Lord Bathurst on the 27th: 'I am grieved to be under the necessity of informing you that the agitation arising out of the protracted illness of the poor Princess Amelia has had within these few days a serious effect upon the mind of the King, and his situation is become truly alarming. Sir Henry Halford and Dr. Baillie see him daily, and Dr. Heberden (who has personally attended the King under similar circumstances) is gone to Windsor at the King's request this evening. As they possess our entire confidence we do not feel much embarrassment in what way we should proceed, though it would be more satisfactory if all our colleagues were in town. The unpleasant symptoms may subside, and it is very desirable not to create alarm before it is absolutely necessary. It has been judged expedient therefore to keep everything as quiet as possible, but as matters appear more unfavourable this morning, and as we cannot write by the post tomorrow, we have judged it best that you and the rest of our colleagues should be apprised of the actual state of things in order that you may hasten your return to town, if it is not particularly inconvenient to you.' (Bathurst MSS.)

And Canning wrote to Mrs Canning on 2 Nov.: 'The truth is that poor old Knobbs is just as mad as ever he was in his life. He has no other complaint. The fever is symptomatic only—and the favourable difference between this and any former time is that he is very tractable. No mad physician has yet been called in. The physicians desire that this may not be done—as yet the *threat* to do it is quite sufficient to keep him in order, and make him do whatever is desired of him.

'Wellesley saw him yesterday. He describes the sight, but still more the *hearing* of him before he went into the room, as most dreadful—a sort of *wailing*, most horrible and heartrending to hear. He knew the Chancellor and talked kindly to him. Formerly he used to be violent against everybody that came near him. He was conscious that the complaint was coming on some days before it actually seized him. He told the D. of York that, *if* he should be ill, he wished to have Heberden and Sir H. Halford and Baillie to attend him. But the D. of Y. had found him out before, from his quoting some expression of Scripture: "If the thing I tell you be true, why will you not believe me and let me go my own way?" or something to that effect, in a conversation upon some indifferent subject—and then adding, "Such-a-one" (mentioning some parson's name) "preached me one of the best sermons upon that I ever heard upon that text. He preached that sermon in the morning, and then in the evening he preached the *damnedest* sermon that ever was heard." From that moment the D. of Y. was convinced that the disease was coming on. To another person he said on Thursday or Friday last, "I am sure I am going to be ill —for I had the same dream last night that I have had every time the night before my illness." Accordingly on Friday night he was taken decidedly ill.

'These are the circumstances that I have picked up from W[ellesley] and from our old Dean, who had some of them from the D. of Y. Since his illness W. tells me he has said, "This is the fourth time that I have been ill. The first time the cause of it was so-and-so; the second so; the third so" (stating the real causes) "and now it is poor Amelia."

'All the three physicians concur in giving the most positive opinion that he will recover. As to the time they do not venture an opinion—but they think it will be short.

'The death of the poor Princess Amelia would probably accelerate it. The one shock would probably do good. It is the lingering suspense and daily leave-taking that have worked upon his feelings and irritated him into madness.' (Harewood MSS.)

APPENDICES

I

CABINET MINUTE, 1 MARCH 1787

4239 CABINET MINUTE, *1 March 1787*[1]

Present: The Lord Chancellor, the Lord President, the Lord Privy Seal, Mr. Pitt, the Marquess of Carmarthen, Lord Howe, Lord Sydney.

It is humbly submitted to your Majesty in consequence of the answer of the twelve Judges to the question proposed by your Majesty's order upon the case of the Dutch mutineers who escaped from the ship Barbestein when lying in the Downs, that the Dutch Minister should be informed that the prisoners will be delivered to the officers whom the States-General may have appointed to receive them, and that proper orders should be sent for delivering them up. (P.R.O., F.O. 95/5)

[1] This Cabinet Minute is not in the Royal Archives: it may have been at one time. Its proper place in this edition would be in Vol. I, page 273.

II

SOME NEW LETTERS FROM
THE ELDON MSS.

4240   THE KING *to* LORD ELDON[1]

[*Kew, 4 May 1801.*] The King never doubted that the title deeds of the houses on Richmond Green were in Craig's Court, but this instance of neglect shews the impropriety of ever trusting gentlemen in that line with concerns they cannot have any reason to be entrusted with. In future his Majesty proposes that all the rents to be received and all business in his Richmond property shall solely be managed by Mr. Strong, of whose tallents and integrity he is most thoroughly convinced.

There seems no objection to naming three trustees to whom Lady Essex's estate shall be conveyed. His Majesty proposes they shall also hold the other purchases he has made in the said manors, viz., his Chancellor Lord Eldon, Lord Kenyon and Sir John Mitford, Speaker of the House of Commons, whose zeal in conducting the Bill as well as attention to obtain a proper title for the purchase of the Capel property, points this mark of confidence as highly proper.

4241   THE KING *to* LORD ELDON[2]

[*Kew, 20 June 1801.*] The King is sorry for the inadvertancy of having wrongly directed and sent the two letters, though from their contents it happens to be of no consequence. That to the Lord Chancellor was a mere acknowledgement of the receipt of the Commission for passing the Bills ready for his assent, and that he shall be at the Queen's Palace on Wednesday[3] in consequence of an application from Lord Hobart that two Judges going to the East Indies may be knighted.[4]

4242   THE KING *to* LORD ELDON[5]

[*Kew, 23 June 1801.*] The King is much pleased with the whole contents of the Lord Chancellor's letter and returns the Commission, having signed it for passing the Bills now ready for the Royal assent. He cannot avoid adding, as he knows it will give pleasure to the person to whom it is addressed, that appetite and good

---

[1] This, and the letters that follow, are in the Eldon MSS. at Encombe House, Dorset, and are printed with the kind permission of Lieut.-Colonel Scott. There are no copies in the Royal Archives. They are too numerous to be conveniently indexed under one number.

In the P.R.O. there is a box of papers relating to the King's purchase of freehold land and the 'capital messuage' at Kew from the 5th Earl of Essex, the deed being dated March 1802. There had been earlier purchases of land at Kew and Richmond, but this deed apparently refers to the purchase of the main Capel property. Frederick, Prince of Wales, purchased the contents of the house at Kew, including, the pictures, in 1731 (information *ex* Miss Langton, and Mr E. K. Timings of the P.R.O.).

[2] See No. 2448.   [3] The 24th.   [4] See No. 2456.   [5] See No. 2451.

sleep is perfectly, by the goodness of Divine Providence, restored, and that no degree of attention shall be wanting to keep those necessary assistants of perfect health.

4243 THE KING *to* LORD ELDON[1]

[*Cuffnals, 1 July 1801, $\underline{m}$ pt. p.m.*] The King received from Lord Glanbervie [*sic*] the Lord Chancellor's letter after giving the Order-in-Council for the prorogation of the Parliament. He has signed the Commission for that purpose and also that for passing the Bills. The prorogation must be renewed previous to the 6th[2] of August, as that now ordered ends then, to enable the Lord Chancellor to issue the new [one] before he closes his own Court for the Long Vacation.

The King can assure the Lord Chancellor he continues daily improving in strength, that his sleep is now very refreshing, and that he trusts when the Lord Chancellor comes to Weymouth he will see a manifest improvement, as medicine is now, by the advice of Doctor Gisborne, entirely laid aside.

4244 THE KING *to* LORD ELDON

[*Weymouth, 31 July 1801.*] The King received yesterday the Lord Chancellor's note and signed the Commission for further proroguing the Parliament to the 1st of September, which will keep the Lord Chancellor more confined this summer than the King had hoped would have been necessary.

4245 THE KING *to* LORD ELDON

[*Weymouth, 15 Aug. 1801.*] The King is happy at finding the Lord Chancellor has at length been able to finish the necessary business of the Court of Chancery, and shall be glad to see him whenever he thinks he can most conveniently absent himself from London.

4246 THE KING *to* LORD ELDON[3]

[*Windsor, 20 Nov. 1801.*] The King forwards to the Lord Chancellor the letter of the Princess of Wales and the draft of his proposed answer on which he is desirous of having the Lord Chancellor's opinion. His Majesty deems it best as this is the beginning of a business that may occasion some altercation, after expressing kindness to the Princess, not to commit himself till by the information he may in future stages obtain through the Lord Chancellor it may fully appear how he ought to act; and the more the Princess may be in the right the more this line of conduct must be conducive to her interest. The Lord Chancellor is fully authorized to consult Mr. Addington on this occasion, who undoubtedly sees in the same light that justice must be done to the Princess of Wales.

[1] The second paragraph is in Jesse, III, 288. See No. 2460.
[2] Altered from the 4th.
[3] *See* No. 2556. The Princess's letter to the King about her uncomfortable financial position (18 Nov.), is in *Corresp. of George, Prince of Wales*, IV, 239.

4247   THE KING to LORD ELDON

[*Windsor, 23 Nov. 1801.*] The King, in consequence of the note[1] he received this morning from the Lord Chancellor, has copied the draft of the letter to the Prince and now encloses it and desires the Lord Chancellor will deliver it as soon as he can find it convenient. The King is ready to come to the Queen's Palace any day this week that either the Lord Chancellor or Mr. Addington will insinuate[2] a wish for it, when he can also clear off any business in Council that may require his attendance. It would be convenient to have notice of it the day before.

4248   THE KING to LORD ELDON[3]

[*Queen's Palace, 24 Feb. 1802.*] The King returns the Commission for giving his assent to the Bills that have passed both Houses of Parliament which he has received this morning from the Lord Chancellor, having in the usual manner signed it.

4249   THE KING to LORD ELDON

[*Queen's Palace, 7 May 1802.*] The King returns the Commission for giving his assent to the Bills now ready for that confirmation which he has signed.

4250   THE KING to LORD ELDON[4]

[*Windsor, 23 May 1802.*] The King returns to the Lord Chancellor the Commission he has signed for passing tomorrow the Bills, as also the Sign Manual for appointing Mr. Leicester to succeed the Solicitor-General as a Welsh Judge.

4251   THE KING to LORD ELDON[5]

[*Windsor, 12 June 1802.*] The King returns the warrant for appointing the Duke of Northumberland Custos Rotulorum for the County of Northumberland which he has signed, and at the same time cannot deny himself the pleasure of expressing approbation at the Lord Chancellor's having calmed the temper of that Duke to see the propriety of his holding in that northern County the employment which his noble fortune points him out as the most proper to sustain.

4252   THE KING to LORD ELDON

[*Weymouth, 17 July 1802.*] The King returns to the Lord Chancellor the two warrants appointing Mr. Manley Attorney-General upon the Chester Circuit and for the Welsh Counties comprised in it, which he has signed.

---

[1] No. 2556 (22 Nov.).   [2] Not 'intimate'.
[3] See IV, 14, note 2, for Eldon's routine note to the King (23 Feb.).
[4] See No. 2628.   [5] See No. 2636.

4253   THE KING to LORD ELDON[1]

[*Queen's Palace, 25 March 1803.*] The King having signed the Commission for passing the Bills this day returns it to the Lord Chancellor. He at the same time expresses his approbation of the granting a Patent of Preceedence [*sic*] in the Courts in the East Indies in favour of Mr. Smith, appointed Advocate-General to the East India Company.

4254   THE KING to LORD ELDON

[*Windsor, 11 Aug. 1803.*] The King returns to the Lord Chancellor the Commission for passing this day the Bills ready for his assent. He had expected to have heard when the business of this Session will be concluded, as he shall certainly come to town for that purpose the day most convenient to both Houses of Parliament.

4255   THE KING to LORD ELDON[2]

[*Windsor, 27 Sept. 1803.*] The King would have wished to have avoided a fresh troubling the Lord Chancellor on the subject of the Earl of Berkeley, but to his great surprize the subject of bringing her to Court has been renewed. The King therefore desires the Lord Chancellor will in his name write to the Earl of Berkeley that till his first marriage is clearly established in the House of Lords he cannot think himself justified in receiving her at Court. The reason of the King's now writing is that he has reason to suspect the Earl of Berkeley will ask an audience on Wednesday to renew his application, and an intimation from the Lord Chancellor will probably prevent it.

4256   THE KING to LORD ELDON[3]

[*Windsor, 27 Sept. 1803, 7.35 p.m.*] The King is perfectly satisfied with the manner the Lord Chancellor has thought most eligible of stating to the Earl of Berkeley the commission with which the King has entrusted him, and consequently the Lord Chancellor is desired to send the letter as prepared to the Earl of Berkeley.

4257   THE KING to LORD ELDON[4]

[*Queen's Palace, 16 May 1804.*] The King has this instant received from the Lord Chancellor the Commission for passing the Bills now ready for his Royal assent. His Majesty is going to Kew for a walk, having, he thanks God, compleated the arrangement of strengthening his Administration by the retreat of no man but those he was desirous of seeing out of office.

The King hopes to see the Lord Chancellor this day at three, as he is most

---

[1] See No. 2720.   [2] See No. 2800.   [3] See No. 2800.   [4] See No. 2859.

thoroughly tired of the unnecessary delays of the Lord Chancellor, and has been desired by Mr. Pitt to go into the country, which is now become necessary for his Majesty's health; after a confinement he never can forget, though on which he must be silent as he cannot, agreable to his own heart, punish, which he ought to do, those who have dared to confine him.

4258   THE KING to LORD ELDON[1]

[*Queen's Palace, 18 May 1804, 10.05 a.m.*] The King having signed the Commission for giving his Royal Assent, returns it to his excellent Lord Chancellor, whose conduct he most thoroughly approves. His Majesty feels the difficulties he has had, both political, and personally to the King, but the uprightness of Lord Eldon's mind, and his attachment to the King, have borne him with credit and honour, and, what the King knows will not be without its due weight, with the approbation of his Sovereign, through an unpleasant labyrinth.

The King is anxious to know when the Message to both Houses of Parliament will be ready for his signature, as his honour as well as the real merit of Mr. Addington call for that measure.

The four thousand each for the five Princesses ought also now to come forward; indeed, why Mr. Addington has been for two years promising it and as constantly forgetting is inexplicable and has not a little incensed the Queen and her children, who all agree in rejoicing at his retreat; indeed he has no friend in this House but the King, who knows the warmth of his heart whilst they only the futility of his measures.

A word from the Lord Chancellor will fix the Vice-Admiralty of Scotland on his friend the Earl of Galway and rid the King of a most unpleasant *Scotch* Lord of his Bedchamber.

The Earl of Aylesford is highly pleased and will come to town the moment his gout will permit.

The King saw Mr. Addington yesterday and communicated to him the letter to Lord Auckland with which he seemed truely pleased and spoke with his former warmth of friendship for the Lord Chancellor. He seems to require quiet, as his mind is perplexed between returning *affection* for Mr. Pitt, and great soreness at the *contemptuous* treatment he met with, the end of the last Session, from one he had ever looked upon as his private friend. This makes the King resolved to keep them for some time asunder.

4259   THE KING to LORD ELDON[2]

[*Kew, 3 July 1804, 7.40 a.m.*] The King having signed the Commission for passing Bills, returns it to the Lord Chancellor. He has just received a note from Mr. Pitt with the favorable account of his having carried his Resolutions on the

---

[1] See No. 2859 (18 May). Part of this important letter is in Twiss, *Eldon*, I, 449. Also among the Eldon MSS. is the King's letter to Castlereagh, 11 June (see Jesse, III, 383; and No. 2879). The King's brief note to Eldon, fixing an appointment (22 June), is in Jesse, III, 384, copied from the Eldon MSS.

[2] See No. 2905.

Civil List, as also the Additional Stamps to compleat the Ways and Means of the year, without any opposition except on the former from Sir Francis Burdett whose seat in Parliament will probably be vacated by the Resolution of the Committee the next week. The whole of this business does great credit to Mr. Pitt but does not reflect the same on his predecessor, who in the most extra-ordinary manner ever did what he should not, and omitted what he ought to have performed.

4260 THE KING to LORD ELDON

[*Windsor Castle, 25 Dec. 1804.*] The King with many compliments on the season sends with infinite pleasure the two letters[1] he has received this morning from Lord Hawkesbury and Mr. Pitt to his Lord Chancellor. This reconciliation will give ease and add much strength to *his Majesty's Administration*, at which no man will more sincerely rejoice than the Lord Chancellor. At the same time the King transmits a very extraordinary letter[2] received the last evening by the D. of Kent from the Earl of Moira enclosing one for his Majesty,[3] to which the Duke of Kent by the King's direction wrote the accompanying answer.[4] The Lord Chancellor is desired to return all the papers communicated to him this day, as his Majesty has no copies.

4261 THE KING to LORD ELDON

[*Windsor Castle, 10 March 1805.*] The King loses no time in returning to the Lord Chancellor the very improper paper[5] and indeed unfair one to the Bishop of Exeter and Lady de Clifford which the Prince of Wales has put into their hands as instructions for their conduct, and as it seems wanting to make them parties in the false statement he chooses to make as to the future residence of his Majesty's granddaughter. The Lord Chancellor is so fully apprised of what has passed that the King authorises him to consult with Mr. Pitt and prepare a proper answer that may keep the business in its true channel, the Lord Chancellor's hands, and exonerate the Bishop and the Governess from any part of the business.

His Majesty must either have the whole care and superintendance of the person and education of the Princess Charlotte, or entirely decline any interference or expense; by this he in no means proposes to interfere with her visiting both the Prince and Princess of Wales when they require it, and will for that purpose fix her the next winter at Kensington for that season, that the Prince and Princess may with less inconvenience visit her or send for her at that season to their respective houses; but Windsor will be her residence for the greatest part of the year, where she will have the advantage of excellent air and a retired garden, which will enable her quietly and with effect, to pursue her studies, which certainly

---

[1] Nos. 2986, 2987. The first sentence of the King's letter is in Twiss, *Eldon*, i, 484.
[2] *Corresp. of George, Prince of Wales*, v, 152 (23 Dec.).
[3] *Ibid.*, v, 151 n.   [4] *Ibid.*, v, 153 n.
[5] See *Corresp. of George, Prince of Wales*, v, 201 (4 March).

as yet have been but little attended to. The Lord Chancellor is desired to take a copy for the King of this returned paper of instructions, and prepare the paper to be transmitted to the Prince of Wales, who certainly means further chicane.

4262 THE KING *to* LORD ELDON

[*Windsor Castle, 12 March 1805.*] The King returns the Commissions [*sic*] for passing the Bills this day, having signed it. He at the same time cannot but approve, previous to the Lord Chancellor and Mr. Pitt's preparing a paper to be sent to the Prince of Wales, that as the business may come to a serious issue, that they should have the sanction of the Cabinet, but his Majesty thinks a prior consultation of the Lord Chief Justice of the King's Bench, perhaps the two other Chiefs, the Attorney and Solicitor-General and the Master of the Rolls, would enable the Cabinet to be more confident in the opinion that may with propriety be given.[1]

4263 THE KING *to* LORD ELDON[2]

[*Kew, 22 March 1805.*] The King has signed the accompanying Commission for passing the Bills now ready for his assent. There cannot be the smallest doubt but that the Lord Chancellor will make a report of the proper mode of proceeding on the very unbecoming line of conduct the Prince of Wales has been ill advised to follow, and therefore his Majesty does by no means press for a speedy but a decisive answer when it can with propriety be given.

The Lord Chancellor's opinion of the sufficiency of Mr. Plumer for the vacancy of a Welsh Judge makes the King desirous the appointment may be immediately executed.

[1] See *Corresp. of George, Prince of Wales*, v, 206 n. The King's letter of the 18th to Eldon on the same subject is in *ibid.*, v, 206, copied from the Dropmore Papers, but in line 2 the MS. reads 'for his Assent'.

[2] See No. 3049.

III

SOME PRE-1784 LETTERS

4264 *Letters from* THE QUEEN *to the* KING

[Q[ueen's] H[ouse], 24 April 1778.] The arrival of Ramus cannot be expected till some hours hence, yet can I not refuse myself the agreable occupation of beginning to scribble by way of conversing with him who takes up the greatest part of my thoughts, a little before ten a clock this morning I thougt your Majesty arrived at Greenwhich & we amused ourselves with hearing the sound of the firing of the canons. I then observed the wind & found it nort [*sic*] east which was a very agreable thing as of course it must naturally carry you sooner to the end of your journey.[1]

In hopes of making my correspondence a little entertaining I tried to get some news that might be depended upon, but to my great mortification that proves to be almost impossible. The only thing that I could learn this morning is that Lord Chatham was somewhat easier last night at eleven o'clock but still very weak.[2] From Sion Hill I have no direct account but was told by the Dutchess of Ancaster[3] that Mrs. Lockhart was to go there today and that she in her opinion thinks that Lord Holderness[4] will not live a fortnight longer.

The newspapers informed us last night of a man being taken up who was suspected of having fixed up the paper about the declaration of war against the French, sighned Effingham. This I hear is really true. The man was examined and said that he was paid *forty* guineas by a gentleman of fortune for doing it. Who this gentleman is, or what induced him to take this step I have not been able to learn as yet, but flatter myself to get some more instructions about it in the course of this evening.

Prince of Wales of Frederick [*sic*] dined with me to day. Both have charged me with their duty to you. At eight o'clock when all their lessons are finish'd they are to make up my commerce party.

[Q. H., 25 April 1778.] Ramus did not return till ten a clock last night just as I was going to supper. He finds the house at Portsmouth extreamly neat. All rooms furnish with very '*elegant cutton beds*' [*sic*]; this is his expression, but

---

[1] The King had set out that morning for Chatham to inspect the fleet. He sailed from Greenwich in the yacht *Augusta*, arriving at Chatham next day.

[2] He died on 11 May.

[3] Peregrine Bertie, third Duke of Ancaster (1714–78), married, as his second wife, Mary, daughter of Thomas Panton. She was Mistress of the Robes to Queen Charlotte, 1761–93 (*d.* 1793). *See* No. 312. Horace Walpole inaccurately described her as the 'natural daughter of Panton, a disreputable horse-jockey of Newmarket'. (*Last Journals*, II, 196 n.).

[4] Robert D'Arcy, sixth Earl of Holdernesse (1718–78), Governor of the Prince of Wales and of Prince Frederick, 1771–6. He died on 16 May.

no bedding for the servants beds. The kitchen so very indifferently stokd [*sic*] with furniture that the greatest part must be taken from hence, Ramus also wishes to know whether the *épargne* from Windsor is to be sent or not, there being no wont of a desert; he is of opinion that would make the table look better. I have taken the copy of the paper which Ramus gave me and shall see Gray as early as possible this morning. Portsmouth town was so full on Thursday night that no more lodgins [*sic*] could be found and a great many of the ladies were obliged to set up all night, the scarcity of post horses immense, it was owing to this that Ramus come so late for he says the poor beasts are so fatigued nobody cant get along with them.[1]

Madame Becker has wrote a letter to a friend of her friends which arrived yesterday; she says Monsieur de Salzas[2] is so much worth [*sic*] that his phisician has ordered him to take the bath of a particular place in Switzerland famous for curing his complaint, but as nobody ever thinks of going there till the beginning of the month of July, I believe we must give up all hopes of seing him this summer.

Mary is very anxious to see your Majesty; she desired me to call *dear papa* but after telling her that could not be, she desired to be lifted up, and she calld for at least half an hour, '*Papa coming, now papa comes*' but seeing she was disapointed by not receiving an answer I desired her to tell me what I should say to the King in case I should write, and she answered '*Minny say goody papa, poor papa*'. Ernest will be delighted when he hears that I did let you know of his behaving well; the two gentlemen attending him were both satisfied with his conduct of yesterday.

It would be very indiscreet to take up your Majesty time any longer with my very bad writing, I do own it is against inclination that I stop here but prudence and discretion is a necessary thing in this world. I hope that your Majesty's orders for me shall be very well executed assuring you that nobody can feel more happy in executing them than your Majesty's very affectionate friend & wife. (36349–51)

[*Q[ueen's] H[ouse], 26 April 1778.*] A thousand thanks unto you for your kind and affectionate letter which arrived last night by a quarter past ten just after my commerce party was broken up. It hath served me as supper and is to keep me company at breakfast this morning when that hours comes, where I shall take an opportunity to rejoice all the little people with your kindness to them. Dear little Minny remains quite uneasy about not finding you anywhere in the house, every coach she sees is papa a coming, and nothing satisfies her hardly but sitting at the window to look for you.

The Duke of Mountague[3] brought yesterday a little before dinner Lord Dal-

[1] Preparations were then being made for the visit of the King and Queen to Portsmouth, 2–9 May 1778.
[2] Horace Walpole wrote in May 1776: 'Lord Hertford told me...that Salgas [*sic*], son of a French refugee, and one of the Prince's tutors, insisted on retiring, too, from the ungovernable temper of the Prince [the Prince of Wales].' (*Last Journals*, I, 558.) M. de Salzas had been private secretary to Lord Holdernesse when Ambassador to The Hague (1749–51). His name is sometimes spelt Salzes.
[3] George Brudenell Montagu, Duke of Montagu and fourth Earl of Cardigan (1712–90). Governor to the Prince of Wales and Prince Frederick, 1776–80; Master of the Horse, 1780, till his death. See No. 238.

keith[1] to the Prince of Wales appartment in order to take leave of him as also to shew him in the uniform of his father's Regiment. He is drest in the Light Infantry cloth, the caps I think are pretty enough. He told me that he must go to Scotland to raise the Regiment, and that he was to do it all himself. Adolphus seeing his sword asked him if it was *sharp*. 'Yes,' says he, 'not much, but sufficient to cut off a Frenchman's head,' so I said, 'but how do you know that so exactly could it not fail wth trial?' 'No! for I know how to frighten a French man away for I try & succeed frequently in frighting my papa's valet de chambre,' he is altogether a fine boy and the very image of his mother and I think the darling of the grandfather.

There was a great fire the night before last broke out in a pack house at Barkley Square, a cabinet maker's house being near threatened the destruction to all they [*sic*] neigbours, but providentially the wind changed all of a sudden and it was soon extinguished. A mews is quite burnt down and the only real sufferer by this fire is a poor labouring man who by his industry had just saved enough to buy himself a horse & a cart to carry about his goods. These riches being there taken care of, are destroy'd & this *honest old man*, for such the inhabitants call him, again return'd to his former fate, that of working hard to carry his goods about when he had the hopes of doing it in an easier way.

There is a report of a match between Lord Waldegrave's eldest son[2] and Lady Louisa Fitzpatrick.[3] It cannot be interest, it must be liking, je ne dispute pas des gouts but such is the truth that I am blind enough not to see her beauty.

How glad do I feel to know that you are pleased and enjoy good health a board your yacht, there is pleasure in doing what is right to do and you will have the benefit by your voyages to put spirit in everybody, to be more known by the world, and if possible more beloved by the people in general. That must be the case, but not equal to the love of her who subscribes herself [etc.].

Gray is to go this afternoon to Windsor. He understands every thing perfectly well, and to prevent all mistakes I sent him to Ramus where he got all the necessary information about the neatness & cleanniness [*sic*] of the house at Portsmouth.

Poor Lady Carlisle[4] is very uneasy by the breaking of a sore breast. I do hear there is no danger in her case, but I think her of so delicate a make that everything would alarm me if I did belong to her.

Thank God they tell me it is not so cold this morning, a little mild air would really not be uncomfortable after our high & cutting wind of yesterday.

To day William is to dine with me, I shall just have made the *tour* of all the children by Tuesday when I hope to be supplied with the company of him who is ever dear to me. You know who that is I am sure. (36352-4)

[1] The Duke of Montagu's grandson (1772-1819). See No. 1320. The Duke's daughter, Elizabeth (1743-1827), married the third Duke of Buccleuch (1746-1812) in 1767, and their 2nd but 1st surviving son, the Earl of Dalkeith, succeeded as fourth Duke in 1812.

[2] The elder son of the third Earl Waldegrave (1718-84), married his cousin, Lady Elizabeth Laura Waldegrave, in May 1782, and succeeded as fourth Earl in Oct. 1784. (1751-89.)

[3] Lady Louisa Fitzpatrick (1755-89), daughter of the first Earl of Upper Ossory, married Lord Shelburne, the Prime Minister, in 1779. Lord Henry Petty, later third Marquess of Lansdowne, was their only son.

[4] The fifth Earl of Carlisle (1748-1825), married, in 1770, Margaret Caroline, daughter of the first Marquess of Stafford (1753-1824).

[*Undated.*] I send your Majesty the Dutchess of Argyle's[1] letter to me, I know there is also one for you. Her indelicacy goes a great way, and I am of opinion with my humble advice that your Majesty would now do better to let the Duke of Manchester[2] acquaint her that her daughter should not come to Court, or be ill received, as letting her come will open the door to others, for though she is not divorced, she has stood a public tryal. I declare I shall neither speak to mother or daughter, and if she leaves my family I shall but get rid of an impertinent person who has always behaved disrespectful to me.

There will be time enough to send to the Duke of Manchester. I shall not answer the Dutchess of Argyle's letter. (36357)

4265 THE KING *to* ? REAR-ADMIRAL DIGBY[3]

[*Late May or early June 1779.*] It is the natural object of a parent eagerly to desire that his children may distinguish themselves in whatever profession their inclination and his reflection may judge right to place them. In the Navy an early introduction is necessary to gain the habits of a style of life, so different from any other. I have therefore thought it proper to send my dearly beloved son Prince William, at so early an age, to make his first trial of the naval profession, and I have thought it proper to entrust him to your care, from a thorough opinion of your skill in that profession as well as of the worth of your personal character.

I should have been inclined not to give you any instructions on this occasion had I not perceived how much you felt the greatness of the trust reposed in you, and therefore concluded that these may be an alleviation to your mind.

1. My dearly beloved son Prince William shall on my receiving notice of the Prince George[4] being compleatly ready for sea be conducted by Major-General de Budé[5] to Portsmouth and be delivered to you at Spithead.

[1] John Campbell, fifth Duke of Argyll (1723–1806) married, in 1759, Elizabeth (1733–90), widow of the sixth Duke of Hamilton, and daughter of John Gunning. Elizabeth (1753–97), her elder daughter by her first marriage, married the 21st Earl of Derby (1752–1834) in 1774. In 1778 she was led into an intrigue with the vicious Duke of Dorset, with whom she lived. Lord Derby would not divorce her, being determined to prevent their marriage. (*G.E.C.*) Horace Walpole wrote, in Nov. 1778: 'About this time became known a quarrel at Court, which had happened the last month...The Duchess of Argyll...had long aimed at being the King's mistress, but I believe never was so, though she had got great weight with him.... The Queen had early been jealous of her, and had used her so ill that she had thought of resigning; but the Duke loved money better than her, and was not jealous. Whether as the Duchess grew old and lost her beauty, or whether, to disguise her own jealousy, the Queen had made her a sort of favourite; but the Duchess was grown so insolent and behaved so familiarly with the King, even at chapel, and behind the Queen's chair, that the latter was determined to affront her; and when she was to go to Warley Camp with the King, and it was the Duchess's turn to wait, the Queen said she would have Lady Egremont go... (*Last Journals*, II, 203; I, 542.) The Duchess was a Lady of the Bedchamber to Queen Charlotte, 1761–84.
[2] George Montagu, fourth Duke of Manchester (1737–88); Lord Chamberlain, 1782–3; Ambassador to Paris, April–Dec. 1783. These dates may give a clue to the date of the letter.
[3] Robert Digby (1732–1815); Lieutenant, 1752; Captain, 1755; Rear-Admiral, 19 March 1779; Admiral, 1794. During the summer of 1779 he was second in command of the Channel fleet under Sir Charles Hardy, and in Dec. was second in command of the fleet which sailed under Rodney for the relief of Gibraltar.   [4] Rear-Admiral Digby's 98-gun flagship.
[5] Major-General Budé (1736?–1818) was a Swiss, with a commission in the Hanoverian army. Later, he became the Duke of York's private secretary. 'His person', wrote Fanny Burney in 1786,

2. You will without loss of time direct the mode in which he is to be taught the theoretical as well as practical part of his profession, as I am very desirous he may in time become an expert navigator.

3. You will direct his being kept exactly to the performance of every duty of the station in which he is placed, and without any indulgence not shewn to others.

4. You will be particularly attentive that a proper Lieutenant be on duty during his watch, that you may be very exactly informed how he has conducted himself.

5. You will be very careful that on all occasions he may shew a due obedience to those above him, and that he may conduct himself with politeness to his equals, and humanity to his inferiors.

6. You will direct him to be treated with civility, but no visible marks of respect, as such you will have it understood that it is not my pleasure that he should receive any visits, and he is to make none; but at any time you wish to shew him any ship he may attend you.

7. He is not to dine on board other ships except that of the Commander-in-Chief, which will of course be seldom.

8. When you shall judge it proper to send him to sail in any small vessel as a better means of learning the art of navigation, you will be careful to appoint a Lieutenant to go with him, who will exactly follow the mode of conduct you have established.

9. The same rule to be followed when you think it proper that he should practice swimming.

10. You will never let him go on shore but when you can accompany him.

11. As I wish the other branches of his education may not be neglected, I have directed the Revd. Mr. Majendie[1] to attend him for the pursuit of his studies, and have ordered such books to be taken, as I think necessary for that purpose; I trust you will see that sufficient hours are allotted for that purpose, and that you will on all occasions inculcate to my dearly beloved son, how much more is expected from him both in the profession he is now entering into, and in every branch of knowledge becoming a gentleman, than from persons who have not had the advantages he may have of education.

12. I trust you will from time to time by letter addressed unto me, report how he conducts himself, and what improvement he makes in nautical knowledge. (Add. Georgian 15/461)

4266   THE KING *to* MAJOR-GENERAL DE BUDÉ

[*Kew, 11 June 1779.*] As my dearly beloved son Prince William is on Monday to join Rear-Admiral Digby under whose direction he is to learn whatever relates to the Naval profession, I have thought it proper that the Revd. Mr. Majendie should attend him, that he may pursue, when not employed in the

'is tall and showy, and his manners and appearance are fashionable. But he has a sneer in his smile that looks sarcastic, and a distance in his manner that seems haughty.'
[1] Henry William Majendie (1754–1830), later Bishop of Chester (1800) and of Bangor (1809). He was appointed preceptor to Prince William in Jan. 1780, at a salary of £200 a year. His father, John James Majendie (1709–83), was tutor to the Prince of Wales and the Duke of York.

business of his profession, those branches of knowledge which are essential to every gentleman; but more so to those in the conspicuous station it hath pleased the Almighty to place him.

Mr. Majendie from his natural modesty must feel anxious on entering into so new a scene of life to be informed how he ought to conduct himself; Major General de Budé is therefore empowered to acquaint him

1. That what I have most at heart is that he should take every proper opportunity of instructing my dearly beloved son Prince William in the Christian religion, to inculcate the habitual reading the Holy Scriptures, and to accompany these with moral reflexions that may counteract the evil he may have but too many opportunities of hearing.

2. That he is to pursue the study of the Latin language, as I am very desirous he should not only read it with ease, but taste its beauties.

3. That he is to practice compositions in English, that a facility may be attained in writing, and a degree of elegance which must be looked upon as essential to the character of a gentleman; the letters of my dearly beloved son to his relations cannot at his early age contain much of a secret nature, therefore it may be proper for Mr. Majendie in the beginning to correct the orthography, and perhaps the style, though the sentiments should not on any account be altered.

4. That the study of the English history will be a pleasant as well as useful occupation, Mr. Majendie should in this first course merely teach him the facts, and omit political reasoning that will take more effect when his mind is more enlightened.

5. That translating from Latin and English into French will be the easiest and best method of acquiring a language now become so universal; Mr. Majendie should as much as possible converse with him in that language, as it will be the only means whilst at sea of not losing the practice; and all books of recreation ought to be in that language, as that will be one of the most pleasing means of learning the language, and at the same time there are more books of that kind void of evil than in his native tongue.

6. That Mr. Majendie will take every opportunity of pointing out when alone to my dearly beloved son the omissions he has remarked in his general conduct, and how much I shall be mortified when he returns from sea, if not void of the little tricks and rudeness which ought to be cast off at an earlier age than he is now arrived at.

7. That Mr. Majendie will pursue these instructions at every opportunity which may occurr, when my dearly beloved son is not either employed in the theoretical or practical branches of his profession; there may not be opportunities for long lessons, but from the frequency of them I trust much information may be acquired; should my son attempt to avoid his lessons, any application from Mr. Majendie to Rear Admiral Digby to enforce the necessity of attending to his studies will I am certain meet with the fullest support.

8. That Mr. Majendie is to omit no opportunity of corresponding with Major General de Budé, that I may be kept constantly informed how these instructions are followed. (Add. Georgian 15/460)

[*Kew, 13 June 1779.*] You are now launching into a scene of life where you may either prove an honour or a disgrace to your family. It would be very unbecoming of the love I have for my children if I did not at this serious moment give you advice how to conduct yourself. Had I taken the common method of doing it in conversation it would soon have been forgot, therefore I prefer this mode, as I trust you will frequently peruse this, as it is dictated from no other motive than the anxious feelings of a parent that his child may be happy and deserve the approbation of men of worth and integrity.

It is highly necessary for every rational being never to lose sight of the certainty that every thought as well as action is known to the All-wise Disposer of the Universe; and that no solid comfort ever in this world can exist without a firm reliance on His protection, and on His power to shield us from misfortunes: but these reflections are still more necessary to be foremost in the minds of those at sea who naturally are exposed to perils peculiar to that element; therefore I strongly recommend the habitual reading of the Holy Scriptures and your more and more placing that reliance on the Divine Creator which is the only real means of obtaining that peace of mind that alone can fit a man for arduous undertakings.

Remember you are now quitting home where it has been the object of those who were placed about you to correct your faults, yet keep them out of the sight of the world; now you are entering into a society of above seven hundred persons who will watch every step you take, will freely make their remarks and communicate them to the whole Fleet; thus what would I hope have been cured must now be instantly avoided, or will be for ever remembered to your disadvantage.

Though when at home a Prince, on board of the Prince George you are only a boy learning the naval profession; but the Prince so far accompanies you, that what other boys might do you must not; it must never be out of your thoughts that more obedience is necessary from you to your superiours in the Navy, more politeness to your equals, and more good nature to your inferiours, than from those who have not been told that these are essential for a gentleman.

Mr. Majendie goes with you to continue the mode of education thought proper; you must consequently take thorough pains, and by your improvement encourage me to continue you in the naval profession.

The Rear-Admiral will direct what regards the theoretical as well as practical parts of the profession; I trust you will take every kind of pains to advance in them.

I shall only add that after the pains Major-General de Budé has taken with you I trust you must feel how much he has your interest at heart, and therefore that you will treasure up in your mind the advice he will give you during the journey, and that you will conduct yourself whilst from home that your parents may receive you with pleasure on your return, and that the General may feel he can with credit continue his care of you whilst on shore.

The Queen has desired me to add every expression of tenderness in her name, and believe me ever [etc.]. (Add. Georgian 21/1/2)

[*From Prince William, off the Land's End, Prince George, Sunday morning, 20 June 1779.*] Sir, I take the opportunity of a vessel sailing to England of writing this letter. I am treated with the greatest kindness by Admiral Digby, & I hope that, being instructed in navigation by the Admiral, in religion & other useful studies by Mr. Majendie, I may be approved of by your Majesty & the Queen. I have received from General de Budé your Majesty's letter; it shall be my constant endeavour, to observe the affectionate directions it contains.

Pray give my respects to the Queen, & my love to my brothers & sisters.

I am very much pleased, Sir, with this new situation in life, in which it is my resolution to shew myself your Majesty's affectionate & dutiful son.[1] (44598–9)

4268   THE QUEEN *to* PRINCE WILLIAM[2]

[*9 July 1779.*] Oh what infinite pleasure does your sweet letter give me! The surprise was the greater as I did not expect it, yet longed very much to hear news from your element. You say that you are happy & well; may you always continue to be so! By experience you will find that to be happy depends very much upon yourself. The fulfilling the duties in that rank and that situation it does please Providence to put you in, & which I hope you will think of doing, will greatly contribute towards it; & the most essential thing of all is to put God always before your eyes & to become a sincere Christian. Believe me no man ever can prove a usefull member to society without being a good Christian. It is religion that should guide your steps; it will assist you in every action of your life and support you in misfortunes & affliction. If you choose this *path*, you must feel comfortable in this world, and be greatly rewarded in the next.

Our first journey to Windsor was, as in general, very pleasing; the weather did not favour us much, being very rainy; but notwithstanding that, our morning drives were performed, and the company of your two elder brothers added great chearfulness to the party. Lord Boston's new house is now furnishing & the family intend to take possession of it in about four weeks. Clifden House is still in the same situation wee [*sic*] left it last year, and it is yet undecided whether some additional rooms are to be build to it, or whether it is to be inhabited in its present ugly situation: in short it is at present everything it should not be, unfurnishd, unfinishd, dirty and uncomfortable to the greatest degree, & does not appear the least chearfull. A thing the most essential in a country place is its being chearfull; for else it is not worth living at it.

Our own habitation at Windsor is just the thing for us, the new building of offices advances very well & the Duke of St. Albans'[3] house will be finished by

---

[1] Admiral Digby's fleet was now cruising in the Channel, the English coast being threatened by the combined French and Spanish fleets. The enemy retired without an encounter.

[2] This letter can be dated 9 July 1779 by the reference to the death of Robert Bertie, fourth Duke of Ancaster, which took place on 8 July. He was Hereditary Lord Great Chamberlain. He died unmarried.

[3] Aubrey, 5th Duke of St. Albans (1740–1802). M.P. for Thetford, 1761–8; for Aldborough, 1768–74. Son of Lord Vere Beauclerk, and grandson of Charles, 1st Duke of St. Albans. Succeeded his father as 2nd Baron Vere, 2 Oct. 1781, and his cousin as Duke, 16 Feb. 1787.

the beginning of Autumn. That being done, our journeys will be, I flatter myself at least, more frequent & attended with less inconveniencies.

The poor Dutchess of Ancaster has met with another very severe stroke in the loss of her only son, the Duke of Ancaster,[1] who died yesterday at seven a clok of a putrid fever. It is to be lamented that this young man with fine talents, a good heart and the advantage of rank did choose to lead so idle a life & to ruin his health by giving himself up to drinking, & to become unfit to be usefull to the world; it was low company which prevented him to shine by this capacity, and in short it was his ruin. This is a good lesson for all young people; pray beware of it at all times. Shun low company, be humane & charitable to your inferiors; but do not make them your confidentes, & be civil & not proud to those who are [the rest is missing]. (Add. Georgian 21/1/3)

4269 *Letters from* PRINCE WILLIAM *to the* KING

[*Torbay, Sunday, 11 July* [*1779*].] I have to return your Majesty my thanks for the gracious letter of the 26th, which I received last Thursday.

I shall always remember that the advice it contains is for my good, & it will be my constant endeavour to observe it as long as I live. I am certain that if I do behave myself in the manner prescribed in your Majesty's two letters, & particularly in that delivered to me by General de Budé, I shall keep up the fame of our illustrious family. With the advice of such tender parents, & with the other assistance I have, I hope to be hereafter of use to my country & a comfort & honour to my parents & relations.

I have been formerly very much displeased with General de Budé. But now I am as much attached to him, & I wish that, if ever I return (for I may be killed) I may give your Majesty & him as much satisfaction as possible.

It will not, I hope, be disagreeable to your Majesty if I should mention what has happened since I had the honour of writing to her Majesty.

The wind being westerly, we were obliged to make for Torbay, where Sr. Charles Hardy[2] made the sig. for anchoring about half after five p.m.

Next day, Admiral Digby gave a great dinner where were present Admirals Darby[3] & Ross,[4] & several Captains. I have been three times on shore with Admiral Digby. He has allowed me to begin to swim, & I have been twice in the water, with which I am very much delighted.

The Hector & Porcupine[5] have taken two Spanish prizes. Sr. Charles Hardy & his son have paid us a visit.

[1] Robert, 4th Duke of Ancaster (1756–79), who succeeded his father in 1778, and who was appointed Lord Lieutenant of Lincolnshire, 12 Feb. 1779, died of scarlet fever.

[2] Admiral Sir Charles Hardy commanded the Channel fleet in 1779.

[3] George Darby (*c.* 1720–90). Lieutenant, 1742; Captain, 1747; Rear-Admiral, 1778; Vice-Admiral, 1779; Commander-in-Chief, Western squadron, 1780–2. A Lord of the Admiralty, 1780–March 1782, M.P. for Plymouth, 1780–4.

[4] Sir John Lockhart Ross (1721–90), 5th son of Sir James Lockhart, 2nd Bart.; took name of Ross in 1760; succeeded brother George as 6th Bart., 1778. Entered navy, 1735; Lieutenant, 1743; Captain, 1756; Rear-Admiral, 19 March 1779; Vice-Admiral, 1787. M.P. for the Linlithgow Burghs, 1761–8; for Lanarkshire, 1768–74.   [5] Carrying 74 and 24 guns respectively.

Last Thursday, there being a court martial on board the Britannia,[1] I attended it, & was interested in it.

Yesterday I dined on board the Victory, & afterwards went on shore & into the water.

Will your Majesty be graciously pleased to thank the Queen in my name for her good wishes, & assure her, that, as I know how she wishes me to behave, I will keep as strictly as I can to her desire.

General de Budé has written me a very affectionate letter, which I am afraid I cannot answer at present, being very much engaged, & the Fleet being expected to sail tomorrow. The same reason prevents me writing to the Prince of Wales, to whom I beg your Majesty to make my excuses.

I wish your Majesty joy of the good accounts from America, & hope that we shall soon send word of a victory. We are all in spirits to sail, for Sr. Charles Hardy has made the sig[nal] for the Fleet to unmoor. We expect to weigh to-morrow & sail.

I conclude my letter by desiring your Majesty to present my duty to the Queen & my love to my brothers & sisters. (44600–1)

[*Prince George, 3 Sept.* [*1779*], *at St Helens.*] Having been detained for some time by contrary winds 30 leagues W.S.W. of Scilly, & in such confusion, I have not been able to write to your Majesty; I am therefore very happy to seize this first opportunity of sending a letter.

Nothing very material happened from the time I wrote last, till we received information from the Southampton of the French & Spanish Fleets being in the Channel. We were, as your Majesty may suppose, very much surprized & al-larmed, being apprehensive of their invading England. We heard at the same time they had taken several small vessels, & I am afraid that Mr. Denoyer,[2] who had letters for us, was among the number. The wind did not favour us till the 27th, when it changed, & we set sail towards England. In the afternoon of the 29th, the Cumberland,[3] being ahead, & to windward withal, let fly her top gallant sheets as a sig[na]l for a Fleet. In the evening of the 30th, we saw some cutters making signals, as was supposed, to the combined Fleets. Next morning we saw from the masthead upwards of sixty sail. We were in a very disagreeable situation all day.

The 1st of this month in the morning off Plymouth Sound, we counted only 31 sail from the masthead: at noon we anchored off the Sound, where we were joined by the Buffalo, Blenheim,[4] Isis,[5] Southampton, & 2 other frigates. About 5 in the afternoon we weighed & set sail, coming to St. Helens, where we dropped anchor this morning, & expect to be joined by the Princess Amelia,[6] Edgar,[7] Alcide, Arrogant,[8] & some frigates.

I wish that the Queen's health may not have been impaired by the anxiety of

[1] A line-of-battle ship carrying 100 guns.
[2] Mr. Denoyer was the Princes' dancing master.
[3] A 74-gun ship.   [4] A 90-gun ship.   [5] A 50-gun ship.
[6] An 80-gun ship.   [7] A 74-gun ship.   [8] A 74-gun ship.

the mind, occasioned by the sudden news of the combined Fleets appearing in the Channel.

I wish your Majesty & the Queen joy for the birthdays of my dear brothers Frederick & the Prince of Wales who I hope will be an honour to our country & a comfort & a credit to our family.

We celebrated the Prince of Wales birthday by firing many great guns & small arms. We had the Captains of our division to dine aboard.

I have nothing more to add, than to beg your Majesty to give my duty to the Queen & my love to my brothers & sisters, & to assure your Majesty that I am [etc.]. (44602–3)

[*Prince George, at Spithead, 18 Oct. 1779.*] As Mr. Majendie had told me that he was writing to the General, I was desirous that a letter of mine to your Majesty might accompany his.

I am afraid that in a former letter your Majesty did not receive the best accounts of my behaviour. In the course of the day I was very sorry for what I had done, & hope that I never shall be in such a temper again. The Admiral & Mr. Majendie gave me a great deal of good advice, which I hope I have followed, but that will be best known by the letter which mine accompanies.

I have lived very pleasantly during the time we have been in port: & particularly since I wrote last to Edward. We have been to the Isle of Wight several times, & twice up Beaulieu River: near the Duke of Mountagu's seat,[1] where the Adml. shot two brace of pheasants; the first time we went without knowing there was game. In our second visit, we went to the gamekeeper's house & he attended us with his dogs. We had to deal with brambles & thorns, & at last got into a swamp. When we returned on board the cutter, we had a fire lighted, & I pulled off my shoes & stockings to dry. As I was sitting by the fire side, a cinder fell out & burnt my foot. This has turned to a sore, which is troublesome & makes me limp a little.

There have been several courts martial upon deserters & mutinous people, most of whom have been condemned to be flogged. I attended one lately, held on board the Britannia, upon Captain Crosby, of the Heart of Oak, armed ship on the impress service. The charge is very heinous; he is accused of having discharged good men, & rated boys as able seamen, sold the stores, detained the men's liquor for his own use, & committed other crimes contrary to the good of your Majesty's service; if these be proved against him, he will be certainly broke.

I have received a letter from my brother Edward, in which he tells me that the family have lived very happily at Windsor: but above all things I am pleased to find that your Majesties have received more satisfaction from him this summer than you have at any time. I am glad that this has been the case, on another account, for it must have given the General pleasure.

We do not hear the accounts that I wish from the West Indies, nor even from North America. However, we must hope for better fortune & depend upon the Sovereign Disposer of all things. We know that fortune is variable, & it would

---

[1] Beaulieu, near Lymington.

be very unbecoming to despond. The fatal end of Captain Farmer[1] shocked me very much, for I had dined with him the day before he set off: he expressed to me the greatest joy upon going, & the expectations of being succesful; but unfortunately met with a melancholy end.

In the present state of affairs your Majesty has great comfort in your family, who, I hope, do all in their power to contribute to your Majesty's ease. I am sure at least they ought if they do not. As for myself, it is & will be my constant endeavour ever to please you.

May I trouble your Majesty to present my duty to the Queen, & my love to my brothers & sisters. (44604–5)

[*Prince George at Spithead, Wednesday, 24 Nov. 1779.*] I suppose that the Fleet is going to be laid up for the winter, & that I shall return home soon to appear before your Majesty again. This will therefore be probably the last letter that I shall write to any of the family this year.

I hope, Sir, that by my conduct it will appear that I have learnt nothing bad. I should be sorry to show any bad example to my brothers, & particularly to my sisters. I hope on the contrary by the accounts your Majesty will receive from the Adl. it may be known that I am in the way of proving an honour to my country & a comfort to my parents: that my moral conduct is not infected by the great deal of vice I have seen, nor my manners more impolite by the roughness peculiar to most seamen.

Upon the whole our private affairs with Mr. Majendie have been but little interrupted; they were sometimes necessarily broken off, particularly when we cleared ship, & whenever anything was done by which I could gain any knowledge in my profession. I have gone three times through the six first books of Euclid, once through part of logarithms, & some more algebra & trigonometry. With Mr. Majendie I have written a short account of the History of England from the Reformation till the Revolution, & am now reading Sully's[2] Memoires. I have translated French, Latin, & English, in all which I hope I am improved. The drawing has not gone on quite so well. I am sensible I have been negligent about it; it is at present more attended to.

By this method of living I have learnt many things in common life I never knew before; amongst others keeping accounts. I have seen the manners practised in the world, & things begin to appear to me in a very different light from what I had seen them before. I have seen martial discipline kept up, & the severity arising from it executed: the manner courts martial are held: the justice that is done in a free country.

I look forward with the greatest pleasure to the time when I shall see all my dear relations again, whose love I am sure to meet with if I deserve it, & till your Majesty thinks proper to send for me home, believe me [etc.]. (44606–7)

[1] George Farmer (*d.* 1779). Lieutenant, 1759; Commander, 1768; Captain, 1771. He was blown up with his ship on 6 Oct. after a desperate engagement with a French frigate with a much more powerful armament.

[2] The Duc de Sully (1560–1641), Henry IV's chief Minister. Two volumes of his *Memoirs* were printed in 1638 and two more in 1662. An English translation was first published in 1756.

[*Prince George, Spithead, 2 Dec. 1779.*] I have received this morning your Majesty's two letters which were brought by General de Budé. I have taken the opportunity of the General's return to send back this answer. Your Majesty's letter alone would have done me real pleasure, but the arrival of the General greatly added to it.

While I was on shore yesterday, I heard that the Prince George was ordered to prepare for foreign service immediately, a thing very little suspected. When I heard it, I thought your Majesty would send for me home; yet it was my desire to go wherever the ship was sent. However, I would have returned home with pleasure if it had been your Majesty's will to send for me. I cannot but say that I am heartily glad to hear of my going to sea in the ship. During the cruize I will do my best towards discharging my duty, & will use my endeavours to improve in the instruction given me.

The General has acquainted me with the arrangement your Majesty has thought proper to appoint for me when I come on shore, for which I am very thankful both to your Majesty & the Queen; & ever be assured that I am [etc.]. (44608)

[*Prince George, at sea, Lat. in 12° 42' North, Sunday, 9 Jan. 1780.*] I am very happy to congratulate your Majesty upon the success of the Fleet under Sr. George Rodney & to give you an account of what I myself saw.[1]

Yesterday morning we fell in with a fleet which proved to be a Spanish fleet of merchantmen bound from St. Sebastian to Cadiz under the convoy of a 64-gun ship, 4 frigates, & 2 sloops, laden with corn & naval stores. They sailed to the number of 27 from St. Sebastian, but four had parted company. We took all the rest & were informed that another convoy was to sail from the same place, bound to Cadiz, & laden with the same commodities, four days after they had.[2]

I have been present at the taking of the first line of battle ship[3] this war, & hope to see such a number of them taken before the end of it, as that our enemies, who have undertaken the war upon such unfair grounds, may suffer for their temerity. This I wish may be the beginning of a successful year.

The Queen & all the family, I am sure, will rejoice at the news; to whom I beg your Majesty to present my best wishes & congratulations on this success; & to believe me [etc.]. (44609–10)

[*Prince George, Gibraltar Bay, 26 Jan. 1780.*] Since my last letter I have an occasion of congratulating your Majesty upon greater & more important success, our squadron having taken most of the ships under the command of Don Juan de Langara.[4]

After the America & the prizes had parted company for England, we made the best of our way to Cape St. Vincent, which we saw on the 16th. We had been informed a few days before by a Dutchman that there was a fleet of Spanish

[1] Rodney's fleet had been ordered to relieve Gibraltar, which was besieged by the Spaniards.

[2] Cf. the Admiralty communiqué, 22 Jan. (*Morning Chronicle*, 24 Jan. 1780); *Annual Register*, 1780 (*Hist. of Europe*, p. 202); John Watkins, *Life of William IV*, I, 38.

[3] Rodney christened this 64-gun ship the *Prince William*.

[4] There is an account of this action in the *Morning Chronicle*, 16 Feb. 1780. Cf. *Annual Register*, 1780 (*Hist. of Europe*, pp. 202–3); Watkins, *Life of William IV*, I, 40.

line of battle ships, cruizing between Cape St. Vincent & Cape St. Mary's, which put us upon our guard. About one o'clock in the forenoon on the 16th, the signal was made for a fleet, & soon afterwards for their being enemies. At about four o'clock the engagement began; soon after the St. Domingo[1] blew up; a most shocking & dreadful sight. Being not certain whether it was an enemy or a friend, I felt a horror all over me. We were three miles astern, & heard no noise, nor saw any of the wreck. The engagement continued till eight, when it began to slacken. At twelve we were coming up fast, & the fire became very brisk. At one the Prince George came into action, & fired four broad sides at a ship which was making her escape & had lost her main top mast. We carried away her main yard, after which she struck. We sent for the Spanish officers, who told us her name was St. Julian, a ship of 70 guns, commanded by the Marquis de Medina, who, being wounded, was excused coming on board. An officer & some men went on board of her. Next morning we parted company from her, & saw her in the course of the next night making signals of distress. We have not seen her since, & are afraid she has fallen into the hands of the Spaniards.[2]

Thus far in the year 80, fortune has crowned us with success. I hope it will go on so thro' the year: that our enemies, who have so unjustly taken up the war to assist rebellious subjects, may feel the effects of our arms.

Two days after our victory we anchored in Gibraltar Bay, where I passed my time very agreeably. I have been three times on shore, & received very affectionately on your Majesty's account. I have walked over all the town & garrison, dined with General Eliot,[3] & have seen the batteries, & Spanish lines. The idea of the Spaniards was to take Gibraltar by famine, but, as long as we keep a superiority at sea it is impossible. To take it by storm would be hardly practicable, for it is too strongly fortified both by nature & art.

This news of our victory will, I am sure, give great pleasure to the Queen, my brothers & sisters, to whom I beg your Majesty to present my best wishes & congratulations; & ever believe me [etc.]. (44611–2)

[*Prince George, Gibraltar Bay, 8 Feb. 1780.*] I did myself the honour of writing to your Majesty by the Childers brig which carried Captain Mc. Bride with Sr. George Rodney's Dispatches for England. But the winds have been so contrary that the vessel has not been able to get through the Straights. I therefore take the first opportunity of the Hyena, which is to carry the Admiral's duplicates, to send a second letter in case the first should miscarry.

Since the time I have been here I have passed my time very agreeably. I have dined several times with General Eliot. The last time the General invited us, Don Juan de Langara, the Spanish Commodore, & the Captains of the Spanish ships, were of the party. I have been up to the top of the Rock, both to the northward & to the southward. The General has been so good as to promise me a plan of the whole, & of the enemy's camp & lines. I have seen that part of your Majesty's Electoral troops which is here under the command of a very worthy, & loyal subject, Major-General de la Motte.

[1] A 70-gun ship, with a crew of 600.   [2] The *San Julian* ran aground.   [3] See No. 9.

Till I have the pleasure of seeing the Queen, my brothers & sisters, will you assure them of my love & attachment for them, & ever believe me [etc.]. (44613–4)

[*Prince George, off Scilly, 3 March 1780.*] Since my last letter to your Majesty dated in Gibraltar Bay, & conveyed to England in the Hyena, the Fleet (under the command of Admiral Digby, since Sr. George Rodney left us[1]) has been further successful in falling in with a French convoy on the 24th of last month, bound to the Isle of France, under the command of the Vicomte de Duchilio in Le Prothée, a 64-gun ship. The convoy consisted of L'Ajax, L'Eléphante, Le Gange (of the same force), La Charmante, a frigate of 20 guns, two armed brigs, & a cutter. We discovered them at two in the afternoon, & chaced them all night. Between one & two next morning the Resolution & Bedford came up & engaged the Prothée for some time, when she struck. She has on board to the value, we are told, of £100,000 of ready money. Two other prizes have been taken, one by the Malborough [*sic*] & another by the Apostle. The Invincible, Bienfaisante & Triton parted company in the chace, but have since joined us off Scilly. Thus far in the year 80 every thing has been successful on our side, as if Providence was resolved to punish our enemies for having begun the war so unjustly.

When I return home, I shall be happy to present your Majesty with the Ensigns, taken from on board the Prince William, the St. Julian & Le Prothée, as trophies of our success over the French, & Spanish.

As to myself since our departure from Spithead, I have been reading astronomy, & have learnt the methods of finding the latitude, longitude & variations of the compass. I have brought home a plan of Gibraltar, which General Eliot obligingly ordered to be made for me, where your Majesty will see the works raised since the last disturbances.

The Queen & all our family must heartily rejoice at the success of our Fleet. I shall defer giving a further account of what I have seen till I have the pleasure of seeing them after my long absence.[2] I intend writing to the Queen by this opportunity, & shall therefore have the pleasure of assuring her Majesty myself of my duty, & respect. (44615–6)

[*Prince George, at sea, 16 June 1780.*] The day after General de Budé left us, we went out with a fair wind: however, soon after the wind changed & we were obliged to beat down Channel. Last night the Admiral bore away for Ushant, but as it became calm this morning Admiral Geary[3] was so civil as to write word to Admiral Digby that about noon he would send a cutter into Falmouth, & it is by this means that your Majesty will receive this letter.

As soon as I came on board, I began the usual course again: in pursuing

---

[1] About the middle of February Rodney, having re-victualled the Gibraltar garrison, sailed for the West Indies, leaving a portion of his fleet under Digby, who escorted his Spanish prizes to England.

[2] He arrived in London, at the Queen's Palace, on 8 March. His furlough was a short one: in May he sailed from Spithead with Admiral Geary, and returned in August.

[3] Admiral Sir Francis Geary (1710?–96). Lieutenant, 1735; Captain, 1741; Rear-Admiral, 1758; Vice-Admiral, 1762; Admiral, 1773. Commander-in-Chief at Portsmouth, 1770; commander of the Channel fleet, May 1780. Baronet, 1782. The *Victory* was his flagship.

astronomy, improving myself in French, Latin & History. Till now I have been happy, & pleased with everything about me. In general Mr. Majendie has expressed his satisfaction of my manner of going on, & I mean to continue in the same way. The Admiral, who has my interest at heart, approves of my conduct, & for this reason, believing me steadier, & more attentive to the duty of the ship than I was last summer, has ordered me to keep a more regular watch.

Whilst we were in port, our time was spent very agreeably; we dined at Sr. Thomas Pye's[1] & on your Majesty's birthday we went to the Dockyard to see the procession of the shipwrights, & afterwards dined on board the Victory, where Admiral Geary gave a dinner to all the Admirals & Captains of the Fleet.

We are all in hopes of meeting some French frigate, & as we are now cruizing near the coast of France, of taking several prizes to make up for our unsuccessful cruize last summer.

I beg your Majesty to present my duty & affection to the Queen. In all affairs that relate to my happiness & advantage, I know the Queen takes the most lively interest. I promise always to use my utmost endeavours to prove myself, Sir, [etc.]. (44617–8)

4270 THE QUEEN *to* PRINCE WILLIAM

[*Kew, 28 July 1780.*] The confirmation of your total recovery by your own letter gave both the King and me great satisfaction, and I am glad to find that your natural good spirits are also so well restored as to make you write so chearfully.

There is however one paragraph in your letter which gives me, if possible, even more pleasure than that of your recovery, I mean that in which you mention the different feelings and struggles you perceived in leaving Kew, and at parting with us. Nothing can be more amiable and commendable in a human mind than the attachment to one's family; both religion and nature require it of us, and it is one of the first Christian principles instilled in a young mind, as the beginning of fulfilling their duty towards God, in paying regard to obedience to one's parents. This I see you considered well when you say you went away reluctantly, but submitted to the King's will with chearfulness. You have met with nothing in your profession hitherto that could set you against it; on the contrary, with every advantage and encouragement possible. You find yourself under the command of an Officer who besides being a very religious and honest man, is possessed of a very amiable character and disposition of temper; he loves you and thinks of nothing so much, after pushing you in your profession, than to make you spend your time happily. You have Mr. Majendie's kind and friendly advice upon every occasion, who loves you also very much, does you justice whenever an opportunity happens; but, like an honest man, is not blind to your faults, and perfectly agrees with the Admiral. Your Fleet also has been, last year and this, rather fortunate; therefore I see everything that should make you delight in your profession,

[1] Admiral Sir Thomas Pye (1713?–85). Entered the navy, 1727; Lieutenant, 1735; Captain, 1741; Rear-Admiral, 1758; Vice-Admiral, 1762; Admiral, 1773. Commander-in-Chief at Portsmouth, 1770–3 and 1777–83. M.P. for Rochester, 1771–4. Knighted, 1773.

particularly as the Navy is one of the greatest supports of this country. And I know you so well that whenever you give your little head time to think, you will glory in being one of the members of that support. In your situation you could not choose better than you have done. A Prince, as well as the rest of the world, is a member of Society, and consequently should try to be as useful as possible. That can never be obtained but by pursuing a regular plan in life, this you do in perfecting yourself in your profession; in which you should try to become all perfection, well considering that the higher your rank the more the world will expect from you; and therefore, I beseech you to endeavour, in everything you undertake, to do better than the rest of the world. I love you so well, that I cannot bear the idea of your being only *mediocre*. Perfection is the thing you should aim at. And that I know you will do when you are persuaded that it will make the King and myself happy.

The report of the King's being reconciled to his brothers is true; it seems to give universal satisfaction in public, but makes no difference in our way of living at Windsor. The Duke of Cumberland comes to Court, and walks Sundays upon the Terrace. The Duke of Glocester's bad state of health will not permit him to do either.

I am glad to find that you feel a pleasure in keeping company with young Stopford and Legg,[1] as both are so amiable and good in their disposition. I hope you will see the benefit arising from keeping good company, and set as good an example to your young companions as you can. Low company is always a ruin to a young mind, but it particularly is the greatest proof of pride a man can give.

In a short time you shall hear again from me. The King sends his love to you, and so does the rest of the family. All at Eastbourn are well. Edward learns to swim and is delighted with this amusement. (Add. Georgian 21/1/9)

4271   *Letters from* PRINCE WILLIAM *to the* KING, *and a reply*

[*Prince George, at sea, Lat. 45° 52′, 6 Aug. 1780.*] I received the 23 of last month by the Marlborough your Majesty's letter of the 20 of June, in which your Majesty expresses your satisfaction at the accounts you have received from the Admiral with respect to me. I hope my conduct has been the same since, for it shall always be my endeavour to do my duty.

As for my studies, I have begun opticks with Mr. Waddington,[2] & am now able to keep the ship's reckoning. I believe I am perfect in euclid, trigonometry & that part of astronomy I have read with him. With Mr. Majendie I am pursuing the usual studies.

I sincerely hope that the Queen enjoys perfect health, & that my brothers & sisters are all well. By the late unfortunate riot[3] of a deluded multitude, I am sensible that the Queen must have been allarmed. I thank God it is at an end, & hope the punishment of the rioters will prove an example for the future.

[1] Probably Sir Arthur Kaye Legge (1766–1835), the 3rd Earl of Dartmouth's brother. Lieutenant, 1789; Commander, 1790; Captain, 1793; Rear-Admiral, 1810; Vice-Admiral, 1814.
[2] Chaplain of the *Prince George*.
[3] The 'No Popery' riots of June, when London was in the hands of a raging mob for several days.

For your Majesty's health & prosperity, as well as those of the Queen, I shall pray to the Divine Providence in terms of a most dutiful [etc.]

P.S. As the wind is now contrary, & it may be some time before we get in, the Admiral is sending in a frigate (her name I have not been able to learn) which will convey this letter to your Majesty, I could not allow the opportunity to slip without writing. (44619–20)

[*The King's reply, Windsor Castle, 22 Aug.*] I have received your letter of the 6th of last month, and this day one of the 6th of this month. I flatter myself your conduct has changed this year much to your advantage, as the accounts from the Admiral as well as those from Mr. Majendie have uniformly given me satisfaction. Indeed I have no objects in life but to do my duty and to see my children turn out an ornament to their country and a comfort to their parents, which can alone be attained by assiduity and imbibing virtuous and honourable principles such as must render them useful members of society and examples to the youth of this country, that may tend to restore the manners of it.

You may easily imagine though ever much in our thoughts that yesterday was kept as a day of festivity; may it ever be so to the latest period of my life, which will be a proof of your conducting yourself praiseworthily, and you will ever find me [etc.].

P.S. I do not mean by my general commendation to include that I understand you have quite conquered your warmth, on any improprieties in your conduct being pointed out, but I trust your good sense will correct that which must arise more from pride than sense. (Add. Georgian 21/1/2)

[*From Prince William, Prince George, in Torbay, 29 Sept.*] It is with the greatest pleasure & satisfaction I congratulate your Majesty on the Queen's safe delivery on the 22d instant, a day already propitious to your Majesty. I received the news of this happy event by a letter from the General, dated that same day, in which he mentions that the Queen was as well as could possibly be expected, & my little brother likewise.[1] I think that, whether it had been a brother or a sister, it would have given equal pleasure; but I confess, as to myself, I am more happy it is a boy, because when he grows up, he may be more useful to his country.

Will your Majesty be so good as to give my duty & my sincere congratulations to the Queen, & my love to all my brothers & sisters.

We attempted to get out of Torbay, but were driven in again by contrary winds; since that time we have had courts martial, held every day, on board the Prince George. A man belonging to the Foudroyant, was sentenced to receive 300 lashes for having struck his officers; & four deserters from the Valiant were condemned to death, not only for their desertion, but for high treason in appearing in open arms against their King & country, having been taken on board a French privateer.

I have nothing more to add than to assure your Majesty of my being [etc.]. (44622)

---

[1] Prince Alfred, born on 22 Sept. 1780, died on 20 Aug. 1782.

[*Hanover, 5 Feb. 1781.*] I delayed writing to your Majesty last post as Monsieur de Hardenberg was so good as to say that he would take charge of my letter. The Field Marechal is in a manner recovered, it was impossible for me to see him till yesterday bedause his phisitian would not permit him to speak as it increased his cough. I found him very chearfull and looking much better, than considering the violence of the disorder one could have expected. Last Tuesday I saw all the horses in the stables. As for the coach horses nothing can be finer for parade, particularly the tall set of creams, though I own I give the preference to the white set over all the others. The travelling sets go at the rate of about six miles an hour. As for the saddle horses I cannot say much in their praise. In general all the stallions are bad, particularly Chance and Soldier. All Chance's breed are heavy shouldered and ugly headed, and in general all the horses have long pasterns. And then they are excessively ill broke. Kemp hangs totally by the bit so that they stick their noses out and depend totally upon the rider's strength, for if he lets the reins loose in the least they must tumble down and by this manner of riding also, their paces are broke, so that there is not hardly a horse that can go any regular pace. There is one little brown mair which has not been long enough under them to be quite spoilt, and there is also a little stone horse which Busch used to ride, they are the only two saddle horses I have yet seen that I think worth speaking of, the little white horse is only fit for the mange.

Permit me, Sir, before I close my letter to desire your Majesty to give my duty to the Queen and my love to Prince of Wales, and all my other brothers and sisters, and be assured, Sir, that nothing shall be wanting on my part to fullfill your Majesty's expectation. (43378–9)

[*Hanover, 27 Feb.*] I cannot let the messenger set out without writing a few lines to thank your Majesty for the two gracious letters which I received last week. I have very little new to communicate to your Majesty except the recovery of the Field Marechal, which I thought very doubtfull. I have seen him very often but I own I thought there was very little chance till within this last week, but the change is so very considerable that I think he will in a very few days be able to go abroad. Our weather here is worse this year than ever it was known before. At one moment it snows and at another it is so windy there is no bearing it. Everybody expected on Friday that we should have gone in sledges the very next day, but in one night the whole was gone. I forgot to acquaint your Majesty that the Landgrave of Hesse Cassel sent one of his Chambelains last week to congratulate me upon my arrival here. Everybody here appears quite happy that your Majesty has been so gracious to give the vacant Regiment to General Friedricks. He has the true look of an old soldier, and I honour him very much for not making any secret that he was a private trooper in our service. He told me himself he was a Private in Wade's[1] Horse which I believe now is the Prince of Wales Dragoon Guards; he owns himself above seventy five and he is thought to be at least eighty.

---

[1] George Wade (1673–1748); Field Marshal, 1743; commanded in Flanders, 1744–5, and against Prince Charles Edward, 1745.

Permit me, Sir, before I conclude my letter to desire your Majesty to present my duty to the Queen and my love to my brothers and sisters and to believe me [etc.]. (43390–1)

[*Hanover, 13 March.*] Since my last letter Monsieur de Hacke acquainted me that he had received your Majesty's orders to construct the stables at the house which you bought for my use, but it will require such total alterations which cannot be begun till after Easter and will take the whole summer that till it is known what your Majesty intends to do with the house after I quit Hanover I begged Mons. de Hacke not to begin, particularly as they are fitting up stables at Mont Brilliant which will be ready before my horses can possibly arrive. If your Majesty intends to keep the house standing afterwards then we must only pull down the inside of the house to make the stables, but if it is your intention to pull it down it will be much better to pull it down now, by which means the Palace will be separated from any other house on that side, and by running the stables up against the wall of the next house, they will be much better and lighter, and they will then be able to break another door into the Opera House which is really of great consequence because at present there is but one passage out, so that if the house was to take fire the people would be either burnt or crushed to pieces.

I have nothing new to acquaint your Majesty with. We have had three shooting parties, in which I have had very great success, because having very good eyes I am already a good shot. Permit me, Sir, before I close my letter to trouble your Majesty with my duty to the Queen and my love to Prince of Wales and my other brothers and sisters. (43395–6)

[*Hanover, 29 March.*] I have a thousand thanks to return your Majesty for the gracious letter which the courier brought me. I cannot describe how much I feel myself flattered by the affectionate manner in which you express yourself hitherto pleased with my conduct. Your Majesty may be thoroughly convinced that nothing shall ever be wanting on my part to fulfill your expectations of me. I shall certainly in the first letter which I write to my brother express as forcibly as I can what your Majesty wishes. As for my studies I am so far advanced with Hograve[1] that I this morning made my first survey. I find the German grow every day more and more easy, so that I now dare begin to talk it a little. I went on Sunday last to see Hernhausen, which to be sure is not in a very good state at present; however, they are repairing it, there is a great deal of room in the house. I cannot conclude my letter without most sincerely congratulating your Majesty on the good news from Sir George Rodney,[2] I hope that in a short time you will receive as good from Admiral Darby. Permit me, Sir, to trouble your Majesty with my love to my brothers and sisters, and to subscribe myself [etc.].

P.S. May I trouble your Majesty to give my humble duty to the Queen, and acquaint her that I intend myself the honor of answering her letter next post? (43400–1)

[1] Captain Hogreve.
[2] Admiral Rodney had recently seized the Dutch West Indian island of St. Eustatius, with merchandise worth more than two millions, but the island was subsequently lost, with a large part of the booty, to De Bouillé.

[*Prince George, off Cape Spartel, 11 April 1781.*] By the date of this letter your Majesty will see that we are at no great distance from Gibraltar. We have not yet met with the success of last year. However I make no doubt that if we were to meet with them, Spanish Fleet [*sic*] we should have a complete victory, for by all accounts they are said to have no more than 32 sail of the line. If an English squadron of 27 sail of the line, of which 9 are 3 deckers, cannot beat 32 Spaniards, they ought not to see England again. The Fleet are in great health & very desirous to meet their enemies, as I hope an English Fleet will ever be.

Since I have been on board this last time, I have begun mechanicks with Mr. Waddington. Everything else goes on as usual.

I beg your Majesty will give my duty to the Queen, & my love to all my brothers & sisters, & ever believe me [etc.]. (44624)

4274 *Letters from* PRINCE FREDERICK *to the* KING

[*Hanover, 7 May 1781.*] I hope your Majesty will pardon my long silence, but not having anything material to write to you by last post, I was desirous of delaying my letter till the departure of the courier. The Count de la Lippe was so polite as to invite me to go tomorrow to Wilhelmstein to see the fortress, which now nobody is allowed to see without a particular permission. As we shall be probably out all day, I am obliged to write now. The Field Marechal has been so good as to settle that I should set out either the eighteenth or nineteenth of this month to see the Hartz, the Solling Herpsberg Furstenberg &c. We shall probably pass ten days or a fortnight in our tour. I shall within a fortnight or three weeks at farthest begin gunnery, having already gone through geometry and the greatest part of trigonometry, there now therefore remains only levelling, and a slight knowledge of conic sections, before I am able to begin with Colonel Trey.[1] I can not sufficiently express to your Majesty how much I am obliged to Captain Hograve, for having rendered this study which is otherwise dry as easy and amusing as possible. I am affraid I have already tresspassed too much upon your Majesty's patience. I shall therefore only entreat you to present my humble duty to the Queen and my love to my brothers and sisters. (43418–9)

[*Hanover, 5 June.*] Though I know how much your Majesty dislikes compliments, yet I hope you will receive my most sincere congratulations upon the anniversary of your birthday,[2] and my most hearty prayers to Heaven to shower down upon you, every blessing both in your publick and private affairs, which it is possible to receive. I went last week to make Prince Earnest[3] a visit at Zelle. The town is extremely ugly but the faubourg where the nobility live is very fine. I went in the evening to see the Mad House. I was told that I should be excessively struck by the appearance of the mad people, but I must confess that I was not half so much struck with them as with the State prisoners. They are perfectly well taken

---

[1] He refers to Colonel Trew in Nos. 273 and 315.   [2] June 4.   [3] The Queen's brother.

care of and the man who is at the head of it is exceedingly attentive and kind to them. I saw Henneberg. He is grown fat, and now wears a wig. They told me that he has had only one fit of madness since he has been there. He is allowed to go about and play, but he is always attended by one of the people belonging to the house. My hand is so far recovered, that both Zimmerman and the surgeon have given me leave to go to the Hartz.[1] I am to set out tomorrow morning. Permit me, Sir, before I conclude my letter, to trouble your Majesty with my duty to the Queen, and my love to my brothers and sisters; and to sign myself [etc.]. (43427-8)

[*Montbrilliant, 3 July.*] Yesterday evening Prince Henry of Prussia[2] passed through here. He only staid supper, and continued his journey to Spa. I cannot say his appearance is much in his favor; he is the very image of Lord Oxford, only the eyes stand much more out of his head; he appears exceedingly high and proud. His Chamberlain, Monsieur de Wrech, is exactly Baddeley[3] when he acts Canton in the Clandestine Marriage.[4] After having said he should arrive at six he never came till half an hour after nine and set out again at twelve. He had said that if he was invited he might possibly stay some days here upon his return. But as I thought your Majesty would not like it, and I confess upon my account I thought that everything in the world should deter me from even the appearance of an acquaintance with such a person, I cautiously avoided giving the least hint on that subject.

I this morning began my first lesson in artillery, Colonel Trey having recommended a Lieutenant Wessel of the Artillery to teach me, as he himself is not master enough either of the French or English languages to be able to do it himself.

I am affraid I tresspass too long upon your Majesty's patience, I shall therefore only add that I have the honor to be [etc.].

P.S. I enclose to your Majesty the letter[5] which I received from Prince Henry, which I believe it was more difficult for me to make out than for his Royal Highness to write. (43435-6)

4275   THE KING *to* PRINCE WILLIAM

[*10 July 1781.*] You are now going for the first time to a foreign Station, and consequently for a very considerable time to a distance from your parents. I avoid taking a long leave for it could only give us both pain and could avail nothing to your advantage; a long conversation of advice might strike you at the moment, but the levity of youth would probably by degrees destroy its having the full effect that must be of utility to you. I have therefore preferred putting down my thoughts on paper and on the cover directing Major-General de Budé to deliver

[1] For his accident, see *Corresp. of George, Prince of Wales*, I, 63 n.
[2] Brother of Frederick the Great. (1726-1802). He married Wilhelmina (1726-1808), daughter of the Landgrave Maximilian of Hesse-Cassel.
[3] Robert Baddeley (1733-94), the Drury Lane actor.   [4] By the Elder Colman.
[5] Missing.

it to you in the presence of Mr. Majendie that you may read it before them both, which is also the clearest method of you as well as Mr. Majendie clearly comprehending my orders; it will also be the best method of your from time to time refreshing your memory as to my sentiments, and enable Mr. Majendie more forcibly to convey any advice that he may think you require. It would be but time thrown away to mention his zeal for your turning out to my comfort, to the credit of yourself and to the advantage of the public, for you know my sentiments on that head and you have expressed yours to me as well.

I should not deal with the openess that I feel my duty, did I not express how much I was pleased, the first days of your return, with the affection and attention towards me and the Queen that marked every step you took, and how sensibly you talked on the improper conduct of one who is dear to all of us; but since that, things have somewhat changed. It has clearly appeared to both of us that you have been more desirous of getting out of the room and perhaps in some degree copying what seemed very properly not to please you when you first came back to us; had your stay been longer I should have mentioned it, but as I knew it could last but for [a] few weeks, I thought it more advisable to wait if any change arose from yourself, or at worst to put it in this letter before your eyes, as an example how with best intentions evil example is catching. I shall say no more on this subject but leave it to your own reflections.

Of course you will feel that I expect an implicit obedience to the directions you will receive from Rear-Admiral Digby, whose care and attention to those he has bred up is very conspicuous from the success [illegible][1] in Lord Longford[2] and Captain Cornwallis, but it is impossible he can attend to more than your improvement in your profession and your behaviour whilst in his presence. On Mr. Majendie therefore I depend for the prosecution of your studies, for instilling those sentiments which may make you a good Christian and a good man; which comprehend every quality that will make you happy in yourself, a comfort to your family and a credit to your country. From youth it has sometimes dropped from you, as if you thought nautical knowledge was the whole expected of you, but you forget that you are a Prince, that it is in the womb of fate whether in futurity you may not be called to the most arduous situation. You must therefore have all the means of doing your duty if that event should happen; besides if you behave as you ought I shall naturally wish to advance you in your profession, and bring you by degrees much earlier forward than any private person can; but that will require on your side not only professional ability but a steadiness and propriety of conduct. You must be from behaviour, from sedateness, fit for my advancing you, or my affection would be conspicuous at the expence of my judgement, and even duty, which you may depend upon never shall be the case; till the world sees you are to be trusted with command, you shall not have it.

As the Admiral may not always be enabled to be so much at sea as he naturally would wish, and as a Port is not a good place for improvement, he has my leave

---

[1] The letters in Add. Georgian 21 are photostats. The original of this letter has clearly been torn across the middle of the page and repaired just where this passage comes. Moreover, the King obviously corrected the word he originally wrote.

[2] Edward Michael, 2nd Baron Longford (1743–92). Succeeded his father in 1766.

to send you at times in frigates for short cruizes, but never without Mr. Majendie accompanying you. I should not have the real affection I have for you if I neglected any means of having you guided through this perilous world. I trust your conduct towards Mr. Majendie will enable him to go through his attendance till you are of an age to have his assistance less necessary; but should that not happen you may depend I shall send some other person to take care of you, for I could not answer it to my conscience to let you proceed in your profession but under a conviction that you have the assistance of a person on whose morals as well as knowledge I can depend that whilst advancing in one branch, you are not neglecting every other, and destroying those principles which alone can make you a good or useful member of society.

You mentioned to me the other day a desire that you might be permitted to write to me without communicating the draughts to anyone. I readily give that permission as far as relates to your writing to the Queen or me, but to any of your brothers or any other person Mr. Majendie must see them, for it is impossible any harm can arise from any confidence you may place in your parents, but in other persons the case is quite different; therefore the same injunction subsists as did on former occasions exclusive of the exceptions now made.

My dear William, I now conclude my epistle with wishing you every degree of health and prosperity, every good inclination to become what both parents so eagerly implore the Divine Providence to effect; and assuring you of the affection of the Queen as well as of him who will ever wish to remain [etc.]. (Add. Georgian 21/1/17)

4276 PRINCE FREDERICK *to the* KING

[*Hanover, 30 July 1781.*] As General Freytag is returning to England I take the opportunity of supplicating your Majesty's permission of serving next campaign in America. I have explained to the General every reason which makes me particularly anxious for it. I must assure your Majesty however that it is not owing in the least to any dislike to this place, for I should be very ungratefull if I was not pleased with my situation here, as everybody does their utmost to render it agreable to me, but from my great desire to serve your Majesty and to learn that profession which I have entered into. On our road back from Pyrmont, where we received every kind of civility and politeness from the Prince of Waldeck, who, to all appearance, is a well wisher to your Majesty's arms, in his heart we saw the field of battle of Hastenbeck.[1] The country is of itself so strong that it is hardly possible to take a bad position, and certainly if it had not been owing to unpardonable neglect the battle must have been ours. When we came to the spot where the fifteen French batallions were drove down the precipice by General Brulenbach with three batallions, the Landrath Bulow, who then served in Freytag's Chasseurs, said that four and twenty years before on that very same day, he was posted in the same place, being first day of the battle, and looked with as

---

[1] On 26 July 1757 the Duke of Cumberland's army was defeated by the French at Hastenbeck, on the Weser, and the Electorate of Hanover was in consequence overrun.

much unconcern upon the canonade in the plain as he did now, as it was then thought impossible for the French to make any attack on the mountain.

The Field Marechal desired me to ask your Majesty's permission to lodge during the camp in one of the villages in the rear, as it would be very inconvenient for me to come every morning from Hanover.

I am affraid I have tresspassed too much upon your Majesty's patience by this long letter. I shall therefore only beg your Majesty to give my duty to the Queen and my love to my brothers and sisters. (43446–7)

4277 THE QUEEN *to the* KING

[*Queen's House, Windsor, 19 Aug. 1781.*] There never was anybody so agreably surprised as I have been an hour ago by the arrival of your Majesty's letter, for which I return you a thousand thanks. I am glad to find that you continue well, and that your journey as far as you are come affords you pleasure, and I look forward with great impatience for Wednesday evening to embrace and congratulate your Majesty upon your return amongst us.[1] A quarter before three I had sent off a letter to town which I ordered to be given to your postillion in order to be delivered to you when the horses were sent for, but the arrival of the messenger 20 minutes past three with so charming a letter is to[o] great a temptation for me to withstand writing a second time. Our news are not of any great importance, I met Lady Sicilia Johnson[2] and her family upon the Terrace last night; the General seems delighted with the thought of your Majesty's seeing his Regiment soon, as we have had plentifull of rain within these three days, the showers have been very partial and very heavy which hath cooled the air wonderfully, and makes the Park look beautifull. Mrs Walsingham[3] hath begun to see her friends on an evening. This is called private, though the number of them is not limited. Neither she nor her daughter[4] have appeared anywhere. Father Paul goes there in order to recruit his spirits, with his coxcomical son, as General Mathews calls him. I am glad that I am not of the party, as I cannot help always dreading to find instead of the *Canon* a *Jesuit*. Mrs Walsingham is rather silent upon her loss, which is, in my opinion, very sensible in her, for if she was to say much upon the subject she must be suspected of hypocrisy.

Lady Juliana Penn[5] hath been for one night at Stoke and from thence is gone

[1] On the 17th the King and the Prince of Wales sailed from Greenwich in different yachts to inspect the dockyard, fortifications and fleet under Vice-Admiral Parker at the Nore. Parker had fought the Dutch, on the Dogger Bank, on 5 August, in an indecisive battle. Horace Walpole wrote: 'The King and Prince have been to thank the Admiral and fleet.' (*Letters* [ed. Toynbee], xii, 40.)

[2] Lady Cecilia West, daughter of the seventh Baron (afterwards first Earl) Delawarr, married (1763) Lieutenant-General James Johnston, Colonel of the Enniskillen Dragoons.

[3] Charlotte, daughter of Sir Charles Hanbury-Williams, married (1759) the Hon. Robert Boyle, fifth son of the first Earl of Shannon. He took the surname of Walsingham on the death of his brother Henry. Walsingham was lost on board the *Thunderer* man-of-war, of which he was commander, in a hurricane in the West Indies in Oct. 1779.

[4] Charlotte, later (1806) Baroness De Ros in her own right (1769–1831). She married Lord Henry Fitzgerald (1761–1829), son of James, first Duke of Leinster, in 1791.

[5] Lady Juliana Penn was the fourth daughter of the first Earl of Pomfret. In 1751 she married Thomas Penn of Stoke Park, Bucks., one of the proprietors of Pennsylvania.

to Harteford, in which neighbourhood she wished to take a house, but not being able to meet with any thing she liked, she hath taken a house belonging to Admiral Forbs[1] near Lady Harriot Cornyes.[2]

The children are, thank God, all in perfect health, and present both their love and duty to you, Octavius[3] in particular wishes much to be with papa, *on board a horse* but not on board a ship. I shall be upon the Terras this evening where I shall make many people happy with the good accounts coming from you, but I am sure nobody's happiness can equal the happiness of her who hath received them, and who subscribes herself with the greatest love and affection [etc.]. (36358–9)

4278   PRINCE FREDERICK *to the* QUEEN

[? *c. 20 Aug. 1781.*] I have a thousand thanks to return your Majesty for the kind and affectionate letter which the courier brought me from you. As for our journey to Brunswic, about which you are so good as to say you are curious to hear the particulars, I must say I found it much more agreable than I thought beforehand I should, as everybody appeared really glad to see me and did everything in their power to render our stay there pleasant to us. I was much afraid I should have to undergo much questioning, but I luckily escaped that. The Duke is exceedingly agreable, and treated me not only with great politeness but also with great affection. As for the Duchess I say nothing about her because your Majesty knows her very well, only that I do not see the least likeness between her and Princess Amelia. As for the Princesses, they are exceedingly polite and agreable. I think I never saw a more beautifull face or figure than Princess Caroline,[4] she is not above thirteen years old, so that she is not allowed to appear in public but of a Sunday evening, and that only for half an hour, so that I could make the least acquaintance with her, but by what I have heard she is very lively and sensible. I cannot however say much in praise of the Hereditary Prince,[5] who is a stupid lubberly boy. He appears one of those kind of beings called a *good-natured* man, which is an expression never made use of when a person has any other good quality to recommend him. I think, Madam, I have now given your Majesty as full an account as I could of the Court of Brunswic. The palace is not yet finished building nor probably ever will be finished. It is of wood; if the whole plan is ever executed it will be in the shape of an A, but at present it to be sure has an odd appearance. The appartments however are exceedingly fine.

I am affraid, Madam, I have already tresspassed too much upon your Majesty's patience. I shall therefore only beg you to give my love to my brothers and sisters and to believe me [etc.]. (43452–3)

---

[1] John Forbes (1714–96), second son of the third Earl of Granard. Lieutenant, 1731; Captain, 1737; Rear-Admiral, 1747; Vice-Admiral, 1755; Admiral, 1758.

[2] Lady Henrietta Fermor (1727–93), daughter of the 1st Earl of Pomfret: married John Conyers, of Copthall, in Essex. He died in 1775.

[3] Prince Octavius, the King's eighth son (1779–83).

[4] Later, Princess of Wales. She had one sister surviving in 1781: Princess Augusta (1764–88), who married Frederick, afterwards King, of Wurtemberg (1754–1816).

[5] Prince Charles of Brunswick-Wolfenbüttel (1766–1806), the Duke's eldest son.

4279 PRINCE WILLIAM *to the* KING

[*Prince George, at sea, 21 Aug. 1781.*] Your Majesty sees by the date of this letter that it was written on the day I was born. The reason I wrote it on this day in particular is because I should naturally think both of what has happened, & what is to be my course of life hereafter. Another reason is, because for some time after my arrival in America my thoughts & time will [be] too much taken up to write long letters.

Since I have been on board this last time, it has been my constant rule to observe in every respect the orders of the Adml. & Mr. Majendie's advice. I have so far succeeded that they are both very well pleased with me. Mr. Majendie has assured [me] that he has written very favourable accounts of my behaviour to your Majesty. The Adml. sent for me this morning to tell me that for the future I should keep my watches regularly like a midshipman upon deck day & night. I am sure I should be very much wanting to your Majesty & the Queen [if] I did not do my utmost, after having received so much encouragement from both my father & mother.

I must own that by nature I always feel a desire of being at home. However, I consider that there are two very good reasons why I should wish now to be absent. The first reason is, because I have an advantage over all others in my situation of life both in seeing the characters of different nations & at making myself acquainted with the service in active scenes. The second reason is, because very unfortunately the Prince of Wales has taken [a] terrible course of life, which he might perhaps (had I been at home) [have] induced me to lead, which would have been very much to my own detriment & very much to yours, Sir, & the Queen's mortification & grief.

Thanks to all those who have been concerned about me, but particularly Mr. Majendie, I have a pretty good sense of religion; which I hope & I am sure will keep me out of many of those vices which are too apt to be practised now a days. It makes me put my trust in the Creator of all things, to whom I pray dayly for Y- M- & the Queen's health & prosperity, & for the whole family's turning out well hereafter.

In my natural disposition, there is not a more obstinate or a more perverse boy; & if it had not been by dint of education I should not be what I am now (which is far from being perfect) for which reason I should always be in duty bound to be grateful to Y. M. & the Queen, & to all those who have had anything to do with such a bad & obstinate disposition as mine.

I beg my duty to the Queen & my love to my brothers & sisters, & ever believe [etc.]. (44628–9)

4280 PRINCE FREDERICK *to the* KING

[*3 Sept. 1781.*] As I had the honor to inform your Majesty in my last we set out last Friday in order to see the field of battle of Minden.[1] The country is not so

---

[1] Ferdinand of Brunswick's Anglo–Hanoverian army defeated the French at Minden on 1 Aug. 1759.

much altered as it was supposed before we set out. We came first to the place where Wangenheim's Corps was encamped, and so passed through one of the openings which were cut for his columns to march to their ground. Though the rest of these openings are planted up, it is easy to perceive where they were as the trees are not yet come to their full growth. We afterwards came to the brow of the hill where the redoubts were placed, of which there are now no vestiges. From thence we went to the place where the great battery of the French was, and from thence to the windmill where our right wing of cavalry was posted, in front of which is the famous fir wood which could not have been above 100 paces long, and fifty wide with a plain on each side of it over which ten squadrons *might* have passed a-breast, and indeed the wood itself is also so excessively thin that it could have been no inconvenience to them. From thence we passed along the side of the morass to the spot where the French had thrown their bridges over, and from thence going over the glacis of the town of Minden we came to the place where the Grenadiers de France were so roughly handled and so back to Thonhausen. The Grand Marechal wished I would write to know your Majesty's commands, as there is a kind of difficulty arisen where to lodge the Duke of Brunswick, who will come here the beginning of next month. As there was none of the family living here, there was an order from the late King to lodge nobody in the Castle, but now that I am here the Grand Marechal says it will look very odd to lodge him, one of the family, out of the Palace, particularly as no other Court in Germany does it, but as the order is so very express he has desired me to ask your Majesty's commands about it. I have received another letter from Prince Henry of Prussia who returns tomorrow thro. here from Spa in which he says he will do us the infinite honor of breakfasting here at ten o'clock.

I am affraid I have already tresspassed too much on your Majesty's patience. I shall therefore only entreat your Majesty to give my duty to the Queen and sign myself [etc.]. (43456–7)

4281   MAJOR-GENERAL RICHARD GRENVILLE[1] *to the* KING

[*Mont Brillant, 11 Sept. 1781.*] I was honoured with your Majesty's letter of ye 31st of last month the day before yesterday, & am very happy to find that my letters give your Majesty so much satisfaction. I hope sincerely I may always have it in my power to send your Majesty the like good accounts. Since I had last the honour of writing to your Majesty, his Royal Highness has been to visit the field of battle at Minden. M.-Genl. du Plat attended his Royal Highness in order to explain to him the several particulars relative to that action, & to shew him the different positions of the two army's on that day. After the Prince had reviewed the whole very attentively he returned to Stoltzenau, where he slept that night, & reached Mont Brillant the next day at dinner time.

His Royal Highness Prince Henry of Prussia stopped here on ye. 4th inst. on his way to Brunswick, & partook of a cold collation; as the company, by his particular desire, was not so numerous as the time before, & much less ceremoni-

---

[1] He accompanied Prince Frederick to Hanover, and for many years was at the head of his Household.

ous, his Royal Highness entered more into conversation, which however ran upon general topics chiefly concerning the society & amusements of Spa. His Royal Highness stayed about three hours, & then proceeded upon his journey to Brunswic, where he proposed resting for four or five days before he set out upon his return to Berlin.

The Artillery encamped here on ye 5th inst., & were reviewed yesterday by the Field Marechal. His Royal Highness proposes to himself much pleasure & instruction for these next twenty days during the time of the camp, & I make no doubt but that it will answer the utmost of his expectation. (43460)

4282   PRINCE FREDERICK *to the* KING

[*Hanover, 21 Sept. 1781.*] I have a thousand excuses to make to your Majesty for not having written to you by the last courier, but as I had written the Tuesday before I did not chuse to trouble your Majesty so soon again with another. The Artillery has been encamped here this fortnight. I have not missed a day attending their exercise which they have done perfectly well particularly considering the length of time since they were last assembled together and the badness of their guns which is such that they have burst one twelve pounder and rendered another useless. I went every morning an hour before they began their exercise in order to learn how to point both cannon and mortars, in which I succeeded pretty well. The body of men is exceedingly fine. Last Tuesday evening after it was dark they were ordered to throw a number of shells into a battery they had erected, some of which were to burst, which succeeded perfectly. We have been terribly affraid all this last week that we should have lost the good Field Marechal. He went last Friday to Hameln to review the 15th Regiment, whither I accompanied him; as we returned home he complained that he had got a diarhea, and begged we would leave him to follow in another carriage, which we would not do but afterwards he chose to stop on the road for a time and so we left him. However, he did not chuse to mention then his true disorder which was a retention of urine encreased to such a degree that he was not able to come on to Hanover that night; he however came on the next morning, but without passing the least water. Every possible remedy was applied without any effect till the afternoon, when by the help of the cathedra he at last past some water. They have tried once to take the cathedra out, but they have been obliged to put it in again, and the surgeons say that it will be a week before they will attempt it again. I was told that it was a very moving seen [*sic*] yesterday morning when the garrison marched out into camp. He ordered them to pass his windows, and when they marched by he burst into tears. Today is the first day the troops begin their manœuvres. They had yesterday a very bad day to march to camp, for it rained the whole day long.

Permit, Sir, before I close my letter to entreat your Majesty to give my duty to the Queen and my love to my brothers and sisters. (43461–2)

[*Commandant's House, New York, 27 Sept. 1781.*] Last Monday about four in the afternoon we anchored without the bar, the tide not being favourable to come up to New York. Next day the wind being not favourable, the ship could not get up. Yesterday morning the Commander-in-Chief, Sr. Henry Clinton, sent down his cutter to fetch the Adl.[1] & myself up to the city.

We arrived at the town about 6 in the afternoon. We were met on the beach by the Generals & Admirals, & walked with them first round the parade, where is the pedestal of the statue of Y.M., & from thence thro' the greater part of the town to Commodore Afflec's[2] house, where I was received by a Captain's guard with colours, which was to have been made up of that fine & brave company of Grenadiers of the 40th Regiment, had they been able to have turned out a sufficient number. But they had suffered too much in the expedition against New London, where brave Arnold[3] commanded. The Genl. did not salute me, because it was sunset.

We dined & past the evening at the Commodore's, & from thence went to Genl. Burch, the Commandant's house, who was so civil as to resign it to us.

When I came on shore I was received by an immense concourse [of] people, who appeared very loyal, continually crying out, '*God bless King George.*' They appear in general very well affected to our Government, but particularly the Dissenters & Quakers.

This morning I walked round the town & about a mile out of the town with Sr. Henry Clinton, & went to see a Hessian Regiment encamped & the 38th on their march to camp, & a fort, called Bunker's Hill. As we were walking thro the city there was a Quaker came up to me & said: *God bless thy father; it is not for want of respect that I do not take my hat off, but because my religion requires it.*

We dined today at Headquarters, & I had there a very pretty concert, consisting principally of officers, & particularly of Hessians. There was at dinner all the English Genls. at New York, except Genl. Arnold, who[m] [I] have not yet seen, but am to see tomorrow, the Adls. of the Fleet; Ld. Lincon[4] & Coll. Conway.[5] The Mayor & Corporation intend to come to me tomorrow morning, with Sr. Henry's leave, to present me with an Address. I dread the thoughts of it. However, the Adl. & Mr. Majendie are very well pleased hitherto. (44630–1)

[1] Admiral Digby.

[2] At this time he was Commissioner of the Port of New York.

[3] Benedict Arnold (1741–1801), the American General who deserted to the British in 1780, and who subsequently commanded expeditions against Richmond in Virginia and New London in Connecticut.

[4] Thomas Pelham Clinton, third son of the 2nd Duke of Newcastle. M.P. for Westminster, 1774–80; for East Retford, 1781–94. Ensign, 1769; Captain, 1770; Lieutenant-Colonel, 1775; Colonel, 1780; Major-General, 1787. Styled Earl of Lincoln from 23 Sept. 1779 to 22 Feb. 1794, when he succeeded his father as 3rd Duke. A.D.C. to General Clinton, 1779–80; and A.D.C. to the King, 1780–87. (1752–95.)

[5] Robert Seymour-Conway (1748–1831), M.P. for Orford, 1771–84; for Wootton Bassett, 1784–90; for Orford, 1794–1807; for Carmarthenshire, 1807–20. Third son of 1st Earl of Hertford. Ensign, 1766; Captain, 1770; Lieutenant-Colonel, 1775; A.D.C. to General Clinton, 1780–1.

[[*New York*,] *28 Sept.*] This morning the Commander-in-Chief presented to me all the Generals & Field Officers of the Army, & the Admirals their Captains & all the Navy Officers that were in the city. Afterwards the Governor, Genl. Robinson, came with the Counsel to present a very loyal Address, of which I send Y.M. a copy, & likewise of my answer to it.

We afterwards went out into the country, to Hell Gates, where I saw a Capn. Robertson, son to the Col. who raised a Provincial Regiment. This young man distinguished himself in Ld. Rawdon's last action, where he was wounded in his left arm & has totally lost the use of it. Afterwards I saw the 69th Reg. disembark from Sr. Samuel Hood's[1] Fleet.

Since we have been here, I have had the pleasure of seeing the famous Genl. Arnold, & that brave Camel who made that gallant defence in Pensicola. Ld. Lincoln is here. Coll. Conway is going home.

The town is built in the Dutch way, with trees before the houses. The streets are in general narrow & very ill paved. There is but one Church, all the others being converted either into magazines or barracks. The regiments in the town are the 38th & 54th of British, & several Hessian regiments. The regiments that are going to the southward are 4 battalions of British & 4 of Hessian Grenadiers, the Light Infantry, the 37th & 43d Reg. & 2 Hessian Regs.

The Fleet are lying some at New York & others at Statten Island in a most wretched condition. They expect to be ready about the 7 or 8 of next month. However I believe they will not be ready so soon as that time, for many ships are lying without lower masts, & there is a great scarcity of lower masts & in short of all stores here.

The inhabitants of the town are in number 25,000. They have 3000 militia, besides which there are about 1000 men raised at their own expence & cloathed & armed.

I hope the family are all well, & that you receive good accounts from my brother Frederick. I beg my duty to the Queen, & my love & best wishes to my brothers & sisters.

I understand the Adl. intends to write to Y.M. so that I need not be particular about myself, but only in assuring you, Sir, that so far I have met with the Adl's. & Mr. Majendie's approbation.

During the voyage, I had a very great cold & pain in my side, which was soon removed by a blister: since which time, I have had my health very well. (44632)

4284   *Letters from* PRINCE FREDERICK *to the* KING

[*Hanover, 28 Sept. 1781.*] I have many thanks to return your Majesty for the gracious letter which I received from you today by the post. Nothing can have been more unlucky than the camp here which broke up today owing to the badness of the weather. None of the officers have been able to pull off a single piece of their cloaths since Tuesday. The wind blew so hard between Tuesday and Wednesday that not a tent was left standing, and at the same time with such a rain as is hardly

[1] He had been created a Baronet on 20 May 1778, on the occasion of the King's visit to Portsmouth.

to be conceived. The troops were only able to manœuvre one day, which altogether succeeded pretty well. The finest Regiment in point of both horses and men is Fredrick's, in which Malhorti is, they have not above fifty horses in the regiment which are not of the country. The finest regiment of infantry is Reden's, though not so much in point of men, but of discipline and air, having been so long in garrison and Hanau that they have much more of the Prussian stile. The ground where the troops were to have exercised is so compleatly spoilt that it would be impossible for them to do anything for a fortnight even if it was now to hold up. I am just returned from seeing the garrison march in; [it] is impossible to describe the figures they cut, but however it must be said to their credit that they appeared in very good humour and spirits. However, one lucky thing is that as yet it is astonishing how very few are sick.

Permit me Sir, to entreat your Majesty to give my duty to the Queen, and my love to my brothers and sisters, and to sign myself [etc.] (43463–4)

[*Hanover, 12 Oct.*] The Duke of Brunswic was so good as to come and make us a visit here last Wednesday. I cannot express to your Majesty how very kind and affectionate his behaviour was to me, and with how much respect and feeling he spoke about your Majesty. The Duke sent me through Grenville a message from the King of Prussia. He said he was charged by the King to say that if I was to come next year to the Reviews at Berlin he should be very glad of having that opportunity of shewing his attachment to his relations. I answered that I begged the Duke would express to his Majesty how much I felt myself honoured by his gracious offer, and that there was nothing I was more desirous of than the honour of being presented to him, but that as I did not as yet know your Majesty's intentions about me next summer I could give no answer.

I have again begun my lessons with Hograve, Wessel and Falk, which had been interrupted by the camp, with Hograve I have just finished my second plan, and with Wessel I have begun to draw cannon. My lessons with Falk become every day more amusing. Part of the time I talk German with him, and the other part we read the history of Germany in German, which I understand without much difficulty; indeed by Falk's agreable manner of teaching I find myself much more advanced in the time I have learnt from him than I thought I should.

Permit me, Sir, before I finish my letter to entreat your Majesty to give my duty to the Queen and my love to my brothers and sisters. (43465–6)

[*Hanover, 28 Oct.*] I have a thousand thanks to return your Majesty for the last gracious letter which I received from you. It shall ever be the studdy of my life to deserve as much as it is in my power, the affection which your Majesty is pleased so strongly to express for me. Captain Hogreve has begged me to send over to your Majesty a plan I have drawn of a starred fort which I could never have thought of troubling your Majesty with if I did not hope it might be a means of shewing your Majesty how very attentive and diligent he has been in teaching me. Lord Apsley has been here two months, he is a very agreable and clever young man, and to all appearance will turn out exceedingly well. Brunswic will be quite stocked with Englishmen, who are gone there to the Academy for their education. The poor Field Marechal continues exactly in the same way; he was taken a few days ago with a violent fever, which however has now quite left him, but his other disorder is not in the least better. However, he is in very good spirits and in all other respects quite well. I never in my life saw such weather, as we have had for the last six weeks; it has not ceased raining a single day so that it is almost impossible to go out. I have been very desirous of going out partridge shooting but it has been hitherto quite out of my power, for the place where the most partridges are is at present a compleat bog.

Permit me, Sir, before I close my letter to entreat your Majesty to give my duty to the Queen and to tell her that I had intended to have done myself the honor of writing to her by this courier, but that I have been unavoidably hindered. (43472-3)

4285 PRINCE WILLIAM *to the* KING

[*Prince George, 10 Nov. 1781, off the Hook.*] Your Majesty will see that we are lying at the Hook, the wind not permitting us to go over the bar. As the packet is soon to sail I take this opportunity of writing.

I wish it had been in our power to have given a good account of the French Fleet: but unfortunately they were so posted to such advantage that we could not attack them without much loss, particularly after having heard of Lord Cornwallis's surrender.[1] I will enclose to your Majesty the proceedings of the two Fleets when in sight of one another; a list of the Army on board the Fleet, of Lord Cornwallis's forces & the combined Army.

Capn. Dundass (a very brave & excellent, but unfortunate officer) dined with us yesterday. He commanded the Bonetta sloop of war which, by the 8th Article of the Convention, was permitted to come to New York with an aide [de] camp from my Lord Cornwallis & such persons as his Lordship should think proper to send to New York. He has brought with him 488 loyal Hessians who were the only remains of the British Legion under the brave Col. Tarleton, & the Queen's Rangers under Simco. He offered to bring away three clergymen; but they refused to come. Accordingly, the next day he saw them chained & put into a cart to go to Williamsburg.

The Brigade of Guards, the Light Infantry & the Legions behaved upon a sally with the greatest coolness & courage in the world. Coll. Abercrombie who commanded the Light Infantry had a very great compliment paid him by Mr. Rochambeau,[2] that if, instead of having 300, he had had 3000, he would have obliged them to have raised the siege, for even with 300 he killed 500 of the enemy & spiked 21 pieces of cannon. He caused such a consternation amongst the enemy that the whole camp was near being evacuated. Another day Coll. Dundass & Coll. Tarleton with 200 cavalry went out against Mr. de Lozun's hussars & all the American horse. We were worsted in that action: but however it was with great difficulty the enemy got the better. Coll. Tarleton was rode down by one of his

[1] At Yorktown, on 19 October.   [2] Commander-in-Chief of the French army. (1725-1807.)

(683)

own men, & during the action Mr. de Lozun rode over Coll. Tarleton's horse & would have killed him had not Coll. Tarleton got under his horse's belly. In short, all the British, both seamen & soldiers, & Hessians behaved with the greatest spirit & resolution. The Anspackers deserted, & all the time behaved infamously.

The Charon was burnt by a red hot shot from the enemy, the Guadaloupe was sunk, the Fairy was broken up, & the Bonetta was the only ship that was above water. All the ships' guns were landed & the seamen & marines served the batteries, which were defended with the greatest vigour. Capn. Symonds deserves great credit for sending down fire ships on the enemy. Two of their ships cut their cables & got on shore on the Spit & lay there for two days. There is a comfort in our ill success that every [one] did their best.

Our loss is reckoned to be between 6 & 700 men; the enemy's between 7 & 800 men. We have had 10 officers killed & as many wounded. Major Cockrain is the only officer of distinction killed. One of the Articles of Capitulation was that a General & Field Officer of every nation should remain with their troops; accordingly our officers drew lots: the General, that stays, I do not know who he is; the Field Officer was Coll. Lake; but Major Gordon, of the 76th Regt. would not allow Coll. Lake to stay as he was a marryed man.

Capn. Dundass told me he went on board the Ville de Paris; she is an over-built ship. The Comte de Grasse[1] was very civil to him: he is a very tall & old man, a very good officer & a man of the greatest honour. He is very much disliked by his captains, but no wonder, for anybody that wants a Frenchman to do his duty must be disliked. For instance, Sir, the officers must be up to see the ship got under way at any time of night. A Frenchman says that 'Cela n'est pas poli'. There is a very great disunion between the French & American officers & men. The French treat the Americans with a great deal of hauteur: there was a very great instance of it the other day. A Continental officer passed a French centry, after being ordered not to do it. Next a French Major ordered this American officer to be tied naked to a gun & receive 24 hard strokes with a sabre.

We are now going on board the Lion: the Prince George is going to winter in Long Island. The Adl. intends passing the winter on shore. (44633)

[*Enclosure*]

Proceedings of the Fleet

[*Sund., 28 Oct. 1781.*] Little wind & clear. At 2 p.m. the Nymphe made the sigl. for a Fleet. Set sail. At 3 saw 3 sail from the mast head. At $\frac{1}{2}$ past 5 saw 29 sail from the mast head at an anchor. Those 3 sail above-mentioned made a vast number of sigls. At 6 the sigl. for all cruizers. During the night the enemy made a number of sigls. on shore. At 6 a.m. saw a stranger off the deck, making sigls. At 12 saw the French Fleet of 37 sail with their top sails loose at an anchor: & 2 sailing about the Bay, one a line of battle ship, the other a frigate.

[1] The Comte de Grasse was decisively defeated by Rodney at the battle of the Saints, 12 April 1782, and was captured in his flagship, the *Ville de Paris*.

[*Mond. 29 Oct.*] Saw the same number of ships in the Bay before dark. Next morning two of the enemy's ships still observing us & making sigls.

[*Tuesd., 30 Oct.*] Bore away with the whole Fleet for New York, where we arrived Nov. 1. (44635)

4286   PRINCE FREDERICK *to the* KING

[*Hanover, 22 Nov. 1781.*] I had intended myself the honor of writing to your Majesty by the last courier, but having been out all the day at a chasse of boars when I returned it was too late then to write. The chasse itself turned out exceedingly well, only we were not successfull in taking the stags; however, tomorrow we have a great chasse at the Hallerbrach where we hope we shall be able to take a good many as by the time the stags set out all the chasse's here will be over for the winter; the Grand Veneur has been so good as to say, that the chasseur, who always goes with me, shall accompany them. I believe there is not a more honest nor a braver fellow living than he is nor nobody more attached to another than he is to me. I hope tomorrow to get into my new apartment, which will be much more comfortable than the one I am at present in. Grenville has received a letter from Fawcett dated at Aix la Chapelle. Your Majesty and the Queen have been so gracious as to send me letters by him as well as a Cheshire cheese, for which I return my most humble thanks. Till within these three days has been the worst and most disagreable I ever felt, continually raining so that the roads about Hanover, not being over fine, it has been no very pleasant thing to go out of the town. I think now one may say that all hopes of the poor Field Marechal's recovery are all over. He may linger on some few days longer, but I hardly think that is possible. When he was told that there was very little hopes left he thanked his family for having had that idea of his fortitude as to tell him the truth, and added that he had always lived a very happy life, and that he was quite resigned to his fate.

I am affraid I have already tresspassed too long upon your Majesty's patience. I shall therefore only entreat your Majesty to give my duty to the Queen and my love to my brothers and sisters. (43476–7)

4287   PRINCE WILLIAM *to the* KING

[*New York, 25 Dec. 1781.*] The Europe will I hope, get home safe, for Capn. Child[1] has been so good as to take charge of my letters. Yesterday we received word that the September packet was taken. I am very sorry to have lost my letters for I understand that Alfred had been very ill. I hope he is recovered.[2] The rest of the family are well I suppose. Frederick is going on as well as he was before I make no doubt; or else he is very undeserving of your Majesty's goodness.

[1] Smith Child (*d.* 1813). Lieutenant, 1755; Captain, 1780; Rear-Admiral, 1799; Vice-Admiral, 1804; Admiral, 1810.
[2] He died on 20 August 1782.

There has nothing public transpired: the Savage is retaken: the Perseverance has taken a very large French cutter: two floating batteries are building, one here, the other at Charlestown. Yesterday a fleet consisting of 15 ships went to Charlestown. The troops are in winter quarters & very healthy.

I am at present in my winter quarters at the Adl's. house: as for my conduct Mr. Majendie has written a very long letter which I hope will satisfy the Queen & you, my dear father; the greatest pleasure I have is to find that I meet with my parent's approbation. The Adl. says he is very well pleased with me in most respects.

Since I have been here I have made acquaintance with Lieut. Sawyer[1] of the Perseverance, a very promising & well behaved young man, of my age exactly. Mr. M. approves of my connection with him vastly.

I am vastly happy & wish to continue in the way I go on at present, for I am sure you will be pleased with that son, who makes it his duty to show his parents that he loves & respects them with that affection & piety, which will enable them to think that he is a virtuous & pious son. (44637)

4288   *Letters from* PRINCE FREDERICK *to the* KING

[*Hanover, 29 Dec. 1781.*] I hope your Majesty will pardon my not having wrote to your [*sic*] by the last courier but as General Fawcett was to set out so soon I thought it better to delay my letter till then. As your Majesty ordered me I have also sent over by General Fawcitt two other plans, the one of tête de ponts, the other, of lines. The objection which your Majesty made to the last plan appeared in the same light to me, but by the rules of fortification here, the Germans are content if the salient angle is of sixty degrees. Last Wednesday three companies of the Sixteenth past through here on their march for Stade; they are the three worst companies, and yet they are considerably finer than those of the Fifteenth Regiment; they even hardly any old men amongst them [*sic*]. The officers are so fully persuaded of the good will of these soldiers that they would not take away their arms from them at night, which was always done when the Fifteenth were on their march. I received by last courier a very sensible letter with which I am sure your Majesty would be exceedingly pleased if you had seen it.

I think I never saw in my life such weather as we have at present here; it is so warm that we are obliged to keep the windows constantly open. The stags will not, I am affraid, not arrive in England so soon as it is to be wished [*sic*], for the master of the ship who was to have transported them refused at last to sail till February, so that in all probability before everything is settled it will take a great deal of time; they are all, however, in very good health.

Permit me, Sir, before I close my letter to desire your Majesty to give my duty to the Queen and my love to my brothers and sisters. (43484–5)

[1] Sir Herbert Sawyer (1765–1833), Admiral Sawyer's eldest son. Lieutenant, 1780; Captain, 1789; Rear-Admiral, 1807; Vice-Admiral, 1811. In 1794 he captured *La Révolutionnaire* French frigate, for which exploit he was knighted.

[*Hanover, 1 Feb. 1782.*] Though I have nothing particular to write to your Majesty yet I do not chuse to let the courier set out without sending a letter.

Malhorti has received a letter from Monsieur de Salzas by which he appears to be in a very melancholy situation, the death of Madame de Fagel seems to have revived his former grief for the loss of his wife which had begun a little to subside, and he writes besides that one of his sisters is in a very dangerous way.

I have very near finished with Hogreve field fortification. We have already gone through so much of sluices and dams as is necessary on fortification and are at present drawing all kinds of fortified posts. In artillery I am finishing my last plan of gun carriages and shall next week begin upon mortars. I find it however much more amusing to draw positions, and posts than to draw cannon.

Our weather is still as bad as ever, for it one day snows, and the next rains and the third freezes, so that there is hardly any possibility of going out.

Permit me, Sir, before I close my letter to desire your Majesty to give my duty to the Queen and my love to my brothers and sisters, and to believe me [etc.].

P.S. Colonel Grenville does not propose himself the honour of writing to your Majesty as he has nothing in particular to communicate. (43489–90)

[*Hanover, 4 Feb. 1782.*] Though I had the honor of writing to your Majesty by the courier who set off last Friday, yet I cannot help troubling you again today in order to express to your Majesty my sincere thanks for your gracious letter and at the same time my joy at your recovery. I confess I was not a little alarmed at the arrival of the last post, when everybody told me of your Majesty's indisposition. However, I cannot sufficiently express how happy I am that it was of so short a continuance. You are too well acquainted with my affection for Lake not to conceive how rejoiced I am at his return after having gained to himself so much credit, and I have no doubt but that he will do everything in his power to make my brother behave in such a manner as to please your Majesty.

I am affaid I have already intruded too much on your Majesty's patience. I shall therefore only entreat you, Sir, to give my duty to the Queen, and sign myself [etc.]. (43491–2)

[*Hanover, 1 March.*] I have many thanks to return to your Majesty for your last gracious letter, as well as for your goodness in sending me William's letter, which I have the honor according to your orders, of returning. I am exceedingly happy that his conduct has met with your approbation, and I have no doubt but that he will turn out a great comfort to your Majesty, and a usefull member of society. Permit me, Sir, to return your Majesty my most hearty thanks for the favor you have conferred upon Lake, by appointing him your Aide de Camp. Your Majesty is too well acquainted with my affection for him not to conceive the joy I felt upon receiving the news of his promotion.

Our weather here is quite altered. Our frost and snow are quite gone and we have the finest weather in the world. I hope your Majesty is content with the stags though I am affraid they must be a little stiff from the length of time they have been in their cases. Your Majesty says in your letter that you are quite surprised that I do not ride oftener, and that I prefer shooting to riding, but that is not quite the case, but as there are only certain times in which I can go out a-shooting, and that I can ride every day, I prefer during those seasons, shooting.

Permit me, Sir, before I close my letter to entreat your Majesty to give my duty to the Queen, and to believe me most sincerely [etc.]. (43494–5)

4289 PRINCE WILLIAM to the KING

[*Admls. House, New York, 28 March 1782.*] It was with the greatest pleasure I received your Majesty's letter by Capn. Edwards. We had not heard from England, before the Narcyssus arrived, about 23 weeks. She made her passage in 63 days, with the loss of her mizen mast & all the rest of her rigging cut to pieces by the violence of the weather. Her ship's company were all ill of the scurvy.

As I was finishing the letter I intended for your Majesty we heard of the capture by the French of St. Kitts on the 22d February, & having mentioned several circumstances which were intended to shew that the capture would not take place so soon, I have been obliged to alter my opinion.

Adl. Kempenfelt's[1] dispersing that French Fleet will be the means of Sr. George Rodney's arriving first in the West Indies, & of making our Fleet superior to theirs. We have 24 sail of the line, the French have 29. I understand Sr. George is to bring with him 12 sail of the line which will make us superior to the French, & I make no doubt of your Majesty's receiving a very good account of those gentry.

Genl. Elliot's sortie at Gibraltar[2] must have been very decisive in our favour. The affairs in the East Indies promise very well for a successful campaign next summer; Genl. Murray[3] at Minorca does not seem to be at all uneasy or afraid of the Spaniards taking St. Philipps.[4] Neither the Dutch or the Spaniards have great reasons to be pleased with the success they have had this war: it is only the French. We shall still do very well if we succeed this summer.

Our cruizers this winter have not been very successful: there have been some with prizes sent in. Capn. Bazely[5] has retaken the Bonetta sloop of war. Last week the cruizer sent in three or four ships pierced for 20 guns. The privateers have been more successful than the men of war.

There is an expedition on foot, for the following regiments are under orders to embark at an hour's warning (the 22d, 38th, 40th & 57th British Legion & Queen's Rangers). They are to be under the command either of Genl. O'Hara[6]

[1] Richard Kempenfelt (1718–82), Rear-Admiral since 1780. He went down with his ship, the *Royal George*, on 29 August, at Spithead.   [2] On 27 November 1781.

[3] James Murray (1719?–94), Governor of Minorca, 1774. Lieutenant-General, 1772; General, 1783. The island had been besieged by a Franco–Spanish force under the Duc de Crillon since August 1781. The disease-stricken garrison had already, in February 1782, been forced to capitulate.

[4] Fort St. Philip.

[5] John Bazeley (d. 1809). Lieutenant, 1760; Captain, 1778; Read-Admiral, 1795; Vice-Admiral, 1799; Admiral, 1805. See No. 57 n.

[6] He was captured, with Cornwallis's army, at Yorktown, 19 October 1781, and remained a prisoner until Feb. 1782, when he was exchanged, and in May he was given the command of reinforcements sent from New York to Jamaica. Cornwallis wrote on 2 Jan. 1784: 'Poor O'Hara is once more driven abroad by his merciless creditors.' (*Cornwallis Corresp.*, 1, 162.)

or Genl. Abercrombie. Some people say they are going to the West Indies because the Grenadier companies of each regiment are to join them. In short it is a secret wherever they are going to.

As to my own private life I regret very much the loss of this whole winter without going to sea. I have continued my studies with Mr. Waddington every morning from ten to twelve in the forenoon. With Mr. Majendie I am writing an extract that he has collected from different people relative to the present state of affairs in this continent.

The French have lost a frigate of 32 guns, called the Diligante. They agree very indifferently with the Americans, who begin to grow jealous of them. At Philadephia [sic] there has been a riot about the heavy taxes, of which the whole nation complain most grievously.

I hope the Queen is in perfect health: I beg my duty to her Majesty & my love to my brothers & sisters & ever believe [etc.]. (44638–9)

4290   *Letters from* PRINCE FREDERICK *to the* KING

[*Hanover, 29 March 1782.*] I have a thousand thanks to return to your Majesty for your last gracious letter which I received by General Fawcett who arrived here on Tuesday last. I am very much vexed to find that your Majesty is not yet recovered from your indisposition, which I was in great hopes would long ago have been passed, but which, the many vexations which your Majesty must have had lately, have, I am affraid, not a little contributed to encrease.

As your Majesty has ordered that a part of the troops here should encamp this summer at Lunenberg, I hope you will pardon me, Sir, if I ask your Majesty's leave if it is practicable to go there.

We have had within this few days such a fall of snow as had not been remembred [sic] ever in the winter for many years pass'd; it is in some places above ten foot deep.

I am very happy to hear that your Majesty has received such very good accounts of William from America, I have no doubt but that he will do his utmost to fit himself for that line of life into which he has entered.

Permit me, Sir, before I close my letter, to repeat how anxious I am to hear of your Majesty's perfect recovery and to sign myself [etc.]. (43506–7)

[*Hanover, 5 April.*] Permit me to sieze the very first opportunity of returning your Majesty my most hearty thanks for your gracious appointment of me to the command of the Horse Grenadiers.[1] This gracious favor which your Majesty has unexpectedly conferred upon me fills my heart with the strongest sentiments of gratitude, and adds a fresh instance to the numberless others of affection which your Majesty has ever been pleased to shew towards me and which it shall ever be the business of my life to deserve. As for the Agency of the troop, which

---

[1] He was Colonel of the 2nd Troop of Horse Grenadier Guards (being styled as such, in the Calendars, as Bishop of Osnaburg), from 23 March 1782 to Oct. 1784, when he was appointed Colonel of the Coldstream Regiment of Foot Guards.

your Majesty seems to wish should be given to Brummell[1] and Bishop,[2] though I had in a manner promised Cox and Mair to be my Agents, yet I shall be very happy even in this small instance to obey your Majesty's commands. I am excessively sorry to find for [sic] your last letter that you are not yet recovered from your late indisposition which I am affraid has not been a little increased by the present state of affairs, but which I hope now that they appear to be some way settled will soon be entirely cured. I confess I shall wait with anxious expectation for the next letters from England, which I hope will bring the news of your Majesty's recovery. My cough, about which you have been pleased to express so much concern, is quite gone, and Dr. Zimmerman has allowed me to do what I like so as not to overheat me.

Permit me Sir, before I close my letter to entreat your Majesty to give my duty to the Queen and to believe me [etc.]. (43510–1)

[*Hanover, 26 April 1782.*] Though I did myself the honor of writing to your Majesty last Friday yet I could not let the quarterly courier set out without again addressing you. I have been desired by the Grand Marechal to bear testimony to your Majesty about the dentist here, who really is exceedingly good and who has saved my teeth, which, though I take all the care I can in the world of them, were in so wretched a plight that in six months more they would have been compleatly spoilt. I do this the more readily because he is not only very knowing in his trade but is at the same time a very harmless inoffensive man, and really has very little to live upon.

I have taken the liberty to send your Majesty the last plan I have drawn of a fortified camp, which closes the whole of my instructions about field fortification. I have only now to go through a little of great fortification, and the attack and defence of places which will not take me up much time, and which will finish the instructions which I at present receive from Captain Hograve, to whom I cannot sufficiently express to your Majesty how much I am obliged for his care and diligence as well as for the agreable manner in which he has given his instructions, *so as even* to render the driest parts amusing. With Monsieur Wissell[3] I have almost finished my second plan of mortars, so that I have not much more than a week's or a fortnight's business with him.

As your Majesty has been graciously pleased to consent to my going to the camp at Lunenburgh I should be exceedingly happy if your Majesty would permit me as I am so near to go and see Hamburgh, which is so remarkable a town in Germany, and from thence to see the fortifications of Harburgh, and at the same time on my return I might go and see your Majesty's stud at the Hoya. I have within these two or three days made a purchase which, if your Majesty pleases to have after you have heard the story, is very much at your service. It is a frame filled with antiques and miniature pictures. The story is as follows. There were four of these frames which belonged to Kings of England. When Charles the

1 William Brummell (*d.* 1794), the father of George Bryan Brummell (1778–1840), 'Beau Brummell'. He had been Lord North's private secretary.
2 Bishop and Co., Army Agents (sometimes spelt Bisshopp).
3 Wessel in other letters.

Second was obliged to quit the Kingdom,[1] he took one of them with him; the other three were left, and are now hanging up at the Queen's House. This was first sold in Holland, and after passing thro. a series of hands at last came to a Lieut. Gronin, who refused twenty thousand crowns for them and who died here about thirty years ago very much in debt, so that they were seized and lodged in the Justitz Cantzley where they have been put up to auction, but were never sold till within these two or three days when I bought them for a mere trifle, 1500 crowns. Permit me, Sir, before I close my letter, to entreat your Majesty to give my duty to the Queen and to sign myself [etc.]. (43516–7)

[*Hanover, 24 May.*] I should not have troubled your Majesty so soon again with a letter if I had not been desired by Prince Earnest[2] to entreat your Majesty to break to the Queen the news of Princess Charles's[3] death, who died here the day before yesterday as well as to inclose to you a letter for the Queen from him. She was taken ill last Monday was sennight with the disorder which reigns here to a violent degree, but what was very surprising, would never take the least medicine or do the least thing which could tend to her cure. The efforts which she made on account of her cough were such as to make her lie in on Sunday evening full six weeks before her time. This made the fever return with redoubled violence and at last killed her on Wednesday morning.

The disorder dayly augments here. Poor Malhorti in spight of all his hopes has caught it, but in the very slightest manner.

Colonel Grenville had purposed writing to your Majesty by this courier to acquaint you with my perfect recovery, but as I informed him that I intended myself to have that honor he did not think it necessary to trouble your Majesty with a letter as he had nothing particular to transmit to you.

Permit me, Sir, before I close my letter to entreat your Majesty to give my duty to the Queen, and to sign myself, Sir [etc.].[4] (43527–8)

---

[1] In 1646.

[2] Queen Charlotte's brother (1742–1814).

[3] She was the daughter of the Landgrave George William of Hesse-Darmstadt, and had married Prince Charles of Mecklenburg-Strelitz in 1768. (1752–82.)

[4] Prince Frederick wrote to his brother William from Hanover on 5 July: 'It is so long since I have heard the least word from you that I am affraid you have quite forgot me. The Queen wrote me word that you complained that I had not answered your letters. I am therefore affraid that some of mine must have been letters taken or lost, as I have not only answered every letter which I have received from you but have also wrote three or four times since. I should have wrote to you sooner if I had not been near a month absent from here, having been first at the Camp at Lunenburgh and afterwards having made a little tour to Hamburgh and Bremen. I suppose you have passed a very quiet winter at New York and will now in all probability be if possible still more so. News you can expect none from us here except our joy at Rodney's success, which has been a fatal blow to the French, and has again restored the British Navy to its former glory, which till now it appeared to have totally lost. I suppose you will already have heard that his Majesty has been so gracious as to appoint me Colonel of the Second Troop of Horse Grenadier Guards, and you may easily conceive how overjoyed I was when I first received the news, which was the more unexpected as I had heard by the post before, that it was supposed the King would give it to another. I have totally forgot to congratulate you upon receiving the Garter. I suppose we shall soon see Edward's punch belly decorated with the Green Ribbon. I hope you have all been well this winter and have not got the terrible disorder which has raged all over Europe, of which many old people have died; I have been ill with it for about three

[*Windsor, 6 Aug. 1782.*] You may easily conceive how much I have been grieved at hearing from the Admiral of the terrible accident you have had on your last cruize, and that I cannot be easy till I hear how far you may recover the use of your arm. All the surgeons I have enquired of here seem to think you must be very cautious how you exert it, and that it will be very hazardous for you to raise above your head, consequently to venture going aloft; but this is a part of your profession you have now practiced three years, therefore I suppose without much detriment it may now be dispensed with.

I should by no means wish you should pass another inactive winter, I have therefore wrote my thoughts on that subject to your Admiral, and trust my plan will be every way advantageous to you. Dear William, now is the time that you are by application to fit yourself for being useful in your profession when arrived to riper years; therefore every hour not applied in acquiring knowledge is lost time; I owne I am anxious you should prove an ornament to your country as well as a comfort to your family and that I may ever have reason to prove myself[1] [etc.]. (Add. Georgian 21/1/24)

4292 REAR-ADMIRAL ROBERT DIGBY *to the* KING

[*New York, 29 Oct. 1782.*] I have receiv'd your Majesty's commands in your letter of the 6th of Augt. to place his R.H. with Ld. Hood who is luckily still here & will (I make no doubt) pay every attention to Prince William possible; but I doubt whether his Ldship wou'd willingly pay quite so much attention to my instructions if he cd. seperate them from your Majesty's as he wd. have done before the very great & merited credit he has got; particularly as we have differ'd in oppinion about a matter too common to differ about (I mean prise money). But I have the greatest oppinion of his abilitys as an officer & I think him a very amiable man in private life, and very much attach'd to your Majy. As I have

weeks but am now thoroughly recovered. In England it is astonishing what a number have died, but thank God neither the King nor the Queen nor any of the family have caught it.

'I think you will be heartily tired with this long letter; I shall therefore only desire you will give my compliments to Majendie.

'P.S.—I hope you will write often, and you may depend upon it, that I shall keep up the correspondence very heartily. Adieu.' (Add. Georgian 21/1/23)

[1] Lord Hood wrote to Budé from New York on 5 Oct.: 'The Warwick with Prince William on board returned here the 27th of last month, with a very large French frigate named La Aigle, which was forced on shore in the Delaware. Her masts were cutt away and attempts made to destroy her without effect: she carries 28, 24-pounders (English guns) on her main deck, and 16, 9-pounders on her quarter deck & forecastle. She came from Rochfort, & had on board several French Generals and other officers, and about £90,000 in money. The former gott ashore, and took the cash with them to about £4,000. La Gloire of 32 guns was with her, but drawing less water, beat over the sand, and escaped to Philadelphia.

'I have not words to express to you, how very much his Royal Highness is improved in every respect. His appearance delighted me most exceedingly, and I really believe has grown a full head since I had the honor of seeing him last year. The very kind, polite, attentive, and manly manner in which his Royal Highness was pleased to receive me was flattering in the extreme. On the 30th my friend and old acquaintance Coll. Musgrave arrived here in the Diomede from Chas. Town, and has brought the Blue Ribbon for Prince William.'

wrote very fully to General Budé it remains only to inform your Majy. that upon considering Mr. Majendie's situation w[it]h Prince William in every respect, I think it as well he shou'd seperate from his R.Hss. now as that he shou'd attend him to the West Indies, which quite corresponds wh. Mr. Majendie's ideas, but I sd. have judg'd Mr. Waddington might have been of use a few months longer. However I thought it much better to yeild to Lord Hood's great aversion to receive him, particularly as I believe his Captain is a good mathematician; but I have positively insisted (tho much contrary to Lord Hood's inclination), upon Captain Napier's[1] attending his R.Hss. as I think it of great consequence that some person sd. be with him, for some time at least that had known him before and I cd. not think of any Lieutt. fit for the charge whose views of quick preferment wd. not have made it difficult to reward him. Captn. Napier is out of employ, having lately been taken by a French frigate; is a man of family, a steady, firm man & a man of honor, has lived much in my family & is the fittest person I know at present to attend Pr. Wm. and is not unpleasing to him, notwithstanding he will not give way too much. This I hope yr. Majy. will approve, as I can assure you, Sir, I have no motive but his R.Hs's. well doing, and nothing but my firm oppinion that this step was of consequence to it (particularly as your Majy. seems to intend he shall return to me) wd. have made me take it, as I think it of no small consequence that Ld. Hood sd. be satisfy'd. And I flatter myself, when Captn. Napier is a little better known to him, he will be of my oppinion, tho I rather think he will not rest till he gets him remov'd. Your Majesty may therefore think it prudent to anticipate his desire, in which case I have only to hope that your Majy. will order Capt. Napier to be promoted to the rank of a Post, otherwise it might fix a stigma upon his character in the service as long as he lives. I have made no provision for Captn. Napier's being paid, but as he was appointed a Master & Commander I shou'd think that the natural provision whilst he remains wh. his R.Hss. I cannot conclude my letter without repeating to your Majy. how much I am oblig'd to Mr. Majendie for his unalterable attention. As your Majy. will soon see him, I shall leave it to him to represent his R.Hss's little foibles and dangers and indulge myself with assuring you, Sir, that he is at present a very fine young man, fond of his profession to a degree, and with more knowledge in it than most officers in ye. service; of a temper to make an excellent officer, & spirits to go thro anything, yet perfectly ready to comply wh. any rules or advice I have ever given him, tho in many respects not so prudent as I cd. wish, but I shou'd be ungratefull if I did not feel great obligation and affection for his R.Hss. for his great attention to me.

I must still trespass a little longer upon your Majy's. time first to recommend to yr. Majy's. favor Captain Elphinston who will be the bearer of my dispatches, and with whom as I have mention'd in former letters, I thought proper to entrust Prince William of which I have no reason to repent. Had I not receiv'd any instructions from your Majesty relative to his R.Hss. before the winter set in, I propos'd to have sent him again under his care & was fitting L'Aigle, the War- wick's prize, for that purpose & had appointed Captn. Elphinston to her, intending that after cruizing some time with another frigate or two under his command he

---

[1] Charles Napier (1731–1807), son of the 5th Lord Napier. Lieutenant, 1754; Captain, 1762.

shou'd have gone to the West Indies to water & refresh & to have return'd in April, and if it sd. be thought hereafter that it wd. be an advantage to his R.Hss. to serve in a frigate I know no Captain I shou'd so readily entrust wh. that charge, have therefore both in manning & appointing this frigate look'd forward to Captain Elphinston's returning to her. But events of some kind or other may probably produce other views. (Add. Georgian 15/719)

4293 LORD HOOD to the KING

[*Barfleur, New York, 30 Oct. 1782.*] Sensible as I am of the very honorable and flattering proof your Majesty has been graciously pleased to give me of perfect confidence and regard in placing Prince William under my care, I am no less so of the great importance of the charge, or how very unequal I feel myself to it; but what I want in abilities I will endeavour most studiously to make up by diligence and attention to his Royal Highnesses benefit.

My eye shall constantly be kept upon his Royal Highness and to the utmost of my power will be watchfull not only to encourage every laudable pursuit, but to check & restrain whatever I may see amiss; in so doing I am very sure I shall in the most effectual manner act up to your Majesty's wishes and such instructions as I may receive from Rear Admiral Digby, and if any example or precept of mine should prove usefull to your Majesty's most amiable and truly beloved son, it will be the pride & glory of my remaining days. (Add. Georgian 15/720)

4294 PRINCE WILLIAM to the KING

[*New York, 1 Nov. 1782.*] I have received your Majesty's of the 3d Sepr. by which I am informed that I am to go with Lord Hood to the West Indies. Having, from the moment of entering into my profession, felt a desire of making a figure in it, I am so much the more obliged to such a tender parent now in particularly, when there is the greatest likelyhood of our falling in with Monsr. de Vaudreuil[1] & his squadron on the passage to the West Indies.

As for promises I shall make none, but will endeavour to behave as an Officer & as a Prince, keeping always before my eyes the prospect of being one day or other a glory to the nation, & a comfort to my parents.

Mr. Majendie, who will have the honour of delivering this letter into your Majesty's hands, has been between 7 & 8 years with me, & particularly for the last three years on board a ship. I trust you will provide for him, & I shall take it as a favour conferred on me by your Majesty. The Admiral has thought proper to appoint the Honble. Capn. Napier, a very deserving & very amiable young man to go with me: he has been lately taken & treated most inhumanely by the French. I hope your Majesty will confer the rank of Post Captain upon him & give him an indemnification for his losses when taken. (44640)

[1] The Marquis de Vaudreuil commanded the French fleet in the West Indies after the spectacular defeat of De Grasse by Rodney on 12 April 1782 off Dominica.

[*Hannover, 22 Nov. 1782.*] Permit me most sincerely to congratulate your Majesty upon the great success which Lord Howe has had in throwing in the supplies into Gibraltar. I believe no object ever occupied the attention of the whole world so much as this siege, and I am certain that there never was more sincere joy shewn than upon the news of its being relieved. We have been so unlucky as to have five posts wanting by the way of Ostend, so that it is almost three weeks since we have had any news from England. We have had for some time past the very worst weather I ever saw in my life, continual rains, and at present a most violent frost. None of the farmers have been able to sow their fields, and in many places the harvest is not yet over. In the county of Hoya, I was assured three days ago that the oats were not carried in. In short, there never was known such a year as this at least in these parts of the country, and if luckily the two last years had not been so very plentifull there would have been a famine here. As for my studies I have finished with Captain Hogreve both field fortification and great fortification as well as a treatise upon mines, and I shall tomorrow begin the attack and defence of places. I cannot sufficiently express to your Majesty how very attentive Hogreve is, and how clear and easy he has made many things which would otherwise have been very difficult and tiresome.

Permit me, Sir, before I close my letter to entreat your Majesty to give my duty to the Queen and to believe me [etc.]. (43542–3)

[*Hannover, 6 Dec.*] Permit me most sincerely to return your Majesty my most humble thanks for the favor you have been pleased to confer on me in promoting me to the rank of Major-General. It was the more pleasure to me as it was totally unexpected. Fawcitt arrived here last Thursday and brought me the letter which your Majesty was so gracious as to write to me, by which I find it is your Majesty's intention that I should go to Brunswic to meet the Princess of Mecklenburgh.[1] I confess I have no small curiosity to see her, she passed thro. here last summer, but unluckily I did not know it till they were gone from hence. This morning five convicts were executed here. I went to hear their sentence declared to them, which was done in the Market Place. It was a very awfull scene, and they appeared exceedingly penitent and resigned. Four were beheaded and one was hanged. I heard afterwards that the execution went off very ill because the executioner hacked them most terribly before he could sever their heads from their bodies. The five who have been executed this morning have accused about twenty others, and have died upon their confession; fourteen of these twenty have not yet been taken. We have had here for the last three weeks a violent frost, which however now appears to be going which is much to be wished by the farmers here as very few of them have got in their harvest. I have received a long letter from William by which I am very happy to find that he is quite recovered.

[1] Frederick Francis, Hereditary Prince of Mecklenburg-Schwerin (1756–1837), who succeeded his uncle as Duke in 1785, married (1775) Louisa (1756–1808), daughter of Prince John Augustus of Saxe-Gotha.

Permit me, Sir, before I close my letter to entreat your Majesty to give my duty to the Queen, and to believe me [etc.]. (43544–5)

[*Hannover, 3 Jan, 1783.*]. The courier who returned last week from Ostend made me very happy by bringing me your Majesty's very gracious letter of the 17th. I am exceedingly sorry to hear of the poor Bishop of Worcester's misfortune; everybody who knows him must esteem him, and so much the more so as the cause of his disorder is owing to his goodness of heart. Poor Arnold, little did I think the last time I saw him, that he would have been in so dreadfull a situation.[1]

Our winter which appeared to have been totally gone is returned, with re-doubled violence. We have already had a violent fall of snow, and it appears as if we should have a great deal more. I am affraid this weather, will be very much felt by the country people here, as the harvest has been so exceedingly bad, and they have not had time to sew their fields.

I am at present very hard at work with Hogreve, at the attack and defence of places. And I can not sufficiently express to your Majesty how very clear he is in all his instructions.

Though I know your Majesty does not like New Year's Day compliments, yet I cannot close my letter without humbly congratulating your Majesty upon the change of the year; that the All Mighty may shower down His blessings upon your Majesty's head, and that he may bestow on you a long and a happy series of years are the constant prayers of [etc.]. (43550–1)

[*Hannover, 17 Jan. 1783.*] The courier who arrived here last Sunday brought me your Majesty's gracious letter of the third of this month in which you order me to send over the estimate of the furnishing the Palace at Osnabruck. I explained to the Grand Marechal as fully as I could your Majesty's intentions about it and he has made an estimate as exact as it was in his power of everything which is absolutely necessary. I hope your Majesty will be pleased with it as he has made it as little expensive as possible. As for guilding we have determined there shall be none. I enclose two papers: the small one marked number 1 is the estimate of the whole such as the furniture, linnen, kitchen furniture &c.; the other is the mere account of the furniture of the house. If your Majesty is pleased with this estimate may I humbly desire that your Majesty would order the money to be remitted to your Chamber of Finances at Hannover, because as everything must be made here, the workmen being so exceedingly bad at Osnabruck it would be very inconvenient if the money was left there, to be continually writing for it. May I at the same time entreat your Majesty in the order which you must give to the Chambers here to add the permission that I may have the things made by the workmen whom I chuse, otherwise, as your Majesty's workmen here have the same trick as those in England of charging twice as much as other workmen, the things would come much dearer and be much worse made.

---

[1] The Rev. William Arnold (*d.* 1802). In 1776 he succeeded Cyril Jackson (later the famous Dean of Christ Church) as Sub-preceptor to the Prince of Wales and Prince Frederick. He became mentally deranged, and died at Leicester.

I hope that by the end of the next week I shall finish with Captain Hogreve my lessons on fortification, which have certainly be [*sic*] rendered as amusing as possible by his attention and manner of teaching.

I am affraid I have already tresspassed to long upon your Majesty's leisure. I shall therefore only entreat your Majesty to give my duty to the Queen, and to tell her that by the next courier I will do myself the honor of writing to her, and sign myself [etc.]. (43552–3)

4296   PRINCE WILLIAM *to the* KING, *and two replies*

[*Port Royal, Barfleur, 15 April, 1783.*] I received your Majesty's letters two days ago, which contain everything that a son can wish to hear from a father he loves so tenderly. Since 4th of last Septr. I had not had a word from home, that my anxiety was very great, but it was relieved by those very affectionate terms in which you was pleased to express your approbation of my conduct: this is the first time I have had that pleasure of receiving a letter from your Majesty as from a tender parent to his son grown up. You was likewise pleased to say I should not return immediately, which is another mark of your great affection, because it is my good fortune to have already served so much of my six years abroad, that it was my wish to stay out till my apprentichip [*sic*] was compleated.

As I have lately so fully wrote to your Majesty about my own affairs, I shall only just add that Lord Hood is satisfied with my conduct. Mr. Majendie has wrote me a long & affectionate letter. I was pleased to hear that your Majesty gave him a flattering reception & promised to provide for him. I take a great interest in his welfare & hope he will soon be rewarded for his many services to me. (44641)

[*From the King, Queen's House, 16 April.*] Your letters of the 22d of December, of the 31st of January and of the 2d of February arrived together the 14th of this month, the two first relating to your voyage from New York to Tiberoon, and therefore require only this acknowledgement of them.

The third shews too strongly a continuation of that unhappy disposition to resist controul which has too much on former occasions appeared, and convinces me that your judgement does not ripen so fast as I could wish; to be fit to command, the knowledge of obedience must first have been obtained, without which self controul cannot be gained.

Had Capt. Napier formed any sinister view he could only attain it by flattery. He on the contrary for your sake has wished to guard you against improprieties; perhaps his zeal may have on your resistance hurried him to some degree of warmth. Ought not you on reflection to have felt this and then esteemed him for it, and by putting more pliancy to his advice have rendered his conduct more pleasing, instead of which by your own letter you have so far forgot yourself as to tell him that he is your *attendant*—certainly not the proper term for an officer placed to advise you, and to be answerable to me for your conduct, therefore any heat he may have shewn on such an assertion from you is perfectly natural.

It certainly is the general opinion that you have acquired as much nautical knowledge as the time you have been at sea will allow; but previous to this I had received from some of the best naval opinions in this Island that perhaps in the seaman you would lose the ideas of the Officer and the Prince.

I shall not go into the various improprieties which appear in your letter as I attribute them to momentary heat, and that you must have been long before this ashamed of them.

Whether Capt. Napier leaves you or remains till your return with Lord Hood to Europe, which cannot be many months, will depend on that able Admiral's decision; but he will have my directions in any case to have a proper Officer always to accompany you, who may be answerable for your behaviour.

You seem to wish to copy Frederick, but there is one very considerable difference; he though two years older is perfectly compliant to every advice the Officers about him give him.

I shall certainly send you to the Continent as soon as you return from sea, that your manners and behaviour may be formed fit for shore, and that you may be in time an Officer. Lord Howe who certainly is a scientific officer assures me that he thinks in our service the attention is carried so long alone to seamanship that few Officers are formed, and that a knowledge of the military is necessary to open the ideas to the directing large Fleets. (Add. Georgian, 21/1/33)

[*From the King, Windsor, 14 June.*] You may easily conceive after an absence of near two years how rejoiced I feel as well as the Queen at the thoughts of seeing you within a day or two; I have sent M.G. de Budé to London that on the first account of the division under Lord Hood arriving at Spithead he may set out for Portsmouth to receive you and bring you here. He has my directions to speak very openly to you; behave as you ought and you will ever have every reason to feel the affection your parents have for you. He will tell you my mind is far from at ease; it has pleased the Allmighty to put an end very unexpectedly of the most amiable as well as attached child a parent could have.[1] May I find those I have as warmly so as he was and I cannot expect more. I will not add more on a subject that very much fills my mind and I own [h]as strongly convinced me how very transitory all enjoyments are in this world, but it the stronger convinces me that the fulfilling every duty is the only real comfort and that our rewards must be looked for in another, not this world. (Add. Georgian 21/1/34)

4297 PRINCE FREDERICK *to the* KING

[*Hannover, 29 June 1783.*] It has been as yet out of my power to acquaint your Majesty with the time of our setting out for Strelitz and Schwerin, as the Duke of Mecklenburgh Strelitz has been so very much incommoded with the rheumatism in his hip as to make us think it would be impossible for us to make him a

---

[1] Prince Octavius (1779–83) died on 3 May 'of an hereditary humour which the Princess Dowager of Wales had brought into the family, and of which she herself and some of her children and grandchildren died'. (Horace Walpole, *Letters*, XIII, 7 n.)

visit, as he would be obliged to set out immediately for a bathing place at a little distance from Berlin, but as he is at present a little recovered, we mean to set out tomorrow for Strelitz, where we mean to stay three days and from thence to go to Ludowick's Lust, and remain there two days, and so return here on Friday sen'night. According to your Majesty's orders I have spoken to your Minister Monsieur de Bussche, who has also consulted Monsieur de Bussche de Hunefeldt and Monsieur d'Ahrenswaldt about the Gentlemen who should compose the Court at Osnabruck, at the same time acquainting them that they should not name more than was absolutely necessary. After having considered the matter thoroughly over, they made out the following list, which I have the honor to enclose to your Majesty, and which I hope will meet with your approbation. Permit me, Sir, to convey to your Majesty's [sic] Colonel Malhortie's humble thanks for the gracious favor you have conferred on him, and may I, Sir, add mine at the same time, as General Freytag has acquainted me that your Majesty has done it on my account, and I am sure your Majesty's favor could not have been conferred on a more deserving person. As General Freytag has also acquainted me that your Majesty intended to give proofs of your favor towards all those who have been about me, may I, Sir, recommend to you, Monsieur Falcke[1] who has instructed me in Civil Law as well as in the Law of the Empire, and who has done everything in his power to render that study otherwise dry and hard, as amusing and easy as possible. His talents and his education have fitted him for places of much more trust and confidence than the one which he at present occupies, for he is the only person now in your Majesty's service who has had the advantage to travel, and to visit all the papers [sic] belonging to the Embassies at Ratisbon and at Vienna, by which means every impartial person will say that he is the only person who is fit to succeed Monsieur Meyer who is at present very old and infirm, though a cabal among the other Secretaries who are jealous of his talent may hinder his name from being mentioned. I am affraid I have tresspassed too much upon your Majesty's leisure. I shall therefore only entreat you, Sir, to give my duty to the Queen and sign myself [etc.]. (43584–5)

4298   THE KING *to* MAJOR-GENERAL DE BUDÉ

[*Windsor, 25 July 1783.*] The propriety of your conduct during the time you have been with my sons made me as soon as I proposed on the Peace to send my dearly beloved son Prince William to Germany determine that he should have the advantage of your advice and experience in a scene quite new to him; but at the same time that he should be acquiring that politeness and decorum which is but little to be met with on service in the Navy, and in Head Quarters on shore, though essential in a Prince, a gentleman, and an officer; yet that he should not omit pursueing the theory of his profession, I have through the recommendation of Lord Hood for that purpose nominated Captain Merrick[2] also to accompany him,

[1] Falk in No. 4284 (12 Oct. 1781).
[2] Captain William Augustus Merrick (*d.* 1785). Lieutenant, 1774; Commander, 1779; Captain, April 1782.

and have placed Captain de Linsingen of my Electoral troops to attend him, whose knowledge of English as well as German and French will render him very useful.

My great object is that my dearly beloved son may learn the German language, the law of nations, the grounds of civil law, engineering, artillery, and military tacticks, which three last branches will open his ideas and enable him to pursue his profession as an officer, not a mere sailor.

As to the rules of conduct to be observed and the etiquettes which the usage of Germany requires, they have been laid down and pursued with so much approbation in the case of my dearly beloved second son Prince Frederick, Bishop of Osnabruck, that I referr you to the instructions I gave to Major-General Grenville, and to the information he will readily give you. I also referr you to my Ober Hoff Marschal de Lichtenstein, who can give you every sort of information concerning the usages of German Courts.

You will lose no opportunity of keeping me apprized of every occurrence that may deserve my notice, and I cannot conclude without expressing my hopes that with the blessing of God my unwearied attention to place my third son in a way to become a respectable character and an useful officer may in the end be crowned with success. (Add. Georgian 15/464)

4299   THE KING *to* PRINCE WILLIAM

[*Windsor, 1 Aug. 1783.*] By the account from Sheerness you have not advanced very rapidly but I trust you landed about yesterday. I shall not be long on this occasion; you must remember you have had many advantages over persons of your rank, you have been early sent to sea by which the common service of a mariner is now known to you. I have taken the first opportunity on the Peace to send you to Germany that you may get quit of the manner of a sailor, acquire those of a Prince and a gentleman, and acquire that knowledge as well as behaviour that may fit you for an Officer and for any other situation that time may require; above all things consider that unless you are a good man you cannot be of utility to your country nor of credit to your family. This may seem an old fashioned language but experience will shew you it is most true. That you may become everything that is estimable is my sincere wish who shall ever remain [etc.]. (Add. Georgian 21/1/36)

4300   PRINCE FREDERICK *to the* QUEEN

[*Hannover, 28 Aug. 1783.*] Permit me to make your Majesty my most humble congratulations upon your happy delivery and to express to you how rejoiced I was to hear that you were perfectly well. I should have done myself the honor of answering by the last courier the kind and affectionate letter which William brought me from your Majesty if I had not thought that my letter would have arrived at a time when it would have been inconvenient to your Majesty to read it.[1] By the end of next week the servant whom his Majesty has ordered over to

Princess Amelia was born on 7 August.

dress him will set out for England. Permit me, Madam, to recommend him to your protection and to entreat you to support him a little. He is a very good honest fellow and I have no doubt will do exceedingly well but he will have no easy task to play as his Majesty's other servants will be set against him, and will do everything in their power to ruin him with the King. I shall set out tomorrow morning at five o'clock for Cassel &c, a tour which will take me about six weeks. The country through which we shall pass is by all accounts the finest in all Germany and we shall just be there during the vintage which will make it exceedingly pleasant.

Your Majesty was pleased to ask me in your last letter what my opinion was of William. I think him much improved in many points, but to be sure he seems very fond of manual jokes. I however really think that he has already begun to lay them a little aside and I have no doubt that his good sense will in a short time make him leave off this kind of behaviour, which certainly is not that of a gentleman. I am affraid I have already tresspassed too long upon your Majesty's leisure. I shall therefore only entreat you, Madam, to give my love to my brothers and sisters and to believe me [etc.]. (43604–5)

4301   THE KING *to* COLONEL HOTHAM

[*Windsor, 12 Sept. 1783.* [*Draft.*]] It is with reluctance I give unpleasant commissions which is encreased when the task falls to your lot; without farther preface an atercation [*sic*] totally subserversive [*sic*] of all propriety having arisen between Mr. Bruyeres[1] and Mr. Farhill which the former very properly instantly communicated to me; which occasioned me the next day writing a memorandum of what had passed and sending it to Mr. Bruyeres. This put his situation in the clearest light and I trusted would have prevented farther disputes when communicated to Mr. Farhill, since which Mr. Bruyeres has acquainted me that subsequent to my paper Mr. Farhill has by letter acquainted him that had he conceived the smallest responsibility would have been expected from him to Mr. Bruyeres he would never have entered into the Establishment; that Mr. Bruyeres chose in his side to let a month elapse to see whether Mr. Farhill would not recall that letter, but not having done it he thought it right to acquaint me how impossible it would be for them both to continue in the same Establishment; I therefore very easily determined that Mr. Farhill should be the one to be removed, for though contented with his assiduity in instructing Edward, yet not thinking his other conduct tended to that subordination without which no regularity can exist in any house, and a young pupil must naturally take advantage of dissentions which must overthrow any plan of education of which any branch of knowledge makes but a part.

You will therefore acquaint Mr. Bruyeres in the first place with this decision, and that he is permitted to mention it to Edward. You will then see Mr. Farhill and after expressing my approbation of the pains he has taken in the branches of

---

[1] Prince Edward's Instructor.

knowledge he has pursued with Edward, acquaint him that I am willing to continue him half his present salary till an opportunity may arise of otherwise employing him.

I desire you will then both to Edward's Establishment and to that of my three other sons explain the situation of the Governor and of the Preceptors which from your conduct and assiduity whilst with my two eldest sons you are fully able to do without farther assistance than the memorandum I alluded to.

Mr. Fisher[1] ought to be told by Mr. Bruyeres that he will be sole preceptor and take Religion, Classical learning and History as his branches of instruction.

You will also mention to Mr. Bruyeres that I intend to appoint Capt. Green instructor in Mathematicks and other branches of military knowledge. He is also to assist him in attending Edward in his exercises. (41804–5)

4302   THE QUEEN *to* MAJOR-GENERAL DE BUDÉ

[*7 Oct. 1783.*] Monsieur, Je vous suis bien obligé de l'information que vous m'avez donné dans votre lettre par rapport a l'affaire de Guillaume et ma niece.[2] J'ai des la premiere lettre de mon fils penetré ses sentiments et jai consequ'ament prevu cet attachement pour la Princesse. Je n'ai non plus manqué d'en avertir mon frere c'est a dire de mes sçoupçons mais ma lettre ne lui est parvenue qu'après son retour de la Saxe ce qui me fache d'autant plus comme je croyoit par la, prevenir les frequentes visites dans sa maison de mon fils pendant son absence. Une permission qu'il faut absolument lui interdire chaque foi qu'il se voit obligé de quiter sa famille quand même il ne fut pas question de la belle passion car ces sortes de libertées sans etre criminelle paroissent imprudente a un monde qui veut parlé et il vaut mieux ne pas s'exposer.

Je convient avec vous Monsieur qu'on doit eviter tous ce qui peut faire un eclat dans cette affaire, mais je craint que notre jeune homme sous l'apparence de la soumission aux arrangements que vous avez prise avec mon frere ne nous joue un mauvais tour et en parle a la Princesse quand l'occasion s'y presente. Il en est bien capable car sa vivacité et ses passions l'emportent toujours sur son jugement, cela vous est connu, aussi bien bien qu'a moi, et cela une foi arrivé, comment ferons nous alors pour empecher cette folie de prendre racine? Je suis donc d'avis que mon frere doit accepter l'offre de sa belle mere pour quelque tems seulement et de lui amener sa fille pour lui tenir compagnie ce qui se peut faire avec toute la decence imaginable comme il y va pour se remarié, et la Princesse Douairiere sera bien aise de l'avoir auprês d'elle vue qu'elle sera toute seule alors. Je ne manquerai pas de representé ceci tellement a mon frere pour qu'il en convient et jusqu'alors il faut tenir ferme aux arrangements faites quils ne se voyent qu'en presence de mon frere et aussie rarement que possible.

Jai ecrit une longue lettre a Guillaume et je l'ai prié de vous la montrer, ayez la bonté de me faire sçavoir quel effet elle a sur lui, et si peut etre vous serez d'oppinion que jauroit du dire plus, faite moi le sçavoir et je le ferai.

---

[1] John Fisher (1748–1825) was responsible for the education of the Duke of Kent, 1780–85, and later of Princess Charlotte.   [2] See Vol. I, Introduction, p. xviii, and No. 164.

Je n'en ferai point mention au Roi qu'aprés avoir reçue votre reponce, que je vous prie de m'envoyér par une enveloppe du General Freytag car comme il execute mille petite commissions la Hagedorn ne me donne ses lettres que quand je suis seule et que je suis a l'abri de toute sorte de question.

Toute la famille restera a la campagne jusqu'aprés Noel. Le Parlement cependant nous fera revoir Londres une foi par semaine, mais pour nous y etablir pour un hyver entier, cela n'arrivera plus. Il faut s'y soumettre de bonne grace. Je vit toujours en esperance de jouir d'un peut plus d'amusement. Ah c'est une exellente chose que l'esperance. Je croi pourtant que pour les Reines elle n'est pas ce qu'elle est pour d'autres gens, car c'est longtems que j'ai esperé sans effet.

Lady Conyers[1] passera son hyver a Londres. Elle est toujours malade a ce qu'on dit et devienne plus maigre de jour en jour, il y a un bruit en ville que je ne tient cependant pas de três bonne main, qu'une separation doit se faire entre elle et son mari, j'en doute, au moins je croi que Lady Holderness s'y opposera.

On pense ou plutot on se flatte que Monsieur Cordon[2] reviendra ici, c'est Monsieur *Scarnafis* qui l'a dit a Paris, se servant de l'expression '*contre son attente*'; ces mots paroissent un enigme pout tout le monde peut etre pouriez vous l'expliqué. Le Colonel Goldsworthy est en service ici, il a eté empeché de nous joindre plutot par violente attaque de la goutte qui lui a duré pour trois jours, il est tres bien a l'heure qu'il est, est bien determiné a se defaire de cette mauvaise connoissance. Lord Spencer[3] vient de mourir a Bath aprés avoir souffert beaucoup. Mrs Harcourt[4] se porte bien et continue sa partialité pour sa campagne.

Voila assez pour aujourdhui, c'est deja vous faire faire penitence Monsieur de lire mon François, je n'ai pas besoin d'ajouter a la longueur de la lettre, car mauvais françois est triste, mais mauvais et long est pis. J'attendroi votre lettre avec impatience. (Add. Georgian 15/470)

4303   THE KING *to* PRINCE WILLIAM

[*Queen's House, 23 Oct. 1783.*] The quarterly messenger has delivered your letter of the 10th mentioning the rejoicings of the town of Hannover on the return of Frederick, which doubly pleases me as it gives a strong mark of the affection for me and family and a consciousness of the propriety of his conduct by which he has acquired the esteem of my very faithful *German* subjects. I am happy to find you are sensible of my care to put you in a way to be of credit to yourself and family and of utility if you make the proper use of it to your country. To be

---

[1] Amelia (1754–84), sole surviving child of the 4th Earl of Holdernesse, and who became *suo jure* Baroness Conyers in 1778 on her father's death, married (29 Nov. 1773) Lord Francis Godolphin Osborne, (1751–99) styled Marquess of Carmarthen, 1761–89, who succeeded his father as 5th Duke of Leeds in 1789. She eloped from her husband on 13 Dec. 1778, and was divorced by Act of Parliament in May 1779. A few days later (9 June) she married John Byron, who died on 2 Aug. 1791, at the age of 35, the father, by a second wife, of Lord Byron, the poet.

[2] The Marquis de Cordon was the Sardinian Minister in London. His chapel in Lincoln's Inn Fields was gutted during the Lord George Gordon riots in 1780. He was succeeded in Oct. 1784 by the Chevalier de Pollon.

[3] John, first Earl Spencer (1734–83), died on 31 October.

[4] See No. 1224.

fit to restore discipline in [the] fleet hereafter which at present is undoubtedly lost in our service you must get a command of yourself; you have the best means of doing that, therefore on yourself alone the blame as well as disadvantage will fall if you do not turn out agreeable to my most sanguine wishes. (Add. Georgian 21/1/41)

4304   *Letters from* PRINCE FREDERICK *to the* KING

[*Hannover, 24 Oct. 1783.*] I now sit down to give your Majesty according to your orders as exact an account as I can of every thing remarkable during our last journey.

We went from hence in one day to Cassel, and were the next morning presented to the Lan[d]grave, at his parade, and were received in a very polite manner. The parade consisted of the whole garrison of Cassel, which is three Batallions of Guards, a squadron of Horse Guards and four Regiments of dismounted Dragoons. They are cloathed in every respect as the Prussians, but there is a terrible difference in their manœuvres and in their appearance. We were presented to the Langravine before dinner. She has one of the finest faces that can be seen though she is thirty eight years old, but her figure does not in the last answer to her face, as she is remarkable fat. During the whole time we were at Cassel we were treated in the kindest manner possible, particularly by Prince Frederick,[1] who is very much altered for the better since he was in England: indeed everybody gives him the best of characters now. The town of Cassel is exceedingly fine and situated in a most beautiful country, the Weissenstein which is a country house belonging to the Langrave is beyond description fine, and the fall of water is wonderful, in order to get up to the top from whence the water falls, one must mount 900 steps. We also saw the field of battle of Wilhelmsdahl, which can be perfectly seen from the top of a small hill in the garden. From Cassel we went to Gotha, I confess I cannot say much in the praise of this Court. The Duke[2] is by all accounts a very good and learned man, but not much a man of the world and as for the Duchess, the best thing one can say for her is that she is a little mad. We also had the honor of finding there the Duke of Meiningen[3] the Duchess of Gotha's brother, who is really worthy of his dearly beloved sister. Hilbourghausen was the next place we visited. The old Duke though past eighty is still exceedingly chearful and received me in the most polite manner possible.[4] He gave us the day after our arrival a great Chasse in which we killed thirty two stags, besides other game, and the next day we killed one hundred and thirty two pheasants and a hundred and sixty hares. Your Majesty can have no idea of the cold in this part of Germany, on account of the neighbourhood of [a] large range of mountains, called the Thuringer Walde. Though it was only the beginning of September

[1] The Landgrave's fourth son (1747–1837).
[2] The Duke of Saxe-Gotha (1745–1804), married (1769) Charlotte (1751–1827), daughter of Anton Ulrich, Duke of Saxe-Meiningen.
[3] George, Duke of Saxe-Meiningen (1761–1803).
[4] Prince Frederick cannot have been referring to the Duke of Saxe-Hildburghausen (1763–1834), who succeeded his father in 1780.

everybody wore pelisses. The difference was the more striking as we came from Gotha where it was very hot and went from Hilbourghausen to Anspach where it was equally warm. The Margrave[1] does not live at Anspach but at a country house about nine miles from Anspach called Triersdorf. He has a wonderful fine stable of horses, though I cannot say that he keeps them in the best order. He is a very good man and remarkably civil. He begged me particularly to express to your Majesty how much he is attached to your person and to your family. We staid two days at Triersdorf and went from thence two [*sic*] Manheim where we staid one day to see everything which is remarkable there. The town is beautiful, it is a perfect square and the streets are quite straight. The Palace is immense but furnished in a very old stile. There is a very fine collection of pictures there. We went in the evening to see the gardens of Schwetzingen, which is a country house belonging to the Elector about ten miles from Manheim. I cannot say the gardens are very fine, they are in the old style, but the buildings are beautiful. The Court of Darmstadt being at Paris we did not stop there but went immediately on to Frankfort, where we staid one day to view the town which is very old and ugly. The fare is very great. From Frankfort we paid our visit to the Court at Hanau, which is very small. We lodged at the Bath of Wilhelmstade which is close to the town, and which is very pretty. On our return to Frankfort we went over the field of battle of Berghen which is very curious. We remained the next day at Frankfort in order to embark our carriages on board the yacht, and were three days in going down the Rhine. There is no expressing the beauty of this country, one passes the whole way through mountains which are covered to the very top with vines. We disembarked at Cologne and from thence made the best of our way to Osnabruck where we staid a week, which was employed in settling everything there, though indeed everything was in such good order that there was not much to arrange. I have now given your Majesty as exact an account as possible of everything which passed during my journey, which has lengthened out my letter to an enormous size. The Prince of Waldeck came here the beginning of this week to make acquaintance with William. He gave me a letter which he desired me to enclose to your Majesty in order that it might arrive safe, which I could not refuse. I cannot help adding that he expressed in the very strongest terms the respect which he bore towards your Majesty. May I entreat your Majesty to give my duty to the Queen and to make my excuses to her for not having wrote to her by this courier, but this long letter will I hope plead my excuse. (43611–4)

[*Hannover, 21 Nov.*] Permit me to return your Majesty my most humble thanks for your gracious letter which I received by the quarterly courier. As your Majesty does not mention your own health I trust that it is at present better, as I confess it has given me for some time no small degree of alarm. We have had last Wednesday a very great chasse in which we killed thirty six boars. William was not of the party as he is not a very great admirer of that amusement, besides which, his shoulder hinders him from ever being a good shot as he cannot bear the least recoil of the gun. Our winter is now set in. We have had for this last week a

---

[1] Charles Alexander, Margrave of Brandenburg-Ansbach (1736–1806).

great deal of rain, and now it begins to snow. If your Majesty has had this same weather in England I am affraid the hunting will not have succeeded. I have my most sincere thanks to return your Majesty for the gracious rescript which you have sent to the Regency here about Falcke and I am certain that if he obtains the place which he is anxious for, your Majesty will not find reason to be displeased with your choice. Permit me, Sir, before I close my letter to entreat your Majesty to give my duty to the Queen. (43621–2)

[*Hannover, 8 Dec. 1783.*] Permit me to return your Majesty my most humble thanks for the gracious letter which I received from you by the courier and to express to you at the same time how much I feel as a fresh mark of your goodness towards me, the manner in which you have been pleased to settle about the four thousand crowns. The affection which your Majesty has ever shewn towards me emboldens me to recommend to your Majesty's consideration the case of a distressed family. Mr. Hanbury, who has been a reputable merchant and ever reckoned the first English House at Hamburgh for upwards of fifty years, has been suddenly drawn upon by his correspondent in England for a very large sum, which correspondent having broke, has availed himself of an Act of Parliament little known to merchants, by which he has refused to pay the bills which Mr. Hanbury had accepted upon his account, and has even refused him to share with the other creditors, by which he is reduced from affluence to be dependent upon his friends' assistance to augment these misfortunes. His son, who was your Majesty's Consul for Lower Saxony, going over to arrange his father's affairs, died of a broken heart. The father is now very anxious to obtain his son's place, and if any small stipend could be added to it, it might serve to alleviate the poor man's distress who being turned of seventy has little hopes of ever recovering any part of his loss, though his friends at Hamburgh have behaved very nobly to him upon the occasion. I am affraid I have already tresspassed too much upon your Majesty's leisure, I shall therefore only entreat your Majesty to give my humble duty to the Queen. (43625–6)

[*Hannover, 18 Dec.*] Permit me to return your Majesty my most humble thanks for your gracious letter which I received by the courier, as well as for the attention you was pleased to pay to my recommendation of Monsieur Falke, who I confess for the sake of your Majesty's service I am sorry did not succeed, as I have no doubt he would have proved himself every way qualified for the post to which he aspired. As I am affraid your Majesty might think it extraordinary in me to recommend to you for that office a person who was unfit for it, I cannot help mentioning that before I would venture to recommend him to your Majesty I inquired of those who were able to judge of his merits infinitely better than I am what their opinion of him was, and they all agreed in giving him the very best of characters both in regard to his talents and learning as well as to his remarkable correctness and goodness of style in writing, and therefore I confess that I was the more astonished at hearing that the only objection that could be made against him was that he was not a good writer by those very persons who had themselves born witness to the contrary. Pardon me also, Sir, if I add that knowing the great jealousy that the other Secretaries had of him and the great party that had been formed in order to obtain the appointment of another, I was not at all astonished at the answer which was sent to your Majesty's gracious orders about him. I would not have dwelt so long upon this subject if I had not thought that your Majesty would have had great reason to be displeased with me if I had strongly recommended to your Majesty's favor a person who was [in] any ways undeserving of it.

I am affraid that I have already tresspassed too long upon your Majesty's leisure. I shall therefore only entreat your Majesty to give my duty to the Queen. (43627–8)

IV

A LETTER FROM QUEEN CHARLOTTE[1]

4305   THE QUEEN *to the* COUNTESS OF MANSFIELD[2]

[*Windsor, 5 Jan. 1801.*] Madam, I have communicated the contents of your letter to his Majesty, who perfectly agrees with you & Mr Greville that the Princes of Orleans, being foreigners of distinction, should have leave to pass through Richmond Park.[3] I should have answered yesterday had I not received the letter too late for the post.

I rejoice to hear that you are so well recovered after your confinement, but tho I do hear that the little boy[4] is equal in beauty to his sister, I hope not to displease when I say that dear sweet little Georgina will bear the prize with me. I beg my compliments to Mr Greville & am my dear Lady Mansfield's affectionate friend. (Liverpool Public Libraries)

[1] This letter reached the Editor too late for inclusion in Vol. III. It is printed by courtesy of the Librarian of the Liverpool Public Libraries.

[2] For Lady Mansfield see Nos. 1539 and 2821.   [3] For their arrival in England, see No. 2102.

[4] Robert Fulke Greville was born in 1800. His sister Georgiana married Lieutenant-Colonel Cathcart, and his sister Louisa married the Rev. Daniel Finch Hatton, brother of the Earl of Winchilsea.

V

COLONEL TAYLOR'S MEMORANDUM RELATIVE TO THE DISPOSAL OF THE KING'S PAPERS

[*Windsor Castle, 23 Dec. 1811.*] The correspondence and papers bearing dates from December 1805 to November 1810 have been progressively arranged by Colonel Taylor and deposited in presses under the windows in the further room of his Majesty's Library in Windsor Castle.

The correspondence for the months of Colonel Taylor's attendance in 1805, namely, since 13th July, were not regularly given to him, but were received in the course of subsequent searches, and, as far as was possible, deposited with the rest, some few loose letters excepted, which were found at more recent periods & deposited in other presses.

An arrangement of papers was made in the summer of 1808, in consequence of a fruitless search for some former correspondence on subjects which had recurred. These papers were delivered to Colonel Taylor by his Majesty, in great number from various presses, table drawers, bureaus, boxes &c,—were of mixed periods and dates, some anterior to his Majesty's reign, & in irregular progress to 1805–6. They are official and private, English, French & German, but the proportion of the latter is small. These were all docketted and arranged by Col. Taylor according to date & deposited in the before-named presses in the Library.

A further arrangement was begun in the months of April and May 1811 of all the papers, official and private of every description & completed after Colonel Taylor's immediate attendance upon his Majesty had ceased. This arrangement comprehended letters and papers of various date which his Majesty had withheld, or which had escaped his notice during the previous searches of the presses &c. in the Lower Apartments; also papers (chiefly German) found in some tables or bureaus in the State Apartments, documents, printed and manuscript, relating to domestic Establishments and Departments, political, financial & military state of foreign countries, Reports from the Electorate of Hanover, military & civil; Returns, English & German & miscellaneous documents of various description; —of mixed periods & dates;—some anterior to his Majesty's reign & progressive with greater or lesser intervals to 1805–6. This search also produced a large proportion of Army & Navy Returns, arranged in portfolios, others loose; also books of various description, plans, maps, prints & architectural drawings, surveys, a small proportion of minerals, medals & coins, some telescopes &c. &c. and five boxes containing deeds & leases.

The whole of these have been arranged with the assistance of Mr. Bott, Junior, Mr Snart & Mr Hely (the Page's son).

The English private & ministerial correspondence, German & French papers & family letters were arranged by Colonel Taylor according to subjects and dates and deposited in a black press of which Colonel Taylor has the only key and which also contains some presents from the Grand Signor, recently unpacked. The family correspondence sealed up.

The Army Returns, including the greater proportion which had been deposited at the Queen's Palace & which are understood to be complete from 1760, were, by his Majesty's command, sent in May 1811 to the Adjutant General's Office down to 1799 inclusive. Those from 1800 to the present period were sorted and arranged by Messrs Snart, Bott and Hely & are deposited in a large deal press, of which Col. Taylor & Mr Bott junior have each a key. This press and another of nearly the same size contain further, such books & prints as were not moved to the Library (while the loan of his Majesty's key afforded access to the Library presses) also a proportion of the architectural & other drawings, surveys, some maps and a variety of printed documents & manuscript books and papers of inferior importance—all sorted & arranged as far as the subjects admitted—also sundry loose articles of various nature which had been withdrawn from other presses during the search for papers.

The deeds were sorted by Mr John Bott, and schedules being made, were replaced in the boxes which originally contained them, of which Mr John Bott has the keys. The number does not correspond with the specification in the original schedules; and it is presumed that Messrs Still & Strong have those wanting.

Some other articles, viz. two Turkish swords, some telescopes &c. &c. are under the charge of Mr Bott Senior. Six Turkish musquets & rifles, recently unpacked, are in the Library.

Hence it will appear that the articles to which Colonel Taylor has access are the contents of the large black press and of the two large deal presses, containing papers, books and other articles, as already described, produced by the last search. These three presses are in the passages leading to the King's private apartments.

Mr John Bott has access to the two large deal presses above-named & to the boxes containing deeds.

The articles under charge of Mr Bott, Senior, are secured in the wardrobe presses to which he has access.

The private presses in the Library are only accessible with the King's private key, now in the Queen's possession.

That key also opens a large book press in the Blue Room, containing chiefly books on agriculture; another smaller one containing Handel's Works, a table with drawers containing the medals, coins & minerals and a few other trifling articles. It opens the several presses and bureaus in his Majesty's bedroom and dressing room, in which there are no papers of much import, excepting the small press nearest the chimney which contains the papers relating to the Enquiry into the Princess of Wales's conduct.

The same key opens every other press throughout the apartments (those in the windows of the dining room and others on that side, containing papers chiefly, German returns & accounts). This key (Col. T. believes) opens also the bureaus in the State Apartment which have been emptied of papers, and the various presses, bureaus &c. in the Great Lodge, in the Queen's House and at Kew.

Those in the Queen's House were emptied by his Majesty's direction, in May last, by Mr. John Bott and the contents brought to Windsor. (50262–4)

COMPREHENSIVE INDEX TO
VOLUMES I TO V

To facilitate reference to the appropriate volume, the numbers included in Volumes II to IV are given at the foot of each double page of the Index.

Abercromby, Sir Ralph (*cont.*)
 successes in West Indies, 1427
 and the 1798 Rebellion, 1709
 resigns his post in Ireland, 1709n, 1720
 his son's marriage, 1900
 to command expedition to Holland (1799),
  1979n, 2011
 given local rank of General, 2037
 question of a peerage for, 2054, 2054n
 his children, 2054n
 idea of sending him to Portugal (1800), 2136
 killed outside Alexandria, 2393n
 his Red Bibbon, 2421, 2421n
Abercromby, Sir Robert (1740–1827), Sir
  Ralph's brother, 384, 700, 1588, 2032,
  2507, 3815
 given a Red Ribbon, 767n
 Commander-in-Chief in India, 791
 why he entered Parliament, 2054n
 and Governorship of Stirling Castle, 2507
 appointed Governor of Edinburgh Castle,
  2507n
 his campaign in America, 4285, 4289
Aberdeen, 3rd Earl of (1722–1801),
 elected a Scottish Representative Peer, 78
Aberdeen, 4th Earl of (1784–1860), 3966n
 letter from, 3607n
 made a K.T., 3607, 3624
Aberdeenshire, 3642
Aberffraw, 4120, 4122
Abergavenny, 4126n
Abergavenny, 1st Earl of (1727–85), 75
Abergavenny, 2nd Earl of (1755–1843),
  2474n, 3966n
Abingdon, Earl of (1740–99), 1983n
Aboukir, battle of, *see* Nile
Aboukir, capture of (1801), 2394n
Aboyne, Earl of, *see* Huntly, 9th Marquess of
Abrams, a convict, 189
Abyssinia, King of, 3773
Achill Head, 1996
Achilles, a 74-gun ship, 4001
Acland, Lieut.-Gen. Sir Wroth Palmer
  (1770–1816), 3801
A'Court, Sir William, Baron Heytesbury
  (1779–1860), 3386
 Sec. of Legation at Naples (1801), 2480
Act of Grace (Ireland), 1790
Active, a 38-gun frigate, 3332
Adair, James (1743?–98), Recorder of Lon-
  don, 19, 159, 335, 508, 530, 532, 1033,
  1185, 1195, 1519, 1550, 1566
 letter from, 1490n
 resigns his Recordership (1789), 532n

Adair, Sir Robert (1763–1855), 3336, 3342,
  3369, 3388, 3440, 3773, 3868, 4110
 Mission to Vienna, 3409
Adam, William (1751–1839), 438, 757, 838,
  878, 894n, 956, 977, 1031, 1033, 2833n,
  2834, 3373, 3420n, 3491, 3617, 3787n,
  3799, 3804, 3804n, 3815, 3818, 3824n,
  3832, 3878n, 4122, 4122n, 4126, 4133,
  4159
 letters to, 934n, 3583n
 his opposition to the War, 983
Adamant, a 50-gun ship, 1672, 1779
Adams, Mrs, nurse to the Princesses, 4155
Adams, Charles (*c.* 1753–1821), 3009n, 4074n
  4138n
 seconds the Address (1805), 3009
Adams, James (1752–1816), 1664n
Adams, John (1735–1826), Pres. of U.S.A.,
  1868n
Adams, William (*c.* 1752–1811), 1546n,
  1664n
Adams, William Dacres (1775–1862), private
  secretary to Pitt and Portland,
 letter from, 4018n
 letters to, 3522n, 4018n
 appointed a Commissioner of Woods and
  Forests, 3970, 3970n
Addington, Henry, Viscount Sidmouth
  (1757–1844), 438, 534, 734, 741, 814,
  1214n, 1250n, 1333, 1337, 1537, 1760,
  1764n, 1793, 1796, 1922, 1932, 1981,
  2092n, 2108n, 2174, 2196n, 2269, 2272–
  3, 2288n, 2290, 2308–9, 2327, 2334n,
  2336n, 2339n, 2346n, 2349, 2357n, 2365,
  2365n, 2368n, 2369n, 2379n, 2386,
  2397, 2409, 2456n, 2461n, 2474n,
  2481, 2483, 2493, 2500, 2504, 2510,
  2510n, 2515n, 2519, 2533, 2536n, 2552,
  2554n, 2556, 2572, 2588, 2589n, 2595n,
  2612, 2614, 2619, 2629, 2635, 2638n,
  2643, 2669, 2673, 2676, 2689n, 2702,
  2702n, 2747, 2757n, 2760, 2772, 2777–8,
  2780n, 2782n, 2785, 2786n, 2789, 2794,
  2794n, 2806n, 2808, 2837n, 2842, 2843n,
  2851n, 2852n, 2857, 2858n, 2870n,
  2871n, 2884n, 2888, 2888n, 2894, 2902,
  2902n, 2907, 2922n, 2983–4, 2986–7,
  2988n, 2990, 2991n, 2993, 2994n, 3002,
  3075n, 3081n, 3105n, 3120n, 3164n,
  3169n, 3174n, 3221n, 3223n, 3283n,
  3394, 3395n, 3417, 3417n, 3426, 3434n,
  3442, 3483n, 3508, 3832n, 3873, 3906n,
  3966n, 3996, 4074, 4092–3, 4142, 4184,
  4204, 4229, 4246–7

Addington, Henry (*cont.*)

letters from, 1764n, 1932n, 2189n, 2330n,
2331, 2334, 2337, 2341, 2350, 2354, 2357,
2369, 2373, 2379, 2405, 2411, 2421, 2427,
2431, 2435, 2439, 2456, 2461, 2467, 2474,
2479, 2482, 2489, 2498, 2498n, 2502,
2515, 2518, 2520, 2529, 2536, 2540n,
2554, 2570, 2572, 2585, 2587, 2589, 2592,
2599, 2606, 2608, 2617, 2620, 2638, 2645,
2650, 2653, 2661, 2665, 2682, 2684, 2689,
2712, 2714, 2719, 2725, 2745, 2752,
2755, 2757n, 2761, 2766, 2780, 2781n,
2782, 2788, 2794n, 2806, 2811, 2824,
2826, 2826n, 2830, 2833, 2835, 2839n,
2851, 2858, 2864, 2888n, 2988, 2988n,
3003n, 3075n, 3081, 3394n, 3431, 3487n,
3559n

letters to, 1357n, 1793n, 2060n, 2264n,
2269n, 2327n, 2331, 2354, 2357, 2357n,
2361, 2365n, 2371, 2371n, 2386n, 2405,
2411, 2428n, 2435, 2445, 2445n, 2456–7,
2461, 2461n, 2467, 2469, 2479n, 2489,
2498, 2500n, 2502, 2515, 2515n, 2518,
2536, 2536n, 2554, 2570, 2573, 2581n,
2585, 2585n, 2587, 2592, 2592n, 2599,
2608, 2608n, 2617, 2620, 2624, 2630,
2640, 2645, 2647, 2648n, 2650, 2653,
2661, 2665, 2682, 2684, 2689, 2699n,
2709, 2714, 2719n, 2735n, 2746n, 2752,
2766, 2788, 2788n, 2806n, 2811, 2812n,
2826, 2828, 2830, 2830n, 2835, 2835n,
2858, 2888n, 2901n, 2902n, 2934n,
2940n, 2984, 3003n, 3221n, 3356n,
3416n, 3431, 3559n, 3590n, 4076n

chosen Speaker of the House of Commons
(1789), 524, 524n

sworn of the Privy Council, 530

influencing persons against Cath. eman.,
2329n

unequal to his position, 2329n, 2777n

formation of his Government, 2350 sqq.

first suggests Bragge-Bathurst as Speaker,
2350n

relations with Dundas (1801), 2363n

given the occupation of the Royal Lodge
in Richmond Park (1801), 2445n

as Speaker of the House of Commons, 2585

and ecclesiastical patronage, 2617

anxious to reduce defence commitments
(1802), 2629

appointed a Governor of the Charterhouse,
2650, 2653

financial measures attacked by Grenville,
2734

independent members still support (1803),
2752n

anxious to get rid of Lord Pelham, 2777n

his soothing manner, 2835n

collapse of his Ministry, 2838n

refuses peerage, pension and office of
Chancellor of Duchy, 2838n, 2839n

his income, 2839n

parliamentary provision for (1804), 2842,
2934n

King grateful to (1804), 2857

his family, 2864

his foolish, undignified conduct (1804),
2881n

loses King's confidence (1804), 2888n

his consequence at an end (1804), 2888n

pension for, 2983

returns to office (1805), 2983–4

reluctance to take a peerage, 2984, 2984n,
3003n

suggestion he should take Chancellorship
of Duchy, 2984n

becomes Lord President, 2984, 2984n, 2991

no intercourse with the Opposition (1804),
2993

his title, 3003, 3003n, 3004, 3006

opposed to Canning's entry into Cabinet
(1805), 3075n

deplores Middleton's appointment as head
of Admiralty, 3075n

resignation of (April 1805) withdrawn,
3081, 3081n, 3085, 3085n

Canning's abuse of, 3085n

resignation (July 1805), 3115n

financial provision for, 3120n

at first refuses office (1806), 3175n

resignation (1807), 3394n

not offered office by Portland, 3410n,
3414n

on results of general election (1807), 3483n

criticises Copenhagen expedition, 3589,
3589n

unpopularity of (1809), 3966

not invited to join Perceval's Govt., 3989,
3989n, 3992

King critical of, 3992, 4258–9

'that fool the Doctor', 4073n

attitude to Perceval Ministry, 4142

Addington, Henry, jun. (1786–1823), 2469,
2469n, 2474

II, 832–1662; III, 1663–2575; IV, 2576–3578

Alessandria, Austrians in possession of, 1973
Armistice signed by Austrians at (1800), 2181, 2185, 2188, 2193, 2198, 2214

Alexander, a 74-gun ship, 1153

Alexander I, Tsar of Russia (1777–1825), 2386, 2395, 2425, 2456n, 2475, 2522, 2566, 2655, 2698, 2791, 3073n, 3101, 3265, 3265n, 3278n, 3318, 3346n, 3369, 3427, 3430, 3432–3, 3459, 3468, 3480, 3484, 3492, 3510, 3513, 3527, 3527n, 3535, 3537, 3539, 3560, 3562, 3566, 3568, 3570, 3610, 3623, 3743, 3746, 3807

Alexander, Henry (c. 1763–1818), 3095, 3105

Alexander, Nathaniel (1760–1840), 2928n, 3035

Alexander, Sir William, Bart (1743–c. 1820), 4038, 4038n

Alexandria, 1841, 2089, 2552, 2829, 3331
occupation of (1807), 3463
abandonment of, 3475, 3475n

Alfieri, the Italian poet (1749–1803), 2633n

Alfred, Prince (1780–2), birth of, 4271, 4287

Algeçiras, 2496, 2972n, 3597, 3689n, 4143

Algerine Ambassador, the, 2549, 2560

Algiers, 2560; Regency of, 229

Alien Office, the, 2860, 3547

Aliens Bill (1793), 819

Aliens, expulsion of (1803), 2790

Alkmaar, 2047, 2051, 2060n

Alkmaar, Convention of (1799), 1979n, 2065, 2065n

Allan, Sir Alexander (c. 1764–1820), 3662, 4074n, 4138n

Allegiance, oath of, 1219

Allen, John, 1691, 1694, 1717n

Allen, John (1771–1843), friend of Lord Holland, 3409

Allen, Joseph, Prebendary of Westminster (1770–1845), 3302

Allerton, Duke of York buys estate at (1786), 285

Alley, *see* Allen

Allonville, Comte d' (1732–1811), 1286, 1289

All Souls, Oxford, 3567

Alnwick Castle, 3462n

Alopeus, M. d' (1748–1822), 2742, 2744, 3380, 3382, 3432, 3452, 3459, 3468, 3480, 3484, 3495, 3513, 3560, 3566, 3581

Alphea, a 10-gun cutter, 3689

Alsace, 977, 998

Altamont, Countess of, *see* Sligo

Altamont, 3rd Earl of, *see* Sligo

Althorp, Visct, later 3rd Earl Spencer (1782–1845), 3302, 3857, 4162

his maiden speech, 3841, 3841n

Alton, 1090

Altona, 3520

Altshausen, 1944

Alvanley, Lord, *see* Arden, Richard Pepper

Alvensleben, M. d' (Prussian Minister at Dresden, nephew of Hanoverian Minister in London), 92, 351

Alvensleben, Baron, Hanoverian Minister in London (d. 1795), 92, 344, 426, 499, 676, 745, 803, 1182, 1198

Alverstoke, 1332

Alvintzy, Baron, Austrian Field-Marshal, General, 924, 957, 1088

Amazon, a 38-gun frigate, 3244

Ambler, Charles (1721–94), the Queen's Attorney-Gen., 1031

Amboyna, conquest of, 1472

Amelia, Archduchess of Austria, sister of Francis II (1780–98), 1848

Amelia (Amalie), a 44-gun captured French frigate, 1699, 2601

Amelia, Princess (1710–86), daughter of George II, 309, 335n, 341n, 1248, 4278
her will, 335, 335n
her house sold for £10,000, 335n
post mortem on, 335

Amelia, Princess (1783–1810), 455n, 799, 1697, 1822, 1860, 1873, 1876, 1921, 2019, 2042, 2064, 2139, 2233, 2927n, 2962n, 3285, 3937, 3943, 3947, 3950, 3954, 3956, 3964, 3972, 3976, 3977n, 3983, 3988, 3991, 3994, 3997, 4001, 4005, 4009, 4012, 4016, 4019, 4021, 4024, 4027, 4029, 4031, 4065, 4077, 4097, 4106, 4123, 4131, 4134, 4154, 4157, 4160, 4163, 4165–9, 4172–3, 4175–6, 4178–81, 4183, 4185–6, 4189–90, 4194, 4197, 4217–18, 4233n, 4236, 4238n
letters from, 1801, 1804, 1807, 1815, 1823, 1858, 1865, 1875, 3929, 3944, 3949, 3955, 3961, 3965, 3974, 3982, 3987, 3990, 3993, 3995, 4000, 4004, 4008, 4017, 4022, 4030, 4049, 4066, 4068, 4078, 4107, 4132, 4155, 4193, 4216
letters to, 3897, 3944, 3949, 3955, 3961, 3965, 3974, 3982, 3987, 3990, 3993, 3995, 4000, 4004, 4008, 4017, 4022, 4049, 4066, 4068, 4078, 4107, 4132, 4155, 4193, 4216
her allowance of £500 p.a., 985, 1388
birth of, 4300
the seaside recommended for, 1784
her partiality for Weymouth, 1601
living at Worthing, 1601
financial provision for, 1929, 1929n

Amelia, Princess (cont.)
  confirmation of, 2091, 2098
  is to live in Dr Heberden's house, 4008–9,
    4012
America, a 64-gun ship, 4269
American Loyalists, the, 111
American Trade Bill (1784), 50, 102
American War, the (1775–82), 399, 1477
Amethyst, a 38-gun frigate, 2738, 2758, 3854
Amherst, Jeffrey, Lord (1717–97), 458, 519,
    829, 921, 975, 983, 989, 991, 996, 1010,
    1019, 1020n, 1051, 1101, 1121, 1150,
    1202, 1231, 1849, 1983n
  letters from, 1135, 1172, 1200
  letter to, 1200
  appointed Comm.-in-Chief in England
    (1793), 829
  superseded by Duke of York, 1198
  to be made a Field-Marshal, 1199n, 1200
  to be given land in Canada, 1200
  death of, 1597, 1604, 1606–7
  and Governorship of Jamaica, 1849n
Amherst, William Pitt, Earl (1773–1857),
    458, 3663, 3674, 3936, 3966n, 4023,
    4039
  and the Bedchamber, 2894n, 2902n, 3000n
Amiens, peace negotiations at, 2544, 2561,
    2597; Treaty signed at (1802), 2600,
    2600n, 2605, 2609, 2615, 2621, 2623,
    2654, 2669, 2674, 2912, 3242n, 3265n
  French and Spanish ratification of, 2621
  Spanish and Dutch ratification of, 2623
Amphion, a 32-gun frigate, 377, 3689
Amphitrite, a 32-gun frigate, 1444, 2409
Amsterdam, 403, 409, 414, 1169, 2046–7,
    2065n
  French occupy (1795), 1197, 1204
Amyot, Thomas (1775–1850), 3412
Ancaster, Mary, Duchess of (d. 1793),
    Mistress of the Robes to the Queen, 312,
    4264, 4268
Ancaster, 4th Duke of (1756–79), death of,
    4268
Ancaster, 5th Duke of (1729–1809), 1983
Ancient Concert, Directors of the, 1013
Andalusia, 3677, 3693, 3695, 3759, 3926n
Andaman Islands, 567
Anderson, Dr, 4229
Anderson, Francis Evelyn (1752–1821), M.P.
    for Grimsby (1774–80) and Beverley
    (1780–4), 57
Anderson, George (1760–96), 255

Anderson, Sir John William, Alderman
    (c. 1736–1813), 564, 1480, 1546, 1855
Andover, 3946, 3964, 4005, 4029–31
Andréossi, Antoine François, Count (1761–
    1828), 2639, 2639n, 2724n, 2730n,
    2735
Andrewes, Rev. Gerrard (1750–1825), Dean
    of Canterbury, 3635, 3996
Andrews, 915
Andrews, Miles Peter (c. 1742–1814), 1546,
    2881n, 2894n
Andromeda, a 32-gun frigate, 475, 525
Aduaga, the Chevalier d', Spanish Minister in
    London, 2981
  his letter of credence, 2730n
Angoulême, Louis Antoine de Bourbon,
    Duc d' (1775–1844), 2512, 3556, 3644
Angoulême, Marie Thérèse, Duchess of
    (1778–1851), 689, 1848, 2512, 3623,
    3644
Anne, Queen (1665–1714), 499, 508, 1215,
    2170, 2174, 2308, 3888n
Anquetil, M. d', 548
  his books, L'Esprit de la Ligue, 548;
    L'Histoire de Louis XIV, 548
Anson, a 40-gun frigate, 3377, 3379n
Anson, Thomas, Visct (1767–1818), M.P. for
    Lichfield (1789–1806), 3966n
  letter to, 1559n
Anspach [Ansbach], 1934, 2185, 4304
  Margrave of (1736–1806), 4304
Anstruther, Sir John, Bart (1753–1811), 670,
    744, 757, 831, 878, 1033, 1122, 1253,
    1255, 1255n, 3787n, 3857, 3873, 3876,
    3878n, 4087n, 4126, 4130, 4133, 4198
  his parliamentary interest, 64n
  departure for India, 1588
  refused a baronetcy (1797), 1588
  Chief Justice at Calcutta, 3163, 3906
  attitude to Perceval Ministry, 3989n
Anstruther, Brigadier-Gen. Robert (1768–
    1809), 1443, 1445, 1768, 1771, 1894,
    2396, 3801
Antelope, the, a 50-gun ship, 3144
Antigua, 3210
Anti-Jacobin, the, 2201
Antraigues, Comte d' (1755–1812), 3492,
    3492n, 3527n, 3748n
Antrim, 1816
  the rebellion in, 1761
Antrobus, Sir Edmund (d. 1826), partner in
    Coutts's Bank, 849

Augustus Frederick (*cont*).

sails for Lisbon (1800), 2297n, 2307

finds Lisbon a disagreeable place, 2370

his Dukedom, 2552, 2565n

abandons Lady Augusta Murray (1801), 2565, 2565n

proposes to join Portuguese Army as a General, 2724

his improved health in Portugal, 2724

wants to join Volunteers at home, 2818

apartments in Kensington Palace for, 2972

his debts, 3680

Aust, George, 8n, 954, 1337

letters from, 52n, 78n, 112n

letter to, 714

denied an Under-Secretaryship (1789), 544n

leaves Foreign Office (1796), 1337n

appointed Chief Muster Master of the Forces, 1337n

Aust, Mrs, 1337n

Austerlitz, battle of, 3146n, 3197

Austin, William, M.D. (1754–93), 528

Austin, William (1802–49), 3279n

Austria, makes peace with France (1797), 1538, 1538n, 1634

Austria, peace treaty signed with (1809), 3773

Austria, Archduchess Maria Louisa of, *see* Maria Louisa

Austria, Archduke of, *see* Ferdinand

Austrian loan, the (1794–5), 1167, 1180, 1198, 1198n; (1797), 1537

Austrian troops inferior to the Prussian, 138

Austrian Netherlands, rebellion in, 560, 564

French invade the, 816

British plan to cede them to Prussia, 1429

Auvergue, Capt. D', 35

Avaray, Comte d', 3552, 3556, 3698

Averne, Thomas, Lieut.-Gen. (*d.* 1805), 2601

Avesnes, 966, 1000

Avignon, disorders in, 674, 816

Avonmore, Lord, *see* Yelverton

Aylesbury, 660, 664

Aylesbury election (1784), 58; (1804), 2921, 2922n

Aylesford, Charlotte, Countess of (1730–1805), death of, 3024n, 3027

Aylesford, 4th Earl of (1751–1812), 6, 10, 2376, 2653, 2853, 2878n, 3024, 3242, 3486, 3966n

letters from, 2874, 2880, 2886, 3027, 3031, 3057, 3530

letters to, 2880, 3027, 3060, 3216

becomes Capt. of the Yeomen of the Guard (1783), 10

choice of Household office (1804), 2850n, 2853n, 2856, 2856n, 4258

and the Garter, 2994, 3014n, 4041n

the Lord Steward, 2880, 3056, 3589

Aylesford, Louisa, Countess of (1760–1832), 2874, 3216

her safe delivery of a son, 2880, 2886

the 'prolific Countess', 2880

Aylmer, Frederick Whitworth William, 6th Baron (1777–1858), 3937

Ayrshire Fencible Cavalry, the 1535, 1616

Babette, a 28-gun ship, 1186

Backhouse, Lieut.-Gen. Thomas Joseph (*d.* 1828), 3368

Bacon, Anthony, senior (*c.* 1717–86), 1496

Bacon, Anthony, junior (*b.* 1772),

unsuccessful election contests, 1496n, 2834n

declines standing for Windsor, 1498

Bacon, Sir Francis, Lord Verulam and Viscount St Albans (1561–1626), 2814

Bacon, John (1738–1816), 3584n

Bacon, John (1777–1859), sculptor, 3584

Baddeley, Robert (1733–94), actor, 4274

Baden, Charles Frederick, Margrave of (1728–1811), 2685

Baden, Princess Wilhelmina of (1788–1836), a possible wife for Duke of Cambridge, 2680, 2685, 2685n

her sisters, 2685n

Badminton, 2502

Bagot, Sir Charles (1781–1843), 3474n, 3552n, 3970n, 4113n

letter from, 3701

asks for an Under-Secretaryship (1807), 3701n

Bagot, Lewis, Bishop of St Asaph (1740–1802), 1983n

Bagot, Louisa, Lady (1787–1816), 3350

Bagot, William, 2nd Lord (1773–1856), 1983n, 3350, 3966n

Bagshaw, Sir William Chambers, High Sheriff of Derbyshire, 3218

Bagshot, 770, 1090

Bagwell, John (*c.* 1754–1816), 2894n

Bagwell, William (*c.* 1776–1826), 2894n

Bahamas, the, 1426, 1464, 1644, 2102n, 2113, 3366

Bailey, Thomas, a militiaman, 2523
Baillie, Matthew (1761–1823), 4049, 4178, 4238n
  letters from, 4166, 4168, 4172, 4175, 4178, 4180
Baily, Captain, 2243
Bainbridge, banker, 4232
Baird, Lieut.-Col., 3201
Baird, General Sir David (1757–1829), 2476, 3140, 3200–1, 3227, 3273, 3291, 3696, 3696n, 3727, 3729, 3745, 3763, 3767, 3769, 3795, 3802, 3851, 3853
Baker, Sir George (1722–1809), 458n, 3164n
  letters from, 465, 468
Baker, William (1743–1824), 4n, 124, 605, 605n, 670, 751, 757, 1329, 3483n
  loses seat for Hertford (1784), 124n
Balam [Balan], Mr, 2660, 3298
Balcarres, 6th Earl of (1752–1825), 972, 983n, 1297, 2389, 3966n
  elected a Scottish Representative Peer (1784), 78
  Lieut.-Gov. of Jamaica, 2220n, 2222
Balderwood Walk (in the New Forest), 3138
Baldon House, near Oxford, 324
Baldwin, 1512
Baldwyn, 335
Balearic Islands, 3689
Balfour, Lieut.-Gen. James (d. 1823), 2527
Balfour, General Nesbitt (c. 1743–1823), 991, 1298, 2802
Balfour, Col. Thomas (d. 1799), 2005
Ball, Rear-Admiral Sir Alexander John, Bart (1757–1809), 2412, 2737
  Civil Commissioner at Malta, 4051
Ball, William, a debtor, 481
Balliol College, Oxford, 2374n, 3996
balloon ascent, a, 124
Balm of Gilead, 372
Baltic, expedition to the (1807), 3471, 3471n, 3479, 3501–3, 3520, 3523, 3537, 3543
Bamberg, 2255, 2312
Banda island, conquest of, 1472
Bandinel, James, Clerk in the Foreign Office, 3194
Bandon election (1808), 3637n
  disaffection in, 1583
Bandon, Francis Bernard, 1st Baron and Visct, and 1st Earl of (1755–1830), 958, 2315, 3637n, 3966n
Banffshire, 2894
Bangalore, capture of (1791), 700
Bangor, Bishop of, *see* Cleaver, William; and Randolph, John

Bank of England, 661, 1475n, 1491n, 1502, 1509, 1509n, 1521, 1537, 3818, 3821, 3869, 4232
  suspends cash payments (1797), 1502, 1507, 1509, 1519, 1546
Bank of Ireland, 3584, 3674n
Bankes, Mrs Frances, wife of Henry Bankes, 3965
Bankes, Henry (1756–1834), 26n, 1180, 1247, 1255, 1509, 2137, 2140, 2752n, 3025, 3071n, 3085, 3105, 3115, 3259, 3444, 3487, 3629, 3675, 3829n, 3832, 3832n, 3834, 3867, 4076, 4076n, 4087n, 4105, 4109, 4116, 4124n, 4126, 4126n, 4138, 4162, 4184, 4205
  his Offices in Reversion Bill (1808), 3613n, 3627, 3629, 3637, 3637n, 3640, 3643; (1809), 3867; (1810), 4076, 4076n, 4097, 4116, 4146
  opposes parliamentary reform (1785), 203
Banks, Sir Joseph (1743–1820), President of the Royal Society, 379, 1299, 1431, 2442, 3076, 3924n
  letters from, 372, 563, 2163, 2569
  letters to, 236, 369, 570, 2093, 2852n
  made a C.B., 1261
  on sheep breeding, 2569
Bantry Bay, French expedition to, 1490–1
  mutiny in the squadron there, 2570, 2570n, 2572
Barbados, 363, 627, 712, 817, 996, 1119, 1331, 3067, 3087–8, 3093, 3104, 3117, 3142, 3174, 3288, 3348
Barbary States, the, 3712
Barbestein, a Dutch ship, 4239
Barclay, 1143n
Barfleur, a 98-gun ship, 194, 393, 536, 3466
Barham, Joseph Foster (1759–1832), 3657, 3904, 4147, 4188
  letter from, 1565
Barham, Lord, *see* Middleton, Sir Charles
Barham Downs, near Canterbury, 1269, 2011, 2029
Baring, Alexander, Lord Ashburton (1774–1848), 3787n, 3828
Baring, Sir Francis (1740–1810), 438, 700–1, 1198, 1897, 2894n, 3828n
Baring, Sir Thomas (1772–1848), 3787n
Barker, Rev. Mr, aspires to be a Prebendary of Worcester, 3645
Barker, Dr John (c. 1727–1808), Master of Christ's College, Cambridge, death of, 3622

Barker, Rev. Samuel, *letter from*, 4233
  sends King October strawberries, 4233
Barker, Thomas, 3233
Barlow, Sir George Hilaro (1762–1846), 3015n, 3255
Barlow, Admiral Sir Robert (1757–1843), 821, 1712n, 3721
Barnard, *see* Bernard
Barnard, Edward (1717–81), Provost of Eton, 4041
Barnard, Frederick, the King's Librarian, 2487, 3121, 3132
  letter to, 3127
Barne, Barne (1754–1828), Commissioner of Taxes, 1685
Barne, Snowdon (1756–1825), a Lord of the Treasury, 4032
Barnes, Sir Edward (1776–1838), appointed Lieut.-Gov. of Dominica, 3664
Barnes, Rev. Frederick, 4076
Barnet, 1269
Barnet, banker, 4232
Baronetcies, applications for, and conferments of, 290, 1054n, 1588, 1666, 2366, 2409, 2465, 2631, 2940, 4038
Baronets higher in rank than K.B.s, 2409n
Barons of the Exchequer (Scotland), 4010
Barrack Office, 2519, 3401
Barracks, inquiry into expenditure on, 1386
Barré, Colonel Isaac (1726–1802), 438, 2357, 2405n
  death of, 2653
Barrington, Admiral Samuel (1729–1800), 591, 609, 616
  death of, 2227
Barrington, Dr Shute, Bishop of Durham (1734–1826), 297, 299, 312n, 688A, 710, 1983n, 3775, 3966n
  letter from, 304
Barrington, Mrs, wife of the Bishop (*d.* 1807), 312n
Barry, James (1741–1806), painter; his *Pandora*, 2577
  has incurred King's displeasure, 2577
Bartenstein, Convention of (1807), 3459
Barthélemi, M., French Chargé d'Affaires in London, 335, 382n, 394, 700, 1301, 1326, 1387
Barwick in Elmet, 4238
Basderadko, *see* Bezborodko
Basingstoke, 713

Basle, Treaty of (1795), 1295, 1304
Basque Roads, 3862, 3865, 3877
Basra, news from, 763, 763n
Bass Strait, proposed settlement at [i.e. in Tasmania], 2691
Bassano, Giacomo (1510–92), 2992
Basset, Sir Francis, Lord De Dunstanville (1757–1835), 438, 751, 838, 1330, 1498n, 3966n
  his borough of Penryn, 1498n
Basseville, M., 824
Basseville, Mme, 824
Bastard, John Pollexfen (1756–1816), 347, 435, 438, 446, 552, 1198, 1223, 1255, 1509, 1724, 3243, 3508
Basule (? Bassilly), 882
Batavian Republic, the, 2733, 2757
Bateman, John, 2nd Visct (1721–1802), 158
Bates, 126
Bates, Joah, a Commissioner of the Customs, (*d.* 1799), 1969, 2483n
Bath, 528, 534, 1160, 1249, 1326, 1382, 1479, 1507n, 1545n, 1840, 1943, 1971, 2049, 2056, 2091, 2106, 2201, 3410n, 3559n, 3777, 4302
  by-election (1804), 3043n
Bath, Elizabeth Cavendish, Lady Weymouth, later Marchioness of (1735–1825), 458n, 465, 2839, 2849
  letters from, 3043
  becomes Marchioness of Bath (1789), 552
  her sons, 2839, 2849
Bath family, the, 2361
Bath, Henrietta Laura Pulteney, Countess of (1766–1808), 1025
Bath, Marquess of, *see* Weymouth
Bath, Order of the, 21, 686, 767n, 1104, 1261, 1370, 1614, 1684, 2421, 2421n, 2434, 2518, 2696, 2706, 2732n, 2739, 2870, 2892–3, 2931, 2944, 2964, 2998n, 3063, 3093, 3093n, 3230, 3372, 3376, 3385, 3387, 3584n, 3607, 3622, 3624, 3707, 3802, 3851, 3853, 3855, 3865, 3938, 4104n, 4143
Bath, Thomas, 2nd Marquess of (1765–1837), 2839, 2849
  declines office of Lord Chamberlain (1804), 2849, 2852
Bath and Wells, Bishop of, *see* Moss, Charles
  Bishopric of, 2617
Bathurst, Mr, a relative of Lord Bathurst, 318
Bathurst, agitator, 1380

Bathurst, Apsley (1769–1816), 3404
Bathurst, Benjamin (1784–1809), diplomatist, 3814, 3912
Bathurst, 1st Earl (1684–1775), 1449n, 4035n
Bathurst, 2nd Earl (1714–94), 291, 297, 313, 318, 4035n
Bathurst, 3rd Earl (1762–1834), 313, 446, 686, 1932n, 1983n, 2746, 2870n, 2994n, 3174n, 3417n, 3445n, 3502, 3603, 3635, 3666, 3673, 3817, 3856n, 3913n, 3966, 3966n, 3985n, 3989, 4007n, 4026, 4028, 4028n, 4032n, 4042, 4046, 4048, 4105n, 4284
  letters from, 2250n, 2851n, 3030n, 3068n, 3523n, 3538n, 3567n, 3824n, 3856n, 3867n, 4011, 4023, 4033, 4035, 4039, 4041n, 4109n
  Minute by, 3613n
  letters to, 1908n, 3068n, 3420n, 3538n, 3832n, 4011, 4023, 4033, 4035, 4039, 4041n, 4112n, 4233n, 4238n
  given reversion of Tellership of the Exchequer (1786), 313
  appointed a Lord of the Treasury (1789), 544
  resigns seat at Treasury Board (1791), 686
  sworn of the Privy Council (1793), 895
  moves the Address (1796), 1449
  his natural diffidence, 1449n
  offered the Petersburg Embassy (1799), 1908
  thought of again for Petersburg Embassy (1800), 2123
  refuses the Mint (1804), 2839n
  accepts the Mint (1804), 2881n; (1807), 3416
  Pres. of the B. of Trade, 3416
  a possible successor to Portland, 3934n, 4028n
  takes Foreign Secretaryship *pro tem.*, 3989
Bathurst, Charles Bragge (c. 1754–1831), 1480, 2354, 2369n, 2648n, 2780, 2817, 2888, 2888n, 2934n, 3041, 3105, 3105n, 3347, 3373, 3373n, 3380, 3435, 3444, 3483n, 3485, 3491, 3505, 3508, 3559n, 3590, 3594, 3821, 3824, 3832, 3832n, 3834, 3841, 3873, 3876, 3878, 3878n, 3906n, 3960n, 3966n, 4046, 4074, 4076, 4076n, 4093, 4102, 4105, 4109, 4122n, 4124, 4133, 4138n, 4174, 4184, 4198, 4205
  letters from, 2796, 2845
  thought of as Solicitor-Gen. to the Queen, 1793, 1793n, 1796
  on Lady Berkeley, 2138n

suggested by Addington as Speaker, 2350n, 2354n, 2554n
Chairman of Ways and Means, 2354n
appointed Treasurer of the Navy (1801), 2554
becomes Sec. at War (1803), 2777, 2777n, 2780n, 2787n, 2845n
re-elected for Bristol (1803), 2787n
thought of as Irish Secretary (1804), 2826n, 2871n
changes his name, 2845n
resigns office (1804), 2845n
office promised for, 2984, 2984n
office not found for him, 3041n, 3075n
refuses office (1807), 3416, 3416n
refuses office under Perceval, 3989, 3992
Bathurst, Henry (1744–1837), Bishop of Norwich, 3016n, 3666, 3966n
Bathurst, Sir James (d. 1850), 3887
Bathurst, Poole, 2845n
Batt, Dr Edward, 648
Battiscombe, Robert, the Windsor apothecary, 4077, 4106, 4160, 4178
Bavaria, 1304, 1526n, 3209
Bavaria, Emp. Joseph II's exchange scheme involving, 178, 211
Bavaria, Charles Theodore, Elector of (1724–99), 99, 178, 1827
  'strong and hale', 97
Bavaria, Maximilian Joseph, Elector of (1756–1825), 178n, 2072, 2161, 2255
Bavay, 957, 962, 979
Baxter, 1594
Baxter, Alexander, 3869n
Bay of Biscay, 1016
Bayham, Lord, *see* Camden, 1st Marquess
Baylen [Bailen], French army surrenders at, 3587n, 3689n
Bayley, Ensign, 920, 923
Bayley, Mr, police magistrate, 1717
Bayley, Sir John (1763–1841), 1968
  becomes a King's Bench Judge, 3656
Bayning, Lord (1728–1810), 1983n, 3623n, 3966n
Bayntum [*sic*], Thomas, 4219
Bayonne, 3672
Bayreuth, 1928
Bazeley, John (d. 1809), 4289
  defeated at Dover (1784), 57n
Beachy Head, 2485, 2989
Beadon, Richard (1737–1824), Master of Jesus College, Cambridge, 428
  becomes Bishop of Gloucester (1789), 516, 1983n

Belle Isle, 2171, 2175n, 2183, 2202–3, 2203n, 2204–5

Belle Poule, capture of the, 3244

Bellerophon, the, a 74-gun ship, 907, 3928n

Bellew, Patrick (*d.* 1799), Lieut.-Col. (1778), Major-Gen. (1793), 1597

appointed Lieut.-Gov. of Quebec, 1619

Bellingham, Mr, 545n

Bellingham, Sir William (?1755–1826), 158

Bellona, a 74-gun ship, 2485

Belmonte, Prince de, Neapolitan Minister in London, 1777

Belville, John, a footman, 652

Belvoir Castle, 2811, 3637n, 3821n, 3857n, 4120n

Bemyowsky, Lieut.-Gen., 957

Ben, M. de, 341

Benevente, 3802

Bengal, Presidency of, 18, 372, 425, 443, 784, 2325n, 3163, 4057, 4072

Benjafield, John (*c.* 1756–1832), 158

Bennet, Richard Henry Alexander (?1742–1814), 2894n

Bennet, Dr William (1746–1820), Bishop of Cork, later of Cloyne, 586, 1158

Bennett, Mrs, 2888n

Bennett, William, Acting Adjutant at the Military College, 2462n

Bennigsen, Count (1745–1826), Russian General, 3342, 3390n, 3492n, 3510, 3510n

Bent, Robert, M.P. for Aylesbury (1802–4), 2921n

Bentheim, 847, 859, 861, 2749

Bentinck, Captain, Governor of St Vincent, 1644

Bentinck, Charles, 3756, 3756n

Bentinck, General, a Count of the Empire (1762–1835), 840

Bentinck, Lord Edward Charles Cavendish (1744–1819), 1119, 1127

Bentinck, Lord Frederick Cavendish (1781–1828), 3015, 3794

Bentinck, Henry, Governor of St Vincent, 2962, and of Demerara, 3756n

Bentinck, Lady Jemima (1767–1839), 4032

Bentinck, John Charles, a Count of the Empire (1763–1833), 4032n

Bentinck, Lady Mary (1778–1843), 1528

Bentinck, Lord Wm. Henry Cavendish (1774–1839), 2581, 3015, 3416n, 3599, 3794, 3960n, 4036, 4036n

a candidate for the Government of Madras, 2581n, 3015n

and the Gov.-Generalship of Bengal, 2581n, 3015, 3015n, 3186, 3905A

Mission to Austrian Army, 3871

thought of as Sec. at War (1809), 3992, 3996, 4007n

declines office, 3998

Bentinck, Lord Wm. Charles Augustus Cavendish (1780–1826), 3794

Bentinck, William Harry Edward, Naval officer at Barbados, 1119, 1127,

Bentinck, Rev. William Harry Edward (1784–1868), Clerk of the Signet, 2777, 3607, 3984

Berar, Raja of, 2808

Berbice, 2810, 2902n;

capture of (1796), 1422; (1803), 2813

Berehaven, 2570, 2572

Beresford, Rev. George de la Poer (1765–1841), Bishop of Clonfert (1801), and (1802) of Kilmore, 2301, 2592

his 'infamous' character, 2592n

Beresford, John (1738–1805), First Commissioner of Revenue [I.], 228, 2301, 2404

Beresford, John Claudius (1766–1846), 2752n, 3657, 3818, 4076n, 4102n

Beresford, Admiral Sir John Poo (*c.* 1769–1844), 3264, 3270

Beresford, Marcus, to be Lieut.-Gen. of the Ordnance [I.], 2245

Beresford, William, Baron Decies, Archbishop of Tuam (1743–1819), 1127, 3815

Beresford, William Carr, Visct Beresford (1768–1854), 3297, 3367, 3526n, 3556, 3926n

captures Madeira, 3587

Beresfords, the, 4105n

Bergen, 1132, 2048, 2054n

Bergen-op-Zoom, 859, 861, 1979n

Berger, Captain, 1326, 1513

Bergues, 903, 920, 923, 943

Berkel, Van, 409

Berkeley, 5th Earl of (1745–1810), 664, 1983n, 2750, 3966n

his controversial marriage, 2138, 2138n, 2800, 4198, 4255–6

Berkeley, Admiral Sir George Cranfield (1753–1818), 2574, 2752n, 3233, 3521

Berkeley, Lieut.-Col. James, 2601

Berkeley, Mary, Countess of (*c.* 1767–1844), 2138, 2138n, 2750, 4255

Berkhamsted, 1311

Berkshire, 3962, 4201

Berkshire election (1784), 62, 158

Berlaiment, 957

Berlin, 339, 351, 355, 361, 370, 387n, 394, 409, 450, 462, 485, 538, 712, 1087, 1212, 1246, 1301, 1326, 1368, 1525, 1563, 1656, 1670, 1750n, 1817, 1845, 1863, 1867, 1879, 1888, 1890, 1894, 1920n, 1933, 1936, 1938, 1943–4, 1948, 1959, 1971, 1985, 1999, 2000, 2009–10, 2012, 2014, 2017, 2032, 2218, 2395, 2672, 2731, 2742, 2744, 2749, 3167, 3226, 3298–9, 3305, 3320, 3866, 4281, 4284, 4297

Berlin, Court of, 178, 221, 382, 663, 769, 838, 1035, 1210, 1233, 1245, 1295, 1304, 1429, 1434, 1661, 1673, 1689, 1693, 1704, 1719, 1725, 1908, 1952, 2082, 2386A, 2522, 2964, 3168, 3209

Berlin Decrees, the, 3359n, 4231

Bermuda, 2969, 3179, 3231, 3576

Bernadotte, General, later Charles XIV, King of Sweden (1764–1844), 1725, 3380, 3704n

Bernard, 1401

Bernard, James, Visct, later 2nd Earl of Bandon (1785–1856), 4074

Bernard, Sir Thomas (1750–1818), 3775

Bernard, Thomas (c. 1769–1834), 4188

Berne, 706, 1184, 2059, 2667

Bernstorff, Andreas Peter, Count (d. ?1797), Danish Foreign Minister, 223, 399

Bernstorff, Andreas Peter, Count, the Danish statesman, 2406

Berri, duc de (1778–1820), 1725, 2214n

Berry, Rear-Admiral Sir Edward (1768–1831), 1892, 3281

Berry, Lieut., R.N., 3542

Berthier, Marshal, Prince of Neuchâtel and Wagram (1753–1815), 3214n

Bertie, General Albemarle, 9th Earl of Lindsey (1744–1818), 2882

Bertie, Captain Peregrine (1741–90), 446

Berwick, 1172, 1298

Berwick, a 74-gun ship, 925; captured by the French, 1229

Berwick, James FitzJames, Duke of (1670–1734), 1148n

Berwick, Thomas, 2nd Baron (1770–1832). 1983n, 3539, 3966n

Berwickshire Fencible Cavalry, 1298

Besborodko, *see* Bezborodko

Bessborough, 2nd Earl of (1704–93), 335

Bessborough, Frederick, Visct Duncannon, later 3rd Earl of (1758–1844), 335, 1983n, 2743n, 3966n

Bessborough, Henrietta Frances, Countess of (1761–1821), 2645n, 3130n, 3556n, 3813n

Best, 59n, 144, 188, 1182, 1331, 1687

Best, William Draper, Lord Wynford (1767–1845), 2833, 2888, 3234

Béthune, 903

Beulwitz, M. de, 211

Beverley election (1784), 57

Bevern, *see* Brunswick-Bevern

Beyerland, 840

Beyme, Karl Friedrich (1765–1838), 1959

Bezborodko, Count Alexander (1747–99), *cr.* Count (1784), Prince (1797), 219, 399

Bicester, 1311

Bic island, in the St Lawrence, 385

Bickerton, Admiral Sir Richard (1727–92), 341, 363, 4139

Bickerton, Admiral Sir Richard Hussey (1759–1832), 2024, 3425, 3500n, 4139

Biddulph, Robert Myddelton (1761–1814), 3487, 3637, 3873, 3876, 3878

Bidwell, John, Foreign Office clerk, 3194

Bidwell, Thomas, Foreign Office clerk and Superintendent of St James's and Hyde Parks (d. 1817), 3194

Bidwell, Thomas, jun., Foreign Office clerk, 3194

Bielfinger, General 2151

Bienfaisant, a French warship, 385, 4269

Biggin, 2693

Bilbao, 563

Binfield, 3764, 3764n

Bingen, 1322

Bingham, Richard, 2nd Earl of Lucan (1764–1839), 605, 2315

Binning, Lady, later Countess of Haddington (1781–1861), 4093n

Binning, Lord, later 9th Earl of Haddington (1780–1858), 2752n, 3867, 3966n, 4093, 4093n, 4105n, 4124n, 4126

letter to, 3970n

his India Board Commissionership (1809), 3867n

Binns, 1380

Binns, John (1772–1860), journalist and politician, arrest of, 1691, 1694, 1717

Bique, *see* Bic

Birch, Mr, 320

Birch, 1332

Bird, and the Coventry election (1784), 57

Bird, William Wilberforce (c. 1758–1836), 1509

Birdwood, Rev. William Ilbert, an adulterer, 2374n

Birmingham, 708, 1380
bread riots in, 2243

Birmingham 'Church and King' riots in (1791), 691–2, 700, 708, 708n

Bischoffswerder, General, 1432

Bishop, Charles, King's Proctor, 2885

Bisshopp and Co., Army Agents, 4290

Bisshopp, Lieut.-Col. Harry, 1607
letter from, 1607n

Blachford, Barrington Pope (d. 1816), 3610
Canning's 'twelfth man', 3610n, 3966n, 4124n

Black, Captain, 543

Black, John, a marine, 3973

Blackburne, John (1754–1833), 27n, 2881n, 3832n

Black Forest, the, 1603, 2478, 2488

Blackheath, 449, 1788, 2455; Princess of Wales living at, 2993, 3490, 3516, 3531
the King at, 3082

Blackstone, Sir William (1723–80), 114, 615
his Commentaries, 615, 648

Blackwood, Vice-Admiral Sir Henry (1770–1832), 3174

Blair, Captain Archibald, 567

Blair, Edward, 3128

Blair, Rev. Hugh (1718–1800), his Sermons, 2313

Blair, Robert (1741–1811), Sol.-Gen. for Scotland, 2313, 3145n, 3262n
declines seat on Scottish Bench (1795), 1351
declines office of Lord Advocate (1801), 2403

Blake, Joachim, the Spanish General, commanding in Galicia, 3727

Blanche, a 38-gun frigate, 2425, 3281

Bland-Burges, see Burges, Bland-

Blandford, 3947

Blandford, Marquess of, later 5th Duke of Marlborough (1766–1840), 665, 3193n, 3966n

Blandford Lodge, 665n

Blane, Sir Gilbert, physician (1749–1834), 2708

Blaney, Benjamin (1728–1801), 1870n

Blankett, Captain John (d. 1801), 229

Blaquiere, Sir John, Lord de Blaquiere (1732–1812), 2315, 3095, 3243, 3259

Blenheim, a 90-gun ship, 4269

Bletchingley, a pocket borough, 4210

Bletchington barracks, 1259n

Bleyswick [Bleyswyk], Peter van, 376, 409

Bligh, Sir Richard Rodney, Admiral (1737–1821), 1153

Bligh, Thomas Cherburgh (c. 1761–1830), 2894n

Bligh, Captain William (1754–1817), Governor of New South Wales, 3076, 3113

Blinkworth, John, convict, 532

Blitterswyk [Blytterswyk], Lynden de, 409; his brother, 409

Blomberg, Rev. Frederick Wm. (1761–1847), Chaplain to Prince of Wales, preferment for, applied for, 3622, 3635

Blonde, a 32-gun frigate, 1049, 1815n

Blount, George, Commissioner of Taxes, 1685

Bloxham, Sir Matthew (1744–1822), 466

Blücher, Prince, Field-Marshal of Prussia (1742–1819), 3334, 3393

Blumfield, James, a Court servant, 1710

Blundell, Peter (1520–1601), merchant, 3245

Blundell's Grammar School, Tiverton 3245

Blyth Bay, Northumberland, 1298

Boadicea, a 38-gun ship, 1838

Board of Accounts, the, 2858n

Board of Admiralty, the, 446, 1109, 1244, 1272, 1274, 1284, 1426, 1437, 1439, 1490, 1530, 1532–3, 1551, 1556, 1558, 1605, 1632, 1736, 1830, 1996, 2055n, 2067, 2090, 2094, 2180n, 2425, 2506, 2555, 2637, 2826, 2861, 2871, 2904, 2908, 2946, 3013, 3019n, 3040, 3053, 3069, 3122, 3160, 3163, 3244, 3417, 3417n, 3418–19, 3425, 3840, 3910, 4010n, 4108, 4236

Board of Agriculture, the, 915, 937, 1166, 1173, 1188, 1264, 1306, 1400, 2212

Board of Control, the India, 253, 372, 425, 582, 1621, 2144n, 2180, 2180n, 2862, 2900, 3255n, 3538n, 3856, 3861, 3861n, 3906, 4010
composition of the, 2180n, 3418, 3420, 3420n

Board of Customs, 1685

Board of Excise, 1685

Board of Green Cloth, the (Lord Steward's Dept.), 1555, 1895, 2269n, 2320, 2464, 2675n, 3057, 3060, 3196, 3679, 3778, 3846, 4149

Board, the Navy, 867, 2416, 3096

Board, the Ordnance, 2444, 2500, 4112

Board of Revenue [I.], 3238n

Bourne, Lieut., 43

Bourne, William Sturges, *see* Sturges-Bourne

Bouverie, Bartholomew (1753–1835), 1255n

Bouverie, Edward (1738–1810), 1255n

Bouverie, Hon. Edward (1760–1824), appointed Groom of the Bedchamber to Prince of Wales (1787), 365n

Bouverie, William Henry (1752–1806), 1255n, 2137, 2288

Bouvines, 891

Bowen, Captain, 3795

Bowles, John, 3869n

Bowman, the King's Page, 2558

Bow Street magistrates, the, 335, 652, 778, 1594, 1927

Bowyer, Henry (1786–1853), 4074n, 4138n

Bowyer, Henry (*d.* 1808),
Lieut.-Col. (1782), Col. (1793), Major-Gen. (1795), Lieut.-Gen. (1801), 1657

Bowyer, Robert (1758–1834), *letter from*, 4085

Box Hill, 3142

Boyd, Captain (*d.* 1807), 2575, 3702

Boyd, James, convict, 2848

Boyd, Lady, 307
her sons Guy and Thomas, 307n

Boyd, General Sir Robert (1710–94), 173, 205, 1104
pension for, 307, 307n

Boydell, Josiah, *letter from*, 2340

Boyle, Sir Courtenay (1769–1844), 3853

Boyle, David, Solicitor-General [S.] (1772–1853), 3834, 4076, 4126, 4133, 4133n

Boyles, Vice-Admiral Charles (*d.* 1816), 4003

Boyne, a 98-gun ship, destroyed by fire, 1244

Brabant, 816, 966, 1880

Brackle, a royal servant, 4024

Braddock, General (1695–1755), 404

Bradford, Sir Henry Bridgeman, 1st Baron (1725–1800), 1983n
his peerage, 1104

Bradford, 2nd Baron and 1st Earl of (1762–1825), 3966n

Bradley, James, the astronomer (1693–1762), 3052

Bradshaw, Augustus Cavendish (1768–1832), 3787n

Bradshaw, Robert Haldane, M.P. for Brackley (1802–32), (*c.* 1760–1835), 2752n

Brady, a mutineer, 1591

Brady, John, a mutineer, 1834

Braga, 3887

Bragge, *see* Bathurst

Bragge-Bathurst, *see* Bathurst

Bramham, Major-Gen. James (*d.* 1786), 317

Bramston, Mr, 4227

Brand, Thomas, 20th Baron Dacre (1774–1851), 3797n, 3834, 3857, 4102, 4122, 4122n, 4170
his Motion of Censure (1807), 3425, 3434–5

Brande, Augustus E., the Queen's apothecary, 3130

Brandis, Professor J. F. (1760–90), 588

Brandling, Charles (1733–1802), 757, 1180, 1198, 1509, 1546

Brandling, Charles John (1769–1826), M.P. for Newcastle (1798–1812), 2752n

Brantz [Brantzer], 409

Braun, Ernest, Capt., R.N., 2413

Brawn [Braun], Robert, the King's barber, 1754, 2413, 2413n

Brawn, a servant, 318

Bray, Lieut. Edward Moore, 3124

Bray, Dr Thomas, Canon of Windsor and Rector of Exeter College, Oxford (*d.* 1785), 194

Braybrooke, Quarter-Master, of the Royal Dragoons, 2216
his wife, 2216

Braybrooke, Richard Aldworth-Neville, 2nd Baron (1750–1825), 458, 458n, 556n, 1461n, 3434n, 3966n
letter from, 2438
Provost Marshal of Jamaica, 2847

Brazil, Prince of, *see* John VI

Brazil, Princess Charlotte of (1775–1830), daughter of Charles IV of Spain, 2443

Bread, the Assize of, 1311

Breadalbane, 4th Earl and 1st Marquess of (1762–1834), 3966n
elected a Scottish Representative Peer, 78

Bread fruit, 372; present of, to the King, 2586

Bread riots, 2243, 2245, 2250, 2278n

Brecknock, Mr, 158

Brecon, 1505

Brecon, Forest of, 3660

Breda, French capture (1793), 840, 843, 859, 861, 866, 1099, 1189

Bremen, 399, 1573, 1633, 1734, 2260, 4290n

Brentford, 856, 2648, 2648n, 3328

Brenton, 924

Brest, 621, 852, 1138, 1307, 1491, 1506, 1760, 1838, 1838n, 1844, 1873, 2003, 2490, 2824, 2924, 3210, 4143

Brickwood, John, 3869n

Bridgwater, borough of, 3645

Bridgwater, 7th Earl of (1753–1823), 3635, 3966n

Bridport, Alexander Hood, 1st Visct (1726–1814), 1186, 1244, 1258n, 1263, 1274, 1284, 1307, 1490–1, 1545, 1613, 1838, 1838n, 1983, 2003–4, 2006, 3966n, 4143
  King critical of, 1284
  made a Viscount, 2131n
  becomes General of Marines, 2227
Brie, Mme de, 1953
Briel, the, 840
Brienz, 706
Brighton, 688n, 921, 1405, 1435, 1784, 1834n, 2768, 2782n, 2889n, 3554
Brilliant, the, a 28-gun frigate, 934
Brin[c]kma[n], M. de, Swedish Minister in London, 3513n, 3581, 3733, 3743, 3780, 3847, 3891, 3912, 4152
Brisbane, Sir Charles (1769–1829), 3377, 3379
Brisbane, Admiral John (*d.* 1807), 4143
Brisk, the, the sloop, 377, 385
Bristol, 754, 1232, 1505, 1511, 1531, 2245, 2453, 2523, 2787, 2792n, 2793, 3760
  Freedom of, for D. of Cumberland, 2792n
  election (1803), 2787
  Bishopric of, 1498, 2271, 2684, 3462, 3465, 3469, 4238
  Prebendaries of, 1498
  Deanery of, 3996
Bristol, Bishop of, *see* Cornewall, Pelham, Luxmoore
Bristol, Mayor of, 1511
Bristol, a 50-gun frigate, 4143
Bristol, 4th Earl of (1730–1803), Bishop of Derry, 120
  his 'daring and indecent conduct', 100n
  'this wicked Prelate', 100
  his alleged plotting in Ireland, 120
  death of, 2778
Bristol, 5th Earl of (1769–1859), 2778, 2778n, 3966n
Bristol, Elizabeth, Countess of (1775–1844), 2778n
Bristow, Captain, 920
Britannia, a 100-gun ship, 3540, 4269
'British Convention', the, 991
British Museum, the, 3194n, 3287, 3446
Brittany, 866, 963, 974, 983, 1266–8, 1270, 1277, 1282, 1289, 3523
Broadstairs, 1607
Brodie, William Douglas, a merchant at Malaga, 777
Brodrick, Charles (1761–1822), Archbishop of Cashel, 1217

translated from Clonfert to Kilmore, 1345, 1347
translated to Cashel, 2546
Brodrick, George, 1st Baron, and Visct Midleton, *see* Midleton
Brodrick, General John (1765–1842), 3727
  appointed Gov. of Martinique, 3898
Brodrick [Broderick], Thomas (1756–95), 471
Brodrick, William (1763–1819), Secretary to the India Board, 2087n, 3373
  appointed a Lord of the Treasury (1807), 3522n
  and the Surveyorship of Woods and Forests, 3522, 3522n
Broglio, Duke of, 1111, 1111n, 1136; his son, 1111, 1136
Broglio, Duchess of, 1136
Brome, Visct, *see* Cornwallis, 2nd Marquess
Brook, a marine, 3122
Brooke, Capt., 120
Brooke, Richard (Lieut.-Col., 1790; Col., 1795), 1464
Brooke, George, 2nd Earl Brooke and Earl of Warwick (1746–1816), 3966n, 4238
Brooke, Henry, 3rd Earl (1779–1853), 4032, 4238
Brooke, General William (*d.* 1843), 3804
Brooks, Joseph, a soldier, 3195
Brooks, Thomas, a mutineer, 1591
Brooks, a messenger, 1620
Brooks' Club, 46n, 193
Broome, *see* Brome
Brougham, Henry, Lord (1778–1868), 3004n, 3260n, 4159, 4182
  letter from, 4034n
Brougham, William, 2nd Baron (1795–1886), 3004n
Broughton, 940
Broughton, Charles R., clerk in the Foreign Office, 3194
Broughton, Wm. Robert (1762–1821), 4001
Browell, Capt. William (1759–1831), 2409
Brown, 1324
Brown, 4103
Brown, Captain, of the *Amphion*, 377
Brown, Dr, 931, 1636
Brown, John, 3233
Brown, Lancelot ['Capability Brown'] (1715–83), the landscape gardener, 1970
Brown, Richard, a mutineer, 1599
Brown, Capt. William, R.N., 3164

Browne, Capt., A.D.C. to Lieut.-Gen. Trigge, 2063

Browne, 3689n

Browne, Denis (c. 1760–1828), 3491n, 4032n, 4037n, 4076

Browne, Isaac Hawkins (1745–1818), 203, 589, 1255, 1330, 1342, 1482, 1546, 1637, 2137, 2189, 2881n, 3105, 3174, 3675, 3834, 3873, 4076, 4159

Browne, Robert, jun., Clerk of Works at Richmond and Kew, 494

Brownlow, 1st Baron (1744–1807), 1983n, 3966n

Brownrigg, General Sir Robert (1759–1833), 1212, 1607, 2060, 2065, 2067, 2396, 3818
letter to, 3959

Bruce, George, Lord (1800–40), son of Lord Elgin, 2430

Bruce, Lieut.-Col. J., appointed Lieut.-Gov. of Dominica (1789), 514, 565, 567

Bruce, Professor John, of Edinburgh (1745–1826), 791
his historical works, 791, 791n

Bruce, Lord, later 1st Marquess of Ailesbury (1773–1856), 648, 980, 2752n, 3428

Bruce, Henrietta Maria, Lady, later Marchioness of Ailesbury (d. 1831), 980, 3428

Bruce, Robert, of Kennet (d. 1785), a Lord of Session, 201

Bruce, Lieut.-Gen. Thomas (c. 1738–97), Major-Gen. (1782), M.P. for Marlborough (1790–6), for Great Bedwin (1796–7), 989, 1657

Bruce-Brudenell, Thomas, 552

Brudenell, George Bridges (?1725–1801), supports Pitt (1784), 15n

Brudenell, Lord (1725–1811), see Cardigan, 5th Earl of

Bruges, 866, 870, 891, 941, 943, 962, 966, 977, 982, 1008, 1022, 1022n, 1029, 1736n

Brughel, 2563

Brulenbach, General, 4276

Brummell, George Bryan (1778–1840), 'Beau' Brummell, 1997

Brummell, William (d. 1794), 4290

Brundrett, Jonathan, a clerk, 3500n

Brune, General, 2059

Brunn, 3901, 3926n

Brunswick, a 74-gun ship, 1377

Brunswick, 355, 716, 1326, 1573, 1670, 1693, 1817, 1863, 1866, 2277, 2655, 2662, 3320, 4278, 4281, 4284, 4295
visit to, contemplated by Prince of Wales (1784), 113–14

Brunswick, Augusta, Duchess of (1737–1813), George III's sister, 135, 207, 334, 351, 355, 361, 370, 558, 679, 1562, 1573, 1817, 1898, 2277, 2655, 2662, 3064, 3307, 3334, 3337n, 3457–8, 3460, 3472, 3481, 3512, 3512n, 3607, 3613, 3811, 3933, 4037, 4150, 4150n, 4278
letters to, 7, 3260, 3310, 3326, 3335, 3337, 3354, 3473, 3516, 3531, 3536, 3859, 3879, 3942, 4123
in her usual high spirits, 679
and the proposed Wurtemberg marriage, 1325n
arrives in England (1807), 3488, 3490
her resemblance to the King, 3490n
pension for, 3531, 3657, 3657n

Brunswick, Prince Augustus of (1770–1820), 339, 344, 613, 3512, 3578, 3607, 3613, 3811, 4037

Brunswick, Augustus William, Duke of (1662–1731), 1708

Brunswick, Prince Charles of (1766–1806), 558, 714, 4278
death of, 3310, 3310n

Brunswick, Charles William Ferdinand, Duke of (1735–1806), 7n, 178, 339, 344, 361, 370, 382, 387n, 390, 394–5, 409, 417n, 455, 546, 558, 613, 679, 685, 785, 802, 816, 993, 998, 1000, 1176, 1212, 1228, 1233, 1246, 1303, 1326, 1331, 1461n, 1513, 1631, 1639, 1656, 1670–1, 1673, 1675, 1693, 1698, 1789, 1817, 1898, 1943–4, 2662, 2680, 3298, 3298n, 3300, 3320n, 3326, 3512n, 4278, 4280, 4284
letters from, 392, 414
letters to, 387n, 414, 1641
defeats the French at Landau, 995
to be offered command of Anglo-Dutch armies on Continent (1794), 1139, 1139n, 1140
his irresolution, 1689
death of, 3326n, 3334–5
his Garter, 3347

Brunswick, Elizabeth Sophia, Duchess of (1683–1767), 1708

Brunswick, Prince Ferdinand of (1721–92), 838, 2756n

Brunswick, Princess Frederica of (1770–1819), wife of Prince Charles, 714
far from handsome, 679

Brunswick, Prince Frederick Augustus of (1740–1805), 847, 854, 859, 861

Brunswick, Prince George of (1769–1811), 3512, 3578, 3607, 3613, 3811, 4037

Brunswick-Bevern, Frederick, Duke of (1729–1809), 3878–9

Brunswick-Oels, Prince Charles of (1804–73), 3607

Brunswick-Oels, Frederick William, Duke of (1771–1815), 3347, 3468, 3512, 3613, 3811, 3871, 3879, 3977, 3977n, 4032, 4037, 4041, 4142, 4147, 4151, 4159, 4159n, 4162
  letters from, 3393, 3578, 3999, 4043
  letter to, 4043
  asks for financial assistance, 3578, 3607
  arrival in England (1809), 3931, 3931n, 3933

Brunswick-Oels, Prince William of (1806–84), 3607

Brussels, 957, 959, 990, 992, 1001, 1007–8, 1014, 1018, 1043, 1047, 1066
  French enter (1792), 816

Brutus, 824

Bruyeres, J., Prince Edward's Instructor, 4301

Bryan, John, 1786

Buccleuch, Henry, 3rd Duke of (1746–1812), 373n, 664, 1174, 1983n, 2455, 2684n, 3016, 3243n, 3425, 4264
  and a Blue Ribbon, 890
  appointed Lord Lieut. of Co. Roxburgh (1804), 2869n

Buccleuch, Earl of Dalkeith, later 4th Duke of (1772–1819), 3417n, 3425, 3425n, 3428, 3628n, 3764n, 3966n, 4264
  moves the Address (1795), 1320

Buccleuch, Elizabeth, Duchess of (1743–1827), 373, 1174, 4264

Buchan, 11th Earl of (1742–1839), 3262n
  letters from, 2577, 3422

Buckingham, 1311

Buckingham, Mary Elizabeth, Marchioness of (d. 1812), 2299
  created Baroness Nugent (1800), 2299n

Buckingham, Marquess of, see Temple, Earl

Buckinghamshire, 3rd Earl of (1731–1804), 1223n, 1983n

Buckinghamshire, 4th Earl of, see Hobart

Buckinghamshire, 4124n
  Militia, the, 1505, 1765–6

Buckner, Admiral Charles (d. 1811), 1545, 1551

Buckner, Dr John (1734–1824), Bishop of Chichester, 1617, 1983n, 3966n

Buckworth, J. F., Commissioner of West India Accounts, 3401

Budberg, Baron de, Russian Minister of Foreign Affairs, 3378, 3459, 3513, 3535, 3537

Budé, General J. (c. 1736–1818), 90, 104, 160, 164, 172, 207, 233, 269, 284, 693, 4265, 4267, 4269, 4275, 4292, 4296
  letters to, 33, 58, 103, 2428, 2438, 4266, 4291n, 4298, 4302

Budget, the (1787), 352; (1792), 735; (1796), 1340; (1802), 2734; (1803), 2755; (1806), 3219; (1807), 3361, 3361n, 3374; (1810), 4162

Buenos Aires, capture of (1806), 3273, 3297, 4228
  loss of, 3356, 3358, 3363, 3367–8, 3528–9, 3558n

Buffalo, frigate, 4269

Buhle, Professor, 357, 484

Bühler, M. de, 2214

Bulkeley, 7th Visct (1752–1822), 416, 3666, 3966n

Buller, Vice-Admiral Sir Edward (1764–1824), 3151

Buller, Sir Francis (1746–1800), 761, 1717, 1740n, 1746

Buller, James (1772–1830), a Lord of the Admiralty, 3425

Buller, Rev. William (1735–96), Bishop of Exeter, 40, 194, 775n, 812, 3462
  appointed Bishop of Exeter, 780

Bülow, 145

Bülow, the Landrath, 4276

Bülow, Lieut. (d. 1793), missing, believed killed, 882

Bülow, Lieut.-Col. (1755–1816), 882

Bülow, Captain, 901, 905, 909

Bulow, M. de, of Denmark, 223

Bulstrode, near Beaconsfield, Duke of Portland's seat, 2581, 2921, 3934

Bunbury, Mr, 158

Bunbury, Henry William (1750–1811), Equerry to Duke of York (1787), 384, 3554n

Bunbury, Sir Thomas Charles (1740–1821), 584, 2804

Bune, General, 3471

Bunker's Hill, 4283

Burch, General, 4283

Burdett, Sir Charles (1728–1803), 1426

Burdett, Charles Sedley (1773–94), 973

Burdett, Sir Francis (1770–1844), 1521, 1559n, 1691, 1701, 1881, 1881n, 1950,

Burdett, Sir Francis (cont.)
2189, 2276, 2648, 2648n, 2652, 2839, 2907, 3487, 3643, 3799, 3804, 3804n, 3827n, 3832, 3857, 3867, 3867n, 3876, 3878, 3878n, 3890, 3890n, 3902, 4048n, 4074, 4076, 4087, 4112, 4120, 4122, 4122n, 4124, 4133, 4151, 4159, 4174, 4201, 4205, 4259
his marriage, 973
and the Middlesex election (1802), 2833, 2839n, 2849n
his motion for parliamentary reform, 3904
committed to the Tower, 4126–7, 4129–30
released from custody, 4213
Burdett, Sir Robert (1716–97), 973
Burdett, Sophia, Lady, Thomas Coutts' daughter (1771–1844), 973, 2648n
Burdon, Rowland (c. 1757–1838), 644, 757, 1180, 1180n, 1198, 1247, 1546, 1654, 1658, 2752n
and Co. Durham election (1790), 619n
Burges, Sir James Bland (1752–1824), 754n, 770n, 783, 886, 917, 940, 1468n, 3300n
letter from, 1316n
letter to, 1316n
and the Under-Secretaryship of State for Foreign Affairs (1789), 544n
his resignation of the Under-Secretaryship, 1316
made a Baronet, 1316
given office of Knight Marshal of the Royal Household (1795), 1316n
Burges, John Smith, Chairman of East India Company, 715
Burgess, Thomas, Bishop of St David's (c. 1756–1837), 2764
Burgh, Major-Gen. H. J. T. De, 1483
Burghersh, Lord, later 11th Earl of Westmorland (1784–1859), 3886, 3893–4, 3894n, 3920
letter from, 3920n
Burgos, 3726, 3763, 3887
Burgoyne, Lieut.-Gen. John (1723–92), 190, 404
death of, 770
Burgoyne, Major-Gen. Sir John, Bart (1739–85), 73
Burke, Edmund (1729–97), 438, 446, 448, 524, 666, 713, 751, 836, 838, 869n, 1125, 3192n
letters from, 1171n, 1507n
his Economical Reform Act (1782), 20, 3873
'Nabob money' financing elections, 72n

his vindication of the 1780–84 Parliament, 89
opposes Pitt's India Bill (1784), 101
Charges against Warren Hastings (1786), 290
and Test and Corporation Acts, 580
anxious for a no-party Govt, 774n, 807n
supports Habeas Corpus Suspension Bill, 1070
offered a pension (1794), 1116, 1116n, 1125n
on Chatham's services at the Admiralty, 1171n
Burke, Mrs (née Nugent), (d. 1812), pension for, 1116n
Burland, John Berkeley (1754–1804), 2881n
Burlington, 3rd Earl of (1694–1753), 552
Burlington House, Duke of Portland's London residence, 1265, 1812n, 3399n
Burlton, Capt., of the Lively frigate, 12
Burney, Charles (1726–1814), 3238n
Burney, Frances (Fanny), Madame d'Arblay (1752–1840), second Keeper of the Robes to the Queen, 458n, 474n, 496n
Burrard, Rev. Sir George (1769–1856), 2058
Burrard, Grace Elizabeth, Lady (c. 1772–1855), 3994–5, 3997
Burrard, Sir Harry (?1707–91), 158
Burrard, Sir Harry (1755–1813), 3511, 3697n, 3699n, 3711, 3785n, 3797, 3801, 3862, 3965, 3994–5, 3997
King's confidence in, 3693
Burrard, John Thomas (1792–1809), 3965
death of, 3994–5, 3997
Burrell, 3342
Burrell, Sir Charles Merrik (1774–1862), 3834, 3886, 4133
Burrell, Lindsay Merrik Peter (1786–1848), 3369
Burroughs, Sir William (?1753–1829), 2940, 2940n
a Judge at Calcutta, 3163
Burrows, J., mutineer, 1613
Burton, Francis (?1744–1832), 14n, 458, 3828, 3828n, 3830
Burton, Sir Francis Nathaniel (1766–1832), 2969, 3763, 3763n
Burton, Maj.-Gen. Napier Christie (1758–1835), put under arrest, 2817
Burton Pynsent, Lady Chatham's home, 253, 333, 2725
Bury St Edmunds, 584
election (1784), 55
Busby, Rev. William Beaumount, 2811, 3764n

Bushby, 1496n
Bushe, Charles Kendal (1767–1843), 3283n
Bushey, 494n
Bushey Park, Rangership of, 1492
Bussche, Captain, 1063, 1322
Bussche, M. de, 145, 277, 315, 321, 473
death of his wife (1786), 321
Bussche, Lieut.-Gen. (d. 1794), 145, 329, 704,
870, 962, 966, 968, 1063, 1066, 1073,
1075, 1079, 1322
his wife, 321
Bussche, Miss, marriage of, 2236
Bussche de Hunefeldt, M. de, 4297
Bute, County, 1400
Bute, 3rd Earl of (1713–92), 733, 733n, 742,
749, 834, 1918
Bute, 4th Earl and 1st Marquess of (1744–
1814), 743, 829n, 967n, 1384, 1676,
1983n, 2106, 2349n, 2972, 3553, 3966n
letters from, 733n, 749, 834, 834n, 894, 1147,
1151, 1378, 1676n, 1918
letters to, 742, 749
his affairs in disorder (1792), 749
resigns office of Lord Lieut. of Glamorgan
to his son, 834n
a Portland Whig, 834n
opinion of Pitt, 834n
would like office (1793), 834n
goes over to Government side (1794),
834n
a 'King's Friend', 894
given a Marquessate (1796), 1378, 1378n
wants office at home, 1676n
would like to be Lord Steward, 1676n
fails to get the Garter, 1918
his second marriage (1800), 2106n
Bute, Frances, Marchioness of (c. 1773–
1832), daughter of Thomas Coutts, 973,
2106n, 3583n
Bute, Mary, Countess of (1718–94), 733n,
742, 834n, 1147, 1151
letters from, 733, 743, 775
letter to, 743
asks for a Bishopric for her son, 775
asks for a Canonry of Windsor for her son
(1793), 834n
death of, 1151
Butler, Charles Harward (1780–1860), 2894n
Butler, James Wandesford (1774–1838), 1st
Marquess of Ormonde, 2894n
Butler, John, Bishop of Oxford and of Hereford (1717–1802), 2684, 2729

Buxhoeveden, Count Friedrich (1750–1811),
the Russian General and conqueror of
Finland, 3342
Buxton, 483
Buxton, C., 3955
Buxton, Mrs, 1823
Buxton, Sir Robert John (1753–1839), 1180,
1247, 1255, 1323, 1724, 2189, 2752n,
3115, 3174
Byam, Sir Ashton Warner (1744–90),
Attorney-Gen. of Grenada, knighted
(1789), 559
Byard, Sir Thomas (d. 1798), 1628
Byerley, Miss J., Princess Amelia's maid,
3964
Byerley, Mrs, Princess Augusta's maid
(d. 1830), 3964n
Byfleet, 3583n
Byland, Count de, 840
Byllingham, *see* Bellingham
Byng, George (1764–1847), 4144, 4208
contest for Middlesex (1784), 72; (1802),
2839n, 2849n
Byng, Gerald Frederick F. (d. 1871), son of
5th Viscount Torrington; clerk in the
Foreign Office, 3194
Byron, Lord (1788–1824), 3966n
Byron, Vice-Admiral John (1723–86), 4229
Byron, Miss Sophia Maria, 4229
Bywater, Henry, soldier, 3128

Cabinet and Departmental boxes, 1459, 1481,
1600, 1638, 1846, 1936, 2034, 2467–8,
2471, 2866n, 2869
Cabinet, 'Grand' (or 'Great' or 'Nominal' or
'Honorary'), 80, 317n, 755n, 1180, 1190,
1211n, 1261, 1978, 2304, 2309, 2328,
2643, 2676, 2781, 2781n, 2881n, 3028n,
3277
Cabinet meetings, regularity of, 275
Cabinet Ministers, Minutes by individual,
3613n
Cabinet Minutes (1784), 67, 78, 147; (1785),
162, 167–8, 173, 204, 256; (1786), 302,
367, 405, 407, 430, 450, 617, 621, 633,
663, 721, 815, 1138, 1199, 1233, 1285,
1300, 1429, 1533, 1576, 1751, 1907–8,
2060, 2072, 2080, 2089, 2120, 2175n,
2176, 2913, 2202, 2209, 2230, 2256, 2297,
2371n, 2373, 2475, 2534, 2572, 2600,
2667, 2807n, 2981, 3088, 3093, 3171,
3204–5, 3209, 3211, 3222, 3226, 3229,

Candia, 2259

Canning, George (1770–1827), 961n, 1044,
1080n, 1223, 1250n, 1320n, 1519, 1764n,
1911, 2108, 2173n, 2199, 2274n, 2288,
2357, 2357n, 2373n, 2714, 2720n, 2881n,
2888, 2888n, 3004n, 3023n, 3030, 3075n,
3085, 3105, 3105n, 3111, 3243, 3256,
3262, 3351, 3351n, 3359, 3373, 3380n,
3394n, 3418n, 3433n, 3435, 3448n, 3471,
3475, 3487, 3504n, 3529n, 3568n, 3569,
3590, 3590n, 3594, 3594n, 3600n, 3610,
3610n, 3613, 3617, 3620, 3628, 3637,
3640, 3643n, 3647n, 3657n, 3665, 3665n,
3675, 3689n, 3701, 3713, 3748n, 3768n,
3773n, 3776n, 3787, 3799, 3804, 3804n,
3813n, 3821, 3821n, 3824, 3828, 3832,
3834, 3860n, 3867, 3873, 3876, 3878n,
3888, 3892, 3906n, 3919, 3925, 3951n,
3952n, 3953, 3958, 3960n, 3962n, 3966,
3966n, 3969n, 3977, 3978n, 3980, 3985–
6, 3986n, 3989n, 3998n, 4007n, 4028,
4028n, 4074, 4076, 4076n, 4087, 4093,
4105, 4122, 4124, 4124n, 4126, 4138,
4142, 4162, 4170, 4170n, 4177, 4184,
4198, 4208

letters from, 1320n, 1337n, 1509n, 1514n,
1519n, 1521n, 1526n, 1620, 1664n,
1713, 1722n, 1739, 1756, 1764n,
1830n, 1849n, 1881n, 1914n, 1932n,
1950n, 1983n, 2065n, 2108n, 2144n,
2180n, 2199n, 2276n, 2288n, 2339n,
2752n, 2940n, 2994n, 3025n, 3068n,
3085n, 3105n, 3130n, 3174n, 3180n,
3259n, 3371n, 3373n, 3410n, 3424,
3427, 3427n, 3430, 3432, 3436, 3440,
3445, 3445n, 3448, 3449n, 3452, 3454,
3454n, 3456, 3459, 3468, 3474, 3476,
3478, 3480, 3484, 3492, 3492n, 3495,
3498, 3501n, 3504, 3507, 3510, 3510n,
3511n, 3513, 3515, 3515n, 3518, 3518n,
3520, 3520n, 3523n, 3524, 3524n,
3527, 3527n, 3528n, 3533, 3533n, 3535,
3535n, 3537, 3537n, 3539, 3539n, 3541,
3545, 3547, 3549, 3552, 3552n, 3557,
3560, 3562, 3564, 3566, 3568, 3570, 3573,
3573n, 3575, 3579, 3581, 3585, 3606,
3618, 3621, 3623, 3626, 3633, 3636, 3639,
3647, 3647n, 3651, 3653, 3655, 3657n,
3658, 3669, 3672, 3677, 3686, 3688, 3690,
3692, 3695, 3698, 3700, 3703, 3706, 3708,
3710, 3714, 3717, 3722, 3724, 3728, 3730,
3730n, 3733, 3736, 3739, 3743, 3746,
3748, 3750, 3759, 3762, 3765, 3768, 3771,
3773, 3776, 3780, 3783, 3798, 3807, 3814,

3823, 3825, 3827, 3831, 3845, 3847, 3858,
3860, 3863, 3866, 3868, 3871, 3878, 3883,
3891, 3896, 3901, 3903, 3905A, 3907,
3912, 3914n, 3915, 3915n, 3918, 3921,
3924, 3924n, 3931, 3933, 3936, 3940,
3946, 3951, 3957, 3970n, 3971, 3979,
3985, 4018n, 4036, 4036n, 4063n, 4073n,
4074n, 4076n, 4080n, 4087n, 4093n,
4105n, 4109n, 4113n, 4124n, 4126n,
4138n, 4159n, 4238n

Minute by, 3613n

Memo. by, 3960

letters to, 1507n, 2180n, 3424, 3427, 3430,
3433, 3436, 3440, 3445, 3445n, 3448, 3454,
3456, 3459, 3468, 3474, 3476, 3478, 3480,
3492, 3492n, 3495, 3498, 3507, 3510, 3513,
3515, 3520, 3524, 3527, 3533, 3535, 3537,
3539, 3541, 3547, 3552, 3554n, 3557,
3560, 3562, 3562n, 3564, 3566, 3568,
3570, 3573, 3575, 3579, 3581, 3581n, 3585,
3606, 3623, 3626, 3633, 3647, 3651, 3653,
3655, 3669, 3672, 3677, 3686, 3688, 3690,
3695, 3698, 3700, 3703, 3706, 3708, 3710,
3714, 3717, 3722, 3724, 3728, 3730, 3733,
3743, 3743n, 3746, 3748, 3750n, 3759,
3765, 3768, 3771, 3773, 3780, 3783,
3786n, 3798, 3807, 3814, 3823, 3825,
3827, 3827n, 3831, 3845, 3847, 3858,
3860, 3863, 3866, 3868, 3871, 3878, 3883,
3891, 3896, 3901, 3903, 3905A, 3907,
3912, 3915, 3915n, 3918, 3921, 3924,
3924n, 3926n, 3931, 3933, 3936, 3940,
3946, 3951, 3951n, 3979, 4036

his opinion of Sylvester Douglas, 994n

on the Habeas Corpus Suspension Bill
debate, 1069n, 1070, 1070n

seconds the Address (1794), 1180

unable to make a projected speech, 1198n

on Prince of Wales's debts (1795), 1238n

marriage, 1297n, 1830n

on composition of King's Speech (1795),
1319n

on Pichegru, 1830n

appointed Under-Secretary of State, 1337n

a great speech from, 1893, 1893n

on Pitt's Union speech, 1914n

his mother, 1914n, 3970n

appointed a member of the India Board
(1799), 1932, 1932n

a brilliant speech on the Union, 1950,
1950n

on the Helder expedition, 2065n

to be joint Paymaster-Gen. (1800), 2144

sworn of the Privy Council (1800), 2144

II, 832-1662; III, 1663-2575; IV, 2576-3578

Caramanico, Prince, 124

Cardigan, 540, 3842

Cardigan, George, 3rd Earl of (d. 1732), 552n

Cardigan, Lord Brudenell, later 5th Earl of (1725–1811), Keeper of the King's Privy Purse, 51, 312n, 597, 651, 856, 1983n, 2045, 2411, 2433, 2441, 3966n

    Constable of Windsor Castle, 312n, 597n, 602, 651

    asks for office of Master of the Robes (1790), 597

Cardiganshire Militia, the, 1506

Cardonnel, Adam de (d. 1719), Marlborough's secretary, 32

Carew, Mrs, 2914n

Carew, Reginald Pole (1753–1835), 524, 670

    to be Under-Secretary of State, 2777n, 2786n, 2790n

    thought of as Irish Secretary (1804), 2871n, 2914n

    a P.C., 3006n

    Harrowby's poor opinion of, 3006n

Carey, Mrs, the Duke of York's mistress, 3821n

Carey, Rev. William (1769–1846), Headmaster of Westminster, 2653, 2665, 3635

    a Prebendary of Westminster, 3819

Carhampton, 2nd Earl of (?1737–1821), 751, 1283, 1552, 2211, 2211n, 3135

    and office of Comm.-in-Chief [I.], 1436

    conspiracy to murder, 1640, 1640n

    A British peerage recomended for, 1640n

    changed views on the Union, 2211n

    resigns office of Master-Gen. of the Ordnance [I.], (1800), 2211

Caribs, the, 2054

Carleton, Sir Guy, 1st Baron Dorchester (1724–1808), 9, 9n, 190, 287, 307, 307n, 404, 539, 555, 3966n

Carleton, Hugh, 1st Visct (1739–1826), Irish Judge, 2201, 2315, 2515n, 2585n, 2635, 3966n

Carleton, Maria, Lady, later Lady Dorchester (1753–1836), 404

Carleton, Thomas, Governor of New Brunswick (?1732–1817), 106

Carlisle, 1172

    See of, 3559, 3567

Carlisle, Margaret Caroline, Countess of (1753–1824), 4264

Carlisle, 5th Earl of (1748–1825), 7, 102, 436, 1983n, 2743, 2743n, 3008, 3489, 3966n, 4087

letter from, 2873n

and a Blue Ribbon, 890

complains of a breach of privilege, 2165, 2165n

an 'adulterous profligate', 2165n

Carlow, 2510, 2575

Carlsruhe, 2680, 2685

Carlton House, 4n, 110, 161, 181, 184, 300n, 310, 360, 364, 366, 683, 686, 753, 798, 801, 805, 1142, 1148n, 1237, 1329, 1405, 1417, 1596, 1655, 2145, 2149, 2939n, 3164n, 4122n

windows of, broken by mob (1784), 46n

an execution expected in, 1374, 3680

Carlton House Party, 2745n, 2914n, 3434n

list of members in 1804, 2894n

Carlyon, Rear-Admiral Wm. (1751–1829), 2310

Carmarthen, 540, 3389

Carmarthenshire, 3842

Carmarthen, Marquess of, later Duke of Leeds (1751–99), 4n, 26n, 35, 35n, 50n, 54n, 68n, 72n, 75n, 130n, 186, 220, 235, 303n, 368, 378, 394, 416, 516, 544n, 644n, 686, 737, 774, 4302, 4302n

letters from, 8, 12, 17, 45, 65, 68, 95, 127, 148, 154, 180, 191, 198, 208, 213, 219, 221, 223, 250, 256, 262, 275, 302, 308, 323, 367, 374, 406, 423, 429, 451n, 462, 499, 505, 509, 513, 538, 558, 560, 564, 1013, 1468, 1468n

letters to, 8, 12, 17, 45, 65, 68, 95, 154, 180, 191, 198, 213, 223, 235n, 241n, 250, 256, 262, 275, 323, 367, 378n, 387, 406n, 423, 455, 499, 503, 558, 564

divorces his wife (1779), 4302n

declines, then accepts Foreign Secretaryship (1783), 8n

succeeds to Dukedom (1789), 499

replaced as Foreign Secretary (1791), 670n, 672

wants office of Groom of the Stole (1796), 1468

unconnected with Party (1794), 1468n

proposing to succeed Pitt as Prime Minister? (1794), 1468n

Carmarthenshire, Sheriff of, see Powell

Carnarvon, Henry Herbert, Earl of Carnarvon (1741–1811), 1983n, 2743n, 3416–17, 3966n

letter fron, 3182n

question of a Cabinet office for, 3193n

appointed Master of the Horse (1806), 3182n

Carnarvon, Henry George, Lord Porchester, later 2nd Earl of (1772–1833), 2714, 2752n, 3643, 3657n, 3787n, 3804, 3867, 4076, 4076n, 4093, 4100, 4112, 4120, 4122, 4124, 4126, 4133, 4170

Carnatic, the, 137, 1493n

Carnatic, Nawab of the, 137, 1493n, 3662

Carnot, member of the French Directory and Minister of War (1753–1823), 1469

Caroline, Queen, wife of George II (1683–1737), portrait of, 2985

Caroline, Princess of Wales (1768–1821), 1126, 1374, 1405, 1409, 1411–12, 1416–17, 1419, 1421, 1495, 1596, 1655, 1660, 1667, 2455, 2556, 2993, 2993n, 2996, 3298n, 3326, 3453, 3553, 3778, 3846, 4045n, 4159n, 4246, 4261

letters from, 1393, 3571, 4150n

letters to, 3490, 3571, 4150

the King's message to, 1652

her beautiful face and figure (1786), 4278

journey to England, 1168, 1168n, 1169, 1176, 1183, 1203, 1224, 1226, 1228

her coronet, 1178

King on her amiable qualities, 1231

her first Drawing Room, 1237

question of her naturalisation, 1238, 1241

her jointure, 1238, 1241, 1247

her income, 1255

brought to bed, 1356

jewels for her wedding, 1371n

breach with the Prince, 1393, 1398, 1405

short of money, 2556n

and her daughter's education, 2993

charges against (1806), 3279

her letter to the King mentioned, 3373n

attends a House of Commons debate, 3628n

Carpenter, Robert, a convict, 189

Carpenter, S., Commissioner of Excise Appeals, 3411

Carr, Sir John (1772–1832), 4231

Carrick, the Special Commission at, 3352

Carrington, Sir Codrington Edmund (1769–1849), M.P. for St Mawes (1826–31), 2456n

Carrington, Lord, *see* Smith, Robert

Carrol, M. de, 399

Cartagena, 3677

Carter, Samuel, 3815, 3820

Carter, Thomas (c. 1761–1835), 4076n

Carteret, George, 2nd Baron, *see* Thynne

Carteret, Henry Frederick, Lord (1735–1826), joint Postmaster-Gen., 10n, 19, 3966n

resigns his office (1789), 544

Carteret, John, Lord (1690–1763), 2114

Cartwright, John (1740–1824), 4070, 4159

Cartwright, General Wm. (c. 1753–1827), 1857, 2717n

Cartwright, William Ralph (1771–1847), 2752n, 3105, 3174, 3174n, 3832n, 3834, 3841, 3867n, 3876, 3878, 4120n

Carty, Patrick, 1640n

Cary, 915

Carysfort, 1st Earl of [I.] (1751–1828), George Grenville's son-in-law, 644, 1643, 2135, 2285n, 2315, 2550, 2743n, 3416, 3966n

given a Green Ribbon, 23

wants a seat in the Commons (1787), 23

supports Pitt's Government, 23n

British Minister in Berlin, 2396

Cashel, Archbishop of, *see* Agar, Charles

Cashel election, 3876, 3876n

Cashman, a seaman, 2506

Cassel, 1574, 1944, 4300, 4304

Cassel, Landgrave of, *see* Hesse-Cassel

Cassillis, 10th Earl of (c. 1730–92), elected a Scottish Representative Peer (1784), 78

Cassillis, 12th Earl of (1770–1846), 3966n

Castanos, General Francisco Xavier de, Duke of Baylen (1756–1852), 3689, 3689n, 4088

Castelcicala, Fabrizio Ruffo, Prince of (d. 1832), Neapolitan Minister in London, 886, 3036, 3287, 3347, 3478, 3636, 3714, 3722, 3748, 3807, 4039, 4222, 4231

Castlebar, the Special Commission of Judges at, 3345, 3349

'Castlebar Races', the, 1816n

Castleford, Rector of, 3630

Castle Hill, royal family's visit to Lord Fortescue's seat, 552

Castlereagh, Robert, Visct (1739–1821), *see* Londonderry, 1st Marquess of

Castlereagh, Visct, *see* Stewart, Robert

Castries, Maréchal de, 1100

Catalonia, 4120n

Cateau Cambrésis, Le, 1040, 1047

Cathcart, Lieut.-Col., 322

Cathcart, Rev. Archibald Hamilton (1764–1841), 3635

Cathcart, Lieut. Charles Allan (1759–88), 93

Cathcart, Elizabeth, Countess (*d.* 1847), 160
pension for, 1154
Cathcart, William Schaw, 1st Earl (1755–
1843), 572, 1154, 1435, 1555, 1595n,
2023, 2462, 3158–9, 3163, 3168, 3362,
3475, 3506, 3511, 3519, 3538, 3538n,
3546, 3565, 3635, 3641, 3966n
candidate for Scottish Representative
Peerage (1784), 78
seconds the Address (1789), 492
Chairman of the Committees of House of
Lords, 1154n
and the Life Guards, 1597
appointed Commander-in-Chief in Ireland
(1803), 2789
and the Green Ribbon, 3155
his Mission in Russia, 3155–6
his expedition to the Baltic (1807), 3471n,
3501, 3509, 3523, 3525–6, 3543, 3550
his U.K. peerage (1807), 3544
Catherine II, Empress (1729–96), 8, 95n, 178,
219, 235, 298, 399, 663, 756, 869n, 970,
1246, 1948n
Catherine, Grand Duchess of Russia (1788–
1819), 3278n
Catholic Petition, the (1805), 3095, 3095n;
(1806), 3238; (1808), 3773n
Commons' debate on, 3665, 3665n; (1810),
4164, 4177, 4188
Lords' debate on (1810), 4200
Catholic question, 1214n, 1916, 2329, 2329n
Pitt and the (1801), 2329n, 2474n; (1804),
2857
the King and the, 2329n, 2331, 2412, 2474n
Duke of York and the, 2356
debates on the (1805), 3092, 3092n, 3094–
5, 3095n; (1807), 3496, 3978, 3992
Catholic Relief Act [Ireland] (1793), 1158;
(1795), 1246
Catholic Relief Bill (1791), 1215; (1807),
3388, 3394–5, 3395n, 3400n, 3403n,
3437
Catley, Miss, 1259n
Causton, Rev. Thomas, Prebendary of West-
minster (*d.* 1842), 1932
Cavalry Bill (1796), 1459
Cavan, 7th Earl of (1763–1837), 920, 2048,
3142
Cavan Co., 2301
Cavan, the Special Commission at, 3357,
3357n
Cave, a convict, 564
Cavendish, Lord Frederick (1729–1803),
1483

Cavendish, Lord George Augustus Henry,
later Earl of Burlington (1754–1834),
1526, 1543, 3876n, 3960n, 3969n
Cavendish, Sir Henry (1732–1804), 3221n
Cavendish, Lord John (1732–96), 3, 3n, 35n
defeated at York (1784), 55
death of, 1483
Cavendish, William (1783–1812), elected
M.P. for Aylesbury, 2921, 4076, 4076n
Cavendishes, the, 358n
Cawdor, John Campbell, Lord (1755–1821),
1033n, 1506, 1510, 1512, 1983n, 2743n,
3966n
Cawsand Bay, near Plymouth, 1085, 1282
Cayenne, 1830n, 4110
Cayler, Brigadier, 900
Censeur, a 74-gun ship, captured by Hotham,
1229
Centaur, the, a 74-gun ship, 3157, 3721
Ceuta, 3443
garrison at, 3266, 3591
Cevallos, Don Pedro, Spanish Minister, 3825,
3858, 3883, 3896, 3903
Ceylon, 372, 1676, 2264, 2388, 2548, 2603,
2709, 2876, 2979, 3407, 3641, 4057, 4207
Ceylon, conquest of, 1422
Chalons-sur-Marne, 689
Chamberlain, office of Lord, 1370
Chamberlain, John, Keeper of the King's
Drawings, 770, 1708, 1923, 2985, 2992
appointed tallywriter in Exchequer Office,
1923
his second son, 770
Chambers, Sir William (1726–96), 127, 494
death of, 1379
Chambré, Sir Alan (1739–1823), appointed a
Baron of the Exchequer, 1974, 3902,
4227
Champagne district, the, 689
Champagné, Col. Josiah, 2388
Champagny, Jean Baptiste Nompère de, Duc
de Cadore (1756–1834), 3743, 3750,
3750n, 3768, 3768n, 3807
Chancellor of the Duchy of Lancaster, office
of, 2852n, 3417
Chancellor of the Exchequer [I.], *see* Parnell,
Sir John
Chancery, Court of, 2859, 4245
Chandos, 3rd Duke of (1731–89), Lord
Steward, 6, 80, 82, 516n, 553, 561
wants a Garter, 297
Channel Fleet, the, 1187
Chant, 159
Chant, Charles, a mutineer, 1591

Chantilly, 1583, 2735
Chapman, 399
Chapman, Lieut.-Col. Sir Thomas, 2013
Chappuis, General, 1061
Charborough, Dorset, 2960n
Charente, the, 3862
Charette, M. de (d. 1796), the Vendéan leader, 1270, 1277n, 1282, 1282n, 1286, 1289, 1294
Charger, a 14-gun brig, 2804
Charity Schools, 2477n
Charlemont, 4th Viscount and 1st Earl of (1728–99), 100, 100n, 410n
Charleroi, 950
Charles, Archduke of Austria (1771–1847), 1018, 1066, 1420n, 1441, 1447, 1526, 1612. 1625, 1907n, 1944, 1948, 1951, 1961, 2041, 2064, 2088, 2115, 2118, 2292, 2303, 2312, 3689, 3901, 3912
   defeated at Wagram, 3926
Charles I (1600–49), 42n, 114, 820, 2672
Charles II, King of Great Britain (1630–85), 1215, 1219, 1248n, 1278n, 4290
Charles III, King of Spain (1716–88), 186, 204, 275, 3036n
Charles IV, King of Spain (1748–1819), 1523, 3649
Charles V, Emperor (1500–58), 2668
Charles VI, Emperor (1685–1740), 32
Charles XIII, King of Sweden (1748–1818), 399, 3912
Charles Edward, the 'Young Pretender' (1720–88), 2633n
Charles Emmanuel, King of Sardinia (1751–1819), 2072, 2936n
Charles Felix, King of Piedmont-Sardinia (1765–1831), 803
Charleston, 4287, 4291n
Charleville, Earl of (1764–1835), 3193n, 3966n
   and a Representative Peerage, 2510, 2510n, 2515, 2515n,
Charlotte, Queen (1744–1818), 16, 30, 41, 58, 87–8, 97, 110, 122–3, 216, 222, 227, 232, 238, 241, 244, 247, 254, 258, 262, 268–9, 283–4, 309, 317, 320, 325, 325n, 328–9, 333–4, 335n, 344, 348–9, 355, 358, 361, 369–70, 388, 465, 468, 473, 480, 488, 489n, 495–7, 547, 550, 622, 625, 634, 641n, 648, 659, 665n, 679, 717, 719, 724, 731, 770, 794, 820, 853, 866, 935, 1009n, 1010, 1017, 1033, 1051, 1178, 1196, 1225,
1232, 1356, 1380n, 1405, 1417, 1423, 1547, 1570, 1582, 1593, 1601, 1622, 1631, 1646–7, 1689–90, 1692, 1697, 1708, 1713, 1716, 1723, 1728, 1728n, 1731, 1735, 1739, 1756, 1793, 1793n, 1801, 1804, 1807, 1815, 1822–3, 1823n, 1858, 1875–6, 1888, 1920, 1952, 1961, 1976n, 1995, 2098, 2160, 2218n, 2233, 2260, 2275, 2303, 2326, 2354, 2368n, 2372n, 2379, 2387, 2388n, 2424, 2435, 2440, 2453, 2545, 2680, 2696, 2704, 2722, 2762, 2768, 2791, 2814, 2835n, 2838n, 2856n, 2873n, 2930n, 2934n, 2962n, 3004, 3028, 3031, 3118, 3121, 3164n, 3194n, 3452, 3285, 3452, 3494, 3580, 3743, 3750n, 3766, 3770, 3903, 3944, 3947, 3977n, 3991, 4000, 4005, 4022, 4027, 4042, 4077–9, 4103, 4107, 4132, 4150, 4150n, 4154, 4170n, 4194, 4197, 4216, 4264n, 4267, 4269, 4271–6, 4279, 4282–4, 4286–90, 4290n, 4295, 4296–7, 4304
letters from, 160, 164, 233, 281, 312, 458n, 476, 533n, 541, 548, 552, 578, 659n, 665, 980, 985, 1230, 1388, 1495, 1636, 1687, 2042–3, 2307n, 2624, 2630, 2639n, 3017, 3064, 3130, 4097, 4209, 4264, 4268, 4270, 4277, 4302, 4305
letters to, 487, 489, 1388n, 2307n, 4167, 4278, 4300
her diary quoted, 1139n, 1156n, 1163n
hurt at Prince of Wales's conduct, 110
criticisms of Prince William, 233, 281
her 'great sense of religion', 265
portraits of, 282
increasing expense of her daughters, 283, 776
her debts (1786), 325
wishes to read Prof. Less's lectures on religion, 541
on the Revolution in France, 548
on *figures intéressantes*, 552
likes Devonshire, 552
at the Opera, 665
her cottage at Windsor, *see* Frogmore
on the Duchess of York, 688n
her dove house, 980
her financial position (1793), 980, 985; (1796), 1388
hit by a stone in her coach (1796), 1365n
comments on progress of currency inflation, 1388
dislikes and distrusts mankind, 1495

II, 832–1662; III, 1663–2575; IV, 2576–3578

II, 832–1662; III, 1663–2575; IV, 2576–3578

II, 832–1662; III, 1663–2575; IV, 2576–3578

Cobentzl, Count Johann Ludwig Joseph, the Imperial Vice-Chancellor and Foreign Minister (1753–1808), 1850, 1854, 1908, 2273, 2281, 2297

Coblenz, 772

Coburg, Prince of, *see* Saxe-Coburg

Cochin, 1285
    capture of, 1376

Cochin China, 372

Cochorn, Col., 3365

Cochrane, Major (*d.* 1781), 4285

Cochrane, Rear-Admiral Sir Alexander Inglis Forrester (1758–1832), 3062, 3157, 3210, 3270, 3276, 3277n, 3281, 3288, 3488, 3598, 3880, 3885

Cochrane, Thomas, Lord, later 10th Earl of Dundonald (1775–1860), 3865, 4089, 4133, 4138, 4208
    his K.B., 3865n
    imprisonment of, 3865n

Cockburn, Archibald, 592

Cockburn, Sir James, 8th Bart (1729–1804), M.P. for the Linlithgow Burghs (1772–84); appointed Secretary to the Prussian Minister in London, as a means of eluding his creditors, 308

Cockburn, Lieut.-Gen. Sir Wm. (1768–1835)
    letter from, 2314

Cockerell, Sir Charles (1755–1837), 4125

Cockpit, the, 2039n, 2330n

Cocks, John Somers, 1st Earl Somers (1760–1841), 666, 738, 2888, 2888n, 3105, 3787n

Codrington, Christopher (1764–1843), 2752n

Coehorn [?], Col., 3365

Coffee houses, 976

Coffin, Admiral Sir Isaac, 1st Bart (1759–1839) [M.P. for Ilchester, 1818–26], 385

Coghlan, Lieut. Jeremiah (?1775–1844), his extraordinary promotion, 2215

Coin, 1955

Coining, execution of a woman by burning, for crime of, 466

Coire, 1964

Coke, Daniel Parker (1745–1825), 1247

Coke, Edward (1758–1837), M.P. for Derby (1780–1807, 1807–18), 1559n, 3387n

Coke, Thomas William, 1st Earl of Leicester (1754–1842), 666, 3387n, 3610n, 3832, 4076n
    supports the Coalition (1783–4), 29

Colborne, Nicholas Wm. Ridley, 1st Baron Colborne (1779–1854), 3882

elected for Appleby (1807), 3500n

Colchester, 1178, 1194, 1196, 1616, 2470, 2481, 2499, 2527, 2789n, 3195

Colchester election (1784), 158

Coldstream Guards, the, 145, 469, 519, 527, 660, 825, 879, 905, 920, 923, 977, 1557–8

Cole, Captain, 1570

Cole, Dr William (1753–1806), death of, 3302

Coleman, 1774

Coleman, George (1732–94), manager of the Haymarket Theatre, 1107

Coleman, George, junior (1762–1836), manager of the Haymarket Theatre, 1107

Coles, Thomas, King's Page, 1806

College of Arms, the, 3165

College of Heralds, the, 1109

Collier, Sir George Ralph, 3532

Colliers, Captain, 850, 860, 872

Collingwood, Vice-Admiral Cuthbert, Lord (1750–1810), 2601, 3088, 3149, 3210, 3331–2, 3363, 3443, 3470, 3573, 3689, 3691, 3693, 3835, 3872, 3966n, 4111, 4139
    pension for (1806), 3176
    appointed Major-Gen. of the Marines, 3777
    death of, 4137

Collingwood, Captain Wilfred (*d.* 1787), 363

Collins, Lieut.-Col. David (1756–1810), Lieut.-Gov. of Tasmania, 2691

Collins, Sir John, 559n

Collins, Richard (1755–1831), miniature painter, 1109

Colloredo, Count Joseph Maria, the Imperial Field-Marshal (1735–1815), 882, 1951

Colman, Edward, the Sergeant-at-Arms, 2483n

Colman, Francis John, the Sergeant-at-Arms (*d.* 1811), 4100, 4100n, 4126, 4129–30, 4159

Cologne, 816, 4304

Cologne, Maximilian Frederick, Archbishop and Elector of, 138, 178, 265

Colombian Republic, the, 3270n

Colombo, 372
    surrender of, 1422

Colpoys, Admiral Sir John (?1742–1821), 243, 1237n, 1490
    made a K.B., 1684
    appointed Treasurer of Greenwich Hospital, 3019
    resigns seat at Admiralty Board (1805), 3019n, 3090n

Dartmouth, Viscount Lewisham, later 3rd
Earl of (1755–1810), 2363n, 2455, 2843,
2856, 2972, 3024, 3060, 3135–6, 3154,
3180n, 3202n, 3259n, 3486, 3530n, 3603,
3754, 3788, 3966n, 4056
letters from, 2846, 2972, 3056, 3063, 3202,
3350, 3553
letters to, 2808, 2846n, 3754n
and the Staffordshire election (1784), 64
appointed Pres. of the B. of Control, 2369
succeeds to Earldom, 2369n
Glenbervie on, 2369n
resigns the Board of Control, 2645n
appointed Lord Steward, 2645, 2645n,
2657n, 2856n
and the Garter, 2994n, 3009, 3014n, 3073n,
4041n
appointed Lord Chamberlain (1804),
2850n, 2853n
Dartmouth, Frances Catherine, Countess of
(*d.* 1805), 2369n
Dashwood, Miss Anna Maria (1785–1857),
one of Queen's Maids of Honour, 4208
Datchet, 1241, 1241n
Dauncey, Philip, 3234
D'Auvergne, see Auvergne, D'
Davenport, Mrs, 4077
Davers, Sir Charles, 6th Bart (1737–1806),
55n
Davidowich, General, 995
Davidson, *see* Davison
Davidson, John, a seaman, 3466
Davies, Dr Jonathan (1736–1809), Provost
of Eton, 729
letters from, 1431, 3032
resigns Canonry of Windsor, 729, 4041
Davis, a locksmith at Windsor, 2467, 2469
Davis, Jack, 2804n
Davis, a mutineer, executed, 1591
Davis, John, a mutineer, 1613
Davis, Thomas, *letter from*, 915
Davison, 1275, 1282
Davison, Alexander (*c.* 1750–1829), Nelson's
friend, question of a knighthood for,
2739
Davout, Marshal of France (1770–1823),
3326n, 3342
Davy, Martin, Vice-Chancellor of Cam-
bridge University (1763–1839), 2781
Dawkins, Henry, 3970n
Dawson, Richard (*c.* 1761–1807), 2447n,
2888n

Day, Sir John, 279n
Day, Lady (*d.* 1811), 279n
Deal, 1026, 1607, 1907n, 2028, 2030, 2037,
2046, 2052, 3214n, 3626n, 3743
Dean, John, printer, 4091
Dean, Richard Betenson, Commissioner of
Customs, 4229
Debiege, Col., 710
De Blaquiere, *see* Blaquiere
Debrett, John (*d.* 1822), 2108n, 2199n
Deccan, the, campaigns in, 2820
Decken, Brig.-Gen. F., 1042, 1661, 2718,
2731, 2742, 2744, 2749, 3727, 3905, 3988
De Dunstanville, Lord, *see* Basset
Dee, Miss, 386
Deer, the, in Richmond Park, 2707
Deerhurst, Visct, later 7th Earl of Coventry
(1758–1831), 3753
Defence Bill, the, *see* Additional Force Bill
'Defenders', the, 1358
Defiance, a 74-gun ship, 1444, 1834, 1838,
4225
De Front, *see* Front
De Hervilly, *see* Hervilly
Deinach, 1728
De Lancey, Major-Gen. Oliver (1749–1822),
2481, 2493, 2511, 2519
letter from, 692
Delany, Mrs (1700–88), *letter from*, 174
Delaval, Lord (1728–1808), 84, 98, 3966n
supports the Coalition (1783), 84n
changes sides and supports Pitt, 84n
Delaware, 3264n
Delaware river, the, 4291n
Del Campo, M., the Spanish Ambassador,
180, 191, 204, 220, 589
Delhi, capture of (1803), 3610
'Delicate Investigation', the, 3279, 3279n
De Lima, Marquis Lorenzo, Portuguese
Minister in London, 2426
De Luc, Jean André (1727–1817), 1639, 1641,
1656, 1670, 1673, 1675, 1689, 1693, 1719
letter from, 1631
De Lynden, Baron, *see* Lynden
Delmé family, the, 665n
Demerara, 3664
capture of (1803), 2810
Demez's, Hartford Bridge, 1595n
Dempster, George, M.P. (1732–1818), 98
Denbigh, 3487n
Denbigh, 6th Earl of (1719–1800), 1983n,
2199n

Denman, Thomas, Lord (1779–1854), 3004n
Denman, William, 2532
Denmark, Court of, 95, 223, 235, 399, 2435, 3340
  ultimatum to (1800), 2230, 2234
  Convention with (1800), 2235
Denmark, Frederick, Prince Royal of, *see* Frederick VI
Denmark, Queen of, *see* Juliana
Denmark, King of, *see* Christian VII
Denoyer, 4269
Dent, John (1760–1826), 838, 1086, 1247, 1475, 1546, 1654, 2367, 2752n, 3966n, 3970n, 4076n, 4093n, 4105n, 4124n
Denton, Thomas, a convict, 532
Deptford, 3252, 3257, 3924, 3924n
Derby, Edward, Earl of (1752–1834), 226, 1223n, 2822, 3508n, 3966n, 4264n
Derby, Elizabeth, Countess of (1753–97), 4264, 4264n
Derbyshire, 3218
Dering, Charles, Commissioner of Taxes, 1685
Derry, Bishop of, *see* Bristol, 4th Earl of
Desars, 2726
Desart, 1st Earl of (1737–1804), 2315
Desart, 2nd Earl of (1788–1820), 4032n, 4087, 4109, 4205
  declines, then accepts seat at Treasury Board, 4032, 4037
deserters from the Navy, 2492
deserters from the Army, 2499
Désirée, a 36-gun frigate, 2425, 4115
Despard, Edward Marcus, traitor (1751–1803), 2699, 2706, 2774
  plot to kill the King, 2676, 2680, 2683
  execution of, 2706n, 2708
Despencer, Baron Le (1766–1831), 3966n
Dessau, Prince de, 298
D'Esté, Augusta Emma, Lady Truro (1801–1866), 1009n
D'Esté, Sir Augustus Frederick (1794–1848), 1009, 1327–8, 1413, 1888, 1990, 1997, 1999, 2010, 2014, 2017, 2023, 2023n, 2145
Detroit, Prince Edward at, 794
Deux Ponts, Duc de (Zweibrücken) (1746–95), 178
Devay, Patrick, a mutineer, 1834
Devaynes, William (c. 1730–1809), 567, 1165
  Deputy Chairman of East India Company, 70, 253
Deventer, 376

Devonshire, 915, 1504, 1767, 1775, 1787, 1803, 2415, 3559n, 3989
  Queen dislikes, 552
Devonshire, Georgiana, Duchess of (1757–1806), 2329n, 2339n, 2346n, 2349n, 2357n, 2367n, 3813n
  eye troubles, 3130n
  death of, 3224, 3226n
Devonshire, 3rd Duke of (1698–1755), 3n
Devonshire, 4th Duke of (1720–64), 1754
Devonshire, 5th Duke of (1748-1811), 774n, 3293n, 3637n, 3966n
  contribution to party funds, 894n
  declines the Privy Seal (Sept. 1796), 1678n
Devonshire House, 2852n, 3130n
  that 'cursed brothel', 1514n
Dewar, Lieutenant (*d.* 1793), 911
Dewes, 174
Dewitz, Stephan Werner von (1726–1800), Principal Minister of Duke of Mecklenburg-Strelitz, 1137, 1687
Diadem, a 74-gun ship, 1815n
Diana, a 38-gun frigate, 1595
Dick, Sir John (*d.* 1804), 127
Dick, Quintin (c. 1777–1858), 3876, 3876n, 3878
Dickie, Andrew (*d.* 1834), clerk, later partner of Coutts's Bank, 3583n
Dickinson, William (1745–1806), 2752n, 3319n
Dickinson, William (1771–1837), 1893, 2276, 2752n, 3834
  letter from, 3319n
  elected for Somerset (1806), 3319n
  and a seat at the Admiralty Board, 3319, 3319n
Dickson, Admiral Archibald (*d.* 1803), 2228, 2230, 2234, 2413
Dickson, William (1745–1804), Bishop of Down, 2928
Dictator, a 74-gun ship, 1815n
Diepholtz, 1633, 1705n
Diepholtz, Count von, the incognito of Princes of Hanover, 1863
Diessenbroick, Major-Gen., 1090, 1099
Diet, the Imperial, 175, 178
Dieu, Isle, *see* Yeu Île d'
Digby, Rev. Charles (1775–1841), 3580, 4238
Digby, Mrs Charlotte Margaret (*d.* 1794), 578
Digby, Edward, 2nd Earl (1773–1856), 1983n, 3622, 3966n
Digby, Capt. George, R.N., 3691
Digby, Henry, 1st Earl (1731–93), 3622, 3914

Digby, Julia (*d.* 1807), a Maid of Honour, 578

Digby, Admiral Robert (1732–1814), 160, 1244, 4267, 4269–71, 4275, 4279, 4283, 4285, 4287, 4291–2

letters from, 598, 3631, 4292

letter to, ?4265

his wife (*d.* 1830), 160

his brother, 598

is refused (1790), the office of Groom of the Bedchamber, 598n

resigns office of Groom of the Bedchamber, 3631

King's instructions to (1779), 4265

Digby, Hon. Stephen (1742–1800), 312, 458n

the Queen's Vice-Chamberlain (to 1792), 980n, 3580

his marriage (1790), 578

Digby, Rev. William, Dean of Durham (1733–88), 578

death of, 483

Diligente, a 32-gun frigate, 4289

Dillon, Capt. (*d.* 1800), of the Falmouth Packet Station, 2117

Dillon, Charles, 12th Visct (1745–1813), 1676, 2693

Dillon, Henry Augustus, 13th Visct (1777–1832), 2693, 2752n, 3095

moves the Address (1805), 3009

Dimsdale, Nathaniel (1748–1811), Baron of the Russian Empire; elected M.P. for Hertford, 605

Dimsdale, Thomas (1712–1800), Baron of the Russian Empire, 605n

Dinant, 972

Diomede, a 44-gun ship, 1794, 1869, 4291n

Directory, the French, 1387, 1449, 1458, 1469, 1484, 1593, 1656, 1691n, 1732n, 1830n, 1961

overthrow of (1799), 2082

Disbrowe, Col. Edward (*c.* 1754–1818), the Queen's Vice-Chamberlain, 2084–5, 2819, 3014n, 3397

Dissenters, the, 692, 1046, 1360, 3394

Distillery Bill (1801), 2570; (1810), 4091, 4093

Division List in H. of Commons, error in, 2606

on 3 June 1803, 2753n

Dixmude, 934, 968

Dixon, Admiral, *see* Dickson

Dixon, James, mutineer, 1605

Dockyards, Report on the (1801), 2349

'Doctor', the, *see* Addington, Henry

Dod, Captain, 574n

Dodd, Capt. Thomas, D. of Kent's secretary, 4034

questions put to, with answers, 4034

Doederlein, Professor, 480

Dogger Bank, the, 4143

Dogmersfield Park (Hants), Sir Henry Mildmay's seat, 2461n

Dogs, tax on, 1390

Dolben, Sir William (1727–1814), 448, 1086, 1198, 1255, 1559, 3095, 3712

supports parliamentary reform, 203

opposes repeal of Test and Corporation Acts (1790), 580

Dolly, *see* Adolphus Frederick

Dolphin, a 44-gun ship, 3103

Domeier, Dr William, Prince Augustus's physician, 1727, 1727n, 1750, 1767, 1775, 1787, 1792, 1803, 1817, 1863, 1867, 1888, 1943, 1998

letters from, 1750n, 1888n

bulletins issued by, 1848, 1863

Domenichino, the painter (1581–1641), 2668

Domett, Admiral Sir Wm. (1754–1828), 2310, 3143

Dominica, a 14-gun sloop, 3348

Dominica, island of, 341, 363, 567, 3062, 3088, 3174n, 3664

Don, Sir Alexander, 1603

Don, General Sir George (1754–1832), 1734, 2011, 3159, 4015, 4025, 4109

a Staff Officer, 1703

Donaghadee, 1586, 1752

Doncaster, Earl of, *see* Buccleuch

Donegal Co., 2301, 3763n

Donegall, 5th Earl and 1st Marquess of (1739–99), given a British peerage, 604

Donegall, 6th Earl and 2nd Marquess of (1769–1844), 3966n

Donegall, Marchioness of (*c.* 1768–1829), 1666

Dönhoff, Countess of, mistress of Frederick William II, 762n

Donington Park, Leics, 2914n

Donnington Grove, near Newbury, 1496

Donoughmore, 2nd Baron, 1st Visct and 1st Earl of (1756–1825), 2315, 2699, 2888n, 3966n

applies for title of Clancarty, 2699n

Dorchester, 541, 1616, 1769, 2051, 2376, 2926, 3128

Downes, Rev. John, 1009, 1024

Downes, William, 1st Baron Downes (1751–1826), 3198

Downie, David, convicted of treason, 1121n

Downing Street, 218, 1247, 1320n, 2155n, 2461n

Downman, Captain Hugh, 3200

Downpatrick, 3095n
    election (1807), 3485n

Downshire, 1st Marquess of (1718–93), 472n, 2575, 2928, 3035
    refused a Dukedom (1791), 561n

Downshire, 2nd Marquess of (1753–1801), 1662, 1913, 1913n, 2309, 2575
    letter to, 2323
    his property plundered, 1540
    his electoral influence in Ireland, 1913n
    dismissed from Privy Council (1800), 2109, 2575
    his sons, 2309, 2575, 2928, 3035, 3129
    death of (7 Sept.), 2580

Downshire, Mary, Marchioness of, and (1802) Baroness Sandys (1764–1836), 2580
    letters from, 2575, 2928, 3035, 3129
    in mourning for her husband, 2580
    her children, 2928
    her son George (1801–79), 2580
    her electoral influence in Co. Down, 3129

Downton, 3428n

Dowson, a draftsman, 2642n

Doyle, Sir Charles William (1770–1842), 3725, 3727, 3887

Doyle, General Sir John (?1756–1834), 479, 882, 911, 1045, 1282, 1289, 1294, 1296n, 1314, 1334, 3380, 3806
    letter to, 1286
    appointed Secretary to Prince of Wales (1791), 723

D'Oyley, Francis (*d.* 1801), Major-Gen. (1794), Lieut.-Gen. (1801), 920, 1630

Draining, improvements in art of, 1173, 1264

Drake, a 14-gun sloop, 978

Drake, Francis, diplomatist, 822, 1234
    his pension, 3319

Drake, Sir Francis Henry (1723–94), Master of the Household, 1181, 2975

Drake, Rev. Thomas, D.D. (1745–1819), 257, 260
    letter from, 260

Drake, William, M.P. for Agmondesham, 595, 644, 757

Draper, a soldier, 835

Drax, Mr, 3994

Drax, Mrs, 3972, 3982–3

Dreadnought, a 98-gun ship, 2824

Dresden, 538, 1198, 1563, 1692, 1817, 1863, 1867, 2672, 3296

Dreyer, M. de, 12

Drichsel, Major, 882

Drinkwater, Lieut.-Col. John, 3390

Driver, a 16-gun ship, 3264n

Drogheda, Marquess of, later Baron Moore (U.K.) (1730–1822), 2315, 3455n, 3483n, 3966n

Droits of the Admiralty, *see* Admiralty

Dromore, See of, 3035

Dropmore, Lord Grenville's seat, 862, 862n, 1098, 1430, 1598, 1719, 1879, 2082, 2100, 2304

Druid, the, 4143

Drummond, Andrew Berkeley (1755–1833),
    letter from, 2945

Drummond, Lieut.-Gen. Andrew John, 1630, 2507, 3693, 3693n, 3844n

Drummond family, the, 1278, 1278n

Drummond, Henry (1730–95), son of 4th Visct Strathallan, and M.P. for Wendover (1774–80) and Midhurst (1780–90), 51n, 109, 116, 126, 129, 133, 139, 141, 144, 188
    letters from, 51, 59, 121, 140
    letters to, 51, 51n, 56, 59, 59n, 140
    his family, 51
    his receipts, 141, 188

Drummond, James, 1st Earl of Perth (c. 1580–1611), son of 3rd Lord Drummond, 1278n

Drummond, James, Lord [G.B.] (*d.* 1800), 1278n

Drummond, Lady Mary (c. 1756–1839), 2945

Drummond, Messrs, bankers, 109, 121, 126, 140, 144, 2915, 2441n, 3970n

Drummond, Robert, banker (1728–1804), 51, 126, 133, 141, 1475, 2411
    his receipt, 188

Drummond, Sir William, diplomatist (c. 1770–1828), 1637, 2371n, 2480, 2901, 3300, 3309, 3386, 3386n, 3539, 3714, 3722
    letter from, 2901n
    moves the Address (1797), 1637
    Chargé d'Affaires at Copenhagen, 2297
    appointed Minister to K. of Naples, 2426
    made a P.C., 2901

Drummond, Sir William (*cont.*)
  wants to buy a seat in Parliament, 2901n
  sent to Palermo, 2901n
Drummond's Bank, 4149
Drury, 915
Drury Lane Theatre, 732, 1365n, 1902, 2092
  attempted assassination of King at, 2152n, 2153
  destruction of, 3824, 3824n, 3826
Dryad, a 36-gun frigate, 3329, 3955
Dryden, John (1631–1700), 3293n
Dublin, 224, 1347, 1490n, 1491, 1640n, 1746, 1776, 1836, 1859, 1869, 1896, 1904n, 1913, 1914n, 1942n, 1958, 2013, 2575, 2779, 2793–4, 3224, 3683, 4038, 4038n
Dublin, Archbishop of, *see* Agar, Charles
Dublin, a 'tumultuous insurrection' in (1784), 67n, 94
  Address from people of, to the King (1784), 94
  Corporation of, 94, 1127
  further troubles in Dublin (1784), 112, 112n
  disturbances in (1795), 1283
  mutiny of garrison in, 1297, 1297n
  Militia, 2519
  Emmet's rebellion in, 2772, 2774, 2780n, 2786, 2790, 2794
Duc de Chartres, a captured French frigate of 20 guns, 85
Duchy of Lancaster, *see* Lancaster
Duchilio [*sic*], Vicomte de, 4269
Ducie, 4th Baron and 1st Earl (1775–1840), 3966n
Duckett, 1795
Duckworth, Admiral Sir John Thomas (1748–1817), 1901, 2018n, 3210, 3215, 3250, 3331, 3443, 3454n
  made a K.B., 2409
  not made a Baronet in 1801, 2409n
  parliamentary provision for, 3219, 3219n, 3604
Du Cret, Madame, 1013
Dudley, Sir Henry Bate, 1st Bart (1745–1824), 158
Dudley and Ward, 3rd Viscount (1870–1823), 1983n, 3966n, 4074
Duelling, execution for, 3702
Du Dresnay, 1294
Duer, Lieut., *see* Dewar
Duff, Capt., 3379
Duff, General Sir James (1753–1839), 968, 1630, 1746, 1765
Duigenan, Patrick (*c.* 1737–1816), 3095, 3657, 3657n, 3665n, 4135

and his seat in Parliament (1801), 2329, 2333, 2333n, 2338
Dukedoms, King's restricted creation of, 4n, 226n, 561n
  applications for, 531, 561, 561n
Dumaresq, Sir John, Lieut.-Bailiff of Jersey, 2721
Dumaresq, Philip, Lieut., R.N., 2496
Dumbarton, Fencible Infantry, 1535
  Governorship of, 1597, 1619
Dumergue, Charles Francis (*d.* 1814), the Royal dentist, 3017
Dumfries, 6th Earl of (1726–1803), 1983n, 2965
  candidate for Scottish Representative Peerage (1784), 78
Dumouriez, Charles François (1739–1823), 792, 802, 816, 859, 864, 866, 3270n
  his treachery, 863n
Dunbar, Sir James (1770–1836), 3353
Duncan, Adam, Visct (1731–1804), Admiral, 1274, 1291, 1291n, 1307n, 1377, 1555, 1563, 1616, 1632, 1634, 1636, 1668n, 1685, 1844n, 1846, 1869, 1965, 1965n, 1983, 1983n, 2011, 2016, 2328n
  given Order of St Alexander, 1614
  victory off Camperdown, 1627–9, 1634, 1653
  gold medal given to (1797), 1653
  annuity for, 1681
  death of, 2924
Duncan, 2nd Visct, later Earl of Camperdown (1785–1859), 3966n
Duncan, Henry, 3233
Duncan, Jonathan, Governor of Bombay (1756–1811), 2974
Duncan, Mrs Mary, 928n
  letter to, 928
Duncannon, Visct, *see* Bessborough, 3rd Earl of
Duncombe, Henry (1728–1818), 647, 878, 1180, 1180n, 1250, 1255
  his Yorkshire contest (1784), 55, 61
  a parliamentary reformer, 203
Dundalk elections, 2329n
Dundas, Captain, 4285
Dundas, Anne, Lady Arniston (*c.* 1705–98), mother of Henry Dundas, 1900
Dundas, Charles, 1st Baron Amesbury (1751–1832), 2752n, 2834n, 3243, 3787n, 3834, 4201
  and the Speakership (1801), 2354n
Dundas, Colonel, a Commissioner of American claimants, 404, 958

Dundas, Sir David, the King's surgeon, 2922, 4077, 4106, 4175, 4189–90
  letter from, 2083
  bulletin issued by, 4165
  his five children, 2922
  his wife, 2922
Dundas, General Sir David (1735–1820), 875, 930, 1060, 1266, 1461, 1709n, 1755n, 2048, 2462, 2805n, 3137, 3841, 3984n, 3935, 3967n, 4015, 4076, 4117–8, 4138, 4159
  letter from, 3959
  letter to, 4117
  his K.B., 2732
  appointed Commander-in-Chief, 3837, 3837n, 3839
Dundas, Lieut.-Col. Francis, 2805n
Dundas, General Francis (*d.* 1824)
  Henry Dundas's nephew, and military commander at the Cape, 891, 2264, 2672
Dundas, George Heneage Lawrence (1778–1834), M.P. for Richmond (1802–6), 2752n
Dundas, Henry, 1st Viscount Melville (1742–1811), 4n, 70n, 89, 93, 93n, 98, 101, 235, 237, 358, 425, 438, 568, 619, 635, 647, 670, 670n, 692, 735, 738, 740, 740n, 744, 751, 754n, 755, 757, 761, 767n, 770n, 774, 789, 793, 829, 831, 836, 839, 862, 912, 974, 977, 990, 998, 1060, 1010–11, 1014, 1020n, 1056, 1064, 1070, 1078, 1085, 1097, 1143, 1150, 1180, 1182, 1193, 1198, 1198n, 1233, 1255, 1277, 1278n, 1286, 1301, 1304, 1326, 1340n, 1342–3, 1351, 1370, 1436, 1464, 1482, 1487, 1507, 1509, 1514, 1535–6, 1543, 1554, 1560, 1621, 1623, 1628, 1658, 1664, 1692, 1702, 1724, 1729, 1736n, 1752n, 1758–9, 1765, 1792–3, 1848, 1880, 1882, 1897, 1903, 1905, 1908n, 1910–11, 1917, 1922, 1932, 1990, 1997, 2008–10, 2013–14, 2017, 2020, 2023, 2029, 2041n, 2067, 2070, 2074, 2079, 2079n, 2108, 2108n, 2135–6, 2204, 2222, 2243, 2276, 2288, 2288n, 2329n, 2331, 2339, 2346, 2357, 2359, 2365n, 2367, 2368n, 2371n, 2373n, 2388, 2416, 2619, 2752n, 2794, 2794n, 2839n, 2899, 2912n, 2947, 2965, 2994n, 3019n, 3068n, 3071n, 3075, 3075n, 3079, 3085, 3105, 3105n, 3115, 3115n, 3178n, 3425n, 3442, 3538n, 3554n, 3824n, 3856, 3906n, 3966n, 4010n, 4105n, 4142

letters from, 286, 443, 691, 700, 708, 710, 713, 715, 734, 746, 754, 760, 763, 767, 770, 771n, 773, 779, 784, 786, 791, 797–8, 814, 818, 827, 842, 857, 892, 900, 921, 928, 949, 953, 956, 961, 963, 969, 972, 975, 983, 989, 991, 994, 997, 1005, 1012, 1019, 1025, 1028, 1036, 1048, 1053, 1058, 1065, 1069, 1077, 1083, 1090, 1092, 1094, 1105, 1121, 1124, 1134, 1138, 1154, 1165, 1175, 1191, 1245, 1258, 1268, 1271, 1273, 1280, 1282, 1285, 1289–90, 1294–5, 1300, 1303, 1305, 1314, 1331, 1334, 1350, 1359, 1366, 1368, 1371, 1422, 1427, 1467, 1488, 1493, 1497, 1518, 1532, 1556, 1588, 1604, 1653, 1715, 1736, 1748, 1771, 1803, 1813, 1874, 1900, 1915, 1939, 1947, 1976, 1979, 1994, 2007, 2011–13, 2023n, 2027, 2030, 2033, 2040, 2051, 2054, 2054n, 2060, 2066, 2068, 2070n, 2073, 2077n, 2087, 2087n, 2112, 2116, 2144n, 2171, 2175, 2178, 2184, 2203, 2205, 2207, 2223, 2229, 2242, 2242n, 2252, 2256, 2256n, 2259, 2264, 2291, 2307n, 2313, 2325, 2346n, 2357n, 2684n, 2839n, 2861, 2866n, 2871, 2890, 2904, 2915, 2924, 2939, 2946, 2959, 2977, 3019, 3069, 3069n, 3410n, 3417n, 3425n, 3996

letters to, 372, 619n, 688A, 691, 700, 708, 710, 713, 734, 746, 758, 760, 763, 763n, 767, 770, 773, 779, 779n, 786, 791, 797, 807n, 857, 864, 867, 880, 887, 900, 902, 919, 921, 946, 949, 956, 958, 969, 972, 975, 983, 991, 1012, 1024–5, 1028, 1053, 1061, 1065, 1069, 1077, 1090, 1121, 1130, 1134, 1138, 1139n, 1145, 1163, 1165, 1226, 1258, 1260, 1280, 1282, 1285, 1288, 1289, 1294, 1303, 1314, 1331, 1334, 1361, 1366n, 1368, 1371, 1376, 1422, 1427, 1467, 1493, 1497, 1497n, 1518, 1532, 1556, 1588, 1604, 1653, 1715, 1736, 1748, 1748n, 1768, 1771, 1803, 1900, 1913n, 1939, 1971, 1976, 1986, 1999, 2007, 2012, 2023n, 2032, 2043, 2051, 2054, 2054n, 2060, 2066, 2073, 2077n, 2082n, 2087, 2112–13, 2116, 2184, 2203, 2203n, 2204n, 2205, 2242, 2247, 2252, 2256, 2291, 2307n, 2313, 2346, 2363, 2757n

supports parliamentary reform, 203
thought of as Foreign Secretary (1791), 670n
appointed Home Sec. *ad int.* (1791), 672, 686

II, 832–1662; III, 1663–2575; IV, 2576–3578

Dundas, Henry (*cont.*)

remains Pres. of India Board of Control (1791), 672

re-elected for Edinburgh (1791), 672n

criticism of his new appointment, 672n

and a Governorship of Charterhouse (1792), 795, 797

his second marriage (1793), 864

to be War Secretary, 1090n, 1091, 1091n

threatens to resign, 1090n

and Gov.-Generalship of Bengal (1797), 1493n

wishes to resign War Secretaryship, 2077n, 2087, 2144n

wishes to see a new head of the Admiralty, 2077n

resigns Treasurership of the Navy (1800), 2144, 2144n

his official house in Somerset Place, 2144

King's wild accusation against, 2329n

relations with Addington (1801), 2363n

and 'management' of Scotland, 2363n, 2965

his peerage (1802), 2684, 2684n

origin of impeachment proceedings against, 2687n, 3068

appointed First Lord of the Admiralty (1804), 2839, 2839n

impeachment charges, 2852n

King's opinion of, 2908, 2912, 2939, 3040, 3047, 3069

his house at Dunira, 2915

salary of his office of Privy Seal of Scotland, 2915

annuity from East India Company, 2915

resigns office after censure motion, 3068–71, 3081n, 3090n

Addresses for his removal from Privy Council, 3077, 3077n

name struck out of list of Privy Councillors, 3089

rejoices at Sidmouth's resignation (1805), 3115n

question of his re-admittance to Privy Council, 3417–18, 3435, 3485

attitude to Perceval Ministry, 3966, 3989, 3996, 3998, 4002, 4007, 4007n, 4010, 4026

refuses an Earldom, 3998n

Dundas, Lady Jane, later Viscountess Melville (1766–1829), 1138, 1999, 2054n, 2144n, 2307n, 2368n, 2839n, 2915, 3417n

letter from, 2769

her marriage to Dundas (1793), 864

Dundas, Lawrence, 1st Earl of Zetland (1766–1839), defeated at Camb. Univ. election (1790), 608n, 2752n

Dundas, Lieut.-Gen. Ralph (*d.* 1814), 2022, 2216

Dundas, Robert (1685–1753), Henry Dundas's father, M.P. for Edinburgh County (1722–37), 1900n

Dundas, Robert, of Arniston, Henry Dundas's nephew, Lord Advocate of Scotland (1758–1819), 991, 997, 1031, 1121, 1380, 2301, 2363n, 2560, 2752n

letter from, 991n

appointed Chief Baron of the Exchequer, Scotland (1801), 2403, 2418

Dundas, Robert Saunders, 2nd Viscount Melville (1771–1851), 773, 2915, 3105, 3115, 3417n, 3485, 3538n, 3582, 3861, 3878n, 3906n, 3966, 3998n, 4028n, 4072, 4089, 4113n, 4122n, 4124, 4130, 4147, 4159, 4164n, 4188, 4229

letters from, 3861n, 3873n, 3878n, 4010n

letters to, 2684n, 3797n, 4072, 4164n

Pres. of India Board, 3418, 3590n

appointed Irish Secretary (1809), 3856n

offered the Colonial Secretaryship, 3985, 3985n, 3989n, 3992, 3998, 4002, 4007, 4007n, 4015

an excellent man of business, 3998n

agrees to return to India Board, 4010, 4015

accepts seat in Cabinet, 4026

declines office of First Lord of Admiralty, 4142, 4142n

Dundas, Sir Thomas, 2nd Bart, later Baron Dundas (1741–1820), 2752n

his peerage (1794), 1104, 1983n, 3966n

Dundas, William (?1762–1845), 2619n, 2752n, 2854, 2881n, 2894, 2933, 2984n, 3020

given a seat on India Board (1797), 1621, 1623

Glenbervie's assessment of, 2263n

resigns seat at India Board (1803), 2852n

sworn of the Privy Council, 2180

becomes Secretary at War (1804), 2845n, 2852

offered but declines Government of Upper Canada (1806), 3174, 3179

Dunira, Dundas's Perthshire seat, 2915

Dunkirk, 405, 896, 898, 903, 916, 920–1, 928–9, 941n, 966, 1456, 1506, 1760, 2496n

failure to capture, 934, 943, 949n, 1043

Dunlo, Lord, *see* Clancarty

Dunlop, Lieut.-Gen. James (*d.* 1832), 2863

Dunmore, Countess of (*d.* 1818), 1009–10, 1017, 1024, 1225, 1999
King's opinion of, 1012

Dunmore, 4th Earl of (1730–1809), 545, 1009–10, 1024
elected a Scottish Representative Peer (1784), 78

Dunn, a mutineer, 1599

Dunn, James, 1640n

Dunn, Terence, a mutineer, 1834

Dunne, General Edward (*c.* 1762–1844), 2008

Dupont, Gainsborough (?1754–97), portrait-painter, 2985

Dupont de L'etang, Pierre, Count (1765–1840), French General, 3587n, 3689n, 3693

Dupré, James (1778–1870), M.P. for Aylesbury (1802–6), 2752n

Dupuis, Lieut.-Col. Richard, 2008, 2028

Durack, John, a mutineer, 1595

Durham, Bishop of, *see* Barrington

Durham, Prebendaries of, 3559

Durham, 812, 3775

Durham Militia, 1298, 1535

Durham County election (1790), 619n

Durham, Rear-Admiral Sir Philip Charles (1763–1845), 327n

During, General, 979

Durlach, 2015

Dursley, William FitzHardinge Berkeley, later 1st Earl FitzHardinge (1786–1857), 4177, 4198

Dusseldorf, 1132

Dutch East Indies, 372

Dutch settlements to be occupied (1795), 1199

Dutch settlements in South America, 2754

Dutch troops in British pay, 2646

Dutheil, M., 1656

Dutton, James (1744–1820), 1st Baron Sherborne, 55

Duval, 399

Duval, the jeweller, 1109, 1178, 1178n

Duval, Dr Philip (*d.* 1808), Canon of Windsor, 3622

Dyer, Sir Thomas, 4034n

Dyneley, Mr, 2318

Dynevor, Lord (1765–1852), 1983n, 3966n

Dyott, Col. William (1761–1847), 2390

Dysart, 5th Earl of (1734–99), candidate for Scottish Representative Peerage (1784), 78

Eamer, Sir John, Sheriff of London, 1235
Lord Mayor, 2157, 2543, 2543n, 2605, 2652

Eardley, Luke, a mutineer, 1605

Earldoms, applications for, 544

Earle, Andrew, a mutineer, 1599

Earnest, gun brig, 3528

Eartham, Huskisson's seat, 4076n

East, Sir Edward Hyde (1764–1847), 1198

Eastbourne, 312, 1784, 2653, 4270

East Friesland, 1304
Prince Ernest in, 1240

East Grinstead, Postmaster at, 2659

East India Establishment, the, 2882

East India Company, the, 70, 93, 128, 136, 206, 253, 274, 274n, 430, 442–3, 580, 669, 784, 1343, 1376, 1881n, 2506, 2745, 2915, 2933n, 3255, 3595, 3832, 3867n, 4072, 4110, 4207–8, 4253
its trade monopoly, 399
proprietors of, 18
Directors of, 18, 67, 136–7, 253, 274n, 286, 430, 442, 567, 701, 715, 734, 784, 791
mutinies in its armies, 4057, 4060
its stock, 253

East India House, the, 18, 132, 149, 253, 322, 477, 763, 779, 1422, 1898, 2394, 2505

East Indian Army, the, 1165

East Indies, 363, 633, 684, 817, 1186, 1288, 1300, 1433, 1588, 2047, 2247, 2476, 2505, 3273, 3574, 4241, 4253
Portuguese settlements in the, 2674
capture of French settlements in (1793), 1005

East London Militia, the, 1557

East Looe, 40n

East Retford, 3435n

East Suffolk Militia, 1607, 1825

Eastern (military) District, the, 3125

Ebony, 372

Echo, the, a 16-gun sloop, 845, 3233

Eckhart, 1884

Eclipse, an 18-gun sloop, 3691

Eden, Catherine Isabella, later Mrs Vansittart (1778–1810), 3258, 3267

Eden, Elizabeth Charlotte, later Lady Godolphin (1780–1847), 2110

Eden, George, 1st Earl of Auckland (1784–1849), 593n, 4105n

Eden, Sir Morton Frederick, 1st Baron Henley (1752–1830), diplomatist, 538, 762n, 1020, 1152, 1162, 1526, 1553, 1563, 1671, 1695, 1727, 1727n, 1750, 1762, 1767,

Eld, Colonel (*d.* 1793), 923
Elderton, Charles, 3815n
Eldon, Lady (*d.* 1831), 3981n, 4045n
Eldon, Lord, *see* Scott, Sir John
Elections, *see* No. 158 *and under* Armagh, Aylesbury, Bandon Bridge, Berkshire, Beverley, Bossiney, Brecknock, Bristol, Bury St Edmunds, Caithness, Cambridgeshire, Cambridge University, Carlow, Cashel, Chipping Wycombe, Colchester, Coventry, Dover, Down Co., Dundalk, Durham County, Gloucestershire, Great Bedwin, Hampshire, Harwich, Hastings, Hedon, Hertford, Kent, Kirkcudbright, Linlithgowshire, London, Lostwithiel, Lymington, Middlesex, Minehead, New Shoreham, Norfolk, Northampton, Northumberland, Old Sarum, Oxfordshire, Queenborough, Reigate, Rochester, Rye, St Albans, Saltash, Somerset, Southwark, Stafford, Staffordshire, Surrey, Tewkesbury, Tipperary, Tregony, Westminster, Wigtonshire, Windsor, Worcestershire, Yarmouth, York, Yorkshire
Election Fund, the Government's, 1674n
Election, General (1807), 3485n
Election Petitions, trial of, 182n, cost of, 2834
Elephant, a 74-gun ship, 3276, 3288, 3540
Elford, Sir William, 1st Bart (1749–1837), 1526, 1550, 1637, 2752n
Elfy [*sic*] Bey, 2819
Elgin, 7th Earl of (1766–1841), 619, 737, 785, 792, 796, 802, 812, 839, 859, 926, 931, 938, 955, 957, 968, 975, 995, 1007, 1014, 1020, 1034, 1066, 1525, 1656, 3966n
letter from, 2430
Envoy to Austrian Netherlands, 769
Minister at Berlin, 1670–1, 1673, 1689, 1693, 1719, 1725, 1791, 1848, 1879, 1920, 1983, 1983n, 2089–90, 2176, 2256n, 2391, 2396, 2476, 2235, 3268, 3564
recalled from Berlin, 1920n
asks for a mark of the King's favour, 2430
Ambassador to Turkey, 2591
Eliot, Caroline, Lady (1765–1818), *letter to*, 4097
Eliot, Edward, Lord (1727–1804), 19, 19n
his seven parliamentary seats, 19n
given office of Receiver-Gen. of Duchy of Cornwall for life (1749), 606
father of Wm. Eliot, 2180, 2180n, 2270n
Eliot, Edward James (1758–97), 248, 1621

death of his wife Lady Harriot (Pitt's sister), 330, 1621n
Eliot, John, Lord, later 2nd Baron Eliot and 1st Earl of St Germans (1761–1823), 670, 2270n, 2752n, 2842n, 3614, 3966n, 4142n
moves the Address (1805), 3008
Eliot, William (1767–1845), later 2nd Earl of St Germans, 718, 1194, 1196, 4097
appointed a Lord of the Admiralty (1800), 2180, 2180n
Marquess of Stafford's son-in-law, 2180
a Lord of the Treasury (1807), 3418
death of his wife Letitia (1810), 4097
Eliott, Francis, 2nd Baron Heathfield (1750–1813), 780
Eliott, George Augustus, 1st Baron Heathfield (1717–90), 9, 614, 1846, 4269, 4289
Elizabeth, Queen (1533–1603), 60
Elizabeth, Mme, Louis XVI's sister (1764–94), 689
Elizabeth, Princess (1713–57), daughter of George II, 309
Elizabeth, Princess (1770–1840), the King's 3rd daughter, 269–70, 273, 312n, 465, 541, 665n, 1976n, 2042, 2377, 2442, 2516, 3388, 3743, 3750n, 4209
letters from, 158n, 2835n
suffering from chickenpox, 868, 875
her stoutness, 2685
Elizabeth, Grand Duchess of Russia (1806–08), birth of, 3369
Elkington, Mr, 1173
his experiments in draining, 1264
parliamentary grant for, 1264n
Ellenborough, Lord, *see* Law, Sir Edward
Elliot, Anna Maria, Lady, later Countess of Minto (1752–1829)
letters from, 46n, 2214n
letter to, 3255n
Elliot, Colonel George, 2084
Elliot, Sir Gilbert, Earl of Minto (1751–1814), 46n, 446, 489n, 493n, 740n, 754n, 1053, 1109, 1184, 1207, 1299, 1311, 1461, 1483, 1670–1, 1893n, 1983n, 2080, 2082, 2107, 2120, 2193, 2214n, 2230, 2270n, 2273, 2321, 2459n, 2502, 2502n, 2505, 2514, 2551, 2743n, 2878n, 3008n, 3172n, 3255, 3966n, 4057, 4072
letters from, 218n, 446n, 1764n, 2357n, 3255n
letters to, 2082n, 3169n, 3402n
opinion of Duke of York (1788), 16n

II, 832–1662; III, 1663–2575; IV, 2576–3578

Exeter, 10th Earl, later 1st Marquess of (1754–1804), 1983n

Exeter, Bishop of, *see* Ross, John; Buller, William; and Fisher, John

Exeter, 2051

Exeter, Deanery of, 40, 2653, 2665
see of, 3462, 3465

Eylau, battle of, 3390, 3510n

Eyre, Col. Anthony Hardolph (1757–1836), 2888n, 4076

Eyre, Sir George, 820

Eyre, Sir James (1734–99), Chief Baron of the Exchequer, 230, 287, 760–1, 761n
appointed Chief Justice of the Common Pleas (1793), 829, 831

Eyre, Lady Mary (*d.* 1801), 648

Eyre, Thomas, 648

Faber, 2139

Fabian, Captain, 4228

Fabri, Major-Gen., 922, 924

Fagan, a French agent, 4083

Fagel, Baron Henry (1765–1838), Dutch Minister in Britain, 1721, 1731, 1744, 1917, 2123, 2278n, 2645
his brothers and sisters, 1731

Fagel, Henry, (*d.* 1790), 49, 49n, 376, 409
grandson of, 1144, 1152, 1189

Fagel, M. de, 3901, 3916

Fagel, Mme. de (*d.* 1782), 4288

Fairfax, Sir William George (1739–1813), knighthood for, 1628

Fairy, warship, 4285

Falcke, [Falk], 4284, 4297, 4304

Falmouth, 1009, 1773, 1830, 2106, 2106n, 2117, 2200, 2594, 3062, 3669, 3725, 3729, 3767, 3769, 4072, 4269

Falmouth, 3rd Visct (1758–1808), 544, 1983n, 1966n
letter from, 2192n
letter to, 1054n
his interest at Tregony, 64
seconds the Address (1784), 83
letters to Pitt mentioned, 270n
appointed Chief Justice in Eyre north of the Trent (1789), 544
resigns Chief Justiceship (1790), 2192
is Capt. of Band of Gentlemen Pensioners, 2192n
is refused office of Chief Justice in Eyre south of the Trent (1800), 2192n

Falsterbo [Falsterborn], 2425

Famars, 882, 891, 992

'Family Compact', the, 399

Fane, John (1751–1824), 2881n, 3622, 4124n

Fane, Col. Thomas (1760–1807), 270

Fanny, Lady, *see* Howard

Farhill, Mr, 4301

Farhills, John, *letter from*, 2078
wants to be Treasurer of the Ordnance, 2078

Farmer, Dr Richard (1735–97), Prebendary of Westminster, Master of Emmanuel College, 1617

Farmer, Captain (*d.* 1779), 4269

Farnall, Capt. Harry, 2417

Farnham, 1090, 1138, 2960n

Farquhar, Sir Walter (1738–1819), 2229, 2264, 2264n, 3383, 4036n

Farr, John, 2804n

Farraby, John, Commissioner of Taxes, 1685

Farrachi, 985

Farrel, John, a mutineer, 1605

Farrington, Dorset, 2376

Fast Days, 1515, 2793, 2868, 3374n, 3376

Fauconberg, 1st Earl (1699–1774), 641

Fauconberg, Henry Belasyse, 2nd Earl (1743–1802), 632, 1983n
letters from, 5, 641, 1471
letters to, 5, 474
votes with the Coalition (1783), 5n
his house (Fauconberg Lodge) at Cheltenham, 458n, 474, 474n
wants to be Groom of the Stole, 1471
death of, 2624

Fauconberg, Jane, Countess (*d.* 1820), 641

Faulknor, Robert, R.N. (*d.* 1795), 1049

Fauquier, William, 1261

Fawcett, Lieut.-Gen. Sir William (1728–1804), 35, 73, 173, 202n, 218, 335, 387, 387n, 392, 394, 397, 449, 502, 519, 581, 691, 722, 838, 1198, 1329, 1424, 1557, 1700, 1774, 1788, 1910, 1910n, 2013, 2022, 2028, 2074n, 2079, 2224, 3192, 4286, 4288, 4290, 4295
letters from, 9, 280, 2026, 2053, 2057, 2061, 2063, 2067, 2070, 2074
letters to, 9, 692, 787, 835, 2068, 2070n
appointed Governor of Chelsea Hospital, 1424n
resigns office of Adjutant-Gen. of the Forces, 1910n

Fawkener, William Augustus (*d.* 1811), Clerk of the Privy Council, son of Sir Everard Fawkener, 927, 2023, 2287
letters from, 755n, 761n

Fawkes, Walter Ramsden (1769–1825), 3380

Feder, Professor, 306n, 346, 357

Feilding, Viscount (1760–99), 417, 417n, 644, 819

Fencibles, definition of, 2070n

Fenwick, Charles, Consul at Elsinore, 2602, 3359

Ferdinand, Archduchess, daughter of Ferdinand I, King of Sicily (1773–1802), 2440

Ferdinand, Archduke of Austria (1754–1806), Leopold II's brother, 639

Ferdinand, Grand Duke of Tuscany, *see* Tuscany

Ferdinand, Princess, *see* Wurtemberg

Ferdinand IV, King of Naples (Ferdinand I, King of the Two Sicilies) (1751–1825), 728n, 1750, 1792, 1905, 1917, 1963n, 1993, 2099, 2483, 3036, 3204, 3236, 3277n, 3287, 3300, 3309, 3316, 3386n, 3478, 3669, 3714, 3827, 4079, 4231
recovers his territory in the South, 1964
Treaty with (1808), 3669

Ferdinand VII, King of Spain (1784–1833), 3649, 3689n, 3733, 3771, 3783, 4079

Ferdinand, Prince Augustus's servant at Berlin, 1997

Ferguson, 425

Ferguson, James (1735–1820), M.P. for Aberdeenshire (1790–1820), 2752n

Ferguson, Sir Ronald Craufurd (1773–1841), 3834, 4076n

Fergusson, Sir Adam, 3rd Bart (1733–1813), thought of for office of Surveyor-Gen. of Crown Lands (1791), 651

Fergusson, Robert Cutlar (c. 1768–1838), 1966

Fergusson, Miss, 4229

Feroner, M. de, 558, 1176

Ferrand, General, 911, 914

Ferrara, 1973

Ferraris, General, 882

Ferras, M., a Portuguese Deputy, 3907

Ferrers, Robert, Earl (1756–1827), 3966n

Ferrers, Lord, *see* Townshend, 2nd Marquess

Ferrier, Capt. John (d. 1836), 2496n

Ferrol, 2202–5, 2291, 2367

Fersen, Count (1719–94), 399

Ferson, Count (1755–1810), 399, 689

Ffrench, Sir Charles, Bart (d. 1784), 1666n

Ffrench, Rose, Baroness (d. 1805), 1666

Ffrench, Thomas, 2nd Baron (c. 1765–1814), 1666

Fidge, Prince William's surgeon, 363, 377

Field-Marshal, the, *see* Freytag and Wallmoden-Gimborn

Fiennes, Rev. Charles, Prebendary of Westminster, 441

Fife, 2nd Earl of (1729–1809), given a British peerage (1790), 604, 3966n

Filewood, Rev. Roger Thomas (?1745–1800), 257, 260
his father's Will, 257n

Fincastle, Visct, later 5th Earl of Dunmore (1762–1836), 2145

Finch, a convict, 655

Finch, Lady Charlotte (1725–1813), Governess to the Royal Nursery, 468
letters to, 2191, 2194

Finch, Rev. Daniel (1757–1840), Lord Aylesford's brother; Prebendary of Gloucester, 2653
his unfortunate shyness, 2665

Finch, Edward (1756–1843), 905, 1329, 2376, 2390, 2564

Finch, George (b. 1804), 2880

Finch, Lady Henrietta Constantia (1769–1814), 3027

Finch, Lady Maria Elizabeth (1766–1848), 3027

Finch, William (1691–1766), 3154

Finckenstein, Count Karl Wilhelm Finck von (1714–1800), Prussian Minister of State, 1863

Fingall, Earl of (1758–1836), leader of the Irish Catholics, 3665n

Finland, 399, 2425, 3568

Firth, a barrister, 3398

Fisgard [*Fishgard*], a 38-gun frigate, 3377, 3379n

Fisher, Lord St Helens' Secretary, 1194

Fisher, at Berlin, 1997

Fisher, Colonel, 1558

Fisher, Dr, 1723

Fisher, John, Commissioner of the Barrack Department, 3401

Fisher, John (1748–1825), 237–8, 2611, 2875n, 3031, 3567, 3764n, 4261
letter from, 3100
tutor to Prince Edward, 237n, 4301, 4301n
Bishop of Exeter, 2764, 3966n
Deputy Clerk of the Closet, 2875n
translation to Salisbury, 3462

Fisher, Professor, of Göttingen, 611, 756

Fishguard, 1503–6, 1510, 1512

Fisk, a stationer in Wigmore Street, 317n

Fitch, Lieut.-Col., 1192

Fitzgerald, Captain, the Duke of York's

Fitzgerald, Captain (*cont.*)
A.D.C. in Helder campaign, 1192, 2048, 2051, 2054n, 2063
Fitzgerald, Lord Edward (1763–98), 472, 1564, 1808, 1828n
Fitzgerald, Lieut.-Col. Henry Gerald, a natural son of Lady Kingston's brother, dismissed from Army, 1630
killed in a duel, 1630n
Fitzgerald, Mrs, 1630
Fitzgerald, Maurice, Knight of Kerry (?1771–1849), 3095, 3095n, 3665, 3834, 4109, 4135, 4188
Fitzgerald, Lord Robert Stephen (1765–1833), 558, 1167, 1783, 2998, 3647n
wants a Ribbon, 2998n
pension for, 3647
Fitzgerald, Wm. Vesey, 2nd Baron Fitzgerald (*c.* 1783–1843), 4037n, 4122, 4135, 4135n, 4205
Fitzgibbon, John, Lord, later Earl of Clare (1748–1802), Lord Chancellor of Ireland, 1158, 1201, 1211, 1686, 1820, 1824, 1839, 2111n, 2285, 2378, 2404, 2510, 2746, 2794
letter from, 2201
appointed Lord Chancellor of Ireland (1789), 511n
Pitt will not remove him, 1156n
speech answering Moira's (1798), 1688n
goes to London to discuss a Union, 1839, 1839n
efforts made to place him in Cabinet (1801), 2378n
his influence over Lord Hobart, 2378n
detests Charles Abbot, 2445n
death of, 2584–5
his Will, 2584
his children, 2584
views on gaming, 2584
Glenbervie's strictures on, 2584n
FitzHarris, Visct, later 2nd Earl of Malmesbury (1778–1841), 2752n, 2888n, 3613n
letters from, 2498n, 3068n, 3071n
letters to, 2794n, 3433n
appointed Under-Secretary of State, 3701n
resigns his Under-Secretaryship (1807), 3474n, 3510n
Fitzherbert, Alleyne, Lord St Helens (1753–1839), diplomatist, 3, 20, 221, 504, 583, 720, 731, 967n, 1043, 1100, 1125, 1140, 1152, 1176, 1183, 1194, 1917, 2386A, 2396, 2473, 2475, 2522, 2566, 2577n, 2639n, 3966n

letters from, 2867, 2985, 2992
appointed Amb. to Russia (1801), 2386, 2396
given a U.K. peerage (1801), 2386, 2386n, 2473, 2473A
recalled from Petersburg for health reasons, 2480
Fitzherbert, Mrs Maria Anne (1756–1837), in Paris, 193
Fitzjames, Duke of (1743–1805), 1148, 1148n, 1448
Fitzmaurice, Hon. Thomas (1742–93), 973
Fitzpatrick, Sir Jeremiah, 1134
Fitzpatrick, Lady Louisa, later Countess of Shelburne (1755–89), 4264
Fitzpatrick, General Richard (1748–1813), 1482, 1950, 2752n, 3254, 3283, 3787n, 3821
letter to, 2114n
Fitzroy, Charles (1762–1831), General, 2926, 3015, 3050
Equerry to Duke of York (1787), 384n
Equerry Extraordinary to the King (1801), 2320
Fitzroy, Lady Charles (1777–1810), death of, 4082
Fitzroy, Lord Charles (1764–1829), 920, 2882, 4082n
Fitzroy, George Ferdinand, later 2nd Baron Southampton (1761–1810), M.P. for Bury St Edmunds (1784–7), 55n
appointed Groom of the Bedchamber to Prince of Wales (1787), 365n
Fitzwilliam, Charlotte, Countess (1747–1822), 3224n
Fitzwilliam, 2nd Earl (1748–1833), 55n, 102, 894n, 1090n, 1190, 1192, 1205–8, 1210–11, 1223, 1235, 1480, 1678, 1686, 1983, 1916n, 2301n, 2339, 2346, 2381, 2743, 2743n, 2746, 2752n, 2774, 2812, 2839n, 3966n, 4205n
letters from, 1179, 1207n, 1243, 3193n
letters to, 774n, 1192n, 1199n, 1201n, 1205n, 1207n, 1208n, 1686n, 3177n, 3182n, 3193n, 3224n, 3380n, 3399n, 4074n
enters a protest about the Dissolution (1784), 83
appointed Lord Lieut. of Ireland, 1155–6, 1156n, 1158, 1177, 1498n
his changes in Ireland, 1198
instructions to, 1201, 1201n
recalled from Ireland, 1208, 2355
question of his remaining in Cabinet, 1208, 1208n, 1211, 1211n

II, 832–1662; III, 1663–2575; IV, 2576–3578

Frederick, Duke of York (*cont.*)

Frederick, Duke of York (*cont.*)

Frederick William III, King of Prussia (1770–1840), 688n, 714, 1610, 1636, 1639, 1641, 1648, 1661, 1670–1, 1673, 1675, 1689, 1696, 1719, 1848, 1863, 1867, 1888, 1908, 1920, 1943–4, 1954–5, 1967, 1973, 1985, 1997, 2000, 2082, 2127, 2395, 2651, 2655, 2658, 2662, 2731, 2744, 2870, 3134, 3209, 3313, 3313n, 3320n, 3324, 3330, 3342, 3356, 3369, 3380, 3393, 3454, 3456, 3459, 3468, 3478, 3504, 3524, 3581n, 3658, 3866n, 3901, 4033, 4042
  letters from, 1642n, 3166, 3303
  letters to, 1642, 3315
  a moral man, 2010
  and Hanover, 2395, 3298
Freeling, Sir Francis (1764–1836), Secretary to the G.P.O., 3062, 3536
  letter to, 1456
Freeman, Henry, a mutineer, 1613
Freiburg, 706
Fréjus, the Roman antiquities at, 648
Fremantle, Rear-Admiral Sir Thomas Francis (1765–1819), 1403
Fremantle, Sir William Henry (1766–1850), 1710, 3174n, 3373, 3444n, 3787n, 3804n, 3821n, 3934n, 4182
  letters from, 2622, 2922n, 3821n, 3828n, 3832n, 4076n, 4120n, 4122n, 4124n, 4142n, 4170n
  letters to, 2962n, 3178n
  his office of Deputy Teller of the Exchequer, 2622n
  joint Sec. of the Treasury (1806), 3178n
French invasion, the last (1797), 1503–7, 1507n
French prisoners removed to Lundy Island (1801), 2493
  behaviour of, 3827n
French West Indies, proposal to retrocede them (1797), 1518
French, *see* Ffrench
French, Arthur (*c.* 1764–1820), 2894
French, Wm. Fry, 3809, 3809n, 3812
Frere, 1710
Frere, Bartholomew (1778–1851), diplomatist, 2981, 3456, 3474n, 3896, 4035, 4088
  Minto's private secretary at Vienna, 2514
  Secretary of Legation at Lisbon, 2514
  Sec. of Embassy at Constantinople, 3459, 3459n
  Sec. of Embassy to Spain, 3896n
Frere, John Hookham (1769–1846), 2082n, 2297, 2940n, 3689n, 3746, 3781, 3783, 3822, 3842, 3860, 3860n, 3868

  letters from, 2101, 2173, 3456
  letters to, 2288n, 2752n, 4063n
  marries Lady Errol, 2010n
  recalled from Madrid, 2918, 2967, 2981, 3006
  becomes a P.C., 3006
  his Special Mission to Spain (1808), 3728, 3733
Freytag, Field-Marshal William von (1711–98), 90, 145, 172, 175, 212, 249, 254, 270, 273, 282, 315, 344, 350, 356, 433, 649, 679, 752, 806, 809, 832, 861, 863, 866, 868, 870, 875–6, 879, 882, 901, 905, 908–9, 914, 920–1, 924, 926, 932, 941, 943, 962, 966, 983, 1003, 1008, 1022, 1029, 1079, 1198, 1335, 1489, 1513, 1573, 1669, 4272, 4274, 4276, 4281–2, 4284, 4286, 4297, 4302
  defeat of, 933–4
  death of, 1669n
Friedberg (Bavaria), 2161
Friedland, battle of (1807), 3492n, 3510n
Friedricks, General, 4272
'Friends of the People' Association, 751, 751n, 991
Friesland, 367, 409, 2011, 2032, 2047
Frith, James, 575
Frith, William, a mutineer, 1599
Froberg [*sic*], 3467
Froggatt, William, 158
Frogmore, the Queen's house at Windsor, 665, 980, 985, 1247, 1388, 2488, 2626, 3494, 3494n, 3977n, 4005
Frognal, Queen visits, 1636
Front, Count St Martin de, the Sardinian Envoy, 2660n, 2956, 3539
Froya, Swedish frigate, 3547n
Fuenza, Duke de la, 2370
Fulham, 1784, 3821n, 3824n
Fullarton, Col. William (1754–1808), M.P. for Plympton Erle (1779–10); for the Haddington Burghs (1787–90); for Horsham (1793–6); for Ayrshire (1796–1803), 303, 438, 446, 1550
  a command recommended for (1801), 2452
  his service in India, 2454
  Commissioner of Trinidad, 2728, 2728n, 3163
  wants to be Governor of Madras, 2728n
  his diplomatic service, 2728n
Fuller, John (*c.* 1756–1834), 2752n, 3085, 3834, 4076, 4087
  creates a 'scene' in House of Commons, 4100, 4100n

(778)

Fundy, Bay of, 377

Furie, a captured Dutch frigate, 1869n

Furnes, 879, 891, 920, 941n, 943, 966, 977
Deanery of, 1158

Fürstenau, 2749

Fürstenbund, the (1785), 178, 235n, 241, 252, 258, 265, 270, 277, 295, 344, 429

Furth, 2300

Fyers, Capt., 2496n

Fyfield, Essex, 4056

Fynes, *see also* Fiennes

Fynes-Clinton, Henry (1781–1852), 3420, 3425

Gaeta, 2018, 3291n

Gage, Henry, Visct (1761–1808), 3966n

Gage, Captain J., 968, 977

Gage, John, Clerk of the Signet, 2777, 3194n

Gaines, a mutineer, 1591

Gainsborough, Thomas, painter (1727–88), 2985n

Galicia, 178, 3676–7, 3710, 3714, 3726, 3759, 3791, 3887

Gallini, Giovanni Andrea Battista (1728–1805), 263

Gallo, Marchese di, Neapolitan Minister at Vienna, 1777

Galloway, 7th Earl of (1736–1806), 619, 619n, 1983n, 3402, 3607n
letters from, 568, 2631
a Lord of the Bedchamber (1783), 10, 2631
wants a Scottish office (1788), 10n
elected a Scottish Representative Peer (1784), 78
wants a G.B. peerage (1790), 619n
resigns office of Lord of the Bedchamber, 2631
withdraws his resignation, 2640, 2640n
the King dislikes, 4258

Galloway, Lord Garlies, later 8th Earl of (1768–1834), 2631, 3259, 3402, 3612, 3966n

Galway Co., 1927n

Galway Volunteers, the, 1816n

Galway [Galwey], Rear-Admiral Edward (d. 1844), 3955

Galway, 4th Visct (1752–1810), 84, 4258
elected for York (1784), 55, 61
Wraxall on, 55n

Gambier, Vice-Admiral James (1723–89), 85

Gambier, James, Lord (1756–1833), 3075n, 3425, 3499, 3506, 3510n, 3519, 3523, 3525–6, 3527n, 3528, 3532, 3543, 3550 3652, 4111
a Lord of the Admiralty (1804), 2861
his U.K. peerage (1807), 3544
to command Channel Fleet, 3648
thought of as First Lord of Admiralty, 4142

Gambier, James, appointed Consul at Lisbon, 2649n, 2727n

Gandersheim, Abbess of (d. 1810), 142, 4123

Gange, Le, see *Le Gange*

Ganges, a 74-gun ship, 3375

Ganges river, the, 3577

Gantheaume, Rear-Admiral (1755–1818), 2453

Garbut, Mrs, 1025

Gardens, the Royal, 2464

Gardiner, General William (1748–1806), 741, 1279, 1826, 1935, 1935n, 2503

Gardner, Sir Alan, 1st Baron (1742–1809), 2504, 2716, 2959, 3075n, 3088, 3777, 3941, 3966n, 4084, 4143
refuses post of Commander-in-Chief at Portsmouth, 2024
thought of as Melville's successor, 3068n
resigns command of Channel Fleet, 3648

Garland, a 28-gun frigate, 1573n

Garland, Joseph, and the Poole election (1807), 3500n

Garlies, Lord, *see* Galloway, 8th Earl of

Garlike, Benjamin, diplomatist (c. 1766–1815), 1434, 1848, 1863, 1883, 2107, 2386A, 2386, 2480, 3365, 3369

Garnett, John, Dean of Exeter (d. 1813), 4076

Garter King of Arms, *see* Heard

Garter, Order of the, 290, 297, 301, 304, 306, 318n, 399, 428, 644–6, 710n, 774n, 782, 890, 926, 1093, 1093n, 1095, 1095n, 1190, 1473, 1479, 1772n, 1918, 1927, 1927n, 2428n, 2806, 2809, 2811, 2837, 2846n, 2854n, 2856n, 2906, 2963, 2994, 2994n, 3000, 3008n, 3009, 3014n, 3056–7, 3073, 3206, 3249, 3347, 3410n, 3414n, 3416, 4041, 4094, 4099, 4290n

Garth, Charles (c. 1734–84), 2132n

Garth, General George (d. 1819), 631, 989, 991, 2132n

Garth, John (1701–64), 2132n

Garth, Major-Gen. Thomas (1744–1829), 1573, 1632, 1769, 2132, 2717n, 2787, 2792, 3947, 3949–50, 3954, 3956, 3961, 3982–3, 4005, 4012, 4022, 4024, 4027

George III (cont.)

his bilious attack (1788), 456, 458n
at Cheltenham (1788), 460
visits Worcester (1788), 473
returns to Windsor, 474
King is unguarded at Cheltenham, 476
neuralgic pains in his head, 482, 482n
views on University discipline, 483
his illness (1788), 485–6
his recovery (1789), 490
remuneration of his physicians, 493n
Windsor his favourite residence, 495
contemplating a visit to Hanover (1789), 496
solicitude for advancement of learning, 497
'not a lover of novelties', 497
criticism of Lords Lieut. of Ireland, 497
on Lord Temple's 'base conduct' in 1783, 502
Spanish sheep sent to, 563
affords relief for Worcester debtors, 566
stoned by a lunatic (1790), 575
on Test and Corporation Acts, 580
dislikes granting offices for life, 602
attitude to French Canadians in Quebec, 655
Herschel's telescopes for, 656
gifts of Shetland sheep to (1791), 668
comments on the 'Church and King' riots (1791), 691
gifts of Spanish sheep to, 720
forced by Pitt to dismiss Thurlow (1792), 755
on Members 'of a venomous disposition', 757
proud of the 'glorious Constitution', 767
his opinion of Chauvelin, 773
difficulty in reading papers at night, 812
against peace negotiations, 871n, 1458n, 1467
on humbling France, 887
opinion of Elector of Hesse-Cassel, 921
on military objectives, 972
good opinion of Prince Adolphus, 1003
opinion of Lady Dunmore, 1012
on useless debates in Parliament, 1044
criticism of Prince of Saxe-Coburg, 1090
praises conduct of Duke of York, 1090, 1138
on the evidence of informers, 1129
alleged plot against his life (1794), 1129
on the 'supine' Dutch, 1138, 1180

on the shameful behaviour of the Dutch, 1189, 1193
criticises Fitzwilliam, 1206, 1210
on the Catholic question, 1208
queries about his Coronation Oath, 1215
refuses Prince of Wales higher rank, 1231
on Princess of Wales's amiable qualities, 1231
on Frederick William II of Prussia, 1246
praises Sir John Warren, 1263, 1263n
criticises Lord Bridport, 1284
objects to sending Foot Guards to West Indies, 1288
criticises Cabinet's strategy, 1288
signs Lord Titchfield's marriage licence, 1299
his farms, 1306
on British military objectives (1795), 1314, 1318n
his coach attacked (1795), 1319n, 1321
on his future son-in-law's brutal and unpleasant qualities, 1325n
hopes for collapse of France in 1796, 1337n
his opinion of Thomas Steele, 1345
against peace negotiations (1796), 1361, 1366n
his coach again attacked (1796), 1365, 1372–3
remarks on the slave trade, 1366n
Opposition's improper parliamentary activities, 1379
believes in submission in women, 1398
advice to Prince on breakdown of his marriage, 1405
and a threatened invasion, 1415n
on English slovenliness, 1477
on Fox's 'malevolence', 1480
on suspension of cash payments, 1507
on the insidious Prussian advances, 1507
against peace negotiations (1797), 1507
rejoices at Malmesbury's failure (1797), 1514
opposed to restoration of conquered possessions, 1518
views on Continental situation (1797), 1526n
disapproves of new peace negotiations (1797), 1528
attitude to naval mutinies (1797), 1530, 1532
Fox 'an open enemy of his country', 1537
and creation of Baronets, 1588

II, 832–1662; III, 1663–2575; IV, 2576–3578

(781)

George III (cont.)

and travelling on Sundays, 1595n
on appointment of Bishops, 1617
visits the Fleet, 1645
on the spread of mutiny, 1665n
is overloaded with boxes, 1670
his voluntary contribution (1798), 1674
contributes to Govt.'s election fund, 1674n
draws no money from Hanover, 1674n
on restoring discipline at Cambridge, 1733n
urges that Cornwallis should replace Camden in Ireland, 1755n
his attachment to Hanover, 1791
views on honours for Nelson, 1844, 1844n
views on choice of Irish Secretary, 1868n
gift of sheep to, 1879
loves plain dealing, 1894
on pensions for Under-Secretaries, 1903
views on State provision for Irish Catholic clergy, 1911n
views on the Irish Union, 1913n
criticism of Frederick William III, 1954
reviews the Kent Volunteers, 1976, 1976n
on Lady Augusta Murray's conduct, 2012
on the Convention of Alkmaar, 2066
gives financial assistance to the Cardinal York, 2082n
views on sheep rearing, 2093
Bonaparte's letter to, 2095, 2095n
on the 'Corsican tyrant', 2095
rejects Bonaparte's peace overture, 2095, 2097, 2097n, 2103n
criticises Sir Sidney Smith, 2120
views on peace terms (1800), 2193, 2232
refuses the Imperial Crown, 2274n, 2305
memo. on the Catholic question (1801), 2381
building programme at Kew, 2121
critical of Paul I, 2123, 2287
on parliamentary reform (1800), 2137n
on Prince Augustus's absurd ideas, 2145
Hadfield's attempt to assassinate (1800), 2153–4
his Spanish sheep, 2163
on Addington as Speaker, 2174
opposes Ministers' military plans, 2203, 2203n, 2204, 2204n, 2205, 2205n
on the Emperor's shameful pusillanimity, 2256, 2261
dislikes stale bread, 2276
on a diet of rice and potatoes, 2276
on preparing rice pudding, 2278
his new style and title, 2305
on appointing to Irish offices for life, 2309

difficulties in reading speeches from the Throne, 2328n
wild accusation against Dundas, 2329n
first signs of derangement (1801), 2329n
influences votes of Household on Catholic question, 2329n
hostility to Cath. eman., 2331, 2412n
in bed with a severe cold (1801), 2361
his illness in 1801, 2368n
on his coronation oath, 2381
high opinion of Lord St Helens, 2386n
thinks of Charles Yorke as Speaker (1801), 2397
advice to Lord Hardwicke as Lord Lieut., 2404, 2408
receives medical advice (1801), 2407
views on the government of Ireland, 2408
on the Irish established Church, 2408
veiled threat to retire to Hanover (1801), 2412n
and his bank account with Coutts's, 2433, 2441n
his Botanic Garden, 2464
on University appointments, 2479n
takes up Botany, 2501
his health, summer of 1801, 2451, 2510n, 2515n, 4242
interferes with ministerial patronage, 2510, 2515
his 'insight into men's characters', 2540n
his Annual Bounty List, 2571
patronage of science and the arts, 2577
views on the Speakership of the Commons, 2585, 2588n
views on the Peace (1802), 2597
suffers from rheumatism, 2651, 2662, 2828, 2830, 3017
and the great Public Schools, 2653
is sent 50 quill pens, 2659
gift of rare coffee to, 2675
Despard's plot to kill, 2676, 2680, 2683, 2710
blunder in reading Speech from Throne (1804), 2922n
Speeches from the Throne, see Speeches
hopes peerage will keep Melville quiet, 2684
thinks captious opposition in Parliament discreditable, 2684
not fond of receiving letters, 2690
his collection of drawings and pictures, 2694
salaries of his Equerries, 2717
his new house at Richmond, 2722

George III (cont.)

on Napoleon, 2735, 2764, 3003n

on evacuation of Hanoverian army (1803), 2754

and the invasion threat, 2786n, 2814

his villa at Richmond, 2799

prefers Gothic to Grecian style of architecture, 2799

his illness (1804), 2835n, 2856n

criticisms of Addington, 2838n

his recovery (1804), 2838n, 2839n

his eyesight (1804), 2839n

vetoes Fox's return to office (1804), 2839n

offers Yorke a peerage (1804), 2839n

his high opinion of Charles Yorke, 2839n

changed his Household (1804), 2843, 2843n

medical opinions on King's health (1804), 2855, 2864n, 2873n, 2894n, 2910n, 2930n

grateful to Addington (1804), 2857

opinion of Lord Hawkesbury, 2870n, 2973n

on the choice of Lords of the Admiralty, 2871

Lord Carlisle on the King's health (1804), 2873n

criticises Lord Pelham, 2987

financial provision for his daughters, 2905, 2905n

on the importance of the Cape, 2912

on the Irish militia, 2912

opinion of Addington, 2934n, 2983

suggests pension for Addington, 2934n, 2983

opinion of Lord Mulgrave, 2991n

his kangaroos, 2921

opinion of Lord Melville, 2908, 2912, 2915, 2939, 3040, 3047, 3069

on Peace of Amiens, 2912

his Scottish revenue, 2915

looking 20 years older, 2922n, 2927n

his glaring eyes, 2927n

and the Cathedral in Co. Down, 2928, 3035

wedding-day anniversary celebrated, 2930n, 2934n

opinion of Sheridan, 2934n

opinion of Bragge-Bathurst, 2934n

flies into a rage, 2934n

and appointment of a new Archbishop (1804), 2978, 2978n, 3014

portraits of, 2985, 3070, 3118

his spectacles, 3004n

sends Eldon a watch, 3013n

insists on nominating Archbishop of Canterbury, 3014

and the dispensing of patronage, 3014n

at Eton, 3014n

his Chaplains, 3031

opposed to his daughters' marrying, 3064

views on Melville's successor, 3068n

on the slave trade, 3086

on the Catholic question (1805), 3094

adverse to a union of parties, 3111n

cataracts in his eyes, 3119n, 3130, 3130n, 3132, 3132n, 3260, 3260n

his tour in West Country postponed (1805), 3119n

his last personally-written letters, 3120, 3139

opinion of Frederick William III, 3168

on future of his Electorate, 3168, 3207

prejudiced against Canning, 3180n, 3501n

changes in his Household (1806), 3182, 3185n, 3202n; (1807), 3410

his library in London, 3186

views on Windham's Army plan, 3221, 3223

on peace negotiations (1806), 3229

on disturbed state of Ireland, 3341

and the Catholic Relief Bill (1807), 3394, 3394n, 3395n

and formation of Portland Ministry, 3399n

well in health (1807), 3400n

views on seizure of Danish fleet (1807), 3501, 3501n, 3502

gives financial aid to his sons (1807–8), 3583

on impropriety of granting peerages to men without property, 3607

a lioness sent to, 3611

views on an expedition to Spanish America, 3649

on the grant to Maynooth College, 3657

views on sending military aid to Spain, 3669

his confidence in the Peninsular Generals, 3693

receives a present of merino sheep (1808), 3700, 3743, 3743n

more sheep offered (1809), 3896, 3903, 3924, 3924n

on peace terms (1808), 3743

accident to his carriage, 3765

II, 832–1662; III, 1663–2575; IV, 2576–3578

George III (cont.)
  his library, 3810
  declines the Golden Fleece, 3825
  criticises preparations for Walcheren expe-
    dition, 3910
  on matrimony, 3914n
  dislikes Lord Wellesley, 3925n, 3966n
  is given a white Indian tiger, 3926
  his affection for Portland, 3960
  and Catholic question (1809), 3960n, 3978
  his Jubilee to be celebrated, 3975, 3977n,
    4002, 4010, 4018
  on Canning's duel, 3966n, 3967n, 3970
  is critical of Addington, 3992, 4258-9
  donation for relief of poor prisoners, 4002,
    4010, 4026
  on Portland's death, 4018
  on the increasing cost of the War, 4041
  his opinion of Lord Gambier, 4142
  attitude to the Reversion Bill, 4146
  receives gift of October strawberries, 4233
George, Prince of Wales (1762–1830), 34, 58,
    103, 125, 146, 181, 181n, 209, 281, 292,
    305, 309, 313, 332, 334, 335n, 341n,
    342-4, 352, 354, 358, 364-6, 370, 393,
    431, 449, 488-9, 489n, 516, 520, 523, 573,
    618n, 683, 686, 705, 798-9, 805n, 807,
    901, 904, 940, 1203, 1224, 1257, 1374,
    1395-6, 1407, 1410, 1416, 1419, 1421,
    1495, 1500, 1596, 1652, 1678n, 1679n,
    1718, 1788, 1983n, 1990, 2009, 2014,
    2017, 2023, 2092n, 2141, 2145, 2149-50,
    2165, 2225, 2462n, 2564, 2794n, 2873n,
    2934n, 2993n, 2994, 3030n, 3063, 3130n,
    3164n, 3202n, 3242n, 3243n, 3464, 3571,
    3622, 3635, 3680, 3763n, 3909, 3977n,
    4005, 4016, 4019, 4021, 4247, 4261-4,
    4269, 4272, 4277n, 4301
  letters from, 1, 110, 113, 117, 161, 181n, 185,
    197, 289, 294, 300, 310, 314, 340, 358n,
    431n, 535, 537, 547, 606, 801, 805, 825,
    828, 830, 913, 941, 1126, 1207n, 1213,
    1222, 1254, 1356, 1374, 1405-6, 1411-12,
    1417, 1655, 1660
  letters to, 1, 110, 192, 192n, 310, 340, 358n,
    360n, 535, 537, 736, 825, 828, 830, 913,
    941, 1126, 1207n, 1231, 1296n, 1356,
    1374, 1405-6, 1417, 1607n, ?1983, 2148,
    2165n
  messages to, 115, 181, 184, 200, 292n, 313n,
    431n
  his 'terrible course of life' (1781), 4279
  takes seat in Lords, 1n
  votes for Fox's India Bill, (1783) 1, 16, 110

  strained relations with the King (1783), 16;
    (1784), 110
  appointments to his Household (1784), 34
  his racing stables, 58n
  plans to go abroad (1784), 110, 113-14, 117
  his 'reprehensible conduct', 110
  his expensive Fêtes at Carlton House, 110
  his 'irregular passions', 110
  his extravagance, 110
  seeks permission to live in Brunswick,
    113-14, 181
  his debts, 110, 114, 119-20, 122, 161, 181,
    181n, 184-5, 192, 192n, 193, 197, 200,
    222, 292n, 294, 300, 310, 314, 343, 352,
    354, 358n, 360, 360n, 362, 370, 753,
    753n, 789, 798, 805
  is forbidden to leave England, 115, 119,
    122, 181, 192
  his 'pride and vanity', 119
  claim to nominate Sheriff of Cornwall
    (1784), 146
  renews application to go abroad, 185
  anxious to join Mrs Fitzherbert in Paris
    (1785), 193, 200
  his 'natural turn for expense', 215
  his neglect of religious duties, 222
  his want of civility to the Queen, 222
  his total disobedience, 222
  dismissal of part of his Household (1786),
    311
  influenced by 'evil and designing people',
    326
  refuses to see the King (1786), 326
  dismisses Col. Hotham, 340, 342, 344
  his Privy Purse account, 360
  expenditure on his stables, 360
  re-establishment of his Household (1787),
    365
  list of Household appointments (1787),
    365n
  influenced by evil-minded people, 375
  his Regt (10th Light Dragoons), 449
  sees the King on his recovery (1789), 488
  conduct during Regency crisis, 547, 550
  has no wish to marry (1791), 688
  changes in his family, 723
  gives up the turf, 753n
  financial situation in 1792, 801
  question of a military command (1793),
    829
  becomes in effect, a Portland Whig (1793),
    830
  wants to serve on Continent (1793), 901
  debts of (1793), 904

George, Prince of Wales (*cont.*)
    drunk at a dinner party, 913n
    his marriage, 1110, 1126, 1176, 1540
    plan to liquidate his debts (1794), 1122
    an account of his debts (1794), 1142, 1142n
    asks for military promotion, 1213, 1230–1
    asks for a military command, 1213
    and the Colonelcy of 10th Dragoons, 1231
    asks to be made a Major-Gen. (1793), 1231
    debts of (1795), 1238, 1238n, 1250, 1253,
      1255, 1255n, 1371, 1374
    an Establishment for (1795), 1238, 1238n,
      1241, 1247, 1250–1, 1251n, 1255
    and the Datchet Canal Bill, 1241n
    his Riding House, 1329
    his Regiment, 1329
    pursued by his creditors, 1371
    breach with the Princess, 1393, 1398, 1405,
      1667
    plans for his daughter's education, 1405
    his representations to Pitt (1796), 1454
    asks to be made a General (1796), 1454
    Memo. on state of Ireland (mentioned),
      1500
    cannot have a separation from his wife,
      1667
    his Regiment, 1788, 1788n
    gives proxy in support of slave trade
      (1799), 1983n
    income from Duchy of Cornwall, 2608n
    his Petition of Right (1802), 2608n, 2625,
      2635, 2714n
    dismisses Lord Dartmouth, 2850n
    interview with the King (1804), 2934n
    his Garter, 3014n
    attends Nelson's funeral, 3153n
    and the formation of Grenville Ministry,
      3202n
    his friends, 3434n, 4105n
    and Brand's Motion (1807), 3434n
    at Weymouth (1809), 3964–5
    his carriage breaks down at Andover, 3964
    sends his carriage to Weymouth for
      Amelia, 4005, 4016, 4019, 4021
    attitude to Perceval Ministry, 4105n, 4133n
George, Capt., instructions to (1800), 2230,
    2232
George, Lady, *see* Murray
George, Sir Rupert, Bart, 2310
Georges, General, 2175n
German Association, the, *see* Fürstenbund, the
German Legion, the, King's, 2929, 2960,

3128, 3142, 3159, 3283, 3298, 3471, 3479,
    3509, 3554, 3576
German Universities, little discipline in the,
    282
Gertruydenburg, French capture (1793), 847,
    861, 866; 1114, 1189
Geusau, Col. de, 331
Ghent, 866, 943, 950, 966, 977, 979, 982, 1008,
    1066
Ghistelles, 966
Gibbon, Edward, (1737–94), 1463, 1463n
    his 'pestilent philosophy', 1463
    his writings corrupt Europe, 1463
Gibbs, a merchant in Naples, 1727
Gibbs, Sir Vicary (1751–1820), 2934n, 3061,
    3115, 3165, 3428, 3558, 3620, 3718,
    3786n, 3815, 3832, 3888, 3917, 4018,
    4034, 4076, 4093, 4126, 4130, 4133, 4142,
    4161, 4187, 4225
    letter from, 4034
    letter to, 4034
    Sol.-Gen. to Prince of Wales, 1660
    Attorney-Gen. (1807), 3418
Gibraltar, 341, 447, 574, 581, 614, 684, 696,
    705, 835, 872, 938, 944, 946, 1016, 1051,
    1300, 1326, 1767, 1775, 1787, 1792, 1803,
    1848, 1871, 1991, 2113, 2184, 2202, 2252,
    2256, 2413, 2572, 2603, 2972n, 3108,
    3142, 3164, 3266, 3543, 3554n, 3557,
    3576, 3587n, 3597, 3615, 3641, 3672,
    3689, 3689n, 3693, 3714, 3722, 3781,
    3800–1, 3844, 3844n, 3887n, 4002, 4143,
    4208, 4269, 4272, 4289, 4295
    Governor of, 2785, 3451
    the magazines at, 166
    high cost of living at, 594
    rapacious Jews at, 594
    garrison at, 9, 519, 581, 1285, 2972n, 3519,
      3591, 4060, 4088
    office of Receiver-General of, 3411
    Duke of Kent and Governorship of, 3597,
      3659
Gibraltar, the, an 80-gun ship, 419
Gibson, Rev. Robert (*c.* 1765–1840), 4056
Giddy, Davies (1767–1839), 3876, 3878,
    4074n, 4076n, 4122, 4122n, 4138n,
    4159, 4170, 4205
Gideon, Sir Sampson, 1st Bart, later Baron
    Eardley (1745–1824), 57n
Gies[e]well, a Page, 3951n
Gieswell, 295
    letters to, 379, 379n, 432, 656

Giffardière, M., *see* Guiffardière

Gijon, 3669, 3743n, 3810

Gilchrist, Lieut., 1506

Gilchrist, Captain, 1248

Gillespie, Sir Robert Rollo (1766–1814), 2916

Gillies, Adam, Lord Gillies (1760–1842), 3262n

Gillross, Mr, 126

Gilpin, Rev. William (*c.* 1726–1804), 2529

Gisborne, Dr Thomas (*d.* 1806), 1344–5, 1347, 1351, 2460n, 3164n, 3202, 4243
  letter from, 2407

Givet, 392

Gladiator, a 44-gun ship, 4050

Glamorganshire, 834, 1510

Glandevese, M. de, 674

Glandore, 2nd Earl of (1752–1815), 2285n, 2315, 3966n

Glasgow, 4th Earl of (1765–1843), 3966n

Glastonbury, James Grenville, Lord (1742–1825), 215, 1983n, 3666, 3966n

Glenbervie, Catherine Anne, Lady (1760–1817), appointed Lady of Bedchamber to Princess of Wales (1807), 3571
  attends a House of Commons' debate, 3628n

Glenbervie, Lord, *see* Douglas, Sylvester

Glencairn, 14th Earl of (1749–91), candidate for Scottish Representative Peerage (1784), 78

Glencairn, 15th Earl of (1750–96), a clergyman, pleading poverty
  letter from, 1281

Glentworth, Lord, *see* Limerick, 1st Earl of

Globe newspaper, 3665n

Glory, a 98-gun ship, 1628, 1859

Gloucester, 1505

Gloucester, Bishop of, *see* Beadon, Hallifax, and Huntingford
  Royal family at (1788), 476
  gaols in, 481

Gloucester, Dean of, *see* Luxmoore
  see of, 2620

Gloucester, Maria, Duchess of (1736–1807), 431n

Gloucester, Duke of, *see* William Frederick, Duke of Gloucester; and William Henry, Duke of Gloucester

Gloucester House, 431, 3135

Gloucester Lodge, Weymouth, 1106n, 1815n, 2246n, 2459n, 2657n

Gloucestershire election (1784), 55
  freeholders of, 4198

Glückstadt, 2758

Glyn, Sir Richard Carr, Bart (1755–1838), 1459, 1550, 2140

Goate, Edward (*d.* 1803), 2748

Goddard, Charles, Collector and Transmitter of State Papers (F.O.), 1316n, 2253, 2258

Godfrey, Capt., 1871

Godfrey, Jacob, mutineer, 2579

Godfrey, Rev. Luke, D.D., wants a Bishopric, 1666

Godolphin House, 3137

Gold coins, new (1801), 2456

'Gold Sticks' (Col. of the 1st House Guards [Life Guards from 1788]; Capt. of the Band of Gentlemen Pensioners; and Capt. of the Yeomen of the Guard), 10, 218n, 2023n, 2850,n 2889, 2889n, 2894, 2894n, 2897, 2897n, 2976

Golden Fleece, Order of the, 3825

Goldie, Lieut.-Gen. Thomas (*d.* 1804), 1757n

Golding, Edward (1746–1818), 3243

Golding, George, 2804n

Goldsmid, Abraham (*c.* 1756–1810), financier, 4232

Goldsmith, Oliver (1728–74), 484

Goldsworthy, Miss Martha Carolina ('Gooly,' 'Goully'), 4107

Goldsworthy, Lieut.-Gen. Philip (*c.* 1737–1801), 152, 215, 480, 500, 1549, 1646, 1723, 1801, 1804, 1823, 1875, 2042, 4302
  letter to, 501

Goliath, a 74-gun ship, 3540

Gooch, Thomas, 2804n

Gooch, Sir Thomas Sherlock (1767–1851), 3873, 4076, 4126, 4133

Goodall, Joseph (1760–1840), Headmaster, later Provost of Eton, 2559, 3622, 4041

Goodenough, George, Commissioner of Taxes, 1685

Goodenough, Samuel, Dean of Rochester and (1808), Bishop of Carlisle (1743–1827), 2638, 3567, 3624, 3764n
  tutor to Duke of Portland's sons, 2638n

Goody, J., a mutineer, 1605

Goold, Manager of the Opera House, 2693

Goold, Thomas, M.P. for Kilbeggan [I.] (*c.* 1766–1846), 2693n

Gordon, 'the rebellious exile from Utrecht', 409

Gordon, 4103

Gordon, Mr, his house on Kew Green, 3285

Gordon, a seaman, 3284

Gordon, Major, 4285

Gordon, Col. A., 137

II, 832–1662; III, 1663–2575; IV, 2576–3578

Gower, Susanna, Countess, later Marchioness of Stafford (*c.* 1743–1805), (?) 1997, (?) 1999, 2010, 3966n
  letters from, 7, 619, 1017
Graeme, Alexander, Admiral (*d.* 1818), 2485
Graevner [?], Prussian Minister at Petersburg, 1997
Grafton, 3rd Duke of (1735–1811), 55n, 483, 497, 890, 1223n, 1362, 3437, 3966n
  letter from, 2841
  refuses Cabinet office (1784), 483n
  resigns Lord Lieutenancy of Suffolk, 542, 542n
  thought of for office of Chancellor of Duchy of Lancaster (1791), 651, 654
  wants a Broad-Bottom Ministry (1804), 2841
Graham, Inspector of Hulks, 3538
Graham, Aaron, the Hatton Garden (later Bow Street) Police Magistrate (?1754–1818), 1544, 2318, 2598, 3826
  letter from, 3826
Graham, Major-Gen. Charles (*d.* 1800), 1265, 1277, 1464, 1819
Graham, D., clerk in Foreign Office, 3194
Graham, Earl, *see* Montrose, James, Duke of
Graham, Hepburn, master's mate on the *St George,* 3348
Graham, James (1753–1825), M.P. for Cockermouth (1802–5), 2752n
Graham, Marquess of, *see* Montrose, Duke of
Graham, Sir Robert, Baron of the Exchequer (1744–1836), 2804, 4227
Graham, Major-Gen. Thomas, Baron Lynedoch (1748–1843), 2752n, 4088, 4145
Gramont, Duc de, 3556
Grammont, 1090
Grampus, a 44-gun ship, 1584, 2510
Granard, Georgiana Augusta, Countess of (1749–1820), *letter from,* 3307
  looks like a prostitute, 3307n
Granard, 6th Earl of (1760–1837), 479, 3247, 3966n
  his four Members in Irish House of Commons, 479n
Grange, the, Prince of Wales's country seat near Alresford, Hants, 1406–7, 1411
Grant, Mrs [*sic*], 3804
Grant, Charles (1746–1823), 3595, 3878n, 4072
  letter from, 4072
Grant, General James (1720–1806), Governor of Stirling Castle, 2507
Grant, Sir James, 8th Bart (1738–1811), 1752

Grant, Sir Lewis Alexander, 5th Earl of Seafield (1767–1840), 670, 740
Grant, Sir William (1752–1832), 670, 1002, 1309n, 1333, 1922, 2023, 2158, 2189, 2327n, 2339
  elected member for Windsor, 1002n, 1076, 1309
  appointed a Welsh Judge, 1002n
  appointed Solicitor-General to the Queen, 1031, 1388
  resigns Court appointment, 1793n
  appointed Solicitor-General, 2023n
  appointed Master of the Rolls, 2357, 2357n, 2432
  Master of the Rolls, 2834, 2891, 3025, 3025n, 3068n, 3085, 3105, 3259, 3259n, 3327, 3371n, 3425, 3483n, 3596, 3794, 3832, 4102n, 4122, 4122n, 4138, 4138n
Grantham, 2nd Baron (1738–86), 20, 927, 3444n
Grantham, 3rd Baron, later Earl De Grey (1781–1859), 3444, 3643, 3787, 3966n
Grantley, 1st Baron (1716–89), 436, 440, 521n
Grantley, William, 2nd Baron (1742–1822), 1983, 1983n, 3966n
Granville, 983n, 4143
Granville-Leveson, *see* Leveson-Gower
Grasse, Comte de (1722–88), the French Admiral, 341
Grasse, Vicomte de, the Admiral's nephew, 341
Grassini, Guiseppa (1773–1850), the Italian singer, 2010
Grattan, Henry (1746–1820), 1158, 1205, 1205n, 1210, 1494, 1691n, 1644n, 3095, 3259, 3259n, 3485n, 3508, 3657, 3657n, 3665, 3665n, 3828, 3867, 3867n, 3878n, 4122, 4126, 4135, 4164, 4188, 4205
  struck off the Irish Privy Council (1798), 1828
Grattan, Major, 477
Graudenz, 3356
Grave (Holland), 847
Grave, M. de, 2106, 2106n
Gravelines, 923, 1760
Graves, 1997
Graves, Richard, Rear-Admiral, 2310
Graves, Admiral Sir Thomas (?1747–1814), 2429
Gravesend, 838, 1168n, 1424, 1554, 1560, 1632, 2779
Gray, 1717
Gray, 4264

II, 832–1662; III, 1663–2575; IV, 2576–3578

Grenville, William Wyndham (*cont.*)

1430, 1446, 1461, 1491, 1540, 1553, 1615, 1638–9, 1670, 1678n, 1708, 1713, 1727n, 1736n, 1768, 1775, 1787, 1790, 1792, 1803, 1817, 1889, 1937, 1973n, 1978, 1983n, 2007, 2011, 2020, 2027, 2097n, 2101, 2173n, 2199, 2203, 2235n, 2242, 2247, 2256, 2256n, 2278n, 2285, 2297n, 2322, 2327n, 2331, 2344n, 2346, 2350n, 2357n, 2371n, 2474n, 2689n, 2743, 2743n, 2746, 2812, 2839n, 2856n, 2906n, 2942n, 3008, 3079n, 3093n, 3094, 3146n, 3172n, 3174n, 3177n, 3178n, 3179n, 3180n, 3186, 3188, 3195n, 3218, 3220, 3228n, 3255n, 3259n, 3262n, 3286–7, 3298, 3298n, 3300n, 3337, 3351n, 3389–90, 3395, 3395n, 3410n, 3414n, 3416n, 3418n, 3483, 3496, 3510n, 3527n, 3589n, 3603, 3603n, 3612, 3674, 3787n, 3788, 3808, 3817, 3866n, 3873, 3873n, 3960n, 3966n, 3969n, 3978n, 3989n, 3992, 4041n, 4048n, 4049n, 4073, 4073n, 4074n, 4076n

letters from, 528, 530, 532, 539, 543, 545, 549, 555, 559, 565, 567, 575, 584–6, 590, 592, 600, 604, 607, 609, 612, 614, 618, 618n, 619n, 627, 630, 632, 636, 646, 652, 655, 657, 660, 664, 667, 669, 677, 690, 693, 697, 701, 703, 707, 720, 725, 730–1, 737, 741, 745, 750, 762, 762n, 766, 769, 777, 781, 783, 785, 792, 796, 800, 802, 810, 812, 822, 839, 841, 844, 858, 862, 871, 873, 886, 899, 912, 917, 931, 936, 940, 948, 951, 954, 967, 970, 981, 988, 1001, 1006, 1011, 1020, 1023, 1035, 1043, 1052, 1067, 1078, 1087, 1096, 1098, 1100, 1102, 1106, 1108, 1137, 1140, 1149, 1152, 1157, 1159, 1162, 1167, 1176, 1183, 1194, 1196, 1203, 1232, 1234, 1239, 1256, 1279, 1316, 1316n, 1318, 1325, 1337, 1367, 1381, 1387, 1418, 1423, 1428, 1434, 1440, 1443, 1445, 1447, 1449, 1451, 1455, 1458, 1466, 1469, 1474, 1481, 1484, 1486, 1516, 1525, 1527, 1529, 1538, 1563, 1585, 1593, 1598, 1600, 1614, 1624, 1647, 1656, 1671, 1673, 1675, 1682, 1689, 1693, 1698, 1704, 1719, 1721, 1725, 1731, 1734, 1762, 1777, 1782, 1791, 1795, 1798, 1814, 1827, 1841, 1843, 1845, 1850, 1854, 1879, 1883, 1886, 1890, 1894, 1898, 1908, 1908n, 1912, 1917, 1923, 1930, 1933, 1936, 1938, 1952, 1954, 1959, 1964, 1973, 1985, 1987, 1995, 2031, 2072, 2080, 2082, 2082n, 2095, 2097, 2100, 2103, 2107, 2120, 2123, 2142, 2176, 2181, 2193, 2202n, 2209, 2218, 2221, 2228, 2230, 2232, 2235, 2237, 2241, 2244, 2246, 2248, 2253, 2258, 2273, 2278, 2281, 2287, 2295, 2297, 2302, 2304, 2319, 2321, 2326, 2344, 2541, 3145n, 3175, 3177, 3190, 3219, 3224n, 3242, 3253, 3255, 3269, 3274, 3277, 3279, 3289, 3293, 3302, 3319, 3346, 3346n, 3361, 3364, 3374, 3384, 3401, 3411, 3485n, 3832n, 3978

letters to, 530, 532, 534, 543, 559, 559n, 567, 584, 586, 590, 592, 600, 604, 607, 609, 612, 614, 618, 627, 630, 632–3, 636, 646, 652, 655, 657, 660, 660n, 664, 669, 677, 690, 693, 701, 703, 707, 711, 718, 720, 725, 731, 741, 745, 748, 750, 766, 769, 792, 796, 800, 802, 812, 816, 844, 862n, 899, 912, 917, 931, 940, 959, 970, 981, 1023, 1052, 1078, 1087, 1098n, 1102, 1106, 1137, 1149, 1152, 1162, 1189, 1196, 1224, 1234, 1279, 1316n, 1340n, 1383, 1428, 1434, 1440, 1443, 1474, 1481, 1527, 1585, 1673, 1682, 1689, 1693, 1698, 1704, 1719, 1721, 1725, 1731, 1734, 1758, 1766, 1777, 1782, 1791, 1795, 1814, 1827, 1841, 1843, 1845, 1854, 1879, 1883, 1886, 1894, 1898, 1908, 1919, 1923, 1930, 1933, 1936, 1938, 1952, 1954, 1959, 1964, 1973, 1985, 1987, 1995, 2003, 2031, 2034, 2072, 2080, 2082, 2090, 2095, 2097, 2099, 2100, 2103, 2107, 2120, 2123, 2142, 2176, 2181, 2193, 2209, 2218, 2221, 2228, 2230, 2232, 2235, 2239, 2242n, 2244, 2246, 2248, 2253, 2261, 2273, 2278, 2281, 2287, 2295, 2297, 2302, 2304, 2319, 2321, 2326, 2344, 3145n, 3175, 3175n, 3177, 3211n, 3219, 3224n, 3226n, 3229n, 3242, 3277, 3279, 3289, 3298n, 3302, 3316n, 3319, 3319n, 3346, 3361, 3364, 3374, 3374n, 3394n, 3396, 3401, 3411, 3411n, 3416n, 3821n, 3828n, 3832n, 3975n, 4076n, 4120n, 4122n, 4124n, 4142n, 4170n

special Mission to Paris (1787), 380, 382, 382n

appointed Home Secretary (1789), 521n

peerage, 635

appointed Foreign Secretary (1791), 670n, 672

appointed Ranger of St James's and Hyde Park (1791), 729

offers to take Home Department (1794), 1090n

his dissenting Minute, 1233

his house in Cleveland Row, 2344n

resignation (1801), 2344

Grey, Charles (*cont*).
3683n, 3773n, 3785n, 3787n, 3797n, 3799n, 3804n, 3821n, 3824n, 3828n, 3873n, 3906n, 3966n, 3967n, 3969n, 3978n, 3989n, 4034n, 4092n, 4133n
his motion on dispute with Spain (1790), 644
motion for parliamentary reform (1797), 1559, 1559n
on restoration of French Monarchy, 2114n
allegedly elected leader of the Opposition (1800), 2288n
motion on the State of the Nation (1801), 2373
succeeds to the Earldom, 3584n
dislikes his father's promotion to the peerage, 2445n
declines the poll in Northumberland (1807), 3462
his disgust at politics, 3665n
overture from Perceval (1809), 3966, 3978, 3985
Grey, Sir George, Bart (1767–1828), son of 1st Earl Grey, 2409, 2413, 2642
Grey, Mary Elizabeth, Countess (1776–1861), 2301n, 3462n, 3590n, 3594n, 3876n
Grey, Major, 1048
Grey, Richard, the King's body coachman, 2854
Grey, Thomas de, *see* Walsingham, 2nd Baron
Grey de Wilton, Lord, *see* Egerton, Sir Thomas
Griffith, John, a mutineer, 1595
Grillion's Hotel, in Albemarle Street, 3549n
Grimshaw, Benjamin, 3917
Grimston, 3rd Visct (1747–1808), given a British peerage (1790), 604, 3966n
Grimston, 4th Visct, and 1st Earl of Verulam (1775–1845), 4073
Grimston, William (1750–1814), M.P. for St Albans (1784–90); for Appleby (1791–6), 604n
Grinfield, General William (*d.* 1803), 916, 920, 923, 960, 966, 1060, 2737, 2754, 2775, 2783n, 2792, 2810, 2813, 2827
death of, 2827n
Grisbach, 1013
Grisons, the, 1959, 1964
Grodno, 3342
Gronin, Lieut., 4290
Gröningen, 367, 409, 2011
Groom of the Stole, the, 1468, 3060

Grose, Sir Nash (1740–1814), Judge of the King's Bench, 618, 618n
Gross Aspern, 3926
Grosvenor, Earl, *see* Belgrave, Lord
Grosvenor, Richard Erle Drax (1762–1819), 2888, 2960n, 3965
Grosvenor, Thomas (1734–95), 89, 524, 589
a member of the St Alban's Tavern Committee (1784), 35n
Grosvenor, General Thomas (1764–1851), 2888, 3821, 4076, 4076n, 4105
Grosvenors, the, 3950
Grote, Baron de, 227
Grubenhagen (Hanover), 2736
Guadaloupe, warship, 4285
Guadaloupe, 341, 363, 1285, 1622, 2804, 3880
capture of (1794), 1051, 1074, 1098, 1098n, 1111
French recover (1794), 1098n
Guardian, the, 484
Guardian, a 44-gun frigate, 587
Guatemala, President of, 204
Guayaquil, 3391
Guelph [*sic*], Charlotte Georgina Mary Ann, a lunatic, 1369
Guercino, the painter (1590–1666), 2668
Guernsey, 983n, 1280, 1300–1, 1535, 1597, 1712n, 1748n, 2060, 2240, 2470, 2531, 3128, 3887, 4143
Guerrier, destruction of French warship, 1859
Guiffardière, Rev. C. de, 2294, 2611
Guildford, 2106n, 3479
Guilford, Anne, Countess of, wife of Lord North (*d.* 1797), 1492
Guilford, 1st Earl of (1704–90), the Queen's Treasurer, 325
Guilford, 2nd Earl of, *see* North, Frederick
Guilford, Francis, 4th Earl of (1761–1817), 2646, 3663, 3966n
Guilford, 3rd Earl of, *see* North
Guilford, Susan, Countess of, *see* Coutts
Guines, Duc de, 687
Guise, 957, 966, 995
Guise, Sir John (1733–94), 481
Gun, Reverend Mr, 1009
Gundersheim, *see* Gandersheim
Gunn, Major, 48, 153, 178
Gunning, Sir George William (1763–1823), M.P. for Hastings (1802–6), 2752n
Gunning, Miss, 665
her mother, 665, 665n
marries Stephen Digby (1790), 578
Gunning, Major-Gen. John, 665
Guntersblum, 1322

(792)

II, 832–1662; III, 1663–2575; IV, 2576–3578

Harman & Hoare, Messrs, 1151

Harper, 3660

Harper, Deputy Clerk of the Council of the Duchy of Lancaster, 3188

Harpy, an 18-gun sloop, 2046

Harrington, 3rd Earl of (1753–1829), 1041, 1365, 2376, 2461n, 3156, 3167, 3696, 3702n, 3829n, 3966n, 4034
  letters from, 2596, 3696
  moves the Address (1787), 416, 416n

Harrington, Sir Edward, Sheriff of Bath, 1249

Harrington, Jane, Countess of (c. 1754–1824), 1365n

Harris, a convict, 287
  his wife, 287

Harris, Lieut., 1646

Harris, James (1709–80), father of Lord Malmesbury, 2446
  a new edition of his *Works*, 2446n

Harris, Sir James, 1st Earl of Malmesbury (1746–1820), 3n, 127, 148n, 250, 256, 266n, 302, 323, 367, 382, 390, 403, 406, 408, 437, 450–3, 455, 457, 688n, 753n, 1043, 1052, 1056, 1078, 1078n, 1090, 1096, 1098, 1176, 1183, 1203, 1223–4, 1228, 1246, 1461, 1469, 1983n, 2346n, 2367n, 2474n, 2498n, 2600n, 2782n, 2888n, 2897n, 2899n, 2902n, 3000n, 3298n, 3394n, 3409n, 3444n, 3448n, 3449n, 3535n, 3537n, 3713n, 3756n, 3966n
  letters from, 2232n, 2446, 2794n, 3107, 3613n
  letters to, 2474n, 3068n, 3071n, 3613n
  peerage for, 451, 451n
  his income (1788), 451
  at the Duke of York's wedding, 714
  his Mission to Berlin, 967
  his Mission to Brunswick, 1239
  Mission to France, 1451, 1455, 1458, 1467, 1484, 1514, 1576, 1598, 1600, 1620
  in poor health, 2031, 2031n
  asks for an Earldom, 2232n
  and the Foreign Secretaryship (1801), 2365n; (1804), 2991n
  his seat, Park Place, near Henley-on-Thames, 3107

Harris, Thomas (d. 1820), 158
  proprietor of Covent Garden Theatre, 2092

Harrison, John (1738–1811), 670, 1342, 1480, 1519, 2359, 2888

Harrowby, Elizabeth, Lady (c. 1729–1804), 2966n, 2991n

Harrowby, Lord, *see* Ryder, Dudley

Harry, Sir, *see* Neale

Hart, Mr, 3520

Hartford Bridge, near Odiham, Hants, 1270, 1277, 1815n, 3943–4, 3947, 4005

Hartlebury, 3121
  Library at, 3127

Hartley, Winchcombe Henry (?1740–94), 647, 751
  and the Berkshire election (1784), 62

Harvey, a Weymouth shopkeeper, 3995

Harvey, Capt., *see* Hervey

Harvey, Rear-Admiral Sir Eliab (1758–1830), 3210, 3889, 4076n, 4111

Harvey, Felton, *see* Hervey, Felton Lionel

Harvey, Admiral Sir Henry (1737–1810), 327, 1282, 1307, 2227, 2310
  destroys a Spanish squadron, 1523

Harward, Rev. Charles, Dean of Exeter (d. 1802), 2653n

Harwich, 1141, 1178, 1456, 1555, 1567n, 1568, 1570, 2396, 2519, 2779, 3506, 3509, 3511, 3547, 3654, 3933, 4037n

Harwich election (1791), 671; (1803), 2689, 2689n

Hastenbeck, battle of, 4276

Hastings, Sir Charles (1752–1823), natural son of 10th Earl of Huntington, 548n

Hastings election, 158, 3876, 3876n

Hastings, Warren (1732–1818), 137, 253, 372, 425, 508
  Charges against (1786), 290; (1788), 436
  Trial of, 829n, 883

Hats, duty on, 1390

Hatsell, John (1743-1820), 19n, 168, 2984
  his *Precedents of Proceedings in the House of Commons*, 168

Hatsell, Mrs, 2665

Hatton, 1435

Hatton, Edward Finch, Under-Sec. of State, 2786n

Hatzfeldt, Comte de (Elector of Mainz's Envoy at Berlin), 546

Haughty, a 14-gun sloop, 1741n

Haugwitz, Count Christian August Heinrich von (1752–1832), 1078, 1078n, 1670, 1673, 1693, 1704, 1863, 1908, 1948n, 1954, 1973, 2651, 2655, 2744, 2749, 3246, 3256

Havana, 2229

Haverfield, Thomas (d. 1804), gardener at Hampton Court, 2975

Hawgill, Capt., 778

Hawick, 4229

Hawke, a servant, 227, 318
Hawke, 2nd Baron (1744–1805), 434
Hawkesbury, Lord, *see* Jenkinson
Hawkesworth, John (?1715–73), 372
Hawkey, Lieut. (*d.* 1809), 3928
Hawkins, Major, 1766n
Hawkins, Charles, surgeon, 468
Hawkins, Sir Christopher (1758–1829), 2881n
  letter from, 1565
Hawkins, Edward, and the Saltash election
  (1784), 158
Hawley, William Tooley, Lieut.-Col., 1657
Hawthorne, Charles Stewart (*c.* 1760–
  c. 1830), 3095, 3095n, 3243
Hay, Charles, Lord Newton, Scottish Judge
  (1747–1811), 3145n, 3203
Hay, James, Lieut.-Col. (1795), Col. (1803),
  Major-Gen. (1810), 1657
Hay, Lieut.-Col. (*d.* 1799), 2027, 2037
  his family, 2027, 2037
Hay, Lord [G.B.], and Earl of Kinnoull [S.]
  (1751–1804), 1983, 1983n
Hayes, Horace, Preceptor to the Princes, 312,
  578
  Commissioner of Taxes, 1685
Hayes, Sir John Macnamara (1750–1809),
  1331
Hayes, Mrs, 312
Hayman, Miss, 3202n
Haymarket Theatre, the, 1107
Hayne, *see* Heyne
Haynes, Charles, a Poor Knight of Windsor,
  2613
Haynes [Haines], John, highwayman, 1927
Hazard, an 18-gun sloop, 3542
Headfort, Earl of Bective, later 1st Marquess
  of (1757–1829), 2315, 3966n
Heard, Sir Isaac (1730–1822), Garter King-
  at-Arms, 318n, 646, 725, 1415, 1872,
  3825
Heart of Oak, an armed ship, 4269
Heath, Rev. Dr George (*c.* 1748–1822), *letter
  from*, 2559
  thought of for a Canonry of Windsor
    (1800), 2196
  appointed to a Canonry, 2272
  his family, 2272n
  application for Bishopric of Bangor, 2272n
  his character, 2272n
  application for an Eton Fellowship, 2259
Heathcote, Sir Gilbert, Bart (1773–1851),
  1546, 2881n

Heathfield, 1st Baron, *see* Eliott, George
  Augustus
Heathfield, Francis Augustus, 2nd Baron
  (1750–1813), 3966n, 4118
Hebe, a 36-gun frigate, 242, 264, 363, 1291
Heberden, William, the elder (1710–1801),
  2949
  his house at Windsor, 2949n, 4001, 4005,
    4008–9, 4012
Heberden, William, the younger (1767–
  1845), the King's physician, 2930n,
  2949n, 3164n, 4238n
  on the King's health, 2855, 2864n, 2934n
Hebrew Professorship at Oxford and Cam-
  bridge, 1870
Hector, a 74-gun ship, 4269
Hector, Comte d', 1294
Hedemann, Capt., Prince Adolphus's Aide-
  de-Camp, 1063, 1335, 2236
  his daughters, 2236
Hedon election (1784), 158
Hedsor, Lord Boston's seat near Beaconsfield
  (Bucks), 279
Heerdt, Baron de, 3249, 3901, 3918, 3921
Heilbronn, 1588, 2015, 2041, 2075
Heine, Professor, *see* Heyne
Helder, expedition to the (1799), 1979n, 1994,
  2011, 2013, 2016, 2016n, 2018n, 2020,
  2027–30, 2032, 2037, 2054n, 2059–60,
  2065, 2065n, 2066, 2066n, 2077n
Heligoland, 3339–40, 3539n, 3831, 3878,
  3901, 3926n, 3931
  capture of (1807), 3528, 3963
Helsingborg, 3356n, 3539n
Helston election (1801), 2585n
Helvoet, 840, 1114, 1168–9, 2704
Helvoetsluys, 840, 845, 861, 1141
Helyar, Wession, Sheriff of Cornwall (1785),
  146n
Hemp production in Ireland, 2301
Henderland, Alexander Murray, Lord (1736–
  1795), death of, 1227
Henderson, 3965
Henderson, Anthony (*c.* 1763–1810), M.P.
  for Brackley (1803–10), 2752n
Henley, Lord, *see* Eden, Sir Morton Frederick
Henneberg, 4274
Henniker, Sir John, Bart and 1st Baron
  Henniker (1724–1803), of Stratford
  House, 1276
Henniker, John, 2nd Baron (1752–1821), 446
Henry VIII (1491–1547), 1870

Hepburn, Dundas's Secretary, 928
  letter to, 928n
Heralds' Office, the, 4130
Heras, M. de las, 3728
Herbert, Charles (1743–1816), *letter from*, 3619
  wants office of Master of the Robes, 3619
Herbert, Elizabeth, Lady (*d.* 1793), 500, 506
Herbert, Henry Arthur (*c.* 1756–1821), 3665, 3787n, 3797, 3834, 4074, 4122, 4126, 4135, 4177
Herbert, George (1788–93), Lord Herbert's son, 500–1
Herbert, George Augustus, Lord, *see* Pembroke, 11th Earl of
Herbert, Thomas, a convict, 655, 657
Herbert, William (1778–1847), 3373
Hercule, a French 74-gun ship, 1735, 1859
Hereford, 1505
  see of, 2684
Herefordshire Militia, the, 1607
Hermann, General, 1979n
Herminegeldo, Spanish warship, 2496
Hermione, a 32-gun frigate, 111, 2186, 2210, 2472, 2512, 2590, 2607, 3312
  re-captured from Spaniards, 2105
Heron, a convict, 584
Herrenhausen, 1335, 1573, 4272
Herries, Charles, 1236
Herries, John Charles (1778–1855), 3966n
Herries, Colonel, 1554
Herschel, Sir William (1738–1822)
  letters from, 236, 369, 379, 379n, 432, 570, 656, 2577
  his plans for a new telescope, 236, 369, 379, 379n, 432, 570, 570n
  his brother, 236
  his sister, 369, 570
Hertford, 1329
Hertford election (1790), 605
Hertford, Francis, 1st Marquess of (1718–94), 890, 3056
  letter from, 319
  letters to, 84n, 319
Hertford, Francis, Lord Beauchamp, later 2nd Marquess of (1743–1822), 228, 819, 831, 899, 912, 936, 938, 940, 948, 1001, 1066, 3230, 3966n
  letters from, 84n, 313n, 3182, 3187
  offers to undertake Embassy to Madrid, 967
  appointed Master of the Horse (1804), 2854
  his dismissal (1806), 3182, 3182n, 3187
  given the Garter (1807), 3182n, 3416

Hertfordshire, 812
Hertfordshire Militia, the, 851
Hertsberg, M. de (1725–95), Prussian War Minister, 252, 455, 485
Hervey [Harvey], 327
Hervey, 708
Hervey, Felton Lionel (*d.* 1785), Remembrancer of the Exchequer, 248
Hervey, John Augustus, Lord (1757–96), Envoy to Tuscany, 531, 860, 897, 1015
  given a pension on his retirement, 1096
Hervey, Lord, *see* Bristol, 5th Earl of
Hervey, Rear-Admiral, *see* Harvey
Hervilly, Comte d' (*d.* 1795), 1258, 1263n, 1294
Heseltine, James, King's Proctor (*d.* 1804), 1010, 2885
Hesse, Prince of, 223
Hesse-Cassel, unrest in (1789), 551, 1526
Hesse-Cassel, Prince Charles of (1744–1836), 1894
Hesse-Cassel, Frederick II, Landgrave of (1720–85), 97, 256, 297, 334, 4272, 4304
Hesse-Cassel, Prince Frederick of (1747–1837), 4304
Hesse-Cassel, Landgravine of (1745–1800), 97, 4304
Hesse-Cassel, Princess Wilhelmina of (1726–1808), 714n
Hesse-Cassel, William VIII, Landgrave of (1682–1760), 344
Hesse-Cassel, William IX, Landgrave of, later Elector of (1743–1821), 256, 344, 351, 355, 387, 387n, 546, 551, 583, 834, 921, 940, 983n, 1210, 1287, 1481, 1943–4, 2692, 3134, 3495, 3871, 4272, 4304
  to be made a K.G., 297, 318n
  detested by his subjects, 334
  his pride and obstinancy, 349
Hesse-Darmstadt, Louis X, Landgrave of (1753–1830), 838, 979, 983n, 986, 1198, 1287
  Subsidy Treaty signed with, 1198n
  strength of his contingent, 1287
  Court of, 4304
Hesse-Homburg, Caroline, Landgravine of (1746–1821), 2704
Hesse-Homburg, Frederick V, Landgrave of (1748–1820), 2704
Hesse-Homburg, Frederick, Hereditary Prince of, later Landgrave (1769–1829), wishes to marry Princess Augusta, 2704
Hesse-Philipstal, 376

Hessian troops arrive in England from New York (1783), 9, 19n, 48
in the Flanders campaign, 921
Hetch, Frederick von (1758–1838), 3059
Heureuse, destruction of French warship, 1859
Hewborough, Robert, a mutineer, 1595
Hewett, General Sir George (1750–1840), 3373
Hewgil [*sic*], Captain, 859
Heyland, Catherine, a convict, 466
Heyne, Professor (1729–1812), 284, 306n, 320, 480, 484
Heytesbury, 14n
Heywood, a grenadier, 778
Heywood, James Modyford (1730–98), appointed a Lord of the Admiralty (1783), 15
Heywood, Captain Peter (1773–1831), 3937, 3955
Heywood, Samuel (1753–1828), 3389
Hibbert, Alderman George (1757–1837), 2094, 3380, 3444, 3605, 3787n, 3834
Hibernia, a 110-gun ship, 3691
Hickes, Robert, Commissioner of Excise Appeals, 3411
Hières, *see* Hyères
Higgins, George, a shopman, 1129, 1136, 1305n
High Wycombe, 2462
Higham Ferrers, 55n
Highlands of Scotland, condition of, 232
Hildesheim, Bishopric of, 1432, 2651, 2655, 2662
Hill, Captain, 778n
Hill, Francis, Secretary of Legation at Copenhagen, 3524
and at Rio, 3581
Hill, Dr George (1750–1819), 928
letter from, 928n
Hill, Sir George Fitzgerald, 2nd Bart (1763–1839), 2124n, 2301, 3095, 4135
Hill, Sir John (?1716–75), 127
Hill, Noel, Lord Berwick (1745–89), his peerage (1784), 55
Hill, Sir Richard, Bart (1733–1808), 89, 438, 838, 878, 1180, 1180n
denied a peerage (1784), 55n
Wraxall on, 89n
Hill, Rowland, 1st Visct (1772–1842), General, 3844
Hill, William, 3rd Baron Berwick (1773–

1842), diplomatist, 3038–9, 3706, 3708, 3827
Hillsborough, the new church at, 3035
Hillsborough Castle, 1540
Hilsea Barracks, near Portsmouth, 9
Hinchcliffe, John (1731–94), Bishop of Peterborough, 483
Hinchingbrooke, Visct, later 5th Earl of Sandwich (1744–1814), 1983n, 3447, 3674
letters from, 3185, 3185n
letters to, 3185, 3185n
retains office of Master of the Buckhounds (1783), 15
resigns the Buckhounds (1806), 3185
Hinchingbrooke, Visct, later 6th Earl of Sandwich (1773–1818), 3622, 3966n
Hinckel, Baron, 1324
Hinckley, 3647, 3970n
Hind, a 28-gun ship, 999
Hind, Rev. Mr, Duke of Marlborough's domestic chaplain, 3635
Hippisley, Sir John Coxe (1747–1825), 1561, 1561n, 1562, 2082, 2752n, 3665, 4076n, 4164
letters from, 1568, 1760
Hirschau, 2488
Hislop, Sir Thomas (1764–1843), Lieut.-Governor of Grenada, 2740
appointed Lieut.-Governor of Trinidad, 2740
Hoare, Harriet, Lady (*c.* 1775–1851), 4037
Hoare, John, a mutineer, 1834
Hoare, Messrs (bankers), 985, 1475
Hobart, George Vere (1761–1802), Lieut.-Governor of Grenada, 2618
death of, 2691
Hobart, Robert, 4th Earl of Buckinghamshire (1760–1816), 584, 751, 994, 997, 1983n, 2332, 2357n, 2365n, 2374, 2378n, 2456n, 2461n, 2474, 2482, 2493, 2498, 2500n, 2612, 2629, 2645, 2700, 2743, 2765n, 2777n, 2789, 2792, 2794, 2808, 2825, 2827, 2838n, 2852n, 2857, 2865n, 2876, 2902, 3003, 3006n, 3417, 3966n, 3989n, 4092, 4241
letters from, 2394, 2412, 2416, 2452, 2454, 2456n, 2483, 2495, 2497, 2505, 2508, 2525, 2586, 2588, 2597, 2618, 2646, 2656, 2669, 2674, 2691, 2711, 2723, 2728, 2737, 2740, 2754, 2760, 2775, 2783, 2785, 2810, 2813, 2819, 2829, 2840, 2847, 2853, 2902n

Hobart, Robert (*cont.*)

letters to, 2383n, 2394, 2412, 2416, 2452, 2454, 2468, 2483, 2497, 2498n, 2505, 2508, 2525, 2597, 2618, 2646, 2656, 2669, 2674, 2691, 2711, 2723, 2728, 2737, 2740, 2754, 2760, 2775, 2783, 2785, 2792, 2810, 2813, 2819, 2829, 2840, 2847, 2850, 2853, 2902n, 3487n

Governor of Madras, 1908n

offered the Petersburg Embassy (1799), 1908, 1908n

Secretary of State for War (1801), 2365, 2365n

and Governor-Generalship of Bengal (1801), 2365n

as Governor of Madras, 2365n

is Wellesley's 'implacable enemy', 2365n

given the Colonial business (1801), 2489

Fitzharris's poor opinion of, 2498n

memo by, *re* the Army of Reserve, 2823

is of little use to Pitt (1804), 2847n

Chancellor of the Duchy (1805), 2853n, 2984, 2984n, 2987, 2991

his seat in the Cabinet, 3003n

refuses office of Captain of the Yeomen of the Guard, 2850n, 2852–3

Charles Long's opinion of, 3006n

not appointed First Lord of the Admiralty, 3075n, 3081n

withdraws his resignation (April 1805), 3081n

resignation of (July 1805), 3115n

excluded from Grenville's Cabinet (1806), 3175n

criticises Copenhagen expedition, 3589

Hobhouse, Sir Benjamin (1757–1831), 1509, 1521, 1546, 1654, 1664, 1724, 2189, 4074n, 4138n

office promised for, 2984, 2984n

Hoburgh, a Page of the Backstairs (*d.* 1761), 1708, 1754

Hoche, an 84-gun French warship, 1838n, 1862, 2124n

Hoche, General (1768–97), 1263n, 1277, 1277n, 1514

his expedition to Ireland, 1494n

Hockless, James, a mutineer, 1591

Hodgson, General John (1757–1846), 3179

Hodgson, Field-Marshal Studholme (1708–98), 3179

Hodgson, Rev. Mr (*d.* 1810), 4238

Hodson, Dr Frodsham, Principal of Brasenose College (1770–1822), 4032n

Hoghton, Sir Henry (1728–95), 838

Hogreve, Captain, 285, 551, 576, 588, 613, 859, 4272, 4274, 4284, 4288, 4290, 4295

his mother, 285

Hohenheim, 1582, 1747

Hohenlinden, battle of (1800), 2292

Hohenlohe-Ingelfingen, Frederick Louis, Prince of (1746–1818), 882, 896, 986, 990, 992–3, 995, 1210, 3320n

Hohentweil, 1988, 1993, 2025, 2147, 2151, 2544

Hohnhorst, M. de, Chamberlain to Duke of Brunswick, 3298, 3298n

Holdernesse, Mary, Countess of (?1721–1801), 4302

letter to, 2110

death of, 2540

Holdernesse, Robert, Earl of (1718–78), 4264

Holding, Peter, a mutineer, 1591

Holdsworth, William, a mutineer, 1613

Holford, George Peter (1767–1839), 4138n

Holland, Definitive Peace Treaty with (1784), 80, 83

Holland, 367, 376, 382, 387n, 390, 392, 395, 403, 406n, 408, 414, 417n

expedition to, contemplated (1787), 398; (1799), 1979, 1979n; (1805), 3158

conquest of, completed, 1210

Treaty with (1787), 1361

Treaty with (1794), 967n

Holland, Elizabeth, Lady (1770–1845), 3594n, 3657n, 3665n, 3773n, 4073n, 4076n

Holland, Henry Fox, 1st Lord (1705–74), 3n

Holland, Henry (?1746–1806), the architect, 805

letter from, 732

Holland, Henry, M.P. for Okehampton (1802–6), 2752n

Holland, Henry Richard, 3rd Lord (1773–1840), 1691n, 1983, 1983n, 3296n, 3356n, 3386n, 3584n, 3612, 3613n, 3614, 3614n, 3966n, 4142n, 4195, 4195n

Hollingbury, Lieut., 1506

Hollingsworth, Mr, 124

Holloway, Major-Gen. Sir Charles, of the Royal Engineers (1749–1827), 2703, 3401

Holloway, Admiral John (c. 1742–1826), 363, 3214

Holloway, William, a convict, 276

Holme-Sumner, George, *see* Sumner

Holmes, Sir Henry, 8th Bart, 3844n

Holmes, Sir Leonard Thomas Worsley (1787–1825), elected for Newport (Isle of Wight), 4099

Holmes, Robert, a mutineer, 1599
Holstein, 2260, 3340, 3497, 3501, 4037
Holstein-Oldenburg, Prince Augustus of (1783–1853), 3278, 3495, 3495n
Holstein-Oldenburg, Prince George of (1784–1812), 3278, 3495, 3495n
Holwood, near Bromley (Kent), Pitt's country seat, 912, 1611n, 1764n, 1985, 2166, 2204
Holyhead, 1357n, 1503, 1995n
Holyrood Palace, 1357, 1995, 2512, 3547, 3552, 3556n, 3623n
Home, Sir Everard (1756–1832), 4193, 4196, 4199
Home Circuit, the, 1968
Home Office, division of work of the, 2777n, 2790n, 2794
Homer, the 'Grenville', 2487
Hompert(?), 1464
Hompesch, Baron Ferdinand de, 2423, 2480
Hondschoote, 932–3, 935, 943
Honiton, 2672
Honywood, Filmer (c. 1745–1809), elected M.P. for Kent (1784), 69n
Honywood, Sir John (c. 1757–1806), 2881n
Hood, Admiral Sir Samuel, 1st Visct (1724–1816), 363, 417, 446, 470, 698, 907, 925, 934n, 942, 942n, 945, 969, 1031n, 1053, 1160, 1229, 1244, 1329, 1983, 3108, 3966n, 4283, 4292
  letters from, 91, 4291n, 4293, 4296, 4298
  his Westminster contest (1784), 64n; (1788), 467, 472, 472n
  Government pays his Westminster election expenses, 64n
  appointed Governor of Greenwich Hospital, 1382
  cr. Visct, 1404
Hood, Sir Samuel, 1st Bart (1762–1814), 2783n, 2931, 3157, 3375, 3526n, 3540, 3604, 3721, 3728, 3733, 3797, 4143
  his K.B., 2892–3, 2927n
  loses his right arm, 3308
Hope, the Amsterdam banker, 843
Hope, General Sir Alexander (1769–1837), 2005n, 2752n, 3818, 4118
  Governor of the Royal Military College, 3945n
Hope, Charles, Lord Granton (1763–1851), 2779, 2894, 3147–8
  letter from, 3262n

appointed Lord Advocate (1801), 2403, 2418, 2684n
Hope, General, 404
Hope, Henry (d. 1789), Lieut.-Governor of Quebec, 543
Hope, General John, later 4th Earl of Hopetoun (1765–1823), 607, 2005, 3685, 3687
Hope, Lieut.-Gen. Sir John (1765–1836), 3727, 3791, 3795, 4091
  his K.B., 3802, 3853
Hope, Rear-Admiral Sir William Johnstone (1766–1831), 363, 419, 2018, 3425
  resigns seat at Admiralty Board (1809), 3840
Hopetoun, Elizabeth, Countess of (1750–93), 921
Hopetoun, 3rd Earl of (1741–1816), 607, 619, 921n, 3262n, 3417n, 3425n
  elected a Scottish Representative Peer (1784), 78
  his brothers, 3262n
  promised a U.K. peerage by Pitt, 3628n
Hopkins, John, a mutineer, 1834
Hopkins, Richard (c. 1728–99)
  declines a seat at Treasury Board (1789), 544
  resigns seat at Admiralty Board (1791), 686
  becomes a Lord of the Treasury (1791), 686
  resigns Treasury office, 1498, 1498n
Hoppner, Richard Belgrave, clerk in the Foreign Office, 3194
Horne, a British agent employed abroad, 3336, 3388, 3863, 3878, 3901, 3940
Horne, Rev. George (1730–92), Bishop of Norwich, 600
Horne, Brigadier-Gen. (d. 1794), 137, 1053
Horner, Francis (1778–1817), 3613n, 3895
Horse Guards, the, 2796, 3245
Horsham, 1801, 2415
Horsley, Samuel, Bishop of Rochester (1733–1806), 1983n, 2418
Hotham, Anne Elizabeth (d. 1862), wife of Rev. Frederick Hotham, 3033
Hotham, Sir Beaumont (d. 1771), 1499
Hotham, Sir Beaumont, 2nd Baron Hotham (1737–1814), 3108
  letter from, 3033
Hotham, Frances (d. 1836), 3033
Hotham, Rev. Frederick (?1772–1854), 3033

Howe, Sophia Charlotte, Baroness (1762–1835), 458n, 2129, 2217

Howe, Sir William, Visct Howe (1729–1814), Earl Howe's brother and Lieut.-General of the Ordnance, 1207, 1207n, 1298, 1557–8, 1616, 1709n, 1755n, 2444
  letters from, 1811, 1871
  declines office of Constable of the Tower (1795), 1207n

Howe family, the, 541

Howick, Visct, *see* Grey, Charles, 2nd Earl Grey

Howley, Wm., Archbishop of Canterbury (1766–1848), 3916, 4007
  becomes Prof. of Divinity at Oxford, 4014

Howth, Earl of (1730–1801), 1345

Hoya, 1610, 4290, 4295

Hoymb, Capt. of the Hanoverian Horse Guards, 172, 215

Huddleston, Major, 930

Hudson, Joseph, a mutineer, 1613

Hughes, a carpenter at Woolwich, 2663

Hughes, a mutineer, 1591

Hughes, John, informer, 1828

Hughes, R., theatre manager at Weymouth, 2042

Hughes, Admiral Sir Richard (?1729–1812), 293

Hughes, Rev. Thomas (?1757–1833), 441, 441n, 461, 480

Hughes, Rev. Mr, of Cheltenham, 481

Hughes, Quarter-Master of the 17th Light Dragoons, 2216

Hugo, Colonel in Hanoverian army, 90

Hugo, M. de, 3459

Hugues, 1622

Hulks, the, 2590
  improved state of, 2598, 2708, 3538

Hull, 1172, 1292, 1616, 3506, 3509, 3547

Hulse, General Sir Samuel (1747–1837), 311, 340, 723, 920, 923, 964, 1060, 1752, 2030, 2526, 3135
  appointed Comptroller of Prince of Wales's Household (1784), 34
  re-appointed (1787), 365n
  appointed Treasurer (1791), 723

Hume, David (1711–76), the historian, 484

Humphrys, George, 3404, 3404n

Humphrys, George, jun., 3404, 3404n

Humphrys, Josiah, 3404, 3404n

Hungary, 1648

Hungary, King of, *see* Francis II, Emperor

Hungary, Maria, Queen of (1745–92), 601

Hunt, Captain, 1570

Hunt, Joseph, a Commissioner of the Transport Office, 1826

Hunter, Elizabeth, 2313

Hunter, John (1728–93), surgeon, 335

Hunter, John, diplomatist, 2649, 2998

Hunter, John (1738–1821), Governor of New South Wales, 1510

Hunter, Lieut.-Gen. Peter (*d.* 1805), 1765, 2882, 3174

Huntingdon, 10th Earl of (1729–89), 548

Huntingdon, 15n

Huntingdonshire, 15n, 23n

Huntingford, Dr George Isaac (1748–1832), Bishop of Gloucester (1802), and Warden of Winchester, 2620, 2643
  thought of for a Bishopric (1800), 2196, 2196n
  not to be appointed Bishop of Bath and Wells, 2617

Huntly, Lord Strathavon, later Earl of Aboyne and 9th Marquess of (1761–1853), 527, 3243n

Huntly, Marquess of, later 5th Duke of Gordon (1770–1836), 2048, 2051, 3417n, 3425, 4091, 4105n
  appointed Lord-Lieut. of Aberdeenshire, 3642

Hünubre, 1574

Hurd, Richard (1720–1808), 237, 273, 297, 4295
  letters from, 152, 234, 238, 257, 260, 299, 320, 381, 460, 480, 566, 739, 1463, 1635, 1876, 2044, 2062, 2069, 2076, 2098, 2133, 2160, 2168, 2275, 2294, 2360, 2436, 2545, 2710, 2715, 2762, 2764, 2814, 2868, 2875, 3021, 3099, 3119, 3121, 3127, 3132, 3139
  letters to, 260, 315n, 2764, 2814, 3119n
  invited to Windsor, 152
  his Warburton lectures, 1463n
  on the authenticity of Book of Daniel, 1463n
  on Gibbon's 'pestilent philosophy', 1463
  feeble physical and mental condition, 2545
  his nephew, 3099
  death of, 3668

Hurst, Robert (*c.* 1750–1843), 2894n

Huskisson, Mrs (*d.* 1856), pension for, 1903

Huskisson, William (1770–1830), 1331, 1368, 1736n, 1903, 2066, 2070n, 2077n, 2087n,

II, 832–1662; III, 1663–2575; IV, 2576–3578

II, 832–1662; III, 1663–2575; IV, 2576–3578

Liston, Sir Robert (1742–1836), diplomatist, 180, 275, 748, 2658, 2754, 2759
offered the Mission to America (1795), 1316n
Litchfield, Henry Charles (1756–1822), the Treasury Solicitor, 3411
Little, Thomas, a seaman, 3329
Littlehales, Sir Edward Baker (1765–1825), Under-Sec. of State [I.], 2515n, 2540, 2575
Littlehampton, 1784
Littlejohn, Capt. (d. 1795), killed in action, 1229
Littleton, near Staines, 3493n
Littleton, see Lyttleton
Littleton, Sir Edward, 4th Bart (c. 1725–1812), 1463, 2044, 2881n
elected for Staffordshire (1784), 64
Littleton, Edward John, 1st Baron Hatherton (1791–1863), 1463n, 2084n, 2153n
Lively, a 38-gun frigate, 1229n, 3062
Liverpool, Catherine, Countess of (1744–1827), 2392n
Liverpool, Earl of, see Jenkinson
Liverpool, 1833, 3124, 3288, 3401, 3617, 4149n
Mayor of, 2779
Livings, number of Church, in England and Wales, 3888
Livingston, E., 1744, 1768, 1771, 1791, 1803, 1813, 1947, 1971, 1986, 1994, 1998–9, 2012, 2014, 2017, 2023n, 2145, 2149
letters from, 1692, 1695, 1727, 1727n, 1750, 1767, 1775, 1787, 1803, 1817, 1848, 1863, 1867, 1888, 1920, 1943, 1992, 2010, 2145
letters to, 1792, 1888, 1888n, 1992, 1997, 2000
to attend Prince Augustus, 1654
his allowance of £500 p.a., 1654
disliked by Prince Augustus, 1945
Livonia, 399
Lizard, the, 1263
Llandaff, Bishop of, see Watson, Richard
Llewenny Hall, near Denbigh, 973
Lloyd, 158
Lloyd, Mr, 1740n
Lloyd, Rev. Evan (d. ?1843), 4120, 4122
Lloyd, Francis (c. 1748–99), 1459
Lloyd, Professor the Rev. Henry (c. 1764–1831), Petition from, 1870
letter from, 1870n
Lloyd, Sir James Martin (1762–1844), 2894n

Lloyd, John (c. 1749–1815), 471, 1643
appointed a Welsh Judge, 540
Lloyds, 715
Lobb, Capt. Wm. Granville, of H.M.S. *L'Aimable*, 1830
Lobo, Don Rafael, 3728
Loch, James, William Adam's nephew (1780–1855), 4122n
Lock, Charles, (1770–1804) 2393
Lockhart, John Ingram (1765–1835), 3834, 4076, 4126, 4138
Lockhart, Mrs, 4264
Lockley, a convict, 287
Lockman, Rev. Dr John (d. 1807), 3580
Loeken (? Lokeren), 866
Löev, M. de, 1573
Loftus, John, Lord, later 2nd Marquess of Ely (1770–1845), 3174
Loftus, William, Gen. (?1751–1831), 418, 1583, 1776, 1819, 2135, 2367, 3256, 4087, 4105, 4124, 4138, 4159
Lombard, Mr, 2655
Lombardy, 1403, 2763
London, a 98-gun ship, 2382, 3244
London, the 'dirty rabble' of, 473
London, Addresses from Corporation of, 1321, 1483, 1855, 2038, 2153, 2265, 3191
London, 2625
a horse patrol for, 3013
London, Addresses from City of, 21, 495, 1360, 1453, 1491, 1499, 1625, 1629, 2153, 2625, 3193, 3437, 3447, 3735, 4020, 4047, 4051, 4051n, 4055n, 4061, 4153
Address from merchants of, 24
Address from Clergy of, 497
Livery of, 1332, 4153
rioting in (1810), 4126–7
London, Bishop of, see Porteus
London, the City Remembrancer of, 1360, 1629, 2254, 2257n, 2262, 2625, 3191, 3632, 4061; see also Tyrrell
London Corresponding Society, the, 1129, 1305n, 1324n, 1405n, 1594, 1691, 1800
London election (1784), 158
London Evening Post, the, 158
London Gazette, 320, 508, 626, 700, 715, 754, 758, 764n, 767n, 1048, 1090, 1202, 1229, 1329, 1336, 1341, 1360, 1365, 1404, 1422, 1453, 1460, 1514n, 1628, 1630, 1748, 1780, 1844, 1846, 2018n, 2041n, 2215n, 2425n, 2499, 2535n, 2663, 2961, 3436, 3438, 3545n, 3627, 3629, 3894

II, 832–1662; III, 1663–2575; IV, 2576–3578

London, Lord Mayor of, *see* Ainslie, John; Clark, Richard; Combe, H. C.; Curtis, Sir William; Eamer, Sir John; Flower, Sir Charles; Perring, Sir John; Perchard, Peter; Price, Sir Charles; Skinner, Thomas; and Watson, Sir Brook

London, Petitions to Parliament from, 878

London, Regiment of Volunteers, 1973n, 2797

London, Sheriffs of, 1235, 1453, 1483, 1499, 1547, 1629, 1855, 2038, 2153, 2254, 2257, 2257n, 2262, 2625, 3191, 3632, 3694, 4061

Londonderry Co., 2301

Londonderry, 1st Marquess of (1739–1821), 1426, 2315, 2575, 3591, 3966n

does not want a U.K. peerage, 2315n

Long, Charles, Lord Farnborough (1760–1838), 740n, 1914n, 1943, 2099, 2339n, 2341, 2752n, 2877n, 2884, 2894n, 2914n, 2931, 3014n, 3137, 3243, 3373n, 3637n, 3786n, 3829, 3832–3, 3844n, 3876n, 3906n, 3966, 3998n, 4045n, 4102n, 4105n, 4162, 4182

letters from, 2339n, 3006n, 3449n, 3966n, 4007n, 4074n, 4076n

appointed Joint Secretary of the Treasury (1791), 651

proposed Mission to Paris (1792), 812

financial position in 1801, 2339n

attitude to Catholic emancipation, 2339n

resignation (1801), 2339n

a Lord of the Treasury (1804), 2844n

opinion of Vansittart, 3006n

appointed Irish Secretary (1805), 3115n, 3140

appointed Joint Paymaster-General, 3416

offered Secretaryship at War, 3992

declines Chancellorship of the Exchequer, 4007

Long (later, North), Dudley (1748–1829), 446n, 2367n

Long, Rev. William, Canon of Windsor, Charles Long's brother (*d.* 1835), 2931

Long, Mrs Amelia, daughter of Sir Abraham Hume (1772–1837), 2339n

Longcroft, Capt., 1506

Longfield, Capt., nephew of Visct Longueville, 2290, 2301, 2318

Longford, Co., 1358

Longford Militia, the, 1816n

Longford, 2nd Baron (1743–92), 4275

Longford, 4th Earl of (1774–1835), 2315, 3966n

Long Island, 4285

Longleat, royal family visits (1789), 552

Longman, Thomas (1730–97), publisher, 158

Long Reach, 1554, 1557

Longueville, Visct (1734–1811), 2301, 2315, 3966n

Lonillac, M. de, 322

Lonsdale, Sir James Lowther, Earl of (1736–1802), 1983n

Lonsdale, Earl of, *see* Lowther, Sir William

Lonsdale, Lord, *see* Lowther

Lonsdale party, the, 358n

Loo, Anglo–Prussian Treaty (1788) signed at, 450n, 455

Lorch, 2419

Lord Advocate of Scotland, *see* Dundas, Robert, of Arniston; Hope, Charles; Erskine, Henry; and Colquhoun

Lord Advocate of Scotland, position of, 3262n

Lord Chamberlain, jurisdiction of the, 3060

Lord Chamberlain's Staff and Gold Key, 2839n, 2843, 2846n, 2849, 2856

Lord Chief Baron of Scotland, *see* Montgomery, Sir James William; and Dundas, Robert

Lord Privy Seal of Scotland, the £3,000 a yr sinecure office of, 2144n

Lord Steward, *see* Chandos, Duke of; and Townshend, George, Earl of Leicester

Lord Steward, change in the office of, 2645, 2856, 2856n

jurisdiction of the, 3060

Lords, House of, *see* House of Lords

L'Orient, 839, 1263, 1307, 3308n, 3880, 3885, 4143

Lorraine, 689

Lostberg, Gen., 344

Lostwithiel election (1784), 158

Lothian, 5th Marquess of (1737–1815), 'Gold Stick', 218

elected a Scottish Representative Peer (1784), 78

his 'Gold Stick' taken away (1789), 218n

Lottery Bill (1810), 4201

Lottery tickets, forging of, 2340

Lottum [*sic*], Gen., 388

Loughborough, 2243

Loughborough, Alexander Wedderburn, Baron, later Earl of Rosslyn (1733–1805), 226, 266n, 436, 440, 774, 827, 831, 1010, 1065, 1117, 1148, 1198, 1221, 1227, 1242, 1250, 1255, 1301, 1313, 1317, 1329, 1374, 1406, 1411, 1413, 1435, 1488,

Loughborough (*cont.*)

1533n, 1561n, 1564, 1608, 1678n, 1680n, 1692, 1746, 1771, 1790, 1792, 1800, 1836, 1966, 1983n, 2010, 2012, 2020, 2023n, 2149, 2158, 2235, 2239, 2242, 2285, 2302, 2304–5, 2308n, 2309, 2333, 2341, 2349n, 2350, 2354

letters from, 1103, 1122, 1215, 1253, 1352–3, 1395, 1405n, 1407, 1414, 1968, 1974, 1981, 1990, 2009, 2014, 2017, 2023, 2145, 2150, 2235n, 2308, 2329, 2342, 2363

letters to, 1253, 1328, 1468n, 1667, 2009, 2014, 2023, 2049, 2056, 2138, 2145, 2150, 2308, 2329

is to support Government (1792), 807

to become Lord Chancellor (1792), 807n, 829, 831

paper on the King's Coronation Oath, 1215

opposes Datchet Canal Bill (1795), 1241n

cr. Baron Loughborough (Oct. 1795), with special remainder to his nephews, 1317

his resignation of the Great Seal, 2357, 2357n

and the Presidentship of the Council, 2357n

becomes Earl of Rosslyn (1801), 2357n, 2481n

Louis, the Dauphin, son of Louis XVI, the titular Louis XVII (1785–95), 689, 1259, 1282n

Louis XIV (1638–1715), 548, 680, 824

Louis XV (1710–74), 824, 951

Louis XVI (1754–93), 341, 399, 423, 503, 546, 558, 560, 800, 820, 824, 914, 961, 1268, 2633

flight to Varennes, 687, 689

execution of, 833

Louis XVIII (1755–1824), ('Monsieur'), 689, 707, 1100, 1282n, 1357, 1673, 1673n, 2936, 3556, 3561, 3565, 3623, 3698

expected arrival in England, 3547, 3549, 3552, 3556n

his family not welcome in England, 3623, 3623n

Louis Philippe, Duke of Orleans (1747–93), 114, 1148n, 2102n, 2106

visits England, 558, 560

Louis Philippe, Duke of Orleans, later King of the French (1773–1850), 2102, 2106, 2106n, 3468, 3634, 3692, 3693n, 3714, 3714n, 3717, 3936, 4023, 4228, 4305

lives at Twickenham, 2102n

his marriage, 4023n, 4079

his sister Adelaide (1777–1847), 3693n, 3714n

Louis, Rear-Admiral Sir Thomas (1759–1807), 3308, 3332

Louisa, Princess (1724–51), daughter of George II, 309

Louisa, Queen of Prussia (1776–1810), 1610, 1689, 1867, 1905, 1905n, 1920, 1943–4

Louisburg (Wurtemberg), *see* Ludwigsburg

Louise, wife of *Monsieur* [Louis XVIII] (1753–1810), 689, 3623, 3644

Louisiana, 2941

Louth, Co. by-election (1804), 2922n

Louvain, 816, 1038

Louvre, the, 2668

Lovaine, Lord, later 5th Duke of Northumberland (1778–1867), 2752n, 3420, 3474n

Loveden, Edward Loveden (*c.* 1750–1822), 446, 644, 647, 1086

Löw, Lieut.-Col. [de], 914, 920, 1326

Lower Canada, Province of, 787, 794, 3412, 3763

Lower Saxon Circle, the, 3570

Lowestoffe, a 32-gun frigate, 574, 574n, 1186

Lowndes, William, Commissioner of Taxes, 1685

Lowndes, William (*c.* 1768–1840), 4124n

Lowten [Lowton], an attorney, 2693, 3500n

Lowth, Dr Robert (1710–87), Bishop of London, 412, 2617

Lowther, Sir James, 5th Bart, Earl of Lonsdale (1736–1802), 534, 2638n

Lowther, James (1753–1837), M.P. for Westmorland (1775–1812), 2752n

Lowther, Sir John, 1st Visct Lonsdale (1655–1700), 3670

his *Memoirs of Reign of James II*, 3670

Lowther, Sir John, 1st Bart (1759–1844), M.P. for Cumberland (1796–1831), 2752n

Lowther, Sir William, Visct Lowther, later Earl of Lonsdale (1757–1844), 2638, 2746, 3399, 3400, 3410, 3414, 3567, 3622, 3635, 3670, 3966n, 3969n, 4010, 4076, 4105n

letters from, 3406n, 4310n, 3414n

letters to, 2922n, 2973n, 2991n, 3014n, 3025n, 3136n, 3395n, 3399n, 3400n, 3410n, 3440n, 3449n, 3734n, 3832n,

Lowther, Sir William (*cont.*)
    3896n, 3966n, 4007n, 4010n, 4074n,
    4076n, 4101n, 4109n, 4124n
    seconds the Address (1796), 1450
    prepares to take non-Departmental office
      (1807), 3410n
    and the Garter, 3410n, 3414n, 4041n
    given an Earldom, 3421
    will support Perceval Ministry, 3969
Lowther, William, Visct, later 2nd Earl of
    Lonsdale (1787–1872), 3635
    letters from, 4010n, 4109n, 4124n
    offered seat at Admiralty Board, 4010
Lowther Castle, 3969n
'Loyalty' Loan (1796), 1475, 1475n, 1478
Lozun, M. de, 4285
Lubbock, Sir John, 1st Bart (1744–1816),
    2894n
    his Baronetcy, 3219
Lübeck, 3334, 3393
Lublin, 3390
Lucan, 2nd Earl of, *see* Bingham, Richard
Lucas family, the, 60
Lucchesini, Marquis de, the Prussian Minister
    (1751–1825), 2393
Lucchesini, M. de, Chamberlain to King of
    Prussia, the bosom friend of Frederick
    the Great, 351
Lucerne, 973, 2059
Ludlow, 1505
Ludlow, Major-Gen. Sir George James, 1st
    Baron Ludlow (1758–1842), 2931
    his K.B., 2944, 2964, 3063
    appointed Equerry to Prince of Wales
      (1784), 34
Ludovick, *see* Orramin
Ludwigsburg, near Stuttgart, 385, 1578, 1612,
    1625, 1663, 1668, 1690, 1706, 1716, 1738,
    1743, 1746, 1763, 1780, 1809, 1835, 1860,
    1873, 1944, 2015, 2041, 2075, 2115, 2121,
    2147, 2214, 2419, 2478, 2544, 2551, 2568,
    2677, 2686, 2722, 2887, 3059, 3118
Lukin, Rev. George William, Prebendary of
    Westminster and Dean of Wells
    (*c.* 1746–1812), 1932, 3412
Lulworth Castle, 2677
Lumsdaile, Lieut.-Gen. James (*d.* 1807), 581
Lumsdale, *see* Lumsdaile
Lunardi, Vincent (1759–1806), *letter from*,
    124
    his balloon ascent (1784), 124
Lundy Island, French prisoners removed to
    (1801), 2493
Lüneburg, 215–6, 227, 247, 269–70, 282, 284,

    301, 301n, 306, 338, 351, 355, 361, 370,
    1372, 1895, 4290, 4290n
Lunéville, 2232, 2297, 2544
Luran, James, a mutineer, 1591
Lushington, Edmund Henry (1766–1839),
    Puisne Judge in Ceylon, 2363
Lushington, Sir Stephen (1744–1801), created
    Bart (1791), 669
Lushington, Stephen (1782–1873), 3380
Lushington, Stephen Rumbold (1776–1868),
    3834
    seconds the Address, 3787
    would have liked office (1809), 3787n
Lushington, Alderman William (1747–1823),
    1323, 1480, 1546, 1658
Lusi, Count (1735–1815), Prussian Minister
    in London, 308
Luton, 894
Luttrell, James (? 1751–88), Lord Carhamp-
    ton's brother, appointed Surveyor-Gen.
    of Ordnance (1784), 57
    'the best of that family', 57
Luttrell, John Fownes (1752–1816), pro-
    prietor of Minehead, 654n
Lutwidge, Admiral Skeffington (?1737–
    1814), 2485
Luxemburg, 816
    capitulation of, 1259
    Prince of, 357
Luxmoore, John, Bishop of Bristol (*c.* 1756–
    1830), 3462n, 3465, 3469, 3673
    translated to Hereford (1808), 3673
Luzac, 409
Luzerne, Marquis de la (1737–91), the French
    Ambassador, 423, 429, 503, 558
Lyceum, the, 2294
Lydiard, Captain Charles, 3377, 3379n
Lyell, a messenger, 2735n
Lygon, William, 1st Earl Beauchamp (1747–
    1816), 3180, 3183, 3966n
    letters from, 3784, 3784n
Lygon, William, 2nd Earl Beauchamp
    (*c.* 1782–1823), 3180
Lymington, 1289
Lymington election (1784), 158
Lynch, frigate, 845
Lynch, Sub.-Lieut., 2976
Lynden, Baron de, Dutch Minister in London
    until 1788, 148, 437n, 452
Lyons, 959, 1760
Lyons, Philip, soldier, 3124
Lys, river, 920, 926, 977, 982, 998, 1059–60,
    1064
Lyte, Henry (*d.* 1791), 311, 340, 360, 362, 683

(820)

Macqueen, Robert, Lord Braxfield (1722–99), 528

Madagascar, 3874

Madan, Spencer (1729–1813), Bishop of Bristol and of Peterborough, 758, 1025, 1983n, 3966n

Maddon, Lieut.-Col., 2068

Madeira, 3062, 3573, 3641, 3801
   British occupation of (1801), 2452, 2454, 2508, 3104; (1807), 3526, 3556, 3573n, 3589, 3871n
   capture of (1808), 3587–8, 3621

Madeweis (?), M. de, 1648

Madocks, William Alexander (1773–1828), 2894n, 3873, 3876, 3876n, 3878, 3878n, 3890, 3904

Madras, Presidency of, 18, 73, 149, 286, 372, 477, 530, 734, 779n, 2581n, 3015n, 4057, 4060, 4072
   a Lieut.-Gen. to be sent to (1784), 67
   a letter from (1784), 137

Madrid, 378, 538, 731, 967, 2649, 2957, 2967, 2972n, 2981, 2998, 3006, 3456, 3597, 3649, 3725, 3763

Magdalen islands, the, 327, 385

Magdeburg, 355, 361, 2749, 3320, 3334, 3866n

Magestie, a messenger, 1620

Magna Carta, 4201

Magnificent, a 74-gun ship, 536, 541

Mahadaji Sindhia, the Maratha Prince (d. 1794), 253

Mahmud II (1785–1839), Sultan of Turkey (1808–39), 4121

Mahon, Lord, later 4th Earl Stanhope (1781–1855), 3380

Mahony, Denis, seaman, 4115

Maida, 3291n

Maidenhead, 1009

Maidstone, 1691n, 1717, 1720
   treason trials at, 1691n, 1726, 1740, 1742

Mainwaring, William (1735–1821), 2648, 2849n, 3243n
   elected for Middlesex (1784), 72, 158

Maisonblanche, 922

Maitland, Col. Frederick (1763–1848), Lieut.-Governor of Grenada, 2999, 3001

Maitland, James, Visct, later 9th Earl of Lauderdale (1784–1860), 3351n

Maitland, Lieut.-Gen. Sir Thomas (1759–1824), 670, 682, 735, 744, 751, 819, 838, 1044, 2171, 2175n, 2184, 2888, 2888n, 3407, 4057
   and Governorship of Ceylon, 2979

Maitland, Lieut., R.N., 1229n

Majendie, Rev. Henry William (1754–1830), Preceptor to Prince William, 194, 2076, 2169, 3984n, 4265–7, 4269–71, 4275, 4279, 4283, 4287, 4289, 4290n, 4292, 4294, 4296
   his marriage (1785), 194, 194n
   appointed Canon of St Paul's, 1617
   Bishop of Chester, 2133, 3966n
   Bishop of Bangor, 3984

Majestic, a 74-gun ship, 907, 2579

Majorca, 3689, 3693

Makan (?), M., 824

Malacca, capture of, 1376

Malaga, 777, 1760, 2579, 3726
   wine, 283

Malcour, M. de, Wurtemberg Chargé d'Affaires in London, 2735n
   recalled, 3214

Maldon, borough of, 4230

Maldonado, 3367–8

Malines, 816

Maling, Capt. John, 3806

Mallet, David (?1705–65), 32

Mallet du Pan, Jacques (1749–1800), 1148

Malmesbury, Countess of (1761–1830), 2214n

Malmesbury, Lord, *see* Harris, Sir James

Malmo, 3356n, 3448

Malortie, Gen. Carl von (1736–98), 90, 252, 258, 270, 277, 282, 284, 295, 315, 326, 334, 361, 486, 554, 1335, 1372, 4284, 4288, 4290, 4297
   Chamberlain in Hanover to the King's sons, 90n
   his son Ferdinand (1771–1847), 252, 258
   his family, 1372
   his pension, 1372
   his death, 1714

Malta, 1805n, 2128, 2256, 2297, 2412, 2483, 2534, 2654, 2674, 2701, 2737, 3161, 3265n, 3378, 3467, 3519, 3634, 3641, 3692, 3814n, 3951n, 3963, 4023n, 4051, 4104n, 4130n, 4235
   French in possession of, 1787, 2251n
   naval store dept. at, 3164

Malta, the Order of the Knights of St John, 1908, 2007
   capture of (1800), 2251, 2251n, 2259–60

Malta, the, a captured French warship, 2307

Malt tax, 2039

Malton, 55n

Man, Admiral Robert (d. 1813), 855

Manby, Capt. Thomas (1769–1834), 3103

Manchester, 1172, 1717, 1720

Manchester, 4th Duke of (1737–88), 8n, 4264

Manchester, 5th Duke of (1771–1843), 653, 3966n
  Governor of Jamaica, 3514, 3899, 4114, 4114n
Manchester, Susan, Duchess of (1774–1828), 3553
Manesty, Samuel, Resident at Basra, 763
Manfredonia, 1692
Manilas, the, 1510
Manley, Commodore, 817, 840, 845
Manley, Mr, 4252
Mann, Major-Gen. Gother (1747–1830), 3123
Mann, Sir Horace, 2nd Bart (1744–1814), 1637, 3815
Manners, John (1752–1826), 2894n
Manners, Gen. Robert (?1758–1823), 158n, 496n, 1329, 1935
  his election expenses at Great Bedwin (1784), 158
  at Northampton (1709), 158n
  an Equerry to the King, 158n
  succeeds Goldsworthy as First Equerry (1801), 2320, 2717n
Manners, Gen. Russell (d. 1800), 2240
Manners–Sutton, Charles (1755–1828), 2978, 3028, 3139, 3355, 3414n, 3420, 3486, 3559, 3603, 3674, 3775, 3788, 3794, 3888, 3966n, 3975, 4010, 4071
  letters from, 2428, 2963
  thought of as Primate of Ireland (1794), 1158
  Bishop of Norwich, 1983n
  Register of Order of the Garter, 2994
  appointed Archbishop of Canterbury, 3014, 3016, 3021
  an anti-Catholic, 3094, 3395n
Manners–Sutton, Charles, 1st Visct Canterbury (1780–1845), 3867, 4014, 4076n
  Judge Advocate General (1809), 3559n, 4010, 4018, 4117, 4201
Manners–Sutton, Sir Thomas, 1st Baron Manners (1756–1842), 2608, 2628, 2683, 2821, 3016, 3018, 3437, 3447, 3455, 4037
  letter from, 2608n
  Solicitor-General to Prince of Wales, 2608n
  appointed Solicitor-General, 2608n
  appointed Lord Chancellor [I.], 3425, 3429, 3455n
Mannheim, 1320, 1322, 1335, 1337, 1835, 2041, 2075, 2088, 4304

Manning, William (1763–1835), 2752n, 3380, 4232
Manningham, Major-Gen. Coote (d. 1809), 1104, 2008, 2397, 2510n, 2717n
Mansel, William Lort, Master of Trinity College, Camb., later Bishop of Bristol (1753–1820), 1733, 3673, 3673n, 4238
Mansell, Capt., 1056
Mansell, Gen. John (d. 1794), 1041, 1056
Mansfield, 1st Earl of (1705–93), 52n, 303, 1155
  letter from, 445
  letter to, 445
  infirm state of (1786), 291
  resigns office of Lord Chief Justice (1788), 445
Mansfield, 2nd Earl of (1727–96), 1n, 29, 102, 274, 416, 436, 440, 516, 1117n, 1156
  letter from, 1155
  letter to, 1155
  votes against Fox's India Bill (1783), 1n
  elected a Scottish Representative Peer, 78, 78n
  appointed President of the Council, 1155, 1158, 1177
  resigns office of Justice-General of Scotland, 1155, 1158, 1217
  death of, 1435
Mansfield, 3rd Earl of (1777–1840), 1983n, 3635, 3966n
  his marriage, 1539
Mansfield, Sir James, Chief Justice of Chester (1734–1821), 2138
  refuses the Great Seal, 3189n
  Chief Justice of the Common Pleas, 4187
Mansfield, Louisa, Countess of (1758–1843), 2821
  letter from, 1539
  letter to, 4305
Mansfield, Notts, 1046
Mansion House, the, 1507, 1507n
Manson, 2629
Manson, William, a seaman, 3292
Mantin, pistol maker, 1691
Mantua, 1993, 2188
Manvers, Earl, *see* Pierrepont, Charles
Marat, Jean Paul (1743–93), 899, 917
Marathas, the, 2808, 2820, 3140
Marchiennes, 891, 916, 955, 960, 966
Marchmont, 3rd Earl of (1708–94), 10n, 568
  candidate for Scottish Representative Peerage (1784), 78, 78n

Marcoff, M. de, *see* Markov
Marcou, *see* St Marcou
Marengo, capture of the, 3244
Marengo, battle of (1800), 2172n, 2181n
Maret, Hughes Bernard, Duc de Bassano, 4083
Margate, 777, 1146, 1691, 3108
Maria, Queen of Portugal (1734–1816), 2371n, 2410n, 2443A, 2443, 3575
Maria Amelia, Duchess of Orleans (1782–1866), 4023
Maria Theresa, Empress (1772–1807), 772, 1848
Maria Theresa, later Queen of Sardinia (1773–1832), 719, 3236
Maria Theresa, Order of, 926
Marie Antoinette, Queen of France (1755–93), 8n, 178, 335n, 399, 689, 783, 917, 957, 961
Marie Louise, Empress, wife of Napoleon I (1791–1847), 4222
Mariensee (Hanover), 2236
Marine [French], Minister of, 3211
Marines, the, 516, 1677, 2317, 2601, 2637
    office of Major-General of, 1091
Marins, Baron de, 3356
Markham, a Lottery Commissioner (*d.* 1801), 2340
Markham, Frederica [Countess of Mansfield], (*c.* 1774–1860), her marriage, 1539
Markham, Rev. George, Dean of York, son of the Archbishop (*d.* 1822), 2592–3, 2599
    his nine children, 2593
Markham, Admiral John (1761–1827), 2357, 2687n, 4076n
Markham, Osborn (1769–1827), 3401, 3401n
Markham, William, Archbishop of York (1719–1807), 1539, 2592
    letter from, 2593
    letter to, 2593
    death of, 3555, 4149n
Markov [Marcoff], M. de, 223, 399
Marlay, Richard (*d.* 1802), Bishop of Clonfert, 1158, 1217
Marlborough, the, 4269, 4271
Marlborough, 1st Duke of (1650–1722), his MSS, 32, 53
Marlborough, 4th Duke of (1739–1817), 15, 665n, 890, 2365n, 2844n, 3635, 3966n, 4105n
    letters from, 14, 22, 53
    letters to, 14, 22
    King's opinion of, 14
    his attachment to the King, 14, 22

his MSS at Blenheim, 32
    his parliamentary interest, 14, 2991n, 4105n
Marlborough, Caroline, Duchess of, wife of 4th Duke (1743–1811), 14, 665n
Marlborough, Sarah, Duchess of (1660–1744), her Will, 32n
Marlborough election (1807), 3428
Marlow, Rev. Michael (*c.* 1759–1828), 3622
Marmont, Auguste Frédéric Louis Viesse de, Duc de Ragusa, Marshal (1774–1852), 3926
Marquessates, applications for, 544
Marquion, 916, 1059, 1079
Marriott, Sir James (*c.* 1730–1803), 1584, 1683
    resigns office of Judge of Court of Admiralty, 1859
    pension for, 1957, 1957n
Marryat, Joseph (1757–1824), 4122
Mars, a 74-gun ship, 1291, 1735
Marsden, Alexander (1761–1834), Under-Sec. [I.], 1820, 2752n, 2794, 2922n
Marsden, William, Secretary of the Admiralty (1754–1836), 2946n, 3149
    letter to, 3260n
Marseilles, 674, 1760
Marsh, Gen. James, death of (1804), 2882
Marsh, John, a Commissioner of the Transport Office, 1826
Marshall, George, a drummer, 3124
Marsham, Charles, 1st Earl of Romney (1744–1811), 35–6, 448, 1976, 1986, 2746, 3966n
    Wraxall on, 35n
    the King's opinion of (1784), 69
    his Earldom (1801), 2445
    resigns office of Lord-Lieut. of Kent, 3663
Marstrand, 3740
Martello towers, 2929, 2989
Martens, G. F. von, 588
Martial Law Bills [Ireland], 1927, 1940, 2447, 2451, 2774
    see also Habeas Corpus Suspension Bills
Martin, Rear-Admiral Sir George (1764–1847), 3689
Martin, Sir Henry, Bart (1733–94), Resident Commissioner at Portsmouth, 283n
Martin, Henry (1763–1839), 3832, 3869, 3873, 4076, 4116, 4124, 4124n, 4126, 4159, 4162, 4205
Martin, James (1738–1810), 89, 347, 446, 448, 580, 595, 757, 1086, 1255, 1509, 1543, 1643, 1654, 2189
    his 'incorruptible integrity', 89n

(824)

Martin, Richard (1754–1834), 3085, 3665
Martin, Sarah, Prince William's attachment to (1786), 283n
Martin, Sir Thomas Byam (1773–1854), 3721, 3740, 3928
Martinique, 341, 363, 1360, 1622, 2045, 2229, 2723, 2737, 3288, 3898
    capture of (1794), 1030, 1037, 1048–9, 1051, 1111
    capture of (1809), 3715, 3852–3
Martyn, J., *letter from*, 2455
Marul (?), Gen., 891
Mary, the yacht, 1632, 2485
Mary, Princess (1723–72), daughter of George II, 309
Mary, Princess, later Duchess of Gloucester (1776–1857), 163, 458n, 2927n, 3445n, 3929, 3944, 3949, 3955, 3961, 3965, 3974, 3977n, 3982, 3987, 3990, 3995, 4000, 4004, 4008, 4017, 4066, 4078, 4107, 4132, 4173, 4193, 4199, 4216, 4264
    letters from, 2388n, 3445n, 3943, 3947, 3950, 3954, 3956, 3964, 3972, 3976, 3983, 3988, 3991, 3994, 3997, 4001, 4005, 4009, 4012, 4016, 4019, 4021, 4024, 4027, 4029, 4031, 4065, 4077, 4106, 4131, 4134, 4154, 4186, 4189, 4194, 4217
    letters to, 3943, 3947, 3950, 3954, 3956, 3964, 3972, 3976, 3983, 3988, 3991, 3994, 3997, 4001, 4005, 4009, 4012, 4019, 4021, 4024, 4027, 4029, 4065, 4077, 4106, 4131, 4134, 4154, 4189, 4194, 4197, 4217
    frequent fainting fits (1788), 468
    removal of a tumour, 468
    her allowance of £1,000 p.a., 985, 1388
    not very robust, 2722
    Prince Frederick of Orange allegedly in love with, 3242n
Marylebone Fields, 1341
Marystow, royal family at, 552
Masnières, 916
Masons, the, 581
Massena, André, Marshal of France (1758–1817), 1944, 1993n, 2172n, 3926
Massey, Gen. Eyre, 1st Baron Clarina (1719–1804), 1351, 1619, 2301
Master, Mr, 3754
Master, Thomas (1744–1823), 55
Master of the Ceremonies, the, 2426A
Master of the Horse, office of, 1895, 2854
Master of the Rolls, *see* Kenyon; Arden, Richard Pepper; and Grant, Sir William

Masterman, W., election expenses at Saltash (1784), 158
Matarrosa, Visct, 3728
Matcham, Catherine, Lord Nelson's sister (1767–1842), 3242
Mathew, Gen. Edward (*d.* 1805), 630, 1248, 3135, 4277
Mathew, Montagu James (1773–1819), 3590, 3590n, 3657, 3665, 3787n, 4126, 4135, 4177
Mathias, Thomas James, Vice-Treasurer of Queen's Household (*c.* 1754–1835), 1388n, 4208–9
Matra, J. Maria, Consul-General at Tangier, 3163
    Consul at Tunis, 3712
Matra, Mrs, 3712
Matson (Glos), royal family at (1788), 476
Matson, F. H., 3961
Matson, Capt. Henry, R.N., 3214n
Matthews, George, 2575
Matthias, 1575
Maubeuge, 903, 938, 950, 952, 957, 992, 995, 1034, 1066
Maulde, 875, 962
Mauritius, the, 322, 1285, 4207, 4237
Mawbey, Sir Joseph (1730–98), 589
Maxwell, 1691
Maxwell, Major, of the Northampton Fencibles, 1435, 3963
Maxwell, Patrick, Secretary to the island of Grenada (*d.* 1789), 545
Maxwell, Lieut.-Col. Patrick, 2243
May, Sir James Edward (*c* 1753–1814), 2894n
May, John, marine, 3872
Mayence (Mainz), 351, 370, 773, 943, 1176, 1322, 2041
    capture of, 912
    Elector of, 546
Mayer, Professor, 306n
Maynard, Visct (1752–1824), 1223n, 1983n, 3966n
Mayne, Edward, Justice of the Common Pleas [I.], 3702
Maynooth, College of, 3657, 3657n
Mayo Co., 2315n
Meade, Lieut.-Col. John (*c.* 1775–1849), 3129
    elected for Co. Down (1805), 3129n
Meadowbank, Allan Maconochie, Lord (1748–1816), 3147–8
Meath, Bishop of, *see* O'Beirne
Meath Co., state of, 1283, 1540

Meath's Liberty, the Earl of, in Dublin, 94
Mecca, 372
Mechlin, 870
Mecklenbourg, Capt., 901, 905, 909
Mecklenburg-Schwerin, Louisa, Duchess of (1756–1808), 4295
Mecklenburg-Strelitz, Adolphus Frederick, Duke of (1738–94), 1687, 1708, 2969, 4297
Mecklenburg-Strelitz, Prince Charles, later, Duke, and Grand Duke of (1741–1816), 164, 258, 265, 268, 393, 714, 1137, 1673, 1687, 1708, 1905n, 3064
Mecklenburg-Strelitz, Prince Charles of (1785–1837), 3064n
Mecklenburg-Strelitz, Princess Charles of (1752–82), 4290
Mecklenburg-Strelitz, Princess Charlotte of (1755–85), death of, 265, 268
Mecklenburg-Strelitz, Princess Charlotte of (1769–1818), Prince William in love with (1783), 164, 4302
Mecklenburg-Strelitz, Elizabeth Albertine, Princess of (1713–61), mother of Queen Charlotte, 3130
Mecklenburg-Strelitz, Prince Ernest of (1742–1814), Queen Charlotte's brother, 306, 4274, 4290
Mecklenburg-Strelitz, Prince George Augustus of (1748–85), 258, 262, 265, 269
Mecklenburg-Strelitz, George, Hereditary Prince of (1779–1860), 1687, 1708
  wishes to marry one of the King's daughters, 3064
Mediator, a fire ship, 3877
Medici family, the, 2668
Medina, Marquis de, 4269
Medini Celi, Duke of, 186
Medows, Edward, Commissioner of Taxes, 1685
Medows, Gen. Sir William (1738–1813), 590, 705, 715, 767, 919, 921, 3135
  given a Red Ribbon, 767n
  returns to England from Madras, 767n
  waives claim to £15,000 prize money, 767n
  appointed Comm.-in-Chief in Ireland (1801), 2369n
Medusa, a 32-gun ship, 2496n, 3835
Mee, Benjamin, Lady Palmerston's brother (d. 1796), *letter to*, 589n
Meer [Mir] Saib, 137
Mehrfeld, *see* Merveldt
Meiringen, 706
Melampus, a 36-gun frigate, 1291, 1862
Melas, Michel, Baron de, Gen., 2188

Melbourne, Visct (1745–1828), appointed a Gentleman of Prince of Wales's Bedchamber (1787), 365n
Meldrum, 1584
Melius, *see* Mylius
Mellish, Capt., 3887
Mellish, Joseph Charles (d. 1823), 3539
Mello, M. de, 951
Melpomene, a 44-gun French frigate (captured), 1461, 1595, 3928n
Melville, Gen. Robert (1723–1809), 565
Melville, Lady, *see* Dundas, Lady Jane
Melville, Visct, *see* Dundas, Henry
Members drunk in House of Commons, 446n
  weeping in House of Commons, 446n
  qualifications of, 1932n
Memel, 2655, 3380, 3454, 3459, 3510, 3524, 3600n
Mendiola, 309
Mendip Hills, the, 915
Mendip, Lord, *see* Ellis, Welbore
Menin, 879, 891, 920, 924, 926, 934, 941n, 943, 960, 962, 964, 966, 1022, 1038, 1040, 1042, 1045, 1056, 1060, 1088
  Dutch defeated at, 940–1, 948n, 957
Menou, Baron de (1750–1810), French General, capitulates in Egypt, 2393, 2394n, 3842
Menzies, Sir John, 4th Bart (d. 1800), 2124
Mercy [Merci], Count (d. 1794), 689, 816, 926, 986, 992, 1007, 1034, 1106, 1108
Meredith, Capt., 2948
Merida, 2981, 3767
Merrick, Capt. William Augustus (d. 1785), 4298
Merry, of Nottinghamshire, 1046
Merry, Anthony, diplomatist, 2209n, 2230, 2609, 2615, 2621, 2656, 2667, 3207, 3537, 3537n, 3539, 3748, 3771, 3773, 3845
Merveldt, Count von, the Austrian General, 2015, 2161
Merystow, *see* Marystow
Messina, 3204, 3236, 3248, 3463
Messines, 943
Methet, Mr, 3285
Methodists, the, 4045n
Methuen, 3955
Methuen, Paul (1723–95), M.P. for Westbury, Warwick and Great Bedwyn, *letter from*, 60
  asks for a peerage, 60
Metternich, M. de, 816
Metternich, Countess, 1951
  'a very pleasant woman', 1948

Mondego Bay, 3696n, 3711n, 3887
river, 3587n
Money, Lieut., R.N., 3994-5
Moniteur, the, 2383n, 2705n, 3562, 3743, 3901
Monke, 399
Monkhouse, Dr (*d.* 1810), 4076
Monmouth, a 64-gun ship, 1571, 1599
Monro, Dr John (1715-91), 317
Monroe, James (1758-1831), 2784, 2941, 3356, 3513, 3515, 3537, 3541, 3653n
Mons, 689, 816, 957, 979, 984, 990, 995, 1003, 1008, 1066
Monsieur, *see* Louis XVIII, *and* 1282n, *and* Artois, Comte d'
Monson, 4th Baron (1785-1809), 3966n
Monson, Lieut.-Col. William (1760-1807), 2709
Montagu, Frederick (1733-1800), 524
Montagu, George, Duke of (1712-90), Master of the Horse, 238, 516n, 541, 596, 4264, 4269
Montagu, Admiral Sir George (1750-1829), 1081, 1085, 2429, 3789
Montagu, Lord, *see* Hussey Montagu
Montagu, Henry James Scott, Lord (1776-1845), 3966n
Montagu, Matthew, 4th Baron Rokeby (1762-1831), 595, 647, 682, 1198, 1247, 1255, 1323, 1379, 3359, 3491, 4109
Montagu, 7th Visct (1728-87), *letter from,* 108
and the borough of Midhurst, 108n
Montagu, 8th Visct (1769-93), 973
Montague, a 74-gun ship, 1595, 1632
Montalembert, Baron, 1473
Montbéliard, Principality of (Wurtemberg territory, 1407-1801), 2544
Mont Brilliant, near Hanover, 1385, 4272
Montego Bay, 1297
Montevideo, 3363, 3367, 3801
capture of (1807), 3438-9
Governor of, 3714
Montferrat, Duke of, *see* Charles Felix
Montfort, Lord (1773-1851), 3966n
Montgomerie, Lieut.-Gen. Sir James (1755-1829), 3664, 3834
Montgomery, Sir Henry Conyngham (1765-1830), 3763n, 4138
Montgomery, Sir James, Lord Advocate of Scotland (1766-1839), 3148
letter from, 3147
letter to, 3145

removal from office (1806), 3262n
Montgomery, Sir James William (1721-1803), resigns his judicial office (1801), 2403
Montgomery Militia, the, 1607
Montgomeryshire, 1459
Montjoye Frohberg, Comte de, the Duke of Brunswick's Chamberlain, 3347, 3354
Montmédy, 689
Montmorin, Comte de (*d.* 1792), 403, 429, 503
Montpensier, Antoine Philippe, Duc de (1775-1807), Louis Philippe's brother, 2102, 2106, 2106n
death of, 3468
Montreal, 404
Montreal, frigate, 4143
Montron, M. de, 3235n
Montrose, James, Marquess of Graham, later 3rd Duke of (1755-1836), 1983n, 2746, 3120n, 3400n, 3416, 3612, 3808, 3966n
proposes Addington as Speaker (1789), 524
appointed Joint Paymaster-General (1789), 544
appointed Master of the Horse (1790), 644
appointed a Commissioner for India (1791), 677
appointed Justice-General of Scotland, 1155n, 1158, 1190, 1217, 2852n
resigns office of Master of the Horse, 1155n, 1158
remains member of the 'Nominal' Cabinet, 1190
and the Foreign Secretaryship (1801), 2365n
refuses office of Lord-Lieut. of Ireland, 2369n
appointed President of Board of Trade and Joint Paymaster-General (1804), 2844n, 2852, 2852n
an excellent Master of the Horse, 2854
Moody, 1373
Moore, Mrs Catherine, wife of the Archbishop, 2010, 3022
Moore, Charles (*c.* 1771-1826), one of Duke of Marlborough's members, 4105n, 4122n
Moore, F., clerk in F.O., 2605, 2667
Moore, Col. Francis, of Bedford militia, 2792
letter from, 2792n
Moore, Admiral Sir Graham (1764-1843), 3rd son of Dr John Moore, 3574, 3884n

Newport, Sir John (*cont.*)
    letter to, 3485n
    Chancellor of Exchequer [I.] (1806–7), 3418
Newport, P., Collector at Dover, 1324, 1613
Newport (Cornwall), 19n
Newport (Isle of Wight), 3844n, 4099n
Newport (South Wales), 4126n
New Ross, 1757, 1765, 1765n
New Shoreham election, 158
New South Wales, 2804, 2848, 3076, 3113, 3850
Newton, Sir Isaac (1642–1727), 1932n
Newtownards Reform Club, the, 100
New Windsor, Vicarage of, 2831
Newry, borough of, 3129
    election committee, 3637n
New York, 9, 190, 2200, 3264, 4283, 4285, 4290n, 4296
Ney, Michel, Marshal of France (1769–1815), 3380, 3791n
Niagara, 768, 787, 794
Nice, 557, 659, 1760
Nicholas, British representative in Heligoland, 3878, 3915n, 3931, 3940
Nicholl, Sir John (1759–1838), the King's Advocate-General, 2318, 2770, 3023, 3270, 3371, 3428n, 3513, 3605, 3683, 3788, 3794, 4089
    resigns office of King's Advocate-General, 3790
Nicholls, John (*c.* 1745–1832), 1507, 1637, 1654, 2135, 2140, 2189, 2276, 2276n
Nicholls, Gen. Oliver (*c.* 1742–1829), 1464, 1833
Nicholls, William, 3815
Nichols, Capt., 2496n
Nicholson, George, 317, 317n
Nicholson, Margaret (?1750–1828), attempted murder of the King, 317
    in Bedlam, 2153n
Nicolay, Baron Paul (1777–1866), 3318, 3378, 3380
Nicolls, Mr, surgeon, 1931
Nienburg, 1326, 2749
Nieuport, 891, 930, 934, 941n, 943, 962, 966, 968, 986, 1038, 1099
Nightingall, Lieut.-Gen. Sir Miles (1768–1829), 3850
Niger, a 32-gun frigate, 1595
Nile, battle of the, 1837, 1841–2, 1844–5, 1923, 1993, 2128, 2366n, 3153n, 3540, 4143
Nillequier, M. de, 689

Nimeguen, 376, 382, 847, 859, 861, 1132, 1141, 1144
Nivelon, the Parisian dancer, 399
Nizam, the, of the Deccan, 137, 567, 586, 590, 715
Noirmoutier, 1270, 1282, 1286, 1294
Nolan (*d.* 1793), 933
Nolcken, Baron Adam (1733–1812), 750, 750n, 796
Nolekin [*sic*], Baroness, 3815
Nooth, Dr, Inspector-General of Hospitals, Quebec, 1818, 1840
Nootka Sound dispute with Spain (1790), 589
Nordheim, 1573
Nördlingen, 2177
Nore, the, 1302, 1545, 1551, 1555, 1560, 1571, 1577, 1597, 1632, 1645, 1965, 2057, 2086, 2485, 2579, 2590, 2716, 3506, 3509, 3511
Norfolk, 735, 812, 1166, 1834n, 1838
    election (1797), 1611; (1807), 3387
    Lord-Lieutenancy of, 3607
Norfolk, 11th Duke of (1746–1815), 6n, 89, 510, 632, 1223n, 1678–9, 1680n, 1691, 1801, 3360, 3590n, 3966n
    letter from, 1680
    Wraxall on, 89n
    dismissed from office of Lord-Lieut. of West Riding of Yorkshire (1798), 1678, 1678n
    very friendly with Duke of York, 1678n
    his uncertain politics, 3008
    is refused the Garter (1804), 3008n
Norfolk House, the Duke's London home, 1678n
Noriega, Don Lorenzo, 3728
Normanton, Earl of, *see* Agar, Charles
Norris, Rev. Charles (*c.* 1743–1833), 1885
North family, the, 994n, 2646n
North, Anne, Lady (*d.* 1797), 121
North, Brownlow (1741–1820), Bishop of Winchester, 1983, 3966n, 4076
North, Dudley, *see* Long
North, Frederick, Lord, later 2nd Earl of Guilford (1732–92), 1n, 3, 3n, 7, 21, 28, 51, 56, 57n, 89, 98, 105, 109, 116, 121, 144, 147, 190, 203, 266n, 307, 383, 670, 2256, 4032
    letters to, 118, 126
    his party, 7
    his office of Lord Warden of the Cinque Ports, 121
    his ill behaviour to the King, 129, 140
    his premature death, 770, 2857

Orange, Princess Wilhelmina, Hereditary Princess of (1774–1837), arrival in England, 1194

birth of her daughter, 4206

Orange, Princess Louisa Marianna of (1810–83), 4206

Orange, William V of, the Stadholder, and a grandson of George II (1748–1806), 256, 367, 376, 382, 392, 409, 414, 546, 812, 840, 843, 846–7, 854, 859, 879, 882, 891, 920, 950, 952, 957, 966, 1006, 1088, 1098–9, 1102, 1139, 1152, 1157, 1161, 1196, 1199, 1199n, 1233, 1290, 1295, 1495, 1719, 1883, 1906, 1908, 1917, 1919, 2011, 2123, 2178n, 2530, 2658, 2950, 3249

letters from, 371, 391, 395, 402, 422, 437, 457, 583, 1144

letters to, 387n, 395, 400, 452

arrival in England (1795), 1194

financial assistance to, 2645, 2647, 2766, 2766n

death of, 3242, 3242n, 3251, 3253

Orange, William, Hereditary Prince of, later King of the Netherlands (1772–1843), 714, 847, 854, 879, 891, 920, 924, 934, 939, 941, 941n, 943, 957, 1139, 1670, 1906, 2032, 2037, 2645, 3369, 3901, 3903, 3921

letters to, 3251, 4206

his absurdities, 923

his 'shameful' behaviour, 926, 943

his ignorance, 950

arrival in England (1795), 1194

succeeds father as Stadholder, 3242

given financial assistance, 3253

Orange, Prince William of (1792–1849), afterwards William II of Holland, 1196, 3903

a possible husband for Princess Charlotte, 3903n

to study at Oxford, 3916

Orchies, 891, 924, 955, 957, 960

Ord, William (1781–1855), 3869, 4164

Orde, Admiral Sir John (1751–1824), 341, 1591, 2055, 2959, 4126

Lieut.-Governor of Dominica, 514, 567

Comm.-in-Chief at Portsmouth, 1584

Orde, John, Attorney-General to Duchy of Lancaster, 4227

Orde, Thomas, Lord Bolton (1746–1807), 3n, 15n, 94, 112, 112n, 120, 168, 176, 182,

224, 231, 246, 248n, 359, 595, 1983, 3966n

called to the Privy Council (1785), 259

appointed Governor of Isle of Wight (1791), 671n

re-elected for Harwich (1791), 671

Order of Christ, the Portuguese, 2974

Orders-in-Council, 2578, 3392, 3496, 3545, 3569, 3596, 3629, 3655, 3683, 3686, 3714, 3724, 3808, 3877, 3909, 4230, 4243

debates on the, 3371, 3596, 3603, 3605, 3617, 3620, 3629, 3653n, 3808, 3817, 3817n

Ordnance Estimates (1787), 420

Department, 867, 3801

O'Reilly, Sir Hugh, 1st Bart (*d. ? c.* 1825), 1772

Orestes, an 18-gun sloop, 1732n

Orford, 3rd Earl of (1730–91), appointed Ranger of the Parks, 15n

Orford, Horatio, 2nd Baron Walpole and 1st Earl of (1723–1809), 3966n

Orford, Horace Walpole, Earl of, *see* Walpole, Horace

Orford Ness (Suffolk), 2485

Orion, a 74-gun ship, 3332, 4143

Orkney Islands, state of the (1785), 232

reported French landing on (1806), 3362

Orleans, Duke of, *see* Louis Philippe

Orleans, island of, near Quebec, 385

Ormonde, 2nd Duke of (1665–1745), 32, 531

Ormonde, 18th Earl of, later Marquess of (1770–1820), 1448, 2315, 3966n

made a K.P. (1798), 1684

Ormsby, Sir Charles Montagu (1767–1818), given a Government seat, 2510

appointed Counsel to the Commissioners of the Revenue [I.] (1801), 2510n

Orpheus, a 32-gun ship, 1186

Orramin Ludovick, Duke of York's footman, 3809n

Osborn, Sir George, 4th Bart (1742–1818), Gen. (1797), 1298, 3135

Osborn, Sir John, 5th Bart (1772–1848), 2752n, 2888, 3435

Osborne, Lord Francis Godolphin, later Lord Godolphin (1777–1850), his marriage, 2110

election for Cambridgeshire, 4142n

Osborne, Lady Mary, later Countess of Chichester (1776–1862), 2110

Osnabrück, Dean of, 138
    Duke of York's Bishopric of, 138, 270, 285,
        351, 355, 588, 716, 1290, 1432, 1633,
        2651, 2655, 2662, 2744, 2749, 4297
    Palace at, 4295, 4304
Ossulston, Lord, later 5th Earl of Tanker-
    ville (1776–1859), 3787n, 4126, 4138
Ostend, 351, 863, 866, 879, 891, 909, 930,
    938–9, 941n, 955, 966, 968, 977, 979,
    983n, 986, 993, 999, 1026, 1041, 1066,
    1085, 1088, 1320, 1456, 4083, 4295
    attack on (1798), 1736n, 1741
Osterman, Count, 219
Osterode, 3342
Ostrolenka, 3365
Oswego, 787, 794
Ottley, Lieut. Edward, R.N. (d. 1807), 3488
Otto, Gen., 882, 960, 995, 1066, 1073
Otto, Louis Guillaume, Comte de Mosloy
    (1754–1817), French Commissioner in
    London, 2228, 2230, 2232, 2235, 2237,
    2244, 2246, 2248, 2261, 2534–5, 2539n,
    2605, 2667, 2678
Otway, Sir Robert Waller (1770–1846), 2382,
    3108, 3927
Oubril, M. d', Russian Minister at Paris, 2941,
    3265
Oudenarde, 943, 1079, 1084
Oudh, 1493n
Oudinot, Charles Nicolas, Duc de Reggio,
    Marshal of France (1767–1847), 1993n
Oughton, Capt. James, 2018, 2032
Ouseley, Sir Gore (1770–1844), 4042, 4110,
    4113, 4224, 4226
Outram, Mrs, 4229
Over Flakkee, 840
Overyssel, 367, 391, 409
Oviedo, 3669, 3677
Owen, Sir Edward William Campbell Rich
    (1771–1849), 3472–3, 3481
Owen[s], George, a convict, 157, 159
Owen, Sir John (c. 1776–1861), 4105, 4122,
    4122n, 4138
Owen, Capt. William Fitzwilliam, 2805n
Oxenstierna, 399
Oxenstierna, Gustavus Adolphus, Swedish
    Chancellor (1583–1654), 399
Oxford, 4th Earl of (1726–90), 428, 4274
Oxford, 5th Earl of (1773–1848), 1983n,
    3966n
Oxford, 14n, 1311, 1973
Oxford, Bishopric of, 2062
Oxford Circuit, the, 1793n, 2138n, 3234
Oxford Gaol, 324

Oxford Militia, 1259, 1607
Oxford Volunteers, 1973
Oxford, University of, 495, 497, 760, 1237,
    1248, 1332, 1870, 1870n, 2153, 2479,
    2487, 3052, 3186, 3410, 3437, 3449, 3916,
    3970, 4007, 4014, 4020
    royal visit to (1785), 257
    election of Chancellor of, 4032, 4040, 4045
Oxfordshire, 3622
Oxfordshire election (1754), 2894
Oxmantown, Visct and (1806), Earl of Rosse,
    see Parsons
Oynhausen [sic], Gen., 1059

Packwood, Rev. Rogers Porter (c. 1775–
    1815), 4238
Padley, William, gardener at Hampton Court,
    2975, 3679
Paget, Sir Arthur (1771–1840), 1827, 2082,
    2099, 2099n, 2426, 2654, 2956, 3454,
    3454n, 3456, 3543, 3573, 3573n
    Chargé d'Affaires at Berlin, 1087
    Secretary of Embassy at Madrid, 1434
    Minister at Vienna, 2391
    nominated K.B., 2870
    applies for a pension, 3409
    and the Vienna Embassy, 3454n
    marries Lady Boringdon, 3813n
Paget, Vice-Admiral Sir Charles (1778–1839),
    1628, 3037, 3215, 3611
    marries Elizabeth Araminta Monck
        (d. 1843), 3037n
Paget, Sir Edward (1775–1849), 3037n, 3887
Paget, Henry, 1st Earl of Uxbridge (1744–
    1812), 1710, 2307n, 3896n, 3966n, 4120
    letter from, 3044
    father of Lady Louisa Erskine, 3037
Paget, Sir Henry William, 2nd Earl of
    Uxbridge and 1st Marquess of Anglesey
    (1768–1854), 2008, 2048, 3791
    marries Lady Charlotte Wellesley, 3896n
Paget, Lady Louisa, see Erskine
Pagets, the, 4105n
Pahlen, Count, 2456n
Painswick, royal family at (1788), 476
Painted Chamber at Westminster, the, 1319n,
    2269, 2269n, 2272
Painter, Charles, mutineer, 1605
Paisley, disaffection in (1794), 991n
Pakenham, Admiral Sir Thomas (c. 1757–
    1836), 1494, 1530
Pakenham, Thomas, Master-General of Ord-
    nance [I.], 2245
Palace Yard, Westminster, 2877

Parnell, Sir John, 2nd Bart (1744–1801), Chancellor of the Exchequer [I.], 1686, 1707, 1824n, 1889
his dismissal (1799), 1686n
Parr, John, Governor of Nova Scotia, 106
Parry, Rev. Gregory (d. 1785), Prebendary of Worcester, 234, 237
Parry, Edward, Chairman of East India Company, 3595
Parsloe's, 2745n
Parsons, John (1761–1819), Vice-Chancellor of Oxford 3916, 3970, 3996
Parsons, Lawrence Harman, 1st Baron and 1st Visct Oxmantown, and (1806), Earl of Rosse (1749–1807), 2301, 2315
Parsons, Sir Lawrence, 2nd Earl of Rosse (1758–1841), on the Union, 2157
Parsons, Thomas Zachariah, a Poor Knight of Windsor, 2574
Partington, a convict, 564
Partition Treaty of 1699, 4076
Party funds, 894n
Pasley, Admiral Sir Thomas, Bart (1734–1808), Lieut. (1757), Capt. (1771), Rear-Adm. (1794), Vice-Adm. (1795), Adm. (1799), Bart (1794), 1577
Passports, 1817, 2089, 2281, 2539A
Paterson, Major, 1510
Patriotic Fund, the, 3325
Patten, Peter Bold (c. 1764–1819), 2746n
his motion of censure (1803), 2752, 2752n, 4124n
Patterson, John (1755–1833), 4076
Patton, Philip (1739–1815), Admiral, 1294
Paul, Father, 4277
Paul, Sir George Onesiphorus, 2nd Bart, Gloucestershire prison reformer (1746–1820), 481, 1311
Paul, Tsar (1754–1801), 1525, 1670, 1817, 1845, 1854, 1888, 1908, 1908n, 1948n, 1961, 1979, 1987, 1997, 2007, 2027, 2072, 2080, 2082, 2123, 2142, 2181, 2287, 2297, 2322, 2566, 3278n
Treaty with (1799), 1960, 1960n, 1987
his embargo on British ships, 2287n
assassination of, 2386n
Paulet, Lady Mary, see Poulett
Pauletts, the, see Pouletts
Pavia, 642
Pavilion, George IV's, at Brighton, 2462n
Payne, Lieut.-Col., 1182
Payne, John Willett, Rear-Admiral (1752–1803), appointed Auditor to Duchy of Cornwall, 723, 1122, 1168n, 1203, 1226

Payne, Sir Ralph, cr. Lord Lavington [Oct. 1795], M.P. for Shaftesbury (1768–71), Camelford (1776–80), Plympton (1780–4), Woodstock (1795–9); Governor of Leeward Islands (1771–5, 1799–1807) (1739–1807), 1283
Payne, Sir William (d. 1831), Col. (1798), Major-Gen. (1805), Lieut.-Gen. (1811), Gen. (1825), Bart. (1812), 1833
Peace negotiations (1796), 1451, 1455, 1458, 1467, 1484–7; (1797), 1528; (1801), 2373, 2514, 2534
preliminary articles, 2534n
preliminaries signed, 2535, 2581n
rupture of (1806), 3318
Peachey, Sir James, Baron Selsey (1723–1808), letter from, 71
applications for a peerage, 71, 71n
given a G.B. peerage (1794), 1104
Master of the Robes, 3593
Pearce, John, seaman, 2513
Pearse, John (c. 1760–1836), Governor of Bank of England, 4232
Pearse, Col. Thomas Deane (d. 1789), 137
Pedro III, King of Portugal (1717–86), 3575n
Peebles, Lieut. George, 3381
Peel, Sir Robert, 1st Bart (1750–1830), 2752n, 2888
Peel, Sir Robert, 2nd Bart (1788–1850), 3876n, 4124, 4126n, 4156
seconds the Address, 4074, 4074n, 4076n
Peerages, applications for, 4n, 55n, 60, 71, 71n, 77, 89n, 531, 544, 561, 568n, 603, 619n, 764, 1174, 1276, 1400–2, 1415n, 1426, 1426n, 1498n, 1626, 1666, 1926n, 2232n, 2270, 2289, 2301n, 2449, 2510, 2567, 2702, 2702n, 2791, 2812n, 2940, 3075n, 3195n, 3224, 3224n, 3438, 3442, 3757, 3784, 3914, 4018, 4076n, 4104n
Peers, impoverished, 20, 1033, 1281, 2638, 3356n
Peers, seniority of new, 2301
Pegasus, a 28-gun frigate, 288, 293, 296, 327, 327n, 341, 346n, 363, 377, 385, 413, 419
Pegge, Sir Christopher (1765–1822), 1973, 2479, 2479n
Peirson, David, Mary Anne Clarke's butler, 3809n
Pelham, Rev. George, Bishop of Bristol and of Exeter (1766–1827), 2684, 3462, 3465, 3966n
Pelham, Mary, Lady (1776–1862), daughter of 5th Duke of Leeds, 2604n, 2713, 2889n, 2897n

(840)

Pelham, Thomas, Lord, later 1st Earl of Chichester (1728–1805), 335, 1355, 1355n, 2192n, 2445, 2794, 2852n
letter to, 2445n
his Earldom, 2445n, 2456n
Pelham, Thomas, Lord Pelham (1801), later 2nd Earl of Chichester (1765–1826), 10, 11, 644, 682, 1292, 1297, 1357–8, 1491, 1494, 1522, 1586, 1662, 1666, 1707, 1709n, 1820, 1824, 2192n, 2357n, 2365n, 2405n, 2456, 2474, 2487, 2487n, 2489, 2498, 2498n, 2507, 2510n, 2578, 2639n, 2645, 2657, 2780n, 2782, 2786n, 2788, 2847n, 2852n, 2888n, 2889, 2894, 2902, 3483n, 3674, 3966n
letters from, 2445n, 2474n, 2500, 2500n, 2512, 2532, 2540, 2546, 2549, 2552, 2557, 2560, 2562, 2574, 2584, 2595, 2598, 2604, 2613, 2619, 2625, 2635, 2643, 2648, 2652, 2659, 2663, 2671, 2676, 2679, 2681, 2683, 2687, 2696, 2699, 2706, 2708, 2713, 2721, 2726, 2732, 2734, 2739, 2743, 2746, 2748, 2757, 2768, 2772, 2774, 2777, 2779, 2781, 2794, 2794n, 2806n, 2878, 2878n, 2889n, 2897n
letters to, 1355n, 1559n, 1868n, 2330n, 2357n, 2456n, 2500, 2540n, 2635, 2648, 2652, 2706, 2748, 2777, 2781n, 2794n, 2894n
could have remained in office (1783), 10n
on the Duchess of York, 688n
to be Irish Secretary, 1214
anxious to resign Irish Secretaryship, 1345–6, 1349, 1349n
agrees to return to Ireland (1796), 1355
his illness, 1701, 1701n
Cornwallis wants him as his Secretary, 1759
question of his returning to Ireland, 1820n, 1824n, 1868n
reluctance to take office (1801), 2350, 2350n, 2357, 2357n, 2456n
and the Board of Control, 2357n
and the War Secretaryship (1801), 2357n
becomes Home Secretary, 2456, 2474n
his peerage (1801), 2456n
refuses a Cabinet office (1801), 2456n
refuses a diplomatic Mission, 2456n
Leader of House of Lords (1801), 2487n
wants to be a Governor of Charterhouse, 2562
out of humour, 2595n

his dissenting Cabinet Minute (1802), 2600n
contemplates resignation (1802), 2600n
his 'disgusting and offensive negligence', 2777n
offered Chancellorship of Duchy of Lancaster and Presidentship of Board of Trade (1803), 2777, 2782n
declines seat in Cabinet (1803), 2788, 2794
becomes Chancellor of Duchy, 2782n, 2794n, 2806, 2806n
and the War Secretaryship, 2794
refuses a Household appointment (1804), 2852n, 2878, 2889, 2894, 2897, 2897n
refuses foreign employment (1804), 2852n
his connection with Prince of Wales, 2852n
memo. by, 2878n
wants Duchy of Lancaster for life, 2878n, 3003n
his political tergiversation, 2897
Joint Postmaster-General (1807), 3416, 3447
applies for a Tellership of the Exchequer, 4076
Pellew, Sir Edward, 1st Visct Exmouth (1757–1833), 1054, 1146, 1315, 2310, 3926
letter from, 1054n
wants a baronetcy, 1054n
Pells, office of Clerk of the, 2839n
Pemberton, Christopher Robert, physician (1765–1822), 1931
Pembroke, 540, 1506, 3843
Pembroke Castle, French prisoners in, 1505–6
Pembroke, Elizabeth, Countess of (1737–1831), 506
letter from, 500
Pembroke, 10th Earl of (1734–94), 501–2
his unjustifiable conduct, 507
Pembroke, Lord Herbert, later Earl of (1759–1827), 500, 507, 924, 1657, 1769, 3966n
letters from, 501, 506, 2283n, 3000, 4112n
letters to, 506, 3000, 4109n
appointed Vice-Chamberlain (1784), 146
refuses a Marquessate, 2283
declines office of Lord Chamberlain (1804), 2856n, 3000n
given a Garter, 2906n, 3000
declines Embassy to Russia (1804), 3000n
his Mission to Vienna (1807), 3440, 3440n, 3454, 3454n, 3541
declines the Ordnance, 4109, 4112, 4112n

Pitcairn, David, M.D. (1749–1809), 1765

Pitfield, John, a debtor, 637, 637n

Pitt, Lady Harriot, Pitt's sister (1758–86), 248n

  death of, 330

Pitt, Mrs Morton (d. 1818), 3965

Pitt, Thomas, 1st Baron Camelford (1737–93), 587

  his peerage, 13

Pitt, William (1759–1806), 3, 3n, 8n, 10n, 11, 15n, 21, 26n, 35, 35n, 37–8, 54n, 55n, 64n, 71, 84n, 91, 93n, 100, 106n, 112n, 130n, 136, 159, 159n, 162, 177, 182n, 183, 210, 224, 237, 251, 253, 256, 275, 303n, 333, 335, 352n, 353, 360n, 367, 401, 417n, 420n, 425, 446n, 488, 489n, 495, 514, 516, 520–1, 545, 555, 558n, 562, 568, 577, 589n, 600, 604, 607n, 630, 636, 655, 670n, 691, 740n, 741, 754, 760n, 770, 773, 784, 797, 805, 812, 830, 839, 845, 859, 869n, 943, 956, 963, 969, 975, 983, 991, 1009n, 1020n, 1053, 1054n, 1077–8, 1078n, 1083, 1090, 1092, 1095n, 1096, 1100, 1124, 1127, 1130, 1138, 1140, 1154–5, 1158, 1167, 1171, 1192n, 1198n, 1200, 1208n, 1211, 1214n, 1251n, 1253–4, 1269, 1277n, 1294–5, 1319n, 1320n, 1337n, 1345, 1347, 1355n, 1358, 1361, 1366n, 1371, 1436, 1467, 1468n, 1475n, 1477, 1481, 1491, 1493n, 1497, 1498n, 1507n, 1509n, 1515, 1519n, 1521n, 1522, 1554, 1560, 1561n, 1565, 1603, 1616, 1656, 1668n, 1671, 1678n, 1680n, 1686n, 1692, 1701, 1719, 1721, 1727, 1750, 1752n, 1766, 1768, 1771, 1782, 1787, 1791–2, 1803, 1814, 1844–5, 1852, 1854, 1880, 1899, 1904, 1908, 1910, 1913n, 1926n, 1932n, 1959, 1985, 1987, 1990, 2005, 2012–3, 2017, 2023n, 2027–8, 2031, 2033, 2054, 2054n, 2055n, 2068, 2070n, 2074, 2082, 2087, 2102n, 2107, 2108n, 2116, 2142, 2158, 2163, 2166, 2166n, 2171, 2180n, 2184, 2189n, 2203, 2205, 2227, 2230, 2235, 2237, 2252, 2264, 2273, 2282, 2285–7, 2288n, 2307n, 2308, 2327n, 2331–2, 2334n, 2336, 2336n, 2339n, 2340–1, 2344, 2344n, 2345–6, 2349n, 2357, 2357n, 2365n, 2368, 2368n, 2371n, 2372n, 2373n, 2381, 2401, 2411, 2412n, 2439, 2459n, 2474n, 2498n, 2536n, 2581n, 2606, 2745n, 2752, 2752n, 2757n, 2782n, 2806n, 2833n, 2837n, 2838–9, 2839n, 2842n, 2843n, 2844n, 2847, 2849, 2850n, 2851n, 2852n, 2853n, 2855n, 2857, 2857n, 2859, 2865n, 2866n, 2867n, 2871n, 2878n, 2881n, 2882, 2884n, 2888n, 2889n, 2891, 2894n, 2897n, 2902n, 2905, 2905n, 2907n, 2912n, 2914n, 2915, 2922n, 2926, 2930n, 2934n, 2940n, 2942n, 2965, 2978n, 2984, 2986, 2990, 2993, 2994n, 2998n, 3002n, 3003n, 3006n, 3014n, 3019n, 3020, 3025n, 3030n, 3049, 3051, 3068n, 3069, 3069n, 3071n, 3073n, 3075n, 3079n, 3081, 3081n, 3082, 3085n, 3093, 3105n, 3115n, 3120, 3120n, 3123, 3137, 3146, 3147n, 3149–50, 3163, 3164n, 3169–73, 3169n, 3174n, 3180, 3186, 3195n, 3283n, 3322n, 3373n, 3380n, 3395n, 3400n, 3410n, 3418n, 3425n, 3440n, 3483n, 3505n, 3584n, 3657n, 3797n, 3809n, 3842, 3869, 3960, 3960n, 3966, 3970, 4018n, 4041n, 4086n, 4105n, 4142, 4229, 4257–62

letters from, 2, 4, 4n, 6, 10, 15, 18, 26, 28, 31, 36, 40, 42, 44, 46, 50, 52, 55, 57, 62, 64, 66, 72, 74, 76, 80, 82, 89, 89n, 93, 98, 101, 105, 107, 112, 120, 128, 143, 146, 150, 155, 169, 171, 176, 179, 182, 187, 190, 194, 199, 203, 217, 228, 231, 235, 237n, 246, 248, 259, 266, 274, 283, 290, 297, 305, 307, 309, 313, 313n, 325, 330, 343, 347, 352, 358, 358n, 360, 362, 364, 366, 368, 373, 378, 380, 382, 387n, 394, 403, 408, 412, 417, 420, 438, 441, 446, 448, 451, 456, 467, 472, 477, 479, 483, 485, 488n, 491, 502, 504, 507, 511, 515, 524, 529, 533, 544, 544n, 553, 556, 561, 568n, 572, 574, 580, 582, 589, 593, 595, 599, 602, 631, 635, 644, 647, 651, 654, 661, 666, 670, 672, 675, 678, 682–3, 686, 690n, 709, 709n, 712, 729, 735, 738, 740, 744, 751, 757, 761, 764, 771, 774, 780, 793, 795, 807, 807n, 819, 829, 831, 836, 838, 848, 856, 865, 869, 878, 883, 890, 895, 904, 927, 934n, 938, 974, 983n, 994n, 1002, 1027, 1031, 1033, 1039, 1044, 1055, 1057, 1070, 1080, 1086, 1091, 1091n, 1093, 1095, 1101, 1104, 1110, 1113, 1116, 1120, 1123, 1125, 1128, 1131, 1139, 1139n, 1158, 1161, 1164, 1170, 1177, 1180, 1185, 1190, 1195, 1198, 1201, 1208, 1210, 1214, 1218, 1223, 1233, 1236, 1238, 1241, 1247, 1250, 1251, 1255, 1266,

II, 832–1662; III, 1663–2575; IV, 2576–3578

Pitt, William (*cont.*)

1270, 1279n, 1293, 1293n, 1296, 1301,
1309, 1313, 1320, 1323, 1330, 1333, 1338,
1340, 1342, 1344, 1349, 1357n, 1370,
1378n, 1379, 1386, 1390, 1394, 1397,
1401, 1425, 1430, 1441, 1446, 1450, 1452,
1459, 1478, 1480, 1482, 1485, 1487, 1491n,
1492, 1496, 1498, 1498n, 1500, 1502, 1507,
1509, 1514, 1517, 1519, 1521, 1526, 1537,
1541, 1543, 1546, 1550, 1559, 1561, 1566,
1580, 1608, 1611, 1617, 1621, 1626, 1637,
1639, 1643, 1649, 1654, 1658, 1664,
1664n, 1670, 1674, 1674n, 1678, 1680n,
1681, 1685, 1686n, 1708, 1722, 1722n,
1724, 1729, 1733, 1744, 1745n, 1755,
1755n, 1759, 1759n, 1764, 1770, 1772n,
1773, 1793, 1793n, 1796, 1826, 1877,
1881, 1885, 1893, 1897, 1903, 1911, 1914,
1922, 1926, 1929, 1932, 1950, 1957, 1960,
1969, 1972, 1980, 2020, 2039, 2045,
2077n, 2079, 2082n, 2108, 2135, 2137,
2140, 2144, 2149, 2165, 2170, 2174, 2180,
2182, 2187, 2189, 2192, 2196, 2199,
2203n, 2204, 2204n, 2263, 2264n, 2269,
2269n, 2272, 2276, 2279, 2283, 2288,
2299, 2309, 2327, 2330, 2339, 2339n,
2359, 2364, 2367, 2372, 2457, 2757n,
2852, 2865n, 2866, 2872–3, 2881, 2884,
2888, 2894, 2907, 2920, 2922, 2927, 2931,
2940, 2942, 2952, 2952n, 2959n, 2961,
2967, 2978, 2987, 2991, 3003, 3003n,
3006, 3009, 3012, 3014, 3016, 3023, 3025,
3030, 3041, 3068, 3071, 3075, 3079, 3085,
3089, 3089n, 3095, 3105, 3111, 3115,
3141, 3146, 3146n, 3152, 3155

letters to, 2, 10, 15, 18, 19n, 23n, 36, 40n,
42, 50, 55, 57, 62, 69, 80, 82, 84, 89, 105,
120, 128, 146, 150, 155, 181, 190, 194,
206, 214, 228, 231, 235, 255, 259, 266n,
274, 283, 290, 292, 297, 309, 313, 325,
343, 354, 358n, 362n, 364, 366, 368, 373,
378, 382, 382n, 383, 387n, 390, 403, 408,
410, 420, 428, 431, 435, 441, 446, 451n,
454, 458, 467, 477, 482n, 483, 485, 494,
502, 507, 524, 526, 533, 542, 552n, 553,
556, 572n, 574, 580, 582, 599, 602, 608,
619n, 629, 631, 640, 644, 651, 666, 686,
712, 729, 735, 738, 751, 757, 757n, 761,
764, 771n, 776, 780, 789, 793, 829, 831,
834n, 838, 846, 856, 862n, 890, 895, 913n,
1002, 1004, 1021, 1027, 1031, 1033, 1039,
1039n, 1044, 1070n, 1086, 1091, 1093n,
1095, 1125, 1142n, 1156, 1164, 1180,
1181, 1185, 1190, 1193, 1198, 1206, 1208,

1210, 1212, 1214n, 1216, 1223, 1228,
1233, 1236, 1238, 1241, 1243, 1247, 1250,
1255, 1275, 1277, 1301, 1309, 1309n,
1313, 1320, 1323n, 1326, 1330, 1333,
1340, 1342, 1344, 1346, 1346n, 1347n,
1349, 1349n, 1370, 1374–5, 1378n, 1379,
1390, 1392, 1394, 1430, 1454, 1459, 1480,
1482, 1487, 1492, 1496, 1498, 1507, 1509,
1514, 1519, 1521, 1526, 1526n, 1537,
1541, 1546, 1562, 1566, 1590, 1608,
1611n, 1617, 1623, 1640n, 1654, 1670,
1676n, 1678n, 1685, 1701n, 1708, 1709n,
1722, 1724, 1727n, 1729, 1744, 1746n,
1757n, 1759n, 1772n, 1773n, 1844n,
1870n, 1903, 1926, 1932, 2011, 2056n,
2077n, 2079, 2079n, 2087n, 2114, 2124n,
2132n, 2135, 2140, 2144, 2144n, 2149,
2155n, 2170, 2174, 2179n, 2187, 2189n,
2192n, 2196, 2199, 2212, 2232n, 2235n,
2250n, 2256n, 2269, 2270n, 2272, 2276,
2279, 2283n, 2285n, 2288, 2301n, 2309,
2315n, 2327n, 2329n, 2330, 2336n, 2339,
2339n, 2344n, 2346n, 2350n, 2357n,
2364n, 2483n, 2638n, 2702n, 2838n,
2839n, 2850n, 2854, 2865n, 2873n, 2881,
2884, 2888, 2894, 2902n, 2907, 2910,
2920, 2922, 2931, 2934n, 2936n, 2940,
2940n, 2942n, 2952, 2961, 2967, 2983–4,
2987, 2991n, 2994, 3004n, 3006, 3006n,
3009, 3015n, 3016, 3016n, 3023, 3025,
3030, 3063n, 3071, 3075n, 3088n, 3090n,
3092n, 3105n, 3111, 3115, 3155, 3159,
3784n

formation of his Ministry (1783–4), 3–4,
4n, 6, 10

abortive negotiations with Whigs (1783), 3n

will not sit in Cabinet with Lord North
(1783), 3n

his India Bill (1784), 18n, 21, 98, 101–2,
425, 2180n

and negotiations for an extended Administration (1784), 36–8, 44

attacked by a mob (1784), 46

and European politics (1784), 68n

his Parliamentary Reform proposals
(1785), 182, 182n, 183, 203

his house in Downing Street, 218

burnt in effigy (1785), 218n

his election forecast (1790), 607n

declines the Garter, 644

strained relations with Thurlow (1791),
672n

appointed Warden of the Cinque Ports
(1792), 771

Portland, 3rd Duke of (*cont.*)

2474, 2479, 2489, 2494, 2498, 2500n, 2510, 2515, 2515n, 2536, 2554, 2574, 2604, 2643, 2645, 2682, 2699n, 2706, 2726, 2782n, 2786n, 2788, 2793–4, 2794n, 2828, 2830, 2881n, 2889n, 2894, 2935, 2937, 2970–1, 2984n, 3171, 3208, 3208n, 3298n, 3395n, 3400, 3408, 3410n, 3413, 3414n, 3416n, 3417, 3417n, 3420n, 3421, 3425n, 3430, 3444n, 3445n, 3448, 3449n, 3501n, 3510, 3522n, 3535n, 3567n, 3607n, 3613n, 3623n, 3629, 3699n, 3753, 3756n, 3763n, 3764n, 3776n, 3836, 3844n, 3856n, 3861n, 3906n, 3914n, 3919, 3925n, 3952–3, 3957n, 3958, 3960, 3962n, 3966, 3966n, 3969n, 3970n, 3971, 3978n, 3979–80, 3984n, 3985–6, 4007, 4028, 4032, 4036, 4036n, 4041, 4041n, 4056, 4076, 4076n, 4149n

letters from, 38, 757n, 774n, 830, 1097, 1109, 1111, 1117, 1119, 1127, 1129, 1136, 1143, 1148, 1169, 1184, 1192, 1192n, 1199n, 1201n, 1205, 1205n, 1207, 1207n, 1211, 1217, 1227, 1235, 1237, 1242, 1246, 1249, 1252, 1259, 1261, 1267, 1283, 1292, 1297, 1299, 1311, 1317, 1319, 1321, 1324, 1329, 1332, 1336, 1339, 1341, 1345, 1347, 1351, 1355, 1355n, 1356n, 1357, 1360, 1362, 1365, 1369, 1373, 1380, 1384, 1402, 1404, 1415, 1420, 1426, 1435, 1442, 1448, 1453, 1457, 1461, 1465, 1473, 1483, 1491, 1494, 1499, 1503, 1506, 1508, 1510, 1512, 1520, 1522, 1528, 1531, 1536, 1450, 1544, 1547, 1552, 1564, 1569, 1581, 1583, 1586, 1594, 1596, 1615, 1627, 1629, 1638, 1640, 1644, 1650, 1662, 1666, 1676, 1678n, 1679, 1684, 1686, 1686n, 1688, 1691, 1694, 1701, 1705, 1707, 1709, 1711, 1717, 1720, 1726, 1740, 1742, 1746, 1753, 1757, 1757n, 1761, 1772, 1776, 1790, 1797, 1800, 1802, 1808, 1812, 1816, 1820, 1824, 1828, 1832, 1836, 1839, 1844n, 1855, 1861, 1868, 1868n, 1872, 1878, 1882, 1889, 1896, 1899, 1904, 1909, 1913, 1916, 1925, 1927, 1940, 1942, 1958, 1962, 1966, 1975, 1978, 1996, 2038, 2094, 2102, 2104, 2109, 2111, 2122, 2124, 2126, 2131, 2143, 2146, 2153, 2157, 2166, 2169, 2179, 2183, 2211, 2220, 2222, 2226, 2231, 2245, 2250, 2254, 2257, 2262, 2265–6, 2268, 2271, 2274, 2285, 2290, 2301, 2306, 2318, 2324, 2328, 2329n, 2343, 2351, 2357n, 2362, 2365n,

2374, 2378, 2385, 2389, 2403, 2418, 2434, 2444, 2447, 2456n, 2459, 2465, 2487, 2578, 2581, 2581n, 2638n, 2688, 2751, 2794n, 2839, 2839n, 2849, 2889n, 2911, 2921, 3005, 3006n, 3007, 3015, 3015n, 3016n, 3039, 3052, 3172, 3186, 3395, 3399, 3400n, 3410, 3414, 3416, 3417n, 3418, 3420, 3425, 3429, 3434, 3447, 3449, 3453, 3462, 3465, 3469, 3502, 3512, 3522, 3544, 3551, 3555, 3559, 3567, 3580, 3583, 3607, 3613, 3622, 3627, 3635, 3635n, 3637n, 3645, 3649, 3663, 3668, 3673, 3673n, 3680, 3707, 3712, 3744, 3757, 3760, 3766, 3775, 3794, 3802, 3811, 3819, 3829, 3833, 3837, 3839, 3851, 3853, 3856, 3856n, 3857n, 3861, 3865, 3867n, 3881, 3884, 3892, 3906, 3906n, 3913, 3913n, 3916, 3925, 3930, 3934, 3938, 3970, 3977, 3984, 4164n

letters to, 733n, 830, 834n, 1096n, 1097, 1109, 1111, 1117, 1119, 1129, 1184, 1192, 1205, 1207, 1211, 1217, 1227, 1237, 1242, 1246, 1249, 1259, 1261, 1283, 1292, 1293n, 1297, 1299, 1311, 1324, 1329, 1332, 1336, 1339, 1345, 1246n, 1347, 1351, 1358, 1490n, 1528, 1596, 2297n, 2328, 2794n, 2889n, 3186, 3405, 3410, 3410n, 3414, 3416, 3417n, 3418, 3420, 3425, 3429, 3434, 3447, 3449, 3453, 3462, 3465, 3502, 3512, 3522, 3544, 3555, 3559, 3567, 3580, 3583, 3607, 3613, 3622, 3627, 3635, 3645, 3649, 3663, 3668, 3673, 3680, 3707, 3712, 3760, 3766, 3775, 3794, 3802, 3811, 3833, 3837, 3839, 3851, 3853, 3856, 3861, 3865, 3881, 3884, 3892, 3906, 3906n, 3913, 3916, 3925, 3930, 3934, 3938, 3957, 3970, 3972n, 3977, 3984, 3996n

Memo. by, 3522n

Minute by, 3613n

Message from the King to, 37

and negotiations for an extended Administration (1784), 37–9, 44

declines the Garter (1792), 774n

attitude to Government (1792), 807, 807n

strength of his Party (1792), 807n

his political creed in 1793, 830

his friends in Parliament, 838

contribution to Party funds, 894n

negotiations with Government (1794), 1090n, 1091

Portland, 3rd Duke of (*cont.*)

declines Foreign Secretaryship (1794), 1090n

given the Garter, 1093, 1093n, 1095, 1095n

elected Recorder of Nottingham, 1119

would like Fitzwilliam to remain in Cabinet (1795), 1208

fractures a rib, 1812, 1812n

suffering from erysipelas, 1872

views on Catholic question, 2329n

appointed President of the Council, 2456, 2491

his private use of public money, 2456, 2459n

his tardy resignation of Home Secretaryship, 2474n, 2487, 2487n

his 'distressed circumstances' (1801), 2487n

dangerous illness of, 2751, 2751n

does not take in *The Times*, 2839

declines office of Lord Chamberlain (1804), 2839, 2852

resigns office of Lord President (1805), 2984n, 2991n, 3003, 3005–6

incapable of attending to business, 2991n

Cabinet Minister without portfolio, 2991, 3006, 3006n, 3007

refuses Duchy of Lancaster, 3003, 3003n, 3006

Chancellor of Oxford University, 3052

advises King to veto Catholic Relief Bill (1807), 3395

to be First Lord of the Treasury, 3399, 3399n, 3408

illness in 1807, 3399n, 3405n, 3406, 3567n

moves from Downing Street, 3590n

his epileptic seizure, 3934, 3934n

resigns Premiership, 3952n, 3966

tenders resignation before Sept. 1809, 3960

'the last of his species', 3960

to remain in Cabinet (Oct. 1809), 3996

death, 4018, 4018n, 4041n, 4195n

his mild disposition, 4041n

Portland, 4th Duke of, *see* Titchfield

Portland Roads, 1595, 2642, 3032

Portland Whigs, the, 3n

Port Louis, 2215n

Portman, Edward Berkeley (1771–1823), 3834, 4126

Portmore, Wm. Charles, 3rd Earl of (*c.* 1747–1823), pension for, 3712, 3744, 3744n

Port Patrick, near Stranraer, 1503, 1586, 1757n

Portsmouth, 3rd Earl of (1767–1853), 1983n, 3966n

Portsmouth, 377, 398, 536, 577, 698, 791, 945, 969, 971, 987, 1083, 1085, 1089–90, 1187, 1265, 1282, 1291, 1302, 1307, 1331, 1363, 1370, 1501, 1530, 1532–3, 1542, 1544, 1546, 1584, 1677, 1752, 1765, 1786, 1965, 2004, 2024, 2210, 2238, 2297, 2415, 2472, 2476, 2481, 2513, 2519, 2524, 2547, 2555, 2564, 2590, 2598, 2601, 2607, 2716, 2912, 2926, 3125–6, 3174, 3276, 3370, 3390, 3528–9, 3538, 3557, 3573, 3615, 3655, 3729, 3742, 3743n, 3769, 3789, 3795, 3801, 3845, 3889, 3910, 3923–4, 3948n, 4119, 4228, 4264–5, 4296

garrison at, 9

defences of, 210

the hulks at, 2598

Portsmouth Division of Marines, the, 43

Portugal, Queen of, *see* Maria

Portugal, assistance for (1797), 1580; (1799), 1960; (1800), 2256; (1801), 2371n, 2410, 2410n; (1806), 3286

Portugal, Prince Regent of, *see* John VI

Convention with (1807), 3545, 3575, 3871

Treaties with, 951

Portuguese settlements in Asia, 2674

Post Horse Bill (1787), 358

Postlethwaite, Thomas (1731–98), appointed Master of Trinity College, Cambridge, 483n

death of, 1733

Postmaster-General, office of, not tenable with seat in House of Commons, 1926

Post Office, *see* General Post Office

Potato crop saves country from famine (1795), 1306

Potocki, Count, 3356

Potsdam, 306, 351, 1863, 1867, 1888, 1920

military manoeuvres at (1785), 252; (1787), 355, 361

Poulett, 4th Earl (1756–1819), 1983n, 3645, 3966n, 3974, 3982, 3988

Poulett, Lady Mary, daughter of 4th Earl Poulett, and later wife of Lord Charles Henry Somerset, 1835

Poulett, Sophia, Countess (*d.* 1811), 3974, 3988

Poulett, Lady Sophia, later Duchess of Cleveland (1785–1859), 3974

Pouletts, the, 3974, 3976

Powell, Mr, 126

Powell, Sir Gabriel, Sheriff of Carmarthenshire, knighted, 2183

Powell, William Samuel (1717–75), 260
Powelson, 2472
Powerful, a 74-gun ship, 1377
Powerscourt, Amelia, Viscountess (*d.* 1831), 1276
Powis, 1st Earl of (1754–1839), 2879, 2888, 3416, 3622, 3662, 3966n
    offered office of Lord-Lieut. of Ireland (Nov. 1805), 3155, 3418n
    declines the office (March 1807), 3418
Powis, George Edward Henry Arthur, 2nd Earl of (1755–1801), 1607, 1983n
Powlett [Poulett], Col. Thomas Norton, appointed Clerk of the Signet, 3533, 3533n
Pownall, Sir George, secretary of Province of Lower Canada, 1384, 3412
Pownall, John, 569
Pownall, Thomas (1722–1805), Governor of Massachusetts, 1384
Powney, Penyston Portlock (?1743–94), 373, 458
    elected for Windsor (1784), 57n, 158; re-elected (1790), 602
    appointed Ranger of Windsor Home Park (1788), 602n, 604
Powys, Thomas, 1st Baron Lilford (1743–1800), 42n, 44, 203, 438, 448, 589, 644, 670, 682, 744, 751, 757, 836, 838, 878, 1033, 1039, 1247, 1255, 1330
    a member of the St Alban's Tavern Committee (1784), 35n
    Wraxall on, 44n
Powys, Rev. Thomas (*c.* 1737–1809), appointed Dean of Canterbury, 1498
    resigns Canonry of Windsor, 1498
Poyntz, Rev. Charles, D.D. (*c.* 1735–1809), 2875
Poyntz, Wm. Stephen (*c.* 1770–1840), M.P. for St Albans, 2315n, 2752n
Praemunire, Statutes of, 1215, 1353, 1365, 1393
Praga, 3342
Prague, 1992, 2118, 2292, 3342, 3390
Pralsamao, Visct de, 3728
Prescott, Sir George William (1748–1801), given a baronetcy, 1164
Prescott, Gen. Robert (*c.* 1726–1815), 1818
President, a captured 38-gun frigate, 3308
Press, liberty of the, 75n
Press, The, an Irish newspaper, 1691n
Pressburg, 3912

Preston, Sir Charles, 5th Bart (*c.* 1735–1800), M.P. for the Dysart Burghs (1784–90), 1728n
Preston, John, a mutineer, 1584
Preston, Sir Robert (1740–1834), M.P. for Dover (1784–90), 57n; for Cirencester (1792–1806), 2752n
Pretyman (later Tomline), Sir George (1750–1827), Pitt's tutor and private secretary, 343, 1983n, 2350n, 2978, 3441n, 3559
    letters from, 3170, 3174n
    letters to 1498n, 2173n, 2329n, 2844n, 3170, 3174n
    given the Living of Sudbourne (1785), 248
    Dean of St Paul's (1787), 343, 1336
    not to be Archbishop of Canterbury, 3014
    Bishop of Lincoln, 3966n
    his wife, 3174n
Prevost, Sir George (1767–1816), 3062, 3174, 3514
Price, Lieut., R.N., 1732n
Price, Sir Charles (1748–1818), Lord Mayor of London (1803), 2670, 2708, 2797, 3867, 4126
Price, William, the Queen's Vice-Chamberlain (from 1792), 312, 312n, 980, 985, 1310, 1353–4, 1414, 1562, 2084n
Price, Mrs, 317
Priestley, Joseph (1733–1804), 691–2
Primate of Ireland, *see* Fowler
Primate of Ireland, *see* Stuart, William
Primrose, an 18-gun sloop, 3691
Prince Edward, the Falmouth packet, 1773n
Prince George, a 98-gun ship, 194, 4265, 4267, 4269, 4271, 4285
Prince Royal of Denmark, *see* Frederick VI
Prince William, a 64-gun ship, captured from Spaniards, 4269
Prince of Orange, packet, 1529n
Prince of Wales, a 98-gun ship, 2227
Princess Amelia, an 80-gun ship, 4269
Princess Augusta, the, yacht, 2409, 2413, 2485
Princess Royal, a 34-gun French frigate, 1186
Princess Royal, a 98-gun ship, 3329
Princess Royal, *see* Charlotte Augusta Matilda
Princesses, increased allowances for the (1804), 2905, 2907
Pringel, Vice-Admiral Thomas (*d.* 1803), 1377
Prisoners to be relieved, poor, 4002, 4010

Privy Council meeting at Weymouth, 2657

Privy Council Minutes, 1009

Privy Purse, the King's, 1674, 1674n, 1678, 2045, 2187, 2411, 2457, 2770, 4002, 4208, 4227

Privy Seal, office of, put in commission (1784), 54n, 150n

Privy Seal of Scotland, office of, 2915

Proby, Rev. Baptist (c. 1726–1807), Dean of Lichfield, death of, 3364

Proclamation against seditious writings (1792), 757, 757n, 807n, 830

Professorship of Divinity at Oxford, 4007

Prometheus, the, 3928n

Property tax, the, 2975

Proserpine, a 28-gun frigate, 1377, 1912n, 1920n, 1930

Provence, Comte de, *see* Louis XVIII

Prowse, Rear-Admiral Wm. (c. 1752–1826), 3835

Prudente, a French warship, 385

Prussia, Treaty with (1794), 967n, 1055–7; (1807), 3424

Prussia, Prince Albert of (1809–72), 4033, 4042

Prussia, Princess Augusta of, later wife of Elector of Hesse-Cassel (1780–1841), 714

Prussia, Elizabeth, Queen Dowager of (1715–97), 714

Prussia, Prince Ferdinand of (1730–1813), 2255

his wife Louise (1738–1820), 2255

Prussia, Frederica, Queen of (1751–1805), 241n, 714, 1920

Prussia, Princess Frederica of, later Duchess of Cumberland, *see* Frederica of Mecklenburg-Strelitz

Prussia, Prince Henry of (1726–1802), 714n, 4274, 4281

Prussia, Prince Henry of (1781–1846), son of Frederick William II, 714

Prussia, Prince Louis of (1773–96), 714

Prussia, Prince Louis Ferdinand of (1772–1806), Frederick the Great's nephew, 1734

killed at Saalfeld, 3320, 3320n

Prussia, Prince William of, son of Frederick William II (1783–1851), 714, 3320n, 4042

Prussia, Princess Louisa of (1808–70), 3658

Prussia, Princess Wilhelmina of (1774–1837), daughter of Frederick William II and wife of Hereditary Prince of Orange, 714

Prussia, King of, *see* Frederick William II *and* Frederick William III

Prussia, Queen of, *see* Louisa, Queen of Prussia

Prussia, Prince of, *see* Frederick William II

Prussia, Prince Royal of, *see* Frederick William III

Prussia, Princess Louis of, *see* Mecklenburg-Strelitz, Princess Frederica of

Prussia, Princess Royal of, *see* Louisa, Queen of Prussia

Prussian subsidy, suspension of the (1794), 1131

Public Ledger, the, 158

Pugachoff, 399

Puisaye, Comte Joseph de, 1258, 1277, 1277n, 1282

Puiter [Peyster], Lieut. de (d. 1793), 920

Pulteney, 1025

Pulteney, Sir James Murray, 7th Bart (c. 1755–1811), Lieut.-Gen., 666, 670, 785, 792, 802, 844, 854, 859, 862–4, 866, 868, 875, 877, 879, 882, 891, 896, 898, 901, 905, 911–12, 914, 916, 921, 932, 943, 947, 952, 963, 966, 977, 979, 981–4, 986, 989, 991, 993, 1000, 1025, 1044, 1459, 1537, 1765, 2136, 2184, 2203–5, 2243, 2246, 2246n, 2252, 2256, 2367, 2526, 2929, 3243, 3256, 3505, 3620, 3643, 3799, 3821, 3832, 3834, 3861, 3906n, 4229

letter from, 3681

letters to, 2843n, 2873n, 2902n

Secretary at War (1807), 3418

Pulteney, Sir William (1729–1805), 1198, 1323, 1480, 1509, 1526, 1537, 1654, 2239, 2833, 4229

letter from, 1565

succeeds as 5th Bart (1794), 438n

Pultusk, 3342

Purefoy, Thomas, acquitted of murder, 519n

Purfleet, 1557–8

Purvis, Rear-Admiral John Child (d. 1825), 3557, 3669, 3682, 3689, 3796

Putney, 3170

Putney Heath, duel on, 1745

Pütter, Professor Johann, one of the Princes' tutors at Göttingen, 351, 484

Pybus, Charles Small (1766–1810), 670, 740

becomes a Lord of the Admiralty (1791), 686

Treasury pays his Dover election expenses, 686n

Pye, Henry James (1745–1813), elected for Berkshire (1784), 62, 158

Pye, James, Mews Keeper at Kensington (d. 1801), 2335

Pye, Sir Thomas (?1713–85), 1090n, 4269

Pylades, a 16-gun sloop, 2086

Quakers, the, 495, 1046, 4283
  reluctant to take part in elections, 76

Quarantine Act, the (1805), 3061

Quebec, 377, 385, 404, 448, 543, 555, 655, 696, 787, 1030, 1051, 1384, 1657, 1818, 3526, 4120n

Quebec Act (1774), 655n

Queen Anne's Bounty, 4056, 4201

Queenborough elections, 3876, 3876n

Queen Charlotte, a 100-gun ship, 591, 1085, 1533n; blows up near Leghorn (1800), 2128

Queensberry, 4th Duke of (1725–1810), 3966n
  letter from, 523
  elected a Scottish Representative Peer (1784), 78
  his politics during Regency crisis, 523
  dismissed from his Household office, 523n

Queen's House, 198, 207, 226, 238, 297, 333, 359, 444, 652, 726–7, 760, 770, 1138, 1141, 1232, 1258, 1261, 1321, 1374, 1495–6, 1541, 1647, 1701, 1725, 1895, 1959, 2116, 2153, 2331, 2334–5, 2337, 2350, 2356n, 2365, 2368n, 2379, 2426A, 2428n, 2445, 2456, 2461, 2474n, 2487, 2536, 2577, 2583, 2630, 2697, 2712, 2726, 2732, 2747n, 2748, 2781n, 2830, 2832, 2834, 2839, 2849, 2859, 2910–11, 2924, 2961, 2962n, 2964, 2973, 2981–2, 2985, 2993, 3002, 3004, 3014, 3023, 3033–4, 3039, 3042, 3049, 3054, 3082, 3094, 3110n, 3113, 3120, 3164n, 3187, 3206, 3216, 3218, 3226, 3232, 3257, 3278, 3283, 3294, 3298, 3317, 3328, 3333, 3347, 3355, 3372, 3385, 3411, 3413, 3415–6, 3418, 3420, 3425, 3430, 3437, 3447, 3449, 3453–4, 3468–9, 3486–8, 3510, 3536–7, 3541, 3545, 3549, 3559, 3591, 3627, 3632, 3635, 3637, 3642, 3653, 3663, 3673, 3678, 3694, 3728, 3733, 3743, 3747–8, 3759, 3839, 3865, 3883, 3903, 3908, 3915, 3918, 3924, 3951n, 3958, 3967, 3977, 3984–5, 4037, 4042, 4099, 4104, 4121, 4150, 4194, 4233n, 4241, 4247, 4290

pictures in the, 2985; medals and drawings at, 770; lunatic in the, 1369

Queen's Lodge, Windsor, 494n, 499

Quesnoy, 943, 948, 957, 962, 992

Quiberon Bay, 1307, 2184

Quiberon Peninsula, expedition to (1795), 1258, 1263, 1263n, 1265, 1270, 1277, 1282, 1289, 1506

Quick, John, the actor (1748–1831), 2042

Quievrain, 882

Quigley [O'Coigly], James (c. 1762–98), 1691, 1694, 1717
  convicted of high treason, 1742, 1742n, 1746
  execution of, 1746n

Quin, Windham Henry Wyndham, 2nd Earl of Dunraven (1782–1850), 4076

Quinn, Mr, Portuguese diplomatist, 3924

Raby, Barony of, 2672

Radetzsky, Count (1766–1858), 3912

Radnor, Jacob, 6th Earl of (1750–1828), 1009n, 1983n, 2743n, 3966n

Radstock, Lord, *see* Waldegrave, William

Rae, 565

Rae, Sir David, Lord Eskgrove (?1724–1804), 201

Raigersfeldt, Baron, 3739

Railleuse, a French frigate, 341

Raine, Jonathan (1763–1831), 2894n, 3025

Rainier, Peter, Admiral (?1741–1808), 1472

Riansford, Gen. Charles (1728–1809), 946, 3135

Raleigh, Lord (Addington's proposed title), 3004, 3006

Rambouillet, 3750

Ramillies, a 74-gun ship, 1377

Ramsay, Lieut., 940

Ramsay, Sir Alexander, 6th Bart (d. 1806), 3219n

Ramsay, Sir Alexander, 1st Bart (1757–1810), 3219

Ramsbottom, 1498

Ramsbottom, Richard, candidature at Windsor, 2834n

Ramsey, Col. William, 2388

Ramsgate, 1368, 3479, 3923

Ramus (of the Treasury), 770

Ramus, Henry, in service of East India Company, 580, 770

Ramus, William (d. 1792), Page of the Backstairs, 580, 4264
  letter to, 279

Ranby, George II's surgeon, 1754

Randolph, John, Bishop of Bangor and of London (1749–1813), 2038, 3881, 3966n, 4007

Raphael, the painter (1483–1520), 2668

Rastatt, 1936, 1948, 1953, 2015
  Congress of (1797), 1642n, 1648, 1704

Ratisbon, 3539, 4297

Rattan island, *see* Roatan

Rattler, a 14-gun sloop, 341, 363

Rattlesnake, a 16-gun sloop, 166

Ravenna, 1963

Ravestein, 1132

Rawdon, Lord, *see* Moira

Rawleigh, 581

Rawlins, Sir William, Sheriff of London and Middlesex, 2625, 3016n

Raynham, John, a convict, 584

Read, James, the Bow Street Police Magistrate, 4187

Reading, 1241, 1241n

Reading Mercury, the, 1241n

Real Carlos, Spanish warship, 2496

Reay, 7th Lord (1773–1847), 3966n

Rebellion, the Great, 60

Recorder of London, *see* Adair, James, and (from July 1789) Rose, J. W., and from 1803, Silvester, John

Recorder's report, the, 19, 159, 335, 444, 530, 612, 655, 746, 1025, 1058, 1103–4, 1261, 1321, 1457, 1473, 1564, 1793, 1797, 1878, 2204, 2456, 2595, 2640, 2643, 2671, 2708, 2748, 2750, 2832, 2881, 2881n, 2885n, 2895n, 2899, 2909n, 2925, 2964, 2973, 3028, 3077, 3113, 3328, 3364, 3782, 3805, 3855
  presented at Windsor, 508; at Kew, 530

Red Ribbons, *see* Bath, Order of the

Rede, Lieut. Thomas William, *letter from*, 2804
  his family, 2804

Reden, 4284

Reden, Mme de, 1953

Reden, M. de, Envoy from Wurtemberg, 1706, 1953

Redern, Count (Prussian Envoy in London), 703, 730, his recall, 769

Redesdale (Northumberland), 2587

Redesdale, Lord, *see* Mitford

Redfern, William, a mutineer, 1613

Reed, David, a mutineer, 1834

Reed, Lady, *see* Reid

Reede, M. de, 409

Regency Bill (1789), 218n

Regius Professor of Civil Law at Oxford, 3970

Rehausen, Baron, Swedish Minister in London, 3080, 3471, 3474, 3476

Reichenberg Forest, 1809

Reid, Lady, 3983, 3987

Reidinger, 2563

Reigate election (1784), 158

Reinhard, 1615

Remembrancer of the Exchequer, office of, 1621, 2250

Rennell, James (1742–1830), 137, 3577

Repnin, Prince, 1563

Report of Committee on waste lands and commons, 1188

Résistance, a 52-gun French warship, 1506

Resolution, a 74-gun ship, 4269

Resource, a 28-gun ship, 377, 385, 404

Retford, 1046

Reuss, Prince, 896, 926, 943, 1000

Revel, 1979, 2425, 3495n

Revel, Prince de, 1111

Revenge, the, a 74-gun ship, 3691

Reventlau [Reventlow], Count, Danish Minister in London, 223

Reventlow, the two Counts, 3371

Revenue Boards, the, 1316n

Reversion Bill, *see* Offices in Reversion Bill

Reynier, defeated at Maida, 3291n

Reynolds, Capt., R.N., 1830

Reynolds, Dr Henry Revell (1745–1811), 2970
  on the King's health, 2855, 2864n
  medical report on Duke of Portland, 2971
  professional services to the King, 3164n

Rheims, Archbishop of, 1192

Rhine, the, 816, 866, 973, 1000, 1064, 1132, 1197, 1223, 1228, 1318, 1319n, 1322, 1324, 1337, 1429, 1610, 1704, 1744, 1949, 2050, 2064, 2139, 2236

Rhode Island, 4143

Rhodes, 2259

Ribblesdale, Lord (1752–1826), 3966n

Rice, increased consumption of, 2278

Rice, Mr, 2796

Rice, William, Clerk of Works at Hampton Court (*d.* 1789), 494

Rich, Sir Thomas (*c.* 1733–1803), Admiral, 1016

Richard II (1367–1400), 1024

Richard, Mr, 1997

Richards, Sir Richard (1752–1823), 2693, 3447

Richmond, 3rd Duke of (1735–1806), 4, 26n, 50n, 54, 54n, 57, 102, 190, 226, 256, 280, 440, 472, 495, 614, 710, 829, 867, 902, 928, 949n, 1554, 1617

letter from, 3074

declines, then accepts, seat in Cabinet (1783), 4n

at Carlton House with Fox, 4n

declines Home Secretaryship (1784), 10n, 54n

'a great acquisition' to the Cabinet, 54n

a difficult Cabinet colleague, 54n

his 'love of County elections', 495

his 'chicanery', 949

removal from Ordnance Dept., 1198

to remain on the Staff, 1198

Richmond, 4th Duke of, *see* Lennox, Charles

Richmond, 500, 616

Richmond, the King's villa at, 2722, 2799

Richmond Green, the King's houses on, 4240

Richmond Park, 494n, 743, 2757n, 2821, 2864, 2864n

the deer in, 2707

Addington removes to, from Downing Street, 2864, 2864n

kangaroos in, 2921

Richpanse, Gen. Antoine (1770–1802), nominated (1802) Commandant of Guadeloupe, 2214

Richter, surgeon at Göttingen, 1348

Ridge, Capt., 2290

Ridley, Rev. Henry, Lord Eldon's brother-in-law, 2657

Ridley, Sir Matthew White (1745–1813), 448, 1543, 2657n

Ridley, Nicholas, Bishop of London (?1500–55), 2657

Rieger, Baron de, 1461, 1474, 1516, 1527, 1561, 1585

Riga, 178, 399

Rigby, Richard (1722–88), 126

letter from, 118

Master of the Rolls [I.] (1759–88), 2285n

Rights, Bill of (1689), 1219

Rio de la Plata, 3273, 3363

Riot Act, the, 4126

Riou, Capt. Edward, R.N., 587

Rist, M. de, 3317, 3371, 3537, 3552

Rivers, 1st Lord (1721–1803), 1983n

Rivers, 2nd Lord (1751–1828), 2965, 3965, 3966n

letter to, 3650

a Lord of the Bedchamber, 2902n, 3650n

Rivers, James (*d.* 1807), Clerk of the Signet, 3533, 3533n

Rivers, Penelope, Lady (?1725–95), 648

Rivière, M., 3211, 3211n, 3221

Roatan island, in West Indies, 191

Robarts, Abraham (*c.* 1745–1816), 2984n

Robbins, John, of the *Warrior*, 2349

Roberton, Corporal George, *letter from*, 928

Roberton, Mrs George, 928

Roberton, Margaret, 928

Roberts, Thomas Sautelle (1760–1826), artist, 2694

Robertson, Dr, his house at Greenwich, 2455

Robertson, Lieut.-Gen. James (*d.* 1788), 57

Robertson, Capt., 4283

Robinson, Mrs Catherine (1750–1834), 927

Robinson, Sir Christopher (*c.* 1766–1833), 3982, 4234

appointed King's Advocate (1809), 3790

Robinson, Frederick (1746–92), 927

Robinson, Frederick John, Visct Goderich and Earl of Ripon (1782–1859), 3444, 3444n, 3643, 3787, 4076n, 4087, 4087n, 4138n

letter from, 3787n

refuses office (1807), 3444n

moves the Address, 3787

appointed an Under-Secretary of State, 3870

Robinson, John (1727–1802), 140, 740n, 770n, 1567n

letters from, 84n, 93n, 109, 126, 133, 139, 141, 144, 358n, 671

letters to, 116, 129, 1932n

forecast of results of 1784 elections, 55n, 57n

appointed Surveyor-General of Woods and Forests (1787), 420

death of, 2689

Robinson, Joseph, a mutineer, 1665n

Robinson, Morris, 3rd Baron Rokeby (1757–1829), 1323

Robinson, Lieut.-Gen. Robert, 4283

Robinson, William, a mutineer, 1595

Robison [*sic*], Lieut., 1811

Robley, Mr, President of Tobago, 2586

Robson, Richard Bateman (*d.* 1827), 2276, 2276n

Robust, a 74-gun ship, 1377

Rochambeau, 382n, 4285

Rose, Sir George Henry (1771–1855), 1087, 2173n, 2881n, 2884n, 3262
 given reversion of office of Clerk of the Parliaments (1795), 1313
 Mission to the U.S.A. (1807–8), 3549, 3653
Rose, Sir John William, Recorder of London (d. 1803), 564, 612, 1025, 1058, 1103–4, 1261, 1321, 1457, 1473, 1564, 1797, 1878, 1927, 2204, 2456, 2543n, 2595, 2640, 2643, 2671, 2708, 2748
 elected Recorder (1789), 532n
Rose, Mrs Mary, 3757
Roseau (Dominica), 341, 363, 3062
Rosebery, 3rd Earl of (1729–1814), candidate for Scottish Representative Peerage (1784), 78
Rosembusch's Hussars, 252
Rosetta, 1866, 2552, 3475n
Ross, Major-Gen. Alexander, Surveyor-General of the Ordnance (1742–1827), 1019, 1597, 1657, 2376, 2376n
Ross, 4036n
Ross, Anna Munro, 4229
Ross, Major-Gen. Charles (c. 1729–97), 173, 202, 202n, 205
Ross, Gen. Sir Charles Lockhart- (?1763–1814), 2575
Ross, John (1719–92), Bishop of Exeter, 775, 780, 3462
Ross, Sir John Lockhart (1721–90), 4269
Rosse, Earl of (1758–1841), 3966n, 4038n
Rosslyn, Sir James St Clair-Erskine, later 2nd Earl of (1762–1837), 105, 670, 751, 1852, 2481, 2486, 3317, 3527n, 3927, 3966n, 4091
 letters from, 3967n, 3989n, 4092n, 4133n
Rosslyn, 1st Earl of, see Loughborough
Rossmore, Lord, see Cuninghame, Gen.
Rostopchin, Count Feodor (1765–1826), Russian Foreign Minister, 2123, 2297
Rottingdean, 1784
Rotterdam, 843, 859, 3926
Roubaix, 920, 1066
Round Tower, Windsor Castle, 495
Rous, the East India Company's solicitor, 438
Rous, Sir John, Baron Rous and 1st Earl of Stradbroke (1750–1827), 1330, 2804n, 3966n
 cr. Baron Rous, 1404
Rousselaere, 943, 1022, 1084
Rowe, Lieut., R.N., 3532
Rowle, Thomas, 3233

Rowley, Samuel Campbell (1774–1846), 2894n
Roxburgh Fencible Cavalry, the, 1298
Roxburghe, 3rd Duke of (1740–1804), 644, 1812, 2199, 2902, 2963
 letter from, 1806
 asks for the Garter (1790), 644
 Groom of the Stole, 2199
 Lord-Lieut. of Co. Roxburgh, 2869n
 the King's 'much-lamented friend', 2869n
Royal African Corps, the, 2947
Royal Charlotte yacht, 1632, 2409, 2413, 2416, 2485
Royal Dukes, payment of debts of (1806), 3225n
Royal Fusiliers, the, 835
Royal Gardens, the, 1462, 3679
Royal George, the, 100-gun ship, 591, 2310
Royal Horticultural Society, 1931n
Royal Hospital for Seamen at Greenwich, see Greenwich
Royal Hotel in Pall Mall, 1529n
Royal Institution, the, 1575
Royal Lodge, Richmond Park, 2445
Royal Marine Mutiny Bill (1805), 3049
Royal Marriages Act (1772), 193, 709, 1010, 1024
Royal Military College at Great Marlow, the, 2462, 2471, 2511, 3945
Royal Society, the, 236, 379
 President of, see Banks, Sir Joseph
Royal Sovereign, the King's yacht, 3937
Royal Sovereign, a 110-gun ship, 1613, 2227, 3132, 3872
Royal Veterinary College, the, 1166
Royal Waggon Train, the, 3195
Royds, Sir John, Judge at Calcutta, 2456n
Royds, John, 1488
Rozendahl, 1099
Rozière, Marquis de la (1733–1808), 1286
Rozzelli, the singer, 1013
Rubens, Peter Paul, the painter (1757–1640), 2668
 pictures by, 3118
Ruhr, the, 816, 1132
Rumbold, Caroline, Lady (d. 1826), 3645, 3645n
Rumbold, Sir George Berriman (1764–1807), 2966
Rumford, 4126
Rumford, Sir Benjamin Thompson, Count (1753–1814), 1827

Rumphius, Georgius Everhardus, 372

Rundell and Bridge, Messrs, the Court jewellers, 1178n, 3970n

Rush, John, Inspector of Military Hospitals, 2152

Rushout, Sir James, grandfather of Lord Northwick (d. 1689), 1426n

Rushout, Sir John, 4th Bart (1685–1775), father of Lord Northwick, 1426n

Rushout, Sir John, Lord Northwick (1738–1800), 1426, 1590, 1983n
letter from, 1426n
asks for a peerage, 1426n
given a peerage, 1590
the family borough (Evesham), 1426n

Rushworth, Edward (1755–1817), 203

Russell, Irish rebel, 2793, 2795

Russell, Sir Henry (1751–1836), 3163

Russell, Lord John, later 6th Duke of Bedford (1766–1839), 757, 1619n

Russell, Admiral Thomas Macnamara (?1740–1824), 3528, 3716

Russell, Lord William (1767–1840), 831, 1195, 1519, 1729, 1950, 2699, 3787n, 3834, 4126

Russell, a 74-gun warship, 1377, 1632, 4143

Russia, rupture with Turkey threatened (1784), 17
France seeks alliance with (1785), 241
Treaty with Great Britain (1799), 1979, 1979n, 1987; (1805), 3045, 3072n

Russia, Emperor of, *see* Paul I and Alexander I

Russia, Empress of, *see* Catherine II and Sophia

Russia, Grand Duchess Anne of (1795–1865), 2698

Russia, Grand Duchess Catherine of (1788–1819), 2698

Russia, Grand Duchess Mary of (1786–1859), a possible wife for Duke of Cambridge, 2698, 2718

Russia, Empress Sophia of, *see* Sophia, Tsarina

Russo-Turkish War (1768–74), 399

Rutherford, John (c. 1748–1834), M.P. for Selkirkshire (1802–6), 2752n, 4034n

Rutland, 1643

Rutland, 4th Duke of (1754–87), 3n, 4n, 26n, 67n, 79, 94, 100, 100n, 101, 120, 120n, 162, 167–8, 171, 179, 182n, 214, 224, 472n, 2774, 2856n
becomes Lord Privy Seal (1783), 4n

appointed Lord-Lieut. of Ireland (1784), 54n, 75n, 150n
devoted to Pitt, 79n
promises Pitt a parliamentary seat for life, 79n
alarming illness of (1784), 155
suggests a Marquessate for Shelbourne (1784), 226n
death of, 410–12

Rutland Fencible Cavalry, the, 2008

Rutland, John Henry, 5th Duke of (1778–1857), 1983, 3243n, 3437, 3447, 3760, 3966n
letters to, 3637n, 3673n, 3857n, 3867n
given the Garter, 2806, 2811
offered office of Lord-Lieut. of Ireland, 3418, 3420
his Members in the Commons, 3821n, 4124n

Rutland, Mary Isabella, Duchess of, wife of 4th Duke (1756–1831), and the Duke of York, 688n
in love with Sir Arthur Paget, 3813n

Ryall, a Weymouth shopkeeper, 3995

Ryan, Nicholas, a mutineer, 1834

Ryde, John, appointed Equerry to Duke of Clarence (1789), 520n

Ryder, Dudley, 1st Earl of Harrowby (1762–1847), 544, 647, 670, 738, 740n, 751, 836, 895, 1198, 1459, 1745n, 1790, 2140, 2143, 2290, 2346n, 2842n, 2856n, 2914n, 2935, 2966, 3068n, 3070, 3166–7, 3168, 3171n, 3522, 3568n, 3808, 3873n, 3900n, 3962, 3966, 3989, 4028, 4076n, 4092, 4105n
letters from, 2870, 2895, 2901, 2913, 2918, 2936, 2936n, 2941, 2951, 2956, 2958, 3002, 3075n, 3188
letters to, 3002, 3188, 3373n, 3380n, 3406n, 3856n, 3913n, 4051n, 4055n, 4072n, 4234n
moves the Address (1787), 417, 417n
becomes Under-Secretary of State for Foreign Affairs (1789), 544n, 895n
given a seat at Board of Control (1790), 582
appointed Joint Paymaster-General (1791), 651n, 654
Vice-President of Board of Trade, 654
Comptroller of the Household (1790), 654n
ceases to be a Commissioner for India (1791), 677
declines Mastership of the Mint (1799), 1932n

Ryder, Dudley (*cont.*)

to be Treasurer of the Navy (1800), 2144

resigns office (Nov. 1801), 2554

his death expected, 2554n

accepts Foreign Secretaryship (1804), 2844n, 2852n

his poor health, 2870n, 2964n, 2966n, 2984n, 3167n

resigns Foreign Secretaryship, 2984n, 2991, 2991n, 2994n, 3002

accident to (1804), 2964n, 2966n, 2991n, 3002n

remains in Cabinet without portfolio, 3002

hopes Pitt will not resign (1805), 3014n

as Treasurer of the Navy, 3068n

declines, then accepts, office of President of India Board, 3856, 3861n, 3913n

given an Earldom, 3913

a possible successor to Portland, 3934n, 4028n

in Cabinet without office, 4026

resigns office, 4026, 2046n

Ryder, Nathaniel, 1st Baron Harrowby (1735–1803), 3913

Ryder, Richard (1766–1832), 2991n, 3105, 3174, 3174n, 3485, 3485n, 3832, 3989n, 4007n, 4010, 4061, 4074, 4076, 4089, 4093, 4105n, 4113n, 4124n, 4126, 4129–30, 4138, 4151, 4153, 4177, 4208

letters from, 3373n, 3380n, 4038, 4047, 4051n, 4052, 4055n, 4061, 4070, 4072, 4072n, 4075, 4090, 4095, 4104, 4127, 4136, 4187, 4192, 4195, 4203, 4211, 4213, 4230, 4234n

letters to, 4038, 4038n, 4047, 4052, 4061, 4070, 4072, 4075, 4090, 4095, 4104, 4127, 4136, 4187, 4192, 4195, 4203, 4211, 4213, 4230

appointed a Welsh Judge, 2914

refuses Irish Secretaryship (1804), 2914n

Lord Stafford's Auditor, 2914n

a Lord of the Treasury (1807), 3522

Judge Advocate-General, 3559, 3559n

becomes Home Secretary, 3559n, 4007n, 4010n, 4014–5

Rye elections, 158, 1932n, 3876, 3876n

Ryland, John, 708

Rymer, a servant, 227, 393

Sack, Dr, 484

Sackville, Visct, 1983n, 3533n, 3966n

Sadleir, Anthony, of Madras (*d.* 1793), 137

Safford, James, 2804n

Sago, production of, 372

Sainbel, Charles Vial de (1753–93), 1166

'Saint', the, 3044

St Alban's Committee, the (1784), 35, 35n, 93n

St Albans, 5th Duke of (1740–1802), 4268

St Albans, 6th Duke of (1765–1815), 3966n

St Albans, 1439

election (1790), 604n, 605; (1800), 2315n

St Amand, 875, 1034, 1050, 1056, 1066

St Andrew, Order of, *see* Thistle

St Andrews, University of, 516, 928

St Anne's Hill, Fox's country home, 3293n

St Asaph, 2779, 3333

St Asaph, Lord, *see* Ashburnham, 3rd Earl of

St Bartholomew, island of, reported cession by France to Sweden (1784), 95; capture of (1801), 2409

St Clair, M., 3722

St Clair, *see* Erskine

St Clair, Sir James, *see* Rosslyn, 2nd Earl of

St Constantine (Sicilian) Order of, 4231

St Croix, capture of (1801), 2409

St Croix, M. de, 800

St Cyr, Gen. Laurent Couvion (1764–1830), later Marshal of France (1812), 1949

St David's, 3888; Bishop of, *see* Stuart, William; and Murray, Lord George

St Dennis, Chevalier, Master of Fortification at the Military College, 2462n

St Domingo, a Spanish warship, 4269

St Fiorenzo, a 42-gun frigate, 1302, 1545, 1838, 1844, 1858, 2004, 3961

St George, the, a 98-gun ship, 2298, 3348

St George, Fort, *see* Madras

St George, Lieut.-Col. Richard (?1759–90), 586

St George's, Hanover Square, 1009–10, 1024

St George's Chapel, Windsor, 1927, 2428, 2532, 3136, 3477, 3964n

St George's Hall, Windsor, 3056–7, 3060

St Germain, Count, 613

St Germans, borough of, 4142n

St Gotthard, the, 2059

St Helena, 921, 2672, 3244n, 3250n

St Helens (Isle of Wight), 1112, 1294, 1363, 4269

St Helens, Lord, *see* Fitzherbert, Alleyne

St James's Chapel, 727, 1178

St James's Chronicle, the, 158

St James's Coffee House, 1348n

Salisbury, 7th Earl (*cont.*)
1730, 1754, 2035, 2092, 2401, (?)2693, (?)2695, 2856
wants a Marquessate, 544; question of the Garter for, 644, 2846n
wants to be a Governor of Charterhouse, 793
removal from office of Lord Chamberlain, 2843, 2843n, 2846, 2846n, 2856n
Salisbury Plain, 2481
Sallust, 484
Salm, Rheingrave of, 2050
Saltash election (1784), 158
Salter, Capt. Elliott, R.N. (?1741–90), 373
Saltersford, Baron, *see* Courtown, Earl of
Saltoun, 16th Baron (1758–93), candidate for Scottish Representative Peerage (1784), 78
Saltpetre, export of, prohibited, 2726
Saltram, royal family's visit to, 550, 550n, 552, 3914n
Saltzburg, Archbishop of, 178
Salusbury, Sir Robert (1756–1817), 4126, 4126n
Salvador del Mundo, a captured Spanish warship, 3542
Sambre river, 947, 1066, 1088
Sandalwood, 372
Sanderson, Sir James (1741–98), 823, 1039
baronetcy for, 1164
Sandfleet, 3905, 3910
Sandford, *see* Sanford
Sandgate, 3818
San Domingo, 1111, 1119, 1134, 1285, 1297, 1359, 1464, 1473, 1622, 2220, 2256, 2548, 2600n, 2923, 3211, 3215, 3641, 4119
French troops land in, 2602
Government of, 2923
Sandon, Capt. Huxley, 3815, 3818
Sandwich, a 98-gun ship, 1437, 1577n, 1591, 1595, 1602
Sandwich, 4th Earl of (1718–92), 15, 434–5, 440, 1431, 2902n
his parliamentary interest, 15n
political views (1783), 15n
resigns his Rangership of the Parks (1783), 15n
votes for Fox's India Bill (1783), 15n
canvassing for the Opposition (1787), 358n
Sandwich, 5th Earl of, *see* Hinchingbrooke
Sandwich Islands, King of the, *letter from*, 4103

Sandy Hook, 3864n
Sanford, William Ayshford (*d.* 1833), 3982, 3988, 3993
Sangro, Don Francisco, a Spanish Deputy, 3728, 3759
San Josef, a 112-gun ship, 2307, 2824
Sankey, Lieut.-Col., 2519
Saragossa, 3725
Sardinia, King of, *see* Victor Amadeus; Charles Emmanuel, and Victor Emmanuel
Sardinia, Queen of, *see* Maria Theresa
Sargent, Mrs Charlotte (*d.* 1841), 2858
Sargent, Isaac, & Co. of Paddington, 3196
Sargent, John (*c.* 1750–1831), Clerk of the Ordnance, 1198, 2821, 2834, 2858
letter from, 2717
thought of as Irish Secretary (1795), 1347, 1349, 1349n, 1355n, 1358
his seat on the Board of Accounts (1806), 2858n
Sataro, M., 3691
Saturn, a 74-gun ship, 1605
Saul, Thomas, a mutineer, 1613
Saumarez, Sir James, Baron de Saumarez (1757–1836), 2485, 2496, 2498, 2504, 2716, 2719, 3684, 3686, 3704, 3716, 3721, 3740, 3928
repeated applications for a Baronetcy, 2366
given a Red Ribbon, 2518
given an annuity, 2719n
statement of his services, 4143
Saumarez, Nicholas, Commissioner of West India Accounts, 3401
Saunders, *see* Dundas
Saunders, a merchant, 327
Saunderson, *see* Sanderson
Saurau, Count, the Imperial Finance Minister, 1848
Saurin, Mrs Mary (*d.* 1840), 4037
Saurin, William (?1757–1839), 1904, 1904n, 4037, 4037n
Savage, a 16-gun sloop, 999, 4287
Savernake Forest, 552
Savoy, 803, 816
Sawbridge, John (1732–95), 589
his Motion on the state of parliamentary representation (1784), 89
his republican principles, 89n
Sawyer, Admiral Herbert (*c.* 1731–98), 229, 377, 385, 404, 419, 475

Sawyer, Sir Herbert (1765–1833), 4287
Saxe-Coburg, Prince Frederick Josias of
(1737–1815), 854, 859, 861, 863–4, 866,
868, 875, 877, 879, 882, 891, 893, 896,
898, 901, 903, 913–14, 916, 920, 926,
938–9, 943, 950, 955, 957, 959–60, 962,
966, 968, 977, 979, 982–4, 986, 990,
992–3, 1000, 1003, 1008, 1014, 1018,
1020n, 1029, 1032, 1039n, 1041–2, 1066
King's criticism of, 1090
Saxe-Gotha, Charlotte, Duchess of (1751–
1827), 4304
Saxe-Gotha, Ernest, Duke of (1745–1804),
2963, 4304
his Garter, 644n, 2906, 3014n
Saxe-Lauenburg, 1304
Saxe-Meiningen, George, Duke of (1761–
1803), 4304
Saxe-Teschen, Duke of, 816
Saxe-Weimar, Charles Augustus, Duke of
(1757–1828), 685, 714, 1603, 3743
Saxe-Weimar, Charles Frederick, Hereditary
Prince, later Grand Duke of (1783–
1853), 1603, 2698, 2718
Saxony, Frederick Augustus III, Elector of,
later King (1750–1827), 138, 235, 1848
alliance with Hanover (1785), 235
Saxton, Sir Charles, 1st Bart (1732–1808),
1244
Saxton, Sir Charles, 2nd Bart (1773–1838),
letter to, 3876n
Saye and Sele, Lord (1769–1844), 1983n,
3966n
Scania, 3543
Scarborough, 1292, 1616, 3547
Scarbrough, 5th Earl of (1753–1807), 3966n
Scarsdale, 1st Baron (1726–1804), letters from,
2702, 2702n
labouring under a dreadful stigma, 2702
Scarsdale, 2nd Baron (1751–1837), 2702,
2702n, 3966n
Scarsdale, 3rd Baron (1781–1856), 2702,
2702n
Scarsdale family, the, 60
Schack-Rathelow, M. de, 223, 275, 399
Schaffhausen, Falls of, 973n, 1944, 1949
Scharnhausen, 1582, 1587, 1603, 1612, 1625,
1668
Scharrenhorst [?Scharnhorst], 1088, 1610
Schaumburg-Lippe, 355; Philip II of (1723–
87), 344
his mother, 344
Countess of, 344, 351
Schaw, John, King's messenger, 2230, 3750

Scheldt, the, 859, 861, 866, 882, 884, 905, 916,
943, 966, 1079, 3910–11
Scheldt expedition, the, see Walcheren
Schérer, Gen. Barthélemy Louis Joseph
(1745–1804), 1949
Schimmelman, Count, 223
Schlieffen, Baron de, 256, 351
Schlunter, Capt., 924
Schomberg, Capt. Isaac (1753–1813), 3721
put under arrest by Prince William (1787),
363
Schonborn, M., 516
Schönbrunn, Treaty of, 3814n, 4042, 4042n,
4046
Schroeder, the German actor, 195
Schroeder, M., a Page of the Backstairs
(d. 1797), 1687, 1708
Schulenburg, Count, 2655
Schulz, mathematician, 484
Schwarzburg-Sonderhausen, Prince Christian
of, 1970, 2680
Schwarzenberg, Prince, 1197
Schwerein, 4297
Schwicheldt, Count Heinrich Ernst von
(1748–1817), 2277
Scilly islands, 4269
Scipio, a 64-gun ship, 616
Scotland, road and bridge construction in,
3240; Act of Union with (1707), 1148,
1201n, 2308–9; disturbances in (1797),
1615
Scotsmen, continuing unpopularity of, 672n
Scott, 991
Scott, Brig., 2533
Scott, Anna Maria, Lady (d. 1809), 3958,
3962, 3966n
Scott, Sir Claude (1742–1830), London
banker, M.P. for Malmesbury (1802–6);
for Dungannon (1809–12), 1297, 1311,
2752n
Scott, Elizabeth (d. 1862), 3991
Scott, George Lewis, 3422
Scott, John, and Major-Gen. Guydickens, 916n
Scott, John, seaman, 3917
Scott, Major John (1747–1819), M.P., 93, 98,
303n, 438
Scott, Sir John, Lord Eldon (1751–1838),
438, 562, 725, 1024, 1033, 1039, 1070,
1086, 1117, 1195, 1216, 1218, 1255, 1330,
1338, 1342, 1365, 1380, 1433, 1509, 1520,
1602, 1605, 1680n, 1686, 1720, 1726,
1742, 1794, 1800, 1832, 1966, 2023, 2158,
2327n, 2332, 2336, 2350n, 2378, 2403,
2427, 2428n, 2456, 2472, 2520, 2588n,

Scott, Sir John (*cont.*)
2592, 2595, 2608n, 2643, 2671, 2683,
2748, 2774, 2794, 2805, 2837n, 2838n,
2839n, 2855n, 2872, 2881n, 2885n, 2899,
2934n, 2935, 2937, 2986n, 2991, 2994,
3013n, 3018, 3034, 3043, 3094, 3119n,
3120, 3147, 3163, 3164n, 3165, 3173,
3189, 3399, 3399n, 3400, 3400n, 3415,
3425, 3447, 3449, 3464, 3502, 3545, 3592,
3603, 3627, 3629, 3705, 3782, 3815, 3821,
3859, 3868, 3888, 3894, 3906n, 3960n,
3962, 3966, 3966n, 3969n, 3985, 3991,
4014, 4061, 4071, 4096, 4238, 4238n
letters from, 2383, 2392, 2392n, 2422, 2432,
2448, 2451, 2460, 2543, 2556, 2595n,
2614, 2616, 2628, 2636, 2644, 2657, 2670,
2673, 2720, 2750, 2767, 2800, 2803, 2831,
2836, 2838, 2838n, 2859, 2873, 2877,
2891, 2903, 2905, 2914, 3046, 3049, 3066,
3282, 3413, 3455, 3548, 3656, 3678, 3747,
3813, 3816, 3820, 3830, 3843, 3909, 3953,
3958, 3981, 3981n, 3984n, 4013, 4040,
4045, 4045n, 4146, 4212, 4221
letters to, 2604n, 3148, 3285, 3455, 3548,
3699n, 3747, 3764n, 3820, 3899, 3948n,
3953, 3958, 4013, 4045, 4146, 4149n,
4240–63
and the Solicitor-Generalship (1784), 55
appointed Solicitor-General (1788), 456n
appointed Lord Chief Justice (1799),
2023n, 2451
resigns Chief Justiceship (May 1801),
2383n
appointed Lord Chancellor (1801), 2357,
2357n, 2364n, 2392n
appointed a Trustee of the King's property
(1801), 2403n
on the King's health (1801), 2451
a Governor of the Charterhouse, 2653
dislikes Broad-Bottom Ministries, 2838n
appointed Lord Chancellor (1807), 3410
unsuccessful candidate for Chancellorship
of Oxford University, 4032, 4040, 4045,
4045n
Scott, John (1774–1805), Eldon's elder son,
2903
Scott, Mrs, wife of John Scott, Nelson's
secretary, 3242
Scott, Sir Samuel, 2nd Bart (1772–1849),
M.P. for Malmesbury (1802–6), 2752n
Scott, Sir William, Lord Stowell (1745–
1836), 1024, 2592, 2770, 2885, 3095,

3278, 3483n, 3513, 3620, 3665n, 3788,
3790, 3794, 3962, 4089, 4177
letter to, 4045n
appointed Judge of the Court of
Admiralty, 1859
Scottish Fencibles, the, 1616
Scottish Pension List, 2645, 2952
Scottish Representative Peers, election of
(1784), 78; (1790), 619; (1802), 2644,
2965, 2965n, 3442, 3483n
Scout, an 18-gun brig, 3691
Scudamore, John (1757–1805), 2894n
Seaford, disturbances at, 1259n
Seaforth, Lord (1754–1815), 3966n
Sea Horse, a 38-gun frigate, 1805n
Searle, Lieut. John Clarke, Commander
(1795), Capt. (1796), 910
Sebastiani, Comte, French General and
diplomatist (1772–1851), 2705n, 3329n,
3454n, 3492n
Sebright, Sir John Saunders (1767–1846),
3821n, 4074, 4074n, 4076, 4133
Secker, Mr, 2834
Secret boxes, 2858, 2866n, 2869
Secret service money, 231, 675, 874, 2082n,
2411, 4018n, 4037
Secret service payments to parliamentary
candidates (1784), 158, 675
Secretary of State (Ireland), office of, 1158
Secretaryship of State, the, 1091n
re-arrangement of duties of (1801), 2489,
2498, 2500
Seditious Meetings Bill (1795), 1323, 1330,
1333, 1338
Seditious Meetings Act (1801), 2392
Sedley, Henry, *letter from*, 3875
Seid Achmet Effendi, Turkish diplomatist,
3703
Seine, a 36-gun frigate, 3288
Selim III, the Turkish Sultan (1761–1807),
2591, 2675, 2675n
Selkirk, 4th Earl of (1722–99), candidate for
Scottish Representative Peerage (1784),
78; (1790), 619n
Selkirk, 5th Earl of (1771–1820), 3207, 3402,
3402n, 3966n
Sellis, Joseph, the Duke of Cumberland's
valet (*d*. 1810), 4184n
Selsey, 1st Baron, *see* Peachey, Sir James
Selsey, 2nd Baron (1749–1816), 3966n
Selwyn, George Augustus (1719–91), death
of, 651

Sheridan, Richard Brinsley (*cont.*)
2888n, 2894n, 2934n, 3041, 3085, 3105,
3228n, 3416–17, 3485n, 3590, 3643,
3824n, 4093n, 4126
Motion to repeal Habeas Corpus Act
Suspension Act, 1185
and Drury Lane Theatre, 2092
Motion for a Call of the House, 2182
Fox's opinion of, 2276n
'plays the devil', 2745n
his office of Treasurer of the Navy (1807),
3416
drunk in House of Commons, 3590n,
3643n
and exclusion of 'strangers' from House of
Commons, 4076
Sheridan, Thomas, R.B. Sheridan's son
(1775–1817), 3228, 3228n
Sheriffs, pricking the (1789), 514; (1790),
632; (1802), 2627n
the Roll of, 3328
nomination of the (1808), 3592
Sherreff [Shirreff], Major Gen. William
(*d.* 1804), Lieut.-Gen. (1798); Gen.
(1803), 1558, 1616
Sherwin, mathematician, 484
Shipley, William (*c.* 1778–1820), 3886, 3894n
Shop tax (1785), 217, 218n; repeal of,
demanded (1788), 438
Shore, Sir John, Lord Teignmouth (1751–
1834), 592, 3163, 3418, 3420, 3420n
appointed Governor-General of Bengal
(1792), 784, 791
declines a Baronetcy (1790), 791; created a
Baronet (1792), 791; his Irish peerage,
1686
Shoreham, 182, 1784
Shorncliffe Camp, near Folkestone, 2929
Shrewsbury, 1505, 2700
Shropshire Militia, 1616
Shum, George (*c.* 1752–1805), 2894n
Sicard, John Jacob, Princess of Wales's maître
d'hôtel, 3778, 3778n, 3846
Sicignano, Duke of (*d.* 1793), 886
Sicily, 3048, 3236, 3248, 3265, 3271, 3274n,
3277n, 3316, 3331, 3386, 3461, 3463,
3475, 3543, 3554, 3554n, 3576, 3591,
3842
British garrison in, 3519, 3641
French threat to, 2483, 3204–5, 3209, 3212
Sicily, King of, *see* Ferdinand IV
Sicily, King and Queen of, *see* under Naples

Sidkey, Effendi [*sic*], 3700
Sidmouth, Visct, *see* Addington, Henry
Sierra Leone Company, 3602, 3602n, 3704
Sigglesthorne, Yorks, 3607
Signet, Clerks of the, 3194n, 3533
Silesia, 613, defences of, 131; Prussian mili-
tary manoeuvres in (1785), 252; (1790),
610
Silverhjelm, Baron, Swedish Minister in
London, 2623n, 2703, 3080, 3084
Silvester, a messenger, *see* Sylvester
Silvester, Sir John (1745–1822), Recorder of
London, 1878, 2885n, 2899, 2925, 2964,
2973, 3028, 3328, 3782, 3855
Simbschen, Joseph Anton von (1746–1820),
Austrian General, 2292
Simcoe, John Graves, Lieut.-Gen. (1752–
1806), 705, 711, 722, 1765, 3527n, 3594,
4285
Simeon, Sir John (1756–1824), 1724, 1897
Simmons, Dr Richard, 2873n
Simmons, Dr Samuel Foart (1750–1813),
2873, 2873n, 3164n
on the King's health, 2855, 2864n
Simolin, M., 8, 12, 17, 95n, 689
Simonbourne, 3682
Simpson, a mutineer, 1605
Simpson, Capt. Slingsby, R.N., 3264n
Sims [?Symes, Richard], Col., 875
Sinclair, Sir John (1754–1835), 915n, 1643,
1881, 1881n, 1885, 1897, 2212
letters from, 668, 937, 1173, 1188, 1262,
1264, 1306, 1400, 1565
letter to, 915
asks for a peerage, 1400
Sindhia, 2808
Siniavin, the Russian Admiral, 3557, 3732,
3740
Sion House, 674
Sirius, a 36-gun frigate, 3835
Sirr, Major Henry Charles (1764–1841), 2793
Sistova, Peace of, ends Austro-Turkish War
(1791), 697
Sixtus V, Pope (1521–90), 813
Skinner, Thomas, Lord Mayor of London
(1795), 1311, 1321
Slade, James, 545n
Slade, Sir John (1762–1859), Gen., 1857
Slave Trade, the, 341, 1366n, 1849n, 3086
Bill to abolish (1807), 3380, 3709
Bill to regulate (1788), 459
Slave Trade Limitation Bill (1799), 1983

II, 832–1662; III, 1663–2575; IV, 2576–3758

II, 832–1662; III, 1663–2575; IV, 2576–3578

Spain (*cont.*)

makes peace with France (1795), 1279, 1282

breach with (1805), 2984, 2998, 3004, 3010

Court of, 147, 180, 186, 204, 220, 229, 378, 399, 816, 1285

Spain, King of, *see* Charles III

Spangenberg, Lieut.-Col., 1060

Spanish-American colonies, future of, 3649

expedition to, contemplated (1808), 3649, 3659, 3667, 3801

Spanish Main, expedition to, abandoned (1797), 1518

Sparke, Dr Bowyer, Edward, Dean of Bristol (*c.* 1759–1836), 3673n, 3760, 3913, 3913n

Sparrow, Bence, 2804n

Sparrow, Robert, 2804n

Spartel, Cape, 852

Speaker, the, *see* Cornwall, Charles Wolfran; Addington, Henry; Abbot, Charles

his Chaplain, 441

contest for the Speakership (1789), 524

heavy expenses of the office of, 2585n

invariably (from 1817 to 1928), accepts a peerage on retirement, 2585n

pension for a retiring, 2983

Spectator, the, 484

Speeches from the Throne, referred to, 80–3, 274, 368, 545, 599, 600, 734, 814, 816, 1091, 1180, 1319, 1450, 1638, 1772, 1877, 1978, 1980, 2020n, 2039, 2039n, 2204–5, 2269, 2276n, 2304, 2309, 2327, 2327n, 2328, 2328n, 2330, 2330n, 2461, 2467, 2546, 2676, 2679, 2781, 2781n, 2812, 2818, 2919–20, 2922, 2922n, 3004, 3006, 3119n, 3120, 3277, 3279, 3346, 3346n, 3449–50, 3483, 3487, 3517, 3589–90, 3606, 3683, 3770, 3786, 3786n, 3787, 3908, 4072, 4201, 4211

Spence, Capt., 3964

Spence, John Clarke, 4103

Spencer, a 74-gun ship, 3375

Spencer, Sir Brent (*c.* 1760–1828), 2603, 3576, 3587, 3591, 3615, 3641, 3659, 3687, 3691, 3693, 4145

letter from, 2553n

appointed an Equerry (1801), 2424, 2553

his K.B., 3802, 3853

Spencer, Lord Charles (1740–1820), 22

letter from, 3751

supports the Coalition (1783–4), 22n

would have liked office of Chief Justice in Eyre south of the Trent (1800), 2192n

suggested as Joint Paymaster-General (1801), 2365n

appointed Joint Postmaster-General (1801), 2365

his position in 1804, 2844n, 2991; in 1805, 3003n

Spencer, Lord Francis Almeric, later 1st Baron Churchill (1779–1845), 2365n, 4093n, 4105n

Spencer, George John, 2nd Earl (1758–1834), 3, 4n, 1158, 1187, 1203, 1208, 1331, 1347n, 1370, 1410, 1461, 1491, 1493n, 1497, 1499n, 1500, 1530n, 1532, 1533n, 1545n, 1570, 1715, 1736n, 1760, 1885, 1924n, 1963n, 1964, 1983, 1983n, 2142, 2176n, 2209, 2235, 2315n, 2329n, 2341, 2346, 2349n, 2350, 2456n, 2474n, 2743, 2743n, 2812, 2839n, 3186, 3194n, 3221n, 3226n, 3259n, 3271, 3289, 3300, 3302, 3317, 3360, 3372, 3388, 3441n, 3841n, 3966, 4074n

letters from, 1170n, 1186, 1208n, 1229, 1237n, 1244, 1263, 1274, 1284, 1291, 1302, 1307, 1315, 1346n, 1364, 1377, 1382, 1403, 1433, 1437, 1439, 1444, 1460, 1472, 1476, 1490, 1501, 1515, 1523, 1533, 1542, 1545, 1551, 1555, 1571, 1577, 1579, 1584, 1591, 1595, 1599, 1602, 1605, 1613, 1618, 1628, 1632, 1665, 1672, 1677, 1683, 1699, 1712, 1732, 1741, 1779, 1781, 1786, 1794, 1805, 1834, 1838, 1844, 1846, 1859, 1862, 1864, 1869, 1892, 1901, 1937, 1963, 1965, 1982, 1991, 2004, 2006, 2016, 2018, 2021, 2024, 2029, 2046, 2055, 2055n, 2071, 2077, 2086, 2105, 2186, 2190, 2208, 2210, 2213, 2215, 2227, 2234, 2238, 2249, 2280, 2284, 2298, 2310, 2317, 2349, 2349n, 2353, 2366, 3181, 3191, 3193, 3198, 3203, 3206, 3218, 3220, 3224, 3228, 3230, 3238, 3240, 3245, 3247, 3254, 3257, 3261, 3278, 3283, 3287, 3294, 3298, 3304, 3316, 3322, 3325, 3328, 3333, 3341, 3345, 3349, 3351n, 3352, 3357, 3362, 3366, 3376, 3383, 3385, 3402

letters to, 1090n, 1186, 1229, 1229n, 1244, 1263, 1263n, 1274, 1284, 1291, 1291n, 1302, 1307, 1307n, 1377, 1382, 1403, 1433, 1437, 1439, 1444, 1472, 1476, 1490, 1501, 1515, 1523, 1530, 1542, 1543n, 1545, 1551, 1555, 1579, 1584, 1591, 1595, 1599, 1602, 1605, 1613, 1618, 1628, 1632, 1672, 1677, 1699, 1741, 1779, 1786, 1805, 1838, 1844, 1846, 1859, 1862, 1869, 1892, 1901, 1924, 1991, 2004, 2006, 2018,

II, 832–1662; III, 1663–2575; IV, 2576–3578

Sullivan, Sir Benjamin, Judge at Madras, 2456n
Sullivan, John (1749–1839), appointed Under-Secretary of State for War (1801), 2412
   King's good opinion of, 2847
   his son, 2847
   a P.C., 3006n
   Harrowby's poor opnion of, 3006n
Sullivan, Margaret, executed for coining (1788), 466
Sullivan's Island, 4143
Sully, Duc de (1560–1641), 4269
Sultan, the Turkish, see Selim III
Sumatra, 372
Sumner, George Holme (1760–1838), 1255, 3834, 4076
Sumner, Humphrey, Vice-Chancellor of Cambridge (c. 1744–1814), 2713
Sun, the, newspaper, 1277
Sunderland, 1298
Superb, a 74-gun ship, 3250
Supremacy, Act of (1559), 1215; Oath of, 1219
Surinam, 3113; capture of (1804), 2892
Surprize, a 24-gun frigate, 2105
Surrey, Earl of, see Norfolk, Duke of
Surrey, 812, 4213
Surrey election (1784), 158
   Magistrates, 2774
Surveillante, a 36-gun frigate, 3284, 3532, 3550
Sussex, 2794, 2940, 2954, 3360, 4100
   measures for defence of, 2485, 2519, 2526
   Fencible Cavalry, 1505
   Militia regiment, 2782n
Sutherland, Capt. Alexander (d. 1793), 891, 965–6
Sutherland Fencibles, the, 1752
Sutton, see Manners-Sutton
Sutton, Capt., 1620
Sutton, Dr R., letter from, 1046
Sutton, Sir Richard (1733–1802), 446, 446n
Sutton, Lieut. Thomas, 3815, 3824n
Sutton-on-Trent, 1046
Suvorov, Marshal Alexander (1729–1800), 1907n, 1959, 1973, 1993n, 2050, 2059, 2072, 2080
Swabia, 1944, 2059, 2115, 2125, 2198, 2206, 2419, 2478
Swallow, an East India Company's packet, 1915
Swallow, an 18-gun sloop, 3353
Swan, a 14-gun sloop, 2249

Swann, Henry (d. 1824), 4124n
Swansea, 1510–11
Sweden, King of, see Gustavus III, and Gustavus IV
   Treaty with France (1784), 95
Sweden, subsidy treaty with (1808), 3579, 3618, 3618n
   British army to defend, 3646
   Commercial Convention with, 3671
Sweden, Princess Albertine of (1753–1829), 399
Sweden, 376; memo. respecting state of, 399
Swedish Pomerania, 2951, 3476
Sweeney, James, a marine, 3239
Swiftsure, a 74-gun ship, 2490
Swinburne, Capt., 1289
Swinden's Academy (Greenwich), 1785
Swinley Camp, 2216
Swinley Lodge, the Duke of York's house near Windsor, 1979, 1981n, 2203, 2203n
Swinley, Rangership of, 3185n
Swinney, Edward, a mutineer, 1834
Switzerland, 1845, 1960; French intervention in (1802), 2667, 2667n
Sydenham, 4028n
Sydney, Lord, see Townshend, John Thomas
Sydney, Elizabeth, Lady (1736–1826), a Lady of the Bedchamber to the Queen, 333, 335
Sydney, 1st Visct (1733–1800), 4n, 10, 10n, 11, 11n, 26n, 28, 37, 50n, 82, 107, 146, 168, 179, 235, 259, 297, 343, 362, 368, 383, 441, 454, 471, 751, 795, 797, 1426, 1983n
   letters from, 11, 13, 19, 21, 23, 29, 35, 39, 54, 67, 70, 73, 78–9, 81, 83, 94, 100, 102, 106, 132, 136, 147, 149, 151, 157, 159, 162, 167, 173, 177, 183, 189, 201, 205, 210, 218, 220, 224, 226, 230, 237, 253, 276, 287, 291, 303, 317, 322, 333, 335, 353, 359, 405, 407, 416, 430, 434, 436, 440, 442, 444, 459, 466, 492, 495, 497, 499, 508, 510, 514, 516, 521
   letters to, 11, 13, 19, 23, 29, 35, 38–9, 54, 67n, 70, 75, 75n, 79, 83, 94, 100, 102, 106, 132, 136, 147, 149, 157, 159, 162, 167, 170, 173, 177, 183, 205, 210, 220, 226, 237, 237n, 240, 253, 272, 287, 291, 303n, 307n, 322, 333, 335, 353, 359, 389, 407n, 411, 442, 444, 459, 482, 492, 495, 497, 499, 508, 514, 516
   his daughter Mary (Lady Chatham), 10n
   idea of his becoming Privy Seal (1784), 10n, 54n

II, 832–1662; III, 1663–2575; IV, 2576–3578

II, 832–1662; III, 1663–2575; IV, 2576–3578

Trigge, Lieut.-Gen. Sir Thomas (*d.* 1814), 1053, 2063, 2518, 2955, 4080, 4138
letter from, 4034n
Trimleston, Anne, Lady (*c.* 1758–1831), 2635n, 4229
Trimleston peerage, the, 2635n, 4229n
Trincomali, 477, 1285
capture of (1795), 1356n, 1359
'Trinette', *see* Wurtemberg, Catherine, Princess of
Trinidad, Government of, 3163
Governor of, 2728, 2740
captured, 1523, 1523n, 2548
Col. Hislop appointed Lieut.-Governor of, 2740
Trinity College, Cambridge, 483, 1733, 1870, 3302, 3673, 4238
Trinity College, Dublin, 1158, 1662, 1975
Trinity House, 1108, 3257
Triple Alliance Treaty (with Prussia and Holland, 1788), 516, 516n
Triscati, 1225
Triton, a 32-gun frigate, 1991, 4269
Trollope, Admiral Sir Henry (1756–1839), 1291, 1628, 1632
Tromp, a 54-gun captured Dutch warship, 1665
Trotter, Capt., 2496n
Trotter, Alexander, Paymaster of the Navy, 2648n, 2852n, 3068, 3068n, 3079, 3085
Trotter, Sir Coutts (1767–1837), partner in Coutts's Bank, 849, 2363n
Trotter, John Bernard (1775–1818), Fox's secretary, 3293n
Troubridge, Sir Thomas, 1st Bart (?1758–1807), 2310, 2357, 2570, 3281
created Baronet (1799), 2018
Trouvé, 'Citizen', 1948, 1948n
Troy, John Thomas (1739–1823), 1283
True Briton, the, 1405, 1405n, 1406
Trulliber, Parson, a character in Fielding's *Joseph Andrews*, 3399n
Tuam, 1816, 2267n, 3815
Archbishop of (Edward Dillon, *d.* 1809), 3966n
Tübingen, University of, 1728, 1902, 1921, 1946
Tucker, Daniel, debtor, 481
Tucker, Major, 3438
Tudela, battle of (1808), 3689n
Tudor, Mr, Assistant-Inspector of Hospitals, 2792
Tuilleries, the, 689
Tullamore, affray at, 3283

Tulmeier, 376, 426
Tunbridge Wells, 921, 1603
Tunis, 1186
Tunisian Minister, 1442, 1457
Turin, 717, 938, 1964, 1973, 1973n, 2672
Turkey, 1648, 2895
rupture with Russia threatened (1784), 17
peace proposals from (1808), 3703
Treaty with (1809), 3868
Turkish Ambassador, 1196, 1585, 1593, 1647
departure of (1800), 2218, 2221, 2225
Turkish medals, wearing of, 2955
Turner, Capt., 3815
Turner, Lieut., R.N., 1031n
Turner, Sir Barnard (*c.* 1742–84), 158
Turner, Chatfield, 158
Turner, Sir Gregory Page (1748–1805), 1027, 1559
Turnhout, 937, 943, 977
Turton, Dr John (1735–1800), 1495
Turton, Sir Thomas (1764–1844), 3359, 3371, 3662, 3675, 3832, 3834, 4076, 4122n, 4124, 4138, 4156, 4188
Tuscany, 2297, 2763
Tuscany, Ferdinand, Grand Duke of (1769–1824), 2151, 2440
letter to, 1015
Tuttlingen, 2147
Tweed, a mutineer, 1595
Tweeddale, George, 7th Marquess of (1753–1804), 1983
Twickenham Park, 1483, 3255n
Tylney-Long, Catherine (1789–1825), 4056
Tynte, J. Kemeys, appointed a Groom of Prince of Wales's Bedchamber (1787), 365n; appointed Comptroller (1791), 723
Tyrawley, Lord (1748–1821), 2315, 2315n, 2515n
Tyrconnell, 2nd Earl of (1750–1805), 688n
Tyrconnell, Sarah, Countess of (1763–1800), and the Duke of York, 688n
Tyrol, the, 1949
Tyrrell, Timothy, Remembrancer of City of London, 2254, 2262, 2265, 2625, 3077, 3632, 3694
Tyrwhitt, Sir Thomas (*c.* 1763–1833), 1643, 2894n, 4122n
Tyttenhanger (Herts), Lord Hardwicke's seat, 2510n

Uhle, 2128
Ukscull, *see* Uxkull
Ulm, 2015, 2161, 3146n

Villiers, George (*cont.*)
  resigns office of Paymaster of Marines, 4063–4
Villiers, Mrs George (1775–1855), Lord Boringdon's sister, 3914n, 3970n, 4063n, 4149
  letter from, 4148
  letter to, 4148
Villiers, John Charles, 7th Earl of Clarendon (1757–1838), 659, 695, 699, 717, 2752n, 2805, 2805n, 3014n, 3765, 3951, 3951n, 4039, 4063n
  Chief Justice in Eyre north of the Trent, 2192n
  his special Mission to Portugal (1808), 3759, 3762, 4055, 4055n, 4058
  arrival from Portugal, 4099
Villiers, Maria Eleanor, later Countess of Clarendon (*c.* 1759–1844), wife of J. C. Villiers, 659, 659n, 3014n
Vimiero, battle of (1808), 3587n, 3730n, 3802, 3935, 3938, 4120n
Vincent, H. D., Duke of Gloucester's Equerry, 386
Vincent, T., the King's barber (*d.* 1798), 1754
Vincent, Dr William, Dean of Westminster (1739–1815), 2638, 2661
Vinegar Hill, Irish rebels defeated at, 1759n
Viper, a 12-gun cutter, 2215n
Vistula, the, 1304, 3342
Vives, Don Miguel de, Governor-General of Balearic Islands, 3689
Vivian, Professor William of Corpus Christi, Oxford (?1727–1801), 2479
Voltaire (1694–1778), 706
Voluntary subscriptions for financing the War, 1674, 1674n, 1678
Volunteers, the, 2884
Volunteers, the Irish, 1158
Votes of Credit, 865, 1055, 1057, 1340, 1342, 1755, 1960, 2192, 2439, 3110, 3508, 3886, 4174, 4208
Vries, Martinus de, 4229
Vukássovich, Baron Joseph Philip von, the Austrian commander, 1955
Vulliamy, 493
Vyse, Gen. Richard (1746–1825), Lieut.-Col. (1781), Major-Gen. (1794), Lieut.-Gen. (1801), M.P. for Beverley (1806–7), Gen. (1812), 1056, 1061
Vyse, Richard William Howard (1784–1853), 3487

Vyvyan, Philip, *letter from*, 25

Waakzaamheid, a captured Dutch frigate, 1869n
Waal, the, 840, 1132, 1176, 1189, 1197, 1233, 3159
Waddingham, Rectory of, 3622
Waddington, Rev. M., Chaplain of the *Prince George*, 4271, 4273, 4289, 4292
Wade, George (1673–1748), Field-Marshal, 4272
Wagner, Lieut., 3831
Wagram, battle of, 3926, 3931n
Wakefield, 4076
Walcheren, 4229
Walcheren expedition (1809), 3905, 3910, 3919, 3922–3, 3926n, 3927, 3937, 3941, 3948, 3959, 3967–8, 4010n, 4015, 4028, 4051n, 4072n
  Parliamentary debates on, and inquiry into the, 4074, 4076, 4080, 4084, 4089, 4091, 4093, 4098, 4100–2, 4109, 4120, 4122, 4124
Waldeck, Prince of (1744–98), 926, 992, 4276, 4304
Waldegrave, Lady Caroline (1765–1831), 312
Waldegrave, Edward William (1787–1809), 3835
Waldegrave, Elizabeth, Countess (1760–1816), *letter from*, 3835
Waldegrave, Lady Elizabeth (1758–1823), Lady of the Bedchamber to the Princess Royal, 312
Waldegrave, 3rd Earl (1817–84), 4264
Waldegrave, 4th Earl (1751–89), 146, 4264
Waldegrave, 5th Earl (1784–94), 3835
Waldegrave, 6th Earl (1785–1835), 3835
Waldegrave, 8th Earl (1788–1859), 3835
Waldegrave, Granville George, 2nd Baron Radstock (1786–1857), 3835
Waldegrave, William, Admiral, Lord Radstock (1753–1825), 3835
  letter from, 817
Waldstein, Count, 3931
Wales, Prince of, *see* George, Prince of Wales
Wales, Princess of, *see* Caroline, Princess of Wales
Walker, Capt., 1628
Walker, Capt. John, 3124
Wallace, Admiral Sir James (1731–1803), 43
Wallace, Thomas, Lord (*c.* 1768–1844), 1333, 3262, 3662, 4156, 4208

Wellesley, Lady Charlotte (1781-1853), 3896n

Wellesley, Rev. Gerald Valerian (1770–1848), 3984, 3984n, 4018

Wellesley, Sir Henry, Lord Cowley (1773–1847), 796, 1600, 3418, 3474n, 3873, 3876, 3876n, 3896, 3951, 3970n, 4062, 4099, 4226, 4228

  letter from, 3844n
  thought of as Envoy to Madrid (1804), but not sent, 2918
  a Lord of the Treasury (1804), 2918n
  declines a Home Office appointment (1804), 2918n; wants a seat at India Board, 2918n
  Secretary of the Treasury (1807), 3418
  divorces his wife, 3896n
  Mission to Spain, 4042
  made a P.C., 4046

Wellesley, Hyacinthe Gabrielle Roland, Marchioness (c. 1759–1816), 2250n

Wellesley, Richard (1787–1831), 2250, 2250n

Wellesley, Richard Colley, Lord Mornington, later Marquess (1760–1842), 340n, 744, 878, 895, 1309, 1626, 1908n, 2041n, 2205, 2242, 2918, 3015n, 3163, 3416n, 3622, 3662, 3665n, 3787n, 3832n, 3861n, 3867n, 3868, 3896, 3951n, 3966, 3966n, 3980, 3989, 4028, 4032, 4051n, 4055n, 4073n, 4076, 4076n, 4092, 4124n, 4126, 4142n, 4204, 4234n, 4238n

  letters from, 913n, 1309n, 2365n, 2808, 2820, 2940n, 3420n, 4042, 4046, 4053, 4055, 4058, 4062, 4067, 4079, 4081, 4083, 4094, 4099, 4110, 4113, 4121, 4125, 4140, 4152, 4158, 4171, 4222, 4224, 4226, 4228, 4231, 4234, 4234n

  letters to, 1664n, 1680n, 1745n, 2250n, 4042, 4046, 4055, 4058, 4067, 4079, 4081, 4083, 4094, 4099, 4110, 4113, 4121, 4125, 4152, 4158, 4171, 4224, 4226, 4228, 4231, 4234

  elected M.P. for Windsor (1787), 373
  re-elected (1790), 602
  sworn of the Privy Council (1793), 895
  is obnoxious to Windsor electors, 1309
  elected for Old Sarum (1796), 1309n
  given a G.B. peerage (1797), 1626
  becomes Governor-General of Bengal, 1626
  his 'double-gilt potato', 2041n
  wants a Dukedom, 2041n
  his office of Remembrancer of the Exchequer, 2250, 2250n
  his Party, 2940n

might succeed Castlereagh as Secretary of State (1807), 3554n
appointed Ambassador to Spain (1809), 3868, 3871
suggested appointment as War Secretary, 3919, 3925, 3957, 3986
accepts Foreign Secretaryship, 3989n, 4028n, 4034–5
a possible successor to Portland, 4028n
arrival in England, 4037, 4039
given the Garter, 4041, 4041n, 4094
resigns Order of St Patrick, 4041, 4094
on need to strengthen Perceval's Government, 4113n

Wellesleys, the, 3978n

Wellesley-Pole, Mrs, later Lady Maryborough (c. 1760–1851), 4028n

Wellesley-Pole, William, Lord Maryborough (1763–1845), 2554n, 3519, 3657, 3721, 3872, 3896n, 4010n, 4028, 4028n, 4032, 4038n, 4126, 4135, 4147, 4205

  letters from, 4028n, 4087n, 4102n, 4105n, 4124n
  and the Irish Secretaryship, 3985n

Wellesley-Pole, William, 4th Earl of Mornington (1788–1857), 4056n

Wellington, Lord, *see* Wellesley, Sir Arthur

Wells, Admiral Sir John (d. 1841), Lieut. (1780), Capt. (1782), Rear-Admiral (1804), Vice-Admiral (1808), 1558

Wells, Deanery of, 1932, 3412

Welsford, J. P., 3325n

Weltje, Louis (d. 1800), the Prince of Wales's Clerk of the Kitchen, 46n, 300n

Wemyss, David Douglas, Gen. (1760–1839), 1765

Wemyss, Lieut.-Gen. Maurice, court-martial on, 1677, 1819

Wendover election (1799), 1932n; (1800), 2144n

Wense, Capt., in the Hanoverian army, 90

Wentworth, Sir John (1737–1820), 1818, 2102

Wentworth, Thomas, Visct (1745–1815), 1983n, 3966n

Weobley, 19n

Werneck [Warneck], *see* Verneck

Wervicq, 943, 966, 1022

Wesel, 403, 816, 866

Weser, the, 1193, 2744, 2749, 3142, 3159, 3392

Wesley, *see* Wellesley, Arthur

Wessel, Lieut., 4274, 4284, 4290

Whitworth, Sir Charles (*cont.*)
2724n, 2730, 2730n, 2732–3, 3063, 3390,
3537
letters from, 1888, 3063n
given Irish peerage, 1987
recalled from Petersburg Embassy, 1908,
1908n, 2123, 2123n
Ambassador to France, 2639
leaves Paris, 2735, 2735n, 2741n, 2743
wants employment (1804), 3063n
Whitworth, Richard (1734–1811), 158
Whyte, Gen. John, 2526
Whyte, Richard (*d.* 1807), Major-Gen.
(1790), Lieut.-Gen. (1797), Gen. (1802),
1464
Wickham (Hants), 1090
Wickham, Mrs Eleanor (*d.* 1836), 1645, 2130,
2134
Wickham, Henry Lewis (1789–1864), 3411,
3411n
Wickham, William (1761–1840), 1167, 1184,
1256, 1387, 1645,
Under-Secretary of State, 1682, 1717, 1740,
1742, 1746, 1790, 1800, 1800n, 1802,
1808, 1816, 1830n, 1836, 1861, 1868n,
1904, 1927, 2072, 2080, 2080n, 2130,
2134, 2151, 2157, 2288, 2516, 2777n,
2779, 2790n, 3411, 3485n
letters from, 2752n, 2757n, 3221n
succeeds Abbot as Irish Secretary, 2585n,
2595n
elected for Heytesbury (1802), 2585n
his division list (1803), 2752n
resigns Irish Secretaryship, 2826
Wicklow Co., 2301, 2694; election (1801),
2301n
Wicklow, Visct (1757–1815), 2315, 3966n
Wiechers, 295
Wigg, Edmund Rush, Attorney-General of
Bahama Islands, 3366
Wigg, Mrs, 3366
Wigley, Edmund (*c.* 1758–1821), 1658
Wigram, Robert (1744–1830), M.P. for
Fowey (1802–6), 2752n
Wigtownshire, 3402
election (1802), 2631
Wilberforce, William (1759–1833), 61, 589,
644, 1185, 1198n, 1223, 1247, 1255,
1320n, 1323, 1339n, 1342, 1459, 1480,
1482, 1509, 1537, 1637, 1643, 1664, 1724,
2189, 2276, 2745n, 2752n, 3105, 3105n,
3174, 3243, 3262, 3347, 3380, 3380n,

3483n, 3487, 3491, 3602n, 3657, 3657n,
3665, 3665n, 3799, 3832, 3832n, 3834,
3876, 3878, 3878n, 4076, 4076n, 4087,
4087n, 4105, 4122, 4122n, 4124n, 4126,
4133, 4135, 4138, 4138n, 4147, 4153,
4156, 4205
letter from, 1251n
elected for Yorkshire (1784), 55; (1807),
3462n
supports parliamentary reform (1785), 203
opposes repeal of Test and Corporation
Acts (1790), 580
favours peace negotiations, 1180, 1198,
1250, 1250n
doubtful about parliamentary reform
(1800), 2137
and attack on Lord Melville, 3068n, 3071n
Wilbraham, E. Bootle, *see* Bootle
Wilbraham, Roger (1743–1829), M.P. for
Helston (1786–90); for Bodmin (1790–
6), 446n
Wildbad, 1728, 1763, 1799, 2478, 2488
Wildernesse, Lord Camden's seat near
Sevenoaks, 2981
Wilford, Major-Gen. Richard Rich (*c.* 1754–
1822), 2524
Wilhelmsdal, 4304
Wilhelmstein, 4274
Wilkes, John (1727–97), 2254
elected for Middlesex (1784), 72
Wilkinson, William, a seaman, 3874
Willaumez, Jean Baptiste Philibert (1763–
1845), the French Rear-Admiral, 3276,
3288
Willemstad, 840, 843, 859
William III, King of England (1650–1702),
1215, 1426n, 3670
William Henry, Duke of Clarence, later
William IV (1765–1837), 58, 172, 194,
216, 242, 285, 309, 349, 541, 547, 638,
688n, 753, 828, 1328, 1411, 1617, 1895,
1983n, 2153, 2165, 2428, 2462n, 3966n,
4012, 4022, 4024, 4027, 4264, 4288, 4290,
4291n, 4292–3, 4295
letters from, 165, 196, 232, 239, 245, 288,
296, 327, 341, 341n, 363, 377, 385, 404,
419, 475, 518, 520, 616, 1410, 4267,
4269, 4271, 4273, 4279, 4283, 4285, 4287,
4289, 4294, 4296
letters to, 104, 142, 160, 164, 207, 233, 243,
281, 2165n, 4267–8, 4270–1, 4275,
4290n, 4291, 4296, 4299, 4303

II, 832–1662; III, 1663–2575; IV, 2576–3578

William Henry, Duke of Clarence (*cont.*)
sent to sea (1779), 4265–7
admits his obstinacy and perverseness (1781), 4279
at New York (1781), 4283
given the Garter, 4290n
to be sent to Germany (1783), 4298
his ungentlemanly behaviour, 4300
his swearing, 90
his debts (1784), 103–4
his love of improper company, 104
King's further criticism of, 142
dislikes life in Hanover, 160, 281
neglect of his education, 160
his attachment to the Queen's niece (1783), 164, 4302
wants to return to sea (1785), 165, 196
would like to go to the East Indies, 165
King displeased with him (1785), 195–6, 207
to be a Lieutenant in Navy, 207
recalled to England, 209, 215
arrives in England, 215n
at sea again (1785), 232
his 'offensive pride', 233
a 'great-little man', 233
his 'little nonsensical volatile head', 233
asks for a ship, 239, 243
is refused a ship, 243, 245
objects to going to America, 281
not allowed to go to the Mediterranean, 281
his vanity, 281
keeps bad company, 281
sent to the Newfoundland station (1786), 283
his attachment to Sarah Martin, 283n
given command of the *Pegasus*, 288
forbidden to visit foreign ports, 293, 293n
to winter in Leeward Islands, 293, 341n
on the Newfoundland station, 327
in a constant round of dissipation, 341n
his allowance too small, 341n
as happy as the day is long, 346n
his illness in West Indies (1787), 363, 475
arrives at Halifax, Nova Scotia (1787), 377
in Canada, 404
in Jamaica, 413
returns home (1787), 413, 419
his violent temper, 419
would like another ship, 419
commands the *Andromeda* frigate (1788), 475
arrives at Halifax, Nova Scotia (1788), 475
has no wish to visit London, 475

in love with the Devonshire Miss Winne, 475n
an additional allowance for (1789), 515, 518
created Duke of Clarence (1789), 516
takes his seat in the House of Lords, 516n
his finances (1789), 517–8, 520, 529, 673
his proposed Establishment (1789), 520, 520n, 533
refuses to go to sea again (1789), 525–6
says smoking is good for sailors, 616
his debts (1791), 673
wants a ship (1793), 821
breaks an arm, 825
his debts (1793), 880
refused employment at sea, 880n
opposes Datchet Canal Bill, 1241n
wants to succeed Spencer as First Lord of Admiralty, 1410
given Rangership of Bushey Park, 1492n
speech in the Lords (1805), 3008
and the Grand Duchess Catherine, 3278n
asks for command of Mediterranean fleet, 3755, 3761
and Miss Tylney-Long, 4056n
William Frederick, Duke of Gloucester (1776–1834), 163n, 386, 1040, 1075, 1213, 1298, 2567, 3135, 3138, 3483n, 3966n
letter to, 2996, 3136
University education for, considered, 386
becomes a Major-Gen. (1795), 1213n
question of a peerage for, 2996
his Regiment, 1285
becomes a Lieut.-Gen. (1799), 2081
becomes Duke of Gloucester (1805), 3135
wishes to be placed on the Staff, 2533
unfit for an important command, 2533, 2533n
votes against Ministers, 3603n
William Henry, Duke of Gloucester (1743–1805), 217, 431n, 545, 751, 977, 1225, 1301, 1405, 1474, 1597, 1619, 1630, 1700, 2013, 2507, 4270
letters from, 2081, 2567, 2996
letters to, 386, 1398, 2165n, 2996
his children, 386
promised an Irish pension, 386
wants a peerage for his son, 2567, 2996
death of, 3135, 3136n, 3137n, 3137–8, 3142
his Garter, 3014n
wishes to be buried at Windsor, 3135–6
his Will, 3135–6
his Keeperships, 3138

(890)

William Tell, the, a French warship, 2128
Williams, 279
Williams, Capt. (*d.* 1793), 923
Williams, Mrs, 4154–5
Williams, Sir Charles Hanbury, diplomatist (1708–59), 2672
Williams, John, Archbishop of York (1582–1650), 2672
Williams, John, and the Windsor election (1802), 2834, 2834n
Williams, Matthew, a mutineer, 1599
Williams, Rev. Philip (the Speaker's Chaplain), 441
Williams, Robert (1735–1814), 3904
Williams, Sir Robert (1764–1830), 3174
Williams, Admiral Sir Thomas (*c.* 1762–1841), 4003
Williamsburg, 4285
Williamson, Comte de, 1280
Williamson, Lieut.-Gen. Sir Adam, Lieut.-Governor of Jamaica (1736–98), 630, 1111, 1299
  nominated Governor of San Domingo, 1119, 1129
  recall of, 1297
Williamson, Nicholas, a mutineer, 1599
Willich, Anthony Florian Madinger, 2273
Willingdon, 2532
Willis, Dr Francis (1718–1807), 2368n, 2451
  letters from, 493, 493n
  pension for, 593
Willis, Henry Norton, 4223
Willis, Dr John (1751–1835), 2368n, 2372n, 2451, 3164n
Willis, Dr Robert Darling (1760–1821), 2368n, 2451, 3164n
Willis, Dr Thomas (1754–1827), 2368n, 2372n
Willoughby, Sir Christopher (1748–1808), *letters from,* 324, 1076
  wants a seat in Parliament, 1076
  given a Baronetcy, 1164
Willoughby, Henry (1780–1849), 3643
Willoughby de Broke, 14th Lord (1738–1816), 1983, 1983n, 2083, 3966n
Wilmot, John (1749–1815), 57n
Wilson, Lieut. of the Royal Artillery, 923
Wilson, Lieut. of the 15th Foot, 2318
Wilson, Lieut.-Col., 3142
Wilson, Rev. Edward (?1739–1804), 40, 194, 330, 1969, 2931n
Wilson, Sir John (1741–93), 760–1

Wilson, Richard, the Duke of Northumberland's Agent (1759–1834), 1678n
Wilson, Sir Robert Thomas (1777–1849), 3510, 3535, 3537, 3562
  a Knight of the Crescent, 3510n
Wilton, Earl of (1749–1814), 3966n
Wiltshire, 399, 915
Wimbledon, 1070n, 1436, 1759, 1788n, 1917, 2070, 3012
Wimpffen, Baron de, Wurtemberg Minister in London, 1325, 1325n, 1516, 1988, 2139
Wimpole Park, Cambs., near Royston, 1166, 4010
Winchelsea borough, 3873n
Winchelsea, a 32-gun frigate, 1112
Winchester, 780, 2074n, 2469, 2926
  French émigré priests at, 791
Winchester Cathedral, 1252, 4076
Winchester College, 2617, 2620
Winchester gaol, 189, 618n, 660n, 2804
Winchester, 13th Marquess of (1764–1843), 3966n
Winchilsea and Nottingham, George Finch, 9th Earl of (1752–1826), 1983n, 3060, 3183, 3186, 3966n
  refuses office of Lord-Lieut. of Ireland, 2369n
  his Garter, 2906n, 3014n, 4041n
Winck, 588
Winckheim [Winckleim], Major-Gen., 911, 957
Windham, William (1750–1810), 89, 438, 589, 644, 740, 751, 757, 807, 819, 831, 838, 878, 1031, 1039, 1057, 1070, 1070n, 1110, 1113, 1118, 1120–1, 1139, 1180, 1185, 1250, 1250n, 1282, 1323, 1386, 1482, 1509, 1514, 1519, 1654, 1686n, 1760, 1849, 1852, 1922, 1932, 1932n, 2023, 2033, 2132, 2143, 2189, 2235n, 2242, 2256, 2288, 2288n, 2329n, 2336n, 2365, 2474n, 2502n, 2535n, 2672, 2714, 2752n, 2780n, 2839n, 2888, 2888n, 2894, 2922n, 3009, 3025n, 3030, 3030n, 3041, 3085, 3095, 3111, 3115, 3169, 3169n, 3174, 3174n, 3186n, 3205, 3243n, 3256, 3259, 3283n, 3331, 3331n, 3358n, 3482, 3485, 3487, 3505, 3558n, 3590, 3594, 3594n, 3596, 3607, 3610n, 3617, 3620, 3625, 3643, 3657, 3665, 3665n, 3675, 3821, 3824, 3832, 3834, 3867, 3867n, 3873, 3876, 3876n, 3978n, 3890, 3902, 4076, 4087, 4087n, 4105, 4122, 4122n, 4124, 4126, 4130, 4133, 4138

II, 832–1662; III, 1663–2575; IV, 2576–3578

(891)

Wöllwarth, Baron de, 2125

Wolverhampton, 691–2

Wood, Sir George (1743–1824), a Baron of the Exchequer, 3455, 3902

Wood, Sir James Athol (1756–1829), 3379

Wood, Sir Mark (c. 1747–1829), 1480, 1724, 2140, 3508
  letter from, 3522n
  wants a Baronetcy, 3522n

Wood, Sir Matthew (1768–1843), 4127

Wood, Robert, harbour-master at Malta, 3963

Wood, Col. Thomas (1777–1860), 3493n, 4138n

Wood, Thomas, a mutineer, 3312

Woodchester Park (Glos), royal family at (1788), 476

Woodfall, William (1746–1803), 2108n, 2199n

Woodford, Mr, 283

Woodford, Capt., 1106

Woodford, Sir Ralph (?1735–1810), created Baronet, 686

Woodhouse, Rev. Dr John Chappell (c. 1749–1833), Dean of Lichfield, 3364

Woodley, Addington's country seat near Reading, 2264n, 2272, 2309, 2536n, 2620

Woodley, Mr, 3965, 3994

Woods and Forests, new arrangement of Office of the, 3970

Woodstock, 14n

Wooldridge, *see* Woolridge

Woolridge, Capt. William, 3877

Woolwich, 1302, 1554–5, 1557–8, 1560, 3538
  the laboratory at, 2663

Worcester, 1505, 1876, 2062, 2138n, 2275, 2814, 2942, 3098, 3121, 4208, 4238
  royal family at (1788), 476

Worcester, Bishop of, *see* Hurd
  Prebend of, 234, 237, 2665, 3645
  Infirmary, 381
  prisoners at, 739

Worcestershire, 915, 1426n, 3753

Worcestershire election (1806), 3180

Workman, William, a debtor, 481

Worm, Gen., 344

Wormhoudt, 922, 924

Woronzow, Count Alexander (1741–1805), the Russian Chancellor, 2609n, 2701

Woronzow, Count Simeon Romanovitch (1744–1832), the Russian Ambassador, 219, 221, 235, 516, 858, 1149, 1256, 1614, 1845, 1850, 1854, 1908, 1908n, 2082,

2123, 2181, 2386, 2698, 2701, 2759, 2770, 2895, 2984, 3101, 3109, 3217, 3222, 3226
  a warm friend to England, 2484
  again Ambassador (1801), 2484
  recall from London (1800), 2142
  continues to live in England (1800), 2181
  recall of, 3232, 3537
  his son, 3232

Worship Street Public Office, 1800n

Worsley, Sir Richard (1751–1805), 670
  appointed Envoy to Venice, 954

Worthing, 1784, 1815

Wortley, *see* Stuart-Wortley

Wraxall, Sir Nathaniel William (1751–1831), 35n, 44n, 55n, 203n, 335n, 410n, 523n, 556n

Wray, Sir Cecil, Bart (1734–1805), his Westminster contest (1784), 64n, 66, 69, 91

Wrech, M. de, 4274

Wright, Francis, upholsterer, 4034

Wright, George, 3412

Wright, John (?1770–1844), book-seller, 2201

Wright, John Atkins [Atkyns], (d. 1822), M.P. Oxford City (1802–7), 2752n

Wright, Lieut.-Col. Robert, 3693n, 3645n, 3689n, 3693n, 3714n, 3844n, 3887n, 4034n

Wright, Sir Sampson (d. 1793), 78, 335, 657, 777n

Wright, Thomas, a proprietor of the *Whitehall Evening Post*, 158

Wright, Thomas, Lord Mayor of London (1786), 335

Wrottesley, Sir John, 1st Baron Wrottesley (1771–1841), 2276

Wroughton, Sir Thomas (d. 1787), 399

Wurmb, Gen., 923, 966, 968

Wurmser, Gen., 943, 992–3, 995, 998, 1000, 1322, 1337

Wurnstorf (Hanover), convent in, 2125

Wurtemberg, 1673, 1792, 3080, 3388
  French invade (1799), 1941, 1946; (1800), 2147, 2177
  French exactions in, 2206, 2214, 2311
  territorial losses during the War, 2544

Wurtemberg, Augusta, Princess of (1764–88), daughter of Charles Wm. Ferdinand, Duke of Brunswick, 1461n, 2685
  her unhappy married life, 1325n

Wurtemberg, Caroline Alexei, Princess of, *cr.* (1807), Baroness von Röttenburg and

II, 832–1662; III, 1663–2575; IV, 2576–3578

II, 832–1662; III, 1663–2575; IV, 2576–3578

Yorke, Charles Philip (*cont.*)
  letters from, 327n, 2397, 2397n, 2399,
    2456n, 2471, 2510n, 2515n, 2554n,
    2595n, 2694, 2771, 2777n, 2780n, 2786,
    2786n, 2790, 2790n, 2793, 2797, 2807,
    2816, 2822, 2832, 2838n, 2839n, 2842,
    2842n, 2852n, 2914n, 2922n, 3075n,
    3169n, 3483n, 3906n, 3989n, 4007n,
    4010, 4076n, 4161, 4225, 4236
  letters to, 2397, 2399, 2447n, 2510n, 2515n,
    2771, 2786, 2786n, 2793, 2842, 2842n,
    2871n, 2881n, 3861n, 3906n, 4076n,
    4161, 4219, 4225, 4236
  Secretary at War in Addington Ministry,
    2388, 2397, 2922n
  King thinks of him as Speaker (1801), 2397
  offered Treasurership of the Navy (1801),
    2554n
  memo. by, 2753
  commands a militia regiment, 2771
  becomes Home Secretary (1803), 2777,
    2780, 2780n, 2782n, 2794
  says the Cabinet is detestable (1803), 2777n
  feels unequal to his new post (1803), 2780n,
    2786n
  re-elected for Cambridgeshire (1803), 2790n
  offered Governor-Generalship of Bengal
    (1802), 2842n
  thought of as Melville's successor, 3068n,
    3075n
  his want of temper and nerves, 3075n
  on Middleton's appointment, 3075n
  would refuse any offer from Pitt (1804),
    2839n, 2842n
  offered a peerage (1804), 2839n
  income less than £1,500, 2839n, 2842n
  declines office in 1807, 3505n
  disapproves of Convention of Cintra, 3786n
  offered but refuses office of President of
    India Board (1809), 3856, 3861n, 3906n
  his wife, 3906n
  refuses office under Perceval (1809), 3966,
    3989n, 4007, 4007n, 4010
  appointed a Teller of the Exchequer, 4076,
    4076n
  elected for St Germans, 4076n
  appointed First Lord of the Admiralty, 4142
Yorke, James, Bishop of Ely (*d.* 1808), 1870,
    3760n, 3966n
Yorke, John (1728–1801), 2520
Yorke, Sir Joseph, Baron Dover, Gen. (1724–
    92), 519, 2404
  letters to, 376, 409
  question of a peerage for (1788), 451

Yorke, Rear-Admiral Sir Joseph Sydney
    (1768–1831), 49, 4076n, 4122n, 4220
  letter to, 327n
  his knighthood (1805), 3073
Yorkshire, 812, 1535, 1616, 1686, 3114, 3489;
    disturbances in (1795), 1283
Yorkshire Address to the King (1784), 57
Yorkshire Association, the, 159n
Yorkshire election (1784), 55, 61; (1807),
    3462, 3462n, 3485n
Youghal, 3637n
Young, Arthur, Secretary of the Board of
    Agriculture (1741–1820), 915n
Young, Rev. Arthur, 1740, 1740n, 1742n
Young, Rev. John, D.D., Prebendary of
    Worcester (*d.* 1786), 297n
Young, Rev. Dr J., of Hawick, 4229
  his daughters, 4229
Young, Rev. Matthew (1750–1800), Bishop
    of Clonfert, 2275n, 2301
Young, Sir William, 2nd Bart (1749–1815),
    438, 448, 644, 647, 670, 878, 1044,
    1255, 1637, 1897, 2137, 2140, 2752n,
    3030, 3174n
  appointed Governor of Tobago, 3372
Young, Vice-Admiral Sir William (1751–
    1821), 2924, 3497, 3793
Ypres, 891, 920, 924, 926, 934, 939, 941,
    943, 966, 968, 1084
Yser, river, 920, 922, 986, 1022, 1040, 1088
Yssel, river, 1182, 1233, 3159
Yucatan, coast of, 539

Zastrow, Prussian Foreign Minister, 3378, 3380
Zealand, 367, 376, 3497, 3501, 3535, 3539n, 3543
Zellada [Zellado], Cardinal (1717–1801), 824
Zelle, 4274
Zeppelin, Count Johann Karl von (1767–
    1801), Wurtemberg Minister, 1383n,
    1418, 1423, 1634, 1873, 1961, 2221
Zetwitz, Lieut., 882
Zimmerman, Dr Jean George, 215, 306, 486,
    676, 4274, 4290
Zoffany, John (or Johann) (1733–1810), 2985
Zouch, Thomas (*c.* 1737–1815), Prebendary
    of Durham, 3559
  refuses Bishopric of Carlisle, 3567
  his sister Anne, 3567n
Zuccarelli, Francesco (1702–88), the Italian
    painter, 2992
Zumsteeg, 1873
Zurich, 1907n, 1973, 2059
Zuyder Zee, the, 2016, 2032, 2037, 2046
Zweibrücken, Duke of, *see* Deux Ponts